INTERNATIONAL MARKETING

Seventh Edition

MICHAEL R. CZINKOTA
Georgetown University

ILKKA A. RONKAINEN
Georgetown University

THOMSON

SOUTH-WESTERN

Australia · Canada · Mexico · Singapore · Spain · United Kingdom · United States

International Marketing, 7e
Michael R. Czinkota and Ilkka A. Ronkainen

Editor-in-Chief:
Jack W. Calhoun

Team Leader:
Melissa S. Acuña

Acquisitions Editor:
Steven W. Hazelwood

Developmental Editor:
Erin Joyner

Marketing Manager:
Nicole Moore

Production Editors:
Amy A. Brooks and Emily Gross

Manufacturing Coordinator:
Diane Lohman

Compositor:
Stratford Publishing Services

Printer:
R.R. Donnelly & Sons Company
Willard, OH

Internal Designer:
Tippy McIntosh

Cover Designer:
Tippy McIntosh

Cover Image:
Photodisk, Inc.

Photography Manager:
John W. Hill

Photo Researcher:
Sam A. Marshall

Domestic Student Edition:
ISBN 0-324-19046-8

International Student Edition:
ISBN 0-324-28289-3 (Not for Sale
in the United States)

Library of Congress Control
Number:
2002116682

To Ilona and Margaret Victoria—MRC
To Susan, Sanna, and Alex—IAR

Preface

Practicing international marketing and writing a text on the subject have some things in common: It is a lot of work, the competition is tough, and it's fun to succeed. It is therefore with great pleasure that we present the seventh edition of *International Marketing* to you. We have made significant revisions in this edition, but our goals continue to be excellence and relevance in content, combined with user-friendliness for both the student and the professor. We have greatly streamlined the text, which now comprises 20 chapters. We have done so to balance the workload for the reader but without taking shortcuts. We have combined topics, eliminated redundancies, and tightened content wherever possible. The result is a shorter, crisper text of better quality.

We now reflect very clearly the ongoing controversies surrounding issues such as globalization or international aid. We paint a broader picture of the implications of a market orientation, and show the effects of competing directions. This includes discussions of the shortcomings encountered in corporate transparency, executive veracity, and international ambitions. We provide much deeper data analysis and support. For example, we now compare the leading economic regions, the United States and Europe, but also offer comparative benchmarks from Japan, China, Australia, Kenya, and Brazil. Overall, we unabashedly admit that this seventh edition of *International Marketing* is the best one yet!

Here are the key reasons why this book is special:

➤ We write about both the theory and the application of international marketing. Based on our personal research record and business experience, we can offer research insights from around the globe and show how corporations are adjusting to the marketplace realities of today.

➤ We acknowledge and give clear examples of how the world has changed in an era of terrorism, hostility, and distrust. We look at the marketing repercussions of these changes on people management, sourcing policies, cargo security, inventory management, and port utilization. However, we also draw on our work with corporations to find new forms of collaboration and network building without compromising safety or security.

➤ We address the concerns of emerging and developing marketing venues throughout the text. We present the issue of underserved markets, with a population of four billion, and also suggest how these people and countries can take on a greater role as contributors to marketing efforts in mainstream markets.

➤ We cover the full spectrum of international marketing, from start-up operations to the formation of virtual alliances. We offer a thorough discussion of the operations of multinational corporations, but also present a specific focus on the activities of small- and medium-sized firms, which are increasingly major players in the international market and will be the employers of many students.

➤ We examine international marketing from a truly global perspective rather than from only the U.S. point of view. By addressing, confronting, and analyzing the existence of different environments, expectations, and market conditions, we highlight the need for awareness, sensitivity, and adaptation.

➤ We also address the growing interaction between government and business. Because of our policy experience, we know how businesses work with governments and what role governmental considerations can play for the international marketer. This policy orientation greatly contributes to the managerial relevance of this book.

➤ We integrate the e-commerce and Web impact on the international marketer. We also offer information access by providing detailed listings of Web sites. We discuss the revolutionary changes in communication between firms and their customers and suppliers, and present the latest consequences for international market research and market entry.

➤ We fully incorporate the important societal dimensions of diversity, environmental concern, ethics, and economic transformation.

Personal Support

Most important, we personally stand behind our product and we will work hard to delight you. Should you have any questions or comments on this book, you can contact us, talk to us, and receive feedback from us.

Michael R. Czinkota
(202) 687-4204
Czinkotm@msb.edu

Ilkka A. Ronkainen
(202) 687-3788
Ronkaii@msb.edu

Organization

The text is designed primarily for the advanced undergraduate student with prior exposure to the marketing field. Because of its in-depth coverage, it also presents an excellent challenge for graduate instruction and executive education.

The text is divided into three parts. First, the core concepts of international marketing are outlined, and the environmental forces that the international marketer has to consider are discussed. The second part focuses on the various activities necessary for international marketing planning and concentrates on the beginning of international marketing activities. Export and import operations are covered here, together with elements of the marketing mix that tend to be most important for firms at an initial level of international experience. The third part discusses strategy and marketing management issues most relevant to the expanded global operations of multinational corporations with a key focus on implementation. We conclude with a chapter on the future of the field and the student.

Both the instructor and the student can work with this text in two ways. One alternative is to cover the material sequentially, progressing from the initial international effort to multinational activities. In this way, marketing dimensions such as distribution, promotion, and pricing are covered in the order in which they are most relevant for the particular level of expertise within the firm. Another approach is to use the text in a parallel manner, by pairing comparable chapters from Parts Two and Three. In this way, the primary emphasis can be placed on the functional approach to international marketing.

Key Features

The seventh edition reflects the highly dynamic international marketplace. We offer a perspective on the shift from marketplace to market space, and the impact of this revolution on international marketers in terms of outreach, research, and competition. Several Internet technology sections are now part of our chapters and *International Marketplace* vignettes, reflecting state-of-the-art corporate practices. We have included links to the Web sites of companies in our vignettes as well as those of our data sources, when practical. We also provide several appendices that list Web addresses for governments, international organizations, and monitors of international marketing issues.

Our focus on the physical environment and geography is strong. Updated maps provide context in terms of social and economic data. An appendix addresses directly the relationship between geography and international marketing. New text components, marketplaces, and several cases focus specifically on the environment and the opportunities, challenges, and ambiguities that it poses to international marketers.

This seventh edition is divided into three parts: The environment, beginning international marketing activities, and advanced international marketing management.

The five chapters of Part One reflect the drivers behind the globalization phenomenon in the cultural, economic, financial, political, and legal areas. Both the established markets in Europe and North America as well as the growth markets of Asia and Latin America are emphasized. We address the response of international marketers to financial crises. Our strong policy orientation continues with an update of the role of international agreements and organizations, as well as their interaction with national and regional policies. The World Trade Organization (WTO), the Doha Round of trade negotiations, the IMF, and the World Bank are discussed, together with the controversies and public debate surrounding these institutions. The section on export controls reflects the realities of the new awareness of terrorism and conflict that reshapes the world. Also covered are newly emerging areas of international policy conflict, such as dumping, country of origin rules, intellectual property rights, the Helms-Burton Act, and the important issues of ethics, bribery, and human rights. We also highlight the importance of corporate virtue, vision, and veracity in determining the future success of marketing around the globe.

Beginning international marketing activities in Part Two are placed in the context of market expansion strategy and the evolutionary nature of the internationalization process. The role of research in this process is highlighted in the chapter on building the knowledge base necessary for initial and more involved marketing activities across borders. Also included is a section on Web sites and Internet information to facilitate direct student access to international data. The discussion of the export process is now followed immediately by a presentation of export intermediaries, licensing, and franchising—thus offering insight into the continuity of the internationalization patterns of firms. Particular attention rests with the expansion of the product life cycle. There is also an increased reflection of marketing theory and practices as emanating from outside North America.

Advanced international marketing activities in Part Three are presented with a strong strategy orientation. The opening chapter is dedicated to the global strategic planning framework, which addresses market choice, competitive strategy, and international marketing segmentation. The foreign direct investment process is more clearly linked to globalization trends and now also covers such investments from the local employee perspective. The product chapter has a new section dealing with brand management and how marketers can build global, regional, and local brands. The services chapter reflects the shift from marketplace to market space and the resulting mobility of corporate activities. Also highlighted is the global imbalance of skilled labor in the information technology field. The logistics chapter has "supply chain management" in its title, reflecting issues such as efficient customer response, the close cooperation between customers and suppliers, and the emerging linkages between logistics and the environment. In the pricing chapter, major emphasis rests with the marketing strategy implications of the euro currency and the implications of greater pricing transparency due to the Internet. Promotional strategies include a discussion of global community relations and the need for corporate preparedness for global crises management. The chapter on organization and control has a section dealing with a firm's ability to leverage resources and strengths across borders and includes approaches such as the Intranet. This part also presents the results of a special delphi study on the future of international marketing that was conducted by the authors with a global panel of experts.

Innovative Learning Tools

Contemporary Realism

Each chapter offers three or more current International Marketplace boxes. They focus on real marketing situations and are intended to help students understand and absorb the presented materials. The instructor can highlight the boxes to exemplify theory or use them as mini-cases for class discussion. Whenever possible, Internet addresses are provided to the companies featured in these boxes, so that students can obtain the latest information.

Research Emphasis

A special effort has been made to provide current research information and data from around the world. Chapter notes are augmented by lists of relevant recommended readings incorporating the latest research findings. In addition, a wide variety of sources and organizations that provide international information are listed in the text. These materials enable the instructor and the student to go beyond the text whenever time permits.

Internet Focus

All chapters now make specific reference to how the Internet, electronic commerce, and the World Wide Web affect international marketing. We highlight how the way of reaching customers and suppliers has changed given the new technology. We also explain the enhanced ability of firms to position themselves internationally in competition with other larger players. We offer insights into the electronic marketing research process and present details of how companies cope with new market realities. Whenever appropriate, we direct readers to Internet resources which can be useful in updating information. Each chapter also provides several Internet questions in order to offer training opportunities that make use of the Internet.

Geography

This edition contains several full-color maps, covering the social, economic, and political features of the world. In addition, several chapters have maps particularly designed for this book, which integrate the materials discussed in the text and reflect a truly "global" perspective. These maps enable the instructor to visually demonstrate concepts such as political blocs and socioeconomic variables. An appendix, dealing specifically with the impact of geography on international marketing, is part of Chapter 1.

Cases

Following each part of the text are a variety of cases, most of which are new or updated especially for this book, that present students with real business situations. Some of our best cases from previous editions are also available on the text support site (**http://czinkota.swlearning.com**) for the instructor's use. All cases address the activities of actual or former companies and cover a broad geographic spectrum. In addition, a number of video cases further assists to enliven classroom activity. Challenging questions accompany each case, permitting in-depth discussion of the materials covered in the chapters.

Ancillary Package

Instructor's Resource CD (IRCD)

The Instructor's Resource CD delivers all the traditional instructor support materials in one handy place: a CD. Electronic files are included on the CD for the complete

Instructor's Manual, Test Bank, computerized Test Bank and computerized Test Bank software (ExamView), and chapter-by-chapter PowerPoint presentation files that can be used to enhance in-class lectures.

Instructor's Manual

The text is accompanied by an in-depth *Instructor's Manual,* devised to provide major assistance to the professor. The Instructor's Manual files are located on the IRCD in Microsoft Word 2000 format. The material in the manual includes the following:

➤ **Teaching Plans**   Alternative teaching plans and syllabi are presented to accommodate the instructor's preferred course structure and varying time constraints. Time plans are developed for the course to be taught in a semester format, on a quarter basis, or as an executive seminar.

➤ **Discussion Guidelines**   For each chapter, specific teaching objectives and guidelines are developed to help stimulate classroom discussion.

➤ **End-of-Chapter Questions**   Each question is fully developed in the manual to accommodate different scenarios and experience horizons. Where appropriate, the relevant text section is referenced. In addition, each chapter has Internet-based exercises in order to offer students the opportunity to explore the application of new technology to international marketing on their own.

➤ **Cases**   A detailed case-chapter matrix is supplied that delineates which cases are most appropriate for each area of the international marketing field. In addition, detailed case discussion alternatives are provided, outlining discussion strategies and solution alternatives.

➤ **Video and Film References**   An extensive listing of video and film materials available from educational institutions, companies, and government agencies is provided. Materials are briefly discussed, possible usage patterns are outlined, and ordering/availability information is supplied. In addition, each adopter of this text can receive the free video cases in international marketing, which contain news stories relevant to issues in international marketing.

Test Bank

The revised and updated Test Bank includes a variety of multiple choice, true/false questions, and cases, which emphasize the important concepts presented in each chapter. The Test Bank questions vary in levels of difficulty so that each instructor can tailor his/her testing to meet his/her specific needs. The Test Bank files are located on the IRCD in Microsoft Word 2000 format.

ExamView (Computerized) Test Bank

The Test Bank is also available on the IRCD in computerized format (ExamView), allowing instructors to select problems at random by level of difficulty or type, customize or add test questions, and scramble questions to create up to 99 versions of the same test. This software is available in DOS, Mac, or Windows formats.

PowerPoint Presentation Slides

The PowerPoint presentation package brings classroom lectures and discussions to life with the Microsoft PowerPoint 2000 presentation tool. Extremely professor friendly, easy to read, and organized by chapter, these presentations provide lecture outlines to serve as a valuable visual teaching tool. The PowerPoint presentation slides are available on the IRCD in Microsoft 2000 format and as downloadable files on the text support site (**http://czinkota.swlearning.com**).

Web Site

Visit the text Web site at **http://czinkota.swlearning.com** to find instructor's support materials as well as study resources that will help students practice and apply the concepts they have learned in class.

Student Resources

> Online quizzes for each chapter are available on the Web site for those students who would like additional study materials. After each quiz is submitted, automatic feedback tells the students how they scored and what the correct answers are to the questions they missed. Students are then able to e-mail their results directly to their instructor if desired.

> Crossword quizzing of glossary terms and definitions arranged by chapter is also available for extra review of key terms found in the text.

> Students can download the PowerPoint presentation slides from the web site.

> Links to news articles and hot marketing topics are provided for extra student research.

Instructor Resources

> Downloadable Instructor's Manual files are available in Microsoft Word 2000 format and Adobe Acrobat format.

> Downloadable PowerPoint presentation files are available in Microsoft PowerPoint 2000 format.

> An online database of cases, contributed by leading professors in the field of International Marketing, is supplied for adopters of the text at the instructor resources page. Go there to find tried and true case studies that have been donated by a multitude of experts internationally. Professors can also opt to submit their *own* "favorite" cases!

Videos

A video package has been prepared to correspond with the key concepts taught in the text. These videos, featuring companies such as Pier One Imports and Whirlpool, coincide with the video cases found at the end of each part in the text. Professors can assign the cases after presenting videos in class or use these cases to simply illustrate a key point.

Acknowledgments

We are deeply grateful to the professors, students, and professionals using this book. Your interest demonstrates the need for more knowledge about international marketing. As our market, you are telling us that our product adds value to your lives. As a result, you add value to ours. Thank you!

We also thank the many reviewers for their constructive and imaginative comments and criticisms, which were instrumental in making this edition even better.

We remain indebted to the reviewers and survey respondents of this and earlier editions of this text:

Sanjeev Agarwal
Iowa State University

Zafar Ahmed
Texas A&M—Commerce

Lyn S. Amine
St. Louis University

Jessica M. Bailey
The American University

Warren Bilkey
University of Wisconsin

S. Tamer Cavusgil
Michigan State University

Shih-Fen Chen
Kansas State University

Alex Christofides
Ohio State University

Robert Dahlstrom
University of Kentucky

Paul Dowling
University of Utah

John Dyer
University of Miami

Luiz Felipe
*IBMEC Business School
(Rio de Janeiro, Brazil)*

Dr. John P. Fraderich
*Southern Illinois University—
Carbondale*

Roberto Friedmann
University of Georgia

Shenzhao Fu
University of San Francisco

Jim Gentry
University of Nebraska

Donna Goehle
Michigan State University

Needlima Gogumala
Kansas State University

Peter J. Gordon
*Southeast Missouri State
University*

Paul Groke
Northern Illinois University

Andrew Gross
Cleveland State University

John Hadjimarcou
University of Texas at El Paso

Hari Hariharan
DePaul University

Braxton Hinchey
University of Lowell

Carol Howard
Oklahoma City University

G. Thomas M. Hult
Florida State University

Basil Janavaras
Mankato State University

Denise Johnson
University of Louisville

Sudhir Kale
Arizona State University

Ceyhan Kilic
DePaul University

Hertha Krotkoff
Towson State University

Kathleen La Francis
Central Michigan University

Trina Larsen
Drexel University

Edmond Lausier
*University of Southern
California*

Bertil Liander
University of Massachusetts

Mushtaq Luqmani
Western Michigan University

Isabel Maignan
Florida State University

James Maskulka
Lehigh University

James McCullouch
Washington State University

Fred Miller
Murray State University

Joseph Miller
Indiana University

Mark Mitchell
*University of South Carolina—
Spartanburg*

Henry Munn
*California State University,
Northridge*

Jacob Naor
University of Maine, Orono

Urban Ozanne
Florida State University

Tony Peloso
*Queensland University of
Technology (Australia)*

Ilsa Penaloza
University of Connecticut

John Ryans
Kent State University

Ray Taylor
Villanova University

John Wilkinson
University of South Australia

Matthew Sim
Temesek Business School (Singapore)

Tyzoon T. Tyebjee
Santa Clara University

Sumas Wongsunopparat
University of Wisconsin— Milwaukee

Robert Underwood
Virginia Polytechnic Institute and State University

James Spiers
Arizona State University

Nittaya Wongtada
Thunderbird

Janda Swinder
Kansas State University

Robert Weigand
University of Illinois at Chicago

Van R. Wood
Texas Tech University

Many thanks to all the faculty members and students who have helped us sharpen our thinking by cheerfully providing challenging comments and questions. In particular, we thank Bernard LaLonde, The Ohio State University; Lyn Amine, St. Louis University; Tamer Cavusgil, Michigan State University; and James Wills, University of Hawaii.

Many colleagues, friends, and business associates graciously gave their time and knowledge to clarify concepts; provide us with ideas, comments, and suggestions; and deepen our understanding of issuses. Without the direct links to business and policy that you have provided, this book could not offer its refreshing realism. In particular, we are grateful to Secretaries Malcolm Baldrige, C. William Verity, Clayton Yeutter, and William Brock for the opportunity to gain international business policy experience and to William Morris, Paul Freedenberg, and J. Michael Farrell for enabling its implementation. We also thank William Casselman of Stairs Dillenbeck Kelly Merle and Finley, Robert Conkling of VSSL Corporation, Lew Cramer of Summit Ventures, Mark Dowd of IBM, David Danjczek of Manufacturers Alliance, and Veikko Jaaskelainen and Reijo Luostarinen of HSE.

Valuable research assistance was provided by our student research elite team. They made important and substantive contributions to this book. They dig up research information with tenacity and relentlessness; they organize and analyze research materials, prepare drafts of vignettes and cases, and reinforce everyone on the third floor of Old North with their can-do spirit. They are Sabrina Nguyen, Angie Kang, Shannon Antonio, Sofina Qureshi, Ruthie Braunstein, and Jessie Sze-Ting Cheung, all of Georgetown University. We appreciate all of your work.

A very special word of thanks to the people at Thomson/South-Western. Michael Roche and Melissa Acuña have the vision but haven't lost their hands-on approach. Erin Joyner supported the lengthy process of writing a text with her input and feedback. Emily Gross helped us in the final stretch of production.

Foremost, we are grateful to our families, who have truly participated in the writing of this book. Only the patience, understanding, and love of Ilona and Margaret Victoria Czinkota and Susan, Sanna, and Alex Ronkainen enabled us to have the energy, stamina, and inspiration to write this book.

Michael R. Czinkota
Ilkka A. Ronkainen
Washington, D.C.
May, 2003

About the Authors

Michael R. Czinkota is on the faculty of marketing and international business of the Graduate School and the Robert Emmett McDonough School of Business at Georgetown University. He has held professorial appointments at universities in Asia, Australia, Europe, and the Americas.

Dr. Czinkota served in the U.S. government as Deputy Assistant Secretary of Commerce. He also served as head of the U.S. Delegation to the OECD Industry Committee in Paris and as senior trade advisor for Export Controls.

Dr. Czinkota's background includes eight years of private sector business experience as a partner in an export-import firm and in an advertising agency. His research has been supported by the U.S. government, the National Science Foundation, the Organization of American States, and the International Council of the American Management Association. He was listed as one of the three most published contributors to international business research in the *Journal of International Business Studies* and has written several books, including *Best Practices in International Marketing* and *Mastering Global Markets* (Thomson). He is also the author of the *STAT-USA/Internet Companion to International Marketing,* an official publication of the U.S. Department of Commerce.

Dr. Czinkota served on the Global Advisory Board of the American Marketing Association and on the Board of Governors of the Academy of Marketing Science. He is on the editorial boards of *Journal of the Academy of Marketing Science, International Marketing Review,* and *Asian Journal of Marketing.* For his work in international business and trade policy, he was named a Distinguished Fellow of the Academy of Marketing Science and a Fellow of the Chartered Institute of Marketing in the United Kingdom. He has been awarded honorary degrees from the Universidad Pontificia Madre y Maestra in the Dominican Republic and the Universidad del Pacifico in Lima, Peru.

Dr. Czinkota serves on several corporate boards and has worked with corporations such as AT&T, IBM, GE, Nestlé, and US WEST. He also serves as advisor to the United Nations' and World Trade Organization's Executive Forum on National Export Strategies. Dr. Czinkota is often asked to testify before Congress and is a sought-after speaker and advisor to corporations.

Dr. Czinkota was born and raised in Germany and educated in Austria, Scotland, Spain, and the United States. He studied law and business administration at the University of Erlangen-Nürnberg and was awarded a two-year Fulbright Scholarship. He holds an MBA in international business and a Ph.D. in logistics from The Ohio State University.

Ilkka A. Ronkainen is a member of the faculty of marketing and international business at the School of Business at Georgetown University. From 1981 to 1986 he served as Associate Director and from 1986 to 1987 as Chairman of the National Center for Export-Import Studies. Currently, he directs Georgetown University's Hong Kong Program.

Dr. Ronkainen serves as docent of international marketing at the Helsinki School of Economics. He was visiting professor at HSE during the 1997–1988 and 1991–1992 academic years and continues to teach in its Executive MBA, International MBA, and International BBA programs. He is currently the chairholder at the Saastamoinen Foundation Professorship in International Marketing.

Dr. Ronkainen holds a Ph.D. and a master's degree from the University of South Carolina as well as an M.S. (Economics) degree from the Helsinki School of Economics.

Dr. Ronkainen has published extensively in academic journals and the trade press. He is a coauthor of a number of international business and marketing texts, including *Best Practices in International Marketing* and *Mastering Global Markets* (Thomson). He serves on the review boards of the *Journal of Business Research, International Marketing Review,* and *Journal of Travel Research* and has reviewed for the *Journal of International Marketing* and the *Journal of International Business Studies.* He served as the North American coordinator for the European Marketing Academy, 1984–1990. He was a member of the board of the Washington International Trade Association from 1981 to 1986 and started the association's newsletter, *Trade Trends.*

Dr. Ronkainen has served as a consultant to a wide range of U.S. and international institutions. He has worked with entities such as IBM, the Rand Organization, and the Organization of American States. He maintains close relations with a number of Finnish companies and their internationalization and educational efforts.

Brief Contents

Preface iv
Acknowledgments x
About the Authors xii

Part One

The International Environment

Chapter 1 ✓   The International Marketing Imperative 2
Chapter 2   International Trade Institutions and Trade Policy 30
Chapter 3   The Cultural Environment 56
Chapter 4   The Economic Environment 88
Chapter 5   The International Political and Legal Environment 130
Cases   "Trick-or-Treat?" Costume Market in Horror as Halloween
                    Approaches 157
                  A Presidential Proclamation on Steel 161
                  Car Financing in China 167
                  IKEA in the USA 174
                  Renaming the Vietnamese Catfish 179
Video Case   Equal Exchange Strives for Equality through Fair Trade 182

Part Two

Beginning International Marketing Activities

Chapter 6   Building the Knowledge Base 186
Chapter 7   Exporting, Licensing, and Franchising 224
Chapter 8   Product Adaptation 246
Chapter 9   Export Pricing Strategies 272
Chapter 10   International Communications 304
Chapter 11   Channels and Distribution Strategies 332
Cases   Exports of Tobacco 368
                  Damar International 374
                  Water from Iceland 376
                  Joemarin Oy 381
                  The Gray Ferrari 386
Video Cases   Global Vendor Relations at Pier 1 Imports 389
                  Lakewood Chopsticks Exports 391

Part Three

Global Marketing Management

Chapter 12   Global Strategic Planning 396
Chapter 13   Global Market Expansion 420
Chapter 14   Product and Brand Management 438
Chapter 15   Services Marketing 464
Chapter 16   Global Pricing Strategies 484
Chapter 17   Logistics and Supply Chain Management 508
Chapter 18   Global Promotional Strategies 536
Chapter 19   Marketing Organization, Implementation, and Control 568
Chapter 20   The Future 598
Cases   Chupa Chups Vending: "Choose Your Flavor" 627
                    Nova Scotia 634
                    Customer Service Online: The HP DesignJet 639
                    The F-18 Hornet Offset 647
                    Kadimi Group of Companies (India): Exports 654
                    Parker Pen Company 659
Video Case   Whirlpool and the Global Appliance Industry 663

References
Glossary
Index

Contents

Preface iv
Acknowledgments x
About the Authors xii

Part One

The International Environment

Chapter 1   The International Marketing Imperative 2

The International Marketplace 1.1: The Two Sides of International
Marketing 3
What International Marketing Is 4
The Importance of World Trade 5
Global Linkages 6
The International Marketplace 1.2: Some Thoughts on Basketball
Competitiveness 7
Domestic Policy Repercussions 8
The International Marketplace 1.3: International Marketing: Bringing
Peace, Fighting Terrorism 10
Opportunities and Challenges in International Marketing 10
The Goals of This Book 14
Summary 15
Key Terms 15
Questions for Discussion 15
Internet Exercises 16
Appendix A: Basics of Marketing 17
Strategic Marketing 17
Target Market Selection 17
Marketing Management 19
The Marketing Process 19
Key Terms 20
Appendix B: Geographical Perspectives on International
Marketing 21
Location 22
Place 22
Natural Features 23
Human Features 24
Interaction 25
Movement 26
Region 28
Key Terms 29

Chapter 2   International Trade Institutions and Trade Policy 30

The International Marketplace 2.1: Who Should Regulate E-Commerce? 31
The Historical Dimension 31
    Global Division 33
Transnational Institutions Affecting World Trade 33
    World Trade Organization (WTO) 33
    International Monetary Fund (IMF) 36
    World Bank 36
The International Marketplace 2.2: World Bank to the Rescue 37
    Regional Institutions 37
Comparing International Trade Positions 38
    A Diagnosis of the U.S. Trade Position 40
The Impact of Trade and Investment 41
    The Effect of Trade 41
    The Effect of International Investment 42
Policy Responses to Trade Problems 44
    Restrictions of Imports 44
    Export Promotion Efforts 48
A Strategic Outlook for Trade and Investment Policies 50
    A U.S. Perspective 50
    An International Perspective 51
The International Marketplace 2.3: A Marketing Approach to Trade 52
    Summary 53
    Key Terms 53
    Questions for Discussion 53
    Internet Exercises 53
    Recommended Readings 54
Appendix A: Members of the U.S. Trade Promotion Coordination Committee (TPCC) 55

Chapter 3   The Cultural Environment 56

The International Marketplace 3.1: Cultural Imperialism Does Not Sell in International Markets 57
Culture Defined 59
The Elements of Culture 61
    Language 61
The International Marketplace 3.2: Euroteens = U.S. Teens? 62
    Nonverbal Language 64
    Religion 65
    Values and Attitudes 68
    Manners and Customs 69
The International Marketplace 3.3: Soup: Now It's Mmmm-Mmmm-Global! 71
    Material Elements 72
    Aesthetics 73
    Education 74
    Social Institutions 74
Sources of Cultural Knowledge 75
Cultural Analysis 77
The Training Challenge 81

The International Marketplace 3.4: Online Cultural Training 84
Making Culture Work for Marketing Success 84
    Summary 86
    Key Terms 86
    Questions for Discussion 86
    Internet Exercises 86
    Recommended Readings 87

Chapter 4   The Economic Environment 88

The International Marketplace 4.1: Markets at the Bottom of the Income
    Pyramid 89
Market Characteristics 94
    Population 95
The International Marketplace 4.2: In Search of the New China 101
    Infrastructure 106
The International Marketplace 4.3: Bringing the New Economy to New
    Markets 108
Impact of the Economic Environment on Social Development 109
Regional Economic Integration 109
    Levels of Economic Integration 110
The International Marketplace 4.4: NAFTA and Wal-Mart: Reshaping the
    Mexican Retail Market 118
    Other Economic Alliances 120
    Economic Integration and the International Marketer 122
Dealing with Financial Crises 124
    Causes of the Crises 125
    Effects of the Crises 125
    Consumer and Marketer Responses 125
    Summary 127
    Key Terms 127
    Questions for Discussion 128
    Internet Exercises 128
    Recommended Readings 128

Chapter 5   The International Political and Legal Environment 130

The International Marketplace 5.1: Is Your French Wine Really from Mexico? 131
Home Country Political and Legal Environment 132
    Embargoes and Sanctions 132
    Export Controls 135
    A New Environment for Export Controls 136
The International Marketplace 5.2: Export Controls: More Harm than Good? 137
    Import Controls 140
    Regulation of International Business Behavior 141
Host Country Political and Legal Environment 144
    Political Action and Risk 144
    Legal Differences and Restraints 149
The International Marketplace 5.3: The *Ehime Maru:* A Clash of Two Cultures 150
    Influencing Politics and Laws 151
The International Environment 153
    International Politics 153

International Law 153
Summary 154
Key Terms 155
Questions for Discussion 155
Internet Exercises 155
Recommended Readings 156

Cases   "Trick-or-Treat?" Costume Market in Horror as Halloween
Approaches 157
A Presidential Proclamation on Steel 161
Car Financing in China 167
IKEA in the USA 174
Renaming the Vietnamese Catfish 179

Video Case   Equal Exchange Strives for Equality through Fair Trade 182

Part Two

Beginning International Marketing Activities

Chapter 6   **Building the Knowledge Base 186**
The International Marketplace 6.1: Welcoming China to International
Marketing Research 187
Defining the Issue 188
International and Domestic Research 188
New Parameters 188
New Environments 188
Number of Factors Involved 189
Broader Definition of Competition 189
Recognizing the Need for Research 189
The Benefits of Research 190
Determining Research Objectives 191
Going International: Exporting 191
Going International: Importing 192
Market Expansion 192
Determining Secondary Information Requirements 193
Sources of Data 193
The International Marketplace 6.2: Secondary Data Sources in Europe 194
Evaluating Data 196
Analyzing and Interpreting Secondary Data 196
Data Privacy 197
The Primary Research Process 197
Determining Information Requirements 198
Industrial versus Consumer Research 198
Determining Research Administration 198
Determining the Research Technique 202
The International Marketplace 6.3: Adapting Research Procedures to
Local Conditions 203
Designing the Survey Questionnaire 205

Developing the Sampling Plan 207
Data Collection 208
Analyzing and Interpreting Primary Data 208
Presenting Research Results 208
Follow-Up and Review 208
Using Web Technology for Research 209
The International Information System 209
Environmental Scanning 210
Delphi Studies 211
Scenario Building 212
Summary 213
Key Terms 214
Questions for Discussion 214
Internet Exercises 214
Recommended Readings 214
Appendix A: Information Sources for Marketing Issues 215
Appendix B: The Structure of a Country Commercial Guide 221

Chapter 7   Exporting, Licensing, and Franchising 224

The International Marketplace 7.1: Tapping Global Markets through
E-Commerce 225
Motivations to Internationalize 226
Proactive Motivations 227
Reactive Motivations 228
Change Agents 230
Internal Change Agents 230
The International Marketplace 7.2: An Accidental Exporter 231
External Change Agents and Export Intermediaries 232
Export Intermediaries 233
International Stages 235
Licensing and Franchising 237
Licensing 237
Assessment of Licensing 237
The International Marketplace 7.3: International Franchising That Will Melt in
Your Mouth 238
Principal Issues in Negotiating Licensing Agreements 239
Trademark Licensing 239
Franchising 240
The Internationalization Process 242
Summary 244
Key Terms 245
Questions for Discussion 245
Internet Exercises 245
Recommended Readings 245

Chapter 8   Product Adaptation 246

The International Marketplace 8.1: Europeanizing Products 247
Product Variables 248
Standardization versus Adaptation 249
Factors Affecting Adaptation 252

The Market Environment 252
    Government Regulations 252
    Nontariff Barriers 254
    Customer Characteristics, Expectations, and Preferences 255
    Economic Development 258
    Competitive Offerings 259
    Climate and Geography 259
Product Characteristics 259
    Product Constituents 260
    Branding 260
    Packaging 261
The International Marketplace 8.2: When There Is More to a Name 262
    Appearance 263
    Method of Operation or Usage 264
    Quality 264
    Service 265
    Country-of-Origin Effects 265
Company Considerations 266
Product Counterfeiting 266
The International Marketplace 8.3: The Phantom Pirates 268
    Summary 270
    Key Terms 270
    Questions for Discussion 270
    Internet Exercises 271
    Recommended Readings 271

Chapter 9   **Export Pricing Strategies 272**
The International Marketplace 9.1: Adjusting to the Currency Squeeze 273
Price Dynamics 274
The Setting of Export Prices 276
    Export Pricing Strategy 277
    Export-Related Costs 278
Terms of Sale 281
The International Marketplace 9.2: Penetrating Foreign Markets by Controlling Export Transport 283
Terms of Payment 284
Getting Paid for Exports 289
The International Marketplace 9.3: Now for the Hard Part: Getting Paid for Exports 292
Managing Foreign Exchange Risk 292
Sources of Export Financing 296
    Commercial Banks 296
    Forfaiting and Factoring 297
    Official Trade Finance 298
Price Negotiations 299
Leasing 300
Dumping 300
    Summary 302
    Key Terms 302
    Questions for Discussion 302

Internet Exercises 302
Recommended Readings 303

Chapter 10   International Communications 304

The International Marketplace 10.1: The Art of Negotiation 305
The Marketing Communications Process 306
International Negotiations 308
Stages of the Negotiation Process 309
How to Negotiate in Other Countries 310
Marketing Communications Strategy 312
Communications Tools 316
Business/Trade Journals and Directories 316
Direct Marketing 318
Internet 320
Trade Shows and Missions 321
The International Marketplace 10.2: At the Fair 326
Personal Selling 326
The International Marketplace 10.3: Automating the Sales Force 329
Summary 330
Key Terms 330
Questions for Discussion 331
Internet Exercises 331
Recommended Readings 331

Chapter 11   Channels and Distribution Strategies 332

The International Marketplace 11.1: Getting the Distribution Job Done in
Latin America 333
Channel Structure 334
Channel Design 336
Customer Characteristics 336
Culture 337
Competition 339
Company Objectives 340
Character 341
Capital 341
Cost 342
Coverage 342
Control 343
Continuity 344
Communication 344
Selection of Intermediaries 345
Types of Intermediaries 345
Sources for Finding Intermediaries 346
Screening Intermediaries 350
The Distributor Agreement 353
Channel Management 355
Factors in Channel Management 355
Gray Markets 357
The International Marketplace 11.2: Country of Origin and Gray Markets 360
Termination of the Channel Relationship 361

E-Commerce 363

The International Marketplace 11.3: E-Commerce in Emerging Markets 365

    Summary 366

    Key Terms 366

    Questions for Discussion 367

    Internet Exercises 367

    Recommended Readings 367

Cases   Exports of Tobacco 368

Damar International 374

Water from Iceland 376

Joemarin Oy 381

The Gray Ferrari 386

Video Cases   Global Vendor Relations at Pier 1 Imports 389

Lakewood Chopsticks Exports 391

Part Three

Global Marketing Management

Chapter 12   **Global Strategic Planning 396**

The International Marketplace 12.1: Appliance Makers on a
Global Quest 397

Global Marketing 398

    Globalization Drivers 399

The International Marketplace 12.2: Born Global 401

The Strategic Planning Process 403

    Understanding and Adjusting the Core Strategy 403

    Formulating Global Marketing Strategy 405

    Global Marketing Program Development 412

    Implementing Global Marketing 414

The International Marketplace 12.3: Finding the Fit Overseas 416

    Summary 417

    Key Terms 418

    Questions for Discussion 418

    Internet Exercises 418

    Recommended Readings 418

Chapter 13   **Global Market Expansion 420**

The International Marketplace 13.1: Buying Domestic? Maybe Not 421

Foreign Direct Investment 421

Major Foreign Investors 422

    Reasons for Foreign Direct Investment 422

The International Marketplace 13.2: The Chinese World Factory 426

A Perspective on Foreign Direct Investors 427

    Types of Ownership 428

The International Marketplace 13.3: One Company Chooses Four Modes of
International Investment 429

Contractual Arrangements 434

Summary 435
Key Terms 436
Questions for Discussion 436
Internet Exercises 436
Recommended Readings 437

Chapter 14   Product and Brand Management 438

The International Marketplace 14.1: Anatomy of a Global Product Launch 439
Global Product Development 441
    The Product Development Process 442
    The Location of R&D Activities 445
The International Marketplace 14.2: Centers of Excellence 447
    The Organization of Global Product Development 448
    The Testing of New Product Concepts 449
    The Global Product Launch 450
Management of the Product and Brand Portfolio 451
    Analyzing the Product Portfolio 451
    Managing the Brand Portfolio 455
The International Marketplace 14.3: Development and Management of a
Global Brand 458
    Summary 462
    Key Terms 462
    Questions for Discussion 462
    Internet Exercises 463
    Recommended Readings 463

Chapter 15   Services Marketing 464

The International Marketplace 15.1: A Global Service: Free Access to
Medical Journals 465
Differences between Services and Goods 465
    Linkage between Services and Goods 467
    Stand-Alone Services 467
The Role of Services in the U.S. Economy 470
The Role of International Services in the World Economy 472
Global Transformation of Services 473
International Trade Problems in Services 474
    Data Collection Problems 474
    Regulation of Services Trade 475
Corporations and Involvement in International Services Marketing 476
    Typical International Services 476
The International Marketplace 15.2: A New Services Industry: Finding
Basketball Players 478
    Starting to Market Services Internationally 479
The International Marketplace 15.3: Accounting after Enron 480
    Strategic Implications of International Services Marketing 481
    Summary 482
    Key Terms 483
    Questions for Discussion 483
    Internet Exercises 483
    Recommended Readings 483

Chapter 16   Global Pricing Strategies 484

The International Marketplace 16.1: A Global Tax War? 485
Transfer Pricing 486
    Use of Transfer Prices to Achieve Corporate Objectives 487
    Transfer Pricing Challenges 488
Pricing within Individual Markets 491
    Corporate Objectives 491
    Costs 493
    Demand and Market Factors 494
The International Marketplace 16.2: Just Do It in a Recession! 494
    Market Structure and Competition 495
    Environmental Constraints 496
Pricing Coordination 496
The Euro and Marketing Strategy 497
The International Marketplace 16.3: Coordinating Prices in Integrating Markets 499
Countertrade 500
    Why Countertrade? 501
Types of Countertrade 502
Preparing for Countertrade 504
    Summary 506
    Key Terms 506
    Questions for Discussion 506
    Internet Exercises 506
    Recommended Readings 507

Chapter 17   Logistics and Supply Chain Management 508

The International Marketplace 17.1: How Does That HP Printer Get to Your Desk? 509
A Definition of International Logistics 509
Supply-Chain Management 511
The Impact of International Logistics 512
    The New Dimensions of International Logistics 513
International Transportation Issues 513
    Transportation Infrastructure 514
    Availability of Modes 514
The International Marketplace 17.2: Port Closure Hurts Production and Produce 515
    Choice of Modes 516
The International Shipment 521
    Documentation 521
    Assistance with International Shipments 523
International Inventory Issues 523
International Storage Issues 525
    Storage Facilities 525
    Foreign Trade Zones 526
International Packaging Issues 527
Management of International Logistics 529
    Centralized Logistics Management 529
    Decentralized Logistics Management 529
    Contract Logistics 530

The Supply Chain and the Internet 530
Logistics and Security 531
Reverse Logistics 532
The International Marketplace 17.3: Happy Returns 533
    Summary 533
    Key Terms 534
    Questions for Discussion 534
    Internet Exercises 534
    Recommended Readings 535

Chapter 18   Global Promotional Strategies 536

The International Marketplace 18.1: Being a Good Sport Globally 537
Planning Promotional Campaigns 538
    The Target Audience 538
    Campaign Objectives 540
    The Budget 540
    Media Strategy 541
The International Marketplace 18.2: The World Wants Its MTV! 547
    The Promotional Message 548
    The Campaign Approach 553
    Measurement of Advertising Effectiveness 558
Other Promotional Elements 558
    Personal Selling 558
    Sales Promotion 559
    Public Relations 562
    Sponsorship Marketing 564
The International Marketplace 18.3: Expanding the Social Vision: Global
    Community Relations 565
    Summary 566
    Key Terms 567
    Questions for Discussion 567
    Internet Exercises 567
    Recommended Readings 567

Chapter 19   Marketing Organization, Implementation, and
              Control 568

The International Marketplace 19.1: Procter & Gamble: Organization 2005 569
Organizational Structure 570
    Organizational Designs 571
Implementation 581
    Locus of Decision Making 581
    Factors Affecting Structure and Decision Making 582
    The Networked Global Organization 583
    Promoting Internal Cooperation 584
The International Marketplace 19.2: Characteristics of Success 587
    The Role of Country Organizations 588
Control 589
    Types of Controls 590
The International Marketplace 19.3: International Best Practice Exchange 591

Exercising Control 594
Summary 595
Key Terms 596
Questions for Discussion 596
Internet Exercises 596
Recommended Readings 596

Chapter 20   The Future 598

The International Marketplace 20.1: Marketing Overseas—Excellent for
  Career Advancement 599
The International Marketing Environment 600
  The Political Environment 600
The International Marketplace 20.2: The Future of East Asian Integration 603
  The International Financial Environment 603
  Population Patterns 604
The International Marketplace 20.3: Migration: A Double Blessing 605
  The Technological Environment 607
The Trade Framework 608
Governmental Policy 609
The Future of International Marketing Management 610
  International Planning and Research 612
  Product and Production Policy 613
  International Communications 616
  Distribution and Logistics Strategies 616
  International Pricing 617
Careers in International Marketing 618
  Further Training 618
  Employment with a Large Firm 618
  Employment with a Small or Medium-Sized Firm 623
  Self-Employment 623
  Opportunities for Women in Global Firms 623
  Summary 625
  Key Terms 625
  Questions for Discussion 625
  Internet Exercises 626
  Recommended Readings 626

Cases   Chupa Chups Vending: "Choose Your Flavor" 627
Nova Scotia 634
Customer Service Online: The HP DesignJet 639
The F-18 Hornet Offset 647
Kadimi Group of Companies (India): Exports 654
Parker Pen Company 659

Video Case   Whirlpool and the Global Appliance Industry 663

References
Glossary
Index

Part One

Chapter 1
The International Marketing
Imperative

Chapter 2
International Trade Institutions
and Trade Policy

Chapter 3
The Cultural Environment

Chapter 4
The Economic Environment

Chapter 5
The International Political and
Legal Environment

Cases

Video Case

INTERNATIONAL MARKETING

The International Environment

Part One introduces the international trade framework and environment. It highlights the need for international marketing activities and explains why the international market is an entirely new arena for a firm and its managers. The chapters devoted to macro-environmental factors explain the many forces to which a firm is exposed. The marketer must adapt to these foreign environments and adeptly resolve conflicts among political, cultural, and legal forces in order to be successful.

chapter 1

The International Marketing Imperative

THE INTERNATIONAL MARKETPLACE   1.1

The Two Sides of International Marketing

Today might be called the triumph of international marketing. There is proof that market economies are more efficient than planned economies. Governments all over the world are encouraging market-based activities. We are witnessing the abolition of state monopolies, the opening of national economies towards the world market, and the ongoing introduction and enforcement of rules to ensure competitive market conditions.

The fastest globalizing nations have enjoyed rates of economic growth up to 50 percent higher than those that have integrated into the world economy more slowly.[i] Linked to this growth, these same countries have also achieved relatively more gains in political freedom, and greater increases in life expectancy, literacy rates, and their overall standard of living.

Firms have benefited substantially from global marketing expansion. With wider market reach and many more customers, firms in the international market produce more and do so more efficiently than do their domestic-only counterparts. As a result, international firms simultaneously achieve lower costs and higher profits both at home and abroad. Market diversification and the stability arising from firms' lack of dependence on any particular market are other positive effects. Firms also learn from their competitors, and can recruit and develop the best talent from all over the world. The cumulative effect of all these dimensions is significant. Research has shown that firms of all sizes and in all industries engaged in international marketing outperformed their strictly domestic counterparts. They grow more than twice as fast in sales and earn significantly higher returns on equity and assets.[ii]

Workers also benefit from international marketing activities. International firms of all sizes pay significantly higher wages than domestic-only firms. Due to their greater profitability and longevity, workplace security is also substantially greater for employees working for international firms than for those working for local firms.[iii] Compelled by global media scrutiny, international firms have become greater practitioners of social responsibility—much to the benefit of their employees around the world. Never before have workers benefited to such a degree from benevolent rules implemented by corporations headquartered far away from their locale. For example, the global working conditions set by Nike for its subcontractors or by Kmart for its suppliers are unique in the annals of global commerce.

Consumers are the greatest beneficiaries of all. They are offered an unprecedented degree of product availability and choice. Furthermore, due to international competition, the prices of these products are usually low and offer a better quality and quantity of life to a broad spectrum of individuals. Rising incomes have assured leaps in purchasing power. For the first time in history, international goods and service availability have gone beyond the reach of the elite and have become, especially in emerging markets, a reasonable expectation for the majority of the population.

Yet, in spite of all these achievements, international marketing faces challenges. Many practitioners refuse to participate in the global market—judging either the market to be too dangerous or themselves too unprepared. This even applies to the most technologically advanced firms. For example, in the United States, most e-tailers do not accept orders from outside their home market, and more than 55 percent of U.S. web-merchants do not even ship to Canada. Similarly, most European firms on the Web do not encourage sales outside of Europe.

The "Battle of Seattle" and the subsequent confrontations in Washington, DC, Davos, Geneva, Quebec, and Genoa have alerted the world to the displeasure vocalized by a variety of groups. Populist messages have turned globalization into a derogatory term and are swaying the sentiments of the general public. For example, after the Seattle summit, a survey found 52 percent of the respondents sympathetic toward the protestors even though they may have been hard-pressed to explain their goals.[iv] Within the United States, many have come to believe that international marketing undermines U.S. labor and living standards. Outside of the United States, international marketing and its agents, the marketers, are derided as exploiters, destroyers, and Americanizers.

No wonder that many people are left confused, skeptical, and ill-informed, which may lead them to make poor decisions. Given that the public in general does not have a great deal of interest in international and trade matters, there is great need for an analysis of the transformational and uplifting capabilities of market forces.

SOURCE: Michael R. Czinkota and Ilkka Ronkainen, "An International Marketing Manifesto," *Journal of International Marketing,* Winter 2003.

REFERENCES:

[i]Global Business Policy Council, *Globalization Ledger* (Washington, DC: A. T. Kearney, 2000), Introduction.

[ii]Charles Taylor and Witold Henisz, *U.S. Manufacturers in the Global Market Place* (New York: The Conference Board, 1994), Report 1058.

[iii]J. David Richardson and Karin Rindal, *Why Exports Matter: More!* Washington, DC: The Institute for International Economics and the Manufacturing Institute, 1996.

[iv]*Business Week Online,* December 22, 1999.

Y OU ARE ABOUT TO BEGIN an exciting, important, and necessary task: the exploration of international marketing. International marketing is exciting because it combines the science and the art of business with many other disciplines. Economics, anthropology, cultural studies, geography, history, languages, jurisprudence, statistics, demographics, and many other fields combine to help you explore the global market. Different business environments will stimulate your intellectual curiosity, which will enable you to absorb and understand new phenomena. International marketing has been compared by many who have been active in the field to the task of mountain climbing: challenging, arduous, and exhilarating.

International marketing is important because the world has become globalized. Increasingly, we all are living up to the claim of the Greek philosopher Socrates, who stated, "I am a citizen, not of Athens or Greece, but of the world." International marketing takes place all around us every day, has a major effect on our lives, and offers new opportunities and challenges, as *The International Market-place 1.1* shows. After reading through this book and observing international marketing phenomena, you will see what happens, understand what happens, and, at some time in the future, perhaps even make it happen. All of this is much better than to stand by and wonder what happened.

International marketing is necessary because, from a national standpoint, economic isolationism has become impossible. Failure to participate in the global marketplace assures a nation of declining economic capability and its citizens of a decrease in their standard of living. Successful international marketing, however, holds the promise of an improved quality of life, a better society, more efficient business transactions, and, as some have stated, even a more peaceful world.

This chapter is designed to increase your awareness of what international marketing is all about. It describes the current levels of world trade activities, projects future developments, and discusses the resulting repercussion on countries, institutions, and individuals worldwide. Both the opportunities and the threats that spring from the global marketplace are highlighted, and the need for an international "marketing" approach on the part of individuals and institutions is emphasized.

This chapter ends with an explanation of the major organizational thrust of this book, which is a differentiation between the beginning internationalist and the multinational corporation. This theme ties the book together by taking into account the concerns, capabilities, and goals of firms that will differ widely based on their level of international expertise, resources, and involvement. The approach to international marketing taken here will therefore permit you to understand the entire range of international activities and allow you easily to transfer your acquired knowledge into practice.

What International Marketing Is

In brief, **international marketing** is the process of planning and conducting transactions across national borders to create exchanges that satisfy the objectives of individuals and organizations. International marketing has forms ranging from export-import trade to licensing, joint ventures, wholly owned subsidiaries, turnkey operations, and management contracts.

As this definition indicates, international marketing very much retains the basic marketing tenets of "satisfaction" and "exchange." International marketing is a tool used to obtain improvement of one's present position. The fact that a transaction takes place across national borders highlights the difference between domestic and international marketing. The international marketer is subject to a new set of macroenvironmental factors, to different constraints, and to quite frequent conflicts resulting from different laws, cultures, and societies. The basic principles of marketing still apply, but their applications, complexity, and intensity may vary substantially. It is in the international marketing field where one can observe most closely the role of marketing as a key agent of societal change and as a key instrument for the development of societally responsive business strategy. When we look, for example, at the emerging market economies of China and Russia, we can see the many new challenges confronting international marketing. How does the marketing concept fit into these societies? How can marketing contribute to economic development and the improvement of society? How should distribution systems be organized? How can we get the price mechanism to work? Similarly, in the international areas of social responsibility and ethics, the international marketer is faced with a multicultural environment with differing expectations and often inconsistent legal systems when it comes to monitoring environmental pollution, maintaining safe working conditions, copying technology or trademarks, or paying bribes.[1] In addition, the long-term repercussions of marketing actions need to be understood and evaluated in terms of their societal impact. These are just a few of the issues that the international marketer needs to address. The capability to master these challenges successfully affords a company the potential for new opportunities and high rewards.

The definition also focuses on international transactions. The use of the term recognizes that marketing internationally is an activity that needs to be pursued, often aggressively. Those who do not participate in the transactions are still exposed to international marketing and subject to its changing influences. The international marketer is part of the exchange, recognizes the changing nature of transactions, and adjusts to a constantly moving target subject to shifts in the business environment. This need for adjustment, for comprehending change, and, in spite of it all, for successfully carrying out transactions highlights the fact that international marketing is as much art as science.

To achieve success in the art of international marketing, it is necessary to be firmly grounded in its scientific aspects. Only then will individual consumers, policymakers, and business executives be able to incorporate international marketing considerations into their thinking and planning. Only then will they be able to consider international issues and repercussions and make decisions based on the answers to such questions as these:

➢ Should I obtain my supplies domestically or from abroad?
➢ What marketing adjustments are or will be necessary?
➢ What threats from global competition should I expect?
➢ How can I work with these threats to turn them into opportunities?
➢ What are my strategic global alternatives?

If all these issues are integrated into each decision made by individuals and by firms, international markets can become a source of growth, profit, needs satisfaction, and quality of life that would not have existed for them had they limited themselves to domestic activities. The purpose of this book is to aid in this decision process.

The Importance of World Trade

World trade has assumed an importance heretofore unknown to the global community. In past centuries, trade was conducted internationally but never before did it have the broad and simultaneous impact on nations, firms, and individuals that it has today. Within three decades, world trade has expanded from $200 billion to almost $7 trillion.[2] Such growth is unique, particularly since, as Figure 1.1 shows, trade growth on a global level has usually outperformed the growth of domestic economies in the past few decades. As a result, many countries and firms have found it highly desirable to become major participants in international marketing.

Figure 1.1 Growth of World Output and Trade, 1990–2003

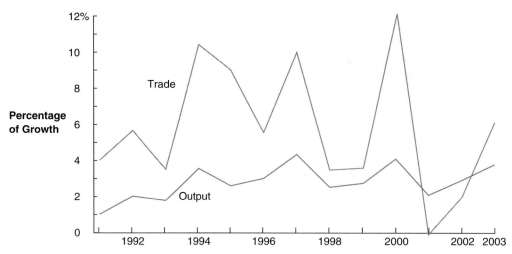

SOURCE: Compiled from World Economics Outlook, Statistical Appendix, Washington, DC: IMF, 2003, **http://www.imf.org** (accessed March 4, 2003).

The Iron Curtain has disintegrated, offering a vast array of new marketing opportunities—albeit amid uncertainty. Firms invest on a global scale, with the result that entire industries shift their locations. International specialization and cross-sourcing have made production much more efficient. New technologies have changed the way we do business, allowing us to both supply and receive products from across the world by using the Internet. As a result, consumers, union leaders, policymakers, and sometimes even the firms themselves are finding it increasingly difficult to define where a particular product was made. There are trading blocs such as the European Union in Europe, NAFTA in North America, Mercosur in Latin America, and ASEAN in Asia. These blocs encourage trade relations between their members, but, through their rules and standards, they also affect the trade and investment flows of nonmember countries.

Individuals and firms have come to recognize that they are competing not only domestically but also globally. World trade has given rise to global linkages of markets, technology, and living standards that were previously unknown and unanticipated. At the same time, it has deeply affected domestic policy-making and has often resulted in the emergence of totally new opportunities as well as threats to firms and individuals. *The International Marketplace 1.2* provides an example.

Global Linkages

World trade has forged a network of global linkages that bind us all—countries, institutions, and individuals—much more closely than ever before. These linkages were first widely recognized during the worldwide oil crisis of 1970, but they continue to increase. A drought in Brazil and its effect on coffee production and prices are felt around the world. The sudden decline of the Mexican peso reverberated throughout Poland, Hungary, and the Czech Republic. The "Asian meltdown" of the 1990s spawned uncertainty and affected businesses on every continent.[3] The Argentine financial crisis of 2002 not only instigated domestic economic hardships of historic proportions, but it also created a financial and political "domino" or, in this case, "tango effect," throughout Latin America and required major rescue actions by the International Monetary Fund (IMF).[4]

These linkages have also become more intense on an individual level. Communication has built new international bridges, be it through music or international programs transmitted by CNN. New products have attained international appeal

THE INTERNATIONAL MARKETPLACE 1.2

Some Thoughts on Basketball Competitiveness

It happens to every great superpower. Over time, complacency sets in, and the drive to innovate and the need to compete decline. The will to expand, renew, and improve seems unnecessary when one is on top, but these desires could not be more important. Eventually, most superpowers slip into this familiar trap of lethargy and decline.

On Wednesday, September 4, 2002, the U.S. basketball team had its 10-year, 58-game winning streak snapped by Argentina in the World Basketball Championship. The U.S. sports word fell into silence as the Dream Team realized its worst nightmare: defeat.

In every industry, competition is the key to success, and it seems the U.S. basketball team stopped competing. The reasons for defeat are complex, but not surprising, and the lesson the team learned can be applied not only to the world of international athletics but also to international business practices.

First, the Dream Team of 2002 was composed of players who could more aptly be called the "Second String Team." It should be no surprise that an organization that is unwilling or unable to send its best players into competition is leaving itself vulnerable to competing powers. Argentina sent the cream of its athletic crop, including half a dozen athletes who play or have played in the NBA.

Second, it is in this instance that the concerns surrounding the spillover of talent, knowledge, and recourses become apparent. Companies in Silicon Valley often face this common dilemma. Once sent overseas, U.S. technological products lose a fraction of the market to overseas domestic producers who decide to generate new technology themselves. The will to compete is natural and encouraged, but the reigning superpower must be prepared to protect its position when rivals begin to catch up. The basketball gap is closing and the rest of the world is adjusting. All competitors, particularly the leader, need to adjust along with the rest of the world.

A third reason for the U.S. defeat is the team's lack of preparation (they practiced as a team for only ten days before the competition). Their rivals had spent years practicing together as a coherent team. In terms of practice alone, the rest of the world has the United States' raw powerhouses beat.

"The simple fact is international teams are getting better. That's it. The bottom line is they're not in awe of us anymore," said former NBA all-star Charles Barkley, a member of the original Dream Team, the first Olympic team to use mainly NBA players.

The key to staying ahead of rising competition: preparation.

Just as U.S. basketball must constantly innovate, recruit better players, and practice harder, international companies must constantly innovate, increase efficiency, and strive to reach markets better and to create relevant products. In both sports and business, competitors must find a way to stay in the game, or they will be forced to leave the competition.

The United States has the most developed and successful professional basketball league in the world, recruiting from around the world for talent and fans alike. With the NBA as a ready source of talent, the United States has the competitive advantage to stay on top of international basketball. But if the World Championship game against Argentina is an indication of its competitive attitude, even raw talent will not be able to save the NBA from the laws of international competition.

SOURCES: Michael Wilbon, "Basketball's New World Order," *The Washington Post*, September 6, 2002, D01; and Steve Wyche, "Team USA Adjust to World Revolution: Embarrassment, 2 Losses, No Medal," *The Washington Post*, September 6, 2002, D, D-4.

and encouraged similar activities around the world—where many of us wear jeans, dance to the same music, and eat kebobs, curry, and sushi. Transportation linkages let individuals from different countries see and meet each other with unprecedented ease. Common cultural pressures result in similar social phenomena and behavior—for example, more dual-income families are emerging around the world, which leads to more frequent, but also more stressful, shopping.[5]

World trade is also bringing about a global reorientation of corporate processes, which opens up entirely new horizons. Never before has it been so easy to gather, manipulate, analyze, and disseminate information—but never before has the pressure been so great to do so. Ongoing global technological innovation in marketing has direct effects on the efficiency and effectiveness of all business activities. Products can be produced more quickly, obtained less expensively from sources around the world, distributed at lower cost, and customized to meet diverse clients' needs. As an example, only a decade ago, it would have been thought impossible for a firm to produce parts for a car in more than one country, assemble the car in yet another country, and sell it in still other nations. Today, such global investment strategies coupled with production and distribution sharing are becoming a matter of routine. Of course, as *The International Marketplace 1.2* explains, these changes increase the level of global competition, which in turn makes it an ongoing effort if one wants to stay in a leadership position.

Advances in technology also allow firms to separate their activities by content and context. Firms can operate in a "market space" rather than a marketplace[6] by keeping the content while changing the context of a transaction. For example, a newspaper can now be distributed globally online rather than house-to-house on paper, thereby allowing outreach to entirely new customer groups.

The level of global investment is at an unprecedented high. The shifts in financial flows have had major effects. They resulted in the buildup of international debt by governments, affected the international value of currencies, provided foreign capital for firms, and triggered major foreign direct-investment activities. For example, well over one-third of the workers in the U.S. chemical industry toil for foreign owners. Many of the office buildings Americans work in are owned by foreign landlords. The opening of plants can take the place of trade. All these developments make us more and more dependent on one another.

This interdependence, however, is not stable. On almost a daily basis, realignments taking place on both micro and macro levels make past trade orientations at least partially obsolete. For example, for the first 200 years of its history, the United States looked to Europe for markets and sources of supply. Today, U.S. two-way trade with Asia far outpaces U.S. trade with Europe.

Not only is the environment changing, but the pace of change is accelerating as well. Atari's Pong was first introduced in the early 1980s; today, action games and movies are made with computerized humans. The first office computers emerged in the mid-1980s; today, home computers have become commonplace. E-mail was introduced to a mass market only in the 1990s; today, many college students hardly ever send personal notes using a stamp and envelope.[7]

These changes and the speed with which they come about significantly affect countries, corporations, and individuals. One change is the role participants play. For example, the United States accounted for nearly 25 percent of world merchandise exports in the 1950s, but by 2001, this share had declined to less than 13 percent. Also, the way countries participate in world trade is shifting. In the past two decades the role of primary commodities in international trade has dropped precipitously, while the importance of manufactured goods has increased. The increase in the volume of services trade has been even higher. In a few decades, international services went from being a nonmeasured activity to a global volume of more than $1.4 trillion in 2000.[8] Figure 1.2 shows how substantial the growth rates for both merchandise and services trade have been. Most important, the growth in the overall volume and value of both merchandise and services trade has had a major impact on firms, countries, and individuals.

Domestic Policy Repercussions

The effects of closer global linkages on the economics of countries have been dramatic. Policymakers have increasingly come to recognize that it is very difficult to isolate domestic economic activity from international market events. Decisions that once were clearly in the domestic purview have now become subject to revision by influences from abroad, and domestic policy measures are often canceled out or counteracted by the activities of global market forces.

A lowering of interest rates domestically may make consumers happy or may be politically wise, but it quickly becomes unsustainable if it results in a major outflow of funds to countries that offer higher interest rates. Agricultural and farm policies, which historically have been strictly domestic issues, are suddenly thrust into the international realm. Any policy consideration must now be seen in light of international repercussions due to influences from global trade and investment.

| Figure 1.2 | The Changing Face of Exporting |

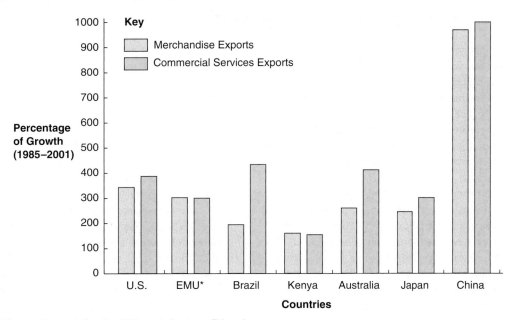

*EMU = EU (minus Denmark, Sweden, UK), excluding intra-EU trade.

SOURCE: Based on statistics from World Bank's 2002 *World Development Indicators*, Washington, D.C., 2002, **http://www.worldbank.org**, accessed September 18, 2002.

The following examples highlight some of these influences in the relationship between the European Union and the United States:

> Over the past decade, the U.S.–EU trade relationship in goods has more than doubled, to approach $400 billion in 2002. A few statistics show its size and diversity: Each month, over 100,000 computer hard drives, $450 million worth of pharmaceuticals, 10 million kilos of California almonds, and $100 million worth of paintings leave the United States to arrive in London, Antwerp, Dublin, Lisbon, Milan, Oslo, or Helsinki; the United States in turn imports $230 million in semiconductors, a million clocks, 70 million tulip bulbs from the Netherlands, 3 million liters of French champagne, 70,000 German cars, and 2,600 German violins.[9]

To some extent, the economic world as we knew it has been turned upside down. For example, trade flows traditionally have been used to determine currency flows and therefore the level of the exchange rate. In the more recent past, **currency flows** took on a life of their own. Independent of trade, they set exchange rates, which are the values of currencies relative to each other. These **exchange rates** in turn have now begun to determine the level of trade. Governments that wish to counteract these developments with monetary policies find that currency flows outnumber trade flows by 100 to 1. Also, private-sector financial flows vastly outnumber the financial flows that can be marshaled by governments, even when acting in concert. Similarly, constant rapid technological change and vast advances in communication permit firms and countries to quickly emulate innovation and counteract carefully designed plans. As a result, governments are often powerless to implement effective policy measures, even when they know what to do.

Policymakers therefore find themselves with increasing responsibilities yet with fewer and less effective tools to carry out these responsibilities. At the same time that more parts of a domestic economy are vulnerable to international shifts and changes, these parts are becoming less controllable. The global market imposes increasingly tight limits on national economic regulation and sovereignty.

THE INTERNATIONAL MARKETPLACE 1.3

International Marketing: Bringing Peace, Fighting Terrorism

One really big surprise of the postwar era has been that historic enemies, such as Germany and France or Japan and the United States, have not had the remotest threat of war between themselves since 1945. Why should they? Anything Japan has that we want, we can buy, and on very easy credit terms, so why fight for it? Why should the Japanese fight the United States and lose all those profitable markets? France and Germany, linked intimately through marketing and the European Union, are now each other's largest trading partners.

Closed systems build huge armies and waste their resources on guns and troops; open countries spend their money on new machines to crank out Barbie dolls or some such trivia. Their bright young people figure out how to run the machines, not how to fire the latest missile. For some reason, they not only get rich fast but also lose interest in military adventures. Japan, that peculiar superpower without superguns, confounds everyone simply because no one has ever seen a major world power that got that way by selling you to death, not shooting you to death.

More recently, political leaders are enlisting international marketing as a key tool in the war against ter-rorism. U.S. trade agreements with Vietnam, Jordan, and Russia and the slashing of tariffs on Pakistani textiles by the European Union showcase the might of international marketing. The expansion of trade creates jobs, improves health and education standards, and raises overall stan-dards of living to impoverished regions—all of which bring a new sense of hope which turns aside the false appeal of terrorism.

Yet, as Harvard economist Jeffery Sachs asserts, much more effort is required from the international commu-nity. Trade-based progress towards global wealth must include extensive health-care and environmental aid, massive debt write-offs, and substantial tariff and quota reductions for steel, textile, and agricultural exports from impoverished regions.

Yet, no matter what the political environment, whether it be yesterday's post–World War II era or today's War on Terrorism, if you trade a lot with someone, why fight?

SOURCES: Adapted from Richard N. Farmer, "Would You Want Your Granddaughter to Marry a Taiwanese Marketing Man?" *Journal of Market-ing* 51 (October 1987): 114–115; and "Trade Craft Is Employed on War's Economic Front," *The Wall Street Journal*, October 29, 2001, A1.

To regain some of their power to influence events, policymakers have sought to restrict the impact of global trade and financial flows by erecting barriers, charg-ing tariffs, designing quotas, and implementing other import regulations. How-ever, these measures too have been restrained by international agreements that regulate trade restrictions, particularly through the World Trade Organization (WTO) (**http://www.wto.org**). Global trade has therefore changed many previously held notions about nation-state sovereignty and extraterritoriality. The same inter-dependence that has made us more affluent has also left us more vulnerable. Be-cause this vulnerability is spread out over all major trading nations, however, some have credited international marketing with being a pillar of international peace, as *The International Marketplace 1.3* shows. Clearly, closer economic relations can result in many positive effects. At the same time, however, interdependence brings with it risks, such as dislocations of people and economic resources and a decrease in a nation's capability to do things its own way. Given the ease—and sometimes the desirability—of blaming a foreign rather than a domestic culprit for economic failure, it may well also be a key task for the international marketer to stimulate societal thinking about the long-term benefits of interdependence.

Opportunities and Challenges in International Marketing

To prosper in a world of abrupt changes and discontinuities, of newly emerging forces and dangers, of unforeseen influences from abroad, firms need to prepare themselves and develop active responses. New strategies need to be envisioned, new plans need to be made, and the way of doing business needs to be changed.

The way to obtain and retain leadership, economically, politically, or morally, is—as the examples of Rome, Constantinople, and London have amply demonstrated—not through passivity but rather through a continuous, alert adaptation to the changing world environment. To help a country remain a player in the world economy, governments, firms, and individuals need to respond aggressively with innovation, process improvements, and creativity.[10]

The growth of global business activities offers increased opportunities. International activities can be crucial to a firm's survival and growth. By transferring knowledge around the globe, an international firm can build and strengthen its competitive position. Firms that heavily depend on long production runs can expand their activities far beyond their domestic markets and benefit from reaching many more customers. Market saturation can be avoided by lengthening or rejuvenating product life cycles in other countries. Production sites once were inflexible, but now plants can be shifted from one country to another and suppliers can be found on every continent. Cooperative agreements can be formed that enable all parties to bring their major strengths to the table and emerge with better products, services, and ideas than they could produce on their own. In addition, research has found that multinational corporations face a lower risk of insolvency and pay higher wages than do domestic companies.[11] At the same time, international marketing enables consumers all over the world to find greater varieties of products at lower prices and to improve their lifestyles and comfort.

International opportunities require careful exploration. What is needed is an awareness of global developments, an understanding of their meaning, and a development of capabilities to adjust to change. Firms must adapt to the international market if they are to be successful.

One key facet of the marketing concept is adaptation to the environment, particularly the market. Even though many executives understand the need for such an adaptation in their domestic market, they often believe that international customers are just like the ones the firm deals with at home. It is here that many firms commit grave mistakes which lead to inefficiency, lack of consumer acceptance, and sometimes even corporate failure.

Firms increasingly understand that many of the key difficulties encountered in doing business internationally are marketing problems. Judging by corporate needs, a background in international marketing is highly desirable for business students seeking employment, not only for today but also for long-term career plans.

Many firms do not participate in the global market. Often, managers believe that international marketing should only be carried out by large multinational corporations. It is true that there are some very large players from many countries active in the world market. But smaller firms are major players, too. For example, 50 percent of German exports are created by firms with 19 or fewer employees.[12] Nearly 97 percent of U.S. exporters are small and medium-sized enterprises.[13] Increasingly we find smaller firms, particularly in the computer and telecommunications industries, that are born global, since they achieve a worldwide presence within a very short time.[14]

Those firms and industries that are not participating in the world market have to recognize that in today's trade environment, isolation has become impossible. Willing or unwilling, firms are becoming participants in global business affairs. Even if not by choice, most firms and individuals are affected directly or indirectly by economic and political developments that occur in the international marketplace. Those firms that refuse to participate are relegated to react to the global marketplace and therefore are unprepared for harsh competition from abroad.

Some industries have recognized the need for international adjustments. Farmers understand the need for high productivity in light of stiff international competition. Car producers, computer makers, and firms in other technologically advanced industries have learned to forge global relationships to stay in the race. Firms in the steel, textile, and leather sectors have shifted production, and perhaps even adjusted their core business, in response to overwhelming onslaughts from abroad.

International Trade as a Percentage of Gross Domestic Product

Total Gross Domestic Product by Region
(in millions of U.S. $)

United States

$10,445,600*

Western Europe

$8,137,318

Japan

$4,841,584

East Asia and Pacific

$2,059,100

Latin America and Caribbean

$2,000,500

China and India

$1,536,938

Eastern Europe and Central Asia

$942,100

Canada

$687,882

Middle East and North Africa

$659,700

South Asia

$596,800

Sub-Saharan Africa

$322,700

*http://www.bea.doc.gov (accessed March 3, 2003).

SOURCE: Based on *The Little Data Book 2002*, The World Bank.

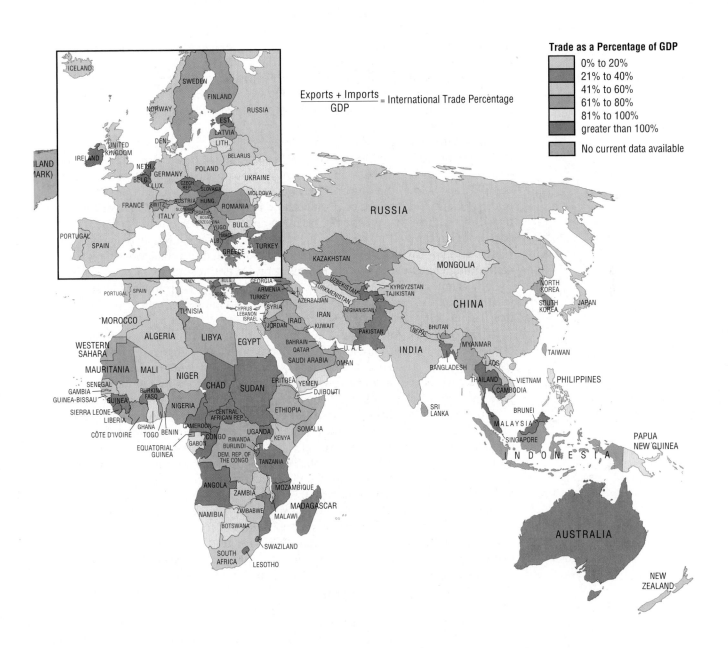

Trade as a Percentage of GDP

- 0% to 20%
- 21% to 40%
- 41% to 60%
- 61% to 80%
- 81% to 100%
- greater than 100%

No current data available

$$\frac{Exports + Imports}{GDP} = International\ Trade\ Percentage$$

Other industries in some countries have been caught unaware and have been unable to adjust. The result is the extinction of firms or entire industries such as VCRs in the United States and coal mining and steel smelting in other countries.

The Goals of This Book

This book aims to make you a better, more successful participant in the international marketplace by providing information about what is going on in international markets and by helping you to translate knowledge into successful business transactions. By learning about both theory and practice, you can obtain a good conceptual understanding of the field of international marketing as well as become firmly grounded in the realities of the global marketplace. Therefore, this book approaches international marketing in the way the manager of a firm does, reflecting different levels of international involvement and the importance of business–government relations.

Firms differ widely in their international activities and needs, depending on their level of experience, resources, and capabilities. For the firm that is just beginning to enter the global market, the level of knowledge about international complexities is low, the demand on time is high, expectations about success are uncertain, and the international environment is often inflexible. Conversely, for a multinational firm that is globally oriented and employs thousands of people on each continent, much more leeway exists in terms of resource availability, experience, and information. In addition, the multinational firm has the option of responding creatively to the environment by shifting resources or even shaping the environment itself. For example, the heads of large corporations have access to government ministers to plead their case for a change in policy, an alternative that is rarely afforded to smaller firms.

To become a large international corporation, however, a firm usually has to start out small. Similarly, to direct far-flung global operations, managers first have to learn the basics. The structure of this text reflects this reality by presenting initially a perspective of the business environment, which covers national marketing and policy issues and their cultural, economic, financial, political, and legal dimensions.

Subsequently, the book discusses in detail the beginning internationalization of the firm. The emphasis is on the needs of those who are starting out and the operational questions that are crucial to success. Some basic yet essential issues addressed are: What is the difference between domestic and international marketing? Does the applicability of marketing principles change when they are transferred to the global environment? How do marketers find out whether there is a market for a product abroad without spending a fortune in time and money on research? How can the firm promote its products in foreign markets? How do marketers find and evaluate a foreign distributor, and how do they make sure that their firm gets paid? How can marketers minimize government red tape yet take advantage of any governmental programs that are of use to them?

These questions are addressed both conceptually and empirically, with a strong focus on export and import operations. We will see how the international commitment is developed and strengthened within the firm.

Once these important dimensions have been covered, we make the transition to the multinational corporation. The focus is now on the transnational allocation of resources, the coordination of multinational marketing activities, and the attainment of global synergism. Finally, emerging issues of challenge to both policymakers and multinational firms, such as countertrade, marketing to economies in transition, and the future outlook of the global market, are discussed.

All the marketing issues are considered in relation to national policies so as to familiarize you with the divergent forces at play in the global market. Governments' increased awareness of and involvement with international marketing require managers to be aware of the role of governments and also to be able to work with them in order to attain marketing goals. Therefore, the continued references in the text to business–government interaction demonstrate a vital link in the development of international marketing strategy. In addition, we give full play to the increased ability of firms to communicate with a global market. Therefore, we develop and offer, for firms both small and large, our ideas and strategies for viable participation in electronic commerce.

We expect that this gradual approach to international marketing will permit you not only to master another academic subject, but also to become well versed in both the operational and the strategic aspects of the field. The result should be a better understanding of how the global market works and the capability to participate in the international marketing imperative.

Summary

Over the past three decades, world trade has expanded from $200 billion to almost $7.6 trillion. As a result, nations are much more affected by international business than in the past. Global linkages have made possible investment strategies and marketing alternatives that offer tremendous opportunities. Yet these changes and the speed of change also can represent threats to nations and firms.

On the policy front, decision makers have come to realize that it is very difficult to isolate domestic economic activity from international market events. Factors such as currency exchange rates, financial flows, and foreign economic actions increasingly render the policymaker powerless to implement a domestic agenda. International interdependence, which has contributed to greater affluence, has also increased our vulnerability.

Both firms and individuals are greatly affected by international trade. Whether willing or not, they are participating in global business affairs. Entire industries have been threatened in their survival as a result of international trade flows and have either adjusted to new market realities or left the market. Some individuals have lost their workplace and experienced reduced salaries. At the same time, global business changes have increased the opportunities available. Firms can now reach many more customers, product life cycles have been lengthened, sourcing policies have become variable, new jobs have been created, and consumers all over the world can find greater varieties of products at lower prices.

To benefit from the opportunities and deal with the adversities of international trade, business needs to adopt the international marketing concept. The new set of macroenvironmental factors has to be understood and responded to in order to let international markets become a source of growth, profit, and needs satisfaction.

Key Terms

international marketing
currency flows
exchange rates

Questions for Discussion

1. Will expansion of world trade in the future be similar to that in the past?
2. Does increased world trade mean increased risk?
3. Is it beneficial for nations to become dependent on one another?
4. Why do more firms from other countries enter international markets than do U.S. firms?
5. Can you think of examples of international marketing contributing to world peace?
6. Describe some opportunities and challenges in international marketing created by new advances in information technology.

Internet Exercises

1. Using World Trade Organization data (**http://www.wto.org**), identify the following: (a) the top ten exporting and importing countries in world merchandise trade and (b) the top ten exporting and importing countries of commercial services.

2. Find the ten largest multinational corporations and briefly explain their key products. Hint: You may wish to use the Web sites of publications such as *Forbes, Fortune,* and *Wirtschaftswoche.*

Appendix A
Basics of Marketing

This appendix provides a summary of the basic concepts in marketing for the reader who wishes to review them before applying them to international marketing.

The American Marketing Association defines *marketing* as "the process of planning and executing the conception, pricing, promotion, and distribution of ideas, goods, and services to create exchanges that satisfy individual and organizational goals."[1] The concepts of satisfaction and exchange are at the core of marketing. For an exchange to take place, two or more parties must come together in person, through the mail, or through technology, and they must communicate and deliver things of perceived value. Potential customers should be perceived as information seekers who evaluate marketers' efforts in terms of their own drives and needs. When the offering is consistent with their needs, they tend to choose the product; if it is not, they choose other alternatives. A key task of the marketer is to recognize the ever-changing nature of needs and wants. Increasingly, the goal of marketing has been expanded from sensing, serving, and satisfying individual customers to taking into consideration the long-term interests of society.

Marketing is not limited to business entities but involves governmental and nonbusiness units as well. Marketing techniques are applied not only to goods but also to ideas (for example, the "Made in the U.S.A." campaign) and to services (for example, international advertising agencies). The term *business marketing* is used for activities directed at other businesses, governmental entities, and various types of institutions. Business marketing accounts for well over 50 percent of all marketing activities.

Strategic Marketing

The marketing manager's task is to plan and execute programs that will ensure a long-term competitive advantage for the company. This task has two integral parts: (1) the determining of specific target markets and (2) marketing management, which consists of manipulating marketing mix elements to best satisfy the needs of individual target markets.

Target Market Selection
Characteristics of intended target markets are of critical importance to the marketer. These characteristics can be summarized by eight Os: occupants, objects, occasions, objectives, outlets, organization, operations, and opposition.[2]

Occupants are targets of the marketing effort. The marketer must determine which customers to approach and also define them along numerous dimensions, such as demographics (age, sex, and nationality, for example), geography (country or region), psychographics (attitudes, interests, and opinions), or product-related variables (usage rate and brand loyalty, for example). Included in this analysis must be the major influences on the occupants during their buying processes.

Objects are what is being bought at present to satisfy a particular need. Included in this concept are physical objects, services, ideas, organizations, places, and persons.

Occasions are moments when members of the target market buy the product or service. This characteristic is important to the marketer because a product's consumption may be tied to a particular time period—for example, imported beer and a festival.

Objectives are the motivations behind the purchase or adoption of the marketed concept. A computer manufacturer markets not hardware but solutions to problems. Additionally, many customers look for hidden value in the product they purchase, which may be expressed, for example, through national origin of the product or through brand name.

Outlets are places where customers expect to be able to procure a product or to be exposed to messages about it. Outlets include not only the entities themselves but also location within a particular place. Although aseptic packaging made it possible to shelve milk outside the refrigerated area in supermarkets, customers' acceptance of the arrangement was not automatic: the product was not where it was supposed to be. In the area of services, outlet involves (1) making a particular service available and communicating its availability and (2) selecting the particular types of facilitators (such as brokers) who bring the parties together.

Organization describes how the buying or acceptance of a (new) idea takes place. Organization expands the analysis beyond the individual consumer to the decision-making unit (DMU). The DMU varies in terms of its size and its nature from relatively small and informal groups like a family to large groups (more than ten people) to formal buying committees. Compare, for example, the differences between a family buying a new home-entertainment center and the governing board at a university deciding which architectural firm to use. In either case, to develop proper products and services, the marketer should know as much as possible about the decision-making processes and the roles of various individuals.

Operations represent the behavior of the organization buying products and services. Increasingly, industrial organizations are concentrating their purchases with fewer suppliers and making longer-term commitments. Supermarkets may make available only the leading brands in a product category, thereby complicating the marketer's attempts to place new products in these outlets.

Opposition refers to the competition to be faced in the marketplace. The nature of competition will vary from direct product-type competition to competition from other products that satisfy the same need. For example, Prince tennis rackets face a threat not only from other racket manufacturers but also from any company that provides a product or service for leisure-time use. Competitive situations will vary from one market and from one segment to the next. Gillette is number one in the U.S. market for disposable razors, with Bic a distant runner-up; however, elsewhere, particularly in Europe, the roles are reversed. In the long term, threats may come from outside the industry in which the marketer operates. As an example, digital watches originated in the electronics industry rather than the watch industry.

Analyzing the eight Os, and keeping in mind other uncontrollable factors in the environment (cultural, political, legal, technological, societal, and economic), the marketer must select the markets to which efforts will be targeted. In the short term, the marketer has to adjust to these environmental forces; in the long term, they can be manipulated to some extent by judicious marketing activity. Consumerism, one of the major forces shaping marketing activities, is concerned with protecting the consumer whenever an exchange relationship exists with any type of organization. Manifestations of the impact of consumerism on marketing exist in labeling, product specifications, promotional campaigns, recycling expectations, and demands for environmentally friendly products.

Because every marketer operates in a corporate environment of scarcity and comparative strengths, the target market decision is a crucial one. In some cases, the marketer may select only one segment of the market (for example, motorcycles of +1,000 cc) or multiple segments (for example, all types of motorized two-wheeled vehicles), or the firm may opt for an undifferentiated product that is to be mass-marketed (for example, unbranded commodities or products that satisfy the same need worldwide, such as Coca-Cola).

Marketing Management

The marketing manager, having analyzed the characteristics of the target market(s), is in a position to specify the mix of marketing variables that will best serve each target market. The variables the marketing manager controls are known as the elements of the marketing mix, or the four Ps: product, price, place, and promotion.[3] Each consists of a submix of variables, and policy decisions must be made on each.

Product policy is concerned with all the elements that make up the good, service, or idea that is offered by the marketer. Included are all possible tangible characteristics (such as the core product and packaging) and intangible characteristics (such as branding and warranties). Many products are a combination of a concrete product and the accompanying service; for example, in buying an Otis elevator, the purchaser buys not only the product but an extensive service contract as well.

Pricing policy determines the cost of the product to the customer—a point somewhere between the floor created by the costs to the firm and the ceiling created by the strength of demand. An important consideration of pricing policy is pricing within the channel of distribution; margins to be made by the middlemen who assist in the marketing effort must be taken into account. Discounts to middlemen include functional, quantity, seasonal, and cash discounts, as well as promotional allowances. An important point to remember is that **price** is the only revenue-generating element of the marketing mix.

Distribution policy covers the **place** variable of the marketing mix and has two components: channel management and logistics management. Channel management is concerned with the entire process of setting up and operating the contractual organization, consisting of various types of middlemen (such as wholesalers, agents, retailers, and facilitators). Logistics management is focused on providing product availability at appropriate times and places in the marketing channel.[4] Place is the most long term of all the marketing mix elements; it is the most difficult to change in the short term.

Communications policy uses **promotion tools** to interact with customers, middlemen, and the public at large. The communications element consists of these tools: advertising, sales promotion, personal selling, and publicity. Because the purpose of all communications is to persuade, this is the most visible and sensitive of the marketing mix elements.

Blending the various elements into a coherent program requires trade-offs based on the type of product or service being offered (for example, detergents versus fighter aircraft), the stage of the product's life cycle (a new product versus one that is being revived), and resources available for the marketing effort (money and personnel), as well as the type of customer at whom the marketing efforts are directed.

The Marketing Process

The actual process of marketing consists of four stages: analysis, planning, implementation, and control.

Analysis begins with collecting data on the eight Os and using various quantitative and qualitative techniques of marketing research. Data sources will vary from secondary to primary, internal to external (to the company), and informal to formal. The data are used to determine company opportunities by screening a plethora of environmental opportunities. The company opportunities must then be checked against the company's resources to judge their viability. The key criterion is competitive advantage.

Planning refers to the blueprint generated to react to and exploit the opportunities in the marketplace. The planning stage involves both long-term strategies and short-term tactics. A marketing plan developed for a particular market includes a situation analysis, objectives and goals to be met, strategies and tactics, and cost and profit estimates. Included in the activity is the formation of a new organizational structure or adjustments in the existing one to prepare for the execution of the plan.

Implementation is the actual carrying out of the planned activity. If the plans drawn reflect market conditions, and if they are based on realistic assessments of the company's fit into the market, the implementation process will be a success. Plans must take into account unforeseeable changes within the company and environmental forces and allow for corresponding changes to occur in implementing the plans.

For this reason, concurrently with implementation, **control mechanisms** must be put into effect. The marketplace is ever dynamic and requires the monitoring of environmental forces, competitors, channel participants, and customer receptiveness. Short-term control tools include annual plan control (such as comparing actual sales to quota), profitability control, and efficiency control. Long-term control is achieved through comprehensive or functional audits to make sure that marketing not only is doing things right but is doing the right things. The results of the control effort provide valuable input for subsequent planning efforts.

These marketing basics do not vary, regardless of the type of market one is planning to enter or to continue operating within. They have been called the "technical universals" of marketing.[5] The different environments in which the marketing manager must operate will give varying emphases to the variables and will cause the values of the variables to change.

Key Terms

product policy	analysis
price	planning
place	implementation
promotion tools	control mechanisms

Geographical Perspectives on International Marketing

The globalization of business has made geography indispensable for the study of international marketing. Without significant attention to the study of geography, critical ideas and information about the world in which business occurs will be missing.

Just as the study of business has changed significantly in recent decades, so has the study of geography. Once considered by many to be simply a descriptive inventory that filled in blank spots on maps, geography has emerged as an analytical approach that uses scientific methods to answer important questions.

Geography focuses on answering "Where?" questions. Where are things located? What is their distribution across the surface of the earth? An old aphorism holds, "If you can map it, it's geography." That statement is true, because we use maps to gather, store, analyze, and present information that answers "Where?" questions. Identifying where things are located is only the first phase of geographic inquiry. Once locations have been determined, "Why?" and "How?" questions can be asked. Why are things located where they are? How do different things relate to one another at a specific place? How do different places relate to each other? How have geographic patterns and relationships changed over time? These are the questions that take geography beyond mere description and make it a powerful approach for analyzing and explaining geographical aspects of a wide range of different kinds of problems faced by those engaged in international marketing.

Geography answers questions related to the location of different kinds of economic activity and the transactions that flow across national boundaries. It provides insights into the natural and human factors that influence patterns of production and consumption in different parts of the world. It explains why patterns of trade and exchange evolve over time. And because a geographic perspective emphasizes the analysis of processes that result in different geographic patterns, it provides a means for assessing how patterns might change in the future.

NOTE: This appendix was contributed by Thomas J. Baerwald. Dr. Baerwald is deputy assistant director for the geosciences at the National Science Foundation in Arlington, Virginia. He is coauthor of *Prentice-Hall World Geography*—a best-selling geography textbook.

SOURCES: Darrell Delamaide, *The New Superregions of Europe* (New York: Dutton, 1994); Joel Garreau, *The Nine Nations of North America* (New York: Houghton Mifflin Co., 1981).

Geography has a rich tradition. Classical Greeks, medieval Arabs, enlightened European explorers, and twentieth-century scholars in the United States and elsewhere have organized geographic knowledge in many different ways. In recent decades, however, geography has become more familiar and more relevant to many people because emphasis has been placed on five fundamental themes as ways to structure geographic questions and to provide answers for those questions. Those themes are (1) location, (2) place, (3) interaction, (4) movement, and (5) region. The five themes are neither exclusive nor exhaustive. They complement other disciplinary approaches for organizing information, some of which are better suited to addressing specific kinds of questions. Other questions require insights related to two or more of the themes. Experience has shown, however, that the five themes provide a powerful means for introducing students to the geographic perspective. As a result, they provide the structure for this discussion.

Location

For decades, people engaged in real estate development have said that the value of a place is a product of three factors: location, location, and location. This statement also highlights the importance of location for international marketing. Learning the location and characteristics of other places has always been important to those interested in conducting business outside their local areas. The drive to learn about other kinds of places, and especially their resources and potential as markets, has stimulated geographic exploration throughout history. Explorations of the Mediterranean by the Phoenicians, Marco Polo's journey to China, and voyages undertaken by Christopher Columbus, Vasco da Gama, Henry Hudson, and James Cook not only improved general knowledge of the world but also expanded business opportunities.

Assessing the role of location requires more than simply determining specific locations where certain activities take place. Latitude and longitude often are used to fix the exact location of features on the earth's surface, but to simply describe a place's coordinates provides relatively little information about that place. Of much greater significance is its location relative to other features. The city of Singapore, for example, is between 1 and 2 degrees North latitude and is just west of 104 degrees East longitude. Its most pertinent locational characteristics, however, include its being at the southern tip of the Malay Peninsula near the eastern end of the Strait of Malacca, a critical shipping route connecting the Indian Ocean with the South China Sea. For nearly 150 years, this location made Singapore an important center for trade in the British Empire. After it attained independence in 1965, Singapore's leaders diversified its economy and complemented trade in its bustling port with numerous manufacturing plants that export products to nations around the world.

An understanding of the way location influences business therefore is critical for the international marketing executive. Without clear knowledge of an enterprise's location relative to its suppliers, to its market, and to its competitors, an executive operates like the captain of a fog-bound vessel that has lost all navigational instruments and is heading for dangerous shoals.

Place

In addition to its location, each place has a diverse set of characteristics. Although many of those characteristics are present in other places, the ensemble makes each place unique. The characteristics of places—both natural and human—profoundly influence the ways that business executives in different places participate in international economic transactions.

Natural Features

Many of the characteristics of a place relate to its natural attributes. **Geologic characteristics** can be especially important, as the presence of critical minerals or energy resources may make a place a world-renowned supplier of valuable products. Gold and diamonds help make South Africa's economy the most prosperous on that continent. Rich deposits of iron ore in southern parts of the Amazon Basin have made Brazil the world's leading exporter of that commodity, while Chile remains a preeminent exporter of copper. Coal deposits provided the foundation for massive industrial development in the eastern United States, in the Rhine River Basin of Europe, in western Russia, and in northeastern China. Because of abundant pools of petroleum beneath desert sands, standards of living in Saudi Arabia and nearby nations have risen rapidly to be among the highest in the world.

The geology of places also shapes its **terrain.** People traditionally have clustered in lower, flatter areas, because valleys and plains have permitted the agricultural development necessary to feed the local population and to generate surpluses that can be traded. Hilly and mountainous areas may support some people, but their population densities invariably are lower. Terrain also plays a critical role in focusing and inhibiting the movement of people and goods. Business leaders throughout the centuries have capitalized on this fact. Just as feudal masters sought control of mountain passes in order to collect tolls and other duties from traders who traversed an area, modern executives maintain stores and offer services near bridges and at other points where terrain focuses travel.

The terrain of a place is related to its **hydrology.** Rivers, lakes, and other bodies of water influence the kinds of economic activities that occur in a place. In general, abundant supplies of water boost economic development, because water is necessary for the sustenance of people and for both agricultural and industrial production. Locations like Los Angeles and Saudi Arabia have prospered despite having little local water, because other features offer advantages that more than exceed the additional costs incurred in delivering water supplies from elsewhere. While sufficient water must be available to meet local needs, overabundance of water may pose serious problems, such as in Bangladesh, where development has been inhibited by frequent flooding. The character of a place's water bodies also is important. Smooth-flowing streams and placid lakes can stimulate transportation within a place and connect it more easily with other places, while waterfalls and rapids can prevent navigation on streams. The rapid drop in elevation of such streams may boost their potential for hydroelectric power generation, however, thereby stimulating development of industries requiring considerable amounts of electricity. Large plants producing aluminum, for example, are found in the Tennessee and Columbia river valleys of the United States and in Quebec and British Columbia in Canada. These plants refine materials that originally were extracted elsewhere, especially bauxite and alumina from Caribbean nations like Jamaica and the Dominican Republic. Although the transport costs incurred in delivery of these materials to the plants is high, those costs are more than offset by the presence of abundant and inexpensive electricity.

Climate is another natural feature that has profound impact on economic activity within a place. Many activities are directly affected by climate. Locales blessed with pleasant climates, such as the Cote d'Azur of France, the Crimean Peninsula of Ukraine, Florida, and the "Gold Coast" of northeastern Australia, have become popular recreational havens, attracting tourists whose spending fuels the local economy. Agricultural production is also influenced by climate. The average daily and evening temperatures, the amount and timing of precipitation, the timing of frosts and freezing weather, and the variability of weather from one year to the next all influence the kinds of crops grown in an area. Plants producing bananas and sugar cane flourish in moist tropical areas, while cooler climates are more conducive for crops such as wheat and potatoes. Climate influences other industries as well. The aircraft manufacturing industry in the United States developed largely in warmer, drier areas, where conditions for test and delivery flights were more beneficial throughout the year. In a similar way, major rocket-launching facilities have been placed in locations where climatic conditions are most favorable. As a result, the primary launch site of the European Space Agency is not in Europe at all, but rather in the South American territory of French Guiana. Climate also affects the length of the work day and the length of economic seasons. For example, in some regions of the world, the construction industry can build only during a few months of the year because permafrost makes construction prohibitively expensive the rest of the year.

Variations in *soils* have a profound impact on agricultural production. The world's great grain-exporting regions, including the central United States, the Prairie Provinces of Canada, the "Fertile Triangle" stretching from central Ukraine through southern Russia into northern Kazakhstan, and the Pampas of northern Argentina, all have been blessed with mineral-rich soils made even more fertile by humus from natural grasslands that once dominated the landscape. Soils are less fertile in much of the Amazon Basin of Brazil and in central Africa, where heavy rains leave few nutrients in upper layers of the soil. As a result, few commercial crops are grown.

The *interplay between climate and soils* is especially evident in the production of wines. Hundreds of varieties of grapes have been bred in order to take advantage of the different physical characteristics of various places. The wines fermented from these grapes are shipped around the world to consumers, who differentiate among various wines based not only on the grapes but also on the places where they were grown and the conditions during which they matured.

Human Features

The physical features of a place provide natural resources and influence the types of economic activities in which people engage, but its human characteristics also are critical. The **population** of a place is important because farm production may require intensive labor to be successful, as is true in rice-growing areas of eastern Asia. The skills and qualifications of the population also play a role in determining how a place fits into global economic affairs. Although blessed with few mineral resources and a terrain and climate that limit agricultural production, the Swiss have emphasized high levels of education and training in order to maintain a labor force that manufactures sophisticated products for export around the world. In recent decades, Japan and smaller nations such as South Korea and Taiwan have increased the productivity of their workers to become major industrial exporters.

As people live in a place, they modify it, creating a **built environment** that can be as important as or more important than the natural environment in economic terms. The most pronounced areas of human activity and their associated structures are in cities. In nations around the world, cities grew dramatically during the twentieth century. Much of the growth of cities has resulted from the migration of people from rural areas. This influx of new residents broadens the labor pool and creates vast new demand for goods and services. As urban populations have grown, residences and other facilities have replaced rural land uses. Executives seeking to conduct business in foreign cities need to be aware that the geographic patterns found in their home cities are not evident in many other nations. For example, in the United States, wealthier residents generally have moved out of cities, and as they established their residences, stores and services followed. Residential patterns in the major cities of Latin America and other developing nations tend to be reversed, with the wealthy remaining close to the city center while poorer residents are consigned to the outskirts of town. A store location strategy that is successful in the United States therefore may fail miserably if transferred directly to another nation without knowledge of the different geographic patterns of that nation's cities.

Interaction

The international marketing professional seeking to take advantage of opportunities present in different places learns not to view each place separately. The way a place functions depends not only on the presence and form of certain characteristics but also on interactions among those characteristics. Fortuitous combinations of features can spur a region's economic development. The presence of high-grade supplies of iron ore, coal, and limestone powered the growth of Germany's Ruhr Valley as one of Europe's foremost steel-producing regions, just as the proximity of the fertile Pampas and the deep channel of the Rio de la Plata combine to make Buenos Aires the leading economic center in southern South America.

Interactions among different features change over time within places, and as they do, so does that place's character and its economic activities. Human activities can have profound impacts on natural features. The courses of rivers and streams are changed as dams are erected and meanders are straightened. Soil fertility can be improved through fertilization. Vegetation is changed, with naturally growing plants replaced by crops and other varieties that require careful management.

Many human modifications have been successful. For centuries, the Dutch have constructed dikes and drainage systems, slowly creating polders—land that once was covered by the North Sea but that now is used for agricultural production. But other human activities have had disastrous impacts on natural features. A large area in Ukraine and Belarus was rendered uninhabitable by radioactive materials leaked from the Chernobyl reactor in 1986. In countless other places around the globe, improper disposal of wastes has seriously harmed land and water resources. In some places, damage can be repaired, as has happened in rivers and lakes of the United States following the passage of measures to curb water pollution in the last three decades, but in other locales, restoration may be impossible.

Growing concerns about environmental quality have led many people in more economically advanced nations to call for changes in economic systems that harm the natural environment. Concerted efforts are under way, for example, to halt destruction of forests in the Amazon Basin, thereby preserving the vast array of different plant and animal species in the region and saving vegetation that can help moderate the world's climate. Cooperative ventures have been established to promote selective harvesting of nuts, hardwoods, and other products taken from natural forests. Furthermore, an increasing number of restaurants and grocers are refusing to purchase beef raised on pastures that are established by clearing forests.

As with so many other geographical relationships, the nature of human–environmental interaction changes over time. With technological advances, people have been able to modify and adapt to natural features in increasingly sophisticated ways. The development of air conditioning has permitted people to function more effectively in torrid tropical environments, thereby enabling the populations of cities such as Houston, Rio de Janeiro, and Jakarta to multiply many times over in recent decades. Owners of winter resorts now can generate snow artificially to ensure favorable conditions for skiers. Advanced irrigation systems now permit crops to be grown in places such as the southwestern United States, northern Africa, and Israel. The use of new technologies may cause serious problems over the long run, however. Extensive irrigation in large parts of the U.S. Great Plains has seriously depleted groundwater supplies. In central Asia, the diversion of river water to irrigate cotton fields in Kazakhstan and Uzbekistan has reduced the size of the Aral Sea by more than one-half since 1960. In future years, business leaders may need to factor into their decisions the additional costs associated with the restoration of environmental quality after they have finished using a place's resources.

Movement

Whereas the theme of interaction encourages consideration of different characteristics within a place, movement provides a structure for considering how different places relate to each other. International marketing exists because movement permits the transportation of people and goods and communication of information and ideas among different places. No matter how much people in one place want something found elsewhere, they cannot have it unless transportation systems permit the good to be brought to them or allow them to move to the location of the good.

The location and character of transportation and communication systems long have had powerful influences on the economic standing of places. Especially significant have been places on which transportation routes have focused. Many ports have become prosperous cities because they channeled the movement of goods and people between ocean and inland waterways. New York became the largest city in North America because its harbor provided sheltered anchorage for ships crossing the Atlantic; the Hudson River provided access leading into the interior of the continent. In eastern Asia, Hong Kong grew under similar circumstances, as British traders used its splendid harbor as an exchange point for goods moving in and out of southern China.

Businesses also have succeeded at well-situated places along overland routes. The fabled oasis of Tombouctou has been an important trading center for centuries because it had one of the few dependable sources of water in the Sahara. Chicago's ascendancy as the premier city of the U.S. heartland came when its early leaders engineered its selection as the termination point for a dozen railroad lines converging from all directions. Not only did much of the rail traffic moving through the region have to pass through Chicago, but passengers and freight passing through the city had to be transferred from one line to another. This process generated numerous jobs and added considerably to the wealth of many businesses in the city.

In addition to the business associated directly with the movement of people and goods, other forms of economic activity have become concentrated at critical points in the transportation network. Places where transfers from one mode of transportation to another were required often were chosen as sites for manufacturing activities. Buffalo was the most active flour-milling center in the United States for much of the twentieth century because it was the point where Great Lakes freighters carrying wheat from the northern Great Plains and Canadian prairies were unloaded. Rather than simply transfer the wheat into rail cars for shipment to the large urban markets of the northeastern United States, millers transformed the wheat into flour in Buffalo, thereby reducing the additional handling of the commodity.

Global patterns of resource refining also demonstrate the wisdom of careful selection of sites with respect to transportation systems. Some of the world's largest oil refineries are located at places like Bahrain and Houston, where pipeliners bring oil to points where it is processed and loaded onto ships in the form of gasoline or other distillates for transport to other locales. Massive refinery complexes also have been built in the Tokyo and Nagoya areas of Japan and near Rotterdam in the Netherlands to process crude oil brought by giant tankers from the Middle East and other oil-exporting regions. For similar reasons, the largest new steel mills in the United States are near Baltimore and Philadelphia, where iron ore shipped from Canada and Brazil is processed. Some of the most active aluminum works in Europe are beside Norwegian fjords, where abundant local hydroelectric power is used to process imported alumina.

Favorable location along transportation lines is beneficial for a place. Conversely, an absence of good transportation severely limits the potential for firms to succeed in a specific place. Transportation patterns change over time, however, and so does their impact on places. Some places maintain themselves because their business leaders use their size and economic power to become critical nodes in newly evolving transportation networks. New York's experience provides a good example of this process. New York became the United States' foremost business center in the early nineteenth century because it was ideally situated for water transportation. As railroad networks evolved later in that century, they sought New York connections in order to serve its massive market. During the twentieth century, a complex web of roadways and major airports reinforced New York's supremacy in the eastern United States. In similar ways, London, Moscow, and Tokyo reasserted themselves as transportation hubs for their nations through successive advances in transport technology.

Failure to adapt to changing transportation patterns can have harmful impacts on a place. During the middle of the nineteenth century, business leaders in St. Louis discouraged railroad construction, seeking instead to maintain the supremacy of river transportation. Only after it became clear that railroads were the mode of preference did St. Louis officials seek to develop rail connections for the city, but by then it was too late; Chicago had ascended to a dominant position in the region. For about 30 years during the middle part of the twentieth century, airports at Gander (Newfoundland, Canada) and Shannon (Ireland) became important refueling points for transatlantic flights. The development of planes that could travel nonstop for much longer distances returned those places to sleepy oblivion.

Continuing advances in transportation technology have effectively "shrunk" the world. Just a few centuries ago, travel across an ocean took harrowing months. As late as 1873, readers marveled when Jules Verne wrote of a hectic journey around the world in 80 days. Today's travelers can fly around the globe in less than 80 hours, and the speed and dependability of modern modes of transport have transformed the ways in which business is conducted. Modern manufacturers have transformed the notion of relationships among suppliers, manufacturers, and markets. Automobile manufacturers, for example, once maintained large stockpiles of parts in assembly plants that were located near the parts plants or close to the places where the cars would be sold. Contemporary auto assembly plants now are built in places where labor costs and worker productivity are favorable and where governments have offered attractive inducements. They keep relatively few parts on hand, calling on suppliers for rapid delivery of parts as they are needed when orders for new cars are received. This "just-in-time" system of production leaves manufacturers subject to disruptions caused by work stoppages at supply plants and to weather-related delays in the transportation system, but losses associated with these infrequent events are more than offset by reduced operating costs under normal conditions.

The role of advanced technology and its effect on international marketing are even more apparent with respect to advances in communications systems. Sophisticated forms of telecommunication that began more than 150 years ago with the telegraph have advanced through the telephone to facsimile transmissions and electronic mail networks. As a result, distance has practically ceased to be a consideration with respect to the transmission of information. Whereas information once moved only as rapidly as the person carrying the paper on which the information was written, data and ideas now can be sent instantaneously almost anywhere in the world.

These communication advances have had a staggering impact on the way that international marketing is conducted. They have fostered the growth of multinational corporations, which operate in diverse sites around the globe while maintaining effective links with headquarters and regional control centers. International financial operations also have been transformed because of communication advances. Money and stock markets in New York, London, Tokyo, and secondary markets such as Los Angeles, Frankfurt, and Hong Kong now are connected by computer systems that process transactions around the clock. As much as any other factor, the increasingly mobile forms of money have enabled modern business executives to engage in activities around the world.

Region

In addition to considering places by themselves or how they relate to other places, regions provide alternative ways to organize groups of places in more meaningful ways. A region is a set of places that share certain characteristics. Many regions are defined by characteristics that all of the places in the group have in common. When economic characteristics are used, the delimited regions include places with similar kinds of economic activity. Agricultural regions include areas where certain farm products dominate. Corn is grown throughout the "Corn Belt" of the central United States, for example, although many farmers in the region also plant soybeans and many raise hogs. Regions where intensive industrial production is a prominent part of local economic activity include the manufacturing belts of the northeastern United States, southern Canada, northwestern Europe, and southern Japan.

Regions can also be defined by patterns of movement. Transportation or communication linkages among places may draw them together into configurations that differentiate them from other locales. Studies by economic geographers of the locational tendencies of modern high-technology industries have identified complex networks of firms that provide products and services to each other. Because of their linkages, these firms cluster together into well-defined regions. The "Silicon Valley" of northern California, the "Western Crescent" on the outskirts of London, and "Technopolis" of the Tokyo region all are distinguished as much by connections among firms as by the economic landscapes they have established.

Economic aspects of movement may help define functional regions by establishing areas where certain types of economic activity are more profitable than others. In the early nineteenth century, German landowner Johann Heinrich von Thünen demonstrated how different costs for transporting various agricultural goods to market helped to define regions where certain forms of farming would occur. Although theoretically simple, patterns predicted by von Thünen can still be found in the world today. Goods such as vegetables and dairy products that require more intensive production and are more expensive to ship are produced closer to markets, while less demanding goods and commodities that can be transported at lower costs come from more remote production areas. Advances in transportation have dramatically altered such regional patterns. Once, a New York City native enjoyed fresh vegetables and fruits only in the summer and early autumn when New Jersey, upstate New York, and New England producers brought their goods to market. Today, New Yorkers buy fresh produce year-round, with new shipments flown in daily from Florida, California, Chile, and even more remote locations during the colder months.

Governments have a strong impact on the conduct of business, and the formal borders of government jurisdictions often coincide with the functional boundaries of economic regions. The divisive character of these lines on the map has been altered in many parts of the world in recent decades. The formation of common markets and free trade areas in Western Europe and North America has dramatically changed the patterns and flows of economic activity, and similar kinds of formal restructuring of relationships among nations likely will continue into the next century. As a result, business analysts increasingly need to consider regions that cross international boundaries.

Some of the most innovative views of regional organization essentially have ignored existing national boundaries. In 1981, Joel Garreau published a book titled *The Nine Nations of North America,* which subdivided the continent into a set of regions based on economic activities and cultural outlooks. Seven of Garreau's nine regions include territory in at least two nations. In the Southwest, "Mexamerica" recognized the bicultural heritage of Anglo and Hispanic groups and the increasingly close economic ties across the U.S.–Mexican border that were spurred by the *maquiladora* and other export-oriented programs. The evolution of this region as a distinctive collection of places has been accelerated by the passage of the North American Free Trade Agreement (NAFTA). Another cross-national region identified by Garreau is "The Islands," a collection of nations in the Caribbean for which Miami has become the functional "capital." Many business leaders seeking to tap into this rapidly growing area have become knowledgeable of the laws and customs of those nations. They often have done so by employing émigrés from those nations who may now be U.S. citizens but whose primary language is not English and whose outlook on the region is multinational.

In a similar vein, Darrell Delamaide's 1994 book entitled *The New Superregions of Europe* divides the continent into ten regions based on economic, cultural, and social affinities that have evolved over centuries. His vision of Europe challenges regional structures that persist from earlier times. Seen by many as a single region known as Eastern Europe, the formerly communist nations west of what once was the Soviet Union are seen by Delamaide as being part of five different "super-regions": "The Baltic League," a group of nations clustered around the Baltic Sea; "Mitteleuropa," the economic heartland of northern Europe; "The Slavic Federation," a region dominated by Russia with a common Slavic heritage; "The Danube Basin," a mélange of places along and near Europe's longest river; and "The Balkan Peninsula," a region characterized by political turmoil and less-advanced economies.

Delamaide's book has been as controversial as Garreau's was a decade earlier. In both cases, however, the value of the ideas they presented was measured not in terms of the "accuracy" of the regional structures they presented, but rather by their ability to lead more people to take a geographic perspective of the modern world and the way it functions. The regions defined by Garreau and Delamaide are not those described by traditional geographers, but they reflect the views of many business leaders who have learned to look across national boundaries in their search for opportunities. As marketing increasingly becomes international, the most successful entrepreneurs will be the ones who complement their business acumen with effective application of geographic information and principles.

For online activities, visit the following Web sites:

http://state.gov
http://www.state.gov/www/regions/independent_states.html

Key Terms

geologic characteristics	climate
terrain	population
hydrology	built environment

chapter 2

International Trade Institutions and Trade Policy

THE INTERNATIONAL MARKETPLACE   2.1

Who Should Regulate E-Commerce?

E-commerce has increasing influence on international trade systems. The value of global business-to-business goods and services trade via the Internet is predicted to reach $12.8 trillion in 2006, compared to only $2.3 trillion in 2002.

Some governments in Europe and Asia believe that regulation and state control will aid in the development of the Internet. Such regulation, they claim, protects Internet consumers from fraud. This point of view is in contradiction to the United States' current policy that the e-commerce market should primarily police itself. U.S. Senator Joseph Lieberman and Representative Ellen Tauscher urged caution in regulating international e-commerce, saying, "The Internet allows for buyers and sellers from different countries to meet and do business to an unprecedented degree, but because the technology is so new, the legal questions created by cross-border business-to-consumer transactions are very much undecided."

As countries begin to adopt an array of different rules and regulations, consistency needs to be established. To solve cross-border disputes in Europe the EU commission has proposed a system that favors the enforcement of the laws of the country in which the transaction originated. However, businesses seem to disagree. While governments throughout the world support varying levels of regulation, an international group of executives has united to oppose Internet taxes and restrictions on data exports. This group, working together as the Global Business Dialogue on Electronic Commerce, has pushed for the adoption of a "seal of approval" for Web sites that protect consumer privacy. It has also advocated third-party arbitration in solving e-commerce disputes.

It seems clear that some supervision is needed to ensure fairness and privacy. What is unclear is who should conduct such supervision—domestic governments, international organizations such as the WTO, or a newly formed supranational group.

SOURCES: Andy Sullivan, "Hands Off e-Commerce, Democratic Lawmakers Say," *Reuters,* March 15, 2001; Victoria Shannon, "CEO's Lobby for E-Commerce; Technology Chiefs Call for Restraint in Regulation of Internet," *The Washington Post,* September 14, 1999, E3; Seminar on Electronic Commerce, Forrester Research, Presentation to the World Trade Organization, Geneva, April 22, 2002.

THE INTERNATIONAL ENVIRONMENT is changing rapidly. Firms, individuals, and policymakers are affected by these changes. As *The International Marketplace 2.1* shows, these changes offer new opportunities but also represent new challenges. Although major economic and security shifts will have a profound impact on the world, coping with them successfully through imagination, investment, and perseverance can produce a new, better world order and an improved quality of life.

This chapter begins by highlighting the importance of trade to humankind. Selected historical developments that were triggered or influenced by international trade are delineated. Subsequently, more recent trade developments are presented, together with the international institutions that have emerged to regulate and facilitate trade.

The chapter will analyze and discuss the position of the United States in the world trade environment and explain the impact of trade on the United States. Various efforts undertaken by governments to manage trade by restricting or promoting exports, imports, technology transfer, and investments will be described. Finally, the chapter will present a strategic outlook for future developments in trade relations.

The Historical Dimension

Many peoples throughout history have gained preeminence in the world through their trade activities. Among them were the Etruscans, Phoenicians, Egyptians, Chinese, Spaniards, and Portuguese. To underscore the role of trade, we will take a closer look at some selected examples.

One of the major world powers in ancient history was the Roman Empire. Its impact on thought, knowledge, and development can still be felt today. Even while expanding their territories through armed conflicts, the Romans placed primary emphasis on encouraging international business activities. The principal approaches used to implement this emphasis were the **Pax Romana,** or the Roman Peace, and the common coinage. The Pax Romana ensured that merchants were able to travel safely on roads that were built, maintained, and protected by the Roman legions and their affiliated troops. The common coinage, in turn, ensured that business transactions could be carried out easily throughout the empire. In addition, Rome developed a systematic law, central market locations through the founding of cities, and an excellent communication system that resembled an early version of the Pony Express; all of these measures contributed to the functioning of the international marketplace and to the reduction of business uncertainty. As a result, economic well-being within the empire rose sharply compared to the outside.

Soon, city-nations and tribes that were not part of the empire wanted to share in the benefits of belonging. They joined the empire as allies and agreed to pay tribute and taxes. Thus, the immense growth of the Roman Empire occurred through the linkages of business rather than through the marching of its legions and warfare. Of course, the Romans had to engage in substantial efforts to facilitate business in order to make it worthwhile for others to belong. For example, when pirates threatened the seaways, Rome, under Pompeius, sent out a large fleet to subdue them. The cost of international distribution, and therefore the cost of international marketing, was substantially reduced because fewer goods were lost to pirates. As a result, goods could be made available at lower prices, which, in turn, translated into larger demand.

The fact that international business was one of the primary factors holding the empire together can also be seen in its decay. When "barbaric" tribes overran the empire, it was not mainly through war and prolonged battles that Rome lost ground. The outside tribes were actually attacking an empire that was already substantially weakened, because it could no longer offer the benefits of affiliation. Former allies no longer saw any advantage in being associated with the Romans and willingly cooperated with the invaders, rather than face prolonged battles.

In a similar fashion, one could interpret the evolution of European feudalism to be a function of trade and marketing. Because farmers were frequently deprived of their harvests as a result of incursions by other (foreign) tribes, or even individuals, they decided to band together and provide for their own protection. By delivering a certain portion of their "earnings" to a protector, they could be assured of retaining most of their gains. Although this system initially worked quite well in reducing the cost of production and the cost of marketing, it did ultimately result in the emergence of the feudal system, which, perhaps, was not what the initiators had intended it to be.

Interestingly, the feudal system encouraged the development of a closed-state economy that was inwardly focused and ultimately conceived for self-sufficiency and security. However, medieval commerce still thrived and developed through export trade. In Italy, the Low Countries, and the German Hanse towns, the impetus for commerce was provided by East–West trade. Profits from the spice trade through the Middle East created the wealth of Venice and other Mediterranean ports. Europe also imported rice, oranges, dyes, cotton, and silk. Western European merchants in turn exported timber, arms, and woolen clothing in exchange for these luxury goods. A remaining legacy of this trade are the many English and French words of Arabic origin, such as divan, bazaar, artichoke, orange, jar, and tariff.[1]

The importance of trade has not always persisted, however. For example, in 1896, the Empress Dowager Tz'u-hsi, in order to finance the renovation of the summer palace, impounded government funds that had been designated for Chinese shipping and its navy. As a result, China's participation in world trade almost came to a halt. In the subsequent decades, China operated in almost total isolation, without any transfer of knowledge from the outside, without major inflow of goods, and without the innovation and productivity increases that result from exposure to international trade.

More recently, the effect of turning away from international trade was highlighted during the 1930s. The Smoot-Hawley Act raised duties to reduce the volume of imports into the United States, in the hopes that this would restore domestic employment. The result, however, was a raising of duties and other barriers to imports by most other trading nations as well. These measures were contributing factors in the subsequent worldwide depression and the collapse of the world financial system, which in turn set the scene for World War II.

International marketing and international trade have also long been seen as valuable tools for foreign policy purposes. The use of economic coercion—for example, by nations or groups of nations—can be traced back as far as the time of the Greek city-states and the Peloponnesian War or, in more recent times, to the Napoleonic wars. Combatants used blockades to achieve their goal of "bringing about commercial ruin and shortage of food by dislocating trade."[2] Similarly, during the Civil War in the United States, the North consistently pursued a strategy of denying international trade opportunities to the South and thus deprived it of export revenue needed to import necessary products. In the 1990s, the Iraqi invasion of Kuwait resulted in a trade embargo of Iraq by the United Nations, with the goal of reversing the aggression. Although such deprivations of trade do not often bring about policy change, they certainly have a profound impact on the standard of living of a nation's citizens.

Global Division

After 1945, the world was sharply split ideologically into West and East, a division that had major implications for trade relations. The Soviet Union, as the leader of the Eastern bloc, developed the Council for Mutual Economic Assistance (CMEA or COMECON), which focused on developing strong linkages among the members of the Soviet bloc and discouraged relations with the West. The United States, in turn, was the leading proponent of creating a "Pax Americana," or American peace, for the Western world, driven by the belief that international trade was a key to worldwide prosperity. Many months of international negotiations in London, Geneva, and Lake Success (New York) culminated on March 24, 1948, in Havana, Cuba, with the signing of the charter for an International Trade Organization (ITO).

This charter, a series of agreements among 53 countries, was designed to cover international commercial policies, domestic business practices, commodity agreements, employment and reconstruction, economic development and international investment, and a constitution for a new United Nations agency to administer the whole. In addition, a General Agreement on Tariffs and Trade was initiated, with the purpose of reducing tariffs among countries, and international institutions such as the World Bank and the International Monetary Fund were created.

Even though the International Trade Organization incorporated many farsighted notions, most nations refused to ratify it, fearing its power, its bureaucratic size, and its threat to national sovereignty. As a result, the most forward-looking approach to international trade never came about. However, other organizations conceived at the time are still in existence and have made major contributions toward improving international trade.

Transnational Institutions Affecting World Trade

World Trade Organization (WTO)[3]

The World Trade Organization has its origins in the General Agreement on Tariffs and Trade (GATT), to which it became the successor organization in January of 1995. In order to better understand the emergence of the WTO, a brief review of the GATT is appropriate. The GATT has been called "a remarkable success story of a postwar international organization that was never intended to become one."[4] It began in 1947 as a set of rules for nondiscrimination, transparent procedures, and settlement of disputes in international trade. One of the most important tools is the Most-Favored Nation (MFN) clause, which calls for each member country of the GATT to grant every other member country the most favorable treatment it accords to any other country with respect to imports and exports. In effect, MFN is the equal opportunity clause of international trade. Over time, the GATT evolved into an institution that sponsored successive rounds of international trade negotiations with a key focus on a reduction of prevailing high tariffs.

Early in its existence, the GATT achieved the liberalization of trade in 50,000 products, amounting to two-thirds of the value of the trade among its participants. In subsequent years, special GATT negotiations such as the Kennedy Round and the Tokyo Round further reduced trade barriers and developed improved dispute-settlement mechanisms, better provisions dealing with subsidies, and a more explicit definition of rules for import controls.

In spite of, or perhaps because of, these impressive gains, GATT became less effective over time. Duties had already been drastically reduced—for example, the average U.S. tariff rate fell from 26 percent in 1946 to an average of 5.4 percent in 2001. Further reductions are therefore unlikely to have a major impact on world trade. Most imports either enter the United States duty free or are subject to low tariffs. The highest tariffs apply mainly to imports of agri-food and tobacco products, as well as clothing, textiles, and footwear. In these industries, tariffs tend to increase with the degree of processing.[5]

Many nations developed new tools for managing and distorting trade flows, nontariff tools that were not covered under GATT rules. Examples are "voluntary agreements" to restrain trade, bilateral or multilateral special trade agreements such as the multifiber accord that restricts trade in textiles and apparel, and other nontariff barriers. Also, GATT, which was founded by 24 like-minded governments, was designed to operate by consensus. With a membership of 144, this consensus rule often led to a stalemate of many GATT activities.

After many years of often contentious negotiations, the Uruguay Round accord was finally ratified in January of 1995. As part of this ratification, a new institution, the World Trade Organization, was created, which now is the umbrella organization responsible for overseeing the implementation of all the multilateral agreements negotiated in the Uruguay Round and those that will be negotiated in the future.[6] The GATT has ceased to exist as a separate institution and has become part of WTO, which also is responsible for the General Agreement on Trade in Services (GATS), agreements on trade-related aspects of intellectual property rights (TRIPS), and trade-related investment measures (TRIMS), and administers a broad variety of international trade and investment accords.

The creation of the WTO has greatly broadened the scope of international trade agreements. Many of the areas left uncovered by the GATT, such as services and agriculture, are now addressed at least to some degree by international rules, speedier dispute settlement procedures have been developed, and the decision-making process has been streamlined. Even though the WTO will attempt to continue to make decisions based on consensus, provisions are now made for decisions to be made by majority vote if such consensus cannot be achieved.

The WTO makes major contributions to improved trade and investment flows around the world. However, a successful WTO may well infringe on the sovereignty of nations. For example, more streamlined dispute settlements mean that decisions are made more quickly and that nations in violation of international trade rules are confronted more often. Negative WTO decisions affecting large trading nations are likely to be received with resentment. Some governments intend to broaden the mandate of the WTO to also deal with social causes and issues such as labor laws, competition, and emigration freedoms. Since many nations fear that social causes can be used to devise new rules of protectionism against their exports, the addition of such issues may become a key reason for divisiveness and dissent within the WTO.[7] Outside groups such as nongovernmental organizations and special interest alliances believe that international trade and the WTO represent a threat to their causes.

In 2001, a new round of international trade negotiations was initiated. Because the agreement to do so was reached in the city of Doha (Qatar), the negotiations are now called the "Doha Round." The aim was to further hasten implementation of liberalization, particularly to help impoverished and developing nations. In addition, the goal was to expand the role of the WTO to encompass more of the trade activities in which there were insufficient rules for their definition and structure. This was due to either purposeful exclusion of governments in earlier negotiations or due to new technology changing the global marketplace. Examples include trade in agricultural goods, antidumping regulations, and electronic commerce. For instance, in the agricultural sector, it was proposed to reduce average global tariffs on farm products from 62 percent to 15 percent and to remove $100 billion in global trade-distorting subsidies. Cutting barriers to trade by a third could boost the world economy by $613 billion, which is like adding an economy the size of Canada's to the world economy.[8]

The beginning of the negotiations was quite slow, because U.S. negotiators did not have "fast track" authority, in which Congress could either approve or disapprove proposed trade agreements but not amend or change them. However, in the summer of 2002, such authority was granted to the president, and prospects for the Doha Round improved rapidly. A conclusion of the round is expected by 2006.

Unless trade advocates and the WTO are supported by their member governments and other outside stakeholders in trade issues, there is unlikely to be major progress on further liberalization of trade and investment. It will therefore be important to have the WTO focus on its core mission, which is the facilitation of international trade and investment, while ensuring that an effective forum exists to afford a hearing and subsequent achievements for concerns surrounding the core.

International Monetary Fund (IMF)[9]

The International Monetary Fund (IMF), conceived in 1944 at Bretton Woods in New Hampshire, was designed to provide stability for the international monetary framework. It obtained funding from its members, who subscribed to a quota based on expected trade patterns and paid 25 percent of the quota in gold or dollars and the rest in their local currencies. These funds were to be used to provide countries with protection against temporary fluctuations in the value of their currency. Therefore, it was the original goal of the IMF to provide for fixed exchange rates between countries.

The perhaps not so unintended result of using the U.S. dollar as the main world currency was a glut of dollar supplies in the 1960s. This forced the United States to abandon the gold standard and devalue the dollar and resulted in flexible or floating exchange rates in 1971. However, even though this major change occurred, the IMF as an institution has clearly contributed toward providing international liquidity and to facilitating international trade.

Although the system has functioned well so far, it is currently under severe pressure. In the 1980s, some of this pressure was triggered by the substantial debts incurred by less-developed countries as a result of overextended development credits and changes in the cost of energy. Since the 1990s, major additional pressure has resulted from the financial requirements of the former socialist countries, which search for funds to improve their economies. In addition, 12 former Soviet republics joined the IMF. Beyond the needs of these new members, major currency fluctuations among old customers have stretched the resources of the IMF to the limit. For example, on September 6, 2002, the International Monetary Fund approved Brazil's request for a 15-month standby credit of US$30.4 billion to support the country's economic and financial program through December 2003.[10] As a result of all these global financial needs, the future role of the IMF may be very different. If the institution can mobilize its members to provide the financial means for an active role, its past accomplishments may pale in view of the new opportunities.

At the same time, however, the newness in orientation also will require a rethinking of the rules under which the IMF operates. For example, it is quite unclear whether stringent economic rules and performance measures are equally applicable to all countries seeking IMF assistance. New economic conditions that have not been experienced to date, such as the privatization of formerly centrally planned economies, may require different types of approaches. Also, perhaps the link between economic and political stability requires more and different considerations, therefore magnifying but also changing the mission of the IMF.

World Bank[11]

The World Bank, whose official name is the International Bank for Reconstruction and Development, has had similar success. It was initially formed in 1944 to aid countries suffering from the destruction of war. After completing this process most successfully, it has since taken on the task of aiding world development. With more and more new nations emerging from the colonial fold of the world powers of the early twentieth century, the bank has made major efforts to assist fledgling economies to participate in a modern economic trade framework. More recently, the bank has begun to participate actively with the IMF to resolve the debt problems of the developing world and may also play a major role in bringing a market economy to the former members of the Eastern bloc.

A major debate, however, surrounds the effectiveness of the bank's expenditures. In the 1970s and 1980s, major funds were invested into infrastructure projects in developing countries, based on the expectation that such investment would rapidly propel the economies of these nations forward. However, in retrospect, it appears that many of these funds were squandered by corrupt regimes, and that many large projects have turned into white elephants—producing little in terms of economic progress. In addition, some projects have had major negative side

THE INTERNATIONAL MARKETPLACE   2.2

World Bank to the Rescue

Poverty is traditionally defined as a situation where a person's consumption or income levels fall below some minimum level necessary to meet basic needs. Extreme economic poverty is defined as living on less than $1 per day. Since "basic needs" vary between countries and evolve as time progresses, the definition of poverty also keeps changing. For example, living standards have risen dramatically. Whereas per capita private consumption growth in developing countries averaged about 1.4 percent a year between 1980 and 1990, the growth rate averaged 2.4 percent per year between 1990 and 1999.

The growing population of developing countries has yielded an increasing number of people being born into poverty. The population of developing countries has risen from 2.9 billion in 1970 to 5.2 billion in 2000. Of these 5.2 billion, 2.8 billion live on less than $2 a day. Analysts predict that total world population will increase by another 1 billion between 2000 and 2015, with 97 percent of this increase occurring in developing countries.

The World Bank attempts to address the multidimensional nature of poverty by taking several factors into consideration: levels of income and consumption, social indicators, and indicators of vulnerability to risks and of socio/political access. There are seven major international development goals regarding the reduction of poverty: (1) to reduce the proportion of people living in extreme poverty by half by 2015; (2) to enroll all children in primary school by 2015; (3) to make progress toward gender equality and empowering women by eliminating gender disparities in primary and secondary education by 2005; (4) to reduce infant and child mortality rates by two-thirds by 2015; (5) to reduce maternal mortality ratios by three-quarters by 2015; (6) to provide access for all who need reproductive health services by 2016; and (7) to implement national strategies for sustainable development by 2005 so as to reverse the loss of environmental resources by 2015. In order to reach these goals, the World Development Report proposes three strategies: promoting opportunity, facilitating empowerment, and enhancing security.

In fiscal year 2002, the World Bank provided more than US$19.5 billion in loans to its client countries. It works with more than 100 developing countries, providing financing and ideas to support poverty reduction. The World Bank's "Bottom-Up Participatory Approach" encourages governments to find the root causes of poverty, thus allowing the appropriate policy prescriptions to be developed. Despite the fact that it has access to vast oil reserves, Nigeria is among the 20 poorest countries in the world, with roughly 66 percent of its population living below the poverty line. Gross national product (GNP) per capita has decreased from US$370 in 1985 to US$260 today. Much of Nigeria's woes stem from economic mismanagement, corruption, and excessive dependence on the oil sector. Nigeria's large reserves of human and natural resources make its potential for overcoming poverty large. In June 2002, the Bank approved loans worth US$237 million to Nigeria for socioeconomic improvement. In total, the World Bank supports ten projects in Nigeria with commitment of about US$783 million in the areas of HIV/AIDS, health, community-driven development, privatization, power transmission, education, water, and economic management capacity building.

SOURCE: World Bank's World Development Report Overview, *Attacking Poverty: Opportunity, Empowerment, and Security,* **http://www.worldbank.org**.

effects for the recipient nations. For example, the highway through the rain forest in Brazil has mainly resulted in the migration of people to the area and an upsetting of a very fragile ecological balance. The World Bank is now trying to reorient its outlook, focusing more on institution building and the development of human capital through investments into education and health. A clearer differentiation of its role as an organization working on the micro level of the economy as opposed to the macro level of the IMF is also likely to redirect the work of the bank. *The International Marketplace 2.2* shows how the bank tries to address the poverty issue. However, it has become clear that there is no single solution for bringing countries out of poverty.

Regional Institutions

The WTO, IMF, and World Bank operate on a global level. Regional changes have also taken place, based on the notion that trade between countries needs to be encouraged. Of particular importance was the formation of **economic blocs** that integrated the economic and political activities of nations.

The concept of regional integration was used more than 100 years ago when Germany developed the Zollverein. Its modern-day development began in 1952 with the establishment of the European Coal and Steel Community, which was designed to create a common market among six countries in coal, steel, and iron. Gradually, these nations developed a Customs Union and created common external tariffs. The ultimate goal envisioned was the completely free movement of capital, services, and people across national borders and the joint development of common international policies. Over time, the goals have been largely attained. The European Union (EU) now represents a formidable market size internally and market power externally, and the well-being of all EU members has increased substantially since the bloc's formation.

Similar market agreements have been formed by other groups of nations. Examples are the North American Free Trade Agreement (NAFTA), the Mercosur in Latin America, and the Gulf Cooperation Council (GCC). These unions were formed for different reasons and operate with different degrees of cohesiveness as appropriate for the specific environment. They focus on issues such as forming a customs union, a common market, an economic union, or a political union. Simultaneous with these economic bloc formations, the private sector has begun to develop international trade institutions of its own. Particularly when governments are not quick enough to address major issues of concern to global marketers, business has taken the lead by providing a forum for the discussion of such issues. One example is the Transatlantic Business Dialogue, which is a nongovernmental organization composed of business leaders from Europe and the United States. Recognizing the inefficiency of competing and often contradictory standards and lengthy testing procedures, this group is working to achieve mutual recognition agreements on an industry basis. The executives of leading international firms that participate in this organization attempt to simplify global marketing by searching for ways to align international standards and regulations in the pharmaceutical and telecommunication sectors.

The activities of all these institutions demonstrate that the joining of forces internationally permits better, more successful international marketing activities, results in an improved standard of living, and provides an effective counterbalance to large economic blocs. Just as in politics, trade has refuted the old postulate of "the strong is most powerful alone." Nations have come to recognize that trade activities are of substantial importance to their economic well-being. Over the long term, the export activities of a nation are the key to the inflow of imports and therefore to the provision of choice, competition, and new insights. In the medium and long run, the balance of payments has to be maintained. In the short run, "an external deficit can be financed by drawing down previously accumulated assets or by accumulating debts to other countries. In time, however, an adjustment process must set in to eliminate the deficit."[12]

The urgency of the adjustment will vary according to the country in question. Some countries find it very hard to obtain acceptance for an increasing number of IOUs. Others, like the United States, can run deficits of hundreds of billions of dollars and are still a preferred borrower because of political stability, perceived economic security, and the worldwide use of the U.S. dollar as a reserve and business reference currency. Such temporary advantages can change, of course. Before the rise of the dollar, the British pound was the reserve currency of choice for many years.

Comparing International Trade Positions

Over the years, international trade positions have changed substantially when measured in terms of world market share. For example, in the 1950s, U.S. exports composed 25 percent of total world exports. Since then, this share has declined precipitously. It is not that U.S. exports have actually dropped during that time. The history of the U.S. success in world market share began with the fact that the U.S. economy was not destroyed by the war. Because other countries had little to export and a great need for imports, the U.S. export position was powerful. Over time, however, as other trade partners entered the picture and aggressively obtained a larger world market share for themselves, U.S. export growth was not able to keep pace with total world export growth. Figure 2.1 shows the world share of exports and imports of various trading countries and regions. Notable is the degree to which U.S. imports exceed exports.

U.S. exports as a share of the GDP are about 11 percent. This level pales when compared with the international trade performance of other nations. The European Monetary Union (EMU), for example, has consistently maintained an export share of close to 30 percent of GDP. Japan, in turn, which is so often maligned as the export problem child in the international trade arena, now exports only about 11 percent of its GDP. China, in turn, has had a very rapid growth in its export proportion. Comparative developments of exports across countries in terms of percentage of GDP can be seen in Table 2.1.

The impact of international trade and marketing on individuals is highlighted when trade is scrutinized from a per-capita perspective. Table 2.2 presents this information on a comparative basis. Among the major industrialized nations, the United States has the lowest exports per capita, amounting to less than one-half of the per-person exports of the EMU. By comparison, imports per capita are relatively high, thus producing major trade deficits for the United States.

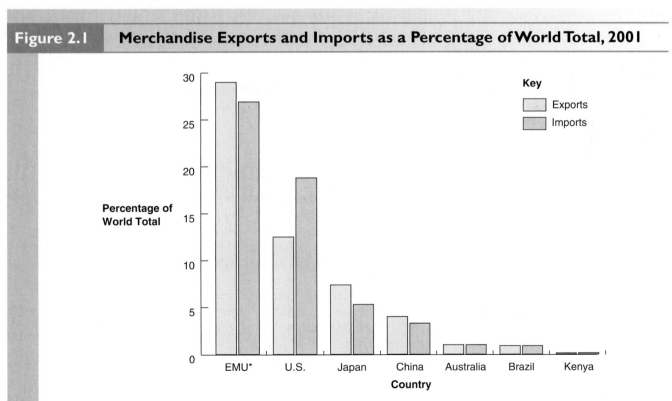

| Figure 2.1 | Merchandise Exports and Imports as a Percentage of World Total, 2001 |

*excludes intra-EMU trade.

SOURCES: Based on World Bank 2002 World Development Indicators, Washington, DC, 2002; WTO International Financial Statistics, 2001, Geneva, 2002.

Table 2.1   Exports of Goods and Services as a Percentage of Gross Domestic Product

Period	U.S.	EMU*	Brazil	Kenya	Australia	Japan	China
1986	7.3	28.2	8.8	25.8	16.3	11.2	11.8
1988	8.8	28.0	10.9	12.9	15.8	9.8	13.1
1990	9.7	28.5	8.2	25.6	16.7	10.4	17.5
1992	10.2	26.7	10.9	26.9	18.0	9.8	19.5
1994	10.4	27.7	9.5	37.0	18.5	9.0	25.3
1996	11.3	29.6	7.1	32.8	19.8	9.7	21.0
1998	11.1	32.6	7.3	24.9	18.8	10.7	21.9
2000	10.9	33.7	10.9	26.5	21.2	10.9	25.9

*excludes intra-EMU trade.

SOURCE: World Bank 2002 World Development Indicators, Washington, DC, 2002.

Table 2.2   Exports and Imports of Goods and Services per Capita for Selected Countries, 2001

Country	Exports per Capita	Imports per Capita
EMU*	$7,434	$7,302
Australia	4,296	4,525
Brazil	379	428
China	222	199
Japan	4,165	3,622
Kenya	91	125
United States	3,794	5,106

*European Monetary Union (EU, except Denmark, Sweden, and United Kingdom); excludes intra-EMU trade.

SOURCE: World Bank 2002 World Development Indicators, Washington, DC, 2002.

A Diagnosis of the U.S. Trade Position

The developments just enumerated foster the question: Why did these shifts occur? We should not attribute changes in U.S. trade performance merely to temporary factors such as the value of the dollar, the subsidization of exports from abroad, or the price of oil. We need to search further to determine the root causes for the decline in U.S. international competitiveness.

Since World War II, it has been ingrained in the minds of American policymakers that the United States is the leading country in world power and world trade. Together with this opinion came the feeling that the United States should assist other countries with their trade performance because without American help, they would never be able to play a meaningful role in the world economy. At the same time, there was admiration for "Yankee ingenuity"—the idea that U.S. firms were the most aggressive in the world. Therefore, the U.S. private sector appeared not to need any help in its international trade efforts.

The result of this overall philosophy was a continuing effort to aid countries abroad in their economic development. At the same time, no particular attention was paid to U.S. domestic firms. This policy was well conceived and well intentioned and resulted in spectacular successes. Books written in the late 1940s describe the overwhelming economic power of the United States and the apparently impossible task of resurrecting foreign economies. Comparing those texts with the economic performance of countries such as Japan and Germany today demonstrates that the policies of helping to stimulate foreign economies were indeed crowned by success.

These policies were so successful that no one wished to tamper with them. The United States continued to encourage trade abroad and not to aid domestic firms throughout the 1960s and the 1970s. Although the policies were well conceived, the environment to which they were applied was changing. In the 1950s and early 1960s, the United States successfully encouraged other nations again to become full partners in world trade. However, U.S. firms were placed at a distinct disadvantage when these policies continued for too long.

U.S. firms were assured that "because of its size and the diversity of its resources, the American economy can satisfy consumer wants and national needs with a minimum of reliance on foreign trade."[13] The availability of a large U.S. domestic market and the relative distance to foreign markets resulted in U.S. manufacturers simply not feeling a compelling need to seek business beyond national borders. Subsequently, the perception emerged within the private sector that exporting and international marketing were too risky, complicated, and not worth it.

This perception also resulted in increasing gaps in international marketing knowledge between managers in the United States and those abroad. Whereas business executives in most countries were forced, by the small size of their markets, to look very quickly to markets abroad and to learn about cultural sensitivity and market differences, most U.S. managers remained blissfully ignorant of the global economy. Similarly, U.S. education did not make knowledge about the global business environment, foreign languages, and cultures an area of major priority.

Given such lack of global interest, inadequacy of information, ignorance of where and how to market internationally, unfamiliarity with foreign market conditions, and complicated trade regulations, the private sector became fearful of conducting international business activities.

However, conditions have begun to change. Most institutions of higher learning have recognized the responsibilities and obligations that world leadership brings with it. Universities and particularly business programs are emphasizing the international dimension, not only in theory but also in practice. Many schools are offering opportunities for study abroad, designing summer programs with global components, and expecting a global orientation from their students.

Managers have also grown more intense in their international commitment. Many newly founded firms are global from the very beginning, giving rise to the term **"born global."** Electronic commerce has made it more feasible to reach out to the global business community, whether the firm be large or small. The U.S. Department of State has begun to offer training in business-government relations to new ambassadors and now instructs them to pay close attention to the needs of the U.S. business community.

In effect, the attention paid to international markets as both an opportunity for finding customers and a source of supplies is growing rapidly. As a result, the need for international marketing expertise can be expected to rise substantially as well.

The Impact of Trade and Investment

The Effect of Trade

Exports are important in a macroeconomic sense, in terms of balancing the trade account. Exports are special because they can affect currency values and the fiscal and monetary policies of governments, shape public perception of competitiveness, and determine the level of imports a country can afford. The steady erosion of the U.S. share of total world exports that took place in the 1960s and 1970s has had more than purely optical repercussions. It has also resulted in a merchandise **trade deficit,** which since 1975 has been continuous. In 1987, the United States posted a then record trade deficit with imports of products exceeding exports by more than $171 billion. Due to increases in exports, the merchandise trade deficit declined in the following years, only to climb again to record heights in 2002 by reaching $458 billion, due to increased imports.[14] Such large trade deficits are unsustainable in the longer run.[15]

These trade deficits have a major impact on the United States and its citizens. They indicate that a country, in its international activities, is consuming more than it is producing. One key way to reduce trade deficits is to increase exports. Such an approach is highly beneficial for various reasons.

One billion dollars worth of exports supports the creation, on average, of 11,500 jobs.[16] Increases in exports can become a major contributor to economic growth. This fact became particularly evident during the economic slowdown of the 1990s, when export growth accounted for most of the domestic economic growth rate and produced most new employment.

Equally important, through exporting, firms can achieve **economies of scale.** By broadening its market reach and serving customers abroad, a firm can produce more and do so more efficiently. As a result, the firm may achieve lower costs and higher profits both at home and abroad. Through exporting, the firm also benefits from market diversification. It can take advantage of different growth rates in different markets and gain stability by not being overly dependent on any particular market. Exporting also lets the firm learn from the competition, makes it sensitive to different demand structures and cultural dimensions, and proves its ability to survive in a less-familiar environment in spite of higher transaction costs. All these lessons can make the firm a stronger competitor at home.[17]

On the import side, firms become exposed to new competition, which may offer new approaches, better processes, or better products and services. In order to maintain their market share, firms are forced to compete more effectively by improving their own products and activities. Consumers in turn receive more choices when it comes to their selection. The competitive pressures exerted by imports also work to keep quality high and prices low.

The Effect of International Investment

International marketing activities consist not only of trade but of a spectrum of involvement, much of which results in international direct investment activities. Such investment activities can be crucial to a firm's success in new and growing markets.

For decades, the United States was the leading foreign direct investor in the world. U.S. multinationals and subsidiaries sprouted everywhere. Of late, however, international firms increasingly invest in the United States. At the same time, investment continues to expand around the globe, following attractive factor conditions and entering new markets.

The extent of **foreign direct investment** in different U.S. industries is shown in Table 2.3. Almost one in seven U.S. manufacturing employees works for a **foreign affiliate,** which is a U.S. firm of which foreign entities own at least 10 percent. However, the foreign ownership is not equally distributed across all industries. Foreign direct investment tends to be concentrated in specific sectors, where the foreign investors believe they are able to contribute the best and benefit the most from their investment. For example, in the U.S. chemical industry, one-third of all employees work for foreign owners, but this is the case for only 3 percent of employees in the retail industry. As a result of foreign investment, some individuals and policymakers may grow concerned about dependency on foreign owners, even though firm proof for the validity of such concern has been difficult to establish.

Table 2.3   Employment by U.S. Affiliates of Foreign Corporations, 2001

Industries	Employees (in thousands)	As Percentage of U.S. Industry Employment
Chemicals	286	32%
Computer and Electronic Products	314	20
Electrical Equipment, Appliances, and Components	123	21
Transportation Equipment	386	21
Primary Metals	93	16
Beverages and Tobacco Products	34	20
Nonmetallic Mineral Products	124	24
Total Manufacturing	2,310	14

SOURCE: BEA, *Survey of Current Business*, August 2002, **http://www.bea.doc.gov/bea/ARTICLES/2002/08August/USAffiliates.pdf**.

Many of these investments take place in the industrialized nations and are carried out by industrialized nations. However, as Figure 2.2 shows, increasingly there is also a large stock of foreign direct investment in countries such as China and Brazil. So while the investors are still mainly from the "rich" countries, their investment targets are becoming increasingly diversified.

To some extent, these foreign direct investments substitute for trade activities. As a result, firms operating only in the domestic market may be surprised by the

Figure 2.2   International Investments in and by the United States

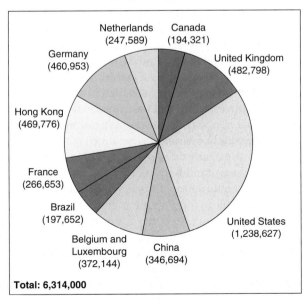

Foreign Direct Investment Inward Stock, 2000, Top 10 (millions of dollars)

Netherlands (247,589)
Canada (194,321)
Germany (460,953)
United Kingdom (482,798)
Hong Kong (469,776)
France (266,653)
Brazil (197,652)
Belgium and Luxembourg (372,144)
China (346,694)
United States (1,238,627)
Total: 6,314,000

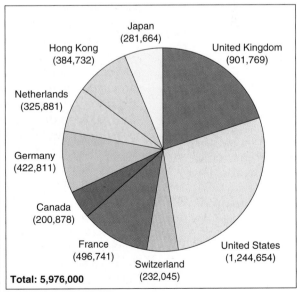

Foreign Direct Investment Outward Stock, 2000, Top 10 (millions of dollars)

Japan (281,664)
Hong Kong (384,732)
United Kingdom (901,769)
Netherlands (325,881)
Germany (422,811)
Canada (200,878)
France (496,741)
Switzerland (232,045)
United States (1,244,654)
Total: 5,976,000

SOURCE: World Investment Report 2001, United Nations Conference on Trade and Development.

onslaught of foreign competition and, unprepared to respond quickly, may lose their domestic market share. However, the substitution for trade is far from complete. In many instances, foreign affiliates themselves are major participants in trade. They may import raw materials or components and export some of their output.

Even though theory suggests an open investment policy that welcomes foreign corporations, some degree of uneasiness exists about the rapid growth of such investment. Therefore, many countries review major incoming investment projects as to their effect and desirability. For example, in the United States, the government review is done by an interagency committee called the Committee for Foreign Investments in the United States (CFIUS). This committee primarily scrutinizes foreign investment activities from the standpoint of their impact on U.S. national security.

A general restriction of foreign investments might well be contrary to the general good of a country's citizens. Domestic industries may be preserved, but only at great peril to the free flow of capital and at substantial cost to consumers. A restriction of investments may permit more domestic control over industries, yet it also denies access to foreign capital and often innovation. This in turn can result in a tightening up of credit markets, higher interest rates, and a decrease in willingness to adapt to changing world market conditions.

Policy Responses to Trade Problems

The word *policy* implies that there is a coordinated set of continuous activities in the legislative and executive branches of government to attempt to deal with U.S. international trade. Unfortunately, such concerted efforts only rarely come about. Policy responses have consisted mainly of political ad hoc reactions, which over the years have changed from deep regret to protectionism. Whereas in the mid-1970s most lawmakers and administration officials simply regretted the lack of U.S. performance in international markets, more recently, industry pressures have forced increased action.

Restrictions of Imports

In light of persistent trade deficits, growing foreign direct investment, and the tendency by some firms and industries to seek legislative redress for failures in the marketplace, the U.S. Congress in the past two decades has increasingly been willing to provide the president with more powers to restrict trade. Many resolutions have also been passed and legislation enacted admonishing the president to pay closer attention to trade. However, most of these admonitions provided only for an increasing threat against foreign importers, not for better conditions for U.S. exporters. The power of the executive to improve international trade opportunities for U.S. firms through international negotiations and a relaxation of rules, regulations, and laws has become increasingly restricted over time.

A tendency has also existed to disregard the achievements of past international negotiations. For example, in Congress an amendment was attached to protectionistic legislation, stipulating that U.S. international trade legislation should not take effect if it is not in conformity with internationally negotiated rules. The amendment was voted down by an overwhelming majority, demonstrating a legislative lack of concern for such international trade agreements. There has also been a tendency to seek short-term political favors domestically in lieu of long-term international solutions. Trade legislation has become increasingly oriented to specific trading partners and specific industries. The United States often attempts to transfer its own trade laws abroad, in areas such as antitrust or export controls, resulting in bilateral conflicts. During international trade negotiations, U.S. expectations regarding production costs, social structure, and cultural patterns are often expected to be adopted in full abroad.

Yet, in spite of all these developments, the United States is still one of the strongest advocates of free trade, to which its large volume of imports and on-going trade deficit attest. Although this advocacy is shared, at least officially, by nations around the world, governments have become very creative in designing and implementing trade barriers, examples of which are listed in Table 2.4.

One typical method consists of "voluntary" import restraints that are applied selectively against trading partners. Such measures have been used mainly in areas such as textiles, automobiles, and steel. Voluntary restrictions, which are, of course, implemented with the assistance of severe threats against trading partners, are intended to aid domestic industries to reorganize, restructure, and re-capture their trade prominence of years past. They fail to take into account that foreign importers may not have caused the economic decline of the domestic industry.

The steel industry provides a good example. World steel production capacity and supply clearly exceed world demand. This is the result both of overly ambitious industrial development projects motivated by nationalistic aspirations and of technological innovation. However, a closer look at the steel industries of developed nations shows that demand for steel has also been reduced. In the automobile industry, for example, fewer automobiles are being produced, and they are being produced differently than ten years ago. Automobiles are more compact, lighter, and much more fuel efficient as a result of different consumer tastes and higher oil prices. The average automobile today weighs 700 pounds less than in the 1970s. Accordingly, less steel is needed for its production. In addition, many components formerly made of steel are now being replaced by components made from other materials such as plastic. Even if imports of steel were to be excluded totally from the markets of industrialized nations, the steel industries could not regain the sales lost from a substantial change in the automotive industry. The case

Table 2.4	**Types of Trade Barriers**

- Import policies (for example, tariffs and other import charges, quantitative restrictions, import licensing, customs barriers)
- Standards, testing, labeling, and certification (including unnecessarily restrictive application of sanitary and phytosanitary standards and environmental measures, and refusal to accept U.S. manufacturers' self-certification of conformance to foreign product standards)
- Government procurement (for example, "buy national" policies and closed bidding)
- Export subsidies (for example, export financing on preferential terms and agricultural export subsidies that displace U.S. exports in third-country markets)
- Lack of intellectual property protection (for example, inadequate patent, copyright, and trademark regimes)
- Services barriers (for example, limits on the range of financial services offered by foreign financial institutions, regulation of international data flows, and restrictions on the use of foreign data processing)
- Investment barriers (for example, limitations on foreign equity participation and on access to foreign government-funded research and development [R&D] programs, local content and export performance requirements, and restrictions on transferring earnings and capital)
- Anticompetitive practices with trade effects tolerated by foreign governments (including anticompetitive activities of both state-owned and private firms that apply to services or to goods, and that restrict the sale of U.S. products to any firm, not just to foreign firms that perpetuate the practices)
- Trade restrictions affecting electronic commerce (for example, tariff and nontariff measures, burdensome and discriminatory regulations and standards, and discriminatory taxation)

SOURCE: Office of the United States Trade Representative, *2002 National Trade Estimate Report on Foreign Trade Barriers,* Washington, DC, September 26, 2002.
For more information, refer to **http://www.ustr.gov/reports/nte/2002/index.htm**.

The Global Environment: A Source of Conflict between Developed and Less-Developed Nations

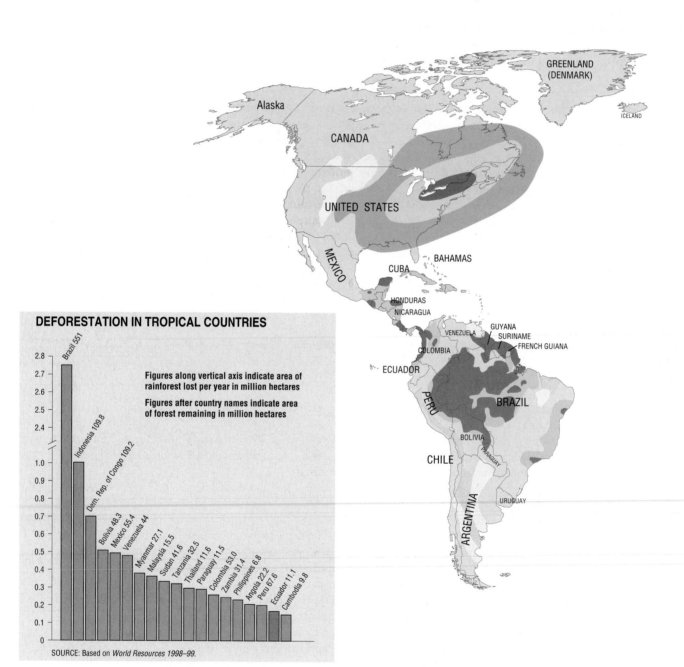

DESERTIFICATION

High degree of desertification hazard
Moderate degree of desertification hazard

DEFORESTATION IN TROPICAL COUNTRIES

Figures along vertical axis indicate area of rainforest lost per year in million hectares

Figures after country names indicate area of forest remaining in million hectares

Brazil 551
Indonesia 109.8
Dem. Rep. of Congo 109.2
Bolivia 48.3
Mexico 55.4
Venezuela 44
Myanmar 27.1
Malaysia 15.5
Sudan 41.6
Tanzania 32.5
Thailand 11.6
Paraguay 11.5
Colombia 53.0
Zambia 31.4
Philippines 6.8
Angola 22.2
Peru 67.6
Ecuador 11.1
Cambodia 9.8

2.8
2.7
2.6
2.5
2.4
1.0
0.9
0.8
0.7
0.6
0.5
0.4
0.3
0.2
0.1
0

SOURCE: Based on *World Resources 1998–99.*

RAINFOREST DESTRUCTION

Present distribution of forest area
Former extent of rainforest

ACID DEPOSITION
Estimated acidity of precipitation in the Northern Hemisphere

Slightly acid rain
Acid rain
Very acid rain

SOURCE: Based on *Environment Atlas*

on the protection of the steel industry (see end of Part One) delineates more of the complexity inherent in the international trade restrictions surrounding this industry.

If countries do not use the subtle mechanism of voluntary agreements, they often resort to old-fashioned tariffs. For example, Japanese heavy motorcycles imported into the United States were assessed a duty of 49.4 percent. This regulation kept the last U.S. producer of motorcycles, the Harley-Davidson Company, in business. Even though these tariffs have since been removed—and one year early at that—and the firm keeps on producing heavy motorcycles, one can rightfully question whether the cost imposed on U.S. consumers who preferred foreign products during the four years of tariff imposition was justified. Even though tariffs have been substantially reduced on average, their specific application can still have a major effect on trade flows.

A third major method by which trade has been restricted is through **nontariff barriers.** Typically, these barriers are much more subtle than tariffs. Compared with tariffs or even subsidies, which are visible and at least force products to compete for market acceptance on dimensions other than price, some nontariff barriers are much more difficult to detect, prove, and quantify. For example, these barriers may be government or private-sector "buy domestic" campaigns, which affect importers and sometimes even foreign direct investors. Other nontariff barriers consist of providing preferential treatment to domestic bidders over foreign bidders, using national standards that are not comparable to international standards, placing emphasis on design rather than performance, and providing for general difficulties in the market entry of foreign products. Most famous in this regard are probably the measures implemented by France. To stop or at least reduce the importation of foreign video recorders, France ruled in 1983 that all of them had to be sent through the customs station at Poitiers. This customshouse is located in the middle of the country, was woefully understaffed, and was open only a few days each week. In addition, the few customs agents at Poitiers insisted on opening each package separately in order to inspect the merchandise. Within a few weeks, imports of video recorders in France came to a halt. The French government, however, was able to point to international agreements and to the fact that officially all measures were in full compliance with the law.

The primary result of all of these trade restrictions is that many actions are taken that are contrary to what we know is good for the world and its citizens. Industries are preserved, but only at great peril to the world trade framework and at substantial cost to consumers. The direct costs of these actions are hidden and do not evoke much public complaint because they are spread out over a multitude of individuals. Yet, these costs are real and burdensome and directly affect the standard of living of individuals and the competitiveness of firms. It has been estimated that each year the total cost to U.S. consumers alone due to import restraints amounts to $70 billion. For example, abolishing import barriers in the apparel industry would let U.S. consumers gain more than $21 billion. Consumer gains would be $3.2 billion for textiles, $1.3 billion for sugar, $1.2 billion for dairy products, and $54 million for peanuts.[18] Even though each specific trade restriction may not be very significant in its impact on individuals, over time and across products these costs accumulate and prevent consumers from spending their hard-earned money on other products of their choice.

Export Promotion Efforts

Many countries provide export promotion assistance to their firms. Key reasons for such assistance are the national need to earn foreign currency, the encouragement of domestic employment, and the increase in domestic economic activity. Many forms of export promotion can also be seen as government distortion of trade since government support simply results in a subsidization of profitability or reduction of risk. Yet, there are instances where such intervention may be justified.

Government support can be appropriate if it annuls unfair foreign practices, increases market transparency and therefore contributes to the better functioning of markets,[19] or helps overcome, in the interest of long-term national competitiveness, the short-term orientation of firms.[20]

The U.S. Department of Commerce provides companies with an impressive array of data on foreign trade and marketing developments. Its Commercial Service provides a link with U.S. businesses in terms of information flow and market assistance. Efforts are made to coordinate the activities of diverse federal agencies. As a result of these efforts, a national network of export assistance centers has been created, capable of providing one-stop shops for exporters in search of export counseling and financial assistance. In addition, an official interagency advocacy network was created that helps U.S. companies win overseas contracts for large government purchases abroad. A variety of agencies have formed the Trade Promotion Coordination Committee in order to continue to improve services to U.S. exporters. A listing of these agencies together with their Web sites is provided in the appendix to this chapter, so that readers can obtain the most up-to-date information about trade policy changes and export assistance.

In terms of comparative efforts, however, U.S. export promotion activities still lag far behind the support provided by other major industrial nations. Many countries also provide substantial levels of private-sector support, which exists to a much lesser degree in the United States. Even more importantly, of the total export promotion expenditures, the largest portion (almost 50 percent) continues to go to the agricultural sector, and relatively few funds are devoted to export counseling and market research.

A new focus has come about in the area of export financing. Policymakers have increasingly recognized that U.S. business may be placed at a disadvantage if it cannot meet the subsidized financing rates of foreign suppliers. The Export-Import Bank of the United States, charged with the new mission of aggressively meeting foreign export-financing conditions, has in recent years even resorted to offering **mixed aid credits.** These take the form of loans composed partially of commercial interest rates and partially of highly subsidized developmental aid interest rates. The bank has also launched a major effort to reach out to smaller-sized businesses and assist in their export success.

Tax legislation that inhibited the employment of Americans by U.S. firms abroad has also been altered to be more favorable to U.S. firms. In the past, U.S. nationals living abroad were, with some minor exclusion, fully subject to U.S. federal taxation. Because the cost of living abroad can often be quite high—rent for a small apartment can approach the range of $4,000-plus per month—this tax structure often imposed a significant burden on U.S. firms and citizens abroad. Therefore, companies frequently were not able to send U.S. employees abroad. However, as the result of a tax code revision that allows a substantial amount of income (up to $78,000 in 2001) to remain tax-free,[21] more Americans can now be posted abroad. In their work they may specify the use of U.S. products and thus enhance the competitive opportunities of U.S. firms.

One other export promotion development was the passage of the Export Trading Company Act of 1982. Intended to be the U.S. response to Japanese *sogoshoshas,* or international trading firms, this legislation permits firms to work together to form **export consortia.** The basic idea was to provide the foreign buyer with a one-stop shopping center in which a group of U.S. firms could offer a variety of complementary and competitive products. By exempting U.S. firms from current antitrust statutes, and by permitting banks to cooperate in the formation of these ventures through direct capital participation and the financing of trading activities, the government hoped that more firms could participate in the international marketplace. Although this legislation was originally hailed as a masterstroke and a key measure in turning around the decline in U.S. competitiveness abroad, it has not attracted a large number of successful firms. It appears that the legislation may not have provided sufficient incentive for banks, export service firms, or exporters to participate. Banks simply may find domestic profit margins to be more attractive and safe; export service firms may be too small; and exporters themselves may be too independent to participate in such consortia.

A Strategic Outlook for Trade and Investment Policies

All countries have international trade and investment policies. The importance and visibility of these policies have grown dramatically as international trade and investment flows have become more relevant to the well-being of most nations. Given the growing links among nations, it will be increasingly difficult to consider domestic policy without looking at international repercussions.

A U.S. Perspective

The U.S. need is for a positive trade policy rather than reactive, ad hoc responses to specific situations. **Protectionistic legislation** can be helpful, provided it is not enacted. Proposals in Congress, for example, can be quite useful as bargaining chips in international negotiations. If passed and signed into law, however, protectionistic legislation can result in the destruction of the international trade and investment framework.

It has been suggested that a variety of regulatory agencies could become involved in administering U.S. trade policy. Although such agencies could be useful from the standpoint of addressing narrowly defined grievances, they carry the danger that commercial policy will be determined by a new chorus of discordant voices. Shifting the power of setting trade and investment policy from the executive branch to agencies or even states could give the term *New Federalism* a quite unexpected meaning and might cause progress at the international negotiation level to grind to a halt. No U.S. negotiator can expect to retain the goodwill of foreign counterparts if he or she cannot place issues on the table that can be negotiated without constantly having to check back with various authorities.

In light of continuing large U.S. trade deficits, there is much disenchantment with past trade policies. The disappointment with past policy measures, particularly trade negotiations, is mainly the result of overblown expectations. Too often, the public has mistakenly expected successful trade negotiations to affect the domestic economy in a major way, even though the issue addressed or resolved was only of minor economic importance. Yet, in light of global changes, U.S. trade policy does need to change. Rather than treating trade policy as a strictly "foreign" phenomenon, it must be recognized that it is mainly domestic economic performance that determines global competitiveness. Therefore, trade policy must become more domestically oriented at the same time that domestic policy must become more international in vision. Such a new approach should pursue at least five key goals. First, the nation must improve the quality and amount of information government and business share to facilitate competitiveness. Second, policy must encourage collaboration among companies in such areas as goods and process technologies. Third, U.S. industry collectively must overcome its export reluctance and its short-term financial orientation. Fourth, the United States must invest in its people, providing education and training suited to the competitive challenges of the twenty-first century. Finally, the executive branch must be given authority by Congress to negotiate international agreements with a reasonable certainty that the negotiation outcome will not be subject to minute amendments. Therefore, the extension of **trade promotion authority,** which still gives Congress the right to accept or reject trade treaties and agreements, but reduces the amendment procedures, was very important. Such authority is instrumental for new, large-scale trade accords such as the Doha Round to succeed.

It will also be necessary to achieve a new perspective on government–business relations. In previous decades, government and business stayed at arm's length, and it was seen as inappropriate to involve the government in private-sector activities. Now, however, closer government–business collaboration is seen as one key to enhanced competitiveness. More mutual listening to each other and joint consideration of the long-term domestic and international repercussions of policy actions and business strategy can indeed pay off. Perhaps it will make both business and government more responsive to each other's needs. At least it will reduce the failures that can result from a lack of collaboration and insufficient understanding of linkages, as described in *The International Marketplace 2.3*.

An International Perspective

From an international perspective, trade and investment negotiations must continue. In doing, so, trade and investment policy can take either a multilateral or bilateral approach. **Bilateral negotiations** are carried out mainly between two nations, while **multilateral negotiations** are carried out among a number of nations. The approach can also be broad, covering a wide variety of products, services, or investments, or it can be narrow in that it focuses on specific problems.

In order to address narrowly defined trade issues, bilateral negotiations and a specific approach seem quite appealing. Very specific problems can be discussed and resolved expediently. However, to be successful on a global scale, negotiations need to produce winners. Narrow-based bilateral negotiations require that there be, for each issue, a clearly identified winner and loser. Therefore, such negotiations have less chance for long-term success, because no one wants to be the loser. This points toward multilateral negotiations on a broad scale, where concessions can be traded off among countries, making it possible for all participants to emerge and declare themselves as winners. The difficulty lies in devising enough incentives to bring the appropriate and desirable partners to the bargaining table.

Policymakers must be willing to trade off short-term achievements for long-term goals. All too often, measures that would be beneficial in the long term are sacrificed to short-term expediency to avoid temporary pain and the resulting political cost. Given the increasing links among nations and their economies, however, such adjustments are inevitable. In the recent past, trade and investment volume continued to grow for everyone. Conflicts were minimized and adjustment possibilities were increased manyfold. As trade and investment policies must be implemented in an increasingly competitive environment, however, conflicts are likely to increase significantly. Thoughtful economic coordination will therefore be required among the leading trading nations. Such coordination will result to some degree in the loss of national sovereignty.

New mechanisms to evaluate restraint measures will also need to be designed. The beneficiaries of trade and investment restraints are usually clearly defined and have much to gain, whereas the losers are much less visible, which will make coalition building a key issue. The total cost of policy measures affecting trade and investment flows must be assessed, must be communicated, and must be taken into consideration before such measures are implemented.

The affected parties need to be concerned and join forces. The voices of retailers, consumers, wholesalers, and manufacturers all need to be heard. Only then will policymakers be sufficiently responsive in setting policy objectives that increase opportunities for firms and choice for consumers.

THE INTERNATIONAL MARKETPLACE 2.3

A Marketing Approach to Trade

U.S. trade negotiations with Japan in the wood-products industry and subsequent results provide an excellent example of American industry's difficulties in understanding and responding to foreign demand. The U.S. General Accounting Office reports that for more than a decade, the United States has negotiated with the Japanese government to allow more U.S. solid wood products to enter the Japanese market, particularly in the construction field. High-level meetings, ongoing negotiations, government financial support, and industry demonstration projects were to achieve that goal.

After all of these efforts, much has been accomplished. Japanese building codes, which, due to fire-code provisions, had prohibited construction of multistory wooden buildings, were changed. Product certification was made less costly and less complicated. Certification authority, previously the exclusive purview of the Ministry of Construction, was delegated to foreign testing organizations such as the American Plywood Association in the United States. Japan's tariffs were lowered for processed solid wood products—for softwood plywood to 10 percent from 16 percent, for glue-laminated beams to 4 percent from 15 percent. To top it all off, the Foreign Agricultural Service spent close to $18 million to promote U.S. wood-product sales in Japan.

Considering these successes, one would expect U.S. leadership in the market for solid wood products in Japan and rapid employment growth back home. Instead, the market leadership belongs to Canada, and job increases in the United States have been marginal.

These are several reasons for this situation. First, Canadian firms were much quicker than U.S. companies to take advantage of the changes. Canadian firms obtained certification much faster and were more aggressive in their marketing. They understand the different specifications and grades of wood products used in Japan, they pay attention to product quality and appearance, and they demonstrate more commitment to market and after-sales service requirements such as the development of manuals in Japanese. By contrast, U.S. firms tend to provide their information in English, tend to be less reliable as long-range suppliers, show little interest in after-sales service, and do not meet Japanese quality and appearance standards.

Second, and of even greater importance, is the U.S. disregard of the Japanese market. American companies try to sell what they produce to the Japanese, rather than producing what the Japanese want to buy. The largest portion of Japan's market for solid wood products is in post and beam construction, not in timber frames. Only 7 percent of new wooden homes are built with U.S. two-by-four products. Most other wooden housing construction uses four-by-four posts and boards for framing and is based on a three-by-six-foot module that fits the standard-sized tatami mats that cover Japanese floors. In other words, U.S. companies have focused all of their energies on increasing their penetration of the smallest part of the market, and have done so with only limited success.

Third, those U.S. firms that do attempt to adjust their products to Japanese market requirements encounter major problems in financing the new equipment and longer export payment terms. They also run into human resource problems when trying to meet Japanese quality standards or searching for international business expertise.

What do U.S. companies need to do differently? As Washington becomes more involved in trade, it should do so in a market-oriented way. The key considerations of U.S. trade policy need to be:

- A focus on market opportunities that make a difference;
- Identification of the needs and desires of foreign customers;
- Industry commitment to government market-opening approaches; and
- A link between trade policy and domestic assistance to firms planning to go abroad.

Washington needs to explicitly recognize that the times when the United States opened foreign markets simply for the well-being of the world are over. Funds should only be expended if the market is large enough to warrant attention and government actions are fully supported and followed up by industry. American trade policy needs to be focused on those issues that make a meaningful difference in terms of jobs and economic activity. After all, that is what funds government operations, provides taxes, reduces adjustment expenditures, and pays for health care.

SOURCE: Michael Czinkota, "Washington Needs a Marketing Approach to Trade," *The Asian Wall Street Journal Weekly,* June 28, 1993, 12.

Summary

International trade has often played a major role in world history. The rise and fall of the Roman Empire and the emergence of feudalism can be attributed to trade. Since 1945, the Western nations have made concerted efforts to improve the trade environment and expand trade activities. In order for them to do so, various multinational organizations, such as the WTO, the IMF, and the World Bank, were founded. In addition, several economic blocs such as the EU, NAFTA, and Mercosur were formed. Many of these organizations have been very successful in their mission, yet new realities of the trade environment demand new types of action.

Over the years, the U.S. international trade position has eroded substantially, and the U.S. share of world exports has declined precipitously from 25 percent in the 1950s. This has occurred mainly because other countries have expanded their trade activities. U.S. firms have been too complacent and disinterested in foreign markets to keep up the pace. However, a new interest in and commitment to international markets bodes well for growing U.S. and global marketing activities.

Successful foreign competitiveness in international trade has resulted in major trade deficits for the United States. Since each billion dollars' worth of exports creates, directly and indirectly, more than 11,500 jobs, it is important for U.S. firms to concentrate on the opportunities the international market has to offer.

Some policymakers intend to enhance trade performance by threatening the world with increasing protectionism. The danger of such a policy lies in the fact that world trade would shrink and standards of living would decline. Protectionism cannot, in the long run, prevent adjustment or increase productivity and competitiveness. It is therefore important to improve the capability of firms to compete internationally and to provide an international trade framework that facilitates international marketing activities.

Key Terms

Pax Romana
economic blocs
born global
trade deficit
economies of scale
foreign direct investment
foreign affiliate

nontariff barriers
mixed aid credits
export consortia
protectionistic legislation
trade promotion authority
bilateral negotiations
multilateral negotiations

Questions for Discussion

1. Why is international trade important to a nation?
2. Give examples of the effects of the "Pax Americana."
3. Discuss the role of "voluntary" import restraints in international marketing.
4. What is meant by multilateral negotiations?
5. How have consumer demands changed international trade?
6. Discuss the impact of import restrictions on consumers.
7. Does foreign direct investment have an effect on trade?

Internet Exercises

1. What is the major role played by the World Bank today? Check **http://www.worldbank.org** to report on key projects.
2. Determine the latest exports per capita for a country of your choice not listed in Table 2.2 (use data from **http://www.imf.org** and **http://www.un.org**).

Recommended Readings

Bowen, Harry, and Abraham Hollander. *Applied International Trade Analysis*. Ann Arbor: University of Michigan Press, 1998.

Business Guide to the World Trading System, 2nd ed. Geneva: International Trade Centre UNCTAD/WTO, 2000.

Das, Bhagirath Lal. *An Introduction to the WTO Agreements*. New York: St. Martin's Press, 1998.

Finger, Michael J. *Institutions and Trade Policy*. Northampton, MA: Edward Elgar, 2002.

Letterman, Gregory G. *Basics of Multilateral Institutions and Multinational Organizations: Economics and Commerce*. Ardsley, NY: Transnational, 2002.

McCue, Sarah S. *Trade Secrets: The Export Answer Book,* 3rd ed. Detroit, MI: Wayne State University Press, 2001.

Messerlin, Patrick A. *Measuring the Costs of Protection in Europe: European Commerical Policy in the 2000s*. Washington, DC: Institute for International Economics, 2001.

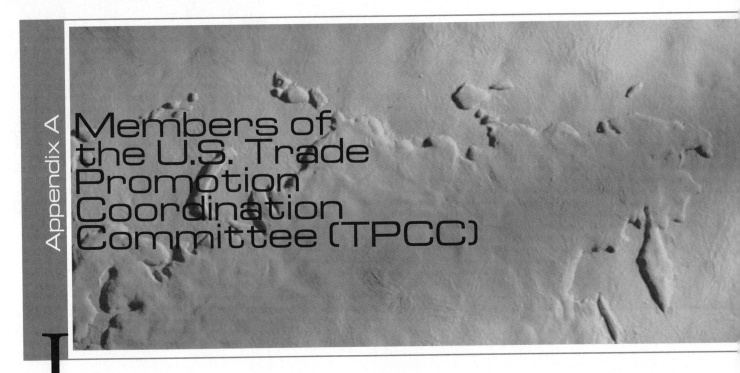

Appendix A
Members of the U.S. Trade Promotion Coordination Committee (TPCC)

Information on both individual TPCC agency programs and the National Export Strategy is available on the Internet. The TPCC's official repository of export promotion information is the National Trade Data Bank available from STAT-USA. Information about individual TPCC agency programs can be obtained by using the following Internet addresses:

- Agency for International Development (**http://www.usaid.gov**)
- Council of Economic Advisers (**http://www.whitehouse.gov/cea**)
- Department of Agriculture (**http://www.fas.usda.gov**)
- Department of Commerce (**http://www.ita.doc.gov**)
- Department of Defense (**http://www.defenselink.mil**)
- Department of Energy (**http://www.osti.gov**)
- Department of Interior (**http://www.doi.gov**)
- Department of Labor (**http://www.dol.gov**)
- Department of State (**http://www.state.gov**)
- Department of Transportation (**http://www.dot.gov**)
- Department of the Treasury (**http://www.ustreas.gov**)
- Environmental Protection Agency (**http://www.epa.gov**)
- Export-Import Bank of the United States (**http://www.exim.gov**)
- National Trade Data Bank (**http://www.stat-usa.gov**)
- National Economic Council (**http://www.whitehouse.gov/nec**)
- Office of Management and Budget (**http://www.whitehouse.gov/omb/circulars**)
- Office of the U.S. Trade Representative (**http://www.ustr.gov**)
- Overseas Private Investment Corporation (**http://www.opic.gov**)
- Small Business Administration (**http://www.sba.gov**)
- U.S. Trade and Development Agency (**http://www.tda.gov**)

SOURCE: National Export Strategy, Fourth Annual Report to the United States Congress, U.S. Government Printing Office, October 1996, 54.

chapter 3
The Cultural Environment

THE INTERNATIONAL MARKETPLACE   3.1

Cultural Imperialism Does Not Sell in International Markets

The dominance of U.S. cultural exports is felt every-where. In *USA Today*'s 2001 list of top movies, U.S. films took 48 of the top 50 places in a list that included only two non-English-language films, *Crouching Tiger, Hidden Dragon* and *Chocolat*. Given the marketing power of Holly-wood, many are worried that diversity will not survive and that the end result of globalization will be "American-ization." Quite the opposite is actually taking place in the entertainment world and international market for popu-lar culture.

In television, during the initial stage of the life cycle, the domestic industry has only fledgling production and cheap imports—primarily from the United States—to fill the time slots. With time, however, homegrown produc-tion develops and its market share increases. The top TV show in South Africa is *Generations* (a soap opera); in France, it is *Julie Lescaut* (a police series); and in Brazil, it is *O Clone* (a soap opera). The more the world global-izes, the more people want entertainment that reflects their own culture. U.S. shows do have their niche, as well. Blockbuster Hollywood action movies, cartoons (easy to dub), and certain hit series travel well across cultural bar-riers. The number one hit among German teenagers is *Buffy im Bann der Dämonen,* while Chinese children enjoy newly introduced Mickey Mouse cartoons. U.S. content providers are having to think about how to refashion their exports.

Art Attack, an art show for Disney Channel (which is seen around the world), included 216 episodes shot in 26 different languages. A single format (a set that features oversized paint pots and paint brushes, in fuchsia pink and lime green) is reshaped for each country to give it a local feel. About three fifths of each show is made up of shared footage: close-ups of the hands of one artist (British). The rest of the show is filmed separately for each country, with the heads and shoulders of local presenters seam-lessly edited in. Even though the local presenters are all flown into one central studio in the United Kingdom, the show costs only one-third of what it would take to pro-duce separately for each country. Local viewers in each place consider the show to be theirs.

In Europe, a number of developments seem to conspire to favor U.S. films. The spread of multiplex cinemas has increased attendance, but the multiplexes tend to show more U.S. movies. Hollywood blockbusters, such as *Spiderman* or *Star Wars: Attack of the Clones,* are made with budgets beyond the Europeans' wildest dreams. Marketing spending, too, has soared, doubling since the mid-1990s to an average of $3.2 million per movie. Finally, U.S. studios have become increasingly dependent on

overseas revenues and are investing more to push their movies in foreign markets. Lately, French moviemakers, who have long resented the overwhelming popularity of Hollywood movies on their home turf, have begun to fight back. *Le Fabuleux Destin d'Amélie Poulain,* a French-made romantic comedy, recently recaptured the French box office to the tune of $37.7 million in receipts. It was one of four French films released in 2001 that sold more than five million tickets, beating a record set in 1947. For the first time in decades, French films stood their ground against American imports. With higher budgets and bet-ter production values, the new films were created by a wave of young directors with Hollywood experience. What is even more interesting is that films that have success in their home markets are also more acceptable to the big-money U.S. market. In 2001, French-language films enjoyed their best year in the United States, gross-ing $28 million—small by overall standards but a huge improvement over $6.8 million in 2000. The boost in U.S. audience for foreign films in general comes squarely from

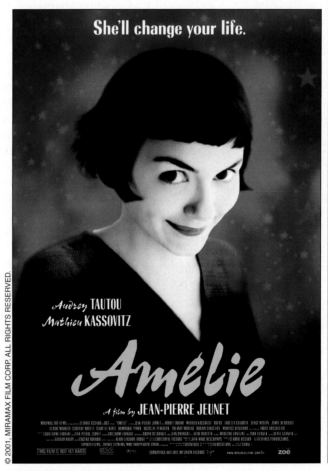

the youth market, a dramatic change from the art-house crowd of the past. To reach this audience, studios use the Internet as a marketing tool, offering prizes as well as trailers and synopses.

Top local programming created around the world is making its way into the United States, too. Most shows on Univision, America's Spanish-language TV network, including the hugely popular telenovelas, are made by Mexico's Televisa. The BBC, while expanding its own programming in the United States, coproduces much of the natural-history content on Discovery. Even Arte, a Franco-German culture channel, is no stranger to American airwaves.

The trade in entertainment is no longer a one-way street making all who watch and listen clones of one another. Much of the U.S. content going abroad is adjusted to its markets, as is the material coming into the United States. Britain's *Bob the Builder* has hammered his way into U.S. homes, but with the loss of his Staffordshire accent; since its introduction in May 2001, 2.9 million videos of this animated series have been sold.

SOURCE: "Think Local: A Survey of Television," *The Economist,* April 13, 2002, 12–14; "Culture in Peril? Mais Oui," *Fortune,* May 13, 2002, 51; "The American Connection," *The Washington Post,* May 25, 2002, E1–E2; "Rebels Without a Cause," *The Economist,* April 27, 2002, 65; "At Vivendi Universal, A French Evolution," *The Washington Post,* April 24, 2002, E1, E3.

THE EVER-INCREASING LEVEL of world trade, opening of markets, enhanced purchasing power of customers, and intensifying competition all have allowed and even forced marketers to expand their operations. The challenge for the marketing manager is to handle the differences in values and attitudes, and subsequent behavioral patterns that govern human interaction, on two levels: first, as they relate to customer behavior and, second, as they affect the implementation of marketing programs within individual markets and across markets.

For years, marketers have been heralding the arrival of the global customer, an individual or entity that would both think and purchase alike the world or region over.[1] These universal needs could then be translated into marketing programs that would exploit these similarities. However, if this approach were based on the premise of standardization, a critical and fatal mistake would be made. Overseas success is very much a function of cultural adaptability: patience, flexibility, and tolerance for others' beliefs.[2]

To take advantage of global markets or global segments, marketers are required to have or attain a thorough understanding of what drives customer behavior in different markets, and to detect the extent to which similarities exist or can be achieved through marketing efforts. After conducting market research throughout Europe, Whirlpool entered the fastest-growing microwave market with a product clearly targeted at the Euroconsumer but that offered various product features with different appeal in different countries.[3]

In expanding their presence, marketers will acquire not only new customers but new partners as well. These essential partners, whose efforts are necessary for market development and penetration, include agents, distributors, other facilitating agents (such as advertising agencies and law firms), and, in many cases, the government. Expansion will also mean new employees or strategic alliance partners whose motivations will either make or break marketing programs. Thus understanding the hot buttons and turnoffs of these groups becomes critical.

In the past, marketing managers who did not want to worry about the cultural challenge could simply decide not to do so and concentrate on domestic markets. In today's business environment, a company has no choice but to face international competition. In this new environment, believing that concern about culture and its elements is a waste of time often proves to be disastrous. An understanding allows marketers to determine when adaptation may be necessary and when commonalities allow for regional or global approaches, as seen in *The International Marketplace 3.1*. Understanding culture is critical not only in terms of getting strategies right but also for ensuring that implementation by local operations is effective.

Cultural differences often are the subject of anecdotes, and business blunders may provide a good laugh. Cultural diversity must be recognized not simply as a fact of life but as a positive benefit; that is, differences may actually suggest better solutions to challenges shared across borders. Cultural competence must be recognized as a key management skill.[4] Adjustments will have to be made to accommodate the extraordinary variety in customer preferences and work practices by cultivating the ability to detect similarities and to allow for differences. Ideally, this means that successful ideas can be transferred across borders for efficiency and adapted to local conditions for effectiveness. For example, in one of his regular trips to company headquarters in Switzerland, the general manager of Nestlé Thailand was briefed on a promotion for a cold coffee concoction called Nescafé Shake. The Thai group swiftly adopted and adapted the idea. It designed plastic containers to mix the drink and invented a dance, the Shake, to popularize the product.[5] Cultural incompetence, however, can easily jeopardize millions of dollars in wasted negotiations, potential purchases, sales and contracts, and customer relations. Furthermore, the internal efficiency of a firm may be weakened if managers, employees, and intermediaries are not "on the same wavelength."

The intent of this chapter is first to analyze the concept of culture and its various elements and then to provide suggestions for meeting the cultural challenge.

Culture Defined

Culture gives an individual an anchoring point—an identity—as well as codes of conduct. Of the more than 160 definitions of culture analyzed by Alfred Kroeber and Clyde Kluckhohn, some conceive of culture as separating humans from non-humans, some define it as communicable knowledge, and some see it as the sum of historical achievements produced by humanity's social life.[6] All the definitions have common elements: Culture is learned, shared, and transmitted from one generation to the next. Culture is primarily passed on by parents to their children but also by social organizations, special-interest groups, the government, the schools, and the church. Common ways of thinking and behaving that are developed are then reinforced through social pressure. Geert Hofstede calls this the "collective programming of the mind."[7] Culture is also multidimensional, consisting of a number of common elements that are interdependent. Changes occurring in one of the dimensions will affect the others as well.

For the purposes of this text, **culture** is defined as an integrated system of learned behavior patterns that are distinguishing characteristics of the members of any given society. It includes everything that a group thinks, says, does, and makes—its customs, language, material artifacts, and shared systems of attitudes and feelings.[8] The definition therefore encompasses a wide variety of elements, from the materialistic to the spiritual. Culture is inherently conservative, resisting change and fostering continuity. Every person is encultured into a particular culture, learning the "right way" of doing things. Problems may arise when a person encultured in one culture has to adjust to another one. The process of **acculturation**—adjusting and adapting to a specific culture other than one's own—is one of the keys to success in international operations.

Edward T. Hall, who has made some of the most valuable studies on the effects of culture on business, makes a distinction between high and low context cultures.[9] In **high context cultures,** such as Japan and Saudi Arabia, context is at least as important as what is actually said. The speaker and the listener rely on a common understanding of the context. In **low context cultures,** however, most of the information is contained explicitly in the words. North American cultures engage in low context communications. Unless we are aware of this basic difference, messages and intentions can easily be misunderstood. If performance appraisals of marketing personnel are to be centrally guided or conducted in a multinational corporation, those involved must be acutely aware of cultural nuances. One of the interesting differences is that the U.S. system emphasizes the individual's development, whereas the Japanese system focuses on the group within which the individual works. In the United States, criticism is more direct and recorded formally, whereas in Japan it is more subtle and verbal. What is not being said can carry more meaning than what is said.

Few cultures today are as homogeneous as those of Japan and Saudi Arabia. Elsewhere, intracultural differences based on nationality, religion, race, or geographic areas have resulted in the emergence of distinct subcultures. The international manager's task is to distinguish relevant cross-cultural and intracultural differences and then to isolate potential opportunities and problems. Good examples are the Hispanic subculture in the United States and the Flemish and the Walloons in Belgium. On the other hand, borrowing and interaction between national cultures may lead to narrowing gaps between cultures. Here the international business entity will act as a **change agent** by introducing new products or ideas and practices. Although this may consist of no more than shifting consumption from one product brand to another, it may lead to massive social change in the manner of consumption, the type of products consumed, and social organization. Consider, for example, that in the 1990s the international portion of McDonald's annual sales grew from 13 percent to 58 percent.[10] In markets such as Taiwan, one of the 119 countries on six continents entered, McDonald's and other fast food entities dramatically changed eating habits, especially of the younger generation.

The example of Kentucky Fried Chicken in India illustrates the difficulties marketers may have in entering culturally complex markets. Even though the company opened its outlets in two of India's most cosmopolitan cities (Bangalore and New Delhi), it found itself the target of protests by a wide range of opponents. KFC could have alleviated or eliminated some of the anti-Western passions by taking a series of preparatory steps. First, rather than opting for more direct control, KFC should have allied with local partners for advice and support. Second, KFC should have tried to appear more Indian rather than using high-profile advertising with Western ideas. Indians are quite ambivalent toward foreign culture, and ideas usable elsewhere do not work well in India. Finally, KFC should have planned for reaction by competition that came from small restaurants with political clout at the local level.[11]

In some cases, the international marketer may be accused of "cultural imperialism," especially if the changes brought about are dramatic or if culture-specific adaptations are not made in the marketing approach. Some countries, such as France, Canada, Brazil, and Indonesia, protect their "cultural industries" (e.g., music and movies) through restrictive rules and subsidies. The WTO agreement that will allow restrictions on exports of U.S. entertainment to Europe is justified by the Europeans as a cultural safety net intended to support a desire to preserve national and regional identities.[12] In June 1998, Canada organized a meeting in Ottawa about U.S. cultural dominance. Nineteen countries attended, including Britain, Brazil, and Mexico; the United States was excluded. At issue were ways of exempting cultural goods from treaties lowering trade barriers, on the view that free trade threatened national cultures. The Ottawa meeting followed a similar gathering in Stockholm, sponsored by the United Nations, which resolved to press for special exemptions for cultural goods in the Multilateral Agreement on Investment.[13]

Even if a particular country is dominant in a cultural sector, such as the United States in movies and television programming, the commonly suggested solution of protectionism may not work. Although the European Union has a rule that 40 percent of the programming has to be domestic, anyone wanting a U.S. program can choose an appropriate channel or rent a video. Quotas will also result in behavior not intended by regulators. U.S. programming tends to be scheduled during prime time, while the 60 percent of domestic programming may wind up being shown during less attractive times. Furthermore, quotas may also lead to local productions designed to satisfy official mandates and capture subsidies that accompany them.

Popular culture is not only a U.S. bastion. In many areas, such as pop music and musicals, Europeans have had an equally dominant position worldwide. Furthermore, no market is only an exporter of culture. Given the ethnic diversity in the United States (as in many other country markets), programming from around the world is made readily available. Many of the greatest successes among cultural products in 1999–2000 in the United States were imports; e.g., in television programming, *Who Wants to Be a Millionaire?* is a British concept, as is the best-seller in children's literature, the Harry Potter series. In cartoons, Pokémon hails from Japan.

The worst scenario for marketers is when they are accused of pushing Western behaviors and values—along with products and promotions—into other cultures, which can result in consumer boycotts and even destruction of property. McDonald's, KFC, Coca-Cola, Disney, and Pepsi, for example, have all drawn the ire of anti-American demonstrators for being icons of globalization.

The Elements of Culture

The study of culture has led to generalizations that may apply to all cultures. Such characteristics are called **cultural universals,** which are manifestations of the total way of life of any group of people. These include such elements as bodily adornments, courtship, etiquette, family gestures, joking, mealtimes, music, personal names, status differentiation, and trade.[14] These activities occur across cultures, but their manifestation may be unique in a particular society, bringing about cultural diversity. Common denominators can indeed be found, but the ways in which they are actually accomplished may vary dramatically.[15] Even when a segment may be perceived to be similar across borders, such as in the case of teenagers and the affluent, cultural differences make marketers' jobs challenging, as shown in *The International Marketplace 3.2.*

Observation of the major denominators summarized in Table 3.1 suggests that the elements are both material (such as tools) and abstract (such as attitudes). The sensitivity and adaptation to these elements by an international firm depends on the firm's level of involvement in the market—for example, licensing versus direct investment—and the product or service marketed. Naturally, some products and services or management practices require very little adjustment, whereas others have to be adapted dramatically.

Language

Language has been described as the mirror of culture. Language itself is multidimensional by nature. This is true not only of the spoken word but also of what can be called the nonverbal language of international business. Messages are conveyed by the words used, by the way the words are spoken (for example, tone of voice), and by nonverbal means such as gestures, body position, and eye contact.

Very often, mastery of the language is required before a person is acculturated to a culture other than his or her own. Language mastery must go beyond technical competency, because every language has words and phrases that can be readily

Table 3.1	Elements of Culture
Language	Manners and customs
• Verbal	Material elements
• Nonverbal	Aesthetics
Religion	Education
Values and attitudes	Social institutions

THE INTERNATIONAL MARKETPLACE   3.2

Euroteens = U.S. Teens?

Marketers have often operated under the notion that young people in developed markets are either North American or they share in the habits and mind-sets of their North American counterparts. However, there may be a number of things wrong with that perception. First, European teens resent being perceived as Americans with an accent and, second, they harbor national loyalties and behaviors that may leave marketers baffled.

Teens in Europe and North America have money to spend. A survey of European teens found that they receive a monthly allowance of €36.74 (compared with $22.68 weekly in the United States). The growing purchasing power of teens around the world is, therefore, of great interest to marketers, given that the full market size in 2001 was $155 billion in the United States and $728 million in the United Kingdom alone.

European teens consume much of the same media as their U.S. counterparts, with television and the Internet topping the list of favorites. But, at the same time, 67.5 percent of European boys and 47.1 percent of European girls call the Internet "too American." Just over a quarter of those surveyed said that they would rather buy a local product over the Internet than a U.S. one.

Promotions and giveaways are effective on both sides of the Atlantic. Promotions will have to be adjusted from one market to another, but the gifts do not have to be as elaborate in Europe as has become the standard in the United States. At fast food outlets, a word puzzle on the menu tray or a small stuffed animal suffices, but giveaways are not of the same complexity as in North America. For example, in 2001, Burger King ran a music-based promotion that offered teens a CD single by one of four popular acts with the purchase of a kid's meal.

Some of the differences are a function of the material elements of culture. Wireless marketing is much more advanced in Europe and U.S. marketers will test ideas to be used later at home. A total of 65 to 70 percent of teens in many EU countries have mobile phones (with the U.S. figure at 25 percent). Fun mobile features such as personalized icons and ring tones are popular. For

© EYEWIRE/GETTY IMAGES INC.

example, Fox Kids Europe sends kids, at their request, information about TV shows they are interested in. Kids are also invited to visit Fox's UK Web site to participate in interactive games they learn about via text messages.

Key considerations in marketing to European teens are the differences in national attitudes that affect how marketing messages are received. For example, while the United Kingdom encourages teens to "Just Say No," the Dutch have decriminalized marijuana and advocate teaching children about drugs at an early age.

SOURCE: "The American Connection," *The Washington Post*, May 25, 2002, E1–E2; "Euroteen Market Grabs U.S. Attention, *Marketing News*, October 22, 2001, 15. See also **http://www.yomag.net**.

understood only in context. Such phrases are carriers of culture; they represent special ways a culture has developed to view some aspect of human existence.

Language capability serves four distinct roles in international marketing.[16] Language is important in information gathering and evaluation efforts. Rather than rely completely on the opinions of others, the manager is able to see and hear personally what is going on. People are far more comfortable speaking their own language, and this should be treated as an advantage. The best intelligence is gathered on a market by becoming part of the market rather than observing it from the outside. For example, local managers of a multinational corporation should be the firm's primary source of political information to assess potential risk. Second, language provides access to local society. Although English may be widely spoken, and may even be the official company language, speaking the local language may make a dramatic difference. For example, firms that translate promotional materials and information are seen as being serious about doing business in the country. Third, language capability is increasingly important in company communications, whether within the corporate family or with channel members. Imagine the difficulties encountered by a country manager who must communicate with employees through an interpreter. Finally, language provides more than the ability to communicate. It extends beyond mechanics to the interpretation of contexts.

The manager's command of the national language(s) in a market must be greater than simple word recognition. Consider, for example, how dramatically different English terms can be when used in Australia, the United Kingdom, or the United States. In negotiations, for U.S. delegates "tabling a proposal" means that they want to delay a decision, whereas their British counterparts understand the expression to mean that immediate action is to be taken. If the British promise something "by the end of the day," this does not mean within 24 hours, but rather when they have completed the job. Additionally, they may say that negotiations "bombed," meaning that they were a success; to a U.S. manager, this could convey exactly the opposite message. Similar challenges occur with other languages and markets. Swedish is spoken as a mother tongue by 8 percent of the population in Finland, where it has idioms that are not well understood by Swedes. Goodyear has identified five different terms for the word *tires* in the Spanish-speaking Americas: *cauchos* in Venezuela, *cubiertas* in Argentina, *gomas* in Puerto Rico, *neumaticos* in Chile, and *llantas* in most of the other countries in the region.[17]

Difficulties with language usually arise through carelessness, which is manifested in a number of translation blunders. The old saying "If you want to kill a message, translate it," is true. A classic example involves GM and its "Body by Fisher" theme; when translated into Flemish, this became "Corpse by Fisher." There is also the danger of sound-alikes. For example, IBM's series 44 computers had a different number classification in Japan than in any other market because the Japanese word for four (*shih*) also sounds like the word for death. The danger of using a translingual homonym also exists; that is, an innocent English word may have strong aural resemblance to a word not used in polite company in another country. Examples in French-speaking areas include Pet milk products and a toothpaste called Cue. A French firm trying to sell pâté to a Baltimore importer experienced a problem with the brand name Tartex, which sounded like a shoe polish. Kellogg renamed Bran Buds in Sweden, where the brand name translated roughly to "burned farmer." In some cases, adjustments may not have to be dramatic to work. For example, elevator marketer Kone wanted to ensure the correct pronunciation of its name and added an accent *aigu* (Koné) to its name in French-speaking countries to avoid controversy.

An advertising campaign presented by Electrolux highlights the difficulties in transferring advertising campaigns between markets. Electrolux's theme in marketing its vacuum cleaners, "Nothing Sucks Like an Electrolux," is interpreted literally in the United Kingdom, but in the United States, the slang implications would interfere with the intended message. In a Lucky Goldstar ad, adaptation into Arabic was carried out without considering that Arabic reads from right to left. As a result, the creative concept in this execution was destroyed.

If a brand name or an advertising theme is to be extended, care has to be taken to make sure of a comfortable fit. Kellogg's Rice Krispies snap, crackle, and pop in most markets; the Japanese, who have trouble pronouncing these words, watch the characters "patchy, pitchy, putchy" in their commercials. To avoid market-by-market differences in the sound of dogs barking (i.e., "woof-woof" in Britain, "bau-bau" in Italy, "vov-vov" in Romania, or "wuff-wuff" in Austria), Pedigree dog food advertisements do not have dogs barking; the ads feature breeders talking about their dogs.[18]

The role of language extends beyond that of a communications medium. Linguistic diversity often is an indicator of other types of diversity. In Quebec, the French language has always been a major consideration of most francophone governments because it is one of the clear manifestations of the identity of the province that separates it from the English-speaking provinces. The Charter of the French Language states that the rights of the francophone collectivity are, among others, the right of consumers to be informed and served in French. The Bay, a major Quebec retailer, spends $8 million annually on its translation operations. It even changed its name to La Baie in appropriate areas. Similarly, in trying to battle English as the *lingua franca,* the French government has tried to ban the use of any foreign term or expression wherever an officially approved French equivalent exists (e.g., *mercatique,* not *un brainstorming*).[19] This applies also to Web sites that bear the ".fr" designation; they have to be in the French language. Similarly, the Hong Kong government is promoting the use of Cantonese rather than English as the language of commerce.

Despite the fact that English is encountered daily by those on the Internet, the "e" in e-business does not translate into "English." In a survey, European users highlighted the need to bridge the culture gap. One third of the senior managers said they will not tolerate English online, while less than 20 percent of the German middle managers and less than 50 percent of the French ones believe they can use English well. Fully three-quarters of those surveyed considered that being forced to use nonlocalized content on the Internet had a negative impact on productivity.[20] A truly global portal works only if online functions are provided in a multilingual and multicultural format.

Dealing with the language problem invariably requires the use of local assistance. A good local advertising agency and a good local market research firm can prevent many problems. When translation is required, as when communicating with suppliers or customers, care should be taken in selecting the translator or translation software. One of the simplest methods of control is **back-translation**—the translating of a foreign language version back to the original language by a different person from the one who made the first translation. This approach may help to detect only omissions and blunders, however. To assess the quality of the translation, a complete evaluation with testing of the message's impact is necessary.[21] In essence this means that international marketers should never translate words but emotion, which then, in turn, may well lead to the use of completely different words.

Language also has to be understood in its historic context. In Germany, Nokia launched an advertising campaign for the interchangable covers for its portable phones using the theme "*Jedem das Seine*" ("to each his own"). The campaign was withdrawn after the American Jewish Congress pointed out that the same slogan was found on the entry portal to Buchenwald, a Nazi-era concentration camp.[22] The Indian division of Cadbury-Schweppes incensed Hindu society by running an advertisement comparing its Temptations chocolate to war-torn Kashmir. The ad carried a tag line: "I'm good. I'm tempting. I'm too good to share. What am I? Cadbury's Temptations or Kashmir?" The ad featured a map of Kashmir to highlight the point, and it also first appeared on August 15th, Indian Independence Day.[23]

Nonverbal Language

Managers must analyze and become familiar with the hidden language of foreign cultures.[24] Five key topics—time, space, material possessions, friendship patterns, and business agreements—offer a starting point from which managers can begin to acquire the understanding necessary to do business in foreign countries. In many parts of the world, time is flexible and not seen as a limited commodity; people come late to appointments or may not come at all. In Hong Kong, for example, it is futile to set exact meeting times, because getting from one place to another may take minutes or hours depending on the traffic. Showing indignation or impatience at such behavior would astonish an Arab, Latin American, or Asian.

In some countries, extended social acquaintance and the establishment of appropriate personal rapport are essential to conducting business. The feeling is that one should know one's business partner on a personal level before transactions can occur. Therefore, rushing straight to business will not be rewarded, because deals are made not only on the basis of the best product or price, but also on the entity or person deemed most trustworthy. Contracts may be bound on handshakes, not lengthy and complex agreements—a fact that makes some, especially Western, businesspeople uneasy.

Individuals vary in the amount of space they want separating them from others. Arabs and Latin Americans like to stand close to people they are talking with. If a U.S. executive, who may not be comfortable at such close range, backs away from an Arab, this might incorrectly be taken as a negative reaction. Also, Westerners are often taken aback by the more physical nature of affection between Slavs—for example, being kissed by a business partner, regardless of sex.

International body language must be included in the nonverbal language of international business. For example, a U.S. manager may, after successful completion of negotiations, impulsively give a finger-and-thumb OK sign. In southern France, the manager will have indicated that the sale is worthless, and in Japan that a little bribe has been asked for; the gesture is grossly insulting to Brazilians. An interesting exercise is to compare and contrast the conversation styles of different nationalities. Northern Europeans are quite reserved in using their hands and maintain a good amount of personal space, whereas Southern Europeans involve their bodies to a far greater degree in making a point.

Religion

In most cultures, people find in religion a reason for being and legitimacy in the belief that they are part of a larger context. To define religion requires the inclusion of the supernatural and the existence of a higher power. Religion defines the ideals for life, which in turn are reflected in the values and attitudes of societies and individuals. Such values and attitudes shape the behavior and practices of institutions and members of cultures.

Religion has an impact on international marketing that is seen in a culture's values and attitudes toward entrepreneurship, consumption, and social organization. The impact will vary depending on the strength of the dominant religious tenets. While religion's impact may be quite indirect in Protestant Northern Europe, its impact in countries where Islamic fundamentalism is on the rise (such as Algeria) may be profound.

Religion provides the basis for transcultural similarities under shared beliefs and behavior. The impact of these similarities will be assessed in terms of the dominant religions of the world: Christianity, Islam, Hinduism, Buddhism, and Confucianism. Other religions may have smaller numbers of followers, such as Judaism with 14 million followers around the world, but their impact is still significant due to the many centuries during which they have influenced world history. While some countries may officially have secularism, such as Marxism-Leninism, as a state belief (for example, China, Vietnam, and Cuba), traditional religious beliefs still remain a powerful force in shaping behavior. International marketing managers must be aware of the differences not only among the major religions but also within them. The impact of these divisions may range from hostility, as in Sri Lanka, to barely perceptible but long-standing suspicion, as in many European countries where Protestant and Catholic are the main divisions. With some religions, such as Hinduism, people may be divided into groups, which determines their status and to a large extent their ability to consume.

Christianity has the largest following among world religions, with more than 2 billion people. While there are many significant groups within Christianity, the major ones are Catholicism and Protestantism. A prominent difference between the two of them is their attitude toward making money. While Catholicism has questioned it, the Protestant ethic has emphasized the importance of work and the

Religions of the World: A Part of Culture

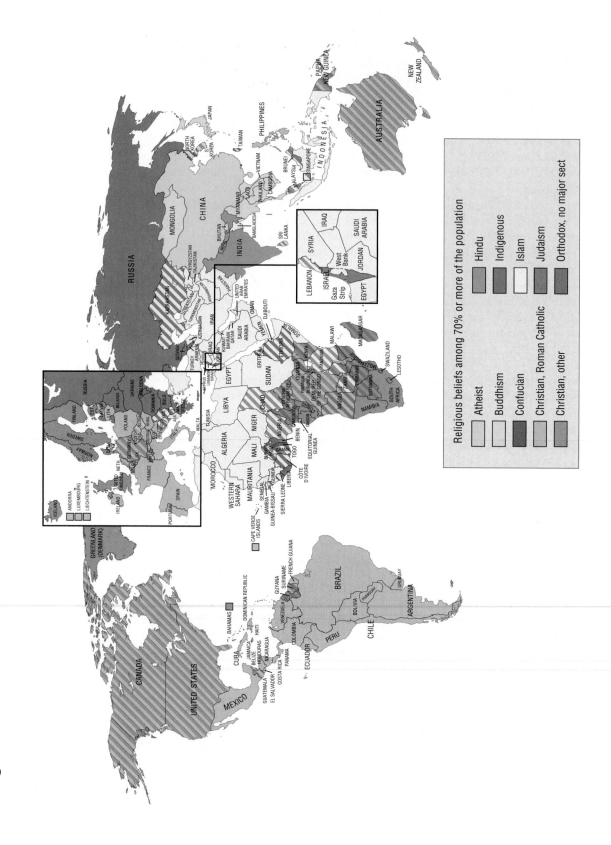

Religious beliefs among 70% or more of the population

- Atheist
- Buddhism
- Confucian
- Christian, Roman Catholic
- Christian, other
- Hindu
- Indigenous
- Islam
- Judaism
- Orthodox, no major sect

SOURCE: Based on *The World Factbook*, 2002.

accumulation of wealth for the glory of God. At the same time, frugality is stressed and the residual accumulation of wealth from hard work formed the basis for investment. It has been proposed that this is the basis for the development of capitalism in the Western world, and for the rise of predominantly Protestant countries to world economic leadership in the twentieth century.

Major holidays are often tied to religion. Holidays will be observed differently from one culture to another, and the same holiday may have different connotations. Christian cultures observe Christmas and exchange gifts on either December 24 or 25, with the exception of the Dutch, who exchange gifts on St. Nicholas Day, December 6. Tandy Corporation, in its first year in the Netherlands, targeted its major Christmas promotion for the third week of December with less than satisfactory results. The international marketing manager must see to it that local holidays are taken into account in the scheduling of events ranging from fact-finding missions to marketing programs.

Islam, which reaches from the west coast of Africa to the Philippines and across a wide band that includes Tanzania, central Asia, western China, India, and Malaysia, has more than 1.2 billion followers.[25] Islam is also a significant minority religion in many parts of the world, including Europe. It plays a pervasive role in the life of its followers, referred to as Muslims, through the *shari'ah* (law of Islam). This is most obvious in the five stated daily periods of prayer, fasting during the holy month of Ramadan, and the pilgrimage to Mecca, Islam's holy city. While Islam is supportive of entrepreneurship, it nevertheless strongly discourages acts that may be interpreted as exploitation. Islam also lacks discrimination, except for those outside the religion. Some have argued that Islam's basic fatalism (that is, nothing happens without the will of Allah) and traditionalism have deterred economic development in countries observing the religion.

The role of women in business is tied to religion, especially in the Middle East, where women are not able to function as they would in the West. The effects of this are numerous; for example, a firm may be limited in its use of female managers or personnel in these areas, and women's role as consumers and influencers in the consumption process may be different. Except for food purchases, men make the final purchase decisions.[26] Access to women in Islamic countries may only be possible through the use of female sales personnel, direct marketing, and women's specialty shops.[27]

Religion affects the marketing of products and service delivery. When beef or poultry is exported to an Islamic country, the animal must be killed in the *halal* method and certified appropriately. Recognition of religious restrictions on products (for example, alcoholic beverages) can reveal opportunities, as evidenced by successful launches of several nonalcoholic beverages in the Middle East. Other restrictions may call for innovative solutions. A challenge for the Swedish firm that had the primary responsibility for building a traffic system to Mecca was that non-Muslims are not allowed access to the city. The solution was to use closed-circuit television to supervise the work. Given that Islam considers interest payments usury, bankers and Muslim scholars have worked to create interest-free banking products that rely on lease agreements, mutual funds, and other methods to avoid paying interest.[28]

Hinduism has 860 million followers, mainly in India, Nepal, Malaysia, Guyana, Suriname, and Sri Lanka. In addition to being a religion, it is also a way of life predicated on the caste, or class, to which one is born. While the caste system has produced social stability, its impact on business can be quite negative. For example, if one cannot rise above one's caste, individual effort is hampered. Problems in workforce integration and coordination may become quite severe. Furthermore, the drive for business success may not be forthcoming because of the fact that followers place value mostly on spiritual rather than materialistic achievement.

The family is an important element in Hindu society, with extended families being the norm. The extended family structure will have an impact on the purchasing power and consumption of Hindu families. Market researchers, in particular, must take this into account in assessing market potential and consumption patterns.

Buddhism, which extends its influence throughout Asia from Sri Lanka to Japan, has 360 million followers. Although it is an offspring of Hinduism, it has no caste system. Life is seen as an existence of suffering, with achieving nirvana, a state marked by an absence of desire, as the solution to suffering. The emphasis in Buddhism is on spiritual achievement rather than worldly goods.

Confucianism has over 150 million followers throughout Asia, especially among the Chinese, and has been characterized as a code of conduct rather than a religion. However, its teachings that stress loyalty and relationships have been broadly adopted. Loyalty to central authority and placing the good of a group before that of the individual may explain the economic success of Japan, South Korea, Singapore, and the Republic of China. It also has led to cultural misunderstandings: In Western societies there has been a perception that the subordination of the individual to the common good has resulted in the sacrifice of human rights. The emphasis on relationships is very evident when developing business ties in Asia. The preparatory stage may take years before the needed level of understanding is reached and actual business transactions can take place.

Values and Attitudes

Values are shared beliefs or group norms that have been internalized by individuals.[29] Attitudes are evaluations of alternatives based on these values. The Japanese culture raises an almost invisible—yet often unscalable—wall against all *gaijin,* foreigners. Many middle-aged bureaucrats and company officials, for example, feel that buying foreign products is unpatriotic. The resistance therefore is not so much against foreign products as it is against those who produce and market them. As a result, foreign-based corporations have had difficulty in hiring university graduates or midcareer personnel because of bias against foreign employers. Dealing in China and with the Chinese, the international marketing manager will have to realize that marketing has more to do with cooperation than competition. The Chinese believe that one should build the relationship first and, if that is successful, transactions will follow. The relationship, or *guanxi,* is a set of exchanges of favors to establish trust.[30]

The more rooted values and attitudes are in central beliefs (such as religion), the more cautiously the international marketing manager has to move. Attitude toward change is basically positive in industrialized countries, whereas in more tradition-bound societies, change is viewed with great suspicion, especially when it comes from a foreign entity. These situations call for thorough research, most likely a localized approach, and a major commitment at the top level for a considerable period of time. For example, Procter & Gamble has made impressive inroads with its products by adopting a long-term, Japanese-style view of profits. The company has gained some 20 percent of the detergent market and made Pampers a household word among Japanese mothers. The struggle toward such rewards can require foreign companies to take big losses for five years or more.

To counter the perceived influence of Mattel's Barbie and Ken dolls on Iranian values, a government agency affiliated with Iran's Ministry of Education is marketing its own Dara and Sara dolls. The new products, a brother and sister, are modeled on Iranian school-book characters. Sara is dressed in a white headscarf covering black or brown curls. A popular outfit is a full-length, flower-dotted chador, which covers the doll from head to toe. One toy seller explained that playing with Mattel's golden-haired, skimpily dressed Barbie may lead girls to grow up into women who reject Iranian values.[31]

Cultural attitudes are not always a deterrent to foreign business practices or foreign goods. Japanese youth, for instance, display extremely positive attitudes toward Western goods, from popular music to Nike sneakers to Louis Vuitton haute couture to Starbuck's lattes. Even in Japan's faltering economy, global brands are able to charge premium prices if they are able to tap into cultural attitudes that revere imported goods. Similarly, attitudes of U.S. youth toward Japanese "cool" have increased the popularity of authentic Japanese "manga" comics and animated cartoons. Pokémon cards, Hello Kitty, and Sony's tiny minidisc players are examples of Japanese products that caught on in the United States almost as quickly as in Japan.[32]

While products that hit the right cultural buttons can be huge successes in foreign markets, not all top brands will translate easily from one culture to another. For example, while the Disneyland concept worked well in Tokyo, it had a tougher time in Paris. One of the main reasons was that while the Japanese have positive attitudes toward American pop culture, the Europeans are quite content with their own cultural values and traditions.[33]

Manners and Customs

Changes occurring in manners and customs must be carefully monitored, especially in cases that seem to indicate narrowing of cultural differences between peoples. Phenomena such as McDonald's and Coke have met with success around the world, but this does not mean that the world is becoming Westernized. Modernization and Westernization are not at all the same, as can be seen in Saudi Arabia, for example.

Understanding manners and customs is especially important in negotiations, because interpretations based on one's own frame of reference may lead to a totally incorrect conclusion. To negotiate effectively abroad, one needs to read correctly all types of communication. U.S. executives often interpret inaction and silence as a negative sign, so Japanese executives tend to expect their U.S. counterparts to lower prices or sweeten the deal if they just say as little as possible. Even a simple agreement may take days to negotiate in the Middle East, because the Arab party may want to talk about unrelated issues or do something else for a while. The abrasive style of Russian negotiators, and their usual last-minute change requests, may cause astonishment and concern on the part of ill-prepared negotiators. And consider the reaction of a U.S. businessperson if a Finnish counterpart were to propose the continuing of negotiations in the sauna. Preparation is needed not only in the business sense but in a cultural sense as well. Some of the potential areas in which marketers may not be prepared include: (1) insufficient understanding of different ways of thinking; (2) insufficient attention to the necessity of saving face; (3) insufficient knowledge and appreciation of the host country—history, culture, government, and image of foreigners; (4) insufficient recognition of the decision-making process and the role of personal relations and personalities; and (5) insufficient allocation of time for negotiations.[34]

One instance when preparation and sensitivity are called for is in the area of gift giving. Table 3.2 provides examples of what to give and when. Gifts are an important part of relationship management during visits and a way of recognizing partners during holidays. Care should be taken with the way the gift is wrapped; for example, it should be in appropriately colored paper. If delivered in person, the actual giving has to be executed correctly; in China, this is done by extending the gift to the recipient using both hands.[35]

Managers must be concerned with differences in the ways products are used. For example, General Foods' Tang is positioned as a breakfast drink in the United States; in France, where orange juice is not usually consumed at breakfast, Tang is positioned as a refreshment. The questions that the international manager must ask are, "What are we selling?" "What are the use benefits we should be providing?" and "Who or what are we competing against?" These questions are highlighted in *The International Marketplace 3.3.* Care should be taken not to assume cross-border similarities even if many of the indicators converge. For example, a jam producer noted that the Brazilian market seemed to hold significant potential because per capita jelly and jam consumption was one-tenth that of Argentina, clearly a difference not justified by obvious factors. However, Argentines consume jam at tea time, a custom that does not exist in Brazil. Furthermore, Argentina's

Table 3.2 When and What to Give as Gifts

China	India	Japan	Mexico	Saudi Arabia
Chinese New Year (January or February)	*Hindu Diwali festival (October or November)*	*Oseibo (Jan. 1)*	*Christmas/New Year*	*Id al-Fitr (December or January)*
✓ Modest gifts such as coffee table books, ties, pens	✓ Sweets, nuts, and fruit; elephant carvings; candleholders	✓ Scotch, brandy, Americana, round fruit such as melons	✓ Desk clocks, fine pens, gold lighters	✓ Fine compasses to determine direction for prayer, cashmere
✗ Clocks, anything from Taiwan	✗ Leather objects, snake images	✗ Gifts that come in sets of four or nine	✗ Sterling silver items, logo gifts, food baskets	✗ Pork and pigskin, liquor

✓ recommended
✗ to be avoided

SOURCE: Kate Murphy, "Gifts without Gaffes for Global Clients," *Business Week* (December 6, 1999): 153.

climate and soil favor growing wheat, leading it to consume three times the amount of bread Brazil does.[36]

Many Western companies have stumbled in Japan because they did not learn enough about the distinctive habits of Japanese consumers. Purveyors of soup should know that the Japanese drink it mainly for breakfast. Johnson & Johnson had relatively little success selling baby powder in Japan until research was conducted on use conditions. In their small homes, mothers fear that powder will fly around and get into their spotlessly clean kitchens. The company now sells baby powder in flat boxes with powder puffs so that mothers can apply it sparingly. Adults will not use it at all. They wash and rinse themselves before soaking in hot baths; powder would make them feel dirty again.

Package sizes and labels must be adapted in many countries to suit the needs of the particular culture. In Mexico, for example, Campbell's sells soup in cans large enough to serve four or five because families are generally large. In Britain, where consumers are more accustomed to ready-to-serve soups, Campbell's prints "one can makes two" on its condensed soup labels to ensure that shoppers understand how to use it.

In the United States, men buy diamond engagement rings for their fiancées. This custom is not global, however. In Germany, for example, young women tend to buy diamond rings for themselves. This precludes the use of global advertising campaigns by a company such as De Beers.

Managers must be careful of myths and legends. One candy company was ready to launch a new peanut-packed chocolate bar in Japan, aimed at giving teenagers quick energy while they crammed for exams. The company then learned about a Japanese folk legend that eating chocolate with peanuts can cause nosebleed. The launch never took place. Approaches that might be rarely taken in the United States or Europe could be recommended in other regions; for example, Conrad Hotels (the international arm of Hilton) experienced low initial occupancy rates at its Hong Kong facility until the firm brought in a feng shui man. These traditional "consultants" are foretellers of future events and the unknown through occult means and are used extensively by Hong Kong businesses, especially for advising about where to locate offices and how to position office equipment.[37] In Conrad's case, the suggestion was to move a piece of sculpture outside of the

THE INTERNATIONAL MARKETPLACE   3.3

Soup: Now It's Mmmm-Mmmm-Global!

In the late 1990s, Campbell Soup aimed to generate half of its revenues outside the U.S. by the twenty-first century. This turned out to be an ambitious goal: Its foreign sales were only a quarter of the total in 2000. Adding to the challenge is the fact that prepared food may be one of the toughest products to sell overseas. It is not as universal or as easily marketed as soap or soft drinks, given regional taste preferences. While an average Pole consumes five bowls of soup a week, 98 percent of Polish soups are homemade.

Campbell has managed to overcome some cultural obstacles in selected countries. In Poland, Campbell advertises to working Polish mothers looking for convenience. Says Lee Andrews, Campbell's new-product manager in Warsaw: "We can't shove a can in their faces and replace Mom."

However, in many regions, Campbell is trying to cook more like her. This means creating new products that appeal to distinctly regional tastes. The approach has been to use test kitchens and taste-testing with consumers. Results have included fiery cream of poblano soup in Mexico as well as watercress and duck-gizzard soup for China. Cream of pumpkin has become Australia's top-selling canned soup.

Asia has traditionally accounted for only 2 percent of Campbell's worldwide sales, but the region—China, in particular—is being targeted as the area with the strongest growth potential. In new markets, Campbell typically

launches a basic meat or chicken broth, which consumers can doctor with meats, vegetables, and spices. Later, more sophisticated soups are brought on line. In China, the real competition comes from homemade soup, which accounts for over 99 percent of all consumption. With this in mind, Campbell's prices have been kept at an attractive level and the product promoted on convenience.

Japan comes in at number two as a soup consumer (after the United States). Campbell teamed with Nakano Vinegar Co., Ltd., to learn the subtle ins and outs of marketing to the Japanese. For example, fish-based products were immediately added to the line. To cater better to local market needs, grassroots research plays a significant role. Campbell has a staff that eats in five restaurants every day. They order soup and then report as fully as possible on the taste, the spices used, and any ingredients they can identify. They describe appearance, texture, color, consistency—even what garnishes are used. These mystery shoppers also interview people and browse store shelves to determine what is popular.

Local ingredients may count, but Campbell draws the line on some Asian favorites. Dog soup is out, as is shark's fin, since most species are endangered. For most other options, including snake, for example, the company keeps an open mind.

Campbell is also finding that ethnic foods are growing in popularity around the world. With its emphasis on vegetables, Asian cuisine benefits from a healthy image in Europe and North America. This means that some new products being presently developed for the Asian consumer may become global favorites in no time.

At the same time, the company has made a strategic shift, acknowledging that outside the U.S. cultural preferences for dry soups are well entrenched. While Campbell is succeeding in developing canned soups for local tastes, its acquisition of dry soup makers like the Anglo-Dutch Unilever will help it truly become a global soup company.

SOURCES: "A Fine Kettle of Fish," *World Trade,* October 2001, 74–76; "Campbell Soup Creates a Stake in the European Market with recent Acquisition," *The Philadelphia Inquirer,* January 30, 2001, A3; "Souping Up Campbell's," *Business Week,* November 3, 1997, 70–72; Linda Grant, "Stirring It Up at Campbell," *Fortune,* May 13, 1996, 80–86; "Ethnic Food Whets Appetites in Europe, Enticing Producers to Add Foreign Fare," *The Wall Street Journal,* November 1, 1993, B5A; "Hmmm, Could Use a Little More Snake," *Business Week,* March 15, 1993, 53; "Canned and Delivered," *Business China,* November 16, 1992, 12; and **http://www.campbellsoup.com**.

hotel's lobby because one of the characters in the statue looked like it was trying to run out of the hotel.[38]

Meticulous research plays a major role in avoiding these types of problems. Concept tests determine the potential acceptance and proper understanding of a proposed new product. **Focus groups,** each consisting of eight to twelve consumers representative of the proposed target audience, can be interviewed and their responses used to check for disasters and to fine-tune research findings. The most sensitive types of products, such as consumer packaged goods, require consumer usage and attitude studies as well as retail distribution studies and audits to analyze the movement of the product to retailers and eventually to households. H.J. Heinz Co. uses focus groups to determine what consumers want in ketchup in the way of taste and image. U.S. consumers prefer a relatively sweet ketchup while Europeans go for a spicier variety. In Central Europe and Sweden, Heinz sells a hot ketchup in addition to the classic variety. In addition to changes in the product, the company may need to promote new usage situations. For example, in Greece this may mean running advertisements showing how ketchup can be poured on pasta, eggs, and cuts of meat. While some markets consider Heinz's U.S. origin a plus, there are others where it has to be played down. In Northern Europe, where ketchup is served as an accompaniment to traditional meatballs and fishballs, Heinz deliberately avoids reminding consumers of its heritage. The messages tend to be health related.[39]

The adjustment to cultural variables in the marketplace may have to be long term and accomplished through trial and error. For example, U.S. retailers have found that Japanese consumers are baffled by the warehouse-like atmosphere of the U.S-style retail outlets. When Office Depot reduced the size of its Tokyo store by a third and crammed the merchandise closer together, sales remained at the same level as before.[40]

Material Elements

Material culture results from technology and is directly related to the way a society organizes its economic activity. It is manifested in the availability and adequacy of the basic economic, social, financial, and marketing **infrastructures.** The basic economic infrastructure consists of transportation, energy, and communications systems. Social infrastructure refers to housing, health, and educational systems. Financial and marketing infrastructures provide the facilitating agencies for the international firm's operation in a given market in terms of, for example, banks and research firms. In some parts of the world, the international firm may have to be an integral partner in developing the various infrastructures before it can operate, whereas in others, it may greatly benefit from their high level of sophistication.

The level of material culture can be a segmentation variable if the degree of industrialization of the market is used as a basis. For companies selling industrial goods, such as General Electric, this can provide a convenient starting point. In developing countries, demand may be highest for basic energy-generating products. In fully developed markets, time-saving home appliances may be more in demand.

While infrastructure is often a good indicator of potential demand, goods sometimes discover unexpectedly rich markets due to the informal economy at work in developing nations. In Kenya, for example, where most of the country's 30 million population live on less than a dollar a day, more than 770,000 people have signed up for mobile phone service during the last two years; wireless providers are scrambling to keep up with demand. Leapfrogging older technologies, mobile phones are especially attractive to Kenya's thousands of small-business entrepreneurs—market stall owners, taxi drivers, and even hustlers who sell on the sidewalks. For most, income goes unreported, creating an invisible wealth on the streets. Mobile phones outnumber fixed lines in Kenya, as well as in Uganda, Venezuela, Cambodia, South Korea, and Chile. This development is attractive for marketers as well, given the expense of laying land lines.

Technological advances have probably been the major cause of cultural change in many countries. For example, the increase in leisure time so characteristic in Western cultures has been a direct result of technological development. Workers in Germany are now pushing for a 35-hour work week. Increasingly, consumers are seeking more diverse products—including convenience items—as a way of satisfying their demand for a higher quality of life and more leisure time. For example, a 1999 Gallup survey in China found that 44 percent of the respondents were saving to buy electronic items and appliances, second only to saving for a rainy day.[41] Marketers able to tailor and market their products to fit the new lifestyle, especially in emerging markets, stand to reap the benefits. Consumers around the world are showing greater acceptance of equipment for personal use, reflected in increased sales of mobile phones and small computers as well as increased Internet use. With technological advancement also comes **cultural convergence.** Black-and-white television sets extensively penetrated the U.S. market more than a decade before they reached similar levels in Europe and Japan. With color television, the lag was reduced to five years. With videocassette recorders, the difference was only three years, but this time the Europeans and the Japanese led the way while U.S. consumers concentrated on cable systems. With the compact disc, penetration rates were even after only one year. Today, with MTV available by satellite around the world, no lag exists at all.[42]

Material culture—mainly the degree to which it exists and how much it is esteemed—will have an impact on marketing decisions. Many exporters do not understand the degree to which U.S. consumers are package-conscious; for example, cans must be shiny and beautiful. On the other hand, packaging problems may arise in other countries due to lack of certain materials, different specifications when the material is available, different line-fill machinery, and immense differences in quality and consistency of printing ink, especially in South America and the Third World. Even the ability of media to reach target audiences will be affected by ownership of radios, television sets, and personal computers.

Aesthetics

Each culture makes a clear statement concerning good taste, as expressed in the arts and in the particular symbolism of colors, form, and music. What is and what is not acceptable may vary dramatically even in otherwise highly similar markets. Sex in advertising is an example. In an apparent attempt to preserve the purity of Japanese womanhood, Japanese advertisers frequently turn to blonde, blue-eyed foreign models to make the point. In introducing the shower soap Fa from the European market to the North American market, Henkel also extended its European advertising campaign to the new market. The main difference was to have the young woman in the waves don a bathing suit rather than be naked, as in the German original.

Color is often used as a mechanism for brand identification, feature reinforcement, and differentiation. In international markets, colors have more symbolic value than in domestic markets. Black, for instance, is considered the color of mourning in the United States and Europe, whereas white has the same symbolic value in Japan and most of the Far East. A British bank interested in expanding its operations to Singapore wanted to use blue and green as its identification colors. A consulting firm was quick to tell the client that green is associated with death there. Although the bank insisted on its original choice of colors, the green was changed to an acceptable shade.[43] Similarly, music used in broadcast advertisements is often adjusted to reflect regional differences.

International firms have to take into consideration local tastes and concerns in designing their facilities. They may have a general policy of uniformity in building or office space design, but local tastes may often warrant modifications. Respecting local cultural traditions may also generate goodwill toward the international marketer. For example, McDonald's painstakingly renovated a seventeenth-century building for its third outlet in Moscow.

Education

Education, either formal or informal, plays a major role in the passing on and sharing of culture. Educational levels of a culture can be assessed using literacy rates and enrollment in secondary or higher education, information available from secondary data sources. International firms also need to know about the qualitative aspects of education, namely, varying emphases on particular skills, and the overall level of the education provided. Japan and the Republic of Korea, for example, emphasize the sciences, especially engineering, to a greater degree than do Western countries.

Educational levels will have an impact on various business functions. Training programs for a production facility will have to take the educational backgrounds of trainees into account. For example, a high level of illiteracy will suggest the use of visual aids rather than printed manuals. Local recruiting for sales jobs will be affected by the availability of suitably trained personnel. In some cases, international firms routinely send locally recruited personnel to headquarters for training.

The international marketing manager may also have to be prepared to fight obstacles in recruiting a suitable sales force or support personnel. For example, the Japanese culture places a premium on loyalty, and employees consider themselves to be members of the corporate family. If a foreign firm decides to leave Japan, employees may find themselves stranded midcareer, unable to find a place in the Japanese business system. University graduates are therefore reluctant to join all but the largest and most well known of foreign firms.[44]

If technology is marketed, the level of sophistication of the product will depend on the educational level of future users. Product adaptation decisions are often influenced by the extent to which targeted customers are able to use the product or service properly.

Social Institutions

Social institutions affect the ways in which people relate to each other. The family unit, which in Western industrialized countries consists of parents and children, in a number of cultures is extended to include grandparents and other relatives. This will have an impact on consumption patterns and must be taken into account, for example, when conducting market research.

The concept of kinship, or blood relations between individuals, is defined in a very broad way in societies such as those in sub-Saharan Africa. Family relations and a strong obligation to family are important factors to be considered in human resource management in those regions. Understanding tribal politics in countries such as Nigeria may help the manager avoid unnecessary complications in executing business transactions.

The division of a particular population into classes is termed **social stratification.** Stratification ranges from the situation in Northern Europe, where most people are members of the middle class, to highly stratified societies such as India in which the higher strata control most of the buying power and decision-making positions.

An important part of the socialization process of consumers worldwide is **reference groups.** These groups provide the values and attitudes that become influential in shaping behavior. Primary reference groups include the family, coworkers, and other intimate groupings, whereas secondary groups are social organizations in which less-continuous interaction takes place, such as professional associations and trade organizations. Besides socialization, reference groups develop an individual's concept of self, which manifests itself, for example, through the use of products. Reference groups also provide a baseline for compliance with group norms through either conforming to or avoiding certain behaviors.

Social organization also determines the roles of managers and subordinates and the way they relate to one another. In some cultures, managers and subordinates are separated explicitly and implicitly by various boundaries ranging from social class differences to separate office facilities. In others, cooperation is elicited through equality. For example, Nissan USA has no reserved parking spaces and no private dining rooms, everyone wears the same type of white coveralls, and the president sits in the same room with a hundred other white-collar workers. The fitting of an organizational culture for internal marketing purposes to the larger context of a national culture has to be executed with care. Changes that are too dramatic may cause disruption of productivity or, at the minimum, suspicion.

While Western business practice has developed impersonal structures for channeling power and influence through reliance on laws and contracts, the Chinese emphasize getting on the good side of someone and storing up political capital with him or her. Things can get done without this capital, or *guanxi,* only if one invests enormous personal energy, is willing to offend even trusted associates, and is prepared to see it all melt away at a moment's notice.[45] For the Chinese, contracts form a useful agenda and a symbol of progress, but obligations come from relationships. McDonald's found this out in Beijing, where it was evicted from a central building after only two years despite having a twenty-year contract. The incomer had a strong *guanxi,* whereas McDonald's had not kept its relationships in good repair.[46]

Sources of Cultural Knowledge

The concept of cultural knowledge is broad and multifaceted. **Cultural knowledge** can be defined by the way it is acquired. Objective or **factual information** is obtained from others through communication, research, and education. **Experiential knowledge,** on the other hand, can be acquired only by being involved in a culture other than one's own.[47] A summary of the types of knowledge needed by the international manager is provided in Table 3.3. Both factual and experiential information can be general or country-specific. In fact, the more a manager becomes involved in the international arena, the more he or she is able to develop a meta-knowledge, that is, ground rules that apply to a great extent whether in Kuala Lumpur, Malaysia, or Asunción, Paraguay. Market-specific knowledge does not necessarily travel well; the general variables on which the information is based do.

In a survey on how to acquire international expertise, managers ranked eight factors in terms of their importance, as shown in Table 3.4. These managers emphasized the experiential acquisition of knowledge. Written materials were indicated to play an important but supplementary role, very often providing general or country-specific information before operational decisions must be made. Interestingly, many of today's international managers have precareer experience in government, the Peace Corps, the armed forces, or missionary service. Although the survey emphasized travel, a one-time trip to London with a stay at a large hotel and scheduled sight-seeing tours does not contribute to cultural knowledge in a

Table 3.3	Types of International Information	

	Type of Information	
Source of Information	**General**	**Country-Specific**
Objective	Examples: • Impact of GDP • Regional integration	Examples: • Tariff barriers • Government regulations
Experiential	Example: • Corporate adjustment to internationalization	Examples: • Product acceptance • Program appropriateness

Table 3.4	Managers' Rankings of Factors Involved in Acquiring International Expertise

Factor	Considered Critical	Considered Important
1. Assignments overseas	85%	9%
2. Business travel	83	17
3. Training programs	28	57
4. Non-business travel	28	54
5. Reading	22	72
6. Graduate courses	13	52
7. Pre-career activities	9	50
8. Undergraduate courses	0.5	48

SOURCE: Data collected by authors from 110 executives by questionnaire, February, 2003. Original study by Stephen J. Kobrin, *International Expertise in American Business* (New York: Institute of International Education, 1984), 38.

significant way. Travel that involves meetings with company personnel, intermediaries, facilitating agents, customers, and government officials, on the other hand, does contribute.

However, from the corporate point of view, the development of a global capability requires experience acquisition in more involved ways. This translates into foreign assignments and networking across borders, for example through the use of multicountry, multicultural teams to develop strategies and programs. At Nestlé, for example, managers shuffle around a region (such as Asia or Latin America) at four- to five-year intervals and may have tours at headquarters for two to three years between such assignments. This allows these managers to pick up ideas and tools to be used in markets where they have not been used or where they have not been necessary up to now. In Thailand, where supermarkets are revolutionizing consumer-goods marketing, techniques perfected elsewhere in the Nestlé system are being put to effective use. These experiences will then, in turn, be used to develop newly emerging markets in the same region, such as Vietnam.

Various sources and methods are available to the manager for extending his or her knowledge of specific cultures. Most of these sources deal with factual information that provides a necessary basis for market studies. Beyond the normal business literature and its anecdotal information, specific country studies are published by governments, private companies, and universities. The U.S. Department of Commerce's (**http://www.ita.doc.gov**) *Country Commercial Guides* cover 133 countries, while the Economist Intelligence Unit's (**http://www.eiu.com**) *Country Reports* cover 180 countries. *Culturegrams* (**http://www.culturegrams.com**) which detail the customs of peoples of 174 countries, are published by the Center for International and Area Studies at Brigham Young University. Many facilitating agencies—such as advertising agencies, banks, consulting firms, and transportation companies—provide background information on the markets they serve for their clients: Runzheimer International's (**http://www.runzheimer.com**) international reports on employee relocation and site selection for 44 countries and the Hong Kong and Shanghai Banking Corporation's (**http://www.hsbc.com**) *Business Profile Series* for 22 countries in the Asia-Pacific to *World Trade* magazine's (**http://www.worldtrademag.com**) "Put Your Best Foot Forward" series, which covers Europe, Asia, Mexico/Canada, and Russia.

Facilitators who specialize in advising clients on the cultural dimensions of marketing are available as well. Their task is not only to avoid cultural mistakes but also to add culture as an ingredient of success in the program. An example of such a service provider is shown in Figure 3.1.

Figure 3.1   An Example of Culture Consulting

If this picture offends you, we apologize. If it doesn't, perhaps we should explain. Because, although this picture looks innocent enough, to the Asian market, it symbolizes death. But then, most people wouldn't be expected to know that.

That's where we come in. Over the last 7 years Intertrend has been guiding clients to the Asian market with some very impressive results. Clients like California Bank & Trust, Disneyland, GTE, JC Penney, Nestlé, Northwest, and The Southern California Gas Company have all profited from our knowledge of this country's fastest growing and most affluent cultural market. And their success has made us one of the largest Asian advertising agencies in the country.

We can help you as well. Give us a call. We can share some more of our trade secrets. We can also show you how we've helped our clients succeed in the Asian market. And that's something that needs no apology.

InterTrend Communications
19191 South Vermont, Suite 400
Torrance, CA 90502
310.324.6313   fax: 310.324.6848

OOOOPS.

© COURTESY OF INTERTREND COMMUNICATIONS

SOURCE: interTrend Communications. See **http://www.intertrend.com**.

Blunders that could have been avoided with factual information about a foreign market are generally inexcusable. A manager who travels to Taipei without first obtaining a visa and is therefore turned back has no one else to blame. Other oversights may lead to more costly mistakes. For example, Brazilians are several inches shorter than the average U.S. consumer, but this was not taken into account when Sears erected American-height shelves that block Brazilian shoppers' view of the rest of the store.

International business success requires not only comprehensive fact finding and preparation, but also an ability to understand and fully appreciate the nuances of different cultural traits and patterns. Gaining this **interpretive knowledge** requires "getting one's feet wet" over a sufficient length of time.

Cultural Analysis

To try to understand and explain differences among cultures and subsequently in cross-cultural behavior, the marketer can develop checklists and models showing pertinent variables and their interaction. An example of such a model is provided in Figure 3.2. This model is based on the premise that all international business activity should be viewed as innovation and as producing change processes.[48] After all, exporters and multinational corporations introduce, from one country to other cultures, marketing practices as well as products and services, which are then perceived to be new and different. Although many question the usefulness of such models, they do bring together, into one presentation, all or most of the

Figure 3.2   A Model of Cross-Cultural Behavior

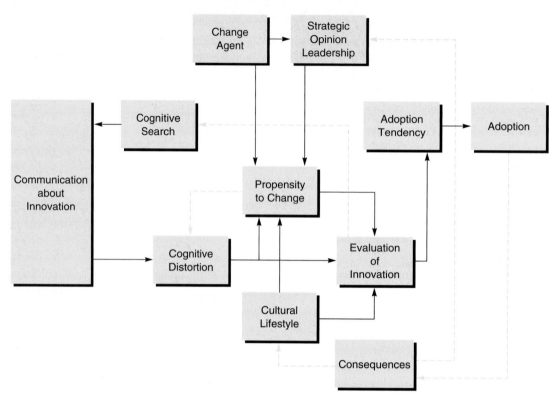

SOURCE: Adapted by permission of the publisher from "A Theory of Cross-Cultural Buying Behavior," by Jagdish N. Sheth and S. Prakash Sethi, in *Consumer and Industrial Buying Behavior*, eds. Arch G. Woodside, Jagdish N. Sheth, and Peter D. Bennett, 1977, 373. Copyright 1977 by Elsevier Science Publishing Co., Inc.

relevant variables that have an impact on how consumers in different cultures may perceive, evaluate, and adopt new behaviors. However, any manager using such a tool should periodically cross-check its results with reality and experience.

The key variable of the model is propensity to change, which is a function of three constructs: (1) cultural lifestyle of individuals in terms of how deeply held their traditional beliefs and attitudes are, and also which elements of culture are dominant; (2) change agents (such as multinational corporations and their practices) and strategic opinion leaders (for example, social elites); and (3) communication about the innovation from commercial sources, neutral sources (such as government), and social sources, such as friends and relatives.

It has been argued that differences in cultural lifestyle can be accounted for by four major dimensions of culture.[49] These dimensions consist of (1) individualism (e.g., "I" consciousness versus "we" consciousness), (2) power distance (e.g., level of equality in a society), (3) uncertainty avoidance (e.g., need for formal rules and regulations), and (4) masculinity (e.g., attitudes toward achievement, roles of men and women). Figure 3.3 presents a summary of twelve countries' positions along these dimensions. A fifth dimension has also been added to distinguish cultural differences: long-term versus short-term orientation.[50] All the high-scoring countries are Asian (e.g., China, Hong Kong, Taiwan, Japan, and South Korea), while most Western countries (such as the United States and Britain) have low scores. Some have argued that this cultural dimension may explain the Japanese marketing success based on market-share (rather than short-term profit) motivation in market development.

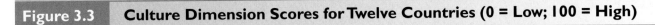

Figure 3.3   Culture Dimension Scores for Twelve Countries (0 = Low; 100 = High)

SOURCE: Data for the figure derived from Geert Hofstede, "Management Scientists Are Human," *Management Science* 40 (no. 1, 1994): 4–13.

Knowledge of a target market's position on these dimensions will help the marketer design a strategy for optimal results. Marketers want to elicit a specific, common, and favorable response from their target markets. Geographic target markets can be segmented along cultural dimensions and subsequently marketing mixes can be developed to exploit the commonalities in these segments. Table 3.5 highlights an example of such cultural segmentation from the European market. Cluster 2, for example, displays the highest uncertainty avoidance and should therefore be targeted with risk-reducing marketing programs such as extended warranties and return privileges.[51] It is important to position the product as a continuous innovation that does not require radical changes in consumption patterns.[52]

Cultural analysis can also provide specific guidelines for marketing-mix development. Since the United States highly regards individualism, promotional appeals should be relevant to the individual. Also, in order to incorporate the lower power distance within the market, copy should be informal and friendly.[53] In opposite situations, marketing communications has to emphasize that the new product is socially accepted. However, if the product is imported, it can sometimes utilize global or foreign cultural positioning. For example, individualism is often used for imported products but almost never for domestic ones.[54] Similarly, channel choice is affected by cultural factors. Firms in societies emphasizing individualism are more likely to choose channel partners based on objective criteria, whereas firms at the opposite end would prefer to deal with other firms whose representatives they consider to be friends.[55] When negotiating in Germany, one can expect a counterpart who is thorough, systematic, very well prepared, but also rather dogmatic and therefore lacking in flexibility and compromise. Great emphasis is

| Table 3.5 | Culture-Based Segmentation |

| | Size (Million) | Cultural Characteristics | | | | Illustrative Marketing Implications |
		Power Distance	Uncertainty Avoidance	Individualism	Masculinity	
Cluster I Austria, Germany, Switzerland, Italy, Great Britain, Ireland	203	Small	Medium	Medium-High	High	Preference for "high-performance" products, use "successful-achiever" theme in advertising, desire for novelty, variety and pleasure, fairly risk-averse market.
Cluster 2 Belgium, France, Greece, Portugal, Spain, Turkey	182	Medium	Strong	Varied	Low-Medium	Appeal to consumer's status and power position, reduce perceived risk in product purchase and use, emphasize product functionality.
Cluster 3 Denmark, Sweden, Finland, Netherlands, Norway	37	Small	Low	High	Low	Relatively weak resistance to new products, strong consumer desire for novelty and variety, high consumer regard for "environmentally friendly" marketers and socially conscious firms.

SOURCE: Sudhir H. Kale, "Grouping Euroconsumers: A Culture-Based Clustering Approach," *Journal of International Marketing* 3 (no. 3, 1995): 42. Reprinted by permission.

placed on efficiency. In Mexico, however, the counterpart may prefer to address problems on a personal and private basis rather than on a business level. This means more emphasis on socializing and conveying one's humanity, sincerity, loyalty, and friendship. Also, the differences in pace and business practices of the region have to be accepted. Boeing found in its annual study on world aviation safety that countries with both low individualism and substantial power distances had accident rates 2.6 times greater than at the other end of the scale. These findings will naturally have an impact on training and service operations of airlines.

Communication about the innovation takes place through the physical product itself (samples) or through a new policy in the company. If a new practice, such as quality circles or pan-regional planning, is in question, results may be communicated in reports or through word-of-mouth by the participating employees. Communication content depends on the following factors: the product's or policy's relative advantage over existing alternatives; compatibility with established behavioral patterns; complexity, or the degree to which the product or process is perceived as difficult to understand and use; trialability, or the degree to which it may be experimented with and not incur major risk; and observability, which is the extent to which the consequences of the innovation are visible.

Before the product or policy is evaluated, information about it will be compared with existing beliefs about the circumstances surrounding the situation. Distortion will occur as a result of selective attention, exposure, and retention. As examples, anything foreign may be seen in a negative light, another multinational company's efforts may have failed, or the government may implicitly discourage the proposed activity. Additional information may then be sought from any of the input sources or from opinion leaders in the market.

Adoption tendency refers to the likelihood that the product or process will be accepted. Examples of this are advertising in the People's Republic of China and equity joint ventures with Western participants in Russia, both unheard of a few years ago. If an innovation clears the hurdles, it may be adopted and slowly diffused into the entire market. An international manager has two basic choices: adapt company offerings and methods to those in the market or try to change market conditions to fit company programs. In Japan, a number of Western companies have run into obstructions in the Japanese distribution system, where great value is placed on established relationships; everything is done on the basis of favoring the familiar and fearing the unfamiliar. In most cases, this problem is solved by joint venturing with a major Japanese entity that has established contacts. On occasion, when the company's approach is compatible with the central beliefs of a culture, the company may be able to change existing customs rather than adjust to them. Initially, Procter & Gamble's traditional hard-selling style in television commercials jolted most Japanese viewers accustomed to more subtle approaches. Now the ads are being imitated by Japanese competitors. However, this should not be interpreted to mean that Japanese advertising will adapt necessarily to the influence of Western approaches. The emphasis in Japan is still on who speaks rather than on what is spoken. That is why, for example, Japan is a market where Procter & Gamble's company name is presented, as well as the brand name of the product, in the marketing communication for a brand rather than using only the product's brand name, which is customary in the U.S. and European markets.[56]

Although models like the one in Figure 3.3 may aid in strategy planning by making sure that all variables and their linkages are considered, any analysis is incomplete without the basic recognition of cultural differences. Adjusting to differences requires putting one's own cultural values aside. James E. Lee proposes that the natural **self-reference criterion**—the unconscious reference to one's own cultural values—is the root of most international business problems.[57] However, recognizing and admitting this are often quite difficult. The following analytical approach is recommended to reduce the influence of one's own cultural values:

1. Define the problem or goal in terms of domestic cultural traits, habits, or norms.
2. Define the problem or goal in terms of foreign cultural traits, habits, or norms. Make no value judgments.
3. Isolate the self-reference criterion influence in the problem and examine it carefully to see how it complicates the problem.
4. Redefine the problem without the self-reference criterion influence and solve for the optimal goal situation.

This approach can be applied to product introduction. If Kellogg Co. wants to introduce breakfast cereals into markets where breakfast is traditionally not eaten or where consumers drink very little milk, managers must consider very carefully how to instill this new habit. The traits, habits, and norms of breakfast are quite different in the United States, France, and Brazil, and they have to be outlined before the product can be introduced. In France, Kellogg's commercials are aimed as much at providing nutrition lessons as they are at promoting the product. In Brazil, the company advertised on a soap opera to gain entry into the market, because Brazilians often emulate the characters of these television shows.

Analytical procedures require constant monitoring of changes caused by outside events as well as the changes caused by the business entity itself. Controlling **ethnocentricism**—the belief that one's own culture is superior to others—can be achieved only by acknowledging it and properly adjusting to its possible effects in managerial decision making. The international manager needs to be prepared and able to put that preparedness to effective use.[58]

The Training Challenge

International managers face a dilemma in terms of international and intercultural competence. U.S. firms' lack of adequate foreign language and international business skills has resulted in lost contracts, weak negotiations, and ineffectual management. A UNESCO study of ten- and fourteen-year-old students in nine countries placed U.S. teens next to last in their comprehension of foreign cultures. Even when cultural awareness is high, there is room for improvement. For example, a survey of European executives found that a shortage of international managers was considered the single most important constraint on expansion abroad.[59] The increase in overall international activity of firms has increased the need for cultural sensitivity training at all levels of the organization. Today's training must take into consideration not only outsiders to the firm but interaction within the corporate family as well. However inconsequential the degree of interaction may seem, it can still cause problems if proper understanding is lacking. Consider, for example, the date 11/12/03 on a message; a European will interpret this as the eleventh of December, but in the United States it is the twelfth of November.

Some companies try to avoid the training problem by hiring only nationals or well-traveled executives for their international operations. This makes sense for the management of overseas operations but will not solve the training need, especially if transfers to a culture unfamiliar to the manager are likely. International experience may not necessarily transfer from one market to another.

To foster cultural sensitivity and acceptance of new ways of doing things within the organization, management must institute internal education programs. These programs may include (1) culture-specific information (e.g., data covering other countries, such as videopacks and culturegrams), (2) cultural general information (e.g., values, practices, and assumptions of countries other than one's own), and (3) self-specific information (e.g., identifying one's own cultural paradigm, including values, assumptions, and perceptions about others).[60] One study found that Japanese assigned to the United States receive mainly language training as preparation for the task. In addition, many companies use mentoring whereby an individual is assigned to someone who is experienced and who will spend the required time squiring and explaining. Talks given by returnees and by visiting lecturers hired specifically for the task round out the formal part of training.[61]

The objective of formal training programs is to foster the four critical characteristics of preparedness, sensitivity, patience, and flexibility in managers and other personnel. These programs vary dramatically in terms of their rigor, involvement, and, of course, cost.[62] A summary of these programs is provided in Figure 3.4. In the 1990s, Korean firms embarked on a mission of *segyehwa,* or globalization, which meant preparing the managers and employees who will be in charge of implementing the program. At Kumho Group, the chairman required all airline and tire maker employees to spend an hour each morning studying a language or learning about foreign cultures. Cards taped up in bathrooms taught a new phrase in English or Japanese each day. Hyundai Motor Co. sent twenty-five managers in their thirties and forties to Cornell University for nearly a year to learn new disciplines and the less rigid U.S. management style.[63]

At Samsung, several special interest groups were formed to focus on issues such as Japanese society and business practices, the Chinese economy, changes in Europe, and the U.S. economy. In addition, groups also explored cutting-edge business issues, such as new technology and marketing strategies. And for the last few years, Samsung has been sending the brightest junior employees abroad for a year.[64]

Environmental briefings and cultural orientation programs are types of **area studies** programs. These programs provide factual preparation for a manager to operate in, or work with people from, a particular country. Area studies should be a basic prerequisite for other types of training programs. Alone, they serve little practical purpose because they do not really get the manager's feet wet. Other, more involved programs contribute the context in which to put facts so that they can be properly understood.

The **cultural assimilator** is a program in which trainees must respond to scenarios of specific situations in a particular country. These programs have been

Figure 3.4	Cross-Cultural Training Methods

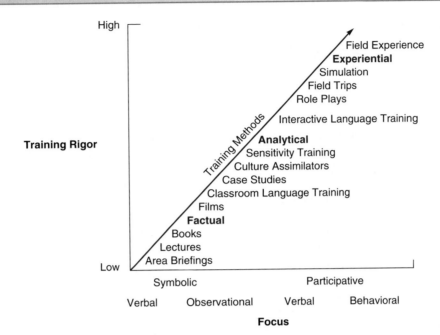

SOURCE: J. Stewart Black and Mark Mendenhall, "A Practical but Theory-Based Framework for Selecting Cross-Cultural Training Methods," in *International Human Resources Management*, eds. Mark Mendenhall and Gary Oddou. Copyright © 1991, p. 188. Reprinted by permission of South-Western College Publishing, a division of Thomson Publishing, Inc.

developed for the Arab countries, Iran, Thailand, Central America, and Greece.[65] The results of the trainees' assimilator experience are evaluated by a panel of judges. This type of program has been used in particular in cases of transfers abroad on short notice.

When more time is available, managers can be trained extensively in language. This may be required if an exotic language is involved. **Sensitivity training** focuses on enhancing a manager's flexibility in situations that are quite different from those at home. The approach is based on the assumption that understanding and accepting oneself is critical to understanding a person from another culture. While most of the methods discussed are best delivered in face-to-face settings, Web-based training is becoming more popular, as seen in *The International Marketplace 3.4*.

Finally, training may involve **field experience,** which exposes a manager to a different cultural environment for a limited amount of time. Although the expense of placing and maintaining an expatriate is high (and, therefore, the cost of failure is high), field experience is rarely used in training. One field experience technique that has been suggested when the training process needs to be rigorous is the host-family surrogate. This technique places a trainee (and possibly his or her family) in a domestically located family of the nationality to which they are assigned.[66]

Regardless of the degree of training, preparation, and positive personal characteristics, a manager will always remain foreign. A manager should never rely on his or her own judgment when local managers can be consulted. In many instances, a manager should have an interpreter present at negotiations, especially if the manager is not completely bilingual. Overconfidence in one's language capabilities can create problems.

THE INTERNATIONAL MARKETPLACE 3.4

Online Cultural Training

The Internet can play an important role in preparing marketing people for the international marketplace. While it cannot replace real-life interaction as an experiential tool, it does provide a number of benefits, including comparisons of behavior in different cultures, and can provide an opportunity to develop the skills needed to interact successfully with people from other cultures. Many companies use online learning as an addition to existing instructor-led programs.

Companies typically rely on the following elements in designing Web-based training:

1. **Detailed Scenarios.** Much of the training material consists of a detailed, realistic story that is tied into elements of the learner's background; i.e., the session becomes more than a briefing. It becomes a narrated experience full of learning moments for participants. This is made possible by the ability of the Web to store and circulate a lot of information instantaneously around the world.

2. **Gradual Delivery.** The ability to control the flow of information to the participant supports the learning process in a number of ways. First, the participant is allowed to fit the training into his or her schedule. Second, the real-life flow of information is mimicked and a higher degree of realism is achieved.

3. **Support.** A set of detailed materials is provided to the participants 24 hours a day. At any hour and at any location, participants can check their perceptions against the materials, reinforce learning from a dimly recalled lesson, or seek feedback on an important point or issue.

4. **Relevant Exercises.** Participants can be provided topical exercises and activities, the level of which can be adjusted depending on how the participant has invested in the training.

5. **Online Discussions.** Sessions can be simulcast to hundreds of participants around the world. The lack of face-to-face interaction can be remedied by having discussion groups where participants can share their experiences with one another. The pooled learning experience is stronger than the experience with one solitary participant.

The following case highlights some of the points made:

Joe Schmed is a marketing representative for a pharmaceutical company. His company has just undertaken a joint venture with a pan-Asian pharmaceutical company based in Kuala Lumpur. In order to develop a successful sales plan, over the next six months Joe will travel to Southeast Asia at least eight times. The first trip will be in two weeks. However, Joe lacks the time to take two full days out of his schedule for a traditional training program. Since his undergraduate major was in Asian studies, Joe feels that his cultural understanding is quite adequate. Nevertheless, he would like to brush up on some of his knowledge and gain a better understanding of Asian business. Logging on, he enters a training course, completing parts of it as he finds time—on airplanes and after work, for example.

SOURCES: "On-Line Learning," Special Advertising Section, *Fortune*, July 1, 2002, S1–S19; Peter T. Burgi and Brant R. Dykehouse, "On-Line Cultural Training: The Next Phase," *International Insight*, Winter 2000, 7–10. See also **http://www.runzheimer.com**.

Making Culture Work for Marketing Success

Culture should not be viewed as a challenge but as an opportunity that can be exploited. This requires, as has been shown in this chapter, an understanding of the differences and their fundamental determinants. Differences can quite easily be dismissed as indicators of inferiority or approaches to be changed; however, the opposite may actually be the case. Best practice knows no one particular origin, nor should it acknowledge boundaries. The following rules serve as a summary of how culture and its appreciation may serve as a tool to ensure marketing success.

➤ **Embrace local culture.** Many corporate credos include a promise to be the best possible corporate citizens in every community operated in.[67] For example, in 3M's plant near Bangkok, Thailand, a Buddhist shrine, wreathed in flowers, pays homage to the spirits that Thais believe took care of the land prior to the plant's arrival. Showing sensitivity to local customs helps local acceptance and builds employee morale. More importantly, it contributes to a deeper understanding of the market and keeps the marketer from inadvertently doing something to alienate constituents.

➤ **Build relationships.** Each market has its own unique set of constituents who need to be identified and nurtured. Establishing and nurturing local ties at the various stages of the market-development cycle develop relationships which can be invaluable in expansion and countering political risk. 3M started its preparations for entering the China market soon after President Nixon's historic visit in 1972. For ten years, company officials visited Beijing and entertained visits of Chinese officials to company headquarters in Minneapolis–St. Paul. Such efforts paid off in 1984, when the Chinese government made 3M the first wholly owned venture in the market. Many such emerging markets require long-term commitment on the part of the marketer.

➤ **Employ locals to gain cultural knowledge.** The single best way to understand a market is to grow with it by developing human resources and business partnerships along the way. Of the 7,500 3M employees in Asia, fewer than ten are from the United States. As a matter of fact, of the 34,000 3M employees outside of the United States, fewer than 1 percent are expatriates. The rest are locals who know local customs and the purchasing habits of their compatriots. In every way possible, locals are made equals with their U.S. counterparts. For example, grants are made available for 3M employees to engage in the product-development process with concept and idea development.

➤ **Help employees understand you.** Employing locals will give a marketer a valuable asset in market development; i.e., in acculturation. However, these employees also need their own process of adjustment (i.e., "corporatization") to be effective. At any given time, more than 30 of 3M's Asian technicians are in the United States, where they learn the latest product and process advances while gaining insight to how the company works. Also, they are able to develop personal ties with people they may work with. Furthermore, they often contribute by infusing their insights into company plans. Similar schemes are in place for distributors. Distributor advisory councils allow intermediaries to share their views with the company.

➤ **Adapt products and processes to local markets.** Nowhere is commitment to local markets as evident as in its product offering. Global, regional, and purely local products are called for, and constant and consistent product-development efforts on a market-by-market basis are warranted to find the next global success. When the sales of 3M's famous Scotchbrite cleaning pads were languishing, company researchers interviewed housewives and domestic help to determine why. They found that traditionally floors are scrubbed with the help of the rough shells of coconuts. 3M responded by making its cleaning pads brown and shaping them like a foot. In China, a big seller for 3M is a composite to fill tooth cavities. In the United States, dentists pack a soft material into the cavity and blast it with a special beam of light, making it as hard as enamel in a matter of seconds. In China, dentists cannot afford this technology. The solution was an air-drying composite that hardens in a matter of minutes, but at a reasonable expense to the dental customer.

➤ **Coordinate by region.** The transfer of best practice is critical, especially in areas that have cultural similarities. When 3M designers in Singapore discovered that customers used its Nomad household mats in their cars, they spread the word to their counterparts throughout Asia. The company encourages its product managers from different parts of Asia to hold regular periodic meetings and share insights and strategies. The goal of this cross-pollination is to come up with regional programs and "Asianize," or even globalize, a product more quickly. Joint endeavors build cross-border esprit de corps, especially when managers may have their own markets' interests primarily at heart.[68]

Summary

Culture is one of the most challenging elements of the international marketplace. This system of learned behavior patterns characteristic of the members of a given society is constantly shaped by a set of dynamic variables: language, religion, values and attitudes, manners and customs, aesthetics, technology, education, and social institutions. An international manager, to cope with this system, needs both factual and interpretive knowledge of culture. To some extent, the factual can be learned; the interpretation comes only through experience.

The most complicated problems in dealing with the cultural environment stem from the fact that we cannot learn culture—we have to live it. Two schools of thought exist in the business world on how to deal with cultural diversity. One is that business is business the world around, following the model of Pepsi and McDonald's. In some cases, globalization is a fact of life; however, cultural differences are still far from converging.

The other school proposes that companies must tailor business approaches to individual cultures. Setting up policies and procedures in each country has been compared to an organ transplant; the critical question centers on acceptance or rejection. The major challenge to the international manager is to make sure that rejection is not a result of cultural myopia or even blindness.

The internationally successful companies all share an important quality: patience. They have not rushed into situations but rather built their operations carefully by following the most basic business principles. These principles are to know your challenger, know your audience, and know your customer.

Key Terms

culture
acculturation
high context cultures
low context cultures
change agent
cultural universals
back-translation
focus groups

infrastructures
cultural convergence
social stratification
reference groups
cultural knowledge
factual information
experiential knowledge
interpretive knowledge

self-reference criterion
ethnocentrism
area studies
cultural assimilator
sensitivity training
field experience

Questions for Discussion

1. Comment on the assumption, "If people are serious about doing business with you, they will speak English."

2. You are on your first business visit to Germany. You feel confident about your ability to speak the language (you studied German in school and have taken a refresher course), and you decide to use it. During introductions, you want to break the ice by asking *"Wie geht's?"* and insisting that everyone call you by your first name. Speculate as to the reaction.

3. What can a company do to culture-sensitize its staff?

4. What can be learned about a culture from reading and attending to factual materials? Given the tremendous increase in international marketing activities, where will companies in a relatively early stage of the internationalization process find the personnel to handle the new challenges?

5. Management at a U.S. company trying to market tomato paste in the Middle East did not know that, translated into Arabic, tomato paste is "tomato glue." How could they have known in time to avoid problems?

6. Give examples of how the self-reference criterion might be manifested.

Internet Exercises

1. Various companies, such as GMC Global Relocation Services, are available to prepare and train international marketers for the cultural challenge. Using their Web site (**http://www.windhamint.com**), assess its role in helping the international marketer.

2. Compare and contrast an international marketer's home pages for presentation and content; for example, Coca-Cola (**http://www.coca-cola.com**) and its Japanese version (**http://www.cocacola.co.jp**). Are the differences cultural?

Recommended Readings

Axtell, Roger E. *Do's and Taboos around the World.* New York: John Wiley & Sons, 1993.

Brislin, R. W., W. J. Lonner, and R. M. Thorndike, *Cross-Cultural Research Methods.* New York: John Wiley & Sons, 1973.

Copeland, Lennie, and L. Griggs. *Going International: How to Make Friends and Deal Effectively in the Global Marketplace.* New York: Random House, 1990.

Elashmawi, Farid, and Phillip R. Harris. *Multicultural Management 2000: Essential Cultural Insights for Global Business Success.* Houston, TX: Gulf, 1998.

Hall, Edward T., and Mildred Reed Hall. *Understanding Cultural Differences.* Yarmouth, ME: Intercultural Press, 1990.

Hoecklin, Lisa. *Managing Cultural Differences.* Workingham, England: Addison-Wesley, 1995.

Hofstede, Geert. *Culture's Consequences.* London: Sage Publications, 1981.

Kenna, Peggy, and Sondra Lacy. *Business Japan: Understanding Japanese Business Culture.* Lincolnwood, IL: NTC, 1994.

Lewis, Richard D. *When Cultures Collide.* London: Nicholas Brealey Publishing, 2000.

Marx, Elizabeth. *Breaking through Culture Shock: What You Need to Succeed in International Business.* London: Nicholas Brealey Publishing, 1999.

O'Hara-Devereux, Mary, and Robert Johansen. *Global Work: Bridging Distance, Culture, and Time.* San Francisco: Jossey-Bass Publishers, 1994.

Parker, Barbara. *Globalization and Business Practice: Managing across Boundaries.* London: Sage Publications, 1999.

Terpstra, Vern, and K. David. *The Cultural Environment of International Business.* Cincinnati, OH: South-Western, 1992.

Trompenaars, Fons, and Charles Hampden-Turner. *Riding the Waves of Culture.* New York: Irwin, 1998.

chapter **4**
The Economic Environment

THE INTERNATIONAL MARKETPLACE   4.1

Markets at the Bottom of the Income Pyramid

Marketers are facing a challenging time at the start of the twenty-first century: domestic markets are not experiencing growth and many of the promising international markets have been struck by recession or by financial crises. The time may have come to consider the 4 billion people in the world who live in poverty, subsisting on less than $1,500 a year (see figure), as potential customers. Despite initial skepticism, marketers are finding that they can make profits while at the same time having a positive effect on the sustainable livelihoods of these people. However, these new ventures will require radical departures from the traditional business models; for example, new partnerships (ranging from local governments to nonprofits) and new pricing structures (allowing customers to rent or lease rather than buy).

The first order of business is to learn about the needs, aspirations, and habits of targeted populations for whom traditional intelligence gathering may not be the most effective. Hewlett-Packard has an initiative called World e-Inclusion which, working with a range of global and local partners, aims to sell, lease, or donate a billion dollars' worth of satellite-powered computer products and services to markets in Africa, Asia, Eastern Europe, Latin America, and the Middle East. To engage with beta communities in Senegal, Hewlett-Packard partnered with Joko, Inc., a company founded by revered Senegalese pop star Youssou n'Dour.

The World Economic Pyramid

Annual per Capita Income*	Tiers	Population in Millions
More Than $20,000	1	75–100
$1,500–$20,000	2 & 3	1,500–1,750
Less Than $1,500	4	4,000

*Based on purchasing power parity in U.S.$.

SOURCE: UN World Development Reports.

In the product area, marketers must combine advanced technology with local insights. Hindustan Lever (part of Unilever) learned that low-income Indians, usually forced to settle for low-quality products, wanted to buy high-end detergents and personal care products, but could not afford them in the quantities available. In response, the company developed extremely low-cost packaging material and other innovations that allowed for a product priced in pennies instead of the $4 to $15 price of the regular containers. The same brand is on all of the product forms, regardless of packaging. Because these consumers do not shop at supermarkets, Lever employs local residents with pushcarts who take small quantities of the sachets to kiosks.

© AFP/CORBIS

Coca-Cola has introduced "Project Mission" in Botswana to launch a drink to combat anemia, blindness, and other afflictions common in poorer parts of the world. The drink, called Vitango, is like the company's Hi-C orange-flavored drink, but it contains 12 vitamins and minerals chronically lacking in the diets of people in developing countries. The project satisfies multiple objectives for the Coca-Cola company. First, it could help boost sales at a time when global sales of carbonated drinks are slowing, and, second, it will help in establishing relationships with governments and other local constituents that will serve as a positive platform for brand Coca-Cola.

Due to economic and physical isolation of poor communities, providing access can lead to a thriving business. In Bangladesh (with income levels of $200), Grameen-Phone Ltd. leases access to wireless phones to villagers. Every phone is used by an average of 100 people and generates $90 in revenue a month—two or three times the revenues generated by wealthier users who own

their phones in urban areas. Similarly, the Jhai Foundation, an American-Lao foundation, is helping villagers in Laos with Internet access. The first step, however, was to develop an inexpensive and robust computer. The computer has no moving and very few delicate parts. Instead of a hard disk, it relies on flash-memory chips, and instead of an energy-guzzling glass cathode ray tube, its screen is a liquid-crystal display.

The emergence of these markets presents a great opportunity for international marketers. It also creates a chance for business, government, and civil society to join together in a common cause to help the aspiring poor to join the world market economy.

SOURCES: "Making the Web Worldwide," *The Economist,* September 28, 2002, 76; C. K. Prahalad and Stuart L. Hart, "The Fortune at the Bottom of the Pyramid," *Strategy and Business,* first quarter, 2002, 35–47; "Drinks for Developing Countries," *The Washington Post,* November 27, 2001, B1, B6; and Dana James, "B2-4B Spells Profits," *Marketing News,* November 5, 2001, 1, 11–12.

T HE ASSESSMENT OF A FOREIGN MARKET ENVIRONMENT should start with the evaluation of economic variables relating to the size and nature of the markets. Because of the large number of worthwhile alternatives, initial screening of markets should be done efficiently yet effectively enough, with a wide array of economic criteria, to establish a preliminary estimate of market potential. One of the most basic characterizations of the world economy is provided in Figure 4.1, which incorporates many of the economic variables pertinent to marketers.

The **Group of Five**—listed in Figure 4.1 as the United States, Britain, France, Germany, and Japan—consists of the major industrialized countries of the world. This group is sometimes expanded to the **Group of Seven** (by adding Italy and Canada) and to the **Group of Ten** (by adding Sweden, the Netherlands, and Belgium). It may also be expanded to encompass the members of the Organization for Economic Cooperation and Development, OECD (which consists of 30 countries: Western Europe, the United States, Australia, Canada, Czech Republic, Hungary, Japan, Mexico, New Zealand, Poland, Slovakia, South Korea, and Turkey).

Important among the middle-income developing countries are the newly industrialized countries (NICs), which include Singapore, Taiwan, Korea, Hong Kong, Brazil, and Mexico (some propose adding Malaysia and the Philippines to the list as well). Some of these NICs will earn a new acronym, RIC (rapidly industrializing country). Over the past 20 years, Singapore has served as a hub, providing critical financial and managerial services to the Southeast Asian markets. Singapore has successfully attracted foreign investment, mostly regional corporate headquarters and knowledge-intensive industries, and has served as one of the main gateways for Asian trade. Its exports have reached well over 300 percent of GDP.[1]

The major oil-exporting countries, in particular the eleven members of the Organization of Petroleum Exporting Countries (OPEC) and countries such as Russia, are dependent on the price of oil for their world market participation. A relatively high dollar price per barrel (as high as $30 in 2002) works very much in these countries' favor.

Figure 4.1   The Global Economy

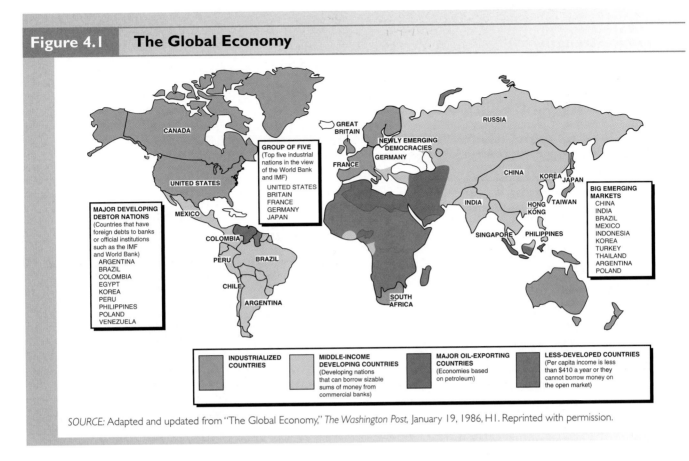

SOURCE: Adapted and updated from "The Global Economy," *The Washington Post,* January 19, 1986, H1. Reprinted with permission.

Many of the emerging economies will depend on the success of their industrialization efforts in the years to come, even in the case of resource-rich countries that may find commodity prices being driven down by humanmade substitutes. China became the second-largest exporter of textiles to the United States after it began increasing production in the 1980s. Despite an image of hopeless poverty, India has over 200 million middle-class consumers, more than Germany. A special group in this category consists of the countries saddled with a major debt burden, such as Egypt and Peru. The degree and form of their participation in the world market will largely depend on how the debt issue is solved with the governments of the major industrialized countries and the multilateral and commercial banks.

In less-developed countries, debt problems and falling commodity prices make market development difficult. Africa, the poorest continent, owes the rest of the world $375 billion, an amount equal to three quarters of its GNP and nearly four times its annual exports. Another factor contributing to the challenging situation is that only 1 percent of the world's private investment goes to sub-Saharan Africa.[2] However, as shown in *The International Marketplace 4.1,* these countries, which constitute the majority of the world's population, may also provide the biggest potential market opportunity for marketers in the twenty-first century.[3]

In the former centrally planned economies, dramatic changes are under way. A hefty capital inflow will be key to modernizing both the newly emerging democracies of Central and Eastern Europe. They are crippled by $60 billion in foreign debt and decades of Communist misrule. Desperately needed will be Western technology, management, and marketing know-how to provide better jobs and put more locally made and imported consumer goods in the shops. Within the groups, prospects vary: The future for countries such as Hungary, the Baltics, the Czech Republic, and Poland looks far better than it does for Russia as they prepare to join the European Union.[4]

Economic Strength

GDP/capita ?

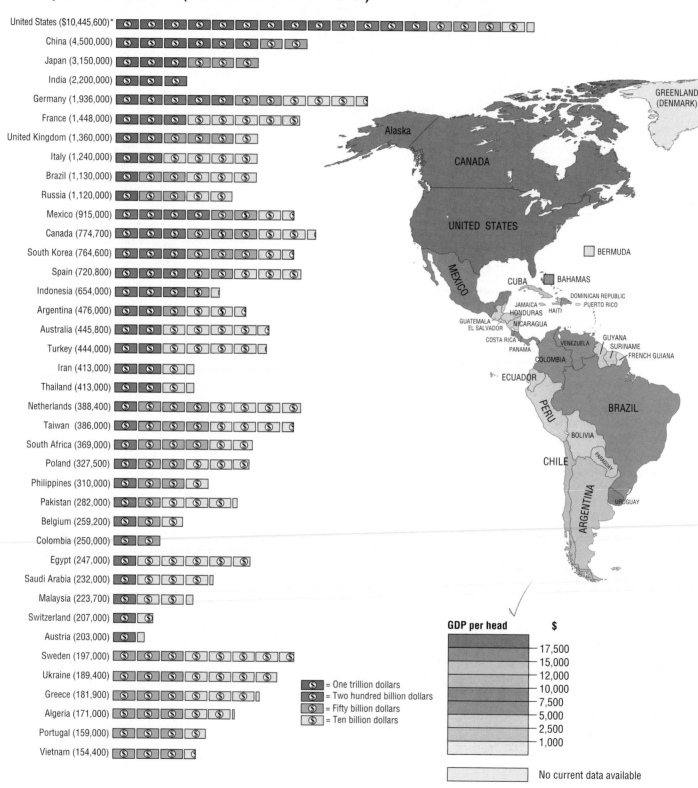

Top World Economies (GDP in million dollars U.S.)

United States ($10,445,600)*

China (4,500,000)

Japan (3,150,000)

India (2,200,000)

Germany (1,936,000)

France (1,448,000)

United Kingdom (1,360,000)

Italy (1,240,000)

Brazil (1,130,000)

Russia (1,120,000)

Mexico (915,000)

Canada (774,700)

South Korea (764,600)

Spain (720,800)

Indonesia (654,000)

Argentina (476,000)

Australia (445,800)

Turkey (444,000)

Iran (413,000)

Thailand (413,000)

Netherlands (388,400)

Taiwan (386,000)

South Africa (369,000)

Poland (327,500)

Philippines (310,000)

Pakistan (282,000)

Belgium (259,200)

Colombia (250,000)

Egypt (247,000)

Saudi Arabia (232,000)

Malaysia (223,700)

Switzerland (207,000)

Austria (203,000)

Sweden (197,000)

Ukraine (189,400)

Greece (181,900)

Algeria (171,000)

Portugal (159,000)

Vietnam (154,400)

⑤ = One trillion dollars
⑤ = Two hundred billion dollars
⑤ = Fifty billion dollars
⑤ = Ten billion dollars

GDP per head　　$

17,500
15,000
12,000
10,000
7,500
5,000
2,500
1,000

No current data available

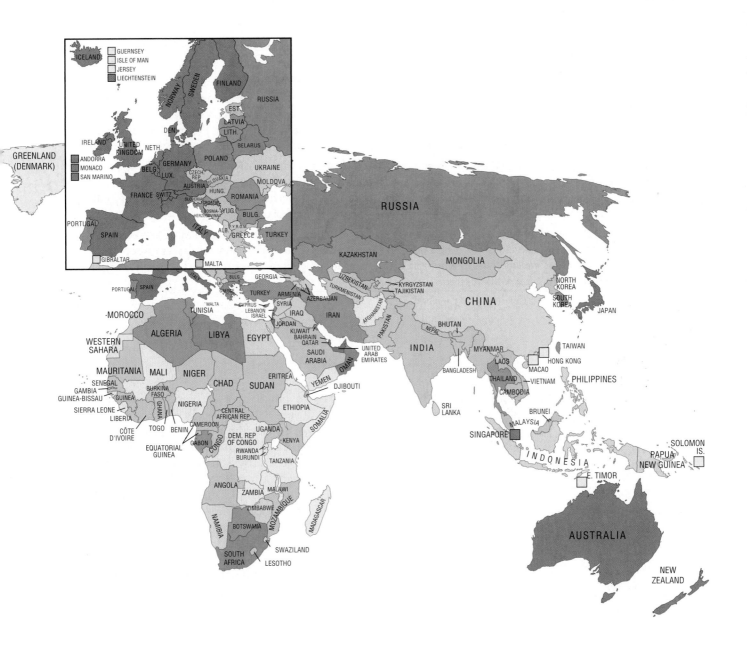

*http://www.bea.doc.gov (accessed March 3, 2003).
SOURCE: Based on The World Almanac, 2003.

| Table 4.1 | Economic Development Variable in Countries' Use of Electricity and Electrical Goods |

Less developed: These countries have primarily agrarian and/or extractive economies. High birthrates, along with limited infrastructures, account for the low per capita income and usage of electricity. Electrification is limited to the main population centers. Generally, basic electrical equipment is imported.

Early developing: These countries have begun initial development of an infrastructure and have infant industries, especially mining and selected cottage manufacturers. Target economic sectors may enjoy high growth rates even though per capita income and electricity consumption are still modest. Progressively more sophisticated electrical equipment is imported, frequently to achieve forward integration of extractive industries.

Semideveloped: These countries have started an accelerated expansion of infrastructure and wide industrial diversification. Thus, per capita income and electricity consumption are growing rapidly. Increased discretionary income and electrification allow greater ownership of autos and electrical appliances among the expanding middle class. Larger quantities of high-technology equipment are imported.

Developed: These countries enjoy well-developed infrastructures, high per capita income and electricity consumption, and large-scale industrial diversification. They are also characterized by low rates of population and economic growth, as well as shifts in emphasis from manufacturing to service industries—notably transportation, communication, and information systems.

SOURCE: Adapted from V. Yorio, *Adapting Products for Export* (New York: Conference Board, 1983), 11.

Classifications of markets will vary by originator and intended use. Marketers will combine economic variables to fit their planning purposes by using those that relate directly to the product and/or service the company markets, such as the market's ability to buy. For example, Table 4.1 provides a summary of an economic classification system for possible use by a marketer in power and electricity generation. This format takes into account both general country considerations—such as population, GNP, geography, manufacturing as a percentage of national product, infrastructure, and per capita income—and narrower industry-specific considerations of interest to the company and its marketing efforts, such as extent of use of the product, total imports, and U.S. or EU share of these imports.

The discussion that follows is designed to summarize a set of criteria that helps identify foreign markets and screen the most opportune ones for future entry or change of entry mode. Discussed are variables on which information is readily available from secondary sources such as international organizations, individual governments, and private organizations or associations.

World Bank and United Nations publications and individual countries' *Statistical Abstracts* provide the starting point for market investigations. The more developed the market, the more data are available. Data are available on past developments as well as on projections of broader categories such as population and income. Euromonitor, for example, publishes *World Consumer Income & Expenditure Patterns,* which covers 71 countries around the world.

Market Characteristics

The main dimensions of a market can be captured by considering variables such as those relating to the population and its various characteristics, infrastructure, geographical features of the environment, and foreign involvement in the economy.

Figure 4.2   World Population: Present and the Shape of Things to Come

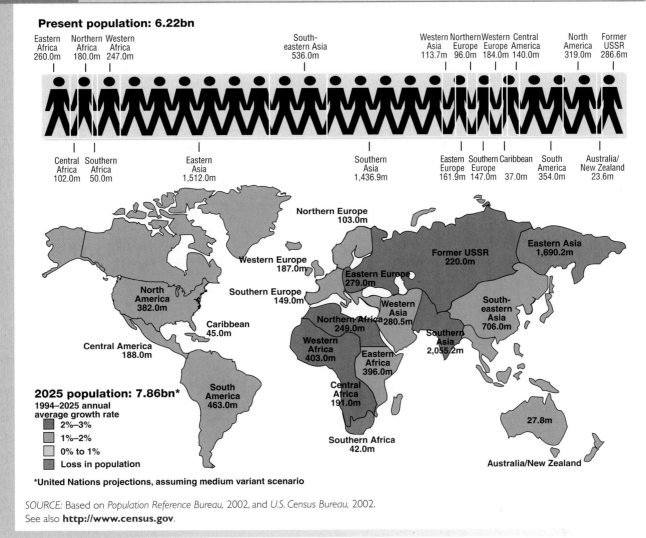

Present population: 6.22bn

| Eastern Africa 260.0m | Northern Africa 180.0m | Western Africa 247.0m | South-eastern Asia 536.0m | Western Asia 113.7m | Northern Europe 96.0m | Western Europe 184.0m | Central America 140.0m | North America 319.0m | Former USSR 286.6m |

| Central Africa 102.0m | Southern Africa 50.0m | Eastern Asia 1,512.0m | Southern Asia 1,436.9m | Eastern Europe 161.9m | Southern Europe 147.0m | Caribbean 37.0m | South America 354.0m | Australia/New Zealand 23.6m |

2025 population: 7.86bn*

1994–2025 annual average growth rate
- 2%–3%
- 1%–2%
- 0% to 1%
- Loss in population

*United Nations projections, assuming medium variant scenario

SOURCE: Based on *Population Reference Bureau,* 2002, and *U.S. Census Bureau,* 2002. See also **http://www.census.gov**.

Population

The total world population exceeded six billion people in 1999. The number of people in a particular market provides one of the most basic indicators of market size and is, in itself, indicative of the potential demand for certain staple items that have universal appeal and are generally affordable. As indicated by the data in Figure 4.2, population is not evenly divided among the major regions of the world; Asia holds over half the world's population.

These population figures can be analyzed in terms of marketing implications by noting that countries belonging to the European Union (EU) constitute 85 percent of the Western European population, and with the expected expansion of the EU in 2004, the percentage will rise to 95. The two largest entities in Asia, China and India, constitute nearly 70 percent of Asia's population. The greatest population densities are also to be found in Europe, providing the international marketer with a strategically located center of operation and ready access to the major markets of the world.

Population figures themselves must be broken down into meaningful categories in order for the marketer to take better advantage of them. Because market entry decisions may lie in the future, it is worthwhile to analyze population projections in the areas of interest and focus on their possible implications. Figure 4.2 includes United Nations projections that point to a population explosion, but mainly in the developing countries. Northern Europe will show nearly zero population growth for the next 30 years, whereas the population of Africa will triple. Even in the low- or zero-growth markets, the news is not necessarily bad for the international marketer. Those in the 25 to 45 age group, whose numbers are increasing, are among the most affluent consumers of all, having formed family units and started to consume household goods in large quantities as they reach the peak of their personal earnings potential. Early in this century, they are expected to start spending more on leisure goods and health care and related services.[5]

To influence population growth patterns, governments will have to undertake, with the help of private enterprise, quite different social marketing tasks. These will range from promoting and providing incentives for larger families (in Scandinavia, for example) to increased family planning efforts (in Thailand, for example). Regardless of the outcome of such government programs, current trends will further accelerate the division of world markets into the "haves" and the "have-nots." More adjustment capability will be required on the part of companies that want to market in the developing countries because of lower purchasing power of individuals and increasing government participation in the marketing of basic products. However, as the life expectancy in a market extends and new target markets become available, international marketers may be able to extend their products' life cycles by marketing them abroad.

Depending on the marketer's interest, population figures can be classified to show specific characteristics of their respective markets. Age distribution and life expectancy correlate heavily with the level of development of the market. Industrialized countries, with their increasing median age and a larger share of the population above 65, will open unique opportunities for international marketers with new products and services. For example, Kimberly-Clark markets its Depend line for those with incontinence problems both in Europe and North America.

Interpretation of demographics will require some degree of experiential knowledge. As an example, which age categories of females should be included in an estimate of market potential for a new contraceptive? This would vary from the very early teens in the developing countries to higher age categories in developed countries, where the maturing process is later.

An important variable for the international marketer is the size of the household. A **household** describes all the persons, both related and unrelated, who occupy a housing unit.[6] Within the EU, the average household size has shrunk from 2.9 to 2.7 persons in the last 25 years and is expected to decline further.[7] One factor behind the overall growth in households, and the subsequent decline in the average size, has been the increase in the numbers of divorced and sole survivor households. One-person households are most common in Norway and Germany. This compares strikingly with countries such as Colombia, where the average household size is six. With economic development usually bringing about more, but smaller-sized, households, international marketers of food products, appliances, and household goods have to adjust to patterns of demand; for example, they may offer single-serving portions of frozen foods and smaller appliances.

The increased urbanization of many markets has distinctly changed consumption patterns. Urban populations as a percentage of the total will vary from a low of 6 percent in Burundi to a high of 97 percent in Belgium. The degree of urbanization often dictates the nature of the marketing task the company faces, not only in terms of distribution but also in terms of market potential and buying habits. Urban areas provide larger groups of consumers who may be more receptive to marketing efforts because of their exposure to other consumers (the demonstration effect) and to communication media. In markets where urbanization is recent and taking place rapidly, the marketer faces additional responsibility as a change agent, especially when incomes may be low and the conditions for the proper use of the products may not be adequate. This is especially true in countries where rapid industrialization is taking place, such as Greece, Spain, and Portugal.

When using international data sources, the international marketer must recognize that definitions of a construct may vary among the many secondary sources. The concept of **urbanization,** for example, has different meanings depending on where one operates. In the United States, an urban area is defined as a place of 2,500 or more inhabitants; in Sweden, it is a built-up area with at least 200 inhabitants with no more than 200 meters between houses; in Mauritius, it is a town with proclaimed legal limits. Comparability, therefore, is concerned with the ends and not the means (or the definition).

Income

Markets require not only people but also purchasing power, which is a function of income, prices, savings, and credit availability.

Apart from basic staple items, for which population figures provide an estimate, income is most indicative of the market potential for most consumer and industrial products and services. For the marketer to make use of information on gross national products of various nations, such as that summarized in Table 4.2, further knowledge is needed on distribution of income. Per capita GNP is often used as a primary indicator for evaluating purchasing power. This figure shows great variation between countries, as indicated by Norway's $38,700 and Ethiopia's $99. The wide use of GNP figures can be explained by their easy availability, but they should nevertheless be used with caution. In industrialized countries, the richest 10 percent of the population consume 20 percent of all goods and services, whereas the respective figure for the developing countries may be as high as 50 percent.[8] In some markets, income distribution produces wide gaps between population groups. The more developed the economy, the more income distribution tends to converge toward the middle class.

Table 4.2	Gross Domestic Product per Capita for Selected Countries, 2000

Highest GDP per Head (in Dollars)

Rank	Country	GDP	Rank	Country	GDP
1	Norway	38,700	18	Taiwan	13,900
2	USA	37,300	19	New Zealand	13,800
3	Switzerland	36,500	20	Greece	12,700
4	Denmark	34,600	21	Portugal	12,200
5	Japan	31,900	22	South Korea	9,530
6	Sweden	28,700	23	Saudi Arabia	8,110
7	Finland	27,200	24	Argentina	7,550
8	Austria	26,100	25	Czech Republic	6,510
9	Germany	25,900	26	Hungary	6,300
10	UK	25,500	27	Mexico	6,110
11	Canada	24,900	28	Venezuela	5,650
12	France	24,600	29	Poland	5,200
13	Italy	21,300	30	Lebanon	4,890
14	Singapore	20,700	31	Chile	4,370
15	Australia	20,400	32	Slovakia	4,160
16	Israel	17,400	33	Malaysia	3,290
17	Spain	16,600	34	Iraq	3,120

(continued on next page)

Table 4.2 continued

Lowest GDP per Head (in Dollars)

Rank	Country	GDP	Rank	Country	GDP
1	Haiti	465	10	Uganda	261
2	Pakistan	425	11	Madagascar	243
3	Vietnam	390	12	Nepal	223
4	Zambia	345	13	Mozambique	193
5	Kenya	344	14	Burkina Faso	186
6	Nigeria	314	15	Malawi	143
7	Cambodia	292	16	Sierra Leone	131
8	Bangladesh	284	17	Ethiopia	99
9	Tanzania	270			

SOURCE: Compiled from *International Marketing Data and Statistics 2002* (London: Euromonitor, 2002), table 1098.

The international marketer can use the following classification as a planning guide:

1. Very low family incomes. Subsistence economies tend to be characterized by rural populations in which consumption relies on personal output or barter. Some urban centers may provide markets. Example: Cameroon.

2. Very low, very high family incomes. Some countries exhibit strongly bimodal income distributions. The majority of the population may live barely above the subsistence level, but there is a strong market in urban centers and a growing middle class. The affluent are truly affluent and will consume accordingly. Examples: India, Mexico.

3. Low, medium, high family incomes. Industrialization produces an emerging middle class with increasing disposable income. The very low and very high income classes tend to remain for traditional reasons of social class barriers. Example: Portugal.

4. Mostly medium family incomes. The advanced industrial nations tend to develop institutions and policies that reduce extremes in income distribution, resulting in a large and comfortable middle class able to purchase a wide array of both domestic and imported products and services. Example: Denmark.

Although the national income figures provide a general indication of a market's potential, they suffer from various distortions. Figures available from secondary sources are often in U.S. dollars. The per capita income figures may not be a true reflection of purchasing power if the currencies involved are distorted in some way. For example, fluctuations in the value of the U.S. dollar may distort real-income and standard-of-living figures. The goods and services in different countries have to be valued consistently if the differences are to reflect real differences in the volumes of goods produced. The use of **purchasing power parities (PPP)** instead of exchange rates is intended to achieve this objective. PPPs show how many units of currency are needed in one country to buy the amount of goods and services that one unit of currency will buy in another country. Table 4.3 provides an example of such data.

Second, using a monetary measure may not be a proper and all-inclusive measure of income. For example, in developing economies where most of the consumption is either self-produced or bartered, reliance on financial data alone would seriously understate the standard of living. Further, several of the service-related items (for example, protective services and travel), characteristic of the industrialized countries' national income figures, do not exist for markets at lower levels of development.

Moreover, the marketer will have to take into consideration variations in market potential in individual markets. Major urban centers in developing countries may have income levels comparable to those in more developed markets, while rural areas may not have incomes needed to buy imported goods.

In general, income figures are useful in the initial screening of markets. However, in product-specific cases, income may not play a major role, and startling scenarios may emerge. Some products, such as motorcycles and television sets in China, are in demand regardless of their high price in relation to wages because of their high prestige value. Some products are in demand because of their foreign origin. As an example, European luxury cars have lucrative markets in countries where per capita income figures may be low but there are wealthy consumers who are able and willing to buy them. For example, Mercedes-Benz's target audience in India is families earning 1 million rupees (approximately $30,000).

Table 4.3 Gross Domestic Product/Purchasing Power Parities

Country	Gross Domestic Product (billions of dollars)				Gross Domestic Product per Capita (dollars)			
	1985	1990	1997	1999	1985	1990	1997	1999
United States	3,967.5	5,392.0	7,783	9,324	16,581	21,449	29,080	33,836
OECD Europe	3,980.2	5,871.0	8,408	8,658	9,857	14,070	18,698	19,038
Austria	81.2	128.0	225	201	10,748	16,620	22,010	24,668
Belgium	106.1	164.0	272	255	10,768	16,405	23,090	24,868
Denmark	62.8	86.0	184	145	12,279	16,765	23,450	27,098
Finland	56.1	82.0	127	118	11,447	16,453	19,660	22,743
France	646.6	984.0	1,542	1,319	11,720	17,431	22,210	22,225
Germany	738.7	1,157.0	2,321	1,974	12,105	18,291	21,170	23,840
Greece	59.7	75.0	122	161	6,010	7,349	12,540	15,154
Ireland	24.4	37.0	65	97	6,901	10,659	17,420	25,427
Italy	624.2	924.0	1,160	1,341	10,927	16,021	20,100	23,261
Netherlands	164.3	236.0	403	412	11,339	15,766	21,300	25,947
Portugal	53.2	82.0	110	168	5,516	8,389	14,180	16,698
Spain	292.5	459.0	570	729	7,597	11,792	15,690	18,231
Sweden	106.3	144.0	232	204	12,727	16,867	19,010	23,038
United Kingdom	624.0	903.0	1,231	1,362	11,020	15,720	20,710	22,882
Norway	58.0	68.0	159	127	13,963	15,921	24,260	28,267
Switzerland	94.3	143.0	305	208	14,440	20,997	26,580	28,697
Turkey	179.7	190.9	199	416	3,547	3,316	6,470	6,338
Australia	184.4	273.0	383	493	11,682	15,951	19,510	25,721
Canada	388.8	509.0	595	826	15,440	19,120	21,750	26,423
Japan	1,425.4	2,179.0	4,812	3,238	11,805	17,634	24,400	25,590
New Zealand	33.1	45.0	60	71	10,126	13,258	15,780	18,532

SOURCE: Adapted from Bureau of the Census, *Statistical Abstract of the United States,* 2001 (Washington, DC: Government Printing Office, 2001), tables 1362 and 1363. **http://www.statusa.gov**.

Earnings at that level are enough for a lifestyle to rival that of a U.S. or European family with an income three times higher due to a much higher level of disposable income.[9] Further, the lack of income in a market may preclude the marketing of a standardized product but, at the same time, provide an opportunity for an adjusted product. A packaged goods company, confronted with considerable disparity in income levels within the same country, adapted a deodorant product to fit two separate target income groups—the regular product version in an aerosol can and the less expensive one in a plastic squeeze bottle. By substituting cheaper parts and materials, successful international marketers can make both consumer and industrial products more affordable in less affluent markets and therefore reach a wider target audience.

Consumption Patterns

Depending on the sophistication of a country's data collection systems, economic data on consumption patterns can be obtained and analyzed. The share of income spent on necessities will provide an indication of the market's development level as well as an approximation of how much money the consumer has left for other purchases. Engel's laws provide some generalizations about consumers' spending patterns and are useful generalizations when precise data are not available. They state that as a family's income increases, the percentage spent on food will decrease, the percentage spent on housing and household operations will be roughly constant, and the amount saved or spent on other purchases will increase. Private expenditure comparisons reveal that the percentage spent on food in 2000 varied from 9.2 percent in the United States to 60 percent in Indonesia (see Table 4.4).

In Western Europe, expenditures on clothing typically account for 5 to 9 percent of all spending, but in poorer countries the proportion may be lower. In some low-wage areas, a significant proportion of clothing is homemade or locally made at low cost, making comparisons not entirely accurate. Eastern European households spend an inordinate proportion of their incomes on foodstuffs but quite a low proportion on housing. The remaining, less absolutely central areas of consumption (household goods, leisure, and transportation) are most vulnerable to short-term cancellation or postponement and thus serve as indicators for the strength of confidence in the market in general.

In large markets, such as China, India, and the United States, marketers need to exercise care in not assuming uniformity across regions. As seen in *The International Marketplace 4.2,* regional differences may be marked. Similar gaps exist between urban and rural populations. In China, the average rural citizen spends $4 on goods other than food and less than $1 on entertainment, while the amount is $10 for both in the cities.

Table 4.4	Consumer Spending by Category, as Percent of Total, 2000

	Food, Beverages, Tobacco	Clothing Footwear, Textiles	House-hold Fuels	House-hold Goods & Services	Housing	Health Goods & Medical Services	Leisure and Education	Transport and Communi-cations	Hotels/ Catering
Argentina	27.8	7.5	4.4	6.7	8.4	8.8	9.5	13.9	7.3
Australia	15.3	3.9	2.0	5.5	17.9	3.7	13.4	14.3	8.5
Brazil	21.4	4.3	2.3	9.6	17.5	7.8	5.2	13.6	8.3
Canada	14.1	6.7	3.1	8.2	21.2	3.5	10.6	17.1	7.5
China	38.1	10.2	4.9	8.6	5.7	5.3	11.4	6.9	4.8
Colombia	32.5	4.7	2.4	5.3	8.6	6.5	5.8	18.0	13.3
Eastern Europe*	40.9	6.7	5.2	5.1	12.4	2.6	6.0	10.3	4.9
European Union/ Western Europe**	20.2	6.4	4.0	6.8	17.5	4.5	9.2	15.8	7.3
India	53.1	5.2	3.2	3.0	6.7	4.4	3.5	13.7	1.4
Indonesia	60.1	5.2	3.8	4.6	8.9	1.9	5.8	3.5	4.3
Israel	21.0	4.7	2.4	8.3	22.3	4.5	10.8	10.9	3.5
Japan	12.1	5.0	2.2	4.4	20.8	11.5	10.7	11.5	4.0
Mexico	28.2	5.1	1.2	9.0	12.1	4.3	6.0	15.2	8.0
Nigeria	56.0	8.1	1.0	4.1	3.7	3.8	4.7	10.9	1.6
Singapore	14.5	4.5	2.5	6.3	15.8	5.8	10.7	20.2	14.7
South Korea	24.5	4.0	3.9	4.6	13.3	7.4	12.4	16.8	6.7
Thailand	31.4	12.0	2.4	6.5	6.7	6.1	7.0	12.6	9.0
United States	9.2	4.8	2.3	5.0	14.7	17.6	11.5	13.5	6.4

*Countries include Belarus, Bulgaria, Croatia, Czech Republic, Estonia, Hungary, Latvia, Lithuania, Poland, Romania, Russia, Slovadia, Slovenia, Ukraine.

**Countries include Austria, Belgium, Denmark, Finland, France, Germany, Greece, Ireland, Italy, Netherlands, Norway, Portugal, Spain, Sweden, Switzerland, Turkey, and United Kingdom.

SOURCE: Compiled from *International Marketing Data and Statistics 2002* (London: Euromonitor, 2002), table 10.3.

THE INTERNATIONAL MARKETPLACE   4.2

In Search of the New China

The complexity and vast changes of the Chinese market have always proved the biggest challenges for Western marketers. Geographically, regional difference is so distinct that China is regarded as a combination of many small markets. The consumption pattern varies significantly between coastal and central regions, and between the south and the north, mainly due to differences in cultural and economic backgrounds. The Gallup Organization conducted a broad range of surveys to better understand Chinese consumers from different regions. For example, there is much heavier consumption of beer in northern China than in other regions. In eastern China, people

mostly read newspapers but do not listen to the radio. This has major implications for how marketers advertise their products.

On the other hand, the dynamics across different industries as well as within each industry also vary drastically. In China's PC market, for example, desktop PCs hold 90 percent of the market share, although the demand for laptop computers is growing quickly. In 2001, a total of 60 percent of PCs sold were sold in the economically developed east, north, and south. In the submarket of PC servers, the share is even higher at 65 percent. Among PC makers, local manufacturers have the majority of the market share. According to International Data Corporation, the domestic IT flagship Legend is the dominator in the PC market, with a market share around 31 percent in 2001. Founder is the second largest seller, with a market share ranging between 7 and 8 percent. And Tsinghua Tongfang follows in third position. Among the overseas

brands, Dell is the largest player, with a market share of 4.6 percent, the fourth largest among all the players.

SOURCES: "A Survey of China," Economist, April 8, 2000, 1–16; "In Search of the New China," Fortune, October 11, 1999, 230–232; "What the Chinese Want," Fortune, October 11, 1999, 233–237; "Sino-Foreign Consultancy Firms to Jointly Launch On-Line Survey," Xinhua, November 15, 2000.

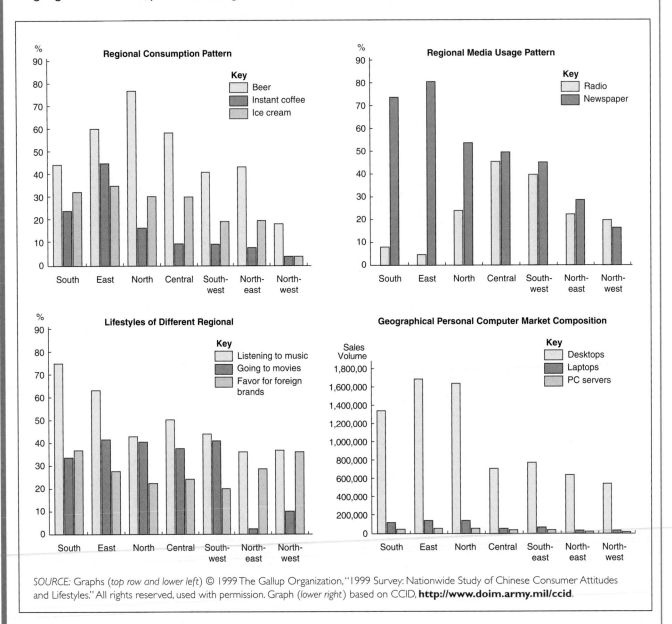

Data on product saturation or diffusion—information on the percentage of households in a market that own a particular product—allow a further evaluation of market potential. Table 4.5 presents the percentage of households that own certain appliances and indicates that saturation levels in the markets for which the data exist are quite high. This does not necessarily indicate lack of market potential; replacement markets or the demand for auxiliary products may offer attractive opportunities to the international marketer. Low rates of diffusion should be approached cautiously, because they can signal a market opportunity or lack thereof resulting from low income levels, use of a substitute product, or lack of acceptance. As an example of lack of acceptance, the time-saving feature of micro-wave ovens may not be as attractive in more tradition-bound societies as it is in the United States or the EU.

General consumption figures are valuable, but they must be viewed with cau-tion because they may conceal critical product-form differences; for example, appliances in European households tend to be smaller than their U.S. counterparts. Information about existing product usage can nevertheless provide indirect help to international marketers. As an example, a large number of telephones, and their even distribution among the population or a target group, may allow market research via telephone interviewing.

A problem for marketers in general is **inflation;** varying inflation rates compli-cate this problem in international markets. Many of the industrialized countries, such as the United States, Germany, and Japan, have recently been able to keep inflation rates at single-digit levels, while some have suffered from chronic infla-tion (Table 4.6). Inflation affects the ability of both industrial customers and con-sumers to buy and also introduces uncertainty into both the marketer's planning process and consumers' buying habits. In high-inflation markets, the marketer may have to make changes in the product (more economical without compromising quality), promotion (more rational), and distribution (more customer involvement) to meet customer needs and maintain demand. In response to rapidly escalating prices, a government will often invoke price controls. The setting of maximum prices for products may cause the international marketer to face unacceptable profit situations, future investments may not be made, and production may even have to be stopped.[10]

Another challenge for international marketers is the **debt problem.** Many of the developing countries are saddled with a collective debt of $1.2 trillion (Figure 4.3). Debt crises crush nations' buying power and force imports down and exports up to meet interest payments. For example, during the Latin American debt crisis, the U.S. trade balance with Latin nations deteriorated from an annual surplus of

Table 4.5		Percentage of Households Owning Selected Appliances, 2000											
	USA	Bel-gium	Den-mark	France	Ger-many	Italy	Nether-lands	Spain	Sweden	Switzer-land	United Kingdom	China	Japan
Car	92.6	78.3	70.9	78.6	89.3	75.9	70.2	73.0	90.3	47.5	73.1	2.7	81.3
CD player	53.7	64.3	85.9	23.8	78.6	12.8	87.4	34.6	80.1	55.1	81.0	1.8	63.4
Dishwasher	53.9	44.1	46.8	35.9	57.9	32.9	39.9	23.1	56.9	71.0	26.5	1.2	54.4
Freezer	34.9	66.8	92.0	49.0	73.4	47.0	70.8	48.4	97.6	66.2	57.4	0.5	32.6
Microwave oven	84.3	79.4	52.4	49.5	33.5	35.1	73.1	37.9	67.9	50.4	87.2	0.4	91.0
Personal computer	63.5	46.5	65.8	34.9	48.5	21.8	64.8	19.5	48.0	54.7	41.1	14.3	35.1
Refrigerator	99.7	99.6	96.8	84.7	87.4	84.8	98.6	87.4	98.3	99.6	98.7	5.9	97.1
Telephone	85.2	91.9	96.3	88.7	98.5	96.7	90.3	81.6	98.7	98.7	93.3	22.8	87.0
Television (color)	99.3	99.2	92.1	95.9	97.0	94.9	98.3	98.2	97.3	97.2	98.2	44.6	99.1
Tumble dryer	70.4	27.1	43.1	25.6	39.0	17.3	58.1	15.8	35.3	36.3	53.5	1.3	34.0
Vacuum cleaner	97.5	98.2	95.1	96.2	99.7	84.8	94.0	69.0	95.6	98.9	10.6	1.5	98.9
VCR	83.2	74.3	83.7	60.5	65.9	67.5	78.1	65.5	78.1	74.4	86.7	0.8	77.2
Washing machine	78.0	88.8	78.5	97.9	97.6	98.3	96.1	92.1	76.3	75.8	93.8	2.2	98.8

SOURCE: Compiled from *International Marketing Data and Statistics* 2002 (London: Euromonitor, 2002), table 15.7.

Table 4.6   Consumer Price Index

Country	1995	1996	1997	1998	1999	2000	2001
United States	2.81	2.93	2.34	1.55	2.19	3.38	2.83
Argentina	3.38	0.16	0.53	0.92	−1.17	−0.94	−1.07
Australia	4.64	2.61	0.25	0.85	1.49	4.45	4.38
Austria	2.25	1.84	1.33	0.90	0.56	2.35	2.66
Bangladash	8.52	4.06	1.73	6.97	8.91	3.92	1.39
Belgium	1.47	2.06	1.63	0.95	1.12	2.55	2.47
Bolivia	10.19	12.43	4.71	7.67	2.16	4.60	1.60
Brazil	66.01	15.76	6.93	3.20	4.86	7.04	6.86
Canada	2.17	1.58	1.62	0.99	1.72	2.75	2.53
Chile	8.24	7.36	6.14	5.11	3.34	3.84	3.57
China (PRC, excl. Hong Kong)	16.90	8.32	2.81	−0.84	−1.41	0.26	0.34
Colombia	20.96	20.24	18.86	20.35	11.21	9.49	8.70
Ecuador	22.89	24.37	30.64	36.10	52.24	96.09	37.68
Egypt	15.74	7.19	4.63	4.18	3.08	2.68	2.27
Finland	0.99	0.62	1.20	1.40	1.16	3.37	2.58
France	1.78	2.01	1.20	0.67	0.53	1.70	1.63
Germany	1.72	1.42	1.90	0.93	0.58	1.95	2.48
Ghana	59.46	46.56	27.89	14.62	12.41	25.19	32.91
Greece	8.94	8.20	5.54	4.76	2.63	3.15	3.36
Guatemala	8.41	11.06	9.23	6.97	4.86	5.98	7.63
India	10.22	8.98	7.16	13.23	4.67	4.01	3.68
Indonesia	9.43	7.97	6.73	57.64	20.49	3.72	11.50
Iran	49.66	28.94	17.35	17.87	20.07	14.48	11.27
Israel	10.04	11.28	9.00	5.43	5.19	1.12	1.12
Italy	5.24	3.97	2.04	1.96	1.66	2.54	2.79
Japan	−0.13	0.14	1.73	0.66	−0.34	−0.67	−0.73
Malaysia	3.45	3.49	2.66	5.27	2.74	1.53	1.42
Mexico	35.00	34.38	20.63	15.93	16.59	9.50	6.36
Netherlands	1.92	2.02	2.16	1.98	2.21	2.52	4.53
Norway	2.46	1.26	2.58	2.26	2.33	3.09	3.03
Pakistan	12.34	10.37	11.38	6.23	4.14	4.37	3.15
Peru	11.13	11.54	8.56	7.25	3.47	3.76	1.98
Philippines	8.03	9.01	5.84	9.72	6.71	4.34	6.11
Portugal	4.12	3.12	2.16	2.78	2.34	2.87	4.35
Romania	32.24	38.83	154.76	59.10	45.80	45.67	34.47
South Africa	8.68	7.35	8.60	6.88	5.18	5.34	5.70
South Korea	4.50	4.92	4.44	7.54	0.82	2.25	4.03
Spain	4.67	3.56	1.97	1.83	2.31	3.43	3.59
Sweden	2.53	0.47	0.52	−0.14	0.45	1.00	2.44
Switzerland	1.80	0.82	0.52	0.10	0.74	1.58	0.95
Thailand	5.80	5.81	5.61	8.07	0.31	1.55	1.66
Turkey	88.11	80.35	85.73	84.64	64.87	54.92	54.40
United Kingdom	3.41	2.45	3.13	3.42	1.56	2.93	1.82
Venezuela	59.92	99.88	50.04	35.78	23.57	16.20	12.53

SOURCE: Compiled data from *International Financial Statistics* (Washington, DC: International Monetary Fund, various editions). © International Monetary Fund; **http://www.imf.org**.

Figure 4.3   Nations in Debt: Debt Outstanding (Millions of Dollars) in 2000

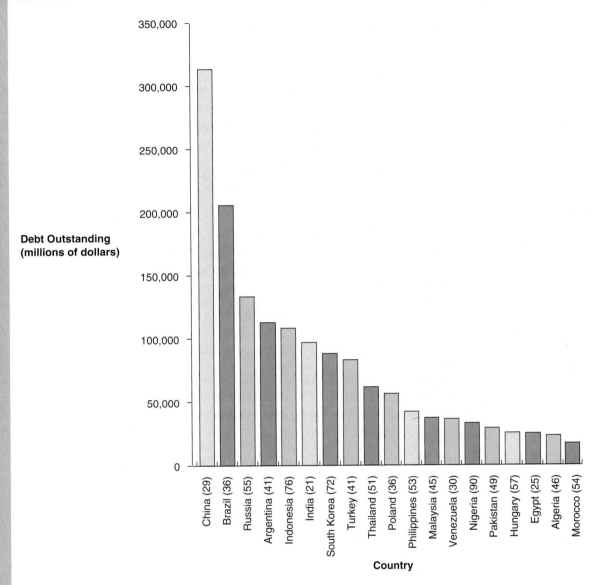

Numbers in parentheses indicate percentages of GDP.

SOURCE: Based on *Global Development Finance 2001* (Washington, DC: World Bank, 2001), 100–107; see also **http://www.worldbank.org**.

$6 billion in 1980 to a deficit of $40.7 billion in 2001. To continue growing, many companies are looking at developing nations because of the potential they see 10 to 15 years ahead. U.S. companies typically face competition in these regions from entities that are often aided by their government's aid grants, as well as by Europeans who do business with the help of government export credits that have interest rates lower than those provided by U.S. entities. Access to these markets can be achieved by helping political leaders provide jobs and by increasing exports. Heinz, for example, operates in many developing countries through joint ventures in which Heinz holds 51 percent. To sell products in these markets, companies may have to engage in countertrade either by accepting payment in goods or by supporting customers' efforts in their international marketing.[11] Many industrialized countries, such as Japan, France, and the United States, are seeking ways to ease the burden facing debtor nations.

Infrastructure

The availability and quality of an infrastructure is critically important in evaluating marketing operations abroad. Each international marketer will rely heavily on services provided by the local market for transportation, communication, and energy as well as on organizations participating in the facilitating functions of marketing: marketing communications, distributing, information, and financing. Indicators such as steel consumption, cement production, and electricity production relate to the overall industrialization of the market and can be used effectively by suppliers of industrial products and services. As an example, energy consumption per capita may serve as an indicator of market potential for electrical markets, provided evenness of distribution exists over the market. Yet the marketer must make sure that the energy is affordable and compatible (in terms of current and voltage) with the products to be marketed.

The existence and expansion of basic infrastructure has contributed significantly to increased agricultural output in Asia and Latin America. The Philippines has allocated 5 percent of agricultural development funds to rural electrification programs. On a similar level, basic roads are essential to moving agricultural products. In many parts of Africa, farmers are more than a day's walk from the nearest road. As a result, measures to improve production without commensurate improvements in transportation and communications are of little use because the crops cannot reach the market. In addition, the lack of infrastructure cuts the farmers off from new technology, inputs, and ideas.

Transportation networks by land, rail, waterway, or air are essential for physical distribution. An analysis of rail traffic by freight tons per kilometer offers a possible way to begin an investigation of transportation capabilities; however, these figures may not always indicate the true state of the system. China's railway system carries five times as much freight as India's does, which is an amazing feat considering that only 20 percent of the network is doubletracked and that it is shared by an ever-growing amount of passenger traffic. In spite of the railway's greater use, the international marketer has to rely on other methods of distribution. The tremendous logistics challenge makes national distribution in China only a dream and slows down expansion from the major urban population centers of Guangzhou, Shanghai, and Beijing.[12] With the same type of caution, the number of passenger cars as well as buses and trucks can be used to analyze the state of road transportation and transportation networks.

Communication is as important as transportation. The ability of a firm to communicate with entities both outside and within the market can be estimated by using indicators of the communications infrastructure: telephones, computers, broadcast media, and print media in use. The countries of the former Eastern bloc possess some of the world's worst telephone systems. Western Europe has 49 main telephone lines per 100 people, while Russia has 12, Hungary has 9, and Poland has 8. Upgrading the telephone system will be expensive (estimated at $50 billion for Central Europe alone) but necessary for competing in the world market and attracting international investors. Official figures may not reveal the quality of the services provided and their possible reach. For example, the telephone system in Egypt, especially in Cairo, is notorious for its frequent breakdowns and lack of capacity. Wireless technology is poised to change the worldwide landscape in many ways. While the number of cellular phones in use in 2000 was estimated at 555 million, the estimated number for 2003 is set at over 900 million (with 150 million in use in North America, 285 million in Europe, 295 million in Asia, 128 million in Latin America, and 44 million in the Middle East and Africa).[13]

The diffusion of Internet technology into core business processes and into the lifestyles of consumers has been rapid, especially in industrialized countries. The number of Internet hosts (computers through which users connect to the network) has increased to 162.1 million by 2003, up from 9.4 million in 1993 and 43.2 million in 1999.[14] While the United States still has the majority of these, Northern Europe is also very active (Table 4.7). The total number of people using the Internet is difficult to estimate. One estimate in September 2002 placed the number at 605.6 million worldwide, with 182.67 million in North America, 190.91 million in Europe, 187.27 million in the Asia-Pacific, 33.35 million in Latin America, 6.31 million in Africa, and 5.12 million in the Middle East.[15] Given the changes expected in the first years of the twenty-first century, all the estimates indicating explosive growth may be low. The number of users will start evening out around the globe, with new technologies assisting. Computers priced at less than $500 will boost global computer ownership and subsequent online activity. Developments in television, cable, phone, and wireless technologies not only will make the market broader but will also allow for more services to be delivered more efficiently. For example, with the advent of third-generation mobile communications technology, systems will have 100-fold increase in data transfer, allowing the viewing of videos on mobile phones.[16] This will create an advantage for both European and Japanese players thanks to their lead over the United States in mobile telephony. Television will also become a mainstream Internet access method of the future. While the interactive TV market served only 3 million viewers in Europe and North America in 1999, the estimates are for 67 million subscribers by 2003.[17] The growth in international opportunities is leading to a rapid internationalization of Internet players, as shown in *The International Marketplace 4.3*.

The careful assessment of infrastructure spells out important marketing opportunities. While 2 billion people in Asia are without electricity and only 16 in 1,000 have access to a telephone, the Asian market is the most keenly watched by marketers. According to one estimate, between 1994 and 2000, Asian countries

Table 4.7	**Network Effect (Internet Hosts per 1,000 Inhabitants in 2001)**		
Country	**Internet Hosts per 10,000 Inhabitants in 2001**	**Country**	**Internet Hosts per 10,000 Inhabitants in 2001**
United States	3,714.01	Singapore	479.18
Iceland	1,904.81	Austria	400.51
Finland	1,707.25	Britain	371.37
Netherlands	1,634.77	Belgium	341.98
Australia	1,183.40	Ireland	333.67
New Zealand	1,049.59	France	312.94
Denmark	1,045.38	Luxembourg	312.42
Canada	931.90	Germany	294.58
Sweden	825.14	Israel	220.77
Switzerland	730.74	Hungary	168.04
Norway	673.82	Spain	133.24
Hong Kong SAR	573.52	Italy	117.28
Japan	559.03		

SOURCE: Compiled from International Telecommunications Union (ITU) data, **http://www.itu.int**.

THE INTERNATIONAL MARKETPLACE   4.3

Bringing the New Economy to New Markets

With the U.S. market crowded with competitors, Yahoo!, Excite, Lycos, and America Online are expanding their plans to establish brands in Asia, Europe, and Latin America before local competitors can create dominant positions of their own. With the non-U.S. share of users increasing, the fastest growth can be secured abroad.

One significant reason for the growth is falling costs. Internet users pay telephone charges on top of Internet access fees to use the Web, but more operators are offering free monthly access, and phone charges are dropping fast across the board.

Yahoo!, with the most worldwide customers, operates 24 overseas sites. Lycos' merger in 2000 with Terra Networks, S.A., boosted Terra Lycos' coverage to 140 sites in 41 countries. AOL, now serving 16 countries, gained access to a rich variety of content through its 2001 merger with media giant Time Warner, while Excite operates 9 international ventures. These sites offer native-language news, shopping links, and other content tailored to the local population. Lycos's German site features tips on brewing beer at home, and Yahoo's Singapore site offers real-time information on haze and smog in Southeast Asia.

The top U.S. players face tough domestic competitors that often have a better sense of the local culture and Internet styles. In many countries, the dominant telephone companies offer portals, giving them a significant competitive advantage with customers who are automat-ically sent to their home pages when they log on. Germany's leading portal, T-Online, is run by Deutsche Telekom, while the leading portal, Wanadoo, is operated by France Telecom.

The danger for U.S. portals is that they might be viewed as "digital colonialists" trying to flex their muscles around the world. In Brazil, AOL was accused by its local competitor, Universo Online, of using a misleading slogan: "We're the biggest because we're the best." The operation has also been hurt because AOL's installation disks altered users' hard drives.

Market resistance may lead to a desire to form partnerships with local outfits that would also help in understanding the local culture. In Japan, Lycos teams up with Sumitomo, an ultra-traditional company with a 250-year history, while in Korea it teamed up with Mirae, a machinery and electronics company.

Direct government interference may also emerge. The Chinese government initially blocked access to Google from Internet providers in China because the search engine helped Chinese users to gain access to forbidden sites. After an outcry from those users, access was restored.

SOURCES: "The Search Goes On," *The Economist,* September 19, 2002, 57; "For Internet Portals, the Next Battleground Is Overseas," *The Wall Street Journal,* March 23, 2000, B1, B4; and "Shopping around the Web," *Economist,* February 26, 2000, 5–54. Access international sites at **http://www.google.com**.

(excluding Japan) spent $1.5 trillion on power, transportation, telecommunications, water supplies, and sanitation.[18] China overtook the United States in pager use by late 1997 mainly because of the low cost of the needed infrastructure to support paging. The big winners will be companies like Motorola that are developing new products for this market such as pagers that play back voice mail. The booming middle class in cities such as Bangkok will ensure that cellular phone sales continue at a record pace. With increasing affluence comes an increasing need for energy. General Electric estimates that China will place orders for 168,000 megawatts in additional power-generating capacity, and India more than 70,000 megawatts; the corresponding figure in the United States is 154,000.

Data on the availability of commercial (marketing-related) infrastructure are often not readily available. Data on which to base an assessment may be provided by government sources, such as Overseas Business Reports; by trade associations, such as the Business Equipment Manufacturers' Association; and by trade publications, such as *Advertising Age.* The more extensive the firm's international involvement, the more it can rely on its already existing support network of banks, advertising agencies, and distributors to assess new markets.

Impact of the Economic Environment on Social Development

Many of the characteristics discussed are important beyond numbers. Economic success comes with a price tag. All the social traumas that were once believed endemic only to the West are now hitting other parts of the world as well. Many countries, including the nations of Southeast Asia, were able to achieve double-digit growth for decades while paying scant attention to problems that are now demanding treatment: infrastructure limits, labor shortages, demands for greater political freedom, environmental destruction, urban congestion, and even the spread of drug addiction.[19]

Because of the close relationship between economic and social development, many of the figures can be used as social indicators as well. Consider the following factors and their significance: share of urban population, life expectancy, number of physicians per capita, literacy rate, percentage of income received by the richest 5 percent of the population, and percentage of the population with access to electricity. In addition to these factors, several other variables can be used as cultural indicators: number of public libraries, registered borrowings, book titles published, and number of daily newspapers. The **Physical Quality of Life Index (PQLI)** is a composite measure of the level of welfare in a country. It has three components: life expectancy, infant mortality, and adult literacy rates.[20] The three components of the PQLI are among the few social indicators available to provide a comparison of progress through time in all of the countries of the world.

Differences in the degree of urbanization of target markets in lesser-developed countries influence international marketers' product strategies. If products are targeted only to urban areas, products need minimal adjustments, mainly to qualify them for market entry. However, when targeting national markets, firms may need to make extensive adaptations to match more closely the expectations and the more narrow consumption experiences of the rural population.[21]

In terms of infrastructure, improved access in rural areas brings with it an expansion of nonfarm enterprises such as shops, repair services, and grain mills. It also changes customs, attitudes, and values. As an example, a World Bank study on the impact of rural roads of Yucatán in Mexico found that roads offered an opportunity for enlarging women's role by introducing new ideas, education, medical care, and economic alternatives to maize cultivation.[22] In particular, women married later, had fewer children, and pursued more nondomestic activities. The same impact has been observed with increased access to radio and television. These changes can, if properly understood and utilized, offer major new opportunities to the international marketer.

The presence of multinational corporations, which by their very nature are change agents, will accelerate social change. If government control is weak, the multinational corporation bears the social responsibility for its actions. In some cases, governments restrict the freedom of multinational corporations if their actions may affect the environment. As an example, the Indonesian government places construction restrictions (such as building height) on hotels in Bali to avoid the overcrowding and ecological problems incurred in Hawaii when that state developed its tourism sector vigorously.

Regional Economic Integration

Economic integration has been one of the main economic developments affecting world markets since World War II. Countries have wanted to engage in economic cooperation to use their respective resources more effectively and to provide larger markets for member-country producers. Some integration efforts have had quite ambitious goals, such as political integration; some have failed as the result

Figure 4.4   Forms of Economic Integration in Regional Markets

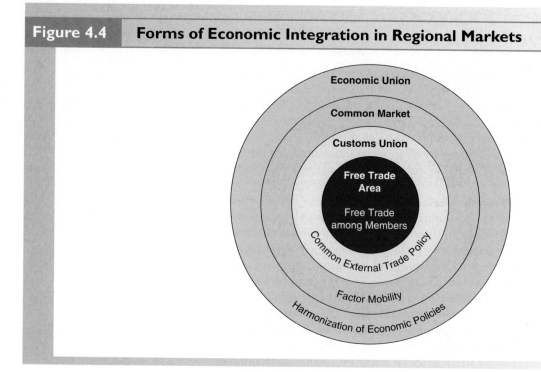

of perceptions of unequal benefits from the arrangement or parting of ways politically. Figure 4.4, a summary of the major forms of economic cooperation in regional markets, shows the varying degrees of formality with which integration can take place. These economic integration efforts are dividing the world into trading blocs. Of the 32 groupings in existence, some have superstructures of nation-states (such as the European Union), some (such as ASEAN Free Trade Area) are multinational agreements that are currently more political than economic. Some are not trading blocs per se, but work to further them. The Free Trade Area of the Americas (FTAA) is a foreign-policy initiative to further democracy in the hemisphere through incentives to capitalistic development and trade liberalization. Blocs are joining bigger blocs as in the case of the Asia Pacific Economic Cooperation, which brings partners together from multiple continents (including NAFTA, AFTA, and individual countries such as Australia, China, Japan, and Russia).[23]

Levels of Economic Integration

Free Trade Area

The **free trade area** is the least restrictive and loosest form of economic integration among nations. In a free trade area, all barriers to trade among member countries are removed. Goods and services are freely traded among member countries. No discriminatory taxes, quotas, tariffs, or other barriers are allowed. Sometimes a free trade area is formed only for certain classes of goods and services. For example, before NAFTA, the United States and Canada already had sectoral free trade agreements such as that for automobiles. A notable feature of free trade areas is that each member country continues to set its own policies in relation to nonmembers. This means that each member is free to set any tariffs or other restrictions that it chooses on trade with countries outside of the free trade area. Among such arrangements are the European Free Trade Area (EFTA) and the North American Free Trade Agreement (NAFTA). As an example of the freedom members have in terms of their policies towards nonmembers, Mexico has signed a number of bilateral free trade agreements with other blocs (the European Union) and nations (Chile) to both improve trade and to attract investment.

Customs Union

The **customs union** is one step further along the spectrum of economic integration. As in the free trade area, members of the customs union dismantle barriers to trade in goods and services among members. In addition, however, the customs union establishes a common trade policy with respect to nonmembers. Typically, this takes the form of a common external tariff, whereby imports from nonmembers are subject to the same tariff when sold to any member country. The Southern African Customs Union is the oldest and most successful example of economic integration in Africa.

Common Market

The **common market** amounts to a customs union covering the exchange of goods and services, the prohibition of duties in exports and imports between members, and the adoption of a common external tariff in respect to nonmembers. In addition, factors of production (labor, capital, and technology) are mobile among members. Restrictions on immigration and cross-border investment are abolished. The importance of **factor mobility** for economic growth cannot be overstated. When factors of production are mobile, then capital, labor, and technology may be employed in their most productive uses.

Despite the obvious benefits, members of a common market must be prepared to cooperate closely in monetary, fiscal, and employment policies. Furthermore, although a common market will enhance the productivity of members in the aggregate, it is by no means clear that individual member countries will always benefit. Because of these difficulties, the goals of common markets have proved to be elusive in many areas of the world, notably Central and South America and Asia. In the mid-1980s, the European Community (EC) embarked on an ambitious effort to remove the barriers between the then twelve member countries to free the movement of goods, services, capital, and people. The process was ratified by the passing of the **Single European Act** in 1987 with the target date of December 31, 1992, to complete the internal market. In December 1991, the EC agreed in Maastricht that the so-called 1992 process would be a step toward cooperation beyond the economic dimension. While many of the directives aimed at opening borders and markets were completed on schedule, some sectors, such as automobiles, took longer to open up.

Economic Union

The creation of a true **economic union** requires integration of economic policies in addition to the free movement of goods, services, and factors of production across borders. Under an economic union, members will harmonize monetary policies, taxation, and government spending. In addition, a common currency is to be used by members. This could be accomplished, de facto, by a system of fixed exchange rates. Clearly, the formation of an economic union requires members to surrender a large measure of their national sovereignty to supranational authorities in communitywide institutions such as the European Parliament. The final step would be a **political union** calling for political unification. The ratification of the Maastricht Treaty in late 1993 by all of the twelve member countries of the EC created the **European Union,** effective January 1, 1994. The treaty (jointly with the Treaty of Amsterdam in 1997) set the foundation for economic and monetary union (EMU) with the establishment of the euro (€) as a common currency by January 1, 1999. Twelve EU countries are currently part of "Euroland" (Austria, Belgium, Finland, France, Germany, Greece, Holland, Ireland, Italy, Luxembourg, Portugal, and Spain). In addition, moves would be made toward a political union with common foreign and security policy as well as judicial cooperation.[24]

European Integration

The most important implication of the freedom of movement for products, services, people, and capital within the EU is the economic growth that is expected

International Groupings

OECD Organization for Economic Cooperation and Development
OPEC Organization of the Petroleum Exporting Countries
Commonwealth

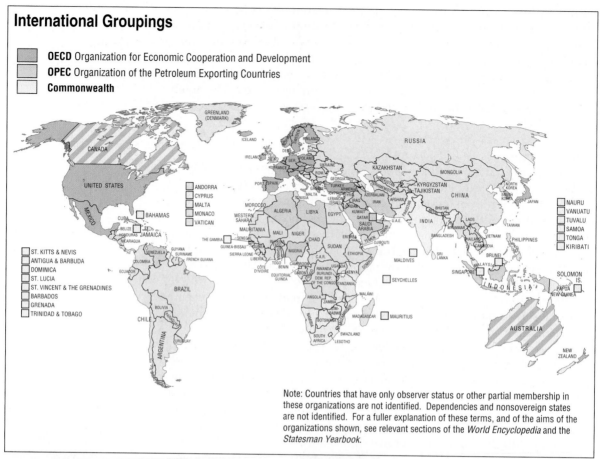

Note: Countries that have only observer status or other partial membership in these organizations are not identified. Dependencies and nonsovereign states are not identified. For a fuller explanation of these terms, and of the aims of the organizations shown, see relevant sections of the *World Encyclopedia* and the *Statesman Yearbook*.

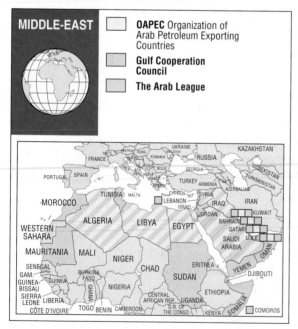

MIDDLE-EAST

OAPEC Organization of Arab Petroleum Exporting Countries
Gulf Cooperation Council
The Arab League

EUROPE

EU European Union
Countries interested in **EU** membership
EU membership by 2004

SOURCES: Based on *Statesman Yearbook; The European Union: A Guide for Americans,* 2000, **http://www.eurounion.org/infores/euguide/euguide.html**; "Afrabet Soup," *The Economist,* February 10, 2001, p. 77, **http://www.economist.com**.

PACIFIC BASIN

- **AFTA** ASEAN (Association of South East Asian Nations) Free Trade Area

AFRICA

- ***Franc Zone** currency linked to the French Franc
- **SADC** Southern African Development Community
- **COMESA** Common Market for East and Southern Africa (formerly **PTA**)
- **ECOWAS** Economic Community of West African States

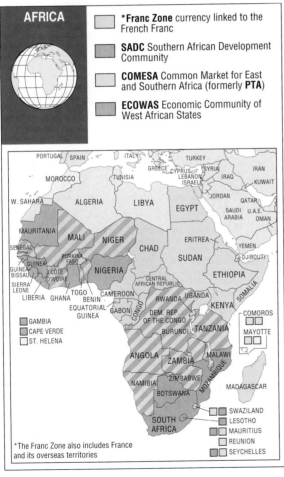

- GAMBIA
- CAPE VERDE
- ST. HELENA

*The Franc Zone also includes France and its overseas territories

AMERICAS

- **NAFTA** North American Free Trade Agreement
- **ANCOM** Andean Common Market
- **MERCOSUR** Southern Common Market
- **CARICOM** Caribbean Community and Common Market
- **CACM** Central American Common Market

- ST. KITTS & NEVIS
- ANTIGUA & BARBUDA
- MONTSERRAT
- DOMINICA
- ST. LUCIA
- ST. VINCENT & THE GRENADINES
- BARBADOS
- GRENADA
- TRINIDAD & TOBAGO

to result. Several specific sources of increased growth have been identified. First, there will be gains from eliminating the transaction costs associated with border patrols, customs procedures, and so forth. Second, economic growth will be spurred by the economies of scale that will be achieved when production facilities become more concentrated. Third, there will be gains from more intense competition among European companies. Firms that were monopolists in one country will now be subject to competition from firms in other member countries. The introduction of the euro is expected to add to the efficiencies, especially in terms of consolidation of firms across industries and across countries. Furthermore, countries in Euroland will enjoy cheaper transaction costs and reduced currency risks, and consumers and businesses will enjoy price transparency and increased price-based competition. Marketer reactions to the euro will be discussed further in Chapter 18.

The enlargement of the EU has become one of the most debated issues. Thirteen countries, especially Central European nations, are eager to join. The earliest date for expansion has been pushed to 2004, with disagreements about agriculture and free movement of labor still persisting. The most likely to join at this stage are those in advanced negotiations with the EU (Cyprus, the Czech Republic, Estonia, Hungary, Poland, and Slovenia) and possibly those just starting (Latvia, Lithuania, Malta, and Slovakia). The agreement on the European Economic Area (EEA) extends the Single Market of the EU to three of the four EFTA countries (Iceland, Liechtenstein, and Norway, with Switzerland opting to develop its relationship with the EU through bilateral agreements).[25]

The integration has important implications for firms within and outside Europe because it poses both threats and opportunities, benefits and costs. There will be substantial benefits for those firms already operating in Europe. These firms will gain because their operations in one country can now be freely expanded into others and their products may be freely sold across borders. In a borderless Europe, firms will have access to approximately 380 million consumers. Substantial economies of scale in production and marketing will also result. The extent of these economies of scale will depend on the ability of the marketers to find pan-regional segments or to homogenize tastes across borders through promotional activity.

For firms from nonmember countries, there are various possibilities depending on the firm's position within the market. Table 4.8 provides four different scenarios with proposed courses of action. Well-established U.S.-based multinational marketers such as H.J. Heinz and Colgate-Palmolive will be able to take advantage of the new economies of scale. For example, 3M plants earlier turned out different versions of the company's products for various markets. Now, the 3M plant in Wales, for example, makes videotapes and videocassettes for all of Europe. Colgate-Palmolive has to watch out for competitors, like Germany's Henkel, in the brutally competitive detergent market. At the same time, large-scale retailers, such as France's Carrefour and Germany's Aldi group, are undertaking their own efforts to exploit the situation with hypermarkets supplied by central warehouses with computerized inventories. Their procurement policies have to be met by companies like Heinz. Many multinationals are developing pan-European strategies to exploit the emerging situation; that is, they are standardizing their products and processes to the greatest extent possible without compromising local input and implementation.

A company with a foothold in only one European market is faced with the danger of competitors who can use the strength of multiple markets. Furthermore, the elimination of barriers may do away with the company's competitive advantage. For example, more than half of the 45 major European food companies are in just one or two of the individual European markets and seriously lag behind broader-based U.S. and Swiss firms. Similarly, automakers PSA and Fiat are nowhere close to the cross-manufacturing presence of Ford and GM. The courses of action include expansion through acquisitions or mergers, formation of strategic alliances (for example, AT&T's joint venture with Spain's Telefonica to produce state-of-the-art microchips), rationalization by concentrating only on business segments in which the company can be a pan-European leader, and finally, divestment.

Table 4.8	Proposed Company Responses to European Integration		
Company Status	**Challenges**		**Response**
Established multinational market/multiple markets	Exploit opportunities from improved productivity Meet challenge of competitors Cater to customers/intermediaries doing same		Pan-European strategy
Firm with one European subsidiary	Competition Loss of niche		Expansion Strategic alliances Rationalization Divestment
Exporter to Europe	Competition Access		European branch Selective acquisition Strategic alliance
No interest	Competition at home Lost opportunity		Entry

SOURCE: Developed from John F. Magee, "1992: Moves Americans Must Make," *Harvard Business Review* 67 (May–June 1989): 78–84.

Exporters will need to worry about maintaining their competitive position and continued access to the market. Small and mid-sized U.S. companies account for more than 60 percent of U.S. exports to the EU. Their success, despite the high value of the dollar making exports more expensive, is based on the relationships they have developed with their customers, especially in high-tech.[26] Companies with a physical presence may be in a better position to assess and take advantage of the developments. Internet systems provider WatchGuard Technologies has almost doubled its staff in Europe, from 12 to 20 in 2002, in the wake of September 11 and increasing concern about viruses. In some industries, marketers do not see a reason either to be in Europe at all or to change from exporting to more involved modes of entry. Machinery and machine tools, for example, are in great demand in Europe, and marketers in these companies say they have little reason to manufacture there.

The term **Fortress Europe** has been used to describe the fears of many, especially U.S. firms, about a unified Europe. The concern is that while Europe dismantles internal barriers, it will raise external ones, making access to the European market difficult for U.S. and other non-EU firms. In a move designed to protect European farmers, for example, the EU has occasionally banned the import of certain agricultural goods from the United States. The EU has also called on members to limit the number of American television programs broadcast in Europe. Finally, many U.S. firms are concerned about the relatively strict domestic content rules passed by the EU. These rules require certain products sold in Europe to be manufactured with European inputs. One effect of the perceived threat of Fortress Europe has been increased direct investment in Europe by U.S. firms. Fears that the EU will erect barriers to U.S. exports and fears of the domestic content rules governing many goods have led many U.S. firms to initiate or expand European direct investment.

North American Integration

Although the EU is undoubtedly the most successful and best-known integrative effort, North American integration efforts, although only a few years old, have gained momentum and attention. What started as a trading pact between two close and economically well-developed allies has already been expanded conceptually to include Mexico, and long-term plans call for further additions. However, North American integration is for purely economic reasons; there are no constituencies for political integration.

The ratification of NAFTA created the world's largest free market with 390 million consumers and a total output of $10 trillion, roughly the same size as the EEA.[27] The pact marked a bold departure: Never before have industrialized countries created such a massive free trade area with a developing-country neighbor.

Since Canada stands to gain very little from NAFTA (its trade with Mexico is 1 percent of its trade with the United States), much of the controversy has centered on the gains and losses for the United States and Mexico. Proponents argue that the agreement will give U.S. firms access to a huge pool of relatively low-cost Mexican labor at a time when demographic trends are resulting in labor shortages in many parts of the United States. At the same time, many new jobs are created in Mexico. The agreement will give firms in both countries access to millions of additional consumers, and the liberalized trade flows will result in higher economic growth in both countries. The top 20 exports and imports between Mexico and the United States are in virtually the same industries, indicating intra-industry specialization and building of economies of scale for global competitiveness.[28] Overall, the corporate view toward NAFTA is overwhelmingly positive.

Opposition to NAFTA centers on issues relating to labor and the environment. Unions in particular worry about job loss to Mexico, given its lower wages and work standards; some estimate that 6 million U.S. workers would be vulnerable to migration of jobs. Similarly, any expansion of NAFTA is perceived as a threat.

Distinctive features of NAFTA are the two side agreements that were worked out to correct perceived abuses in labor and the environment in Mexico. The North American Agreement on Labor Cooperation (NAALC) was set up to hear complaints about worker abuse, and the Commission on Environmental Compliance was established to act as a public advocate on the environment. These side agreements have had little impact, however, mainly because the mechanisms have almost no enforcement power.[29]

After a remarkable start in increased trade and investment, NAFTA suffered a serious setback due to a significant devaluation of the Mexican peso in 1995 and its negative impact on trade. Critics argue that too much was expected too fast of a country whose political system and economy were not ready for open markets. In response, advocates argue that there was nothing wrong with the Mexican real economy and that the peso crisis was a political one that would be overcome with time.

Trade among Canada, Mexico, and the United States has increased by 50 percent since NAFTA took effect, exceeding $612 billion in 2001.[30] Reforms have turned Mexico into an attractive market in its own right. Mexico's gross domestic product has been expanding by more than 3 percent every year since 1989, and exports to the United States have doubled since 1986 to $131.3 billion in 2001. By institutionalizing the nation's turn to open its markets, the free trade agreement has attracted considerable new foreign investment ($85 billion since NAFTA began). The United States has benefited from Mexico's success. U.S. exports to Mexico ($101.3 billion) surpass those to Japan at $57.4 billion. While the surplus of $1.3 billion in 1994 had turned to a deficit of $30.0 billion in 2001, these imports have helped Mexico's recovery and will, therefore, strengthen NAFTA in the long term. Furthermore, U.S. imports from Mexico have been shown to have much higher U.S. content than imports from other countries.[31] Cooperation between Mexico and the United States is expanding beyond trade and investment. For example, binational bodies have been established to tackle issues such as migration, border control, and drug trafficking.[32]

Among the U.S. industries to benefit are computers, autos and auto parts, petrochemicals, financial services, and aerospace. Aerospace companies such as Boeing, Honeywell, Airbus Industrie, and GE Aircraft Engines have recently made Mexico a center for both parts manufacture and assembly. Aerospace is now one of Mexico's largest industries, second only to electronics, with 10,000 workers employed.[33] In Mexico's growth toward a more advanced society, manufacturers of consumer goods will also stand to benefit. NAFTA has already had a major impact on the emergence of new retail chains, many of which were developed to handle new products from abroad.[34] Not only have U.S. retailers, such as Wal-Mart, expanded to and in Mexico, but Mexican retailers, such as Grupo Gigante, have entered the U.S. market.[35] Wal-Mart's use of lower tariffs, physical proximity, and buying power are changing the Mexican retail landscape, as shown in *The International Marketplace 4.4.*

Free trade produces both winners and losers. Although opponents concede that the agreement is likely to spur economic growth, they point out that segments of the U.S. economy will be harmed by the agreement. It is likely that wages and employment for unskilled workers in the United States will decrease because of Mexico's low-cost labor pool. U.S. companies have been moving operations to Mexico since the 1960s. The door was opened when Mexico liberalized export restrictions to allow for more so-called **maquiladoras,** plants that make goods and parts or process food for export to the United States. The supply of labor in the maquiladoras was plentiful, the pay and benefits low, and the work regulations lax by U.S. standards. In the last two decades, maquiladoras evolved from low-end garment or small-appliance assembly outfits to higher-end manufacturing of big-screen TVs, computers, and auto parts. The factories shipped $76.8 billion worth of goods (half of Mexican exports), almost all of it to the United States. But the arrangement is in trouble. The NAFTA treaty required Mexico to strip maquiladoras

THE INTERNATIONAL MARKETPLACE   4.4

NAFTA and Wal-Mart: Reshaping the Mexican Retail Market

Wal-Mart saw the promise of the Mexican market in 1991 when it stepped outside of the United States for the first time by launching Sam's Clubs in 50–50 partnership with Cifra, Mexico's largest retailer. The local partner was needed to provide operational expertise in a market significantly different in culture and income from Wal-Mart's domestic one. Within months, the first outlet—a bare-bones unit that sold bulk items at just above wholesale prices—was breaking all Wal-Mart records in sales. While tariffs still made imported goods pricey, "Made in the USA" merchandise also started appearing on the shelves.

After NAFTA took effect in 1994, tariffs tumbled, unleashing pent-up demand in Mexico for U.S.-made goods. The trade treaty also helped eliminate some of the transportation headaches and government red tape that had kept Wal-Mart from fully realizing its competitive advantage. NAFTA resulted in many European and Asian manufacturers setting up plants in Mexico, giving the retailer cheaper access to more foreign brands.

Wal-Mart's enormous buying power has kept it ahead of its Mexican competitors who are making similar moves. Because Wal-Mart consolidates its orders for all goods it sells outside of the United States, it can wring deeper discounts from suppliers than its local competitors. Wal-Mart Mexico has repeatedly exploited NAFTA and other economic forces to trigger price wars. For example, rather than pocket the windfall that resulted when tariffs on Lasko brand floor fans fell from 20 percent to 2 percent, price cuts took place equal to the tariff reductions.

Behind Wal-Mart's success are increasingly price-conscious consumers. The greater economic security of NAFTA has helped tame Mexico's once fierce inflation. The resulting price stability has made it easier for Mexican consumers to spot bargains. In addition, Wal-Mart's clean, brightly lit interiors, orderly and well-stocked aisles, and consistent pricing policies are a relief from the chaotic atmosphere that still prevails in many local stores.

Wal-Mart's aggressive tactics have resulted in complaints as well. In 2002, Mexico's Competition Commission was asked to probe into reports that Wal-Mart exerts undue pressure on suppliers to lower their prices. Local retailers, such as Comerci, Gigante, and Soriana, have seen their profits plummet but are forced to provide prices competitive to Wal-Mart's. In addition, they have engaged in aggressive rehauls of their operations. Soriana, for example, invested $250 million in new stores in 2002. It took out ads in local newspapers warning about "foreign supermarkets" when regulators fined a Wal-Mart in Monterrey because a shelf price did not match the price on the checkout receipt.

Wal-Mart's success continues as Mexico's number one retailer. It already has 579 grocery stores, wholesale-club outlets, and restaurants in Mexico, and has budgeted $600 million to open 63 new Mexican units by mid-2003. Sales are expected to top $10 billion in 2002.

SOURCES: "War of the Superstores," *Business Week*, September 23, 2002, 60; "How Well Does Wal-Mart Travel?" *Business Week*, September 3, 2001, 82–84; "How NAFTA Helped Wal-Mart Reshape the Mexican Market," *The Wall Street Journal*, August 31, 2001, A1–A2; and Vijay Govindarajan and Anil K. Gupta, "Taking Wal-Mart Global: Lessons from Retailing's Giant," *Strategy and Business*, fourth quarter, 1999, 45–56.

© CORBIS/SYGMA

of their duty-free status by 2001. Tariff breaks formerly given to all imported parts, supplies, equipment, and machinery used by foreign factories in Mexico now apply only to inputs from Canada, Mexico, and the United States. This effect is felt most by Asian factories because they still import a large amount of components from across the Pacific (for example, 97 percent of components for TVs assembled in Tijuana are imported, most from Asia). There is a lesser effect on Europeans because of Mexico's free trade agreement with the EU, which will eliminate tariffs gradually by 2007.[36] Wages have also been rising to $3.52 an hour (up from $2.29 in 1997), resulting in some low-end manufacturers of apparel and toys moving production to Asia.[37] While the Mexican government is eager to attract maquiladora investment, it is also keen to move away from using cheap labor as a central element of competitiveness.

Despite U.S. fears of rapid job loss if companies would send business south of the border, recent studies have declared the job gain or loss almost a washout. The good news is that free trade will create higher-skilled and better-paying jobs in the United States as a result of growth in exports. As a matter of fact, jobs in U.S. exporting firms tend to pay 10 to 15 percent more than the jobs they have replaced. Losers have been U.S. manufacturers of auto parts, furniture, and household glass; sugar, peanut, and citrus growers; and seafood and vegetable producers. The U.S. Labor Department has certified 316,000 jobs as threatened or lost due to trade with Mexico and Canada. At the same time, the U.S. economy has added some 20 million jobs in the years since NAFTA. The fact that job losses have been in more heavily unionized sectors has made these losses politically charged. In most cases, high Mexican shipping and inventory costs will continue to make it more efficient for many U.S. industries to serve their home market from U.S. plants. Outsourcing of lower-skilled jobs is an unstoppable trend for developed economies such as the United States. However, NAFTA has given U.S. firms a way of taking advantage of cheaper labor while still keeping close links to U.S. suppliers. Mexican assembly plants get 82 percent of their parts from U.S. suppliers, while factories in Asia are using only a fraction of that.[38] Without NAFTA, entire industries might be lost to Asia rather than just the labor-intensive portions.

Integration pains extend to other areas as well. Approximately 85 percent of U.S.–Mexican trade moves on trucks. Under NAFTA, cross-border controls on trucking were to be eliminated by the end of 1995, allowing commercial vehicles to move freely in four U.S. and six Mexican border states. But the U.S. truckers, backed by the Teamsters Union, would have nothing of this, arguing that Mexican trucks were dangerous and exceeded weight limits. The union also worried that opening of the border would depress wages, because it would allow U.S. trucking companies to team up with lower-cost counterparts in Mexico. In 2001, however, the NAFTA Arbitration Panel ruled that Mexican trucks must be allowed to cross U.S. borders and the U.S. Senate approved a measure that allows Mexican truckers to haul cargo provided they meet strict inspection and safety rules.[39]

Countries dependent on trade with NAFTA countries are concerned that the agreement would divert trade and impose significant losses on their economies. Asia's continuing economic success depends largely on easy access to the North American markets, which account for more than 25 percent of annual export revenue for many Asian countries. Lower-cost producers in Asia are likely to lose some exports to the United States if they are subject to tariffs but Mexican firms are not and may, therefore, have to invest in NAFTA.[40] Similarly, many in the Caribbean and Central America have always feared that the apparel industries of these regions will be threatened as would much-needed investments.

NAFTA may be the first step toward a hemispheric bloc, although nobody expects it to happen anytime soon. It took more than three years of tough bargaining to reach an agreement between the United States and Canada—two countries with parallel economic, industrial, and social systems. The challenges of expanding free trade throughout Latin America will be significant. However, many of Latin America's groupings are making provisions to join in a hemispheric free trade area by 2005. Such a regime faces difficulties. As a first step, Chile was scheduled to join as a fourth member in 1997. However, the membership has not materialized due to U.S. political maneuvering, and Chile has since entered into bilateral trade agreements with both Canada and Mexico and joined Mercosur as an associate member. This has meant that U.S. marketers are reporting trade deals lost to Canadian competitors, who are free of Chile's 11 percent tariffs.[41] Overall, many U.S. marketers fear that Latin Americans will start moving closer to Europeans if free trade discussions are not seen to progress. For example, both Mercosur and Mexico have signed free-trade agreements with the EU.[42]

Other Economic Alliances

Perhaps the world's developing countries have the most to gain from successful integrative efforts. Because many of these countries are also quite small, economic growth is difficult to generate internally. Many of these countries have adopted policies of **import substitution** to foster economic growth. An import substitution policy involves developing industries to produce goods that were formerly imported. Many of these industries, however, can be efficient producers only with a higher level of production than can be consumed by the domestic economy. Their success, therefore, depends on accessible export markets made possible by integrative efforts.

Integration in Latin America

Before the signing of the U.S.–Canada Free Trade Agreement, all the major trading bloc activity had taken place elsewhere in the Americas. However, none of the activity in Latin America has been hemispheric; that is, Central America had its structures, the Caribbean nations had theirs, and South America had its own different forms. However, for political and economic reasons, these attempts have never reached set objectives. In a dramatic transformation, these nations sought free trade as a salvation from stagnation, inflation, and debt. In response to these developments, Brazil, Argentina, Uruguay, and Paraguay set up a common market called Mercosur (Mercado Commun del Sur).[43] Despite their own economic challenges and disagreements over trade policy, the Mercosur members and the two associate members, Bolivia and Chile, have agreed to economic-convergence targets similar to those the EU made as a precursor to the euro. These are in areas of inflation, public debt, and fiscal deficits. Bolivia, Colombia, Ecuador, Peru, and Venezuela have formed the Andean Common Market (ANCOM). Many Latin nations are realizing that if they do not unite, they will become increasingly marginal in the global market. In approaching the EU with a free trade agreement, Mercosur members want to diversify their trade relationships and reduce their dependence on U.S. trade.

The ultimate goal is a free trade zone from Point Barrow, Alaska, to Patagonia under a framework called the **Free Trade Area of the Americas (FTAA).** The argument is that free trade throughout the Americas would channel investment and technology to Latin nations and give U.S. firms a head start in those markets. Ministerials held since 1994 have established working groups to gather data and make recommendations in preparation for the FTAA negotiations and an agreement by 2005. The larger countries have agreed to consider giving smaller and lesser-developed countries more time to reduce tariffs, to open their economies to foreign investment, and to adopt effective laws in areas such as antitrust, intellectual property rights, bank regulation, and prohibitions on corrupt business practices. At the same time, the less-developed countries have agreed to include labor and environmental standards in the negotiations.[44]

Changes in corporate behavior have followed. Free market reforms and economic revival have had marketers ready to export and to invest in Latin America. For example, Brazil's opening of its computer market has resulted in Hewlett-

Packard establishing a joint venture to produce PCs. In the past, Kodak dealt with Latin America through eleven separate country organizations, but has since streamlined its operations to five "boundaryless" companies organized along product lines and taking advantage of trading openings, and has created centralized distribution, thereby making deliveries more efficient and decreasing inventory carrying costs.[45]

Integration in Asia

Development in Asia has been quite different from that in Europe and in the Americas. While European and North American arrangements have been driven by political will, market forces may force more formal integration on Asian politicians. The fact that regional integration is increasing around the world may drive Asian interest to it for pragmatic reasons. First, European and American markets are significant for the Asian producers, and some type of organization or bloc may be needed to maintain leverage and balance against the two other blocs. Second, given that much of the Asian trade growth is from intraregional trade, having common understandings and policies will become necessary. Future integration will most likely use the frame of the most established arrangement in the region, the Association of Southeast Asian Nations (ASEAN). Before late 1991, ASEAN had no real structures, and consensus was reached through informal consultations. In October 1991, ASEAN members announced the formation of a customs union called Asean Free Trade Area (AFTA). The ten member countries have agreed to reduce tariffs to a maximum level of 5 percent by 2003 and to create a customs union by 2010.

The Malaysians have pushed for the formation of the East Asia Economic Group (EAEG), which would add Hong Kong, Japan, South Korea, and Taiwan to the membership list. This proposal makes sense, because without Japan and the rapidly industrializing countries of the region such as South Korea and Taiwan, the effect of the arrangement would be nominal. Japan's reaction has been generally negative toward all types of regionalization efforts, mainly because it has the most to gain from free trade efforts. However, part of what has been driving regionalization has been Japan's reluctance to foster some of the elements that promote free trade, for example, reciprocity.[46] Should the other trading blocs turn against Japan, its only resort may be to work toward a more formal trade arrangement in the Asia-Pacific area.

Another formal proposal for cooperation would start building bridges between two emerging trade blocs. Some individuals have publicly called for a U.S.-Japan common market. Given the differences on all fronts between the two countries, the proposal may be quite unrealistic at this time. Negotiated trade liberalization will not open Japanese markets because of major institutional differences, as seen in many rounds of successful negotiations but totally unsatisfactory results. The only solution, especially for the U.S. government, is to forge better cooperation between the government and the private sector to improve competitiveness.[47]

In 1988, Australia proposed the Asia Pacific Economic Cooperation (APEC) as an annual forum to maintain a balance in negotiations. The proposal calls for ASEAN members to be joined by Australia, New Zealand, Japan, South Korea, Canada, Chile, Mexico, and the United States. Originally, the model for APEC was not the EU, with its Brussels bureaucracy, but the Organization for Economic Cooperation and Development (OECD), which is a center for research and high-level discussion. However, APEC has now established an ultimate goal of achieving free trade in the area among its 21 members by 2010.[48]

Economic integration has also taken place on the Indian subcontinent. In 1985, seven nations of the region (India, Pakistan, Bangladesh, Sri Lanka, Nepal, Bhutan, and the Maldives) launched the South Asian Association for Regional Cooperation (SAARC). Cooperation has been limited to relatively noncontroversial areas, such as agriculture and regional development, and is hampered by political disagreements.

Integration in Africa and the Middle East

Africa's economic groupings range from currency unions among European nations and their former colonies to customs unions between neighboring states. In addition to wanting to liberalize trade among members, African countries want to gain better access to European and North American markets for farm and textile products. Given that most of the countries are too small to negotiate with the other blocs, alliances have been the solution. In 1975, sixteen West African nations attempted to create a megamarket large enough to interest investors from the industrialized world and reduce hardship through economic integration. The objective of the Economic Community of West African States (ECOWAS) was to form a customs union and eventually a common market. Although many of its objectives have not been reached, its combined population of 160 million represents the largest economic entity in sub-Saharan Africa. Other entities in Africa include the Common Market for Eastern and Southern Africa (COMESA), the Economic Community of Central African States (CEEAC), the Southern African Customs Union, the Southern African Development Community (SADC), and some smaller, less globally oriented blocs such as the Economic Community of the Great Lakes Countries, the Mano River Union, and the East African Community (EAC). Most member countries are part of more than one block (for example, Tanzania is a member in both the EAC and SADC). The blocs, for the most part, have not been successful due to small memberships and lack of economic infrastructure to produce goods to be traded within the blocs. Moreover, some of the blocs have been relatively inactive for substantial periods of time while their members endure internal political turmoil or even warfare amongst each other.[49] In 2002, African nations established the African Union (AU) for regional cooperation. Eventually, plans call for a pan-African parliament, a court of justice, a central bank, and a shared currency.[50]

Countries in the Arab world have made some progress in economic integration. The Arab Maghreb Union ties together Algeria, Libya, Mauritania, Morocco, and Tunisia in northern Africa. The Gulf Cooperation Council (GCC) is one of the most powerful of any trade groups. The per capita income of its six member states (Bahrain, Kuwait, Oman, Qatar, Saudi Arabia, and the United Arab Emirates) is well over $15,000. The GCC was formed in 1980 mainly as a defensive measure due to the perceived threat from the Iran-Iraq war. Its aim is to achieve free trade arrangements with the European nations.

A listing of the major regional trade agreements is provided in Table 4.9.

Economic Integration and the International Marketer

Regional economic integration creates opportunities and potential problems for the international marketer. It may have an impact on a company's entry mode by favoring direct investment because one of the basic rationales of integration is to generate favorable conditions for local production and intraregional trade. By design, larger markets are created with potentially more opportunity. Because of harmonization efforts, regulations may be standardized, thus positively affecting the international marketer.

The international marketer must, however, make integration assessments and decisions from four points of view.[51] The first task is to envision the outcome of the change. Change in the competitive landscape can be dramatic if scale opportunities can be exploited in relatively homogeneous demand conditions. This could be the case, for example, for industrial goods, consumer durables such as cameras and watches, and professional services. The international marketer will have to take into consideration varying degrees of change readiness within the markets themselves; that is, governments and other stakeholders, such as labor unions, may oppose the liberalization of competition, especially when national champions such as airlines, automobiles, energy, and telecommunications are concerned. However, with deregulation, monopolies have had to transform into competitive industries. In Germany, for example, the price of long-distance calls has fallen

Table 4.9	Major Regional Trade Agreements

AFTA **ASEAN Free Trade Area**
Brunei, Indonesia, Laos, Malaysia, Myanmar, Philippines, Singapore, Thailand, Vietnam

ANCOM **Andean Common Market**
Bolivia, Colombia, Ecuador, Peru, Venezuela

APEC **Asia Pacific Economic Cooperation**
Australia, Brunei, Canada, Chile, China, Hong Kong, Indonesia, Japan, Malaysia, Mexico, New Zealand, Papua New Guinea, Peru, Philippines, Russia, Singapore, South Korea, Taiwan, Thailand, Vietnam, United States

CACM **Central American Common Market**
Costa Rica, El Salvador, Guatemala, Honduras, Nicaragua

CARICOM **Caribbean Community**
Antigua and Barbuda, Bahamas, Barbados, Belize, Dominica, Grenada, Guyana, Jamaica, Montserrat, St. Kitts–Nevis, St. Lucia, St. Vincent and the Grenadines, Suriname, Trinidad-Tobago

ECOWAS **Economic Community of West African States**
Benin, Burkina Faso, Cape Verde, Gambia, Ghana, Guinea, Guinea-Bissau, Ivory Coast, Liberia, Mali, Mauritania, Niger, Nigeria, Senegal, Sierra Leone, Togo

EFTA **European Free Trade Association**
Iceland, Liechtenstein, Norway, Switzerland

EU **European Union**
Austria, Belgium, Denmark, Finland, France, Germany, Greece, Ireland, Italy, Luxembourg, Netherlands, Portugal, Spain, Sweden, United Kingdom

GCC **Gulf Cooperation Council**
Bahrain, Kuwait, Oman, Qatar, Saudi Arabia, United Arab Emirates

LAIA **Latin American Integration Association**
Argentina, Bolivia, Brazil, Chile, Colombia, Cuba, Ecuador, Mexico, Paraguay, Peru, Uruguay, Venezuela

MERCOSUR **Southern Common Market**
Argentina, Brazil, Paraguay, Uruguay

NAFTA **North American Free Trade Agreement**
Canada, Mexico, United States

SAARC **South Asian Association for Regional Cooperation**
Bangladesh, Bhutan, India, Maldives, Nepal, Pakistan, Sri Lanka

SACU **Southern African Customs Union**
Botswana, Lesotho, Namibia, South Africa, Swaziland

For information, see **http://www.aseansec.org**; **http://www.apec.org**; **http://www.caricom.org**; **http://www.eurunion.org**; **http://www.mercosur.org.uy**; and **http://www.nafta-sec-alena.org**.

40 percent, forcing the former monopolist, Deutsche Telekom, to streamline its operations and seek new business abroad. By fostering a single market for capital, the euro is pushing Europe closer to a homogeneous market in goods and services, thereby exerting additional pressure on prices.[52]

The international marketer will then have to develop a strategic response to the new environment to maintain a sustainable long-term competitive advantage. Those companies already present in an integrated market should fill in gaps in European product/market portfolios through acquisitions or alliances to create a regional or global company. It is increasingly evident that even regional presence is not sufficient and companies need to set their sights on presence beyond that. In industries such as automobiles, mobile communications, and retailing, blocs in the twenty-first century may be dominated by two or three giants, leaving room only for niche players. Those with currently weak positions, or no presence at all, will have to create alliances for market entry and development with established firms. General Mills created Cereal Partners Worldwide with Nestlé to establish itself in Europe and to jointly develop new-market opportunities in Asia. An additional option for the international marketer is to leave the market altogether if it cannot remain competitive because of new competitive conditions or the level of investment needed. For example, Bank of America sold its operations in Italy to Deutsche Bank after it discovered the high cost of becoming a pan-European player.

Whatever changes are made, they will require company reorganization.[53] Structurally, authority will have to become more centralized to execute regional programs. In staffing, focus will have to be on individuals who understand the subtleties of consumer behavior across markets and are therefore able to evaluate the similarities and differences between cultures and markets. In developing systems for the planning and implementation of regional programs, adjustments have to be made to incorporate views throughout the organization. If, for example, decisions on regional advertising campaigns are made at headquarters without consultation with country operations, resentment from the local marketing staff could lead to less-than-optimal execution. The introduction of the euro will mean increased coordination in pricing as compared to the relative autonomy in price setting enjoyed by country organizations in the past. Companies may even move corporate or divisional headquarters from the domestic market to be closer to the customer or centers of innovation. For example, after Procter & Gamble's reorganization, its fabric and home care business unit is headquartered in Brussels, Belgium.

Finally, economic integration will create its own powers and procedures similar to those of the EU commission and its directives. The international marketer is not powerless to influence both of them; as a matter of fact, a passive approach may result in competitors gaining an advantage or it may put the company at a disadvantage. For example, it was very important for the U.S. pharmaceutical industry to obtain tight patent protection as part of the NAFTA agreement; therefore, substantial time and money were spent on lobbying both the executive and legislative branches of the U.S. government. Often, policymakers rely heavily on the knowledge and experience of the private sector to carry out its own work. Influencing change will therefore mean providing industry information, such as test results, to the policymakers. Many marketers consider lobbying a public relations activity and therefore go beyond the traditional approaches. Lobbying will usually have to take place at multiple levels simultaneously; within the EU, this means the European Commission in Brussels, the European Parliament in Strasbourg, or the national governments within the EU. Marketers with substantial resources have established their own lobbying offices in Brussels, while smaller companies get their voices heard through joint offices or their industry associations. In terms of lobbying, U.S. firms have an advantage because of their experience in their home market; however, for many European firms, lobbying is a new, yet necessary, skill to be acquired. At the same time, marketers operating in two or more major markets (such as the EU and North America) can work to produce more efficient trade through, for example, mutual recognition agreements (MRAs) on standards.[54]

Dealing with Financial Crises

A series of currency crises shook all emerging markets in the 1990s. The devaluation of the Mexican peso in 1994, the Asian crisis of July 1997, the Russian ruble collapse of August 1998, the fall of the Brazilian real in January 1999, and the Argentine default in 2001, have all provided a spectrum of emerging market economic failures, each with its own complex causes and unknown outlooks.

Causes of the Crises

Both the Mexican and Thai cases of currency devaluation led to regional effects in which international investors saw Mexico and Thailand as only the first domino in a long series of failures to come. For example, the historically stable Korean won fell from Won 900/US$ to Won 1,100/US$ in one month. The reasons for the crises were largely in three areas allowing comparison: corporate socialism, corporate governance, and banking stability and management. In 1997, business liabilities exceeded the capacities of government to bail businesses out, and practices such as lifetime employment were no longer sustainable. Many firms in the Far East were often controlled by families or groups related to the governing party of the country. The interests of stockholders and creditors were secondary in an atmosphere of cronyism. With the speculative investments made by many banks failing, banks themselves had to close, severely hampering the ability of businesses to obtain the necessary capital financing needed for operations. The pivotal role of banking liquidity was the focus of the International Monetary Fund's bail-out efforts.

The Asian crisis had global impact. What started as a currency crisis quickly became a region-wide recession.[55] The slowed economies of the region caused major reductions in world demand for many products, especially commodities. World oil markets, copper markets, and agricultural products all saw severe price drops as demand kept falling. These changes were immediately noticeable in declined earnings and growth prospects for other emerging economies. The problems of Russia and Brazil were reflections of those declines. In Argentina, the government defaulted on its debt, blocked Argentines from paying obligations to foreigners, and stopped pegging the peso to the U.S. dollar.

Effects of the Crises

The collapse of the ruble in Russia and of Russia's access to international capital markets has brought into question the benefits of a free-market economy, long championed by the advocates of Western-style democracy. While Russia is the sixth-most populous nation, a nuclear power, and the holder of a permanent seat in the Security Council of the United Nations, its economic status is that of a developing country. There was a growing middle class, particularly in the largest cities. Some Russian businesses had revealed glimmerings of respect for shareholders, staff, and customers. Higher standards were encouraged by a growing international business presence. Many of these positive changes are being lost or are in jeopardy.

In Brazil, similar effects are being felt. A total of 30 million consumers have left the middle class. Many of the free-trade experiments within Mercosur are being reevaluated or endangered, especially by Brazilian moves in erecting tariff barriers. Many of the key sectors, such as automobiles, are hit by layoffs and suspended production.[56] In Argentina, the supply of most foreign-made goods was choked off.

Consumer and Marketer Responses

Changes in the economic environment affect both consumers and marketers. Consumer confidence is eroded and marketers have to weigh their marketing strategies carefully. Some of these adjustments are summarized in Table 4.10.

Recessions have an impact on consumer spending. For example, the 30 million Brazilians who, as a result of the real crisis, were no longer able to consume in a middle-class tradition were also lost to many marketers, such as McDonald's. Rather than buying hamburgers, they would consume more traditional and therefore less expensive meals. Similarly, some consumption may turn not only toward local alternatives but even to generics. Especially hard hit may be big-ticket purchases, such as cars, furniture, and appliances, that may be put on long-term hold.

Marketers' responses to these circumstances have varied from abandoning markets to substantially increasing their efforts. While Daihatsu pulled out of Thailand, GM has decided to stay, with a change in the car model to be produced and

Table 4.10   Consumer and Marketer Adjustment to Financial Crisis

Consumer Adjustment to Financial Hardship	Marketer Adjustment to Financial Hardship

• General reactions
    Reduce consumption and wastefulness
    More careful decision making
    More search for information
	• Marketing-mix strategies
	    Withdraw from weak markets
	    Fortify in strong markets
	    Acquire weak competitors
	    Consider youth markets
	    Resale market for durables

• Product adjustments
    Necessities rather than luxuries
    Switch to cheaper brands or generics
    Local rather than foreign brands
    Smaller quantities/packages
	• Product strategies
	    Prune weak products
	    Avoid introducing new products in gaps
	    Flanker brands
	    Augment products with warranties
	    Adaptive positioning

• Price adjustments
    Life-cycle costs—durability/value
    Emphasis on economical prices
	• Pricing strategies
	    Improve quality while maintaining price
	    Reduce price while maintaining quality
	    Consider product life-cycle pricing

• Promotion adjustments
    Rational approach
    Reduced attraction to gifts
    Information rather than imagery
	• Promotion strategies
	    Maintain advertising budget
	    Focus on print media
	    Assurances through rational appeals
	    Expert endorsements
	    Advisory tone
	    Customer loyalty programs
	    Train sales force to handle objections

• Shopping adjustments
    Increased window shopping
    Preference for discount stores
    Fewer end-of-aisle purchases
	• Distribution strategies
	    Location is critical
	    Sell in discount and wholesale centers
	    Prune marginal dealers
	    Alternative channels

SOURCE: Compiled from Swee Hoon Ang, Siew Meng Leong, and Philip Kotler, "The Asian Apocalypse: Crisis Marketing for Consumers and Businesses," Long Range Planning 33 (February 2000): 97–119.

reduced production volume. Returning to a market having once abandoned it may prove to be difficult. For example, distribution channels may be blocked by competition, or suspicion about the long-term commitment of a returnee may surface among local partners. Deere & Co. would sell its farm equipment in Argentina only if payment was in US$ or to customers with bank accounts abroad.[57] Manipulating the marketing mix is also warranted. Imported products are going to be more expensive, sometimes many times what the local versions cost. Therefore, emphasizing the brand name, the country of origin, and other benefits may convince the consumer of a positive value-price relationship. Adaptive positioning means recasting the product in a new light rather than changing the product itself. For example, Michelin changed its positioning from "expensive, but worth it" to "surprisingly affordable" in Asian markets affected by the crisis.[58] If the perceived prices are too high, the product and/or its packaging may have to be changed by making the product smaller or the number of units in a pack fewer. For example, Unilever reduced the size of its ice-cream packs, making them cheaper, and offers premiums in conjunction with the purchase of soap products (for example, buy three, get one free).[59]

While marketers from North America and Europe may be faced by these challenges, local companies may have an advantage, not only at home but in international markets as well. Their lower prices give them an opportunity to expand outside their home markets or aggressively pursue expansion in new markets. Similarly, companies with sourcing in markets hit by currency crises may be able to benefit from lower procurement costs.

The most interesting approach in the face of challenges is to increase efforts in building market share. A number of U.S. companies in Mexico, such as Procter & Gamble, have decided to invest more due to decreasing competition (which resulted from some competitors leaving) and the increased buying power of their currencies. This strategy is naturally based on the premise that the market will rebound in the foreseeable future, thus rewarding investments made earlier.

Summary

Economic variables relating to the various markets' characteristics—population, income, consumption patterns, infrastructure, geography, and attitudes toward foreign involvement in the economy—form a starting point for assessment of market potential for the international marketer. These data are readily available but should be used in conjunction with other, more interpretive data because the marketer's plans often require a long-term approach. Data on the economic environment produce a snapshot of the past; in some cases, old data are used to make decisions affecting operations two years in the future. Even if the data are recent, they cannot themselves indicate the growth and the intensity of development. Some economies remain stagnant, plagued by natural calamities, internal problems, and lack of export markets, whereas some witness booming economic development.

Economic data provide a baseline from which other more market/product–specific and even experiential data can be collected. Understanding the composition and interrelationships between economic indicators is essential for the assessment of the other environments

and their joint impact on market potential. The international marketer needs to understand the impact of the economic environment on social development.

The emergence of economic integration in the world economy poses unique opportunities and challenges to the international marketer. Eliminating barriers between member markets and erecting new ones vis-à-vis nonmembers will call for adjustments in past strategies to fully exploit the new situations. In the late 1980s and early 1990s, economic integration increased substantially. The signing of the North American Free Trade Agreement produced the largest trading bloc in the world, whereas the Europeans are moving in their cooperation beyond the pure trade dimension.

Economic crises have hit many of the world's markets in the last ten years, especially countries that are emerging as the markets of the twenty-first century. In such a challenging environment, effective market planning and implementation take on additional significance. While withdrawal may be a feasible alternative, international marketers have found ways to grow market share even under adverse circumstances.

Key Terms

Group of Five	inflation
Group of Seven	debt problem
Group of Ten	Physical Quality of Life Index (PQLI)
household	free trade area
urbanization	customs union
purchasing power parities (PPP)	common market

factor mobility
Single European Act
economic union
European Union
Fortress Europe

maquiladoras
import substitution
Free Trade Area of the Americas
    (FTAA)
political union

Questions for Discussion

1. Place these markets in the framework that follows.

a. Indonesia	g. Turkey	m. Peru
b. Mozambique	h. Spain	n. Jamaica
c. India	i. Singapore	o. Poland
d. Bangladesh	j. Nigeria	p. United Kingdom
e. Niger	k. Algeria	q. Iraq
f. Brazil	l. Zambia	r. Saudi Arabia

	Income Level		
	Low	**Middle**	**High**
TRADE STRUCTURE			
Industrial			
Developing			
• Semi-Industrial			
• Oil-Exporting			
• Primary Producing			
• Populous South Asia			
• Least Developed			

2. Using available data, assess the market potential for (a) power generators and (b) consumer appliances in (1) the Philippines, (2) Jordan, and (3) Portugal.

3. From the international marketer's point of view, what are the opportunities and problems caused by increased urbanization in developing countries?

4. Comment on this statement: "A low per capita income will render the market useless."

5. What can a marketer do to advance regional economic integration?

6. Explain the difference between a free trade area and a common market. Speculate why negotiations were held for a North American Free Trade Agreement rather than for a North American Common Market.

Internet Exercises

1. The euro will be either a source of competitive advantage or disadvantage for marketers. Using "Euro case study: Siemens," available at **http://news.bbc.co.uk/hi/english/events/the_launch_of_emu**, assess the validity of the two points of view.

2. Compare and contrast two different points of view on expanding NAFTA by accessing the Web sites of America Leads on Trade, an industry coalition promoting increased access to world markets (**http://www.fasttrack.org**), and the AFL–CIO, American Federation of Labor–Congress of Industrial Organizations (**http://www.aflcio.org**).

Recommended Readings

The Arthur Andersen North American Business Sourcebook. Chicago: Triumph Books, 1994.

Business Guide to Mercosur. London: Economist Intelligence Unit, 1998.

Clement, Norris C., ed. *North American Economic Integration: Theory and Practice*. London: Edward Elgar Publications, 2000.

Current issues of *Country Monitor, Business Europe, Business East Europe, Business Asia, Business Latin America, Business China*.

The European Union: A Guide for Americans, 2002 edition. Available at **http://www.eurunion.org/infores/euguide/Chapter1.htm**.

International Marketing Data and Statistics 2002. London: Euromonitor, 2002.

Marber, Peter. *From Third World to World Class: The Future of Emerging Markets in the Global Economy*. New York: Perseus Books, 1998.

Ohmae, Kenichi. *The Borderless World: Power and Strategy in the Interlinked Economy*. New York: Harper Business, 1999.

Ryans, John K., and Pradeep A. Rau. *Marketing Strategies for the New Europe: A North American Perspective on 1992*. Chicago: American Marketing Association, 1990.

Sueo, Sekiguchi, and Noda Makito, eds. *Road to ASEAN-10: Japanese Perspectives on Economic*

Integration. Tokyo: Japan Center for International Exchange, 2000.

Venables, Anthony, Richard E. Baldwin, and Daniel Cohen, eds. *Market Integration, Regionalism and the Global Economy*. Cambridge, England: Cambridge University Press, 1999.

The World in Figures. London: Economist Publications, 2002.

World Development Report 2002. New York: Oxford University Press, 2002.

Yearbook of International Trade Statistics. New York: United Nations, 2002.

chapter 5

The International Political and Legal Environment

THE INTERNATIONAL MARKETPLACE   5.1

Is Your French Wine Really from Mexico?

To declare a product's country of origin, importers in the United States must evaluate the import under two rulings. First, they must adhere to the Gibson-Thomson ruling of 1940, which states that a product must be marked as originating in the country in which it has undergone a "substantial transformation." Thus, the labeling will communicate to consumers where the product was finished rather than where its materials originated. However, companies must also consider the rulings set forth in the North American Free Trade Agreement (NAFTA) of 1992. Under NAFTA rules, a product will be marked as originating from the country in which it was converted from one product classification to another. Thus, U.S. marketers must mark products coming from NAFTA and non-NAFTA countries differently.

While the "substantial transformation" ruling seems to make logical sense, it may yield misleading labeling. A "substantial transformation" may be different depending on who is making the judgment; that is, various members of the supply chain may disagree regarding the place of the product's transformation. For example, Florida orange juice, if blended with 1 percent Brazilian orange juice, must be labeled "Made in Brazil." Similarly, the U.S. company Bestfoods had to label its Skippy brand peanut butter "Made in Canada," even though it was made in Arkansas with ingredients that were 90 percent from the United States. In an appeal to the U.S. Court of International Trade, Bestfoods successfully argued that since no more than 7 percent of the value of the product was due to Canadian ingredients, Skippy warranted a "Made in the U.S.A." label, yet the rulings remain open to exploitation. Mexican wine blended with a small percentage of wine from France could be marketed as French wine.

SOURCES: Jack Lucentini, "A Sticky Case," July 17, 2000, *The Journal of Commerce* Web site, **http://www.joc.com**, accessed April 12, 2001; Neville, Peterson, Williams, "Country-of-Origin Rules Are Tangled," *The Journal of Commerce*, November 17, 1999, 10; and Cam Simpson, "Made in Korea Fraud Snares Area Firm," *The Chicago Sun-Times*, October 30, 1999, NWS 1.

MUCH AS MOST MANAGERS would like to ignore them, political and legal factors often play a critical role in international marketing activities. In addition, the interpretation and application of regulations can sometimes lead to conflicting and even misleading results, as *The International Marketplace 5.1* shows. Even the best business plans can go awry as a result of unexpected political or legal influences, and the failure to anticipate these factors can be the undoing of an otherwise successful business venture.

Of course, a single international political and legal environment does not exist. The business executive must be aware of political and legal factors on a variety of levels. For example, although it is useful to understand the complexities of the host country legal system, such knowledge does not protect against a home country imposed export embargo.

The study of the international political and legal environment must therefore be broken down into several subsegments. Many researchers do this by separating the legal from the political. This separation—although perhaps analytically useful—is somewhat artificial because laws are generally the result of political decisions. Here no attempt will be made to separate legal and political factors, except when such a separation is essential.

Instead, this chapter will examine the political-legal environment from the manager's point of view. In making decisions about his or her firm's international marketing activities, the manager will need to concentrate on three areas: the political and legal circumstances of the home country; those of the host country; and the bilateral and multilateral agreements, treaties, and laws governing the relations between host and home countries.

Home Country Political and Legal Environment

No manager can afford to ignore the policies and regulations of the country from which he or she conducts international marketing transactions. Wherever a firm is located, it will be affected by government policies and the legal system.

Many of these laws and regulations may not be designed specifically to address international marketing transactions, yet they can have a major impact on a firm's opportunities abroad. Minimum wage legislation, for example, affects the international competitiveness of a firm using production processes that are highly labor intensive. The cost of domestic safety regulations may significantly affect the pricing policies of firms in their international marketing efforts. For example, U.S. legislation that created the **Environmental Superfund** requires payment by chemical firms based on their production volume, regardless of whether the production is sold domestically or exported. As a result, these firms are at a disadvantage internationally when exporting their commodity-type products because they must compete against foreign firms that are not required to make such a payment in their home countries and therefore have a cost advantage.

Other legal and regulatory measures, however, are clearly aimed at international marketing activities. Some may be designed to help firms in their international efforts. The lack of enforcement of others may hurt the international marketer. For example, many firms are quite concerned about the lack of safeguards for **intellectual property rights** in China. Not only may counterfeiting result in inferior products and damage to the reputation of a company, but it also reduces the chances that an innovative firm can recoup its investment in research and development and spawn new products.

Violations of intellectual property rights can occur anywhere. As an example, in 1988, Anheuser-Busch agreed with Czechoslovak authorities to settle a trademark dispute with Budjovicky Budvar over the use of the name Budweiser. Anheuser-Busch agreed to give the Czech brewery a $15 million package, $10.3 million in brewing equipment and $4.7 million in cash, in return for which the two firms agreed to a division of the world into specified exclusive and shared markets. Chapter 8 will provide further in-depth discussions of intellectual property rights problems and ways to protect a firm from infringement.

Another area in which governments may attempt to aid and protect the international marketing efforts of companies is **gray market** activities. Gray market goods are products that enter markets in ways not desired by their manufacturers. Companies may be hurt by their own products if they reach the consumer via uncontrolled distribution channels. Gray market activities will be discussed in detail later in the book.

Apart from specific areas that result in government involvement, the political environment in most countries tends to provide general support for the international marketing efforts of the country's firms. For example, a government may work to reduce trade barriers or to increase trade opportunities through bilateral and multilateral negotiations. Such actions will affect individual firms to the extent that they affect the international climate for free trade.

Often, however, governments also have specific rules and regulations restricting international marketing. Such regulations are frequently political in nature and are based on the fact that governments believe commerce to be only one objective among others, such as foreign policy and national security. Four main areas of governmental activities are of major concern to the international marketer here: embargoes or trade sanctions, export controls, import controls, and the regulation of international business behavior.

Embargoes and Sanctions

The terms **trade sanctions** and **embargoes** as used here refer to governmental actions that distort the free flow of trade in goods, services, or ideas for decidedly adversarial and political, rather than strictly economic, purposes. To understand them better, we need to examine the auspices and legal justifications under which they are imposed.

Trade sanctions have been used quite frequently and successfully in times of war or to address specific grievances. For example, in 1284, the Hansa, an association of north German merchants, felt that its members were suffering from several injustices by Norway. On learning that one of its ships had been attacked and pillaged by the Norwegians, the Hansa called an assembly of its members and resolved on an economic blockade of Norway. The export of grain, flour, vegetables, and beer was prohibited on pain of fines and confiscation of the goods. The blockade was a complete success. Deprived of grain from Germany, the Norwegians were unable to obtain it from England or elsewhere. As a contemporary chronicler reports: "Then there broke out a famine so great that they were forced to make atonement." Norway was forced to pay indemnities for the financial losses that had been caused and to grant the Hansa extensive trade privileges.[1]

The League of Nations set a precedent for the international legal justification of economic sanctions by subscribing to a covenant that provided for penalties or sanctions for breaching its provisions. The members of the League of Nations did not intend to use military or economic measures separately, but the success of the blockades of World War I fostered the opinion that "the economic weapon, conceived not as an instrument of war but as a means of peaceful pressure, is the greatest discovery and most precious possession of the League."[2] The basic idea was that economic sanctions could force countries to behave peacefully in the international community.

The idea of the multilateral use of economic sanctions was again incorporated into international law under the charter of the United Nations, but greater emphasis was placed on the enforcement process. Once decided upon, sanctions are mandatory, even though each permanent member of the Security Council can veto efforts to impose sanctions. The charter also allows for sanctions as enforcement action by regional agencies such as the Organization of American States, the Arab League, and the Organization of African Unity, but only with the Security Council's authorization.

The apparent strength of the United Nations enforcement system was soon revealed to be flawed. Stalemates in the Security Council and vetoes by permanent members often led to a shift of emphasis to the General Assembly, where sanctions are not enforceable. Further, concepts such as "peace" and "breach of peace" are seldom perceived in the same way by all members, and thus no systematic sanctioning policy developed in the United Nations.[3]

Over the years, economic sanctions and embargoes have become an often-used foreign policy tool for many countries. Frequently, they have been imposed unilaterally in the hope of changing a country's government or at least changing its policies. Reasons for the impositions are varied, ranging from human rights to nuclear nonproliferation to antiterrorism. The range of sanctions imposed can be quite broad. Table 5.1 lists the series of economic sanctions that are triggered under different U.S. laws if a country is placed on the list of state sponsors of terrorism. The restrictions include export and import curtailment, elimination of credits, and prohibition of financial transactions. The intent is to bring commercial interchange to a complete halt. Unilateral imposition of sanctions, however, tends to have major negative effects on the firms in the country that is exercising sanctions, mainly due to simple shifts in trade.

Another key problem with unilateral imposition of sanctions is that they typically do not produce the desired result. Sanctions may make the obtaining of goods more difficult or expensive for the sanctioned country, yet achievement of the purported objective almost never occurs. In order to work, sanctions need to be imposed multilaterally. Only when virtually all nations in which a product is produced agree to deny it to a target can there be a true deprivation effect. Without such denial, sanctions do not have much bite. Yet to get all producing nations

Table 5.1	U.S. Sanctions against State Sponsors of Terrorism

- Restrictions on export licenses (or a general ban) for dual-use items or critical technology (under the Export Administration Act of 1979)
- Ban on sales or licenses for items on the U.S. Munitions Control List (under the Arms Export Control Act)
- Ban on U.S. foreign assistance including Export-Import Bank credits and guarantees (under the Foreign Assistance Act of 1961)
- Authorization for the president to restrict or ban imports of goods and services from designated terrorist countries (under the International Security and Development Cooperation Act of 1985)
- Prohibition of financial transactions by U.S. persons with the governments of designated terrorist countries (under the Antiterrorism and Effective Death Penalty Act of 1996)
- Requirement that U.S. representatives at international financial institutions vote against loans or other financial assistance to that country (under the International Financial Institutions Act of 1977)
- Ineligibility for the Generalized System of Preferences (GSP, under the Trade Act of 1974)

SOURCE: Gary Clyde Hufbauer, Jeffrey J. Schott, and Barbara Oegg, "Using Sanctions to Fight Terrorism," **http://www.iie.com/policybriefs/ news01–11.htm**, accessed September 10, 2002.

to agree can be quite difficult. Typically, individual countries have different relationships with the country subject to the sanctions due to geographic or historic reasons, and therefore cannot or do not want to terminate trade relations.

Yet global cooperation can be achieved. For example, when Iraq invaded Kuwait in August of 1990, virtually all members of the United Nations condemned this hostile action and joined a trade embargo against Iraq. Both major and minor Iraqi trading partners—including many Arab nations—honored the United Nations trade embargo and ceased trade with Iraq in the attempt to force it to withdraw its troops from Kuwait. Agreements were made to financially compensate those countries most adversely affected by the trade measures.

The attacks of September 11, 2001, and the subsequent multinational collaboration have strengthened the sanctioning mechanism of the United Nations greatly. It may well be that sanctions will reemerge as a powerful and effective international political tool in the world. When we consider that sanctions may well be the middle ground between going to war and doing nothing, their effective functioning can represent a powerful arrow in the quiver of international policy measures. Economic sanctions can be used to extend political control over foreign companies operating abroad, with or without the support of their local government.[4]

One key concern with sanctions is the fact that governments often consider them as being free of cost. However, even though they may not affect the budget of governments, sanctions imposed by governments can mean significant loss of business to firms. One estimate claims that the economic sanctions held in place by the United States annually costs the country some $20 billion in lost exports and that the success rate of all U.S. sanctions where the United States was part of a sanction coalition remained in the 25 percent range.[5]

Due to these costs, the issue of compensating the domestic firms and industries affected by these sanctions needs to be raised. Yet, trying to impose sanctions slowly or making them less expensive to ease the burden on these firms undercuts their ultimate chance for success. The international marketing manager is often caught in this political web and loses business as a result. Frequently, firms try to anticipate sanctions based on their evaluations of the international political climate. Even when substantial precautions are taken, firms may still suffer substantial losses due to contract cancellations. However, this can be seen as the cost of one's government's support for an open global trading and investing environment.

Export Controls

Many nations have **export control systems,** which are designed to deny or at least delay the acquisition of strategically important goods by adversaries. Most of these systems make controls the exception, rather than the rule, with exports considered to be independent of foreign policy. The United States, however, differs substantially from this perspective in that exports are considered to be a privilege rather than a right, and exporting is seen as an extension of foreign policy.

The legal basis for export controls varies across nations. For example, in Germany, armament exports are covered in the so-called War Weapons List, which is a part of the War Weapons Control Law. The exports of other goods are covered by the German Export List. **Dual-use items,** which are goods useful for both military and civilian purposes, are then controlled by the Joint List of the European Union.[6]

The U.S. export control system is based on the Export Administration Act, administered by the Department of Commerce, and the Munitions Control Act, administered by the Department of State. The Commerce Department focuses on exports in general, while the State Department covers products designed or modified for military use, even if such products have commercial applicability. The determinants for controls are national security, foreign policy, short supply, and nuclear nonproliferation.

U.S. laws control all exports of goods, services, and ideas. It is important to note here that an export of goods occurs whenever goods are physically transferred from the United States. Services and ideas, however, are deemed exported whenever transferred to a foreign national, regardless of location. Permitting a foreign national from a controlled country to have access to a highly sensitive computer program in the United States is therefore deemed to be an export. The effect of such a perspective can be major, particularly on universities and for international students.

In order for any export from the United States to take place, the exporter needs to obtain an export license. The administering government agencies have, in consultation with other government departments, drawn up a list of commodities whose export is considered particularly sensitive. In addition, a list of countries differentiates nations according to their political relationship with the United States. Finally, a list of individual firms that are considered to be unreliable trading partners because of past trade-diversion activities exists for each country.

After an export license application has been filed, government specialists match the commodity to be exported with the commerce control list, a file containing information about products that are either particularly sensitive to national security or controlled for other purposes. The product is then matched with the country of destination and the recipient company. If no concerns regarding any of the three exist, an export license is issued. Control determinants and the steps in the decision process are summarized in Figure 5.1.

This process may sound overly cumbersome, but it does not apply in equal measure to all exports. Most international business activities can be carried out under NLR conditions, which stands for "no license required." NLR provides blanket permission to export. Products can be freely shipped to most trading partners provided that neither the end user nor the end use involved are considered sensitive. However, the process becomes more complicated and cumbersome when products incorporating high-level technologies and countries not friendly to the United States are involved. The exporter must then obtain an **export license,** which consists of written authorization to send a product abroad.

The international marketing repercussions of export controls are important. It is one thing to design an export control system that is effective and that restricts those international business activities subject to important national concerns. It is, however, quite another when controls lose their effectiveness and when one country's firms are placed at a competitive disadvantage with firms in other countries whose control systems are less extensive or even nonexistent. *The International Marketplace 5.2* highlights some of the controversy surrounding export controls.

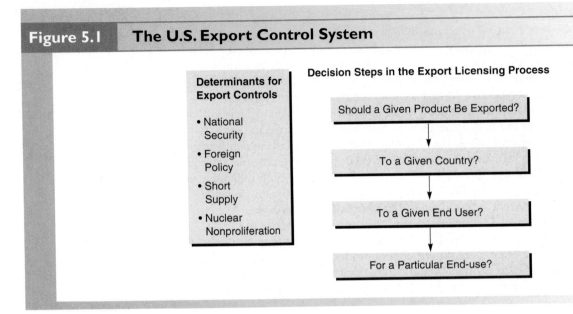

Figure 5.1   The U.S. Export Control System

Determinants for Export Controls

- National Security
- Foreign Policy
- Short Supply
- Nuclear Nonproliferation

Decision Steps in the Export Licensing Process

Should a Given Product Be Exported?

↓

To a Given Country?

↓

To a Given End User?

↓

For a Particular End-use?

A New Environment for Export Controls

The attacks of terrorists have again highlighted the importance of export controls. Restricting the flow of materials can be crucial in avoiding the development of weapons of mass destruction; restricting technology can limit the ability to target missiles; restricting the flow of funds can inhibit funding of terrorist training.

Nowadays, the principal focus of export controls must rest on the Third World. Quite a number of countries from this region want chemical and nuclear weapons and the technology to make use of them. For example, a country such as Libya can do little with its poison gas shells without a suitable delivery system. As a result, export controls have moved from a "strategic balance" to a "tactical balance" approach.

Major change has also resulted from the increased **foreign availability** of high-technology products. In the past decade, the number of participants in the international trade field has grown rapidly. In earlier decades, industrializing countries mainly participated in world trade due to wage-based competition. Today, they are increasingly focused on technology-based competition. As a result, high-technology products are available worldwide from many sources. The broad availability makes any denial of such products more difficult to enforce. If a nation does control the exports of widely available products, it imposes a major competitive burden on its firms.

The speed of change and the rapid dissemination of information and innovation around the world also has shifted. Enormous technical progress is accompanied by a radical change in computer architecture. Instead of having to replace a personal computer or a workstation with a new computer, it is possible now to simply exchange microprocessors or motherboards with new, more efficient ones. Furthermore, today's machines can be connected to more than one microprocessor and users can customize and update configurations almost at will. A user simply acquires additional chips from whomever and uses expansion slots to enhance the capacity of his or her computer.

The question arises as to how much of the latest technology is required for a country to engage in "dangerous" activity. For example, nuclear weapons and sophisticated delivery systems were developed by the United States and the Soviet Union long before supercomputers became available. Therefore, it is reasonable to assert that researchers in countries working with equipment that is less than state-of-the-art, or even obsolete, may well be able to achieve a threat capability that can result in major destruction and affect world safety.

THE INTERNATIONAL MARKETPLACE 5.2

Export Controls: More Harm than Good?

The U.S. government finds itself in a battle between economic prosperity and national security. On September 11, 2001, the whole world watched in awe as the New York World Trade Center buildings collapsed. The United States, along with the rest of the world, was forced to address weaknesses in security policies. Of the many measures suggested to fortify national and international security, an improved export control regime is among the most widely discussed.

An important factor in containing the capabilities of threats to national and international security is a successful multilateral agreement regarding export controls. While one country can prohibit the sales of certain products, it does little for security measures if other countries willingly export the same product. Furthermore, increasing globalization connects countries of the world in a web of trade and interdependence. Due to the close relationships among the economies of all members of the international community, financially debilitating attacks on one state will be felt by all states. A failure to uphold export control standards by one link in the international chain will affect the economic and security conditions of everyone else.

In an effort to coordinate efforts towards export controls, U.S. policymakers have met with close allies, like the U.K., and potential adversaries, like China. Unfortunately, not all international agreements have been successful. For example, in January 2002, the State Department imposed sanctions against China after the discovery that Beijing firms were selling sensitive items to Iran. By taking a firm stance against trade to Iran, the United States addressed the necessity for a multilateral effort towards export controls.

If countries aren't receiving goods from the United States, they can easily obtain them elsewhere, namely from U.S. allies. Take the satellite industy, as an example: Its companies have been very much affected by tight export control regulations. California's commercial satellite industry formerly dominated the world market, accounting for 75 percent of all satellites in orbit for the past decade. As a result of export curbs, the U.S. satellite companies' share of the global market declined 30 percentage points in 2000 to an all-time low of 45 percent, resulting in losses of $1.2 billion in revenue and more than 1,000 jobs. Loral Space in California serves as a compelling example of economic losses resulting from a demanding export control regime. In 1998, the State Department suspended a license to China for the purchase of a satellite from the firm. The Chinese are still waiting for the license to be reissued, and Loral, in the meantime, is praying that it won't lose the $145 million deal. Many customers have already grown weary with the long and difficult licensing process. The losses to the U.S. satellite industry are gains to the European industry. According to a study conducted by the Satellite Industry Association, in the year 2000, European companies, such as Alcatel and Astrium, outstripped U.S. companies in geo-satellite orders for the first time.

As a result of different views on export control practices, serious potential for conflict exists. For example, during a conference on U.S.–European defense relations in February 2002, the NATO general secretary warned that "the gap in defense technology between the United States and its NATO allies will become 'unbridgeable' if Washington does not ease restrictions on technology transfer and relax export controls." In establishing such perceived barriers to trade, the United States risks alienating more than its adversaries; it shuts off its market to allies and limits itself while its competitors trade freely.

While the events of September 11 have emphasized the need for stringent security measures, the losses to the U.S. economy cannot be ignored. Furthermore, while allies are being shut off from the U.S. market, and while adversaries are still obtaining sensitive goods from friends and foes alike, one wonders if a multilateral effort is at all possible, and if such an effort will help the United States to achieve its national security goals.

SOURCES: Bill Gertz, "U.S. Hits China with Sanctions over Arms Sales," *The Washington Times,* January 25, 2002; and Peter Pae, "Satellite-Export Curbs Hurting U.S. Makers, Study Says," *The Los Angeles Times,* February 6, 2001.

From a control perspective, there is also the issue of equipment size. Due to their size, supercomputers and high-technology items used to be fairly difficult to hide and any movement of such products was easily detectable. Nowadays, state-of-the-art technology has been miniaturized. Much leading-edge technological equipment is so small that it can fit into a briefcase, and most equipment is no larger than the luggage compartment of a car. Given these circumstances, it has become difficult to closely supervise the transfer of such equipment.

There is a continuing debate about what constitutes military-use products, civilian-use products, and dual-use products and the achievement of multilateral

Patterns of Global Terrorism outside the United States, 2001

SOURCE: Based on *U.S. Department of State*, 2001; see also
http://www.state.gov/s/ct/rls/pgtrpt/2001/html/10273.htm.

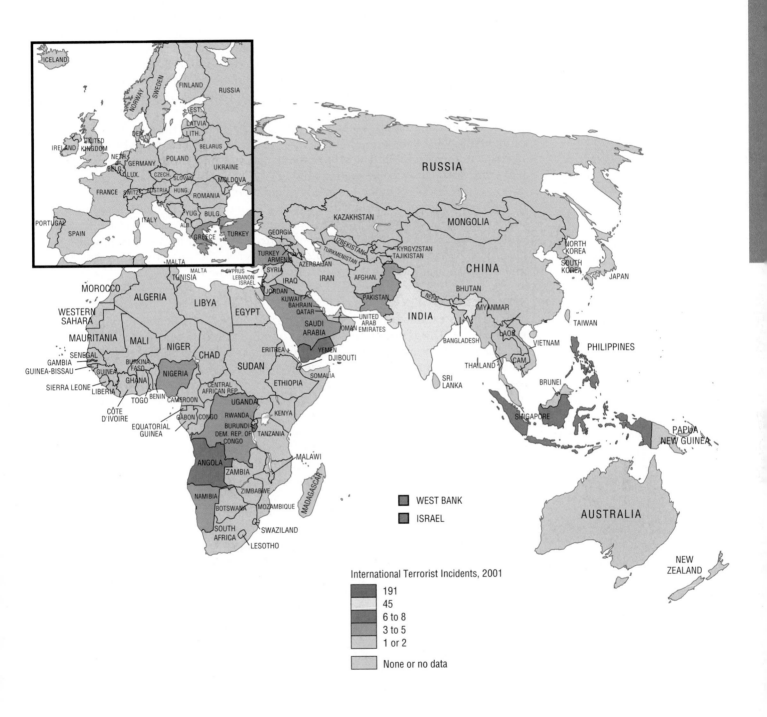

	International Terrorist Incidents, 2001
	191
	45
	6 to 8
	3 to 5
	1 or 2
	None or no data

WEST BANK

ISRAEL

agreement on such classifications. Increasingly, goods are of a dual-use nature, meaning that they are commercial products which have potential military applications.[7] Examples are exported trucks that can be used to transport troops or the exports of supplies to a pesticide factory that, some years later, is revealed to be a poison gas factory.[8] It is difficult enough to define weapons clearly. It is even more problematic to achieve consensus among nations regarding dual-use goods.

Conflicts can result from the desire of nations to safeguard their own economic interests. Due to different industrial structures, these interests vary across nations. For example, Germany, with a strong world market position in machine tools, motors, and chemical raw materials, will think differently about controls than a country such as the United States, which sees computers as an area of its competitive advantage.

The terrorist attacks on Washington, D.C., and New York have led to a renewal of international collaboration in the export control field. Policies are being scrutinized as to their sensibility in light of the dangers of proliferation and international terrorism. Such closer collaboration among countries has resulted in an easing of export control policies in the technology field.[9] Determined to bring U.S. economic as well as military power to bear in the fight against terrorism, the Bush administration has also used policy both as a stick and a carrot by deploying preferential trade measures, the removal of existing controls coupled with loans to reward allies, and new sanctions to intimidate adversaries.[10] The role of export controls and their sophistication can therefore be expected to increase.

Import Controls

Many nations exert substantial restraints on international marketers through import controls. This is particularly true of countries that suffer from major balance-of-trade deficits or major infrastructural problems. In these countries, either all imports or the imports of particular products are controlled through mechanisms such as tariffs, voluntary restraint agreements, or **quota systems** that result in quantitative import restraints. On occasion, countries cut off imports of certain products entirely in order to stimulate the development of a domestic industry.

For the international marketer, such restrictions may mean that the most efficient sources of supply are not available because government regulations restrict importation from those sources. The result is either second-best products or higher costs for restricted supplies. This in turn means that the customer receives inferior service and often has to pay significantly higher prices and that the firm is less competitive when trying to market its products internationally.

Policymakers are faced with several problems when trying to administer import controls. First, most of the time such controls exact a huge price from domestic consumers. Even though the wide distribution of the burden among many consumers may result in a less obvious burden, the social cost of these controls may be damaging to the economy and subject to severe attack by individuals. However, these attacks are counteracted by pressures from protected groups that benefit from import restrictions. For example, although citizens of the European Union may be forced—because of import controls—to pay an elevated price for all agricultural products they consume, agricultural producers in the region benefit from higher levels of income. Achieving a proper trade-off is often difficult, if not impossible, for the policymaker.

A second major problem resulting from import controls is the downstream change in import composition that results from these controls. For example, if the import of copper ore is restricted, either through voluntary restraints or through quotas, firms in copper-producing countries may opt to shift their production systems and produce copper wire instead, which they then export. As a result, initially narrowly defined protectionist measures may have to snowball in order to protect one downstream industry after another.

A final major problem that confronts the policymaker is that of efficiency. Import controls that are frequently designed to provide breathing room to a domestic industry either to grow or to recapture its competitive position often turn out not to work. Rather than improve the productivity of an industry, such controls provide it with a level of safety and a cushion of increased income yet let the drive for technological advancement fall behind. Alternatively, supply may respond to artificial stimulation and grow far beyond demand.

Regulation of International Business Behavior

Home countries may implement special laws and regulations to ensure that the international business behavior of their firms is conducted within the legal, moral, and ethical boundaries considered appropriate. The definition of appropriateness may vary from country to country and from government to government. Therefore, such regulations, their enforcement, and their impact on firms can differ substantially among nations.

Several major areas in which nations attempt to govern the international marketing activities of its firms are **boycotts,** whereby firms refuse to do business with someone, often for political reasons; antitrust measures, wherein firms are seen as restricting competition; and corruption, which occurs when firms obtain contracts with bribes rather than through performance. Arab nations, for example, have developed a blacklist of companies that deal with Israel. Even though enforcement of the blacklisting has decreased, some Arab customers still demand from their suppliers assurances that the source of the products purchased is not Israel and that the company does not do any business with Israel. The goal of these actions clearly is to impose a boycott on business with Israel. The U.S. government in turn, because of U.S. political ties to Israel, has adopted a variety of laws to prevent U.S. firms from complying with the Arab boycott. These laws include a provision to deny foreign income tax benefits to companies that comply with the boycott and also require notification of the U.S. government in case any boycott requests are received. U.S. firms that comply with the boycott are subject to heavy fines and denial of export privileges.

Boycott measures put firms in a difficult position. Caught in a web of governmental activity, they may be forced either to lose business or to pay fines. This is particularly the case if a firm's products are competitive yet not unique, so that the supplier can opt to purchase them elsewhere. Heightening of such conflict can sometimes force companies to withdraw operations entirely from a country.

The second area of regulatory activity affecting international marketing efforts of firms is antitrust laws. These can apply to the international operations of firms as well as to domestic business. In the European Union, for example, the commission watches closely when any firm buys an overseas company, engages in a joint venture with a foreign firm, or makes an agreement with a competing firm. The commission evaluates the effect these activities will have on competition and has the right to disapprove such transactions. However, given the increased globalization of national economies, some substantial rethinking is going on regarding the current approach to antitrust enforcement. One could question whether any country can still afford to define the competition only in a domestic sense or whether competition has to be seen on a worldwide scale. Similarly, one can wonder whether countries will accept the infringement on their sovereignty that results from the extraterritorial application of any nation's law abroad. There are precedents for making special allowances for international marketers with regard to antitrust laws. In the United States, for example, the Webb-Pomerene Act of 1918 excludes from antitrust prosecution those firms that are cooperating to develop foreign markets. This act was passed as part of an effort to aid U.S. export efforts in the face of strong foreign competition by oligopolies and monopolies. The exclusion of international marketing activity from antitrust regulation was further enhanced by the Export Trading Company Act of 1982, which does not expose cooperating firms to the threat of treble damages. It was specifically designed to assist small and medium-sized firms in their export efforts by permitting them to join forces in their international market development activities. Due to ongoing globalization of production, competition, and supply and demand, it would appear that over time the application of antitrust laws to international marketing activities must be revised to reflect global rather than national dimensions.

A third area in which some governments regulate international marketing actions concerns bribery and corruption. The United States has taken a lead on this issue. U.S. firms operating overseas are affected by U.S. laws against *bribery* and *corruption*. In many countries, payments or favors are a way of life, and "a greasing of the wheels" is expected in return for government services. In the past, many U.S. companies doing business internationally routinely paid bribes or did favors for foreign officials in order to gain contracts. In the 1970s, major national debts erupted over these business practices, led by arguments that U.S. firms should provide ethical and moral leadership, and that contracts won through bribes do not reflect competitive market activity. As a result, the Foreign Corrupt Practices Act was passed in 1977, making it a crime for U.S. firms to bribe a foreign official for business purposes.

A number of U.S. firms have complained about the act, arguing that it hinders their efforts to compete internationally against companies from countries that have no such antibribery laws. In-depth research supports this claim by indicating that in the years after the antibribery legislation was enacted, U.S. business activity in those countries in which government officials routinely received bribes declined significantly.[11] The problem is one of the ethics versus practical needs and also, to some extent, of the amounts involved. For example, it may be difficult to draw the line between providing a generous tip and paying a bribe in order to speed up a business transaction. Many business managers argue that the United States should not apply its moral principles to other societies and cultures in which bribery and corruption are endemic. If they are to compete internationally, these managers argue, they must be free to use the most common methods of competition in the host country. Particularly in industries that face limited or even shrinking markets, such stiff competition forces firms to find any edge possible to obtain a contract.

On the other hand, applying different standards to management and firms, depending on whether they do business abroad or domestically, is difficult to envision. Also, bribes may open the way for shoddy performance and loose moral standards among managers and employees and may result in a spreading of generally unethical business practices. Unrestricted bribery could result in a concentration on how best to bribe rather than on how best to produce and market products.

The international manager must carefully distinguish between reasonable ways of doing business internationally—including compliance with foreign expectations—and outright bribery and corruption. To assist the manager in this task, revisions were made in the 1988 Trade Act to clarify the applicability of the Foreign Corrupt Practices legislation. These revisions clarify when a manager is expected to know about violation of the act, and a distinction is drawn between the facilitation of routine governmental actions and governmental policy decisions. Routine actions concern issues such as obtaining permits and licenses, processing governmental papers such as visas and work orders, providing mail and phone service, and loading and unloading cargo. Policy decisions refer mainly to situations in which obtaining or retaining contracts is at stake. One researcher differentiates between **functional lubrication** and individual greed. With regard to functional lubrication, he reports the "express fee" charged in many countries, which has several characteristics: the amount is small, it is standardized, and it does not stay in the hands of the official who receives it but is passed on to others involved in the processing of the documents. The express service is available to anyone, with few exceptions. By contrast, in the process driven by "individual greed," the amount depends on the individual official and is for the official's own personal use.[12] Although the facilitation of routine actions is not prohibited, the illegal influencing of policy decisions can result in the imposition of severe fines and penalties.

Currently, the issue of global bribery has taken on new momentum. In 1995, the Organization of American States (OAS) (**http://www.oas.org**) officially condemned bribery. The Organization for Economic Cooperation and Development (OECD) (**http://www.oecd.org**) in 1999 agreed to change the bribery regulations among its member countries not only to prohibit the tax deductibility of improper payments, but to prohibit such payments altogether. Similarly, the World Trade Organization has, for the first time, decided to consider placing bribery rules on its agenda. A good portion of this progress can be attributed to the public work done by Transparency International (TI). This nonprofit organization regularly publishes information about the perception of corruption in countries around the globe. In addition, TI also reports on countries whose firms are most and least likely to offer bribes—as shown in Table 5.1.

A major issue that is critical for international marketers is that of general standards of behavior and ethics. Increasingly, public concerns are raised about such issues as global warming, pollution, and moral behavior. However, these issues are not of the same importance in every country. What may be frowned on or even illegal in one nation may be customary or at least acceptable in others. For example, cutting down the Brazilian rain forest may be acceptable to the government of Brazil, but scientists, concerned consumers, and environmentalists may object vehemently because of the effect of global warming and other climatic changes. The export of U.S. tobacco products may be legal but results in accusations of exporting death to developing nations. China may use prison labor in producing products for export, but U.S. law prohibits the importation of such products. Mexico may permit the use of low safety standards for workers, but the buyers of Mexican products may object to the resulting dangers. In the area of moral behavior, firms are increasingly not just subject to government rules, but are also held accountable by the public at large. For example, issues such as child labor, inappropriately low wages, or the running of sweat shops are raised by concerned individuals and communicated to customers. Firms can then be subject to public scorn, consumer boycotts, and investor scrutiny if their actions are seen as

---

Table 5.1   The Transparency International Bribe Payers Index 2002

835 business experts in 15 leading emerging market countries were asked: In the business sectors with which you are most familiar, please indicate how likely companies from the following countries are to pay or offer bribes to win or retain business in this country.

A perfect score, indicating zero perceived propensity to pay bribes, is 10.0, and thus the ranking below starts with companies from countries that are seen to have a low propensity for foreign bribe paying. All the survey data indicated that domestically owned companies in the 15 countries surveyed have a very high propensity to pay bribes—higher than that of foreign firms.

Rank		Score	Rank		Score
1	Australia	8.5	12	France	5.5
2	Sweden	8.4	13	United States	5.3
	Switzerland	8.4		Japan	5.3
4	Austria	8.2	15	Malaysia	4.3
5	Canada	8.1		Hong Kong	4.3
6	Netherlands	7.8	17	Italy	4.1
	Belgium	7.8	18	South Korea	3.9
8	United Kingdom	6.9	19	Taiwan	3.8
9	Singapore	6.3	20	People's Republic of China	3.5
	Germany	6.3	21	Russia	3.2
11	Spain	5.8		*Domestic companies*	1.9

SOURCE: Transparency International, Berlin, Germany, May 14, 2002. Reprinted by permission.

reprehensible and run the danger of losing much more money than they gained by engaging in such practices.

International marketers are "selling" the world on two key issues: one is the benefit of market forces which result in the interplay of supply and demand. This interplay in turn uses price signals instead of government fiat to adjust activities, thrives on competition, and works within an environment of respect for profitability and private property. The second key proposition is that international marketers will do their best to identify market niches and bring their products and services to customers around the globe. Since these activities take up substantial financial resources, they provide individuals with the opportunity to invest their funds in the most productive and efficient manner.

Key underlying dimensions of both of these issues are managerial and corporate virtue, vision, and veracity. Unless the world can believe in what marketers say they do, and trust the global activities of international marketers, it will be hard, even impossible, to forge a global commitment between those doing the marketing and the ones being marketed to. It is therefore of vital interest to marketers to ensure that corruption, bribery, lack of transparency, and the misleading of consumers, investors, and employees are systematically relegated to the history books where they belong. It will be the extent to which openness, responsiveness, long-term thinking, and truthfulness rule that will determine the degrees of freedom for international marketers'.

Host Country Political and Legal Environment

The host country environment, both political and legal, affects the international marketing operations of firms in a variety of ways. A good manager will understand the country in which the firm operates so that he or she is able to work within the existing parameters and can anticipate and plan for changes that may occur.

Political Action and Risk

Firms usually prefer to conduct business in a country with a stable and friendly government, but such governments are not always easy to find. Managers must therefore continually monitor the government, its policies, and its stability to determine the potential for political change that could adversely affect corporate operations.

There is political risk in every nation, but the range of risks varies widely from country to country. **Political risk** is defined as the risk of loss when investing in a given country caused by changes in a country's political structure or policies, such as tax laws, tariffs, expropriation of assets, or restriction in repatriation of profits. For example, a company may suffer from such loss in the case of expropriation or tightened foreign exchange repatriation rules, or from increased credit risk if the government changes policies to make it difficult for the company to pay creditors.[13] In general, political risk is lowest in countries that have a history of stability and consistency. Political risk tends to be highest in nations that do not have this sort of history. In a number of countries, however, consistency and stability that were apparent on the surface have been quickly swept away by major popular movements that drew on the bottled-up frustrations of the population. Three major types of political risk can be encountered: **ownership risk,** which exposes property and life; **operating risk,** which refers to interference with the ongoing operations of a firm; and **transfer risk,** which is mainly encountered when attempts are made to shift funds between countries. Political risk can be the result of government action, but it can also be outside the control of government. The type of actions and their effects are classified in Figure 5.2.

Figure 5.2	Exposure to Political Risk

Loss May Be the Result of:

Contingencies May Include:	The actions of legitimate government authorities	Events caused by factors outside the control of government
The involuntary loss of control over specific assets without adequate compensation	• Total or partial expropriation • Forced divestiture • Confiscation • Cancellation or unfair calling of performance bonds	• War • Revolution • Terrorism • Strikes • Extortion
A reduction in the value of a stream of benefits expected from the foreign-controlled affiliate	• Nonapplicability of "national treatment" • Restriction in access to financial, labor, or material markets • Controls on prices, outputs, or activities • Currency and remittance restrictions • Value-added and export performance requirements	• Nationalistic buyers or suppliers • Threats and disruption to operations by hostile groups • Externally induced financial constraints • Externally imposed limits on imports or exports

SOURCE: José de la Torre and David H. Neckar, "Forecasting Political Risks for International Operations," in H. Vernon-Wortzel and L. Wortzel, *Global Strategic Management: The Essentials,* 2nd ed. (New York: John Wiley and Sons, 1990), 195. Copyright © 1990 John Wiley and Sons. Reprinted by permission of John Wiley and Sons, Inc.

A major political risk in many countries involves conflict and violent change. A manager will want to think twice before conducting business in a country in which the likelihood of such change is high. To begin with, if conflict breaks out, violence directed toward the firm's property and employees is a strong possibility. Guerrilla warfare, civil disturbances, and terrorism often take an anti-industry bent, making companies and their employees potential targets. For example, in the spring of 1991, Detlev Rohwedder, chairman of the German Treuhand (the institution in charge of privatizing the state-owned firms of the former East Germany), was assassinated at his home in Germany by the Red Army Faction because of his "representation of capitalism."

International terrorists target U.S. facilities, operations, and personnel for attack in order to strike a blow against the United States and capitalism. Abroad, U.S. firms are prominent symbols of the United States' culture and government and by their nature they cannot have the elaborate security and restricted access of U.S. diplomatic offices and military bases. As a result, U.S. businesses are the primary target of terrorists worldwide and remain the most vulnerable targets in the future.[14] These targets, however, may really be domestic rather than American in nature. For example, when we see pictures of a burning McDonald's establishment, it is typically the domestic franchisee and the local employees and investors who are suffering the most. But then, destruction and terrorism are not known for their thoughtfulness and logic. The methods used by terrorists against business facilities include bombing, arson, hijacking, and sabotage. To obtain funds, the terrorists resort to kidnapping, armed robbery, and extortion.[15] The frequencies of

Figure 5.3 | **International Terrorist Incidents over Time, 1979–2001**

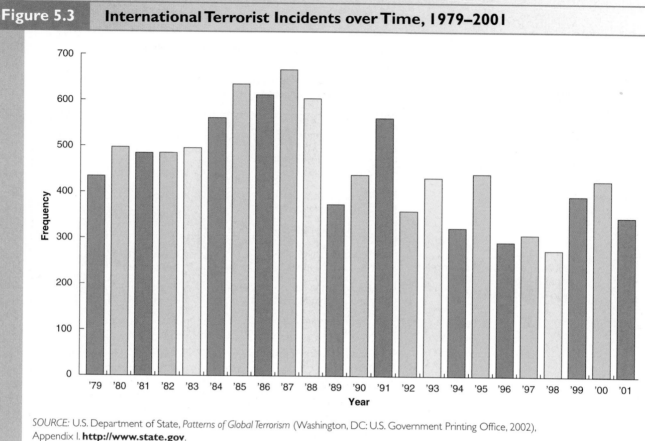

SOURCE: U.S. Department of State, *Patterns of Global Terrorism* (Washington, DC: U.S. Government Printing Office, 2002), Appendix I. **http://www.state.gov**.

such incidents around the world are shown in Figure 5.3. To reduce such international terrorism, recent experience has demonstrated that it is imperative to collaborate internationally in identifying and tracking terrorist groups and to systematically reduce their safe havens and financial support.

In many countries, particularly in the developing world, coups d'état can result in drastic changes in government. The new government may attack foreign multinational corporations as remnants of the Western-dominated colonial past, as has happened in Cuba, Nicaragua, and Iran. Even if such changes do not represent an immediate physical threat to firms and their employees, they can have drastic effects. The past few decades have seen such coups in the countries of Ghana, Ethiopia, and Venezuela, to name a few. These coups have seriously impeded the conduct of international marketing.

Less dramatic but still worrisome are changes in government policies that are caused not by changes in the government itself but by pressure from nationalist or religious factions or widespread anti-Western feeling. The aware manager will work to anticipate these changes and plan ways to cope with them.

What sort of changes in policy result from the various events described? The range of possible actions is broad. All of them can affect international marketing operations, but not all are equal in weight. We have learned that companies have to fear violence against employees, and that violence against company property is quite common. Also common are changes in policy that take a strong nationalist and antiforeign investment stance. The most drastic steps resulting from such policy changes are usually confiscation and expropriation.

An important governmental action is **expropriation,** which is the seizure of foreign assets by a government with payment of compensation to the owners. Expropriation has appealed to some countries because it demonstrated nationalism and immediately transferred a certain amount of wealth and resources from foreign companies to the host country. It did have costs to the host country, however, to the extent that it made other firms more hesitant to invest in the country. Expropriation does provide compensation to the former owners. However, compensation negotiations are often protracted and result in settlements that are frequently unsatisfactory to the owners. For example, governments may offer compensation in the form of local, nontransferable currency or may base the compensation on the book value of the firm. Even though firms that are expropriated may deplore the low levels of payment obtained, they frequently accept them in the absence of better alternatives.

The use of expropriation as a policy tool has sharply decreased over time. Apparently, governments have come to recognize that the damage inflicted on themselves through expropriation exceeds the benefits.[16]

Confiscation is similar to expropriation in that it results in a transfer of ownership from the foreign firm to the host country. However, its effects are even harsher in that it does not involve compensation for the firm. Some industries are more vulnerable than others to confiscation and expropriation because of their importance to the host country economy and their lack of ability to shift operations. For this reason, sectors such as mining, energy, public utilities, and banking have been targets of such government actions.

Confiscation and expropriation constitute major political risks for foreign investors. Other government actions, however, are nearly as damaging. Many countries are turning from confiscation and expropriation to more subtle forms of control, such as **domestication.** The goal of domestication is the same, to gain control over foreign investment, but the method is different. Through domestication, the government demands partial transfer of ownership and management responsibility and imposes regulations to ensure that a large share of the product is locally produced and a larger share of the profit is retained in the country.

Domestication can have profound effects on the international marketer for a number of reasons. First, if a firm is forced to hire nationals as managers, poor cooperation and communication can result. If the domestication is imposed within a very short time span, corporate operations overseas may have to be headed by poorly trained and inexperienced local managers. Further, domestic content requirements may force a firm to purchase supplies and parts locally, which can result in increased costs, inefficiency, and lower-quality products, thus further damaging a firm's interest. Export requirements imposed on companies may also create havoc for the international distribution plan of a corporation and force it to change or even shut down operations in other countries. Finally, domestication will usually shield the industry within one country from foreign competition. As a result, inefficiencies will be allowed to grow due to a lack of market discipline. In the long run, this will affect the international competitiveness of an operation abroad and may become a major problem when, years later, the removal of domestication is considered by the government.

Most businesses operating abroad face a number of other risks that are less dangerous, but probably more common, than the drastic ones already described. Host governments that face a shortage of foreign currency sometimes will impose controls on the movement of capital in and out of the country. Such controls may make it difficult for a firm to remove its profits or investments from the host country. Sometimes, exchange controls are also levied selectively against certain products or companies in an effort to reduce the importation of goods that are considered to be a luxury or unnecessary. Such regulations are often difficult to deal with because they may affect the importation of parts, components, or supplies that are vital for production operations. Restrictions on such imports may force a firm either to alter its production program or, worse yet, to shut down its entire plant. Prolonged negotiations with government officials may be necessary in order to reach a compromise agreement on what constitutes a "valid" expenditure of foreign currency resources. Because the goals of government officials and corporate managers may often be quite different, such compromises, even when they can be reached, may result in substantial damage to the international marketing operations of a firm.

Countries may also raise the tax rates applied to foreign investors in an effort to control the firms and their capital. On occasion, different or stricter applications of the host country's tax codes are implemented for foreign investors. The rationale for such measures is often the seeming underpayment of taxes by such investors, when comparing their payments to those of long-established domestic competitors. Overlooked is the fact that new investors in foreign lands tend to **"over-invest"** by initially buying more land, space, and equipment than is needed immediately and by spending heavily so that facilities are state-of-the-art. This desire to accommodate future growth and to be highly competitive in the early investment stages will, in turn, produce lower profits and lower tax payments. Yet over time, these investment activities should be very successful, competitive, and job-creating. Selective tax increases for foreign investors may result in much-needed revenue for the coffers of the host country, but they can severely damage the operations of the foreign investors. This damage, in turn, may result in decreased income for the host country in the long run.

The international marketing manager must also worry about **price controls.** In many countries, domestic political pressures can force governments to control the prices of imported products or services, particularly in sectors that are considered to be highly sensitive from a political perspective, such as food or health care. If a foreign firm is involved in these areas, it is a vulnerable target of price controls because the government can play on its people's nationalistic tendencies to enforce the controls. Particularly in countries that suffer from high inflation and frequent devaluations, the international marketer may be forced to choose between shutting down the operation or continuing production at a loss in the hope of recouping that loss once the government chooses to loosen or remove its price restrictions. How a firm can adjust to price controls is discussed in greater detail later in the book.

Managers face political and economic risk whenever they conduct business overseas, but there may be ways to lessen the risk. Obviously, if a new government that is dedicated to the removal of all foreign influences comes into power, a firm can do little. In less extreme cases, however, managers can take actions to reduce the risk if they understand the root causes of the host country policies. Most important is the accumulation and appreciation of factual information about a country's history, political background, and culture before making a long-term investment decision. Also, a high degree of sensitivity by a firm and its employees to country-specific approaches and concerns are important dimensions that help a firm to blend into the local landscape rather than stand out as a foreign object.

Adverse governmental actions are usually the result of a host country's nationalism, desire for independence, and opposition to colonial remnants. If a country's citizens feel exploited by foreign firms, government officials are more likely to take antiforeign action. To reduce the risk of government intervention, a firm needs to demonstrate that it is concerned with the host country's society and that it considers itself an integral part of the host country rather than simply an exploitative foreign corporation. Ways to do this include intensive local hiring and training practices, good pay, more charity, and more societally useful investment. In addition, a company can form joint ventures with local partners to demonstrate a willingness to share its benefits with nationals. Although such actions will not guarantee freedom from risk, they will certainly lessen the exposure.

Corporations can also protect against political risk by closely monitoring political developments. Increasingly, private-sector firms offer assistance in such monitoring activities, permitting the overseas corporation to discover potential trouble spots as early as possible and react quickly to prevent major losses. Firms can also take out insurance to cover losses due to political risk. Most industrialized countries offer insurance programs for their firms doing business abroad. In Germany, for example, Hermes Kreditanstalt provides exporters with insurance. In the United States, the Overseas Private Investment Corporation (OPIC) can cover three types of risk: currency inconvertibility insurance, which covers the inability to convert profits, debt service, and other remittances from local currency into U.S. dollars; expropriation insurance, which covers the loss of an investment due to expropriation, nationalization, or confiscation by a foreign government; and political violence insurance, which covers the loss of assets or income due to war, revolution, insurrection, or politically motivated civil strife, terrorism, and sabotage.[17] Rates vary by country and industry, but for $100 of coverage per year for a manufacturing project, the base rate is $0.45 for protection against inconvertibility, $0.50 to protect against expropriation, and $0.70 to protect against political violence.[18] Usually, insurance policies do not cover commercial risks and, in the event of a claim, cover only the actual loss—not lost profits. In the event of a major political upheaval, however, risk insurance can be critical to a firm's survival.

Clearly, the international marketer must consider the likelihood of negative political factors in making decisions on conducting business overseas. On the other hand, host country political and legal systems can have a positive impact on the conduct of international business. Many governments, for example, encourage foreign investments, especially if they believe that the investment will produce economic and political benefits domestically. Some governments have opened up their economy to foreign investors, placing only minimal constraints on them, in the hope that such policies will lead to rapid economic development. Others have provided for substantial subsidization of new investment activities in the hope that investments will generate additional employment. The international marketer, in his or her investment decision, can and should therefore also pay close attention to the extent and forms of incentives available from foreign governments. Although international marketing decisions should be driven by market forces, the basic economies of these decisions may change depending on incentives offered.

In this discussion of the political environment, laws have been mentioned only to the extent that they appear to be the direct result of political changes. However, each nation has laws regarding marketing, and the international manager must understand their effects on the firm's efforts.

Legal Differences and Restraints

Countries differ in their laws as well as in their use of these laws. For example, the United States has developed into an increasingly litigious society, in which institutions and individuals are quick to take a case to court. As a result, court battles are often protracted and costly, and simply the threat of a court case can reduce marketing opportunities. In contrast, Japan's legal tradition tends to minimize the role of the law and of lawyers. Some possible reasons include the relatively small number of courts and attorneys, the delays, the costs and the uncertainties associated with litigation, the limited doctrines of plaintiffs' standing and rights to bring class action suits, the tendency of judges to encourage out-of-court settlements, and the easy availability of arbitration and mediation for dispute resolution.

Some estimates suggest that the number of lawyers in the United States is as much as 48 times higher than in Japan, based on the fact that Japan has only about 12,500 fully licensed lawyers. However, comparisons can be misleading because officially registered lawyers in Japan perform a small fraction of the duties performed by American lawyers. After accounting for the additional roles of American lawyers, the number of "lawyers" in Japan appears to be approximately one-fifth of that in the United States.[19] *The International Marketplace 5.3* shows how different perceptions and legal practices can lead to substantially different approaches to communication.

Over the millennia of civilization, many different laws and legal systems emerged. King Hammurabi of Babylon codified a series of judges' decisions into a body of law. Hebrew law was the result of the dictates of God. Legal issues in many African tribes were settled through the verdicts of clansmen. A key legal

THE INTERNATIONAL MARKETPLACE   5.3

The *Ehime Maru:* A Clash of Two Cultures

The USS *Greeneville,* a Los Angeles–class submarine, is one of the most advanced and versatile warships. The 7,000-ton submarine is 360 feet long and equipped with a Tomahawk cruise missile system. It can operate at depths over 800 feet and reach speeds of over 20 knots per hour.

The 499-ton *Ehime Maru* was a Japanese research vessel from Uwajima Fisheries High School in Ehime Prefecture. It had 35 people on board—high school students, teachers, and crew members—and was cruising off the coast of Hawaii. The purpose of this expedition was to conduct tuna research.

On February 9, 2001, under the command of Commander Scott Waddle, the USS *Greeneville* conducted an emergency surfacing procedure for training purposes. At 1:50 P.M., a tragedy occurred nine miles south of Diamond Head, Honolulu, Hawaii. The USS *Greeneville* collided with the *Ehime Maru.* While the *Greeneville* was barely dented, on the *Ehime Maru,* the power went out and water began to quickly flood the engine room. The boat split in half and sank within ten minutes. The submarine contacted the search and rescue center at Pearl Harbor, and the U.S. Coast Guard was sent immediately to the accident site. Twenty-six occupants of the *Ehime Maru* were rescued, but four high school students, three teachers, and two crew members were killed.

Within a few days after the incident, Commander Waddle came under criminal investigation for possible negligence. He anticipated a court martial and retained an attorney. In order not to prejudice his case, Waddle was advised not to make any public comments. At the end of February 2001, special U.S. Navy envoy Admiral William J. Fallon went to Japan to apologize to the family members of the nine victims. He also delivered a letter of apology from President George W. Bush to Japanese Prime Minister Yoshiro Mori. At the same time, Commander Waddle issued a personal statement expressing his regret that the tragedy had happened. However, on the advice of his lawyers, Commander Waddle refrained from giving an outright apology. It was believed that a speedy apology would have seemed like an admission of guilt and made a court martial more likely.

In the months to follow, U.S. lawyers considered Commander Waddle to have handled the situation well, in allowing the courts to find a resolution. When the threat of a court martial was finally dismissed, Commander Waddle gave a formal apology that was long overdue. From a Japanese perspective, his actions were deemed as disrespectful to Japanese culture.

This is an example of conflict between contrasting cultural values. In the United States, resolutions are often achieved under the legal system. In Japan, resolutions are found through personal actions from the individual himself. Since Japan and the United States have different approaches to achieving resolutions, a conflict was inevitable. The inability to understand and consider cultural values in international relations can either enhance relations between countries, or, as in this instance, weaken them—even though all participants want to do what is right.

SOURCES: Joseph Coleman, "Japanese Demand Traditional Apology from Sub Commander," **http://NCTimes.net** (February 23, 2001): 3 pp., accessed July 6, 2001; "Aggressive PR Saves Waddle," *O'Dwyer's PR Daily* (April 23, 2001): 5 pp., accessed July 6, 2001; "Japanese PM to Visit Sub Collision Site," **http://CNN.com** (March 20, 2001): 4 pp., accessed June 1, 2001; and Doug Struck and Akiko Yamamoto, "Sub Commander Tries to Heal Wounds," *The Washington Post,* December 16, 2002, A1.

---

perspective that survives today is that of **theocracy,** which has faith and belief as its key focus and is a mix of societal, legal, and spiritual guidelines. Examples are Hebrew law and Islamic law, or the *shari'ah,* which are the result of scripture, prophetic utterances and practices, and scholarly interpretations.[20]

While these legal systems are important to society locally, from an international business perspective the two major legal systems worldwide can be categorized into common law and code law. **Common law** is based on tradition and depends less on written statutes and codes than on precedent and custom. Common law originated in England and is the system of law found today in the United States.

On the other hand, **code law** is based on a comprehensive set of written statutes. Countries with code law try to spell out all possible legal rules explicitly. Code law is based on Roman law and is found in the majority of the nations of the world. In general, countries with the code law system have much more rigid laws than those with the common law system. In the latter, courts adopt precedents and customs to fit the cases, allowing the marketer a better idea of the basic judgment likely to be rendered in new situations.

Although wide in theory, the differences between code law and common law and their impact on the international marketer, are not always as broad in practice. For example, many common law countries, including the United States, have adopted commercial codes to govern the conduct of business.

Host countries may adopt a number of laws that affect a company's ability to market. To begin with, there can be laws affecting the entry of goods, such as tariffs and quotas. Also in this category are **antidumping laws,** which prohibit below-cost sales of products, and laws that require export and import licensing. In addition, many countries have health and safety standards that may, by design or by accident, restrict the entry of foreign goods. Japan, for example, has particularly strict health standards that affect the import of pharmaceuticals. Rather than accepting test results from other nations, the Japanese government insists on conducting its own tests, which are time consuming and costly. It claims that these tests are necessary to take into account Japanese peculiarities. Yet some importers and their governments see these practices as thinly veiled protectionist barriers.

A growing global controversy surrounds the use of genetic technology. Governments are increasingly devising new rules that affect trade in genetically modified products. For example, Australia introduced a mandatory standard for foods produced using biotechnology, which prohibits the sale of such products unless the food has been assessed by the Australia New Zealand Food Authority.

Other laws may be designed to protect domestic industries and reduce imports. For example, Russia charges a 20 percent value-added tax on most imported goods; assesses high excise taxes on goods such as cigarettes, automobiles, and alcoholic beverages; and provides a burdensome import licensing and quotas regime for alcohol and products containing alcohol to depress Russian demand for imports.[21]

Very specific legislation may also exist to regulate where a firm can advertise or what constitutes deceptive advertising. Many countries prohibit specific claims by marketers comparing their product to that of the competition and restrict the use of promotional devices. Some countries regulate the names of companies or the foreign language content of a product's label. Even when no laws exist, the marketer may be hampered by regulations. For example, in many countries, governments require a firm to join the local chamber of commerce or become a member of the national trade association. These institutions in turn may have internal regulations that set standards for the conduct of business and may be seen as quite confining to the international marketer.

Finally, the enforcement of laws may have a different effect on national and on foreign marketers. For example, the simple requirement that an executive has to stay in a country until a business conflict is resolved may be a major burden for the international marketer.

Influencing Politics and Laws

To succeed in a market, the international marketer needs much more than business know-how. He or she must also deal with the intricacies of national politics and laws. Although a full understanding of another country's legal and political system will rarely be possible, the good manager will be aware of the importance of this system and will work with people who do understand how to operate within the system.

Many areas of politics and law are not immutable. Viewpoints can be modified or even reversed, and new laws can supersede old ones. Therefore, existing political and legal restraints do not always need to be accepted. To achieve change, however, there must be some impetus for it, such as the clamors of a constituency. Otherwise, systemic inertia is likely to allow the status quo to prevail.

The international marketer has various options. One approach may be to simply ignore prevailing rules and expect to get away with it. Pursuing this option is a high-risk strategy because of the possibility of objection and even prosecution. A second, traditional option is to provide input to trade negotiators and expect any problem areas to be resolved in multilateral negotiations. The drawback to this option is, of course, the quite time-consuming process involved.

A third option involves the development of coalitions or constituencies that can motivate legislators and politicians to consider and ultimately implement change. This option can be pursued in various ways. One direction can be the recasting or redefinition of issues. Often, specific terminology leads to conditioned though inappropriate responses. For example, before China's accession to the World Trade Organization in 2001, the country's trade status with the United States was highly controversial for many years. The U.S. Congress had to decide annually whether to grant "Most Favored Nation" (MFN) status to China. The debate on this decision was always very contentious and acerbic and was often framed around the question why China deserved to be treated the "most favored way." Lost in the debate was the fact that the term "most favored" was simply taken from WTO terminology and indicated only that trade with China would be treated like that with any other country. Only in late 1999 was the terminology changed from MFN to NTR, or "normal trade relations." Even though there was still considerable debate regarding China, the controversy about special treatment had been eliminated.[22]

Beyond terminology, marketers can also highlight the direct linkages and their cost and benefit to legislators and politicians. For example, the manager can explain the employment and economic effects of certain laws and regulations and demonstrate the benefits of change. The picture can be enlarged by including indirect linkages. For example, suppliers, customers, and distributors can be asked to participate in delineating to decision makers the benefit of change. Such groups can be quite influential. For example, it has been suggested that it was the community of Indian businesses working as information technology suppliers to U.S. firms that exerted substantial pressure on their government to find a resolution to the Kashmiri conflict. If so, this is an encouraging example of the benefits of globalization.[23]

Developing such coalitions is not an easy task. Companies often seek assistance in effectively influencing the government decision-making process. Such assistance usually is particularly beneficial when narrow economic objectives or single-issue campaigns are needed. Typical providers of this assistance are lobbyists. Usually, these are well-connected individuals and firms that can provide access to policy-makers and legislators.

Many countries and companies have been effective in their lobbying in the United States. The number of U.S. lobbyists working on behalf of foreign entities is estimated to be in the thousands. As an example, Brazil has held on average nearly a dozen contracts per year with U.S. firms covering trade issues. Brazilian citrus exporters and computer manufacturers have hired U.S. legal and public relations firms to provide them with information on relevant U.S. legislative activity. The Banco do Brasil lobbied for the restructuring of Brazilian debt and favorable banking regulations. A key factor in successful lobbying, however, is the involvement of U.S. citizens and companies.

U.S. firms also have representation in Washington, DC, as well as state capitals. Often, however, they are less adept at ensuring proper representation abroad. For example, a survey of U.S. international marketing executives found that knowledge and information about trade and government officials were ranked lowest among critical international business information needs. This low ranking appears to reflect the fact that many U.S. firms are far less successful in their interaction with governments abroad and are far less intensive in their lobbying attempts than are foreign entities in the United States.[24]

Although representation of the firm's interests to government decision makers and legislators is entirely appropriate, the international marketer must also consider any potential side effects. Major questions can be raised if such representation becomes very strong. In such instances, short-term gains may be far outweighed by long-term negative repercussions if the international marketer is perceived as exerting too much political influence.

The International Environment

In addition to the politics and laws of both the home and the host countries, the international marketer must consider the overall international political and legal environment. Relations between countries can have a profound impact on firms trying to do business internationally.

International Politics

The effect of politics on international marketing is determined by both the bilateral political relations between home and host countries and the multilateral agreements governing the relations among groups of countries.

The government-to-government relationship can have a profound effect, particularly if it becomes hostile. Numerous examples exist of the linkage between international politics and international marketing. The premier example is perhaps U.S.–Iranian relations following the 1979 Iranian revolution. Although the internal political and legal changes in the aftermath of that revolution would certainly have affected international marketing in Iran, the deterioration in U.S.–Iranian political relations that resulted from the revolution had a significant impact. U.S. firms were injured not only by physical damage caused by the violence but also by the anti-American feelings of the Iranian people and their government. The clashes between the two governments completely destroyed any business relationships, regardless of corporate feelings or agreements on either side. It took more than 20 years to reopen governmental dialogue between the two countries.

A more recent example of government-to-government conflict was presented by the Helms-Burton Act. Passed in response to the shooting down of two unarmed small planes by the Cuban Air Force, this U.S. legislation granted individuals the right to sue, in U.S. courts, subsidiaries of those foreign firms that had invested in properties confiscated by the Cuban government in the 1960s. In addition, managers of these firms were denied entry into the United States. Many U.S. trading partners strongly disagreed with this legislation. In response, Canada proposed suing U.S. firms that had invested in properties taken from royalists in 1776, and the European Union threatened to permit European firms to countersue subsidiaries of U.S. firms in Europe and to deny entry permits to U.S. executives.

International political relations do not always have harmful effects on international marketers. If bilateral political relations between countries improve, business can benefit. A good example is the thawing of relations between the West and the countries of the former Soviet bloc. Political warming has opened up completely new frontiers for U.S. international marketers in Hungary, Poland, and Russia, just to name a few countries. Activities such as selling computers, which would have been considered treasonous only a few years ago, are now routine.

The international marketer needs to be aware of political currents worldwide and attempt to anticipate changes in the international political environment, good or bad, so that his or her firm can plan for them. Sometimes, however, management can only wait until the emotional fervor of conflict has subsided and hope that rational governmental negotiations will let cooler heads prevail.

International Law

International law plays an important role in the conduct of international business. Although no enforceable body of international law exists, certain treaties and agreements respected by a number of countries profoundly influence international business operations. As an example, the World Trade Organization (WTO) defines internationally acceptable economic practices for its member nations. Although it does not directly affect individual firms, it does influence them indirectly by providing a more stable and predictable international market environment.

A number of efforts have been made to simplify the legal aspects of business procedures. For example, firms wanting to patent their products in the past had to register them separately in each country in order to have protection. In response to the chaos and expense of such procedures, several multilateral simplification efforts have been undertaken. European countries have been at the forefront of such efforts with the European Patent Convention and the Community Patent Convention.

Similar efforts have been undertaken with regard to trademarks so that firms can benefit from various multilateral agreements. The two major international conventions on trademarks are the International Convention for the Protection of Industrial Property and the Madrid Arrangement for International Registration of Trademarks. Several regional conventions include the Inter-American Convention for Trademark Protection and a similar agreement in French West Africa.

In addition to multilateral agreements, firms are affected by bilateral treaties and conventions. The United States, for example, has signed bilateral treaties of friendship, commerce, and navigation (FCN) with a wide variety of countries. These agreements generally define the rights of U.S. firms doing business in the host country. They normally guarantee that the U.S. firms will be treated by the host country in the same manner in which domestic firms are treated. Although these treaties provide for some stability, they can be canceled when relationships worsen.

The international legal environment also affects the marketer to the extent that firms must concern themselves with jurisdictional disputes. Because no single body of international law exists, firms usually are restricted by both home and host country laws. If a conflict occurs between contracting parties in two different countries, a question arises concerning which country's laws will be followed. Sometimes the contract will contain a jurisdictional clause, which settles the matter. If not, the parties to the dispute can follow either the laws of the country in which the agreement was made or those of the country in which the contract will have to be fulfilled. Deciding on the laws to be followed and the location to settle the dispute are two different decisions. As a result, a dispute between a U.S. exporter and a French importer could be resolved in Paris with the resolution based on New York State law.

The parties to a business transaction can also choose either arbitration or litigation. Litigation is usually avoided for several reasons. It often involves extensive delays and is very costly. In addition, firms may fear discrimination in foreign countries. Companies therefore tend to prefer conciliation and arbitration because these processes result in much quicker decisions. Arbitration procedures are often spelled out in the original contract and usually provide for an intermediary who is judged to be impartial by both parties. Frequently, intermediaries will be representatives of chambers of commerce, trade associations, or third-country institutions. For example, the rules of the international chamber of commerce in Paris are frequently used for arbitration purposes.

Summary

The political and legal environment in the home country, the environment in the host country, and the laws and agreements governing relationships among nations are all important to the international marketer. Compliance with them is mandatory in order to do business abroad successfully. Such laws can control exports and imports both directly and indirectly and can also regulate the international business behavior of firms, particularly in the areas of boycotts, antitrust, corruption, and ethics.

To avoid the problems that can result from changes in the political and legal environment, the international marketer must anticipate changes and develop strategies for coping with them. Whenever possible, the manager must avoid being taken by surprise and thus not let events control business decisions.

On occasion, the international marketer may be caught between clashing home and host country laws. In such instances, the firm needs to conduct a dialogue with the governments in order to seek a compromise solution. Alternatively, managers can encourage their government to engage in government-to-government negotiations to settle the dispute. By demonstrating the business volume at stake and the employment that may be lost through such governmental disputes, government negotiators can often be motivated to press hard for a settlement of such intergovernmental difficulties. Finally, the firm can seek redress in court. Such international legal action, however, may be quite slow and, even if resulting in a favorable judgment for the firm, may not be adhered to by the government against which the judgment is rendered.

In the final analysis, a firm conducting business internationally is subject to the vagaries of political and legal changes and may lose business as a result. The best the manager can do is to be aware of political influences and laws and strive to adopt them as far as possible.

Key Terms

Environmental Superfund
intellectual property rights
gray market
trade sanctions
embargoes
export control systems
dual-use items
export license
foreign availability
quota systems
boycotts
functional lubrication
political risk

ownership risk
operating risk
transfer risk
expropriation
confiscation
domestication
overinvest
price controls
theocracy
common law
code law
antidumping laws

Questions for Discussion

1. Discuss this statement: "High political risk requires companies to seek a quick payback on their investments. Striving for such a quick payback, however, exposes firms to charges of exploitation and results in increased political risk."
2. How appropriate is it for governments to help drum up business for their companies abroad? Should commerce be completely separate from politics?
3. Discuss this statement: "The national security that our export control laws seek to protect may be threatened by the resulting lack of international competitiveness of U.S. firms."
4. After you hand your passport to the immigration officer in country X, he misplaces it. A small "donation" would certainly help him find it again. Should you give him money? Is this a business expense to be charged to your company? Should it be tax deductible?
5. Discuss the advantages and disadvantages of common versus code law for the international marketer.
6. The United States has been described as a "litigious" society. How does frequent litigation affect the international marketer, particularly in comparison with the situation in other countries?
7. What are your views on lobbying efforts by foreign firms?
8. Discuss how changes in technology have affected the effectiveness of U.S. export control policy.

Internet Exercises

1. Summarize the U.S. export licensing policy toward Cuba. (Go to **http://www.bis.doc.gov**.)
2. What are the key components of the anticorruption agreements passed by the European Union, the

Organization of American States, and the United Nations? (Go to **http://www.oecd.org/daf/ nocorruptionweb**.)

Recommended Readings

Export Administration Annual Report 2002 Report on Foreign Policy Export Controls. Washington, DC: U.S. Department of Commerce, Bureau of Export Administration, 2002.

A Global Forum on Fighting Corruption. Washington, DC: Bureau for International Narcotics and Law Enforcement Affairs, U.S. Department of State, September 2001.

Haass, Richard, and Meghan L. O'Sullivan, *Honey and Vinegar: Incentives, Sanctions, and Foreign Policy.* Washington, DC: Brookings Institution, 2000.

Hirschhorn, Eric. *Export Controls Handbook.* New York: Oceana, 2000.

Hufbauer, Gary C., Jeffrey J. Schott, and Kimberly Ann Elliott. *Economic Sanctions Reconsidered: History and Current Policy,* 3rd ed. Washington, DC: Institute for International Economics, 2002.

The OECD Guidelines for Multinational Enterprises. Paris: Organization for Economic Cooperation and Development, 2001.

"Trick-or-Treat?" Costume Market in Horror as Halloween Approaches

You know those flimsy polyester costumes everyone buys before Halloween, and then throws away? Well, would you ever consider wearing one to a formal affair, as a gown or a tuxedo? The U.S. Customs Service has decided you could do just that, according to a new classification of textile costumes as "fancy dress" that could raise the price of these playthings by as much as 50 percent.

In a large and growing industry, this seemingly minor issue could have large consequences for consumers and producers alike. In 2000, Americans spent $6 billion on Halloween-related goods, from costumes to candy to decorations, making it the second largest consumer holiday after Christmas. Of those sales, $1.5 billion are attributed to costume purchases, according to a report by *Business Week*.

The 2000 American Express Retail Index reports that 2000 costume sales—$27 per consumer—are up from 1999 levels of $22 per consumer. Overall budgets for Halloween goods in 2000 averaged $84, $14 down from 1999, but above the 1998 average of $81.

SOURCES: This case was written by Ruth L. Braunstein and Michael R. Czinkota © 2003 using the following sources: Department of the Treasury, United States Customs Service, "Receipt of Domestic Interested Party Petition Concerning Tariff Classification of Textile Costumes," December 22, 1997; Jennifer Gill, "This Year's Halloween Hit: To Be a Hero," *BusinessWeek Magazine*, September 16, 2001; and Neil King, Jr., "Costume Drama: Is a 'Scream' Robe Really as 'Fancy' as a Tux? Judge Says Yes, Slapping Duties on Cheap Halloween Wear; Mr. Beige Is in the Pink," *Wall Street Journal*, March 15, 2002.

Fighting Imports

In 1997, an American producer of Halloween costumes decided that he was not getting a large enough piece of that $1.5 billion market pie. In the grand tradition of Halloween trickery, Rubie's Costume Co. of New York petitioned the U.S. Customs Service for a change in the classification of his foreign competitors' goods.

Is this just another example of a losing marketplace competitor seeking victory in the halls of justice rather than through a superior product? Or does Rubie's petition give voice to a genuine concern?

Imported costumes used to be classified under subheading 9505 of the Harmonized Tariff Schedule of the United States (HTSUS) as "flimsy festive articles" and were allowed to enter the U.S. duty-free under the subheading of "Festive, carnival or other entertainment articles, including magic tricks and practical joke articles; parts and accessories thereof: Other: Other: Other" (Figure 1).

The precedent for this classification can be found in the November 1994 case of *Traveler Trading Co. v. United States* (Civil Action, #91-02-00084). In its ruling, "Customs stated that it had agreed to classify as festive articles in subheading 9505.90.6090, HTSUS, costumes of a flimsy nature and construction, lacking in durability, and generally recognized as not being normal articles of apparel."

The petition filed by Rubie's in December 1997 claims that the costumes should rightfully be filed under Chapter 61 or 62 of the HTSUS, as "fancy dress, of textiles," which would make the imported goods subject to not only import duties,

Figure 1

Harmonized Tariff Schedule of the United States (2002) (Rev.4)
Annotated for Statistical Reporting Purposes

XX
95-4

Heading/ Subheading	Stat. Suf- fix	Article Description	Unit of Quantity	Rates of Duty 1 General	Rates of Duty 1 Special	2
9505		Festive, carnival or other entertainment articles, including magic tricks and practical joke articles; parts and accessories thereof:				
9505.10		Articles for Christmas festivities and parts and accessories thereof:				
		Christmas ornaments:				
9505.10.10	00	Of glass	X	Free		60%
		Other:				
9505.10.15	00	Of wood	X	Free		20%
9505.10.25	00	Other	X	Free		20%
9505.10.30	00	Nativity scenes and figures thereof	X	Free		80%
		Other:				
9505.10.40		Of plastics	. . . .	Free		60%
	10	Artificial Christmas trees	No.			
	20	Other	X			
9505.10.50		Other	. . . .	Free		90%
	10	Artificial Christmas trees	No.			
	20	Other	X			
9505.90		Other:				
9505.90.20	00	Magic tricks and practical joke articles; parts and accessories thereof	X	Free		70%
9505.90.40	00	Confetti, paper spirals or streamers, party favors and noisemakers; parts and accessories thereof . .	X	Free		45%
9505.90.60	00	Other	X	Free		25%

SOURCE: "Harmonized Tariff Schedule of the United States (2002) (Annotated)." Basic Edition plus Revision 4—July 12, 2002. Chapter 95. United States International Trade Commission.

but also quota and visa restraints that would drive up the prices of the costumes. The crux of Rubie's argument was based on the simple fact that the imported costumes are made of fabric composed of man-made or natural fibers.

In its petition, Rubie's cited a precedent set by a decision of the Canadian International Trade Tribunal, in which a distinction is made between costumes that are "arranged or made to suit the wearer's fancy to represent fictitious characters" and costumes composed of "goods [that] are more indicative of face disguises than of actual clothing." The Tribunal decided that subheading 9505 of the HTSUS covered the latter, but not the former.

In July 1998, the U.S. Customs Office denied Rubie's petition and "affirmed that the four textile costumes in question were classified as festive articles in subheading 9505.90.6090 (now 9505.90.6000), HTSUS, because they were found to be flimsy, nondurable, and not normal articles of wearing apparel."

Turning the Tide

In February 2002, the tide turned in favor of Rubie's petition. A judge in the U.S. Court of International Trade agreed to reclassify the costumes as "fancy dress," inciting a near-panic in importers who now believe the flimsy, throw-away costumes will be too expensive for most consumers to consider buying. (See Appendix 1.)

According to one importer interviewed by *The Wall Street Journal,* this ruling "could disrupt $250 million in sales of imported Halloween costumes and could increase retail prices by as much as 50 percent."

The only company that will *not* be devastated by this ruling is Rubie's. The domestic manufacturer—which actually produces the majority of its costumes in Mexico—is exempt from paying import tariffs thanks to the North American Free Trade Agreement.

The textiles industry has faced a long history of debate within the World Trade Organization (WTO) and, previously, with the General Agreement on Tariffs and Trade (GATT). It has been a generally accepted principle that domestic producers that are able to demonstrate they are being seriously damaged due to rapidly increasing imports should be protected by either traditional tariffs or a quota system. But what characterizes "serious damage" to a domestic firm or industry?

It is also important to acknowledge the effect of such actions on the consumer, who could, in the wake of the U.S. decision regarding Halloween costumes, be faced with nearly monopolistic competition led by Rubie's, and thus, very high prices.

Therefore, the question still remains: Is this ruling a trick or a treat for the $2.5-billion Halloween industry? Perhaps the WTO needs to rule on the clothing of future Halloween monsters.

Appendix 1

Department of the Treasury
Customs Service
[T.D. 02–]

Notice of Decision of the United States Court of International
Trade Sustaining Domestic Interested Party Petition Concerning
Tariff Classification of Textile Costumes

AGENCY: Customs Service, Department of the Treasury.

ACTION: Notice of a decision of the United States Court of International Trade sustaining domestic interested party petition concerning tariff classification of textile costumes.

SUMMARY: On February 9, 2002, the United States Court of International Trade (CIT) issued the decision in *Rubie's Costume Company v. United States* which held that imported costumes are fancy dress of textile and, therefore, classifiable as wearing apparel. This decision sustained the petition of a domestic interested party under the provisions of section 516, Tariff Act of 1930, as amended (19 U.S.C. 1516). This document provides notice of the court decision and informs the public that imported textile costumes of the character covered by the Customs decision published in the **Federal Register** on December 4, 1998, will be subject to classification and assessment of duty in accordance with the CIT decision.

EFFECTIVE DATES: Imported textile costumes of the character covered by the Customs decision published in the **Federal Register** on December 4, 1998, which are entered for consumption or withdrawn from warehouse for consumption after [insert date of publication of this document in the **Federal Register**] are to be classified when entered as wearing apparel in accordance with the CIT decision in *Rubie's Costume Company v. United States*. The Committee for the Implementation of Textile Agreements (CITA) intends to apply quota and visa requirements to these goods exported on and after April 1, 2002.

FOR FURTHER INFORMATION CONTACT: For questions regarding operations, Dick Crichton, Office of Field Operations, (202) 927-0162; for

SOURCE: "Notice of Decision of the United States Court of International Trade Sustaining Domestic Interested Party Petition Concerning Tariff Classification of Textile Costumes," Customs Service, Department of the Treasury.

legal questions, Rebecca Hollaway, Office of Regulations and Rulings, (202) 927-2394.

SUPPLEMENTARY INFORMATION:
BACKGROUND

On June 2, 1997, in response to a domestic manufacturer's request, Customs issued a decision, Headquarters Ruling (HQ) 959545, determining that four costumes and their accessories would be classified under subheading 9505.90.6090, Harmonized Tariff Schedule of the United States (HTSUS), which provides for "Festive carnival or other entertainment articles, including magic tricks and practical joke articles; parts and accessories thereof; Other: Other: Other." This provision provided for duty-free entry under the general column one rate of duty. (Effective August 1, 1997, the provision was amended and now reads as follows: 9505.90.6000, HTSUS, "Festive, carnival or other entertainment articles, including magic tricks and practical joke articles; parts and accessories thereof: Other: Other," which provides for duty-free entry under the general column one rate of duty.)

In July 1997, and in accordance with the procedures of 19 U.S.C. 1516 and 19 CFR Part 175, a domestic interested party petition was filed on behalf of an American manufacturer of textile costumes. The petitioner contended that virtually identical costumes to those manufactured by petitioner were being imported into the United States and some of these textile costumes were being erroneously classified by Customs, duty-free, under subheading 9505.90.6090, HTSUS. The petitioner claimed that all imported textile costumes should be classified as wearing apparel in Chapters 61 or 62, HTSUS, are therefore dutiable, and may be subject to quota and visa restraints. Petitioner asserted that all textile costumes are excluded from classification under subheading 9505.90.6090, HTSUS, pursuant to Note 1(e), chapter 95.

Notice of the domestic interested party petition was published in the **Federal Register** on December 27, 1997 (62 FR 66891). After reviewing comments submitted in response to the notice that were supportive of and opposed to Customs classification position, Customs, in HQ 961447, dated July 22, 1998, denied the petition and affirmed the classification determination set forth in HQ 959545. The decision rejected the domestic interested party petition's argument that all imported costumes made of textiles should be classified under Chapters 61 and 62, HTSUS, as items of apparel.

On July 23, 1998, the domestic manufacturer filed written notice of its desire to contest Customs decision in HQ 961447 (19 U.S.C. 1516(c); 19 CFR 175.23). Subsequently, Customs published in the **Federal Register** (63 FR 67170; December 4, 1998) a notice of its classification decision and of the domestic manufacturer's desire to contest the decision. On June 25, 1999, Customs notified the domestic manufacturer that an entry of a costume had been liquidated in accordance with HQ 961447 on that date (19 U.S.C. 1516(c); 19 CFR 175.25(h)). On June 29, 1999, the domestic manufacturer commenced an action in the United States Court of International Trade (CIT) to challenge Customs classification decision.

The CIT, in *Rubie's Costume Company v. United States,* No. 99-06-00388, Slip Op. 02-14, (CIT Feb. 19, 2002), ruled, on a motion for summary judgment decided in favor of plaintiff domestic manufacturer, that the costumes constitute "fancy dress" and are thus excluded from classification in Chapter 95, HTSUS, by virtue of Note 1(e) to Chapter 95, HTSUS. Thus, the court held that the costumes are wearing apparel classifiable in Chapter 61, HTSUS. (To view the court's decision, go to *http://www.uscit.gov.* Note also that the *Rubie's* decision will be published in the *Customs Bulletin* issued on March 6, 2002.)

By publication of this notice in the **Federal Register,** Customs notifies the public, in accordance with 19 U.S.C. 1516(f) and 19 CFR 175.31, of the court's decision in *Rubie's*. Customs also informs the public that, effective on the day after publication of this notice in the **Federal Register,** merchandise of the character covered by the Customs decision published in the **Federal Register** on December 4, 1998, which is entered for consumption or withdrawn from warehouse for consumption will be subject to classification in accordance with the court's decision. Also, as tariff subheadings under Chapters 61 and 62, HTSUS, are subject to quota and visa restraints, Customs notes that CITA intends to apply applicable quota and visa requirements to merchandise of the character covered by the Customs decision published in the **Federal Register** on December 4, 1998, that is exported on and after April 1, 2002.

Dated: Acting Assistant Commissioner
                Office of Regulations and Rulings

A Presidential Proclamation on Steel

The White House
For Immediate Release
Office of the Press Secretary
March 5, 2002

To Facilitate Positive Adjustment to Competition From Imports of Certain Steel Products by the President of the United States of America a Proclamation

1. On December 19, 2001, the United States International Trade Commission (ITC) transmitted to the President a report on its investigation . . . with respect to imports of certain steel products.

2. The ITC reached affirmative determinations under section 202(b) of the Trade Act that the following products are being imported into the United States in such increased quantities as to be a substantial cause of serious injury, or threat of serious injury, to the domestic industries producing like or directly competitive articles. . .

6. The ITC commissioners voting in the affirmative under section 202(b) of the Trade Act also transmitted to the President their recommendations made pursuant to section 202(e) of the Trade Act (19 U.S.C. 2252(e)) with respect to the actions that, in their view, would address the serious injury, or threat thereof, to the domestic industries and be most effective in facilitating the efforts of those industries to make a positive adjustment to import competition.

. . .

9. Pursuant to section 203 of the Trade Act (19 U.S.C. 2253), the actions I have determined to take shall be safeguard measures in the form of:
(a) a tariff rate quota on imports of slabs described in paragraph 7, imposed for a period of 3 years plus 1 day, with annual increases in the within-quota quantities and annual reductions in the rates of duty applicable to goods entered in excess of those quantities in the second and third years; and
(b) an increase in duties on imports of certain flat steel, other than slabs (including plate, hot-rolled steel, cold-rolled steel and coated steel), hot-rolled bar, cold-finished bar, rebar, certain welded tubular products, carbon and alloy fittings, stainless steel bar, stainless steel rod, tin mill products, and stainless steel wire, as described in paragraph 7, imposed for a period of 3 years plus 1 day, with annual reductions in the rates of duty in the second and third years, as provided in the Annex to this proclamation.

. . .

11. These safeguard measures shall apply to imports from all countries, except for products of Canada, Israel, Jordan, and Mexico.

12. These safeguard measures shall not apply to imports of any product described in paragraph 7 of a developing country that is a member of the World Trade Organization (WTO), as long as that country's share of total imports of the product, based on imports during a recent representative period, does not exceed 3 percent . . .

. . .

SOURCE: This case was written by Professor Michael R. Czinkota and Armen S. Hovhannisyan, a graduate student.

IN WITNESS WHEREOF, I have hereunto set my hand this fifth day of March, in the year of our Lord two thousand two, and of the Independence of the United States of America the two hundred and twenty-sixth.

GEORGE W. BUSH

Background

Steel has traditionally been a very important industry worldwide. On the strategic side, weapons, buildings, and ships consume lots of steel. Among industrial products, cars are the major absorbers of steel production. Steel is therefore an important ingredient and symbol of an economy. As a result, governments around the world have tended to be highly protective of their steel industries.

Steel production quantity and location shift constantly. The use of steel (and hence production) tends to increase when economies are growing. Global consumption of steel rose from 28 million tons at the beginning of the twentieth century to 780 million tons at the end—an average increase of 3.4 percent per year for the century. In 1900, the United States was producing 37 percent of the world's steel. One hundred years later, Asia accounts for almost 40 percent, Europe produces 36 percent, and North America 14.5 percent[1] (Figures 1 and 2).

Since the late 1960s the rate of growth in steel production has leveled off, primarily because of greater efficiency in the use of steel and reduced waste. In addition, the auto industry has switched to plastics for many parts. Steel-making processes have also shown significant progress, from the invention of the Bessemer Converter at the turn of the century to the introduction of oxygen conversion processes in the 1950s and continuous casting in the 1960s. Steel is one of the most recycled of all industrial materials, even after decades of use. Recycled steel is processed in minimills that use steel scrap as a raw material. Generally these minimills, which use electrical power, are more productive than traditional steel casting in coal-heated furnaces.

The production costs of steel tend to differ greatly from one country to another. Steel industry wages account for the major price differential. Until 1968, steel wages in the United States were in line with average wages in the manufacturing sector. Starting in the late 1960s and continuing through the mid-1980s, steel firms provided their workers with very generous wages and pensions. In 1976, U.S. steel companies required import controls to get back on their feet. Twenty-six years later, the same steelmakers were in trouble again.

Tens of billions of dollars worth of quotas, tariffs, subsidies, and the like that had been provided to the steel companies had obviously had little effect.

In the early 2000s the supply of steel in the world continued to outstrip the demand, while pushing prices to their lowest level in 20 years. World steel demand was expected to decline from 741 million metric tons in 2001 to 736 million metric tons in 2002. Production was expected to fall from 838 million metric tons to 828 million metric tons, but likely to remain significantly ahead of consumption.[2]

The Asian financial crisis cut the demand for steel in Japan and other nations. That left the United States as one of the few places for foreign manufacturers to sell their steel. In the period between 1999 and 2002, 31 U.S. steel companies filed for bankruptcy protection—mostly the older, integrated steelmakers such as Bethlehem Steel Corporation and LTV Corporation, which use huge, coal-fired blast furnaces to turn ore into metal.

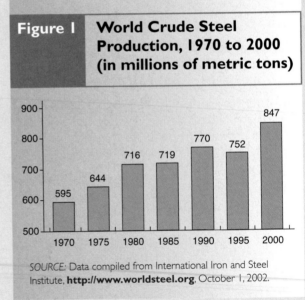

Figure 1 **World Crude Steel Production, 1970 to 2000 (in millions of metric tons)**

SOURCE: Data compiled from International Iron and Steel Institute, **http://www.worldsteel.org**, October 1, 2002.

The Evolution of the Issue

During the 2000 election, presidential candidate George W. Bush campaigned energetically to gain votes from the steelworkers in swing states such as West Virginia, Ohio, and Pennsylvania. Vice-presidential candidate Dick Cheney promised West Virginia's steelworkers that the administration would not forget them; in August 2001, then-president George W. Bush told steelworkers in Pittsburgh that their product was "an important

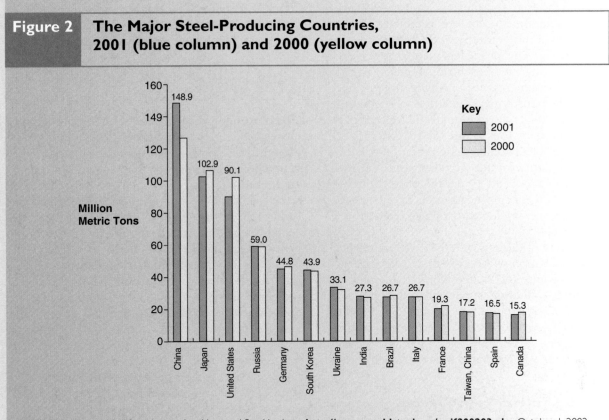

Figure 2   **The Major Steel-Producing Countries, 2001 (blue column) and 2000 (yellow column)**

Million Metric Tons

Key
2001
2000

China 148.9
Japan 102.9
United States 90.1
Russia 59.0
Germany 44.8
South Korea 43.9
Ukraine 33.1
India 27.3
Brazil 26.7
Italy 26.7
France 19.3
Taiwan, China 17.2
Spain 16.5
Canada 15.3

SOURCE: Data compiled from International Iron and Steel Institute, **http://www.worldsteel.org/wsif200203.php**, October 1, 2002.

national security issue."[3] In light of the crisis in the world steel industry, President Bush had asked the U.S. International Trade Commission (ITC) in June 2001 to determine whether a surge in imports had seriously damaged the U.S. steel industry. At the same time, he ordered trade officials to launch negotiations with foreign governments aimed at cutting overproduction and government subsidies.

In November 2001, the ITC found that the U.S. industry had sustained serious injury from imports. It recommended that the president impose some combination of import quotas and tariffs ranging from 15 percent to 40 percent, depending on the type of steel. Substantial tariffs on steel imports would raise U.S. domestic steel prices and would give the industry the financial breathing room to consolidate into fewer, larger, and more modern producers.

The Major Argument for Tariffs[4]

The United States is the world's largest steel consumer and its demand is growing. U.S. steel producers claim that after years of massive investment, technological improvements, and reductions in their workforce, they are the most advanced and the most productive in the world. Yet, 31 U.S. steel producers are in bankruptcy, partly because most of the steel imported into the United States today is selling at subsidized low prices.

These subsidized steel imports are a bargain for U.S. consumers, because the price of imports is below that of domestic steel. But in the long term, subsidized imports may destroy a vital American industry and eliminate high-paid, high-quality U.S. jobs. The United States may become dependent on Russia, Japan, China, Brazil, and developing countries for its steel. A century ago, this issue was framed by Abraham Lincoln in the following terms: "If we purchase a ton of steel rails from England for $20, then we have the rails and England the money. But if we buy a ton of steel rails from an American for $25, then America has both the rails and the money."[5]

Legacy Costs

U.S. steel companies won numerous antidumping cases in the previous decades. This could serve as evidence that the industry was not modernized or restructured sufficiently. Europe suffered similar problems in the early 1990s, but as a result of job cuts and industry consolidation, it now has very large and highly efficient steel producers. There is an important difference between Europe and the United States: European steel manufacturers do not pay for their retirees' health benefits, since that is their governments' responsibility. In the United States, the industry pays such "legacy costs" to its retired workers, who outnumber actively employed steel workers by four to one (600,000 to 150,000).[6] The United Steelworkers Association puts the aggregate figure for these costs at about $1 billion annually (on average, $9 per ton of steel produced in the United States). Legacy costs over the actuarial lifetimes of workers and retirees are said to total $13 billion.[7]

One way of dealing with the problem might be the consolidation of the industry into fewer but bigger producers. U.S. Steel Corp., the largest and most profitable of the surviving integrated steelmakers, proposed to buy Bethlehem Steel and as many as three other rivals, if the federal government agreed to assume some of the health care and pension obligations to the companies' retirees.

The Case for Free Trade

Without protection and support, nearly 60,000 U.S. steel workers may lose their jobs.[8] However, increasing tariffs to protect steelworkers is costly. A 20 percent increase will cost consumers $7 billion over four years. Consumers would pay more than an average of $326,000 per worker.[9]

Steel consumers, such as automakers and construction companies, far outnumber steelmakers (9 million to 150,000).[10] Protection of steel manufacturers will increase prices and hurt businesses that rely on steel as an input. Facing the prospect of tariffs that could raise domestic steel prices by as much as 10 percent, steel-consuming industries—the makers of tractors, washing machines, airplane fasteners, and auto parts—argue that they would lose sales if they were forced to pay more than foreign competitors for a key raw material.

A bailout for the steel industry sets a dangerous precedent and may invite similar demands from other industries, such as textiles and wood products, that have also been hard hit by imports. There is also a question of the feasibility of "rewarding" old-line unionized companies that got into trouble in the first place due to overly generous health and retirement plans.

Imposing tariffs on steel imports goes against U.S. initiatives for trade liberalization and could possibly lead to a trade war, as EU officials and companies have warned. An agreement to cut global production levels by 100 million metric tons

annually, reached by major steel producing nations in Paris late in 2001, was conditional on the United States keeping its tariffs unchanged.[11]

The Decision

Tariffs on steel create winners and losers, shifting jobs and incomes among companies, industries, regions, and countries. President Bush faced a difficult choice. If he did too little, he could trigger another round of steel company bankruptcies and layoffs, jeopardize passage of trade-liberalizing legislation, sacrifice control of the House of Representatives, and perhaps endanger prospects for his own reelection in 2004. On the other hand, if he did too much, it could cause a trade war with Europe, create new entitlements for American workers, raise prices for steel-using companies, and invite other industries to demand similar trade barriers and government bailouts.

On March 5, 2002, President Bush decided to impose tariffs of up to 30 percent on most imported steel. Under the plan, steel imported from Canada and Mexico would be exempt from custom duties, under NAFTA agreements. Japan, China, South Korea, Russia, Ukraine, and Brazil would be among the nations subject to the tariffs. Developing countries such as Argentina, Thailand, and Turkey would be exempt because they account for less than 3 percent of total imports. Administration officials said the purpose of the tariffs was to encourage U.S. companies to shift, at least temporarily, from buying foreign steel to U.S. steel, and in the process raise prices in the U.S. market from their 20-year lows. The tariffs are set to decline in the second and third years, subject to a review after 18 months by the president.[12]

This was the most aggressive action taken by a president to protect a domestic industry from imports since Ronald Reagan imposed steel import restraints in the mid-1980s. President Bush said it was an appropriate exception in the face of years of unfair trading practices by foreign countries that had "resulted in bankruptcies, serious dislocation and job losses" in the United States.[13]

According to political observers, administrating the pursuit of trade liberalization always involves striking a politically delicate balance between the demands of domestic constituencies on the one hand and trading partners on the other. They argue that whatever damage the temporary tariffs might inflict on the political cause of free trade, it is nothing compared with the damage that would have been caused if half of the U.S. steel industry were forced to shut down.[14] They calculate that as many as six House seats—exactly the number it would take for Democrats to take control of the chamber— hinged on the fallout from the steel decision.

Private economists predicted that the tariff regime will increase domestic prices by 6 percent to 8 percent in the first year. If fully passed on to consumers—not a sure thing by any means—that would raise the price of a $30,000 car by about $50 or a washing machine by less than $5. Such increases are probably not enough to substantially affect sales.

The International Reaction

As expected, the introduction of the tariff was immediately criticized by leading steel-producing countries. World leaders took turns pointing out what they viewed as U.S. hypocrisy. The United States' largest trading partner, the EU, threatened to retaliate with its own tariffs. Japan, Australia, South Korea, and Brazil promised to take the United States to a WTO arbitration panel—despite protests from a U.S. official that the tariffs comply with rules allowing just such temporary "safeguards." "The international market isn't the Wild West where everyone acts as he pleases," said the EU's trade commissioner, Pascal Lamy. German Chancellor Gerhard Schroeder declared the Bush decision "against free world markets," while French President Jacques Chirac called the move "serious and unacceptable."[15]

China's Foreign Trade Ministry declared Beijing's "strong displeasure" at the U.S. action, while a top South Korean trade official called it a "tragedy" for that country's economy. Japan's trade minister, Hiranuma, condemned the U.S. move as "deeply regrettable" and warned it could well trigger "compound retaliations."[16]

Russians said the tariff would have a serious impact on the relations between the two countries. Russian officials claimed that it would not help with the war on terrorism if the United States struck a blow to one of Russia's major export industries. In early March, Russia announced it would not issue import permits for U.S. poultry because of health concerns about the use of antibiotics in the animals. Russia's decision signaled the beginning of a low-level trade war.

Thomas Dawson, external relations director at the International Monetary Fund (IMF), said, "The fund clearly believes that lowering, not raising, trade barriers is the appropriate policy for our members, developed and developing, to follow." The IMF was concerned that the U.S. action could hamper its effort to persuade developing countries to reduce their trade barriers.[17] However, the United States targeted the steel tariffs in such a way that virtually all developing countries are exempt from the action.

Implications

EU companies account for a major share of the goods hit by the 30 percent import tariffs that took effect March 20, 2002. But those exports amount to only 2.5 percent of the EU's 160 million metric tons in annual steel production. The tariffs also aren't high enough to block all EU sales to the United States, partly because the strong dollar continues to give European companies a competitive advantage over their U.S. competitors. The biggest fear among European steelmakers is not reduced exports to the United States but a flood of cheap imports diverted into Europe by nations such as Japan, South Korea, and Russia, which are blocked by the new tariffs from selling as much steel to the United States as they have in the past.[18]

Expecting to face a surge in steel imports, Europe may adopt the same remedy of protective tariffs. The damage may possibly spread to other kinds of trade, and a good part of the cost will end up with developing-country producers, while the leaders of Europe and the United States preach liberal trade to the rulers of the developing world and promise better access to their own markets.

Some claim that in a global economy, local issues are important. When it comes to trade, expectations of a perfect track record may be the enemy of good achievements. Trade is only one component of the mosaic of mankind's activity. Policy needs to reflect the broad scope of human desires and needs, and the steel decision needs to be seen in such a context. There is a political price-tag associated with strong U.S. support of free trade. The rare and limited protection of a domestic industry with much leverage is such a price.[19]

Notes

1. International Iron and Steel Institute, **http://www.worldsteel.org**.

2. Peter Marsh, "Outlook for Steel 'Highly Adverse,'" *Financial Times,* January 21, 2002.

3. "Romancing Big Steel: George Bush's Promise to Help Is Coming Back to Haunt Him," *Economist,* February 16, 2002.

4. For more on this, see: American Iron and Steel Institute, **http://www.steel.org**; International Iron and Steel Institute, **http://www.iisi.org**. See also: Gary Clyde Hufbauer and Ben Goodrich, *Time for a Grand Bargain in Steel?* Institute for International Economics, January 2002.

5. Frank Swoboda, "U.S. Steel Seeks to Team with Its Rivals; Foreign Firms Would Still Outstrip Domestic Giant," *The Washington Post,* December 5, 2001, E1.

6. Leslie Wayne, "Rivals and Others Criticize Steel Makers' Bid for U.S. Aid," *The New York Times,* December 6, 2001, C9.

7. Gary Clyde Hufbauer and Ben Goodrich, *Time for a Grand Bargain in Steel?* Institute for International Economics, January 2002.

8. Number according to Thomas Usher, CEO of U.S. Steel Corporation, quoted by Leslie Wayne, "Parched, Big Steel Goes to Washingotn Well," *The New York Times,* January 20, 2002, section 3, page 1.

9. Figures from Gary Clyde Hufbauer, 2002.

10. Leslie Wayne, "Rivals and Others Criticize Steel Makers' Bid for U.S. Aid," *The New York Times,* December 6, 2001, C9.

11. Peter Marsh, "U.S. Urges Drop in Steel Production: Officials to Embark on Worldwide Tour in Effort to Stave Off Financial Crises in Sector," *Financial Times,* November 23, 2001.

12. Mike Allen and Steven Pearlstein, "Bush Settles on Tariff for Steel Imports," *The Washington Post,* March 5, 2002, A1.

13. Steven Pearlstein, "Bush Sets Tariffs on Steel Imports: President Opts for Compromise on Free Trade," *The Washington Post,* March 6, 2002, E1.

14. George F. Will, "Bending for Steel," *The Washington Post,* March 7, 2002, A21.

15. Steven Pearlstein and Clay Chandler, "Reaction Abroad on Steel Is Harsh; Bush Decision to Impose Tariffs Called Setback to Free-Trade Effort," *The Washington Post,* March 7, 2002, E1.

16. Ibid.

17. Edward Alden and Michael Mann, "EU Hits at U.S. 'Unilateralism' on Steel: Trade Dispute Pascal Lamy Says Tariffs Contradict Bush Administration's Rhetoric on Free Trade," *Financial Times,* March 14, 2002.

18. Geoff Winestock and Philip Shishkin, "EU Tempers Anger at U.S. Steel Tariffs: While Spurring Threats, Levies Seem Unlikely to Bring Harsh Action," *Wall Street Journal,* March 8, 2002, A8.

19. Michael R. Czinkota, "Free Trade Carries a Price," special to *The Japan Times,* March 18, 2002.

Car Financing in China

In China, car financing is a lot like the unification of North and South Korea. Just about everyone wants it to happen. But before that can happen, first you need to sweep away the landmines.

—Mike Dunne, *Automotive News*, 2000

China and the WTO

After 15 years of negotiations, China formally became a member of the World Trade Organization (WTO) on December 11, 2001. During this time China had been gradually liberalizing most of its trade and investment policies, making the official admission largely symbolic. More than anything, WTO membership signals China's commitment to establish clear and enforceable nondiscriminatory rules to conduct business in and with the country. For example, China's trademark and copyright laws were brought in line with international standards in October 2001. In a similar fashion, many companies established their strategies in the 1990s based on the assumption that China would gain entry into the WTO and are now ready to execute those plans.

Given China's unwillingness to show progress on political reform, the commitment to structural economic reforms has been particularly noteworthy. A constitutional amendment in 1999 legitimized private capital and granted private firms the same legal rights as state-owned enterprises, which laid a foundation for sustained, market-based growth. The private sector has grown to 40 percent of GDP with over 30 percent of the workforce. New jobs created in the private sector account for 38 percent of all new formal employment, rising to 56 percent in urban areas. The significance of this is more pronounced given layoffs in the state-owned enterprise sector.

China has been the fastest growing economy in the last ten years, with annual real GDP growth averaging 10.8 percent. While average national GDP per capita is under $1,000, urban populations (such as those in Shanghai and Guangzhou) enjoy incomes of over $3,000 (a point at which consumption increases dramatically). This has meant that urban households can afford color TVs (96 percent have them), phones (76 percent), and mobile phones (28 percent). Similar wealth is gradually (albeit slowly) spreading to rural areas as well. Furthermore, purchasing on credit is gaining acceptance among young urban consumers.

SOURCES: This case was compiled by Ilkka A. Ronkainen using publicly available materials. These include: "Motor Nation," *Business Week,* June 17, 2002, 44–45; Gong Zhenzheng, "Auto Price Wars Start to Rev Up," *China Daily,* January 22, 2002, 5; Joe Studwell, *The China Dream* (New York: Atlantic Monthly Press, 2002), chapter 7, note 29; "China's Carmakers Flattened by Falling Tariffs," *Business Week,* December 3, 2001; Mike Dunne, "Car Loans: Ready, Set, Go?" *Automotive News International,* September 1, 2000, 33; "Why Auto Financing Is Difficult in China," *Access Asia,* November 24, 2001; "Shanghai Leads in Efforts to Build Personal Credit for Chinese," Xinhua News Agency, July 20, 2000; "First Auto-Finance Firms to Be Launched in Early 2002," *Access Asia,* December 6, 2001; "China's Carmakers: Flattened by Falling Tariffs," *Business Week,* December 3, 2001, 51; and Danny Hakim, "All That Easy Credit Haunts Detroit Now," *The New York Times,* January 6, 2002, section 3, page 1. For further information, see **http://www.gmacfs.com** and **http://www.fordcredit.com**.

China's integration into the world economy has resulted in spectacular numbers both in trade and in investment. China's trade with the world quadrupled in the 1990s to $474 billion, including $100 billion with the United States (in 2001, China retained its spot as the country with the largest trade imbalance with the United States at $83 billion). While the lowering of trade barriers may permit more sales of foreign goods in China in the future, the rush by many companies from the Americas and Europe to manufacture in China for export may maintain China's trade imbalance with these trading partners. With Asian countries, however, China has been running a trade deficit since 2000 and will continue to be a source of demand as markets liberalize.

China received more foreign direct investment (FDI) in the 1990s than any country in the world except for the United States. The inflows have amounted to over $60 billion per year in the last five years, as shown in Figure 1. China's FDI has not only come at the expense of the rest of Asia, however. FDI inflows go to areas (within a region and a country) with comparative advantages—some to areas with abundant labor, some to areas with technological skills. With China leading in terms of inward investment flows, it may emerge as a hub for interregional demand for goods and services. Countries such as Japan will have to reorient themselves to focus on research and development, design, software, and high-precision manufactured goods.

Of economic significance is China's effort to stabilize its currency in the last five years. While officially described as a managed float, the currency (*yuan renminbi*) is effectively pegged to the U.S. dollar. This has resulted in China being immune to currency fluctuations that have wreaked havoc among emerging markets such as Mexico, Indonesia, Russia, Brazil, and Argentina. However, due to China's increasing foreign exchange reserves, strong capital inflows, and current account surplus, as well as pressure from Asian countries (especially Japan), the currency has come under appreciation pressure. However, with trade liberalization due to WTO membership, the higher value of the *renminbi* would aggravate the shock on domestic companies that compete with imports as well as on exporters who must compete in the global market (often on the basis of price). Chinese authorities have acknowledged the need for financial and currency liberalization, but the damaging impact of rising currency in the short term will most likely keep the currency regime unchanged. This will naturally result in low currency risk for investors.

It has been widely assumed that large corporations in particular from around the world would benefit from the liberalization measures undertaken and committed to by China (Table 1). For

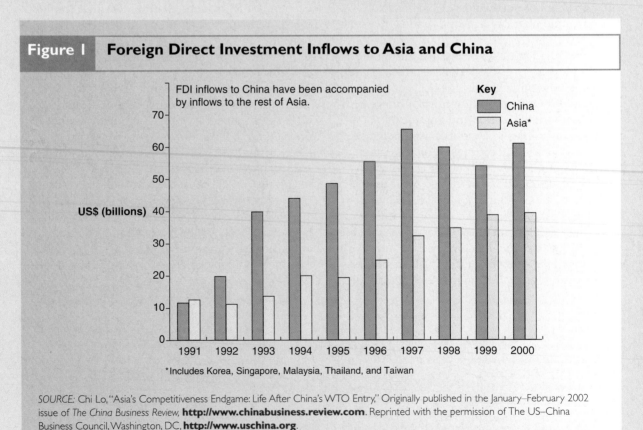

Figure 1   Foreign Direct Investment Inflows to Asia and China

FDI inflows to China have been accompanied by inflows to the rest of Asia.

Key: China, Asia*

US$ (billions)

*Includes Korea, Singapore, Malaysia, Thailand, and Taiwan

SOURCE: Chi Lo, "Asia's Competitiveness Endgame: Life After China's WTO Entry," Originally published in the January–February 2002 issue of *The China Business Review,* **http://www.chinabusiness.review.com**. Reprinted with the permission of The US–China Business Council, Washington, DC, **http://www.uschina.org**.

Table 1   China's WTO Obligations

- **2001:** After membership, China will open new cities to foreign banks for local currency business.
- **2002:** China will eliminate restrictions on where foreign law firms may operate and the number of offices that can be opened.
- **2004:** Foreign companies permitted to provide health and group insurance to Chinese.
- **2005:** U.S. to eliminate Chinese textile quotas but adopt measures to prevent import surges.
- **2006:** China to reduce auto tariffs to 25% from current 80% to 100%.
- **2007:** Foreign companies can hold 49% in telecom services (voice) joint ventures.

SOURCE: "China Begins Career as a WTO Member," *The Washington Post*, December 11, 2001, A14.

example, the Motion Picture Association estimated that lifting the barriers to film distribution would result in $80 million in revenues, in addition to another $120 million from sales and rentals of videos (which would no longer be plagued by rampant piracy). Some sectors, such as banking and insurance, are expected to make especially strong moves as markets open up. Foreign insurers can now operate beyond the two cities they have been limited to and expect nationwide access by 2005. Majority ownership in Chinese companies is now possible, as is the choice of joint venture partners.

Because many imports now face no tariff barriers (and the remaining ones are to be eliminated by 2010) or nontariff barriers (many quotas were eliminated on accession and the rest are due by 2005), and because trading and distribution rights are expected, business questions focus on the timetable for change. Most business leaders have been quite realistic in not expecting substantive changes immediately but have committed to long-term planning. In some sectors, competition has already heated up given consumer expectations of more and less expensive choices.

China's transformation must be seen in the context of political change, which is slow in countries such as China. Adverse effects of WTO membership are expected in terms of output and employment in sectors such as agriculture, financial services, and in general "less-competitive industries" which are typically dominated by state-owned enterprises. For example, agricultural employment is forecast to fall by 11 million, while a

substantial share of the 1.7 million workers in the four largest state-owned banks are in jeopardy. These factors have contributed to the government wanting to move with caution in allowing for change in the post-WTO environment. Furthermore, any dramatic change will probably face opposition from regional or local government officials who may see themselves as protectors of local interests.

There are already examples of the challenges to be faced as the WTO agreement is implemented at industrial and regional levels. Companies wanting to exploit the world's largest mobile telecommunications market were promised a 49 percent stake in domestic operators. But to obtain this, companies have found that waiting periods for official approval are between 270 to 310 days and that any local partner must put up 75 percent of 1 billion *renminbi* before permission is granted. This will mean that the number of joint-venture partners is considerably smaller than expected, and is possibly limited to state-owned entities. In a similar fashion, banks have found their aspirations dampened. Under the WTO agreement, foreign banks were to be able to offer *renminbi* banking services to Chinese corporate clients in 2004 and Chinese consumers starting in 2007. New regulations stipulate that foreign banks can only open one branch per year which, given that many are starting from scratch (only 158 branches of foreign banks existed in 2001) and given the tens of thousands of branches currently held by local entities (for example, the Bank of China has 15,200), creates a daunting task. Foreign branches are required to have 1 billion *renminbi* in operating capital to conduct a full range of services, an amount considered discriminatory by those hoping to develop the sector. Exporters have found delays in certifications for their products to enter the China market, especially in areas that are sensitive, such as agriculture.

The expectation is that disputes and problems will emerge but will be solved over time. A parallel can be drawn between the United States and its trading partners (such as the European Union and Canada), which continue to have disagreements within the WTO framework. The extent of the challenges will depend on China's economic health and its ability to absorb the competitive shocks of WTO membership. Of concern for politicians will be the growing gap between the haves and the have-nots (especially the urban and the rural) and the costs of reforming the state sector causing social unrest and challenging the legitimacy of the political structures.

The western world has had a commercial fascination with China for the last 2,000 years. The latest wave of interest started in 1979 with the official opening of China, culminating in the official acceptance of China as the 143rd member of the WTO. Companies will continue to speculate on what sales might be achieved if only a fraction of the Chinese population would buy its products or services.

China's economic stature will undoubtedly continue to grow. Increased investment will make China a production base for the world as global companies put their best practices to work in the largest emerging market in the world. For the United States, this may mean losses of more than 600,000 jobs and a widening trade deficit with China which, in turn, may result in growing tensions between two world superpowers. At the corporate level, the huge investments have meant that while efforts in China may be profitable, they are not earning their cost of capital (which many multinationals calculate at 15 percent).

Those companies interested in entering China primarily to exploit its domestic market may have more freedom to do so (such as having control of their own distribution or the ability to provide financing) but will continue to face the same challenges as before the WTO agreement. It is no longer enough to extend products and services (however famous their brand names may be) without adjusting to local market conditions. While foreign players are dominant in sectors such as beverages, film, and personal care, local companies still dominate in televisions, refrigerators, and washing machines despite the presence of multinational companies. Multinationals may bring their best practices to China, but local firms are quick to copy those practices and with their inherent advantages are able to compete effectively. While some doubt these Chinese companies will be competitive in global markets due to the lack of success factors such as global brands, some companies are already dominant in commodity-based sectors. Qingdao-based appliance maker Haier already has a 40 percent market share in small refrigerators and is planning to expand its base in the United States to, among other things, learn to be more effective at home.

Changes in the Chinese Car Market

A full-scale price war between car makers in China broke out in the first months of 2002. The phenomenon was a result of Chinese consumers' delays in buying cars throughout 2001 as well as increased imports following China's tariff cuts as part of the WTO agreement. The slashing of tariffs in the car sector was the biggest in any sector

(from 80 percent to 50 percent now and down to 25 percent by 2006).

Consumers had been waiting for cheaper cars for years, and this dream became a reality through the effects of the WTO agreement. For example, the Buick Sail's pre-WTO price was $13,855 but dropped to $12,040, with further decreases possible as domestic makers lower their prices to maintain competitive advantage. The price war was ignited on January 12 when Tianjin Automotive Industry Group slashed prices of all of its Xiali compact cars by 9,000 to 23,000 yuan ($1,084–$2,771). More than 3,600 are reported to have been sold during the first four days after the price cut. Chang'an Suzuki, a joint venture between Chongqing-based Chang'an Motor and Japan's Suzuki Motors, cut its prices by 20 percent. Analysts estimated that domestic car makers of vehicles priced at less than 150,000 yuan ($18,070) would have to reduce prices, although car makers such as Shanghai General Motors and Shanghai Volkswagen would try to hold on and let dealers engage in price promotions. Even with the price decreases, comparable cars cost far less in Europe, a fact not lost on the Chinese consumer.

Car makers already producing in China are bracing for intense competition. As the Chinese government phases out regulations as to what models to produce, General Motors (GM), Volkswagen (VW), Ford, Honda, and Toyota all plan to launch models aimed at quality- and cost-conscious consumers. For example, Ford will launch a compact in 2003 based on its Ikon model, now made in India at a price below $12,000. With the new market freedoms, car makers will have to focus on customer desires more than ever before.

Eventually, lower prices and wider choice should create a thriving auto industry. Experts predict car sales to increase to 900,000 units in 2002 and hit the 2-million unit mark by 2005. It should be noted that planned capacity as early as 1999 exceeded 2.75 million units (with actual sales only reaching 565,000 units).

Current Market Structure for Car Financing in China

In the calendar year 2000, approximately 600,000 cars were sold in China; only 16 percent were financed. Two-thirds of that 16 percent were business-to-business loans between banks and taxi companies, which leaves 25,000 units financed by individuals and private enterprises. In comparison, GM and Ford—by themselves—provided auto financing to approximately the same number of individuals and private enterprises in the state of Maryland in 2000. In contrast, U.S. auto purchasers finance between 65 to 93 percent of all units purchased, depending on make.

China is currently a very small market for auto financing and for consumer credit in general. There are a number of the reasons behind the small market size. Auto financing was not permitted by the government before 1998. Currently, only four state-owned and two private banks are authorized by the Chinese government to provide loans with interest rates regulated by the government. These include Bank of China, China's oldest bank, as well as China Construction Bank. These institutions have onerous requirements to gain approval for a loan, including: (1) collateral other than the car (home, deposits at the bank) valued at 100 to 120 percent of the amount of the loan, (2) a guarantor, (3) proof of income and tax payments (not onerous in and of itself, but many Chinese underreport income and taxes to an extent that verifiable income is insufficient for loan repayment), (4) a marriage certificate, (5) an official estimate of the value of the vehicle, and (6) mandated vehicle purchase through an "approved" retailer. This has meant that nearly one-third of car buyers have opted to quit the process rather than complete it. Even with the onerous requirements, initial results have not been promising: default rates in 1998 ranged from 10 to 30 percent.

In addition, the infrastructure is not yet developed for car financing. Most vehicle regulatory agencies do not allow liens or security interests in autos that are registered for personal use. Laws and regulations are not consistently in place to protect insurance companies when investing in loans or underwriting loan risks. Repossession procedures are not generally codified. Where rules exist, the Public Security Bureau must effect repossession and will decide resale value on repossessed vehicles.

Regional differences are significant. While the industry is still in its infancy, Shanghai is the most advanced both in terms of amounts of consumer credit and the systems in place. The urban populations of the east will play a major role in the change process because of their increasing wealth and nontraditional attitudes toward buying on credit. Foreign interest in the market for car financing is predicated on the long-term potential of the market influenced by China's membership in the WTO. While government rules made market entry possible prior to January 2002, setting up operations is still challenging. For example, government rules mandate loans denominated in *renminbi* (the local currency, "people's money").

But *renminbi* funding sources are scarce, and foreign banks do not have access to funding in *renminbi*. Furthermore, foreign entities can count on local competition from existing and new government-owned institutions as well as private entities. The State Development Planning Commission (SDPC) has disclosed that China will launch its first auto financing company in early 2002. Yafei Auto Chain General Store—with default rates at less than 2 percent and 90 percent regional market share—is a chain of auto dealerships that gets preferential treatment from the Beijing government and enjoys exclusive underwriting support from the China People's Life Insurance Company.

The WTO agreement will cause a drop in the tariffs of imported cars from a range of 70 to 80 percent of the list price to 50 to 60 percent. In 2002, sedan imports are expected to leap 50 percent to 120,000 units. By 2006, duties are to sink another 25 percent—enough to put cars within the reach of China's upper middle class.

Expected Market Changes in Car Financing in China

All indications are that auto financing in China in the 21st century will be a lucrative business both at the macro level and the micro level. Only 1 percent of China's total consumption was made through consumer credit in 1999. In an effort to fuel economic growth, Chinese officials have stated that they are working toward percentages of consumption from credit more in line with the western world. Most of the western economies average between 20% and 25% of consumption through consumer credit.

Average household income in China's 35 largest cities is in excess of US$2,172, with GDP per capita in those cities in excess of $1,100. GDP per capita in Shanghai, Beijing, and Guangzhou exceeds $2,000. Most experts agree that automotive purchases generally and automotive finance specifically expand rapidly after crossing the $2,000 per capita GDP threshold.

Consensus estimates for the car financing market—both for personal and business use—in 2002 were 20% of the 830,000 expected unit sales (166,000 units). This number is expected to increase by 40 to 60% over a five-year period, resulting in a $3.25 billion market. While this is still not large by western standards, it does provide sufficient scale to mirror other world market characteristics (such as those in Brazil) and allow for a fairly precise prediction of the costs to develop the market.

All indications are that Chinese consumers' aversion to debt is waning—at least in the cities of the south and east. Estimates for consumer lending in general can be extrapolated from analogous evidence. In 1995, 15,000 individuals in Shanghai borrowed 570 million *yuan* worth of mortgages, and in 1999, 680,000 individuals in Shanghai borrowed 54 billion *yuan* worth of mortgages.

The industry is dependent on accurate and timely information as well as a transparent system of operation. Shanghai Credit Information Services is maturing as a reliable source of credit information for more than 1 million Chinese. Rules for recording liens and repossession and remarketing of vehicles are now in place in Shanghai and Beijing (albeit in their infancy and open to local interpretation).

Options for Market Entry and Development

There are four ways that auto finance companies can set up in China:

- Automakers can launch an auto-financing services subsidiary;
- Banks (Chinese) can set up special auto financing institutions;
- Nonbanking financial institutions owned by enterprise groups can form an auto financing company; or
- Existing lending consortia can provide financing services for auto companies' sales divisions.

Draft rules for foreign investment are currently being circulated. The foreign firms that have submitted an application for license to do business include VW Credit, Ford Motor Credit, Peugeot/Citroen Credit, and GMAC. Of the firms listed above, those that have traditionally undertaken diversified lending activities outside the area of auto financing have been the most aggressive in terms of new market entry and pricing once they have entered a market.

GMAC's Competitive Position

GMAC and the other financing arms of carmakers are at an obvious disadvantage in relation to home-country institutions because the market was reserved for Chinese institutions until January 2002. GMAC previously acted in an advisory capacity to GM's Shanghai JV manufacturing facility, which, in turn, has set up relationships with official government lending institutions (such as China Construction Bank and the Bank of Shanghai). Currently, GMAC has one person in Shanghai with the task of market investigation and support of GM activities.

GMAC's competitive position vis-à-vis the other foreign companies applying for entry appears to be solid for a number of reasons:

- GM is the largest corporate FDI contributor to China in the world and has a substantial partnership with the government;
- GMAC has numerous manufacturing partners to leverage—SGM, Jinbei GM (which produces the Chevrolet S-10 pickup and Blazer SUV), and Wuling (GM has an equity stake in the largest producer of mini-cars for the Chinese market). These partners deliver the second highest number of FDI autos in the market—just behind VW and far ahead of Ford Motor Credit and Peugeot; and
- GMAC has numerous GM-network partners to leverage (Isuzu, Suzuki, Fiat, Fuji Heavy Industries).

GMAC's expertise in auto lending generally and in the following ancillary areas critical to doing business in China should allow for the business to get up and running. It has extensive experience in auto lending in developing markets without efficient infrastructure; for example, it has experience in India, which has no credit bureaus and state involvement in repossession and remarketing. Partnering with other private and quasi-state-run institutions such as Fannie Mae, GMAC subsidiaries (GMAC Mortgage, GMAC Commercial Mortgage and Residential Funding Corporation) has developed expertise in profitable loan securitization, profitable (mortgage) loan servicing, and profitable receivables (purchase and sale), giving it the necessary skills to work together with third parties and governmental units. Finally, market presence in many other countries in the Asia-Pacific region gives GMAC the human resources necessary for China expansion. These offices are staffed with a broad array of third country expatriates from China and other cultures who have better insight into the Chinese market than do GMAC's U.S.-based staff.

Despite the overwhelming external and internal opportunities, challenges exist as well. Ford's and GM's credit ratings were downgraded by Moody's and Standard & Poor's in 2001, forcing the automakers out of commercial paper and into other, more expensive forms of funding. Their no- or low-interest loans and cheap leases intended to pump up sales in 2001 have threatened the financial health of the carmakers' credit arms. For example, GMAC North America's huge success with 0 percent financing during 2001 Q4's "Keep America Rolling" campaign ate up significant resources. Effectively, GMAC may be out of cash for big market-entry investments and equity investment from the parent company, when GM as a whole faces an unfunded pension liability and reduced cash flow that is critical for reinvestment into future product programs. Ford Motor Credit is facing even bigger problems given its more aggressive lending practices in the recent past.

Implications for Global Operations

A carmaker's captive financing arm exists for two reasons: to assist in delivering additional cars and trucks to consumers, and to provide a superior return on investment and cash flow to its sole stockholder. While still extremely risky and lacking in short-term profit, the China market is still valued by carmakers because of its market potential for sales and because of the potential it displays for their financing arms in terms of auto finance and mortgages. The question is how to deliver on the promise and the mandate. Ford Motor Company, for one, has adopted a wait-and-see attitude.

Questions for Discussion

1. Suggest reasons for GMAC to enter or not to enter the Chinese market for auto financing.
2. What is the most prudent mode of entry and market development for GMAC should it choose to enter the market?
3. If it enters, where should GMAC make its moves and with what type of products?
4. What should GMAC do to influence the positive change in China in its favor?

IKEA in the USA

IKEA, the world's largest home furnishings retail chain, was founded in Sweden in 1943 as a mail-order company and opened its first showroom ten years later. From its headquarters in Almhult, IKEA has since expanded to worldwide sales of $11 billion from 175 outlets in 32 countries (see Table 1). In fact, the second store that IKEA built was in Oslo, Norway. Today, IKEA operates large warehouse showrooms in Sweden, Norway, Denmark, Holland, France, Belgium, Germany, Switzerland, Austria, Canada, the United States, Saudi Arabia, and the United Kingdom. It has smaller stores in Kuwait, Australia, Hong Kong, Singapore, the Canary Islands, and Iceland. A store near Budapest, Hungary, opened in 1990, followed by outlets in Poland, the Czech Republic, and the United Arab Emirates in 1991 and Slovakia in 1992, followed by Taiwan in 1994, Finland and Malaysia in 1996, and mainland China in 1998. IKEA first appeared on the Internet in 1997 with the World Wide Living Room Web site. The first store in Russia opened in March of 2000 and in Israel in 2001. Plans call for opening two stores in Japan by 2006. The IKEA Group's new organization has three regions: Europe, North America, and Asia-Pacific.

The international expansion of IKEA has progressed in three phases, all of them continuing at the present time: Scandinavian expansion, begun in 1963; West European expansion, begun in 1973; and North American expansion, begun in 1976. Of the individual markets, Germany is the largest, accounting for 21.6 percent, followed by the U.S. at 13 percent of company sales. The phases of expansion are detectable in the worldwide sales shares depicted in Figure 1. "We want to bring the IKEA concept to as many people as possible," IKEA officials have said. The company estimates that over 260 million people visit its showrooms annually.

The IKEA Concept

Ingvar Kamprad, the founder, formulated as IKEA's mission to "offer a wide variety of home furnishings of good design and function at prices so low that the majority of people can afford to buy them." The principal target market of IKEA, which

SOURCES: This case, prepared by Ilkka A. Ronkainen, is based on Lisa Margonelli, "How IKEA Designs Its Sexy Price Tags," *Business 2.0*, October 2002, 108; "Furnishing the World," *Economist*, November 19, 1994, 79; Richard Norman and Rafael Ramirez, "From Value Chain to Value Constellation: Designing Interactive Strategy," *Harvard Business Review* 71 (July/August 1993): 65–77; "IKEA's No-Frills Strategy Extends to Management Style," *Business International*, May 18, 1992, 149–150; Bill Saporito, "IKEA's Got 'Em Lining Up," *Fortune*, March 11, 1991, 72; Rita Martenson, "Is Standardization of Marketing Feasible in Culture-Bound Industries? A European Case Study," *International Marketing Review* 4 (Autumn 1987): 7–17; Eleanor Johnson Tracy, "Shopping Swedish Style Comes to the U.S.," *Fortune*, January 27, 1986, 63–67; Mary Krienke, "IKEA—Simple Good Taste," *Stores*, April 1986, 58; Jennifer Lin, "IKEA's U.S. Translation," *Stores*, April 1986, 63; "Furniture Chain Has a Global View," *Advertising Age*, October 26, 1987, 58; Bill Kelley, "The New Wave from Europe," *Sales & Marketing Management*, November 1987, 46–48. Updated information available from **http://www.ikea.com**.

Table 1	IKEA's International Expansion				

Year	Outlets[a]	Countries[a]	Coworkers[a]	Catalog Circulation	Turnover in Swedish Crowns[c]
1954	1	1	15	285,000	3,000,000
1964	2	2	250	1,200,000	79,000,000
1974	10	5	1,500	13,000,000	616,000,000
1984	66	17	8,300	45,000,000	6,770,000,000
1988	75	19	13,400	50,535,000	14,500,000,000
1990	95	23	16,850	n.a.	19,400,000,000
1995	131	27	30,500	n.a.	38,557,000,000
1998	150	28	40,400	n.a.	56,645,000,000
2002	175	32	65,000	110,000,000[b]	99,200,000,000

[a]Stores/countries being opened by 2002.
[b]Estimate.
[c]Corresponding to net sales of the IKEA group of companies.

SOURCE: IKEA U.S., Inc.

is similar across countries and regions in which IKEA has a presence, is composed of people who are young, highly educated, liberal in their cultural values, white-collar workers, and not especially concerned with status symbols.

IKEA follows a standardized product strategy with a universally accepted assortment around the world. Today, IKEA carries an assortment of thousands of different home furnishings that range from plants to pots, sofas to soup spoons, and wine glasses to wallpaper. The smaller items are carried to complement the bigger ones. IKEA has limited manufacturing of its own but designs all of its furniture. The network of subcontracted manufacturers numbers nearly 2,000 in over 55 countries. The top five purchasing countries are China (14 percent), Sweden (14 percent), Poland (8 percent), Germany (6 percent), and Italy (6 percent).

IKEA's strategy is based on cost leadership secured by contract manufacturers, many of whom are in low-labor-cost countries and close to raw materials, yet accessible to logistics links. High-volume production of standardized items allows for significant economies of scale. In exchange for long-term contracts, leased equipment, and technical support from IKEA, the suppliers manufacture exclusively at low prices for IKEA. IKEA's designers work with the suppliers to build savings-generating features into the production and products from the outset. IKEA has acquired some of its own production capacity in the last few years, constituting 10 percent of its total sales. While new facilities were opened in 2000 in Latvia, Poland, and Romania to bring the total number to 30, IKEA plans to have its own production not exceed 10 percent, mainly to secure flexibility.

Manufacturers are responsible for shipping the components to large distribution centers, for example, to the central one in Almhult. These twelve distribution centers then supply the various stores, which are in effect miniwarehouses.

IKEA consumers have to become "prosumers"—half producers, half consumers—because most products have to be assembled. The final distribution is

Figure 1	IKEA'S Worldwide Sales Expressed as Percentages of Turnover by Market Unit

North America 18%

Middle East, Australia, Asia 6%

Europe 76%
• Germany 21%
• United Kingdom 12%
• France 9%
• Sweden 7%
• Other 27%

the customer's responsibility as well. Although IKEA expects its customers to be active participants in the buy-sell process, it is not rigid about it. There is a "moving boundary" between what consumers do for themselves and what IKEA employees will do for them. Consumers save the most by driving to the warehouses themselves, putting the boxes on the trolley, loading them into their cars, driving home, and assembling the furniture. Yet IKEA can arrange to provide these services at an extra charge. For example, IKEA cooperates with car rental companies to offer vans and small trucks at reasonable rates for customers needing delivery service. Additional economies are reaped from the size of the IKEA outlets; for example, the Philadelphia store is 169,000 square feet (15,700 square meters). IKEA stores include baby-sitting areas and cafeterias and are therefore intended to provide the value-seeking, car-borne consumer with a complete shopping destination. IKEA managers state that their competitors are not other furniture outlets but all attractions vying for the consumers' free time. By not selling through dealers, the company hears directly from its customers.

Management believes that its designer-to-user relationship affords an unusual degree of adaptive fit. IKEA has "forced both customers and suppliers to think about value in a new way in which customers are also suppliers (of time, labor information, and transportation), suppliers are also customers (of IKEA's business and technical services), and IKEA itself is not so much a retailer as the central star in a constellation of services." Figure 2 provides a presentation of IKEA's value chain.

Although IKEA has concentrated on company-owned, larger-scale outlets, franchising has been used in areas in which the market is relatively small or where uncertainty may exist as to the response to the IKEA concept. These markets include Hong Kong and the United Arab Emirates. IKEA uses mail order in Europe and Canada but has resisted expansion into the United States, mainly because of capacity constraints.

IKEA offers prices that are 30 to 50 percent lower than fully assembled competing products. This is a result of large-quantity purchasing, low-cost logistics, store location in suburban areas, and the do-it-yourself approach to marketing. IKEA's prices do vary from market to market, largely because of fluctuations in exchange rates and differences in taxation regimes, but price positioning is kept as standardized as possible.

IKEA's promotion is centered on the catalog. The IKEA catalog is printed in 42 editions in 17 languages and has a worldwide circulation of well over 110 million copies. The catalogs are uniform in layout except for minor regional differences. The company's advertising goal is to generate word-of-

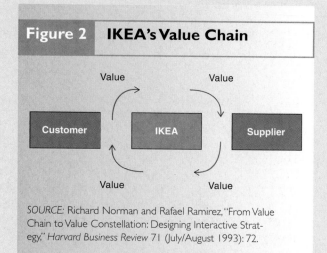

Figure 2   IKEA's Value Chain

SOURCE: Richard Norman and Rafael Ramirez, "From Value Chain to Value Constellation: Designing Interactive Strategy," *Harvard Business Review* 71 (July/August 1993): 72.

Table 2	The IKEA Concept
Target Market:	"Young people of all ages"
Product:	IKEA offers the same products, which are distinctively Swedish/Scandinavian in design, worldwide. The number of active articles is 12,000. Each store carries a selection of these 12,000, depending on outlet size. The core range is the same worldwide. Most items have to be assembled by the customer. The furniture design is modern and light.
Distribution:	IKEA has built its own distribution network. Outlets are outside the city limits of major metropolitan areas. Products are not delivered, but IKEA cooperates with car rental companies that offer small trucks. IKEA offers mail order in Europe and Canada.
Pricing:	The IKEA concept is based on low price. The firm tries to keep its price-image constant.
Promotion:	IKEA's promotional efforts are mainly through its catalogs. IKEA has developed a prototype communications model that must be followed by all stores. Its advertising is attention-getting and provocative. Media choices vary by market.

mouth publicity through innovative approaches. The IKEA concept is summarized in Table 2.

IKEA in the Competitive Environment

IKEA's strategic positioning is unique. As Figure 3 illustrates, few furniture retailers anywhere have engaged in long-term planning or achieved scale economies in production. European furniture retailers, especially those in Sweden, Switzerland, Germany, and Austria, are much smaller than IKEA. Even when companies have joined forces as buying groups, their heterogeneous operations have made it difficult for them to achieve the same degree of coordination and concentration as IKEA. Because customers are usually content to wait for the delivery of furniture, retailers have not been forced to take purchasing risks.

The value-added dimension differentiates IKEA from its competition. IKEA offers limited customer assistance but creates opportunities for consumers to choose (for example, through informational signage), transport, and assemble units of furniture. The best summary of the competitive situation was provided by a manager at another firm: "We can't do what IKEA does, and IKEA doesn't want to do what we do."

IKEA in the United States

After careful study and assessment of its Canadian experience, IKEA decided to enter the U.S. market in 1985 by establishing outlets on the East Coast and, in 1990, one in Burbank, California. In 2002, a total of 17 stores (eight in the Northeast, seven in California, one in Seattle, and one in Texas) generated sales of over $1.5 billion. The stores employ 6,000 workers. The overwhelming level of success in 1987 led the company to invest in a warehousing facility near Philadelphia that receives goods from Sweden as well as directly from suppliers around the world. Plans call for two to three additional stores annually over the next 25 years, concentrating on the northeastern United States and California.

Success today has not come without compromises. "If you are going to be the world's best furnishing company, you have to show you can succeed in America, because there is so much to learn here," said Goran Carstedt, head of North American operations. Whereas IKEA's universal approach had worked well in Europe, the U.S. market proved to be different. In some cases, European products conflicted with American tastes and preferences. For example, IKEA did not sell matching bedroom suites that consumers wanted.

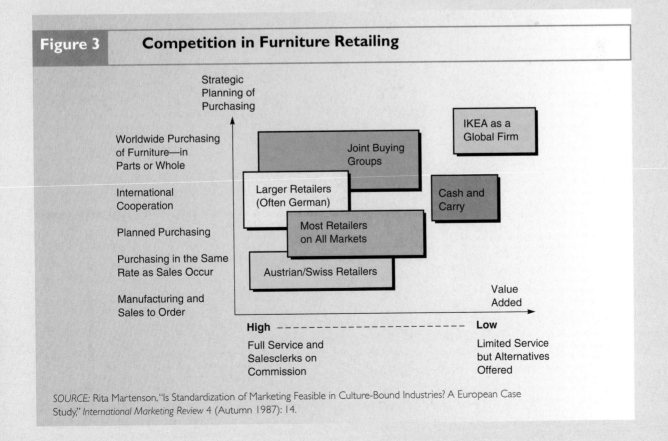

Figure 3 Competition in Furniture Retailing

SOURCE: Rita Martenson, "Is Standardization of Marketing Feasible in Culture-Bound Industries? A European Case Study," *International Marketing Review* 4 (Autumn 1987): 14.

Kitchen cupboards were too narrow for the large dinner plates needed for pizza. Some Americans were buying IKEA's flower vases for glasses.

Adaptations were made. IKEA managers adjusted chest drawers to be an inch or two deeper because consumers wanted to store sweaters in them. Sales of chests increased immediately by 40 percent. In all, IKEA has redesigned approximately a fifth of its product range in North America. Today, 45 percent of the furniture in the stores in North America is produced locally, up from 15 percent in the early 1990s. In addition to not having to pay expensive freight costs from Europe, this has also helped to cut stock-outs. And because Americans hate standing in lines, store layouts have been changed to accommodate new cash registers. IKEA offers a more generous return policy in North America than in Europe, as well as next-day delivery service.

In hindsight, IKEA executives are saying they "behaved like exporters, which meant not really being in the country. . . . It took us time to learn this." IKEA's adaptation has not meant destroying its original formula. Their approach is still to market the streamlined and contemporary Scandi-

navian style to North America by carrying a universally accepted product range but with a mind on product lines and features that appeal to local preferences. The North American experience has caused the company to start remixing its formula elsewhere as well. Indeed, now that Europeans are adopting some American furnishing concepts (such as sleeper sofas), IKEA is transferring some American concepts to other markets such as Europe.

Questions for Discussion

1. What has allowed IKEA to be successful with a relatively standardized product and product line in a business with strong cultural influence? Did adaptations to this strategy in the North American market constitute a defeat to its approach?
2. Which features of the "young people of all ages" are universal and can be exploited by a global/regional strategy?
3. Is IKEA destined to succeed everywhere it cares to establish itself?

Renaming the Vietnamese Catfish

The cultivation of water plants and animals for human use began thousands of years ago. Globally, aquaculture's growth has more than doubled in the 1990s (to more than 35 million tons a year). To meet the demand for improved quality protein sources, scallops, oysters, salmon, and catfish are being raised in controlled environments. Farm-raised fish have high quality and, unlike ocean-caught fish, are available all year long.

U.S. aquaculture production has grown more than 49 percent since 1991.[1] Aquaculture is the fastest growing segment of agriculture in the United States. Farmed seafood makes up about a third of the seafood consumed in the United States. About two-thirds of the shrimp and salmon and almost all of the catfish and trout consumed by Americans are raised in ponds.[2]

Thick-skinned, whiskered, wide-mouthed catfish can be found in the wild in channels and rivers of the southern United States. Wild catfish are typically described as pungent, bony, and muddy. However, as a result of aquaculture technology, catfish are now an economical farm-raised fish with a mild flavor. They are raised in clay-based ponds filled with fresh water pumped from underground wells, and fed an enriched, high-protein, grain-based food. Their firm, white flesh can convey strong flavors and stands up to a variety of cooking techniques, which makes them suit virtually any ethnic cuisine.[3]

Americans consumed about 275 million kilograms (more than 600 million pounds) of catfish in 2000,[4] most of which came from 150,000 acres of catfish ponds in the United States, mainly located in Mississippi, Arkansas, and Louisiana. The U.S. catfish industry is estimated to turn over $4 billion worth of fish product a year. Catfish are especially popular in Southern dishes, but their use has been growing also in the Midwest. Filets are now available in New York supermarkets and fish stores. One recent poll placed catfish as the country's third favorite fish, beaten only by shrimp and lobster.[5]

The Issue

The United States is the leading market for Vietnamese catfish (followed by Hong Kong, the EU, and Australia). In 2001, the United States produced 270.5 million kilograms (597 million pounds) and imported about 3.7 million kilos (8.2 million pounds) of catfish, out of which 90 percent, about 3.2 million kilograms (7 million pounds), came from Vietnam. By the end of 2001 prices for U.S. catfish had dropped to 50 cents a pound, about 15 cents below the cost of production and about 330 cents below the price of 2000. U.S. producers blamed the Vietnamese for the falling prices.[6]

Vietnamese catfish exporters and importers in turn blame U.S. producers for dragging down prices. They say that the Americans are mainly at fault for expanding inventories up to 30 percent, a figure obtained from the National Agricultural Statistics Service (**http:www.usda.gov/nass**). Vietnamese fish importers also claim that American

SOURCE: This case was written by Professor Michael R. Czinkota, Georgetown University McDonough School of Business, and graduate student Armen S. Hovhannisyan, Georgetown University School of Foreign Service.

catfish growers are to blame for their own difficulties because they sell the domestic fish in only
a few states. "It is the failure to adequately market
the product effectively throughout the United
States," says Andrew Forman, president of Boston-
based Infinity Seafood LLC. According to a report
by Consulting Trends International, a California-
based consulting firm, the price drop is "primarily
the result of higher domestic catfish inventories
in the United States, which will depress prices
through the end of 2001 and 2002."

The American catfish industry has almost tripled
in size from 1985 to 2001. Hugh Warren, vice president of the Catfish Institute of America, says that
this growth is strictly due to the industry's marketing effort of $50 million. He feels that as importers,
the Vietnamese get a free ride.[7] The U.S. industry
offers 15,000 jobs that earn $8 an hour in the
poorest parts of America. These jobs are being
"stolen" by cheap Vietnamese imports.[8]

In an attempt to change this situation, American
catfish farmers, industry associations, and supporting organizations came to Washington, DC, to call
on officials at the State Department, the Commerce
Department, the Food and Drug Administration
(FDA), and Congress (which in July 2000 signed a
bilateral agreement with Vietnam to foster free
trade) for help. They waged an advertising campaign against their Vietnamese competitors in
order to convince the public that Vietnamese catfish are low quality and raised in dirty waters.[9]

Congressional Reaction

The support from Congress was swift. In December 2001 an amendment was added to an appro-
priations bill that barred the FDA from spending
money "to allow admission of fish or fish products
labeled in whole or in part with the term 'catfish'
unless the fish is from the Ictaluridae family." The
senators from the South, who introduced a labeling bill, claimed Vietnamese fish to be as different
scientifically from catfish "as a cow from a yak."[10]
Supporting a different view, Senator Phil Gramm
(R-Tex.) characterized the Vietnamese catfish as
follows: "Not only does it look like a catfish, but
it acts like a catfish. And the people who make a
living in fish science call it a catfish. Why do we
want to call it anything other than a catfish?"[11] This
meant that the FDA needed to identify different
kinds of catfish.

In January 2002 under Congress's direction, the
FDA published "Guidance for Industry" regulations
on how the imported fish should be labeled.
Under the regulation, Flat Whiskered Fish is an
acceptable substitute for the Flat Whiskered Catfish; but Katfish or Cat Fish are not. Instead, importers, restaurants, and grocery stores will have
to call the fish "basa," which is another name for
catfish from the Pangasius (Pangasiidae) family.
U.S. producers were counting on such labels to
discourage the sales of imported fish.

About 30 percent of U.S. seafood restaurants
serve Vietnamese catfish, which are slightly milder
and softer than the American variety. The amendment and the regulation were not good news for
them. As the owner of Piazza's Seafood World, a
New Orleans–based importer, put it: "Nobody in
the United States owns the word 'catfish.'"[12] However, Vietnam is still free to export catfish to the
United States, as long as they are called something
other than catfish.

When Is a Catfish a Catfish?

In order to identify different kinds of catfish, the
FDA sought expert help. Before promulgating its
regulation, it consulted Dr. Carl J. Ferraris of the
ichthyology department at the California Academy
of Sciences. Dr. Ferraris's response was that there
was no scientific justification to treat or rename
catfish from Vietnam differently from those from
the United States.[13]

According to U.S. catfish farmers, the only true
catfish belongs to the family with the Latin name
Ictaluridae. The Vietnamese variety is in the family
Pangasiidae, which are "freshwater catfishes of
Africa and southern Asia." Vietnamese catfish
farmers claim that they have created a new agricultural industry, turning their rice and soybean
fields into profitable fish farms in the poor regions
of the country. By giving up crops, they gave up
heavy use of chemical fertilizers and pesticides,
which is good for the environment. They also
gave up agriculture subsidies at a time when
lawmakers wanted to get the government out of
farming.[14]

U.S. catfish farmers say their catfish are raised
in purified water ponds, which have to be tested
by federal agencies and meet the standards of the
Catfish Institute. The U.S. catfish industry must
go through inspections from 17 federal agencies
(including the Department of Commerce, the FDA,
and the Environmental Protection Agency). By
contrast, the Vietnamese imports have to meet
only FDA approval.[15] The Vietnamese catfish are
raised in cages that float in marshes in the Mekong
river; some of the senators from the South talk
about the possibility of toxins from Vietnam in
that "dirty" river.[16]

The Issue and Free Trade

Vietnam's catfish industry provides a useful example of how global cooperation can enhance

participation in global business. An Australian importer, for example, taught the Vietnamese how to slice catfish fillet, French researchers worked with a local university on low-cost breeding techniques, and Vietnam's leading catfish exporters depended on American industrial equipment from the United States.[17] However, a stumbling U.S. economy has made American farmers, along with many others in a number of industries, very sensitive to surging imports, and the catfish dispute represents a case of domestic politics aligning against free market forces.[18] Critics in both Vietnam and the United States say that the catfish issue is an example of protectionism and hypocrisy, undermining the free trade policies most recently espoused by the United States at the World Trade Organization talks in Doha.

"After spending years encouraging the Vietnamese that open trade is a win-win situation, it would be a shame if immediately after the trade agreement is signed the United States shifts to a protectionist 'we win, you lose' approach on catfish," says Virginia Foote, president of the U.S.-Vietnam Trade Council in Washington.[19]

In the ongoing dispute of how to manage global trade, agriculture and its cousin aquaculture are very sensitive issues. Industrial nations use farm policy not only to promote their agribusinesses overseas but also to protect their markets and farmers at home. For example, European countries have used their agricultural subsidies to defend their countryside from urban invasion. Developing countries, on the other hand, try to raise their standard of living by breaking into new markets with less expensive products.

Questions for Discussion

1. Is it fair for the Vietnamese catfish importers to step in and capture market share while the market has been expanded due to the significant efforts and investments of the domestic industry? How should quality (if quality differences exist) considerations be reconciled?

2. The label ban would probably make consumers pay a higher price than they would have paid otherwise. Is this right?

3. Can any industry in the United States influence lawmakers to make decisions in their favor?

Notes

1. Catfish Institute—**http://catfishinstitute.com**.

2. Elizabeth Becker, "Delta Farmers Want Copyright on Catfish," *The New York Times,* January 16, 2002, Section A1.

3. Meredith Petran, "Catfish," *Restaurant Business,* February 1, 2000.

4. Margot Cohen and Murray Hiebert, "Muddying the Waters," *Far Eastern Economic Review,* December 6, 2001.

5. "The Vietnamese Invade: Catfish in the South." *The Economist,* October 6, 2001.

6. Philip Brasher, "When Is a Catfish Not a Catfish," *The Washington Post,* December 27, 2001.

7. James Toedman, "Fighting Like Cats and Dogs Over Fish; It's U.S. vs. Vietnamese as Trade Battle Goes Global," *Newsday,* March 10, 2002, F02.

8. "The Vietnamese Invade: Catfish in the South."

9. "One of these negative advertisements, which ran in the national trade weekly *Supermarket News,* tells us in shrill tones, 'Never trust a catfish with a foreign accent!' This ad characterizes Vietnamese catfish as dirty and goes on to say, 'They've grown up flapping around in Third World rivers and dining on whatever they can get their fins on. . . . Those other guys probably couldn't spell U.S. even if they tried.'" Quoted in Senator John McCain's December 18, 2001 press release, **http://mccain.senate.gov/catfish.htm**.

10. Philip Brasher, "When Is a Catfish Not a Catfish."

11. Ibid.

12. Margot Cohen and Murray Hiebert, "Muddying the Waters."

13. Elizabeth Becker, "Delta Farmers Want Copyright on Catfish."

14. Ibid.

15. Tim Brown, "South and Southeast, Vietnam Embroiled in Catfish Controversy," *Marketing News,* October 22, 2001.

16. "The Vietnamese Invade: Catfish in the South."

17. Ibid.

18. James Toedman, "Fighting Like Cats and Dogs Over Fish; It's U.S. vs. Vietnamese as Trade Battle Goes Global."

19. Margot Cohen and Murray Hiebert, "Muddying the Waters."

Equal Exchange Strives for Equality through Fair Trade

When you sip your cup of morning coffee—whether it's in your dorm room or in the trendy coffee shop down the street—you probably don't think about where it came from. Even if you're familiar with the jargon—*arabica beans, varietals, dark roast*—and even if you can name the major coffee-producing countries, such as Costa Rica and Colombia, you probably aren't thinking about the people who grow the beans thousands of miles away. But, the coffee-growing business is so important in Central and South America that it provides many jobs for people who otherwise would be unemployed. When you buy a pound of gourmet coffee at $8 to $9 per pound, about 40 cents actually reaches the farmers who grew it. Where does the rest of the money go? To agents who offer the lowest possible price to buyers who then put their own brand labels on the coffee. The 20 million coffee farmers who are left in poverty call these middlemen "coyotes" because they are perceived to be preying on the poor.

Equal Exchange Inc., a gourmet coffee company founded in 1986 in Canton, Massachusetts, is working to change these practices by engaging in its own ethically and socially responsible way of doing business. By adopting the concept of "fair trade," Equal Exchange buys coffee directly from the growers themselves, eliminating the middlemen. As a result, the growers gain as much as 50 cents more per pound. Because coffee is the leading source of foreign currency in Latin America, this arrangement is significant to the economy of

SOURCE: Adapted from the video case (of the same name) by Louis E. Boone and David L. Kurtz, *Contemporary Business,* 10th ed. (Forth Worth, TX: Harcourt College Publishers, 2002), 80.

the region. It is also significant to each individual coffee farmer. "We used to live in houses made of corn husks," recalls Don Miguel Sifontes, who operates a farm in El Salvador. "Now we have better work, better schools, homes of adobe, and a greater brotherhood of decision makers."

The concept of fair trade, first adopted in Europe about 15 years ago, illustrates the idea that businesses are responsible and accountable to their employees, their customers, and the general public. Equal Exchange growers receive better prices under exclusive agreements with farming cooperatives, customers are guaranteed high-quality coffee at fair prices, and the general public in the growers' regions benefits from projects that the farm cooperatives have undertaken with the additional income they make. Typical projects are reforestation programs, training for doctors and nurses, and the building of new schools. Equal Exchange follows a strict set of fair trade guidelines in its purchase of coffee:

- *Buy directly from small farmer cooperatives.* These cooperatives are owned and run by the farmers themselves. Each cooperative governs the even distribution of income and services, such as education and healthcare. Buying direct means that profits go to the farmers rather than agents or other middlemen, reducing the need for growers to engage in more profitable activities, such as growing marijuana and other illegal endeavors, in order to survive.
- *Pay a fair price.* Equal Exchange pays a guaranteed minimum price for its coffee, regardless of how low the coffee market

itself may drop. This price assures that farmers will be able to make a living wage during downturns. Of course, the price rises as the market rises.

- *Provide advance credit to growers.* Equal Exchange makes credit available to its farmers. Historically, credit was unavailable or offered only at extremely high rates, trapping farmers in debt. "When we sign a contract with producers, we pay up to 60 percent of the contract six months in advance," notes marketing manager Erbin Crowell. "If a hurricane hits, we share the risk." In fact, several years ago, a hurricane did hit—"Mitch" slammed into Nicaragua, causing deaths, injuries, and millions of dollars in damage. Equal Exchange worked with Lutheran World Relief to raise funds for residents who suffered because of the hurricane.

- *Encourage ecologically sustainable farming practices.* Equal Exchange helps growers use environmentally friendly farming methods, protecting both the local environment and consumers from toxic chemicals. In this way, the company demonstrates social responsibility not only to the health of workers and consumers but also to the local environment. The company pays a premium price for certified organic and shade-grown coffee, both of which are better for the environment.

Not surprisingly, Equal Exchange is also ethical in its conduct toward competitors. Recently, when specialty coffee giants Starbucks and Green Mountain announced that they were entering into fair trade agreements with farmers, Equal Exchange publicly congratulated them. "Believe it or not, we want more, not less competition," says Equal Exchange cofounder and coexecutive director Rink Dickinson. "That's because we know these farmers and their struggles. They urgently need more importers to pay a just price. So we encourage our fellow roasters to expand on the modest fair trade programs they've announced so far." With this statement, Dickinson raised the bar of ethical standards in the coffee business—knowing that his company can clear it with ease.

Questions for Discussion

1. Is Equal Exchange trying to contravene the effect of market forces? Is it likely to succeed in the longer term?

2. Suppose Dickinson discovered that one of Equal Exchange's cooperatives was growing illegal products, selling coffee to competitors, or not paying fair wages to workers. What do you think he should do?

3. Visit Equal Exchange's Web site at **http://www.equalexchange.com** to learn about the company. What characteristics of the company do you think are most appealing to consumers?

Part Two

INTERNATIONAL MARKETING

Chapter 6
Building the Knowledge Base
Chapter 7
Exporting, Licensing, and Franchising
Chapter 8
Product Adaptation
Chapter 9
Export Pricing Strategies
Chapter 10
International Communications
Chapter 11
Channels and Distribution Strategies
Cases
Video Cases

Beginning International Marketing Activities

Part Two focuses on the company that is considering whether to fill an unsolicited export order, on the manager who wants to find out how the current product line can be marketed abroad, and on the firm searching for ways to expand its currently limited international activities. It concentrates on low-cost, low-risk international expansion, which permits a firm to enter the global market without an extraordinary commitment of human and financial resources. The reader will share the concerns of small and medium-sized firms—those that need international marketing assistance most and that supply the largest employment opportunities—before progressing to the advanced international marketing activities described in Part Three.

© PHOTODISC, VOL. 22

chapter 6

Building the Knowledge Base

© PHOTODISC/GETTY IMAGES

THE INTERNATIONAL MARKETPLACE   6.1

Welcoming China to International Marketing Research

China's entry into the World Trade Organization was a major step in the transition from a planned economy to a free market system. However, China did not drop its planned approach to the economy overnight—rather, it has been moving steadily toward a free market system for over a decade. During this period, an indigenous marketing research industry also developed in response to the need of industries to understand consumers.

Marketing research firms have proliferated all over China, with the epicenter of research activity in Guangzhou. In 1985, Guangzhou Soft Science Co. set up a marketing department with the help of the Chinese government. From this department, Guangzhou Market Research Co. (GMR), China's first marketing research firm, emerged in 1988.

GMR served as the starting point and model for future marketing research firms. Ex-employees of GMR started new firms, such as South China Marketing Research Co. Ltd., Far-East Marketing Research Co., East Marketing Research Co. Ltd., Guangdong General Marketing Research Ltd., and Market Insight. The birth of GMR and its offspring would not have been possible without the aid of U.S. firm Procter & Gamble (P&G). Support from P&G came in several forms: technology (both software and hardware), professional training, and revenue (P&G was the source of more than 90 percent of GMR's revenues in the early 1990s).

Today, the Chinese marketing research industry has grown to include about 400 firms. While the industry has expanded immensely, most of the firms are small, with almost half of them bringing in annual revenues between $10,000 and $50,000. Total research revenue for 2000 was $181 million, with the majority of projects coming from state-sponsored (government or university) firms.

With the growing sophistication of the Chinese consumer, companies must increasingly rely on marketing research in order to obtain up-to-date information. International firms, eager to appeal to China's massive consumer population, will look to its marketing research sector for insight into local traditions and trends. This will provide an opportunity for rapid growth of China's competitive marketing research industry. The presence of international marketing research firms, such as Gallup and ACNielsen, brings capital and new research techniques to the region. Today, the Chinese marketing research industry may be considered small by world standards. Yet, given sufficiently trained and supported local talent combined with low wages, Chinese marketing research has the potential to grow into a global competitor.

SOURCE: Adapted from Barton Lee, Soumya Saklani, and David Tatterson, "Growing in Guangzhou," *Marketing News*, American Marketing Association, June 10, 2002, 12.

EVEN THOUGH MOST managers recognize the need for domestic marketing research, the single most important cause for failure in the international marketplace is insufficient preparation and information. Major mistakes often occur because the firm and its managers do not have an adequate understanding of the business environment. Hindsight, however, does not lead to an automatic increase in international marketing research. Many firms either do not believe that international market research is worthwhile or face manpower and resource bottlenecks that impede such research. The increase in international marketing practice is also not reflected in the orientation of the articles published in key research journals.[1] Yet building a good knowledge base is a key condition for subsequent marketing success. To do so, one needs to accumulate data and information through research. Two basic forms of research are available to the firm: primary research, where data are collected for specific research purposes, and secondary research, where data that have already been collected are used. This chapter will first outline secondary research issues, focusing primarily on ways to obtain basic information quickly, ensuring that the information is reasonably accurate, and doing so with limited corporate resources. Later, primary research and its ways of answering more in-depth questions for the firm are covered, together with the development of a decision-support system.

Defining the Issue

The American Marketing Association (AMA) defines marketing research as "the function that links the consumer, customer, and public to the marketer through information—information used to identify and define marketing opportunities and problems; generate, refine, and evaluate marketing actions; monitor marketing performance; and improve understanding of marketing as a process. Marketing research specifies the information required to address these issues, designs the method for collecting information, manages and implements the data collection process, analyzes the results, and communicates the findings and their implications."[2]

This very broad statement highlights the fact that research is the link between marketer and market, without which marketing cannot function. It also emphasizes the fact that marketing actions need to be monitored and outlines the key steps of the research process.

A more recent definition states that marketing research is the "systematic and objective identification, collection, analysis and dissemination for the purpose of improving decision making related to the identification and solution of problems and opportunities in marketing."[3] This statement is more specific to research activities for several reasons: It highlights the need for systematic work, indicating that research should be the result of planned and organized activity rather than coincidence. It stresses the need for objectivity and information, reducing the roles of bias, emotions, and subjective judgment. Finally, it addresses the need for the information to relate to specific problems. Marketing research cannot take place in a void; rather, it must have a business purpose.

International marketing research must also be linked to the decision-making process within the firm. The recognition that a situation requires action is the factor that initiates the decision-making process. The problem must then be defined. Often, symptoms are mistaken for causes; as a result, action determined by symptoms may be oriented in the wrong direction.

International and Domestic Research

The tools and techniques of international marketing research are said by some to be exactly the same as those of domestic marketing research, and only the environment differs. However, the environment is precisely what determines how well the tools, techniques, and concepts apply to the international market. Although the objectives of marketing research may be the same, the execution of international research may differ substantially from the process of domestic research. As a result, entirely new tools and techniques may need to be developed. The four primary differences are new parameters, new environments, an increase in the number of factors involved, and a broader definition of competition.

New Parameters

In crossing national borders, a firm encounters parameters not found in domestic marketing. Examples include duties, foreign currencies and changes in their value, different modes of transportation, international documentation, and port facilities. A firm that has done business only domestically will have had little or no prior experience with these requirements and conditions. Information about each of them must be obtained in order for management to make appropriate business decisions. New parameters also emerge because of differing modes of operating internationally. For example, a firm can export, it can license its products, it can engage in a joint venture, or it can carry out foreign direct investment.

New Environments

When deciding to go international in its marketing activities, a firm exposes itself to an unfamiliar environment. Many of the assumptions on which the firm was founded and on which its domestic activities were based may not hold true internationally. Firms need to learn about the culture of the host country, understand its political system, determine its stability, and appreciate the differences in societal structures and language. In addition, they must fully comprehend pertinent legal issues in the host country to avoid operating contrary to local legislation. They should also incorporate the technological level of the society in the marketing plan and understand the economic environment. In short, all the assumptions formulated over the years in the domestic market must be reevaluated. This crucial point has often been neglected, because most managers were born into the environment of their domestic operations and have subconsciously learned to understand the constraints and opportunities of their business activities. The process is analogous to learning one's native language. Being born to a language makes speaking it seem easy. Only in attempting to learn a foreign language do we begin to appreciate the complex structure of languages, the need for rules, and the existence of different patterns.

Number of Factors Involved

Going international often means entering into more than one market. As a result, the number of changing dimensions increases geometrically. Even if every dimension is understood, management must also appreciate the interaction between them. Because of the sheer number of factors, coordination of the interaction becomes increasingly difficult. The international marketing research process can help management with this undertaking.

Broader Definition of Competition

By entering the international market, the firm exposes itself to a much greater variety of competition than existed in the domestic market. For example, when expanding the analysis of an island's food production from a local to an international level, fishery products compete not only with other fishery products but also with meat or even vegetarian substitutes. Similarly, firms that offer labor-saving devices in the domestic marketplace may suddenly face competition from cheap manual labor abroad. Therefore, the firm must, on an ongoing basis, determine the breadth of the competition, track the competitive activities, and, finally, evaluate the actual and potential impact on its own operations.

Recognizing the Need for Research

To serve a market efficiently, firms must learn what customers want, why they want it, and how they go about filling their needs. To enter a market without conducting marketing research places firms, their assets, and their entire operation at risk. Even though most firms recognize the need for domestic marketing research, this need is not fully understood for international marketing activities. Often, decisions concerning entry and expansion in overseas markets and the selection and appointment of distributors are made after a cursory subjective assessment of the situation. The research done is less rigorous, less formal, and less quantitative than for domestic marketing activities. Many business executives appear to view foreign market research as relatively unimportant.

A major reason that firms are reluctant to engage in international marketing activities is the lack of sensitivity to differences in consumer tastes and preferences. Managers tend to assume that their methods are both best and acceptable to all others. This is fortunately not true. What a boring place the world would be if it were!

A second reason is a limited appreciation for the different marketing environments abroad. Often, managers are insufficiently informed about the effect of geographic boundaries and do not understand that even national boundaries need not always coincide with culturally homogeneous societies.[4] In addition, firms are not prepared to accept that distribution systems, industrial applications and uses, the availability of media, or advertising regulations may be entirely different from those in the home market. Barely aware of the differences, many firms are unwilling to spend money to find out about them.

A third reason is the lack of familiarity with national and international data sources and the inability to use them if obtained. As a result, the cost of conducting international marketing research is seen as prohibitively high and therefore not a worthwhile investment relative to the benefits to be gained.[5] However, as *The International Marketplace 6.1* shows, international marketing research is conducted in a growing number of countries. There is wider information collection and more data availability, and the expanding research base also includes more countries than those traditionally researched in marketing, namely the United States and Europe. In addition, the Internet makes international marketing research much easier and much less expensive. Therefore, growing access to the Internet around the world will make research more accessible as well.

Finally, firms often build up their international marketing activities gradually, frequently on the basis of unsolicited orders. Over time, actual business experience in a country or with a specific firms may be used as a substitute for organized research.

Yet, international marketing research is important. It permits management to identify and develop strategies for internationalization. This task includes the identification, evaluation, and comparison of potential foreign market opportunities and subsequent market selection. Second, research is necessary for the development of a marketing plan. The requirements for successful market entry and market penetration need to be determined. Subsequently, the research should define the appropriate marketing mix for each international market and should maintain continuous feedback in order to fine-tune the various marketing elements. Finally, research can provide management with foreign market intelligence to help it anticipate events, take appropriate action, and prepare for global changes.

The Benefits of Research

To carry out international research, firms require resources in terms of both time and money. For the typical smaller firm, those two types of resources are its most precious and scarce commodities. To make a justifiable case for allocating resources to international marketing research, management must understand what that value of research will be. This is even more important for international market research than for domestic market research because the cost tends to be higher. The value of research in making a particular decision may be determined by applying the following equation:

$$V(dr) - V(d) > C(r)$$

where

$V(dr)$ is the value of the decision with the benefit of research;
$V(d)$ is the value of the decision without the benefit of research;

and

$C(r)$ is the cost of research.

Obviously, the value of the decision with the benefit of research should be greater than the value of the decision without research, and the value increase should exceed the cost of the research. Otherwise, international marketing research would be a waste of resources. It may be difficult to quantify the individual values because often the risks and benefits are not easy to ascertain. Realistically, companies and their marketing researchers are often quite pragmatic: their research decisions are guided by research objectives, but constrained by resources.[6] The use of decision theory permits a comparison of alternative research strategies.[7]

Determining Research Objectives

Research objectives will vary from firm to firm because of the views of management, the corporate mission, and the marketing situation. In addition, the information needs of firms are closely linked with the level of existing international expertise. The firm may therefore wish to start out by determining its internal level of readiness to participate in the global market. This includes a general review of corporate capabilities such as personnel resources and the degree of financial exposure and risk that the firm is willing and able to tolerate. Existing diagnostic tools can be used to compare a firm's current preparedness on a broad-based level.[8] Knowing its internal readiness, the firm can then pursue its objectives with more confidence.

Going International: Exporting

The most frequent objective of international market research is that of **foreign-market opportunity analysis.** When a firm launches its international activities, basic information is needed to identify and compare key alternatives. The aim is not to conduct a painstaking and detailed analysis of the world on a market-by-market basis but instead to utilize a broad-brush approach. Accomplished quickly at low cost, this can narrow down the possibilities for international marketing activities.

Such an approach should begin with a cursory analysis of general market variables such as total and per capita GDP, mortality rates, and population figures. Although these factors in themselves will not provide detailed market information, they will enable the researcher to determine whether the corporation's objectives might be met in those markets. For example, expensive labor-saving consumer products may not be successful in the People's Republic of China because their price may be a significant proportion of the annual salary of the customer, and the perceived benefit to the customer may be only minimal. Such cursory evaluation will help reduce the number of markets to be considered to a more manageable number—for example, from 200 to 25.

Next, the researcher will require information about each individual market for a preliminary evaluation. This information typically identifies the fastest-growing markets, the largest markets for a particular product, market trends, and market restrictions. Although precise and detailed information for each product probably cannot be obtained, it is available for general product categories.

Governmental restrictions on markets must be considered as well. As an example, we can determine that Iraq represents a fast-growing market for computer hardware and software. However, an inspection of export licensing regulations may reveal that computer trade with Iraq is prohibited. Again, this overview will be cursory but will serve to evaluate markets quickly and reduce the number of markets subject to closer investigation.

At this stage, the researcher must select appropriate markets. The emphasis will shift to focus on market opportunities for a specific product or brand, including existing, latent, and incipient markets. Even though the aggregate industry data have already been obtained, general information is insufficient to make company-specific decisions. For example, the market demand for medical equipment should not be confused with the potential demand for a specific brand. In addition, the research should identify demand-and-supply patterns and evaluate any regulations and standards. Finally, a competitive assessment needs to be made that matches markets with corporate strengths and provides an analysis of the best market potential for specific products. Figure 6.1 offers a summary of the various stages in the determination of market potential.

Figure 6.1   A Sequential Process of Researching Foreign Market Potentials

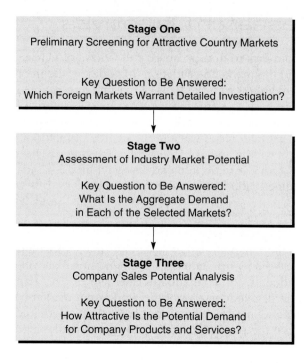

SOURCE: S. Tamer Cavusgil, "Guidelines for Export Market Research," Reprinted with permission from *Business Horizons* 28 (November–December 1985): 29. Copyright 1985 by the Trustees at Indiana University, Kelley School of Business.

Going International: Importing

When importing, firms shift their major focus from supplying to sourcing. Management must identify markets that produce desired supplies or materials or that have the potential to do so. Foreign firms must be evaluated in terms of their capabilities and competitive standing.

The importer needs to know, for example, about the reliability of a foreign supplier, the consistency of its product or service quality, and the length of delivery time. Information obtained through the subsidiary office of a bank or through one's embassy can be very helpful. Information from business rating services and recommendations from current customers are also very useful in evaluating the potential business partner.

In addition, government rules must be scrutinized as to whether exportation from the source country is possible. For example, India may set limits on the cobra handbags it allows to be exported, and laws protecting cultural heritage may prevent the exportation of pre-Columbian artifacts from Latin American countries. The international manager must also analyze domestic restrictions and legislation that may prohibit the importation of certain goods into the home country. Even though a market may exist in the United States for foreign umbrella handles, for example, quotas may restrict their importation in order to protect domestic industries. Similarly, even though domestic demand may exist for ivory, its importation may be illegal because of worldwide legislation enacted to protect wildlife.

Market Expansion

Research objectives may include obtaining detailed information for penetrating a market, for designing and fine-tuning the marketing mix, or for monitoring the political climate of a country so that the firm can expand its operation successfully. The better defined the research objective is, the better the researcher will be able to determine the information requirements and thus conserve time and financial resources of the firm.

Determining Secondary Information Requirements

Using the research objective as a guide, the researcher will be able to pinpoint the type of information needed. For example, if only general initial market information is required, perhaps macro data such as world population statistics will be sufficient. If research is to identify market restraints, then perhaps information is required about international accords and negotiations in the WTO. Alternatively, broad product category, production, and trade figures may be desired in order to pinpoint general market activities. For the fine-tuning of a marketing mix, very specific detailed product data may be necessary. This often entails gathering data on both a macro and micro level. On the macro level, these are typically tariff and nontariff information, and data on government trade policy. On the micro level, these tend to be data on local laws and regulations, local standards and specifications, distribution systems, and competitive activities.

[handwritten margin note: Why do countries want FDI?]

Sources of Data

Secondary data for international marketing research purposes are available from a wide variety of sources. The major ones are briefly reviewed here. In addition, Appendix A to this chapter lists a wide variety of publications and organizations that monitor international issues.

Governments

Of all data sources, governments typically have the greatest variety of data available. Typically, the information provided by governments addresses either macro or micro issues or offers specific data services. Macro information includes population trends, general trade flows between countries, and world agricultural production. Micro information includes materials on specific industries in a country, their growth prospects, and their foreign trade activities. Specific data services might provide custom-tailored information responding to the detailed needs of a firm. Alternatively, some data services may concentrate on a specific geographic region. More information about selected government publications and research services is presented in Appendix A to this chapter. *The International Marketplace 6.2* explains some of the information services offered by the European Union.

   Most countries have a wide array of national and international trade data available. Increasingly these data are available on the Internet, which makes them much more current than ever before. Closer collaboration between governmental statistical agencies also makes the data more accurate and reliable, since it is now much easier to compare data such as bilateral exports and imports to each other. These information sources are often available at embassies and consulates, whose mission includes the enhancement of trade activities. The commercial counselor or commercial attaché can provide the information available from these sources.

International Organizations

International organizations often provide useful data for the researcher. The *Statistical Yearbook* produced by the United Nations (UN) contains international trade data on products and provides information on exports and imports by country. Because of the time needed for worldwide data collection, the information is often dated. Additional information is compiled and made available by specialized substructures of the UN. Some of these are the UN Conference on Trade and Development (**http://www.unctad.org**), which concentrates primarily on international issues surrounding developing nations, such as debt and market access, the UN Center on Transnational Corporations, and the International Trade Centre

THE INTERNATIONAL MARKETPLACE 6.2

Secondary Data Sources in Europe

With the expanding economic and political union within Europe, official information resources are becoming more centralized. A short sampling of government sources of information helpful to international managers targeting the EU are reviewed below. All of them are accessible through EUROPA (**http://europa.eu.int**), which is the portal site of the European Union.

News

"News" is aimed principally at journalists and other people professionally involved in the information industry. It contains links to the virtual press rooms of the various EU institutions and information on major forthcoming events.

Activities

"Activities" sets out the Union's activities by subject, giving an overview of the policies as well as more detailed information for students and professionals.

Institutions

"Institutions" provides a general introduction to each of the institutions and to European decision-making procedures. It also contains links to the institutions' homepages.

The EU at a Glance

"The EU at a Glance" is aimed at the general public and sets out to provide clear answers to key questions concerning such things as the objectives of the European Union, European citizens' rights, and the history of the EU.

Official Documents

"Official Documents" provides access to the conclusions of European Councils, the General Report on the activities of the European Union, and the Bulletin of the European Union. Other documents, such as the Official Journal, the Treaties, and documents on current legislation and legislation under preparation may be obtained via EUR-Lex.

Information Sources

"Information Sources" is a gateway to various databases, information services, and official publications about the European Union. It also provides access to the latest statistics and the list of information relays in the European Union.

SOURCE: EUROPA—Frequently Asked Questions (FAQs), **http://europa.eu.int/abouteuropa/faq/q4/index_en.htm**, accessed October 8, 2002.

(**http://www.intracen.org**). The *World Atlas* published by the World Bank (**http://www.worldbank.org**) provides useful general data on population, growth trends, and GNP figures. The World Trade Organization (**http://www.wto.org**) and the Organization for Economic Cooperation and Development (OECD) (**http://www.oecd.org**) also publish quarterly and annual trade data on their member countries. Organizations such as the International Monetary Fund (**http://www.imf.org**) and the World Bank publish summary economic data and occasional staff papers that evaluate region- or country-specific issues in depth.

Service Organizations

A wide variety of service organizations that may provide information include banks, accounting firms, freight forwarders, airlines, and international trade consultants. Frequently, they are able to provide data on business practices, legislative or regulatory requirements, and political stability as well as basic trade data. Although some of this information is available without charge, its basic intent is to serve as an "appetizer." Much of the initial information is quite general in nature; more detailed answers often require an appropriate fee.

Trade Associations

Associations such as world trade clubs and domestic and international chambers of commerce (for example, the American Chamber of Commerce abroad) can provide valuable information about local markets. Often, files are maintained on international trade issues and trends affecting international marketers. Useful information can also be obtained from industry associations. These groups, formed to represent entire industry segments, often collect from their members a wide variety of data that are then published in an aggregate form. The information provided is often quite general in nature because of the wide variety of clientele served. It can provide valuable initial insights into international markets, since it permits a benchmarking effort through which the international marketer can establish how it is faring when compared to its competition. For example, an industry summary that indicates firm average exports to be 10 percent of sales, and export sales growth to take place mainly in Asia, allows a better evaluation of a specific firm's performance by the international marketer.

Directories and Newsletters

Many industry directories are available on local, national, and international levels. These directories primarily serve to identify firms and to provide very general background information such as the name of the chief executive officer, the address and telephone number, and some information about a firm's products. The quality of a directory depends, of course, on the quality of input and the frequency of updates. Some of the directories are becoming increasingly sophisticated and can provide quite detailed information to the researcher.

Many newsletters are devoted to specific international issues such as international trade finance, international contracting, bartering, countertrade, international payment flows, and customs news. Published by banks or accounting firms in order to keep their clientele current on international developments, newsletters usually cater to narrow audiences but can provide important information to the firm interested in a specific area.

Electronic Information Services

When information is needed, managers often cannot spend a lot of time, energy, or money finding, sifting through, and categorizing existing materials. Consider laboring through every copy of a trade publication to find out the latest news on how environmental concerns are affecting marketing decisions in Mexico. With electronic information services, search results can be obtained almost immediately. International online computer database services, numbering in the thousands, can be purchased to supply information external to the firm, such as exchange rates, international news, and import restrictions. Most database hosts do not charge any sign-up fee and request payment only for actual use. The selection of initial database hosts depends on the choice of relevant databases, taking into account their product and market limitations, language used, and geographical location.

A large number of databases and search engines provide information about products and markets. Many of the main news agencies through online databases provide information about events that affect certain markets. Some databases cover extensive lists of companies in given countries and the products they buy and sell. A large number of databases exist that cover various categories of trade statistics. The main economic indicators of the UN, IMF, OECD, and EU are available online. Standards institutes in most of the G7 nations provide online access to their databases of technical standards and trade regulations on specific products.

Compact Disk/Read-Only Memory (CD-ROM) technology allows for massive amounts of information (the equivalent of 300 books of 1,000 pages each, or 1,500 floppy disks) to be stored on a single 12-centimeter plastic disk. The technology increasingly is used for storing and distributing large volumes of information, such as statistical databases. Typically, the user pays no user fees but instead invests in a CD-ROM "reader" and purchases the actual CDs.

A CD-ROM service widely used in the United States is the National Trade Data Bank (NTDB), a monthly product issued by the U.S. Department of Commerce. The NTDB includes more than 170,000 documents, including full-text market research reports, domestic and foreign economic data, import and export statistics, trade information and country studies, all compiled from 26 government agencies. The NTDB can also provide profiles of screened businesses that are interested in importing U.S. products.

Using data services for research means that researchers do not have to leave their offices, going from library to library to locate the facts they need. Many online services have late-breaking information available within 24 hours to the user. These research techniques are cost-effective as well. Stocking a company's library with all the books needed to have the same amount of data that is available online or with CD-ROM would be too expensive and space-consuming. However, there are also drawbacks. In spite of the ease of access to data on the Internet, search engines cover only a portion of international publications. Also, they are heavily biased toward English-language publications. As a result, sole reliance on electronic information may cause the researcher to lose out on valuable input.[9] Electronic databases should therefore be seen as only one important dimension of research scrutiny.

Other Firms

Often, other firms can provide useful information for international marketing purposes. Firms appear to be more open about their international than about their domestic marketing activities. On some occasions, valuable information can also be obtained from foreign firms and distributors.

Evaluating Data

Before obtaining secondary data, the researcher needs to evaluate their appropriateness for the task at hand. As the first step of such an evaluation, the quality of the data source needs to be considered with a primary focus on the purpose and method of the original data collection. Next, the quality of the actual data needs to be assessed, which should include a determination of data accuracy, reliability, and recency. Obviously, outdated data may mislead rather than improve the decision-making process. In addition, the compatibility and comparability of the data need to be considered. Since they were collected with another purpose in mind, we need to determine whether the data can help with the issue of concern to the firm. In international research it is also important to ensure that data categories are comparable to each other, in order to avoid misleading conclusions. For example, the term *middle class* is likely to have very different implications for income and consumption patterns in different parts of the world.

Analyzing and Interpreting Secondary Data

After the data have been obtained, the researcher must use his or her research creativity to make good use of them. This often requires the combination and cross tabulation of various sets of data or the use of proxy information in order to arrive at conclusions that address the research objectives. A **proxy variable** is a substitute for a variable that one cannot directly measure. For example, the market penetration of television sets may be used as a proxy variable for the potential market demand for DVD players. Similarly, in an industrial setting, information about plans for new port facilities may be useful in determining future containerization requirements. Also, the level of computerization of a society may indicate the future need for software.

The researcher must go beyond the scope of the data and use creative inferences to arrive at knowledge useful to the firm. However, such creativity brings risks. Once the interpretation and analysis have taken place, a consistency check must be conducted. The researcher should always cross-check the results with other possible sources of information or with experts.

In addition, the researcher should take another look at the research methods employed and, based on their usefulness, determine any necessary modifications for future projects. This will make possible the continuous improvement of international market research activities and enables the corporation to learn from experience.

Data Privacy

The attitude of society toward obtaining and using both secondary and primary data must be taken into account. Many societies are increasingly sensitive to the issue of data privacy, and the concern has grown exponentially as a result of e-business. Readily accessible databases may contain information valuable to marketers, but they may also be considered privileged by individuals who have provided the data.

In 2002, the European Union passed a directive on privacy and electronic communications. Extending earlier legislation, it maintains high standards of data privacy to ensure the free flow of data throughout the 15 member states. The new directive requires member states to block transmission of data to non-EU countries if these countries do not have domestic legislation that provides for a level of protection judged as adequate by the European Union. The EU has a strict interpretation of its citizens' rights to privacy. There is an opt-in approach for unsolicited e-mails: online marketing firms and other Internet operators can send commercial e-mails only after the customer has specifically asked them to do so. The placement of invisible data-tracking devices such as "cookies" on a computer is prohibited until after a user has been provided with adequate information about their purpose.

The directive also reflects a EU compromise in light of the September 11 attacks and the growing frequency of cybercrime. Due to requests by key e-commerce partners, such as the United States, revisions were made to EU policy to accommodate criminal investigation. Under the new directive, companies in the EU will still have to erase information immediately after the one- to-two month period needed for billing purposes. However, governments can now require operators to store data for longer periods of time, if deemed necessary for security reasons.[10]

In order to settle conflicts between divergent government policies, companies are increasingly likely to adapt global privacy rules for managing information online and to get certified by watchdog groups, which tell users when a site adheres to specific privacy guidelines.[11] Overall, the international marketer must pay careful attention to the privacy laws and expectations in different nations and to possible consumer reactions to the use of data in the marketing effort.

The Primary Research Process

Primary research is conducted to fill specific information needs. The research may not actually be conducted by the firm with the need, but the work must be carried out for a specific research purpose. Primary research therefore goes beyond the activities of secondary data collection, which often cannot supply answers to the specific questions posed. Conducting primary research internationally can be complex due to different environments, attitudes, and market conditions. Yet, it is precisely because of these differences that such research is necessary. Nonetheless, at this time, marketing research is still mainly concentrated in the industrialized nations of the world. Global marketing research expenditures were estimated to be $15.9 billion in 2002. Of that amount, about three-quarters were spent in the United States and the European Union.[12]

Primary research is essential for the formulation of strategic marketing plans. One particular area of research interest is international market segmentation. Historically, firms segmented international markets based on macro variables such as income per capita or consumer spending on certain product categories. Increasingly, however, firms recognize that segmentation variables, such as lifestyles, attitudes, or personality, can play a major role in identifying similar consumer groups in different countries, which can then be targeted across borders. One such group could consist, for example, of educationally elite readers who read *Scientific American, Time, Newsweek, The Financial Times,* and *The Economist.* Members in this group are likely to have more in common with one another than with their fellow citizens.[13] Alternatively, in marketing to women, it is important to understand the degree to which they have entered the workforce in a country and how women in different economic segments make or influence purchase decisions. In order to identify these groups and to devise ways of meeting their needs, primary international market research is indispensable.

Determining Information Requirements

Specific research questions must be formulated to determine precisely the information that is sought. The following are examples of such marketing questions:

- ➤ What is the market potential for our furniture in Indonesia?
- ➤ How much does the typical Nigerian consumer spend on soft drinks?
- ➤ What will happen to demand in Brazil if we raise our product price along monthly inflation levels?
- ➤ What effect will a new type of packaging have on our "green" consumers in Germany, France, and England?

Only when information requirements are determined as precisely as possible will the researcher be able to develop a research program that will deliver a useful product.

Industrial versus Consumer Research

The researcher must decide whether to conduct research with consumers or with industrial users. This decision will in part determine the size of the universe and respondent accessibility. For example, consumers are usually a very large group and can be reached through interviews at home or through intercept techniques. On the other hand, the total population of industrial users may be smaller and more difficult to reach. Further, cooperation by respondents may be quite different, ranging from very helpful to very limited. In the industrial setting, differentiating between users and decision makers may be much more important because their personality, their outlook, and their evaluative criteria may differ widely.

Determining Research Administration

The major issues in determining who will do the research are whether to use a centralized, coordinated, or decentralized approach and whether to engage an outside research service.

Degree of Research Centralization

The level of control that corporation headquarters exercises over international marketing research activities is a function of the overall organizational structure of the firm and the nature and importance of the decision to be made. The three major approaches to international research organization are the centralized, coordinated, and decentralized approaches.

The centralized approach clearly affords the most control to headquarters. All **research specifications** such as focus, thrust, and design are directed by the home office and are forwarded to the local country operations for implementation. The subsequent analysis of gathered information again takes place at headquarters. Such an approach can be quite valuable when international marketing research is intended to influence corporate policies and strategy. It also ensures that all international market studies remain comparable to one another. On the other hand, some risks exist. For example, headquarters management may not be sufficiently familiar with the local market situation to be able to adapt the research appropriately. Also, headquarters cultural bias may influence the research activities. Finally, headquarters staff may be too small or insufficiently skilled to provide proper guidance for multiple international marketing research studies.

A coordinated research approach uses an intermediary such as an outside research agency to bring headquarters and country operations together. This approach provides for more interaction and review of the international marketing research plan by both headquarters and the local operations and ensures more responsiveness to both strategic and local concerns. If the intermediary used is of high quality, the research capabilities of a corporation can be greatly enhanced through a coordinated approach.

The decentralized approach requires corporate headquarters to establish the broad thrust of research activities and to then delegate the further design and implementation to the local countries. The entire research is then carried out locally under the supervision of the local country operation, and only a final report is provided to headquarters. This approach has particular value when international markets differ significantly, because it permits detailed adaptation to local circumstances. However, implementing research activities on a country-by-country basis may cause unnecessary duplication, lack of knowledge transference, and lack of comparable results.

Local country operations may not be aware of research carried out by corporate units in other countries and may reinvent the wheel. This problem can be avoided if a proper intracorporate flow of information exists so that local units can check whether similar information has already been collected elsewhere within the firm. Corporate units that operate in markets similar to one another can then benefit from the exchange of research findings.

Local units may also develop their own research thrusts, tools, and analyses. A researcher in one country may, for example, develop a creative way of dealing with a nonresponse problem. This new technique could be valuable to company researchers who face similar difficulties in other countries. However, for the technique to become widely known, systems must be in place to circulate information to the firm as a whole.

Finally, if left to their own devices, researchers will develop different ways of collecting and tabulating data. As a result, findings in different markets may not be comparable, and potentially valuable information about major changes and trends may be lost to the corporation.

International marketing research activities will always be carried out subject to the organizational structure of a firm. Ideally, a middle ground between centralization and decentralization will be found, one that permits local flexibility together with an ongoing exchange of information within the corporation. As the extent of a firm's international activities grows, the exchange of information becomes particularly important, because global rather than local optimization is the major goal of the multinational corporation.

Outside Research Services

One major factor in deciding whether or not to use outside research services is, of course, the size of the international operations of a firm. No matter how large a firm is, however, it is unlikely to possess specialized expertise in international marketing research for every single market it currently serves or is planning to serve. Rather than overstretch the capabilities of its staff or assert a degree of expertise that does not exist, a corporation may wish to delegate the research task to outside groups. This is particularly the case when corporate headquarters have little or no familiarity with the local research environment. Figure 6.2 provides an example of such a situation. The use of outside research agencies may be especially appropriate for large-scale international marketing research or when highly specialized research skills are required. Increasingly, marketing research agencies operate worldwide, in order to accommodate the research needs of their clients. Table 6.1 provides information about the top 25 global research organizations and their international activities.

The selection process for outside research providers should emphasize the quality of information rather than the cost. Low price is no substitute for data pertinence or accuracy.

Before a decision is made, the capabilities of an outside organization should be carefully evaluated and compared with the capabilities available in-house and from

Figure 6.2   Research Agencies Understand the Importance of Cultural Adaptation

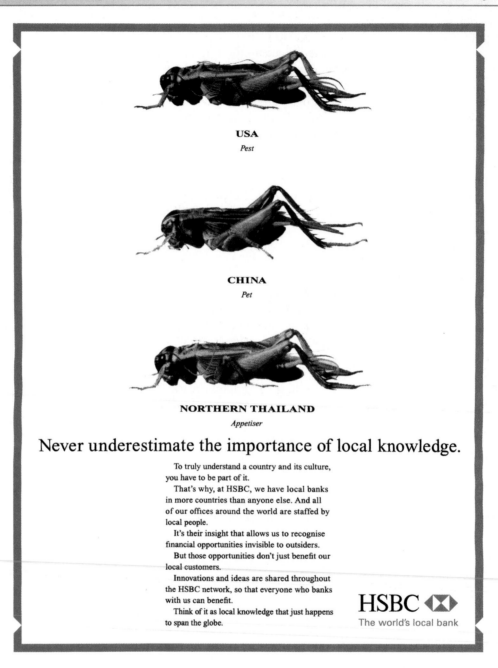

SOURCE: Advertisement issued by HSBC Holdings PLC.

competing firms. Although general technical capabilities are important, the prime selection criterion should be previous research experience in a particular country and a particular industry. Some experience is transferable from one industry or country to another; however, the more the corporation's research needs overlap an agency's past research accomplishment, the more likely it is that the research task will be carried out satisfactorily. Although the research may be more difficult to administer, multinational corporations should consider subcontracting each major international marketing research task to specialists, even if research within one country is carried out by various international marketing research agencies as a

Table 6.1   Top 25 Global Research Organizations

Rank	Organization	Headquarters	Parent country	Web site	No. of countries with subsidiaries/ branch offices[1]	Global research revenues[2] (U.S. $ in millions)	Percent of global revenues from outside home country
1	VNU NV	Haarlem	Netherlands	www.vnu.com	81	$2,400.0	100.0%
2	IMS Health Inc.	Fairfield, Conn.	U.S.	imshealth.com	74	1,171.0	60.0
3	WPP plc	London	U.K.	wpp.com	62	1,006.9	68.9
	The Kantar Group	Fairfield, Conn.	U.K.	www.kantargroup.com	62	962.3	68.9
	Icon Branc Navigation	Nuremberg, Germany	U.K.	Icon-brand-navigation.com	6	44.6	23.2
4	Taylor Nelson Sofres plc	London	U.K.	www.tnsofres.com	50	813.2	78.6
5	Information Resources Inc.	Chicago	U.S.	www.infores.com	20	555.9	24.4
6	GfK Group	Nuremberg, Germany	Germany	www.gfk.com	48	479.6	61.9
7	NFO WorldGroup Inc.	Greenwich, Conn.	U.S.	www.nfow.com	40	452.9	64.0
8	Ipsos Group SA	Paris	France	www.ipsos.com	28	429.9	82.7
9	NOP World	London	U.K.	www.nopworld.com	7	324.7	52.9
	NOP World	London	U.K.	www.nopworld.com	7	249.9	64.2
	Roper Starch Worldwide	New York	U.S.	www.roperasw.com	2	74.8	16.9
10	Westat Inc.	Rockville, Md.	U.S.	www.westat.com	1	285.8	0.0
11	Synovate	London	U.K.	www.aegisplc.com	43	266.5	97.0
12	Arbitron Inc.	New York	U.S.	arbitron.com	2	227.5	3.5
13	Maritz Research	Fenton, Mo.	U.S.	www.maritzresearch.com	5	181.7	30.7
14	Video Research Ltd.	Tokyo	Japan	www.videor.cojp	3	162.2	1.0
15	Opinion Research Corp.	Princeton, N.J.	U.S.	www.opinionresearch.com	8	133.6	31.6
16	J.D. Power and Associates	Westlake Village, Calif.	U.S.	jdpa.com	5	128.0	14.5
17	INTAGE inc.	Tokyo	Japan	www.intage.cojp	2	108.5	3.4
18	The NPD Group Inc.	Port Washington, N.Y.	U.S.	npd.com	11	101.7	12.9
19	Jupiter Media Metrix Inc.	New York	U.S.	jmm.com	7	85.8	20.0
20	Dentsu Research Inc.	Tokyo	Japan	www.dentsuresearch.co.jp	1	78.4	0.3
21	Harris Interactive Inc.	Rochester, N.Y.	U.S.	www.harrisinteractive.com	11	75.4	13.9
22	Abt Associates Inc.	Cambridge, Mass.	U.S.	abtassociates.com	3	62.8	15.0
23	Sample Institut GmbH & Co.KG	Molin	Germany	inra.de	5	59.2	57.6
24	IBOPE Group	Rio de Janeiro	Brazil	www.ibope.com.br	13	56.1	33.2
25	MORPACE International Inc.	Farmington Hills, Mich.	U.S.	morpace.com	3	48.3	32.9
25	Nikkei Research Inc.	Tokyo	Japan	nikkeiresearch.com	4	48.3	5.0
	Total					**$9,743.9**	**63.3%**

1. Includes countries which have subsidiaries with an equity interest or branch offices or both.
2. Total revenues that include nonresearch activities for some companies are significantly higher. This information is given in the individual company profits.

SOURCE: *Marketing News*, August 19, 2000, H4.

result. To have experts working on a problem is usually more efficient than to conserve corporate resources by centralizing all research activities with one service provider, who is only marginally familiar with key aspects of the research. However, if different firms carry out the research, it becomes very important to ensure that data are comparable. Otherwise, the international firm will not be able to transfer lessons learned from one market to another.

Determining the Research Technique

Selection of the research technique depends on a variety of factors. First, the objectivity of the data sought must be determined. Standardized techniques are more useful in the collection of objective data than of subjective data. *Unstructured data* will require more open-ended questions and more time than structured data. Since the willingness and ability of respondents to spend the time and provide a free-form response are heavily influenced by factors such as culture and education, the prevailing conditions in the country and segments to be studied need to be understood in making these decisions. Whether the data are to be collected in the real world or in a controlled environment also must be decided. Finally, a decision needs to be made as to whether the research is to collect historical facts or gather information about future developments. This is particularly important for consumer research because firms frequently desire to determine consumers' future intentions to purchase a certain product.

Cultural and individual preferences, which vary significantly among nations, play a major role in determining research techniques. U.S. managers frequently prefer to gather large quantities of hard data through surveys, which provide numbers that can be manipulated statistically and directly compared to other sets of data. In some other countries managers appear to prefer the "soft" approach. For example, much of Japanese-style market research relies heavily on two kinds of information: soft data obtained from visits to dealers and other channel members and hard data about shipments, inventory levels, and retail sales.

Once the structure of the type of data sought has been determined, a choice must be made among the types of research instruments available. Each provides a different depth of information and has its unique strengths and weaknesses.

Interviews   Interviews with knowledgeable persons can be of great value to a corporation desiring international marketing information. Because bias from the individual may be part of the findings, the intent should be to obtain in-depth information rather than a wide variety of data. Particularly when specific answers are sought to very narrow questions, interviews can be most useful.

Focus Groups   Focus groups are a useful research tool resulting in interactive interviews. A group of knowledgeable persons is gathered for a limited period of time (two to four hours). Usually, the ideal size for a focus group is seven to ten participants. A specific topic is introduced and thoroughly discussed by all group members. Because of the interaction, hidden issues are sometimes raised that would not have been addressed in an individual interview. The skill of the group leader in stimulating discussion is crucial to the success of a focus group. Discussions are often recorded on tape and subsequently analyzed in detail. Focus groups, like in-depth interviews, do not provide statistically significant information; however, they can be helpful in providing information about perceptions, emotions, and other nonovert factors. In addition, once individuals are gathered, focus groups are highly efficient in terms of rapidly accumulating a substantial amount of information. With the advances occurring in the communications field, focus groups can also be carried out internationally, with interaction between groups.

When conducting international research via focus groups, the researcher must be aware of the importance of culture in the discussion process. Not all societies encourage frank and open exchange and disagreement among individuals. Status

THE INTERNATIONAL MARKETPLACE   6.3

Adapting Research Procedures to Local Conditions

Globalization has brought marketing research to new regions of the world. A key challenge is to adapt research procedures to the local environment. Just as understanding culture is important to the development of marketing strategy, it is equally important to keep local traditions and constraints in mind when initiating marketing research efforts.

The distinct cultural environment of Middle Eastern countries requires changes in traditional Western-style approaches to marketing research. One such change concerns gender roles. For example, focus groups are typically a popular way for researchers to obtain information about local consumers. By gathering a random group of people together, the researcher hopes to obtain ideas about which products are popular and which marketing tactics are successful. However, traditional Muslim culture favors male dominance and strict interpretation of Islam demands segregation of the sexes. As a result, mixed-gender focus groups are difficult, if not illegal, to congregate. Even when permissible in the most Westernized countries, such as Egypt, mixed focus groups tend to suffer from male dominance, which makes their insights unbalanced: women will often defer to men and allow them to speak on their behalf. Also, female marketing researchers will encounter difficulties in countries such as Saudi Arabia, where women are barred from assuming professional roles.

The growing need to use technology in international marketing research also proves problematic in Muslim countries. For one, the postal system is often unreliable and Internet access is limited. Because governments restrict access to Western ideas via the Internet, Web-based surveys also have to be ruled out as a widely used method of information collection. The small percentage of the population that does have access to the Internet is composed of the upper class; thus Internet surveys would yield skewed results and fail to represent the population as a whole.

As a result of barriers to communication, research efforts in Muslim countries tend to take much longer than those in Western countries. Researchers must rely on word-of-mouth in order to recruit participants, which in itself is difficult due to the unfamiliarity of the general public with the concept of marketing research. Furthermore, word-of-mouth contacts can lead to collection of information from a small range of participants: if each person is recruited by someone they know, chances are that variety in opinion and experiences is not great.

SOURCE: Adapted from Steve Jarvis, "Western-Style Research in the Middle East," *Marketing News*, American Marketing Association, April 29, 2002, 37.

consciousness may result in situations in which the opinion of one is reflected by all other participants. Disagreement may be seen as impolite, or certain topics may be taboo.

The International Marketplace 6.3 explains in more detail how research processes need to adjust to cultural constraints.

Observation   Observation techniques require the researcher to play the role of a nonparticipating observer of activity and behavior. Observation can be personal or impersonal—for example, mechanical. Observation can be obtrusive or inobtrusive, depending on whether the subject is aware or unaware of being observed. In international marketing research, observation can be extremely useful in shedding light on practices not previously encountered or understood. This aspect is particularly valuable for the researcher who is totally unfamiliar with a market or market situation and can be quickly achieved through, for example, participation in a trade mission. Observation can also help in understanding phenomena that would have been difficult to assess with other techniques. For example, Toyota sent a group of its engineers and designers to southern California to unobtrusively observe how women get into and operate their cars. They found that women with long fingernails have trouble opening the door and operating various knobs on the dashboard. Based on their observations, Toyota engineers and designers were able to observe the women's plight and redraw some of the automobile exterior and interior designs.[14]

Conducting observations can also have its pitfalls. For example, people may react differently to the discovery that their behavior has been observed. The degree to which the observer has to be familiarized or introduced to other participants may vary. The complexity of the task may differ due to the use of multiple languages. To conduct in-store research in Europe, for example, store checks, photo audits of shelves, and store interviews must be scheduled well in advance and need to be preceded by a full round of introductions of the researchers to store management and personnel. In some countries, such as Belgium, a researcher must remember that four different languages are spoken and their use may change from store to store.

The research instruments discussed so far—interviews, focus groups, and observation—are useful primarily for gathering **qualitative data.** The intent is not to amass data or to search for statistical significance, but rather to obtain a better understanding of given situations, behavioral patterns, or underlying dimensions. The researcher using these instruments must be cautioned that even frequent repetition of the measurements will not lead to a statistically valid result. Yet, statistical validity often is not the major focus of corporate international marketing research. Rather, it is the better understanding, description, and prediction of events that have an impact on marketing decision making. When **quantitative data** are desired, surveys are appropriate research instruments.

Surveys

Survey research is useful in providing the opportunity to quantify concepts. In the social sciences, the cross-cultural survey is generally accepted as a powerful method of hypothesis testing. Surveys are usually conducted via questionnaires that are administered personally, by mail, or by telephone. Use of the survey technique presupposes that the population under study is able to comprehend and respond to the questions posed. Also, particularly in the case of mail and telephone surveys, a major precondition is the feasibility of using the postal system or the widespread availability of telephones. In many countries, only limited records are available about dwellings, their location, and their occupants. In Venezuela, for example, most houses are not numbered but rather are given individual names like "Casa Rosa" or "El Retiro." In some countries, street maps are not even available. As a result, it becomes virtually impossible to reach respondents by mail.

In other countries, obtaining a correct address may be easy, but the postal system may not function well. The Italian postal service, for example, repeatedly has suffered from scandals that exposed such practices as selling undelivered mail to paper mills for recycling.

Telephone surveys may also be inappropriate if telephone ownership is rare. In such instances, any information obtained would be highly biased even if the researcher randomizes the calls. In some instances, telephone networks and systems may also prevent the researcher from conducting surveys. Frequent line congestion and a lack of telephone directories are examples. There are also great variations between countries or regions of countries in terms of unlisted telephone numbers. For example, the percentage of households with unlisted telephone numbers varies widely by country and even city.

Surveys can be hampered by social and cultural constraints. Recipients of letters may be illiterate or may be reluctant to respond in writing. In some nations, entire population segments—for example, women—may be totally inaccessible to interviewers. One must also assess the purpose of the survey in the context of the population surveyed. It has been argued, for example, that one should not rely on consumer surveys for new product development information. Key reasons are the absence of responsibility—the consumer is sincere when spending but not when talking; conservative attitudes—ordinary consumers are conservative and tend to react negatively to a new product; vanity—it is human nature to exaggerate and put on a good appearance; and insufficient information—the research results depend on the product characteristics information that is given to survey participants and that may be incomplete or unabsorbed.[15]

In spite of all these difficulties, however, the survey technique remains a useful one because it allows the researcher to rapidly accumulate a large quantity of data amenable to statistical analysis. Even though quite difficult, **international comparative research** has been carried out very successfully between nations, particularly if the environments studied are sufficiently similar so that the impact of uncontrollable macrovariables is limited. However, even in environments that are quite dissimilar, in-depth comparative research can be carried out.[16] Doing so may require a country-by-country adjustment of details while preserving the similarity of research thrust. For example, researchers have reported good results in mail surveys conducted simultaneously in Japan and the United States after adjusting the size of the return envelope, outgoing envelope, address style, signature, and cover letter to meet specific societal expectations.[17] With constantly expanding technological capabilities, international marketers will be able to use the survey technique more frequently in the future. Figure 6.3 provides an overview of the extent of the technology available to help the international research process.

Designing the Survey Questionnaire

International marketing surveys are usually conducted with questionnaires. These questionnaires should contain questions that are clear and easy to comprehend by the respondents, as well as easy for the data collector to administer. Much attention must therefore be paid to question format, content, and wording.

Question Format

Questions can be structured or unstructured. Unstructured or open-ended questions permit the capture of more in-depth information, but they also increase the potential for interviewer bias. Even at the cost of potential bias, however, "the use of open-ended questions appears quite useful in cross-cultural surveys, because they may help identify the frame of reference of the respondents, or may even be designed to permit the respondent to set his own frame of reference."[18]

Another question format decision is the choice between direct and indirect questions. Societies have different degrees of sensitivity to certain questions. Questions related to the income or age of a respondent may be accepted differently in different countries. Also, the social desirability of answers may vary. In some cultures, questions about employees, performance, standards, and financing are asked directly of a respondent, while in others, particularly in Asia or the Middle East, these questions are thought to be rude and insulting.[19] As a result, the researcher must be sure that the questions are culturally acceptable. This may mean that questions that can be asked directly in some cultures will have to be asked indirectly in others. For example, rather than ask "How old are you?" one could ask "In what year were you born?"

The researcher must also be sure to adapt the complexity of the question to the level of understanding of the respondent. For example, a multipoint scaling method, which may be effectively used in a developed country to discover the attitudes and attributes of company executives, may be a very poor instrument if used among rural entrepreneurs. It has been found that demonstration aids are useful in surveys among poorly educated respondents.[20]

The question format should also ensure data equivalence in international marketing research. This requires categories used in questionnaires to be comparatively structured. In a developed country, for example, a white-collar worker may be part of the middle class, whereas in a less-developed country, the same person would be part of the upper class. Before using categories in a questionnaire, the researcher must therefore determine their appropriateness in different environments. This is particularly important for questions that attempt to collect attitudinal, psychographic, or lifestyle data, since cultural variations are most pronounced in these areas.

Figure 6.3 Internet Service Providers around the Globe

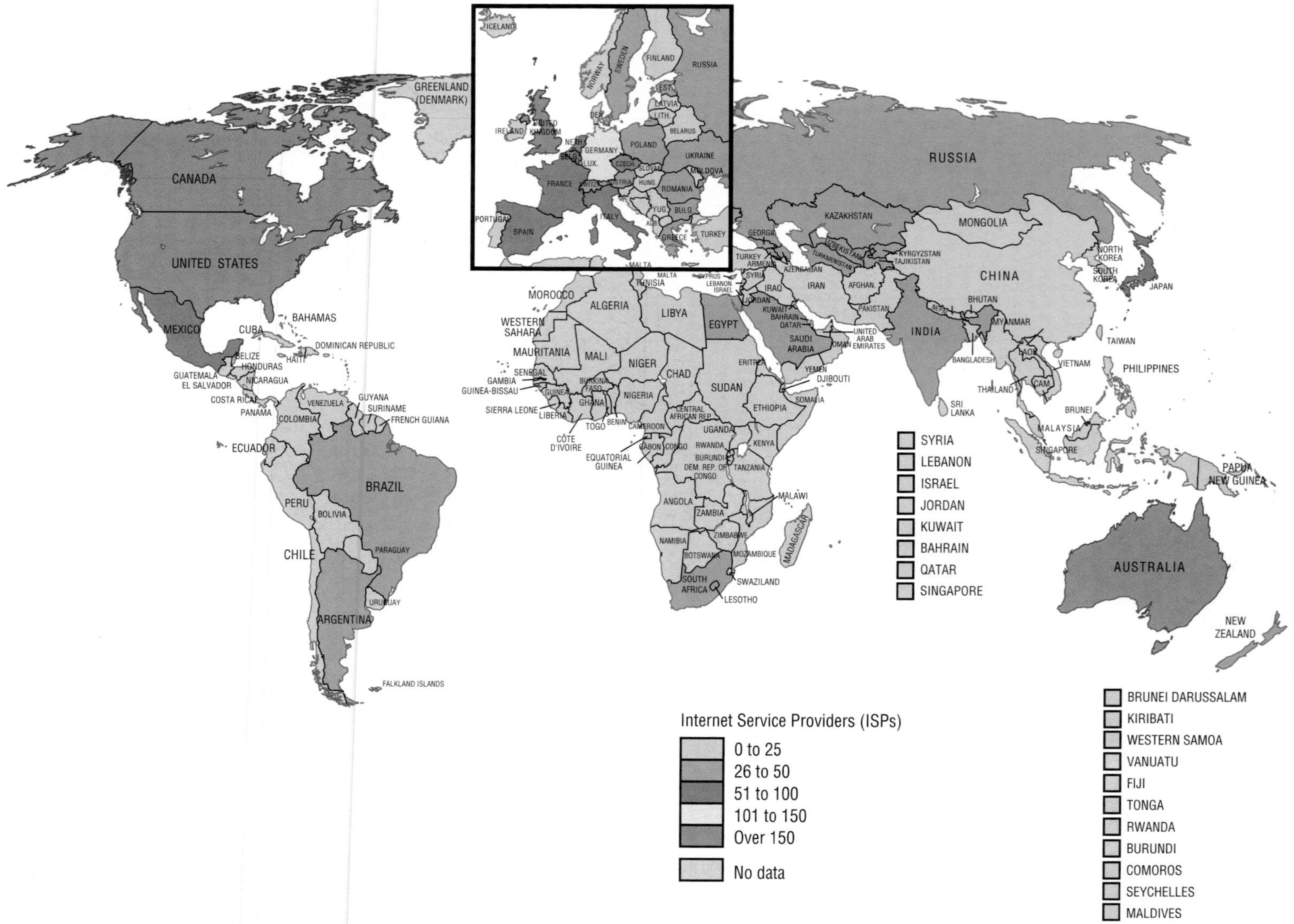

Internet Service Providers (ISPs)

0 to 25
26 to 50
51 to 100
101 to 150
Over 150
No data

SYRIA
LEBANON
ISRAEL
JORDAN
KUWAIT
BAHRAIN
QATAR
SINGAPORE

BRUNEI DARUSSALAM
KIRIBATI
WESTERN SAMOA
VANUATU
FIJI
TONGA
RWANDA
BURUNDI
COMOROS
SEYCHELLES
MALDIVES

SOURCE: Based on Geographics: The World's Online Population, 2003.

Question Content

Major consideration must be given to the ability and willingness of respondents to supply the answers. The knowledge and information available to respondents may vary substantially because of different educational levels and may affect their ability to answer questions. Further, societal demands and restrictions may influence the willingness of respondents to answer certain questions. For various reasons, respondents may also be motivated to supply incorrect answers. For example, in countries where the tax collection system is consistently eluded by taxpayers, questions regarding level of income may deliberately be answered inaccurately. Distrust in the researcher, and the fear that research results may be passed on to the government, may also lead individuals to consistently understate their assets. Because of government restrictions in Brazil, for example, individuals will rarely admit to owning an imported car. Nevertheless, when we observe the streets of Rio de Janeiro, a substantial number of foreign cars are seen. The international market researcher is unlikely to change the societal context of a country. The objective of the content planning process should therefore be to adapt the questions to societal constraints.

Question Wording

The impact of language and culture is of particular importance when wording questions. The goal for the international marketing researcher should be to ensure that the potential for misunderstandings and misinterpretations of spoken or written words is minimized. Both language and cultural differences make this issue an extremely sensitive one in the international marketing research process. As a result, attention must be paid to the translation equivalence of verbal and nonverbal questions that can change in the course of translation. One of this book's authors, for example, used the term *group discussion* in a questionnaire for Russian executives, only to learn that the translated meaning of the term was "political indoctrination session."

The key is to keep questions clear by using simple rather than complex words, by avoiding ambiguous words and questions, by omitting leading questions, and by asking questions in specific terms, thus avoiding generalizations and estimates.[21] To reduce problems of question wording, it is helpful to use a **translation-retranslation approach.** The researcher formulates the questions, has them translated into the language of the country under investigation, and subsequently has a second translator return the foreign text to the researcher's native language. Through the use of this method, the researcher can hope to detect possible blunders. An additional safeguard is the use of alternative wording. Here the researcher uses questions that address the same issue but are worded differently and that resurface at various points in the questionnaire in order to check for consistency in question interpretation by the respondents.

In spite of superb research planning, a poorly designed instrument will yield poor results. No matter how comfortable and experienced the researcher is in international research activities, an instrument should always be pretested. Ideally, such a pretest is carried out with a subset of the population under study. At least a pretest with knowledgeable experts and individuals should be conducted. Even though a pretest may mean time delays and additional cost, the risks of poor research are simply too great for this process to be omitted.

Developing the Sampling Plan

To obtain representative results, the researcher must reach representative members of the population under study. Many methods that have been developed in industrialized countries for this purpose are useless abroad. For example, address directories may simply not be available. Multiple families may live in one dwelling. Differences between population groups living, for example, in highlands and lowlands may make it imperative to differentiate these segments. Lack of basic demographic information may prevent the design of a sampling frame. In instances in which comparative research addresses very different countries, for example China and North America, it may be virtually impossible to match samples.[22]

The international marketing researcher must keep in mind the complexities of the market under study and prepare his or her sampling plan accordingly. Often, samples need to be stratified to reflect different population groups, and innovative sampling methods need to be devised in order to assure representative and relevant responses. For example, a survey concerning grocery shopping habits might require data from housewives in one country, but from maids in another.[23]

Data Collection

The international marketing researcher must check the quality of the data collection process. In some cultures, questionnaire administration is seen as useless by the local population. Instruments are administered primarily to humor the researcher. In such cases, interviewers may cheat quite frequently. Spot checks on the administration procedures are vital to ensure reasonable data quality. A **realism check** of data should also be used. For example, if marketing research in Italy reports that very little spaghetti is consumed, the researcher should perhaps consider whether individuals responded to their use of purchased spaghetti rather than homemade spaghetti. The collected data should therefore be compared with secondary information and with analogous information from a similar market in order to obtain a preliminary understanding of data quality.

Analyzing and Interpreting Primary Data

Interpretation and analysis of accumulated information are required to answer the research questions that were posed initially. The researcher should, of course, use the best tools available and appropriate for analysis. The fact that a market may be in a less-developed country does not preclude the collection of good data and the use of good analytical methods. On the other hand, international researchers should be cautioned against using overly sophisticated tools for unsophisticated data. Even the best of tools will not improve data quality. The quality of data must be matched with the quality of the research tools to achieve appropriately sophisticated analysis and yet not overstate the value of the data.

Presenting Research Results

The primary focus in the presentation of research results must be communication. In multinational marketing research, communication must take place not only with management at headquarters but also with managers in the local operations. Otherwise, little or no transference of research results will occur, and the synergistic benefits of a multinational operation are lost. To minimize time devoted to reading reports, the researcher must present results clearly and concisely. In the worldwide operations of a firm, particularly in the communication efforts, lengthy data and analytical demonstrations should be avoided. The availability of data and the techniques used should be mentioned, however, so that subsidiary operations can receive the information on request.

The researcher should also demonstrate in the presentation how research results relate to the original research objective and fit with overall corporate strategy. At least schematically, possibilities for analogous application should be highlighted. These possibilities should then also be communicated to local subsidiaries, perhaps through a short monthly newsletter. A newsletter format, ideally distributed through an intranet, can be used regardless of whether the research process is centralized, coordinated, or decentralized. The only difference will be the person or group providing the input for the newsletter. It is important to maintain such communication in order for the entire organization to learn and to improve its international marketing research capabilities.

Follow-Up and Review

Although the research process may be considered to be at an end here, from a managerial perspective, one more stage is important. Now that the research has been carried out, appropriate managerial decisions must be made based on the research, and the organization must absorb the research. For example, if it has been found that a product needs to have certain attributes to sell well in Latin America, the manager must determine whether the product development area is aware of this finding and the degree to which the knowledge is now incorporated into new product projects. Without such follow-up, the role of research tends to become a mere "staff" function, increasingly isolated from corporate "line" activity and lacking major impact on corporate activity. If that is the case, research will diminish and even be disregarded—resulting in an organization at risk.

Using Web Technology for Research

The growing use of technology has given rise to new marketing research approaches that allow consumers to be heard more often and permit firms to work much harder at their listening skills. Two primary research approaches are rapidly growing in their use: Web-based research and e-mail–based surveys.

The increasing degree to which the World Wide Web truly lives up to its name is making it possible for international marketers to use this medium in their research efforts. The technology allows them to reach out in a low-cost fashion and provides innovative ways to present stimuli and collect data. For example, on a Web site, product details, pictures of products, brands, and the shopping environment can be portrayed with integrated graphics and sound—thus bringing the issues to be researched much closer to the respondent. In addition, the behavior of visitors to a site can be traced and interpreted regarding interest in products, services, or information.[24]

Surveys can be administered either through a Web site or through e-mail. If they are posted on a site, surveys can be of the pop-up nature, where visitors can be targeted specifically. An e-mail survey format eliminates the need for postage and printing. As a result, larger and geographically much more diverse audiences can be the focus of an inquiry. Research indicates that there is a higher and faster response rate to such electronic inquiries. In addition, the process of data entry can be automated so that responses are automatically fed into data analysis software.[25]

However, it would be too simplistic to assume that the digitalization of survey content is all that it takes to go global on the Web. There are cultural differences that must be taken into account by the researcher. Global visitors to a site should encounter research that is embedded in their own cultural values, rituals, and, symbols, and testimonials or encouragement should be delivered by culture-specific heroes. For example, a Web site might first offer a visitor from Korea the opportunity to become part of a product user community. A low-context visitor from the United States may in turn be exposed to product features immediately.[26]

Such electronic research suffers from a lack of confidentiality of the participants because e-mails disclose the identity of the sender. This issue, in turn, triggers concerns and rules of data privacy which may limit the use of these tools in some nations or regions. Also, the opportunity to overuse a tool may result in the gradual disenchantment of its audience. Therefore, current high response rates may well decline over time.

Nonetheless, the new technology offers international marketers an entire array of new opportunities which will grow rather than diminish. As stated by a leading marketing research expert, Web-based survey research will become the norm, not the exception, in the not too distant future.[27]

The International Information System

Many organizations have data needs going beyond specific international marketing research projects. Most of the time, daily decisions must be made, and there is neither time nor money for special research. An information system already in place is needed to provide the decision maker with basic data for most ongoing decisions. Corporations have responded by developing marketing decision support systems. Defined as "an integrated system of data, statistical analysis, modeling, and display formats using computer hardware and software technology," such a system serves as a mechanism to coordinate the flow of information to corporate managers for decision-making purposes.[28]

To be useful to the decision maker, the system needs various attributes. First, the information must be *relevant*. The data gathered must have meaning for the manager's decision-making process. Only rarely can corporations afford to spend large amounts of money on information that is simply "nice to know." Second, the information must be *timely*. It is of little benefit to the manager if decision information help that is needed today does not become available until a month from now. To be of use to the international decision maker, the system must therefore feed from a variety of international sources and be updated frequently. For multinational corporations, this means a real-time linkage between international subsidiaries and a broad-based ongoing data input operation.

Third, information must be *flexible*—that is, it must be available in the forms needed by management. A marketing decision support system must therefore permit manipulation of the format and combining of the data. Therefore, great effort must be expended to make diverse international data compatible with and comparable to each other. Fourth, information contained in the system must be *accurate*. This attribute is particularly relevant in the international field because information quickly becomes outdated as a result of major changes. Obviously, a system is of no value if it provides incorrect information that leads to poor decisions. Fifth, the system's information bank must be reasonably *exhaustive*. Because of the interrelationship between variables, factors that may influence a particular decision must be appropriately represented in the information system. This means that the marketing decision support system must be based on a broad variety of factors. Finally, to be useful to managers, the system must be *convenient*, both to use and to access. Systems that are cumbersome and time-consuming to reach and to use will not be used enough to justify corporate expenditures to build and maintain them.

More international information systems are being developed successfully due to progress in computer technology in both hardware and software, increased familiarity with technology, and the necessity of dealing with increasing shifts in market conditions. To build an information system, corporations use the internal data that are available from divisions such as accounting and finance and also from their subsidiaries. In addition, many organizations put mechanisms in place to enrich the basic data flow. Three such tools are environmental scanning, Delphi studies, and scenario building.

Environmental Scanning

Any changes in the business environment, whether domestic or foreign, may have serious repercussions on the marketing activities of the firm. Corporations therefore should understand the necessity for tracking new developments and obtaining continuous updates. To carry out this task, some large multinational organizations have formed environmental scanning groups.

Environmental scanning activities are useful to continuously receive information on political, social, and economic affairs internationally; on changes of attitudes held by public institutions and private citizens; and on possible upcoming alterations in international markets.

The precision required for environmental scanning varies with its purpose. Whether the information is to be used for mind stretching or for budgeting, for example, must be taken into account when constructing the framework and variables that will enter the scanning process. The more immediate and precise the exercise is to be in its application within the corporation, the greater the need for detailed information. At the same time, such heightened precision may lessen the utility of environmental scanning for the strategic corporate purpose, which is more long-term in its orientation.

Environmental scanning can be performed in various ways. One method consists of obtaining factual input regarding many variables. For example, the U.S. Census Bureau collects, evaluates, and adjusts a wide variety of demographic, social, and economic characteristics of foreign countries. Estimates for all countries of the world are developed, particularly on economic variables, such as labor force statistics, GDP, and income statistics, but also on health and nutrition variables. Similar factual information can be obtained from international organizations such as the World Bank or the United Nations.

Frequently, corporations believe that such factual data alone are insufficient for their information needs. Particularly for forecasting future developments, other methods are used to capture underlying dimensions of social change. One significant method is **content analysis.** This technique investigates the content of communication in a society and entails literally counting the number of times preselected words, themes, symbols, or pictures appear in a given medium. It can be used productively in international marketing to monitor the social, economic, cultural, and technological environment in which the marketing organization is operating.

Corporations can use content analysis to pinpoint upcoming changes in their line of business, and new opportunities, by attempting to identify trendsetting events. For example, the Alaska oil spill by the tanker *Exxon Valdez* resulted in entirely new international concern about environmental protection and safety, reaching far beyond the incident itself.

Environmental scanning is conducted by a variety of groups within and outside the corporation. Frequently, small corporate staffs are created at headquarters to coordinate the information flow. In addition, subsidiary staff can be used to provide occasional intelligence reports. Groups of volunteers are also formed to gather and analyze information worldwide and feed individual analyses back to corporate headquarters, where they can be used to form the "big picture."

Although environmental scanning is perceived by many corporations as quite valuable for the corporate planning process, there are dissenting voices. For example, it has been noted by researchers "that in those constructs and frameworks where the environment has been given primary consideration, there has been a tendency for the approach to become so global that studies tend to become shallow and diffuse, or impractical if pursued insufficient depth."[29] This presents one of the major continuous challenges faced by corporations in their international environmental scanning. There is a trade-off between the breadth and the depth of information. The continuous evolution of data processing capabilities may reduce the scope of the problem. Yet the cost of data acquisition and the issue of actual data use will continue to be major restraints on the development of environmental scanning systems.

Finally, it should be kept in mind that internationally there may be a fine line between tracking and obtaining information, and misappropriating corporate secrets. With growing frequency, governments and firms claim that their trade secrets are being obtained and abused by foreign competitors. The perceived threat from economic espionage has led to accusations of government spying networks trying to undermine the commercial interests of companies.[30] Information gatherers must be sensitive to these issues in order to avoid conflict or controversy.

Delphi Studies

To enrich the information obtained from factual data, corporations resort to the use of creative and highly qualitative data-gathering methods. Delphi studies are one such method. These studies are particularly useful in the international marketing environment because they are "a means for aggregating the judgments of a number of . . . experts . . . who cannot come together physically."[31] This type of research approach clearly aims at qualitative rather than quantitative measures by aggregating the information of a group of experts. It seeks to obtain answers from those who know instead of seeking the average responses of many with only limited knowledge.

Typically, Delphi studies are carried out with groups of about 30 well-chosen participants who possess particular in-depth expertise in an area of concern, such as future developments in the international trade environment. These participants are asked via mail to identify the major issues in the area of concern. They are also requested to rank their statements according to importance and explain the rationale behind the order. Next, the aggregated information is returned to all participants, who are encouraged to state clearly their agreements or disagreements with the various rank orders and comments. Statements can be challenged, and in another round, participants can respond to the challenges. After several rounds of challenge and response, a reasonably coherent consensus is developed.

The Delphi technique is particularly valuable because it uses the mail or facsimile method of communication to bridge large distances and therefore makes individuals quite accessible at a reasonable cost. It does not suffer from the drawback of ordinary mail investigations: lack of interaction among the participants. One drawback of the technique is that it requires several steps, and therefore months may elapse before the information is obtained. Even though the increasing availability of electronic mail may hasten the process, the researcher must be cautious to factor in the different penetration and acceptance levels of such technology. One should not let the research process be driven by technology to the exclusion of valuable key informants who utilize less sophisticated methods of communication.

Also, substantial effort must be expended in selecting the appropriate participants and in motivating them to participate in this exercise with enthusiasm and continuity. When obtained on a regular basis, Delphi information can provide crucial augmentation to the factual data available for the marketing information system. For example, a large portion of the last chapter of this book was written based on an extensive Delphi study carried out by the authors. Since the study focused on the future of international marketing, and since we wanted to obtain interactive input from around the world, the Delphi method was one of the few possible research alternatives, and it produced insightful results.

Scenario Building

Some companies use **scenario analysis** to look at different configurations of key variables in the international market. For example, economic growth rates, import penetration, population growth, and political stability can be varied. By projecting such variations for medium- to long-term periods, companies can envision completely new environmental conditions. These conditions are then analyzed for their potential domestic and international impact on corporate strategy.

Of major importance in scenario building is the identification of crucial trend variables and the degree of their variation. Frequently, key experts are used to gain information about potential variations and the viability of certain scenarios.

A wide variety of scenarios must be built to expose corporate executives to multiple potential occurrences. Ideally, even far-fetched variables deserve some consideration, if only to build worst-case scenarios. A scenario for Union Carbide Corporation, for example, could have included the possibility of an environmental disaster such as occurred in Bhopal. Similarly, oil companies need to work with scenarios that factor in dramatic shifts in the supply situation, precipitated by, for example, regional conflict in the Middle East, and that consider major alterations in the demand picture, due to, say, technological developments or government policies.

Scenario builders also need to recognize the nonlinearity of factors. To simply extrapolate from currently existing situations is insufficient. Frequently, extraneous factors may enter the picture with a significant impact. Finally, in scenario building, the possibility of joint occurrences must be recognized because changes may not come about in an isolated fashion but may be spread over wide regions. An example of a joint occurrence is the indebtedness of developing nations. Although the inability of any one country to pay its debts would not present a major problem for the international banking community, large and simultaneous indebtedness may well pose a problem of major severity. Similarly, given large technological advances, the possibility of "wholesale" obsolescence of current technology must also be considered. For example, quantum leaps in computer development and new generations of computers may render obsolete the technological investment of a corporation or even a country.

For scenarios to be useful, management must analyze and respond to them by formulating contingency plans. Such planning will broaden horizons and may prepare management for unexpected situations. Familiarization in turn can result in shorter response times to actual occurrences by honing response capability. The difficulty, of course, is to devise scenarios that are unusual enough to trigger new thinking yet sufficiently realistic to be taken seriously by management.[32]

The development of an international information system is of major importance to the multinational corporation. It aids the ongoing decision process and becomes a vital corporate tool in carrying out the strategic planning task. Only by observing global trends and changes will the firm be able to maintain and increase its international competitive position. Many of the data available are quantitative in nature, but attention must also be paid to qualitative dimensions. Quantitative analysis will continue to improve as the ability to collect, store, analyze, and retrieve data increases through the use of high-speed computers. Nevertheless, qualitative analysis should remain a major component of corporate research and strategic planning.

Summary

Constraints of time, resources, and expertise are the major inhibitors of international marketing research. Nevertheless, firms need to carry out planned and organized research in order to explore global market alternatives successfully. Such research needs to be closely linked to the decision-making process.

International market research differs from domestic research in that the environment, which determines how well tools, techniques, and concepts apply, is different abroad. In addition, the manager needs to deal with new parameters, such as duties, exchange rates, and international documentation, a greater number of interacting factors, and a much broader definition of the concept of competition.

Given the scarcity of resources, companies beginning their international effort often need to use data that have already been collected, that is, secondary data. Such data are available from governments, international organizations, directories, trade associations, or online databases.

To respond to specific information requirements, firms frequently need primary research. The researcher needs to select an appropriate research technique to collect the information needed. Sensitivity to different international environments and cultures will guide the researcher in deciding whether to use interviews, focus groups, observation, surveys, or experimentation as data collection techniques. The same sensitivity applies to the design of the research instrument, where issues such as question format, content, and wording are decided. Also, the sampling plan needs to be appropriate for the local environment in order to ensure representative and useful responses.

Once the data have been collected, care must be taken to use analytical tools appropriate for the quality of data collected so that management is not misled about the sophistication of the research. Finally, the research results must be presented in a concise and useful form so that management can benefit in its decision making, and implementation of the research needs to be tracked.

To provide ongoing information to management, an international information support system is useful. Such a system will provide for the systematic and continuous gathering, analysis, and reporting of data for decision-making purposes. It uses a firm's internal information and gathers data via environmental scanning, Delphi studies, or scenario building, thus enabling management to prepare for the future and hone its decision-making skills.

Key Terms

foreign-market opportunity analysis
proxy variable
research specifications
qualitative data
quantitative data

international comparative research
translation-retranslation approach
realism check
content analysis
scenario analysis

Questions for Discussion

1. Discuss the possible shortcomings of secondary data.
2. Why would a firm collect primary data in its international marketing research?
3. Discuss the trade-offs between centralized and decentralized international marketing research.
4. How is international market research affected by differences in language?
5. Compare the use of telephone surveys in the United States and in Egypt.
6. What are some of the crucial variables you would track in an international information system?
7. How has information technology affected international marketing research?

Internet Exercises

1. What were the industries and countries against which the United States filed antidumping actions last year? (Check **http://www.usitc.gov**.)
2. Where would it be most difficult to conduct business due to a high degree of corruption? (Check **http://www.transparency.de**.)

Recommended Readings

Brookes, Richard. *Marketing Research in a .com Environment.* Amsterdam: ESOMAR, 2002.

Churchill, Gilbert A., and Dawn Iacobucci. *Marketing Research: Methodological Foundations,* 8th ed. Mason, OH: South-Western, 2002.

Coyle, James. *Internet Resources and Services for International Marketing.* Westport, CT: Oryx, 2002.

Craig, Samuel C., and Susan P. Douglas. *International Marketing Research: Concepts and Methods,* 2nd ed. Chichester: John Wiley and Sons, 2000.

Directory of Online Databases. Santa Monica, CA: Cuadra Associates, published annually.

Export Programs Guide. Trade Information Center, U.S. Department of Commerce, Washington, DC, 2002, **http://www.usatrade.gov**.

Forrest, Edward. *Internet Marketing Intelligence.* New York: McGraw-Hill, 2003.

International Trade Centre. *Selected Bibliography of Published Market Research.* Geneva, 2002.

Predicasts Services. Cleveland, OH, published monthly.

Information Sources for Marketing Issues

European Union

EUROPA
The umbrella server for all
   institutions
http://www.europa.eu.int

CORDIS
Information on EU research
   programs
http://www.cordis.lu

Council of the European Union
Information and news from the
   Council with sections covering
   Common Foreign and Security
   Policy (CFSP) and Justice and
   Home Affairs
http://ue.eu.int

Court of Auditors
Information notes, annual reports,
   and other publications
http://www.eca.eu.int

Court of Justice
Overview, press releases, publications, and full-text proceedings
   of the court
**http://europa.eu.int/cj/en/
   index.htm**

Citizens Europe
Covers rights of citizens of EU
   member states
http://citizens.eu.int

Delegation of the European Commission to the United States Press

releases, EURECOM: Economic
   and Financial News, EU-U.S. relations, information on EU policies
   and Delegation programs
http://www.eurunion.org

Euro
The Single Currency
http://euro.eu.int

EUDOR (European Union Document Repository)
Bibliographic database
http://www.europa.eu.int/eur-lex

EUROPARL
Information on the European
   Parliament's activities
http://www.europarl.eu.int

European Agency for the Evaluation
   of Medicinal Products
Information on drug approval procedures and documents of the
   Committee for Proprietary Medicinal Products and the Committee
   for Veterinary Medicinal Products
http://www.emea.eu.int

European Bank for Reconstruction
   and Development
One Exchange Square
London EC2A 2EH
United Kingdom
http://www.ebrd.com

European Centre for the Development of Vocational Training

Information on the Centre and
   contact information
http://www.cedefop.gr

European Community Information
   Service
200 Rue de la Loi
1049 Brussels, Belgium
and
2100 M Street NW, 7th Floor
Washington, DC 20037

European Environment Agency
Information on the mission, products and services, and organizations and staff of the EEA
http://www.eea.eu.int

European Investment Bank
Press releases and information on
   borrowing and loan operations,
   staff, and publications
http://www.eib.org

European Monetary Institute
Name: European Central Bank
http://www.ecb.int

EuroStat
**http://europa.eu.int/comm/
   eurostat**

European Training Foundation
Information on vocational educa-
   tion and training programs in
   Central and Eastern Europe and
   Central Asia
http://www.etf.eu.int

European Union
200 Rue de la Loi
1049 Brussels, Belgium
and 2100 M Street NW 7th Floor
Washington, DC 20037
http://www.eurunion.org

Office for Harmonization in the
Internal Market
Guidelines, application forms, and
other information to registering
an EU trademark
**http://www.oami.eu.int/en/
default.htm**

United Nations

http://www.un.org

Conference of Trade and Development
Palais des Nations
1211 Geneva 10
Switzerland
http://unctad.org

Department of Economic and Social
Development
I United Nations Plaza
New York, NY 10017
http://www.un.org/ecosocdev/

Industrial Development Organization
1660 L Street NW
Washington, DC 20036
and
Post Office Box 300
Vienna International Center
A-1400 Vienna, Austria
http://www.unido.org

International Trade Centre
UNCTAD/WTO
54–56 Rue de Mountbrillant
CH-1202 Geneva
Switzerland
http://www.intracen.org

United Nations Educational, Scientific and Cultural Organization
2 United Nations Plaza, Suite 900
New York, NY 10017
http://www.unesco.org

UN Publications
Room 1194
1 United Nations Plaza
New York, NY 10017
**http://www.un.org/pubs/sales.
htm**

U.S. Government

Agency for International Development
Office of Business Relations
Washington, DC 20523
http://www.usaid.gov

Customs Service
1301 Constitution Avenue NW
Washington, DC 20229
http://www.customs.ustreas.gov

Department of Agriculture
12th Street and Jefferson Drive SW
Washington, DC 20250
http://www.usda.gov

Department of Commerce
Herbert C. Hoover Building
14th Street and Constitution Avenue
NW
Washington, DC 20230
http://www.commerce.gov

Department of State
2201 C Street NW
Washington, DC 20520
http://www.state.gov

Department of the Treasury
15th Street and Pennsylvania
Avenue NW
Washington, DC 20220
http://www.ustreas.gov

Federal Trade Commission
6th Street and Pennsylvania Avenue
NW
Washington, DC 20580
http://www.ftc.gov

FedStats
http://www.fedstats.gov

Global Trends 2015
**http://www.cia.gov/cia/
publications/globaltrends2015**

International Trade Commission
500 E Street NW
Washington, DC 20436
http://www.usitc.gov

Small Business Administration
409 Third Street SW
Washington, DC 20416
http://www.sbaonline.sba.gov

U.S. Census Bureau
http://www.census.gov

U.S. House of Representatives Law
Library
http://lectlaw.com/in11/1.htm

U.S. Trade and Development
Agency
1621 North Kent Street
Rosslyn, VA 22209
http://www.tda.gov

World Fact Book
**http://www.odci.gov/cia/
publications/factbook/index.
html**

World Trade Centers Association
60 East 42nd Street
Suite 1901
New York, NY 10165
http://www.wtca.org

Council of Economic Advisers—
http://www.whitehouse.gov/cea

Department of Defense—
http://www.dod.gov

Department of Energy—
http://www.energy.gov

Department of Interior—
http://www.doi.gov

Department of Labor—
http://www.dol.gov

Department of Transportation—
http://www.dot.gov

Environmental Protection Agency—
http://www.epa.gov

National Trade Data Bank—
http://www.stat.usa.gov

National Economic Council—
http://www.whitehouse.gov/nec

Office of Management and Budget—
**http://www.whitehouse.gov/
omb**

Office of the U.S. Trade
Representative—
http://www.ustr.gov

Overseas Private Investment
Corporation—
http://www.opic.gov

Selected Organizations

Academy for Educational
Development
1401 New York Avenue NW
Suite 1100
Washington, DC 20005
http://www.aed.org

American Bankers Association
1120 Connecticut Avenue NW
Washington, DC 20036
http://www.aba.com

American Bar Association
Section of International Law and
Practice
750 N. Lake Shore Drive
Chicago, IL 60611
and
1800 M Street NW
Washington, DC 20036
**http://www.abanet.org/intlaw/
home.html**

American Management Association
440 First Street NW
Washington, DC 20001
http://www.amanet.org

American Marketing Association
311 S. Wacker Drive, Suite 5800
Chicago, IL 60606
**http://www.marketingpower.
com**

American Petroleum Institute
1220 L Street NW
Washington, DC 20005
http://www.api.org

Asia-Pacific Economic Cooperation
Secretariat
438 Alexandra Road
#41–00, Alexandra Road
Singapore 119958
http://www.apecsec.org.sg

Asian Development Bank
2330 Roxas Boulevard
Pasay City, Philippines
http://www.adb.org

Association of South East Asian
Nations (ASEAN)
Publication Office
c/o The ASEAN Secretariat
70A, Jalan Sisingamangaraja
Jakarta 11210
Indonesia
http://www.asean.or.id

Better Business Bureau
http://www.bbb.org

Canadian Market Data
http://www.strategis.ic.gc.ca

Chamber of Commerce of the
United States
1615 H Street NW
Washington, DC 20062
http://www.uschamber.org

Commission of the European
Communities to the United States
2100 M Street NW
Suite 707
Washington, DC 20037
http://www.eurunion.org

Conference Board
845 Third Avenue
New York, NY 10022
and
1755 Massachusetts Avenue
NW Suite 312
Washington, DC 20036
**http://www.conference-board.
org**

Deutsche Bundesbank
Wilhelm-Epstein-Str. 14
P.O.B. 10 06 02
D-60006 Frankfurt am Main
http://www.bundesbank.de

Electronic Industries Alliance
2001 Pennsylvania Avenue NW
Washington, DC 20004
http://www.eia.org

Export-Import Bank of the United
States
811 Vermont Avenue NW
Washington, DC 20571
http://www.exim.gov

Federal Reserve Bank of New York
33 Liberty Street
New York, NY 10045
http://www.ny.frb.org

Gallup Organization
http://www.gallup.com

Greenpeace
http://www.greenpeace.org

Iconoculture
http://iconoculture.com

Inter-American Development Bank
1300 New York Avenue NW
Washington, DC 20577
http://www.iadb.org

International Bank for Reconstruction
and Development (World Bank)
1818 H Street NW
Washington, DC 20433
http://www.worldbank.org

International Monetary Fund
700 19th Street NW
Washington, DC 20431
http://www.imf.org

International Telecommunication
Union
Place des Nations
Ch-1211 Geneva 20
Switzerland
http://www.itu.int

IRSS (Institute for Research in Social
Science)
**http://www.irss.unc.edu/data_
archive/home.asp**

LANIC (Latin American Network
Information Center)
http://www.lanic.utexas.edu

Marketing Research Society
111 E. Wacker Drive, Suite 600
Chicago, IL 60601

Michigan State University global
EDGE
**http://globaledge.msu.edu/ibrd/
ibrd.asp**

National Association of Manufacturers
1331 Pennsylvania Avenue
Suite 1500
Washington, DC 20004
http://www.nam.org

National Federation of Independent
Business
600 Maryland Avenue SW
Suite 700
Washington, DC 20024
http://www.nfib.org

Organization for Economic Cooperation and Development
2 rue Andre Pascal
75775 Paris Cedex Ko, France
and
2001 L Street NW, Suite 700
Washington, DC 20036
http://www.oecd.org

Organization of American States
17th and Constitution Avenue NW
Washington, DC 20006
http://www.oas.org

The Roper Center for Public
Opinion Research
**http://www.ropercenter.uconn.
edu**

Roper Starch Worldwide
http://www.roper.com

Transparency International
Otto-Suhr-Allee 97–99
D-10585 Berlin
Germany
http://www.transparency.org

Indexes to Literature

Business Periodical Index
H.W. Wilson Co.
950 University Avenue
Bronx, NY 10452

New York Times Index
University Microfilms International
300 N. Zeeb Road
Ann Arbor, MI 48106
http://www.nytimes.com

Public Affairs Information Service
Bulletin
11 W. 40th Street
New York, NY 10018

Wall Street Journal Index
University Microfilms International
300 N. Zeeb Road
Ann Arbor, MI 48106
http://www.wsj.com

Directories

American Register of Exporters and
Importers
38 Park Row
New York, NY 10038

Arabian Year Book
Dar Al-Seuassam Est. Box 42480
Shuwahk, Kuwait

Directories of American Firms
Operating in Foreign Countries
World Trade Academy Press
Uniworld Business Publications Inc.
50 E. 42nd Street
New York, NY 10017

The Directory of International
Sources of Business Information
Pitman
128 Long Acre
London WC2E 9AN, England

Encyclopedia of Associations
Gale Research Co.
Book Tower
Detroit, MI 48226

Polk's World Bank Directory
R.C. Polk & Co.
2001 Elm Hill Pike
P.O. Box 1340
Nashville, TN 37202

Verified Directory of Manufacturer's
Representatives
MacRae's Blue Book Inc.
817 Broadway
New York, NY 10003

World Guide to Trade Associations
K.G. Saur & Co.
175 Fifth Avenue
New York, NY 10010

Encyclopedias, Handbooks, and Miscellaneous

A Basic Guide to Exporting
U.S. Government Printing Office
Superintendent of Documents
Washington, DC 20402

Doing Business In . . . Series
Price Waterhouse
1251 Avenue of the Americas
New York, NY 10020

Economic Survey of Europe
United Nations Publishing Division
1 United Nations Plaza
Room DC2–0853
New York, NY 10017

Economic Survey of Latin America
United Nations Publishing Division
1 United Nations Plaza
Room DC2–0853
New York, NY 10017

Encyclopedia Americana,
International Edition
Grolier Inc.
Danbury, CT 06816

Encyclopedia of Business
Information Sources
Gale Research Co.
Book Tower
Detroit, MI 48226

Europa Year Book
Europa Publications Ltd.

18 Bedford Square
London WCIB 3JN, England

Export Administration Regulations
U.S. Government Printing Office
Superintendent of Documents
Washington, DC 20402

Exporters' Encyclopedia—World
Marketing Guide
Dun's Marketing Services
49 Old Bloomfield Rd.
Mountain Lake, NJ 07046

Export-Import Bank of the United
States Annual Report
U.S. Government Printing Office
Superintendent of Documents
Washington, DC 20402

Exporting for the Small Business
U.S. Government Printing Office
Superintendent of Documents
Washington, DC 20402

Exporting to the United States
U.S. Government Printing Office
Superintendent of Documents
Washington, DC 20402

Export Shipping Manual
U.S. Government Printing Office
Superintendent of Documents
Washington, DC 20402

Foreign Business Practices: Mate-
rials on Practical Aspects of
Exporting, International Licens-
ing, and Investing
U.S. Government Printing Office
Superintendent of Documents
Washington, DC 20402

A Guide to Financing Exports
U.S. Government Printing Office
Superintendent of Documents
Washington, DC 20402

Handbook of Marketing Research
McGraw-Hill Book Co.
1221 Avenue of the Americas
New York, NY 10020

Periodic Reports, Newspapers, Magazines

Advertising Age
Crain Communications Inc.
740 N. Rush Street
Chicago, IL 60611
http://www.adage.com

Advertising World
Directories International Inc.
150 Fifth Avenue, Suite 610
New York, NY 10011

American Demographics
**http://www.americandemo
graphics.com**

Arab Report and Record
84 Chancery Lane
London WC2A 1DL, England

Asian Demographics
**http://www.asiandemograph
ics.com**

Barron's
University Microfilms International
300 N. Zeeb Road
Ann Arbor, MI 48106
http://www.barrons.com

Business America
U.S. Department of Commerce
14th Street and Constitution Avenue
 NW
Washington, DC 20230
http://www.doc.gov

Business International
Business International Corp.
One Dag Hammarskjold Plaza
New York, NY 10017

Business Week
McGraw-Hill Publications Co.
1221 Avenue of the Americas
New York, NY 10020
http://www.businessweek.com

Commodity Trade Statistics
United Nations Publications
1 United Nations Plaza
Room DC2–0853
New York, NY 10017

Conference Board Record
Conference Board Inc.
845 Third Avenue
New York, NY 10022

Customs Bulletin
U.S. Customs Service
1301 Constitution Avenue NW
Washington, DC 20229

The Dismal Scientist
http://www.economy.com/dismal

Dun's Business Month
Goldhirsh Group
38 Commercial Wharf
Boston, MA 02109

The Economist
Economist Newspaper Ltd.
25 St. James Street
London SWIA 1HG, England
http://www.economist.com

Europe Magazine
2100 M Street NW Suite 707
Washington, DC 20037

The Financial Times
Bracken House
10 Cannon Street
London EC4P 4BY, England
http://www.ft.com

Forbes
Forbes, Inc.
60 Fifth Avenue
New York, NY 10011
http://www.forbes.com

Fortune
Time, Inc.
Time & Life Building
1271 Avenue of the Americas
New York, NY 10020
http://www.fortune.com

Global Trade
North American Publishing Co.
401 N. Broad Street
Philadelphia, PA 19108

Industrial Marketing
Crain Communications, Inc.
740 N. Rush Street
Chicago, IL 60611

*International Encyclopedia of the
 Social Sciences*
Macmillan and the Free Press
866 Third Avenue
New York, NY 10022

International Financial Statistics
International Monetary Fund
Publications Unit
700 19th Street NW
Washington, DC 20431
http://www.imf.org

Investor's Daily
Box 25970
Los Angeles, CA 90025

Journal of Commerce
100 Wall Street
New York, NY 10005
http://www.joc.com

Lexis-Nexis Legal Express Info
 Service
http://www.michie.com

Sales and Marketing Management
Bill Communications Inc.
633 Third Avenue
New York, NY 10017

Tomorrow
Global Environment Business
http://www.tomorrow-web.com

Wall Street Journal
Dow Jones & Company
200 Liberty Street
New York, NY 10281
http://www.wsj.com

World Agriculture Situation
U.S. Department of Agriculture
Economics Management Staff
http://www.econ.ag.gov

Pergamon Press Inc.
Journals Division
Maxwell House
Fairview Park
Elmsford, NY 10523

Trade Finance
U.S. Department of Commerce
International Trade Administration
Washington, DC 20230
http://www.doc.gov

*World Trade Center Association
 (WTCA) Directory*
60 East 42nd Street
Suite 1901
New York, NY 10048
http://www.wtca.com

*Media Guide International: Busi-
 ness/Professional Publications*
Directories International Inc.
150 Fifth Avenue, Suite 610
New York, NY 10011

World Wide Web Virtual Law Library
http://www.law.indiana.edu/v-lib

Selected Trade Databases

News agencies
Comline-Japan Newswire
Database Omninews
Dow Jones News
Lexis-Nexis
Nikkei Shimbun News
Reuters Monitor
UPI

Trade Publication References with Bibliographic Keywords

Agris
Biocommerce Abstracts & Directory
Findex
Frost (short) Sullivan Market
Research Reports
Marketing Surveys Index
McCarthy Press Cuttings Service
Paperchem
PTS F & S Indexes
Trade and Industry Index

Trade Publication References with Summaries

ABI/Inform
Arab Information Bank
Asia-Pacific
BFAI
Biobusiness
CAB Abstracts
Chemical Business Newbase
Chemical Industry Notes
Caffeeline
Delphes
InfoSouth Latin American Information System
Management Contents
NTIS Bibliographic Data Base
Paperchem
PIRA Abstract
PSTA
PTS Marketing & Advertising Reference Service
PTS PromtRapra Abstracts
Textline
Trade & Industry ASAP
World Textiles

Full Text of Trade Publications

Datamonitor Market Reports
Dow Jones News
Euromonitor Market Direction
Federal News Service
Financial Times Business Report File
Financial Times Fulltext
Globefish
ICC Key Notes Market Research
Investext
McCarthy Press Cuttings Service
PTS Promt

Textline
Trade & Industry ASAP

Statistics

Agrostat (diskette only)
Arab Information Bank
ARI Network/CNS
Comext/Eurostat
Comtrade
FAKT-German Statistics
Globefish
IMF Data
OECD Data
Piers Imports
PTS Forecasts
PTS Time Series
Reuters Monitor
Trade Statistics
Tradstat World Trade Statistics
TRAINS (CD-ROM being developed)
U.S. I/E Maritime Bills of Lading
U.S. Imports for Consumption
World Bank Statistics

Price Information

ARI Network/CNS
Chemical Business Newsbase
COLEACP
Commodity Options
Commodities 2000
Market News Service of ITC
Nikkei Shimbun News Database
Reuters Monitor
UPI
U.S. Wholesale Prices

Company Registers

ABC Europe Production Europe
Biocommerce Abstracts & Directory
CD-Export (CD-ROM only)
Company Intelligence
D&B Duns Market Identifiers (U.S.A.)
D&B European Marketing File
D&B Eastern Europe
Dun's Electronic Business Directory
Firmexport/Firmimport
Hoppenstedt Austria
Hoppenstedt Benelux
Hoppenstedt Germany
Huco-Hungarian Companies
ICC Directory of Companies
Kompass Asia/Pacific
Kompass Europe (EKOD)
Mexican Exporters/Importers

Piers Imports
Polu-Polish Companies
SDOE
Thomas Register
TRAINS (CD-ROM being developed)
UK Importers
UK Importers (DECTA)
U.S. Directory of Importers
U.S. I/E Maritime Bills of Lading
World Trade Center Network

Trade Opportunities, Tenders

Business
Federal News Service
Huntech-Hungarian Technique
Scan-a-Bid
Tenders Electronic Daily
World Trade Center Network

Tariffs and Trade Regulations

Celex
ECLAS
Justis Eastern Europe (CD-ROM only)
Scad
Spearhead
Spicer's Centre for Europe
TRAINS (CD-ROM being developed)
U.S. Code of Federal Regulations
U.S. Federal Register
U.S. Harmonized Tariff Schedule

Standards

BSI Standardline
Noriane/Perinorm
NTIS Bibliographic Data Base
Standards Infodisk ILI (CD-ROM only)

Shipping Information

Piers Imports
Tradstat World Trade Statistics
U.S. I/E Maritime Bills of Lading

Others

Fairbase
Ibiscus

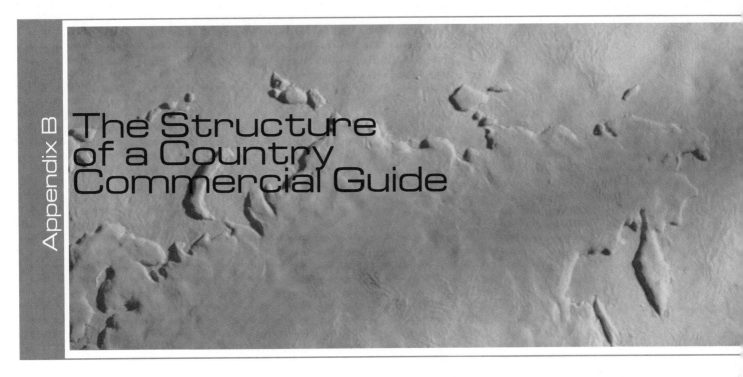

The Structure of a Country Commercial Guide

The U.S. Commercial Service

The following is an example of governmental research made available to firms. Country commercial guides provide a condensed and business-focused overview of business customs, conditions, contacts, and opportunities. Using such guides can be of major help in getting started in unfamiliar territory.

Guide for Austria

Table of Contents

Chapter 1   **Executive Summary**

Chapter 2   **Economic Trends and Outlook**
- **A.** Major Trends and Outlook
- **B.** Government Role in the Economy
- **C.** Balance of Payments Situation
- **D.** Infrastructure Situation

Chapter 3   **Political Environment**
- **A.** Nature of Political Relationship with the United States
- **B.** Major Political Issues Affecting the Business Climate
- **C.** The Civil Society
- **D.** Synopsis of the Political System.

Chapter 4   **Marketing U.S. Products and Services**
- **A.** Distribution and Sales Channels
- **B.** Product Pricing Structures
- **C.** Retail Trends
- **D.** Use of Agents/Distributors; Finding a Partner
- **E.** Franchising
- **F.** Joint Ventures and Licensing
- **G.** Steps to Establishing an Office
- **H.** Selling Factors and Techniques
- **I.** Advertising and Trade Promotion
- **J.** Pricing Products

Additional guides can be found at **http://www.usatrade.gov**.

K. Sales Services and Customer Support

L. Selling to the Government

M. Protecting Your Product from IPR Infringement

N. Need for a Local Attorney

Chapter 5   Leading Sectors for U.S. Exports

A. Best Prospects for Non-Agricultural Products

B. Best Prospects for Agricultural Products

Chapter 6   Trade Regulations, Customs, and Standards

A. Customs Regulations and Tariff Rates

B. Non-Tariff Trade Barriers

C. Import Taxes Including Value Added Taxes

D. Import License Requirements

E. Temporary Goods Entry Requirements

F. Special Import/Export Requirements

G. Labeling Requirements

H. Prohibited Imports

I. Warranty and Non-Warranty Repairs

J. Export Controls

K. Standards

L. Free Trade Zones/Warehouses

M. Membership in Free Trade Agreements

N. Customs Contact Information

Chapter 7   Investment Climate

A. Openness to Foreign Investment

B. Conversion and Transfer Policies

C. Expropriation and Compensation

D. Dispute Settlement

E. Performance Requirements/Incentives

F. Right to Private Ownership and Establishment

G. Protection of Property Rights

H. Transparency of the Regulatory System

I. Efficient Capital Markets and Portfolio Investment

J. Political Violence

K. Corruption

L. Bilateral Investment Agreements

M. OPIC and Other Investment Insurance Programs

N. Labor

O. Foreign Trade Zones/Free Ports

P. List of Major Foreign Investors

Chapter 8   Trade and Project Financing

A. Synopsis of Banking System

B. Foreign Exchange Controls Affecting Trading

C. General Financing Ability

D. How to Finance Exports/Methods of Payment

E. Types of Available Export Financing and Insurance

F. Project Financing Available

G. List of Banks with Correspondent U.S. Banking Arrangements

Chapter 9   Business Travel

A. Business Customs

B. Travel Advisory and Visas

C. Holidays

D. Business Infrastructure

Chapter 10   Economic and Trade Statistics

Appendix A. Country Data

Appendix B. Domestic Economy

Appendix C. Trade

Appendix D. Foreign Direct Investment

Chapter 11   U.S. & Austrian Contacts
- **A.** Austrian Government Agencies
- **B.** Austrian Trade Associations/Chambers of Commerce
- **C.** Austrian Market Research Firms
- **D.** Austrian Commercial Banks
- **E.** U.S. Commercial Service
- **F.** U.S.–Based Multipliers
- **G.** Washington-Based U.S. Government Contacts

Chapter 12   Market Research
- **A.** Foreign Agriculture Service
  Commodity Reports/Market Briefs
- **B.** Department of Commerce Industry Subsector Analyses

Chapter 13   Trade Event Schedule
- **A.** Scheduled Agricultural/Food Trade Events
- **B.** Scheduled Trade Events—U.S. Commercial Service Vienna

chapter **7**

Exporting, Licensing, and Franchising

© PHOTODISC, VOL. 22

© EYEWIRE/GETTY IMAGES

224

THE INTERNATIONAL MARKETPLACE   7.1

Tapping Global Markets through E-Commerce

How does a small business tap into the worldwide markets that demand its products? How does a sales staff of only three people serve clients across the globe with efficiency and a personal touch? The answer comes in the form of e-commerce, the digital-age solution to international marketing.

Evertek Computer Corporation is a San Diego–based company that sells new and refurbished computers and parts in more than 80 countries worldwide. While the 12-year-old company has undertaken some export sales since beginning, these sales now comprise 20 percent of its total revenues.

The key to Evertek's success has been its well-established sales network, whose centerpiece is an e-commerce Web site that loads rapidly, provides real-time inventory, and allows potential new distributors to fill out an online application. The success of this site relies on the hands-on sales approach of John Ortley, Evertek's international sales manager, who writes countless personal e-mails a day to current and potential clients and spends hours on the phone fostering relationships with every one of his clients.

Ortley enhanced his already thriving sales network by becoming a member of BuyUSA.com, an e-commerce Web site backed by the powerful guarantee of the U.S. government. The Web site—which represents many U.S. businesses interested in promoting their products and services abroad—serves 90 countries and over 20,000

customers. BuyUSA.com also promotes Evertek at overseas trade shows in the information technology sector.

Evertek currently requires that buyers pay in advance before their products can be shipped. However, many of Evertek's customers operate within emerging markets, and cannot afford to pay in advance and risk losing that money. BuyUSA.com, backed by the U.S. government, promises customers that their investment will not be lost. If they do not receive the promised goods, they can contact their local U.S. Embassy's Commercial Section for help.

Evertek has established a successful sales network and has grown its revenues considerably thanks to export sales. This has all been due, in large part, to the growing global demand for Evertek's competitively priced computers and parts. Evertek's products would not be available were it not for the appropriate sales strategy it has adopted: Clients worldwide, from developing to industrialized nations, are quickly connecting to the Internet, taking advantage of the convenience and reliability of e-commerce Web sites like BuyUSA.com. Says Ortley: "We are an e-commerce business and we're thriving. The world is shrinking, and it's getting easier and less expensive to do business on a global basis."

SOURCE: "A San Diego Company Uses the Internet to Go Global," U.S. Commercial Service, About What's New, **http://www.usatrade.gov**, accessed October 25, 2002.

PARTICIPATION IN THE INTERNATIONAL MARKETPLACE is increasingly within the grasp of firms both large and small, as *The International Marketplace 7.1* shows. Doing so can be very rewarding and may turn out to be the key to prosperity for both corporations and employees. Research has found that firms that export grow faster, are more productive, and, equally important, have employees who tend to earn more.[1] But most firms cannot simply jump into international marketing and expect to be successful. New activities in an unfamiliar environment also increase a firm's risk. Therefore, companies must prepare their activities and adjust to the needs and opportunities of international markets in order to become long-term participants.

Because most firms start their international involvement with exporting, and most exporters are small and medium-sized firms, this chapter will discuss the export process by addressing the activities that take place within the firm preparing to enter the international marketplace. It will focus on the basic stimuli for exporting and will discuss the change agents, both internal and external, that activate these stimuli. In addition, the concerns and preoccupations of firms as they begin their international marketing operations will be discussed. Finally, a model of the export development process and strategic issues within the firm will be presented.

Managers must understand what "sells" to owners and decision makers in the firm so that they can aid in the move toward internationalization. Current and prospective employees must be able to assess the strategic direction of the firm. An awareness of the inherent attributes that make firms international can aid students in selecting the best environment in which to become active in international marketing.

Motivations to Internationalize

Many researchers have worked on determining the reasons why firms go international. A key factor is apparently the type and quality of management. Dynamic management is important when firms take their first international steps. Over the long term, management commitment and management's perceptions and attitudes are also good predictors of export success.[2]

To a large extent, this conclusion has been formulated by reverse deduction: The managers of firms that are unsuccessful or inactive in the international marketplace usually exhibit a lack of determination to or preparation for international marketing. International markets cannot be penetrated overnight—to succeed in them requires substantial market development activity, market research, and the identification of and response to foreign market factors. It can take as long as two years for a novice firm to successfully complete its first export order.[3] Therefore, a high level of export commitment is crucial. This commitment must be able to endure stagnation and sometimes even setbacks and failure. To obtain such a commitment, it is important to involve all levels of management early on in the export planning process and to impress on all players that the effort will only succeed with a commitment that is companywide. Planning and execution of an export venture must be incorporated into the firm's strategic management process. A firm that sets no strategic goals for its export venture is less likely to make the venture a long-term success.[4]

In addition to broad commitment, it is also important to establish a specific export structure in which someone has the responsibility for exporting. Without some specified responsibility center, the focus that is necessary for success is lost. Just one person assigned part time to international marketing activities can begin exploring and entering international markets, but it is crucial to assign the export responsibility to a specific person.

In most business activities, one factor alone rarely accounts for any given action. Usually a mixture of factors results in firms taking steps in a given direction. This is true of internationalization; there are a variety of motivations both pushing and pulling firms along the international path. Table 7.1 provides an overview of the major motivations to go international. They are differentiated into proactive and reactive motivations. Proactive motivations represent stimuli to attempt strategic change. Reactive motivations influence firms that are responsive

Table 7.1	Why Firms Go International
PROACTIVE MOTIVATIONS	**REACTIVE MOTIVATIONS**
• Profit advantage	• Competitive pressures
• Unique products	• Overproduction
• Technological advantage	• Declining domestic sales
• Exclusive information	• Excess capacity
• Managerial urge	• Saturated domestic markets
• Tax benefit	• Proximity to customers and ports
• Economies of scale	

to environmental changes and adjust to them by changing their activities over time. In other words, proactive firms go international because they want to, while reactive ones go international because they have to.

Proactive Motivations

The most stimulating proactive motivation to become involved in international marketing is the profit advantage. Management may perceive international sales as a potential source of higher profit margins or of more added-on profits. Of course, the perceived profitability when planning to enter into international markets is often quite different from profitability actually attained. The actual initial profitability of international start-up operations may be quite low,[5] mainly due to relatively high start-up costs. The gap between perception and reality may be particularly large when the firm has not previously engaged in international market activities. Despite thorough planning, imponderable influences often shift the profit picture substantially. For example, a sudden shift in exchange rates may drastically alter profit forecasts even though they were based on careful market evaluation.

A second major stimulus results either from unique products or from a technological advantage. A firm may produce goods or services that are not widely available from international competitors or may have made technological advances in a specialized field. Again, real and perceived advantages should be differentiated. Many firms believe that theirs are unique products or services, even though this may not be the case in the international market. If products or technology are unique, however, it can certainly provide a competitive edge and result in major business success abroad. The intensity of marketing's interaction with the research and development function, as well as the level of investment into R&D, has been shown to have a major effect on the success of exported products.[6]

One issue to consider is how long such a technological or product advantage will continue. Historically, a firm with a competitive edge could count on being the sole supplier to international markets for years to come. This type of advantage, however, has shrunk dramatically because of competing technologies and a frequent lack of intellectual property rights protection.

Exclusive market information is another proactive stimulus. This includes knowledge about foreign customers, marketplaces, or market situations that is not widely shared by other firms. Such special knowledge may result from particular insights based on a firm's international research, special contacts a firm may have, or simply being in the right place at the right time (for example, recognizing a good business situation during a vacation trip). Although exclusivity can serve well as an initial stimulus for international marketing activities, it will rarely provide prolonged motivation because competitors—at least in the medium run—can be expected to catch up with the information advantage of the firm, particularly in light of the growing ease of global information access.

Managerial urge is a motivation that reflects the desire, drive, and enthusiasm of management toward international marketing activities. This enthusiasm can exist simply because managers like to be part of a firm that operates internationally. (It sounds impressive.) Further, it can often provide a good reason for international travel—for example, to call on a major customer in the Bahamas during a cold winter month. Often, however, the managerial urge to internationalize is simply the reflection of general entrepreneurial motivation—of a desire for continuous growth and market expansion.[7]

Tax benefits have historically also played a major motivating role. Many countries offer tax concessions to their firms in order to encourage export activities. In the United States, a tax mechanism called the **Exterritorial Income Tax Exclusion (ETI)** provides exporting firms with certain tax deferrals, thus making international marketing activities potentially more profitable. However, the rules of the World Trade Organization prohibit the subsidy of exports by all but the poorest countries. For example, the ETI mechanism of the United States was found to be in violation of WTO regulations, and the United States was advised to terminate such benefits. It can therefore be expected that tax benefits will play a decreasing role in future motivations to export.

A final major proactive motivation is economies of scale. Becoming a participant in international marketing activities may enable the firm to increase its output and therefore slide down more rapidly on the learning curve. Ever since the Boston Consulting Group showed that a doubling of output can reduce production costs up to 30 percent, this effect has been very much sought. Increased production for the international market can therefore also help in reducing the cost of production for domestic sales and make the firm more competitive domestically as well.[8] This effect often results in seeking market share as a primary objective. At an initial level of internationalization this may mean an increased search for export markets; later on, it can result in the opening of foreign subsidiaries and foreign production facilities. These latter effects are discussed in Chapter 13 of this book.

Reactive Motivations

A second type of motivation, primarily characterized as reactive, influences firms to respond to changes and pressures in the business environment rather than attempt to blaze trails.

A prime form of such motivation is the reaction to competitive pressures. A firm may fear losing domestic market share to competing firms that have benefited from the effect of the economies of scale gained by international marketing activities. Further, it may fear losing foreign markets permanently to domestic competitors that decide to focus on these markets. Observing that domestic competitors are beginning to internationalize, and knowing that market share is most easily retained by the firm that obtains it initially, firms frequently enter the international market head over heels. Quick entry may result in similarly quick withdrawal once the firm recognizes that its preparation has been insufficient.

Similarly, overproduction can serve as a major reactive motivation. Historically, during downturns in the domestic business cycle, markets abroad were initially unaffected because of time lags. They provided an ideal outlet for inventories that were significantly above desired levels. Frequently, however, international market expansion motivated by overproduction did not represent full commitment by management, but rather **safety-valve activity** designed for short-term activities only. Instead of developing an international marketing perspective by adjusting the marketing mix to needs abroad, firms using this strategy typically stimulate export sales with short-term price cuts.[9] As soon as the domestic market demand returns to previous levels, international marketing activities are curtailed or even terminated. Firms that have used such a strategy once may encounter difficulties when trying to employ it again because many foreign customers are not interested in temporary or sporadic business relationships. This reaction from abroad, together with the lessons learned about the danger of large inventories—and the fact that the major industrial economies appear to be increasingly synchronized, may well lead to a decrease in the importance of this motivation over time.

Stable or declining domestic sales, whether measured in sales volume or market share, have a similar motivating effect. Products marketed by the firm domestically may be at the declining stage of the product life cycle. Instead of attempting a push-back of the life cycle process at home, or in addition to such an effort, firms may opt to prolong the product life cycle by expanding the market. In the past, such efforts often met with success because customers in many countries only gradually reached a level of need and sophistication already attained by customers in industrialized nations. Increasingly, however, if lag times exist at all in foreign markets, they are quite short. Nevertheless, this motivation is still a valid one, particularly in the context of developing nations, which often still have very good use for products for which the demand in the industrialized world is already on the decline. This holds particularly true for high-technology products that are outdated by the latest innovations. Such "just-dated" technology can be highly useful to economic development and offer vast progress in the manufacturing or services sectors.

Excess capacity can also be a powerful motivation. If equipment for production is not fully utilized, firms may see expansion into the international market as an ideal possibility for achieving broader distribution of fixed costs. Alternatively, if all fixed costs are assigned to domestic production, the firm can penetrate international markets with a pricing scheme that focuses mainly on variable costs. Although such a strategy may be useful in the short term, it may result in the offering of products abroad at a cost lower than at home, which in turn may trigger dumping charges. In the long run, fixed costs have to be recovered to ensure replacement of production equipment that growing international marketing activities may overtax. Market penetration strategy based on variable cost alone is therefore not feasible over the long term.

The reactive motivation of a saturated domestic market is similar in results to that of declining domestic sales. Again, firms in this situation can use the international market to prolong the life cycle of their product and of their organization.

A final major reactive motivation is proximity to customers and ports. Physical closeness to the international market can often play a major role in the export activities of a firm. For example, Canadian firms established near the U.S. border may not even perceive of their market activities in the United States as international marketing. Rather, they are simply an extension of domestic activities, without any particular attention being paid to the fact that some of the products go abroad. Except for some firms close to the Canadian or Mexican border, however, this factor is much less prevalent in North America than in many other countries. Unlike European firms, most American firms are situated far away from foreign countries. Consider the radius of domestic activity of many U.S. firms, which may be 200 miles. When applying such a radius to a European scenario, most European firms automatically become international marketers simply because their neighbors are so close. As an example, a European company operating in the heart of Belgium needs to go only 50 miles to be in multiple foreign markets.

In this context, the concept of psychic or **psychological distance** needs to be understood. Geographic closeness to foreign markets may not necessarily translate into real or perceived closeness to the foreign customer. Sometimes cultural variables, legal factors, and other societal norms make a foreign market that is geographically close seem psychologically distant. For example, research has shown that U.S. firms perceive Canada to be much closer psychologically than Mexico. Even England, mainly because of the similarity in language, is perceived by many U.S. firms to be much closer than Mexico or other Latin American countries, despite the geographic distances. However, in light of the reduction of trade barriers as a result of the North American Free Trade Agreement (NAFTA), and a growing proportion of the U.S. population with Hispanic background, this long-standing perception may be changing rapidly.

It is important to remember two major issues in the context of psychological distance. First, some of the distance seen by firms is based on perception rather than reality. For example, German firms may view the Austrian market simply as an extension of their home market due to so many superficial similarities, just as many U.S. firms may see the United Kingdom as psychologically very close due to the similarity in language. However, the attitudes and values of managers and customers may vary substantially between markets. Too much of a focus on the similarities may let the firm lose sight of the differences. Many Canadian firms have incurred high costs in learning this lesson when entering the United States.[10] At the same time, closer psychological proximity does make it easier for firms to enter markets. Therefore, for firms new to international marketing it may be advantageous to begin this new activity by entering the psychologically closer markets first in order to gather experience before venturing into markets that are farther away.[11]

An overall contemplation of these motivations should also consider the following factors. First, firms that are most successful in exporting are motivated by proactive—that is, firm-internal—factors. Second, the motivations of firms do not seem to shift dramatically over the short term but are rather stable. For the student who seeks involvement in international markets and searches for firms most likely to provide good opportunities, an important consideration should be whether a firm is proactive or reactive.

The proactive firm is also more likely to be service-oriented than are reactive firms. Further, it is frequently more marketing- and strategy-oriented than reactive firms, which have as their major concern operational issues. The clearest differentiation between the two types of firms can probably be made after the fact by determining how they initially entered international markets. Proactive firms are more likely to solicit their first international marketing order, whereas reactive firms frequently begin international marketing activities after receiving an unsolicited order from abroad.

All these considerations lead to the questions of how the activities of firms can be changed and, ideally, how the student and future employee can be part of this change.

Change Agents

For change to take place, someone or something within the firm must initiate it and shepherd it through to implementation. This intervening individual or variable is here called a **change agent.** Change agents in the internationalization process are shown in Table 7.2.

Internal Change Agents

A primary change agent internal to the firm is enlightened management. The key factor leading to such performance-enhancing enlightenment is the international experience and exposure of management.[12] Examples are when the current management of a firm discovers and understands the value of international markets and decides to pursue international marketing opportunities. Such insights are frequently triggered by foreign travel, during which new business opportunities are discovered, or by information that leads management to believe that such opportunities exist. Managers who have lived abroad, have learned foreign languages, or are particularly interested in foreign cultures are likely, sooner rather than later, to investigate whether international marketing opportunities would be appropriate for their firm.

A second set of major internal change agents consists of new management or new employees. Often, managers enter a firm having already had some international marketing experience in previous positions and try to use this experience to further the business activities of their new firm. Also, in developing their goals in

Table 7.2	**Change Agents in the Internationalization Process**

FIRM INTERNAL	FIRM EXTERNAL
• Enlightened management	• Demand
• New management	• Other firms
• Significant internal event	• Domestic distributors
	• Banks
	• Chambers of commerce
	• Governmental activities
	• Export intermediaries
	– Export management companies
	– Trading companies

THE INTERNATIONAL MARKETPLACE   7.2

An Accidental Exporter

Maynard Sauder, president and CEO of ready-to-assemble furniture maker Sauder Woodworking Company of Archbold, Ohio, thought for the longest while that exporting was not for him. The do-it-yourself household furnishings market in the United States had been gathering steam in the late 1980s. Sauder Woodworking was a supplier to national general merchandisers such as Wal-Mart, Kmart, Sears, and J.C. Penney. It was supplying retailers with products in the $19 to $399 range and had just reached a sales volume of $200 million. Annual growth was humming at 12 to 15 percent. Exports at this time were negligible and occurred almost by accident. For instance, the firm started to sell products in the Caribbean because a salesman vacationed there.

How times have changed. Today, Sauder Woodworking does business in more than 70 countries worldwide, with corporate revenues of over $700 million annually. Domestic volume has gone flat, while international accounts have posted an average annual increase of 30 percent. It wasn't until Jerry Paterson, a former export manager for Owens-Corning Fiberglass Corp., caught Sauder's attention that the company became serious about exporting. "I questioned our ability to compete in foreign markets," Sauder says today. "I wasn't sure we could make it on price, and then I wondered if customers outside the United States would accept our designs." But the cost-benefit analysis, plus Paterson's presence, made it worth a

try. "If Jerry Paterson can bring our export sales up to $2 million a year, it will more than pay his expenses," Sauder recalls. "It took us three to four years to reach a critical mass in exporting, but I knew after a year or so that we were going to give our program full support, and that we were in it for the long pull, not casually and not lukewarm."

Paterson quickly went to work, and allayed Sauder's initial fears about jumping into exporting. Soon he realized that the company's proximity to particleboard suppliers in central Ohio would help keep prices competitive worldwide. Concerns over decor preferences also evaporated. "Our styles and colors have proved very acceptable, especially in France, where our penetration has been remarkable. But we're doing very well in Turkey, too." Add to this a positive outlook for sales in India and plans to ship to China via Hong Kong.

"We proved in a very short time that we can compete anywhere in the world," Sauder says. Many U.S. exporters are discovering that American labor can compete with workers anywhere in the world, thanks to increased efficiency and the higher quality of the finished product. "[Our made-in-the-U.S.A. products] are a great sales booster for us the world over."

SOURCES: Daniel McConville, "An Accidental Exporter Turns Serious," *World Trade*, March 1996, 28; and Sauder Company Web site, **http://www.sauder.com**, accessed November 3, 2002.

the new job, managers frequently consider an entirely new set of options for growth and expansion, one of which may be international marketing activities. *The International Marketplace 7.2* shows how a firm can start its initial international involvement through serendipity and later on expand into full-fledged export activity due to expertise from a new employee.

A significant internal event can be another major change agent. A new employee who firmly believes that the firm should undertake international marketing may find ways to motivate management. The development of a new product useful abroad can serve as such an event, as can the receipt of new information about current product uses. As an example, a manufacturer of hospital beds learned that beds it was selling domestically were being resold in a foreign country. Further, the beds it sold for $600 each were resold overseas for approximately $1,300. This new piece of information served to trigger a strong interest on the part of the company's management in entering international markets.

In small and medium-sized firms (firms with fewer than 250 employees), the initial decision to export is usually made by the president, with substantial input provided by the marketing department. The carrying out of the decision—that is, the initiation of actual international marketing activities and the implementation of these activities—is then primarily the responsibility of marketing personnel. Only in the final decision stage of evaluating international marketing activities does the major emphasis rest again with the president of the firm. In order to influence a firm internally, it therefore appears that the major emphasis should be placed first on convincing the president to enter the international marketplace and then on convincing the marketing department that international marketing is an important activity. Conversely, the marketing department is a good place to be if one wants to become active in international business.

External Change Agents and Export Intermediaries

The primary outside influence on a firm's decision to become international is foreign demand. Expressions of such demand through, for example, inquiries from abroad have a powerful effect on initial interest in entering the international marketplace. Unsolicited orders from abroad are one major factor that encourages firms to begin exporting. In the United States, for example, such unsolicited orders have been found to account for more than half of all cases of export initiation by small and medium-sized firms. Due to the growth of corporate Web sites, firms can become unplanned participants in the international market even more often. For example, customers from abroad can visit a Web site and place an international order, even though a firm's plans may have been strictly domestic. Of course, a firm can choose to ignore foreign interest and lose out on new markets. Alternatively, it can find itself unexpectedly an exporter.[13] Such firms can be called **accidental exporters.** While good fortune may have initiated the export activity, over the longer term the firm must start planning how to systematically increase its international expansion or, at least, how to make more of these accidents happen.

Other major outside influences are the statements and actions of other firms in the same industry. Information that an executive in a competing firm considers international markets to be valuable and worthwhile to develop easily captures the attention of management. Such statements not only have source credibility but also are viewed with a certain amount of fear because a successful competitor may eventually infringe on the firm's business. Formal and informal meetings among managers from different firms at trade association meetings, conventions, or business roundtables therefore often serve as a major change agent.

A third, quite influential, change agent consists of domestic distributors. Often, such distributors are engaged, through some of their other business activities, in international marketing. To increase their international distribution volume, they encourage purely domestic firms also to participate in the international market. This is true not only for exports but also for imports. For example, a major customer of a manufacturing firm may find that materials available from abroad, if used in the domestic production process, would make the product available at lower cost. In such instances, the customer may approach the supplier and strongly encourage foreign sourcing.

Banks and other service firms, such as accountants, can serve as major change agents by alerting domestic clients to international opportunities. Although these service providers historically follow their major multinational clients abroad, increasingly they are establishing a foreign presence. They frequently work with domestic clients on expanding their market reach in the hope that their services will be used for any international transactions that result.

Chambers of commerce and other business associations that interact with firms locally can frequently heighten international marketing interests. In most instances, these organizations function only as secondary intermediaries, because true change is brought about by the presence and encouragement of other managers.

Governmental efforts on the national or local level can also serve as a major change agent. In light of the contributions exports make to growth, employment, and tax revenue, governments increasingly are becoming active in encouraging and supporting exports. As was explained in Chapter 2, export promotion has become an integral part of most nations' trade policies.

In the United States, the Department of Commerce is particularly involved in encouraging exports. Its district offices are charged with increasing the international marketing activities of U.S. firms. Frequently, district officers, with the help of voluntary groups such as district export councils, visit firms and attempt to analyze their international marketing opportunities.

Increasingly, other governmental entities are also actively encouraging firms to participate in the international market. This takes place primarily on the state and local levels. Many states have formed economic development agencies that assist companies by providing information, displaying products abroad, and sometimes even helping with financing. Trade missions and similar activities are also being carried out by some of the larger cities. Although it is difficult to measure the effects of these efforts, it appears that due to their closeness to firms, such state and local government authorities can become major factors in influencing firms to go international.

Export Intermediaries

Firms that do not care to export can still participate in international marketing by making use of international market intermediaries. One obvious possibility is the selling of merchandise to a domestic firm that in turn sells it abroad. For example, many products are sold to multinational corporations that use them as input for their foreign sales. Similarly, products sold to the U.S. Department of Defense may ultimately be shipped to military outposts abroad. Alternatively, an exporter may buy products domestically to round out an international product line or a buyer from abroad may purchase goods during a visit.

Frequently firms also enter the international market with the help of market intermediaries who specialize in bringing firms or their goods and services to the global market. Often, they have detailed information about the competitive conditions in certain markets or they have personal contacts with potential buyers abroad. They can also evaluate credit risk, call on customers abroad, and manage the physical delivery of the product. Two key intermediaries are export management companies and trading companies.

Export Management Companies

Export management companies (EMCs) are domestic firms that specialize in performing international marketing services as commission representatives or as distributors for several other firms. Most EMCs are quite small. They are frequently formed by one or two major principals with experience in international marketing or in a particular geographic area. Their expertise enables them to offer specialized services to domestic corporations.

EMCs have two primary forms of operation. They either take title to goods and operate internationally on their own account, or they perform services as agents. In the first instance, the EMC offers a conventional export channel in that it does not have any form of geographic exclusivity and tends to negotiate price with suppliers on every transaction. As an agent, an EMC is likely to have either an informal or a formal contractual relationship, which specifies exclusivity agreements and, often, sales quotas. In addition, price arrangements and promotional support payments are agreed on, which simplifies ongoing transactions.[14] Because EMCs often serve a variety of clients, their mode of operation may vary from client to client and from transaction to transaction—that is, an EMC may act as an agent for one client, whereas for another client, or even for the same one on a different occasion, it may operate as a distributor.

When serving as an agent, the EMC is primarily in charge of developing foreign marketing and sales strategies and establishing contacts abroad. Because the EMC does not share in the profits from a sale, it depends heavily on a high sales volume, on which it charges commission. It may therefore be tempted to take on as many products and as many clients as possible in order to obtain a high turnover. The risk in this is that the EMC will spread itself too thin and cannot adequately represent all the clients and products it carries. This risk is particularly great for small EMCs.

When operating as a distributor, the EMC purchases products from the domestic firm, takes the title, and assumes the trading risk. Selling in its own name offers the opportunity to reap greater profits than does acting as an agent. The potential for greater profitability is appropriate because the EMC has drastically reduced the risk for the domestic firm while increasing its own risk. The burden of the merchandise acquired provides a major motivation to complete an international sale successfully. The domestic firm selling to the EMC is in the comfortable position of having sold its merchandise and received its money without having to deal with the complexities of the international market. On the other hand, the firm is unlikely to gather much international marketing expertise and therefore relegates itself to some extent to remaining a purely domestic firm.

For the concept of an export management company to work, both parties must fully recognize the delegation of responsibilities; the costs associated with these activities; and the need for information sharing, cooperation, and mutual reliance. On the manufacturer's side, use of an EMC should be viewed as a major channel commitment. This requires a thorough investigation of the intermediary and the advisability of relying on its efforts, a willingness to cooperate on a prolonged basis, and a willingness to reward it properly for these efforts. The EMC in turn must adopt a flexible approach to managing the export relationship. As access to the Internet is making customers increasingly sophisticated, export management companies must ensure that they continue to deliver true value added. They must acquire, develop, and deploy resources such as new knowledge about foreign markets or about export processes, in order to lower their client firm's export-related transaction costs and therefore remain useful intermediaries.[15] By doing so, the EMC can clearly let the client know that the cost is worth the service.

Trading Companies

Another major intermediary is the trading company. The concept was originated by the European trading houses such as the Fuggers and was soon formalized by the monarchs. Hoping to expand their imperial powers and wealth, kings chartered traders to form corporate bodies that enjoyed exclusive trading rights and protection by the naval forces in exchange for tax payments. Today, the most famous trading companies are the **sogoshosha** of Japan. Names like Sumitomo, Mitsubishi, Mitsui, and C. Itoh have become household words around the world. These general trading companies play a unique role in world commerce by importing, exporting, countertrading, investing, and manufacturing. Because of their vast size, they can benefit from economies of scale and perform their operations at very low profit margins.

Four major reasons have been given for the success of the Japanese sogoshosha. First, by concentrating on obtaining and disseminating information about market opportunities and by investing huge funds in the development of information systems, these firms now have the mechanisms and organizations in place to gather, evaluate, and translate market information into business opportunities. Second, economies of scale permit them to take advantage of their vast transaction volume to obtain preferential treatment by, for example, negotiating transportation rates or even opening up new transportation routes. Third, these firms serve large internal markets, not only in Japan but also around the world, and can benefit from opportunities for barter trade. Finally, sogoshosha have access to vast quantities of capital, both within Japan and in the international capital markets. They can therefore carry out many transactions that are larger and riskier than is feasible for other firms. In the 1990s, as more Japanese firms set up their own global networks, the share of Japan's trade handled by the sogoshosha declined. However, three giants continue to survive by shifting their strategy to expand their domestic activities in Japan, entering more newly developing markets, increasing their trading activities between countries, and forming joint ventures with non-Japanese firms.

For many decades, the emergence of trading companies was commonly believed to be a Japan-specific phenomenon. Over time, however, prodded by government legislation, successful trading companies have also emerged in countries as diverse as Brazil, South Korea, and Turkey.

Export trading company (ETC) legislation designed to improve the export performance of small and medium-sized firms has also been implemented in the United States. Bank participation in trading companies was permitted and the antitrust threat to joint export efforts was reduced through precertification of planned activities by the U.S. Department of Commerce. Businesses were encouraged to join together to export, or offer export services, by passage of the Export Trading Company Act.

Permitting banks to participate in ETCs was intended to allow ETCs better access to capital and therefore to more trading transactions and easier receipt of title to goods. The relaxation of antitrust provisions in turn was to enable firms to form joint ventures more easily. The cost of developing and penetrating international markets would then be shared, with the proportional share being, for many small and medium-sized firms, much easier to bear. As an example, in case a warehouse is needed to secure foreign-market penetration, one firm alone does not have to bear all the costs. A consortium of firms can jointly rent a foreign warehouse. Similarly, each firm need not station a service technician abroad at substantial cost. Joint funding of a service center by several firms makes the cost less prohibitive for each one. The trading company concept also offers a one-stop shopping center for both the firm and its foreign customers. The firm can be assured that all international functions will be performed efficiently by the trading company, and at the same time, the foreign customer will have to deal with fewer individual firms.

Although ETCs seem to offer major benefits to U.S. firms wishing to penetrate international markets, they have not been used very extensively. By 2002 only 186 individual ETCs had been certified by the U.S. Department of Commerce. Yet these certificates covered more than 5,000 firms, mainly because various trade associations had applied for certification for all of their members.[16] Perhaps the greatest potential of ETCs lies with trade associations. It may also be a worthwhile concept for firms and banks to consider.

Banks need to evaluate whether the mentalities of bankers and traders can be made compatible. Traders, for example, are known for seizing an opportunity, whereas bankers often appear to move more slowly. A key challenge will be to find ways to successfully blend business entrepreneurship with banking regulations.

Firms participating in trading companies by joining or forming them should be aware of the difference between product- and market-driven ETCs. Firms may have a strong tendency to use their trading company primarily to dispose of their merchandise. International sales, however, depend primarily on the demand and the market. An ETC must therefore accomplish a balance between the demands of the market and the supply of the members in order to be successful.

The trading company itself must solicit continuous feedback on foreign market demands and changes in these demands so that its members will be able to maintain a winning international product and service mix. Substantial attention must be paid to gathering information on the needs and wants of foreign customers and disseminating this information to the participating U.S. firms. Otherwise, lack of responsiveness to foreign market demands will result in a decline of the ETC's effectiveness.

International Stages

For many firms, internationalization is a gradual process. Particularly in a market as large as the United States, firms are rarely formed expressly to engage in international marketing activities. In small markets, however, firms may very well be *born global,* founded for the explicit purpose of marketing abroad because of the recognized importance of international marketing and because the domestic economy may be too small to support their activities. It appears that in some countries more than a third of exporting firms commenced their export activities within two years of establishment.[17] Such **innate,** or start-up, **exporters** may have a distinct role to play in an economy's international trade involvement.

In addition, firms with a strong e-commerce focus may also be gaining rapid global exposure due to the ease of outreach and access. Such rapid exposure, however, should not be confused with internationalization, since it may often take a substantial amount of time to translate exposure into international business activities.

In most instances today, firms begin their operations in the domestic market. From their home location, they gradually expand, and, over time, some of them become interested in the international market. The development of this interest typically appears to proceed in several stages. In each one of these stages, firms are measurably different in their capabilities, problems, and needs.[18] Initially the vast majority of firms are not at all interested in the international marketplace. Frequently, management will not even fill an unsolicited export order if one is received. Should unsolicited orders or other international market stimuli continue over time, however, a firm may gradually become a **partially interested exporter.** Management will then fill unsolicited export orders.

Prime candidates among firms to make this transition from uninterested to partially interested are those companies that have a track record of domestic market expansion.[19] In the next stage, the firm gradually begins to explore international markets, and management is willing to consider the feasibility of exporting. After this **exploratory stage,** the firm becomes an **experimental exporter,** usually to psychologically close countries. However, management is still far from being committed to international marketing activities.

At the next stage, the firm evaluates the impact that exporting has had on its general activities. Here, of course, the possibility exists that a firm will be disappointed with its international market performance and will withdraw from these activities. On the other hand, frequently, it will continue to exist as an experienced small exporter. The final stage of this process is that of **export adaptation.** Here a firm is an experienced exporter to a particular country and adjusts its activities to changing exchange rates, tariffs, and other variables. Management is ready to explore the feasibility of exporting to additional countries that are psychologically farther away. Frequently, this level of adaptation is reached once export transactions comprise 15 percent of sales volume. Just as parking ticket income, originally seen as unexpected revenue, gradually became incorporated into city budgets, the income from export marketing may become incorporated into the budget and plans of the firm. In these instances, the firm can be considered a strategic participant in the international market.

The population of exporting firms within these stages does not remain stable. Researchers of U.S. firms have found that in any given year, 15 percent of exporters will stop exporting by the next year, while 10 percent of nonexporters will enter the foreign market. The most critical junctures for the firm are the points at which it begins or ceases exporting.[20]

As can be expected, firms in different stages are faced with different problems. Firms at an export awareness stage—partially interested in the international market—are primarily concerned with operational matters such as information flow and the mechanics of carrying out international business transactions. They understand that a totally new body of knowledge and expertise is needed and try to acquire it. Companies that have already had some exposure to international markets begin to think about tactical marketing issues such as communication and sales effort. Finally, firms that have reached the export adaptation phase are mainly strategy- and service-oriented, which is to say that they worry about longer-range issues such as service delivery and regulatory changes. Utilizing the traditional marketing concept, one can therefore recognize that increased sophistication in international markets translates into increased application of marketing knowledge on the part of firms. The more they become active in international markets, the more firms recognize that a marketing orientation internationally is just as essential as it is in the domestic market.

Licensing and Franchising

In addition to exporting, licensing and franchising are alternatives open to and used by all types of firms, large and small. They offer flexibility in the international market approach, reflecting the needs of the firm and the circumstances in the market. A small firm, for example, may choose to use licensing to benefit from a foreign business concept or to expand without much capital investment. A multinational corporation may use the same strategy to rapidly enter foreign markets in order to take advantage of new conditions and foreclose some opportunities to its competition. It is important to recognize licensing and franchising as additional opportunities for market expansion. These options can be used both in lieu of or in addition to the export strategy discussed previously. Another set of options—consisting of foreign direct investment and its subforms, such as joint ventures and management contracts—will be addressed later in the book.

Licensing

Under a licensing agreement, one firm, the licensor, permits another to use its intellectual property in exchange for compensation designated as a royalty. The recipient firm is the licensee. The property might include patents, trademarks, copyrights, technology, technical know-how, or specific marketing skills. For example, a firm that has developed new packaging for liquids can permit other firms abroad to use the same process. Licensing therefore amounts to exporting and importing intangibles. As *The International Marketplace 7.3* shows, licensing has great potential that may increase for a long time to come.

Assessment of Licensing

Licensing has intuitive appeal to many potential international marketers. As an entry strategy, it may require neither capital investment nor knowledge and marketing strength in foreign markets. By earning royalty income, it provides an opportunity to obtain an additional return on research and development investments already incurred. After initial costs, the licensor can reap benefits until the end of the contract period. Licensing reduces risk of exposure to government intervention in that the licensee is typically a local company that can provide leverage against government action. Licensing will help to avoid host country regulations that are focused on equity ventures. It may also serve as a stage in the internationalization of the firm by providing a means by which foreign markets can be tested without major involvement of capital or management time. Similarly, licensing can be used as a strategy to preempt a market before the entry of competition, especially if the licensor's resources permit full-scale involvement only in selected markets. A final reason that licensing activities are increasing is the growing global protection of intellectual property rights. In many countries, pirated technology, processes, and products are still abundant. However, progress by the World Trade Organization (WTO) has improved the protection of intellectual property and the enforcement of such protection by governments. With greater protection of their proprietary knowledge, companies are more willing to transfer such knowledge internationally.[21] In instances of high levels of piracy, a licensing agreement with a strong foreign partner may also add value because now the partner becomes a local force with a distinct interest in rooting out unlicensed activities.

THE INTERNATIONAL MARKETPLACE 7.3

International Franchising That Will Melt in Your Mouth

The United Arab Emirates (UAE) is a federation of seven independent states located in the southeastern corner of the Arabian Peninsula. It is bordered by the Persian Gulf to the north, Saudi Arabia to the south and west, and Oman and the Gulf of Oman to the east. Rich in oil, the region has enjoyed rapid growth and modernization. An estimated 86 percent of the country's population is urban. The city of Abu Dhabi—the federal capital and largest city of the UAE—serves as the financial, transportation, and communications center of this major petroleum-producing area. The city embodies the unique blend of traditional and modern life that marks the region.

Those who have visited the growing metropolis of Abu Dhabi will not associate the city's name with huge billboards advertising a Colorado-based, women-owned chocolate factory. But that is exactly what a visitor would find ever since a master franchise licensing agreement was signed between the Rocky Mountain Chocolate Factory, Inc., and the family-owned Al Muhairy Group, which operates franchises in the UAE, Saudi Arabia, Oman, Kuwait, Bahrain, and Qatar.

Rocky Mountain Chocolate Factory, Inc., is a confectionary manufacturer that produces an extensive line of chocolate and other confectionary candies in old-fashioned Victorian candy kitchens using traditional American candy-making methods. The company touts its reputation for its "entertaining fudge-making demonstrations, old-fashioned caramel apples, and larger-than-life handmade chocolates." In addition, it is also an international franchiser with 228 retail locations in the United States and Canada. Most recently, Rocky Mountain has added the Middle East to its repertoire, thanks to a franchising agreement with the Al Muhairy Group.

Greg Pope, Rocky Mountain's vice president of franchise development, states: "We are learning that Europeans and Middle Eastern cultures are keen on our theme of in-store candy preparation. . . . Chocolate has a universal appeal and is considered a gourmet luxury. Rocky Mountain's dark chocolates, Butter English Toffee, and Rocky Pop are particular favorites of the UAE consumers."

So how did the market entry come about? Rocky Mountain's owners decided to enlist the aid of the Commercial Service—a global network of international trade experts from the U.S. Commerce Department who help small and mid-sized U.S. companies succeed in global markets. The firm sent marketing packets to Commercial Service offices around the world and attended a franchising trade show in Milan, Italy. An advertisement in the American Business Information Center in Abu Dhabi caught the eye of Sanjay Duggal, a local entrepreneur, who came for a visit to Rocky Mountain's headquarters in Durango, Colorado.

In May 2000, the Al Muhairy Group, which had become the master franchise license holder for the Gulf Region, opened a Rocky Mountain Chocolate Factory franchise in Al Muhairy Centre, an upscale shopping center in Abu Dhabi. Within a few months, the venture was a success and Rocky Mountain hosted a Chocoholics Evening for 120 locals and expatriates in its new Middle Eastern hometown.

SOURCES: Rocky Mountain Chocolate Factory Web site, **http://www. rmcf.com**, accessed September 3, 2002; and Sandra Necessary and Nancy Charles-Parker, "Chocolate-Covered Exports: Colorado Firm Finds Sweet Tooth in Mideast," *Export America—Success Stories* 2 (January 2001).

Licensing has nevertheless come under criticism from supranational organizations, such as the United Nations Conference on Trade and Development (UNCTAD). It has been alleged that licensing provides a mechanism by which older technology is capitalized on by industrialized-country multinational corporations (MNCs). Licensees may often want labor-intensive techniques or machinery, however. Guinness Brewery, for example, in order to produce Guinness Stout in Nigeria, imported licensed equipment that had been used in Ireland at the turn of the twentieth century. Even though this equipment was obsolete by Western standards, it had additional economic life in Nigeria because it presented a good fit with Nigeria's needs.

Licensing offers a foreign entity the opportunity for immediate market entry with a proven concept. It therefore reduces the risk of R&D failures, the cost of designing around the licensor's patents, or the fear of patent infringement litigation. Furthermore, most licensing agreements provide for ongoing cooperation and support, thus enabling the licensee to benefit from new developments. Licensing may also enable the international marketer to enter a foreign market that is closed to either imports or direct foreign investments.

Licensing is not without disadvantages. To a large degree, it may leave the international marketing functions to the licensee. As a result, the licensor may not gain sufficient international marketing expertise to ready itself for subsequent world market penetration. Moreover, the initial toehold in the foreign market may not be a foot in the door. Depending on the licensing arrangement, quite the opposite may take place. In exchange for the royalty, the licensor may create its own competitor not only in the markets for which the agreement was made but also in third markets.

Principal Issues in Negotiating Licensing Agreements

The key issues in negotiating licensing agreements include the scope of the rights conveyed, compensation, licensee compliance, dispute resolution, and the term and termination of the agreement.[22] The more clearly these are spelled out, the more trouble-free the association between the two parties can be.

The rights conveyed are product and/or patent rights. Defining their scope involves specifying the technology, know-how, or show-how to be included, the format, and guarantees. An example of format specification is an agreement on whether manuals will be translated into the licensee's language.

Compensation issues may be heavily disputed and argued. The costs the licensor wants to cover are (1) **transfer costs,** which are all variable costs incurred in transferring technology to a licensee and all ongoing costs of maintaining the agreement, (2) **R&D costs** incurred in researching and developing the licensed technology, and (3) **opportunity costs** incurred in the foreclosure of other sources of profit, such as exports or direct investment. To cover these costs, the licensor wants a share of the profits generated from the use of the license.

Licensees usually do not want to include allowances for opportunity costs, and they often argue that R&D costs have already been covered by the licensor through the profit from previous sales. In theory, royalties can be seen as profit sharing; in practice, royalties are a function of both the licensor's minimum necessary return and the cost of the licensee's next-best alternative.

The methods of compensating the licensor can take the form of running royalties, such as 5 percent of the licensee sales, and/or up-front payments, service fees, and disclosure fees (for proprietary data). Sometimes, government regulations pose an obstacle to the collection of royalty payments. In such instances, the know-how transferred can be capitalized as part of a cooperative venture, where a specific value is attributed to the information. Payments are then received as profits or dividends.

Licensee compliance on a number of dimensions must be stipulated in the agreement: (1) export control regulations, (2) confidentiality of the intellectual property and technology provided, and (3) record keeping and provisions for licensor audits, which are done periodically, usually a minimum of once a year.

Finally, the term, termination, and survival of rights must be specified. Government regulations in the licensee's market will have to be studied, and if the conditions are not favorable (for example, in terms of the maximum allowable duration), a waiver should be applied for.

Trademark Licensing

For companies that can trade on their names and characters, **trademark licensing** has become a substantial source of worldwide revenue. The names or logos of designers, literary characters, sports teams, and movie stars appear on merchandise such as clothing, games, foods and beverages, gifts and novelties, toys, and home furnishings. British designer Laura Ashley started the first major furniture program, licensing her name to Henredon Furniture Industries. Coca-Cola licensed its name to Murjani to be used on blue jeans, sweatshirts, and windbreakers. The licensors are likely to make millions of dollars with little effort, whereas the licensees can produce a branded product that consumers will recognize immediately. Fees can range between 7 and 12 percent of net sales for merchandising license agreements.[23]

Both licensor and licensee may run into difficulty if the trademark is used for a product too far removed from the original success or if the licensed product casts a shadow on the reputation of the licensor. In licensing a trademark, consumer perceptions have to be researched to make sure the brand's positioning will not change. As an example, when Löwenbräu was exported to the United States, it was the number-one imported beer sold in the market. However, when the product name was licensed to Miller Brewing Company for domestic production, the beer's positioning (and subsequently its target audience) changed drastically in the minds of the consumers, resulting in a major decline in sales.

Franchising

In franchising, a parent company (the franchiser) grants another, independent entity (the franchisee) the right to do business in a specified manner. This right can take the form of selling the franchiser's products or using its name, production, preparation and marketing techniques, or its business approach. Usually, franchising involves a combination of these elements. The major forms of franchising are manufacturer-retailer systems (such as car dealerships), manufacturer-wholesaler systems (such as soft drink companies), and service firm–retailer systems (such as lodging services and fast food outlets). One can differentiate between product/trade franchising, in which the major emphasis rests on the product or commodity to be sold, and business format franchising, in which the focus is on ways of doing business. Even though many franchising firms are large, franchising can be a useful international market expansion method for any business operation with international appeal.

Franchising origins are in Bavaria, but it has been adopted by various types of businesses in many countries. In 2002, global franchise sales by almost 16,000 franchisors and more than 1 million franchisees were estimated to be close to $1.5 trillion.[24] Figure 7.1 shows an example of a U.S. fast food franchise that has successfully entered the Hungarian market. Non-U.S. franchisers are penetrating international markets as well and are doing so quite aggressively. For example, 24 percent of British franchisers and 30 percent of French franchisers are active outside their home countries.[25] In the Vietnamese market one can encounter several Asian-owned franchises such as the South Korean–based Burger Khan, Thailand's Five Star Chicken, and Japan's Lotto Burger.[26]

The typical reasons for the international expansion of franchise systems are market potential, financial gain, and saturated domestic markets. From a franchisee's perspective, the franchise is beneficial because it reduces risk by implementing a proven concept. In Malaysia, for example, the success rate in the franchise business is 90 percent, compared to the 80 percent failure rate of all new businesses.[27]

Franchising agreements are usually also beneficial from a governmental perspective. From a source-country view, franchising does not replace exports or export jobs. From a recipient-country view, franchising requires little outflow of foreign exchange, and the bulk of the profit generated remains within the country.[28]

With all its benefits, franchising also encounters some problems. One key issue is that companies first need to find out what their special capabilities are. This requires that there be an identification and codification of knowledge assets in firms—that "they know what they have."[29] After such an investigation, companies can then launch an aggressive program to share knowledge.

Figure 7.1	Fast Food in Hungary

SOURCE: Copyright © Ilona Czinkota.

A second concern is the need for a great degree of standardization. Without such standardization, many of the benefits of the transferred know-how are lost. Typically, such standardization will include the use of a common business name, similar layout, and similar production or service processes. Apart from leading to efficient operations, all of these factors will also contribute to a high degree of international recognizability. At the same time, however, standardization does not mean 100 percent uniformity. Adjustments may be necessary in the final end product so that local market conditions can be taken into account. For example, fast-food outlets in Europe often need to serve beer and wine to be attractive to the local clientele. In order to enter the Indian market, where cows are considered sacred, McDonald's has developed nonbeef burgers. Key to success is the development of a franchising program that maintains a high degree of recognizability and efficiency benefits while being responsive to local cultural preferences.

Another key issue is the protection of the total business system that a franchise offers. Once a business concept catches on, local competition may emerge quite

Table 7.3	Key Impediments to International Franchising

- Meeting and training qualified and reliable franchisees overseas
- Security and protection of industrial property and trademarks in foreign countries
- Keeping current with market prospects overseas
- Familiarity with business practices overseas
- Foreign government regulations on business operations
- Foreign regulations or limitations on royalty fees
- Negotiation with foreign franchisees
- Foreign regulations or limitations on entry of franchise business
- Collection and transfer of franchise fee
- Control of quality or quantity of product or service
- Providing technical support overseas
- Pricing franchise for a foreign market
- Promotion and advertising opportunities for franchise overseas
- Sourcing and availability of raw materials, equipment, and other products
- Shipping and distribution of raw materials required to operate a foreign franchise
- Financing franchise operations overseas
- Shipping and handling of equipment needed to operate a foreign franchise

SOURCE: Adapted from Ben L. Kedia, David J. Ackerman, and Robert T. Justis, "Changing Barriers to the Internationalization of Franchising Operations: Perceptions of Domestic and International Franchisors," *The International Executive* 37 (July/August 1995): 329–348.

quickly with an imitation of the product, the general style of operation, and even with a similar name.

Government intervention can also represent major problems. For example, government restrictions on the type of services to be offered or on royalty remissions can prevent franchising arrangements or lead to a separation between a company and its franchisees.

Selection and training of franchisees present another key concern. Many franchise systems have run into difficulty by expanding too quickly and granting franchises to unqualified entities. Although the local franchisee knows the market best, the franchiser still needs to understand the market for product adaptation purposes and operational details. The franchiser should be the conductor of a coordinated effort by the individual franchisees—for example, in terms of sharing ideas and engaging in joint marketing efforts, such as cooperative advertising. However, even here difficulties can emerge consisting mostly of complications in selecting appropriate advertising media, effective copy testing, effective translation of the franchiser's message, and the use of appropriate sales promotion tools. Table 7.3 summarizes research findings regarding the challenges faced in international franchising.

To encourage better-organized and more successful growth, many companies turn to the **master franchising system,** wherein foreign partners are selected and awarded the rights to a large territory in which they in turn can subfranchise. As a result, the franchiser gains market expertise and an effective screening mechanism for new franchises, without incurring costly mistakes.[30]

The Internationalization Process

Linking the various decision components and characteristics discussed so far facilitates an understanding of the process that a firm must undergo in its internationalization efforts. Figure 7.2 presents a model of the internationalization process. The

Figure 7.2   A Model of the Internationalization Process

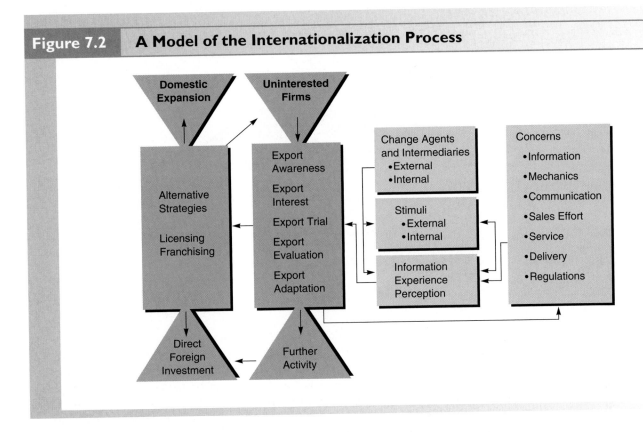

model demonstrates the interaction between components and shows how a firm gradually grows into becoming a full participant in the global arena. With the help of this model, both management and the prospective employee can determine the firm's stage in the process and the changes needed to attain continued progress. A deeper insight into the international level of the firm permits a better understanding of what needs to be done to propel the firm forward in its internationalization. In addition, current or future employees can also use the internationalization process in order to position themselves best for employment or advancement in the firm.

As a firm becomes international, unusual things can happen to both risk and profit. In light of the gradual development of expertise, the many concerns about engaging in a new activity, and a firm's uncertainty with the new environment it is about to enter, management's perception of risk exposure grows. Domestically, the firm has gradually learned about the market and therefore managed to decrease its risk. In the course of new international expansion, the firm now encounters new and unfamiliar factors, exposing it to increased risk. At the same time, because of the investment needs required by a serious international expansion effort, immediate profit performance may slip. In the longer term, increasing familiarity with international markets and the benefits of serving diversified markets will decrease the firm's risk below the previous "domestic only" level and increase profitability as well. For the most part, the more advanced and experienced the firm, the lower the perception of the costs and risks of exporting and the higher the perceived benefits.[31] In the short term, however, managers may face an unusual, and perhaps unacceptable, situation: rising risk accompanied by decreasing profitability. In light of this reality, which is depicted in Figure 7.3, many executives are tempted to either not initiate international activities or discontinue them.[32]

Understanding the internationalization process together with the behavior of risk and profitability can help management overcome the seemingly prohibitive cost of going international by understanding that the negative developments are only short-term. Success does require the firm to be a risk taker, and firms must

Figure 7.3   Profit and Risk During Early Internationalization

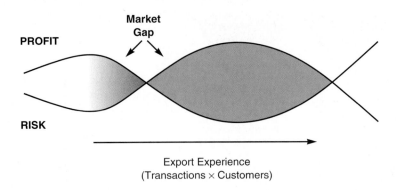

SOURCE: Michael R. Czinkota, "A National Export Assistance Policy for New and Growing Businesses," *Best Practices in International Business,* eds. M. Czinkota and I. Ronkainen (Mason, OH: South-Western, 2001), 35–45.

realize that to get there will take time. This satisfactory performance can be achieved in three ways: international effectiveness, efficiency, and competitive strength. Effectiveness is characterized by the acquisition of market share abroad and by increased sales. Efficiency is manifested later by rising profitability. Competitive strength refers then to the firm's position compared to other firms in the industry and is, due to the benefits of international market experience, likely to grow. The international marketer must appreciate the time and performance dimensions associated with going abroad in order to overcome short-term setbacks for the sake of long-term success.

Summary

Firms do not become experienced globalists overnight but rather progress gradually through an international development process. This process is the result of different motivations to internationalize, varying managerial and corporate characteristics of the firm, the influence of change agents, and the capability of the firm to overcome barriers.

The motivations can be either proactive or reactive. Proactive motivations are initiated by the firm's management and can consist of a perceived profit advantage, technological advantage, product advantage, exclusive market information, or managerial urge. Reactive motivations are the responses of management to environmental changes and pressures. Typical are competitive pressures, overproduction, declining domestic sales, or excess capacity. Firms that are primarily stimulated by proactive motivations are more likely to enter international markets aggressively and successfully.

An international orientation can also be brought about by change agents both external and internal to the firm. Typically, these are individuals and institutions that, due to their activities or goals, highlight the benefits of international activities. They can be managers who have traveled abroad or have carried out success-

ful international marketing ventures, banks, or government agencies. International intermediaries such as export management companies or trading companies can also be a key factor in bringing a firm's offering to the international market.

Over time, firms will progress through stages of international expertise and activity. In each one of these stages, firms are likely to have a distinct level of interest in the international market and require different types of information and help. Their outlook toward international markets is likely to progress gradually from purely operational concerns to a strategic international orientation. Only at that level will the firm have become a truly commited exporter. Firms may also expand internationally via licensing and franchising. The basic advantage of licensing is that it requires relatively less capital investment or knowledge of foreign markets than most other forms of international involvement. The major disadvantage is that licensing agreements typically have time limits, often prescribed by foreign governments, and may even result in creating a competitor. The reasons for global franchising expansion are typically market potential, financial gain, and saturated domestic markets. Franchisers must strike a balance between the need to adapt to local environments and the need to standardize to maintain international recognizability.

In spite of temporary unfavorable conditions for risk and profit, management must understand that export activities only develop gradually through the internationalization stages, and that satisfactory international performance consists of the three dimensions of growing sales and market share, higher profitability, and an improved competitive position.

Key Terms

Exterritorial Income Tax Exclusion (ETI)
safety-valve activity
psychological distance
accidental exporters
sogoshosha

export trading company (ETC)
innate exporters
partially interested exporter
exploratory stage
experimental exporter
export adaptation

transfer costs
R&D costs
opportunity costs
trademark licensing
master franchising system

Questions for Discussion

1. How might advances in information technology encourage a potential exporter to pursue international sales?
2. Discuss the difference between a proactive and a reactive firm, focusing your discussion on the international market.
3. Explain the benefits that international sales can have for domestic market activities.
4. Discuss the benefits and the drawbacks of treating international market activities as a safety valve mechanism.
5. What is meant by the concept of "psychological or psychic distance"?

6. How can an export intermediary avoid circumvention by a client or customer?
7. Comment on this statement: "Licensing is really not a form of international involvement because it requires no substantial additional effort on the part of the licensor."
8. Suggest reasons for the explosive international expansion of franchise systems.
9. What benefits could a potential franchiser receive from joining the International Franchise Association (**http://www.franchise.org**)?

Internet Exercise

1. What programs does the Ex-Im bank (**http://www.exim.gov**) offer that specifically benefit small businesses trying to export? What benefits can be derived from each?

2. Carefully examine the Overseas Private Investment Corporation Web site (**http://www.opic.gov**). Describe the type of country-specific information an exporter can gather using this Web site.

Recommended Readings

Alon, Ilan. *The Internationalization of U.S. Franchising Systems*. New York: Garland Publishing, 2000.

Goldman, Steven M., and Richard M. Asbill. *Fundamentals of International Franchising*. Chicago: American Bar Association, 2001.

International Trade Centre. *Export Quality Management: An Answer Book for Small and Medium-Sized Exporters*. Geneva: ITC, 2001.

International Trade Centre. *World Directory of Importer's Associations*. Geneva: ITC, 2002.

Johnson, Thomas E. *Export/Import Procedures*. New York: AMACOM, 2002.

Joyner, Nelson T. *How to Build an Export Business*, 2nd ed. Reston, VA: Federation of International Trade Associations, 2000.

McCue, Sarah. *Trade Secrets: The Export Answer Book*. Geneva: ITC, 2001.

Mendelsohn, Martin. *The Guide to Franchising*, 6th ed. New York: Cassell Academic, 2000.

Noonan, Chris. *Cim Handbook of Export Marketing*. Boston: Butterworth-Heinemann, 2000.

Woznick, Alexandra, and Edward G. Hinkelman. *A Basic Guide to Exporting*, 3rd ed. Novato, CA: World Trade Press, 2000.

chapter 8

Product Adaptation

THE INTERNATIONAL MARKETPLACE   8.1

Europeanizing Products

Murray, Inc. has had to change the way it has made lawn mowers for decades. Its riding and walking models are now quieter because of new noise standards imposed by the European Union (EU). "We had to slow down the fan blade to cut noise," says Ray Elmy, vice president for design engineering. "However, it will not exhaust and bag grass as well, and our costs have increased." In spite of increased production costs, the company made the changes because a significant portion of its $1 billion in sales comes from European customers. Furthermore, over half of the 35 countries exported to by Murray are in Europe.

Murray's changes are not unique. For regulated products, that is, products covered by directive, the EU has developed single sets of requirements that must be met in order to sell products in the 15 member countries of the EU. With the European Economic Area (EEA) agreement in force January 1, 1994, the number of countries affected increased to 18. The expected expansion of the EU in 2004 will add another ten countries to the group (two of which Murray has already started exports to because they have harmonized their requirements with those of the EU). Many different categories of products are regulated—toys, construction products, pressure vessels, gas appliances, medical devices, telecommunications terminal equipment, and machinery, among others. Overall, approximately half the annual $159 billion of U.S. goods exported to the EU falls within the regulated product category. The harmonization of technical standards focuses essentially on health and safety aspects of products, with minimum levels being established. Compliance with the standards means that goods may circulate freely throughout the EEA and bear the "CE" safety mark, if needed.

For unregulated products, that is, those not covered by Europewide directives, such as paper and furniture, mutual recognition of national standards applies. This means that a U.S. exporter can certify to U.S. standards, and if these standards are accepted by at least one member country, they will be accepted throughout the EEA. For example, a French charter airline was refused certification for a new model Boeing 737 because no French standard for the model existed. The airline registered the aircraft in Ireland, and because the Irish Department of Transport had accepted U.S. requirements as an Irish standard, the airliner was then able to operate throughout Europe, including France.

A word of caution is in order. The "CE" mark is a minimal requirement and not the only one the exporter may be asked to meet. The "Geprüfte Sicherheit" (GS) mark has never been officially mandatory for goods sold in Germany, although in many cases an insurance company may require its client to buy only products that have this mark. German consumers also look for this mark in much the same way as U.S. consumers look for the *Good Housekeeping* Seal of Approval." Products without the GS mark can certainly be placed in the market but they might not be bought.

Although U.S. firms need to comply with European standards, it is more challenging to participate in their development. However, many U.S. firms have their personnel participate in international standardization programs. For example, executives from Bison Gear & Engineering take part in the Transatlantic Business Dialog, a government–industry effort to harmonize product standards. Furthermore, Mutual Recognition Agreements (MRAs) reached in 1998 allow for product assessments such as testing, inspecting, and certifying to be performed in the United States to EU standards and regulations, and vice versa. Thus, companies will be able to gain access to markets without regulatory delays.

Overall, the standards do come with these significant benefits:

- Companies that had to make as many as 18 versions of their products for Europe because of differing national standards now are able to produce just one.
- Marketing should prove more efficient. Approval in one country will serve as an EEA passport permitting the sale throughout the market.
- U.S. manufacturers may be forced to improve the quality of all of their products, a benefit to U.S. customers and U.S. competitiveness. To ensure that EU standards are not violated inadvertently through sloppy manufacturing, some product rules require adoption of an overall quality system approved by the International Organization for Standardization (ISO).

SOURCES: "European Union Gets Ready to Grow," *The Wall Street Journal*, October 10, 2002, A12–A13; "The Secret of U.S. Exports: Great Products," *Fortune*, January 10, 2000, 154(A-J); Erika Morphy, "CE-ing, and Believing," *Export Today* 14 (March 1998): 52–57; "U.S./Mutual Recognition Agreements," *USIS Washington Files*, June 23, 1997; Walter Poggi, "Trans-Atlantic Recognition," *Export Today* 12 (March 1996): 61; Paul Jensen, "Europe: The Uncommon Market," *Export Today* 10 (June 1994): 20–27; Erika Morphy, "American Labs and Foreign Approvals," *Export Today* 10 (June 1994): 29–32; Stephen C. Messner, "Adapting Products to Western Europe," *Export Today* 10 (March/April 1994): 16–18; Phillippe Bruno, "EC Product Standards Will Be Headache Relief," *Export Today* 9 (June 1993): 33–36; and Patrick Oster, "Europe's Standards Blitz Has Firms Scrambling," *The Washington Post*, October 18, 1992, H1–H4; **http://www.murray.com**; **http://www.eurunion.org/websites**; **http://www.bisongear.com**.

BECAUSE MEETING AND SATISFYING customer needs and expectations is the key to successful marketing, research findings on market traits and potential should be used to determine the optimal degree of customization needed in products and product lines relative to incremental cost of the effort. Even if today's emerging market trends allow this assessment to take place regionally or even globally, as seen in *The International Marketplace 8.1,* both regulations and customer behavior differences require that they and the severity of their impact be taken into consideration. Adapting to new markets should be seen not only in the context of one market but also as to how these changes can contribute to operations elsewhere. A new feature for a product or a new line item may have applicability on a broader scale, including the market that originated the product in the first place.[1]

Take the Boeing 737, for example. Due to saturated markets and competitive pressures, Boeing started to look for new markets in the Middle East, Africa, and Latin America for the 737 rather than kill the program altogether. To adjust to the idiosyncrasies of these markets, such as softer and shorter runways, the company redesigned the wings to allow for shorter landings and added thrust to the engines for quicker takeoffs. To make sure that the planes would not bounce even if piloted by less experienced captains, Boeing redesigned the landing gear and installed low-pressure tires to ensure that the plane would stick to the ground after initial touchdown. In addition to becoming a success in the intended markets, the new product features met with approval around the world and made the Boeing 737 the best-selling commercial jet in history.

This chapter is concerned with how the international marketer should adjust the firm's product offering to the marketplace, and it discusses the influence of an array of both external and internal variables. A delicate balance has to be achieved between the advantages of standardization and those of localization to maximize export performance. The challenge of intellectual property violation will be focused on as a specialty topic. International marketers must be ready to defend themselves against theft of their ideas and innovations.

Product Variables

The core of a firm's international operations is a product or service. This product or service can be defined as the complex combination of tangible and intangible elements that distinguishes it from the other entities in the marketplace, as shown in Figure 8.1. The firm's success depends on how good its product or service is and on how well the firm is able to differentiate the product from the offerings of competitors. Products can be differentiated by their composition, by their country of origin, by their tangible features such as packaging or quality, or by their augmented features such as warranty. Further, the positioning of the product in consumers' minds (for example, Volvo's reputation for safety) will add to its perceived value. The **core product**—for example, the ROM BIOS component of a personal computer or the recipe for a soup—may indeed be the same as or highly similar to those of competitors, leaving the marketer with the other tangible and **augmented features** of the product with which to achieve differentiation. Winnebago Industries, a leading exporter of motor homes, is finding increased interest in Europe for its "American-styled" recreation vehicles, or RVs, that offer more features and options than those made available by local competitors, such as automatic transmission and air conditioning. The only significant modifications made today are the conversion of the electrical system and installation of European-made kitchen appliances familiar to the customer. Furthermore, European buyers are assured

Figure 8.1	Elements of a Product

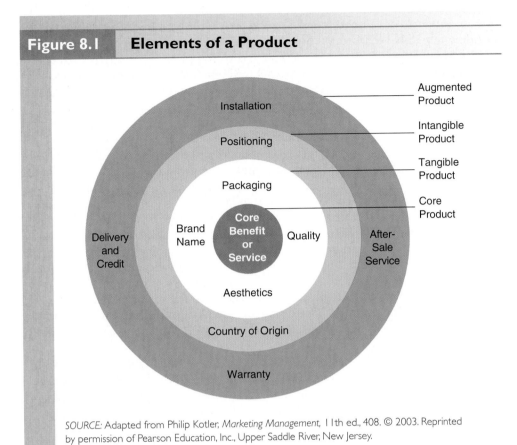

SOURCE: Adapted from Philip Kotler, *Marketing Management,* 11th ed., 408. © 2003. Reprinted by permission of Pearson Education, Inc., Upper Saddle River, New Jersey.

that they will receive the same quality of product and service as customers in the United States.[2]

To the potential buyer, a product is a complete cluster of value satisfactions. A customer attaches value to a product in proportion to its perceived ability to help solve problems or meet needs. This will go beyond the technical capabilities of the product to include intangible benefits sought. In Latin America, for example, great value is placed on products made in the United States. If packaging is localized, then the product may no longer have the *"Hecho in E.E.U.U."* appeal that motivates customers to choose the product over others, especially over local competitors. In some cases, customer behavior has to be understood from a broader perspective. For example, while Chinese customers may view Japanese products quite positively regarding their quality, historic animosity toward Japan may prevent them from buying Japanese goods or cause them to prefer goods from other sources.[3] Given such dramatic variation from market to market, careful assessment of product dimensions is called for.

Standardization versus Adaptation

The first question, after the internationalization decision has been made, concerns the product modifications that are needed or warranted. A firm has four basic alternatives in approaching international markets: (1) selling the product as is in the international marketplace, (2) modifying products for different countries and/or regions, (3) designing new products for foreign markets, and (4) incorporating all the differences into one product design and introducing a global product. Different approaches for implementing these alternatives exist. For example, a firm may identify only target markets where products can be marketed with little or no modification. A large consumer products marketer may have in its product line for any given markets global products, regional products, and purely local products. Some of these products developed for one market may later be introduced elsewhere, including the global marketer's "home" market. The Dockers line of casual wear originated at Levi Strauss's Argentine unit and was applied to loosely cut pants by Levi's Japanese subsidiary. The company's U.S. operation later adopted both, making Dockers the number-one brand in the category in the United States. Similar success has followed in over 40 country markets entered since.[4] Occasionally, the international marketplace may want something that the domestic market discards. By exporting chicken cuts that are unpopular (e.g., dark meat) or would be hauled off to landfills (such as chicken feet), U.S. poultry producers earn well over $1 billion annually from Russian and Chinese markets.[5]

The overall advantages and drawbacks of standardization versus adaptation are summarized in Table 8.1. The benefits of standardization—that is, selling the same product worldwide—are cost savings in production and marketing. In addition to these economies of scale, many point to economic integration as a driving force in making markets more unified. As a response to integration efforts around the world, especially in Europe, many international marketers are indeed standardizing many of their marketing approaches, such as branding and packaging, across markets. Similarly, having to face the same competitors in the major markets of the world will add to the pressure of having a worldwide approach to international marketing. However, in most cases, demand and usage conditions vary sufficiently to require some changes in the product or service itself.

Coca-Cola, Levi's jeans, and Colgate toothpaste have been cited as evidence that universal product and marketing strategy can work. Yet the argument that the world is becoming more homogenized may actually be true for only a limited number of products that have universal brand recognition and minimal product knowledge requirements for use.[6] Although product standardization is generally increasing, there are still substantial differences in company practices, depending on the products marketed and where they are marketed. As shown in Figure 8.2, industrial products such as steel, chemicals, and agricultural equipment tend to be less culturally grounded and warrant less adjustment than consumer goods. Similarly, marketers in technology-intensive industries such as scientific instruments or medical equipment find universal acceptability for their products.[7] Within consumer products, luxury goods and personal care products tend to have high levels of standardization while food products do not.

Adaptation needs in the industrial sector may exist even though they may not be overt. As an example, capacity performance is seen from different perspectives in different countries. Typically, the performance specifications of a German product are quite precise; for example, if a German product is said to have a lifting capacity of 1,000 kilograms, it will perform precisely up to that level. The U.S. counterpart, however, is likely to maintain a safety factor of 1.5 or even 2.0, resulting in a substantially higher payload capacity. Buyers of Japanese machine tools have also found that these tools will perform at the specified level, not beyond them, as would their U.S.-made counterparts.

Table 8.1   Standardization versus Adaptation

Factors Encouraging Standardization	Factors Encouraging Adaptation
• Economies of scale in production	• Differing use conditions
• Economies in product R&D	• Government and regulatory influences
• Economies in marketing	• Differing consumer behavior patterns
• "Shrinking" of the world marketplace/economic integration	• Local competition
• Global competitions	• True to the marketing concept

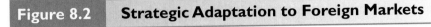

Figure 8.2   Strategic Adaptation to Foreign Markets

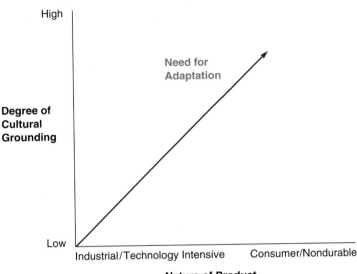

SOURCES: Adapted from W. Chan Kim and R. A. Mauborgne, "Cross-Cultural Strategies," *Journal of Business Strategy* 7 (Spring 1987): 31; and John A. Quelch and Edward J. Hoff, "Customizing Global Marketing," *Harvard Business Review* 64 (May–June 1986): 92–101.

Consumer goods generally require product adaptation because of their higher degree of cultural grounding. The amount of change introduced in consumer goods depends not only on cultural differences but also on economic conditions in the target market. Low incomes may cause pressure to simplify the product to make it affordable in the market. For example, Unilever learned that low-income Indians, usually forced to settle for low-quality products, wanted to buy high-end detergents and personal care products but could not afford them in available formats. In response, the company developed extremely low-cost packaging material and other innovations that allowed the distribution of single-use sachets costing the equivalent of pennies rather than the $5 regular-sized containers. Having the same brand on both product formats builds long-term loyalty for the company.[8]

Beyond the dichotomy of standardization and adaptation exist other approaches. The international marketer may design and introduce new products for foreign markets in addition to the firm's relatively standardized "flagship" products and brands. Some of these products developed specifically for foreign clients may later be introduced elsewhere, including in the domestic market. For example, IKEA introduced sleeper sofas in the United States to cater to local tastes but has since found demand for the concept in Europe as well.

Even companies that are noted for following the same methods worldwide have made numerous changes in their product offering. Some products, like Coca-Cola Company's Hi-C Soy Milk in Hong Kong, may be restricted to markets for which they were specifically developed. Although Colgate toothpaste is available worldwide, the company also markets some products locally, such as a spicy toothpaste formulated especially for the Middle East. McDonald's serves abroad the same menu of hamburgers, soft drinks, and other foods that it does in the United States, and the restaurants look the same. But McDonald's has also tried to tailor its product to local styles; for example, in Japan, the chain's trademark character, known as Ronald McDonald in the United States, is called Donald McDonald because it is easier to pronounce that way. Menu adjustments include beer in Germany and wine in France, mutton burgers in India, and rye-bread burgers in Finland.

Increasingly, companies are attempting to develop global products by incorporating differences regionally or worldwide into one basic design. This is not pure standardization, however. To develop a standard in the United States, for example, and use it as a model for other markets is dramatically different from obtaining inputs from the intended markets and using the data to create a standard. What is important is that adaptability is built into the product around a standardized core. For example, IBM makes more than 20 different keyboards for its relatively standardized personal computers to adjust to language differences in Europe alone. The international marketer attempts to exploit the common denominators, but local needs are considered from product development to the eventual marketing of the product. Car manufacturers like Ford and Nissan may develop basic models for regional, or even global, use, but they allow for substantial discretion in adjusting the models to local preferences.

Factors Affecting Adaptation

In deciding the form in which the product is to be marketed abroad, the firm should consider three sets of factors: (1) the market(s) that have been targeted, (2) the product and its characteristics, and (3) company characteristics, such as resources and policy. For most firms, the key question linked to adaptation is whether the effort is worth the cost involved—in adjusting production runs, stock control, or servicing, for example—and the investigative research involved in determining, for example, features that would be most appealing. For most firms, the expense of modifying products should be moderate. In practice, this may mean, however, that the expense is moderate when modifications are considered and acted on, whereas modifications are considered but rejected when the projected cost is substantial.

Studies on product adaptation show that the majority of products have to be modified for the international marketplace one way or another. Changes typically affect packaging, measurement units, labeling, product constituents and features, usage instructions, and, to a lesser extent, logos and brand names.[9]

There is no panacea for resolving questions of adaptation. Many firms are formulating decision-support systems to aid in product adaptation, and some consider every situation independently. Figure 8.3 provides a summary of the factors that determine the need for either **mandatory** or **discretionary product adaptation.** All products have to conform to the prevailing environmental conditions, over which the marketer has no control. These relate to legal, economic, and climatic conditions in the market. Further adaptation decisions are made to enhance the exporter's competitiveness in the marketplace. This is achieved by matching competitive offers, catering to customer preferences, and meeting demands of local distribution systems.

The adaptation decision will also have to be assessed as a function of time and market involvement. The more exporters learn about local market characteristics in individual markets, the more they are able to establish similarities and, as a result, standardize their marketing approach. This market insight will give the exporters legitimacy with the local representatives in developing a common understanding of the extent of standardization versus adaptation.[10]

The Market Environment

Government Regulations

Government regulations often present the most stringent requirements. Some of the requirements may serve no purpose other than political (such as protection of domestic industry or response to political pressures). Because of the sovereignty of nations, individual firms need to comply but can influence the situation by lobbying, directly or through their industry associations, for the issue to be raised during

Figure 8.3   Factors Affecting Product-Adaptation Decisions

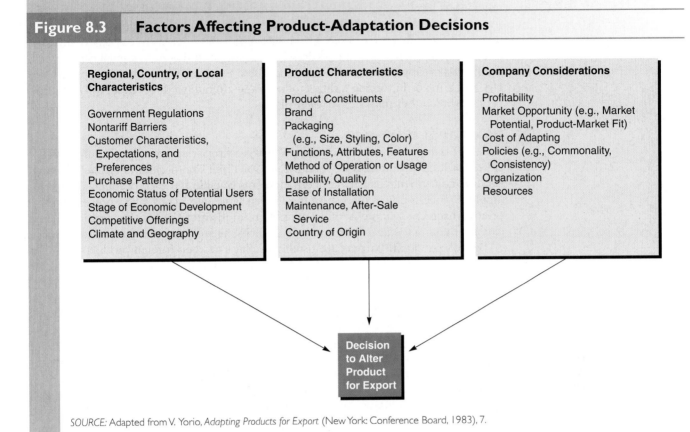

SOURCE: Adapted from V. Yorio, *Adapting Products for Export* (New York: Conference Board, 1983), 7.

trade negotiations. Government regulations may be spelled out, but firms need to be ever vigilant in terms of changes and exceptions.

Sweden was the first country in the world to enact legislation against most aerosol sprays on the grounds that they may harm the atmosphere. The ban, which went into effect January 1, 1979, covers thousands of hair sprays, deodorants, air fresheners, insecticides, paints, waxes, and assorted sprays that use Freon gases as propellants. It does not apply to certain medical sprays, especially those used by people who suffer from asthma. The Swedish government, which has one of the world's most active environmental protection departments, was the first to take seriously warnings by scientists that continued release of these chemicals could eventually degrade the earth's ozone layer. As a matter of fact, certain markets, such as Sweden and California, often serve as precursors of changes to come in broader markets and should, therefore, be monitored by marketers.

Although economic integration usually reduces discriminatory governmental regulation (as seen in *The International Marketplace 8.1*), some national environmental restrictions may stay in place. For example, a ruling by the European Court of Justice let stand Danish laws that require returnable containers for all beer and soft drinks. These laws seriously restrict foreign brewers, whose businesses are not on a scale large enough to justify the logistics system necessary to handle returnables.[11] A poll of 4,000 European companies found that burdensome regulatory requirements (e.g., need to ensure that products confirm to national requirements) affecting exports made the United Kingdom the most difficult market to trade with in the EU.[12]

Government regulations are probably the single most important factor contributing to product adaptation and, because of bureaucratic red tape, often the most cumbersome and frustrating factor to deal with. In some cases, government regulations have been passed and are enforced to protect local industry from competition from abroad. In early 2000, the EU decided to limit the use of older commercial aircraft that have "hush kit" mufflers on their engines to cut down airplane noise. U.S. marketers saw a two-dimensional threat in this new regulation: what the EU was really trying to do was keep out U.S. goods (hush kits are typically U.S. made) and, in forcing airlines to buy new aircraft, to direct them to buy European Airbus rather than U.S. Boeing planes.[13]

Nontariff Barriers

Nontariff barriers include product standards, testing or approval procedures, subsidies for local products, and bureaucratic red tape. The nontariff barriers affecting product adjustments usually concern elements outside the core product. For example, France requires the use of the French language in any offer, presentation, or advertisement whether written or spoken, in instructions for use, and in specification or guarantee terms for goods or services, as well as for invoices and receipts.

Because nontariff barriers are usually in place to keep foreign products out and/or to protect domestic producers, getting around them may be the toughest single problem for the international marketer. The cost of compliance with government regulations is high. The U.S. Department of Commerce estimates that a typical machine manufacturer can expect to spend between $50,000 and $100,000 a year on complying with foreign standards. For certain exports to the European Union, that figure can reach as high as $200,000.[14] As an example, Mack International has to pay $10,000 to $25,000 for a typical European engine certification. Brake system changes to conform with other countries' regulations run from $1,500 to $2,500 per vehicle. Wheel equipment changes will cost up to $1,000 per vehicle. Even with these outlays and the subsequent higher price, the company is still able to compete successfully in the international marketplace.

Small companies with limited resources may simply give up in the face of seemingly arbitrary harassment. For example, product testing and certification requirements have made the entry of many foreign companies into Japanese markets quite difficult, if not impossible.[15] Japan requires testing of all pharmaceutical products in Japanese laboratories, maintaining that these tests are needed because the Japanese may be physiologically different from Americans or Swiss. Similarly, foreign ski products were kept out because Japanese snow was somehow unique. Many exporters, rather than try to move mountains of red tape, have found ways to accommodate Japanese regulations. U.S. cookie marketers, for example, create separate product batches to meet Japanese requirements and avoid problems with the Japanese Health and Welfare Agency.

With a substantial decrease in tariff barriers, nontariff forms of protectionism have increased. On volume alone, agriculture dominates the list. The United States and the EU have fought over beef produced with the aid of hormones. Although it was declared safe for consumption by UN health authorities, the Europeans have banned the importation of such beef and demand appropriate labeling as a precondition for market entry. In a similar debate, an international trade agreement was reached in 2000 that requires the labeling of genetically modified food in the world market. This will mean that U.S. farmers have to separate the increasingly controversial foods from the overall supply.[16]

One way to keep a particular product or producer out of a market is to insist on particular standards. Since the EU chose ISO 9000 as a basis to harmonize varying technical norms of its member states, some of its trading partners have accused it of erecting a new trade barrier against outsiders.[17] ISO 9000, created by the International Organization for Standardization (ISO), is a set of technical standards designed to offer a uniform way of determining whether manufacturing plants and service organizations implement and document sound quality procedures. The ISO itself does not administer or regulate these standards; that job is left to the 143 countries that have voluntarily adopted them. The feeling that ISO registration is a trade barrier comes from the Europeans' earlier start and subsequent control of the program. Of the 570,616 registrations made by 2001, Europe accounts for 269,950, while North American companies have reached 50,894.[18] Growth has been dramatic in the United States, from about 500 companies in 1992 to over 37,000 at present. Studies show that over half the U.S. companies with ISO 9000 registration have fewer than 500 employees, and one-quarter have fewer than 150. There is no legal requirement to adopt the standards; however, many agree that these guidelines are already determining what may be sold to and within the EU and increasingly around the world. This is especially true for products for which there are safety or liability issues, or that require exact measurements or calibration, such as medical or exercise equipment.

The International Organization for Standardization also issued the first standards on environmental management, the ISO 14000 series in 1996. The standards, which basically require that a firm design an environmental management system, do provide benefits for the adopters such as substantial efficiencies in pollution control (e.g., packaging) and a better public image.[19] However, these standards can also serve as a nontariff barrier if advanced nations impose their own requirements and systems on developing countries that often lack the knowledge and resources to meet such conditions. The adoption rate has increased more rapidly in the last few years to 36,765 in 2001, with Europe accounting for 49.62 percent and North America for 7.35 percent of the total.

Customer Characteristics, Expectations, and Preferences

The characteristics and behavior of intended customer groups are as important as governmental influences on the product adaptation decision. Even when the benefits sought are quite similar, the physical characteristics of customers may dictate product adaptation. Quaker Oats' extension of the Snapple soft drink product to Japan suffered from lack of fit on three dimensions: the glass bottles the drink comes in are almost twice the size that Japanese customers are used to; the product itself was too sweet for the palate; and the Japanese did not feel comfortable with the sediment that characteristically collects at the bottom of the bottle.[20] GE Medical Systems has designed a product specifically for Japan in addition to computerized tomography scanners produced for the U.S. market. The unit is smaller because Japanese hospitals are smaller than most U.S. facilities but also because of the smaller size of Japanese patients. Similarly, Tefal, the world leader in cookware, makes available pans with detachable handles in Japan enabling storage in the traditionally tighter spaces of Japanese kitchens. The general expectation is that products are economical in purchase, use, and maintenance.[21]

Product decisions of consumer-product marketers are especially affected by local behavior, tastes, attitudes, and traditions—all reflecting the marketer's need to gain customers' approval. This group of variables is critical in that it is the most difficult to quantify but is nevertheless essential in making a go/no-go decision. The reason most Europeans who wear western boots buy those made in Spain may be that U.S. footwear manufacturers are unaware of style-conscious Europeans' preference for pointed toes and narrow heels. They view U.S.-made boots as "practical, but not interesting." Similarly, the U.S. Mint has been unable to penetrate the Asian market with its gold coins, which are 22 carat (.916 pure), because customers there value pure gold (i.e., 24 carat, .999 pure).

Three groups of factors determine cultural and psychological specificity in relation to products and services: consumption patterns, psychosocial characteristics, and general cultural criteria. The types of questions asked in Table 8.2 should be answered and systematically recorded for every product under consideration. Use of the list of questions will guide the international marketer through the analysis, ensuring that all the necessary points are dealt with before a decision is made.

Because Brazilians are rarely breakfast eaters, Dunkin' Donuts is marketing doughnuts in Brazil as snacks and desserts and for parties. To further appeal to

Table 8.2　Cultural and Psychological Factors Affecting Product Adaptation

I. Consumption Patterns
   A. Pattern of Purchase
      1. Is the product or service purchased by relatively the same consumer income group from one country to another?
      2. Do the same family members motivate the purchase in all target countries?
      3. Do the same family members dictate brand choice in all target countries?
      4. Do most consumers expect a product to have the same appearance?
      5. Is the purchase rate the same regardless of the country?
      6. Are most of the purchases made at the same kind of retail outlet?
      7. Do most consumers spend the same amount of time making the purchase?
   B. Pattern of Usage
      1. Do most consumers use the product or service for the same purpose or purposes?
      2. Is the product or service used in different amounts from one target area or country to another?
      3. Is the method of preparation the same in all target countries?
      4. Is the product or service used along with other products or services?

II. Psychosocial Characteristics
   A. Attitudes toward the Product or Service
      1. Are the basic psychological, social, and economic factors motivating the purchase and use of the product the same for all target countries?
      2. Are the advantages and disadvantages of the product or service in the minds of consumers basically the same from one country to another?
      3. Does the symbolic content of the product or service differ from one country to another?
      4. Is the psychic cost of purchasing or using the product or service the same, whatever the country?
      5. Does the appeal of the product or service for a cosmopolitan market differ from one market to another?
   B. Attitudes toward the Brand
      1. Is the brand name equally known and accepted in all target countries?
      2. Are customer attitudes toward the package basically the same?
      3. Are customer attitudes toward pricing basically the same?
      4. Is brand loyalty the same throughout target countries for the product or service under consideration?

III. Cultural Criteria
      1. Does society restrict the purchase and/or use of the product or service to a particular group?
      2. Is there a stigma attached to the product or service?
      3. Does the usage of the product or service interfere with tradition in one or more of the targeted markets?

SOURCE: Adapted from Steuart Henderson Britt, "Standardizing Marketing for the International Market," *Columbia Journal of World Business* 9 (Winter 1974): 32–40. Copyright © 1974 Columbia Journal of World Business. Reprinted with permission.

Brazilians, the company makes doughnuts with local fruit fillings like papaya and guava. Campbell Soup Company failed in Brazil with its offerings of vegetable and beef combinations, mainly because Brazilians prefer the dehydrated products of competitors such as Knorr and Maggi; Brazilians could use these products as soup starters but still add their own flair and ingredients. The only way of solving this problem is through proper customer testing, which can be formidably expensive for a company interested only in exports.

Often, no concrete product changes are needed, only a change in the product's **positioning.** Positioning refers to consumers' perception of a brand as compared with that of competitors' brands, that is, the mental image that a brand, or the company as a whole, evokes. For example, Gillette has a consistent image worldwide as a masculine, hardware, sports-oriented company. A brand's positioning,

| Figure 8.4 | Diet Coke Marketed as Coke Light in Japan |

SOURCE: Courtesy of Coca Cola Inc.

however, may have to change to reflect the differing lifestyles of the targeted market. Coca-Cola Company took a risk in marketing Diet Coke in Japan, because trying to sell a diet drink is difficult in a nation where "diet" is a dirty word and the population is not overweight by Western standards. The problem was addressed by changing the name of the drink to Coke Light and subtly shifting the promotion theme from "weight loss" to "figure maintenance." Japanese women do not like to admit that they are dieting by drinking something clearly labeled "diet" (Figure 8.4). Coca-Cola positioned its product as a soft drink that would help people feel and look their best rather than one solely centered around weight loss. The company hoped that consumers would perceive these characteristics just by looking at the product's graphics regardless of the name it bore.

On occasion, market realities may cause a shift in the product's positioning. Panda, a northern European chocolate and candy maker, had to place its licorice products in the United Kingdom in healthcare stores after finding traditional channels at British daily-goods retailers blocked by competition.

Health- and beauty-care products often rely on careful positioning to attain a competitive advantage. Timotei shampoo, which is Unilever's brand leader in that category, has a natural-looking image with a focus on mildness and purity. Because people around the world have different hair, Timotei's formula varies, but it always has the same image. The selling of "lifestyle" brands is common for consumer goods for which differentiation may be more difficult. Lifestyles may be more difficult for competitors to copy, but they are also more susceptible to changes in fashion.[22]

The influence of culture is especially of concern where society may restrict the purchase of the product, or when the product or one of its features may be subject to a stigma. A symbol in packaging may seem fully appropriate in one culture yet be an insult elsewhere. Dogs, for example, were alleged to have eaten one of Mohammed's regiments and therefore are considered signs of bad luck and uncleanliness in parts of North Africa. A U.S. cologne manufacturer discovered this after launching a product featuring a man and his dog in a rural setting.

Even the export of TV culture, which is considered by many as a local product, can succeed abroad if concepts are adjusted to reflect local values. By 2002, Muppets were being seen in over 140 countries, including 20 coproductions reflecting local languages, customs, and educational needs.[23] The Russian version of *Sesame Street* is 70 percent locally produced and features Aunt Dasha, a quintessential Russian character who lives in a traditional cottage and spouts folklore and homespun wisdom. In China, new characters were added for local color (such as Little Berry, "Xiao Mei"). The creators of the joint Israeli–Palestinian production, called *Sesame Stories,* hope that the exploits of Dafi, a purple Israeli Muppet, and Haneen, an orange Palestinian one, will help teach mutual respect and understanding by exposing children to each other's culture and breaking down stereotypes.

Economic Development

Management must take into account the present stage of economic development of the overseas market. As a country's economy advances, buyers are in a better position to buy and to demand more sophisticated products and product versions. With broad country considerations in mind, the firm can determine potentials for selling certain kinds of products and services. This means managing affordability in a way that makes the marketer's products accessible. For example, C&A, an apparel retailer from Holland, has been able to build a successful business in Latin American countries because it offers reasonable-quality goods at various price points—the best $10, $20, $30 dresses on the market. In Brazil, two-thirds of its sales are to families with incomes below $8,000 per year.[24] In some cases, the situation in a developing market may require **backward innovation;** that is, the market may require a drastically simplified version of the firm's product due to lack of purchasing power or usage conditions.

Economic conditions will affect packaging in terms of size and units sold in a package. In developing markets, products such as cigarettes and razor blades are often sold by the piece so that consumers with limited incomes can afford them. Soft drink companies have introduced four-can packs in Europe, where cans are sold singly even in large stores. On the other hand, products oriented to families, such as food products, appear in larger sizes in developing markets. Pillsbury packages its products in six- and eight-serving sizes for developing countries, whereas the most popular size in the North American market is for two.

Economic conditions may change rapidly, thus warranting change in the product or the product line. During the Asian currency crisis, McDonald's replaced french fries with rice in its Indonesian restaurants due to cost considerations. With the collapse of the local rupiah, potatoes, the only ingredient McDonald's imports to Indonesia, quintupled in price. In addition, a new rice and egg dish was introduced to maintain as many customers as possible despite the economic hardship.[25]

Competitive Offerings

Monitoring competitors' product features, as well as determining what has to be done to meet and beat them, is critical. Competitive offerings may provide a baseline against which the firm's resources can be measured—for example, what it takes to reach a critical market share in a given competitive situation. An analysis of competitors' offerings may reveal holes in the market or suggest avoiding certain market segments. American Hospital Supply, a Chicago-based producer of medical equipment, adjusts its product in a preemptive way by making products that are hard to duplicate. As a result, the firm achieved increases of about 40 percent per year in sales and earnings in Japan over a ten-year period. The products are so specialized that it would be hard for Japanese firms to duplicate them on a mass production basis.

In many markets, the international marketer is competing with global players and local manufacturers and must overcome traditional purchasing relationships and the certainty they provide. What is needed is a niche-breaking product that is adjusted to local needs. TeleGea has had success in Japan because its technology (which has been adjusted to support Asian languages) automates the service-fulfillment process for telecom companies, cutting their delivery costs more than 30 percent.[26]

Climate and Geography

Climate and geography will usually have an effect on the total product offering: the core product; tangible elements, mainly packaging; and the augmented features. Some products, by design, are vulnerable to the elements. Marketing of chocolate products is challenging in hot climates, which may restrict companies' options. Cadbury Schweppes has its own display cases in shops, while Toblerone has confined its distribution to air-conditioned outlets. Nestlé's solution was to produce a slightly different Kit Kat chocolate wafer for Asia with reduced fat content to raise the candy's melting point. The international marketer must consider two sometimes contradictory aspects of packaging for the international market. On the one hand, the product itself has to be protected against longer transit times and possibly for longer shelf life; on the other hand, care has to be taken that no non-allowed preservatives are used. One firm experienced this problem when it tried to sell Colombian guava paste in the United States. Because the packaging could not withstand the longer distribution channels and the longer time required for distribution, the product arrived in stores in poor condition and was promptly taken off the shelves. If a product is exposed to a lot of sunshine and heat as a result of being sold on street corners, as may be the case in developing countries, marketers are advised to use special varnishing or to gloss the product wrappers. Without this, the coloring may fade and make the product unattractive to the customer.

Product Characteristics

Product characteristics are the inherent features of the product offering, whether actual or perceived. The inherent characteristics of products and the benefits they provide to consumers in the various markets make certain products good candidates for standardization, others not. Consumer nondurables, such as food products, generally show the highest amount of sensitivity toward differences in national tastes and habits. Consumer durables, such as cameras and home electronics, are subject to far more homogeneous demand and more predictable adjustment (for example, adjustment to a different technical system in television sets and videotape recorders). Industrial products tend to be more shielded from cultural influences. However, substantial modifications may sometimes be required—in the telecommunications industry, for example—as a result of government regulations and restraints.

Product Constituents

The international marketer must make sure products do not contain ingredients that might be in violation of legal requirements or religious or social customs. As an example, DEP Corporation, a Los Angeles manufacturer with $19 million annual sales of hair and skin products, takes particular pains to make sure that no Japan-bound products contain formaldehyde—an ingredient commonly used in the United States but illegal in Japan. To ensure the purity of the Japanese batches, the company repeatedly cleans and sterilizes the chemical vats, checks all ingredients for traces of formaldehyde, and checks the finished product before shipment. When religion or custom determines consumption, ingredients may have to be replaced in order for the product to be acceptable. In Islamic countries, for example, animal fats have to be replaced by ingredients such as vegetable shortening. In deference to Hindu and Muslim beliefs, McDonald's "Maharaja Mac" is made with mutton in India.

Branding

Brand names convey the image of the product or service. The term **brand** refers to a name, term, symbol, sign, or design used by a firm to differentiate its offerings from those of its competitors. Brands are one of the most easily standardized items in the product offering; they may allow further standardization of other marketing elements such as promotional items. The brand name is the vocalizable part of the brand, the brand mark the nonvocalizable part (for example, Camel's "camel"). The brand mark may become invaluable when the product itself cannot be promoted but the symbol can be used. As an example, Marlboro cannot be advertised in most European countries because of legal restrictions on cigarette advertising; however, Philip Morris features advertisements showing only the Marlboro cowboy, who is known throughout the world. Unfortunately, most brands do not have such recognition. The term *trademark* refers to the legally protected part of the brand, indicated by the symbol ®. Increasingly, international markets have found their trademarks violated by counterfeiters who are illegally using or abusing the brand name of the marketer.

The international marketer has a number of options in choosing a branding strategy. The marketer may choose to be a contract manufacturer to a distributor (the generics approach) or to establish national, regional, or worldwide brands. The use of standardization in branding is strongest in culturally similar markets; for example, for U.S. marketers this means Canada and the United Kingdom. Standardization of product and brand do not necessarily move hand in hand; a regional brand may well have local features, or a highly standardized product may have local brand names.[27]

The establishment of worldwide brands is difficult; how can a consumer marketer establish world brands when it sells 800 products in more than 200 countries, most of them under different names? This is Gillette's situation. A typical example is Silkience hair conditioner, which is sold as Soyance in France, Sientel in Italy, and Silkience in Germany. Many companies have, however, massive standardization programs of brand names, packaging, and advertising.[28] Standardizing names to reap promotional benefits can be difficult, because a particular name may already be established in each market and the action may raise objections from local constituents. Despite the opposition, globalizing brands presents huge opportunities to cut costs and achieve new economies of scale.[29]

The psychological power of brands is enormous. Brands are not usually listed on balance sheets, but they can go further in determining success than technological breakthroughs by allowing the marketer to demand premium prices.[30] Brand loyalty translates into profits despite the fact that favored brands may not be superior by any tangible measure. New brands may be very difficult and expensive to build, and as a result, the company may seek a tie-in with something that the customer feels positively toward. For instance, a small Hong Kong–based company markets a product line called American No. 1 because the market prefers U.S. products.

Brand names often do not travel well. Semantic variations can hinder a firm's product overseas. Even the company name or the trade name should be checked out. For instance, Mirabell, the manufacturer of the genuine Mozart Kugel (a chocolate ball of marzipan and nougat), initially translated the name of its products as "Mozart balls" but has since changed the name to the "Mozart round."[31] Most problems associated with brands are not as severe but require attention nevertheless. To avoid problems with brand names in foreign markets, NameLab, a California-based laboratory for name development and testing, suggests these approaches:[32]

1. Translation. Little Pen Inc. would become La Petite Plume, S.A., for example.
2. Transliteration. This requires the testing of an existing brand name for connotative meaning in the language of the intended market. Flic Pen Corporation, for example, would be perceived in France as a manufacturer of writing instruments for the police because the slang term *flic* connotes something between "cop" and "pig." In other instances, positive connotations are sought, as shown in *The International Marketplace 8.2.*
3. Transparency. This can be used to develop a new, essentially meaningless brand name to minimize trademark complexities, transliteration problems, and translation complexities. (Sony is an example.)
4. Transculture. This means using a foreign-language name for a brand. Vodkas, regardless of where they originate, should have Russian-sounding names or at least Russian lettering, whereas perfumes should sound French.

Brands are powerful marketing tools; for example, the chemicals and natural ingredients in any popular perfume retailing for $140 an ounce may be worth less than $3.

In some markets, brand name changes are required by the government. In Korea, unnecessary foreign words are barred from use; for example, Sprite has been renamed Kin. The same situation has emerged in Mexico, where local branding is primarily required to control foreign companies in terms of the marketing leverage they would have with a universal brand.

Packaging

Packaging serves three major functions: protection, promotion, and user convenience. The major consideration for the international marketer is making sure the product reaches the ultimate user in the form intended. Packaging will vary as a function of transportation mode, transit conditions, and length of time in transit. Because of the longer time that products spend in channels of distribution, firms in the international marketplace, especially those exporting food products, have had to use more expensive packaging materials and/or more expensive transportation modes. The solution of food processors has been to utilize airtight, reclosable containers that reject moisture and other contaminants.

Pilferage is a problem in a number of markets and has forced companies to use only shipping codes on outside packaging.[33] With larger shipments, containerization has helped alleviate the theft problem. An exporter should anticipate inadequate, careless, or primitive loading methods. The labels and loading instructions should be not only in English but also in the market's language as well as in symbols.

The promotional aspect of packaging relates mostly to labeling. The major adjustments concern bilingual legal requirements, as in the case of Canada (French and English), Belgium (French and Flemish), and Finland (Finnish and Swedish).

THE INTERNATIONAL MARKETPLACE 8.2

When There Is More to a Name

Products in Asia often carry brand names that are translated from their original names. They are either direct translations (which result in a different-sounding but same-meaning name in the local language) or phonetic (which result in the same sound but likely different meaning). Given the globalization of markets, marketers not only need to decide whether to translate their brand names but also must consider the form, content, style, and image of such translations.

In Europe and the Americas, brand names such as Coca-Cola and Sharp have no meaning in themselves, and few are even aware of the origins of the name. But to Chinese-speaking consumers, brand names include an additional dimension: meaning. Coca-Cola means "tasty and happy" and Sharp stands for "treasure of sound."

Chinese and Western consumers share similar standards when it comes to evaluating brand names. Both appreciate a brand name that is catchy, memorable, and distinct, and says something indicative of the product. But, because of cultural and linguistic factors, Chinese consumers expect more in terms of how the names are spelled, written, and styled and whether they are considered lucky. When Frito-Lay introduced Cheetos in the Chinese market, it did so under a Chinese name that translates as "Many Surprises"; in Chinese *qi duo*— roughly pronounced "chee-do."

A name is like a work of art, and the art of writing (*shu fa*—calligraphy) has had a long tradition all over Asia. Reading Chinese relies more on the visual processes, whereas reading English is dominated by phonological processes (affecting, for example, the processing of features such as font style and color). A name has to look good and be rendered in appealing writing, thereby functioning like a logo or trademark. Companies will consequently have to take into account this dimension of Chinese and Chinese-based languages such as Korean, Japanese, and Vietnamese when they create corporate and brand names and related communications strategies.

In a study of Fortune 500 companies in China and Hong Kong, the vast majority of marketers were found to localize their brand names using, for the most part, transliteration (such as that used by Cheetos).

百事可乐
(A hundred happy things)

(Treasure of sound)

SOURCES: Nader Tavassoli and Jin K. Han, "Auditory and Visual Brand Identifiers in Chinese and English," *Journal of International Marketing* 10 (no. 2, 2002): 13–28; F. C. Hong, Anthony Pecotich, and Clifford J. Schultz, "Brand Name Translation: Language Constraints, Product Attributes, and Consumer Perceptions in East and Southeast Asia," *Journal of International Marketing* 10 (no. 2, 2002): 29–45; June N. P. Francis, Janet P. Y. Lam, and Jan Walls, "The Impact of Linguistic Differences on International Brand Name Standardization," *Journal of International Marketing* 10 (no. 1, 2002): 98–116; Eugene Sivadas, "Watching Chinese Marketing, Consumer Behavior," *Marketing News*, July 20, 1998, 10; "The Puff, the Magic, the Dragon," *The Washington Post*, September 2, 1994, B1, B3; and "Big Names Draw Fine Line on Logo Imagery," *South China Morning Post*, July 7, 1994, 3.

IMAGE CREDITS: Used with permission of PepsiCo; used with permission of Sharp.

Even when the same language is spoken across markets, nuances will exist requiring labeling adaptation. Ace Hardware's Paint Division had to be careful in translating the world "plaster" into Spanish. In Venezuela, *friso* is used, while Mexicans use *yeso*. In the end, *yeso* was used for the paint labels, because the word was understood in all of Latin America.[34] Governmental requirements include more informative labeling on products. Inadequate identification, failure to use the needed languages, or inadequate or incorrect descriptions printed on the labels may cause problems. If in doubt, a company should study foreign competitors' labels.

Package aesthetics must be a consideration in terms of the promotional role of packaging. This mainly involves the prudent choice of colors and package shapes. African nations, for example, often prefer bold colors, but flag colors may be alternately preferred or disallowed. Red is associated with death or witchcraft in some countries. Color in packaging may be faddish. White is losing popularity in industrialized countries because name brands do not want to be confused with generic products, usually packaged in white. Black, on the other hand, is increasingly popular and is now used to suggest quality, excellence, and "class." Package shapes may serve an important promotional role as well. When Grey Goose, a French brand of vodka, researched its international market entry, the development of the bottle took center stage. The company finally settled on a tall (taller than competition) bottle that was a mélange of clear glass, frosted glass, a cutaway of geese in flight, and the French flag.[35]

Package size varies according to purchasing patterns and market conditions. For instance, a six-pack format for soft drinks may not be feasible in certain markets because of the lack of refrigeration capacity in households. Quite often, overseas consumers with modest or low discretionary purchasing power buy smaller sizes or even single units in order to stretch a limited budget. The marketer also has to take into consideration perceptions concerning product multiples. In the West, the number 7 is considered lucky, whereas 13 is its opposite. In Japan, the ideogram for the number 4 can also be read as "death." Therefore, consumer products in multiples of four have experienced limited sales. On the other hand, 3 and 5 are considered lucky numbers.

Marketers are wise to monitor packaging technology developments in the world marketplace. A major innovation was in aseptic containers for fruit drinks and milk. Tetra Pak International, the $6.5-billion Swedish company, converted 40 percent of milk sales in Western Europe to its aseptic packaging system, which keeps perishables fresh for five months without refrigeration. The company claimed 5 percent of the fruit juice packaging market and 20 percent of the fruit drink market in the United States. Today, it markets its technologies in over 160 countries.[36]

Finally, the consumer mandate for marketers to make products more environmentally friendly also affects the packaging dimension, especially in terms of the 4 Rs: redesign, reduce, recycle, and reuse. The EU has strict policies on the amounts of packaging waste that are generated and the levels of recycling of such materials.[37] Depending on the packaging materials (20 percent for plastics and 60 percent for glass), producers, importers, distributors, wholesalers, and retailers are held responsible for generating the waste. In Germany, which has the toughest requirements, all packaging must be reusable or recyclable, and packaging must be kept to a minimum needed for proper protection and marketing of the product. Exporters to the EU must find distributors who can fulfill such requirements and agree how to split the costs of such compliance.

Appearance

Adaptations in product styling, color, size, and other appearance features are more common in consumer marketing than in industrial marketing. Color plays an important role in the way consumers perceive a product, and marketers must be aware of the signal being sent by the product's color.[38] Color can be used for brand identification—for example, the yellow of Hertz, red of Avis, and green of National. It can be used for feature reinforcement; for example, Honda adopted the color black to give its motorcycles a Darth Vader look, whereas Rolls Royce uses a dazzling silver paint that denotes luxury. Colors communicate in a subtle way in developed societies; they have direct meaning in more traditional societies. For instance, in the late 1950s, when Pepsi Cola changed the color of its coolers and vending machines from deep regal blue to light ice blue, the result was catastrophic in Southeast Asia. Pepsi had a dominant market share, which it lost to Coca-Cola because light blue is associated with death and mourning in that part of the world. AVG Inc., a California-based provider of technology for theme-park rides, had to change the proposed colors of a ride it designed for a park outside Beijing because the client felt they conveyed the wrong attitude for the ride. Instead the client wanted the colors to be "happy" ones.[39] The only way companies can protect themselves against incidents of this kind is through thorough on-site testing, or, as in AVG's case, on-site production.

Method of Operation or Usage

The product as it is offered in the domestic market may not be operable in the foreign market. One of the major differences faced by appliance manufacturers is electrical power systems. In some cases, variations may exist even within a country, such as Brazil. An exporter can learn about these differences through local government representatives or various trade publications such as the U.S. Department of Commerce publication *Electric Current Abroad*. However, exporters should determine for themselves the adjustments that are required by observing competitive products or having their product tested by a local entity.

Many complicating factors may be eliminated in the future through standardization efforts by international organizations and by the conversion of most countries to the metric system. Some companies have adjusted their products to operate in different systems, for example, VCR equipment that will record and play back on different color systems.

Different operating systems and environments can also provide new opportunities. When Canada adopted the metric system in 1977–1978, many U.S. companies were affected. Perfect Measuring Tape Company in Toledo, for example, had to convert to metric if it wanted to continue selling disposable paper measuring tape to textile firms in Canada. Once the conversion was made, the company found an entire world of untapped markets. It was soon shipping nearly 30 percent of its tape to overseas markets as disparate as Australia and Zimbabwe. More than 2,000 U.S. businesses use the metric system in research and development (e.g., Eastman Kodak) and marketing (e.g., Procter & Gamble's Scope mouthwash is sold in incremental liter bottles) to take advantage of global economies of scale.[40]

Products that rely heavily on the written or spoken language have to be adapted for better penetration of the market. For example, SPSS, Inc., the marketer of statistical software, localizes both DOS and Windows for German, English, Kanji, and Spanish. Producing software in the local language has also proven to be a weapon in the fight against software piracy.

An exporter may also have to adapt the product to different uses. MicroTouch Systems, which produces touch-activated computer screens for video poker machines and ATMs, makes a series of adjustments in this regard. Ticket vending machines for the French subway need to be waterproof, since they are hosed down. Similarly, for the Australian market, video poker screens are built to take a beating because gamblers there take losing more personally than anywhere else.[41]

The international marketer should be open to ideas for new uses for the product being offered. New uses may substantially expand the market potential of the product. For example, Turbo Tek, Inc., which produces a hose attachment for washing cars, has found that foreign customers have expanded the product's functions. In Japan, Turbo-Wash is used for cleaning bamboo, and the Dutch use it to wash windows, plants, and the sidings of their houses.[42] To capture these phenomena, observational research, rather than asking direct questions, may be the most appropriate approach. This is especially true in emerging and developing markets in order to understand how consumers relate to products in general and to the marketer's offer in particular.[43]

Quality

Many Western exporters must emphasize quality in their strategies because they cannot compete on price alone. Many new exporters compete on value in the particular segments in which they have chosen to compete. In some cases, producers of cheaper Asian products have forced international marketers to reexamine their strategies, allowing them to win contracts on the basis of technical advantage. To maintain a position of product superiority, exporting firms must invest in research and development for new products as well as manufacturing methods. For example, Sargent and Burton, a small Australian producer of high-technology racing boats, invested in CAD/CAM technology to develop state-of-the-art racing boats that have proven successful in international competition against sophisticated overseas entries.[44]

Marketers themselves may seek endorsement of their efforts from governmental or consumer organizations. Many car exporters to the United States have become popular in the market by doing well in J.D. Power and other car rankings, a fact that may then be used in promotional efforts.

Increasingly, many exporters realize that they have to meet international quality standards to compete for business abroad and to win contracts from multinational corporations. Foreign buyers, especially in Europe, are requiring compliance with international ISO 9000 quality standards. For example, German electronics giant Siemens requires ISO compliance in 50 percent of its supply contracts and is encouraging other suppliers to conform. This has helped eliminate the need to test parts, which saves time and money. DuPont began its ISO drive after losing a big European order for polyester films to an ISO-certified British firm. However, many exporters still have grave misunderstandings about the certification process and its benefits.[45]

Many exporters may overlook the importance of product quality especially when entering a developing market. While Fedder, the largest U.S. manufacturer of room air conditioners, had planned to market its most up-to-date air conditioners in China, it quickly discovered that even that was not going to be enough. The reason was that many Chinese buyers want a more sophisticated product than the standard unit sold in the United States. In China, it is a major purchase, and therefore often a status symbol. The Chinese also want special features such as remote control and an automatic air-sweeping mechanism.[46]

Service

When a product sold overseas requires repairs, parts, or service, the problem of obtaining, training, and holding a sophisticated engineering or repair staff is not easy. If the product breaks down, and the repair arrangements are not up to standard, the image of the product will suffer. In some cases, products abroad may not even be used for their intended purpose and may thus require modifications not only in product configuration but also in service frequency. For instance, snow plows exported from the United States are used to remove sand from driveways in Saudi Arabia. Closely related to servicing is the issue of product warranties. Warranties not only are instructions to customers about what to do if the product fails within a specified period of time but also are effective promotional tools.

Country-of-Origin Effects

The country of origin of a product, typically communicated by the phrase "Made in (country)," has a considerable influence on the quality perceptions of a product. The manufacture of products in certain countries is affected by a built-in positive or negative sterotype of product quality. These stereotypes become important when important dimensions of a product category are also associated with a country's image.[47] For example, if an exporter has a positive match of quality and performance for its car exports, the country of origin should be a prominent feature in promotional campaigns. If there is a mismatch, the country of origin may have to be hidden or the product sold with the help of prestigious partners whose image overshadows concerns about negative country-of-origin perceptions. This issue may be especially important to developing countries, which need to increase exports, and for importers, who source products from countries different from those where they are sold.[48] In some markets, however, there may be a tendency to reject domestic goods and embrace imports of all kinds.

Some products have fared well in the international marketplace despite negative country-of-origin perceptions. For example, Belarus tractors (manufactured both in Belarus and Russia) have fared well in Europe and the United States not only because of their reasonable price tag but also because of their ruggedness. Only the lack of an effective network has hindered the company's ability to penetrate Western markets to a greater degree.[49]

Country-of-origin effects lessen as customers become more informed. Also, as more countries develop the necessary bases to manufacture products, the origin of the products becomes less important. This can already be seen with so-called hybrid products (for example, a U.S. multinational company manufacturing the product in Malaysia). The argument has been made that with the advent of more economic integration, national borders become less important.[50] However, many countries have started strategic campaigns to improve their images to promote exports and in some cases to even participate in joint promotional efforts. In some cases, this means the development of new positive associations rather than trying to refute past negative ones.[51]

Company Considerations

Before launching a product in the international marketplace, the marketer needs to consider organizational capabilities as well as the nature of the product and the level of adaptation needed to accommodate various market-related differences between domestic and international markets.

The issue of product adaptation most often climaxes in the question "Is it worth it?" The answer depends on the firm's ability to control costs, correctly estimate market potential, and finally, secure profitability, especially in the long term. While new markets, such as those in central Europe, may at present require product adaptation, some marketers may feel that the markets are too small to warrant such adjustments and may quite soon converge with western European ones, especially in light of their pending EU membership. While sales of a standard product may be smaller in the short term, long-term benefits will warrant the adoption of this approach.[52] However, the question that used to be posed as "Can we afford to do it?" should now be "Can we afford not to do it?"

The decision to adapt should be preceded by a thorough analysis of the market. Formal market research with primary data collection and/or testing is warranted. From the financial standpoint, some firms have specific return-on-investment levels to be satisfied before adaptation (for instance, 25 percent), whereas some let the requirement vary as a function of the market considered and also the time in the market—that is, profitability may be initially compromised for proper market entry.

Most companies aim for consistency in their marketing efforts. This translates into the requirement that all products fit in terms of quality, price, and user perceptions. An example of where consistency may be difficult to control is in the area of warranties. Warranties can be uniform only if the use conditions do not vary drastically and if the company is able to deliver equally on its promise anywhere it has a presence.

A critical element of the adaptation decision has to be human resources, that is, individuals to make the appropriate decisions. Individuals are needed who are willing to make risky decisions and who know about existing market conditions. Many companies benefit from having managers from different (types of) countries, giving them the experience and the expertise to make decisions between standardization and adaptation.

Product Counterfeiting

Counterfeit goods are any goods bearing an unauthorized representation of a trademark, patented invention, or copyrighted work that is legally protected in the country where it is marketed. The International Trade Commission estimated that U.S. companies lose a total of $60 billion every year because of product counterfeiting and other infringement of intellectual property. Hardest hit are the most innovative, fastest-growing industries, such as computer software, pharmaceuticals, and entertainment. In 2001, the software, publishing, and distribution industries lost more than $10.97 billion due to software theft.[53] Worldwide, more than 40 percent of all software is illegally copied, with the percentage rising to over 90 percent in countries such as Vietnam.

The practice of product counterfeiting has spread to high-technology products and services from the traditionally counterfeited products: high-visibility, strong-brandname consumer goods. In addition, previously the only concern was whether a company's product was being counterfeited; now, companies have to worry about whether the raw materials and components purchased for production are themselves real.[54] The European Union estimates that trade in counterfeit goods now accounts for 2 percent of total world trade. The International Chamber of Commerce estimates the figure at close to 5 percent. In general, countries with lower per capita incomes, higher levels of corruption in government, and lower levels of involvement in the international trade community tend to have higher levels of intellectual property violation.[55]

Counterfeiting problems occur in three ways and, depending on the origin of the products and where they are marketed, require different courses of action. Approximately 75 percent of counterfeit goods are estimated to be manufactured outside the United States, and 25 percent are either made in this country or imported and then labeled here. Problems originating in the United States can be resolved through infringement actions brought up in federal courts. Counterfeit products that originate overseas and that are marketed in the United States should be stopped by the customs barrier. Enforcement has been problematic because of the lack of adequate personnel and the increasingly high-tech character of the products. When an infringement occurs overseas, action can be brought under the laws of the country in which it occurs. The sources of the largest number of counterfeit goods are China, Brazil, Taiwan, Korea, and India, which are a problem to the legitimate owners of intellectual property on two accounts: the size of these countries' own markets and their capability to export. For example, Nintendo estimates its annual losses to video-game piracy at $700 million, with the origin of the counterfeits mainly China and Taiwan.[56] Countries in Central America and the Middle East are typically not sources but rather markets for counterfeit goods. Counterfeiting is a pervasive problem in terms not only of geographic reach but of the ability of the counterfeiters to deliver products, and the market's willingness to buy them, as shown in *The International Marketplace 8.3*.

The first task in fighting intellectual property violation is to use patent application or registration of trademarks or mask works (for semiconductors). The rights granted by a patent, trademark, copyright, or mask work registration in the United States confer no protection in a foreign country. There is no such thing as an international patent, trademark, or copyright. Although there is no shortcut to worldwide protection, some advantages exist under treaties or other international agreements. These treaties, under the World Intellectual Property Organization (WIPO), include the Paris Convention for the Protection of Industrial Property, the Patent Cooperation Treaty, the Berne Convention for the Protection of Literary and Artistic Works, and the Universal Copyright Convention, as well as regional patent and trademark offices such as the European Patent Office. Applicants are typically granted international protection throughout the member countries of these organizations.[57]

After securing valuable intellectual property rights, the international marketer must act to enforce, and have enforced, these rights. Four types of action against counterfeiting are legislative action, bilateral and multilateral negotiations, joint private sector action, and measures taken by individual companies.

In the legislative arena, the Omnibus Tariff and Trade Act of 1984 amended Section 301 of the Trade Act of 1974 to clarify that the violation of intellectual property rights is an unreasonable practice within the statute. The act also introduced a major carrot-and-stick policy: The adequacy of protection of intellectual property rights of U.S. manufacturers is a factor that will be considered in the designation

THE INTERNATIONAL MARKETPLACE   8.3

The Phantom Pirates

Video pirates moved faster than a speeding pod racer to release the first *Star Wars* prequel, *The Phantom Menace: Episode One,* in Southeast Asia. The first copies appeared in Malaysia only two days after the U.S. opening, with videodisc copies also reaching other parts of Asia, Europe, South Africa, and Latin America. "This shows how amazingly efficient this industry has become," said Michael Ellis, the Asia antipiracy chief of the Motion Picture Association. "They have gotten it down to a sophisticated science."

With advances in technology and continued demand for U.S. films abroad, pirate-video making has become big business. The Motion Picture Association of America estimates that worldwide piracy costs Hollywood $3 billion annually. Asia remains by far the biggest producer and consumer of pirate versions.

The three main types of copies of *The Phantom Menace* in Asia each have their own distinctive marks and character, depending on how and when they were filmed. The "Z" Species, named for the computer-generated letter that dances across the screen's edge, was filmed in a crowded theater and is marked by a loud scream of "Yeah, wooo!" throughout the opening sequence, and frequent applause for Yoda. "The Shakes" features shaky camera work, with audience members getting up to go to the bathroom during the important Darth Maul scene. The "Flying Horse" version is also called "AB" for the blinking letters on the screen and a flying horse on the package cover. It features audience noise and frequent flash bulbs from viewers taking pictures.

It is unclear how the smugglers got the disks to market so quickly. Most of the copies sold in Asia appear to have come from the three master versions, which had been shipped via air courier to Malaysia and Hong Kong, where they were transferred to VCD-production lines in Malaysia. New technologies have facilitated the process as well. Whereas a pirated VCR tape has to be recorded in real time, taking up to two hours for each copy, a videodisc can be stamped out in three seconds and quite inexpensively. Consumers can buy a VCD player for under $100, and movies are typically less than $5.

Officials suspect that most of the copies were produced in Malaysia. With its lax law enforcement, low labor costs, and central location in Asia, Malaysia has become the new hub of the pirate CD industry. Whereas Hong Kong and Macau used to be the capital for this activity,

© AFP/CORBIS

crackdowns have chased the industry away. Malaysian officials have been repeatedly told of the violations, but little action has been taken. Experts say most of the factories producing the films are legitimate CD makers that produce pirate products on the side.

Moviemaking is a risky proposition in that only one in ten movies ever retrieves its investment from domestic exhibition. In 2000, the average movie cost $55 million to produce with an additional $27 million to market. The protection of the intellectual property in such endeavors is therefore critical to the industry. As the movie industry becomes digitalized, the challenges of infringement become manifold.

SOURCE: "Video Pirates Rush Out 'Phantom Menace,' " *The Wall Street Journal,* May 28, 1999, B1, B4; and **http://www.mpaa.org**.

of **Generalized System of Preferences (GSP)** benefits to countries. The United States has denied selected countries duty-free treatment on goods because of lax enforcement of intellectual property laws.

The Trademark Counterfeiting Act of 1984 made trading in goods and services using a counterfeit trademark a criminal rather than a civil offense, establishing stiff penalties for the practice. The Semiconductor Chip Protection Act of 1984 clarified the status and protection afforded to semiconductor masks, which determine the capabilities of the chip. Protection will be available to foreign-designed masks in the United States only if the home country of the manufacturer also maintains a viable system of mask protection. The Intellectual Property Rights Improvement Act requires the U.S. Trade Representative to set country-specific negotiating objectives for reciprocity and consideration of retaliatory options to assure intellectual property protection. The United States imposed punitive tariffs on $39 million of Brazilian imports to retaliate against Brazil's refusal to protect U.S. pharmaceutical patents.

The U.S. government is seeking to limit counterfeiting practices through bilateral and multilateral negotiations as well as education. A joint International Trade Administration and Patent and Trademark Office action seeks to assess the adequacy of foreign countries' intellectual property laws and practices, to offer educational programs and technical assistance to countries wishing to establish adequate systems of intellectual property protection, to offer educational services to the industry, and to review the adequacy of U.S. legislation in the area. Major legislative changes have occurred in the past few years in, for example, Taiwan and Singapore, where penalties for violations have been toughened. The WTO agreement includes new rules on intellectual property protection, under the Trade-Related Aspects of Intellectual Property Rights (TRIPS) agreement. Under them, trade-related intellectual property will enjoy 20 years of protection. More than 100 countries have indicated they will amend their laws and improve enforcement. Violators of intellectual property will face retaliation not only in this sector, but in others as well.[58] Similarly, the NAFTA agreement provides extensive patent and copyright protection.

A number of private-sector joint efforts have emerged in the battle against counterfeit goods. In 1978, the International Anti-Counterfeiting Coalition was founded to lobby for stronger legal sanctions worldwide. The coalition consists of 375 members. The International Chamber of Commerce established the Counterfeit Intelligence and Investigating Bureau in London, which acts as a clearinghouse capable of synthesizing global data on counterfeiting.

In today's environment, companies are taking more aggressive steps to protect themselves. The victimized companies are losing not only sales but also goodwill in the longer term if customers believe they have the real product rather than a copy of inferior quality. In addition to the normal measures of registering trademarks and copyrights, companies are taking steps in product development to prevent knockoffs of trademarked goods. For example, new authentication materials in labeling are extremely difficult to duplicate. Some companies, such as Disney, have tried to legitimize offenders by converting them into authorized licenses. These local companies would then be a part of the fight against counterfeiters, because their profits would be the most affected by fakes.

Many companies maintain close contact with the government and the various agencies charged with helping them. Computer makers, for example, loan testing equipment to customs officers at all major U.S. ports, and company attorneys regularly conduct seminars on how to detect pirated software and hardware. Other companies retain outside investigators to monitor the market and stage raids with the help of law enforcement officers. For example, when executives at WD-40 Co., the maker of an all-purpose lubricant, realized a counterfeit version of their product was being sold in China, they launched an investigation and then approached local authorities about the problem. Offending retailers were promptly raided and, in turn, led police to the counterfeiter.[59]

The issue of intellectual property protection will become more important for the United States and the EU in future years. It is a different problem from what it was a decade ago, when the principal victims were manufacturers of designer items. Today, the protection of intellectual property is crucial in high technology, one of the strongest areas of U.S. competitiveness in the world marketplace. The ease with which technology can be transferred and the lack of adequate protection of the developers' rights in certain markets make this a serious problem.[60]

Summary

Marketers may routinely exaggerate the attractiveness of international markets, especially in terms of their similarity. Despite the dramatic impact of globalization as far as market convergence is concerned, distances, especially cultural and economic, challenge the marketer to be vigilant.[61] The international marketer must pay careful attention to variables that may call for an adaptation in the product offering. The target market will influence the adaptation decision through factors such as government regulation and customer preferences and expectations. The product itself may not be in a form ready for international market entry in terms of its brand name, its packaging, or its appearance. Some marketers make a conscious decision to offer only standardized products; some adjust their offerings by market.

Like the soft drink and packaged-goods marketers that have led the way, the newest marketers of world brands are producing not necessarily identical products, but recognizable products. As an example, the success of McDonald's in the world marketplace has been based on variation, not on offering the same product worldwide. Had it not been for the variations, McDonald's would have limited its appeal unnecessarily and would have been far more subject to local competitors' challenges.

Firms entering or participating in the international marketplace will certainly find it difficult to cope with the conflicting needs of the domestic and international markets. They will be certain to ask whether adjustments in their product offerings, if the marketplace requires them, are worthwhile. There are, unfortunately, no magic formulas for addressing the problem of product adaptation. The answer seems to lie in adopting formal procedures to assess products in terms of the markets' and the company's own needs.

The theft of intellectual property—ideas and innovations protected by copyrights, patents, and trademarks—is a critical problem for many industries and countries, accelerating with the pace of market globalization. Governments have long argued about intellectual property protection, but the lack of results in some parts of the world has forced companies themselves to take action on this front.

Key Terms

core product
augmented features
mandatory product adaptation
discretionary product adaptation
positioning

backward innovation
brand
Generalized System of Preferences
   (GSP)

Questions for Discussion

1. Comment on the statement "It is our policy not to adapt products for export."
2. What are the major problems facing companies, especially smaller ones, in resolving product adaptation issues?
3. How do governments affect product adaptation decisions of firms?

4. Are standards like those promoted by the International Organization for Standardization (see **http://www.iso.ch**) a hindrance or an opportunity for exporters?
5. Is any product ever the same everywhere it is sold?
6. Propose ways in which intellectual property piracy could be stopped permanently.

Internet Exercises

1. How can marketers satisfy the 4 Rs of environmentally correct practice? See, for example, the approaches proposed by the Duales System Deuschland (**www.gruener-punkt.de/e/**).

2. The software industry is the hardest hit by piracy. Using the Web site of the Business Software Alliance (**http://www.bsa.org**), assess how this problem is being tackled.

Recommended Readings

Gorchels, Linda. *The Product Manager's Handbook: The Complete Product Management Resource.* New York: McGraw-Hill, 2000.

Keegan, Warren J., and Charles S. Mayer. *Multinational Product Management.* Chicago: American Marketing Association, 1977.

Lasalle, Diane, and Terry A. Britton. *Priceless: Turning Ordinary Products into Extraordinary Experiences.* Boston, MA: Harvard Business School Press, 2002.

Levitt, Theodore. *The Marketing Imagination.* New York: Free Press, 1986.

Lorenz, C. *The Design Dimension: Product Strategy and the Challenge of Global Markets.* New York: Basil Blackwell, 1996.

Nelson, Carl A. *Exporting: A Manager's Guide to the Export Market.* Mason, OH: International Thomson Business Press, 1999.

Papadopoulos, Nicolas, and Louise A. Heslop. *Product-Country Images.* Binghamton, NY: International Business Press, 1993.

Renner, Sandra L., and W. Gary Winget. *Fast-Track Exporting.* New York: AMACOM, 1991.

Rodkin, Henry. *The Ultimate Overseas Business Guide for Growing Companies.* Homewood, IL: Dow Jones–Irwin, 1990.

Tuller, Lawrence W. *Exporting, Importing, and Beyond: How to "Go Global" with Your Small Business.* Avon, MA: Adams Media Corporation, 1997.

Urban, Glen L, and John Hauser. *Design and Marketing of New Products.* Englewood Cliffs, NJ: Prentice-Hall, 1993.

Webber, Robert. *The Marketer's Guide to Selling Products Abroad.* Westport, CT: Quorum Books, 1989.

chapter **9**

Export Pricing Strategies

THE INTERNATIONAL MARKETPLACE   9.1

Adjusting to the Currency Squeeze

Between 1997 and 2002, the surging dollar, up 50 percent or more against Asian currencies and up 20 percent against European ones, had many U.S. exporters worried and scrambling for creative marketing alternatives. Small exporters, especially those with ties to big-ticket infrastructure projects, saw their customer base dry up in Korea, Malaysia, and Thailand and across the Pacific Rim. Their products got too pricey compared with those of overseas rivals. But rather than complain about their fate, these marketers adapted their operations by taking a number of steps to ensure long-term success.

Chicago's Aerotek International, which makes hydraulic hose repair systems used in industrial construction and mining, cut 50 of its Asian distributors and then set up a company in Singapore to market its product directly. In addition to showing long-term commitment to the marketplace, the direct approach allowed Aerotek to weed out financially weakened customers and avoid possibly unstable intermediaries. Besides developing their own distribution networks, many U.S. exporters also insisted on bank-backed agreements to reduce losses on receivables. In effect, they abandoned open-account financing in which a business relies on its customers to pay up in good faith.

Smaller exporters also redirected or shifted their emphases from Asia to healthier markets in Europe as well as Central and South America. However, while they can reduce their presence in Asia, U.S. exporters cannot avoid competing with Asian rivals and their heavily discounted prices. In Latin America, U.S. toolmakers have countered 15 to 20 percent price cuts on Korean and Japanese products with more value-added services and the "made-in-the USA" image.

Protected at least partly from the dollar swings are U.S. exporters that occupy niche and specialty markets. In many high-tech markets customers commit to solutions because of what the supplier can do, not necessarily what is being charged for it. For example, semiconductor producers enjoyed growth averaging 15 percent during this time. Farm equipment maker John Deere's exports rose 30 percent thanks to strong agricultural economies in Europe, Australia, and South Africa. Diebold, a maker of automatic teller machines, stepped up shipments to Latin America and Asia by 40 percent.

The strong dollar not only was a challenge but may also have opened strategic opportunities as well. U.S. marketers have expanded the assembly work they do in Asia to take advantage of the more economical factors of production there and the lower costs for raw materials ranging from oil to resin. Some exporters engage in strategies that eliminate the effects of currency swings. For example, Vermeer Manufacturing, which makes industrial and agricultural equipment, invoices its dealers abroad in the local currency and then uses the proceeds to pay for supplies and services bought locally. Billing in dollars may be perceived as a method of eliminating currency risk, but it also means that someone else, a competitor, is taking advantage of that currency movement and offering a lower-priced product.

By the end of 2002, however, the dollar had declined nearly 15 percent from its high level vis-à-vis the euro. This gives many U.S. exporters strategic flexibility regarding what to do with the savings; i.e., whether to pass them through to customers in lower prices or enjoy higher profitability. In general, companies are reluctant to change prices too often, especially when many analysts expect the dollar to turn around and start strengthening again with a U.S. economic recovery.

SOURCES: James Sroades, "The Dollar as a War Target," *World Trade*, September 2002, 16; Gordon Platt and Paula L. Green, "Living with a Weak Dollar," *Global Finance* 16 (July/August 2002): 36–38; "For U.S. Small Biz, Fertile Soil in Europe," *Business Week*, April 1, 2002, 57; "Competitive Exports, Sky-High Imports," *Financial Mail*, October 2, 1998, 19; "Turning Small into a Big Advantage," *Business Week*, July 13, 1998, 42–44; Erika Morphy, "Dollar Daze," *Export Today*, September 1998, 27–33; "How Sweet It Is for Europe's Exporters," *Business Week*, May 5, 1997, 52–53; **http://www.deere.com**; **http://www.diebold.com**; and **http://www.vermeer.com**.

T HIS CHAPTER WILL FOCUS on the pricing decision from the exporter's point of view: the setting of export price, terms of sale, and terms of payment. The setting of export prices is complicated by factors such as increased distance from the markets, currency fluctuations, governmental policies such as duties, and typically longer and different types of channels of distribution. In spite of new factors influencing the pricing decision, the objective remains the same: to create demand for the marketer's offerings and to do so profitably in the long term. In achieving this, financing arrangements for export transactions are critical for two reasons:

to secure sales and to combat various types of risk. Two special considerations in export pricing—leasing and dumping—are discussed at the end of this chapter. Foreign market pricing (by subsidiaries) and intracompany transfer pricing, that is, pricing for transactions between corporate entities, will be discussed in Chapter 16.

Price Dynamics

Price is the only element of the marketing mix that is revenue generating; all the others are costs. It should therefore be used as an active instrument of strategy in the major areas of marketing decision making, as seen in *The International Marketplace 9.1*. Price serves as a means of communication with the buyer by providing a basis for judging the attractiveness of the offer. It is a major competitive tool in meeting and beating close rivals and substitutes. Competition will often force prices down, whereas intracompany financial considerations have an opposite effect. Prices, along with costs, will determine the long-term viability of the enterprise.

Price should not be determined in isolation from the other marketing mix elements. It may be used effectively in positioning the product in the marketplace—for example, JLG, the world leader in self-propelled aerial work platforms used at construction sites, is able to charge premium prices because its products are powered by nonpolluting hydrogen fuel cells.[1] The feasibility range for price setting established by demand, competition, costs, and legal considerations may be narrow or wide in a given situation (for example, the pricing of a commodity versus an innovation). Regardless of how narrow the gap allowed by these factors, however, pricing should never be considered a static element. The marketer's ultimate goal is to make the customer as inelastic as possible; i.e., the customer should prefer the marketer's offer even at a price premium.

Similarly, pricing decisions cannot be made in isolation from the other functions of the firm. Effective financial arrangements can significantly support the marketing program if they are carefully formulated between the finance and marketing areas. Sales are often won or lost on the basis of favorable credit terms to the buyer. With large numbers of competent firms active in international markets, financing packages—often put together with the help of governmental support—have become more important. Customers abroad may be prepared to accept higher prices if they can obtain attractive credit terms.

A summary of international pricing situations is provided as a matrix in Figure 9.1. Pricing challenges—such as pricing for a new market entry, changing price either as an attack strategy or in response to competitive changes, and multiple-product coordination in cases of related demand—are technically the same as problems encountered in domestic markets. The scope of these pricing situations will vary according to the degree of foreign involvement and the type of market encountered.

In first-time pricing, the general alternatives are (1) skimming, (2) following the market price, and (3) penetration pricing. The objective of **skimming** is to achieve the highest possible contribution in a short time period. For an exporter to use this approach, the product has to be unique, and some segments of the market must be willing to pay the high price. As more segments are targeted and more of the product is made available, the price is gradually lowered. The success of skimming depends on the ability and speed of competitive reaction.

If similar products already exist in the target market, **market pricing** can be used. The final customer price is determined based on competitive prices, and then both production and marketing must be adjusted to the price. This approach requires the exporter to have a thorough knowledge of product costs, as well as confidence that the product life cycle is long enough to warrant entry into the market. It is a reactive approach and may lead to problems if sales volumes never rise to sufficient levels to produce a satisfactory return. Although firms typically

Figure 9.1	**International Pricing Situations**

Pricing Situation	International Involvement		
	Exporting	Foreign-Market Pricing	Intracompany Pricing
First-Time Pricing			
Changing Pricing			
Multiple-Product Pricing			

SOURCES: Elements of the model adopted from Howard Forman and Richard A. Lancioni, "International Industrial Pricing Strategic Decisions and the Pricing Manager: Some Key Issues," *Professional Pricing Society*, October 9, 1999, at **http://www.pricing-advisor. com/jour_article2.htm**; and Helmut Becker, "Pricing: An International Marketing Challenge," in *International Marketing Strategy*, eds. Hans Thorelli and Helmut Becker (New York: Pergamon Press, 1980): 203–215.

use pricing as a differentiation tool, the international marketing manager may have no choice but to accept the prevailing world market price.

When **penetration pricing** is used, the product is offered at a low price intended to generate volume sales and achieve high market share, which would compensate for a lower per-unit return. One company found, for example, that a 20 percent reduction in average pricing roughly doubled the demand for its product.[2] This approach typically requires mass markets, price-sensitive customers, and decreasing production and marketing costs as sales volumes increase. The basic assumption of penetration pricing is that the lower price will increase sales, which may not always be the case. This approach can also be used to discourage other marketers from entering the market.

Price changes are called for when a new product is launched, when a change occurs in overall market conditions (such as a change in the value of the billing currency), or when there is a change in the exporter's internal situation, such as costs of production. An exporter may elect not to change price even though the result may be lower profitability. However, if a decision is made to change prices, related changes must also be considered. For example, if an increase in price is required, it may at least initially be accompanied by increased promotional efforts. Price changes usually follow changes in the product's stage in the life cycle. As the product matures, more pressure will be put on the price to keep the product competitive despite increased competition and less possibility of differentiation.

With multiple-product pricing, the various items in the line may be differentiated by pricing them appropriately to indicate, for example, an economy version, a standard version, and the top-of-the-line version. One of the products in the line may be priced to protect against competitors or to gain market share from existing competitors. The other items in the line are then expected to make up for the lost contribution of such a "fighting brand."

Although foreign market pricing and intracompany pricing are discussed later in conjunction with multinational pricing challenges, they do have an impact on the exporter as well. For example, distributors in certain markets may forgo certain profit margins in exchange for exclusivity. This may mean that the exporter will have to lower prices to the distributor and take less profit to ensure sales and to remain competitive, or, if the market conditions warrant it, to move into more direct distribution.[3] Similarly, the exporter, in providing products to its own sales offices abroad, may have to adjust its transfer prices according to foreign exchange fluctuations.

The Setting of Export Prices

In setting the export price, a company can use a process such as the one summarized in Figure 9.2. The setting of export price is influenced by both internal and external factors, as well as their interaction.[4] Internal factors include the company's philosophy, goals, and objectives; the costs of developing, producing, and marketing the export product; and the nature of the exporter's product and industry. External factors relate to international markets in general or to a specific target market in particular and include such factors as customer, regulatory, competitive, and financial (mainly foreign exchange) characteristics. The interaction of these elements causes pricing opportunities and constraints in different markets. For example, company management may have decided to challenge its main foreign competitor in the competitor's home market. Regulation in that market requires expensive product adaptation, the cost of which has to be absorbed now for the product to remain competitive.

As in all marketing decisions, the intended target market will establish the basic premise for pricing. Factors to be considered include the importance of price in customer decision making (in particular, the ability to pay), the strength of perceived price-quality relationships, and potential reactions to marketing-mix manipulation by marketers. For example, an exporter extending a first-world product to

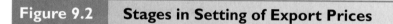

Figure 9.2 | **Stages in Setting of Export Prices**

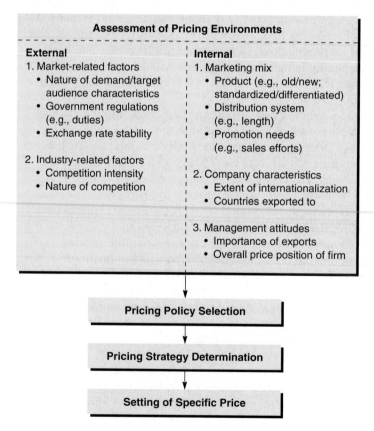

SOURCES: Elements of model adopted from Barbara Stöttinger, "Strategic Export Pricing: A Long and Winding Road," *Journal of International Marketing* 9 (no. 1, 2001): 40–63; S. Tamer Cavusgil, "Pricing for Global Markets," *Columbia Journal of World Business* 31 (Winter 1996): 66–78; and Alfred R. Oxenfeld, "Multistage Approach to Pricing," *Harvard Business Review* 38 (July/August 1960): 120–132.

an emerging market may find its potential unnecessarily limited and thus opt for a new version of a product that costs a fraction of the original version. Customers' demands will also have to be considered in terms of support required by the intermediary. The marketing mix must be planned to match the characteristics of the target market. Pricing will be a major factor in determining the desired brand image as well as the distribution channels to be used and the level of promotional support required. Conversely, mix elements affect pricing's degrees of freedom. If the use of specialty channels is needed to maintain product positioning, price will be affected.

Pricing policies follow from the overall objectives of the firm for a particular target market and involve general principles or rules that a firm follows in making pricing decisions.[5] Policies include profit maximization, market share, survival, percentage return on investment, and various competitive policies such as copying competitors' prices, following a particular competitor's prices, or pricing so as to discourage competitors from entering the market. For example, an exporter entering a new market may allow wholesalers and retailers above-normal profit margins to encourage maximum sales volume, geographic distribution, and loyalty. Loctite Corporation, in marketing adhesives for industrial uses, requires a highly technical selling effort from distributors and uses higher-than-average compensation packages to secure their services. These types of demands are common especially in the early stages of the export effort and may have to be satisfied to gain market penetration. They should be phased out later on, however, with sales volume increases making up for the difference.[6]

Export Pricing Strategy

Three general price-setting strategies in international marketing are a standard worldwide price; dual pricing, which differentiates between domestic and export prices; and market-differentiated pricing. The first two methods are cost-oriented pricing methods that are relatively simple to establish and easy to understand. The third strategy is based on demand orientation and may thus be more consistent with the marketing concept. However, even the third approach has to acknowledge costs in the long term.

The **standard worldwide price** may be the same price regardless of the buyer (if foreign product or foreign marketing costs are negligible) or may be based on average unit costs of fixed, variable, and export-related costs.

In **dual pricing,** domestic and export prices are differentiated, and two approaches to pricing products for export are available: cost-driven and market-driven methods. If a cost-based approach is decided upon, the marketer can choose between the **cost-plus method** and the **marginal cost method.** The cost-plus strategy is the true cost, fully allocating domestic and foreign costs to the product. Although this type of pricing ensures margins, the final price may be so high that the firm's competitiveness is compromised. This may cause some exporters to consider a flexible cost-plus strategy, which allows for variations in special circumstances.[7] Discounts may be granted, depending on the customer, the size of the order, or the intensity of competition. Changes in prices may also be put into effect to counter exchange rate fluctuations. Despite these allowances, profit is still a driving motive, and pricing is more static as an element of the marketing mix.

The marginal cost method considers the direct costs of producing and selling products for export as the floor beneath which prices cannot be set. Fixed costs for plants, R&D, and domestic overhead as well as domestic marketing costs are disregarded. An exporter can thus lower export prices to be competitive in markets that otherwise might have been beyond access. On certain occasions, especially if the exporter is large, this may open a company to dumping charges, because determination of dumping may be based on average total costs, which are typically considerably higher. A comparison of the cost-oriented methods is provided in Table 9.1. Notice how the rigid cost-plus strategy produces the highest selling price by full-cost allocation.

Table 9.1   Export Pricing Alternatives

Production Costs	Standard	Cost Plus	Marginal Cost
Materials	2.00	2.00	2.00
Fixed costs	1.00	1.00	0.00
Additional foreign product costs	0.00	0.10	0.10
Production overhead	0.50	0.50	0.00
Total production costs	3.50	3.60	2.10
U.S. marketing costs	1.50	0.00	0.00
General and administrative	0.75	0.75	0.00
Foreign marketing	0.00	1.00	1.00
Other foreign costs	0.00	1.25	1.25
Subtotal	5.75	6.60	4.35
Profit margin (25%)	1.44	1.65	1.09
Selling price	7.19	8.25	5.44

SOURCE: Adapted from Lee Oster, "Accounting for Exporters," *Export Today* 7 (January 1991): 28–33.

Market-differentiated pricing calls for export pricing according to the dynamic conditions of the marketplace. For these firms, the marginal cost strategy provides a basis, and prices may change frequently due to changes in competition, exchange rate changes, or other environmental changes. The need for information and controls becomes crucial if this pricing alternative is to be attempted. Exporters are likely to use market-based pricing to gain entry or better penetration in a new market, ignoring many of the cost elements, at least in the short term.

While most exporters, especially in the early stages of their internationalization, use cost-plus pricing, it usually does not lead to desired performance.[8] It typically leads to pricing too high in weak markets and too low in strong markets by not reflecting prevailing market conditions. But as experience is accumulated, the process allows for more flexibility and is more market-driven.

Interestingly, exporters have been found to differ in their pricing approaches by their country of origin. For example, Korean firms price more competitively in international markets than domestically, while U.S. firms seem to consider costs and profits more in setting their export prices.[9]

Overall, exporters see the pricing decision as a critical one, which means that it is typically taken centrally under the supervision of top-level management. In addition to product quality, correct pricing is seen as the major determinant of international marketing success.[10]

Export-Related Costs

In preparing a quotation, the exporter must be careful to take into account and, if possible, include unique export-related costs. These are in addition to the normal costs shared with the domestic side. They include the following:

1. The cost of modifying the product for foreign markets
2. Operational costs of the export operation: personnel, market research, additional shipping and insurance costs, communications costs with foreign customers, and overseas promotional costs
3. Costs incurred in entering the foreign markets: tariffs and taxes; risks associated with a buyer in a different market (mainly commercial credit risks and political risks); and risks from dealing in other than the exporter's domestic currency—that is, foreign exchange risk

The combined effect of both clear-cut and hidden costs results in export prices that far exceed domestic prices. The cause is termed **price escalation.** In the case of Geochron, the marketer of world time indicators, the multilayered distribution system with its excessive markups makes the price of a $1,300 clock exceed $3,800 in Japan.[11]

Four different export scenarios are compared with a typical domestic situation in Table 9.2. The first case is relatively simple, adding only the CIF (cost, insurance, freight) and tariff charges. The second adds a foreign importer and thus lengthens the foreign part of the distribution channel. In the third case, a **value-added tax (VAT)**, such as those used within the European Union, is included in the calculations. This is imposed on the full export selling price, which represents the "value added" to or introduced into the country from abroad. In Italy, for example, where most food items are taxed at 2 percent, processed meat is taxed at 18 percent because the government wants to use the VAT to help reduce its trade deficit. The fourth case simulates a situation typically found in less-developed countries where distribution channels are longer. Lengthy channels can easily double the landed (CIF) price.

Complicating price escalation in today's environment may be the fact that price increases are of different sizes across markets. If customers are willing to shop

Table 9.2   Export Price Escalation

International Marketing Channel Elements and Cost Factors	Domestic Wholesale-Retail Channel	CASE 1 Same as Domestic with Direct Wholesale Import CIF/Tariff	CASE 2 Same as 1 with Foreign Importer Added to Channel	CASE 3 Same as 2 with VAT Added	CASE 4 Same as 3 with Local Foreign Jobber Added to Channel
Manufacturer's net price	6.00	6.00	6.00	6.00	6.00
+ Insurance and shipping cost (CIF)	—	2.50	2.50	2.50	2.50
= Landed cost (CIF value)	—	8.50	8.50	8.50	8.50
+ Tariff (20% on CIF value)	—	1.70	1.70	1.70	1.70
= Importer's cost (CIF value + tariff)	—	10.20	10.20	10.20	10.20
+ Importer's margin (25% on cost)	—	—	2.55	2.55	2.55
+ VAT (16% on full cost plus margin)	—	—	—	2.04	2.04
= Wholesaler's cost (= importer's price)	6.00	10.20	12.75	14.79	14.79
+ Wholesaler's margin (33⅓% on cost)	2.00	3.40	4.25	4.93	4.93
+ VAT (16% on margin)	—	—	—	.79	.79
= Local foreign jobber's cost (= wholesale price)	—	—	—	—	20.51
+ Jobber's margin (33⅓% on cost)	—	—	—	—	6.84
+ VAT (16% on margin)	—	—	—	—	1.09
= Retailer's cost (= wholesale or jobber price)	8.00	13.60	17.00	20.51	28.44
+ Retailer's margin (50% on cost)	4.00	6.80	8.50	10.26	14.22
+ VAT (16% on margin)	—	—	—	1.64	2.28
= Retail price (what consumer pays)	12.00	20.40	25.50	32.41	44.94
Percentage price escalation over domestic		70%	113%	170%	275%
Percentage price escalation over Case 1			25%	59%	120%
Percentage price escalation over Case 2				27%	76%
Percentage price escalation over Case 3					39%

SOURCE: Helmut Becker, "Pricing: An International Marketing Challenge," in *International Marketing Strategy*, eds. Hans Thorelli and Helmut Becker (New York: Pergamon Press, 1980), 215.

around before purchasing, the problem of price differentials will make distributors unhappy and could result in a particular market's being abandoned altogether.

Price escalation can be overcome through creative strategies, depending on what the demand elasticities in the market are. Typical methods, such as the following, focus on cost cutting:

1. Reorganize the channel of distribution. The example in Figure 9.3, based on import channels for spaghetti and macaroni in Japan, shows how the flow of merchandise through the various wholesaling levels has been reduced to only an internal wholesale distribution center, resulting in savings of 25 percent and increasing the overall potential for imports. Shortening of channels may, however, bring about other costs such as demands for better discounts if a new intermediary takes the role of multiple previous ones.

2. Adapt the product. The product itself can be reformulated by including less expensive ingredients or unbundling costly features, which can be made optional. Remaining features, such as packaging, can also be made less expensive. If price escalation causes price differentials between markets, the product can be altered to avoid cross-border price shopping by customers. For example, Geochron alters its clocks' appearance from one region to another.

3. Use new or more economical tariff or tax classifications. In many cases, products may qualify for entry under different categories that have different charges levied against them. The marketer may have to engage in a lobbying effort to get changes made in existing systems, but the results may be considerable savings. For example, when the U.S. Customs Service ruled that multipurpose vehicles were light trucks and, therefore, subject to 25 percent tariffs (and not the 2.5 percent levied on passenger cars), Britain's Land Rover had to argue that its $56,000 luxury vehicle, the Range Rover, was not a truck. When the United States introduced a luxury tax (10 percent of the part of a car's price that exceeded $33,000), Land Rover worked closely with the U.S.

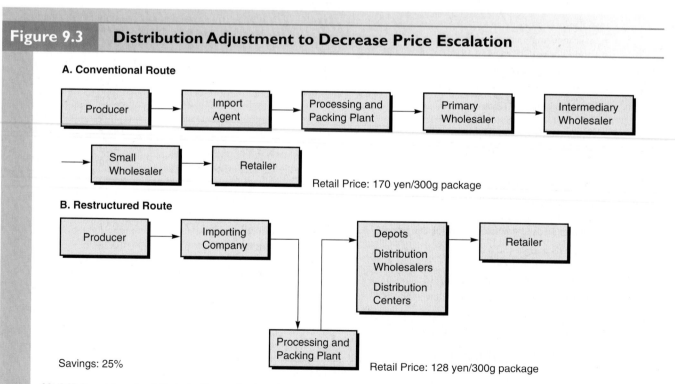

Figure 9.3   Distribution Adjustment to Decrease Price Escalation

A. Conventional Route

Producer → Import Agent → Processing and Packing Plant → Primary Wholesaler → Intermediary Wholesaler → Small Wholesaler → Retailer

Retail Price: 170 yen/300g package

B. Restructured Route

Producer → Importing Company → Processing and Packing Plant / Depots (Distribution Wholesalers, Distribution Centers) → Retailer

Savings: 25%

Retail Price: 128 yen/300g package

Internal Revenue Service to establish that its vehicles were trucks (since trucks were free of such tax). Before it got its way, however, it had to make slight adjustments in the vehicle, since the IRS defines a minimum weight for trucks at 6,000 lbs. Land Rover's following year model weighed in at 6,019 lbs.[12]

4. Assemble or produce overseas. In the longer term, the exporter may resort to overseas sourcing or eventually production. Through foreign sourcing, the exporter may accrue an additional benefit to lower cost: **duty drawbacks.** An exporter may be refunded up to 99 percent of duties paid on imported goods when they are exported or incorporated in articles that are subsequently exported within five years of the importation.[13] Levi Strauss, for example, imports zippers from China that are sewn into the company's jackets and jeans in the United States. The amount that Levi's reclaims can be significant, because the duty on zippers can climb to 30 percent of the product's value.[14]

If the marketer is able to convey a premium image, it may then be able to pass the increased amounts to the final price.

Appropriate export pricing requires the establishment of accounting procedures to assess export performance. Without such a process, hidden costs may bring surprises. For example, negotiations in the Middle Eastern countries or Russia may last three times longer than the average domestic negotiations, dramatically increasing the costs of doing business abroad. Furthermore, without accurate information, a company cannot combat phenomena such as price escalation.

Terms of Sale

The responsibilities of the buyer and the seller should be spelled out as they relate to what is and what is not included in the price quotation and when ownership of goods passes from seller to buyer. **Incoterms** are the internationally accepted standard definitions for terms of sale set by the International Chamber of Commerce (ICC) since 1936. The Incoterms 2000 went into effect on January 1, 2000, with significant revisions to better reflect changing transportation technologies and the increased use of electronic communications.[15] Although the same terms may be used in domestic transactions, they gain new meaning in the international arena. The terms are grouped into four categories, starting with the term whereby the seller makes the goods available to the buyer only at the seller's own premises (the "E"-terms), followed by the group, whereby the seller is called upon to deliver the goods to a carrier appointed by the buyer (the "F"-terms). Next are the "C"-terms, whereby the seller has to contract for carriage but without assuming the risk of loss or damage to the goods or additional costs after the dispatch, and finally the "D"-terms, whereby the seller has to bear all costs and risks to bring the goods to the destination determined by the buyer. The most common of the Incoterms used in international marketing are summarized in Figure 9.4. Incoterms are available in 31 languages.

Prices quoted *ex-works (EXW)* apply only at the point of origin, and the seller agrees to place the goods at the disposal of the buyer at the specified place on the date or within the fixed period. All other charges are for the account of the buyer.

One of the new Incoterms is *free carrier (FCA),* which replaced a variety of FOB terms for all modes of transportation except vessel. FCA (named inland point) applies only at a designated inland shipping point. The seller is responsible for loading goods into the means of transportation; the buyer is responsible for all subsequent expenses. If a port of exportation is named, the costs of transporting the goods to the named port are included in the price.

Free alongside ship (FAS) at a named U.S. port of export means that the exporter quotes a price for the goods, including charges for delivery of the goods alongside a vessel at the port. The seller handles the cost of unloading and wharfage; loading, ocean transportation, and insurance are left to the buyer.

Figure 9.4 Selected Trade Terms (Incoterms)

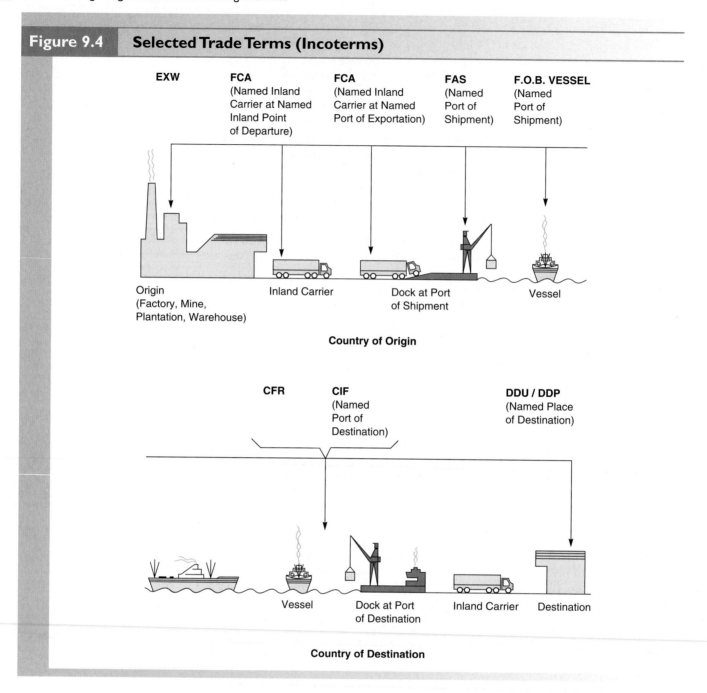

EXW

FCA (Named Inland Carrier at Named Inland Point of Departure)

FCA (Named Inland Carrier at Named Port of Exportation)

FAS (Named Port of Shipment)

F.O.B. VESSEL (Named Port of Shipment)

Origin (Factory, Mine, Plantation, Warehouse)

Inland Carrier

Dock at Port of Shipment

Vessel

Country of Origin

CFR

CIF (Named Port of Destination)

DDU / DDP (Named Place of Destination)

Vessel

Dock at Port of Destination

Inland Carrier

Destination

Country of Destination

Free on board (FOB) applies only to vessel shipments. The seller quotes a price covering all expenses up to, and including, delivery of goods on an overseas vessel provided by or for the buyer.

Under *cost and freight (CFR)* to a named overseas port of import, the seller quotes a price for the goods, including the cost of transportation to the named port of debarkation. The cost of insurance and the choice of insurer are left to the buyer.

With *cost, insurance, and freight (CIF)* to a named overseas port of import, the seller quotes a price including insurance, all transportation, and miscellaneous charges to the point of debarkation from the vessel. If other than waterway transport is used, the terms are *CPT* (carriage paid to) or *CIP* (carriage and insurance paid to).

With *delivered duty paid (DDP),* the seller delivers the goods, with import duties paid, including inland transportation from import point to the buyer's premises. With *delivered duty unpaid (DDU),* only the destination customs duty and taxes are paid by the consignee. Ex-works signifies the maximum obligation for the buyer; delivered duty paid puts the maximum burden on the seller.

Careful determination and clear understanding of terms used, and their acceptance by the parties involved, are vital if subsequent misunderstandings and disputes are to be avoided not only between the parties but also within the marketer's own organization.[16]

These terms are also powerful competitive tools. The exporter should therefore learn what importers usually prefer in the particular market and what the specific transaction may require. An inexperienced importer may be discouraged from further action by a quote such as ex-plant Jessup, Maryland, whereas CIF Helsinki will enable the Finnish importer to handle the remaining costs because they are incurred in a familiar environment.

Increasingly, exporters are quoting more inclusive terms. The benefits of taking charge of the transportation on either a CIF or DDP basis include the following: (1) exporters can offer foreign buyers an easy-to-understand "delivered cost" for the deal; (2) by getting discounts on volume purchases for transportation services, exporters cut shipping costs and can offer lower overall prices to prospective buyers; (3) control of product quality and service is extended to transport, enabling the exporter to ensure that goods arrive to the buyer in good condition; and (4) administrative procedures are cut for both the exporter and the buyer.[17] These benefits are highlighted in *The International Marketplace 9.2*.

THE INTERNATIONAL MARKETPLACE   9.2

Penetrating Foreign Markets by Controlling Export Transport

Companies that once sought short-term customers to smooth out recessions are searching for every means to get an edge over rivals in foreign markets. To achieve that, they are increasingly concerned about controlling quality and costs at every step, including the transportation process.

International transport costs are far higher than domestic shipping expenses. International ocean transport typically accounts for 4 to 20 percent of the product's delivered cost but can reach as high as 50 percent for commodity items. That makes transport a factor in situations in which a single price disadvantage can cause a sale to be lost to a competitor.

Still, most U.S. companies continue to abdicate responsibility for export shipping—either because they lack sophistication or simply because they do not want to be bothered. Increasingly, however, companies like Deere & Co. are paying for, controlling, and often insuring transport from their factories either to foreign ports or to the purchasing companies' doorsteps. This means that they are shipping on a DDP basis.

Deere exports premium-quality farm and lawn equipment worldwide. For years, it has insisted on overseeing transportation because it boosts sales, cuts costs, and ensures quality. "We have a long-term relationship with our dealers. It is in our best interest to do the transport job," says Ann Salaber, an order control manager in the export order department.

One goal of Deere's approach to transportation is to ensure that equipment is delivered to customers in good condition—a factor that Deere considers central to its image as a quality producer. The goal is to avoid cases like the one in which an inexperienced customer insisted on shipping a tractor himself. The tractor was unwittingly put on a ship's deck during a long, stormy sea voyage and arrived in terrible shape.

The process also helps when Deere tractor windows are inadvertently broken during transport. Because Deere closely monitors the tractors, it can quickly install new windows at the port and avoid the huge cost of flying replacements to a customer as far away as Argentina.

Cost is an important consideration as well. Depending on where a $150,000 combine is shipped, transport costs can range between $7,500 and $30,000, or between 5 and 20 percent of delivered cost. Deere's ability to buy steamship space in volume enables it to reduce transport costs by 10 percent. That in turn enables it to cut the combine's delivered cost by between $750 and $3,000. "That adds up," says Salaber. Because of those savings, "you do not have to discount so much, and Deere gets more profit."

SOURCES: Toby B. Gooley, "Incoterms 2000: What the Changes Mean to You," *Logistics Management and Distribution Report* 39 (January 2000): 49–51; "How Badly Will the Dollar Whack the U.S.?" *Business Week*, May 5, 1997; Gregory L. Miles, "Exporter's New Bully Stick," *International Business*, December 1993, 46–49; **http://www.iccwbo.org**; and **http://www.deere.com**.

When taking control of transportation costs, however, the exporter must know well in advance what impact the additional costs will have on the bottom line. If the approach is implemented incorrectly, exporters can be faced with volatile shipping rates, unexpected import duties, and restive customers. Most exporters do not want to go beyond the CIF quotation because of uncontrollables and unknowns in the destination country. Whatever terms are chosen, the program should be agreed to by the exporter and the buyer(s) rather than imposed solely by the exporter.

Freight forwarders are useful in determining costs, preparing quotations, and making sure that unexpected changes do not cause the exporter to lose money. Freight forwarders are useful to the exporter not only as facilitators and advisors but also in keeping down some of the export-related costs. Rates for freight and insurance provided to freight forwarders may be far more economical than to an individual exporter because of large-volume purchases, especially if export sales are infrequent. Some freight forwarders can also provide additional value-added services, such as taking care of the marketer's duty-drawback receivables.

Terms of Payment

Export credit and terms add another dimension to the profitability of an export transaction. The exporter has in all likelihood already formulated a credit policy that determines the degree of risk the firm is willing to assume and the preferred selling terms. The main objective is to meet the importer's requirements without jeopardizing the firm's financial goals. The exporter will be concerned over being paid for the goods shipped and will therefore consider the following factors in negotiating terms of payment: (1) the amount of payment and the need for protection, (2) terms offered by competitors, (3) practices in the industry, (4) capacity for financing international transactions, and (5) relative strength of the parties involved.[18] If the exporter is well established in the market with a unique product and accompanying service, price and terms of trade can be set to fit the exporter's desires. If, on the other hand, the exporter is breaking into a new market or if competitive pressures call for action, pricing and selling terms should be used as major competitive tools. Both parties have their own concerns and sensitivities; therefore, this very basic issue should be put on the negotiating table at the very beginning of the relationship.

The basic methods of payment for exports vary in terms of their attractiveness to the buyer and the seller, from cash in advance to open account or consignment selling. Neither of the extremes will be feasible for longer-term relationships, but they do have their use in certain situations. For example, in the 1999–2000 period very few companies were exporting into Russia except on a cash-in-advance basis, due to the country's financial turmoil. A marketer may use multiple methods of payment with the same buyer. For example, in a distributor relationship, the distributor may purchase samples on open account, but orders have to be paid for with a letter of credit. These methods are depicted in the risk triangle presented in Figure 9.5.

The most favorable term to the exporter is **cash in advance** because it relieves the exporter of all risk and allows for immediate use of the money. It is not widely used, however, except for smaller, first-time transactions or situations in which the exporter has reason to doubt the importer's ability to pay. Cash-in-advance terms are also found when orders are for custom-made products, because the risk to the exporter is beyond that of a normal transaction. In some instances, the importer may not be able to buy on a cash-in-advance basis because of insufficient funds or government restrictions.

A **letter of credit** is an instrument issued by a bank at the request of a buyer. The bank promises to pay a specified amount of money on presentation of documents stipulated in the letter of credit, usually the bill of lading, consular invoice, and a description of the goods.[19] Letters of credit are one of the most frequently used methods of payment in international transactions. Figure 9.6 summarizes the process of obtaining a letter of credit and the relationship between the parties involved.

Figure 9.5 Methods of Payment for Exports

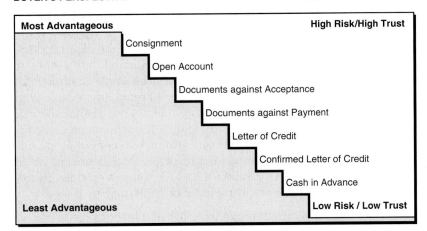

BUYER'S PERSPECTIVE   SELLER'S PERSPECTIVE

Most Advantageous   High Risk/High Trust

Consignment

Open Account

Documents against Acceptance

Documents against Payment

Letter of Credit

Confirmed Letter of Credit

Cash in Advance

Least Advantageous   Low Risk / Low Trust

SOURCE: Adapted from Chase Manhattan Bank, *Dynamics of Trade Finance* (New York: Chase Manhattan Bank, 1984), 5.

Figure 9.6 Letter of Credit: Process and Parties

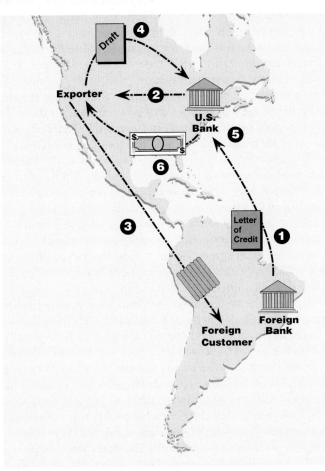

1. L/C opened by foreign customer at local bank and sent to U.S. bank.

2. L/C confirmed by U.S. bank and sent to exporter.

3. Exporter approves terms and conditions of L/C. Exporter ships goods against L/C.

4. Exporter sends shipping documents to U.S. bank and a draft for payment.

5. Bank examines documents for discrepancies.

6. If documents match terms and conditions of L/C, U.S. bank pays exporter for goods.

SOURCE: Based on Faren L. Foster and Lynn S. Hutchins, "Six Steps to Quicker Collection of Export Letters of Credit," *Export Today* 9 (November–December 1993): 26–30.

Letters of credit can be classified among three dimensions:

1. Irrevocable versus revocable. An irrevocable letter of credit can neither be canceled nor modified without the consent of the beneficiary (exporter), thus guaranteeing payment. According to the new rules drawn by the International Chamber of Commerce, all letters of credit are considered irrevocable unless otherwise stated.[20]

2. Confirmed versus unconfirmed. In the case of a U.S. exporter, a U.S. bank might confirm the letter of credit and thus assume the risk, including the transaction (exchange) risk. The single best method of payment for the exporter in most cases is a confirmed, irrevocable letter of credit. Banks may also assume an advisory role but not assume the risk; the underlying assumption is that the bank and its correspondent(s) are better able to judge the credibility of the bank issuing the letter of credit than is the exporter.

3. Revolving versus nonrevolving. Most letters of credit are nonrevolving, that is, they are valid for the one transaction only. In case of established relationships, a revolving letter of credit may be issued.

Figure 9.7 provides an example of a letter of credit.

The letter of credit provides advantages to both the exporter and the importer, which explains its wide use. The approach substitutes the credit of the bank for the credit of the buyer and is as good as the issuing bank's access to dollars. In custom-made orders, an irrevocable letter of credit may help the exporter secure pre-export financing. The importer will not need to pay until the documents have arrived and been accepted by the bank, thus giving an additional float. The major caveat is that the exporter has to comply with all the terms of the letter of credit.[21] For example, if the documents state that shipment is made in crates measuring $4 \times 4 \times 4$ and the goods are shipped in crates measuring $4 \times 3 \times 4$, the bank will not honor the letter of credit. If there are changes, the letter of credit can be amended to ensure payment. Importers have occasionally been accused of creating discrepancies to slow down the payment process or to drive down the agreed-upon price.[22] In some cases, the exporter must watch out for fraudulent letters of credit, especially in the case of less-developed countries. In these cases, exporters are advised to ship only on the basis of an irrevocable letter of credit, confirmed by their bank, even after the credentials of the foreign contact have been established.

With the increasing amount of e-commerce, things will have to change. Solutions include online issuance and status reporting on letters of credit, creating a worldwide network of electronic trade hubs, and offering a smart card that will allow participating companies to transact financial business online.[23] For example, TradeCard is an online service for B2B (business-to-business) exchanges. Once an exporter and importer have agreed on the terms, the buyer creates an electronic purchase order, which specifies the terms and conditions. Once it is in electronic format, the seller formally agrees to the contract. The purchase order is stored in TradeCard's database. The system then creates both a commercial invoice and a packing list, and a promise of payment is included with the invoice for the seller. A third-party logistics provider sends proof of delivery electronically to TradeCard, which then debits the buyer's account and credits the seller's account.[24]

The letter of credit is a promise to pay but not a means of payment. Actual payment is accomplished by means of a **draft,** which is similar to a personal check. Like a check, it is an order by one party to pay another. Most drafts are documentary, which means that the buyer must obtain possession of various shipping documents before obtaining possession of the goods involved in the transaction. Clean drafts—orders to pay without any other documents—are mainly used by multinational corporations in their dealings with their own subsidiaries and in well-established business relationships.

In **documentary collection** situations, the seller ships the goods, and the shipping documents and the draft demanding payment are presented to the importer

Figure 9.7   Letter of Credit

First Union National Bank
International Division

IRREVOCABLE LETTER OF CREDIT
DECEMBER 05, 20___

SAMPLE COPY

ABC EXPORTERS, LTD.
9876 FIRST STREET
ANYWHERE, JAPAN

LETTER OF CREDIT NO.
L000000

WE HEREBY OPEN OUR IRREVOCABLE LETTER OF CREDIT IN YOUR FAVOR, FOR THE ACCOUNT
OF XYZ IMPORTERS, INC 1234 MAIN STREET, ANYWHERE, U.S.A. 54321 IN THE
AGGREGATE AMOUNT OF: USD100,000.00 (UNITED STATES DOLLARS ONE HUNDRED THOUSAND
AND 00/100) AVAILABLE WITH ANY BANK BY NEGOTIATION OF YOUR DRAFTS AT 90 DAYS
OF BILL OF LADING DATE ON FIRST UNION NATIONAL BANK WHEN ACCOMPANIED BY THE
FOLLOWING DOCUMENTS:

1. COMMERCIAL INVOICE IN TRIPLICATE
2. CERTIFICATE OF ORIGIN
3. PACKING LIST IN DUPLICATE
4. FULL SET CLEAN "ON BOARD" OCEAN BILL OF LADING ISSUED TO ORDER OF FIRST
   UNION NATIONAL BANK MARKED NOTIFY XYZ IMPORTERS, INC AND MARKED FREIGHT
   "COLLECT"

COVERING MERCHANDISE AS PER P.O. NUMBER 10205 DATED NOVEMBER 25, 20___

PARTIAL SHIPMENTS ALLOWED / TRANSHIPMENTS PROHIBITED

SHIPMENT FROM: FOB ANY JAPANESE PORT   FOR TRANSPORTATION TO: USA PORT
LATEST SHIPMENT DATE: JANUARY 15, 20 ___
EXPIRY DATE: JANUARY 31, 20___

SPECIAL CONDITIONS:
1. IF DOCUMENTS PRESENTED DO NOT COMPLY WITH THE TERMS AND CONDITIONS OF THIS
CREDIT, A DISCREPANCY FEE FOR EACH SET OF DOCUMENTS WILL BE DEDUCTED FROM ANY
REMITTANCE MADE TO THE BENEFICIARY UNDER THE CREDIT.
2. DOCUMENTS MUST BE PRESENTED FOR NEGOTIATION WITHIN 15 DAYS OF SHIPMENT
DATE, BUT WITHIN THE VALIDITY OF THE CREDIT.
3. DRAFT(S) DRAWN UNDER THIS CREDIT MUST STATE ON THEIR FACE "DRAWN UNDER
FIRST UNION NATIONAL BANK IRREVOCABLE LETTER CREDIT NUMBER L000000 DATED
DECEMBER 05, 20___" AND DATED SAME DATE AS ON BOARD DATE OF BILL OF LADING.

WE HEREBY ENGAGE WITH DRAWERS, ENDORSERS, AND BONA FIDE HOLDERS OF DRAFTS
DRAWN UNDER AND IN COMPLIANCE WITH THE TERMS AND CONDITIONS OF THIS CREDIT,
THAT THE SAME SHALL BE HONORED ON DUE PRESENTATION AND DELIVERY OF DOCUMENTS
TO THE DRAWEE. THE AMOUNT OF ANY DRAFT(S) DRAWN UNDER THIS CREDIT MUST,
CONCURRENTLY WITH NEGOTIATION, BE ENDORSED BY THE NEGOTIATING BANK ON THE
REVERSE HEREOF.

UNLESS EXPRESSLY STATED HEREIN, THIS CREDIT IS SUBJECT TO UNIFORM CUSTOMS AND
PRACTICES FOR DOCUMENTARY CREDITS PUBLICATION NO. 500.

DIRECT ALL INQUIRIES TO FIRST UNION NATIONAL BANK, INTERNATIONAL DIVISION,
301 SOUTH TRYON STREET/T-7, CHARLOTTE, NC 28288-0742.

SINCERELY,   **SAMPLE COPY**

AUTHORIZED SIGNATURE
FIRST UNION NATIONAL BANK
CHARLOTTE, NORTH CAROLINA

SOURCE: **http://www.firstunion.com**.

Figure 9.8 Documentary Collection

```
                (1)                    (2)                      (3)
U.S. $ 500,000.00          Anywhere, Japan          December 17, 20 00

AT        Sight        (4)                      (5)
                            DAYS AFTER ----------------------------------
                                            (6)
PAY TO THE ORDER OF        ABC Exporters, Ltd.


        Five Hundred Thousand and 00/100 U.S. --(7)------------------ DOLLARS
VALUE RECEIVED AND CHARGE THE SAME TO THE ACCOUNT OF:
            (9)                              (8)   "Drawn under First Union National Bank
TO:  First Union National Bank                     Irrevocable L/C No. L000000 dated
     Charlotte, N.C.                               December 4, 2000"

                                                    (10)   ABC Exporters, Ltd.

NO.     (11)   ABC35                                              (12)
                                                          _____
                                                            (AUTHORIZES SIGNATURE)
```

```
                (1)                    (2)                      (3)
U.S. $ 100,000.00          Anywhere, Japan          December 17, 2000

AT  90 Days of B/L Date    (4)                  (5)
                            DAYS AFTER ----------------------------------
                                            (6)
PAY TO THE ORDER OF        ABC Exporters, Ltd.


        One Hundred Thousand and 00/100 U.S. ---(7)----------------- DOLLARS
VALUE RECEIVED AND CHARGE THE SAME TO THE ACCOUNT OF:
            (9)                              (8)   "Drawn under First Union National Bank
TO:  First Union National Bank                     Irrevocable L/C No. L000000 dated
     Charlotte, N.C.                               December 5, 2000"

                                                    (10)   ABC Exporters, Ltd.

NO.     (11)   ABC18                                              (12)
                                                          _____
                                                            (AUTHORIZES SIGNATURE)
```

SOURCE: **http://www.firstunion.com**.

through banks acting as the seller's agent. The draft, also known as the bill of exchange, may be either a sight draft or a time draft (Figure 9.8). A sight draft documents against payment and is payable on presentation to the drawee, that is, the party to whom the draft is addressed. A time draft documents against acceptance and allows for a delay of 30, 60, 90, 120, or 180 days. When a time draft is drawn on and accepted by a bank, it becomes a **banker's acceptance,** which is sold in the short-term money market. Time drafts drawn on and accepted by a business firm become trader's acceptances, which are normally not marketable. A draft is presented to the drawee, who accepts it by writing or stamping a notice of acceptance on it. With both sight and time drafts, the buyer can effectively extend the period of credit by avoiding receipt of the goods. A date draft requires payment on a specified date, regardless of the date on which the goods and the draft are accepted by the buyer.

To illustrate, an exporter may have a time draft accepted by Citibank for $1 million to be paid in 90 days. Like many exporters who extend credit for competitive reasons, the firm may have immediate need for the funds. It could contact an acceptance dealer and sell the acceptance at a discount, with the rate depending on the market rate of interest. If the annual interest rate was 6 percent, for example, the acceptance could be sold for $985,222 ($1 million divided by 1.015).

Even if the draft is not sold in the secondary market, the exporter may convert it into cash by **discounting.** To discount the draft simply means that the draft is sold to a bank at a discount from face value. If the discounting is with recourse, the exporter is liable for the payment to the bank if the importer defaults. If the discounting is without recourse, the exporter will not be liable even if the importer does not pay the bank. Discounting without recourse is known as factoring or, in the case of higher credit risk and longer-term receivables, forfaiting.

The normal manner of doing business in the domestic market is **open account** (open terms). The exporter selling on open account removes both real and psychological barriers to importing. However, no written evidence of the debt exists, and the exporter has to put full faith in the references contacted. Worst of all, there is no guarantee of payment. If the debt turns bad, the problems of overseas litigation are considerable. Bad debts are normally easier to avoid than to rectify. In less-developed countries, importers will usually need proof of debt in the application to the central bank for hard currency, which will not allow them to deal on an open-account basis. Again, open account is used by multinationals in their internal transactions and when there is implicit trust among the partners.

The most favorable term to the importer is **consignment selling,** which allows the importer to defer payment until the goods are actually sold. This approach places all the burden on the exporter, and its use should be carefully weighed against the objectives of the transaction. If the exporter wants entry into a specific market through specific intermediaries, consignment selling may be the only method of gaining acceptance by intermediaries. The arrangement will require clear understanding as to the parties' responsibilities—for example, which party is responsible for insurance until the goods have actually been sold. If the goods are not sold, returning them will be costly and time-consuming; for example, there is getting through customs or paying, avoiding paying, or trying to get refunds on duties. Due to its burdensome characteristics, consignment is not widely used.

Getting Paid for Exports

The exporter needs to minimize the risk of not being paid if a transaction occurs. The term **commercial risk** refers primarily to the insolvency of, or protracted payment default by, an overseas buyer. Commercial defaults, in turn, usually result from deterioration of conditions in the buyer's market, fluctuations in demand, unanticipated competition, or technological changes. These naturally emerge domestically as well, but the geographic and cultural distances in international markets make them more severe and more difficult to anticipate. In addition, non-commercial or **political risk** is completely beyond the control of either the buyer or the seller. For example, the foreign buyer may be willing to pay but the local government may use every trick in the book to delay payment as far into the future as possible.

These challenges must be addressed through actions by either the company itself or support systems. The decision must be an informed one, based on detailed and up-to-date information in international credit and country conditions. In many respects, the assessment of a buyer's creditworthiness requires the same attention to credit checking and financial analysis as for domestic buyers; however, the assessment of a foreign private buyer is complicated by some of the following factors:

1. Credit reports may not be reliable.
2. Audited reports may not be available.
3. Financial reports may have been prepared according to a different format.
4. Many governments require that assets be annually reevaluated upward, which can distort results.

5. Statements are in local currency.

6. The buyer may have the financial resources in local currency but may be precluded from converting to dollars because of exchange controls and other government actions.

More than one credit report should be obtained (from sources such as the two in Figure 9.9), and it should be determined how each credit agency obtains its reports. They may use the same correspondent agency, in which case it does the exporter no good to obtain the same information from two sources and to pay for it twice. Table 9.3 provides a summary of the major sources of credit information. Where private-sector companies (such as Dun & Bradstreet or Veritas) are able to provide the needed credit information, the services of the U.S. Department of Commerce's International Company Profiles (ICP) are not available. However, currently 50 countries are still served by the ICP. Local credit reporting agencies, such as Profancresa in Mexico, may also provide regional services (in this case, throughout Latin America). With the growth of e-commerce, a company may want to demonstrate its creditworthiness to customers and suppliers in a rapid and secure fashion. The Coface Group (of which Veritas is the information arm in the Americas) introduced the "@rating" system, available on the World Wide Web and designed to assess a company's performance in paying its commercial obligations.[25]

Beyond protecting oneself by establishing creditworthiness, an exporter can match payment terms to the customer. In the short term, an exporter may require payment terms that guarantee payment. In the long term, the best approach is to establish a relationship of mutual trust, which will ensure payment even if complications arise during a transaction.[26] Payment terms need to be stated clearly and followed up effectively. If prompt payment is not stressed and enforced, some customers will assume they can procrastinate, as we see in *The International Marketplace 9.3.*

Figure 9.9	**Providers of International Credit Information**

SOURCE: Courtesy of the U.S. Commercial Service (**http://www.usatrade.gov**); copyright © Dun & Bradstreet and The Guild Group.

Table 9.3	Sources of International Credit Information

	Response Time	Service Offerings	Presence	Remarks
Dun & Bradstreet http://www.dnb.com	Many nonsubscription-based reports, in electronic copies, readily available for U.S. customers by online purchase; shipment delays on printed reports depending on location; non-U.S. customers can access online database by subscription; certain delays on customized information	• Credit information, both standardized and customized • Country risk reports available online, costing from $75 to $630	8,000 employees worldwide (including all other D&B business), covering 75 million companies in 214 countries	Core strength in small and medium-size enterprises, with 80% of active files in its U.S. database being small companies with less than 10 staff; industry standard, with the largest worldwide company coverage
FCIB-NACM http://www.fcibnacm.com	Same day for already-available reports (excluding shipment); customized credit reports can take from a few days to three weeks; no online database	• Country risk reports cost $100 each for members and $125 for nonmembers • Credit reports • Business credit magazines • Seminars and conferences for export groups	Two main offices in the United States and UK, with country representatives in Europe, Canada, and Mexico	Services focus on exports business; membership costs $840, fees for industry-focus export groups range from $125 to $515
@rating http://www.cofacerating.com	Online focus, instantaneous access of information	• Free online check of company's reliability and financial soundness • Free country risk assessment and rating • Fee-based information reports • Fee-based @rating quality labeling service	Presence in 99 countries, 5 continents, covering 41 million companies	Most efficient and least costly resource, but analysis may lack depth; aim to become standard Web-based rating system, supported by the EU
International Company Profiles http://www.ita.doc.gov	About 10 days of processing time, depending on complexity of information and availability from existing database; no online service, thus adding delays from shipment, depending on locations	• Company background check, including financial status, management profile, and company potential • $500 for each company report	151 international offices in 83 countries, with 1,800 employees	Focus on serving small and mid-sized companies in the United States; analysis is U.S.-centric because service provider is part of U.S. Department of Commerce
Local Credit Agencies or Trade Councils	Varies	• Focus on information of local companies	Locally	Quality varies, with limited scope in international marketing
Bank Reports	Slow	Company background	None (client)	Limited in scope

SOURCE: Interviews with company and organization personnel, October 2002.

THE INTERNATIONAL MARKETPLACE   9.3

Now for the Hard Part: Getting Paid for Exports

Smaller exporters often do not have the luxury that big corporations have to weigh risks of doing business abroad and to investigate the creditworthiness of foreign customers. The result may be a hard lesson about the global economy: Foreign sales do not help much when you cannot collect the bill.

More often than not, exporters will do less checking on an international account than they will on a domestic customer. For example, a U.S. fan blade manufacturer with less than $10 million in revenue was left with an overdue payment of $127,000 owed by an African customer. Before shipping the goods, the company had failed to call any of the customer's credit references. These turned out to be nonexistent—just like the company itself.

The simple guideline of selling only in countries where you are most likely to get paid may not be enough, given that collection periods for some of the more attractive markets may be long (see table). However, in many cases, basic information about the economic and political conditions in markets may be enough to warrant caution. Old World Industries Inc., a midsized maker of antifreeze fluid and other automotive products, found that out after selling 500,000 gallons of antifreeze to a customer in a newly emerging market. After two years, Old World is still waiting to be paid in full, because the foreign bank it is dealing with has trouble obtaining U.S. dollars despite the country's strengthening foreign reserve position.

The length of time required for U.S. companies in different industries to collect on the average bill varies dramatically. The data in the table are for the second half of 2002 as reported by members of the Foreign Credit Interchange Bureau. The number of days for Argentina increased dramatically in 2002 due to currency restrictions placed on importers. For some countries, such as Pakistan, no number is available because all transactions are on a cash-in-advance or letter-of-credit basis.

Country	Number of Days
Argentina	173
Brazil	113
Kenya	102
Italy	89
Taiwan	78
Mexico	77
Japan	65
United Kingdom	59
Finland	56
Switzerland	51
Germany	47
Canada	31

SOURCES: Data updated by interview with FCIB, October 30, 2002; "Congratulations, Exporter! Now about Getting Paid . . ." *Business Week,* January 17, 1994, 98; and "Small Firms Hit Foreign Obstacles in Billing Overseas," *The Wall Street Journal,* December 8, 1992, B2.

Should a default situation occur in spite of the preparatory measures discussed above, the exporter's first recourse is the customer. Communication with the customer may reveal a misunderstanding or error regarding the shipment. If the customer has financial or other concerns or objections, rescheduling the payment terms may be considered. Third-party intervention through a collection agency may be needed if the customer disputes the charges. For example, the Total Credit Management Group, a cooperative of leading credit and collection companies in 46 countries, can be employed. Only when further amicable demands are unwarranted should an attorney be used.[27]

Managing Foreign Exchange Risk

Unless the exporter and the importer share the same currency (as is the case in the 12 countries of Euroland), exchange rate movements may harm one or the other of the parties. If the price is quoted in the exporter's currency, the exporter will get exactly the price it wants but may lose some sales due to lack of customer orientation. If the exporter needs the sale, the invoice may be in the importer's currency, and the exchange risk will be the burden of the exporter. Some exporters, if they are unable to secure payment in their own currency, try to minimize the risk by negotiating shorter terms of payment, such as 10 or 15 days. Exchange risks may be a result of an appreciating or depreciating currency or result from a revaluation or devaluation of a currency by a central bank. Assume that a U.S. importer bought $250,000 or €250,000 worth of goods from a German company, which agreed to accept U.S. dollars for payment in 90 days. At the time of the quotation, the exchange rate for $1 was €1.00, whereas at the time of payment, it had changed to €0.97. This means that the German exporter, instead of receiving €250,000, winds up with €242,500.

Two types of approaches to protect against currency-related risk are proposed: (1) risk shifting, such as foreign currency contractual hedging, and/or (2) risk modifying, such as manipulating prices and other elements of a marketing strategy.

When invoicing in foreign currencies, an exporter cannot insulate itself from the problems of currency movements, but it can at least know how much it will eventually receive by using the mechanism of the **forward exchange market.** In essence, the exporter gets a bank to agree to a rate at which it will buy the foreign currency the exporter will receive when the importer makes payment. The rate is expressed as either a premium or a discount on the current spot rate. The risk still remains if the exchange rate does not move as anticipated, and the exporter may be worse off than if it had not bought forward. Although forward contracts are the most common foreign currency contractual hedge, other financial instruments and derivatives, such as currency options and futures, are available. An **option** gives the holder the right to buy or sell foreign currency at a prespecified price on or up to a prespecified date. The difference between the currency options market and the forward market is that the transaction in the former gives the participant the right to buy or sell, whereas a transaction in the forward market entails a contractual obligation to buy or sell. This means that if an exporter does not have any or the appropriate amount of currency when the contract comes due, it would have to go into the foreign exchange markets to buy the currency, potentially exposing itself to major losses if the currency has appreciated in the meanwhile. The greater flexibility in the options contract makes it more expensive, however. The currency **futures** market is conceptually similar to the forward market; that is, to buy futures on the British pound sterling implies an obligation to buy in the future at a prespecified price. However, the minimum transaction sizes are considerably smaller on the futures market. Forward quotes apply to transactions of $1 million or more, whereas on the futures market transactions will typically be well below $100,000. The market, therefore, allows relatively small firms engaged in international trade to lock in exchange rates and lower their risk. Forward contracts, options, and futures are available from banks, the Chicago Mercantile Exchange, and the Philadelphia Stock Exchange.

U.S. exporters have faced both high and low values of the dollar with respect to other currencies in the past ten years: low values in the early to mid-1990s and high values since then until early 2002. When the exporter's domestic currency is weak, strategies should include stressing the price advantage to customers and expanding the scale and scope of the export operation. Sourcing can be shifted to domestic markets and the export price can be subjected to full-costing. However, under the opposite scenario, the exporter needs to engage in nonprice competition, minimizing the price dimension as much as possible. Costs should be reduced by every means, including enhancing productivity. At this time, the exporter should prioritize efforts to markets that show the greatest returns. Marketers may also attempt to protect themselves by manipulating leads and lags in export and import payments or receivables in anticipation of either currency revaluations and devaluations. This, however, will require thorough market knowledge and leverage over overseas partners. Alternatives available to marketers under differing currency conditions are summarized in Table 9.4.

Whatever the currency movements are, the marketer needs to decide how to adjust pricing to international customers in view of either a more favorable or an unfavorable domestic currency rate. A U.S. exporter, during a strong dollar, has three alternatives. First, making no change in the dollar price would result in a less favorable price in foreign currencies and, most likely, lower sales, especially if no corrective marketing steps are taken. Second, the export price could be decreased

Table 9.4 — Exporter Strategies under Varying Currency Conditions

Weak	Strong
1. Stress price benefits	1. Nonprice competition
2. Expand product line	2. Improve productivity/cost reduction
3. Shift sourcing to domestic market	3. Sourcing overseas
4. Exploit all possible export opportunities	4. Prioritize exports
5. Cash-for-goods trade	5. Countertrade with weak currency countries
6. Full-costing	6. Marginal-cost pricing
7. Speed repatriation	7. Slow collections
8. Minimize expenditure in local currency	8. Buy needed services abroad

SOURCE: Adapted from S. Tamer Cavusgil, "Unraveling the Mystique of Export Pricing," *Business Horizons* 31 (May–June 1988): 54–63.

in conjunction with increases in the value of the dollar to maintain stable export prices in foreign currencies. This first alternative is an example of **pass-through,** while the second alternative features the **absorption** approach; i.e., the increase in the price is absorbed into the margin of the product, possibly even resulting in a loss. For pass-through to work, customers have to have a high level of preference for the exporter's product. In some cases, exporters may have no choice but to pass most of the increase to the customer due to the cost structure of the firm. Exporters using the absorption approach have as their goal long-term market-share maintenance, especially in a highly competitive environment.

The third alternative is to pass through only a share of the increase, maintaining sales if possible while at the same time preserving profitability. According to a study on exporter responses to foreign-exchange rate changes over a period of 1973 to 1997, Japanese exporters have the highest tendency to dampen the effects of exchange-rate fluctuations in foreign-currency export prices in both directions by adjusting their home-currency prices.[28] Furthermore, Japanese exporters put a larger emphasis on stabilizing the foreign currency prices of their exports during a weak yen than when the yen is strong. German exporters display completely the opposite behavior. The data in Table 9.5 for German and Japanese auto exports support these findings for the period in the early 1990s, when the dollar appreciated against the German mark and the Japanese yen.

Table 9.5 — Absorption versus Pass-Through: Japanese and German Automarketer Behavior

Model	Real Dollar Appreciation	Real Retail Price Change in U.S. Market
Honda Civic 2-Dr. Sedan	39%	−7%
Nissan 200 SX 2-Dr.	39	−10
Toyota Cressida 4-Dr.	39	6
BMW 320i 2-Dr. Sedan	42	−8
BMW 733i 4-Dr. Sedan	42	−17
Mercedes 300 TD Sta. Wgn.	42	−39

SOURCE: Joseph A. Gagnon and Michael M. Knetter, "Markup Adjustment and Exchange Rate Fluctuations: Evidence from Panel Data on Automobile Exports," *Journal of International Money and Finance* 14 (no. 2, 1995): 289–310. Copyright © 1995, with permission from Elsevier.

The strategic response depends on market conditions and may result in different strategies for each market or product. Destination-specific adjustment of mark-ups in response to exchange-rate changes have been referred to as **pricing-to-market.**[29] For example, a mark-up change will be more substantial in a price-sensitive market and/or product category. In addition, the exporter needs to consider the reactions of local competitors, who may either keep their prices stable (hoping that price increases in imports will improve their position) or increase their prices along with those of imports in search of more profits. U.S. automakers were criticized for raising their domestic prices at a time when Japanese imports were forced up by the higher value of the yen during the mid-1990s. Instead of trying to capture more market share, the automakers went for more profits.[30] If the exporter faces a favorable domestic currency rate, pass-through means providing international customers with a more favorable price, while absorption means that the exporter keeps the export price stable and pockets a higher level of profits.

Some exporters prefer price stability to the greatest possible degree and allow mark-ups to vary in maintaining stable local currency prices. Harley-Davidson, for example, maintains its price to distributors as long as the spot exchange rate does not move more than plus or minus 5 percent from the rate in effect when the quote was made. If the movement is an additional 5 percentage points in either direction, Harley and its distributors will share the costs or benefits. Beyond that the price will have to be renegotiated to bring it more in line with current exchange rates and the economic and competitive realities of the market.[31] During times of exchange-rate gains, rather than lower the price, some exporters use other support tools (such as training and trade deals) with their distributors or customers, on the premise that increasing prices after a future currency swing in the opposite direction may be difficult.

Beyond **price manipulation,** other adjustment strategies exist. They include the following:

1. Market refocus. If lower values of the target market currencies make exporting more difficult by, for example, making collections times longer, marketers may start looking at other markets for growth. For example, U.S. construction industry sales to Mexico grew by nearly 150 percent in 1998 after markets in Thailand and Indonesia dried up.[32] In some cases, the emphasis may switch to the domestic market, where market share gain at the expense of imports may be the most efficient way to grow. Currency appreciation does not always lead to a dire situation for the exporter. Domestic competitors may depend very heavily on imported components and may not able to take advantage of the currency-related price pressure on the exporter. The manufacturing sectors of Indonesia, Malaysia, Philippines, and Thailand use over 30 percent imported parts and raw materials in the production process.[33]

2. Streamlined operations. The marketer may start using more aggressive methods of collection, insisting on letters of credit and insurance to guarantee payments. Some have tightened control of their distribution networks by cutting layers or taking over the responsibility from independent intermediaries. On the product side, marketers may focus on offerings that are less sensitive to exchange-rate changes.

3. Shift in production. Especially when currency shifts are seen as long-term, marketers will increase direct investment. With the high value of the yen, Japanese companies shifted production bases to lower-cost locations or closer to final customers. Matsushita Electric, for example, moved a substantial share of its production to Southeast Asian countries, while earthmoving-equipment maker Komatsu launched a $1 billion joint venture with Texas-based Dresser Industries to build equipment in the United States. Remaining units in Japan will focus on research and development, design, software, and high-precision manufactured goods.[34]

In some cases, even adverse developments in the currency market have not had an effect on international markets or marketers. During the currency crisis in Asia, U.S. oil toolmakers and oil-field service companies were never hurt by the high value of the dollar because their expertise was in demand. Similarly, many U.S. firms such as IBM did not suffer because their exported products are both built and sold in other countries. In some cases, imported goods may be in demand because no domestic production exists, which is the case in the United States with consumer goods such as electronics and cameras.

Sources of Export Financing

Except in the case of larger companies that may have their own financing entities, most international marketers assist their customers abroad in securing appropriate financing. Export financing terms can significantly affect the final price paid by buyers. Consider, for example, two competitors for a $1 million sale. Exporter A offers an 8 percent interest rate over a ten-year payment period, while B offers 9 percent for the same term. Over the ten years, the difference in interest is $55,000. In some cases, buyers will award a contract to the provider of cheaper credit and overlook differences in quality and price.

Financing assistance is available from both the private and the public sectors. The international marketer should assess not only domestic programs but also those in other countries. For example, Japan and Taiwan have import financing programs that provide exporters added potential in penetrating these significant markets.[35]

Commercial Banks

Commercial banks the world over provide trade financing depending on their relationship with the exporter, the nature of the transaction, the country of the borrower, and the availability of export insurance. This usually means that financing assistance is provided only to first-rate credit risks, leaving many U.S. exporters to report major problems in enlisting assistance from U.S. commercial banks. Furthermore, some U.S. banks do not see international trade finance as part of their core competence. Although the situation has improved, exporters still continue to complain about lack of export financing as it pertains to developing countries, financing high technology, or lending against foreign receivables. Many exporters complain that banks will not deal with them without a guarantee from the Ex-Im Bank of rock-solid collateral, such as property and/or equipment.

However, as the share of international sales and reach of companies increases, banking relationships become all the more important, a fact that is also noted by banks themselves. Many banks offer enhanced services, such as electronic services, which help exporters monitor and expedite their international transactions to customers who do a certain amount of business with them. As with all suppliers, the more business done with a bank, the higher the level of service usually at a better price. As the relationship builds, the more comfortable bankers feel about the exporter's business and the more likely they will go out of their way to help, particularly with difficult transactions. For example, Silicon Valley Bank in San José finances fledgling technology exporters, while Capitol Bank in Los Angeles provides export and import financing to companies doing business in Taiwan and South Korea. It is clear that the development of an effective credit policy requires teamwork between the company's marketing and finance staffs and its bankers.

In addition to using the types of services a bank can provide as a criterion of choice, an exporter should assess the bank's overseas reach.[36] This is a combination of the bank's own network of facilities and correspondent relationships. While money-center banks can provide the greatest amount of coverage through their own offices and staff, they still use correspondents in regions outside the main banking or political centers of foreign markets. For example, Citibank has a worldwide correspondent network of 5,000 institutions in addition to its facilities in more than 100 countries.

Some banks have formed alliances to extend their reach to markets that their customers are entering. Wachovia, a super-regional bank from North Carolina, has developed relationships with global banks that have strong correspondent networks in place in emerging markets. Regional banks, such as Bank One, which have no intention of establishing branches abroad, rely only on strong alliances with foreign banks. Foreign banks can provide a competitive advantage to exporters because of their home country connections and their strong global networks. For example, Commerzbank, Germany's third largest bank, has branches in the Far East, Latin America, South America, and Eastern Europe to support its international trade financing activities in the NAFTA area.[37] Regardless of the arrangement, the bank's own branches or correspondents play an important role at all stages of the international transaction, from gathering market intelligence about potential new customers to actually processing payments. Additional services include reference checks on customers in their home markets and suggestions for possible candidates to serve as intermediaries.

Forfaiting and Factoring

Forfaiting provides the exporter with cash at the time of the shipment. In a typical forfait deal, the importer pays the exporter with bills of exchange or promissory notes guaranteed by a leading bank in the importer's country. The exporter can sell them to a third party (for example, Citicorp) at a discount from their face value for immediate cash. The sale is without recourse to the exporter, and the buyer of the notes assumes all the risks. The discount rate takes into account the buyer's creditworthiness and country, the quality of the guaranteeing bank, and the interest cost over the term of the credit.

The benefits to the exporter are the reduction of risk, simplicity of documentation (because the documents used are well known in the market), and 100 percent coverage, which official sources such as export-import banks do not provide. In addition, forfaiting does not involve either content or country restrictions, which many of the official trade financing sources may have.[38] The major complaints about forfaiting center on availability and cost. Forfaiting is not available where exporters need it most, that is, the high-risk countries. Furthermore, it is usually a little more expensive than public sources of trade insurance.

Certain companies, known as **factoring** houses, may purchase an exporter's receivables for a discounted price (2 to 4 percent less than face value). Factors do not only buy receivables but also provide the exporter with a complete financial package that combines credit protection, accounts-receivable bookkeeping, and collection services to take away many of the challenges that come with doing business overseas.[39] Arrangements are typically with recourse, leaving the exporter ultimately liable for repaying the factor in case of a default. Some factors accept export receivables without recourse but require a large discount.

The industry is dominated by a dozen major players, most of which are subsidiaries of major banks. Leaders include the CIT Group, 80 percent owned by Dai-Ichi Kangyo Bank of Japan and 20 percent owned by Chase Manhattan, and Bank of America Commercial Finance/Factoring, which has won the President's "E" Award for its excellence in export service.[40] However, with the increase in companies looking for factoring services, independent factors are also emerging. Factors can be found through the Commercial Finance Association or through marketing facilitators whose clients use factors.

Although the forfaiting and factoring methods appear similar, they differ in three significant ways: (1) factors usually want a large percentage of the exporter's business, while most forfaiters work on a one-shot basis; (2) forfaiters work with medium-term receivables (over 180 days to 5 years), while factors work with short-term receivables; and (3) factors usually do not have strong capabilities in the developing countries, but since forfaiters usually require a bank guarantee, most are willing to deal with receivables from these countries. Furthermore, forfaiters work with capital goods, factors typically with consumer goods.[41]

Official Trade Finance[42]

Official financing can take the form of either a loan or a guarantee, including credit insurance. In a loan, the government provides funds to finance the sale and charges interest on those funds at a stated fixed rate. The government lender accepts the risk of a possible default. In a guarantee, a private-sector lender provides the funds and sets the interest rate, with the government assuring that it will reimburse the lender if the loan is unpaid. The government is providing not funds but rather risk protection. The programs provide assurance that the governmental agency will pay for a major portion of the loss should the foreign buyer default on payment. The advantages are significant: (1) protection in the riskiest part of an exporter's business (foreign sales receivables), (2) protection against political and commercial risks over which the exporter does not have control, (3) encouragement to exporters to make competitive offers by extending terms of payment, (4) broadening of potential markets by minimizing exporter risks, (5) the possibility of leveraging exporter accounts receivable, and (6) through the government guarantee, the opportunity for commercial banks to remain active in the international finance arena.[43]

Because credit has emerged as an increasingly important component in export selling, governments of most industrialized countries have established entities that insure credit risks for exports. Officially supported export credit agencies (ECAs), such as the French Coface or German Hermes, are organizations whose central purpose is to promote national trade objectives by providing financial support for national exports. ECAs benefit from varying degrees of explicit or implicit support from national governments. Some ECAs are divisions of government trade missions. Other ECAs operate as autonomous or even private institutions, but most require a degree of recourse to national government support.

The Export-Import Bank of the United States (Ex-Im Bank) was created in 1934 and established as an independent U.S. government agency in 1945. The purpose of the bank is "to aid in financing and facilitating exports." Since its inception, Ex-Im Bank has supported more than $400 billion in U.S. export sales. The Ex-Im Bank supports short-, medium-, and long-term financing to creditworthy international customers (both in the private and public sectors) as well as working capital guarantees to U.S. exporters. Special initiatives exist for environmental exports, small business, and lending directly to municipalities in certain countries.

The data and examples in Table 9.6 highlight the programs available for exporters—pre-export, short term, medium term, and long term. One of the greatest impediments small businesses experience in attempting to fulfill export orders is a lack of working capital to build necessary inventory for the export order. If the local bank is reluctant to make such financing available (because the exporter might have reached its borrowing limit, for example), the Working Capital Guarantee Program is available.

The ability to offer financing or credit terms is often critical in competing for, and winning, export contracts. Increasingly, foreign buyers expect suppliers to offer open account or unsecured credit terms rather than requiring letters of credit, which may be expensive. Yet for small exporters, extending credit terms to foreign customers may represent an unacceptable risk, especially when the exporter's bank is unwilling to accept foreign receivables as collateral for working lines of credit. The solution is export credit insurance, wherein, for a reasonable premium, an institution (e.g., an insurance company or an ECA) guarantees payment to the seller if the buyer defaults. The short-term credit-insurance business is dominated by five major players, which account for more than 75 percent of the world market: Coface, Euler, Gerling, Hermes, and NCM.[44]

Ex-Im Bank also guarantees to provide repayment protection for private-sector loans to creditworthy buyers of U.S. goods and services. Guarantees, both for the

| Table 9.6 | Examples of Ex-Im Projects |

Exports	Appropriate Program	Example
Pre-export	Working Capital Guarantee	Pragmatic Environmental Solutions of Roanoke, Virginia, received a $100,000 loan from Suntrust Bank that enabled it to make an export sale of pollution control equipment to Wren Oil Co. of Australia.
Short term	Export Credit Insurance	Wildflower International of Santa Fe, New Mexico, expanded its export sales of software to Mexico, Israel, and Saudi Arabia by offering 90- and 180-day open account credit terms and insuring them with Ex-Im.
Medium term	Guarantees	Senstar Capital Group provided a four-year $400,000 loan to Ecopreneur, S.A. of Buenos Aires to purchase water-treatment equipment from six U.S. small-business water-treatment suppliers.
Long term	Direct Loans	$49.7 million loan to sponsor Ormat Leyte Co., Ltd. to build, own, and operate four geothermal plants in the Philippines with significant inputs from U.S. suppliers.

SOURCE: Examples courtesy of Craig O'Connor, Export-Import Bank of the United States.

medium and long term, are backed in full by the U.S. government. The fee schedule is determined by country risk and repayment terms of the transaction. Medium-term (not to exceed seven years) guarantees are typically used by commercial banks that do not want exposure in a certain country or that have reached their internal exposure limit in a given country. For long-term guarantees, projects are usually large (in excess of $100 million), and commercial banks may not want such exposure for long periods of time in one country or in a particular industry sector. Ex-Im may act as a lender directly to the foreign buyer. The majority (typically 85 percent or more) of the project must be U.S.-produced goods and services.

Price Negotiations

The final export price is negotiated in person or electronically. Since pricing is the most sensitive issue in business negotiations, the exporter should be ready to discuss price as part of a comprehensive package and should avoid price concessions early on in the negotiations.[45]

An importer may reject an exporter's price at the outset in the hopes of gaining an upper hand or obtaining concessions later on. These concessions include discounts, an improved product, better terms of sales/payment, and other possibly costly demands. The exporter should prepare for this by obtaining relevant information on the target market and the customer, as well as by developing counter-proposals for possible objections. For example, if the importer states that better offers are available, the exporter should ask for more details on such offers and try to convince the buyer that the exporter's total package is indeed superior. In the rare case that the importer accepts the initial bid without comment, the exporter should make sure the extended bid was correct by checking the price calculations and the Incoterm used. Furthermore, competitive prices should be revisited to ascertain that the price reflects market conditions accurately.

During the actual negotiations, pricing decisions should be postponed until all of the major substantive issues have been agreed upon. Since quality and reliability of delivery are the critical dimensions of supplier choice (in addition to price), especially when long-term export contracts are in question, the exporter may want to reduce pressure on price by emphasizing these two areas and how they fit with the buyer's needs.

Leasing

Organizational customers frequently prefer to lease major equipment, making it a $208 billion industry. About 30 percent of all capital goods (50 percent of commercial aircraft) are leased in the United States, with eight out of ten companies involved in leasing.[46] Although a major force in the United States, Japan, and Germany, leasing has grown significantly elsewhere as well; for example, one of the major international trade activities of Russia, in addition to shipping and oil, is equipment leasing. The Russians view leasing not only as a potential source of hard currency but also as a way of attracting customers who would be reluctant to buy an unfamiliar product.

Trade liberalization around the world is expected to benefit lessors both through expected growth in target economies and through the eradication of country laws and regulations hampering outside lessors. For example, the NAFTA agreement and the pent-up demand for machinery, aircraft, and heavy equipment for road building provide a promising opportunity for U.S. leasing companies in Mexico.[47]

For the marketing manager who sells products such as printing presses, computers, forklift trucks, and machine tools, leasing may allow penetration of markets that otherwise might not exist for the firm's products if the firm had to sell them outright. Balance-of-payment problems have forced some countries to prohibit or hinder the purchase and importation of equipment into their markets; an exception has been made if the import is to be leased. In developing countries, the fact that leased products are serviced by the lessor may be a major benefit because of the shortage of trained personnel and scarcity of spare parts. At present, leasing finances over $40 billion in new vehicles and equipment each year in developing countries. The main benefit for the lessor is that total net income, after charging off pertinent repair and maintenance expenses, is often higher than it would be if the unit was sold.

In today's competitive business climate, traditional financial considerations are often only part of the asset-financing formula. Many leasing companies have become more than a source of capital, developing new value-added services that have taken them from asset financiers to asset managers or forming relationships with others who can provide these services. In some cases, lessors have even evolved into partners in business activities. El Camino Resources International, which has leased assets of $836 million (half of it outside the United States), targets high-growth, technology-dependent companies such as Internet providers and software developers for their hardware, software, and technical services needs, including e-commerce as well as Internet and intranet development.[48]

Dumping

Inexpensive imports often trigger accusations of dumping—that is, selling goods overseas for less than in the exporter's home market or at a price below the cost of production, or both. Charges of dumping range from those of Florida tomato growers, who said that Mexican vegetables were being dumped across the border, to those of the Canadian Anti-Dumping Tribunal, which ruled that U.S. firms were dumping radioactive diagnostic reagents in Canada. Such disputes have become quite common, especially in highly competitive industries such as computer chips, ball bearings, and steel. From 1999 to 2000, U.S. steelmakers faced increasing competition from abroad, especially from Asia, with many foreign competitors selling at subsidized low prices. As a result the U.S. government imposed tariffs of 30 percent on imports.[49] Similarly, the European Union was asked to investigate dumping of made fibers by Asian producers, which grew 56 percent in 1998 alone to account for 12 percent of the market. The concern by the European fiber industry was that Asian producers were selling their product in the European market below cost of production, simply to generate cash flow for their beleaguered domestic operations.[50]

Dumping ranges from predatory dumping to unintentional dumping. **Predatory dumping** refers to a tactic whereby a foreign firm intentionally sells at a loss in another country in order to increase its market share at the expense of domestic producers, which amounts to an international price war. **Unintentional dumping** is the result of time lags between the dates of sales transaction, shipment, and arrival. Prices, including exchange rates, can change in such a way that the final sales price turns out to be below the cost of production or below the price prevailing in the exporter's home market. It has been argued that current dumping laws, especially in the United States, do not take into adequate account such developments as floating exchange rates, which make dumping appear to be more widespread.[51]

In the United States, domestic producers may petition the government to impose antidumping duties on imports alleged to be dumped. The duty is imposed if the International Trade Administration within the Department of Commerce determines that sales have occurred at less than fair market value and if the U.S. International Trade Commission finds that domestic industry is being, or is threatened with being, materially injured by the imports. The remedy is an **antidumping duty** equal to the dumping margin. International agreements and U.S. law provide for **countervailing duties,** which may be imposed on imports that are found to be subsidized by foreign governments and which are designed to offset the advantages imports would otherwise receive from the subsidy. The prevalence of anti-dumping actions has increased sharply. The WTO reports a total of 163 anti-dumping measures taken in 2001 (with India and the United States in the lead with over 30 actions each), whereas the total number five years earlier was 84.[52] As more developing and emerging markets are reducing tariffs to comply with WTO agreements, they are switching to antidumping penalties to protect domestic players. For example, U.S. exporters are facing 90 active investigations and 89 penalty tariffs in markets such as China.[53]

Governmental action against dumping and subsidized exports violating WTO may result in hurting the very industries seeking relief. Action against Russian or Brazilian steel, for example, could result in retaliatory measures against U.S. steelmakers, who themselves export billions of dollars' worth of steel products. European governments have also threatened to retaliate against U.S. exports of other products. Furthermore, imposing tariffs on imports such as steel may cause hardship to other industries. For example, steel tariffs will cause the costs of producing automobiles in the United States to rise.

In some cases, dumping suits have strong competitive motivations, for example, to discourage an aggressive competitor by accusing it of selling at unfair prices. Antidumping and unfair subsidy suits have led in some cases to formal agreements on voluntary restraints, whereby foreign producers agree that they will supply only a certain percentage of the U.S. market. One such arrangement is the semiconductor trade agreements signed by the United States and Japan, which required the Japanese to stop selling computer chips below cost and to try to increase sales of foreign-made computer chips in Japan.

To minimize the risk of being accused of dumping (as well to be protected from dumping), the marketer can focus on value-added products and increase differentiation by including services in the product offering. If the company operates in areas made sensitive by virtue of the industry (such as electronics) or by the fact that local competition is economically vulnerable yet powerful with respect to the government, it may seek to collaborate with local companies in gaining market access, for example.[54]

Summary

The status of price has changed to that of a dynamic element of the marketing mix. This has resulted from both internal and external pressures on business firms. Management must analyze the interactive effect that pricing has on the other elements of the mix and how pricing can assist in meeting the overall goals of the marketing strategy.

The process of setting an export price must start with the determination of an appropriate cost baseline and should include variables such as export-related costs to avoid compromising the desired profit margin. The quotation needs to spell out the respective responsibilities of the buyer and the seller in getting the goods to the intended destination. The terms of sale indicate these responsibilities but may also be used as a competitive tool. The terms of payment have to be clarified to ensure that the exporter will indeed get paid for the products and services rendered. Facilitating agents such as freight forwarders and banks are often used to absorb some of the risk and uncertainty in preparing price quotations and establishing terms of payment.

Exporters also need to be ready to defend their pricing practices. Competitors may petition their own government to investigate the exporter's pricing to determine the degree to which it reflects costs and prices prevailing in the exporter's domestic market.

Key Terms

skimming
market pricing
penetration pricing
standard worldwide pricing
dual pricing
cost-plus method
marginal cost method
market-differentiated pricing
price escalation
value-added tax (VAT)
duty drawbacks
Incoterms

cash in advance
letter of credit
draft
documentary collection
banker's acceptance
discounting
open account
consignment selling
commercial risk
political risk
forward exchange market
option

futures
pass-through
absorption
pricing-to-market
price manipulation
forfaiting
factoring
predatory dumping
unintentional dumping
antidumping duty
countervailing duties

Questions for Discussion

1. Propose scenarios in which export prices are higher/lower than domestic prices.
2. What are the implications of price escalation?
3. Discuss the use of the currency of quotation as a competitive tool.
4. Argue for the use of more inclusive shipping terms from the marketing point of view.
5. Suggest different importer reactions to a price offer and how you, as an exporter, could respond to them.
6. Who is harmed and who is helped by dumping?

Internet Exercises

1. Assess the international trade financing commitment of different commercial banks, such as Citibank (**http://www.citibank.com**), Bank One (**http://www.bankone.com**), and Silicon Valley Bank (**http://www.svb.com**).
2. The International Trade Administration monitors cases filed against U.S. exporters on charges of dumping, to assist them in the investigations and their subsequent defense. Using their data on such cases (**http://www.ita.doc.gov/import_admin/ records/**), focus on a few countries (e.g., EU, Canada, South Africa, Japan) and assess what industries seem to come under the most scrutiny.

Recommended Readings

Contino, Richard M., and Tony Valmis, eds. *Handbook of Equipment Leasing: A Deal Maker's Guide*. New York: AMACOM, 1996.

Hinkelman, Edward G., and Molly Thurmond. *A Short Course in International Payments*. New York: World Trade Press, 1998.

Jackson, John H., and Edwin A. Vermulst, eds. *Antidumping Law and Practice*. Ann Arbor: University of Michigan Press, 1989.

Jagoe, John R., and Agnes Brown. *Pricing Your Products for Export & Budgeting for Export*. Minneapolis, MN: The Export Institute, 1998.

Johnson, Thomas E. *Export/Import Procedures and Documentation*. New York: AMACOM, 1997.

Lowell, Julia, and Loren Yager. *Pricing and Markets: U.S. and Japanese Responses to Currency Fluctuations*. Santa Monica, CA: Rand Corporation, 1994.

Monroe, Kent B. *Pricing: Making Profitable Decisions*. New York: McGraw-Hill, 2003.

Nagle, Thomas T., and Reed K. Holden. *The Strategy and Tactics of Pricing: A Guide to Profitable Decision Making*. Englewood Cliffs, NJ: Prentice-Hall, 2002.

Palmer, Howard. *International Trade Finance and Pre-Export Finance*. London: Euromoney Publications, 1999.

Ramberg, Jan. *ICC Guide to Incoterms*. Paris: ICC Publishing, Inc., 2000.

U.S. Department of Treasury. *A Basic Guide to Importing*. Lincolnwood, IL: NTC Business Books, 1995.

Venedikian, Harry M., and Gerald A. Warfield. *Export-Import Financing*. New York: John Wiley & Co., 1996.

Woznick, Alexandra, and Edward G. Hinkelman. *A Basic Guide to Exporting*. New York: World Trade Press, 2000.

© PHOTODISC, VOL. 22

chapter 10

International Communications

© EYEWIRE/GETTY IMAGES

THE INTERNATIONAL MARKETPLACE   10.1

The Art of Negotiation

Nation-states and firms do not make deals; individuals do that for them. In most cases, successful deals are a result of multiple negotiations for which preparation must be extensive, particularly in understanding cross-cultural differences. Imbedded in these differences are national culture, organizational factors, as well as the personality traits of the individuals carrying out the negotiations. Understanding one's counterpart may not suffice; understanding one's own cultural "baggage" may be critical as well.

One such interaction occurred between representatives of Atacs Products, Inc.—a Seattle-based supplier of aircraft repair systems—and Aviation Transactions Conseils, which stocks those supplies, in Juilly, France, during an international trade exhibition in Seattle.

Terry Cooney, Atacs's sales manager, discovered a mutual interest during a chance meeting with ATC's Pierre-Jean Back, president, and Patrick Naumann, sales manager. Cooney then arranged a more formal meeting, and they reconvened with Andrew Thibault, an interpreter.

Cooney began his presentation—speaking slowly and clearly, but without condescension—on technical fronts. During the product demonstration for a heat-sensitive device, Cooney took care to speak in terms of ambient temperature in Bordeaux instead of just saying "72 degrees." And Naumann understood English well enough to laugh at Cooney's references to misuse of the product causing "permanently curly hair." Throughout the presentation, Thibault softly translated, primarily for Back's benefit. Occasionally, the demonstration slowed if either had a question. After the demonstration, Cooney explained Atacs's stance on foreign distributors. "If you start losing business," he joked, "I'm in the Irish mafia."

He mentioned several sales techniques, whom to contact, and the latitude of offers ATC would be able to make to customers. Naumann and Back conferred in French, and then Thibault presented Back's objection: What would prevent Atacs from ending its agreement once ATC had nurtured the territory?

Cooney said he didn't "know how to overcome" that objection. Then, force of personality began to transcend language. "I can be the biggest (expletive) you ever met," Cooney said, "but I'm honest. I don't even cheat in tennis against my sons."

Cooney closed with two more appeals, posed vehemently yet calmly. One mentioned the amount of dollars it could cost ATC not to accept the arrangement. The other: "If you place an order, you still have 90 days for payment, unless the dollar drops against the franc. Then we'll give you 120 days." They all laughed at that remark, but ATC's representatives still did not agree. Cooney said, "That's all I've got to say."

After the meeting, Back said in an interview, "I'm not suspicious of this gentleman, in particular, but it's the general manner of doing business in the American way. In general, when working with Americans, when things are going fine, there's no problem. But when the market starts to go down, Americans tend to bail out. Good business relationships take time to develop. . . . You know that relations are really good when there are problems with money and they'll still allow you to operate.

"However, I would not trust a large American company. There's such a turnover rate in employees that from one day to another it changes completely, so it's really hard to have continuous relations. The best prospects for American businesses to operate in France is with small businesses because there's a more personal relationship."

It would have been useful for Cooney to know about the French as negotiating partners. U.S.-centric references should be avoided, especially self-congratulatory ones, which are perceived as arrogant. Any notion of superiority or the attitude that "We are Number 1" can rub a French businessperson the wrong way. U.S. speakers often try to export baseball, football, or golf metaphors they use at home but that are mostly unknown abroad. However, if one is speaking in France or to the French, relating sports metaphors to World Cup soccer (and especially to the French success in 1998) is appropriate. Throughout the preliminary and middle stages of negotiating, the French manager will judge counterparts carefully on their intellectual skills and their ability to react quickly and with authority. In many ways, the French still embrace the art of diplomatic negotiation invented in France in the fourteenth century. As one French manager put it: "Sometimes I am more impressed by brilliant savvy than by a well-reasoned argument." Because French education stresses mathematics and logic, doing business is a highly intellectual process for French managers. One study found that the style of French negotiators was the most aggressive of thirteen diverse cultural groups analyzed.

SOURCES: Bill Hory, "Building International Relationships," *World Trade*, November 2002, 47–49; "Splitting the Difference," *Global Business*, July 2000, 50; Raymond Saner, Lichia Yiu, and Mikael Sondergaard, "Business Diplomacy Management: A Core Competency for Global Companies," *Academy of Management Executive*, February 1, 2000, 80–92; Sherrie Zhan, "Trade Shows Mean Big Business," *World Trade*, September 1999, 88; John L. Graham, "Vis-à-Vis International Business Negotiations," in *International Business Negotiations*, eds. Jean-Claude D. Usunier and Pervez N. Ghauri (London: The Dryden Press, 1996), chapter 7; "Negotiating in Europe," *Hemispheres*, July 1994, 43–47; David Jacobson, "Marketers Swap More Than Goodwill at Trade Show," *Business Marketing* 75 (September 1990): 48–51; and **http://www.atacs.com**.

EFFECTIVE COMMUNICATION IS PARTICULARLY IMPORTANT in international marketing because of the geographic and psychological distances that separate a firm from its intermediaries and customers. By definition, communication is a process of establishing a "commonness" of thought between a sender and a receiver.[1] This process extends beyond the conveying of ideas to include persuasion and thus enables the marketing process to function more effectively and efficiently. Ideally, marketing communication is a dialogue that allows organizations and consumers to achieve mutually satisfying exchange agreements. This definition emphasizes the two-way nature of the process, with listening and responsiveness as integral parts. A relationship has to be established from the beginning and deepened over time. The majority of communication is verbal, but nonverbal communication and the concept of silent languages must also be considered because they often create challenges for international marketers, as seen in *The International Marketplace 10.1*.

This chapter will include an overview of the principles of marketing communications in international markets. Because face-to-face, buyer–seller negotiations are possibly the most fundamental marketing process,[2] guidelines for international business negotiations are discussed first. Second, the chapter will focus on the management of the international communications mix from the exporter's point of view. Because the exporter's alternatives may be limited by the entry mode and by resources available, the tools and the challenges are quite different from those of the multinational entity. We discuss the promotional approaches used by global marketers in Chapter 20.

The Marketing Communications Process

As shown in the communications model presented in Figure 10.1, effective communications requires three elements—the sender, the message, and the receiver—connected by a message channel. The process may begin with an unsolicited inquiry from a potential customer or as a planned effort by the marketer. Whatever the goal of the communications process, the sender needs to study receiver characteristics before encoding the message in order to achieve maximum impact. **Encoding** the message simply means converting it into symbolic form that is properly understood by the receiver. This is not a simple task, however. For example, if a Web site's order form asks only for typical U.S.-type address information, such as a zip code, and does not include anything for other countries, the would-be buyer abroad will interpret this as unwillingness to do business outside the United States. Similarly, if an export price is quoted on an ex-works basis (which includes only the cost of goods sold in the price), the buyer may not be interested in or be able to take responsibility for the logistics process and will go elsewhere.

The message channel is the path through which the message moves from sender (source) to receiver. This link that ties the receiver to the sender ranges from sound waves conveying the human voice in personal selling to transceivers or intermediaries such as print and broadcast media. Although technological advances (for example, fax, video conferencing, and the Internet) may have made buyer–seller negotiations more efficient, the fundamental process and its purpose have remained unchanged. Face-to-face contact is still necessary for two basic reasons. The first is the need for detailed discussion and explanation, and the second is the need to establish the rapport that forms the basis of lasting business relationships. Technology will then support in the maintenance of the relationship.

Figure 10.1   The Marketing Communications Process

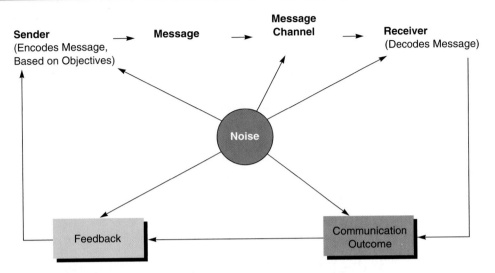

SOURCE: Adapted from Terence A. Shimp, *Advertising, Promotion, and Supplemental Aspects of Integrated Marketing Communications* (Mason, OH: South-Western, 2003), 82. Reprinted by permission.

The message channel also exists in mass communications. Complications in international marketing may arise if a particular medium does not reach the targeted audience, which is currently the case for Internet communications, for example, due to varying online penetration rates around the world.[3] Other examples of complications are the banning of advertising for certain product categories, such as for cigarettes in most of Europe, and the fact that some marketing practices may not be allowed, such as direct selling in China.

Once a sender has placed a message into a channel or a set of channels and directed it to the intended destination, the completion of the process is dependent on the receiver's **decoding**—that is, transforming the message symbols back into thought. If there is an adequate amount of overlap between sender characteristics and needs reflected in the encoded message and receiver characteristics and needs reflected in the decoded message, the communications process has worked.

A message moving through a channel is subject to the influence of extraneous and distracting stimuli, which interfere with the intended accurate reception of the message. This interference is referred to as **noise.** In the international marketing context, noise might be a bad telephone connection, failure to express a quotation in the inquirer's system of currency and measurement, or lack of understanding of the recipient's environment, for example, having only an English-language Web site. A U.S. company got a complaint from its Thai client complaining of an incomplete delivery: an order of 85,000 units was four short! When the U.S. company shipped in bulk, the number of units was estimated by weight. In Thailand, however, labor is cheap and materials expensive, allowing the client to hand count shipments. The solution was to provide a slight overage in each shipment without incurring a major expense but achieving customer satisfaction.[4] Similarly, a valid inquiry from overseas may not be considered seriously by an international marketer because of noise consisting of low-quality paper, grammatical errors, or a general appearance unlike domestic correspondence.

The international marketer should be most alert to cultural noise. The lack of language skills may hinder successful negotiations, whereas translation errors may render a promotional campaign or brochure useless. Similarly, nonverbal language and its improper interpretation may cause problems. While eye contact in North

America and Europe may be direct, the cultural style of the Japanese may involve markedly less eye contact.[5]

The success of the **outcome** is determined by how well objectives have been met in generating more awareness, a more positive attitude, or increased purchases. For example, the development of sales literature in the local language and reflective of the product line offered may result in increased inquiries or even more sales.

Regardless of whether the situation calls for interpersonal or mass communications, the collection and observation of **feedback** is necessary to analyze the success of the communications effort. The initial sender–receiver relationship is transposed, and interpretative skills similar to those needed in developing messages are needed. To make effective and efficient use of communications requires considerable strategic planning. Examples of concrete ways in which feedback can be collected are inquiry cards and toll-free numbers distributed at trade shows to gather additional information. Similarly, the Internet allows marketers to track traffic flows and to install registration procedures that identify individuals and track their purchases over time.[6]

International Negotiations

When international marketers travel abroad to do business, they are frequently shocked to discover the extent to which the many variables of foreign behavior and custom complicate their efforts.[7] Given that most negotiations are face to face, they present one of the most obvious and immediate challenges to be overcome. This means that international marketers have to adjust their approaches to establishing rapport, information exchange, persuasion, and concession making if they are to be successful in dealing with their clients and partners, such as intermediaries.[8]

The two biggest dangers faced in international negotiations are parochialism and stereotyping. Parochialism refers to the misleading perception that the world of business is becoming ever more American and that everyone will behave accordingly. This approach leads to stereotyping in explaining remaining differences. Stereotypes are generalizations about any given group, both positive and negative. For example, a positive stereotype has a clear influence on decisions to explore business options, whereas a negative stereotype may lead to a request to use a low-risk payment system, such as a letter of credit.[9] In a similar fashion, seemingly familiar surroundings and situations may lull negotiators into a false sense of security. This may be true for a U.S. negotiator in the United Kingdom or Australia thinking that the same language leads to the same behavioral patterns, or even in a far-off market if the meeting takes place in a hotel belonging to a large multinational chain.

The level of adjustment depends on the degree of cultural familiarity the parties have and their ability to use that familiarity effectively.[10] For example, in China, the ideal negotiator is someone who has an established relationship with the Chinese and is trusted by them. This is especially true in making the initial contact or stepping in if problems emerge. However, Chinese-Americans or overseas Chinese may be less effective in leading a negotiation. Where the Chinese are often willing to make an exception for visitors, they will expect ethnic Chinese to accept the Chinese way of doing things. The ideal team would, therefore, include a non-Chinese who understands the culture and an ethnic-Chinese individual. Together, the two can play "good guy–bad guy" roles and resist unreasonable demands.[11] If neither party is familiar with the counterpart's culture, outside facilitators should be employed.

With the increased use of the Internet, the question arises as to its use in international negotiations. Using the e-dimension does allow the exporter to overcome distances, minimize social barriers (e.g., age, gender, status), obtain instant feedback, negotiate from a home base, and do so with a number of parties simultaneously. However, it cannot be used in isolation given the critical role of building trust in negotiations. Additionally, its extensive use may restrict much of the interaction to focusing mostly on price. The Internet is effective in the exchange of information and for possible clarification during the course of the process.[12] It should be noted that technology is only gradually making its way to such use; lack of the necessary tools and mind-set may challenge the Internet's use for this purpose.

Stages of the Negotiation Process

The process of international business negotiations can be divided into five stages: the offer, informal meetings, strategy formulation, negotiations, and implementation.[13] Which stage is emphasized and the length of the overall process will vary dramatically by culture. The negotiation process can be a short one, with the stages collapsing into one session, or a prolonged endeavor taking weeks. The differences between northern and southern Europe highlight this. Northern Europe, with its Protestant tradition and indoor culture, tends to emphasize the technical, the numerical, and the tested. Careful prenegotiations preparations are made. Southern Europe, with its Catholic background and open-air lifestyle, tends to favor personal networks, social contexts, and flair. Meetings in the South are often longer, but the total decision process may be faster.[14]

The offer stage allows the two parties to assess each other's needs and degree of commitment. The initiation of the process and its progress are determined to a great extent by background factors of the parties (such as objectives) and the overall atmosphere (for example, a spirit of cooperativeness). As an example, many European buyers may be skittish about dealing with a U.S. exporter, given the number of U.S. companies that are perceived to be focused on short-term gains or that leave immediately when the business environment turns sour.

After the buyer has received the offer, the parties meet to discuss the terms and get acquainted. In many parts of the world (Asia, the Middle East, southern Europe, and Latin America), informal meetings may often make or break the deal. Foreign buyers may want to ascertain that they are doing business with someone who is sympathetic and whom they can trust. For example, U.S. exporters to Kuwait rank the strength of the business relationship ahead of price as the critical variable driving buying decisions.[15] In some cases, it may be necessary to utilize facilitators (such as consultants or agents) to establish the contact.

Both parties have to formulate strategies for formal negotiations. This means not only careful review and assessment of all the factors affecting the deal to be negotiated but also preparation for the actual give-and-take of the negotiations. For example, U.S. negotiators were found to express more satisfaction with the outcome if it maximized joint gain, while Hong Kong Chinese negotiators are happier when they achieve outcome parity. This is evidence that cultural values (e.g., harmonious relationships for the Chinese) create the environment in which negotiation tactics are selected.[16] Thus, managers should consciously and carefully consider competitive behaviors of clients and partners. Especially in the case of governmental buyers, it is imperative to realize that public-sector needs may not necessarily fit into a mold that the marketer would consider rational. Negotiators may not necessarily behave as expected; for example, the negotiating partner may adjust behavior to the visitor's culture.

The actual face-to-face negotiations and the approach used in them will depend on the cultural background and business traditions prevailing in different countries. The most commonly used are the competitive and collaborative approaches.[17] In a competitive strategy, the negotiator is concerned mainly about a favorable outcome at the expense of the other party, while in the collaborative approach focus is on mutual needs, especially in the long term. For example, an exporter accepting a proposal that goes beyond what can be realistically delivered (in the hopes of market entry or renegotiation later) will lose in the long term. To deliver on the contract, the exporter may be tempted to cut corners in product quality or delivery, eventually leading to conflict with the buyer.

The choice of location for the negotiations plays a role in the outcome as well. Many negotiators prefer a neutral site. This may not always work, for reasons of resources or parties' perceptions of the importance of the deal. The host does enjoy many advantages, such as lower psychological risk due to familiar surroundings. Guests may run the risk of cultural shock and being away from professional and personal support systems. These pressures are multiplied if the host chooses to manipulate the situation with delays or additional demands. Visiting teams are less likely to walk out; as a matter of fact, the pressure is on them to make concessions. However, despite the challenges of being a guest, the visitor has a chance to see firsthand the counterpart's facilities and resources, and to experience culture in that market. In addition, visiting a partner, present or potential, shows commitment to the effort.[18]

Negotiator characteristics (e.g., gender, race, or age) may work for or against the exporter in certain cultures. It is challenging to overcome stereotypes, but well-prepared negotiators can overcome these obstacles or even make them work to their advantage. For example, a female negotiator may use her uniqueness in male-dominated societies to gain better access to decision makers.[19]

How to Negotiate in Other Countries[20]

A combination of attitudes, expectations, and habitual behavior influences negotiation style. Although some of the following recommendations may go against the approach used at home, they may allow the negotiator to adjust to the style of the host-country negotiators.

1. *Team assistance.* Using specialists will strengthen the team substantially and allow for all points of view to be given proper attention. Further, observation of negotiations can be valuable training experience for less-experienced participants. Whereas Western teams may average two to four people, a Chinese negotiating team may consist of up to ten people.[21] A study on how U.S. purchasing professionals conduct negotiations abroad revealed that while the vast majority believed a small team (two to five individuals) was ideal, they also said their teams were often outnumbered by their international counterparts.[22] Even if there are intragroup disagreements during the negotiations, it is critical to show one face to the counterparts and handle issues within the team privately, outside the formal negotiations.

2. *Traditions and customs.* For newcomers, status relations and business procedures must be carefully considered with the help of consultants or local representatives. For example, in highly structured societies, such as Korea, great respect is paid to age and position.[23] It is prudent to use informal communication to let counterparts know, or ask them about, any prestigious degrees, honors, or accomplishments by those who will be facing one another in negotiations. What seem like simple rituals can cause problems. No first encounter in Asia is complete without an exchange of business cards. Both hands should be used to present and receive cards, and respect should be shown by reading them carefully.[24] One side should be translated into the language of the host country.

3. *Language capability.* Ideally, the international marketing manager should be able to speak the customer's language, but that is not always possible. A qualified individual is needed as part of a marketing team to ensure that nothing gets lost in the translation, literally or figuratively. Whether the negotiator is bilingual or an interpreter is used, it might be a good gesture to deliver the first comments in the local language to break the ice. The use of interpreters allows the negotiator longer response time and a more careful articulation of arguments. If English is being used, a native speaker should avoid both jargon and idiomatic expressions, avoid complex sentences, and speak slowly and enunciate clearly.[25] An ideal interpreter is one who briefs

the negotiator on cultural dimensions, such as body language, before any meetings. For example, sitting in what may be perceived as a comfortable position in North America or Europe may be seen by the Chinese as showing a lack of control of one's body and, therefore, of one's mind.

4. *Determination of authority limits.* Negotiators from North America and Europe are often expected to have full authority when they negotiate in the Far East, although their local counterparts seldom if ever do. Announcing that the negotiators do not have the final authority to conclude the contract may be perceived negatively; however, if it is used as a tactic to probe the motives of the buyer, it can be quite effective. It is important to verify who does have that authority and what challenges may be faced in getting that decision. In negotiating in Russia, for example, the international marketer will have to ascertain who actually has final decision-making authority—the central, provincial, or local government—especially if permits are needed.

5. *Patience.* In many countries, such as China, business negotiations may take three times the amount of time that they do in the United States and Europe. Showing impatience in countries such as Brazil or Thailand may prolong negotiations rather than speed them up. Also, U.S. executives tend to start relatively close to what they consider a fair price in their negotiations, whereas Chinese negotiators may start with "unreasonable" demands and a rigid posture.[26]

6. *Negotiation ethics.* Attitudes and values of foreign negotiators may be quite different from those that a U.S. marketing executive is accustomed to. Being tricky can be valued in some parts of the world, whereas it is frowned on elsewhere. For example, Western negotiators may be taken aback by last-minute changes or concession requests by Russian negotiators.[27]

7. *Silence.* To negotiate effectively abroad, a marketer needs to read correctly all types of communication. U.S. businesspeople often interpret inaction and silence as a negative sign. As a result, Japanese executives tend to expect that they can use silence to get them to lower prices or sweeten the deal. Finns may sit through a meeting expressionless, hands folded and not moving much. There is nothing necessarily negative about this; they show respect to the speaker with their focused, dedicated listening.[28]

8. *Persistence.* Insisting on answers and an outcome may be seen as a threat by negotiating partners abroad. In some markets, negotiations are seen as a means of establishing long-term commercial relations, not as an event with winners and losers. Confrontations are to be avoided because minds cannot be changed at the negotiation table; this has to be done informally. Face is an important concept throughout the Far East.

9. *Holistic view.* Concessions should be avoided until all issues have been discussed, so as to preclude the possibility of granting unnecessary benefits to the negotiation partners. Concessions traditionally come at the end of bargaining. This is especially true in terms of price negotiations. If price is agreed on too quickly, the counterpart may want to insist on too many inclusions for that price.

10. *The meaning of agreements.* What constitutes an agreement will vary from one market to another. In many parts of the world, legal contracts are still not needed; as a matter of fact, reference to legal counsel may indicate that the relationship is in trouble. For the Chinese, the written agreement exists mostly for the convenience of their Western partners and represents an agenda on which to base the development of the relationship.[29]

When a verbal agreement is reached, it is critical that both parties leave with a clear understanding of what they have agreed to. This may entail only the relatively straightforward act of signing a distributor agreement, but in the case of large-scale projects, details must be explored and spelled out. In contracts that call for cooperative efforts, the responsibilities of each partner must be clearly specified. Otherwise, obligations that were anticipated to be the duty of one contracting party may result in costs to another. For example, foreign principal contractors may be held responsible for delays that have been caused by the inability of local subcontractors (whose use might be a requisite of the client) to deliver on schedule.

Marketing Communications Strategy

The international marketing manager has the responsibility of formulating a communications strategy for the promotion of the company and its products and services. The basic steps of such a strategy are outlined in Figure 10.2.

Few, if any, firms can afford expenditures for promotion that is done as "art for art's sake" or only because major competitors do it. The first step in developing communications strategy is therefore assessing what company or product characteristics and benefits should be communicated to the export market. This requires constant monitoring of the various environments and target audience characteristics. For example, Volvo has used safety and quality as its primary themes in its worldwide promotional campaigns since the 1950s. This approach has provided continuity, repetition, and uniformity in positioning Volvo in relation to its primary competitors: Mercedes-Benz (prestige) and BMW (sportiness).

Absolut, which is owned by the Swedish government, in 1979 started exporting its vodka into the United States with 45,000 cases and an introductory promotion effort by its distributor, Carillon Importers, Ltd. At the time, import vodka sales were almost nonexistent and Absolut's brand name unknown. With a very small budget ($750,000) and the capability to do only print advertising, Carillon's agency TBWA set about to establish brand awareness. Since then the ads have featured a full-page shot of the bottle and a two-word headline.[30] Absolut is now the third largest international spirits brand worldwide, the second largest brand of premium vodka in the United States, and the largest imported vodka brand in the United States. In 20 years, Absolut has grown to number ten in volume and number three in revenue in the U.S. spirits category. In addition to a strong marketing effort, Absolut has also benefited from changing U.S. drinking habits.[31] Vodkas are now the largest category in the distilled spirits business, with Absolut ruling the high-class vodka crowd. Certain rules of thumb can be followed in evaluating resources

---

Figure 10.2   Steps in Formulating Marketing Communications Strategy

Step One	Assess Marketing Communications Opportunities
Step Two	Analyze Marketing Communications Resources
Step Three	Set Marketing Communications Objectives
Step Four	Develop/Evaluate Alternative Strategies
Step Five	Assign Specific Marketing Communications Tasks

SOURCE: Framework adapted from Wayne DeLozier, *The Marketing Communication Process* (New York: McGraw-Hill, 1976), 272.

COURTESY OF ABSOLUT VODKA

to be allocated for export communications efforts. A sufficient commitment is necessary, which means a relatively large amount of money. The exporter has to operate in foreign markets according to the rules of the marketplace, which in the United States, for example, means high promotional costs—perhaps 30 percent of exports or even more during the early stage of entry. With heavily contested markets, the level of spending may even have to increase. For example, Absolut's media expenditures in 2001 were $31 million in measured media.[32]

Because of monetary constraints that most exporters face, promotional efforts should be concentrated on key markets. For example, European liquor marketers traditionally concentrate their promotional efforts on the United States, where volume consumption is greatest, and Great Britain, which is considered the world capital of the liquor trade. A specific objective might be to spend more than the closest competitors do in the U.S. market. In the United States, for example, this would require a new import brand, aimed at the lower-price segment, to spend at the minimum $10 million during the rollout year.[33] In some cases, an exporter will have to limit this to one country, even one area, at a time to achieve set goals with the available budget. International campaigns require patient investment; the market has to progress through awareness, knowledge, liking, preference, and favorable purchase intentions before payback begins. Payback periods of one or two years cannot be realistically expected. For many exporters, a critical factor is the support of the intermediary. Whether a distributor is willing to contribute a $3 million media budget or a few thousand dollars makes a big difference. In some cases, intermediaries take a leading role in the promotion of the product in a market. In the case of Absolut, for example, Carillon Importers has been credited with the creative advertising widely acknowledged as a primary reason for the brand's success. In most cases, however, the exporter should retain some control of the campaign rather than allow intermediaries or sales offices a free hand in the various markets operated. Although markets may be dissimilar, common themes and common objectives need to be incorporated into the individual campaigns. For example, Duracell, the world leader in alkaline batteries, provides graphics—such as logos and photos—to country operations. Although many exporters do not exert pressure to conform, overseas distributors take advantage of annual meetings to discuss promotional practices with their head office counterparts.

Alternative strategies are needed to spell out how the firm's resources can be combined and adapted to market opportunities. The tools the international marketer has available to form a total communications program for use in the targeted markets are referred to as the **promotional mix.** They consist of the following:

1. *Advertising:* Any form of nonpersonal presentation of ideas, goods, or services by an identified sponsor, with predominant use made of *mass* communication, such as print, broadcast, or electronic media, or *direct* communication that is pinpointed at each business-to-business customer or ultimate consumer using computer technology and databases.

2. *Personal selling:* The process of assisting and persuading a prospect to buy a good or service or to act on an idea through use of person-to-person communication with intermediaries and/or final customers.

3. *Publicity:* Any form of nonpaid, commercially significant news or editorial comment about ideas, products, or institutions.

4. *Sales promotion:* Direct inducements that provide extra product value or incentive to the sales force, intermediaries, or ultimate consumers.

5. *Sponsorship:* The practice of promoting the interests of the company by associating it with a specific event (typically sports or culture) or a cause (typically a charity or a social interest).

The use of these tools will vary by company and by situation. Although all Harley-Davidson motorcycles are on allocation in overseas markets, their promotion focuses on postpurchase reinforcement. Owners, in turn, become a powerful promotional tool for Harley-Davidson through word-of-mouth communication. The company also sells "motor clothes," illustrated in catalogs. Copies are made for overseas dealers, who cannot afford to translate and reprint them, and they pass them on to their customers with notes that not all items are available or permissible in their markets.[34]

The choice of tools leads to either a push or a pull emphasis in marketing communications. **Push strategies** focus on the use of personal selling. Despite its higher cost per contact, personal selling is appropriate for the international marketing of industrial goods, which have shorter channels of distribution and smaller target populations than do consumer goods. Governmental clients are typically serviced through personal selling efforts. Some industries, such as pharmaceuticals, traditionally rely on personal selling to service the clientele.

On the other hand, **pull strategies** depend on mass communications tools, mainly advertising. Advertising is appropriate for consumer-oriented products with large target audiences and long channels of distribution. Of its promotional budget, Absolut spends 85 percent in print media in the United States, with the balance picked up by outdoor advertising, mainly billboards. The base of the advertising effort is formed by magazines such as *Sports Illustrated, Vanity Fair, Business Week, Rolling Stone, Esquire, Time,* and *Newsweek.*

No promotional tool should be used in isolation or without regard to the others; hence, we see a trend toward **integrated marketing communications.** Promotional tools should be coordinated according to target market and product characteristics, the size of the promotional budget, the type and length of international involvement, and control considerations. As an example, industrial purchasing decisions typically involve eight to eleven people. Because a salesperson may not reach all of them, the use of advertising may be necessary to influence the participants in the decision-making process. In addition, steps must be taken to have information readily available to prospects who are interested in the exporter's products. This can be achieved with the development of a Web site and participating in trade shows.

Figure 10.3 provides an example of an advertising campaign for a disk-drive exporter. While the company's ads in its home market focus on product benefits and technical excellence, the approach taken in Asia was much softer. Under the theme "Unique ideas are often the most enduring," the objective was to increase original equipment makers' awareness of the company's products and the fact that

Figure 10.3   Advertising Campaign for a Disk-Drive Exporter

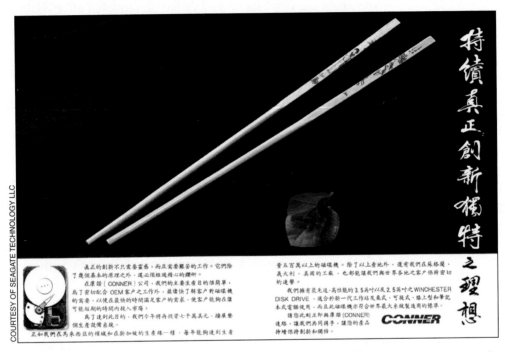

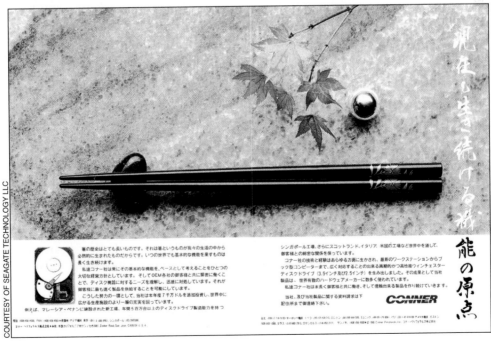

COURTESY OF SEAGATE TECHNOLOGY LLC

it designed them in close cooperation with its customers. The Chinese ad pictured bone Chinese chopsticks on black cloth, while the Japanese version showed enameled Japanese (pointed) chopsticks on a marble slab to appeal to different aesthetics.

Finally, specific marketing communications tasks must be assigned, which may require deciding on a division of labor with foreign intermediaries or with other exporters for cooperative communications efforts. For example, Ernie Ball, the maker of Gauge, Slinky, and Earthwood guitar strings, cooperates closely with its distributors in the marketing of its products. Local distributors have adapted U.S. programs to their markets, such as Battle of Bands for Europe, which is the largest live music promotion in the industry. The company also uses the Internet for contest promotions such as the best guitarist and the best bassist.[35] Cooperative programs allow the exporter control of the promotional effort while getting distribution partners to contribute to the effort financially.

In cases in which the locally based intermediaries are small and may not have the resources to engage in promotional efforts, the exporter may suggest dealer-participatory programs. In exchange for including the intermediaries' names in promotional material without any expense to them—for example, in announcing a sweepstakes—the exporter may request increased volume purchases from the intermediaries.

Communications Tools

The main communications tools used by exporters to communicate with the foreign marketplace from their domestic base are business and trade journals, directories, direct advertising, the Internet, trade fairs and missions, and personal selling. If the exporter's strategy calls for a major promotional effort in a market, it is advisable either to use a domestic agency with extensive operations in the intended market or to use a local agency and work closely with the company's local representatives in media and message choices.

Because the promoter–agency relationship is a close one, it may be helpful if the exporter's domestic agency has an affiliate in the target foreign market. The management function and coordination can be performed by the agency at home, while the affiliate can execute the program as it seems appropriate in that market. An exporter, if it has a sufficient budget, may ask its domestic agency to set up a branch overseas. Some exporters, especially those that have a more significant presence overseas, leave the choice of the agency to local managers. If a local agency is to be chosen, the exporter must make sure that coordination and cooperation between the agency and the exporter's domestic agency can be achieved. Whatever the approach used, the key criterion must be the competence of the people who will be in charge of the creation and implementation of the promotional programs.

Business/Trade Journals and Directories

Many varied business and trade publications, as well as directories, are available to the exporter. Some, such as *Business Week, Fortune, The Economist, The Wall Street Journal,* and *Financial Times,* are standard information sources worldwide. Extensions of these are their regional editions; for example, *The Asian Wall Street Journal* or *Business Week—Europe.* Trade publications can be classified as (1) horizontal, which cater to a particular job function cutting across industry lines, such as *Purchasing World* or *Industrial Distribution,* and (2) vertical, which deal with a specific industry, such as *Chemical Engineering* or *International Hospital Supplies.* These journals are global, regional, or country-specific in their approaches. Many U.S.-based publications are available in national language editions, with some offering regional buys for specific export markets—for example, the Spanish edition of *Feed Management,* titled *Alimentos Balanceados Para Animales.*

The exporter should also be aware of the potential of government-sponsored publications. For example, *Commercial News USA,* published by the U.S. Department of Commerce, is an effective medium for the marketer interested in making itself and its products known worldwide for a modest sum. For less than $500, an exporter can reach 140,000 potential buyers in 152 countries through the publication, distributed to recipients free of charge 12 times a year.[36]

Directories provide a similar tool for advertising efforts. Many markets feature exporter yellow pages, some of which offer online versions in addition to the traditional print ones. For example, MyExports.com (formerly the *U.S. Exporters' Yellow Pages*) offers U.S. firms a means to promote their businesses worldwide at no cost (if they just want to be listed), and at low cost for an advertisement or link to their e-mail or homepage. Some of the directories are country-specific. For example, BellSouth's *Guia Internacional* allows exporters to showcase their products to 425,000 Latin American and Caribbean importers.[37] A number of online directories, such as *Internet International Business Exchange* (**http://www.imex.com**), provide the exporter the opportunity to have banner ads (i.e., ads placed on frequently visited Web sites) for $150 to $1,000 a month. Examples of international trade publications and directories are provided in Figure 10.4.

The two main concerns when selecting media are effectiveness in reaching the appropriate target audience(s) and efficiency in minimizing the cost of doing so, measured in terms of cost per thousand. If the exporter is in a position to define the target audience clearly (for example, in terms of demographics or product-related variables), the choice of media will be easier. In addition, consideration should be given to how well a given medium will work with the other tools the exporter wishes to employ. For example, advertisements in publications and directories may have the function of driving customers and prospects to the exporter's Web site.[38]

Figure 10.4	**Examples of International Trade Publications and Directories**

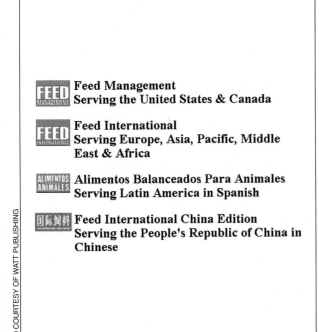

Feed Management
Serving the United States & Canada

Feed International
Serving Europe, Asia, Pacific, Middle East & Africa

Alimentos Balanceados Para Animales
Serving Latin America in Spanish

Feed International China Edition
Serving the People's Republic of China in Chinese

© COURTESY OF WATT PUBLISHING

SOURCES: **http://www.wattmm.com**; and **http://www.guiaexport.bellsouth.com**.

In deciding which publications to use, the exporter must apply the general principles of marketing communications strategy. Coverage and circulation information is available from Standard Rate & Data Service (**http://www.srds.com**). SRDS provides a complete list of international publications in the International Section of the *Business Publication,* and audit information similar to that on the U.S. market is provided for the United Kingdom, Italy, France, Austria, Switzerland, Germany, Mexico, and Canada. Outside these areas, the exporter has to rely on the assistance of publishers or local representatives. Actual choices are usually complicated by lack of sufficient funds and concern over the information gap. The simplest approach may be to use U.S. publishers, in which the exporter may have more confidence in terms of rates and circulation data. If a more localized approach is needed, a regional edition or national publication can be considered. Before advertising is placed in an unfamiliar journal, the marketer should analyze its content and overall quality of presentation.

Direct Marketing

The purpose of direct marketing is to establish a relationship with a customer in order to initiate immediate and measurable responses.[39] This is accomplished through direct-response advertising, telemarketing, and direct selling.

Direct mail is by far the dominant direct-response medium, but some advertising is also placed in mass media, such as television, magazines, and newspapers. Direct mail can be a highly personalized tool of communication if the target audience can be identified and defined narrowly. Ranging from notices to actual samples, it allows for flexibility in the amount of information conveyed and in its format. Direct mail is directly related in its effectiveness to the availability and quality of the mailing lists. Mailing lists may not be available around the world in the same degree that they are in, say, the United States. However, more and better lists are surfacing in Asia, Latin America, and the Middle East. In addition, reliable, economical, global postal service has become available.[40] Magnavox CATV, which markets cable television equipment, has boosted its international mailings to support its broad schedule of trade shows, many of which are in developing regions.

Even when mailing lists are available, they may not be as up-to-date or as precise as the international marketer would desire. In China, for example, lists are available to send literature directly to factories, ministries, professional societies, research institutes, and universities. However, such mailings can be extremely costly and produce few results. An effective and efficient direct-mail campaign requires extensive market-by-market planning of materials, format, and mode of mailing.

Catalogs are typically distributed to overseas customers through direct mail, although many catalogs have online versions as well. Their function is to make the exporter's name known, generate requests for further information, stimulate orders, and serve as a reminder between transactions. Catalogs are particularly useful if a firm's products are in a highly specialized field of technology and if only the most highly qualified specialists are to be contacted. In many markets, especially the developing ones, people may be starving for technology information and will share any mailings they receive. Due to this unsatisfied demand, a very small investment can reach many potential end users.

The growing mail-order segment is attracting an increasing number of foreign entrants to markets previously dominated by local firms. However, because consumers are wary of sending orders and money to an unknown company overseas, the key to market penetration is a local address. In Japan, L. L. Bean, the U.S. outdoor clothing merchandiser, works through McCann Direct, the specialized direct-marketing division of McCann-Erickson Hakuhodo Inc., Japan's largest foreign advertising agency. Bean places ads for its catalogs in Japanese media, orders for catalogs are sent to McCann Direct, and McCann Direct then forwards the addresses to Bean's headquarters in Maine, where all the orders for catalogs or goods are filled.[41] Despite the economic promise of emerging markets such as

China, India, and Russia, the development of direct marketing is constrained by negative attitudes toward Western business practices and problems with distribution networks and marketing support systems, as well as bureaucratic obstacles.[42]

Traditional direct mail is undergoing major change. New types of mail services (e.g., the Mexican Post Office's Buzon Espresso) will enable companies to deal with their customers more efficiently when customers buy through catalogs or electronic means. New electronic media will assume an increasing share in the direct-response area. However, direct marketing will continue to grow as a function of its targetability, its measurability, and the responsiveness of consumers to direct marketing efforts.

In the past, U.S. marketers thought that country-specific offices were almost essential to bringing their companies closer to overseas customers. Now with functioning telecommunication systems and deregulation in the industry, **telemarketing** (including sales, customer service, and help-desk-related support) is flourishing throughout the world. A growing number of countries in Latin America, Asia, and Europe are experiencing growth in this area as consumers are becoming more accustomed to calling toll-free numbers and more willing to receive calls from marketers.

In Europe, companies using this service publicize their assigned local phone numbers on television or print ads, direct mailings, catalogs, or Web sites, and then the calls are routed to a call center. The number and location of such call centers will depend on a variety of issues, such as what the distribution area of the product is, what the fulfillment logistics are, how important local presence is, and how important certain capabilities are, such as language and the ability to handle calls from various time zones.[43] Costa Rica is the choice for Central and Latin American call center operations, Australia for the Asia-Pacific, and Singapore for Asia itself, while Belgium, Holland, Ireland, and Portugal are leading locations in Europe (Figure 10.5).[44] If only one center is used in Europe, for example, access to

| Figure 10.5 | **An Example of an International Call Center** |

a multilingual workforce is a major factor in selecting the location. When a call comes in, the name of the country in which the call originates is displayed above the switchboard so that it can be taken by an operator who speaks the language(s) native to that country.[45]

Call center activity has developed more slowly in Asia than it has in North America and Europe, mostly because of infrastructural reasons and cultural resistance to the new form of communicating with business. However, new technologies are helping to overcome such resistance. **Database marketing** allows the creation of an individual relationship with each customer or prospect. For example, a call center operator will know a customer's background with the company or overall purchasing habits.[46] The development of the needed databases through direct mail or the Internet will advance the use of telemarketing.

Some exporters see the use of call centers as a preliminary step to entering an international market with a deeper presence such as a sales office.

Internet[47]

Having a Web site is seen as necessary if for no other reason than image; lack of a Web presence may convey a negative image to the various constituents of the marketer. The Web site should be linked to the overall marketing strategy and not just be there for appearance's sake. This means having a well-designed and well-marketed site.[48] Quality is especially critical if customers use the Web site to find more information or clarification, as triggered by the exporter's other communications efforts, such as advertisements or telemarketing efforts.

Having a Web presence will support the exporter's marketing communications effort in a number of ways. First, it allows the company to increase its presence in the marketplace and to communicate its overall mission and information about its marketing mix. Second, the Internet will allow 24-hour access to customers and prospects. Providing important information during decision making can help the customer clarify the search. The potential interactivity of the Web site (e.g., in providing tailor-made solutions to the customer's concerns) may provide a competitive advantage as the customer compares alternative sites. For example, the Web site for apparel marketer Lands' End allows consumers to identify their body type and then mix and match clothing items that suit them.[49] Interactivity is also critical when the site is designed, in determining what features to include (e.g., should sites adjust to different dialects of a language in a region?).

Third, the Internet can improve customer service by allowing customers to serve themselves when and where they choose. This is an area where an exporter's Web presence can reduce overall communications costs in the most significant way. Naturally, the exporter must have the necessary capacity to serve all interested customers through the Web site, especially if there is an increase in interest and demand. An important dimension of customer service is after-sales service to solve consumer problems and to facilitate the formation of consumer groups. A Web forum where customers can exchange news and views on product use will not only facilitate product research, but it also will build loyalty among consumers.

The fourth advantage is the ability of the exporter to gather information, which has its uses not only in research but also in database development for subsequent marketing efforts. While the data collected may be biased, they are also very inexpensive to collect. If the data are used to better cater to existing customers, then data collected through Internet interaction are the best possible.

The fifth advantage of the Internet is the opportunity to actually close sales. This function is within the realm of e-commerce. It will require a significant commitment on the part of the exporter in terms of investment in infrastructure to deliver not only information but also the product to the customer. E-commerce is discussed in more detail in Chapter 11.

In addition to communications with customers, the Internet provides the possibility to communicate with internal constituents. Exporters may have part of their Web sites set up with detailed product and price information that only their agents, representatives, or distributors have access to. Especially when changes are called for, this is an efficient way of communicating about them without having to mail or fax each and every overseas party.[50] Web sites can also be used in the recruitment of intermediaries and partners. P&D Creative, a manufacturer of environmentally safe cleaning products, uses its site (**http://www.pdcreative.pair.com**) to attract intermediaries. The company promotes its site in search engines and internationally oriented newsgroups and provides information of special interest to intermediaries.

Internet strategy is not restricted to the exporter's own Web site. The exporter needs to determine with which portals, such as AOL (**http://www.aol.com**) or Yahoo! (**http://www.yahoo.com**), or with what type of hyperlinks with related products or services, such as Internet International Business Exchange (**http://www.imex.com**), to negotiate for banner advertising on those sites.

The challenges faced by exporters in Internet-based communications are related to the newness of the medium and the degree to which adjustments need to be made for each market served. A very large portion of the world population has yet to adopt the Internet, and its users have a distinct profile. In some cases this might match the exporter's intended target market (such as for online music); however, in many cases Internet diffusion has yet to reach the targeted customer.

While English-only Web sites can deliver information and support to some international customers, having local-language sites and registering with local search engines demonstrate appropriate market and cultural sensitivity. The choice of languages will depend on the target audience. The most popular languages are French, Spanish, German, Japanese, and Chinese. For some, a dialect must be specified; for example, Spanish has three main variants: European, Mexican, and South American. The exporter needs also to determine which pages have to be modified. Pages that emphasize marketing, sales, and corporate identity are normally the ones chosen.[51]

While the exporter's local Web sites may (and for global product or service offerings, should) be quite similar in terms of aesthetics, adjustments should also be made for such dimensions as depth of product line and level of market presence. Customers who are familiar with the Internet may access information about products and services before purchasing them and may visit sites in several countries. Second-generation technology is increasing the interactivity of advertising on the Web. Given that individuals around the world have different information needs, varying levels of company and product familiarity, and different user capabilities, exporters can adjust their Web sites' content and develop paths tailored to each group of customers or even to an individual customer. Overall, the incorporation of the Internet into the exporter's marketing strategy will enhance market orientation, marketing competence, and eventually marketing performance.[52]

Marketers using the Web as an advertising medium will have to be concerned about market-by-market differences in regulations. For example, Germany sued Benetton (**http://www.benetton.com**) for "exploiting feelings of pity" with one of its "United Colors of Benetton" campaigns.[53] Finally, online communications strategy should also include provisions for technological development. For example, a full-color site with lots of text will not be legible or attractive on the monochrome screens of smart phones using WAP (wireless application protocol) technology, already in use in Northern Europe.

Trade Shows and Missions

Marketing goods and services through trade shows is a European tradition that dates back to A.D 1240. After sales force costs, trade shows are one of the most significant cost items in marketing budgets. Although they are usually associated with industrial firms, some consumer-products firms are represented as well. Typically, a trade show is an event at which manufacturers, distributors, and other vendors display their products or describe their services to current and prospective customers, suppliers, other business associates, and the press.[54] The International

Trade and Travel Networks

Civilization depends on trade for growth and travel makes this
possible. Shipping is the most important method of world transport
but economic progress and mobility are constantly being improved
by the development of new routes and new methods of transport.

Road and Rail

Integrated road and rail networks are the basis
of industrial society. Containerization and
the extension of modern highway systems
have increased flexibility and reduced the
emphasis on railways transporting freight.

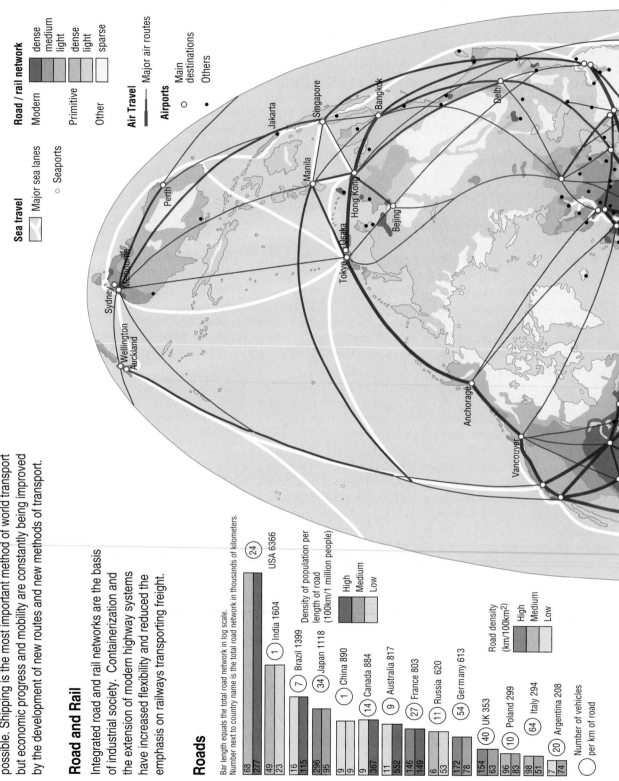

Roads

Bar length equals the total road network in log scale.
Number next to country name is the total road network in thousands of kilometers.

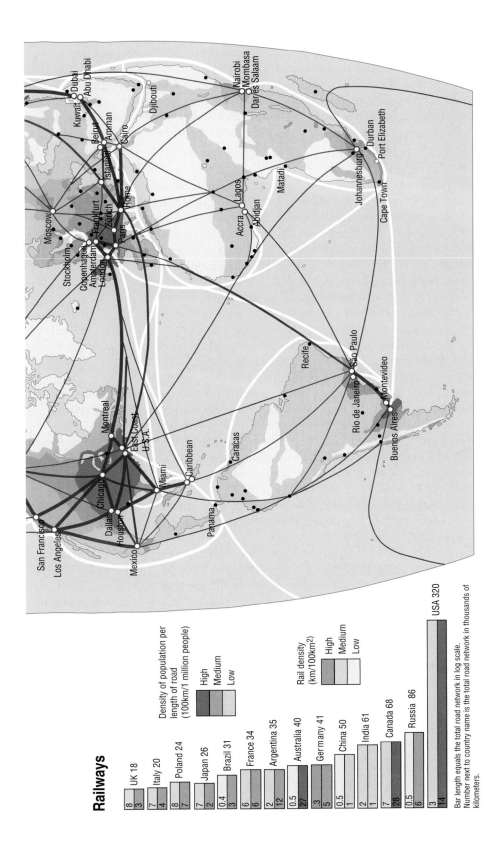

Railways

8 / 3	UK 18
7 / 4	Italy 20
8 / 7	Poland 24
7 / 2	Japan 26
0.4 / 3	Brazil 31
6 / 6	France 34
2 / 12	Argentina 35
0.5 / 27	Australia 40
.3 / 5	Germany 41
0.5 / 1	China 50
2 / 1	India 61
7 / 28	Canada 68
0.5 / 6	Russia 86
3 / 14	USA 320

Density of population per
length of road
(100km/1 million people)

High	Medium	Low

Rail density
(km/100km²)

High	Medium	Low

Bar length equals the total road network in log scale.
Number next to country name is the total road network in thousands of
kilometers.

Air and Sea Routes

A complex network of primary air routes
centered on the Northern Hemisphere provides
rapid transit across the world for mass travel,
mail, and urgent freight.

Ships also follow these principal routes,
plying the oceans between major ports and
transporting the commodities of world trade
in bulk.

Journey Time

The Suez Canal cuts 3,600 nautical miles
off the London–Singapore route, while
the Concorde halves the London–New
York journey time.

Concorde
3½ hours

Jet
7 hours

Propeller
12 hours

First Flight
4½ days

Singapore ◄——► London ——► New York

Sail (via Cape)
164 days

Steam (via Cape)
43 days

Steam (via Suez)
28 days

Supertanker (via Cape)
28 days

Diesel (via Suez)
15 days

SOURCE: Bartholomew, 1993

Automotive Services Industries Show and the International Coal Show, for example, run eight hours for three days, plus one or two preview days, and register 25,000 attendees. In the consumer goods area, expositions are the most common type of show. Tickets are usually sold; typical expositions include home/garden, boat, auto, stereo, and antiques. Although a typical trade show or typical participant does not exist, an estimated $73,000 is allocated for each show, and the median manufacturer or distributor attends nine or ten shows annually.

Whether an exporter should participate in a trade show depends largely on the type of business relationship it wants to develop with a particular country. More than 16,000 trade shows create an annual $50 billion in business worldwide.[55] A company looking only for one-time or short-term sales might find the expense prohibitive, but a firm looking for long-term involvement may find the investment worthwhile. Arguments in favor of participation include the following:

1. Some products, by their very nature, are difficult to market without providing the potential customer a chance to examine them or see them in action. Trade fairs provide an excellent opportunity to introduce, promote, and demonstrate new products. Auto shows, such as the ones in Detroit, Geneva, and Tokyo, feature "concept" cars to gauge industry and public opinion. Recently, many of these new models have been environmentally friendly, such as being 90 percent recyclable.

2. An appearance at a show produces goodwill and allows for periodic cultivation of contacts. Beyond the impact of displaying specific products, many firms place strong emphasis on "waving the company flag" against competition. This facet also includes morale boosting of the firm's sales personnel and distributors.

3. The opportunity to find an intermediary may be one of the best reasons to attend a trade show. A show is a cost-effective way to solicit and screen candidates to represent the firm, especially in a new market. Copylite Products of Ft. Lauderdale used the CeBIT computer-and-automation show in Hannover, Germany, to establish itself in Europe. The result was a distribution center in Rotterdam and six distributors covering eight countries. Its $40,000 investment in the trade show has reaped millions in new business.[56]

4. Attendance is one of the best ways to contact government officials and decision makers, especially in China. For example, participation in the Chinese Export Commodities Fair, which is held twice a year in Guangzhou, China, is "expected" by the host government.

5. Trade fairs provide an excellent chance for market research and collecting competitive intelligence. The exporter is able to view most rivals at the same time and to test comparative buyer reactions. Trade fairs provide one of the most inexpensive ways of obtaining evaluative data on the effectiveness of a promotional campaign.

6. Exporters are able to reach a sizable number of sales prospects in a brief time period at a reasonable cost per contact. According to research by Hannover Messe, more than 86 percent of all attendees represent buying influences (managers with direct responsibility for purchasing products and services). Of equal significance is the fact that trade show visitors are there because they have a specific interest in the exhibits.[57] Similarly, suppliers can be identified. One U.S. apparel manufacturer at the International Trade Fair for Clothing Machinery in Cologne paid for its participation by finding a less expensive thread supplier.[58]

On the other hand, the following are among the reasons cited for nonparticipation in trade fairs:

1. High costs. These can be avoided by participating in events sponsored by the U.S. Department of Commerce or exhibiting at U.S. trade centers or export development offices. An exporter can also lower costs by sharing expenses with distributors or representatives. Further, the costs of closing a

sale through trade shows are estimated to be much lower than for a sale closed through personal representation.

2. Difficulty in choosing the appropriate trade fairs for participation. This is a critical decision. Because of scarce resources, many firms rely on suggestions from their foreign distributors on which fairs to attend and what specifically to exhibit. Caterpillar, for example, usually allows its foreign dealers to make the selections for themselves. In markets where conditions are more restricted for exporters, such as China, Caterpillar in effect serves as the dealer and thus participates itself.

3. For larger exporters with multiple divisions, the problem of coordination. Several divisions may be required to participate in the same fair under the company banner. Similarly, coordination is required with distributors and agents if joint participation is desired, which requires joint planning.

Trade show participation is too expensive to be limited to the exhibit alone. A clear set of promotional objectives would include targeting accounts and attracting them to the show with preshow promotion using mailings, advertisements in the trade journals, or Web site information. Contests and giveaways are effective in attracting participants to the company's exhibition area. Major customers and attractive prospects often attend, and they should be acknowledged, for example, by arranging for a hospitality suite.[59] Finally, a system is needed to evaluate post-show performance and to track qualified leads.

Exporters may participate in general or specialized trade shows. General trade fairs are held in Hannover, Germany (see *The International Marketplace 10.2*) and Milan, Italy. An example of a specialized one is Retail Solutions, a four-day trade show on store automation held in London. Participants planning to exhibit at large trade shows may elect to do so independently or as part of a national pavilion. For small and medium-sized companies the benefit of a group pavilion is in both cost and ease of the arrangements. These pavilions are often part of governmental export-promotion programs. Even foreign government assistance may be available; for example, the Japanese External Trade Organization (JETRO) helps non-Japanese companies participate in the country's two largest trade shows.

Other promotional events that the exporter can use are trade missions, seminar missions, solo exhibitions, video/catalog exhibitions, and virtual trade shows. **Trade missions** can be U.S. specialized trade missions or industry-organized, government-approved (IOGA) trade missions, both of which aim at expanding the sales of U.S. goods and services and the establishment of agencies and representation abroad. The U.S. Department of Commerce is actively involved in assistance of both types. **Seminar missions** are events in which eight to ten firms are invited to participate in a one- to four-day forum, during which the team members conduct generic discussions on technological issues—that is, follow a soft-sell approach. This is followed up by individual meetings with end users, government agencies, research institutions, and other potentially useful contacts. Individual firms may introduce themselves to certain markets by proposing a technical seminar there. Synopses of several alternative proposed lectures, together with company details and the qualifications of the speakers, must be forwarded to the proper body, which will circulate the proposals to interested bodies and coordinate all the arrangements. The major drawback is the time required to arrange for such a seminar, which may be as much as a year. **Solo exhibitions** are generally limited to one, or at the most, a few product themes and are held only when market conditions warrant them. **Video/catalog exhibitions** allow exporters to publicize their products at low cost. They consist of 20 to 35 product presentations on videotapes, each lasting five to ten minutes. They provide the advantage of actually showing the product in use to potential customers. **Virtual trade shows** enable exporters to promote their products and services over the Internet and to have electronic presence without actually attending a trade show. Trade leads and international sales interests are collected and forwarded by the sponsor to the

THE INTERNATIONAL MARKETPLACE   10.2

At the Fair

CeBIT is the Olympic Games of industrial exposition. With more than 4,000,000 square feet (360,000 square meters) of indoor exhibition space and 7,000 exhibitors, the Hannover-based event is ten times as large as most trade shows anywhere in the world. It is superbly organized, with its own train station, post office, over 30 restaurants, and 600 permanent staff. While the range of exhibits covers everything available in information technology and communications, the 2003 fair focused particularly on the convergence of technologies. This included, for example, the entire spectrum of digital products for home automation.

The sheer magnitude of the fair and the technology displayed there are impressive, but are not necessarily the most significant aspects of the event. Rather, it is the opportunity it presents for people from everywhere in the world to view the latest developments and learn an incredible amount about their potential. Most important, it provides the opportunity to meet hundreds of people who can become invaluable future resources, if not necessarily direct sources of future business. More than 670,000 visitors attended in 2002, including 137,000 from abroad (26,800 from Asia, 9,000 from the Americas, 4,200 from Africa, and 1,800 from the Asia-Pacific region). Over 11,000 journalists from 70 countries cover the event annually.

A total of 7,074 exhibitors from 65 countries booked space for 2003, of which 2,767 (39 percent) were from outside Germany. Asia and Australia constituted 42 percent of the foreign exhibitor contingent. The worldwide participation numbers are significant, especially considering that, in addition to Hannover, regional CeBIT fairs are

© COURTESY OF DEUTSHE MESSE AG

also available for exhibitors in Istanbul; Long Beach; New York; Shanghai; and Sydney.

For the first time in 2003, the fair was preceded by a summit meeting of the industry's key decision makers and influencers. "ICT World Forum @ CeBIT 2003" brought together many of the world's leading players in the information technology and telecommunications industries to discuss new trends and formulate new strategies.

SOURCES: Press releases available at **http://presse.messe.de**; "Hannover Fair 2002 Delivers As Expected," *Control Engineering* 49 (May 2002): 17; Hannover's Trade Fair: The Week of the Widget," *The Washington Post*, April 29, 1996, A13; Valerio Giannini, "The Hannover Messe," *Export Today* 9 (July–August 1993): 29–32; **http://www.cebit.de**; and **http://www.ictwf.com**.

companies for follow-up. The information stays online for 365 days for one flat fee. For example, BuyUSA (an online environment sponsored by the U.S. Department of Commerce) offers exporters the opportunity to show their company profile, logo, product listings, Web site link, and catalog in a virtual trade zone. The virtual trade zone is promoted heavily at the trade shows actually attended by the department, giving buyers at the show a chance to review company information for possible contact.[60]

Personal Selling

Personal selling is the most effective of the promotional tools available to the marketer; however, its costs per contact are high. The average cost of sales calls may vary from $200 to $1,100, depending on the industry and the product or service. Personal selling allows for immediate feedback on customer reaction as well as information on markets.

The exporter's sales effort is determined by the degree of internationalization in its efforts, as shown in Table 10.1. As the degree of internationalization advances, so will the exporter's own role in carrying out or controlling the sales function.

Table 10.1   Levels of Exporter Involvement in International Sales

Type of Involvement	Target of Sales Effort	Level of Exporter Involvement	Advantage/ Disadvantage
Indirect exports	Home-country-based intermediary	Low	+No major investment in international sales −Minor learning from/control of effort
Direct exports	Locally based intermediary	Medium	+Direct contact with local market −Possible gatekeeping by intermediary
Integrated exports	Customer	High	+Generation of market-specific assets −Cost/risk

SOURCE: Framework adapted from Reijo Luostarinen and Lawrence Welch, *International Operations of the Firm* (Helsinki, Finland: Helsinki School of Economics, 1990), chapter 1.

Indirect Exports

When the exporter uses indirect exports to reach international markets, the export process is externalized; in other words, the intermediary, such as an EMC, will take care of the international sales effort. While there is no investment in international sales by the marketer, there is also no, or very little, learning about sales in the markets that buy the product. The sales effort is basically a domestic one directed at the local intermediary. This may change somewhat if the marketer becomes party to an ETC with other similar producers. Even in that case, the ETC will have its own sales force and exposure to the effort may be limited. Any learning that takes place is indirect; for example, the intermediary may advise the marketer of product adaptation requirements to enhance sales.

Direct Exports

At some stage, the exporter may find it necessary to establish direct contact with the target market(s), although the ultimate customer contact is still handled by locally based intermediaries, such as agents or distributors. Communication with intermediaries must ensure both that they are satisfied with the arrangement and that they are equipped to market and promote the exporter's product appropriately. Whatever the distribution arrangement, the exporter must provide basic selling aid communications, such as product specification and data literature, catalogs, the results of product testing, and demonstrated performance information—everything needed to present products to potential customers. In some cases, the exporter has to provide the intermediaries with incentives to engage in local advertising efforts. These may include special discounts, push money, or cooperative advertising. Cooperative advertising will give the exporter's product local flavor and increase the overall promotional budget for the product. However, the exporter needs to be concerned that the advertising is of sufficient quality and that the funds are spent as agreed.

For the marketer–intermediary interaction to work, four general guidelines have to be satisfied.[61]

1. Know the sales scene. Often what works in the exporter's home market will not work somewhere else. This is true especially in terms of compensation schemes. In U.S. firms, incentives and commission play a significant role, while in most other markets salaries are the major share of compensation.

The best way to approach this is to study the salary structures and incentive plans in other competitive organizations in the market in question.

2. Research the customer. Customer behavior will vary across markets, meaning the sales effort must adjust as well. ECA International, which sells marketing information worldwide based on a membership concept (companies purchase memberships to both participate in information gathering and receive appropriate data), found that its partners' sales forces could not sell the concept in Asia. Customers wanted instead to purchase information piece by piece. Only after research and modification of the sales effort was ECA able to sell the membership idea to customers.

3. Work with the culture. Realistic objectives have to be set for the salespeople based on their cultural expectations. This is especially true in setting goals and establishing measures such as quotas. If either of these is set unrealistically, the result will be frustration for both parties. Cultural sensitivity also is required in situations where the exporter has to interact with the intermediary's sales force—in training situations, for example. In some cultures, such as those in Asia, the exporter is expected to act as a teacher and more or less dictate how things are done, while in some others, such as in Northern Europe, training sessions may be conducted in a seminar-like atmosphere of give and take.

4. Learn from your local representatives. If the sales force perceives a lack of fit between the marketer's product and the market, as well as inability to do anything about it, the result will be suboptimal. A local sales force is an asset to the exporter, given its close contact with customers. Beyond daily feedback, the exporter is wise to undertake two additional approaches to exploit the experience of local salespeople. First, the exporter should have a program by which local salespeople can visit the exporter's operations and interact with the staff. If the exporter is active in multiple markets of the same region, it is advisable to develop ways to put salespeople in charge of the exporter's products in different markets to exchange ideas and best practice. Naturally, it is in the best interest of the exporter also to make regular periodic visits to markets entered.

An approach that requires more commitment from the exporter is to employ its own sales representatives, whose main function is to represent the firm abroad to existing and potential customers and to seek new leads. It is also important to sell with intermediaries, by supporting and augmenting their efforts. This type of presence is essential at some stage of the firm's international involvement. Other promotional tools can facilitate foreign market entry, but eventually some personal selling must take place. A cooperative effort with the intermediaries is important at this stage, in that some of them may be concerned about the motives of the exporter in the long term. For example, an intermediary may worry that once the exporter has learned enough about the market, it will no longer need the services of the intermediary. If these suspicions become prevalent, sales information may no longer flow to the exporter in the quantity and quality needed.

Integrated Exports

In the final stage of export-based internationalization, the exporter internalizes the effort through either a sales office in the target market or a direct contact with the buyer from home base. This is part of the exporter's perceived need for increased **customer relationship management,** where the sales effort is linked to call-center technologies, customer-service departments, and the company's Web site. This may include also automating the sales force as seen in *The International Marketplace 10.3.* The establishment of a sales office does not have to mean an end to the use of intermediaries; the exporter's salespeople may be dedicated to supporting intermediaries' sales efforts.

At this stage, expatriate sales personnel, especially those needed to manage the effort locally or regionally, may be used. The benefits of expatriates are their better

THE INTERNATIONAL MARKETPLACE   10.3

Automating the Sales Force

In the early 1990s, Dataram Corp. saw its sales shriveling and its distributor-based sales struggling to meet the needs of a rapidly changing market. To survive, Dataram executives decided the company had to go directly to its worldwide customers. However, with only a few in-house sales representatives and inadequate mechanisms to track leads and service customers, the Princeton, New Jersey–based supplier of storage and memory products for high-end computers faced an uphill battle against formidable odds.

The most critical decision in Dataram's change of approach was to automate its sales force. The company's sales representatives and managers worldwide now are equipped with Dell notebook computers listing vital information about their clients and the company's products and services. The system is used to manage database marketing activity, such as lead generation and tracking, trade shows, telemarketing, advertising tracking, product support, and customer service. Management can also spot emerging trends, avert impending disasters, and forecast sales with the help of the system. "When a sales rep can answer a question in 15 minutes instead of three days, the company is perceived as a consultant as much as a vendor," say company officials. Recruiting salespeople may be easier when a company can offer state-of-the-art support. Futhermore, if turnover takes place, important customer information is not lost but preserved in the database.

Sales force automation (SFA), like anything else in marketing, is subject to the realities of the international environment: borders, time zones, languages, and cultures. Sales professionals may see their customer accounts as proprietary and may not be willing to share information for fear of losing their leverage. Furthermore, in markets in which personal relationships drive sales practices, such as in Latin America, technological wizardry may be frowned upon. Representatives in every country may want to do things slightly differently, which means that a system that can be localized is needed. This localization may be as comprehensive as complete language translations or as minor as changing address fields in the database. Another issue to be considered is cost—hardware costs are higher in Europe, and telecommunications costs have to be factored in. Finally, with transoceanic support needs, the company may want to look for local support or invest in keeping desk personnel on board at off-hours.

A significant concern is the cost. A Latin American company may face a price tag of $2 million for a large company or $700,000 for a midsized or small firm. However, according to a recent study, automated companies have realized sales increases of 10 to 30 percent, and in some cases as much as 100 percent.

Complaints are also heard. While initial reactions to the use of technology are normally high, six months after implementation some companies report negative job-related perceptions by salespeople, some even going so far as to reject the technology. Poor results are especially likely when salespeople feel that their jobs or role is being threatened. These facts need to be incorporated into the implementation plan of any SFA program.

SOURCES: Cheri Speier and Viswanath Venkatesh, "The Hidden Minefields in the Adoption of Sales Force Automation Techniques," *Journal of Marketing* 66 (July 2002): 98–111; "Increasing Sales Force Performance," *Industrial Distribution*, July 2002, 30; Kathleen V. Schmidt, "Why SFA Is a Tough Sell in Latin America," *Marketing News*, January 3, 2000; Steven Barth, "Building a Global Infrastructure," *World Trade*, April 1999, S8–S10; Eric J. Adams, "Sales Force Automation: The Second Time Around," *World Trade*, March 1996, 72–74; "Risky Business," *World Trade*, December 1995, 50–51; and "Power Tool," *World Trade*, November 1993, 42–44.

---

understanding of the company and its products, and their ability to transfer best practice to the local operation. With expatriate management, the exporter can exercise a high amount of control over the sales function. Customers may also see the sales office and its expatriate staff as a long-term commitment to the market. The challenges lie mostly in the fit of the chosen individual to the new situation. The cost of having expatriate staff is considerable, approximately 2.5 times the cost at home, and the availability of suitable talent may be a problem, especially if the exporting organization is relatively small.[62]

The role of personal selling is greatest when the exporter sells directly to the end user or to governmental agencies, such as foreign trade organizations. Firms selling products with high price tags (such as Boeing commercial aircraft) or companies selling to monopsonies (such as Seagrams liquor to certain Northern European countries, where all liquor sales are through state-controlled outlets) must rely heavily on person-to-person communication, oral presentations, and direct-marketing efforts. Many of these firms can expand their business only if their markets are knowledgeable about what they do. This may require corporate advertising and publicity generation through extensive public relations efforts.

Whatever the sales task, effectiveness is determined by a number of interrelated factors. One of the keys to personal selling is the salesperson's ability to adapt to the customer and the selling situation.[63] This aspect of selling requires cultural knowledge and empathy; for example, in the Middle East, sales presentations may be broken up by long discussions of topics that have little or nothing to do with the transaction at hand. The characteristics of the buying task, whether routine or unique, have a bearing on the sales presentation. The exporter may be faced by a situation in which the idea of buying from a foreign entity is the biggest obstacle in terms of the risks perceived. If the exporter's product does not provide a clear-cut relative advantage over that of competitors, the analytical, interpersonal skills of the salesperson are needed to assist in the differentiation. A salesperson, regardless of the market, must have a thorough knowledge of the product or service. The more the salesperson is able to apply that knowledge to the particular situation, the more likely it is that he or she will obtain a positive result. The salesperson usually has front-line responsibility for the firm's customer relations, having to handle conflict situations such as the parent firm's bias for domestic markets and thus the possibility that shipments of goods to foreign clients receive low priority.

Summary

Effective communication is essential in negotiating agreements. To maximize the outcome of negotiations with clients and partners from other cultural backgrounds, international marketers must show adjustment capability to different standards and behaviors. Success depends on being prepared and remaining flexible, whatever the negotiation style in the host country.

Effective and efficient communication is needed for the dual purpose of (1) informing prospective customers about the availability of products or services and (2) persuading customers to opt for the marketer's offering over those of competitors. Within the framework of the company's opportunities, resources, and objectives, decisions must be made about whether to direct communications to present customers, potential customers, the general public, or intermediaries. Decisions must be made on how to reach each of the intended target audiences without wasting valuable resources. A decision also has to be made about who will control the communications effort: the exporter, an agency, or local representatives. Governmental agencies are the best sources of export promotion support, which is essential in alleviating the environmental threats perceived by many exporters.

The exporting international marketer must also choose tools to use in the communications effort. Usually, two basic tools are used: (1) mass selling through business and trade journals, direct mail, the Internet, trade shows and missions, and (2) personal selling, which brings the international marketer face-to-face with the targeted customer.

Key Terms

encoding
decoding
noise
outcome
feedback
promotional mix
push strategies
pull strategies
integrated marketing communications

telemarketing
database marketing
trade missions
seminar missions
solo exhibitions
video/catalog exhibitions
virtual trade shows
customer relationship management

Questions for Discussion

1. What is potentially harmful in going out of one's way to make clients feel comfortable by playing down status distinctions such as titles?
2. Discuss this statement: "Lack of foreign-language skills puts U.S. negotiators at a disadvantage."
3. Compare and contrast the usefulness to a novice exporter of elements of the promotional mix.
4. Why do exporters usually choose U.S.-based services when placing advertisements to boost export sales specifically?
5. Some exporters report that they value above all the broad exposure afforded through exhibiting at a trade show, regardless of whether they are able to sell directly at the event. Comment on this philosophy.
6. What specific advice would you give to an exporter who has used domestic direct marketing extensively and wishes to continue the practice abroad?

Internet Exercises

1. Many traditionalists do not foresee that virtual trade shows will become a major threat to the actual shows themselves. Their view is that nothing can replace the actual seeing or touching of a product in person. Visit **http://www.buyusa.com** and develop arguments for and/or against this view.
2. The U.S. Exporters' Yellow Pages changed to www.myEXPORTS.COM in 2000. Will the fact that it is now an Internet-based service add to its ability to "offer U.S. firms a means to promote their businesses worldwide" and "attract appropriate foreign customers"? The service is available at **http://www.myexports.com**.

Recommended Readings

Handbook of International Direct and E-Marketing. London: Kogan Page Ltd., 2001.

Hendon, Donald W., Rebecca A. Hendon, and Paul Herbig. *Cross-Cultural Business Negotiations.* New York: Praeger, 1999.

Hodge, Sheida. *Global Smarts: The Art of Communicating and Deal Making Anywhere in the World.* New York: John Wiley and Sons, 2000.

Jagoe, John R., and Agnes Brown. *Export Sales and Marketing Manual.* Washington, DC: Export Institute, 2001.

Monye, Sylvester O. *The Handbook of International Marketing Communications.* Malden, MA: Blackwell Publishers, 2000.

Reedy, Joel, Shauna Schullo, and Kenneth Zimmerman. *Electronic Marketing.* Mason, OH: South-Western, 2003.

Schuster, Camille P., and Michael J. Copeland. *Global Business: Planning for Sales and Negotiations.* Mason, OH: International Thomson Publishing, 1997.

Shimp, Terence A. *Advertising, Promotion, and Supplemental Aspects of Integrated Marketing Communications.* Mason, OH: South-Western, 2003.

Tussie, Diane, ed. *The Environment and International Trade Negotiations.* London: St. Martin's Press, 1999.

Zeff, Robbin Lee, and Brad Aronson. *Advertising on the Internet.* New York: John Wiley and Sons, 1999.

Zimmerman, Jan, and Hoon Meng Ong. *Marketing on the Internet.* New York: Maximum Press, 2002.

chapter 11
Channels and Distribution Strategies

THE INTERNATIONAL MARKETPLACE 11.1

Getting the Distribution Job Done in Latin America

Changing market conditions from the Rio Grande to Tierra del Fuego are making U.S., European, and Japanese companies reassess their distribution strategies in South and Central America. Regional trade pacts and free trade are enabling companies both to consider entry and to reformulate their strategies in the region. But Latin America is not one homogeneous area (due to, for example, language differences), and three primary markets have emerged: Brazil, Mexico, and Argentina.

In the past, the infrastructure for effective and efficient distribution was largely missing. Underdeveloped and monopolistic distributor networks saw as their primary jobs distributing sales literature, cutting through red tape, and charging invariably high fees.

Times are changing for these intermediaries, however. Outside competition has forced distributors to add value to what they do, for example, by carrying inventory, providing specialized packaging, participating in the logistics infrastructure, handling shipments when they arrive, or otherwise serving the customers' needs. And if locals do not measure up, companies are willing to look for other solutions, such as using outside captive distribution systems or putting their own people in place.

There are no standard answers as to distribution system design. In many cases, companies have found that a mix of techniques yields the best results and allows greater responsiveness to customer requests, as shown by the following four examples.

Motorola in Brazil   Motorola's subsidiary combines in-house systems with an independent distributor network. It uses an in-house sales force to service large manufacturing clients and major end users of its line of imported and domestic semiconductors and portable radios, as well as wireless telephones and pagers. Other customers are served through four large distribution firms. Subrepresentatives are contracted by distributors to provide coverage in areas where they do not have a direct presence. The company has determined that sales made via a distributor at this level are cheaper than direct sales. Distributors can offer fast delivery because in-house inventories are maintained.

ICI in Mexico   ICI markets agrochemicals, explosives, paints, specialty chemicals, and dyes and chooses a distribution approach based on the size of sales and need for technical assistance. The company prefers to sell industrial products directly when possible due to the technical service they require. For example, the firm trains mining clients in explosives and provides on-site studies to determine appropriate blasting methods. The paint business in Mexico City is handled by in-house sales representatives that sell directly to retail stores. ICI products are oriented toward the high-quality, high-price market.

Management takes pains to ensure the quality of retail service, with sales representatives monitoring outlets. Even when independents handle products, the company's sales department continuously assesses the performance of the distribution chain.

Eveready in Argentina   Battery makers sell a large share of their product through small retailers. In Argentina, which is one of the 160 countries in which Energizer and Eveready brands are available, kiosks are one of the most important outlets and product turnover is high. Eveready reaches thousands of kiosks by selling to some 600 independent distributors throughout the country. Distributors are attracted to the firm because of the high product turnover rate and its strong name recognition. Eveready reaches distributors through a national shipping company that carries products to remote markets.

AOL in Brazil, Mexico, and Argentina   With the domestic market overcrowded with competition, AOL has sought growth abroad by establishing 12 international ventures, including Latin America. AOL chose as its partner the Cisneros Group of Companies from Venezuela to understand and exploit the culturally different environment. Partners also provide much of the capital needed to get the service off the ground, while AOL provides the technology and established brand name. In regional expansion, however, care must be taken to choose a partner that can provide support across countries. AOL has had some difficulties in this regard in Brazil because its partner's relationships and influence have been built mostly in Spanish-speaking countries.

SOURCES: Roger Morton, "Latin American Business Is Looking Up," *Transportation & Distribution* 41 (October 2000): 51–54; "AOL Latin America: Off to a Strong Start," *Business Week,* October 2, 2000, 6; "Empire Building: The Slow Track," *Business Week,* September 11, 2000, 126E3; Judi E. Loomis, "Shipping to Latin America," *World Trade,* November 1999, 62–68; Erika Morphy, "Pan-American Byways," *Export Today,* December 1996, 20–28; Joseph V. Barks, "Penetrating Latin America," *International Business,* February 1994, 76–80; "Choosing the Right System: Direct Sales vs. Independents," *Business International,* January 13, 1992, 12; "Winning Approaches to Distribution in LA," *Business International,* January 13, 1992, 12–13; **http://www.motorola.com**; **http://www.ici.com**; **http://www.eveready.com**; and **http://www.aoltimewarner.com**.

CHANNELS OF DISTRIBUTION provide the essential linkages that connect producers and customers. The links are intracompany and extracompany entities that perform a number of functions. Optimal distribution systems are flexible and are able to adjust to market conditions, as seen in *The International Marketplace 11.1*. In general, companies use one or more of the following distribution systems: (1) the firm sells directly to customers through its own field sales force or through electronic commerce; (2) the company operates through independent **intermediaries,** usually at the local level; or (3) the business depends on an outside distribution system that may have regional or global coverage. For example, a number of Asian and European computer makers use the services of Merisel, Inc., a $5 billion technology products company based in California, to reach resellers throughout the North American market in addition to their own direct efforts.

A channel of distribution should be seen as more than a sequence of marketing institutions connecting producers and consumers; it should be a team working toward a common goal.[1] Too often intermediaries are mistakenly perceived as temporary market-entry vehicles and not the partners with whom marketing efforts are planned and implemented. In today's marketing environment, being close to customers, be they the final consumer or intermediary, and solving their problems are vital to bringing about success. When its office supplies superstore customer kicked off a joint venture in Australia, 3M dispatched two employees to its Australian subsidiary to educate that division on the special needs of a superstore.

Since most marketers cannot or do not want to control the distribution function completely, structuring channel relationships becomes a crucial task. The importance of this task is further compounded by the fact that the channel decision is the most long-term of the marketing mix decisions in that, once established, it cannot easily be changed. In export marketing, a new dimension is added to the task: the export channel decision in addition to making market-specific decisions. An experienced exporter may decide that control is of utmost importance and choose to perform tasks itself and incur the information collection and adaptation costs. An infrequent exporter, on the other hand, may be quite dependent on experienced intermediaries to get its product to markets. Whether export tasks are self-performed or assigned to export intermediaries, the distribution function should be planned so that the channel will function as one rather than as a collection of different or independent units.

The decisions involved in the structuring and management of the export channel of distribution are discussed first. The chapter will end with a discussion of the steps needed in preparation for e-commerce. Logistics issues will be discussed in detail in Chapter 17.

Channel Structure

A generalization of channel configurations for consumer and industrial products as well as services is provided in Figure 11.1. Channels can vary from direct, producer-to-consumer types to elaborate, multilevel channels employing many types of intermediaries, each serving a particular purpose. For example, Canadian software firms enter international markets by exporting directly from Canada (40 percent), opening their own sales offices (14 percent), by entering into cooperative arrangements with other exporters (15 percent), by using a local distributor or a value-adding reseller (13 percent), or by a mixture of modes (17 percent).[2] British firms, on the other hand, exported directly in 60 percent of the cases, 8 percent opened a foreign sales office, 5 percent used an agent, and the remainder entered

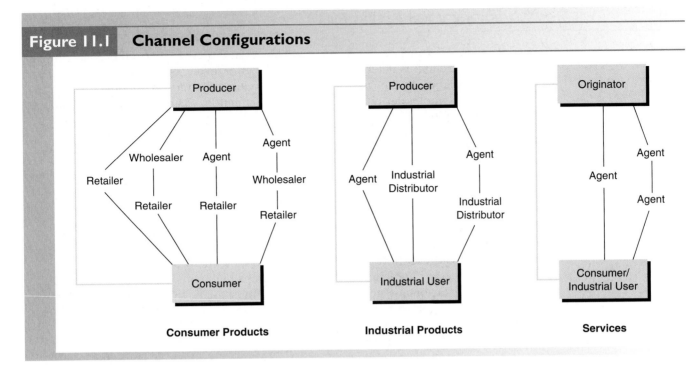

Figure 11.1   Channel Configurations

a cooperative export effort such as piggybacking, in which the exporter uses another company's channel to enter a foreign market.[3]

Channel configurations for the same product will vary within industries, even within the same firm, because national markets quite often have unique features. This may mean dramatic departures from accepted policy for a company. For example, to reach the British market, which is dominated by a few retailers such as J. Sainsbury, Tesco, and ASDA, marketers such as Heinz may have to become suppliers to these retailers' private-label programs in addition to making their own efforts.[4] A firm's international market experience will also cause variation in distribution patterns. AMPAK, a manufacturer of packaging machinery, uses locally based distributors in markets where it is well established. Others are entered indirectly by using domestically based intermediaries: either by using the services of trading companies or through selling to larger companies, which then market the products alongside their own.

The connections made by marketing institutions are not solely for the physical movement of goods. They also serve as transactional title flows and informational communications flows. Rather than unidirectional, downward from the producer, the flows are usually multidirectional, both vertical and horizontal. As an example, the manufacturer relies heavily on the retailer population for data on possible changes in demand. Communications from retailers may be needed to coordinate a cooperative advertising campaign instituted by a manufacturer. The three flows—physical, transactional, and informational—do not necessarily take place simultaneously or occur at every level of the channel. Agent intermediaries, for example, act only to facilitate the information flow; they do not take title and often do not physically handle the goods. Similarly, electronic intermediaries, such as amazon.com, have to rely on facilitating agents to perform the logistics function of their operation.

Because only a few products are sold directly to ultimate users, an international marketer has to decide on alternative ways to move products to chosen markets. The basic marketing functions of exchange, physical movement, and various facilitating activities must be performed, but the marketer may not be equipped to handle them. Intermediaries can therefore be used to gain quick, easy, and relatively low-cost entry to a targeted market.

Channel Design

The term *channel design* refers to the length and the width of the channel employed.[5] Length is determined by the number of levels, or different types, of intermediaries. In the case of consumer products, the most traditional is the producer-wholesaler-retailer-customer configuration. Channel width is determined by the number of institutions of each type in the channel. An industrial goods marketer may grant exclusive distribution rights to a foreign entity, whereas a consumer goods marketer may want to use as many intermediaries as possible to ensure intensive distribution.

Channel design is determined by factors that can be summarized as the 11 Cs, listed in Table 11.1. These factors are integral to both the development of new marketing channels and the modification and management of existing ones. Their individual influences will vary from one market to another, and seldom, if ever, can one factor be considered without the interactive effects of the others. The marketer should use the 11 Cs checklist to determine the proper approach to reach intended target audiences before selecting channel members to fill the roles. The first three factors are givens, since the firm must adjust to the existing structures. The other eight are controllable to a certain extent by the international marketer.

Customer Characteristics

The demographic and psychographic characteristics of targeted customers will form the basis for channel design decisions. Answers to questions such as what customers need—as well as why, when, and how they buy—are used to determine ways in which the products should be made available to generate a competitive advantage. As an example, Anheuser-Busch entered Japan when Suntory, one of the country's largest liquor distillers, acquired the importing rights. Suntory's marketing plan stressed distribution of Budweiser in discos, pubs, and other night spots where Japan's affluent, well-traveled youth gather. Young people in Japan are influenced by U.S. culture and adapt themselves more readily to new products than do older Japanese. Taking advantage of this fact, Suntory concentrated its efforts on one generation, and on-premise sales led to major off-premise (retail outlet) sales as well.

In the early stages of product introduction, the international marketer may concentrate efforts on only the most attractive markets and later, having attained a foothold, expand distribution. When Kronenbourg, the best-selling beer in Europe, entered the U.S. market, distribution was initiated in New York City and then extended to the metropolitan area. The reason was the area's prominence in both domestic and imported beer consumption. The national rollout took place five years later. In the industrial sector, certain industries cluster geographically, allowing the international marketer to take a more direct approach.

Table 11.1	Determinants of Channel Structure and Relationships
EXTERNAL	**INTERNAL**
Customer characteristics	Company objectives
Culture	Character
Competition	Capital
	Cost
	Coverage
	Control
	Continuity
	Communication

Customer characteristics may cause the same product to be distributed through two different types of channels. Many industrial goods marketers' sales, such as those of Caterpillar, are handled by individual dealers, except when the customer might be the central government or one of its entities, in which case sales are direct from the company itself. Furthermore, primary target audiences may change from one market to another. For example, in Japan, McDonald's did not follow the U.S. pattern of locating restaurants in the suburbs. The masses of young pedestrians that flood Japanese cities were more promising than affluent but tradition-minded car owners in the suburbs.

In business-to-business marketing, the adoption of e-commerce provides new opportunities for international marketers. New export markets can be accessed by expanding network and customer bases. Six sectors are forecast to leading the way in business-to-business online transactions by 2003: retail, motor vehicles, shipping, industrial equipment, technological products, and government.[6] At the same time, the explosive growth of the Internet poses a direct threat and challenge to traditional intermediaries, leading possibly to elimination, or disintermediation.[7]

Culture

In planning a distribution system, the marketer must analyze existing channel structures, or what might be called **distribution culture.** As an example, the manner in which Japanese channels of distribution are structured and managed presents one of the major reasons for the apparent failure of foreign firms to establish major market penetration in Japan.[8] In any case, and in every country, international marketers must study distribution systems in general and the types of linkages between channel members for their specific type of product. Usually, the international marketer has to adjust to existing structures to gain distribution. For example, in Finland, 95 percent of all distribution of nondurable consumer goods is through four wholesale chains. Without their support, no significant penetration of the market is possible.

In addition to structure, functions performed by the various types of intermediaries have to be outlined. Retailers in Japan demand more from manufacturers and wholesalers than do U.S. retailers; for example, they expect returns of merchandise to be fully accepted even if there is no reason other than lack of sales. Retailers also expect significant amounts of financing and frequent delivery of products. Retailers, on their part, offer substantial services to their clientele and take great pains to build close relationships with their customers. As can be seen in Table 11.2, which lists channel members in the Japanese cosmetics industry, functions

Table 11.2	**Examples of Function Performance in the Channel System for the Japanese Cosmetics Industry**	
	Channel Member	
Manufacturer	**Intermediary**	**Retail**
Production	Order taking	Selling
Advertising	Inventory maintenance	Organizing consumers
National sales promotion	Space control at the retail level	In-store promotion
Dealer aids	Product assortment	
Education of dealers	Dispatching of sales support personnel	
Financing	Area marketing	
	Financing	

SOURCE: Michael R. Czinkota, "Distribution of Consumer Products in Japan: An Overview," in *International Marketing Strategy: Environmental Assessment and Entry Strategies,* Michael R. Czinkota and Ilkka A. Ronkainen, eds. (Ft. Worth, TX: The Dryden Press, 1994), 293–307.

are—and should be—clearly delineated. Manufacturers concentrate mainly on production and promotional activities; intermediaries work on logistics activities, financing, and communication with manufacturers and retailers; retailers focus on sales and promotional activities.

Changing existing distribution systems may be quite difficult. Porsche tried to change the way it sold automobiles in the United States from traditional independent franchised dealers to a "dealerless system." Whereas dealers buy cars for resale, Porsche would have instituted agents who would order cars as they sold them and work on an 8 percent commission rather than the normal 16 to 18 percent margin. After a dealer uproar, Porsche abandoned the plan. Toys 'Я' Us, which opened its first outlet in Japan in the 1990s, initially had a difficult time getting Japanese toy manufacturers to sell to it directly (as happens in the United States) rather than through multiple layers of distributors. Wal-Mart, on its part, has caused significant changes in supplier operating procedures with its demand that vendors forgo all other amenities and quote the lowest price. This has been traumatic in markets such as the United Kingdom where suppliers and competitors have used the regulatory environment to exist in a less-competitive environment.[9] Wal-Mart will, however, work with suppliers on cost reduction. Similarly, direct sales by marketers through the Internet are raising concerns among distributors who feel that they lose out on these opportunities. Regardless of whether these are completely new sales or come from customers who would have used traditional channels before, intermediaries should be compensated for these sales in some way, such as through e-credits on their next purchase from the marketer, to acknowledge their role in developing the local market.

Additionally, an analysis is needed of the relationships between channel members—for example, the extent of vertical integration. The linkage can be based on ownership, contract, or the use of expert or referent power by one of the channel members. The Japanese distribution system often financially links producers, importers, distributors, and retailers, either directly or through a bank or a trading company. Interdependence in a number of southern European markets is forged through family relationships or is understood as an obligation.

Foreign legislation affecting distributors and agents is an essential part of the distribution culture of a market. For example, legislation may require that foreign firms be represented only by firms that are 100 percent locally owned. Before China's entry into the WTO in late 2001, foreign companies were barred from importing their own products, distributing them, or providing after-sales service. These functions were to be performed by Chinese companies or Sino–foreign joint ventures. Now, these restrictions will all be phased out within three years. This means that General Motors China Group will regain control over its marketing. Up to now, Chinese companies have handled the importing, distributing, and selling, and GM's cars have often passed through four different entities before customers see them. In the future, GM wants to build a consistent network of dealers and start providing financing, which also becomes allowed.[10]

While distribution decisions have been mostly tactical and made on a market-by-market basis, marketing managers have to be cognizant of globalization in the distribution function as well. This is taking place in two significant ways.[11] Distribution formats are crossing borders, especially to newly emerging markets. While supermarkets accounted only for 8 percent of consumer nondurable sales in urban areas in Thailand in 1990, the figure today is over 50 percent. Other such formats include department stores, minimarts, and supercenters. The second globalization trend is the globalization of intermediaries themselves either independently or through strategic alliances. Entities such as Toys 'Я' Us from the United States, Galeries Lafayette from France, Marks & Spencer from the United Kingdom, and Takashimaya and Isetan from Japan have expanded to both well-developed and newly emerging markets. Within the European Union, a growing number of EU-based retailers are merging and establishing a presence in other EU markets. For example, the merger of France's Carrefour and Promodes in 1999 created the world's second largest retailer after Wal-Mart. The merger was partly in response to Wal-Mart's European expansion.[12] Some intermediaries are entering foreign markets by acquiring local entities (e.g., Germany's Tengelmann and Holland's Ahold acquiring the U.S. chains A&P and Giant, respectively) or forming alliances. For example, in Mexico, joint ventures between Wal-Mart and Cifra, Fleming Cos. and Gigante, and Price/Costco and Comercial Mexicana are changing the distribution landscape by concentrating retail power. Beyond opportunity for marketers for more and broader-based sales, these entities are applying the same type of margin pressure marketers find in more developed markets. In many cases, marketers are providing new technologies to these intermediaries and helping to train them with the hope of establishing solid relationships that will withstand competition, especially from local entities that typically start beefing up their own operations.[13] The strategic options chosen by retailers are presented in Table 11.3.

Competition

Channels used by competitors may be the only product distribution system that is accepted by both the trade and consumers. In this case, the international marketer's task is to use the structure effectively and efficiently, or even innovatively. This may mean, for example, that the exporter chooses a partner capable of developing markets rather than one who has existing contacts. The most obvious distributors may be content with the status quo in the market and be ready to push products that are the most profitable for them regardless of who made them. Two approaches may be applicable if those serving major customer prospects with similar product lines are not satisfactory. First, the exporter may form jointly owned sales companies with distributors (or with other exporters) to exercise more control. Second, the approach may be to seek a good company fit in terms of goals and objectives. In Asia, Lycos chose partners for their overall influence in the local market. In Japan, it teamed up with Sumitomo, an ultra-traditional trading company with a 250-year history, and in Korea with Mirae, a machinery and electronics firm.[14] Should a new approach be chosen, it must be carefully analyzed and tested against the cultural, political, and legal environments in which is to be introduced.

In some cases, the international marketer cannot manipulate the distribution variable. For example, in Sweden and Finland, all alcoholic beverages must be distributed through state monopoly–owned outlets. In Japan, the Japan Tobacco & Salt Public Corporation is a state monopoly that controls all tobacco imports and charges a 20 percent fee for distribution. In other cases, all feasible channels may be blocked by domestic competitors either through contractual agreements or through other means. U.S. suppliers of soda ash, which is used in glass, steel, and

Table 11.3	Internationalization of Retailers	
Approach	**Objective**	**Example**
Business exporter	Reconfigure retailing approach across markets with consistent core and focus on scale	Carrefour, IKEA, Makro, Wal-Mart
Concept exporter	Export concept but let local partners execute	Benetton
Skills exporter	Export unique skills (rather than entire concepts)	Price/Costco
Superior operator	Focus on operating capability; implemented through acquisition	Ahold, Tengelmann

SOURCES: Jody Evans, Alan Treadgold, and Felix T. Mavondo, "Psychic Distance and the Performance of International Retailers," *International Marketing Review* 17 (nos. 4 and 5, 2000): 373–391; and Denise Incandela, Kathleen McLaughlin, and Christiana Smith, "Retailers to the World," *The McKinsey Quarterly* 35 (no. 3, 1999): 84–97.

chemical products, have not been able to penetrate the Japanese market even though they offer a price advantage. The reason is the cartel-like condition developed by the Japan Soda Industry Association, which allegedly sets import levels, specifies which local trading company is to deal with each U.S. supplier, and buys the imports at lower U.S. prices for resale by its members at higher Japanese prices. Efforts by U.S. producers to distribute directly or through smaller, unaffiliated traders have faced strong resistance. The end users and traders fear alienating the domestic producers, on whom their business depends.

Company Objectives

A set of management considerations will have an effect on channel design. No channel of distribution can be properly selected unless it meets the requirements set by overall company objectives for market share and profitability. In distribution, this often calls for a compromise between cost and control objectives. While integrated channels (exporter owned and operated) may be preferred because they facilitate the protection of knowledge-based assets and provide needed high levels of customer service, the cost may be 15 to 35 percent of sales, whereas using distributors may drop the expense to 10 to 15 percent.

Often the use of multiple channels arises with the need to increase sales volume.[15] For example, in France, Xerox set up a chain of retail outlets in large cities to support its copier sales. To cover rural areas and smaller towns, Xerox withdrew its direct sales force and replaced it with independent distributors, concessionaires, who work on an exclusive basis. Rapid expansion can also be achieved through partnerships as shown by the Starbucks example in Figure 11.2. Partnerships can

Figure 11.2   Distribution Expansion through Partnerships

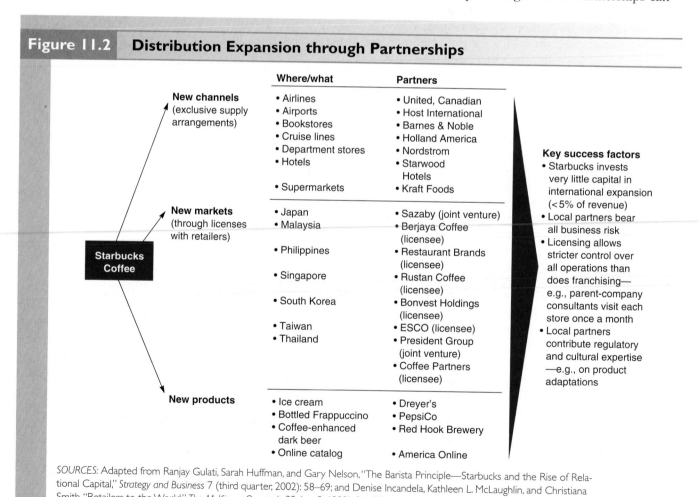

	Where/what	Partners
New channels (exclusive supply arrangements)	• Airlines • Airports • Bookstores • Cruise lines • Department stores • Hotels • Supermarkets	• United, Canadian • Host International • Barnes & Noble • Holland America • Nordstrom • Starwood Hotels • Kraft Foods
New markets (through licenses with retailers)	• Japan • Malaysia • Philippines • Singapore • South Korea • Taiwan • Thailand	• Sazaby (joint venture) • Berjaya Coffee (licensee) • Restaurant Brands (licensee) • Rustan Coffee (licensee) • Bonvest Holdings (licensee) • ESCO (licensee) • President Group (joint venture) • Coffee Partners (licensee)
New products	• Ice cream • Bottled Frappuccino • Coffee-enhanced dark beer • Online catalog	• Dreyer's • PepsiCo • Red Hook Brewery • America Online

Key success factors
• Starbucks invests very little capital in international expansion (<5% of revenue)
• Local partners bear all business risk
• Licensing allows stricter control over all operations than does franchising—e.g., parent-company consultants visit each store once a month
• Local partners contribute regulatory and cultural expertise—e.g., on product adaptations

SOURCES: Adapted from Ranjay Gulati, Sarah Huffman, and Gary Nelson, "The Barista Principle—Starbucks and the Rise of Relational Capital," *Strategy and Business* 7 (third quarter, 2002): 58–69; and Denise Incandela, Kathleen L. McLaughlin, and Christiana Smith, "Retailers to the World," *The McKinsey Quarterly* 35 (no. 3, 1999): 84–97. See also **http://www.starbucks.com**.

be undertaken if appropriate controls are in place to secure expansion with relatively little investment. If expansion is too rapid and the adjustments made to local market conditions too extensive, a major asset—standardization and economies of scale and scope—can be lost.

Character

The nature of the product, its character, will have an impact on the design of the channel. Generally, the more specialized, expensive, bulky, or perishable the product and the more after-sale service it may require, the more likely the channel is to be relatively short. Staple items, such as soap, tend to have longer channels.

The type of channel chosen must match the overall positioning of the product in the market. Changes in overall market conditions, such as currency fluctuations, may require changes in distribution as well. An increase in the value of the billing currency may cause a repositioning of the marketed product as a luxury item, necessitating an appropriate channel (such as an upper-grade department store) for its distribution.

Rules of thumb aside, particular products may be distributed in a number of ways even to the same target audience, as shown in Figure 11.3 for the PC industry. A dual channel may be used in which both intermediaries and a direct contact with customers are used. In some cases, a channel may extend beyond having one tier of distributors and resellers to include importers or agents. Another alternative, hybrid channels, features sharing of marketing functions, with the manufacturer handling promotion and customer generation, and the intermediaries, sales and distribution. The hybrid strategy is based more on cooperation and partnership, while the dual channel may result in conflict if disagreements arise as to who is to handle a specific customer.

Capital

The term *capital* is used to describe the financial requirements in setting up a channel system. The international marketer's financial strength will determine the type of channel and the basis on which channel relationships will be built. The stronger the marketer's finances, the more able the firm is to establish channels it

| Figure 11.3 | Distribution Alternatives: PCs in Europe |

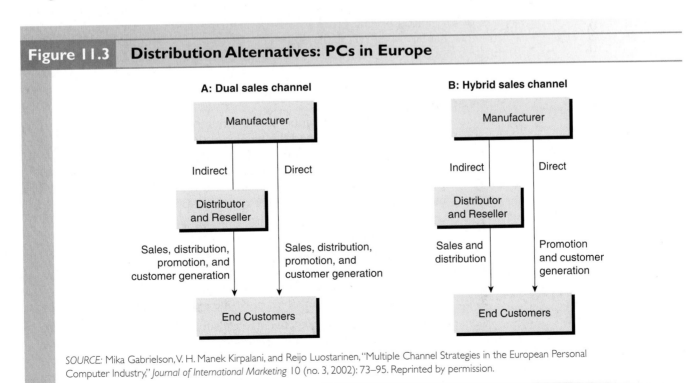

SOURCE: Mika Gabrielson, V. H. Manek Kirpalani, and Reijo Luostarinen, "Multiple Channel Strategies in the European Personal Computer Industry," *Journal of International Marketing* 10 (no. 3, 2002): 73–95. Reprinted by permission.

either owns or controls. Intermediaries' requirements for beginning inventories, selling on a consignment basis, preferential loans, and need for training all will have an impact on the type of approach chosen by the international marketer. For example, an industrial goods manufacturer may find that potential distributors in a particular country lack the capability of servicing the product. The marketer then has two options: (1) set up an elaborate training program at headquarters or regionally or (2) institute company-owned service centers to help distributors. Either approach will require a significant investment, but is necessary to ensure customer trust through superior execution of marketing programs.

Cost

Closely related to the capital dimension is cost—that is, the expenditure incurred in maintaining a channel once it is established. Costs will naturally vary over the life cycle of a relationship with a particular channel member as well as over the life cycle of the products marketed. An example of the costs involved is promotional money spent by a distributor for the marketer's product. A cooperative advertising deal between the international marketer and the intermediary would typically split the costs of the promotional campaign executed in the local market.

Costs will vary in terms of the relative power of the manufacturer vis-à-vis its intermediaries. The number of European retailers accounting for 75 percent of consumer sales has decreased from 132 in 1980 to 40 in 2002. This consolidation includes not only large retailers such as Ahold and Migros but also smaller retailers that have joined forces to form buying groups. One of the most significant is Expert Global, which has a total of 7,400 participating retailers in 22 European, North American, South American, and Pacific countries. The concentrated distribution systems being developed by these giants are eroding the marketing strength of manufacturers, which lay in their networks of distribution depots that delivered direct to stores. Now, retailers want delivery to their central distribution centers. In addition, they are pushing stockholding costs to manufacturers by demanding more frequent deliveries, in smaller, mixed loads, with shorter delivery time.[16]

Costs may also be incurred in protecting the company's distributors against adverse market conditions. A number of U.S. manufacturers helped their distributors maintain competitive prices through subsidies when the exchange rate for the U.S. dollar caused pricing problems. Extra financing aid has been extended to distributors that have been hit with competitive adversity. Such support, although often high in monetary cost, will pay back manyfold through a faultless manufacturer–distributor relationship.

Coverage

The term *coverage* is used to describe both the number of areas in which the marketer's products are represented and the quality of that representation. Coverage is therefore two-dimensional in that horizontal coverage and vertical coverage need to be considered in channel design. The number of areas to be covered depends on the dispersion of demand in the market and also on the time elapsed since the product's introduction to the market. Three different approaches are available:

1. Intensive coverage, which calls for distributing the product through the largest number of different types of intermediaries and the largest number of individual intermediaries of each type
2. Selective coverage, which entails choosing a number of intermediaries for each area to be penetrated
3. Exclusive coverage, which involves only one entity in a market

Generally, intensive and selective coverage calls for longer channels using different types of intermediaries, usually wholesalers and agents. Exclusive distribution is conducive to more direct sales. For some products, such as ethnic or industrial products, customers are concentrated geographically and allow for more intensive distribution with a more direct channel. A company typically enters a market with

Table 11.4	Advantages of a Single Distributor

1. One corporate presence eliminates confusion among buyers and local officials.
2. The volume of business that results when exports are consolidated will attract a larger/more qualified distributor. The distributor will thus have greater influence in its local business community.
3. Communication is less plagued by noise. This will have a positive effect in many areas, from daily information flows to supervising and training.
4. More effective coordination of the sales and promotional effort can be achieved through mutual learning.
5. Logistics flows are more economical.
6. A stronger presence can be maintained in smaller markets or markets in which resources may dictate a holding mode, until more effective penetration can be undertaken.
7. Distributor morale and the overall principal–intermediary relationship are better through elimination of intrabrand competition.

SOURCE: Adapted from Business International Corporation, *201 Checklists: Decision Making in International Operations* (New York: Business International Corporation, 1980), 26–27.

one local distributor, but as volume expands, the distribution base often has to be adjusted. The advantages of a single distributor are listed in Table 11.4.

Expanding distribution too quickly may cause problems. Benetton, one of Italy's major exporters of clothing, had planned to have 1,000 stores in the United States by 1990. The plan was abandoned because of concerns about oversaturation of certain urban areas and overprojection of retail sales. Rather, more emphasis is being put on customer service, and the number of stores in major North American cities was 150 in 2001.[17] Similarly, expanding distribution from specialty outlets to mass distribution may have an impact on the product's image and the after-sales service associated with it. The impact on channel relations may be significant if existing dealers perceive loss of sales as a result of such a move. This may be remedied by keeping the product lines in mass-distribution outlets different or possibly developing a different brand for the new channels.

Control

The use of intermediaries will automatically lead to loss of some control over the marketing of the firm's products.[18] The looser the relationship is between the marketer and intermediaries, the less control the marketer can exert. The longer the channel, the more difficult it becomes for the marketer to have a final say in pricing, promotion, and the types of outlets in which the product will be made available.

In the initial stages of internationalization or specific market entry, an intermediary's specialized knowledge and working relationships are needed, but as exporters' experience base and sales in the market increase, many opt to establish their own sales offices. Use of intermediaries provides quick entry using an existing system in which complementary products provide synergistic benefits. Furthermore, payments are received from one entity rather than from multiple customers.

The issue of control correlates heavily with the type of product or service being marketed. In the case of industrial and high-technology products, control will be easier to institute because intermediaries are dependent on the marketer for new products and service. Where the firm's marketing strategy calls for a high level of service, integrated channels are used to ensure that the service does get performed.[19] Later on, an exporter may want to coordinate programs across markets on a regional basis, which is much easier if the channel is controlled.

The marketer's ability and willingness to exercise any type of power—whether reward, coercive, legitimate, referent, or expert—determines the extent of control. The exercise of control causes more incidents of conflict in channels of distribution than any other activity in the relationship. This points to the need for careful communication with foreign intermediaries about the marketer's intentions and also the need for certain control measures. These might include the marketer's need to be the sole source of advertising copy or to be in charge of all product-modification activities. Generally, the more control the marketer wishes to have, the more cost is involved in securing that control.

Continuity

Channel design decisions are the most long-term of the marketing mix decisions. Utmost care must therefore be taken in choosing the right type of channel, given the types of intermediaries available and any environmental threats that may affect the channel design. Occasionally, however, unpredictable events may occur. As an example, Cockspur, the largest distiller of rum in Barbados, negotiated an arrangement with one of the largest distributors in the United States. Almost immediately, the distributor was acquired by a company that thought liquor distribution did not fit its mission and thus eliminated the products and reassigned the salespeople. Years later, Cockspur was still without substantial distribution in the United States.[20]

Nurturing continuity rests heavily on the marketer because foreign distributors may have a more short-term view of the relationship. For example, Japanese wholesalers believe that it is important for manufacturers to follow up initial success with continuous improvement of the product. If such improvements are not forthcoming, competitors are likely to enter the market with similar, lower-priced products, and the wholesalers of the imported product will turn to the Japanese suppliers.

The U.S. manufacturers of Odoreaters experienced such a development. After three years of costly market development efforts together with a Japanese wholesaler, the firm had reached a sales level of 3.8 million pairs. However, six months after product introduction, 12 comparable Japanese products had already been introduced. Because Odoreaters was not able to improve its product substantially over time, its wholesaler made an exclusive agreement with a competing firm—Scholl Inc.—and terminated the relationship with Odoreaters. Even though Odoreaters managed to find a new distributor, its sales dropped significantly.[21]

Continuity is also expressed through visible market commitment. Industries abroad may be quite conservative; distributors will not generally support an outsider until they are sure it is in the market to stay. Such commitments include sending in technical or sales personnel or offering training, and setting up wholly-owned sales subsidiaries from the start—and staffing them with locals to help communicate that the company is there for the long term.[22] Investment in distributors may be literal (resulting in co-ownership in the future) or abstract (resulting in more solid commitment in the relationship).

Communication

Communication provides the exchange of information that is essential to the functioning of the channel. Communication is an important consideration in channel design, and it gains more emphasis in international distribution because of various types of distances that may cause problems. In the buyer–seller relationships in international markets, the distance that is perceived to exist between a buyer and a seller has five aspects, all of which are amplified in the international setting:[23]

1. Social distance: the extent to which each of the two entities in a relationship is familiar with the other's ways of operating
2. Cultural distance: the degree to which the norms, values, or working methods between the two entities differ because of their separate national characteristics
3. Technological distance: the differences between the product or process technologies of the two entities

4. Time distance: the time that must elapse between establishing contact or placing an order and the actual transfer of the product or service involved

5. Geographical distance: the physical distance between the locations of the two entities

All these dimensions must be considered when determining whether to use intermediaries and, if they are to be used, what types to use.

Communication, if properly utilized, will assist the international marketer in conveying the firm's goals to the distributors, in solving conflict situations, and in marketing the product overall. Communication is a two-way process that does not permit the marketer to dictate to intermediaries. Cases are well known in which the marketer is not able to make the firm's marketing program functional. Prices may not be competitive; promotional materials may be obsolete or inaccurate and not well received overall. This may be compounded if the exporter tries to transplant abroad procedures and programs used domestically.[24] Solving these types of problems is important to the welfare of both parties.

Channels of distribution, because of their sequential positioning of the entities involved, are not conducive to noiseless communication. The marketer must design a channel and choose intermediaries that guarantee good information flow. Proper communication involves not only the passage of information between channel members but also a better understanding of each party's needs and goals. This can be achieved through personal visits, exchange of personnel, or distribution advisory councils. Consisting of members from all channel participants, advisory councils meet regularly to discuss opportunities and problems that may have arisen.

Selection of Intermediaries

Once the basic design of the channel has been determined, the international marketer must begin a search to fill the defined roles with the best available candidates and must secure their cooperation.

Types of Intermediaries

Two basic decisions are involved in choosing the type of intermediaries to serve a particular market. First, the marketer must determine the type of relationship to have with intermediaries. The alternatives are distributorship and agency relationship. A **distributor** will purchase the product and will therefore exercise more independence than agencies. Distributors are typically organized along product lines and provide the international marketer with complete marketing services. **Agents** have less freedom of movement than distributors because they operate on a commission basis and do not usually physically handle the goods. This, in turn, allows the marketer control to make sure, for example, that the customer gets the most recent and appropriate product version. In addition to the business implications, the choice of type will have legal implications in terms of what the intermediary can commit its principal to and the ease of termination of the agreement.

Second, the international marketer must decide whether to utilize indirect exporting, direct exporting, or integrated distribution in penetrating a foreign market.[25] **Indirect exporting** requires dealing with another domestic firm that acts as a sales intermediary for the marketer, often taking over the international side of the marketer's operations. The benefits, especially in the short term, are that the exporter can use someone else's international channels without having to pay to set them up. But there may be long-term concerns in using this strategy if the marketer wants to actively and aggressively get into the markets itself. Indirect exporting is only practiced by firms very early on in their internationalization process. With **direct exporting,** the marketer takes direct responsibility for its products abroad by either selling directly to the foreign customer or finding a local representative to sell its products in the market. The third category of export marketing strategy, **integrated distribution,** requires the marketer to make an investment into the foreign market for the purpose of selling its products in that market or more broadly. This investment could be the opening, for example, of a German or EU sales office, a distribution hub, or even an assembly operation or manufacturing facility. Although the last set of strategies indicates longer-term commitment to a market, it is riskier than the first two because the marketer is making a major financial investment. For example, if the exporter moves from an agency agreement to a sales office, its costs for that market are now fixed costs (i.e., will be incurred even if no sales are made) instead of the previous variable costs. Setting up even a modest office may be expensive.[26] The cost of an office manager and a secretary can easily reach $100,000, while a full-scale sales office will cost $500,000 on an annual basis. Real estate costs can be substantial if the office is in a main business district.

The major types of intermediaries are summarized in Table 11.5. Care should be taken to understand conceptual differences that might exist from one market to another. For example, a **commissionario** may sell in his or her own name (as a distributor would) but for an undisclosed principal (an agency concept). Similarly, a **del credere agent** guarantees the solvency of the customer and may therefore be responsible to the supplier for payment by the customer.[27]

The respective strengths and weaknesses of various export intermediary types were discussed in Chapter 7.

Sources for Finding Intermediaries

Firms that have successful international distribution attest to the importance of finding top representatives.[28] This undertaking should be held in the same regard as recruiting and hiring within the company because an ineffective foreign distributor can set an exporter back years; it is almost better to have no distributor than a bad one in a major market.

The approach can be either passive or active. Foreign operations for a number of smaller firms start through an unsolicited order; the same can happen with foreign distribution. Distributors, wherever they are, are always on the lookout for product representation that can be profitable and status enhancing. The initial contact may result from an advertisement or from a trade show the marketer has participated in. For example, Timberland has traditionally expanded to new markets by responding to intermediaries who have approached it.[29]

Table 11.5	International Channel Intermediaries

Agents	
Foreign (Direct)	**Domestic (Indirect)**
Brokers	Brokers
Manufacturer's representatives	Export agents
Factors	EMCs
Managing agents	Webb-Pomerene associations
Purchasing agents	Commission agents

Distributors	
Distributors/dealers	Domestic wholesalers
Import jobbers	EMCs
Wholesalers/retailers	ETCs
	Complementary marketing

SOURCES: Peter B. Fitzpatrick and Alan S. Zimmerman, *Essentials of Export Marketing* (New York: American Management Association, 1985), 20; Bruce Seifert and John Ford, "Export Distribution Channels," *Columbia Journal of World Business* 24 (Summer 1989): 16; and **http://www.usatrade.gov**.

The marketer's best interest lies in taking an active role. The marketer should not simply use the first intermediary to show an interest in the firm. The choice should be a result of a careful planning process. The exporter should start by gaining an understanding of market conditions in order to define what is expected of an intermediary and what the exporter can offer in the relationship. At the same time, procedures need to be set for intermediary identification and evaluation.[30] The exporter does not have to do all of this independently; both governmental and private agencies can assist the marketer in locating intermediary candidates.

Governmental Agencies

The U.S. Department of Commerce has various services that can assist firms in identifying suitable representatives abroad. Some have been designed specifically for that purpose. A firm can subscribe to the department's Trade Opportunities Program (TOP), which matches product interests of over 70,000 foreign buyers with those indicated by the U.S. subscribers. The Country Directories of International Contacts (CDIC) provides the names and contact information for directories of importers, agents, trade associations, and government agencies on a country-by-country basis.[31] The government also provides a mechanism by which the marketer can indicate its interest in international markets. *The U.S. Exporters Yellow Pages* is a directory that includes information and display advertisements on more than 11,000 U.S. companies interested in exporting. *Commercial News USA* is a catalog-magazine featuring advertisements by U.S. producers distributed worldwide 12 times each year.

Two services are specifically designed for locating foreign representatives. The Agent/Distributor Service (ADS) locates foreign firms that are interested in export proposals submitted by U.S. firms and determines their willingness to correspond with the U.S. firm. Both U.S. and foreign commercial service posts abroad supply information on up to six representatives who meet these requirements. The International Company Profile (ICP) is a valuable service, especially when the screening of potential candidates takes place in markets where reliable data are not readily available. ICPs provide a trade profile of specific foreign firms. They also provide a general narrative report on the reliability of the foreign firm. All of the services are available for relatively small fees; for example, the cost for an ADS application is $250 per country.[32] An example of an ICP is provided in Figure 11.4. Furthermore, individual state agencies provide similar services. These are all available on an online basis.

Private Sources

The easiest approach for the firm seeking intermediaries is to consult trade directories. Country and regional business directories such as Kompass (Europe), Bottin International (worldwide), Nordisk Handelskalendar (Northern Europe), and the Japan Trade Directory are good places to start. Company lists by country and line of business can be ordered from Dun & Bradstreet, Reuben H. Donnelly, Kelly's Directory, and Johnston Publishing. Telephone directories, especially the yellow page sections or editions, can provide distributor lists. The Jaeger and Waldmann International Telex Directory can also be consulted. Although not detailed, these listings will give addresses and an indication of the products sold.

The firm can solicit the support of some of its facilitating agencies, such as banks, advertising agencies, shipping lines, and airlines. All these have substantial international information networks and can put them to work for their clients. The services available will vary by agency, depending on the size of its foreign operations. Some of the major U.S. flagship carriers—for example, Northwest Airlines—have special staffs for this purpose within their cargo operations. Banks usually have the most extensive networks through their affiliates and correspondent banks. Similarly, the exporter may solicit the help of associations or chambers of commerce. For example, interest in China may warrant contacting American Chambers of Commerce in Hong Kong and Shanghai.

Figure 11.4   Sample Report from the International Company Profile

I. FOREIGN COMPANY CONTACT and SIZE INFORMATION:

China Power
Rm. 2301, Saxson Road
Beijing 1000301, China
Mr. Sam, President
Tel: 86-10-6606-3072
Fax: 86-10-6606-3071
1992
Sales: RMB 100,000,000
Employees: 80 including 15 at the headquarters

II. BACKGROUND AND PRODUCT INFORMATION:

Operation
The firm is mainly engaged in selling industrial automation products. It is also engaged in contracting factory automation system projects which consist of system design, programming, installation, and pre-sales service. The firm started to provide services for machine tools refitting in the United States in 1996.

Company Background/History:
The firm is a wholly foreign owned enterprise registered in June of 1992 with the Municipal Administration for Industry & Commerce. The registered capital was USD 1,250,000. The firm is a subsidiary of Can International Ltd., who owns 100% of the firm.

Business Size: small

Major Subsidiaries:
Name: China Power
Add: Rm. 22, Saxson Road, Beijing
Tel: 86-10-6606-3072
Ownership: 80% owned by the firm

Parent Company:
Name: ABZ Ltd., Hong Kong
Line of Business: Investment

Public Record:
According to management, an introduction to the firm and its products was included in editions of the following publications: The People's Daily Overseas Edition, the Science & Technology Daily, the Industrial & Commercial Times, the Worker's Daily, and the Computer World.

Location:
A site visit was made on September 19, 1996. The firm is located in a prime commercial area. It rents office space of 130 square meters at the address shown above. It occupies one floor in a ten-story building, the condition of which is good.

Key Company Officials:
Mr. Sam, President, born on October 24, 1958, is a graduate of Oxford University in 1982. He is now active in the firm's day to day operation in charge of the overall management. Prior to joining the firm, he was employed by the Ministry of Communications from 1982–1989 and China Harbor Engineering Co. 1989–1992.
Mr. Taylor, Vice President, was born in 1948. He joined the firm in 1995 and is currently active in the day to day operations responsible for marketing and sales. Prior to joining the firm, he was employed as Chief Representative from 1984–1995 by CROWE, a foreign plastic company merged by Miller Automation.
Ms. Young, Vice President, is currently active in the firm's day to day operations in charge of finance.

III. REFERENCES:

Foreign Firms Represented:
MILLER AUTOMATION for industrial automation products.
WILDWORLD WARE for Ministry of Machinery's industrial software.
ZXC for low voltage electrical components.
CONTON for industrial computer.
TBP for analyzing instruments.
TINNER for power station meter & instruments.

Bank References: The firm maintains banking relationships with the Industrial & Commercial Bank of China Beijing Branch. However, Mr. Sam declined to provide the account number.

Local Chamber/Trade Association:
Under current investigation, the firm is not known to be a member of any local chambers or trade associations. However, President Sam is a member of China Harbor Association and China Material Handling Association.

Trade References:
PURCHASE TERRITORY:
International: 100%
Import from 90% from the U.S.A., 10% from Germany, Sweden and other countries
SALES TERRITORY: Local and International
Local: 95%; International: 5%
Exporting to South Africa
CUSTOMER TYPE:
Manufacturers: 100%
Major customers include Glass Bulb Co., Ltd.

Other customers include Iron & Steel Corporation.
PURCHASING AND SELLING ITEMS:
Purchasing Terms: L/C at sight T/T
Selling Terms: T/T
IMPORT & EXPORT: YES

IV. FINANCIAL DATA/CREDIT WORTHINESS INFORMATION:

Financial Highlights of the firm for the period January 1 to December 31, 1995 is shown below:
AMOUNT IN RMB
Sales   100,000,000
Total Assets   30,000,000
The firm declined to provide its financial statement due to "tax concerns."

V. MARKET INFORMATION AND OUTLOOK:

According to Mr. Sam, the firm is the sole "Gold Partner" of Miller Automation. Note: To be a "Gold Partner," the firm's sales volume should be more than 50 percent in the China market.

VI. SPECIAL REQUEST INFORMATION: n/a

VII. REPUTATION: Unknown

VIII. POST COMMENTS/ EVALUATION:

As far as can be seen from the information supplied, the firm seems to be a satisfactory contact. EAJ Inc. may, however, wish to contact USFCS Hong Kong to obtain more information of China Power's parent company, Can International Ltd.

IX. SOURCES OF INFORMATION:

Dun & Bradstreet Report
NOTE: The information in this report has been supplied to the United States Government by commercial and government sources in the countries covered and its intended for the sole use of the purchaser. You are requested to honor the trust of these sources by not making secondary distribution of the data. While every effort is made to supply current and accurate information, the U.S. Government assumes no responsibility or liability for any decision based on the content of the ICP.

SOURCE: Example provided by Export Promotion Services, International Trade Administration, U.S. Department of Commerce.

The marketer can take an even more direct approach by buying space to solicit representation. Advertisements typically indicate the type of support the marketer will be able to give to its distributor. An example of an advertisement for intermediaries placed in a trade medium is provided in Figure 11.5. For example, Medtech International, an exporter of surgical gloves, advertises for intermediaries in magazines such as *International Hospital Supplies.* Trade fairs are an important

Figure 11.5	Advertisement for an Intermediary

forum to meet potential distributors and to get data on intermediaries in the industry. Increasingly, marketers are using their Web sites to attract international distributors and agents. For example, P&D Creative, Inc. uses its Web page to solicit distribution for its line of environmentally safe cleaning products. It promotes its site in search engines and internationally oriented newsgroups and provides pricing and product information of interest to intermediaries.[33] The marketer may also deal directly with contacts from previous applications, launch new mail solicitations, use its own sales organization for the search, or communicate with existing customers to find prospective distributors. The latter may happen after a number of initial (unsolicited) sales to a market, causing the firm to want to enter the market on a more formal basis. If resources permit, the international marketer can use outside service agencies or consultants to generate a list of prospective representatives.

The purpose of using the sources summarized in Table 11.6 is to generate as many prospective representatives as possible for the next step, screening.

Screening Intermediaries

In most firms, the evaluation of candidates involves both what to look for and where to go for the information. At this stage, the international marketer knows the type of distributor that is needed. The potential candidates must now be compared and contrasted against determining criteria. Although the criteria to be used vary by industry and by product, a good summary list is provided in Table 11.7. Especially when various criteria are being weighed, these lists must be updated to reflect changes in the environment and the marketer's own situation. Some criteria can be characterized as determinant, in that they form the core dimensions along which candidates must perform well, whereas some criteria, although important, may be used only in preliminary screening. This list should correspond closely to the exporter's own determinants of success—all the things that have to be done better to beat out competition.

Table 11.6	Sources for Locating Foreign Intermediaries

1. Distributor inquiries
2. Home government (e.g., U.S. Department of Commerce)
   Trade Opportunities Program
   Commercial Service International Contacts
   Country Directories of International Contacts
   Agent/Distributor Service
   International Company Profile
3. Host government
   Representative offices
   Import promotion efforts
4. Trade sources
   Magazines, journals
   Directories
   Associations and Chambers of Commerce
   Banks, advertising agencies, carriers
5. Field sales organizations
6. Customers
7. Direct-mail solicitation/contact of previous applicants
8. Trade fairs
9. Web sites
10. Independent consultants

Table 11.7	Selection Criteria for Choosing an International Distributor

Characteristics	Weight	Rating
Goals and strategies	—	—
Size of the firm	—	—
Financial strength	—	—
Reputation	—	—
Trading areas covered	—	—
Compatibility	—	—
Experience in products/with competitors	—	—
Sales organization	—	—
Physical facilities	—	—
Willingness to carry inventories	—	—
After-sales service capability	—	—
Use of promotion	—	—
Sales performance	—	—
Relations with local government	—	—
Communications	—	—
Overall attitude/commitment	—	—

Before signing a contract with a particular agent or a distributor, international marketers should satisfy themselves on certain key criteria. A number of these key criteria can be easily quantified, thereby providing a solid base for comparisons between candidates, whereas others are qualitative and require careful interpretation and confidence in the data sources providing the information.

Performance

The financial standing of the candidate is one of the most important criteria, as well as a good starting point. This figure will show whether the distributor is making money and is able to perform some of the necessary marketing functions such as extension of credit to customers and risk absorption. Financial reports are not always complete or reliable, or they may lend themselves to interpretation differences, pointing to a need for third-party opinion. Many Latin American intermediaries lack adequate capital, a situation that can lead to more time spent managing credit than managing marketing strategy. Therefore, at companies like Xerox, assessment focuses on cash flow and the intermediary's ability to support its operations without outside help.[34]

Sales are another excellent indicator. What the distributor is presently doing gives an indication of how he or she could perform if chosen to handle the international marketer's product. The distributor's sales strength can be determined by analyzing management ability and the adequacy and quality of the sales team. If the intermediary is an importer or wholesaler, its ability to provide customer service to the next channel level is a critical determinant of future sales. Pernod Ricard selects its distribution partners based on their ability to have every needed product on hand and on time at retail locations.[35]

The distributor's existing product lines should be analyzed along four dimensions: competitiveness, compatibility, complementary nature, and quality. Quite often, international marketers find that the most desirable distributors in a given market are already handling competitive products and are therefore unavailable. In that case, the marketer can look for an equally qualified distributor handling related products. The complementary nature of products may be of interest to both parties, especially in industrial markets, where ultimate customers may be in the market for complete systems or one-stop shopping. The quality match for products is important for product positioning reasons; a high-quality product may suffer unduly from a questionable distributor reputation. The number of product lines handled gives the marketer an indication of the level of effort to expect from the distributor. Some distributors are interested in carrying as many products and product lines as possible to enhance their own standing, but they have the time and the willingness to actively sell only those that bring the best compensation. At this time, it is also important to check the candidate's physical facilities for handling the product. This is essential particularly for products that may be subject to quality changes, such as food products. The assessment should also include the candidate's marketing materials, including a possible Web site, for adequacy and appropriateness.

The distributor's market coverage must be determined. The analysis of coverage will include not only how much territory, or how many segments of the market, are covered, but also how well the markets are served. Again, the characteristics of the sales force and the number of sales offices are good quantitative indicators. To study the quality of the distributor's market coverage, the marketer can check whether the sales force visits executives, engineers, and operating people or concentrates mainly on purchasing agents. In some areas of the world, the marketer has to make sure that two distributors will not end up having territorial overlaps, which can lead to unnecessary conflict.

Professionalism

The distributor's reputation must be checked. This rather abstract measure takes its value from a number of variables that all should help the marketer forecast fit and effectiveness. The distributor's customers, suppliers, facilitating agencies, competitors, and other members of the local business community should be contacted for information on the business conduct of the distributor in such areas as buyer–seller relations and ethical behavior. This effort will shed light on variables that may be important only in certain parts of the world; for example, variables such as political clout, which is essential in certain developing countries.

The marketer must acknowledge the distributor as an independent entity with its own goals. The distributor's business strategy must therefore be determined, particularly what the distributor expects to get from the relationship and where the international marketer fits into those plans. Because a channel relationship is long term, the distributor's views on future expansion of the product line or its distribution should be clarified. This phase will also require a determination of the degree of help the distributor would need in terms of price, credit, delivery, sales training, communication, personal visits, product modification, warranty, advertising, warehousing, technical support, and after-sales service. Leaving uncertainties in these areas will cause major problems later.

Finally, the marketer should determine the distributor's overall attitude in terms of cooperation and commitment to the marketer. An effective way of testing this, and weeding out the less interested candidates, is to ask the distributor to assist in developing a local marketing plan or to develop one. This endeavor will bring out potential problem areas and will spell out which party is to perform the various marketing functions. It is important that both parties commit to two-way communication to ensure long-term success, especially in cases of considerable distances.[36]

A criteria list is valuable only when good data are available on each and every criterion. Although the initial screening can take place at the firm's offices, the three to five finalists should be visited. No better method of assessing distributors exists than visiting them, inspecting their facilities, and interviewing their various constituents in the market. A number of other critical data sources are important for firms without the resources for on-site inspection. The distributor's suppliers or firms not in direct competition can provide in-depth information. A bona fide candidate will also provide information through a local bank. Credit reports are available through the National Association of Credit Management, Dun & Bradstreet, and local credit-reporting agencies as discussed in Chapter 9.

The Distributor Agreement

When the international marketer has found a suitable intermediary, a foreign sales agreement is drawn up.[37] The agreement can be relatively simple, but given the numerous differences in the market environments, certain elements are essential. The checklist presented in Table 11.8 is the most comprehensive in stipulating the nature of the contract and the respective rights and responsibilities of the marketer and the distributor.

Table 11.8	Elements of a Distributor Agreement

A. Basic Components
   1. Parties to the agreement
   2. Statement that the contract supersedes all previous agreements
   3. Duration of the agreement (perhaps a three- or six-month trial period)
   4. Territory:
      a. Exclusive, nonexclusive, sole
      b. Manufacturer's right to sell direct at reduced or no commission to local government and old customers
   5. Products covered
   6. Expression of intent to comply with government regulations
   7. Clauses limiting sales forbidden by U.S. Export Controls or practices forbidden by the Foreign Corrupt Practices Act
B. Manufacturer's Rights
   1. Arbitration:
      a. If possible, in the manufacturer's country
      b. If not, before international Chamber of Commerce or American Arbitration Association, or using the London Court of Arbitration rules
      c. Definition of rules to be applied (e.g., in selecting the arbitration panel)
      d. Assurance that award will be binding in the distributor's country
   2. Jurisdiction that of the manufacturer's country (the signing completed at home); if not possible, a neutral site such as Sweden or Switzerland
   3. Termination conditions (e.g., no indemnification if due notice given)
   4. Clarification of tax liabilities
   5. Payment and discount terms
   6. Conditions for delivery of goods
   7. Nonliability for late delivery beyond manufacturer's reasonable control
   8. Limitation on manufacturer's responsibility to provide information
   9. Waiver of manufacturer's responsibility to keep lines manufactured outside the United States (e.g., licensees) outside of covered territory
   10. Right to change prices, terms, and conditions at any time
   11. Right of manufacturer or agent to visit territory and inspect books
   12. Right to repurchase stock
   13. Option to refuse or alter distributor's orders
   14. Training of distributor personnel in the United States subject to:
      a. Practicality
      b. Costs to be paid by the distributor
      c. Waiver of manufacturer's responsibility for U.S. immigration approval
C. Distributor's Limitations and Duties
   1. No disclosure of confidential information
   2. Limitation of distributor's right to assign contract
   3. Limitation of distributor's position as legal agent of manufacturer
   4. Penalty clause for late payment

(continued)

Table 11.8	Elements of a Distributor Agreement (*continued*)

5. Limitation of right to handle competing lines
6. Placement of responsibility for obtaining customs clearance
7. Distributor to publicize designation as authorized representative in defined area
8. Requirement to move all signs or evidence identifying distributor with manufacturer if relationship ends
9. Acknowledgment by distributor of manufacturer's ownership of trademark, trade names, patents
10. Information to be supplied by the distributor:
    a. Sales reports
    b. Names of active prospects
    c. Government regulations dealing with imports
    d. Competitive products and competitors' activities
    e. Price at which goods are sold
    f. Complete data on other lines carried (on request)
11. Information to be supplied by distributor on purchasers
12. Accounting methods to be used by distributor
13. Requirement to display products appropriately
14. Duties concerning promotional efforts
15. Limitation of distributor's right to grant unapproved warranties, make excessive claims
16. Clarification of responsibility arising from claims and warranties
17. Responsibility of distributor to provide repair and other services
18. Responsibility to maintain suitable place of business
19. Responsibility to supply all prospective customers
20. Understanding that certain sales approaches and sales literature must be approved by manufacturer
21. Prohibition of manufacture or alteration of products
22. Requirement to maintain adequate stock, spare parts
23. Requirement that inventory be surrendered in event of a dispute that is pending in court
24. Prohibition of transshipments

SOURCE: Adapted from "Elements of a Distributor Agreement," *Business International,* March 29, 1963, 23–24. Some of the sections have been changed to reflect the present situation.

Contract duration is important, especially when an agreement is signed with a new distributor. In general, distribution agreements should be for a specified, relatively short period (one or two years). The initial contract with a new distributor should stipulate a trial period of either three or six months, possibly with minimum purchase requirements. Duration should be determined with an eye on the local laws and their stipulations on distributor agreements. These will be discussed later in conjunction with distributor termination.

Geographic boundaries for the distributor should be determined with care, especially by smaller firms. Future expansion of the product market might be complicated if a distributor claims rights to certain territories. The marketer should retain the right to distribute products independently, reserving the right to certain customers. For example, many marketers maintain a dual distribution system, dealing directly with certain large accounts. This type of arrangement should be explicitly stated in the agreement. Transshipments, sales to customers outside the agreed-upon territory or customer type, have to be explicitly prohibited to prevent the occurrence of parallel importation.

The payment section of the contract should stipulate the methods of payment as well as how the distributor or agent is to draw compensation. Distributors derive compensation from various discounts, such as the functional discount, whereas agents earn a specific commission percentage of net sales (such as 15 percent). Given the volatility of currency markets, the agreement should also state the currency to be used. The international marketer also needs to make sure that none of the compensation forwarded to the distributor is in violation of the Foreign Corrupt Practices Act or the OECD guidelines. A violation occurs if a payment is made to influence a foreign official in exchange for business favors, depending on the nature of the action sought. So-called grease or **facilitating payments,** such as a small fee to expedite paperwork through customs, are not considered violations.[38]

Product and conditions of sale need to be agreed on. The products or product lines included should be stipulated, as well as the functions and responsibilities of the intermediary in terms of carrying the goods in inventory, providing service in conjunction with them, and promoting them. Conditions of sale determine which party is to be responsible for some of the expenses involved, which will in turn have an effect on the price to the distributor. These conditions include credit and shipment terms.

Effective means of communication between the parties must be stipulated in the agreement if a marketer–distributor relationship is to succeed. The marketer should have access to all information concerning the marketing of his or her products in the distributor's territory, including past records, present situation assessments, and marketing research concerning the future. Communication channels should be formal for the distributor to voice formal grievances. The contract should state the confidentiality of the information provided by either party and protect the intellectual property rights (such as patents) involved.

Channel Management

A channel relationship can be likened to a marriage in that it brings together two independent entities that have shared goals. For the relationship to work, each party must be open about its expectations and openly communicate changes perceived in the other's behavior that might be contrary to the agreement. The closer the relationship is to a distribution partnership, the more likely marketing success will materialize. Conflict will arise, ranging from small grievances (such as billing errors) to major ones (rivalry over channel duties), but it can be managed to enhance the overall channel relationship. In some cases, conflict may be caused by an outside entity, such as gray markets, in which unauthorized intermediaries compete for market share with legitimate importers and exclusive distributors. Nevertheless, the international marketer must solve the problem.

The relationship has to be managed for the long term. An exporter may in some countries have a seller's market situation that allows it to exert pressure on its intermediaries for concessions, for example. However, if environmental conditions change, the exporter may find that the channel support it needs to succeed is not there because of the manner in which it managed channel relationships in the past.[39] Firms with harmonious relationships are typically those with more experience abroad and those that are proactive in managing the channel relationship. Harmonious relationships are also characterized by more trust, communication, and cooperation between the entities and, as a result, by less conflict and perceived uncertainty.[40]

As an exporter's operations expand, the need for coordination across markets may grow. Therefore, the exporter may want to establish distributor advisory councils to help in reactive measures (e.g., how to combat parallel importation) or proactive measures (e.g., how to transfer best practice from one distributor to another). Naturally, such councils are instrumental in building esprit de corps for the long-term success of the distribution system.

Factors in Channel Management

An excellent framework for managing channel relationships is shown in Figure 11.6. The complicating factors that separate the two parties fall into three categories: ownership; geographic, cultural, and economic distance; and different rules

Figure 11.6 Performance Problems and Remedies When Using Overseas Distributors

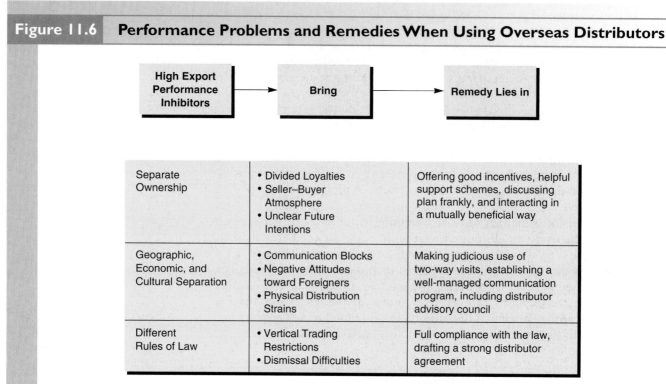

High Export Performance Inhibitors	→ Bring	→ Remedy Lies in
Separate Ownership	• Divided Loyalties • Seller–Buyer Atmosphere • Unclear Future Intentions	Offering good incentives, helpful support schemes, discussing plan frankly, and interacting in a mutually beneficial way
Geographic, Economic, and Cultural Separation	• Communication Blocks • Negative Attitudes toward Foreigners • Physical Distribution Strains	Making judicious use of two-way visits, establishing a well-managed communication program, including distributor advisory council
Different Rules of Law	• Vertical Trading Restrictions • Dismissal Difficulties	Full compliance with the law, drafting a strong distributor agreement

SOURCE: Adapted from Philip J. Rosson, "Success Factors in Manufacturer-Overseas Distributor Relationships in International Marketing," in *International Marketing Management*, ed. Erdener Kaynak (New York: Praeger, 1984), 91–107.

of law. Rather than lament their existence, both parties need to take strong action to remedy them. Often, the major step is acknowledgment that differences do indeed exist.

In international marketing, manufacturers and distributors are usually independent entities. Distributors typically carry the products of more than one manufacturer and judge products by their ability to generate revenue without added expense. The international marketer, in order to receive disproportionate attention for its concerns, may offer both monetary and psychological rewards.

Distance, whether it is geographic, psychological, economic, or a combination, can be bridged through effective two-way communication. This should go beyond normal routine business communication to include innovative ways of sharing pertinent information. The international marketer may place one person in charge of distributor-related communications or put into effect an interpenetration strategy—that is, an exchange of personnel so that both organizations gain further insight into the workings of the other.[41] The existence of cross-cultural differences in people's belief systems and behavior patterns have to be acknowledged and acted on for effective channel management. For example, in markets where individualism is stressed, local channel partners may seek arrangements that foster their own self-interest and may expect their counterparts to watch out for themselves. Conflict is seen as a natural phenomenon. In societies of low individualism, however, a common purpose is fostered between the partners.[42]

Economic distance manifests itself in exchange rates, for example. Instability of exchange rates can create serious difficulties for distributors in their trading activities, not only with their suppliers but also with their domestic customers. Manufacturers and distributors should develop and deploy mutually acceptable mechanisms that allow for some flexibility in interactions when unforeseen rate fluctuations occur.[43] For example, Harley Davidson has instituted a system of risk sharing in which it will maintain a single foreign currency price as long as the spot exchange rate does not move beyond a mutually agreed-upon rate. Should it happen, Harley Davidson and the distributor will share the costs or benefits of the change.

Laws and regulations in many markets may restrict the manufacturer in terms of control. For example, in the European Union, the international marketer cannot prevent a distributor from reexporting products to customers in another member country, even though the marketer has another distributor in that market. EU law insists on a single market where goods and services can be sold throughout the area without restriction. In 1998, VW was fined €90 million and in 2000 GM €43 million for taking steps to limit intra-EU imports. Even monitoring parallel imports may be considered to be in restraint of trade.

Most of the criteria used in selecting intermediaries can be used to evaluate existing intermediaries as well. If not conducted properly and fairly, however, evaluation can be a source of conflict. In addition to being given the evaluation results in order to take appropriate action, the distributor should be informed of the evaluative criteria and should be a part of the overall assessment process. Again, the approach should be focused on serving mutual benefits. For example, it is important that the exporter receive detailed market and financial performance data from the distributor. Most distributors identify these data as the key sources of power in distribution and may, therefore, be inherently reluctant to provide them in full detail. The exchange of such data is often the best indicator of a successful relationship.[44]

A part of the management process is channel adjustment. This can take the form of channel shift (eliminating a particular type of channel), channel modification (changing individual members while leaving channel structure intact), or role or relationship modification (changing functions performed or the reward structure) as a result of channel evaluation. The need for channel change should be well established and not executed hastily because it will cause a major distraction in the operations of the firm. Some companies have instituted procedures that require executives to consider carefully all of the aspects and potential results of change before execution.

Gray Markets

Gray markets, or **parallel importation,** refer to authentic and legitimately manufactured trademark items that are produced and purchased abroad but imported or diverted to the United States by bypassing designated channels.[45] The value of gray markets in the United States has been estimated at $20 billion at retail. Gray marketed products vary from inexpensive consumer goods (such as chewing gum) to expensive capital goods (such as excavation equipment). The phenomenon is not restricted to the United States; Japan, for example, has witnessed gray markets because of the high value of the yen and the subsidization of cheaper exports through high taxes. Japanese marketers thus often found it cheaper to go to Los Angeles to buy export versions of Japanese-made products.

An example of the phenomenon is provided in Figure 11.7, which shows the flow of Seiko watches through authorized and unauthorized channels. Seiko is a good example of a typical gray market product in that it carries a well-known trademark. Unauthorized importers, such as Progress Trading Company in New York, and retailers, such as Kmart or Gem of the Day, buy Seiko watches around the world at advantageous prices and then sell them to consumers at substantial discounts over authorized Seiko dealers. Seiko has fought back, for example, by advertising warnings to consumers against buying gray market watches on the grounds that these products may be obsolete or worn-out models and that consumers might have problems with their warranties. Many gray marketers, however, provide their own warranty-related service and guarantee watches sold through them. Since watches have strong commercial potential online due to the power of their brand identities, gray-market watch Web sites are having the most impact on higher-priced watch lines selling for $1,000 retail. Authorized retailers are being forced to take bigger discounts to keep from losing sales.[46]

Figure 11.7 Seiko's Authorized and Unauthorized Channels of Distribution

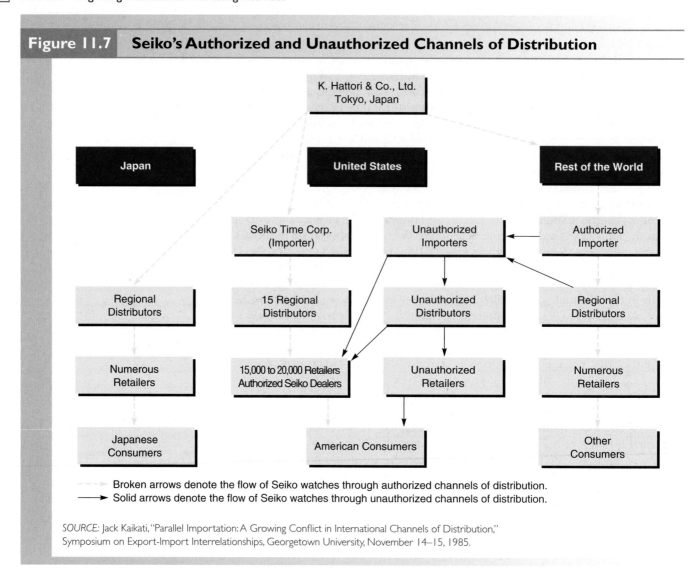

Broken arrows denote the flow of Seiko watches through authorized channels of distribution.
Solid arrows denote the flow of Seiko watches through unauthorized channels of distribution.

SOURCE: Jack Kaikati, "Parallel Importation: A Growing Conflict in International Channels of Distribution," Symposium on Export-Import Interrelationships, Georgetown University, November 14–15, 1985.

Various conditions allow unauthorized resellers to exist. The most important are price segmentation and exchange rate fluctuations. Competitive conditions may require the international marketer to sell essentially the same product at different prices in different markets or to different customers.[47] Because many products are priced higher in, for example, the United States, a gray marketer can purchase them in Europe or the Far East and offer discounts between 10 and 40 percent below list price when reselling them in the U.S. market. Exchange rate fluctuations can cause price differentials and thus opportunities for gray marketers. For example, during the Asian financial crisis, gray marketers imported Caterpillar, Deere, and Komatsu construction and earth-moving equipment no longer needed for halted projects in markets such as Thailand and Indonesia—and usually never used—for as little as 60 percent of what U.S. dealers paid wholesale.[48] In some cases, gray markets emerge as a result of product shortages. For example, at one time, many U.S. computer manufacturers had to turn to gray marketers to secure their supply of DRAMs or else watch their production lines grind to a halt.[49] However, in these cases, the gray market goods typically cost more than those usually available through authorized suppliers. In other cases, if there are multiple production sites for the same product, gray markets can emerge due to negative perceptions about the country of origin, as seen in the case highlighted in *The International Marketplace 11.2.*

Gray market flows have increased as current barriers to trade are being eliminated. The European Union has significant parallel importation due to significant price differentials in ethical drugs, which are in turn the result of differences in regulation, insurance coverage, medical practice, and exchange rates. Of the fifteen member countries, only Denmark grants manufacturers the freedom to price their ethical drugs. The share of parallel trade is estimated at 15 percent and is expected to grow since the European Commission is supporting the practice.[50] A similar controversy has emerged in the United States, where prescription drugs are priced at 34 percent higher than in Canada and where some are advocating the reimportation of these drugs from Canada to the United States.

Opponents and supporters of the practice disagree on whether the central issue is price or trade rights. Detractors typically cite the following arguments: (1) the gray market unduly hurts the legitimate owners of trademarks; (2) without protection, trademark owners will have little incentive to invest in product development; (3) gray marketers will "free ride" or take unfair advantage of the trademark owners' marketing and promotional activities; and (4) parallel imports can deceive consumers by not meeting product standards or their normal expectations of after-sale service. The bottom line is that gray market goods can severely undercut local marketing plans, erode long-term brand images, eat up costly promotion funds, and sour manufacturer–intermediary relations. The opponents scored a major victory when the European Court of Justice ruled in 2001 against Tesco, which imported cheap Levi jeans from the United States and sold them at prices well below those of other retailers. The decision backed Levi's claim that its image could be harmed if it lost control of import distribution. Tesco can continue sourcing Levi's products within the EU from the cheapest provider, but not from outside it.[51]

Proponents of parallel importation approach the issue from an altogether different point of view. They argue for their right to "free trade" by pointing to manufacturers that are both overproducing and overpricing in some markets. The main beneficiaries are consumers, who benefit from lower prices and discount distributors, with whom some of the manufacturers do not want to deal and who have now, because of gray markets, found a profitable market niche.

In response to the challenge, manufacturers have chosen various approaches. Despite the Supreme Court ruling in May 1988 to legitimize gray markets in the United States,[52] foreign manufacturers, U.S. companies manufacturing abroad, and authorized retailers have continued to fight the practice. In January 1991, the U.S. Customs Service enacted a new rule whereby trademarked goods that have been authorized for manufacture and sale abroad by U.S. trademark holders will no longer be allowed into the United States through parallel channels.[53] Those parallel importing goods of overseas manufacturers will not be affected. Recently, courts have taken exception to cases that have shown evidence of deception. For example, Lever Brothers won a long case to stop discounters from selling Sunlight brand dishwashing detergent, produced for the British market, in the United States. Because tap water is generally harder in Britain, formulation of the product there is different from Lever's U.S. version, which produces more lather. Lever reported lost sales and complaints from customers who bought the British brand and were disappointed.

The solution for the most part lies with the contractual relationships that tie businesses together. In almost all cases of gray marketing, someone in the authorized channel commits a diversion, thus violating the agreements signed. One of the standard responses is therefore disenfranchisement of such violators. This approach is a clear response to complaints from the authorized dealers who are being hurt by transshipments. Tracking down offenders is quite expensive and time-consuming, however. Some of the gray marketers can be added to the authorized dealer network if mutually acceptable terms can be reached, thereby increasing control of the channel of distribution.[54]

THE INTERNATIONAL MARKETPLACE 11.2

Country of Origin and Gray Markets

Since the Russian currency crisis of 1998, global oil prices have fueled a boom that has not only replenished government coffers, but also boosted wages across the board and given many Asian, European, and North American marketers reason to look at the market. While expenditures by businesses and consumers tend to be modest by international standards (e.g., annual expenditure on Procter & Gamble products in Russia is $3 annually vs. $77 in the United States), the buyers are extremely quality aware and brand-conscious. Making erroneous assumptions in this regard may be costly, as Canon found with its operations.

As part of a strategic initiative to relocate products and transfer technology, Canon moved the production of its basic model 1215 copier to China. One of the world's leading manufacturers of cameras, optical products, imaging equipment, and computer peripherals, Canon believes in being an organization that undertakes optimal production activities worldwide. It does so through its 120 subsidiaries around the globe.

The change of country of origin from Japan to China was not expected to affect buyers. However, in Russia, Canon found quite the opposite to be true. In many high-technology product categories, both Russian trade and retail customers divided products into three categories: "white" ones, made in Europe or the United States, the best made and subsequently premium priced; "red" ones, assembled in Russia and considered with suspicion; and "yellow" ones, from Asia and rated somewhere in between red and white. However, in China's case, the perception among Russians has traditionally been that technology flows there from Russia but not vice versa, and that nothing interesting in terms of technology can originate from China.

The problem was identified relatively quickly—within three months of the change in source of supply—and the sourcing was redirected back to Japan. However, in the meantime, many intermediaries in Dubai, Hong Kong, and Singapore identified an opportunity and offered Russian customers "made in Japan" versions of the same product while the official channel was stuck with the "made in China" counterparts.

In a worst-case scenario, Canon would have been forced to sell the copiers at any price. However, it undertook the following campaign, which resulted in the swift sale of all the Chinese-made copiers:

1. It developed an "officially imported" hologram, which was attached to every Canon product acquired through official channels in Russia
2. It offered to profile dealers as authorized resellers through a dealer-participatory campaign in which their names were included in the advertisements
3. It offered final customers a premium, a Canon BP-7 camera.

The accompanying advertisement appeared in Russian trade magazines to deliver this message. It portrays the hologram and states the following benefits of buying from official dealers (while implicitly warning readers not to buy from other sources): technical support and training, Russian-language instructions and manuals, product support, and local service.

SOURCES: Example courtesy of Jouko Tuominen, Oy Canon Ab, "To Russia with Love: The Multinationals' Song," *Business Week*, September 16, 2002, 54; and "Laptops from Lapland," *The Economist*, September 6, 1997, 67–68; **http://www.canon.com**.

A one-price policy can eliminate one of the main reasons for gray markets. This means choosing the most efficient of the distribution channels through which to market the product, but it may also mean selling at the lowest price to all customers regardless of location and size. A meaningful one-price strategy must also include a way to reward the providers of other services, such as warranty repair, in the channel.

Other strategies have included producing different versions of products for different markets. For example, Minolta Camera Company markets an identical camera in the United States and Japan but gives it different names and warranties. Some companies have introduced price incentives to consumers. Hasselblad, the Swedish camera manufacturer, offers rebates to purchasers of legally imported, serial-numbered camera bodies, lenses, and roll-fill magazines. Many manufacturers promote the benefits of dealing with authorized dealers (and, thereby, the dan-

gers of dealing with gray market dealers). For example, Rolex's message states that authorized dealers are the only ones who are capable of providing genuine accessories and can ensure that the customer gets an authentic product and the appropriate warranty.

Termination of the Channel Relationship

Many reasons exist for the termination of a channel relationship, but the most typical are changes in the international marketer's distribution approach (for example, establishing a sales office) or a (perceived) lack of performance by the intermediary. On occasion, termination may result from either party not honoring agreements; for example, by selling outside assigned territories and initiating price wars.[55]

Channel relationships go through a life cycle. The concept of an international distribution life cycle is presented in Figure 11.8. Over time, the manufacturer's

Figure 11.8 International Distribution Life Cycle

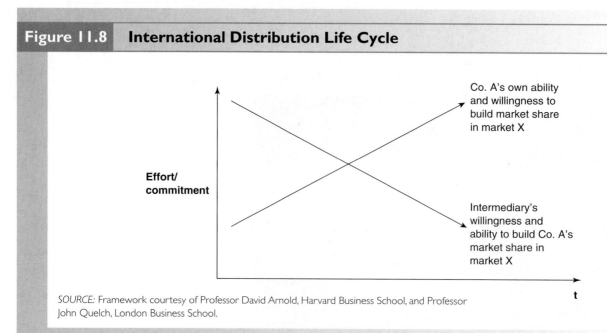

SOURCE: Framework courtesy of Professor David Arnold, Harvard Business School, and Professor John Quelch, London Business School.

marketing capabilities increase while a distributor's ability and willingness to grow the manufacturer's business in that market decreases. When a producer expands its market presence, it may expect more of a distributor's effort than the distributor is willing to make available. Furthermore, with expansion, the manufacturer may want to expand its product line to items that the distributor is neither interested in nor able to support. In some cases, intermediaries may not be interested in growing the business beyond a certain point (e.g., due to progressive taxation in the country) or as aggressively as the principal may expect (i.e., being more of an order-taker than an order-getter). As a marketer's operations expand, it may want to start to coordinate operations across markets for efficiency and customer-service reasons or to cater to global accounts—thereby needing to control distribution to a degree that independent intermediaries are not willing to accept, or requiring a level of service that they may not be able to deliver. If termination is a result of such a structural change, the situation has to be handled carefully. The effect of termination on the intermediary has to be understood, and open communication is needed to make the transition smooth. For example, the intermediary can be compensated for investments made, and major customers can be visited jointly to assure them that service will be uninterrupted.

Termination conditions are one of the most important considerations in the distributor agreement, because the just causes for termination vary and the penalties for the international marketer may be substantial. Just causes include fraud or deceit, damage to the other party's interest, or failure to comply with contract obligations concerning minimum inventory requirements or minimum sales levels. These must be spelled out carefully because local courts are often favorably disposed toward local businesses. In some countries, termination may not even be possible. In the EU and Latin America, terminating an ineffective intermediary is time-consuming and expensive. One year's average commissions are typical for termination without justification. A notice of termination has to be given three to six months in advance. In Austria, termination without just cause and/or failure to give notice of termination may result in damages amounting to average commissions for between 1 and 15 years.

The time to think about such issues is before the overseas distribution agreement is signed. It is especially prudent to find out what local laws say about termination and to check what type of experience other firms have had in the particular country. Careful preparation can allow the exporter to negotiate a termination without litigation. If the distributor's performance is unsatisfactory, careful documentation and clearly defined performance measures may help show that the distributor has more to gain by going quietly than by fighting.

E-Commerce

At the beginning of a new century, the majority of firms still see a Web site as a marketing and advertising tool without expanding it to order-taking capabilities.[56] That is changing rapidly. As shown in Table 11.9, e-commerce, the ability to offer goods and services over the Web (both business to consumer [B2C] and business to business [B2B]) is expected to reach a compound annual growth rate of 100 percent in the next few years around the world. While the United States accounts for the majority of e-commerce activity, the non-U.S. portion is expected to double in the next few years, with Western Europe providing the most significant growth. A survey by KPMG Management Consulting showed 500 European-based large and medium-sized companies getting about 2 percent of their total sales from e-commerce, and expecting it to be 20 percent by 2003.[57] The biggest engine of growth for B2B e-commerce is expected to be global transactions.

Many companies willing to enter e-commerce will not have to do it on their own. Hub sites (also known as virtual malls, e-marketplaces, or digital intermediaries) will bring together buyers, sellers, distributors, and transaction payment processors in one single marketplace, making convenience the key attraction. With 1,400 of them in place,[58] entities such as Compare.net (**http://www.compare.net**), Priceline.com (**http://www.priceline.com**), eBay (**http://www.ebay.com**), ECnet (**http://ecnet.com**), and VerticalNet (**http://www.verticalnet.com**) are leading the way.[59]

As soon as customers have the ability to access a company through the Internet, the company itself has to be prepared to provide 24-hour order taking and customer service, to acquire the regulatory and customs-handling expertise to deliver internationally, and to develop an in-depth understanding of marketing environments for the further development of the business relationship. The instantaneous interactivity users' experience will also be translated into an expectation of expedient delivery of answers and products ordered. Many people living outside the United States who want to purchase online expect U.S.-style service. However, in many cases, they may find that shipping is not even available outside the United States.

The challenges faced in terms of response and delivery capabilities can be overcome by outsourcing services or by building international distribution networks. Air express carriers such as DHL, FedEx, and UPS offer full-service packages that leverage their own Internet infrastructure with customs clearance and

Table 11.9	Worldwide E-Commerce Revenue by Region (in $ billions)		
Region	**2001**	**2006**	**Compound Annual Growth**
United States	255.8	1,917.8	49.6%
Western Europe	153.7	1,985.3	66.8%
Japan	99.0	602.5	43.5%
Asia/Pacific	37.4	892.7	88.6%
Rest of World	52.0	335.6	45.2%
Share of B2B	81.8%	89.3%	

SOURCE: From IDC Internet Commerce Market Model, Version 8.3; **http://www.idc.com**.

e-mail shipment notification. If a company needs help in order fulfilment and customer support, logistics centers offer warehousing and inventory management services as well as same-day delivery from in-country stocks. DHL, for example, has seven express logistics centers and 45 strategic parts centers worldwide, with key centers in Bahrain for the Middle East, Brussels for Europe, and Singapore for Asia-Pacific. Some companies elect to build their own international distribution networks. Both QVC, a televised shopping service, and amazon.com, an online retailer of books and consumer goods, have distribution centers in Britain and Germany to take advantage of the European Internet audience and to fulfill more quickly and cheaply the orders generated by their Web sites.

Transactions and the information they provide about the buyer allow for greater customization and for service by region, by market, or even by individual customer. One of the largest online sellers, Dell Computer, builds a Premier Page for its corporate customers with more than 400 employees, which is linked to the customer's intranet and thus allows approved employees to configure PCs, pay for them, and track their delivery status. Premier Pages also provide access to instant technical support and Dell sales representatives. Presently there are 5,000 companies with such service, and $5 million worth of Dell PCs are ordered every day.[60]

Although English has long been perceived as the lingua franca of the Web, the share of non-English speakers worldwide increased to 65 percent in 2002. It has also been shown that Web users are three times more likely to buy when the offering is made in their own language.[61] However, not even the largest of firms can serve all markets with a full line of their products. Getting a Web site translated and running is an expensive proposition and, if done correctly, time-consuming as well. If the site is well developed, it will naturally lead to expectations that order fulfillment will be of equal caliber. Therefore, any worldwide Web strategy has to be tied closely with the company's overall growth strategy in world markets.

A number of hurdles and uncertainties are keeping some companies out of global markets or preventing them from exploiting these markets to their full potential. Some argue that the World Wide Web does not live up to its name, since it is mostly a tool for the United States and Europe. Yet, as Internet penetration levels increase in the near future, due to technological advances, improvements in many countries' Web infrastructures, and customer acceptance, e-business will become truly global. As a matter of fact, in some cases emerging markets may provide a chance to try out new approaches, because the markets and the marketers in them are not burdened by history, as seen in *The International Marketplace 11.3*.

The marketer has to be sensitive to the governmental role in e-commerce. No real consensus exists on the taxation of e-commerce, especially in the case of cross-border transactions. While the United States and the EU have agreed not to impose new taxes on sales through the Internet, there is no uniformity in the international taxation of transactions.[62] Other governments believe, however, that they have something to gain by levying new e-taxes. Until more firm legal precedents are established, international marketers should be aware of their potential tax liabilities and prepare for them, especially if they are considering substantial e-commerce investments. One likely scenario is an e-commerce tax system that closely resembles sales taxes at physical retail outlets. Vendors will be made responsible for collecting sales taxes and forwarding them to the governments concerned, most likely digitally. Another proposal involves the bit-tax, a variation of the Internet access tax.[63]

In addition, any product traded will still be subject to government regulations. For example, Virtual Vineyards has to worry about country-specific alcohol regulations, while software makers such as Softwareland.com Inc. have to comply with U.S. software export regulations. Dell Computer was fined $50,000 by the U.S. Department of Commerce for shipping computers online to Iran, a country on the sanctions list due to its sponsorship of terrorism.

Governments will also have to come to terms with issues related to security, privacy, and access to the Internet.[64] The private sector argues for the highest

THE INTERNATIONAL MARKETPLACE   11.3

E-Commerce in Emerging Markets

Consumers today are increasingly interested in the Internet to make car shopping and ownership easier and more convenient. A total of 8 to 10 million consumers surf the Internet for information to help them buy new cars. Expanding the use beyond providing information (e.g., owner handbooks, recall announcements, and maintenance) has proved to be challenging, however.

Although the United States has the greatest potential for online buying due to its large customer base, channel culture prevents General Motors from realizing it. The U.S. retail system consists of 20,000 dealers protected in many cases by state franchise laws that stand in the way of Internet sales. Additionally, automakers' production facilities cannot accommodate real-time Internet orders. As a result, GM and Ford are focusing more on the supplier side of their e-operations.

GM is testing electronic commerce strategies in overseas markets such as Taiwan, where it already sells 10 percent of its vehicles through the Internet and plans to build cars to order. "Emerging markets are a lab for us," said Mark Hogan, who heads the new E-GM unit. "We do not have a lot of bricks and mortar in these markets, so they provide perfect conditions for us to learn from." The company hopes to sell about 30 percent of units online in upcoming years.

However, in many of the emerging markets, especially Asia and Latin America, both GM and Ford have factories that are more flexible and will allow for build-to-order programs to operate at a much faster pace. Furthermore, and more importantly, automakers do not have existing retail systems that need to be overhauled. In some cases, such as GM in Taiwan, the firms own a significant share of the retail operations. Ford is experimenting with Internet sales in markets such as the Philippines, where it has set up an e-commerce system that links consumers, dealers, the manufacturer, and suppliers to create a seamless e-business.

In addition to buying cars online, Taiwanese customers can make service appointments through the GM Web site. The company will come to the owner's house or office, pick up the car, and return it within hours or overnight after completing the service.

Retailers are also getting on the bandwagon. Internet malls are mushrooming in Korea, for example. To gain access to products, Web retailer Libero teamed up with 100 traditional car dealers. Profits for the cyber dealers are slim—as little as $180 on each car. In addition, carmakers and dealers have threatened to sue their Web competitors for selling vehicles at low prices which disrupt the traditional way of doing business.

SOURCES: "Car Makers Rev Up to New E-Commerce Initiatives," *Network World*, September 2, 2002, 1, 16; "Follow-Through," *Forbes*, December 24, 2001, 48; "Ford and GM Unveil E-Commerce Alliances," *E-Commerce Times*, January 10, 2000, at **www.ecommercetimes.com/perl/printer/ 2169/**; "Asia Awakes to E-Commerce, *Industry Week.com*. January 5, 2000, at **http://www.industryweek.com/CurrentArticles/asp/articles. asp?ArticleID=808**; "GM Tests E-Commerce Plans in Emerging Markets," *The Wall Street Journal*, October 25, 1999, B6; **http://www.gm.com**; **http://www.GMBuyPower.com**; **http://www.gmautoworld. com.tw**; and **http://www.libero.co.kr**.

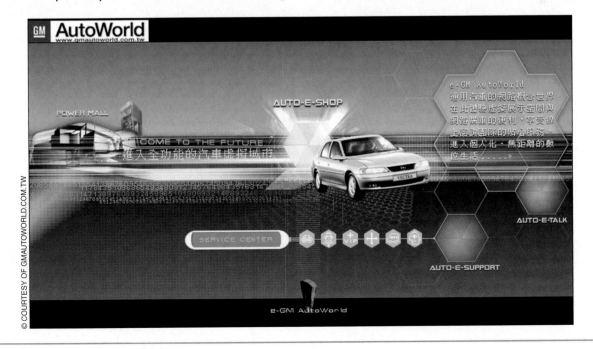

possible ability to safeguard its databases, to protect cross-border transmission of confidential information, and to conduct secure financial transactions using global networks. This requires an unrestricted market for encryption products that operate globally. However, some governments, especially the United States, fear that encryption will enable criminals and terrorist organizations to avoid detection and tracking. Therefore, a strong argument is made in favor of limiting the extent of encryption.

Privacy issues have grown exponentially as a result of e-business. In 1998, the European Union passed a directive that introduced high standards of data privacy to ensure the free flow of data throughout its 15 member states. Each individual has the right to review personal data, correct them, and limit their use. But more importantly, the directive also requires member states to block transmission of data to countries, including the United States, if those countries' domestic legislation does not provide an adequate level of protection. The issue between the United States and the EU will most likely be settled by companies, such as IBM, adopting global privacy policies for managing information online and getting certified by groups, such as Better Business Bureaus or Trust-E, that are implementing privacy labeling systems to tell users when a site adheres to their privacy guidelines.[65] A register of such companies will also then have to be developed.

A related concern is the content of material on the Internet. While freedom of information across international lines is encouraged and easily achieved, some countries (such as China and Saudi Arabia) regulate information and others have quotas on domestically produced broadcasting. Regulations on advertising are also implemented.

For industries such as music and motion pictures, the Internet is both an opportunity and a threat.[66] It provides a new and efficient method of distribution and customization of products. At the same time, it can be a channel for intellectual property violations, through unauthorized postings on Web sites from which protected material can be downloaded. In addition, the music industry is concerned about a shift in the balance of economic power: if artists can deliver their works directly to customers via technologies such as MP3, what will be the role of labels and distributors?

Summary

Channels of distribution consist of the marketing efforts and intermediaries that facilitate the movement of goods and services. Decisions that must be made to establish an international channel of distribution focus on channel design and the selection of intermediaries for the roles that the international marketer will not perform. The channel must be designed to meet the requirements of the intended customer base, coverage, long-term continuity of the channel once it is established, and the quality of coverage to be achieved. Having determined the basic design of the channel, the international marketer will then decide on the number of different types of intermediaries to use and how many of each type, or whether to use intermediaries at all, which would be the case in direct distribution using, for example, sales offices or e-commerce. The process is important because the majority of international sales involve distributors, and channel decisions are the most long-term of all marketing decisions. The more the channel operation resembles a team, rather than a collection of independent businesses, the more effective the overall marketing effort will be.

Key Terms

intermediaries
distribution culture
distributor
agent

indirect exporting
direct exporting
integrated distribution
commissionario

del credere agent
facilitating payments
parallel importation

Questions for Discussion

1. Relate these two statements: "A channel of distribution can be compared to a marriage." "The number one reason given for divorce is lack of communication."

2. Channels of distribution tend to vary according to the level of economic development of a market. The more developed the economy, the shorter the channels tend to be. Why?

3. If a small exporter lacks the resources for an onsite inspection, what measures would you propose for screening potential distributors?

4. The international marketer and the distributor will have different expectations concerning the relationship. Why should these expectations be spelled out and clarified in the contract?

5. One method of screening candidates is to ask distributors for a simple marketing plan. What items would you want included in this plan?

6. Is gray marketing a trademark issue, a pricing issue, or a distribution issue?

Internet Exercises

1. Using the Web site of the U.S. Commercial Service (**http://www.usatrade.gov**), assess the types of help available to an exporter in establishing distribution channels and finding partners in this endeavor.

2. The Anti-Gray Market Alliance (**http://www. antigraymarket.org**) has as its primary purpose to "mitigate gray marketing and counterfeiting of high-technology products." Is it appropriate to equate the two? Are the arguments by this industry coalition convincing?

Recommended Readings

Hutt, Michael D., and Thomas W. Speh. *Business Marketing Management,* 8th ed. Mason, OH: South-Western, 2004.

International Chamber of Commerce. *The ICC Agency Model Contract.* New York: ICC Publishing Corp., 1999.

International Chamber of Commerce. *Incoterms 2000.* New York: ICC Publishing Corp., 2000.

Rosenbloom, Bert. *Marketing Channels: A Management View,* 6th ed. Mason, OH: South-Western, 1999.

U.S. Customs Service, *A Basic Guide to Importing,* 3rd ed. New York: McGraw-Hill, 1996.

Exports of Tobacco

Tobacco and its related products have traditionally played an important role in the U.S. economy. In 2001, tobacco had a farm value of $1.9 billion, making it the United States' eighth largest cash crop. The United States is fourth behind China, Brazil, and India in world production, and second behind Brazil in exports. Twenty-three U.S. states and Puerto Rico grow tobacco, twenty-one states manufacture tobacco products, thirty-three states export tobacco, and all fifty states are engaged in the marketing of tobacco products.

In 1964, the *Surgeon General's Report* documented the adverse health effects of smoking. Since then, many medical experts have repeatedly warned the public that smoking causes lung cancer, low birth weights, and other health problems. Today the World Health Organization (WHO) attributes about 4 million deaths a year to tobacco use, a figure expected to rise to about 10 million deaths a year by 2030. As a result of increased awareness of the consequences of smoking, U.S. cigarette consumption, as well as other forms of tobacco use, have been gradually decreasing. Al-

though health considerations played an important role in discouraging smoking, other factors such as higher cigarette prices, steeper federal and local taxes, and governmental restrictions on smoking in public places also contributed to this decline. Since reaching a peak in 1981, total U.S. cigarette consumption declined by nearly 25 percent, and per capita consumption by 32 percent. In 2000, U.S. cigarette consumption was more than 435 billion cigarettes, accounting for over $68 billion in sales.

The Importance of Tobacco for the U.S. Economy

Taxes on tobacco products contribute significantly to government income and help reduce the budget deficit. As the number of smokers has declined, the government has raised the cigarette tax in order to preserve the level of tax revenues from smoking. The cigarette tax was raised from 8 cents per pack of twenty cigarettes in the period between 1951 and 1982 to 16 cents from 1983 to 1990. In January 2002, the federal cigarette excise tax was raised five cents to 39 cents per pack of twenty cigarettes. In 1999, the tobacco production and related industries contributed over $34 billion to government revenues in excise, sales, personal income, and corporate taxes. Of this amount, well over $5 billion was generated by the federal excise tax on tobacco and over $12 billion by state and local taxes. This means that almost 50 percent of the retail price of tobacco products in the U.S.

SOURCES: This study was prepared by Michael R. Czinkota and Ruth L. Braunstein, using the following background material: Foreign Agricultural Service statistics; "World Cigarette Situation" by the FAS; "Tobacco Industry Profile 1995" by the Tobacco Institute; Glenn Frankel, "U.S. Aided Cigarette Firms in Conquests Across Asia," *Washington Post,* November 17, 1996; Saundra Torry and John Schwartz, "Contrite Tobacco Executives Admit Health Risks Before Congress," *Washington Post,* January 30, 1998: A14; Chip Jones, "Cigarette Farmers to Buy Less Leaf," *Richmond Times-Dispatch,* December 3, 1997: A1; John M. Broder, "Cigarette Makers Reach $368 Billion Accord," *New York Times,* June 21, 1997.

Figure I

Federal Excise and Sales Tax Collections on Domestic Tobacco Sales (in Millions of Dollars)

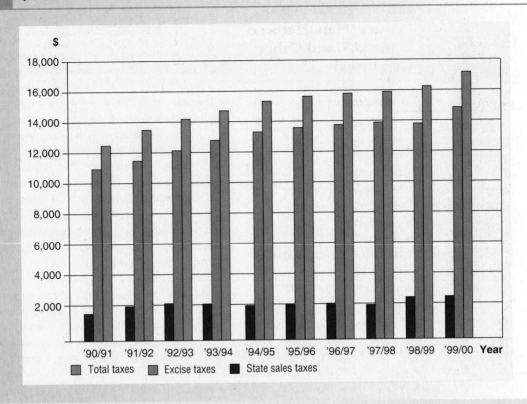

Total taxes   Excise taxes   State sales taxes

ends up in the treasuries of the federal and local governments (see Figure 1).

According to a study conducted by Tobacco USA, the tobacco industry, including growers, manufacturers, distributors, and core suppliers, employed over 600,000 people in 1999. In addition, another 759,000 jobs were generated as a result of the tobacco industry's expenditures on promotion and transportation.

The Importance of Tobacco Exports

In the face of their diminishing domestic market, U.S. tobacco companies are vigorously promoting cigarette exports. Developing countries are the home to most of the world's smokers and are therefore the number one target for cigarette exports (see Table 1). The international cigarette market is dominated by U.S. brands (see Table 2). However, U.S. companies would be able to sell even more cigarettes in developing countries if their products were free of import restrictions.

In the peak year of 1996, the U.S. tobacco industry produced 754 billion pieces of cigarettes. In the same year cigarette exports totaled about 241 billion pieces. The exports of tobacco and trade manufactures resulted in a $5.3 billion surplus in the 1996 trade balance for this group of products, about one-fourth of the surplus in all agricultural products.

In 2002, cigarette production declined by 1 to 2 percent to 570 billion pieces. Exports in 2002 fell by 3 percent from 2001 levels of 133.9 billion pieces, while imports rose almost 53 percent from

Table I

Estimated Number of Smokers (in Millions of Persons)

	Men	Women
Developed Countries	200	100
Developing Countries	700	100

Table 2	Leading International Brands Sold Outside the North American Market (Manufactured in the U.S. and Other Countries)	
Brand	**Producer**	
Marlboro	Philip Morris	
Mild Seven	Japan Tobacco	
Winston	R.J. Reynolds	
L&M	Philip Morris	
Camel	R.J. Reynolds	
Benson & Hedges	PM/BAT/AB	
Gaulloise	Gaulloise	
Bond Street	Philip Morris	
SE555	British American Tobacco	
Philip Morris	Philip Morris	

2001 levels of 14.7 billion pieces. This created a shrinking trade surplus that can be attributed mainly to lower demand and higher levels of off-shore production by domestic manufacturers. Also, the relatively expensive U.S. leaf tobacco is being replaced in many recessionary countries by lesser-grade tobacco leaf grown abroad. Even though the U.S. is still the third leading exporter of leaf tobacco, countries are demonstrating their willingness to sacrifice quality for lower prices by buying leaf tobacco from Brazil, Zimbabwe, and Malawi. U.S. firms exported to 106 countries in 2002. In 2002, the leading destinations for these exports were Belgium-Luxembourg (from there, cigarettes are distributed to individual EU countries), Japan, Saudi Arabia, South Korea, Lebanon, and Israel.

A study conducted by the Economic Research Service of the U.S. Department of Agriculture shows the effects of an excise tax increase of $1-per-pack on the demand for tobacco products. Government revenues would rise by $13.7 billion, and gross revenue to tobacco farmers would fall by $6.2 billion. Wholesale, transportation, and retail businesses would lose $1.5 billion of income and manufacturers would lose $3.9 billion. The study also estimates that the $1 increase in excise tax could cost an estimated 74,700 jobs in the manufacturing, farming, distribution, storage, and sales industries—15,100 of these jobs would be lost in farming. In retail and wholesale establishments, 43,400 jobs could be in jeopardy. Furthermore, 12,800 jobs could be at risk in such related industries as supply paper, packaging, chemicals, equipment, and machinery. Such a domino effect could more than offset the increase in government revenues supplied by the excise tax.

U.S. Trade Policy

Tobacco-related revenue is an important source of income for the governments of many countries. As a result, many nations have traditionally blocked the import of cigarettes by imposing high import tariffs, discriminatory taxes, and restrictive marketing and distribution practices. Japan, China, South Korea, and Thailand even set up state monopolies to produce cigarettes. Throughout the 1980s, the Asian tigers ran huge trade surpluses with the United States. When the U.S. annual trade deficit reached a record high of $123 billion in 1984, the Reagan administration turned to the Office of the U.S. Trade Representative (USTR), a federal agency under the Executive Office of the president. Section 301 of the 1974 Trade Act empowered the USTR to investigate unfair trading practices by foreign countries toward U.S. exporters and required that the U.S. government impose sanctions on a culpable foreign government if its trade policy toward U.S. firms was not changed within one year.

As U.S. tobacco products were among the most restricted goods, the USTR turned its attention to this case of foreign trade discrimination. The scrutiny was aided by the fact that Japan, South Korea, and Thailand were signatories to the General Agreement on Tariffs and Trade (GATT), and Taiwan was interested in joining as well. By their discriminatory policies toward U.S. cigarette imports, these countries violated the free trade principles they had agreed to respect under the GATT. In September 1985, the White House filed a complaint with the USTR under the Section 301 against Japanese restrictions on the sale of cigarettes. After a series of negotiations and mounting pressure from the U.S. government, in September 1986, Japan gave in and allowed imports of U.S. cigarettes. Almost immediately, cigarettes rose from the fortieth to the second most-advertised product on Tokyo television. Imported brands currently control 24.7 percent of the Japanese market with 82.1 billion in annual sales. In 2001, the U.S. share accounted for 95.7 percent of the import market.

China is the world's largest cigarette producer and consumer. In 2001, there were 320 million smokers in China who burned up nearly one-third of the annual 5.43 trillion world cigarette consumption. Although per capita use is slowly declining, overall Chinese consumption is increasing due to the growing population. All Chinese cigarettes are produced by a state monopoly.

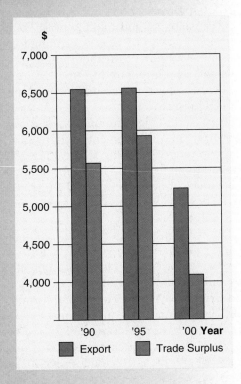

| Figure 2 | U.S. Trade in Tobacco and Tobacco Manufactures (SITC Product Group No. 12) (in Millions of Dollars) |

SOURCE: Bureau of the Census. February 2001.

Asia in the 1980s, U.S. companies are welcomed here as contributors of new technology and scarce investment funds. As part of the privatization process in the formerly communist countries, U.S. cigarette producers were able to buy previously state-owned cigarette factories and are quickly gaining ground in these new markets. Also, these producers are developing infrastructure in these countries with the long-term goal of moving production there due to a more advantageous cost structure and more supportive tax regulations. Some analysts project that over the next decade, Western tobacco manufacturers will gain control over the entire Eastern European cigarette market, which will more than make up for the revenues lost at home.

In addition to these market developments, the European Union agreed to cut export subsidies and reduce tariffs on both unmanufactured and manufactured tobacco, Japan promised to maintain zero duty on cigarettes and to lower duty on cigars, and New Zealand reduced its tariff on cigarettes. Finally, with China's accession to the WTO in February 2001, the decrease in tariffs and quotas allowed tobacco exports to enter the Chinese cigarette market.

Government Support of the Tobacco Industry

The U.S. Department of Agriculture (USDA) administers laws to stabilize tobacco production and prices. According to the Tobacco Institute, without this regulation, more tobacco would be produced and prices would be lower. In 2000, the Commodity Credit Corporation, an agency established in 1933 to administer commodity stabilization programs for the USDA, made new loans to tobacco farmers of an estimated $395 billion. These loans are to be repaid with interest as collateral tobacco is sold. The only direct cost incurred to the taxpayers is the administrative cost of this program, which is estimated at $15 million for 2001.

Until the late 1980s, the U.S. government was in strong support of the tobacco industry. It funded three export promotion programs: the Foreign Market Development Program (also known as the Cooperator Program), the Targeted Export Assistance Program, and the Export Credit Guarantee programs. The most important of these were the Export Credit Guarantee Programs administered by the Commodity Credit Corporation (CCC) of the Department of Agriculture. Under these programs, the CCC underwrote credit extended by the private banking sector in the United States to approved foreign banks, to pay for tobacco and

Because the Chinese government is eager to acquire advanced technology and marketing know-how from the West, it offered limited partnerships to a few foreign cigarette producers, including R.J. Reynolds and Philip Morris. Taxes from cigarette sales raise 12 percent of the Chinese government's annual revenue. As a consequence, the government wants to continue to protect its state monopoly from foreign competition. In 1992, the USTR negotiated an agreement under which China promised to eliminate tariffs and other trade barriers on U.S. cigarette imports within two years. The Chinese government, however, has not enforced the agreement.

With the opening of the markets of the former Soviet Union and Eastern Europe at the beginning of the 1990s, U.S. tobacco manufacturers found new opportunities for expansion. With 60 percent of their populations smoking, Hungary, Poland, Bulgaria, the former Yugoslav republics, the Czech Republic, and Slovakia are among the top ten nations in per capita cigarette consumption. Armenia, Georgia, Azerbaijan, Russia, Ukraine, and Moldova rank among the top twenty. Unlike in other agricultural products sold by U.S. firms to foreign buyers. Between October 1985 and September 1989, sixty-six companies received guarantees of credits under these programs for the sale of 127 million pounds of tobacco with a market value of $214 million. The Targeted Export Assistance Program's purpose was to counteract the adverse effects of subsidies, import quotas, or other unfair trade practices on U.S. agricultural products. Under this program, Tobacco Associates, a private organization entrusted to carry out this endeavor, received $5 million in funding in 1990 to provide certain countries with the technical know-how, training, and equipment to manufacture cigarettes that use U.S. tobacco. In addition, Tobacco Associates received funds from the USDA to promote market development activities for U.S. tobacco products.

During the Clinton administration, the U.S. government discontinued all export promotion programs related to tobacco and tobacco manufacturers. Under the Bush administration, the U.S. government's anti-tobacco stance has softened. U.S. trade officials opposed South Korea's 40 percent duty on imported cigarettes. They objected to this discriminatory trade practice, arguing the duty was aimed at protecting domestic brands rather than promoting health.

Conflicting Objectives

The past involvement of the U.S. government in furthering the export of tobacco has generated controversy within the United States. The U.S. government, spearheaded by the Department of Health and Human Services, has been actively discouraging smoking on the domestic scene. In addition, the United States is a strong supporter of the worldwide antismoking movement. The Department of Health and Human Services serves as a collaborating headquarters for the United Nations World Health Organization and maintains close relationships with other health organizations around the world in sharing information on the detrimental health effects of smoking.

The government has not initiated any concrete steps to reduce U.S. tobacco exports and U.S. investment in cigarette production abroad. This is partly due to the fact that many in government believe that U.S. tobacco products are merely capturing an existing market share now or previously controlled by state monopolies. In contrast to this claim, the National Bureau of Economic Research estimated that U.S. entry in the 1980s into countries previously closed to cigarette imports pushed up the average per capita cigarette consumption by almost 10 percent in the targeted countries. This occurred due to increased advertising and price competition caused by the entry of U.S. products.

This situation reflects a conflict between morality and economics. Projections show that the declining U.S. cigarette consumption can be easily replaced by foreign markets over the next decade. Thus, by pursuing an antismoking policy only at home, the U.S. government is not risking too much. On the contrary, a smaller number of U.S. smokers will significantly reduce the U.S. health system's expenditures on the treatment of smoking-related illnesses. However, the U.S. policy of permissiveness toward cigarette exports is at odds with government's involvement in the worldwide campaign to reduce smoking for health reasons. Conflicting opinions can be heard from different representatives of the government. While Representative Henry A. Waxman of California and former U.S. Surgeon General C. Everett Koop continue to be staunch supporters of the antismoking campaign and principal opponents of U.S. tobacco exports, Governor Paul E. Patton of Kentucky, who established the Governor's Tobacco Marketing and Export Advisory Council, and former Senator Jesse Helms of North Carolina continue to fight against government regulation of tobacco sales and are key supporters of tobacco exports.

The dividing force is economics: In 2001, North Carolina (where flue-cured tobacco is grown) was the number-one tobacco-growing state with annual production of tobacco crops averaging 386 million pounds. Kentucky (where burley is grown) comes in at a close second with tobacco production topping 254 million pounds. Together, North Carolina and Kentucky account for 64.7 percent of the total U.S. tobacco crop.

Questions for Discussion

1. Should U.S. exports of tobacco products be permitted in light of the domestic campaign against smoking?

2. Should the U.S. government be involved in tearing down foreign trade barriers to U.S. tobacco? Should the personal preference of the president affect U.S. trade policy?

3. Should export promotion support be provided to U.S. tobacco producers? What about such support for the export of U.S. beef, which may cause obesity abroad?

4. To what degree should ethics influence government policy or corporate decision-making in the case of tobacco exports?

Sources

ERS/USDA Key Topics: Tobacco. **http://www.ers. usda.gov/Topics/view.asp?T=101226**, accessed October 25, 2002.

"Economic Impact of the United States' Tobacco Industry-(AEG)," TMA Tobacco USA Revised December 1, 2000.

"Tobacco Price Support: An Overview of the Program," Congressional Research Service of the Library of Congress, CRS Report for Congress. Updated August 29, 2000.

Global Tobacco Prevention and Control, National Center for Chronic Disease Prevention and Health Promotion. **http://www.cdc.gov/tobacco/global/index.htm**, accessed September 20, 2002.

"World Kicking Cigarette Habit," Worldwatch Issue Alert Data & Graphs, May 9, 2000. **http://www. worldwatch.org/chairman/issue/000509d.html**, accessed October 25, 2002.

Pete Burr, Tobacco Analyst, FAS/USDA, interviewed March 23, 2001.

Thomas Capehart, Senior Tobacco Analyst, Economic Research Service, USDA, interviewed March 21, 2001.

Amelia Trent, Tobacco Analyst, FAS/USDA, interviewed March 19, 2001.

Nagahama, Masaoki, "Japan Tobacco Annual—Revised 2000." FAS, USDA, May 5, 2000. **http://www.fas. usda.gov/gainfiles/200005/25677628.pdf**, accessed March 16, 2001.

Commonwealth of Kentucky, Office of the Governor, **http://www.kyagpolicy.com/Start.htm**, accessed March 19, 2001.

"Most Frequently Used Tables," ERS/USDA Tobacco Briefing Room, **http://www.ers.usda.gov/Briefing/ Tobacco/**, accessed October 25, 2002.

"Crop Production," Agricultural Statistics Board, NASS, USDA, May 2000.

H. Frederick Gale Jr., Linda Foreman, and Thomas Capehart, "Tobacco and the Economy: Farms, Jobs, and Communities." Agricultural Economic Report No. 789. November 2000.

Economic Research Service, U.S. Department of Agriculture. **http://www.ers.usda.gov/publications/ aer789/aer789c.pdf**, accessed September 20, 2002.

"Big Tobacco Cut Down to Size, Yet Again," *The Economist,* March 27, 2002, 1. *ABI/Inform Global,* accessed August 27, 2002.

Marc Kaufman, "U.S. Helps Tobacco in Trade Case," *Washington Post,* June 26, 2001.

Damar International

amar International, a fledgling firm importing handicrafts of chiefly Indonesian origin, was established in Burke, Virginia, a suburb of Washington, DC. Organized as a general partnership, the firm is owned entirely by Dewi Soemantoro, its president, and Ronald I. Asche, its vice president. Their part-time, unsalaried efforts and those of Soemantoro's relatives in Indonesia constitute the entire labor base of the firm. Outside financing has been limited to borrowing from friends and relatives of the partners in Indonesia and the United States.

Damar International estimates that its current annual sales revenues are between $20,000 and $30,000. Although the firm has yet to reach the break-even point, its sales revenues and customer base have expanded more rapidly than anticipated in Damar's original business plan. The partners are generally satisfied with results to date and plan to continue to broaden their operations.

Damar International was established to capitalize on Soemantoro's international experience and contacts. As the daughter of an Indonesian Foreign Service officer, Soemantoro spent most of her youth and early adulthood in western Europe and has for the past 18 years resided in the United States. Her immediate family, including her mother, now resides in Indonesia. In addition to English and Malay, Soemantoro speaks French, German, and Italian. Although she has spent the past four years working in information management in the Washington area, first for MCI and currently for Records Management Inc., her interest in import-ing derives from the six years she spent as a management consultant. In this capacity, she was frequently called on to advise clients about importing clothing, furniture, and decorative items from Indonesia. At the urging of family and friends, she decided to start her own business. While Soemantoro handles the purchasing and administrative aspects of the business, Asche is responsible for marketing and sales.

Damar International currently imports clothing, high-quality brassware, batik accessories, wood carvings, and furnishings from Indonesia. All of these items are handcrafted by village artisans working in a cottage industry. Damar International estimates that 30 percent of its revenues from the sale of Indonesian imports are derived from clothing, 30 percent from batik accessories, and 30 percent from wood carvings, with the remainder divided equally between brassware and furnishings. In addition, Damar markets in the eastern United States comparable Thai and Philippine handcrafted items imported by a small California firm. This firm in turn markets some of Damar's Indonesian imports on the West Coast.

Most of Damar's buyers are small shops and boutiques. Damar does not supply large department stores or retail chain outlets. By participating in gift shows, trade fairs, and handicraft exhibitions, the firm has expanded its customer base from the Washington area to many locations in the eastern United States.

In supplying small retail outlets with handcrafted Indonesian artifacts, Damar is pursuing a niche strategy. Although numerous importers market similar mass-produced, manufactured Indonesian items chiefly to department stores and chain

SOURCE: This case was prepared by Michael R. Czinkota and Laura M. Gould.

retailers, Damar knows of no competitors that supply handcrafted artifacts to boutiques. Small retailers find it difficult to purchase in sufficient volume to order directly from large-scale importers of mass-produced items. More important, it is difficult to organize Indonesian artisans to produce hand-crafted goods in sufficient quantity to supply the needs of large retailers.

Damar's policy is to carry little if any inventory. Orders from buyers are transmitted by Soemantoro to her family in Indonesia, who contract production to artisans in the rural villages of Java and Bali. Within broad parameters, buyers can specify modifications of traditional Indonesian wares. Frequently, Soemantoro cooperates with her mother in creating designs that adapt traditional products to American tastes and to the specifications of U.S. buyers. Soemantoro is in contact with her family in Indonesia at least once a week by telex or phone to report new orders and check on the progress of previous orders. In addition, Soemantoro makes an annual visit to Indonesia to coordinate policy with her family and maintain contacts with artisans.

Damar also fills orders placed by Soemantoro's family in Indonesia. The firm, in essence, acts as both an importer and an exporter despite its extremely limited personnel base. In this, as well as in its source of financing, Damar is highly atypical. The firm's great strength, which allows it to fill a virtually vacant market niche with extremely limited capital and labor resources, is clearly the Soemantoro family's nexus of personal connections. Without the use of middlemen, this single bicultural family is capable of linking U.S. retailers and Indonesian village artisans and supplying products that, while unique, are specifically oriented to the U.S. market.

Damar's principal weakness is its financing structure. There are limits to the amount of money that can be borrowed from family and friends for such an enterprise. Working capital is necessary because the Indonesian artisans must be paid before full payment is received from U.S. buyers. Although a 10 percent deposit is required from buyers when an order is placed, the remaining 90 percent is not due until 30 days from the date of shipment F.O.B. Washington, DC. Yet, the simplicity of Damar's financing structure has advantages: To date, it has been able to operate without letters of credit and their concomitant paperwork burdens.

One major importing problem to date has been the paperwork and red tape involved in U.S. customs and quota regulations. Satisfying these regulations has occasionally delayed fulfillment of orders. Furthermore, because the Indonesian trade office in the United States is located in New York rather than Washington, assistance from the Indonesian government in expediting such problems has at times been difficult to obtain with Damar's limited personnel. For example, an order was once delayed in U.S. customs because of confusion between the U.S. Department of Commerce and Indonesian export authorities concerning import stamping and labeling. Several weeks were required to resolve the difficulty.

Although Damar received regulatory information directly from the U.S. Department of Commerce when it began importing, its routine contact with the government is minimal because regulatory paperwork is contracted to customs brokers.

One of the most important lessons that the firm has learned is the critical role of participating in gift shows, trade fairs, and craft exhibitions. Soemantoro believes that the firm's greatest mistake to date was not attending a trade show in New York. In connecting with potential buyers, both through trade shows and "walk-in scouting" of boutiques, Damar has benefited greatly from helpful references from existing customers. Buyers have been particularly helpful in identifying trade fairs that would be useful for Damar to attend. Here too, the importance of Damar's cultivation of personal contacts is apparent.

Similarly, personal contacts offer Damar the possibility of diversifying into new import lines. Through a contact established by a friend in France, Soemantoro is currently planning to import handmade French porcelain and silk blouses.

Damar is worried about sustained expansion of its Indonesian handicraft import business because the firm does not currently have the resources to organize large-scale cottage-industry production in Indonesia. Other major concerns are potential shipping delays and exchange rate fluctuations.

Questions for Discussion

1. Evaluate alternative expansion strategies for Damar International in the United States.
2. Discuss Damar's expansion alternatives in Indonesia and France and their implications for the U.S. market.
3. How can Damar protect itself against exchange rate fluctuations?
4. What are the likely effects of shipment delays on Damar? How can these effects be overcome?

Water from Iceland

tan Otis was in a contemplative mood. He had just hung up the phone after talking with Roger Morey, vice president of Citicorp. Morey had made him a job offer in the investment banking sector of the firm. The interviews had gone well, and Citicorp management was impressed with Stan's credentials from a major northeastern private university. "I think you can do well here, Stan. Let us know within a week whether you accept the job," Morey had said.

The three-month search had paid off well, Stan thought. Yet an alternative plan complicated the decision to accept the position.

Stan had returned several months before from an extended trip throughout Europe, a delayed graduation present from his parents. Among other places, he had visited Reykjavik, Iceland. Even though he could not communicate well, he found the island enchanting. What particularly fascinated him was the lack of industry and the purity of the natural landscape. In particular, he felt the water tasted extremely good. Returning home, he began to consider making this water available in the United States.

SOURCES: This study was prepared by Michael R. Czinkota, using the following background material: International Bottled Water Association, Beverage Marketing Corporation, Beverage Aisle, 2002. The author is grateful for the input from Prof. Ingjaldur Hannibalsson and the students of his class at the University of Iceland.

The Water Market in the United States

In order to consider the possibilities of importing Icelandic water, Stan knew that he first had to learn more about the general water market in the United States. Fortunately, some former college friends were working in a market research firm. Owing Stan some favors, these friends furnished him with a consulting report on the water market.

The Consulting Report

Bottled water has more than a 16 percent market share of total beverage consumption in the United States. The overall distribution of market share is shown in Figure 1. Primary types of water available for human consumption in the United States are treated or processed water, mineral water, sparkling or effervescent water, and spring well water.

Treated or processed water comes from a well stream or central reservoir supply. This water usually flows as tap water and has been purified and fluoridated.

Mineral water is spring water that contains a substantial amount of minerals, which may be injected or occur naturally. Natural mineral water is obtained from underground water strata or a natural spring. The composition of the water at its source is constant, and the source discharge and temperature remain stable. The natural content of the water at the source is not modified by an artificial process.

Figure I — Per Capita Consumption of Beverage Products in United States, 2001

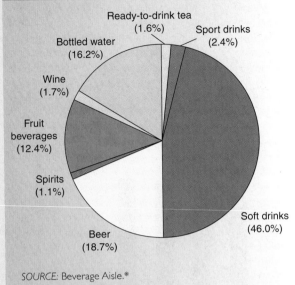

- Ready-to-drink tea (1.6%)
- Sport drinks (2.4%)
- Bottled water (16.2%)
- Wine (1.7%)
- Fruit beverages (12.4%)
- Spirits (1.1%)
- Beer (18.7%)
- Soft drinks (46.0%)

SOURCE: Beverage Aisle.*

Table I — U.S. Beverage Consumption, 2001

	Retail Receipts (in Billions of Dollars)	Per Capita Consumption (in Gallons)
Soft drinks	55.9	55.4
Beer	58.1	22.5
Spirits	38.1	1.3
Fruit beverages	19.5	15.0
Wine	18.9	2.0
Bottled water	7.7	19.5
Sports drinks	3.7	2.9
Ready-to-drink tea	2.8	1.9

SOURCE: Beverage Aisle.* Table and graph data taken from Beverage Aisle, 11 (no. 8): 38, August 15, 2002. Figures are determined based upon industry contracts with the help of Adams Business Media.

Sparkling or effervescent water is water with natural or artificial carbonation. Some mineral waters come to the surface naturally carbonated through underground gases but lose their fizz on the surface with normal pressure. Many of these waters are injected with carbon dioxide later on.

Minerals are important to the taste and quality of water. The type and variety of minerals present in the water can make it a very healthy and enjoyable drink. The combination of minerals present in the water determines its relative degree of acidity. The level of acidity is measured by the pH factor. A pH 7 rating indicates a neutral water. A higher rating indicates that the water contains more solids, such as manganese calcium, and is said to be "hard." Conversely, water with a lower rating is classified as "soft." Most tap water is soft, whereas the majority of commercially sold waters tend to be hard.

Water Consumption in the United States

Tap water has generally been inexpensive, relatively pure, and plentiful in the United States. Traditionally, bottled water has been consumed in the United States by the very wealthy. In the past several years, however, bottled water has begun to appeal to a wider market. The four main reasons for this change are:

1. An increasing awareness among consumers of the impurity of city water supplies
2. Increasing dissatisfaction with the taste and odor of city tap water
3. Rising affluence in society
4. An increasing desire to avoid excess consumption of caffeine, sugar, and other substances present in coffee and soft drinks.

Bottled water consumers are found chiefly in the states of California, Texas, Florida, New York and Arizona. Consumers in California, Texas, Florida, New York, and Arizona account for 70 percent of the bottled water consumption in the United States, with California consuming the most. Nationwide, per capita consumption is estimated to be nearly 20 gallons (19.5). The volume of bottled water sold rose from only 354.3 million gallons in 1976 to nearly 5.5 billion gallons in 2001, more than a fifteen-fold increase. Since 1995, there has been growth of nearly 74 percent, gaining market share on soft drinks, tea, beer, and spirits. Volume

Table 2 — U.S. Bottled Water Market Volume, 1976–2005

Year	Millions of Gallons	Year	Millions of Gallons
1976	354	1995	3,167
1980	605	2002	5,033
1985	1,214	2005	7,200
1990	2,237		

SOURCE: Beverage Marketing Corporation of New York.

Figure 2 — U.S. Bottled Water Market, 1990–2001

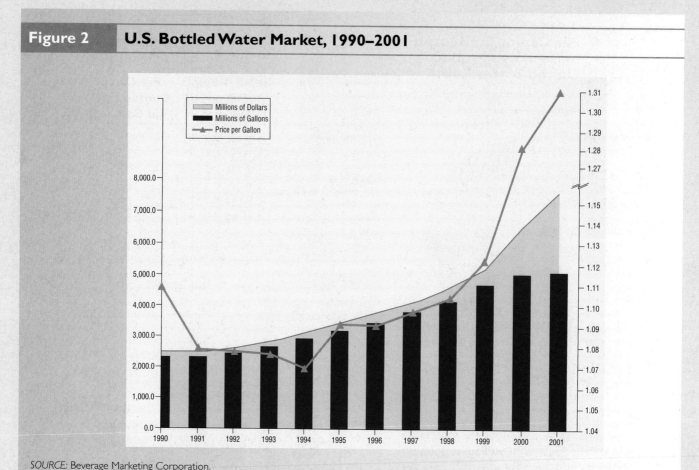

Legend:
- Millions of Dollars
- Millions of Gallons
- Price per Gallon

SOURCE: Beverage Marketing Corporation.

Figure 3 — Market Share of Bottled Water by Segment in 2001 (Based on Volume)

Domestic sparkling (2.74%)

Imports (2.86%)

Domestic nonsparkling (94.6%)

SOURCE: Beverage Marketing Corporation.

is expected to increase to 7.2 billion gallons in 2005, a 43 percent increase from 2000 levels.

In 2001, the industry's receipts totaled $6.5 billion on wholesale and $7.7 billion retail, a 30 percent increase in retail sales from 1999. While the volume of total bottled water more than doubled between 1990 and 2000, consumption of nonsparkling bottled water increased 90 percent as consumption of sparkling water declined by 20 percent.

Though between 1998 and 2000 the volume of imported bottled water decreased 16 percent, imports have almost doubled since 1990 (see Table 3). The leading country importing water to the U.S. is France, with a 53.1 percent share of total bottled water imports. Canada is second with 20.8 percent market share. Ranked ninth, bottled water from Iceland holds 0.05 percent market share (see Figure 4).

Among producers, Perrier is a strong leader with a 30.5 percent market share. The Perrier Group's top four selling bottled water brands are Arrowhead, Poland Spring, Ozarka, and Zephyr-hills — all among the top-ten selling brands in the United States. Suntory Water Group has 9.7 per-

Figure 4 — 2001 Bottled Water Imports by Country (by volume)

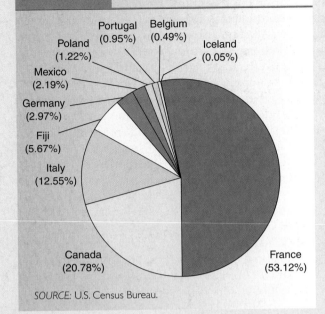

Portugal (0.95%)
Belgium (0.49%)
Poland (1.22%)
Iceland (0.05%)
Mexico (2.19%)
Germany (2.97%)
Fiji (5.67%)
Italy (12.55%)
Canada (20.78%)
France (53.12%)

SOURCE: U.S. Census Bureau.

cent and McKesson has 8.0 percent of the market share, with both companies comprised of many relatively small brands.

Overall, a cursory analysis indicates good potential for success for a new importer of bottled water in the United States. This is especially true if the water is exceptionally pure and can be classified as mineral water.

Additional Research

Further exploring his import idea, Stan Otis gathered information on various other marketing facets. One of his main concerns was government regulations.

Bottled Water Regulations in the United States

The bottled water industry in the United States is regulated and controlled at two levels—by the federal government and by various state governments. Some states, such as California and Florida, impose even stricter regulations on bottled water than they are required to follow under the federal regulations. Others, such as Arizona, do not regulate the bottled water industry beyond the federal requirements. About 75 percent of bottled water is obtained from springs, artesian wells, and drilled wells. The other 25 percent comes from municipal water systems, which are regulated by the Environmental Protection Agency (EPA). All bottled water is considered food and is thus regulated by the Food and Drug Administration (FDA). Under the 1974 Safe Drinking Water Act, the FDA adopted bottled water standards compatible with EPA's standards for water from public water systems. As the EPA revises its drinking water regulations, the FDA is required to revise its standards for bottled water or explain in the Federal Register why it decided not to do so. The FDA requires bottled water products to be clean and safe for human consumption, processed and distributed

Table 3 — U.S. Bottled Water Market by Segments, 1990–2000

Year	Non-Sparkling Volume*	Change	Sparkling Volume*	Change	Imports Volume*	Change	Total Volume*	Change
1990	1,987.7	8.2%	176.0	28.4%	73.9	32.9%	2,237.6	10.3%
1991	2,042.8	2.8%	172.3	−2.1%	71.4	−3.4%	2,286.5	2.2%
1992	2,163.4	5.9%	172.3	0.0%	86.3	20.9%	2,422.0	5.9%
1993	2,356.7	8.9%	174.7	1.4%	92.5	7.2%	2,623.9	8.3%
1994	2,623.1	11.3%	174.8	0.1%	104.0	12.4%	2,901.9	10.6%
1995	2,906.2	10.8%	164.2	−6.1%	97.1	−6.7%	3,167.5	9.2%
1996	3,178.5	9.4%	159.0	−3.2%	111.8	15.2%	3,449.3	8.9%
1997	3,472.9	9.3%	153.8	−3.3%	149.1	33.4%	3,775.8	9.5%
1998	3,839.1	10.5%	146.1	−5.0%	160.8	7.9%	4,146.0	9.8%
1999	4,349.0	13.3%	146.0	−0.1%	151.1	−6.1%	4,646.1	12.1%
2000	4,751.1	9.2%	144.2	−1.2%	137.8	−8.8%	5,033.2	8.3%

*Millions of gallons.

SOURCE: Beverage Marketing Corporation, 2002.

under sanitary conditions, and produced in compliance with FDA good manufacturing practices. In addition, domestic bottled water producers engaged in interstate commerce are subject to periodic, unannounced FDA inspections.

In 1991, an investigation by the U.S. House Energy and Commerce Committee found that 25 percent of the higher-priced bottled water comes from the same sources as ordinary tap water, another 25 percent of producers were unable to document their sources of water, and 31 percent exceeded limits of microbiological contamination. The Committee faulted the FDA with negligent oversight. In response, the FDA established, in November 1995, definitions for artesian water, groundwater, mineral water, purified water, sparkling bottled water, sterile water, and well water in order to ensure fair advertising by the industry. These results went into effect in May 1996. They include specification of the mineral content of water that can be sold as mineral water. Previously, mineral water was not regulated by the FDA, which resulted in varying standards for mineral water across states. In addition, under these rules, if bottled water comes from a municipal source, it must be labeled to indicate its origin.

The Icelandic Scenario

Iceland is highly import-dependent. In terms of products exported, it has little diversity and is dangerously dependent on its fish crop and world fish prices. The government, troubled by high inflation rates and low financial reserves, is very interested in diversifying its export base. An Icelandic Export Board has been created and charged with developing new products for export and aggressively promoting them abroad.

The Ministry of Commerce, after consulting the Central Bank, has the ultimate responsibility in matters concerning import and export licensing. The Central Bank is responsible for the regulation of foreign exchange transactions and exchange controls, including capital controls. It is also responsible for ensuring that all foreign exchange due to residents is surrendered to authorized banks. All commercial exports require licenses. The shipping documents must be lodged with an authorized bank. Receipts exchanged for exports must be surrendered to the Central Bank.

All investments by nonresidents in Iceland are subject to individual approval. The participation of nonresidents in Icelandic joint venture companies may not exceed 49 percent. Nonresident-owned foreign capital entering in the form of foreign exchange must be surrendered.

Iceland is a member of the United Nations, the European Free Trade Association, and the World Trade Organization. Iceland enjoys "most favored nation" status with the United States. Under this designation, mineral and carbonated water from Iceland is subject to a tariff of 0.33 cents per liter, and natural (still) water is tariff-free.

Questions for Discussion

1. Is there sufficient information to determine whether importing water from Iceland would be a profitable business? If not, what additional information is needed to make a determination?
2. Is the market climate in the United States conducive to water imports from Iceland?
3. What are some possible reasons for the fluctuation in the market share held by imports over the past ten years?
4. Should the U.S. government be involved in regulating bottled water products?

Joemarin Oy

inland's first customers in the sailboat business are generally believed to have been the Vikings. More recently, ships and boats were exported as partial payment for World War II reparations. This long tradition in building sailboats is due, no doubt, to Finland's proximity to the sea, long coastline, and its 60,000 lakes. Among luxury sailing yachts, the Swan boats of Nautor Oy and the Finnclippers of Fiskars Oy are internationally known and admired. There are, however, over 100 other boat builders in Finland that turn out 10,000 sailing yachts yearly.

Although most of the Finnish sailboat companies are situated on the coast, for obvious reasons, Joemarin Oy is located in the town of Joensuu, roughly 450 kilometers northeast of Helsinki. Joemarin was founded in the town that lends part of its name to the company because of the efforts of Kehitysaluerahasto, which is the Development Area Foundation of the Finnish government. Kehitysaluerahasto provided a loan of 4 million Finnish marks to Joemarin, a privately owned company, to start its operations in the Joensuu area because of the town's high rate of unemployment.

The present product line consists of three types of fiberglass sailboats. The Joemarin 17 is a coastal sailing yacht with a new design approach (Figure 1). This approach is to provide a craft that enables a family to make weekend and holiday cruises in coastal waters and also offers exciting sailing. The sailboat is very fast. The Finnish Yacht Racing

Association stated in its test in which the Joemarin 17 was judged to be the best in her class: "She is delicate, lively, spacious, and easy to steer. She is well balanced and has a high-quality interior. She is especially fast on the beat and lively to handle in a free wind."

The Joemarin 17, a small day cruiser with berths for two adults and two children, has a sail area of 130 square feet, weighs one-half ton, and has an overall length of a little over 17 feet. The hull is made of glass-reinforced plastic (GRP), and the mast and boom are made of aluminum. The boat has a drop keel that is useful when negotiating shallow anchorages or when lifting the boat on a trailer for transportation. The layout of the boat is shown in Figure 2.

The Joemarin 34 is a relatively large motor sailer that sleeps seven people in three separate compartments. The main saloon contains an adjustable dining table, a complete galley, and a navigator's compartment. The main saloon is separated from the fore cabin by a folding door. The aft cabin, which is entered by a separate companionway, contains a double berth, wardrobe, wash basin, and lockers. The toilet and shower are situated between the fore cabin and the main saloon. The boat has a sail area of 530 square feet, weighs about five tons, and has an overall length of 33 feet 9 inches. A significant feature of the craft is that she is equipped with a 47 horsepower diesel engine.

The Joemarin 34 has the same design approach as the 17. She is well appointed, with sufficient space for seven people to live comfortably. An important feature is that the three separate living compartments allow for considerable privacy. In

SOURCE: This case was prepared by James H. Sood of the American University. Reprinted with permission.

381

Figure 1 Joemarin 17: Ideal for Family Cruising as Well as Exciting Racing

addition, however, the modern hull is quite sleek, making her an excellent sailing yacht.

The Joemarin 36 was designed for a different purpose. Whereas the 17 and 34 are oriented toward a family approach to sailing—combining the features of safety and comfortable accommodations with good sailing ability—the 36 is first and foremost a sailing craft. It does have two berths, a small galley, and toilet facilities, but the emphasis is on sailing and racing rather than comfort. The boat has a sail area of 420 square feet, weighs a little less than four tons, and has an overall length of 35 feet 10 inches. The boat is also equipped with a small (7 horsepower) diesel

Figure 2 The Layout of the Joemarin 17

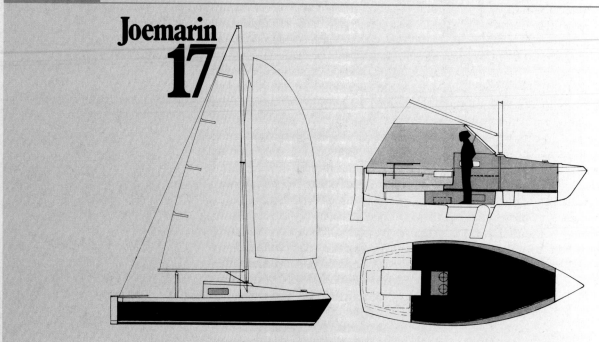

Joemarin
17

engine for emergency power situations. The Joemarin 36 is a traditional Swedish design and, therefore, is directed almost solely to the Swedish market.

The company was established in order to manufacture sailboats for export. The Finnish sailboat market is small because of the short sailing season. Nevertheless, the company has been successful in marketing the 17 in Finland, although this was difficult in the beginning because of the lack of boat dealers. To circumvent this problem, Joemarin persuaded a number of new car dealers throughout the country to handle the Joemarin 17 on an agency basis. This involved the company's providing one boat to each car dealer, who placed it in the showroom. The dealer then marketed the sailboats for a 15 percent sales commission.

Although many people scoffed at this idea, the system produced reasonable sales and also made the company known throughout Finland. This contributed to an arrangement with one of the largest cooperative wholesale-retail operations in Finland. Like most cooperatives, this organization began with agricultural products; however, the product range of the company now includes virtually every conceivable consumer product. The present contract states that the cooperative will purchase 80 Joemarin 17 boats per year for the next three years.

The Swedish market is served by a selling agent, although this representative has not been particularly effective. Because Sweden is also the home of many sailboat builders, the company has tried to market only the 36 in that country. In Denmark, France, Holland, Germany, and the United Kingdom, Joemarin has marketed the 34 through importers. These importers operate marinas in addition to new sailboat dealerships. They purchase the boats from Joemarin for their own accounts and mark up the price by about 20 percent. In return for exclusive marketing rights in their respective countries, they agree to purchase a minimum number (usually three or four) of the 34 design per year. None of these importers is interested in marketing the 17 or the 36; the shipping cost for the 17 is too high compared with the value of the boat, and there is little customer interest in the 36.

Joemarin is planning to introduce a new sailboat. Whereas the present products were designed by people in the company who were relatively unknown (to the customers), the hull of the new sailboat has been designed by an internationally known boat designer. The cost of these design services was a $30,000 initial fee plus a $3,000 royalty fee to be paid for each boat produced. The new sailboat, the Joemarin 29, has an interior quite similar to that of the Joemarin 34. This is not unexpected because the same Joemarin people designed the interiors and decks of both sailboats.

The new boat is a motor sailer that sleeps six people in three separate compartments, is 28 feet 9 inches long, weighs 4 tons, and has a joined cabin space and a separate aft cabin, small galley, toilet and shower facilities, and a 12 horsepower diesel engine. Because of a new construction technique that greatly reduces the amount of fiberglass required, the variable costs to construct the boat are only 60 percent of the costs for the 34. With a preliminary selling price of €97,500, the Joemarin 29 is receiving favorable attention, and the company is concerned that sales may have an adverse effect on sales of the 34.

The company categorizes the marketing expenses as fixed costs because allocating these expenses to specific products is difficult. The major element of the program is participation in international boat shows in London, Paris, Hamburg, Amsterdam, Copenhagen, and Helsinki. The initial purpose of participating in these shows was to locate suitable importers in the target markets; however, this effort is maintained in order to support the marketing programs of the importers. The importers are also supported by advertising in the leading yachting magazines in the national markets. Joemarin's personal selling effort consists primarily of servicing the importers and agents and staffing the exhibitions at the boat shows. Most of the sales promotion costs are the result of the elaborate sales brochures that the company has developed for each boat. These brochures are printed in four colors on three folded pages of high-quality paper. The costs are greatly increased, however, by having to print a relatively small number of each brochure in Finnish, French, English, German, and Swedish. The brochures are provided to the agents and importers and are used at the boat shows.

The company is in the process of preparing its production and marketing plan for the coming year in order to arrange financing. The president is strongly committed to the continued growth of the company, and the market indications suggest that there is a reasonably strong demand for the 17 in Finland and for the 34 in most of the other national markets. The sales results of the previous and present years are shown in Table 1; the profit statement for the present year is shown in Table 2.

The main problem in developing the plan for next year is determining the price for each sailboat in each market. In previous years, Joemarin had established its prices in Finnish marks, on an ex-factory basis. Management has become convinced, however, that it must change the terms of its

Table 1 — Joemarin Sales

	Last Year			Present Year		
	No.	Average Price[a]	Revenue	No.	Average Price[a]	Revenue
JIM-17	200	13,500	2,700,000	240	14,850	3,564,000
JIM-29	—	—	—	—	—	—
JIM-34	30	162,000	4,860,000	36	178,000	6,408,000
JIM-36	4	94,500	378,000	5	103,950	519,750
			7,938,000			10,491,750

[a]All prices are manufacturer's prices; prices and revenues are in euros: 1.00 € = U.S. $1.00.

Table 2 — Joemarin Profit Statement for Present Year

	In Finnmarks	As a Percentage of Sales
Sales revenue	10,491,750[a]	
Variable costs (direct labor and materials)	6,755,000	65.0%
Fixed costs:		
Production (building expenses, production management salaries)	472,500	4.5
Product design costs (salaries, prototypes, testing, consultants)	661,500	6.4
Administration costs (salaries, insurance, office expenses)	324,000	3.1
Marketing costs (salaries, advertising, boat shows, sales promotion, travel expenses)	1,142,000	11.0
Total fixed costs	2,600,000	25.0%
Profit before taxes	1,136,750	10.0

[a]All prices are manufacturer's prices; prices and revenues are in euros; 1.00 € = U.S. $1.00.

prices in order to meet competition in the foreign markets. Thus, the company has decided to offer CIF prices to its foreign customers in the currency of the foreign country. The use of truck ferries between Finland and Sweden, Denmark, and Germany is expected to make this pricing approach more competitive.

Joemarin would also like to assure its agents and importers that the prices will remain in effect for the entire year, but the financial manager is concerned about the possible volatility of exchange rates because of the varying rates of inflation in the market countries. The present exchange rates, the expected inflation rates in the market countries, and the estimated costs to ship the Joemarin 36 to Stockholm and the Joemarin 29 and 34 to the other foreign marinas are shown in Table 3.

A second difficulty in pricing the product line in Joemarin is to establish a price for the 29 that will reflect the value of the boat but will not reduce the sales of the 34. There are three schools of thought concerning the pricing of motor sailers. The predominant theory is that price is a function of the overall length of the sailboat. A number of people, however, believe that the overall weight of the craft is a much more accurate basis. The third opinion argues that price is a function of the special features and equipment. Figure 3, which was prepared by a Swiss market research firm, shows the relationship between present retail prices and the length of new motor sailers in the West European market.

Questions for Discussion

1. Determine the optimal manufacturer's selling price in the Finnish market for the four Joemarin sailboats for the coming year.

Table 3   **Shipping Costs for Joemarin 36 to Sweden, and for Joemarin 29 and 34 to Other Countries**

Country	Present Exchange Rates in €	Expected Inflation Rates	Estimated Freight and Insurance Costs per Boat
Denmark	Danish Kroner = 0.1350	2.1%	€6,750
France	€	1.9	€9,500
Holland	€	4.0	€8,500
Sweden	Swedish Kroner = 0.1105	2.3	€5,000
United Kingdom	English Pound = 1.5798	1.1	€11,000
Germany	€	1.7	€8,500
Finland	—	2.2	—

SOURCE: Eurostat Newsrelease, October 16, 2002.

Figure 3   **Retail Price in the European Market of Sailing Yachts as a Function of Overall Length**

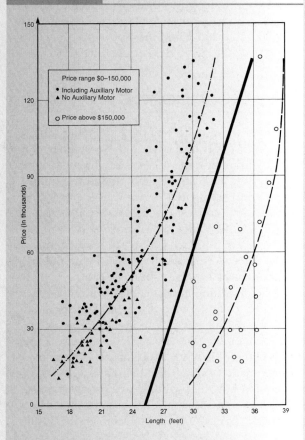

NOTE: All yachts to the right of the bold dividing line are priced above 150,000.

2. Determine the CIF prices for the Joemarin 36 to the final customer in Sweden for the coming year. The agent's commission is 15 percent of the final selling price, and the final selling price should be in Swedish kroner.

3. Recommend a course of action for the company to take in regard to the Joemarin 36.

4. Determine the CIF prices, in the foreign currencies, for the Joemarin 29 and 34 to the importers in Denmark, France, Holland, the United Kingdom, and Germany for the coming year.

5. Develop a production and marketing plan for Joemarin for the coming year. What steps can the company take to ensure that the plan is in line with the demand for its products in its foreign markets?

The Gray Ferrari

We can put a man on the moon, but we can't retrofit a Ferrari. It's crazy!

—Robert L. Johnson, founder and CEO of Black Entertainment Television

It all got started when Robert L. Johnson had dinner at Mr. K's Chinese restaurant with Michael Jordan of the Washington Wizards and David Falk, the leading sports agent. When the discussion turned to cars, Johnson mentioned his interest in getting a Ferrari. Both Falk and Jordan recommended their respective dealers but Johnson found the going tough. Only a select number of Ferraris are made annually, and the automaker limits how many are sold through U.S. dealers to about 1,000 units. In practice, anyone placing an order would have to wait over two years for delivery for a car that would cost $200,000 to $300,000 depending on the model. A New Jersey dealer had

a Ferrari available, but, at $300,000, Johnson felt the price was too high. Michael Jordan's dealer had a 360 Modena available for $160,000. Although he bought it, it was not exactly what he had wanted because the Modena is not a convertible. Franco Nuschese, the owner of Georgetown's Café Milano, referred Johnson to a dealer in Munich who had Ferrari 360 Spiders available at $190,000. Johnson wired the money to Munich and expected to have delivery within days.

The Standards

Only after the purchase of the 360 Spider did Johnson discover that it needed to conform to certain government standards, mainly those relating to emissions and safety (a fact that led to Johnson's Ferrari sitting in a dealer warehouse for months). The greatest obstacles were in satisfying the rules of the Office of Vehicle Safety Compliance (OVSC), a branch of the National Highway Traffic Safety Administration (NHTSA) in the Department of Transportation (DOT).

Nonconforming import cars (from outside the United States and Canada) have to be reported to the OVSC by registered importers (RI) on behalf of the buyer. In 2002, the NHTSA reported 23 registered importers who "specialize in European or gray-market cars." The RI submits a petition explaining how they will replace foreign parts with U.S. parts and adjust the engineering. The bumpers, for example, are thicker on the North

SOURCES: This case was written by Ilkka A. Ronkainen using publicly available materials. These include: Department of Transportation, "Decision That Nonconforming 2001 Ferrari 360/550 Passenger Cars Are Eligible for Importation," *Federal Register* 67 (April 10, 2002): 17479–17486; Alec Klein, "Life in the Stalled Lane," *The Washington Post*, January 6, 2002, A1, A5; and Bob Gritzinger, "Ferrari NA Wants to Block Gray Imports," *AutoWeek*, August 19, 2001, 45–46. For general information on gray-market imports, see The Better Business Bureau/New York at **http://www.newyork.bbb.org/library/publications/subrep45.html**, and Anti-Gray Market Alliance at **http://www.antigraymarket.org**.

Figure 1   Vehicle Importation Guidelines

The following provides information concerning the importation of a passenger car, truck, trailer, motorcycle, moped, bus, or MPV built to comply with the standards of a country other than the United States or Canada. Importers or motor vehicles must file form HS-7 (available at ports of entry) at the time a vehicle is imported to declare whether the vehicle complies with DOT requirements. As a general rule, a motor vehicle less than 25 years old must comply with all applicable Federal motor vehicle safety standards (FMVSS) to be imported permanently. Vehicles manufactured to meet the FMVSS will have a certification label affixed by the original manufacturer in the area of the driver-side door. To make importation easier, when purchasing a vehicle certified to the U.S. standards abroad, a buyer should have the sales contract verify that the label is attached and present this document at time of importation.

A vehicle without this certification label must be imported as a nonconforming vehicle. In this case, the importer must contract with a DOT-Registered Importer (RI) and post a DOT bond for one and a half times the vehicle's dutiable value.

This bond is in addition to the normal Customs entry bond. Copies of the DOT bond and the contract with an RI must be attached to the HS-7 form.

Under the contract, the RI will modify and certify that the vehicle conforms with all applicable FMVSS. Before an RI can modify a vehicle NHTSA must have determined that the vehicle is capable of being modified to comply with the FMVSS. If no determination has been made, the RI must petition NHTSA to determine whether the vehicle is capable of being modified to comply with the FMVSS. If the petitioned vehicle is not similar to one sold in the United States, this process becomes very complex and costly. A list of vehicles previously determined eligible for importation may be obtained from an RI or from the NHTSA Web site.

Since the cost of modifying a nonconforming vehicle, or the time required to bring it into conformance, may affect the decision to purchase a vehicle abroad, we strongly recommend discussing these aspects with an RI before buying and shipping a vehicle to the United States.

SOURCE: National Highway Transportation Safety Administration at **http://www.nhtsa.dot.gov/cars/rules/import/gray_01072003.html.**

American versions; seat-belt warning systems have to be added; and speedometers must be adjusted from kilometers to miles. Petitions are available for public comment, although they are extremely rare. From 1991 to 2001, fewer than ten objections were filed.

There has been a substantial increase in the number of nonconforming vehicles entering the United States. An ever-growing gray market for automobiles, especially luxury models, has emerged. Gray-market goods are defined as items manufactured abroad and imported into the United States without the consent of trademark holders. Gray-market goods are not counterfeits; however, differences may exist between these goods and those goods produced for U.S. or North American sale. In 2001, a total of 199,431 nonconforming vehicles were imported (up 15 percent from 173,841 in 2000). The number of RIs has also increased as a result. Automakers, while aware of the practice, could not look away as they had done in the past. The interest in gray-market Ferraris was the result of the low number of cars authorized for import and the high value of the dollar (from 1997 to early 2002). The strong dollar meant savings of 30 to 40 percent in most cases.

Ferrari's Response

In late June 2001, Ferrari took the unprecedented step of asking the DOT to halt importation of 2001 model Ferrari Modenas and 550 Maranellos until the company could prepare its objections to gray-market imports. On August 6, Ferrari's formal brief stated that gray-market imports differ from their North American counterparts in "hundreds" of ways and cannot be readily modified to meet U.S. requirements. This meant a request for federal intervention in denying imports of Ferraris not originally intended for the United States.

In the technical documentation provided by Ferrari, a total of 234 parts, with a suggested retail price of $56,584, are needed to bring a 2001 non-U.S. model 550 into compliance. A total of 306 parts ($68,021) are needed for a 360. As a result, Ferrari had serious reservations about whether modifications to non-U.S. cars proposed by RIs would be sufficient to meet needed emission and safety requirements. For example, the RI's petition may state that doors on all 550s are identical, but doors on non-U.S. cars are not fitted with side-impact protection bars. Enzo Francesconi, Ferrari NA's director of technical services, said the company was not taking the action for business reasons but because it was concerned about safety.

In a related move, Ferrari informed potential buyers of its limited-production $258,000 550 Brachetta that they would be required to sign an agreement prohibiting them from reselling the car to anyone but their Ferrari dealer within the first year of ownership. The reported rationale is to prevent speculation in these exotic cars.

Ferrari alleges that gray imports have no impact on authorized dealers' profits and that the actions taken are really to protect the company's reputation. It categorically rejects owners and dealer complaints about allegations of control for profit.

The Reaction

Reaction from RIs as well as (would-be) owners was swift and vehement. Rich Goings, a Ferrari owner and chairman of Tupperware Corporation, filed a letter with OVSC stating: "The case currently being presented by Ferrari NA is nothing more than an attempt to continue to artificially influence market demand to support inflated profit margins. Should this continue, I feel compelled to leverage the influence of companies such as mine with the legislative branch to launch an investigation." In a letter to his congressional representative, Doug Pirrone, president of Berlinetta Motocars in Huntington, New York, alleged that Ferrari's goal "is to control the market, ensure a monopoly, fix the prices, and eliminate all competition."

In the meantime, many RIs have felt the strangling effect of Ferrari's action on their businesses. "It's on life-support now," said Lois Joyeusaz, CEO of J.K. Technologies, one of the RIs registered with the DOT. The dealer had to start storing cars, such as Mercedes-Benzes, Porches, and Ferraris, on a remote farm 90 miles away during its wait for government approval.

Government in the Middle

The OVSC found itself caught in a predicament between Ferrari owners and Ferrari itself. Kenneth Weinstein, associate administrator for safety assurance at the NHTSA who oversees the OVSC, stated that the office "wanted to give everyone the right opportunity to make their points" even if that caused delays in approvals and owners getting possession of their cars. As far as RIs' complaints about ever-growing inventories of imports that could not be delivered to rightful owners, Weinstein stated: "We are doing our job, and if they made a financial commitment that we would be done reviewing their petitions by a particular time, that is not the government's responsibility."

A Side Note

In a rare comment from the public during the petition processes, the head of Original Automobile Manufacturers' Association, John Linder, has taken exception to many of the RIs' comments. Upon investigation by a number of parties, records show no evidence of any such association nor of a person called John Linder. A person calling himself John Linder contacted *The Washington Post* and stated as his motive that he was not too keen on the idea of rich people trying to bring in luxury cars, which he deems are in violation of safety standards. He vowed no affiliation with Ferrari or with authorized dealers.

The Decision

On April 10, 2002, the following announcement was made by the NHTSA and became effective immediately: "This notice announces the decision by NHTSA that 2001 Ferrari 360 passenger cars not originally manufactured to comply with all applicable Federal motor vehicle safety standards are eligible for importation into the United States because they are substantially similar to vehicles originally manufactured for importation into and sale in the United States and certified by their manufacturer as complying with the safety standards, and are capable of being readily altered to conform to the standards." The same decision was made with respect to the 550 model.

The landmark petition on which the decision was based was made by J.K. Technologies and generated 21 responses, of which 19 were in favor and 2 against. Mr. Linder's comment was not responded to given that he proved to be a "fictitious entity." Ferrari suffered a setback with this decision.

Questions for Discussion

1. Gary Roberts, a Costa Mesa, California, importer stated: "Ferrari's control freaks ought to cooperate with importers and let the free market take care of itself." Comment.

2. Does Ferrari's case prove that requiring that products be delivered only through approved distribution channels ensures the highest quality for the customer?

3. Given its loss, what alternative actions are open to Ferrari?

Global Vendor Relations at Pier 1 Imports

Over 200,000 pieces of stainless steel flatware are just sitting in a Pier 1 Imports warehouse. Where did these come from? Most recently they were stocked in Pier 1 stores—that is until a couple of customers informed store managers that the stainless steel pieces rusted. The company response? After a very rapid testing process that confirmed the customers' observations, the offending product was pulled from all stores and sent to its "resting place"—all within a two-week period.

The people in merchandising at company headquarters in Fort Worth, Texas, and the local Pier 1 agent in China now have ascertained that while there are 47 different types of stainless steel, only one—referred to as 18–8—can be used to make serviceable flatware that won't rust. This newly recognized quality specification has been quickly communicated to all other company agents who purchase flatware, assuring that this product quality issue will not arise again.

It is John Baker's responsibility to oversee the network of corporate buyers and on-site agents who are directly responsible for finding, choosing, and assuring the quality of merchandise imported from around the world. Baker, the Senior Manager of Merchandise Compliance, accepted a position at Pier 1 Imports over 20 years ago after working for various department stores purchasing "table-top" and kitchen wares. When he first came on board as a buyer, he spent nearly six months of the year on the road, working with the agent network and finding new vendors for Pier 1 merchandise. Today, Baker also handles the increasingly complex area of government regulations of merchandise.

Because such a high percentage of Pier 1 Imports' merchandise is imported (over 85 percent), it is especially critical that U.S. government regulations regarding various product categories be studied and communicated to the manufacturers in other countries. These government regulations form one of the two measures of quality assurance for Pier 1 products. The second is that the products must conform to aesthetic standards that guarantee that the product fits the Pier 1 image and Pier 1 customer desires. It is in large part the buyer's expertise that assures that these standards are met.

What is the process for finding and selecting vendors in countries other than the United States? First of all, Pier 1 depends upon a well- and long-established network of agents in every country from which they import. In some lesser-developed regions, Pier 1 agents work with governments to help locate professional exporters. Some exporters are found at international trade fairs as well. The bulk of Pier 1 agents are native to the country in which they work, and some have been in place for as long as 30 years, with their children now taking over the local positions.

The agents' jobs include finding local producers of handcrafted items that fit Pier 1 customer needs. Buyers look for new sources of products at local craft fairs and even flea markets. Right now, for example, local agents in several countries are looking for sources of wooden furniture—primarily

SOURCE: Adapted from *Contemporary Business,* 9th ed., by Louis E. Boone and David L. Kurtz, *Contemporary Business,* 10th ed., published by Harcourt College Publishers, Fort Worth, TX.

chests and tables—because Pier 1 would like to add to this in-store category. Based upon the location of raw materials, in this case in Italy, South America, Indonesia, and Thailand, agents are searching for just the right manufacturers to be brought to the buyers' attention.

Because it is the agents based within the various exporting countries who must enforce quality requirements, it is critical that John Baker and his colleagues carefully communicate both governmental and aesthetic product requirements to the agents. The agents can then "sit down at the table" with the manufacturers and work out the quality issues. If misunderstandings occur, Pier 1 is always ready to accept some of the responsibility because they view their manufacturers and agents as their partners in this business.

Because Pier 1 Imports has carefully carved out a unique niche in the specialty retail store industry, buyers are hard to hire from outside the company. As Baker noted, "The bulk of our staff has come out of our stores. It is easy for a buyer to move from Macy's to Hudson's—the products are the same, as are most of the vendors. The Pier 1 buyer, however, must understand the Pier 1 store in order to be able to effectively and efficiently buy for it." These Pier 1 buyers, along with their agents on-site around the globe, serve as the company's primary link to product quality.

Questions for Discussion

1. What are the implications for sales, customer satisfaction, and profits for companies like Pier 1 (**http://www.pier1.com**) when low-quality merchandise is not identified early in the purchasing process?
2. Do you think that Pier 1 might have avoided this problem if it had a very aggressive quality assurance program (i.e., ISO 9000) in place?

Lakewood Chopsticks Exports

Since the 1970s, the United States has had a merchandise trade deficit with the rest of the world. Up to 1982, this deficit mattered little because it was relatively small. As of 1983, however, the trade deficit increased rapidly and became, due to its size and future implications, an issue of major national concern. Suddenly, trade moved to the forefront of national debate. Concurrently, a debate ensued on the issue of the international competitiveness of U.S. firms. The onerous question here was whether U.S. firms could and would achieve sufficient improvements in areas such as productivity, quality, and price to remain successful international marketing players in the long term.

The U.S.–Japanese trade relation took on particular significance because it was between those two countries that the largest bilateral trade deficit existed. In spite of trade negotiations, market-opening measures, trade legislation, and other governmental efforts, it was clear that the impetus for a reversal of the deficit through more U.S. exports to Japan had to come from the private sector. Therefore, the activities of any U.S. firm that appeared successful in penetrating the Japanese market were widely hailed. One company whose effort to market in Japan aroused particular

interest was Lakewood Forest Products in Hibbing, Minnesota.

Company Background

In 1983, Ian J. Ward was an export merchant in difficulty. Throughout the 1970s his company, Ward, Bedas Canadian Ltd., had successfully sold Canadian lumber and salmon to countries in the Persian Gulf. Over time, the company had opened four offices worldwide. However, when the Iran–Iraq war erupted, most of Ward's long-term trading relationships disappeared within a matter of months. In addition, the international lumber market began to collapse. As a result, Ward, Bedas Canadian Ltd. went into a survivalist mode and sent employees all over the world to look for new markets and business opportunities. Late that year, the company received an interesting order. A firm in Korea urgently needed to purchase lumber for the production of chopsticks.

Learning about the
Chopstick Market

In discussing the wood deal with the Koreans, Ward learned that in the production of good chopsticks, more than 60 percent of the wood fiber is wasted. Given the high transportation cost involved, the large degree of wasted materials, and his need for new business, Ward decided to explore the Korean and Japanese chopstick industry in more detail.

He quickly determined that chopstick making in the Far East is a fragmented industry, working

SOURCES: This case was written by Michael R. Czinkota based on the following sources: Mark Clayton, "Minnesota Chopstick Maker Finds Japanese Eager to Import His Quality Waribashi," *Christian Science Monitor,* October 16, 1987, 11; Roger Worthington, "Improbable Chopstick Capitol of the World," *Chicago Tribune,* June 5, 1988, 39; Mark Gill, "The Great American Chopstick Master," *American Way,* August 1, 1987, 34, 78–79; "Perpich of Croatia," *The Economist,* April 20, 1991, 27; and personal interview with Ian J. Ward, president, Lakewood Forest Products.

with old technology and suffering from a lack of natural resources. In Asia, chopsticks are produced in very small quantities, often by family organizations. Even the largest of the 450 chopstick factories in Japan turns out only 5 million chopsticks a month. This compares with an overall market size of 130 million pairs of disposable chopsticks a day. In addition, chopsticks represent a growing market. With increased wealth in Asia, people eat out more often and therefore have a greater demand for disposable chopsticks. The fear of communicable diseases has greatly reduced the utilization of reusable chopsticks. Renewable plastic chopsticks have been attacked by many groups as too newfangled and as causing future ecological problems.

From his research, Ward concluded that a competitive niche existed in the world chopstick market. He believed that if he could use low-cost raw materials and ensure that the labor-cost component would remain small, he could successfully compete in the world market.

The Founding of Lakewood Forest Products

In exploring opportunities afforded by the newly identified international marketing niche for chopsticks, Ward set four criteria for plant location:

1. Access to suitable raw materials.
2. Proximity of other wood product users who could make use of the 60 percent waste for their production purposes.
3. Proximity to a port that would facilitate shipment to the Far East.
4. Availability of labor.

In addition, Ward was aware of the importance of product quality. Because people use chopsticks on a daily basis and are accustomed to products that are visually inspected one by one, he would have to live up to high quality expectations in order to compete successfully. Chopsticks could not be bowed or misshapen, have blemishes in the wood, or splinter.

To implement his plan, Ward needed financing. Private lenders were skeptical and slow to provide funds. This skepticism resulted from the unusual direction of Ward's proposal. Far Eastern companies have generally held the cost advantage in a variety of industries, especially those as labor-intensive as chopstick manufacturing. U.S. companies rarely have an advantage in producing low-cost items. Further, only a very small domestic market exists for chopsticks.

Yet Ward found that the state of Minnesota was willing to participate in this new venture. Since the decline of the mining industry, regional unemployment had been rising rapidly in the state. In 1983, unemployment in Minnesota's Iron Range peaked at 22 percent. Therefore, state and local officials were eager to attract new industries that would be independent of mining activities. Of particular help was the enthusiasm of Governor Rudy Perpich. The governor had been boosting Minnesota business on the international scene by traveling abroad and receiving many foreign visitors. He was excited about Ward's plans, which called for the creation of over 100 new jobs within a year.

Hibbing, Minnesota, turned out to be an ideal location for Ward's project. The area had an abundance of aspen wood, which, because it grows in clay soil, tends to be unmarred. The fact that Hibbing was the hometown of the governor also did not hurt. In addition, Hibbing boasted an excellent labor pool, and both the city and the state were willing to make loans totaling $500,000. Further, the Iron Range Resources Rehabilitation Board was willing to sell $3.4 million in industrial revenue bonds for the project. Together with jobs and training wage subsidies, enterprise zone credits, and tax increment financing benefits, the initial public support of the project added up to about 30 percent of its start-up costs. The potential benefit of the new venture to the region was quite clear. When Lakewood Forest Products advertised its first 30 jobs, more than 3,000 people showed up to apply.

The Production and Sale of Chopsticks

Ward insisted that in order to truly penetrate the international market, he would need to keep his labor cost low. As a result, he decided to automate as much of the production as possible. However, no equipment was readily available to produce chopsticks because no one had automated the process before.

After much searching, Ward identified a European equipment manufacturer that produced machinery for making popsicle sticks. He purchased equipment from this Danish firm in order to better carry out the sorting and finishing processes. Since aspen wood is quite different from the wood the machine was designed for, as was the final product, substantial design adjustments had to be made. Sophisticated equipment was also purchased to strip the bark from the wood and peel it into long, thin sheets. Finally, a computer vision system was acquired to detect defects in the chopsticks. This system rejected over 20 percent of the production, and yet some of the chopsticks that passed inspection were splintering. Yet Ward firmly believed that further fine-tuning of the equipment and training of the new workforce would gradually take care of the problem.

Given this fully automated process, Lakewood Forest Products was able to develop capacity for up to 7 million pairs of chopsticks a day. With a unit manufacturing cost of $0.03 per pair and an anticipated unit selling price of $0.057, Ward expected to earn a pretax profit of $4.7 million in 1988.

Due to intense marketing efforts in Japan and the fact that Japanese customers were struggling to obtain sufficient supplies of disposable chopsticks, Ward was able to presell the first five years of production quite quickly. By late 1987, Lakewood Forest Products was ready to enter the international market. With an ample supply of raw materials and an almost totally automated plant, Lakewood was positioned as the world's largest and least labor-intensive manufacturer of chopsticks. The first shipment of six containers with a load of 12 million pairs of chopsticks was sent to Japan in October 1987.

Questions for Discussion

1. Is Lakewood Forest Products ready for exports? Using the export-readiness framework developed by the U.S. Department of Commerce and available through various sites such as **http://www.tradeport.org** (from "Trade Expert" go to "Getting Started" and finally to "Assess Your Export Readiness"), determine whether Lakewood's commitment, resources, and product warrant the action they have undertaken.

2. What are the environmental factors that are working for and against Lakewood Forest Products both at home in the United States and in the target market, Japan?

3. New-product success is a function of trial and repurchase. How do Lakewood's chances look along these two dimensions?

Part Three

INTERNATIONAL MARKETING

Chapter 12
Global Strategic Planning

Chapter 13
Global Market Expansion

Chapter 14
Product and Brand Management

Chapter 15
Services Marketing

Chapter 16
Global Pricing Strategies

Chapter 17
Logistics and Supply Chain Management

Chapter 18
Global Promotional Strategies

Chapter 19
Marketing Organization, Implementation, and Control

Chapter 20
The Future

Cases

Video Case

Global Marketing Management

Part Three deals with advanced international marketing activities. The core marketing concerns of the beginning internationalist and the multinational corporation are the same. Yet multinational firms face challenges and opportunities that are different from those encountered by smaller firms. They are able to expend more resources on international marketing efforts than are small and medium-sized firms. In addition, their perspective can be more globally oriented. Multinational corporations also have more impact on individuals, economies, and governments. Therefore, they are much more subject to public scrutiny and need to be more concerned about repercussions of their activities. Yet their very size often enables them to be more influential in setting international marketing rules.

© PHOTODISC, VOL. 22

chapter 12
Global Strategic Planning

© EYEWIRE/GETTY IMAGES

THE INTERNATIONAL MARKETPLACE   12.1

Appliance Makers on a Global Quest

The $70 billion (expected to grow to $120 billion by 2010) home appliance market is undergoing major consolidation and globalization. Many U.S.-based manufacturers are faced in their home markets with increased competition from foreign companies, such as the world's largest appliance maker, Electrolux, and newcomers such as China's Haier and Kelon. In addition, industry fundamentals in the United States are rather gloomy: stagnating sales, rising raw material prices, and price wars. On the other hand, markets abroad are full of opportunities. The European market, for example, is growing quite fast, and the breakdown of barriers within the European Union has made establishing business there even more attractive. Market potential is significant as well: While 65 percent of U.S. homes have dryers, only 18 percent of Europeans have them. Markets in Latin America and Asia are showing similar trends as well; for example, only 15 percent of Brazil's households own microwave ovens compared with 91 percent in the United States. However, expansion was slowed down considerably by the crises of 1997–2002.

To take advantage of this growth, appliance makers have formed strategic alliances and made acquisitions. General Electric entered into a joint venture with Britain's General Electric PLC, and in its strategic shift to move the company's "center of gravity" from the industrialized world to Asia and Latin America, joint ventures were established in India with Godrej and in Mexico with Mabe. A strictly North American manufacturer before 1989, Whirlpool purchased the appliance business of Dutch giant N. V. Phillips. Whirlpool's move gave it ten plants on the European continent and some popular appliance lines, which is a major asset in a region characterized by loyalty to domestic brands. Today, Whirlpool is third in European market share after Electrolux and Bosch-Siemens. The company ranks first in the Americas, and while it only has a 1 percent market share in Asia, it is the region's largest Western appliance maker. Whirlpool's advantage in Brazil, for example, is the strong loyalty it has earned in 40 years of operations (which it lacks in some Asian markets). In the last five years, Whirlpool has expanded its operations in Eastern and Central Europe as well as South Africa, thus extending its total reach to 170 countries worldwide.

Product differences present global marketers with a considerable challenge. The British favor front-loading washing machines, while the French swear by top-loaders. The French prefer to cook their food at high temperatures, causing grease to splatter onto oven walls, which calls for self-cleaning ovens. This feature is in less demand in Germany, where lower temperatures are traditionally used. Manufacturers are hoping that European integration will bring about cost savings and product standardization. The danger to be avoided is the development of compromise products that in the end appeal to no one. Joint ventures present their share of challenges to the global marketers. For example, in Whirlpool's Shanghai facility, teams of American, Italian, and Chinese technicians must work through three interpreters to set up production.

Although opportunities do exist, competition is keen. Margins have suffered as manufacturers (more than 300 in Europe alone) scrape for business. The major players have decided to compete in all the major markets of the world. "Becoming a global appliance player is clearly the best use of our management expertise and well-established brand line-up," Whirlpool executives have said. Whirlpool's long-term goal is to leverage its global manufacturing and brand assets strategically across the world.

Not everyone has succeeded, however. In its move toward globalization, Maytag acquired Chicago Pacific Corporation, best known for its Hoover appliances. The products have a strong presence in the United Kingdom and Australia but not on the European continent, where Maytag ended up essentially trying to introduce new products to new markets. After six years, Maytag sold its

COURTESY OF HAIER AMERICA

European operations to an Italian manufacturer at a loss of $135 million in 1995. In early 2000, Maytag entered into an alliance with Sanyo Electric Co. to develop and market home appliances for the Japanese and Pacific Rim markets. Maytag's $325 million acquisition of Amana Appliances in 2001 is expected to solidify the company's position in the top three appliance makers in North America. Major sales growth is planned for Canada and Mexico, where Maytag products have long been under-represented.

The most recent entrants into the global home appliance markets are China's Haier and Kelon, both mainly in refrigerators and air conditioners, industries in which China's technology is up to world standards. Haier's market share globally is still small (2.8 percent) compared to Whirlpool's (11.3 percent) and Electrolux's (8.2 percent), but the company is on an ambitious growth trajectory. While no foreign brand has made it big in the U.S. major-appliance market (mainly due to lack of brand recognition and distribution presence), Haier is currently selling 250 models of appliances through big retailers such as Wal-Mart and Costco and over 1,000 independent dealers. The company claims to have 50 percent of the U.S. market for small refrigerators (for offices and dorm rooms). The approach is to build brands with lower prices and dependable quality and move upscale with time. Haier is already the second largest maker of refrigerators in the world and ranks sixth in overall appliance sales.

SOURCES: Joshua Kurlantzick, "Making It in China," *U.S. News & World Report*, October 7, 2002, 44–49; Jonathan Sprague, "Haier Reaches Higher," *Fortune*, September 16, 2002, 43–46; "Chinese Multinationals Aim to Be Just That," *The Wall Street Journal*, January 28, 2002, A1; "The Repairman in Charge of Fixing Maytag," *Business Week*, November 19, 2001, 35–36; Russell Flannery, "China Goes Global," *Forbes*, August 6, 2001, 35–38; "Maytag's Share Price Falls on Earnings Warning," *The Wall Street Journal*, February 15, 2000, B8; "Chinese Brands out of the Shadows," *The Economist*, August 28, 1999, 78–81; "Whirlpool's in the Wringer," *Business Week*, December 14, 1998, 83–84; **http://www.whirlpool.com**; **http://www.ge.com**; **http://www.maytag.com**; and **http://www.haieramerica.com**.

Global Marketing

Many marketing managers have to face the increasing globalization of markets and competition described in *The International Marketplace 12.1*. The rules of survival have changed since the beginning of the 1980s when Theodore Levitt first coined the phrase *global marketing*.[1] Even the biggest companies in the biggest home markets cannot survive on domestic sales alone if they are in global industries such as cars, banking, consumer electronics, entertainment, pharmaceuticals, publishing, travel services, or home appliances. They have to be in all major markets to survive the shakeouts expected to leave three to five players per industry at the beginning of the twenty-first century.

Globalization reflects a business orientation based on the belief that the world is becoming more homogeneous and that distinctions between national markets are not only fading but, for some products, will eventually disappear. As a result, companies need to globalize their international strategy by formulating it across markets to take advantage of underlying market, cost, environmental, and competitive factors. This has meant, for example, that Chinese companies (in categories ranging from auto parts and appliances to telecommunications) have entered the main markets of the world such as Europe and North America to become global powerhouses.[2] Having a global presence ensures viability against other players in the home market as well.

As shown in Figure 12.1, globalization can be seen as a result of a process that culminates a process of international market entry and expansion. Before globalization, marketers utilize a country-by-country multidomestic strategy to a great extent, with each country organization operated as a profit center. Each national entity markets a range of different products and services targeted to different customer segments, utilizing different marketing strategies with little or no coordination of operations between countries.

However, as national markets become increasingly similar and scale economies become increasingly important, the inefficiencies of duplicating product development and manufacture in each country become more apparent and the pressure to leverage resources and coordinate activities across borders gains urgency. Similarly, the increasing number of customers operating globally, as well as the same or similar competitors faced throughout the major markets, adds to the need for strategy integration.

Figure 12.1 Global Marketing Evolution

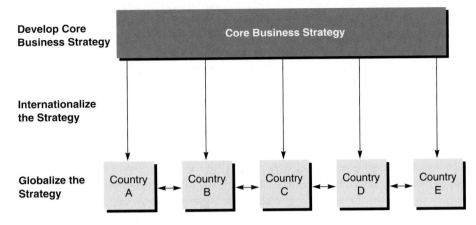

SOURCE: George S. Yip, *Total Global Strategy II* © 2002. Reprinted by permission of Pearson Education, Inc., Upper Saddle River, NJ.

Globalization Drivers[3]

Both external and internal factors will create the favorable conditions for development of strategy and resource allocation on a global basis. These factors can be divided into market, cost, environmental, and competitive factors.

Market Factors

The world customer identified by Ernst Dichter more than 40 years ago has gained new meaning today.[4] For example, Kenichi Ohmae has identified consumers in the **triad** of North America, Europe, and the Asia-Pacific region, whom marketers can treat as a single market with similar consumption habits.[5] Over a billion in number, these consumers have similar educational backgrounds, income levels, lifestyles, use of leisure time, and aspirations. One reason given for the similarities in their demand is a level of purchasing power (ten times greater than that of LDCs or even emerging economies) that translates into higher diffusion rates for certain products. Another reason is that developed infrastructures—diffusion of telecommunication and common platforms such as Microsoft Windows and the Internet—lead to attractive markets for other goods and services. Products can be designed to meet similar demand conditions throughout the triad. These similarities also enhance the transferability of other marketing elements.

At the same time, channels of distribution are becoming more global; that is, a growing number of retailers are now showing great flexibility in their strategies for entering new geographic markets.[6] Some are already world powers (e.g., Benetton and McDonald's), whereas others are pursuing aggressive growth (e.g., ALDI, Toys 'Я' Us, and IKEA). Also noteworthy are cross-border retail alliances, which expand the presence of retailers to new markets quite rapidly. The presence of global and regional channels makes it more necessary for the marketer to rationalize marketing efforts.

Cost Factors

Avoiding cost inefficiencies and duplication of effort are two of the most powerful globalization drivers. A single-country approach may not be large enough for the local business to achieve all possible economies of scale and scope as well as synergies, especially given the dramatic changes in the marketplace. Take, for example, pharmaceuticals. In the 1970s, developing a new drug cost about $16 million and took four years. The drug could be produced in Britain or the United States and eventually exported. Now, developing a drug costs as much as $500 million and takes as long as 12 years, with competitive efforts close behind. For the leading companies, annual R&D budgets can run to $5 billion. Only global products for global markets can support that much risk.[7] Size has become a major asset, which partly explains the many mergers and acquisitions in industries such as aerospace, pharmaceuticals, and telecommunications. The paper industry underwent major regional consolidation between 1998 and 2002, as shown in Table 12.1, as companies from North America and Europe in particular consolidated their positions in a scale-driven sector.[8] In the heavily contested consumer goods sectors, launching a new brand may cost as much as $100 million, meaning that companies such as Unilever and Procter & Gamble are not going to necessarily spend precious resources on one-country projects.

In many cases, expanded market participation and activity concentration can accelerate the accumulation of learning and experience. General Electric's philosophy is to be first or second in the world in a business or to get out. This can be seen, for example, in its global effort to develop premium computed tomography (CT), a diagnostic scanning system. GE swapped its consumer electronics business with the French Thomson for Thomson's diagnostic imaging business. At the same time, GE established GE Medical Systems Asia in Tokyo, anchored on Yokogawa Medical Systems, which is 75 percent owned by GE.

Environmental Factors

As shown earlier in this text, government barriers have fallen dramatically in the last years to further facilitate the globalization of markets and the activities of marketers within them. For example, the forces pushing toward a pan-European market are very powerful: The increasing wealth and mobility of European consumers (favored by the relaxed immigration controls), the accelerating flow of information across borders, the introduction of new products where local preferences are not well established, and the common currency.[9] Also, the resulting removal of physical, fiscal, and technical barriers is indicative of the changes that are taking place around the world on a greater scale.

At the same time, rapid technological evolution is contributing to the process. For example, Ford Motor Company is able to accomplish its globalization efforts by using new communications methods, such as teleconferencing, intranet, and

---

Table 12.1 **Consolidation in the Paper Industry, 1998–2002**

Acquirer	Target	Value	Date Announced
MeadWestvaco (U.S.)*	Mead (U.S.)*	$3.2 billion	8/29/01
Norske Skogindustrier (Norway)	Fletcher Challenge Paper (New Zealand)	$2.5 billion	4/03/00
Smurfit-Stone (U.S.)	St. Laurent Paperboard (Canada)	$1.0 billion	2/23/00
Stora Enso (Finland)	Consolidated Papers (U.S.)	$3.9 billion	2/22/00
International Paper (U.S.)	Champion Int'l (U.S.)	$5.7 billion	2/17/00
Abitibi-Consol. (Canada)	Donohue (Canada)	$4.0 billion	2/11/00
Weyerhaeuser (U.S.)	MacMillan Bloedel (Canada)	$2.3 billion	6/21/99
Int'l Paper (U.S.)	Union Camp (U.S.)	$5.9 billion	11/24/98
Stora (Sweden)*	Enso Oyj (Finland)*	Undisclosed	6/02/98

*Merger of equals

SOURCES: "Paper Merger Attains Size without Adding Huge Debt," *The Wall Street Journal*, August 30, 2001, B4; and "Stora Enso to Buy Consolidated Papers," *The Wall Street Journal*, February 23, 2000, A3, A8. See also **http://www.storaenso.com**; and Robert Frank, "The Emerging Global Paper Industry," **http://www.worldleadersinprint.com**, accessed April 25, 2001.

CAD/CAM links, as well as travel, to manage the complex task of meshing car companies on different continents.[10] Newly emerging markets will benefit from advanced communications by being able to leapfrog stages of economic development. Places that until recently were incommunicado in China, Vietnam, Hungary, or Brazil are rapidly acquiring state-of-the-art telecommunications, especially in mobile telephony, that will let them foster both internal and external development.[11]

A new group of global players is taking advantage of today's more open trading regions and newer technologies. "Mininationals" or "Born Globals" (newer companies with sales between $200 million and $1 billion) are able to serve the world from a handful of manufacturing bases, compared with having to build a plant in every country as the established multinational corporations once had to do. Their smaller bureaucracies have also allowed these mininationals to move swiftly to seize new markets and develop new products—a key to global success.[12] This phenomenon is highlighted in *The International Marketplace 12.2*.

THE INTERNATIONAL MARKETPLACE 12.2

Born Global

Exports account for 95 percent of Cochlear's $40 million sales after a real annual compounded rate of 25 percent throughout the last ten years. Cochlear is a company specializing in the production of implants for the profoundly deaf. Based in Australia, it maintains a global technological lead through its strong links with hospitals and research units around the world and through its collaborative research with a network of institutions around the world.

Cochlear is a prime example of small to medium-sized firms that are remaking the global corporation of the future. The term "mininational" has been coined to reflect their smaller size compared to the traditional multinationals. Sheer size is no longer a buffer against competition in markets where customers are demanding specialized and customized products. With the advent of electronic process technology, mininationals are able to compete on price and quality—often with greater flexibility. By taking advantage of today's more open trading regions, they can serve the world from a handful of manufacturing bases, sparing them from the necessity of building a plant in every country. Developments in information technology have enabled mininationals to both access data throughout most of the world and to run inexpensive and responsive sales and service operations across languages and time zones. An empirical study of exporting firms established in the last ten years found that more than half could be classified as "Born Globals."

The smaller bureaucracies of the mininationals allow them to move swiftly in seizing new markets and developing new products, typically in focused markets. In many cases, these new markets have been developed by the mininationals themselves. For example, Symbol Technolo-gies, Inc. of Bohemia, New York, invented the field of handheld laser scanners and now dominates this field. In a field that did not even exist fifteen years ago, Cisco Systems, Inc. of Menlo Park, California, grew from a mininational to an entity that has over 35,278 employees in more than 200 offices in 66 countries. Other mininationals continue to focus on their core products and services, growing and excelling at what they do best.

The lessons from these new-generation global players are to (1) keep focused and concentrate on being number one or number two in a technology niche; (2) stay lean by having small headquarters to save on costs and to accelerate decision making; (3) take ideas and technologies to and from wherever they can be found; (4) take advantage of employees regardless of nationality to globalize thinking; and (5) solve customers' problems by involving them rather than pushing standardized solutions on them. As a result of being flexible, they are better able to weather storms such as the Asian crisis by changing emphases in the geographical operations.

SOURCES: Øystein Moen and Per Servais, "Born Global or Gradual Global? Examining the Export Behavior of Small and Medium-Sized Enterprises," *Journal of International Marketing* 10 (no. 3, 2002): 49–72; Øystein Moen, "The Born Globals: A New Generation of Small European Exporters," *International Marketing Review* 19 (no. 2, 2002): 156–175; Gary Knight, "Entrepreneurship and Marketing Strategy: The SME Under Globalization," *Journal of International Marketing* 8 (no. 2, 2000): 12–32; "Corporate Profile," available at **http://www.cisco.com**; "Turning Small into an Advantage," *Business Week*, July 13, 1998, 42–44; Michael W. Rennie, "Born Global," *The McKinsey Quarterly* (no. 4, 1993): 45–52; "Mininationals Are Making Maximum Impact," *Business Week*, September 6, 1993, 66–69; **http://www.cochlear.com**; and **http://www.cisco.com**.

Competitive Factors

Many industries are already dominated by global competitors that are trying to take advantage of the three sets of factors mentioned earlier. To remain competitive, the marketer may have to be the first to do something or to be able to match or preempt competitors' moves. Products are now introduced, upgraded, and distributed at rates unimaginable a decade ago. Without a global network, a marketer may run the risk of seeing carefully researched ideas picked off by other global players. This is what Procter & Gamble and Unilever did to Kao's Attack concentrated detergent, which they mimicked and introduced into the United States and Europe before Kao could react.

With the triad markets often both flat in terms of growth and fiercely competitive, many global marketers are looking for new markets and for new product categories for growth. Nestlé, for example, is setting its sights on consumer markets in fast-growing Asia, especially China, and has diversified into pharmaceuticals by acquiring Alcon and by becoming a major shareholder in the world's number-one cosmetics company, the French L'Oreal. Between 1985 and 2000, Nestlé spent $26 billion on acquisitions, and another $18 billion from 2001 to 2002.[13]

Market presence may be necessary to execute global strategies and to prevent others from having undue advantage in unchallenged markets. Caterpillar faced mounting global competition from Komatsu but found out that strengthening its products and operations was not enough to meet the challenge. Although Japan was a small part of the world market, as a secure home base (no serious competitors), it generated 80 percent of Komatsu's cash flow. To put a check on its major global competitor's market share and cash flow, Caterpillar formed a heavy-equipment joint venture with Mitsubishi to serve the Japanese market.[14] Similarly, when Unilever tried to acquire Richardson-Vicks in the United States, Procter & Gamble saw this as a threat to its home market position and outbid its archrival for the company. International Paper prevented Finland's United Paper Mills from acquiring Champion International to protect its market position as the leading paper maker in North America and the world.

The Outcome

The four globalization drivers have affected countries and industrial sectors differently. While some industries are truly globally contested, such as paper and soft drinks, some others, such as government procurement, are still quite closed and will open up as a decades-long evolution. Commodities and manufactured goods are already in a globalized state, while many consumer goods are accelerating toward more globalization. Similarly, the leading trading nations of the world display far more openness than low-income countries, thus advancing the state of globalization in general. The expansion of the global trade arena is summarized in Figure 12.2. The size of the market estimated to be global in the early twenty-first century is well over $21 billion, boosted by new sectors and markets that will become available. For example, while financially unattractive in the short to medium term, low-income markets may be beneficial in learning the business climate, developing relationships, and building brands for the future. Hewlett-Packard, through its e-Inclusion initiative, is looking at speech interfaces for the Internet, solar applications, and cheap devices that connect with the Web.[15]

Leading companies by their very actions drive the globalization process. There is no structural reason why soft drinks should be at a more advanced stage of globalization than beer and spirits, which remain more local, except for the opportunistic behavior of Coca-Cola. Similarly, Nike and Reebok have driven their businesses in a global direction by creating global brands, a global customer segment, and a global supply chain. By creating a single online trading exchange for all their parts and suppliers, General Motors, Ford, and DaimlerChrysler created a worldwide market of $240 billion in automotive components.[16]

Figure 12.2   The Global Landscape by Industry and Market

Industry

Country		Commodities and scale-driven goods	Consumer goods and locally delivered goods and services	Government services
Triad*		Established arena Globalized in 1980s		
Emerging countries†		Growing arena Globally contestable today		
Low-income countries‡		Closed arena Still blocked or lacking significant opportunity		

Global ←——————————————————————→ Local

More globalized ↑ ... ↓ Less globalized

* 30 OECD countries from North America, Western Europe, and Asia; Japan and Australia included
† 70 countries with middle income per capita, plus China and India
‡ 100 Countries of small absolute size and low income per capita

SOURCE: Adapted and updated from Jane Fraser and Jeremy Oppenheim, "What's New about Globalization," *The McKinsey Quarterly* 33 (no. 2, 1997): 173; and Jagdish N. Sheth and Atul Parkatiyar, "The Antecedents and Consequences of Integrated Global Marketing," *International Marketing Review* 18 (no. 1, 2001): 16–29.

The Strategic Planning Process

Given the opportunities and challenges provided by the new realities of the marketplace, decision makers have to engage in strategic planning to match markets with products and other corporate resources more effectively and efficiently to strengthen the company's long-term competitive advantage. While the process has been summarized as a sequence of steps in Figure 12.3, many of the stages can occur simultaneously. Furthermore, feedback as a result of evaluation and control may restart the process at any stage.

It has been shown that for globally committed marketers, formal strategic planning contributes to both financial performance and nonfinancial objectives.[17] These benefits include raising the efficacy of new-product launches, cost reduction efforts, and improving product quality and market share performance. Internally, these efforts increase cohesion and improve on understanding different units' points of view.

Understanding and Adjusting the Core Strategy

The planning process has to start with a clear definition of the business for which strategy is to be developed. Generally, the strategic business unit (SBU) is the unit around which decisions are based. In practice, SBUs represent groupings based on product-market similarities based on (1) needs or wants to be met, (2) end user customers to be targeted, or (3) the product or service used to meet the needs of specific customers. For a global marketer such as Black & Decker, the options may be to define the business to be analyzed as the home improvement business, the do-it-yourself business, or the power tool business. Ideally, these SBUs should have primary responsibility and authority in managing their basic business functions.

This phase of the planning process requires the participation of executives from different functions, especially marketing, production, finance, distribution, and procurement. Geographic representation should be from the major markets

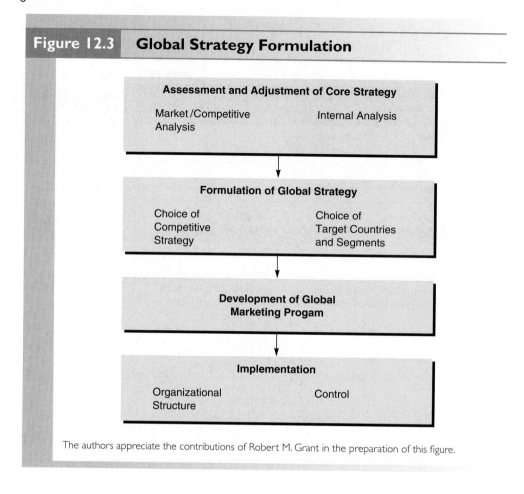

Figure 12.3 | **Global Strategy Formulation**

Assessment and Adjustment of Core Strategy

Market/Competitive
Analysis

Internal Analysis

Formulation of Global Strategy

Choice of
Competitive
Strategy

Choice of
Target Countries
and Segments

**Development of Global
Marketing Progam**

Implementation

Organizational
Structure

Control

The authors appreciate the contributions of Robert M. Grant in the preparation of this figure.

or regions as well as from the smaller, yet emerging, markets. With appropriate members, the committee can focus on product and markets as well as competitors whom they face in different markets, whether they are global, regional, or purely local. Heading this effort should be an executive with highest-level experience in regional or global markets; for example, one global firm called on the president of its European operations to come back to headquarters to head the global planning effort. This effort calls for commitment by the company itself both in calling on the best talent to participate in the planning effort and later in implementing their proposals.

It should be noted that this assessment against environmental realities may mean a dramatic change in direction and approach. For example, the once-separate sectors of computing and mobile telephony will be colliding and the direction of future products is still uncertain. The computer industry believes in miniaturizing the general-purpose computer, while the mobile-phone industry believes in adding new features (such as photo-messaging, gaming, and location-based information) to its existing products.[18] The joint venture between Ericsson and Sony aims at taking advantage of this trend, something that neither party could have done on its own.

Market and Competitive Analysis

For global marketers, planning on a country-by-country basis can result in spotty worldwide market performance. The starting point for global strategic planning is to understand that the underlying forces that determine business success are common to the different countries that the firm competes in. Planning processes that focus simultaneously across a broad range of markets provide global marketers with tools to help balance risks, resource requirements, competitive economies of scale, and profitability to gain stronger long-term positions.[19] On the demand side this requires an understanding of the common features of customer requirements and choice factors. In terms of competition, the key is to understand the structure of the global industry in order to identify the forces that will drive competition and determine profitability.[20]

For Ford Motor Company, strategy begins not with individual national markets, but with understanding trends and sources of profit in the global automobile market. What are the trends in world demand? What are the underlying trends in lifestyles and transportation patterns that will shape customer expectations and preferences with respect to safety, economy, design, and performance? What is the emerging structure of the industry, especially with regard to consolidation among both automakers and their suppliers? What will determine the intensity of competition between the different automakers? The level of excess capacity (currently about 40 percent in the worldwide auto industry) is likely to be a key influence.[21] If competition is likely to intensify, which companies will emerge as winners? An understanding of scale economies, the state of technology, and the other factors that determine cost efficiency is likely to be critically important.

Internal Analysis

Organizational resources have to be used as a reality check for any strategic choice in that they determine a company's capacity for establishing and sustaining competitive advantage within global markets. Industrial giants with deep pockets may be able to establish a presence in any market they wish, while more thinly capitalized companies may have to move cautiously. Human resources may also present a challenge for market expansion. A survey of multinational corporations revealed that good marketing managers, skilled technicians, and production managers were especially difficult to find. This difficulty is further compounded when the search is for people with cross-cultural experience to run future regional operations.[22]

At this stage it is imperative that the company assess its own readiness for the necessary moves. This means a rigorous assessment of organizational commitment to global or regional expansion, as well as an assessment of the product's readiness to face the competitive environment. In many cases this has meant painful decisions of focusing on certain industries and leaving others. For example, Nokia, the world's largest manufacturer of mobile phones, started its rise in the industry when a decision was made at the company in 1992 to focus on digital cellular phones and to sell off dozens of other product lines (such as personal computers, automotive tires, and toilet tissue). By focusing its efforts on this line, the company was able to bring to market new products quickly, build scale economies into its manufacturing, and concentrate on its customers, thereby communicating a commitment to their needs. Nokia's current 40 percent market share allows it the best global visibility of and by the market.[23]

Formulating Global Marketing Strategy

The first step in the formulation of global strategy is the choice of competitive strategy to be employed, followed by the choice of country markets to be entered or to be penetrated further.

Choice of Competitive Strategy

In dealing with the global markets, the marketing manager has three general choices of strategies, as shown in Figure 12.4: (1) cost leadership, (2) differentiation, or (3) focus.[24] A focus strategy is defined by its emphasis on a single industry segment within which the orientation may be toward either low cost or differentiation. Any one of these strategies can be pursued on a global or regional basis, or the marketer may decide to mix and match strategies as a function of market or product dimensions.

Figure 12.4 Competitive Strategies

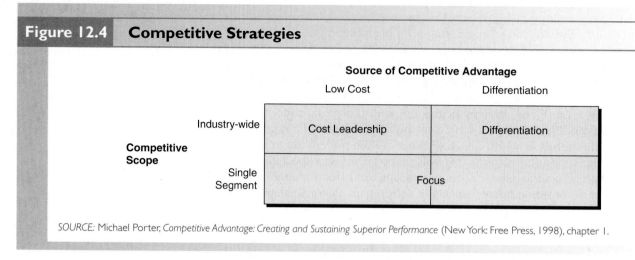

SOURCE: Michael Porter, *Competitive Advantage: Creating and Sustaining Superior Performance* (New York: Free Press, 1998), chapter 1.

In pursuing cost leadership, the global marketer offers an identical product or service at a lower cost than competition. This often means investment in scale economies and strict control of costs, such as overhead, research and development, and logistics. Differentiation, whether it is industry-wide or focused on a single segment, takes advantage of the marketer's real or perceived uniqueness on elements such as design or after-sales service. It should be noted, however, that a low-price, low-cost strategy does not imply a commodity situation.[25] Although Japanese, U.S., and European technical standards differ, mobile phone manufacturers like Motorola and Nokia design their phones to be as similar as possible to hold down manufacturing costs. As a result, they can all be made on the same production line, allowing the manufacturers to shift rapidly from one model to another to meet changes in demand and customer requirements. In the case of IKEA, the low-price approach is associated with clear positioning and a unique brand image focused on a clearly defined target audience of "young people of all ages." Similarly, marketers who opt for high differentiation cannot forget the monitoring of costs. One common denominator of consumers around the world is their quest for value for their money. With the availability of information increasing and levels of education improving, customers are poised to demand even more of their suppliers.

Most global marketers combine high differentiation with cost containment to enter markets and to expand their market shares. Flexible manufacturing systems using mostly standard components and total quality management measures that reduce the occurrence of defects are allowing marketers to customize an increasing amount of their production while at the same time saving on costs. Global activities will in themselves permit the exploitation of scale economies not only in production but also in marketing activities, such as advertising.

Country-Market Choice

A global strategy does not imply that a company should serve the entire globe. Critical choices relate to the allocation of a company's resources between different countries and segments.

The usual approach is first to start with regions and further split the analysis by country. Many marketers use multiple levels of regional groupings to follow the organizational structure of the company, e.g., splitting Europe into northern, central, and southern regions that display similarities in demographic and behavioral traits. An important consideration is that data may be more readily available if existing structures and frameworks are used.[26]

Figure 12.5   Example of a Market-Portfolio Matrix

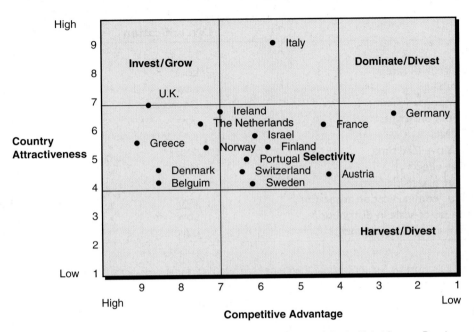

SOURCE: Adapted from Gilbert D. Harrell and Richard O. Kiefer, "Multinational Market Portfolios in Global Strategy Development," *International Marketing Review* 10 (no. 1, 1993): 60–72.

Various portfolio models have been proposed as tools for this analysis. They typically involve two measures—internal strength and external attractiveness.[27] As indicators of internal strength, the following variables have been used: relative market share, product fit, contribution margin, and market presence, which would incorporate the level of support by constituents as well as resources allocated by the company itself. Country attractiveness has been measured using market size, market growth rate, number and type of competitors, and governmental regulation, as well as economic and political stability.

An example of such a matrix is provided in Figure 12.5. The 3 × 3 matrix on country attractiveness and company strength is applied to the European markets. Markets in the invest/grow position will require continued commitment by management in research and development, investment in facilities, and the training of personnel and the country level. In cases of relative weakness in growing markets, the company's position may have to be strengthened (through acquisitions or strategic alliances) or a decision to divest may be necessary. For example, General Mills signed a complementary marketing arrangement with Nestlé to enter the European market dominated by its main global rival, Kellogg's. This arrangement allowed General Mills effective market entry and Nestlé more efficient utilization of its distribution channels in Europe, as well as entry to a new product market. The alliance has since resulted in the formation of Cereal Partners Worldwide, which has a combined worldwide market share of 21 percent.[28]

It is critical that those involved in the planning process consider potential competitors and their impact on the markets should they enter. For example, rather than license software for their next-generation mobile phones from Microsoft, the largest makers (with a combined market share of 80 percent of the mobile handset market) established a software consortium called Symbian to produce software of their own. This will allow the participants to try out many different designs

Table 12.2   Factors Affecting the Choice between Concentration and Diversification Strategies

Factor	Diversification	Concentration
MARKET		
Market growth rate	Low	High
Sales stability	Low	High
Sales response function	Decreasing	Increasing
Extent of constraints	Low	High
MARKETING		
Competitive lead time	Short	Long
Spillover effects	High	Low
Need for product adaptation	Low	High
Need for communication adaptation	Low	High
Economies of scale in distribution	Low	High
Program control requirements	Low	High

SOURCE: Adapted from Igal Ayal and Jehiel Zif, "Marketing Expansion Strategies in Multinational Marketing," *Journal of Marketing* 43 (Spring 1979): 89.

without having to start from scratch every time or be dependent on a potential competitor.[29]

In choosing country markets, a company must make decisions beyond those relating to market attractiveness and company position. A market expansion policy will determine the allocation of resources among various markets. The basic alternatives are **concentration** on a small number of markets and **diversification,** which is characterized by growth in a relatively large number of markets. Expansion strategy is determined by market-, mix-, and company-related factors, listed in Table 12.2. Market-related factors determine the attractiveness of the market in the first place. With high and stable growth rates only in certain markets, the firm will likely opt for a concentration strategy, which is often the case for innovative products early in their life cycle. If demand is strong worldwide, as the case may be for consumer goods, diversification may be attractive. If markets respond to marketing efforts at increasing rates, concentration will occur; however, when the cost of market share points in any one market becomes too high, marketers tend to begin looking for diversification opportunities.

The uniqueness of the product offering with respect to competition is also a factor in expansion strategy. If lead time over competition is considerable, the decision to diversify may not seem urgent. Very few products, however, afford such a luxury. In many product categories, marketers will be affected by spillover effects. Consider, for example, the impact of satellite channels on advertising in Europe or in Asia, where ads for a product now reach most of the market. The greater the degree to which marketing mix elements can be standardized, the more diversification is probable. Overall savings through economies of scale can then be utilized in marketing efforts. Finally, the objectives and policies of the company itself will guide the decision making on expansion. If extensive interaction is called for with intermediaries and clients, efforts are most likely to be concentrated because of resource constraints.

The conventional wisdom of globalization requires a presence in all of the major triad markets of the world. In some cases, markets may not be attractive in their own right but may have some other significance, such as being the home market of the most demanding customers, thereby aiding in product development, or being the home market of a significant competitor (a preemptive rationale). For example, Procter & Gamble rolled its Charmin bath tissue into European markets in 2000 to counter an upsurge in European paper products sales by its global rival Kimberly-Clark.[30] European PC makers, such as Germany's Maxdata and Britain's Tiny, are taking aim at the U.S. market based on the premise that if they can compete with the big multinationals (Dell, Hewlett-Packard, and Gateway) at home, there is no reason why they cannot be competitive in North America as well.[31]

Therefore, for global marketers three factors should determine country selection: (1) the stand-alone attractiveness of a market (e.g., China in consumer products due to its size), (2) global strategic importance (e.g., Finland in shipbuilding due to its lead in technological development in vessel design), and (3) possible synergies (e.g., entry into Latvia and Lithuania after success in the Estonian market given the market similarities).

Segmentation

Effective use of segmentation, that is, the recognition that groups within markets differ sufficiently to warrant individual marketing mixes, allows global marketers to take advantage of the benefits of standardization (such as economies of scale and consistency in positioning) while addressing the unique needs and expectations of a specific target group. This approach means looking at markets on a global or regional basis, thereby ignoring the political boundaries that define markets in many cases. The identification and cultivation of such intermarket segments is necessary for any standardization of marketing programs to work.[32]

The emergence of segments that span markets is already evident in the world marketplace. Global marketers have successfully targeted the teenage segment, which is converging as a result of common tastes in sports and music fueled by their computer literacy, travels abroad, and, in many countries, financial independence.[33] Furthermore, a media revolution is creating a common fabric of attitudes and tastes among teenagers. Today satellite TV and global network concepts such as MTV are both helping create this segment and providing global marketers access to the teen audience around the world. For example, Reebok used a global ad campaign to launch its Instapump line of sneakers in the United States, Germany, Japan, and 137 other countries. Given that teenagers around the world are concerned with social issues, particularly environmentalism, Reebok has introduced a new ecological climbing shoe made from recycled and environmentally sensitive materials. Similarly, two other distinct segments have been detected to be ready for a pan-regional approach. One includes trendsetters who are wealthier and better educated and tend to value independence, refuse consumer stereotypes, and appreciate exclusive products. The second one includes Europe's businesspeople who are well-to-do, regularly travel abroad, and have a taste for luxury goods.

Despite convergence, global marketers still have to make adjustments in some of the marketing mix elements for maximum impact. For example, while Levi's jeans are globally accepted by the teenage segment, European teens reacted negatively to the urban realism of Levi's U.S. ads. Levi's converted its ads in Europe, drawing on images of a mythical America.[34] Similarly, segment sizes vary from one market to another even in cohesive regions such as Europe. The value-oriented segment in Germany accounts for 32 percent of the grocery sales but only 9 percent in the United Kingdom and 8 percent in France.[35]

The greatest challenge for the global marketer is the choice of an appropriate base for the segmentation effort. The objective is to arrive at a grouping or groupings that are substantial enough to merit the segmentation effort (for example, there are nearly 230 million teenagers in the Americas, Europe, and the Asia-Pacific with the teenagers of the Americas spending nearly $60 billion of their own money yearly) and are reachable as well by the marketing effort (for example, the majority of MTV's audience consists of teenagers).

Figure 12.6   Bases for Global Market Segmentation

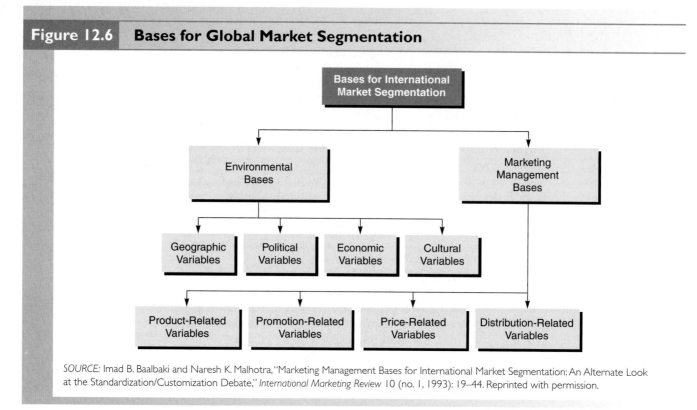

SOURCE: Imad B. Baalbaki and Naresh K. Malhotra, "Marketing Management Bases for International Market Segmentation: An Alternate Look at the Standardization/Customization Debate," *International Marketing Review* 10 (no. 1, 1993): 19–44. Reprinted with permission.

The possible bases for segmentation are summarized in Figure 12.6. Marketers have traditionally used environmental bases for segmentation. However, using geographic proximity, political system characteristics, economic standing, or cultural traits as a stand-alone basis may not provide relevant data for decision making. Using a combination of them, however, may produce more meaningful results. One of the segments pursued by global marketers around the world is the middle-class family. Defining the composition of this global middle class is tricky, given the varying levels of development among nations in Latin America and Asia. However, some experts estimate that 25 percent of the world population enjoy middle-class lives, some 250 million in India alone.[36] Using household income alone may be quite a poor gauge of class. Income figures ignore vast differences in international purchasing power. Chinese consumers, for example, spend less than 5 percent of their total outlays on rent, transportation, and health, while a typical U.S. household spends 45 to 50 percent. Additionally, income distinctions do not reflect education or values—two increasingly important barometers of middle-class status. A global segmentation effort using cultural values is provided in Table 12.3.

It has also been proposed that markets that reflect a high degree of homogeneity with respect to marketing mix variables could be grouped into segments and thereby targeted with a largely standardized marketing strategy.[37] Whether bases related to product, promotion, pricing, or distribution are used, their influence should be related to environmentally based variables. Product-related bases include the degree to which products are culture-based, which stage of the life cycle they occupy, consumption patterns, and attitudes toward product attributes (such as country of origin), as well as consumption infrastructure (for example, telephone lines for modems). The growth of microwave sales, for example, has

Table 12.3   Global Segments Based on Cultural Values

Segment	Characteristics	Geographics
Strivers	More likely to be men; place more emphasis on material and professional goals	One-third of people in developing Asia; one-quarter in Russia and developed Asia
Devouts	22 percent of adults; women more than men; tradition and duty are paramount	Africa, Asia, Middle East; least common in Europe
Altruists	18 percent of adults; larger portion of females; interested in social issues and welfare of society; older	Latin America and Russia
Intimates	15 percent of population; personal relationships and family take precedence	Europeans and North Americans
Fun Seekers	12 percent of population; youngest group	Disproportionately more in developed Asia
Creatives	10 percent worldwide; strong interest in education, knowledge, and technology	Europe and Latin America

SOURCE: Tom Miller, "Global Segments from 'Strivers' to 'Creatives,'" *Marketing News*, July 20, 1998, 11. Reprinted with permission. See also **http://www.roper.com**.

been surprising in low-income countries; however, microwaves have become status symbols and buying them more of an emotional issue. Many consumers in these markets also want to make sure they get the same product as available in developed markets, thereby eliminating the need in many cases to develop market-specific products. Adjustments will have to made, however. Noticing that for reasons of status and space, many Asian consumers put their refrigerators in their living rooms, Whirlpool makes refrigerators available in striking colors such as red and blue.

With promotion, customers' values and norms set the baseline for global vs. regional vs. local solutions. The significant emphasis on family relationships among many Europeans and North Americans creates a multiregional segment that can be exploited by consumer-goods and consumer-services marketers (such as car marketers or telecommunications service providers). On the pricing side, dimensions such as customers' price sensitivity may lead the marketer to go after segments that insist on high quality despite high price in markets where overall purchasing power may be low to ensure global or regional uniformity in the marketing approach. Affordability is a major issue for customers whose buying power may fall short for at least the time being. Offering only one option may exclude potential customers of the future who are not yet part of a targeted segment. Companies like Procter & Gamble and Gillette offer an array of products at different price points to attract them and to keep them as they move up the income scale.[38] As distribution systems converge, for example, with the increase of global chains, markets can also be segmented by outlet types that reach environmentally defined groups. For example, toy manufacturers may look at markets not only in terms of numbers of children but by how effectively and efficiently they can be reached by global chains such as Toys 'Я' Us, as opposed to purely local outlets.

Global Marketing Program Development

Decisions need to be made regarding how best to utilize the conditions set by globalization drivers within the framework of competitive challenges and the resources of the firm. Marketing-related decisions will have to be made in four areas: (1) the degree of standardization in the product offering, (2) the marketing program beyond the product variable, (3) location and extent of value-adding activities, and (4) competitive moves to be made.

Product Offering

Globalization is not equal to standardization except in the case of the core product or the technology used to produce the product. The components used in a personal computer may to a large extent be standard, with the localization needed only in terms of the peripherals; for example, IBM produces 20 different keyboards for Europe alone. Product standardization may result in significant cost savings upstream. For example, Stanley Works' compromise between French preferences for handsaws with plastic handles and "soft teeth" and British preferences for wooden handles and "hard teeth"—to produce a plastic-handled saw with "hard teeth"—allowed consolidation for production and results in substantial economies of scale. At Whirlpool, use of common platforms allows European and American appliances to share technology and suppliers to lower cost and to streamline production. Many of the same components are procedures used for products that eventually are marketed to segments looking for top-of-the-line or no-frills versions.[39] Similar differences in customer expectations have Bestfoods selling 15 versions of minestrone soup in Europe. Shania Twain's double CD *Up!* is an example of catering to multiple segments at the same time: both disks contain the same 19 tracks, but one with the effects pop fans appreciate, and the other with country dimensions. A third disk with "an Asian, Indian vibe" replaces the country disk in Europe.[40]

Marketing Approach

Nowhere is the need for the local touch as critical as in the execution of the marketing program. Uniformity is sought especially in elements that are strategic (e.g., positioning) in nature, whereas care is taken to localize necessary tactical elements (e.g., distribution). This approach has been called **glocalization.** For example, Unilever achieved great success with a fabric softener that used a common positioning, advertising theme, and symbol (a teddy bear) but differing brand names (e.g., Snuggle, Cajoline, Kuschelweich, Mimosin, and Yumos) and bottle sizes. Gillette Co. scored a huge success with its Sensor shaver when it was rolled out in the United States, Europe, and Japan with a common approach based on the premise that men everywhere want the same thing in a shave. Although the language of its TV commercials varied, the theme ("the best a man can get") and most of the footage were the same. A comparison of the marketing mix elements of two global marketers is given in Table 12.4. Notice that adaptation is present even at Coca-Cola, which is acknowledged to be one of the world's most global marketers.

Location of Value-Added Activities

Globalization strives to reduce costs by pooling production or other activities or exploiting factor costs or capabilities within a system. Rather than duplicating activities in multiple, or even all, country organizations, a firm concentrates its activities. For example, Texas Instruments has designated a single design center and manufacturing organization for each type of memory chip. To reduce high costs and to be close to markets, it placed two of its four new $250-million memory chip plants in Taiwan and Japan. To reduce high R&D costs, it has entered into a strategic alliance with Hitachi. Many global marketers have established R&D

| Table 12.4 | Globalization of the Marketing Mix | | | |

Marketing Mix Elements	Adaptation		Standardization	
	Full	Partial	Full	Partial
Product design			C	N
Brand name			C	N
Product positioning		N	C	
Packaging				C/N
Advertising theme		N	C	
Pricing		N		C
Advertising copy	N		C	C
Distribution	N	C		
Sales promotion	N	C		
Customer service	N	C		

Key: C = Coca-Cola; N = Nestlé.

SOURCE: Adapted from John A. Quelch and Edward J. Hoff, "Customizing Global Marketing," *Harvard Business Review*, May–June 1986 (Boston: Harvard Business School Publishing Division), 61.

centers next to key production facilities so that concurrent engineering can take place every day on the factory floor. To enhance the global exchange of ideas, the centers have joint projects and are in real-time contact with each other.

The quest for cost savings and improved transportation and transfer methods has allowed some marketers to concentrate customer service activities rather than having them present in all country markets. For example, Sony used to have repair centers in all the Scandinavian countries and Finland; today, all service and maintenance activities are actually performed in a regional center in Stockholm, Sweden. Similarly, MasterCard has teamed up with Mascon Global in Chennai, India, where MasterCard's core processing functions—authorization, clearing, and settlement—for worldwide operations are handled.[41]

Competitive Moves

A company with regional or global presence will not have to respond to competitive moves only in the market where it is being attacked. A competitor may be attacked in its profit sanctuary to drain its resources, or its position in its home market may be challenged.[42] When Fuji began cutting into Kodak's market share in the United States, Kodak responded by drastically increasing its advertising in Japan and created a new subsidiary to deal strictly with that market.

Cross-subsidization, or the use of resources accumulated in one part of the world to fight a competitive battle in another, may be the competitive advantage needed for the long term.[43] One major market lost may mean losses in others, resulting in a domino effect. Jockeying for overall global leadership may result in competitive action in any part of the world. This has manifested itself in the form of "wars" between major global players in industries such as soft drinks, automotive tires, computers, and cellular phones. The opening of new markets often signals a new battle, as happened in the 1990s in Russia, in Mexico after the signing of the North American Free Trade Agreement, and in Vietnam after the normalization of relations with the United States. Given their multiple bases of operation, global marketers may defend against a competitive attack in one country by countering in another country or, if the competitors operate in multiple businesses, countering in a different product category altogether. In the cellular phone category, the winners in the future will be those who can better attack less mature markets with cheaper phones, while providing Internet-based devices elsewhere.[44]

In a study of how automakers develop strategies that balance the conflicting pressures of local responsiveness and regional integration in Europe, Japanese marketers were found to practice standardization in model offerings but selectively respond to differences in market conditions by manipulating prices and advertising levels.[45]

Implementing Global Marketing

The successful global marketers of the future will be those who can achieve a balance between local and regional/global concerns. Marketers who have tried the global concept have often run into problems with local differences. Especially early on, global marketing was seen as a standardized marketing effort dictated to the country organizations by headquarters. For example, when Coca-Cola re-entered the Indian market in 1993, it invested most heavily in its Coke brand, using its typical global positioning, and saw its market leadership slip to Pepsi. Recognizing the mistake, Coke re-emphasized a popular local cola brand (Thums Up) and refocused the Coke brand advertising to be more relevant to the local Indian consumer.[46] In the past ten years, Coca-Cola has been acquiring local soft-drink brands (such as Inca Cola in Peru), which now account for 10 percent of company sales.[47]

Challenges of Global Marketing

Pitfalls that handicap global marketing programs and contribute to their suboptimal performance include market-related reasons, such as insufficient research and a tendency to overstandardize, as well as internal reasons, such as inflexibility in planning and implementation.

If a product is to be launched on a broader scale without formal research as to regional or local differences, the result may be failure. An example of this is Lego A/S, the Danish toy manufacturer, which decided to transfer sales promotional tactics successful in the U.S. market unaltered to other markets, such as Japan. This promotion included approaches such as "bonus packs" and gift promotions. However, Japanese consumers considered these promotions wasteful, expensive, and not very appealing.[48] Going too local has its drawbacks as well. With too much customization or with local production, the marketer may lose its import positioning. For example, when Miller Brewing Company started brewing Löwenbräu under license in the United States, the brand lost its prestigious import image. Often, the necessary research is conducted only after a product or a program has failed.

Globalization by design requires a balance between sensitivity to local needs and deployment of technologies and concepts globally. This means that neither headquarters nor independent country managers can alone call the shots. If country organizations are not part of the planning process, or if adoption is forced on them by headquarters, local resistance in the form of the **not-invented-here syndrome (NIH)** may lead to the demise of the global program or, worse still, to an overall decline in morale. Subsidiary resistance may stem from resistance to any idea originating from the outside or from valid concerns about the applicability of a concept to that particular market. Without local commitment, no global program will survive.

Localizing Global Marketing

The successful global marketers of the new century will be those who can achieve a balance between country managers and global product managers at headquarters. This balance may be achieved by a series of actions to improve a company's ability to develop and implement global strategy. These actions relate to management processes, organization structures, and overall corporate culture, all of which should ensure cross-fertilization within the firm.[49]

Management Processes   In the multidomestic approach, country organizations had very little need to exchange ideas. Globalization, however, requires transfer of information between not only headquarters and country organizations but also between the country organizations themselves. By facilitating the flow of information, ideas are exchanged and organizational values strengthened. Information exchange can be achieved through periodic meetings of marketing managers or through worldwide conferences to allow employees to discuss their issues and local approaches to solving them. IBM, for example, has a Worldwide Opportunity Council, which sponsors fellowships for employees to listen to business cases from around the world and develop global platforms or solutions. IBM has found that some country organizations find it easier to accept input of other country organizations than that coming directly from headquarters. The approach used at Levi Strauss & Co. is described in *The International Marketplace 12.3*.

Part of the preparation for becoming global has to be personnel interchange. Many companies encourage (or even require) midlevel managers to gain experience abroad during the early or middle stages of their careers. The more experience people have in working with others from different nationalities—getting to know other markets and surroundings—the better a company's global philosophy, strategy, and actions will be integrated locally.

The role of headquarters staff should be that of coordination and leveraging the resources of the corporation. For example, this may mean activities focused on combining good ideas that come from different parts of the company to be fed into global planning. Many global companies also employ world-class advertising and market research staffs whose role should be to consult subsidiaries by upgrading their technical skills and to focus their attention not only on local issues but also on those with global impact.

Globalization calls for the centralization of decision-making authority far beyond that of the multidomestic approach. Once a strategy has been jointly developed, headquarters may want to permit local managers to develop their own programs within specified parameters and subject to approval rather than forcing them to adhere strictly to the formulated strategy. For example, Colgate Palmolive allows local units to use their own ads, but only if they can prove they beat the global "benchmark" version. With a properly managed approval process, effective control can be exerted without unduly dampening a country manager's creativity.

Overall, the best approach against the emergence of the NIH syndrome is utilizing various motivational policies such as (1) ensuring that local managers participate in the development of marketing strategies and programs for global brands, (2) encouraging local managers to generate ideas for possible regional or global use, (3) maintaining a product portfolio that includes local as well as regional and global brands, and (4) allowing local managers control over their marketing budgets so that they can respond to local customer needs and counter global competition (rather than depleting budgets by forcing them to participate only in uniform campaigns). Acknowledging this local potential, global marketers can pick up successful brands in one country and make them cross-border stars. Since Nestlé acquired British candy maker Rowntree Mackintosh, it has increased its exports by 60 percent and made formerly local brands, such as After Eight dinner mints, into pan-European hits. When global marketers get their hands on an innovation or a product with global potential, rolling it out in other regions or worldwide is important.

THE INTERNATIONAL MARKETPLACE   12.3

Finding the Fit Overseas

Twice a year, Levi Strauss & Co. calls together managers from its worldwide operations for a meeting of the minds. In sessions that could be described as a cross between the United Nations general assembly and MTV, the participants brainstorm and exchange ideas on what seems to work in their respective markets, regionally or globally. If a marketing manager finds an advertising campaign appealing, he or she is encouraged to take it back home to sell more Levi's blue jeans.

All told, Levi's marketing approach epitomizes a slogan that is becoming popular among companies around the world: Think globally, act locally. Levi's has deftly capitalized on the Levi's name abroad by marketing it as an enshrined piece of Americana, and foreign consumers have responded by paying top dollar for the product. An Indonesian commercial shows Levi's-clad teenagers cruising around Dubuque, Iowa, in 1960s convertibles. In Japan, James Dean serves as a centerpiece in virtually all Levi's advertising. Overseas, Levi's products have been positioned as an upscale product, which has meant highly satisfactory profit margins. To protect the image, Levi's has avoided the use of mass merchants and discounters in its distribution efforts.

Levi's success turns on its ability to fashion a global strategy that does not stifle local initiative. It is a delicate balancing act, one that often means giving foreign managers the freedom needed to adjust their tactics to meet the changing tastes of their home markets. In Brazil, Levi's prospers by letting local managers call the shots on distribution. For instance, Levi's penetrated the huge, fragmented Brazilian market by launching a chain of 400 Levi's Only stores, some of them in tiny rural towns. Levi's is also sensitive to local tastes in Brazil, where it developed the Feminina line of jeans exclusively for women, who prefer ultratight jeans. What Levi's learns in one market can often be adopted in another. The Dock-

ers line of chino pants and casual wear originated in the company's Argentine unit and was applied to loosely cut pants by Levi's Japanese subsidiary. The company's U.S. operation adopted both in 1986, and the line now generates significant North American as well as European revenues. In 2002, Dockers unveiled its Go Khaki with Stain Defender line in the United States with quick roll-out in other major markets to follow.

Headquarters managers exercise control where necessary. To protect Levi's cherished brand identity and image of quality, the company has organized its foreign operations as subsidiaries rather than relying on a patchwork of licensees. It is important for a brand to have a single face; it cannot be controlled if there are 20 to 25 licensees around the world interpreting it in different ways. The company also keeps ahead of its competition by exporting its pioneering use of computers to track sales and manufacturing.

The company has also launched a reorganization to focus more on consumer needs. Levi's Web site has been redesigned to feature a virtual dressing room, custom-tailored jeans ordering, and virtual salespeople who offer tips on matching outfits.

Levi's continues to focus on global sales with its three divisions: the Americas (NAFTA plus Latin America); Europe, Middle East, and Africa; and Asia-Pacific. In 2001, the Americas contributed 68 percent of its sales; Europe, the Middle East, and Africa 26 percent; and Asia-Pacific 6 percent of $4.3 billion total sales.

SOURCES: Michele Orecklin, "Look, Ma, No Stains," *Time*, December 9, 2002, 64–65; "Levi Strauss & Co. Fiscal 2001 Financial Results," at **http://www.levistrauss.com**; Alice Z. Cuneo, "Levi Strauss Begins 1st Online Sales Effort," *Advertising Age*, November 23, 1998, 18; "For Levi's, a Flattering Fit Overseas," *Business Week*, November 5, 1990, 76–77; and **http://www.levistrauss.com**.

Organization Structures   Various organization structures have emerged to support the globalization effort. Some companies have established global or regional product managers and their support groups at headquarters. Their tasks are to develop long-term strategies for product categories on a worldwide basis and to act as the support system for the country organizations. This matrix structure focused on customers, which has replaced the traditional country-by-country approach, is considered more effective in today's global marketplace according to companies that have adopted it.

Whenever a product group has global potential, firms such as Procter & Gamble, 3M, and Henkel create strategic-planning units to work on the programs. These units, such as 3M's EMATs (European Marketing Action Teams), consist of members from the country organizations that market the products, managers from both global and regional headquarters, and technical specialists.

To deal with the globalization of customers, marketers are extending national account management programs across countries typically for the most important customers.[50] In a study of 165 multinational companies, 13 percent of their revenues came from global customers (revenues from all international customers were 46 percent). While relatively small, these 13 percent come from the most important customers who cannot be ignored.[51] AT&T, for example, distinguishes between international and global customers and provides the global customers with special services, including a single point of contact for domestic and international operations and consistent worldwide service. Executing **global account management** programs builds relationships not only with important customers but also allows for the development of internal systems and interaction.

Corporate Culture   Whirlpool's corporate profile states the following: "Beyond selling products around the world, being a global home-appliance company means identifying and respecting genuine national and regional differences in customer expectations, but also recognizing and responding to similarities in product development, engineering, purchasing, manufacturing, marketing and sales, distribution, and other areas." Companies that exploit the efficiencies from these similarities will outperform others in terms of market share, cost, quality, productivity, innovation, and return to shareholders. In truly global companies, very little decision making occurs that does not support the goal of treating the world as a single market. Planning for and execution of programs take place on a worldwide basis.

An example of a manifestation of the global commitment is a global identity that favors no specific country (especially the "home country" of the company). The management features several nationalities, and whenever terms are assembled, people from various country organizations get represented. The management development system has to be transparent, allowing nonnational executives an equal chance for the fast track to top management.[52]

In determining the optimal combination of products and product lines to be marketed, a firm should consider choices for individual markets as well as transfer of products and brands from one region or market to another. This will often result in a particular country organization marketing product lines and products that are a combination of global, regional, and national brands.

Decisions on specific targeting may result in the choice of a narrowly defined segment in the countries chosen. This is a likely strategy for marketers of specialized products to clearly definable markets, for example, ocean-capable sailing boats. Catering to multiple segments in various markets is typical of consumer-oriented companies that have sufficient resources for broad coverage.

Summary

Globalization has become one of the most important strategy issues for marketing managers in the last ten years. Many forces, both external and internal, are driving companies to globalize by expanding and coordinating their participation in foreign markets. The approach is not standardization, however. Marketers may indeed occasionally be able to take identical technical and marketing concepts around the world, but most often, concepts must be customized to local tastes. Internally, companies must make sure that country organizations around the world are ready to launch global products and programs as if they had been developed only for their markets. Firms that are able to exploit commonalities across borders and do so with competent marketing managers in country organizations are able to see the benefits in their overall performance.[53]

Marketing managers need to engage in strategic planning to better adjust to the realities of the new marketplace. Understanding the firm's core strategy (i.e., what business they are really in) starts the process, and this assessment may lead to adjustments in what business the company may want to be in. In formulating global strategy for the chosen business, the decision makers have to assess and make choices about markets and competitive strategy to be used in penetrating them. This may result in the choice of one particular segment across markets or the exploitation of multiple segments in which the company has a competitive advantage. In manipulating and implementing the marketing mix for maximum effect in the chosen markets, the old adage, "think globally, act locally," becomes a critical guiding principle both as far as customers are concerned and in terms of country organization motivation.

Key Terms

triad
concentration
diversification
glocalization

cross-subsidization
not-invented-here syndrome (NIH)
global account management

Questions for Discussion

1. What is the danger in oversimplifying the globalization approach? Would you agree with the statement that "if something is working in a big way in one market, you better assume it will work in all markets"?

2. In addition to teenagers as a global segment, are there possibly other such groups with similar traits and behaviors that have emerged worldwide?

3. Suggest ways in which a global marketer is better equipped to initiate and respond to competitive moves.

4. Why is the assessment of internal resources critical as early as possible in developing a global strategic plan?

5. What are the critical ways in which the multidomestic and global approaches differ in country-market selection?

6. Outline the basic reasons why a company does not necessarily have to be large and have years of experience to succeed in the global marketplace.

Internet Exercises

1. Using the material available at Unilever's Web site (**http://www.unilever.com**), suggest ways in which Unilever's business groups can take advantage of global and regional strategies due to interconnections in production and marketing.

2. Bestfoods is one of the largest food companies in the world, with operations in more than 60 countries and products sold in 110 countries in the world. Based on the brand information given at its Web site (**http://www.bestfoods.com**), what benefits does a company derive from having a global presence?

Recommended Readings

Birkinshaw, Julian. *Entrepreneurship in the Global Firm*. Thousand Oaks, CA: Sage Publications, 2000.

The Economist Intelligence Unit. *151 Checklists for Global Management*. New York: The Economist Intelligence Unit, 1993.

Feist, William R., James A. Heely, Min H. Lau, and Roy L. Nersesian. *Managing a Global Enterprise*. Westport, CT: Quorum, 1999.

Grant, Robert M., and Kent E. Neupert. *Cases in Contemporary Strategy Analysis*. Oxford, England: Blackwell, 1999.

Irwin, Douglas A. *Free Trade under Fire*. Princeton, NJ: Princeton University Press, 2002.

Kanter, Rosabeth Moss. *World Class*. New York: Simon & Schuster, 1995.

Lindsey, Brink. *Against the Dead Hand: The Uncertain Struggle for Global Capitalism*. New York: John Wiley & Sons, 2001.

Prahalad, C. K., and Yves L. Doz. *The Multinational Mission: Balancing Local and Global Vision*. New York: Free Press, 1987.

Rosensweig, Jeffrey. *Winning the Global Game: A Strategy for Linking People and Profits*. New York: Free Press, 1998.

Schwab, Klaus, Michael Porter, and Jeffrey Sachs. *The Global Competitiveness Report 2001–2002*. Oxford, England: Oxford University Press, 2002.

Scott, Allen J. *Regions and the World Economy: The Coming Shape of Global Production, Competition, and Political Order*. Oxford, England: Oxford University Press, 2000.

Soros, George. *George Soros on Globalization*. New York: Public Affairs, 2002.

Stiglitz, Joseph E. *Globalization and Its Discontents*. New York: W.W. Norton & Co., 2002.

Global Market Expansion

THE INTERNATIONAL MARKETPLACE 13.1

Buying Domestic? Maybe Not

As the United States becomes an ever more global market, the national affiliation of many products is becoming murky. For example, many American car firms are owned by European companies. How American is a Jeep when it is made by the German firm DaimlerChrysler? Many of the products Americans assume to be "American" are actually owned by large international firms who invested hundreds of billions of dollars in the U.S. economy during the long boom of the 1990s. The money has come from Britain, Germany, France, the Netherlands, Italy, Ireland, Scandinavia, and other parts of Western Europe. The Commerce Department reports that in 2000, European investment in the United States reached nearly $900 billion and that U.S. investment in Europe topped $650 billion. In an economic sense, this huge surplus in direct investment inflow helps to offset the ever-widening U.S. trade deficit in international trade.

This massive direct investment in each other's nations has naturally led to U.S. ownership of traditionally European firms and European ownership of what have typically been thought of as American brands. For example, Volvo, Jaguar, and Land Rover are three highly recognizable car brands long considered to be European which are now owned by Ford, the most American of car companies. Conversely, the *American Heritage Dictionary* is owned by Vivendi, a French media colossus who also owns Universal Studios. RCA Records, once part of Radio Corporation of America, is now owned by the German publishing giant Bertelsmann. Even the phrase "as American as apple pie" is no longer true; Mott's apple pie filling, along with its apple juice and applesauce, are British-owned.

European investments are not only in autos and food products. The Royal Bank of Scotland owns more than 15 U.S. banking institutions and Deutsche Bank of Germany has made significant investments in the United States.

The reaction of Americans to this influx of European investment is in sharp contrast to reaction to similar investment by Japanese firms in the mid- to late 1980s. American are either unaware of the large investments by these European firms or have started to accept foreign ownership of American brands. Perhaps growing public awareness of the process of globalization makes Americans more accepting of foreign direct investment. It is also possible, however, that U.S. consumers are less concerned about European ownership because their culture and business practices are perceived to be closer to those of Americans as compared to Japanese firms.

SOURCE: T. R. Reid, "Buying American? Maybe Not," *The Washington Post,* May 18, 2002, E1.

ALL TYPES OF FIRMS, large and small, can carry out global market expansion through foreign direct investment or management contracts, and they are doing so at an increasing pace. Key to the decision to invest abroad is the existence of specific advantages that outweigh the disadvantages and risk of operating so far from home. Since foreign direct investment often requires substantial capital and a firm's ability to absorb risk, the most visible players in the area are large multinational corporations. These firms invest to enter markets or to assure themselves of sources of supply. *The International Marketplace 13.1* shows how the national affiliation of products is becoming increasingly murky. In this chapter, the section on foreign direct investment strategies focuses on the rationale for such investment and on investment alternatives such as full ownership, joint ventures, and strategic alliances. The section on contractual arrangements then focuses on the potential and the benefits and drawbacks of such arrangements.

Foreign Direct Investment

Foreign direct investment represents one component of the international investment flow. The other component is portfolio investment, which is the purchase of stocks and bonds internationally. Portfolio investment is a primary concern to the international financial community. The international marketer, on the other hand, makes foreign direct investments to create or expand a permanent interest in an enterprise. They imply a degree of control over the enterprise.

Foreign direct investments have grown tremendously. The total global value of such investment, which in 1967 was estimated to be $105 billion, had climbed to an estimated $6.3 trillion by 2001.[1] Among global investors, U.S. firms are major players due to significant investments in the developed world and in some developing countries. In 2001, the stock of foreign direct investment abroad by U.S. firms amounted to $6.97 trillion at market value. Major foreign direct investment activity has also been carried out by firms from other countries, many of which decided to invest in the United States. In 2001, the stock of direct investment by foreign firms in the United States totaled approximately $9.17 trillion, up from $6.9 billion in 1960.[2] Foreign direct investment has clearly become a major avenue for foreign market entry and expansion.

Major Foreign Investors

Multinational corporations are defined by the United Nations as "enterprises which own or control production or service facilities outside the country in which they are based."[3] As a result of this definition, all foreign direct investors are multinational corporations. Yet large corporations are the key players. Table 13.1 lists the 40 largest corporations around the world. They come from a wide variety of countries, depend heavily on their international sales, and, in terms of sales, are larger than many countries. As these firms keep growing, they appear to benefit from greater abilities to cope with new, unfamiliar situations.[4] Yet it also appears that there is an optimal size that, when exceeded, increases the costs of operations.[5]

Many of the large multinationals operate in well over 100 countries. For some, their original home market accounts for only a fraction of their sales. For example, the Dutch company Philips, the Swedish SKF, and the Swiss Nestlé sell less than 5 percent of their total sales in their home country of origin. In some firms, even the terms *domestic* and *foreign* have fallen into disuse. Others are working to consider issues only from a global perspective. For example, in management meetings of ABB (Asea Brown Boveri), individuals get fined $100 every time the words *foreign* and *domestic* are used.

Through their investment, multinational corporations bring economic vitality and jobs to their host countries and often pay higher wages than the average domestically oriented firms.[6]

At the same time, however, trade follows investment. This means that foreign direct investors often bring with them imports on an ongoing basis. The flow of imports in turn may contribute to the weakening of a nation's international trade position.

Reasons for Foreign Direct Investment

Firms expand internationally for a wide variety of reasons. Table 13.2 provides an overview of the major determinants of foreign direct investment.

Marketing Factors

Marketing considerations and the corporate desire for growth are major causes for the increase in foreign direct investment. This is understandable since growth typically means greater responsibilities and more pay for those who contribute to it. Even large domestic markets present limitations to growth. Today's competitive demands require firms to operate simultaneously in the "triad" of the United States, Western Europe, and Japan and most other markets of the world as well. Corporations therefore need to seek wider market access in order to maintain and increase their sales. This objective can be achieved most quickly through the acquisition of foreign firms. Through such expansion, the corporation also gains ownership advantages consisting of political know-how and influence.

| Table 13.1 | The World's 40 Largest Corporations (Ranked by Revenues) |

Global Rank	Company	Country of Headquarters	Revenues ($ millions)
1	Wal-Mart Stores	US	219,812
2	Exxon Mobil	US	191,581
3	General Motors	US	177,260
4	BP	UK	174,218
5	Ford Motor	US	162,412
6	DaimlerChrysler	Germany	136,897
7	Royal Dutch/Shell Group	UK/Netherlands	135,211
8	General Electric	US	125,913
9	Toyota Motor	Japan	120,814
10	Citigroup	US	112,022
11	Mitsubishi	Japan	105,813
12	Mitsui	Japan	101,205
13	Chevron Texaco	US	99,699
14	Total Fina Elf	France	94,311
15	Nippon Telegraph & Telephone	Japan	93,424
16	Itochu	Japan	91,176
17	Allianz	Germany	85,929
18	Intl. Business Machines	US	85,866
19	ING Group	Netherlands	82,999
20	Volkswagen	Germany	79,287
21	Siemens	Germany	77,358
22	Sumitomo	Japan	77,140
23	Philip Morris	US	72,944
24	Marubeni	Japan	71,756
25	Verizon Communications	US	67,190
26	Deutsche Bank	Germany	66,839
27	E. ON	Germany	66,453
28	U.S. Postal Service	US	65,834
29	AXA	France	65,579
30	Credit Suisse	Switzerland	64,204
31	Hitachi	Japan	63,931
32	Nippon Life Insurance	Japan	63,827
33	American Intl. Group	US	62,402
34	Carrefour	France	62,224
35	American Electric Power	US	61,257
36	Sony	Japan	60,608
37	Royal Ahold	Netherlands	59,633
38	Duke Energy	US	59,503
39	AT&T	US	59,142
40	Honda Motor	Japan	58,882

SOURCE: Global 500, adapted from **http://www.fortune.com**, accessed November 13, 2002.

Another incentive is that foreign direct investment permits corporations to circumvent current barriers to trade and operate abroad as a domestic firm, unaffected by duties, tariffs, or other import restrictions. For example, research on Japanese foreign direct investment in Europe found that a substantial number of firms have invested there in order to counteract future trade friction.[7]

Table 13.2   Major Determinants of Direct Foreign Investment

A. Marketing Factors
1. Size of market
2. Market growth
3. Desire to maintain share of market
4. Desire to advance exports of parent company
5. Need to maintain close customer contact
6. Dissatisfaction with existing market arrangements
7. Export base

B. Trade Restrictions
1. Barriers to trade
2. Preference of local customers for local products

C. Cost Factors
1. Desire to be near source of supply
2. Availability of labor
3. Availability of raw materials
4. Availability of capital/technology
5. Lower labor costs
6. Lower production costs other than labor
7. Lower transport costs
8. Financial (and other) inducements by government
9. More favorable cost levels

D. Investment Climate
1. General attitude toward foreign investment
2. Political stability
3. Limitation on ownership
4. Currency exchange regulations
5. Stability of foreign exchange
6. Tax structure
7. Familiarity with country

E. General
1. Expected higher profits

SOURCE: International Investment and Multinational Enterprises (Paris: Organization for Economic Cooperation and Development, 1983), 41; **http://www.oecd.org**.

In addition to government-erected barriers, restrictions may be imposed by customers through their insistence on domestic goods and services, either as a result of nationalistic tendencies or as a function of cultural differences. Having the origin of a product associated with a specific country may also bring positive effects with it, particularly if the country is known for the particular product category; for example, an investment in a Swiss dairy firm by a cheese producer. Further, local buyers may wish to buy from sources that they perceive to be reliable in their supply, which means buying from local producers. After the border-crossing delays caused by the attacks of September 11, 2001, many firms in the United States, for example, prefer that their suppliers be located in close proximity rather than far away.[8]

Still another incentive is the cost factor, with corporations attempting to obtain low-cost resources and ensure their sources of supply. Finally, once the decision is made to invest internationally, the investment climate plays a major role. Corporations will seek to invest in those geographic areas where their investment is most protected and has the best chance to flourish.

These determinants will have varying impact on the foreign direct investment decision, depending on the characteristics of the firm and its management, on its objectives, and on external conditions. Firms have been categorized as resource seekers, market seekers, and efficiency seekers.[9] **Resource seekers** search for either natural resources or human resources. Natural resources typically are based on mineral, agricultural, or oceanographic advantages and result in firms locating in areas where these resources are available. The alternatives open to firms therefore depend on the availability of the natural resources sought. Companies seeking human resources are likely to base their location decision on the availability of low-cost labor that matches their needs in terms of output quality. Alternatively, companies may select an area because of the availability of highly skilled labor. If natural resources are not involved, the location decision can be altered over time if the labor advantage changes. When the differential between labor costs in different locales becomes substantial, a corporation, in continuing to improve its human resource access, may relocate to take advantage of the "better" resources. A good example of such shifts was observed in Europe. In the 1980s, many non-European firms decided to gain their foothold in Europe by investing in the low-wage countries of Portugal, Spain, and Greece. In light of the major political changes of the 1990s, however, the investment interest shifted and began to focus on Hungary, the former East Germany, and the Czech Republic. Similarly, the implementation of the North American Free Trade Agreement (NAFTA) precipitated major investment flows from the United States into Mexico, led by firms seeking to obtain a key, low-cost Mexican factor endowment—labor.

Corporations primarily in search of better opportunities to enter and expand within markets are **market seekers.** Particularly when markets are closed or access is restricted, corporations have a major incentive to locate in them. **Efficiency seekers** attempt to obtain the most economic sources of production. They frequently have affiliates in multiple markets with highly specialized product lines or components and exchange their production in order to maximize the benefits to the corporation. The reasons why firms engage in foreign investment can change over time. As *The International Marketplace 13.2* shows, firms entering China may have done so originally as market seekers, but many of them have been converted into resource seekers over time.

Derived Demand

A second major cause for the increase in foreign direct investment is the result of **derived demand,** where demand abroad is the result of the move abroad by established customers. As large multinational firms move abroad, they are quite interested in maintaining their established business relationships with other firms. Therefore, they frequently encourage their suppliers to follow them and continue to supply them from a foreign location. Many Japanese automakers have urged their suppliers in Japan to begin production in the United States in order for the new U.S. plants to have easy access to their products. As a result, a few direct investments can gradually form an important investment preference for subsequent investment flows and even lead to centers of excellence. The same phenomenon holds true for service firms. Advertising agencies often move abroad to service foreign affiliates of their domestic clients. Similarly, engineering firms, insurance companies, and law firms are often invited to provide their services abroad. Yet not all of these developments are the result of co-optation by client firms. Often, suppliers invest abroad out of fear that their clients might find good sources abroad and therefore begin to import the products of services they currently supply. Many firms therefore invest abroad in order to forestall such a potentially dangerous development.

Government Incentives

A third major cause for the increase in foreign direct investment is government incentives. Governments are increasingly under pressure to provide jobs for their

THE INTERNATIONAL MARKETPLACE   13.2

The Chinese World Factory

The 1980s brought prospective companies to China in droves, drawn primarily by what they saw as an immense and untapped market for their products. Accompanied by an environment of cheap labor, companies believed they had found the Promised Land. What they did not see at the time was that the low wages on which they depended as manufacturers translated into extremely low purchasing power for Chinese consumers. The Chinese people could not buy the goods that they produced. After having spent millions setting up shop in China, what were these producers to do?

The resounding answer: Export! Most companies were not willing to give up the extremely low-cost labor that sustained their Chinese manufacturing facilities. Thus, they made China their base of manufacturing, and then exported the goods to markets across the globe. In the 21st century, few multinationals can afford not to consider sourcing products from China, creating a "Made in China" phenomenon that has swept the world.

Foreign investment in China has reached upwards of $600 billion over the past 20 years. This investment brought modern manufacturing techniques and technology, which increased productivity and continued to lower costs. Low-cost labor and relatively high levels of productivity proved to be a winning combination.

In 2001, half of China's exports, totaling $266.2 billion, came from foreign manufacturers or their joint ventures in China. With such massive amounts of goods flowing from its ports, China has become the fourth-largest exporter, behind the United States, Japan, and Germany. Here are some examples of China's production power:

Product	Percentage of Global Market
Metal cigarette lighters	70%
Cameras	50
Air conditioners	30
Televisions	30
Washing machines	25
Refrigerators	20

The largest market for these low-cost (and thus low-price) goods is the United States. The flood of products entering the U.S. market from China has affected most industries. In July 2002, the United States imported $1.2 billion of Chinese-made electronic products, up 12.5 percent from the month before. U.S. imports of high-tech products from China are up 47 percent from 2001 levels, reflecting a troublesome trend for many who believe the United States had established a competitive advantage in high-tech production.

Imports from China are rising in nearly every industry. Between 1998 and 2001, televisions and audio equipment imports rose 13 percent per year to a 2001 level of $6 billion. Tools and hardware imports are up 23 percent from 2000, topping $1.5 billion in 2001. Sporting goods are also up 16 percent to a 2001 level of $2 billion. Due to these imports, the retail prices of these goods are dropping considerably, leaving domestic producers to wonder how they can compete in this China-dominated market.

While the displacement of U.S. workers in import competing industries has been an unavoidable byproduct of the increased trade between the United States and China, American consumers have clearly benefited. The influx of low-cost Chinese goods has driven consumer prices down, while the variety and quality of goods have increased dramatically.

So what is next for the Chinese producers? If Chinese firms continue to establish themselves as high-quality and low-price producers, consumers worldwide may begin to see private Chinese companies exporting under their own names, rather than under the name of a foreign partner. American consumers may soon perhaps be demanding Chinese brands instead of the well-established American brands.

SOURCES: Karby Leggett and Peter Wonacott, "The World's Factory: Surge in Exports from China Jolts Global Industry," *The Wall Street Journal*, October 10, 2002; *Asia & Pacific Review World of Information*, Comment & Analysis; Country Profile; Statistics; Forecast, October 9, 2002, 1; and "How China Is Impacting on World Trade," *Asia Today*, August 2002.

citizens. Over time, many have come to recognize that foreign direct investment can serve as a major means to increase employment and income. Countries such as Ireland have been promoting government incentive schemes for foreign direct investment for decades. Increasingly, state and local governments are also participating in investment promotion activities. Some states are sending out investment missions on a regular basis, and others have opened offices abroad in order to inform local businesses about the beneficial investment climate at home.

Government incentives are mainly of three types: fiscal, financial, and nonfinancial. **Fiscal incentives** are specific tax measures designed to serve as an attraction to the foreign investor. They typically consist of special depreciation allowances, tax credits or rebates, special deductions for capital expenditures, tax holidays, and other reductions of the tax burden on the investor. **Financial incentives** offer special funding for the investor by providing land or buildings, loans, loan guarantees, or wage subsidies. Finally, **nonfinancial incentives** can consist of guaranteed government purchases; special protection from competition through tariffs, import quotas, and local content requirements; and investments in infrastructure facilities.

Incentives are designed primarily to attract more industry and create more jobs. They may slightly alter the advantage of a region and therefore make it more palatable for the investor to choose to invest in that region. By themselves, they are unlikely to spur an investment decision if proper market conditions do not exist. Consequently, when individual states or regions within a country offer special incentives to foreign direct investors, they may be competing against each other for a limited pie rather than increasing the size of the pie. Furthermore, a question exists about the extent to which new jobs are actually created by foreign direct investment. Because many foreign investors import equipment, parts, and even personnel, the expected benefits in terms of job creation may often be either less than initially envisioned or only temporary. One additional concern arises from the competitive position of domestic firms already in existence. Since their "old" investment typically does not benefit from incentives designed to attract new investment, established firms may encounter problems when competing against the newcomer.

A Perspective on Foreign Direct Investors

All foreign direct investors, and particularly multinational corporations, are viewed with a mixture of awe and dismay. Governments and individuals praise them for bringing capital, economic activity, and employment, and investors are seen as key transferers of technology and managerial skills. Through these transfers, competition, market choice, and competitiveness are enhanced.

At the same time, many have negative views of dependence on multinational corporations. Just as the establishment of a corporation can create all sorts of benefits, its disappearance can also take them away again. Very often, international direct investors are accused of actually draining resources from their host countries. By employing the best and the brightest, they are said to deprive domestic firms of talent, thus causing a **brain drain.** Once they have hired locals, multinational firms are often accused of not promoting them high enough, and of imposing many new rules on their employees abroad.

By raising money locally, multinationals are seen to starve smaller capital markets. By bringing in foreign technology, they are viewed either as discouraging local technology development or as perhaps transferring only outmoded knowledge. By increasing competition, they are declared the enemy of domestic firms. There are concerns about foreign investors' economic and political loyalty toward their host government and a fear that such investors will always protect only their own interests and those of their home governments. And, of course, their sheer size, which sometimes exceeds the financial assets that the government controls, makes foreign investors suspect.

Clearly, a love–hate relationship frequently exists between governments and the foreign direct investor. As the firm's size and investment volume grow, the benefits it brings to the economy increase. At the same time, the dependence of the economy on the firm increases as well. Given the many highly specialized activities of firms, their experts are often more knowledgeable than government employees and are therefore able to circumvent government rules. Particularly in developing countries, the knowledge advantage of foreign investors may offer opportunities for exploitation. There seems to be a distinct "liability of foreignness" to which multinational firms are exposed. Such disadvantages can result from governmental resentment of greater opportunities by multinational firms. But they can also be the consequences of corporate actions, such as the decision to have many expatriates rotate in top management positions, which may weaken the standing of the subsidiary and its local employees.[10]

In light of the desire for foreign investment and the accompanying fear of it, a substantial array of guidelines for corporate behavior abroad has been publicized by organizations such as the United Nations, the Organization for Economic Cooperation and Development, and the International Labor Organization. Typically, these recommendations address the behavior of foreign investors in areas such as employment practices, consumer and environmental protection, political activity, and human rights. Corporations may not be legally bound by the guidelines, but they should consider their implications for corporate activities. While the social acceptability of certain practices may vary among nations, the foreign investor should transfer the best business practices across nations. The multinational firm can and should be a leader in improving economic and business practices and standards of living around the world. It will be managerial virtue, vision, and veracity combined with corporate openness, responsiveness, long-term thinking, and truthfulness that will determine the degrees of freedom and success of global business in the future.[11]

Types of Ownership

In carrying out its foreign direct investment, a corporation has a wide variety of ownership choices, ranging from 100 percent ownership to a minority interest. The different levels of ownership will result in varying degrees of flexibility for the corporation, a changing ability to control business plans and strategy, and differences in the level of risk assumed. In some instances, firms appear to select specific foreign ownership structures based on their experience with similar structures in the past.[12] In other words, these firms tend to keep using the same ownership model. However, it may be better to have the ownership decision be either a strategic response to corporate capabilities and needs or a necessary consequence of government regulation. *The International Marketplace 13.3* explains how one firm used three different ownership approaches to its expansion in Asia.

Full Ownership

For many firms, the foreign direct investment decision is, at least initially, considered in the context of 100 percent ownership. Sometimes, this is the result of ethnocentric considerations, based on the belief that no outside entity should have an impact on corporation management. At other times, the issue is one of principle.

To make a rational decision about the extent of ownership, management must evaluate the extent to which total control is important for the success of its international marketing activities. Often, full ownership may be a desirable, but not a necessary, prerequisite for international success. At other times, it may be necessary, particularly when strong linkages exist within the corporation. Interdependencies between and among local operations and headquarters may be so strong that anything short of total coordination will result in a benefit to the firm as a whole that is less than acceptable. This may be the case if central product design, pricing, or advertising is needed, as the following example illustrates:

> The Crane Company manufactures plumbing fixtures, pumps, and valves, and similar equipment which is used in oil refineries, paper mills, and many other types of installations. The firm sells to design engineers throughout the world; these engineers may not be actual buyers, but they design equipment into the plants they build, and so they at least recommend the equipment to be used.

THE INTERNATIONAL MARKETPLACE   13.3

One Company Chooses Four Modes of International Investment

In the early 1990s, Fedders International, the largest U.S. manufacturer of room air conditioners, decided that the best way to grow was to venture abroad. The company concluded that China was the best option for investment.

The initial entrance of Fedders into the Chinese market in 1995 was organized through a joint venture with a struggling Chinese air conditioning company, Ningbo General Air Conditioning Factory. The agreement was that Ningbo General would increase production to 500,000 units in three years, and Fedders would handle all exporting. In March 2001, Fedders announced plans by its subsidiary, Envirco Corporation, to establish a 100 percent–owned factory in China, as well as a new R&D facility to service Fedders' worldwide operations.

While stepping up production in China, Fedders has applied two other strategies to entering the foreign market. One consisted of a greenfield investment, when the Indian Foreign Investment Promotion Board granted Fedders approval to set up a wholly owned facility for manufacturing of air conditioners in India. In the second most populous country in the world, air conditioners are the fastest-growing category of consumer durables. Due to the hot climate of India, Fedders officials are highly optimistic about their new manufacturing site in Asia.

ABB Koppel Inc., in the Philippines, marks Fedders' third approach to expanding its product line and establishing a manufacturing base in Asia, this time through acquisition.

A fourth approach consists of international acquisition in order to obtain a distribution and sales base. Fedders has used this strategy in Europe in buying Polenz GmbH of Germany as its platform for further expansion in Europe.

The use of mixed strategies seems to be working. In 2002, Fedders reported international sales of almost $70 million. Not bad for a company that just ten years before had virtually no global reach!

SOURCES: "Fedders Obtains Indian Government Approval for Wholly Owned Manufacturing Facility in India," Fedders press release, June 8, 1999; "Fedders Acquires Air Conditioning Company," Fedders press release, January 18, 2000; "Fedders to Step Up China Investments," March 20, 2001; and **http://www.fedders.com**, accessed November 14, 2002.

In advertising to this important segment of the international market, Crane recognizes that the design engineer in São Paolo reads engineering journals published in the United States, Great Britain, and perhaps Germany or France, as well as Latin America. So Crane wants its advertising in these journals to be consistent. Therefore, it does not let its foreign subsidiaries conduct their own advertising without advice and clearance from the New York headquarters. If Crane were to use joint ventures abroad, the partner would have to yield advertising authority to New York. This could conceivably lead to discontent on the part of the local partner. To avoid arguments on advertising policies, Crane insists on full ownership.[13]

As this example shows, corporations sometimes insist on full ownership for major strategic reasons. Even in such instances, however, it is important to determine whether these reasons are important enough to warrant such a policy or whether the needs of the firm can be accommodated with other ownership arrangements. In many countries the international environment is quite hostile to full ownership by multinational firms.

Many governments exert political pressure to obtain national control of foreign operations. Commercial activities under the control of foreigners are frequently believed to reflect the wishes, desires, and needs of headquarters abroad much more than those of the domestic economy. Governments fear that domestic economic policies may be counteracted by such firms, and employees are afraid that little local responsibility and empathy exist at headquarters. A major concern is the "fairness" of **profit repatriation,** or transfer of profits, and the extent to which firms operating abroad need to reinvest in their foreign operations. Governments often believe that transfer pricing mechanisms are used to amass profits in a place most advantageous for the firm and that, as a consequence, local operations often show very low levels of performance. By reducing the foreign control of firms, they hope to put an end to such practices.

Ownership options can be limited either through outright legal restrictions or through measures designed to make foreign ownership less attractive—such as limitations on profit repatriation. The international marketer is therefore frequently faced with the choice either of abiding by existing restraints and accepting a reduction in control or of losing the opportunity to operate in the country.

In addition to the pressure from host governments, general market instability can also serve as a major deterrent to full ownership of foreign direct investment. Instability may result from political upheavals or changes in regimes. More often, it results from threats of political action, complex and drawn-out bureaucratic procedures, and the prospect of arbitrary and unpredictable alterations in regulations after the investment decision has been made.[14]

Joint Ventures

Joint ventures are a collaboration of two or more organizations for more than a transitory period.[15] In this collaboration, the participating partners share assets, risks, and profits. Equality of partners is not necessary. In some joint ventures, each partner holds an equal share; in others, one partner has the majority of shares. The partners' contributions to the joint venture can also vary widely. Contributions may consist of funds, technology, know-how, sales organizations, or plant and equipment.

Advantages of Joint Ventures   The two major reasons for carrying out foreign direct investments in the form of joint ventures are governmental and commercial. Governments often pressure firms either to form or accept joint ventures or to forgo participation in the local market. Such restrictions are designed to reduce the extent of control that foreign firms can exercise over local operations. As a basis for defining control, most countries have employed percentage levels of ownership. Over time, countries have shown an increasing tendency to reduce the thresholds of ownerships that define control. This tendency developed as it became apparent that even small, organized groups of stockholders may influence control of an enterprise, particularly if overall ownership is widely distributed. At the same time, however, many countries are also recognizing the beneficial effects of foreign direct investment in terms of technological progress and international competitiveness and are permitting more control of local firms by foreign entities.

Another reason may be the economic orientation of governments and a resulting requirement for joint venture collaboration. Joint ventures can help overcome existing market access restrictions and open up or maintain market opportunities that otherwise would not be available.

Equally important to the formation of joint ventures are commercial considerations. If a corporation can identify a partner with a common goal, and if the international activities do not infringe on the autonomy of the individual partner, joint ventures may represent the most viable vehicle for international expansion. The following is an example of a nearly ideal joint venture:

> The Trailmobile Company of Cincinnati, Ohio, produces truck trailers. It now participates in 27 joint ventures abroad. Truck trailers do not move in international markets in significant numbers because transportation costs are high and, more importantly, because tariffs typically serve to insulate the markets from each other. Therefore, pricing can be decided at the level of the joint venture, because one joint venture cannot invade the market of another. Each joint venture serves its own local market, and these differ from each other in significant ways; hence, the marketing policy decisions are made at the local level. Only a modest part of the total cost of manufacturing the trailer is represented by components bought from Trailmobile. Thus, the interdependencies are limited, decision making can be delegated to the level of the joint venture, and conflicts can be minimized.[16]

Joint ventures are valuable when the pooling of resources results in a better outcome for each partner than if each attempted to carry out its activities individually. This is particularly the case when each partner has a specialized advantage in areas that benefit the joint venture. For example, a firm may have new technology available, yet lack sufficient capital to carry out foreign direct investment on its own. By joining forces with a partner, the technology can be used more quickly and market penetration is easier. Similarly, one of the partners may have a distribution system already established or have better access to local suppliers, either of which permits a greater volume of sales in a shorter period of time.

Joint ventures also permit better relationships with local organizations—government, local authorities, or labor unions. Government-related reasons are the major rationale for joint ventures in developing countries. If the local partner can bring political influence to the undertaking, the new venture may be eligible for tax incentives, grants, and government support and may be less vulnerable to political risk. Negotiations for certifications or licenses may be easier because authorities may not perceive themselves as dealing with a foreign firm. Relationships between the local partner and the local financial establishment may enable the joint venture to tap local capital markets. The greater experience—and therefore greater familiarity—with the culture and environment of the local partner may enable the joint venture to be more aware of cultural sensitivities and to benefit from greater insights into changing market conditions and needs.

Disadvantages of Joint Ventures   Problem areas in joint ventures, as in all partnerships, involve implementing the concept and maintaining the relationship. Many governments that require a joint venture formation are inexperienced in foreign direct investment. Therefore, joint venture legislation and the ensuing regulations are often subject to substantial interpretation and arbitrariness. Frequently, different levels of control are permitted depending on the type of product and the shipment destination. In some instances, only portions of joint venture legislation are made public. Other internal regulations are communicated only when necessary. Such situations create uncertainty, which increases the risk for the joint venture participants.

Major problems can also arise in assuring the maintenance of the joint venture relationship. Many joint ventures have been found to fall short of expectations and/or are disbanded. The reasons typically relate to conflicts of interest, problems with disclosure of sensitive information, and disagreement over how profits are to be shared; these are typically the result of a lack of communication before, during, and after the formation of the venture. In some cases, managers are interested in launching the venture but are too little concerned with actually running the enterprise. In other instances, managers dispatched to the joint venture by the partners may feel differing degrees of loyalty to the venture and its partners. Reconciling such conflicts of loyalty is one of the greatest human resource challenges for joint ventures.[17] Many of the problems encountered by joint ventures stem from a lack of careful, advance consideration of how to manage the new endeavor. A partnership works on the basis of trust and commitment, or not at all.

Areas of possible disagreement include the whole range of business decisions covering strategy, management style, accounting and control, marketing policies and practices, production, research and development, and personnel.[18] The joint venture may, for example, identify a particular market as a profitable target, yet the headquarters of one of the partners may already have plans for serving this market, plans that would require competing against its own joint venture.

Similarly, the issue of profit accumulation and distribution may cause discontent. If one partner supplies the joint venture with a product, that partner will prefer that any profits accumulate at headquarters and accrue 100 percent to one firm rather than at the joint venture, where profits are partitioned according to equity participation. Such a decision may not be greeted with enthusiasm by the other partner. Further, once profits are accumulated, their distribution may lead to dispute. For example, one partner may insist on a high payout of dividends because of financial needs, whereas the other may prefer the reinvestment of profits into a growing operation.

Strategic Alliances One special form of joint ventures consists of strategic alliances, or partnerships. The result of growing global competition, rapid increases in the investment required for technological progress, and growing risk of failure, strategic alliances are informal or formal arrangements between two or more companies with a common business objective. They are more than the traditional customer–vendor relationship, but less than an outright acquisition. The great advantage of such alliances is their ongoing flexibility, since they can be formed, adjusted, and dissolved rapidly in response to changing conditions. In essence, strategic alliances are networks of companies, which collaborate in the achievement of a given project or objective. However, partners for one project may well be fierce competitors for another.

Alliances can take forms ranging from information cooperation in the market development area to joint ownership of worldwide operations. For example, Texas Instruments has reported agreements with companies such as IBM, Hyundai, Fujitsu, Alcatel, and L. M. Ericsson using such terms as "joint development agreement," "cooperative technical effort," "joint program for development," "alternative sourcing agreement," and "design/exchange agreement for cooperative product development and exchange of technical data."

There are many reasons for the growth in such alliances. Market development is one common focus. Penetrating foreign markets is a primary objective of many companies. In Japan, Motorola is sharing chip designs and manufacturing facilities with Toshiba to gain greater access to the Japanese market. Some alliances are aimed at defending home markets. Another focus is spreading the cost and risk inherent in production and development efforts. Texas Instruments and Hitachi have teamed up to develop the next generation of memory chips. The costs of developing new jet engines are so vast that they force aerospace companies into collaboration; one such consortium was formed by United Technologies' Pratt & Whitney division, Britain's Rolls Royce, Motoren-und-Turbinen Union from Germany, Fiat of Italy, and Japanese Aero Engines (made up of Ishikawajima Heavy Industries and Kawasaki Heavy Industries). Some alliances are also formed to block or co-opt competitors.[19] For example, Caterpillar formed a heavy equipment joint venture with Mitsubishi in Japan to strike back at its main global rival, Komatsu, in its home market.

Of course, companies must carefully evaluate the effects of entering such a coalition. Depending on the objectives of the other partners, companies may wind up having their strategy partially driven by their competitors. Partners may also gain strength through coalitions and transfers of technology. As a result, they might become unexpected competitors. The most successful alliances are those that match the complementary strengths of partners to satisfy a joint objective. Often the partners have different product, geographic, or functional strengths, which the alliance can build on in order to achieve success with a new strategy or in a new market. Table 13.3 shows how some firms have combined their individual strengths to achieve their joint objective. In light of growing international competition and the rising cost of innovation in technology, strategic alliances are likely to continue their growth in the future.

Recommendations The first requirement when forming a joint venture is to find the right partner. Partners should have a commonality of orientation and goals, possess relatively similar organizational cultures,[20] and should bring complementary and relevant benefits to the joint venture. The venture makes little sense if the expertise of both partners is in the same area—for example, if both have production experience but neither has distribution know-how. Similarly, bringing a good distribution system to the joint venture may be of little use if the established system is in the field of consumer products and the joint venture will produce industrial products.

Second, great care needs to be taken in negotiating the joint venture agreement. In these negotiations, extensive provisions must be made for contingencies. Questions such as profit accumulation and distribution and market orientation must be

Table 13.3   Complementary Strengths Create Value

Partner Strength . . .	+ Partner Strength . . .	= Joint Objective
Pepsico *marketing clout for canned beverages*	**Lipton** *recognized tea brand and customer franchise*	*To sell canned iced tea beverages jointly*
Philips *consumer electronics innovation and leadership*	**Levi Strauss** *fashion design and distribution*	*Outdoor wear with integrated electronic equipment for fashion-conscious consumers*
KFC *established brand and store format, and operations skills*	**Mitsubishi** *real estate and site-selection skills in Japan*	*To establish a KFC chain in Japan*
Siemens *presence in range of telecommunications markets worldwide and cable-manufacturing technology*	**Corning** *technological strength in optical fibers and glass*	*To create a fiber-optic-cable business*
Ericsson *technological strength in public telecommunications networks*	**Hewlett-Packard** *computers, software, and access to electronics-channels*	*To create and market network management systems*

SOURCES: "Portable Technology Takes the Next Step: Electronics You Can Wear," *The Wall Street Journal,* August 22, 2000, B1, B4; Joel Bleeke and David Ernst, "Is Your Strategic Alliance Really a Sale?" *Harvard Business Review* 73 (January–February 1995); 97–105; and Melanie Wells, "Coca-Cola Proclaims Nestea Time for CAA," *Advertising Age,* January 30, 1995, 2. See also **http://www.pepsico.com**; **http://www.kfc.com**; **http://www.corningcablesystems.com**; **http://www.ericsson.com**; and **http://www.hp.com**.

addressed in the initial agreement; otherwise, they may surface as points of contention over time. A joint venture agreement, although comparable to a marriage contract, should contain the elements of a divorce contract. Changing business conditions and priorities may make a dissolution necessary. Agreements should therefore cover issues such as conditions of termination, disposition of assets and liabilities, protection of proprietary information and property, rights over sales territories, and obligations to customers. In addition, it is important to plan for the continued employment or termination of the people working in a dissolved joint venture.[21]

Finally, joint ventures operate in dynamic business environments and therefore must be able to adjust to changing market conditions. The agreement should provide for changes in the original concept so that the venture can grow and flourish.

Government Consortia

One form of cooperation takes place at the industry level and is typically characterized by government support or even subsidization. Usually, it is the reflection of escalating cost and a governmental goal of developing or maintaining global leadership in a particular sector. A new drug can cost $200 million to develop and bring to market; a new mainframe computer or a telecommunications switch can require $1 billion. To combat the high costs and risks of research and development, **research consortia** have emerged in the United States, Japan, and Europe. Since the passage of the Joint Research and Development Act of 1984 (which allows both domestic and foreign firms to participate in joint basic research efforts without the fear of antitrust action), well over 100 consortia have been registered in the United States. These consortia pool their resources for research into technologies ranging from artificial intelligence and electric car batteries to semiconductor manufacturing. The Europeans have several mega-projects to develop new technologies registered under the names BRITE, COMET, ESPRIT, EUREKA, RACE, and SOKRATES. Japanese consortia have worked on producing the world's highest-capacity memory chip and advanced computer technologies. On the manufacturing side, the formation of Airbus Industries secured European production of commercial jets. The consortium, now backed by the European Aeronautic Defence and Space Company (EADS), which emerged from the link-up of the German DaimlerChrysler Aerospace AG, the French Aerospatiale Matra, and CASA of Spain[22] has become a prime global competitor.

Contractual Arrangements

One final major form of international market participation is contractual arrangements. Firms have found this method to be a useful alternative or complement to other international options, since it permits the international use of corporate resources and can also be an acceptable response to government ownership restrictions.

Such an arrangement may focus on cross-marketing, where the contracting parties carry out complementary activities. For example, Nestlé and General Mills had an agreement whereby Honey Nut Cheerios and Golden Grahams were made in General Mills's U.S. plants and shipped in bulk to Europe for packaging at a Nestlé plant.[23] This alliance evolved into a joint venture, Cereal Partners Worldwide, which markets both companies' products in Europe and Asia. Firms also can have a reciprocal arrangement whereby each partner provides the other access to its market. The New York Yankees and Manchester United sell each others' licensed products and develop joint sponsorship programs. International airlines have started to share hubs, coordinate schedules, and simplify ticketing. Alliances such as Star (joining airlines such as United and Lufthansa) or Oneworld (British Airways and American Airlines) provide worldwide coverage for their customers both in the travel and shipping communities. Other contractual arrangements exist for outsourcing. For example, General Motors buys cars and components from South Korea's Daewoo, and Siemens buys computers from Fujitsu. As corporations look for ways to grow simultaneously and focus on their competitive advantage, outsourcing has become a powerful new tool for achieving these goals. Firms increasingly also develop arrangements for contract manufacturing, which allows the corporation to separate the physical production of goods from the research, development, and marketing stages, especially if the latter are the core competencies of the firm. Such contracting has become particularly popular in the footwear and garment industries.

In a **management contract,** the supplier brings together a package of skills that will provide an integrated service to the client without incurring the risk and benefit of ownership. The activity is quite different from other contractual arrangements because people actually move and directly implement the relevant skills and knowledge in the client organization.[24] Management contracts can be used by the international marketer in various ways. When equity participation, in the form of either full ownership or a joint venture, is not possible or must be relinquished, a management contract can serve to maintain participation in a venture. Depending on the extensiveness of the contract, it may even permit some measure of control. As an example, the manufacturing process might have to be relinquished to foreign firms, yet international distribution is needed for the product. A management contract could serve to maintain a strong hold on the operation by ensuring that all the distribution channels remain firmly controlled.

Yet management contracts should not be seen as a last line of defense. Whenever lack of expertise exists in a particular venture, management contracts can be a most useful tool to help overcome barriers to international marketing activities. This is particularly useful if an outside party has specialized knowledge that is crucial to international marketing success, whether in the area of distribution technology, marketing know-how, or worldwide contacts. Some companies in the service sector have independent entities that specialize in delivering management services. For example, the German airline Lufthansa manages the operations of many airlines by handling the accounting system, setting salary and customer-service levels, and providing training programs.

A management contract can also be the critical element in the success of a project. Such a contract and a lender's faith in the contractor may be crucial in obtaining financial support for a project, particularly in the early planning stages.

One specialized form of management contract is the **turnkey operation.** Here, the arrangement permits a client to acquire a complete operational system, together with the skills investment sufficient to allow unassisted maintenance and operation of the system following its completion.[25] The client need not search for individual contractors and subcontractors or deal with scheduling conflicts and difficulties in assigning responsibilities and blame. Instead, a package arrangement permits the accumulation of responsibility in one hand and greatly eases the negotiation and supervision requirements and subsequent accountability issues for the client.

Management contracts have clear benefits for the client. They can provide organizational skills that are not available locally, expertise that is immediately available rather than built up, and management assistance in the form of support services that would be difficult and costly to replicate locally. In addition, the outside involvement is clearly limited. When a turnkey project is online, the system will be totally owned, controlled, and operated by the customer. As a result, management contracts are seen by many governments as a useful alternative to foreign direct investment and the resulting control by nondomestic entities.

Similar advantages exist for the supplier. The risk of participating in an international venture is substantially lowered because no equity capital is at stake. At the same time, a significant amount of operational control can be exercised. Clearly, being on the inside represents a strategic advantage in influencing decisions. In addition, existing know-how that has been built up with significant investment can be commercialized. Frequently, the impact of fluctuations in business volume can be reduced by making use of experienced personnel who otherwise would have to be laid off. In industrialized countries like the United States, with economies that are increasingly service based, accumulated service knowledge and comparative advantage should be used internationally. Management contracts permit a firm to do so.

From the client's perspective, the main drawbacks to consider are the risks of overdependence and loss of control. For example, if the management contractor maintains all international relationships, little if any expertise may be passed on to the local operation. Instead of a gradual transfer of skills leading to increasing independence, the client may have to rely more and more on the performance of the contractor.

On the contractor's side, the major risks to consider are (1) the effects of the loss or termination of a contract and the resulting personnel problems, and (2) a bid made without fully detailed insight into actual expenses. Winning a management contract could result in Pyrrhic victories, with the income not worth the expense.

Summary

Foreign direct investment represents a major market-expansion alternative. Although such investment can be carried out by any type of firm, large or small, it typically occurs after some experience has been gathered with alternative forms of internationalization, such as exporting. The most visible and powerful players in the foreign direct investment field are larger-sized firms and multinational corporations. Market factors, barriers to trade, cost factors, and investment climate are the major causes of foreign direct investment, with market factors usually playing the major role.

Different ownership levels of foreign investments are possible, ranging from wholly owned subsidiaries to joint ventures. Although many firms prefer full ownership in order to retain full control, such a posture is often not possible because of governmental regulations.

It may not even be desirable. Depending on the global organization and strategic needs of the firm, joint ventures with only partial ownership may be a profitable alternative.

In a joint venture, the partners can complement each other by contributing the strengths and resources that each is best equipped to supply. Joint ventures offer significant benefits in terms of closeness to markets, better acceptance by the foreign environment, and a lessening of the risks involved, but they also pose new problems due to potential clashes of corporate cultures, business orientations, and marketing policies. It is therefore important to select the appropriate joint venture partner and to design an agreement that ensures the long-term approval of all participants.

Strategic alliances, or partnerships, are a special form of joint venture in which the participants, at either the industry or the corporate level, join forces in order to make major strategic progress toward technology development and competitiveness. Given the complexities and cost of technological progress, the number of these alliances, sometimes encouraged through government-sponsored consortia, is rapidly growing.

As countries increasingly develop a service-based economy, the usefulness of contractual arrangements grows. Such contracts can enable the involvement of the international marketer in a project when equity participation is not possible or desirable. They also permit a client to acquire operational skills and turnkey systems without relinquishing ownership of a project. Because management assistance, service delivery, and project planning are increasingly important, international marketers can use management contracting to carve out a profitable market niche.

Key Terms

resource seekers
market seekers
efficiency seekers
derived demand
fiscal incentives
financial incentives

nonfinancial incentives
brain drain
profit repatriation
research consortia
management contract
turnkey operation

Questions for Discussion

1. Will the Internet encourage or discourage foreign direct investments?
2. As a government official, would you prefer the foreign direct investment of a resource seeker, efficiency seeker, or market seeker?
3. Give some reasons why a multinational corporation might insist on 100 percent ownership abroad.
4. At what level of ownership would you consider a firm to be foreign controlled?
5. Do investment-promotion programs of state governments make sense from a national perspective?
6. How can a management contractor have more control than the client? What can the client do under such circumstances?
7. Discuss the benefits and drawbacks of strategic partnerings at the corporate level.

Internet Exercises

1. The Bureau of Economic Analysis (**http://www.bea.doc.gov**) and Stat-USA (**http://www.statusa.gov**) provide a multitude of information about the current state of the U.S. economy. Using the International Investment Tables (D-57), find the current market value of direct investment abroad as well as the value of direct investment in the United States.

2. Find the Fortune Global 500 listing of the world's largest corporations on the *Fortune* Web site (**http://www.fortune.com**). What are the largest corporations in your region? Compare their sales to the GDP of some nations of your choice.

Recommended Readings

Bamford, James, Benjamin Gomes-Casseres, and Michael Robinson. *Mastering Alliance Strategy: A Comprehensive Guide to Design, Management, and Organization.* San Francisco: Jossey-Bass, 2002.

Buckley, Peter J., and Pervez N. Ghauri. *The Global Challenge for Multinational Enterprises.* New York: Pergamon Press, 2000.

Culpan, Refik. *Global Business Alliances: Theory and Practice.* New York: Quorum, 2002.

Gutterman, Alan. *International Joint Ventures: Negotiating, Forming, and Operating the International Joint Venture.* Novato, CA: World Trade Press, 2001.

Hood, Neil, and Stephen Young. *The Globalization of Multinational Enterprise Activity and Economic Development.* New York: Macmillan, 2000.

Rosenbloom, Arthur H. *Due Diligence for Global Deal Making: The Definitive Guide to Cross-Border Mergers and Acquisitions, Joint Ventures, Financings, and Strategic Alliances.* New York: Bloomberg Press, 2002.

Spekman, Robert E., Lynn A. Isabella, and Thomas C. MacAvoy. *Alliance Competence: Maximizing the Value of Your Partnerships.* New York: Wiley, 2000.

chapter 14

Product and Brand Management

THE INTERNATIONAL MARKETPLACE   14.1

Anatomy of a Global Product Launch

By the end of the 1980s, with disposable razors taking up 50 percent of the market, executives at Gillette, the $9.3 billion Boston-based consumer products marketer, decided to break out of what they saw as a dead-end strategy. With disposables, the razor had become a commodity, and the buying decision was based solely on price and convenience. Gillette needed a differentiator, a product upon which the brand could be elevated and market share substantially increased. Rather than compete on the existing playing field, management decided to create a new category, the shaving system, and take control of it.

In 1990, after 10 years of research and development, Gillette introduced its Sensor twin-bladed shaving system. The design not only produced a markedly better shave but also brought the company back into an indisputable leadership position. The next step was to see whether three blades could do a better job than two. In order to ensure that consumers did not simply scoff at three blades as a marketing gimmick, the result—and the communication about it—had to be demonstrably better.

A group, code-named the 225 Task Force, worked for five full years in concert with R&D to produce and orchestrate the introduction of a new product, Mach3. They concentrated as much on developing a great new brand as on developing a great new product. The five years were characterized by ceaseless product improvement, constant product testing around the world, and, eventually, creation of a marketing strategy not only to press the new value propositions but also to substantiate the claims. The marketing strategy was to look at the world as one market and rely on the following premises:

- Because the product would probably take off immediately, manufacturing had to ensure that it had enough capacity to avoid shortages at the outset.
- To facilitate smooth global introduction, all packaging, point-of-sale, and other promotional material had to be the same, simply translated into 30 languages. The company purposefully keeps the number of words on the front of the package to a minimum to avoid the need for design alterations.
- All marketing and advertising was based on a single campaign that was released in every market, again with minor local adjustments and translations. The European introduction was delayed by two months to September 1st to accommodate Europeans on their traditional summer holiday.
- Pricing needed built-in elasticity, but by carefully testing the concept with consumers, Gillette fixed a profitable

price point based on the expected number of blades per user per year.

By 2000, Mach3 had become the success its developers and marketers had planned for. It had captured more than 20 percent of the global blade and razor market. Moreover, market share varied from 13 to 16 percent in all the markets in which it had been launched. Its success is underscored by the introduction of copycats, especially British retailer Asda's Tri-Flex, retailing on the average for $1.00 less than Mach3.

In 2001, Gillette introduced Gillette for Women Venus, backed by a global marketing push similar to that for Mach3. The campaign, "Reveal the goddess is you," included TV, print, outdoor, and Internet advertising. Gillette spent $300 million to bring Venus to market, with extensive worldwide consumer testing. First-year sales exceeded $300 million.

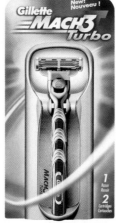

In October 2001, Gillette announced the launch of two new shaving systems, Mach3Turbo and Venus Crystal Clear. Both feature antifriction blades for an easier razor glide and a patented lubrication system for a gentler shave. The global advertising campaign created by BBDO for Mach3Turbo's launch exceeded $200 million. In response, Shick announced the launch of its version, Xtreme 3.

SOURCES: Jack Neff, "Gillette to Break New Shaving Campaign," *Advertising Age*, February 25, 2002, 38; "New Razor Blade Technology Turbo-Charges Product Sales," *DSN Retailing Today*, February 11, 2002, 5; "No New CEO, But Gillette Does Have a New Product," *Advertising Age*, November 6, 2000, 25; "Gillette Unveils Major Global Product Launch," *Marketing Week*, October 26, 2000, 5; Glenn Rifkin, "Mach3: Anatomy of Gillette's Latest Global Launch," *Strategy & Business* (no. 2, 1999): 34–41; "Gillette Flays Asda over 'Inferior' Tri-Flex Razor," *Marketing Week*, June 10, 1999, 9; Hamantha S. B. Herath and Chan S. Park, "Economic Analysis of R&D Projects: An Options Approach," *The Engineering Economist* 44 (no. 1, 1999): 1–35; **http://www.gillette.com**; **http://www.mach3.com**; and **http://www.gillettevenus.com**.

Product Development Summary for Mach3

Patents	35 patent protections on Mach3 and manufacturing processes
Development time	10 years
R&D costs	$200 million
Capital investments	$550 million
Advertising and marketing	$300 million
Launch dates	North America and Israel— July 1, 1998 Europe—September 1998 Worldwide—1999
Retail price	Razor, 2 cartridges, and organizer: $6.49–$6.99 Four-pack cartridges: $6.29–$6.79

IMAGE SOURCE: Courtesy of the Gillette Company.

DEVELOPING AND MANAGING a product portfolio in the global marketplace is both a great challenge and an attractive opportunity, as shown in *The International Marketplace 14.1*. While market conditions may warrant changes in individual product features, products and product lines should be managed for the greatest possible effect globally, regionally, and locally. Global and regional products have to utilize best practice across borders, while local products should be monitored for possible use in other markets.

This chapter is divided into two parts to highlight these issues. The first part will focus on how the product development process can take into account the globalization of markets without compromising dimensions considered essential by local markets. To a large extent this means that the process is market-driven rather than determined by cost or convenience of manufacture. For example, Germany's Volkswagen operated for years under the philosophy that one car was good enough for the whole world, while U.S. marketing executives tried in vain to secure items such as cup holders or seatback release levers in cars destined for the U.S. market. Similarly, Japanese product-development engineers fought against the concept of a third row of seats for a sport utility vehicle, which is preferred by U.S. customers.[1]

The second half of the chapter features a discussion of product management, especially how marketers can utilize resources on a worldwide basis to exploit opportunities in product markets. Unilever, one of the world's largest food companies, often has to take a local view, given differences in the daily diet. Similarly, detergent formulas may have to differ between markets because washing habits, machines, clothes, and water quality vary. However, many strategic product decisions, such as branding, will benefit from worldwide experience and exposure applied to the local context. Some categories cross national borders quite well, such as ice cream, tea, and personal wash products, and translate to opportunities with a standard approach.[2]

Global Product Development

Product development is at the heart of the global marketing process. New products should be developed, or old ones modified, to cater to new or changing customer needs on a global or regional basis. At the same time, corporate objectives of technical feasibility and financial profitability must be satisfied.

To illustrate, Black & Decker, manufacturer of power tools for do-it-yourself household repairs, had done some remodeling of its own. The company in the 1980s was the consummate customizer: the Italian subsidiary made tools for Italians, the British subsidiary for the British. At the same time, Japanese power tool makers, such as Makita Electric Works Ltd., saw the world differently. Makita was Black & Decker's first competitor with a global strategy. Makita management did not care that Germans prefer high-powered, heavy-duty drills and that U.S. consumers want everything lighter. They reasoned that a good drill at a low price will sell from Baden-Baden to Brooklyn. Using this strategy, Makita effectively cut into Black & Decker's market share. As a result, Black & Decker unveiled 50 new models—each standardized for world production. The company's current objective is to "establish itself as the preeminent global manufacturer and marketer" in its field.[3]

With competition increasingly able to react quickly when new products are introduced, worldwide planning at the product level provides a number of tangible benefits. A firm that adopts a worldwide approach is better able to develop products with specifications compatible on a worldwide scale. A firm that leaves product development to independent units will incur greater difficulties in transferring its experience and technology.

In many multinational corporations, each product is developed for potential worldwide usage, and unique multinational market requirements are incorporated whenever technically feasible. Some design their products to meet the regulations and other key requirements in their major markets and then, if necessary, smaller markets' requirements are met on a country-by-country basis. For example, Nissan develops lead-country models that can, with minor changes, be made suitable for local sales in the majority of markets. For the remaining situations, the company also provides a range of additional models that can be adapted to the needs of local segments. Using this approach, Nissan has been able to reduce the number of basic models from 48 to 28.[4] This approach also means that the new product can be introduced concurrently into all the firm's markets. Companies like 3M and Xerox develop most of their products with this objective in mind.

Some markets may require unique approaches to developing global products. At Gillette, timing is the only concession to local taste. Developing markets, such as Eastern Europe and China, are first weaned on older, cheaper products before they are sold up-to-date versions.[5] In a world economy where most of the growth is occurring in developing markets, the traditional approach of introducing a global product may keep new products out of the hands of consumers due to their premium price. As a result, Procter & Gamble figures out what consumers in various countries can afford and then develops products they can pay for. For example, in Brazil, the company introduced a diaper called Pampers Uni, a less-expensive version of its mainstream product. The strategy is to create price tiers, hooking customers early and then encouraging them to trade up as their incomes and desire for better products grow.[6]

The main goal of the product development process, therefore, is not to develop a standard product or product line but to build adaptability into products and product lines that are being developed to achieve worldwide appeal. To accomplish the right balance, marketers need to develop basic capability for capturing consumer information within their country organizations. If consumers are willing to talk about their preferences, traditional approaches such as focus groups and interviews work well. Procter & Gamble, for example, generates Chinese consumer information using a 30-person market research team.[7]

The Product Development Process

The product development process begins with idea generation. Ideas may come from within the company—from the research and development staff, sales personnel, or almost anyone who becomes involved in the company's efforts. Intermediaries may suggest ideas because they are closer to the changing, and often different, needs of international customers. In franchising operations, franchisees are a source of many new products. For example, the McFlurry, McDonald's ice-cream dessert, was the brainchild of a Canadian operator.[8] Competitors are a major outside source of ideas. A competitive idea from abroad may be modified and improved to suit another market's characteristics. As an example, when the president of d-Con returned from a trip to Europe, he brought with him what would seem in the United States to be an unusual idea for packaging insecticides. In a market dominated by aerosols, the new idea called for offering consumers insect repellent in a "felt-tip pen."

For a number of companies, especially those producing industrial goods, customers provide the best source of ideas for new products.[9] Many new commercially important products are initially thought of and even prototyped by users rather than manufacturers. They tend to be developed by **lead users**—companies, organizations, or individuals who are ahead of trends or have needs that go beyond what is available at present. For example, a car company in need of a new braking system may look for ideas at racing teams or even at the aerospace industry, which has a strong incentive to stop its vehicles before they run out of runway.[10] Of the 30 products with the highest world sales in the 1990s, 70 percent trace their origins to manufacturing and marketing (rather than laboratories) via customer input.[11] Many companies work together with complementary-goods producers in developing new solutions; Whirlpool and Procter & Gamble developed new solutions for keeping people's clothes clean. With the increased diffusion of the Internet, chat rooms about products and features will become an important source of information pertinent to product development and adjustment. For example, Sony set up a Web site to support hackers who are interested in exploring and developing new types of games that could be played on the Sony PlayStation. In the field of industrial products, users are invited to use toolkits to design products and services that fit their own needs precisely.[12]

For some companies, procurement requisitions from governments and supranational organizations (for example, the United Nations) are a good source of new product ideas. When the United Nations Children's Fund (UNICEF) was looking for containers to transport temperature-sensitive vaccines in tropical climates, Igloo Corporation noticed that the technology from its picnic coolers could be used and adapted for UNICEF's use.[13] Facilitating agents, such as advertising agencies or market research organizations, can be instrumental in scanning the globe for new ideas. For example, DDB Worldwide uses U.S. research company Market Access for "search-and-reapply" operations to keep clients informed about new ideas around the world, ranging from half-frozen mineral water in Korea to Argentine yogurt drinks containing cereal and fruit chunks.[14]

Most companies develop hundreds of ideas every year; for example, 3M may have 1,000 new product ideas competing for scarce development funds annually. Product ideas are screened on market, technical, and financial criteria: Is the market substantial and penetrable, can the product be mass produced, and if the answer to both of these questions is affirmative, can the company produce and market it profitably? Too often, companies focus on understanding only the current demand of the consumer. A repositioning of the concept may overcome an initial negative assessment; for example, in countries with no significant breakfast habit, cereal marketers present their products as snacks. Procter & Gamble created the perception that dandruff—traditionally a nonissue for the Chinese—is a social stigma and offered a product (Head & Shoulders antidandruff shampoo) to solve the problem. Today, P&G controls more than half the shampoo market in China.[15]

A product idea that at some stage fails to earn a go-ahead is not necessarily scrapped. Most progressive companies maintain data banks of "miscellaneous opportunities." Often, data from these banks are used in the development of other products. One of the most famous examples concerns 3M. After developing a new woven fabric some 50 years ago, 3M's Commercial Office Supply Company did not know what to do with the technology. Among the applications rejected were seamless brassiere cups and disposable diapers. The fabric was finally used to make surgical and industrial masks.

All the development phases—idea generation, screening, product and process development, scale-up, and commercialization—should be global in nature with inputs into the process from all affected markets. If this is possible, original product designs can be adapted easily and inexpensively later on. The process has been greatly facilitated through the use of **computer-aided design (CAD).** Some companies are able to design their products so that they meet most standards and requirements around the world, with minor modifications on a country-by-country basis. The product development process can be initiated by any unit of the organization, in the parent country or abroad. If the initiating entity is a subsidiary that lacks technical and financial resources for implementation, another entity of the firm is assigned the responsibility. Most often this is the parent and its central R&D department.

Larger multinational corporations naturally have development laboratories in multiple locations that can assume the task. Gillette, for example, maintains two toiletries laboratories, one in the United States and the other in the United Kingdom. In these cases, coordination and information flow between the units are especially critical.

Global companies may have an advantage in being able to utilize the resources from around the world. Otis Elevator Inc.'s product for high-rises, the Elevonic, is a good example of this. The elevator was developed by six research centers in five countries. Otis' group in Farmington, Connecticut, handled the systems integration, Japan designed the special motor drives that make the elevators ride smoothly, France perfected the door systems, Germany handled the electronics, and Spain took care of the small-geared components. The international effort saved more than $10 million in design costs and cut the development cycle from four years to two.[16]

In some cases, the assignment of product development responsibility may be based on a combination of special market and technical knowledge. When a major U.S. copier manufacturer was facing erosion of market share in the smaller copier segment in Europe because of Japanese incursions, its Japanese subsidiary was charged with developing an addition to the company's product line. This product, developed and produced outside the United States, has subsequently been marketed in the United States.

Even though the product development activity may take place in the parent country, all the affected units actively participate in development and market planning for a new product. For example, a subsidiary would communicate directly with the product division at the headquarters level and also with the international staff, who could support the subsidiary on the scene of the actual development activity. This often also involves the transfer of people from one location to another for such projects. For example, when Fiat wanted to build a car specifically for emerging markets, the task to develop the Palio was given to a 300-strong team which assembled in Turin, Italy. Among them were 120 Brazilians, ranging from engineers to shop-floor workers, as well as Argentines, Turks, and Poles.[17]

The activities of a typical global program are summarized in Figure 14.1. The managing unit has prime responsibility for accomplishing: (1) single-point worldwide technical development and design of a new product that conforms to the global design standard and global manufacturing and procurement standards as well as transmittal of the completed design to each affected unit; (2) all other activities necessary to plan, develop, manufacture, introduce, and support the

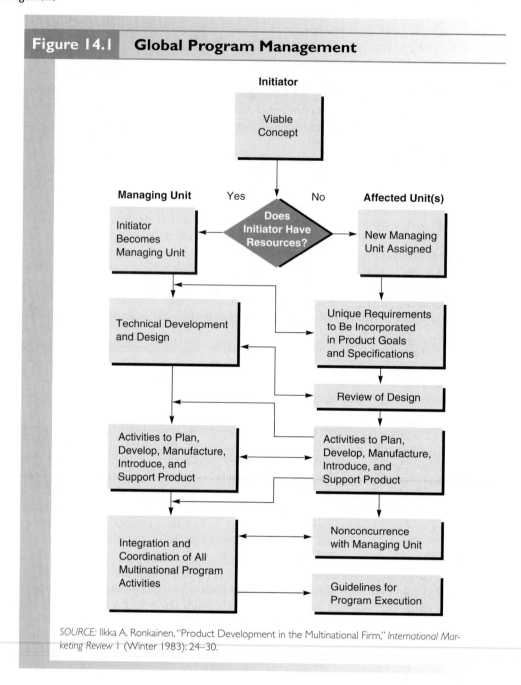

Figure 14.1   Global Program Management

SOURCE: Ilkka A. Ronkainen, "Product Development in the Multinational Firm," *International Marketing Review* 1 (Winter 1983): 24–30.

product in the managing unit as well as direction and support to affected units to ensure that concurrent introductions are achieved; and (3) integration and coordination of all global program activities.

The affected units, on the other hand, have prime responsibility for achieving: (1) identification of unique requirements to be incorporated in the product goals and specifications as well as in the managing unit's technical effort; (2) all other activities necessary to plan, manufacture, introduce, and support products in affected units; and (3) identification of any nonconcurrence with the managing unit's plans and activities.

During the early stages of the product development process, the global emphasis is on identifying and evaluating the requirements of both the managing unit and the affected units and incorporating them into the plan. During the later stages, the emphasis is on the efficient development and design of a global product with a minimum of configuration differences and on the development of supporting systems capabilities in each of the participating units. The result of the interaction and communication is product development activity on a global basis, as well as products developed primarily to serve world markets. For example, Fiat's Palio is designed for the rough roads of the Brazilian interior rather than the smooth motorways of Italy. The car was also deliberately overengineered, because market research revealed that customers' future preferences were developing that way.

This approach effectively cuts through the standardized-versus-localized debate and offers a clear-cut way of determining and implementing effective programs in several markets simultaneously. It offers headquarters the opportunity to standardize certain aspects of the product while permitting maximum flexibility, whenever technically feasible, to differing market conditions. For instance, in terms of technical development, members of subsidiaries' staffs take an active part in the development processes to make sure that global specifications are built into the initial design of the product.[18]

The process has to be streamlined in terms of duration as well. In industries characterized by technological change, coming to market nine to twelve months late can cost a new product half its potential revenues. To cut down on development time, companies like NEC and Canon use multidisciplinary teams that stay with the project from start to finish, using a parallel approach toward product launch. Designers start to work before feasibility testing is over; manufacturing and marketing begin gearing up well before the design is finished. Such teams depend on computer systems for designing, simulating, and analyzing products. Toyota Motor Company estimates that it will, sometime in the future, develop a new automobile in one year (its RAV4 mini sport utility vehicle was brought to market in 24 months), whereas some of its competitors may spend as much as five years on the process.[19] However, with new uncertain technologies for which market response is not clear, longer development cycles are still common and advisable.[20]

Firms using worldwide product management are better able to develop products that can be quickly introduced into any market.[21] Foreign market introduction can take the form of either production or marketing abroad. In general, the length of the lag will depend on (1) the product involved, with industrial products having shorter lags because of their more standardized general nature; (2) degree of newness; (3) customer characteristics—both demographics and psychographics; (4) geographic proximity; (5) firm-related variables—the number and type of foreign affiliations as well as overall experience in global marketing; and (6) degree of commitments of resources.

While research and development is a highly centralized function in a firm, many allow their research centers to devote part of their time purely to their own endeavors. These initiatives are both effective for the motivation of the local personnel and incubators for future regional and global products. For example, the current research and development activities of consumer-product companies, which tend to be centralized near world headquarters, will have to shift to take into account the increasing numbers of customers who live in emerging markets.

The Location of R&D Activities

Most multinational corporations have located most of their product development operations within the parent corporation. Recently, however, a number of experts have called for companies to start using foreign-based resources to improve their ability to compete internationally. At Asea Brown Boveri, for example, 90 percent of R&D is done in worldwide business units rather than in an isolated business laboratory.[22] Dutch electronics giant Philips once funded all its R&D centrally, but now 70 percent of its funding comes from business units.[23] The benefits are accrued from acquiring international contacts and having R&D investments abroad as ways to add new items to the company's existing product line, thus increasing chances for global success.[24] Although the costs are high and recruitment difficult, W. R. Grace opened an $8 million R&D center in Japan. Japan provides the company heightened awareness of and access to technological developments that can be used to be more responsive not only to local markets but to global markets as well. The R&D center is part of Grace's triad approach involving the three leading areas for diffusion of technology: the United States, Europe, and Japan. A dozen other companies, including DuPont, Upjohn, Campbell, and Eastman Kodak, have launched similar centers.[25] For example, Campbell's R&D center in Hong Kong was initially set up to adjust the company's product offering to the Chinese market. It has since acquired a new role of transferring product concepts developed for the Asian market to the Americas and Europe, due to an increasing interest in ethnic foods. Savi Technology, a provider of real-time solutions for managing supply chains, established its R&D Center for IT Logistic Excellence in Singapore, because the city-state is a major starting point for many supply chains and Savi's major customers operate from there.[26]

Investments for R&D abroad are made for four general reasons: (1) to aid technology transfer from parent to subsidiary, (2) to develop new and improved products expressly for foreign markets, (3) to develop new products and processes for simultaneous application in world markets of the firm, and (4) to generate new technology of a long-term exploratory nature. The commitment of the firm to international operations increases from the first type of investment to the third and fourth, in which there is no or little bias toward headquarters performing the job.[27]

A survey of 209 multinationals in Europe, Japan, and North America shows that the trend towards internationalization of R&D is growing. The Japanese have the lowest degree of internationalization in their R&D efforts compared to their European and North American counterparts; the Europeans give their country operations abroad more responsibilities in product development.[28] In most cases, companies want to be closer to the customers they intend to serve. In some industries, such as pharmaceuticals, having localized R&D efforts is necessary due to heavy regulatory efforts by local or regional governments.

In truly global companies, the location of R&D is determined by the existence of specific skills. At Ford Motor Company, development of a specific car or component will be allotted to whichever technical center has the greatest expertise, as seen in *The International Marketplace 14.2*. Placing R&D operations abroad may also ensure access to foreign scientific and technical personnel and information, either in industry or at leading universities. Investment in R&D facilities in the United States by non-U.S. companies is heavily concentrated in California's Silicon Valley, New Jersey, and North Carolina's Research Triangle Park.[29] The location decision may also be driven by the unique features of the market. For example, most of the major carmakers have design centers in California to allow for the monitoring of the technical, social, and aesthetic values of the fifth-largest car market in the world. Furthermore, the many technological innovations and design trends that have originated there give it a trendsetting image. Working with the most demanding customers (on issues such as quality) will give companies assurance of success in broader markets.[30]

Given the increasing importance of emerging markets, many marketers believe that an intimate understanding of these new consumers can be achieved only through proximity. Consequently, Unilever has installed a network of innovation centers in 19 countries, many of which are emerging markets (such as Brazil, China, and Thailand). Hewlett-Packard's eInclusion division, which focuses on rural markets, established a branch of its HP Labs in India charged with developing products and services explicitly for that market.[31]

Many companies regionalize their R&D efforts; for example, U.S.-based multinational corporations often base their European R&D facilities in Belgium because of its central location and desirable market characteristics, which include serving as headquarters for the European Union and providing well-trained personnel. Regional centers may also be needed to adequately monitor customer trends around the world. Sharp, one of Japan's leading electronics companies, has set up centers in Hamburg, Germany, and Mahwah, New Jersey, in addition to its two centers at home.[32]

THE INTERNATIONAL MARKETPLACE   14.2

Centers of Excellence

Local markets are absorbing bigger roles as marketers scan the world for ideas that will cross borders. The consensus among marketers is that many more countries are now capable of developing products and product solutions that can be applied on a worldwide basis. This realization has given birth to centers of excellence. A center of excellence is defined as an organizational unit that incorporates a set of capabilities that have been identified as an important source of value creation with the explicit intention that these capabilities be leveraged by and/or disseminated to other parts of the firm.

Colgate-Palmolive has set up centers of excellence around the world, clustering countries with geographic, linguistic, or cultural similarities to exploit the same marketing plans. Unilever is extending the innovation centers it opened for personal care products to its food businesses, starting with ice cream. In addition to innovation centers for oral care in Milan and hair care in Paris, there are now similar centers for developing product ideas, research, technology, and marketing expertise for ice-cream products in Rome; Hamburg; London; Paris; and Green Bay, Wisconsin; and in Bangkok for the Asian market.

Countries have an edge if there is strong local development in a particular product category, such as hair care in France and Thailand, creating an abundance of research and development talent. Local management or existing products with a history of sensitivity to the core competence also helps win a worldwide role for a country unit. For example, ABB Strömberg in Finland was assigned as a worldwide center of excellence for electric drivers, a category for which it is a recognized world leader.

Ford's centers of excellence have been established with two key goals in mind: to avoid duplicating efforts and to capitalize on the expertise of specialists on a worldwide basis. Located in several countries, the centers will work on key components for cars. One will, for example, work on certain kinds of engines. Another will engineer and develop common platforms—the suspension and other undercarriage components—for similar-sized cars. Designers in each market will then style exteriors and passenger compartments to appeal to local tastes. Each car will usually be built on the continent where it is sold. Ford of Europe introduced the Focus, originally intended

to replace the Escort. The one-year time lag between the two continents was to allow the same team of engineers to direct factory launches in both in Europe and North America. Five Ford design studios had to compromise on design proposals that ranged from a soft, rounded body to a sharply angular one. Although European operations maintained a leadership role, key responsibilities were divided. The U.S. side took over automatic transmissions, with Europe handling the manual version. "If we didn't do it this way, the Americans and the Europeans would have done their own vehicles," says Jacques Nasser, CEO of Ford. "What we have is a shortage of product-development resources, mainly engineering people, and this uses them more efficiently."

Centers of excellence do not necessarily have to be focused products or technologies. For example, Corning has established a Center for Marketing Excellence where sales and marketing staff from all Corning's businesses from glass to television components to electronic communications displays will be able to find help with marketing intelligence, strategies, new product lines, and e-business.

Whatever the format, centers of excellence have as the most important tasks to leverage and/or to transfer their current leading-edge capabilities, and to continually fine-tune and enhance those capabilities so that they remain state-of-the-art. Centers of excellence provide country organizations a critical tool by which to develop subsidiary-specific advantages to benefit the entire global organization.

SOURCES: Tony Frost, Julian Birkinshaw, and Prescott Ensign, "Centers of Excellence in Multinational Corporations," *Strategic Management Journal* 23 (November 2002): 997–1018; Karl J. Moore, "A Strategy for Subsidiaries: Centers of Excellence to Build Subsidiary-Specific Advantages," *Management International Review* 41 (third quarter, 2001): 275–290; Erin Strout, "Reinventing a Company," *Sales and Marketing Management* 152 (February 2000): 86–92; Karl Moore and Julian Birkinshaw, "Managing Knowledge in Global Service Firms: Centers of Excellence," *Academy of Management Executive* 12 (November 1998): 81–92; Laurel Wentz, "World Brands," *Advertising Age International,* September 1996, i1–i21; "Ford to Merge European, North American Car Units," *The Washington Post,* April 22, 1994, G1–2; "Percy Barnevik's Global Crusade," *Business Week Enterprise 1993,* 204–211; **http://www.colgate.com**; **http://www.abb.com**; **http://www.ford.com**; and **http://www.corning.com**.

R&D centers are seen as highly desirable investments by host governments. Developing countries are increasingly demanding R&D facilities as a condition of investment or continued operation, to the extent that some companies have left countries where they saw no need for the added expense. Countries that have been known to have attempted to influence multinational corporations are Japan, India, Brazil, and France. The Chinese government has maintained a preference for foreign investors who have promised a commitment to technology transfer, especially in the form of R&D centers. Volkswagen's ability to develop its business in China is largely due to its willingness to do so. Some governments, such as Canada, have offered financial rewards to multinational corporations to start or expand R&D efforts in host markets. In addition to compliance with governmental regulation, local R&D efforts can provide positive publicity for the company involved. Internally, having local R&D may boost morale and elevate a subsidiary above the status of merely a manufacturing operation.[33]

In many multinational corporations that still employ multidomestic strategies, product development efforts amount to product modifications—for example, making sure that a product satisfies local regulations. Local content requirements may necessitate major development input from the affected markets. In these cases, local technical people identify alternate, domestically available ingredients and prepare initial tests. More involved testing usually takes place at a regional laboratory or at headquarters.

The Organization of Global Product Development

The product development activity is undertaken by specific teams, whose task is to subject new products to tough scrutiny at specified points in the development cycle to eliminate weak products before too much is invested in them and to guide promising prototypes from labs to the market.[34] Representatives of all the affected functional areas serve on each team to ensure the integrity of the project. A marketing team member is needed to assess the customer base for the new product, engineering to make sure that the product can be produced in the intended format, and finance to keep costs in control. An international team member should be assigned a permanent role in the product development process and not simply called in when a need arises. Organizational relationships have to be such that the firm's knowledge-based assets are easily transferable and transferred.[35]

In addition to having international representation on each product development team, some multinational corporations hold periodic meetings of purely international teams. A typical international team may consist of five members, each of whom also has a product responsibility (such as cable accessories) as well as a geographical responsibility (such as the Far East). Others may be from central R&D and domestic marketing planning. The function of international teams is to provide both support to subsidiaries and international input to overall planning efforts. A critical part of this effort is customer input before a new product design is finalized. This is achieved by requiring team members to visit key customers throughout the process. A key input of international team members is the potential for universal features that can be used worldwide as well as unique features that may be required for individual markets.

Such multidisciplinary teams maximize the payoff from R&D by streamlining decision making; that is, they reduce the need for elaborate reporting mechanisms and layers of committee approvals. With the need to slash development time, these teams can be useful. For example, in response to competition, Honeywell set up a multidisciplinary "tiger team" to build a thermostat in twelve months rather than the usual four years.[36]

Challenges to using teams or approaches that require cooperation between R&D centers are often language and cultural barriers. For example, pragmatic engineers in the United States may distrust their more theoretically thinking European counterparts. National rivalries may also inhibit the acceptance by others of solutions developed by one entity of the organization. Many companies have solved these problems with increased communication and exchange of personnel.

With the costs of basic research rising and product life cycles shortening, many companies have joined forces in R&D. The U.S. government and many U.S.-based multinational corporations have seen this approach as necessary to restore technological competitiveness. In 1984, the United States passed the National Cooperative

Research Act, which allows companies to collaborate in long-term R&D projects without the threat of antitrust suits. Since then, more than seventy **R&D consortia** have been established to develop technologies ranging from artificial intelligence to those needed to overtake the Japanese lead in semiconductor manufacturing. The major consortia in those fields are *Microelectronics* and *Computer Technology Corporation* and *Sematech,* both founded to match similar Japanese alliances. *The Consortium for Automotive Research* was set up by GM, Ford, and DaimlerChrysler to work on new concepts for use in the automotive sector, such as new battery technology and safety features. A group of consumer goods (e.g., Unilever and Kimberly-Clark) and technology firms (such as Intermec and Marconi) formed a consortium to speed up movement of goods in supply chains at rates faster than allowed by bar codes.[37] Similar consortia in the European Union are often heavily supported by the European Commission.

These consortia can provide the benefits and face the challenges of any strategic alliance. Countering the benefits of sharing costs and risks are management woes from mixing corporate cultures as well as varying levels of enthusiasm by the participants. As long as participants work on core technologies which each can then apply in their own way in their own fields, these consortia can work very effectively.

The Testing of New Product Concepts

The final stages of the product development process will involve testing the product in terms of both its performance and its projected market acceptance. Depending on the product, testing procedures range from reliability tests in the pilot plant to minilaunches, from which the product's performance in world markets will be estimated. Any testing will prolong full-scale commercialization and increase the possibility of competitive reaction. Further, the cost of test marketing is substantial—on the average, $1 to $1.5 million per market.

Because of the high rate of new product failure (estimated at 67–95 percent[38] and usually attributed to market or marketing reasons), most companies want to be assured that their product will gain customer acceptance. They therefore engage in testing or a limited launch of the product. This may involve introducing the product in one country—for instance, Belgium or Ireland—and basing the go-ahead decision for the rest of Europe on the performance of the product in that test market. Some countries are emerging as test markets for global products. Brazil is a test market used by Procter & Gamble and Colgate before rollout into the Latin American market. Unilever uses Thailand for a test market for the Asian market.

In many cases, companies rely too much on instinct and hunch in their marketing abroad, although in domestic markets they make extensive use of testing and research. Lack of testing has led to a number of major product disasters over the years. The most serious blunder is to assume that other markets have the same priorities and lifestyles as the domestic market. After a failure in introducing canned soups in Italy in the 1960s, Campbell Soup Company repeated the experience by introducing them in Brazil in 1979. Research conducted in Brazil after the failure revealed that women fulfill their roles as homemakers in part by such tasks as making soups from scratch. A similar finding had emerged in Italy more than 20 years earlier. However, when Campbell was ready to enter the Eastern and Central European markets in the 1990s, it was prepared for this and was careful to position the product initially as a starter or to be kept for emergencies.

Other reasons for product failure are a lack of product distinctiveness, unexpected technical problems, and mismatches between functions.[39] Mismatches between functions may occur not only between, for example, engineering and marketing, but within the marketing function as well. Engineering may design features in the product that established distribution channels or selling approaches cannot exploit. Advertising may promise the customer something that the other functions within marketing cannot deliver.

The trend is toward a complete testing of the marketing mix. All the components of the brand are tested, including formulation, packaging, advertising, and pricing. Test marketing is indispensable because prelaunch testing is an artificial situation; it tells the researcher what people say they will do, not what they will actually do. Test marketing carries major financial risks, which can be limited only if the testing can be conducted in a limited area. Ideally, this would utilize localized advertising media—that is, broadcast and print media to which only a limited region would be exposed. However, localized media are lacking even in developed markets such as Western Europe.

Because test marketing in Europe and elsewhere is risky or even impossible, researchers have developed three research methods to cope with the difficulty. **Laboratory test markets** are the least realistic in terms of consumer behavior over time, but this method allows the participants to be exposed to television advertisements, and their reactions can be measured in a controlled environment. **Microtest marketing** involves a continuous panel of consumers serviced by a retail grocery operated by the research agency. The panelists are exposed to new products through high-quality color print ads, coupons, and free samples. Initial willingness to buy and repeat buying are monitored. **Forced distribution tests** are based on a continuously reporting panel of consumers, but they encounter new products in normal retail outlets. This is realistic, but competitors are immediately aware of the new product. An important criterion for successful testing is to gain the cooperation of key retailing organizations in the market. Mars Confectionery, which was testing a new chocolate malted-milk drink in England, could not get distribution in major supermarkets for test products. As a result, Mars changed its approach and focused its marketing on the home delivery market.[40]

The Global Product Launch[41]

The impact of an effective global product launch can be great, but so can the cost of one that is poorly executed. High development costs as well as competitive pressures are forcing companies to rush products into as many markets as possible. But at the same time, a company can ill afford new products that are not effectively introduced, marketed, and supported in each market the company competes in.

A global product launch means introducing a product into countries in three or more regions within a narrow time frame. To achieve this, a company must undertake a number of measures. The country managers should be involved in the first stage of product strategy formulation to ensure that local and regional considerations are part of the overall corporate and product messages. More important, intercountry coordination of the rollout preparations will ultimately determine the level of success in the introduction. A product launch team (consisting of product, marketing, manufacturing, sales, service, engineering, and communication representatives) can also approach problems from an industry standpoint, as opposed to a home country perspective, enhancing product competitiveness in all markets.

Adequate consideration should be given to localization and translation requirements before the launch. This means that right messages are formulated and transmitted to key internal and external audiences. Support materials have to take into account both cultural and technical differences. The advantage of a simultaneous launch is that it boosts the overall momentum and attractiveness of the product by making it immediately available in key geographic markets.

Global product launches typically require more education and support of the sales channel than do domestic efforts or drawn-out efforts. This is due to the diversity of the distribution channels in terms of the support and education they may require before the launch.

A successfully executed global launch offers several benefits. First, it permits the company to showcase its technology in all major markets at the same time. Setting a single date for the launch functions as a strict discipline to force the entire organization to gear up quickly for a successful worldwide effort. A simultaneous worldwide introduction also solves the "lame duck" dilemma of having old models available in some markets while customers know of the existence of the new product. If margins are most lucrative at the early stages of the new product's life cycle, they should be exploited by getting the product to as many markets as possible from the outset. With product development costs increasing and product life cycles shortening, marketers have to consider this approach seriously. An additional benefit of a worldwide launch may be added publicity to benefit the marketer's efforts, as happened with the introductions worldwide of Microsoft's Windows 95, 98, 2000, and XP versions.

Management of the Product and Brand Portfolio

Most marketers have a considerable number of individual items in their product portfolios, consisting of different product lines, that is, grouping of products managed and marketed as a unit. The options for a particular portfolio (or multiple portfolios) are to expand geographically to new markets or new segments and add to existing market operations through new product lines or new product business. The marketer will need to have a balanced product and market portfolio—a proper mix of new, growing, and mature products to provide a sustainable competitive advantage.[42]

The assessment of the product portfolio will have to take into account various interlinkages both external and internal to the firm. Geographic interlinkages call attention to market similarities, especially to possibilities of extending operations across borders. Product-market interlinkages are manifested in common customers and competitors. Finally, the similarities in present-day operations should be assessed in terms of product lines, brands, and brand positionings. As a result of such an analysis, Mars has stayed out of the U.S. chocolate milk market, despite a product-company fit, because the market is dominated by Hershey and Nestlé. However, it has entered this particular market elsewhere, such as Europe.

Analyzing the Product Portfolio

The specific approach chosen and variables included will vary by company according to corporate objectives and characteristics as well as the nature of the product market. A product portfolio approach based on growth rates and market share positions allows the analysis of business entities, product lines, or individual products. Figure 14.2 represents the product-market portfolio of Company A, which markets the same product line in several countries. The company is a leader in most of the markets in which it has operations, as indicated by its relative market shares. It has two cash cows (United States and Canada), four stars (Germany, Great Britain, France, and Spain), and one "problem child" (Brazil). In the mature U.S. market, Company A has its largest volume but only a small market share advantage compared with competition. Company A's dominance is more pronounced in Canada and in the EU countries.

At the same time, Company B, its main competitor, although not a threat in Company A's major markets, does have a commanding lead in two fast-growing markets: Japan and Brazil. As this illustration indicates, an analysis should be conducted not only of the firm's own portfolio but also of competitors' portfolios, along with a projection of the firm's and the competitors' future international products—market portfolios. Building future scenarios based on industry estimates will allow Company A to take remedial long-term action to counter Company B's advances. In this case, Company A should direct resources to build market share in fast-growing markets such as Japan and Brazil.

In expanding markets, any company not growing rapidly risks falling behind for good. Growth may mean bringing out new items or lines or having to adjust existing products. Between 1996 and 2000, General Motors invested a total of $4 billion

Figure 14.2   Example of a Product-Market Portfolio

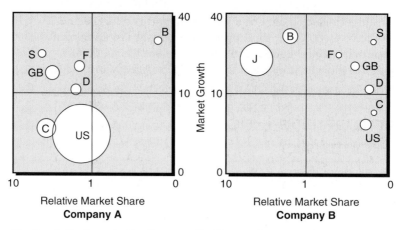

(B = Brazil, C = Canada, D = Germany, F = France, GB = Great Britain, J = Japan, S = Spain, US = United States)

SOURCE: Adapted from Jean-Claude Larréché, "The International Product-Market Portfolio," in *1978 AMA Educators' Proceedings* (Chicago: American Marketing Association, 1978), 276.

in the Brazilian car market, which is the eighth largest in the world. While production capacity of the world's two dozen carmakers is more than double the expected demand of 1.1 million cars and all makers were losing money in 1998–1999, GM, with its investments and new models, has positioned itself to take advantage of significant growth rates projected for the future. Volkswagen and Fiat have seen their market shares fall, mainly because they have been milking the market with old models: Volkswagen with the 18-year-old Golf and Fiat with the Uno, which dates back to 1984.[43] GM is not going to be left unchallenged, however. Fiat, for example, is hoping to regain lost ground with the Palio.

Portfolios should also be used to assess market, product, and business interlinkages.[44] This effort will allow the exploitation of increasing market similarities through corporate adjustments in setting up appropriate strategic business units (SBUs) and the standardization of product lines, products, and marketing programs.

The presentation in Figure 14.3 shows a market-product-business portfolio for a food company, such as Nestlé or Unilever. The interconnections are formed by common target markets served, sharing of research and development objectives, use of similar technologies, and the benefits that can be drawn from sharing common marketing experience. The example indicates possibilities within regions and between regions; frozen foods both in Europe and the United States, and ice cream throughout the three mega-markets.

Such assessments are integral in preparing future strategic outlines for different groups or units. For example, at Nestlé, ice cream was identified as an area of global development since the company already had a presence in a number of market areas and had identified others for their opportunity. The U.S. operations had to be persuaded to get more involved; they classified ice cream as a dairy product, whereas corporate planners saw it more as a frozen confectionery. U.S. operations produced machines and cones, and licensed brands to dairies, while corporate planners wanted to move over to self-manufacture and direct store delivery. Currently, Nestlé in the United States ranks second in the impulse–ice cream segment, and the machinery and cone businesses have been sold.[45]

Figure 14.3   Example of Market-Product-Business Portfolio

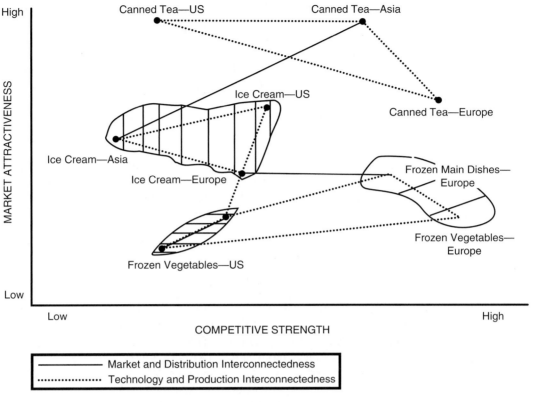

SOURCE: Adapted from Susan P. Douglas and C. Samuel Craig, "Global Portfolio Planning and Market Interconnectedness," *Journal of International Marketing* 4 (no. 1, 1996): 93–110.

Advantages of the Product Portfolio Approach

The major advantages provided by the product portfolio approach are as follows:

1. A global view of the competitive structure, especially when longer-term considerations are included
2. A guide for the formulation of a global marketing strategy based on the suggested allocation of scarce resources between product lines
3. A guide for the formulation of marketing objectives for specific markets based on an outline of the role of each product line in each of the markets served—for example, to generate cash or to block the expansion of competition
4. A convenient visual communication goal, achieved by integrating a substantial amount of information in an appealingly simple format including assessment of interlinkages between units and products

Before making strategic choices based on such a portfolio, the global marketer should consider the risks related to variables such as entry mode and exchange rates; management preferences for idiosyncratic objectives, such as concentrating on countries with similar market characteristics; and marketing costs. For example, the cost of entry into one market may be less because the company already has a presence there in another product category and the possibility exists that distribution networks may be shared. Similarly, ideas for new products and marketing programs can be leveraged across geographies based on both market characteristics and company position in those markets.[46]

The portfolio assessment also needs to be put into a larger context. The Korean market and Korean automakers may not independently warrant urgent action on the part of the leading companies. However, as part of the global strategic setting in the auto industry, both the market and its companies become critically important. Asia is expected to account for 70 percent of the growth in the world auto market between 2000 and 2004. Korea, along with China and Japan, is one of the three most important vehicle markets in Asia and can be considered an ideal platform for exporting to other parts of the continent. While Korean automakers, such as Daewoo Motor Co. and Samsung Motors, are heavily in debt, acquiring them would carry some benefits. Both Ford and GM wanted to acquire Daewoo to attain the top-producer position in the world. Renault, which wanted to acquire Samsung, saw synergistic benefits in that Samsung relies heavily on technology from Nissan, acquired by Renault earlier. There were also other indirect benefits; whoever acquired Daewoo would gain the number-one spot in Poland, long deemed crucial for tapping growth in Central Europe.[47] Renault acquired a 70 percent stake in Samsung, and GM completed the deal for Daewoo in late 2002 and plans to use its low-cost automobiles to supplement its lineup in Asia and Europe.

Disadvantages of the Product Portfolio Approach

The application of the product portfolio approach has a number of limitations. International competitive behavior does not always follow the same rules as in the firm's domestic market; for example, the major local competitor may be a government-owned firm whose main objective is to maintain employment. With European integration, many believed that the continent's $20 billion appliance business would consolidate into a handful of companies. Whirlpool was the major non-EU company that wanted to take advantage of the emerging opportunity and was expected to gain 20 percent of the market. However, its 12 percent share is testimony that local companies are not standing still while foreigners invade their turf. They have shifted their orientation from local and regional to global by laying off workers, building up core businesses, and focusing on profits.[48]

The relationship between market share and profitability may be blurred by a number of factors in the marketing environment. Government regulations in every market will have an impact on the products a company can market. For instance, major U.S. tobacco manufacturers estimate they could capture 30 percent of Japan's cigarette market of $10 billion a year if it were not for restrictions that apply only to non-Japanese producers.

Product lines offered will also be affected by various local content laws—those stipulating that a prescribed percentage of the value of the final product must be manufactured locally. Market tastes have an important impact on product lines. These not only may alter the content of a product but also may require an addition in a given market that is not available elsewhere. The Coca-Cola Company has market leadership in a product category unique to Japan: coffee-flavored soft drinks. The market came into existence some 20 years ago and grew rapidly, eventually accounting for 10 percent of soft-drink sales. The beverage is packaged like any other soft drink and is available through vending machines, which dispense hot cans in the winter and cold servings during warm weather. Although Coca-Cola executives have considered introducing "Georgia" in the United States, they are skeptical about whether the product would succeed, mainly because of declining coffee consumption and the lack of a vending machine network. Also, adoption of the concept by U.S. consumers is doubtful.

The fact that multinational firms produce the same products in different locations may have an impact on consumer perceptions of product risk and quality. If the product is produced in a developing country, for example, the global marketer has to determine whether a well-known brand name can compensate for the concern a customer might feel. The situation may be more complicated for retailers importing from independent producers in developing nations under the retailer's private labels. In general, country-of-origin effects on product perceptions are more difficult to determine since the introduction of hybrid products.

Managing the Brand Portfolio

Branding is one of the major beneficiaries of a well-conducted portfolio analysis. Brands are important because they shape customer decisions and, ultimately, create economic value. Brand is a key factor behind the decision to purchase in both consumer and business-to-business situations, as shown in the results of a worldwide study summarized in Figure 14.4. On the average, brand was responsible for 18 percent of total purchase decisions, and the majority of the studies revealed a brand-loyal segment of individuals for whom the brand was the major influencing factor. In addition, strong brands are able to charge a price premium of 19 percent.[49] Gillette's Mach3, although priced more than 50 percent above its predecessor (Sensor Excel), has been able to increase sales by 30 percent since rollout.[50] Research into the connection of brand strength and corporate performance at 130 multinational companies revealed that strong brands generate total returns to shareholders that are 1.9 percent above the industry average, while weaker brands lag behind the average by 3.1 percent.[51]

Figure 14.4   Importance of Brand in Decision Making

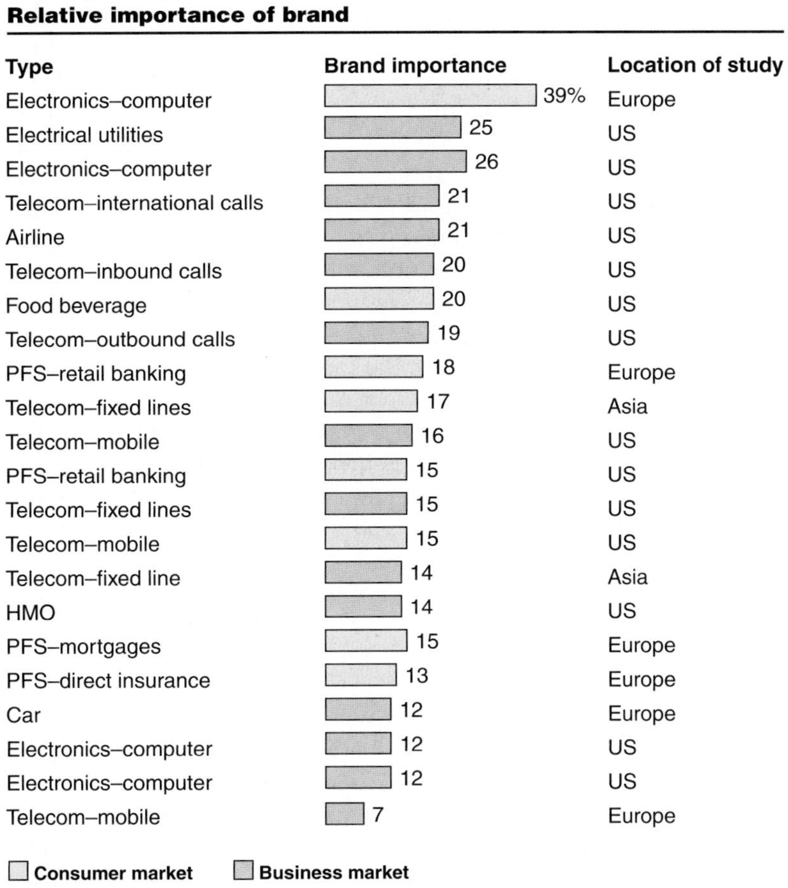

Relative importance of brand

Type	Brand importance	Location of study
Electronics–computer	39%	Europe
Electrical utilities	25	US
Electronics–computer	26	US
Telecom–international calls	21	US
Airline	21	US
Telecom–inbound calls	20	US
Food beverage	20	US
Telecom–outbound calls	19	US
PFS–retail banking	18	Europe
Telecom–fixed lines	17	Asia
Telecom–mobile	16	US
PFS–retail banking	15	US
Telecom–fixed lines	15	US
Telecom–mobile	15	US
Telecom–fixed line	14	Asia
HMO	14	US
PFS–mortgages	15	Europe
PFS–direct insurance	13	Europe
Car	12	Europe
Electronics–computer	12	US
Electronics–computer	12	US
Telecom–mobile	7	Europe

☐ Consumer market   ▨ Business market

SOURCE: Adapted from David Court, Anthony Freeling, Mark Leiter, and Andre J. Parsons, "Uncovering the Value of Brands," *The McKinsey Quarterly* 32 (no. 4, 1996): 176.

Brands are a major benefit to the customer as well. They simplify everyday choices, reduce the risk of complicated buying decisions, provide emotional benefits, and offer a sense of community. In technology (e.g., computer chips), where products change at an ever-increasing pace, branding is critical—far more so than in packaged goods, where a product may be more understandable because it stays the same or very similar over time. "Intel Inside," which derived from Intel's ad agency recommending "Intel, the Computer Inside" and the Japanese operation's "Intel In It," increased the company's brand awareness from 22 percent to 80 percent within two years of its introduction.[52]

The benefit of a strong brand name is, in addition to the price premium that awareness and loyalty allow, the ability to exploit the brand in a new market or a new product category. In a global marketplace, customers are aware of brands even though the products themselves may not be available. This was the case, for example, in many of the former Soviet Republics, before their markets opened up. Starbucks has relied on the strength of its brand in breaking into new markets, including Vienna, Europe's café capital.[53]

Market power is usually in the hands of brand-name companies that have to determine the most effective use of this asset across markets. The value of brands can be seen in recent acquisitions where prices have been many times over the book value of the company purchased. Nestlé, for example, paid five times the book value for the British Rowntree, the owner of such brands as Kit Kat and After Eight. Many of the world's leading brands command high brand equity values, in other words, the price premium the brand commands times the extra volume it moves over what an average brand commands.[54]

An example of global rankings of brands in provided in Table 14.1. This Interbrand-sponsored study rates brands on their value and their strength. Each ranked brand had to be global in nature, deriving 20 percent or more of sales from the home market. The brand value has been determined using publicly available financial information and market analysis. Brand strength is scored using seven attributes: market, stability, leadership, support, trend, geography, and protection. GE has introduced the tagline "Imagination at work," across all its marketing communications, and it has set up a number of co-branding and co-marketing agreements with other known brands as a means of leveraging its brand value and ensuring that the GE umbrella covers more. The dot.coms have also appeared on the list despite the recent beating they have taken in markets due to economic conditions: AOL is at 63 ($4.3 billion), Yahoo at 67 ($3.9 billion), and amazon.com at 80 ($3.2 billion). Of the top 100 global brands in terms of value, 24 are European, 6 Asian, and the rest U.S.-based. This analysis looks at brands, not companies, which means that companies that are all one brand have a better chance of being featured. An assessment has also been made of the portfolio brands; the top five are Johnson & Johnson ($68 billion), Procter & Gamble ($45 billion), Nestlé ($41 billion), Unilever ($38 billion), and L'Oreal ($18 billion).[55]

Brand Strategy Decisions

Global marketers have three choices of branding within the global, regional, and local dimensions: brands can feature the corporate name, have family brands for a wide range of products or product variations, or have individual brands for each item in the product line. With the increase in strategic alliances, co-branding, in which two or more well-known brands are combined in an offer, has also become popular. Examples of these approaches include Heinz, which has a policy of using its corporate name in all its products, Procter & Gamble, which has a policy of stand-alone products or product lines, and Nestlé, which uses a mixture of Nestlé and Nes-designated brands and stand-alones. In the case of marketing alliances, the brand portfolio may be a combination of both partners' brands. General Mills' alliance with Nestlé in cereals, Cereal Partners Worldwide, features General Mills brands such as Trix and Nestlé brands such as Chocapic.[56]

Table 14.1	World's Most Valuable Brands 2002

Rank	Brand Name	Industry	Brand Value ($US Billions)	Country of Origin
1	Coca-Cola	beverages	69.637	US
2	Microsoft	software	64.091	US
3	IBM	computers	51.188	US
4	GE	diversified	41.311	US
5	Intel	computers	30.861	US
6	Nokia	telecoms	29.970	Finland
7	Disney	entertainment	29.256	US
8	McDonald's	food	26.375	US
9	Marlboro	tobacco	24.151	US
10	Mercedes	automotive	21.010	Germany
11	Ford	automotive	20.403	US
12	Toyota	automotive	19.448	Japan
13	Citibank	financial services	18.066	US
14	Hewlett-Packard	computers	16.776	US
15	American Express	financial services	16.287	US
16	Cisco	networking	16.222	US
17	AT&T	telecoms	16.059	US
18	Honda	automotive	15.064	Japan
19	Gillette	personal care	14.959	US
20	BMW	automotive	14.425	Germany
21	Sony	electronics	13.899	Japan
22	Nescafé	beverages	12.843	Switzerland
23	Oracle	software	11.510	US
24	Budweiser	beverages	11.349	US
25	Merrill Lynch	financial services	11.230	US
26	Morgan Stanley	financial services	11.205	US
27	Compaq	computers	9.803	US
28	Pfizer	pharmaceuticals	9.770	US
29	JPMorgan	financial services	9.693	US
30	Kodak	imaging	9.671	US
31	Dell	computers	9.237	US
32	Nintendo	entertainment	9.219	Japan
33	Merck	pharmaceuticals	9.138	US
34	Samsung	electronics	8.310	S. Korea
35	Nike	apparel	7.724	US

SOURCES: Adapted from "The Top 100 Brands," *Business Week*, August 5, 2002. See also **http://www.interbrand.com** for methodology of the rankings.

Branding is an integral part of the overall identity management of the firm.[57] Therefore, it is typically a centralized function to exploit to the fullest the brand's assets as well as to protect the asset from dilution by, for example, extending the brand to inappropriate new lines. The role of headquarters, strategic business unit management, global teams, or global managers charged with a product is to provide guidelines for the effort without hampering local initiative at the same time.[58] An example of this effort is provided in *The International Marketplace 14.3*. In addition to the use of a global brand name from the very beginning, many marketers are consolidating their previously different brand names (often for the same or similar products) with global or regional brand names. For example, Mars

THE INTERNATIONAL MARKETPLACE   14.3

Development and Management of a Global Brand

In 1992, Black & Decker launched a new range of professional portable power tools under the DeWalt brand, in response to a global competitive threat from the Japanese Makita that had increased its market share in the fast-growing professional tool market. The company had determined that the quality of Black & Decker professional tools was not what was causing them to lose share to Makita. Instead, the reason was the brand-name perception of Black & Decker among professional contractors. Contractors did not believe in the performance of tools made by the same company that made toaster ovens, popcorn makers, and consumer-grade power tools.

After the successful launch of DeWalt in the United States, the same approach has been used in Australia, Canada, Europe, Latin America, and Asia. A set of guidelines govern the marketing of the brand, which now exceeds $1 billion in worldwide sales. Some of the areas covered in the guidelines include the brand's position, logo/color, industrial design, brand extensions, and packaging and catalog numbering. In addition to ensuring consistencies, these guidelines also enable country managers to share their best-practice ideals with others in the system. A global team has been set up to monitor these policies as well as to ensure exchange of ideas on the brand.

The DeWalt brand is positioned as the premier brand of tools and accessories for people who make their living using professional-grade power tools. This adroit positioning allows efficient target marketing. Although do-it-yourselfers are not part of the targeted effort, they very often choose products used by professionals, thereby broadening the market. As part of this positioning, DeWalt is never combined with Black & Decker products in

marketing communication programs. All of this allows DeWalt to charge a premium price for its products.

The visual identity program for DeWalt is used to project clearly the image the company wants to project worldwide. The DeWalt logo (shown below) uses bold, capital letters and a solid color (yellow) to project strength. The purpose of this guideline is not only to ensure consistency but also to ensure appropriate legal protection for the brand.

Part of the consistency dimension relates to controlling the industrial design of the tools. The three design centers located in Towson, Maryland; Idstein, Germany; and Spennymoet, England have to adhere to agreed-upon rules, with any deviation requiring approval from the global team. Similarly, extending the brand to new products or categories needs approval to avoid dilution of the brand.

As both customers (such as large contractors) and intermediaries (such as Home Depot or Hagebau) are becoming more global, packaging standards will have to change. This means one global packaging execution per tool using icon packaging with a country-specific sticker attached. DeWalt is also using one catalog number for each product for all geographic regions.

SOURCE: Courtesy of David Klatt, Black & Decker, March 2000; **http://www.dewalt.com**; and **http://www.blackanddecker.com**.

IMAGE SOURCE: © DeWalt Power Tools and Accessories.

replaced its Treets and Bonitas names with M&M worldwide and renamed its British best-seller, Marathon, with the Snickers name it uses in North and South America. The benefits in global branding are in marketing economies and higher acceptance of products by consumers and intermediaries. The drawbacks are in the loss of local flavor, especially when a local brand is replaced by a regional or global brand name. At these times, internal marketing becomes critical to instill ownership of the global brands in the personnel of the country organizations.[59]

An example of a brand portfolio is provided in Figure 14.5. It indicates four levels of brands at Nestlé: worldwide corporate and strategic brands, regional strategic brands, and local brands. The worldwide brands are under the responsibility of SBU and general management, which establish a framework for each in the form of a planning policy document. These policies lay out the brand's positioning, labeling standards, packaging features, and other related marketing mix issues, such as a communications platform. The same principle applies to regional brands

Figure 14.5 Nestlé's Branding Tree

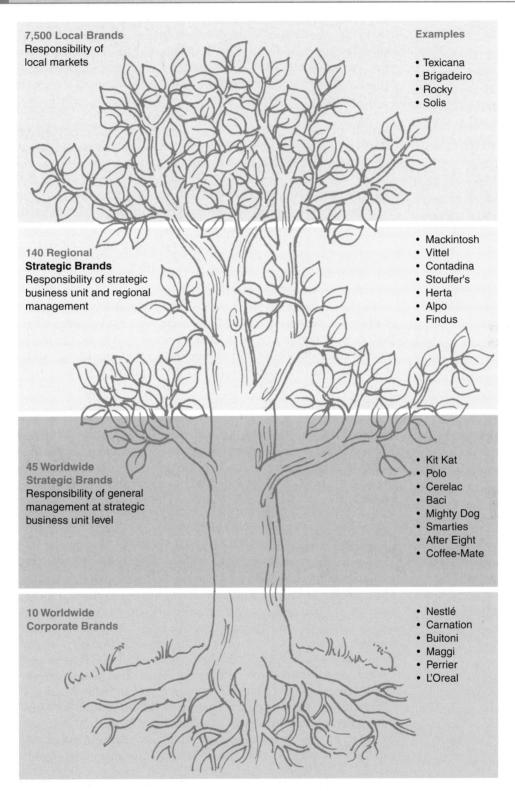

7,500 Local Brands
Responsibility of
local markets

Examples

- Texicana
- Brigadeiro
- Rocky
- Solis

140 Regional
Strategic Brands
Responsibility of strategic
business unit and regional
management

- Mackintosh
- Vittel
- Contadina
- Stouffer's
- Herta
- Alpo
- Findus

45 Worldwide
Strategic Brands
Responsibility of general
management at strategic
business unit level

- Kit Kat
- Polo
- Cerelac
- Baci
- Mighty Dog
- Smarties
- After Eight
- Coffee-Mate

10 Worldwide
Corporate Brands

- Nestlé
- Carnation
- Buitoni
- Maggi
- Perrier
- L'Oreal

SOURCE: Adapted from Andrew J. Parsons, "Nestlé: The Visions of Local Managers," *The McKinsey Quarterly* (no. 2, 1996): 5–29; see also **http://www.nestle.com/html/brands/index.asp**.

where guidelines are issued and decisions made by SBU and regional management. Among the 7,500 local brands are 700 local strategic brands, such as Brigadeiro in Brazil, which are monitored by the SBUs for positioning and labeling standards. Nestlé is consolidating its efforts behind its corporate and strategic brands. This is taking place in various ways. When Nestlé acquired Rowntree, which had had a one-product one-brand policy, it added its corporate name to some of the products, such as Nestlé Kit Kat. Its refrigerated products line under the Chambourcy brand is undergoing a name change to Nestlé. Some of the products that do not carry the corporate name feature a Nestlé Seal of Guarantee on the back. About 40 percent of the company's sales come from products covered by the corporate brand.[60] L'Oreal is managed independently due to the fact that Nestlé is only a 49-percent owner in the corporation that in itself markets brands such as Maybelline, Helena Rubinstein, Garnier, and Soft Sheen.[61]

Carefully crafted brand portfolios allow marketers to serve defined parts of specific markets. At Whirlpool, the Whirlpool brand name will be used as the global brand to serve the broad middle market segment, while regional and local brands will cover the others. For example, throughout Europe, the Bauknecht brand is targeted at the upper end of the market seeking a reputable German brand. Ignis and Laden are positioned as price value brands, Ignis Europe-wide, Laden in France. This approach applies to Whirlpool's other markets as well: in Latin America, Consul is the major regional brand.[62]

The brand portfolio needs to periodically and regularly assessed. A number of global marketers are focusing their attention on A brands with the greatest growth potential. By continuing to dispose of noncore brands, the marketer can concentrate on the global ones and reduce production, marketing, storage, and distribution costs. It is increasingly difficult for the global company to manage purely local brands. The surge of private label products has also put additional pressure on B brands.[63]

However, before disposing of a brand, managers need to assess it in terms of current sales, loyalty, potential, and trends. For example, eliminating a local brand that may have a strong and legal following, has been created by local management, and shows potential to be extended to nearby markets is not necessarily in the best interests of the company. Three approaches for purely local brands may work: a penetration price approach, a cultural approach positioning the product as a true defender of local culture, and a "chameleon" approach, in which the brand tries not to look local.[64] The number-one chewing gum brand in France for the past 25 years has been Hollywood.

Private Brand Policies

The emergence of strong intermediaries has led to the significant increase in private brand goods, that is, the intermediaries' own branded products or "store brands." Two general approaches have been used: umbrella branding, where a number of products are covered using the same brand (often the intermediary's name), and separate brand names for individual products or product lines.

With price sensitivity increasing and brand loyalty decreasing, private brand goods have achieved a significant penetration in many countries. The overall penetration of private brand goods in the United Kingdom is 30 percent, in Germany 23 percent, in Switzerland 23 percent, and in France 20 percent. Over the past 20 years, private brand sales in the United States have averaged 14 percent of supermarket sales. As both the trade and consumers become more sophisticated, private brands' market share is expected to reach U.K. levels in many parts of Europe and the world.

While private brand success can be shown to be affected strongly by economic conditions and the self-interest of retailers who want to improve their bottom lines through the contribution of private label goods, new factors have emerged to make the phenomenon more long-lived and significant in changing the product choices worldwide. The level of private brand share will vary by country and by product category reflecting variations in customer perceptions, intermediary strength, and behavior of leading branders.[65]

The improved quality of private brand products and the development of segmented private brand products have been major changes in the last ten years. While 60 percent of consumers still state that they prefer the comfort, security, and value of a manufacturer's brand over a private brand, as found in a DDB Needham survey,[66] a McKinsey survey found most consumers preferring such products also had no hesitation in buying the private brand.[67] Encouraged by this, private brands have been expanding to new product categories with the hope of increased acceptance by consumers.[68] Beyond just offering products, many retailers are focusing on a broader approach. For example, Tesco in the United Kingdom has focused on the design of its own-label products with the goal of projecting a more uniform image across product categories. Some premium private brand products have been developed to reposition manufacturer's brands. In Canada, for example, Loblaw's President's Choice brand and its regular private brand line squeeze national brands in between the two. Some U.S. chains have also started carrying this line of premium products.

European supermarket chains have had enormous success with private brands mainly due to their power over manufacturers. While the five largest operators in the United States command only 21 percent of supermarket sales, the figure in the United Kingdom is 62 percent, and in Finland the four leading wholesaler-led chains control over 90 percent. With the emergence of new types of intermediaries, such as mass merchandisers and warehouse clubs, this phenomenon will expand as these players exercise their procurement clout over manufacturers. Furthermore, many retailers believe that strong private brand programs can successfully differentiate their outlets and solidify shoppers' loyalty, thereby strengthening their position vis-à-vis manufacturers, and resulting in increasing profitability.[69]

The internationalization of retailers carrying or even focusing solely on private labels has given an additional boost to the phenomenon, such as German ALDI, which sells only its own private label goods in its stores throughout Europe, the United States (with 578 stores in 2002), and Australia.[70] ALDI's focus is on cutting costs rather than quality, permitting it to drive out low-quality brands that trade only on price.

With the increasing opportunities in the private brand categories, the marketing manager will have to make critical strategic choices, which are summarized in Table 14.2. If the marketer operates in an environment where consumers have an absolute preference for manufacturers' brands and where product innovation is a critical factor of success, the marketer can refuse to participate. Brand leaders can

Table 14.2	**Private Brand Strategies**	
Strategy	**Rationale**	**Circumstance**
No participation	Refusal to produce private label	Heavily branded markets; high distinctiveness; technological advantage
Capacity filling	Opportunistic	
Market control	Influence category sales	High brand shares where distinctiveness is less; more switching by consumers
Competitive leverage	Stake in both markets	
Chief source of business	Major focus	Little or no differentiation by consumers
Dedicated producer	Leading cost position	

SOURCES: Adapted from Sabine Bonnot, Emma Carr, and Michael J. Reyner, "Fighting Brawn with Brains," *The McKinsey Quarterly* 40 (no. 2, 2000): 85–92; and François Glémet and Rafael Mira, "The Brand Leader's Dilemma," *The McKinsey Quarterly* 33 (no. 2, 1993): 4.

attack private brands and thereby direct their ambitions on smaller competitors, which often may be local-only players. The argument for strategic participation is that since the phenomenon cannot be eliminated, it is best to be involved. For example, Nestlé sells ice cream called Grandessa for ALDI through a newly acquired unit called Scholler.[71] Reasons include capacity filling, economies of scale, improved relationships with trade, and valuable information about consumer behavior and costs. The argument that profits from private brand manufacture can be used for promotion of the manufacturer's own brands may be eliminated by the relatively thin margins and the costs of having to set up a separate private brand manufacturing and marketing organization. Participation in the private brand category may, however, be inconsistent with the marketer's global brand and product strategy by raising questions about quality standards, by diluting management attention, and by affecting consumers' perception of the main branded business. Many marketers pursue a mixture of these strategies as a function of marketing and market conditions. Wilkinson Sword, for example, produces private brand disposable razors for the most dominant chain in Finland, the K-Group, thereby enabling it to compete on price against other branded products (especially the French Bic) and increasing its share of shelf space. While H.J. Heinz produces insignificant amounts for private brand distributors in the United States, most of its U.K. production is for private brand.

Summary

The global product planning effort must determine two critical decisions: (1) how and where the company's products should be developed, and (2) how and where the present and future product lines should be marketed.

In product development, multinational corporations are increasingly striving toward finding common denominators to rationalize worldwide production. This is achieved through careful coordination of the product development process by worldwide or regional development teams. No longer is the parent company the only source of new products. New product ideas emerge throughout the system and are developed by the entity most qualified to do so.

The global marketer's product line is not the same worldwide. The standard line items are augmented by local items or localized variations of products to better cater to the unique needs of individual markets. External variables such as competition and regulations often determine the final composition of the line and how broadly it is marketed.

Global marketers will also have to determine the extent to which they will use one of their greatest asset, brands, across national markets. Marketers will have to choose among global brands, regional brands, and purely local approaches as well as forgoing their own branding in favor of becoming a supplier for private brand efforts of retailers. Efficiencies of standardization must be balanced with customer preferences and internal issues of motivation at the country-market level.

Key Terms

lead users

computer-aided design (CAD)

R&D consortia

laboratory test markets

microtest marketing

forced distribution tests

Questions for Discussion

1. How can a company's product line reflect the maxim "think globally, act locally"?

2. Will a globally oriented company have an advantage over a multidomestic, or even a domestic, company in the next generation of new product ideas?

3. What factors should be considered when deciding on the location of research and development facilities?

4. What factors make product testing more complicated in the international marketplace?

5. What are the benefits of a coordinated global product launch? What factors will have to be taken into consideration before the actual launch?

6. Argue for and against the use of the corporate name in global branding.

Internet Exercises

1. Using the list of the world's leading brands (available at **http://www.interbrand.com**), evaluate why certain brands place high, some lower. Speculate on the future of, for example, the dot.coms.

2. Using the Mach3 as an example, evaluate how the different country Web sites of Gillette (accessible through **http://www.gillette.com**) support its worldwide brand effort.

Recommended Readings

Aaker, David A. *Building Strong Brands*. New York: The Free Press, 1996.

Aaker, David, and Erich Joachimsthaler. *Brand Leadership: The Next Level of Brand Revolution*. New York: The Free Press, 2000.

Bedbury, Scott. *A Brand New World: Eight Principles for Achieving Brand Leadership in the 21st Century*. New York: Viking Press, 2002.

Cooper, Robert G. *Product Leadership: Creating and Launching Superior New Products*. New York: Perseus Books, 2000.

Cooper, Robert G. *Winning at New Products: Accelerating the Process from Idea to Launch*. New York: Perseus Books, 2001.

Deschamps, Jean-Philippe, and P. Raganath Nayak. *Product Juggernauts: How Companies Mobilize to Generate a Stream of Market Winners*. Boston: Harvard Business School Press, 1995.

Gorchels, Linda. *The Product Manager's Handbook: The Complete Product Management Resource*. New York: McGraw-Hill, 2000.

Gregory, James R., and Jack G. Wiechman. *Branding across Borders: A Guide to Global Brand Marketing*. New York: McGraw-Hill, 2001.

Kapferer, Jean-Noël. *Strategic Brand Management*. New York: The Free Press, 1992.

Keller, Kevin L. *Strategic Brand Management: Building, Measuring, and Managing Brand Equity*. Upper Saddle River, NJ: Prentice Hall, 2002.

Kitcho, Catherine. *High Tech Product Launch*. Mountain View, CA: Pele Publications, 1999.

Kotabe, Masaaki. *Global Sourcing Strategy: R&D, Manufacturing, and Marketing Interfaces*. Greenwich, CT: Greenwood Publishing Group, 1992.

Macrae, Chris. *The Brand Chartering Handbook*. Harlow, England: Addison-Wesley, 1996.

Ries, Laura, and Al Ries. *The 22 Immutable Laws of Branding: How to Build a Product or Service into a World-Class Brand*. New York: HarperCollins, 1998.

Schmitt, Bernd, and Alexander Simonson. *Marketing Aesthetics: The Strategic Management of Brands, Identity and Image*. New York: The Free Press, 1997.

chapter 15

Services Marketing

THE INTERNATIONAL MARKETPLACE   15.1

A Global Service: Free Access to Medical Journals

In mid-2001, the World Health Organization (WHO) and six of the world's largest medical publishers came to an agreement concerning access to biomedical journals for nearly 100 of the world's developing countries. Until then medical journals were priced uniformly worldwide, often "pricing out" developing nations. This led to a widening of the gap in medical knowledge between richer and poorer countries and made it nearly impossible for poor countries to access the newest scientific information. The cost of the journals was simply too high.

The agreement is a part of the Health InterNetwork initiative unveiled at the United Nations Millennium Summit by UN Secretary-General Kofi Annan. The project's goal is to strengthen public health service by providing health professionals in the developing world with relevant information through Internet portals. Access to the journals is now based on a tiered-pricing approach; countries whose per capita gross national product (GNP) is less than $1,000 a year will receive access to the journals for free; countries whose GNP is between $1,000 and $3,000 will receive access to the journals for a minimal charge. It is also hoped that the program will help spread the idea of "evidence-based" medicine throughout Africa and the rest of the developing world. The program is scheduled to last three years and will be monitored for progress. The WHO hopes that "decisions about how to proceed after the initiative will grow from the precedents it sets and will be informed by the working relationships which have developed among the partners."

There are, however, some limitations on the free access to medical journals. Publishers reserve the right to protect existing business. In practice this means that nations where a publisher has significant sales or a local sales agent can be excluded from the agreement. India, with a per capita GNP of $440 in 1999, meets the WHO criteria for free access to the journals, but publishers also have sales and local sales agents in India. The WHO says that it is "still negotiating with the publishers on an alternative arrangement for these countries, but [that they] have not yet reached an agreement."

SOURCES: David Brown, "Free Access to Medical Journals to Be Given to Poor Countries," *The Washington Post,* July 9, 2001, A12; WHO Press Release, July 9, 2001, **http://www.who.int/**, accessed September 6, 2002; and N. Gopal Raj, "Free Access to Medical Journals," *The Hindu,* February 28, 2002, **http://www.hinduonnet.com/thehindu/seta/2002/02/28/stories/2002022800050300.htm**, accessed November 8, 2002.

I NTERNATIONAL SERVICES MARKETING is a major component of world business. As *The International Marketplace 15.1* shows, services can be crucial globally. This chapter will highlight marketing dimensions that are specific to services, with particular attention given to their international aspects. A discussion of the differences between the marketing of services and of goods will be followed by insights on the role of services in the United States and in the world economy. The chapter will explore the opportunities and new problems that have arisen from the increase in international services marketing, focusing particularly on the worldwide transformations of industries as a result of profound changes in the environment and in technology. The strategic responses to these transformations by both governments and firms will be described. Finally, the chapter will outline the initial steps that firms need to undertake in order to offer services internationally—and will look at the future of international services marketing.

Differences between Services and Goods

We rarely contemplate or analyze the precise role of services in our lives. Services often accompany goods, but they are also, by themselves, an increasingly important part of our economy, domestically and internationally. One writer has contrasted services and products by stating that "a good is an object, a device, a thing;

Services as a Portion of Gross Domestic Product

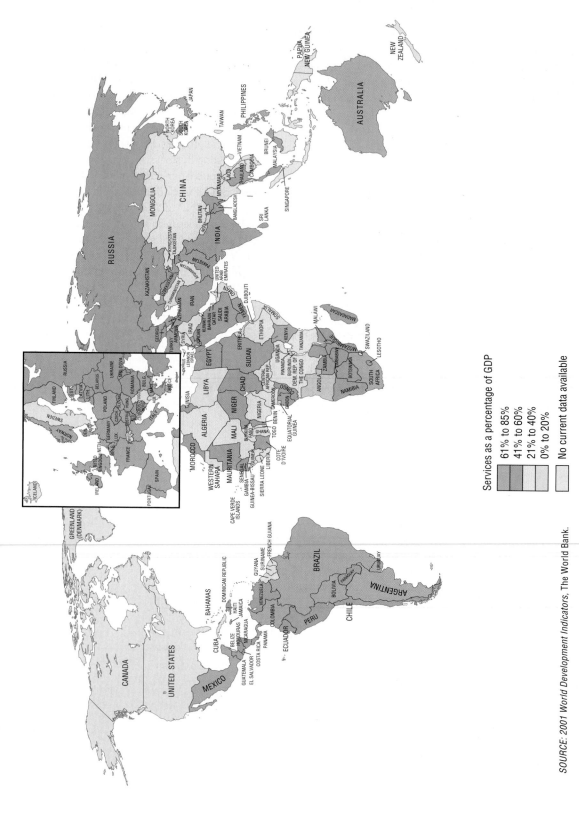

Services as a percentage of GDP

- 61% to 85%
- 41% to 60%
- 21% to 40%
- 0% to 20%
- No current data available

SOURCE: 2001 World Development Indicators, The World Bank.

a service is a deed, a performance, an effort."[1] This definition, although quite general, captures the essence of the difference between goods and services. Services tend to be more intangible, personalized, and custom-made than goods. Services are also often marketed differently from goods. While goods are typically distributed to the customer, services can be transferred across borders or originated abroad, and the service provider can be transferred to the customer or the customer can be transferred to the service territory. Services also typically use a different approach to customer satisfaction. It has been stated that "service firms do not have products in the form of preproduced solutions to customers' problems; they have processes as solutions to such problems."[2]

Services are the fastest-growing sector of world trade, far outpacing the growth in the trade of goods. These major differences add dimensions to services that are not present in goods and thus call for a major differentiation.

Linkage between Services and Goods

Services may complement goods; at other times, goods may complement services. Offering goods that are in need of substantial technological support and maintenance may be useless if no proper assurance for service can be provided. For this reason, the initial contract of sale often includes important service dimensions. This practice is common in aircraft sales. When an aircraft is purchased, the buyer often contracts not only for the physical good—namely, the plane—but also for training of personnel, maintenance service, and the promise of continuous technological updates. Similarly, the sale of computer hardware is critically linked to the availability of proper servicing and software.

This linkage between goods and services can make international marketing efforts quite difficult. A foreign buyer, for example, may wish to purchase helicopters and contract for service support over a period of ten years. If the sale involves a U.S. firm, both the helicopter and the service sale will require an export license. Such licenses, however, are issued only for an immediate sale. Therefore, over the ten years, the seller will have to apply for an export license each time service is to be provided. Because the issuance of a license is often dependent on the political climate, the buyer and seller are haunted by uncertainty. As a result, sales may be lost to firms in countries that can unconditionally guarantee the long-term supply of support services.

Services can be just as dependent on goods. For example, an airline that prides itself on providing an efficient reservation system and excellent linkups with rental cars and hotel reservations could not survive without its airplanes. As a result, many offerings in the marketplace consist of a combination of goods and services. A graphic illustration of the tangible and intangible elements in the market offering of an airline is provided in Figure 15.1.

The simple knowledge that services and goods interact, however, is not enough. Successful managers must recognize that different customer groups will frequently view the service/goods combination differently. The type of use and usage conditions will also affect evaluations of the market offering. For example, the intangible dimension of "on-time arrival" by airlines may be valued differently by college students than by business executives. Similarly, a 20-minute delay will be judged differently by a passenger arriving at her final destination than by one who has just missed an overseas connection. As a result, adjustment possibilities in both the service and the goods area can be used as strategic tools to stimulate demand and increase profitability. For different offerings, service and goods elements may vary substantially. The marketer must identify the role of each and adjust all of them to meet the desires of the target customer group.

Stand-Alone Services

Services do not always come in unison with goods. Increasingly, they compete against goods and become an alternative offering. For example, rather than buy an in-house computer, the business executive can contract computing work to a local

Figure 15.1   Tangible and Intangible Offerings of Airlines

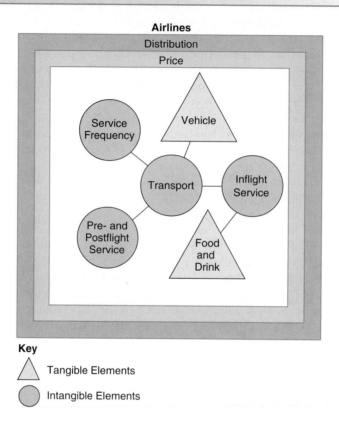

Airlines

Distribution

Price

Service Frequency

Vehicle

Transport

Inflight Service

Pre- and Postflight Service

Food and Drink

Key

△ Tangible Elements

◯ Intangible Elements

SOURCE: Adapted from G. Lynn Shostack, "Breaking Free from Product Marketing," in *Services Marketing,* ed. Christopher H. Lovelock (Englewood Cliffs, NJ: Prentice-Hall, 1984), 40.

or foreign service firm. Similarly, the purchase of a car (a good) can be converted into the purchase of a service by leasing the car from an agency.

Services may also compete against each other. As an example, a store may have the option of offering full service to consumers who purchase there or of converting to the self-service format. With automated checkout services, consumers may self-serve all activities such as selection, transportation, packaging, and pricing.

Services differ from goods most strongly in their **intangibility:** They are frequently consumed rather than possessed. Even though the intangibility of services is a primary differentiating criterion, it is not always present. For example, publishing services ultimately result in a tangible good, namely, a book or an article. Similarly, construction services eventually result in a building, a subway, or a bridge. Even in those instances, however, the intangible component that leads to the final product is of major concern to both the producer of the service and the recipient of the ultimate output because it brings with it major considerations that are nontraditional to goods.

One major difference concerns the storing of services. Because of their nature, services are difficult to inventory. If they are not used, the "brown around the edges" syndrome tends to result in high services **perishability.** Unused capacity in the form of an empty seat on an airplane, for example, becomes nonsaleable quickly. Once the plane has taken off, selling an empty seat is virtually impossible—except for an inflight upgrade from coach to first class—and the capacity cannot be stored for future usage. Similarly, the difficulty of keeping services in inventory makes it troublesome to provide service backup for peak demand. To maintain **service capacity** constantly at levels necessary to satisfy peak demand would be very expensive. The marketer must therefore attempt to smooth out demand levels through price or promotion activities in order to optimize the use of capacity.

For many service offerings, the time of production is very close to or even simultaneous with the time of consumption. This fact points toward close **customer involvement** in the production of services. Customers frequently either service themselves or cooperate in the delivery of services. As a result, the service provider often needs to be physically present when the service is delivered. This physical presence creates both problems and opportunities, and it introduces a new constraint that is seldom present in the marketing of goods. For example, close interaction with the customer requires a much greater understanding of and emphasis on the cultural dimension. A good service delivered in a culturally unacceptable fashion is doomed to failure. Sensitivity to culture, beliefs, and preferences is imperative in the services industry. In some instances, the need to be sensitive to diverse customer groups in domestic markets can assist a company greatly in preparing for international market expansion. A common pattern of internationalization for service businesses is therefore to develop stand-alone business systems in each country. At the same time, however, some services have become "delocalized" as advances in modern technology have made it possible for firms to delink production and service processes and switch labor-intensive service performance to countries where qualified, low-cost labor is plentiful.

The close interaction with customers also points toward the fact that services often are custom-made. This contradicts the desire of a firm to standardize its offering; yet at the same time, it offers the service provider an opportunity to differentiate the service from the competition. The concomitant problem is that in order to fulfill customer expectations, **service consistency** is required. As with anything offered online, however, consistency is difficult to maintain over the long run. The human element in the service offering therefore takes on a much greater role than in the offering of goods. Errors can enter the system, and nonpredictable individual influences can affect the outcome of the service delivery. The issue of quality control affects the provider as well as the recipient of services. Efforts to increase such control through uniformity may sometimes be seen by customers as a reduction in service choices.

Buyers have more problems in observing and evaluating services than goods. This is particularly true when a shopper tries to choose intelligently among service providers. Even when sellers of services are willing and able to provide more **market transparency** where the details of the service are clear, comparable, and available to all interested parties, the buyer's problem is complicated: Customers receiving the same service may use it differently and service quality may vary for each delivery. Since production lines cannot be established to deliver an identical service each time, and the quality of a service cannot be tightly controlled, the problem of service heterogeneity emerges,[3] meaning that services may never be the same from one delivery to another. For example, a teacher's counsel, even if it is provided on the same day by the same person, may vary substantially depending on the student. Over time, even for the same student, the counseling may change. As a result, service offerings are not directly comparable, which makes quality measurements quite challenging. Therefore, the reputation of the service provider plays an overwhelming role in the customer choice process.

Services often require entirely new forms of distribution. Traditional channels are often multitiered and long and therefore slow. They often cannot be used because of the perishability of services. A weather news service, for example, either reaches its audience quickly or rapidly loses its value. As a result, direct delivery and short distribution channels are often required. When they do not exist—which is often the case domestically and even more so internationally—service providers need to be distribution innovators in order to reach their market.

All these aspects of services exist in both international and domestic settings. Their impact, however, takes on greater importance for the international marketer.

For example, because of the longer distances involved, service perishability that may be an obstacle in domestic business becomes a barrier internationally. Similarly, the issue of quality control for international services may be much more difficult to deal with due to different service uses, changing expectations, and varying national regulations.

Because services are delivered directly to the user, they are frequently much more sensitive to cultural factors than are products. Sometimes their influence on the individual may even be considered with hostility abroad. For example, the showing of U.S. films in cinemas or television abroad is often attacked as an imposition of U.S. culture. National leaders who place strong emphasis on national cultural identity frequently denounce foreign services and attempt to hinder their market penetration. Similarly, services are subject to many political vagaries occurring almost daily. Yet coping with these changes can become the service provider's competitive advantage.

The Role of Services in the U.S. Economy

Since the industrial revolution, the United States has seen itself as a primary international competitor in the area of production of goods. In the past few decades, however, the U.S. economy has increasingly become a service economy, as Figure 15.2 shows. The service sector now produces 80 percent U.S. GDP[4] and 62.6 percent of the GDP throughout the world.[5] The service sector accounts for most of the growth in total nonfarm employment. More than 55 percent of U.S. personal consumption expenditures was spent on services in 2002.[6]

Only a limited segment of the total range of services is sold internationally. Fed-

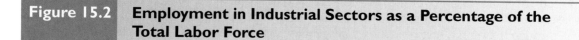

Figure 15.2   **Employment in Industrial Sectors as a Percentage of the Total Labor Force**

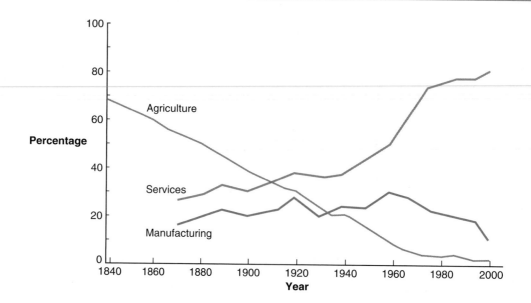

SOURCES: Bureau of Labor Statistics, *Employment Situation*, Historical Data for the A Series, **http://www.bls.gov**, November 7, 2002, Coalition of Service Industries, and Office of Service Industries, U.S. Department of Commerce, July 2002; Quarterly Labor Force Statistics, Paris, Organization for Economic Cooperation and Development, 1996, no. 2; and J. B. Quinn, "The Impacts of Technology on the Services Sector," *Technology and Global Industry: Companies and Nations in the World Economy*, by the National Academy of Sciences, Washington, DC.

Table 15.1   U.S. Balances of Trade in Goods and Services, 2002 (in billions)

Exports of Goods and Services		$973
Goods		683
As a percentage of total exports	70	
Services		290
As a percentage of total exports	30	
Imports of Goods and Services		$1,408
Goods		1,167
As a percentage of total imports	83	
Services		241
As a percentage of total imports	17	
Balance on Goods Trade		−484
Balance on Services		49
Balance on Goods and Services		−435

SOURCE: U.S. Department of Commerce, Bureau of Economic Analysis, **http://www.economicindicators.gov**, accessed March 3, 2003.

eral, state, and local government employees, for example, sell few of their services to foreigners. U.S. laundromats only occasionally service foreign tourists, yet many service industries that do market abroad often have at their disposal large organizations, specialized technology, or advanced professional expertise. Strength in these characteristics has enabled the United States to become the world's largest exporter of services. Total U.S. services exported grew from $6 billion in 1958 to $290 billion in 2002.[7] The contribution of services to the U.S. balance of payments is highlighted in Table 15.1. It shows that the U.S. services trade balance is producing a substantial surplus and makes up for a part of the huge deficits in merchandise trade.

International service trade has had very beneficial results for many firms and industries. Most of the large management consulting firms derive more than half their revenue from international sources. The largest advertising agencies serve customers around the globe, some of them in 107 countries. Table 15.2 shows

Table 15.2   Top Ten Mutual Life and Health Insurance Agencies

Rank	Agency	Home Country	Revenues ($ million)	Employees	No. of Countries
1	Nippon Life Insurance	Japan	63,827.2	72,895	9
2	Dai-ichi Mutual Life Insurance	Japan	43,145.2	57,731	14
3	Asahi Mutual Life Insurance	Japan	33,142.8	27,062	7
4	Sumitomo Life Insurance	Japan	32,548.5	53,821	5
5	New York Life Insurance	United States	25,678.2	7,400	12
6	Meiji Life Insurance	Japan	25,295.5	38,446	12
7	TIAA-CREF	United States	24,230.6	6,385	n/a
8	Mitsui Mutual Life Insurance	Japan	21,655.7	18,034	n/a
9	Mass. Mutual Life Insurance	United States	19,339.6	10,929	n/a
10	Standard Life Assurance	Britain	18,415.7	13,112	8

SOURCE: Fortune.com—Global 500: Industry Snapshot, **http://www.fortune.com**, accessed September 30, 2002. Reprinted by permission.

how the top mutual life and health insurance agencies serve global markets. Bechtel, one of the largest U.S. engineering and construction firms, had more than 34 percent of its work outside North America.[8]

Large international growth, however, is not confined to U.S. service exports. The import of services into the United States is also increasing dramatically. Total services imported into the U.S. in 2002 were $241 billion.[9] Competition in international services is rising rapidly at all levels. Hong Kong, Singapore, and Western Europe are increasingly active in service industries such as banking, insurance, and advertising. For example, businesses are increasingly routing their software projects to India, China, and Central Europe.

The Role of International Services in the World Economy

The rise of the service sector is a global phenomenon. Services contribute an average of more than 60 percent to the gross national product of industrial nations. Services are also rapidly moving to the forefront in many other nations as well, accounting for 66 percent of GDP in Argentina, 69 percent in Mexico, 66 percent in South Africa, and about 50 percent in Thailand.[10] Even in the least developed countries, services typically contribute at least 45 percent of GDP. With growth rates higher than other sectors such as agriculture and manufacturing, services are instrumental in job creation in these countries.[11] Table 15.3 shows the importance of the service sector across the world. Within these countries, the names of such

Table 15.3	Services across the World	
Country	**Services as Percentage of GDP**	**Percentage of Workforce in Services**
United States	80%	83%
Canada	69	74
Brazil	59	53
Australia	72	73
Japan	62	65
Kenya	63	n/a
European Union	69	70
Austria	69	67
Belgium	74	73
Denmark	75	79
Finland	69	76
France	71	71
Germany	71	63
Greece	64	59
Ireland	58	64
Italy	67	63
Luxembourg	69	90
The Netherlands	70	73
Portugal	65	60
Spain	68	64
Sweden	69	74
United Kingdom	73	74

SOURCE: *The World Factbook 2002*, **http://www.cia.gov**, accessed October 28, 2002.

firms as American Express, McDonald's, Club Med, Thomas Cook, Mitsubishi, and Hilton have become widely familiar.

Global Transformation of Services

The rapid rise in international services marketing has been the result of major shifts in the business environment and innovations in technology. One primary change in the past decade has been the reduction of governmental regulation of services. This **deregulation** is clearly seen within the United States. In the mid-1970s, a philosophical decision was made to reduce government interference in the marketplace, in the hope that this would enhance competitive activity. As a consequence, some service sectors have benefited, and others have suffered, from the withdrawal of government intervention. The primary deregulated industries in the United States have been transportation, banking, and telecommunications. As a result, new competitors participate in the marketplace. Regulatory changes were initially thought to have primarily domestic effects, but they have rapidly spread internationally. For example, the 1984 deregulation of AT&T has given rise to the deregulation of Japan's telecommunications monopoly, NT&T. European deregulation followed in the mid-1990s.

Similarly, deregulatory efforts in the transportation sector have had international repercussions. New air carriers have entered the market to compete against established trunk carriers and have done so successfully by pricing their services lower both nationally and internationally. In doing so, these airlines also affected the regulatory climate abroad. Obviously, a British airline can count only to a limited extent on government support to remain competitive with new low-priced fares offered by other carriers also serving the British market. As a result, the deregulatory movement has spread internationally and has fostered the emergence of new competition and new competitive practices. Because many of these changes resulted in lower prices, demand has been stimulated, leading to a rise in the volume of international services trade.

Another major change has been the decreased regulation of service industries by their industry groups. For example, business practices in fields such as health-care, law, and accounting are becoming more competitive and aggressive. New economic realities require firms in these industries to search for new ways to attract market share. International markets are one frequently untapped possibility for market expansion and have therefore become a prime target for such service firms.

Technological advancement is another major factor in increasing service trade. Progress in technology offers new ways of doing business and permits businesses to expand their horizons internationally. For example, Ford Motor Company uses one major computer system to carry out its new car designs in both the United States and Europe. This practice not only lowers expenditures on hardware but also permits better utilization of existing equipment and international design collaboration by allowing design groups in different time zones to use the equipment around the clock. This development could, however, take place only after advances in data transmission procedures.

In a similar fashion, more rapid transmission of data has permitted financial institutions to expand their service delivery through a worldwide network. Again, were it not for advances in technology, such expansion would rarely have been possible or cost-effective.

Another result of these developments is that service industry expansion has not been confined to the traditional services that are labor-intensive and could therefore have been performed better in areas of the world where labor possesses a comparative advantage because of lower prices. Rather, technology-intensive services are the sunrise industries of the new century. Increasingly, firms can reconfigure their service delivery in order to escape the location-bound dimension. Banks, for example, can offer their services through automatic teller machines or telephone banking. Consultants can advise via video conferences, and teachers can teach the world through multimedia classrooms. Physicians can perform operations in a distant country if proper computer linkages can drive roboticized medical equipment.

As a result, many service providers have the opportunity to become truly global marketers. To them, the traditional international market barrier of distance no longer matters. Knowledge, the core of many service activities, can offer a global reach without requiring a local presence. Service providers therefore may have only a minor need for local establishment, since they can operate without premises. You don't have to be there to do business! The effect of such a shift in service activities is major. Insurance and bank buildings in the downtowns of the world may soon become obsolete. Talented service providers see the demand for their performance increase while less capable ones will suffer from increased competition. Most important, consumers and society have a much broader range and quality of service choices available, and often at a lower cost.

International Trade Problems in Services

Together with the increasing importance of service marketing, new problems have beset the service sector. Even though many of these problems have been characterized as affecting mainly the negotiations between nations, they are of sufficient importance to the firm in its international activities to merit a brief review.

Data Collection Problems

The data collected on service trade are quite poor. Service transactions are often "invisible" statistically as well as physically. The fact that governments have precise data on the number of trucks exported, down to the last bolt, but little information on reinsurance flows reflects past governmental inattention to services.

Only recently has it been recognized that the income generated and the jobs created through the sale of services abroad are just as important as income and jobs resulting from the production and exportation of goods. As a result, many governments are beginning to develop improved measuring techniques for the services sector. For example, the U.S. government has improved its estimates of services by covering more business, professional, and technical services and incorporating improved measurement of telecommunications services and insurance services. New data are also developed on travel and passenger fares, foreign students' expenditures in the United States, repairs and alterations of equipment, and noninterest income of banks.

It is easy to imagine how many data collection problems are encountered in countries lacking elaborate systems and unwilling to allocate funds for such efforts. The gathering of information is, of course, made substantially more difficult because services are intangible and therefore more difficult to measure and to trace than goods. The lack of service homogeneity does not make the task any easier. In an international setting, of course, an additional major headache is the lack of comparability between services categories as used by different national statistical systems. For example, while gas and electricity production and distribution are classified as goods by most governments, they are classified as services in the United States.[12]

Insufficient knowledge and information have led to a lack of transparency. As a result, governments have great difficulty gauging the effect of service transactions internationally or influencing service trade. Consequently, international services negotiations progress only slowly, and governmental regulations are often put into place without precise information as to their repercussions on actual trade performance.

Regulation of Services Trade

Typical obstacles to services trade can be categorized into two major types: barriers to entry and problems in performing services. Governments often justify **barriers to entry** by referring to **national security** and economic security. For example, the impact of banking on domestic economic activity is given as a reason why banking should be carried out only by nationals or indeed be operated entirely under government control. Sometimes, the protection of service users is cited, particularly of bank depositors and insurance policyholders. Some countries claim that competition in societally important services is unnecessary, wasteful, and should be avoided. Another justification for barriers is the frequently used **infant industry** argument: "With sufficient time to develop on our own, we can compete in world markets." Often, however, this argument is used simply to prolong the ample licensing profits generated by restricted entry. Impediments to services consist of either tariff or nontariff barriers. Tariff barriers typically restrict or inhibit market entry for the service provider or consumer, while nontariff barriers tend to impede service performance. Yet, defining a barrier to service marketing is not always easy. For example, Germany gives an extensive written examination to prospective accountants (as do most countries) to ensure that licensed accountants are qualified to practice. Naturally, the examination is given in German. The fact that few U.S. accountants read and write German does not necessarily constitute a barrier to trade in accountancy services.

Even if barriers to entry are nonexistent or can be overcome, service companies have difficulty in performing effectively abroad once they have achieved access to the local market. One reason is that rules and regulations based on tradition may inhibit innovation. A more important reason is that governments aim to pursue social or cultural objectives through national regulations. Of primary importance here is the distinction between **discriminatory** and **nondiscriminatory regulations.** Regulations that impose larger operating costs on foreign service providers than on the local competitors, that provide subsidies to local firms only, or that deny competitive opportunities to foreign suppliers are a proper cause for international concern. The discrimination problem becomes even more acute when foreign firms face competition from government-owned or government-controlled enterprises, which are discussed in more detail in a later chapter. On the other hand, nondiscriminatory regulations may be inconvenient and may hamper business operations, but they offer less opportunity for international criticism.

For example, barriers to services destined for the U.S. market result mainly from regulatory practices. The fields of banking, insurance, and accounting provide some examples. These industries are regulated at both federal and state levels, and the regulations often pose formidable barriers to potential entrants from abroad. The chief complaint of foreign countries is not that the United States discriminates against foreign service providers but rather that the United States places more severe restrictions on them than do other countries. These barriers are, of course, a reflection of the decision-making process within the U.S. domestic economy and are unlikely to change in the near future. A coherent approach toward international commerce in services is hardly likely to emerge from the disparate decisions of agencies such as the Interstate Commerce Commission (ICC), the Federal Communications Commission (FCC), the Securities and Exchange Commission (SEC), and the many licensing agencies at the state level.

All these regulations make it difficult for the international service marketer to penetrate world markets. At the governmental level, services frequently are not recognized as a major facet of world trade or are viewed with suspicion because of a lack of understanding, and barriers to entry often result. To make progress in tearing them down, much educational work needs to be done. However, advances are visible. The Council for Trade in Services met in early 2000 to start negotiations on services. In November 2001, the Doha Ministerial Conference set January 1, 2005, as the deadline for the conclusion of the negotiations.[13]

Corporations and Involvement in International Services Marketing

Services and E-Commerce

Electronic commerce has opened up new horizons for global services reach and has drastically reduced the meaning of distance. For example, when geographic obstacles make the establishment of retail outlets cumbersome and expensive, firms can approach their customers via the World Wide Web. Government regulations that might be prohibitive to a transfer of goods may not have any effect on the international marketing of services. Also, regardless of size, companies are finding it increasingly easy to appeal to a global marketplace. The Internet can help service firms develop and transitional economies overcome two of the biggest tasks they face: gaining credibility in international markets and saving on travel costs. Little-known firms can become instantly "visible" on the Internet. Even a small firm can develop a polished and sophisticated Web presence and promotion strategy. Customers are less concerned about geographic location if they feel the firm is electronically accessible. An increasing number of service providers have never met their foreign customers except "virtually," online.[14]

Nonetheless, several notes of caution must be kept in mind. First, the penetration of the Internet has occurred at different rates in different countries. There are still many businesses and consumers who do not have access to electronic business media. Unless they are to be excluded from a company's focus, more traditional ways of reaching them must be considered. Also, firms need to prepare their Internet presence for global visitors. For example, the language of the Internet is English—at least as far as large corporations are concerned. Yet, many of the visitors coming to Web sites either may not have English as their first language or may not speak English at all. A study by International Data Corporation (IDC) shows that while 85 percent of all Web pages are in English, only 45 percent of current online users speak the language.[15]

Many companies do not permit any interaction on their Web sites, thus missing out on feedback or even order placement from visitors. Some Web sites are so culture-bound that they often leave their visitors bewildered and disappointed. Yet over time, increasing understanding about doing business in the global marketplace will enable companies to be more refined in their approach to their customers.

Typical International Services

Although many firms are already active in the international service arena, others often do not perceive their existing competitive advantage. Numerous services have great potential for internationalization.

Financial institutions can offer some functions very competitively in the international field of banking services. Increased mergers and acquisitions on a global basis have led to the emergence of financial giants in Europe, Japan, and the United States. With the increased reach made possible by electronic commerce, they can develop direct linkages to clients around the world, offering tailor-made financial services and reduction in intermediation cost. Figure 15.3 provides an example of the international positioning of a bank.

Another area with great international potential is construction, design, and engineering services. Economies of scale work not only for machinery and material but also for areas such as personnel management and the overall management of projects. Particularly for international projects that are large scale and long term, the experience advantage could weigh heavily in favor of seasoned firms. The economic significance of these services far exceeds their direct turnover because they encourage subsequent demand for capital goods. For example, having an engineering consultant of a certain nationality increases the chances that contracts for the supply of equipment, technology, and know-how will be won by an enterprise

| Figure 15.3 | **Financial Services Firm Positions Itself** |

EN ESPAÑA SOMOS ESPAÑOLES.

IN DEUTSCHLAND SIND WIR DEUTSCHE.

IN AUSTRALIA, WE ARE AUSTRALIAN.

日本では、日本人。

IN CANADA, WE ARE CANADIAN.

IN NEDERLAND ZIJN WE NEDERLANDS.

IN ENGLAND, WE ARE ENGLISH.

IN DER SCHWEIZ SIND WIR SCHWEIZER.

在香港我們是中國人。

IN AMERICA, WE ARE AMERICAN.

DI SINGAPURA KAMI IALAH ORANG SINGAPURA.

EN FRANCE, NOUS SOMMES FRANÇAIS.

AROUND THE WORLD WE ARE THE
CS FIRST BOSTON GROUP.

Announcing a worldwide investment banking firm that draws its strength from established investment banks in the world's financial capitals.

Operating as First Boston in the Americas, Credit Suisse First Boston in Europe and the Middle East, and CS First Boston Pacific in the Far East and Asia, the CS First Boston Group – together with Credit Suisse – offers unparalleled expertise in capital raising, mergers and acquisitions, securities sales, trading and research, asset management, and merchant banking.

So regardless of what language you speak, the words for powerful investment banking are the same all over the world – CS First Boston Group.

| **CS First Boston Group** | First Boston | Credit Suisse First Boston | CS First Boston Pacific |

SOURCE: Courtesy Credit Suisse First Boston LLC; **http://www.csfb.com.**

of the same nationality, given the advantages enjoyed in terms of information, language, and technical specification.[16]

Firms in the fields of legal and accounting services can aid their domestic clients abroad through support activities; they can also aid foreign firms and countries in improving business and governmental operations. In computer and data services, international potential is growing rapidly. Knowledge of computer operations, data manipulations, data transmission, and data analysis are insufficiently exploited internationally by many small and medium-sized firms. For example, India is increasingly participating in the provision of international data services. Although some aspects of the data field are high-technology intensive, many operations still require skilled human service input. The coding and entering of data often has to be performed manually because appropriate machine-readable forms may be unavailable or not usable. Because of lower wages, Indian companies can offer data-entry services at a rate much lower than in more industrialized countries. As a result, data are transmitted in raw form to India where they are encoded on a proper medium and returned to the ultimate user. To some extent, this transformation can be equated to the value-added steps that take place in the transformation of a raw commodity into a finished product. Obviously, using its comparative advantage for this labor-intensive task, India can compete in the field of international services. In 2001, India's software industry exports reached $7.65 billion. Sixty-four percent of exports went to the United States and Canada with another 23 percent exported to the European Union.[17]

Many opportunities exist in the field of teaching services. Both the academic and the corporate education sector have concentrated their work in the domestic market. Yet the teaching of knowledge is in high global demand and offers new opportunities for growth. Technology allows teachers to go global via video conferences, e-mail office hours, and Internet-relayed teaching materials. Removing the confinement of the classroom may well trigger the largest surge in learning that humankind has ever known.

Management consulting services can be provided by firms to institutions and corporations around the globe. Of particular value is management expertise in areas where firms possess global leadership, be it in manufacturing or process activities. For example, companies with highly refined transportation or logistics activities can sell their management experience abroad. Yet consulting services are particularly sensitive to the cultural environment, and their use varies significantly by country and field of expertise. *The International Marketplace 15.2* provides examples of how an international service provider can help locate basketball talent from around the world.

All domestic service expenditures funded from abroad by foreign citizens also represent a service export. This makes tourism an increasingly important area of services trade. For example, every foreign visitor who spends foreign currency in a country contributes to an improvement in that nation's current account. The natu-

THE INTERNATIONAL MARKETPLACE 15.2

A New Services Industry: Finding Basketball Players

Tall kids in countries around the world are finding golden opportunities on American basketball courts. The number of foreign players on U.S. college and professional basketball teams has jumped from 144 to 243 in a four-year period, and American recruiters can't seem to get enough of the foreign imports. Hakeem Olajuwon, an NBA star from Nigeria, has achieved the status of folk hero among many fans around the globe. Many credit his success with the current rush to recruit players from abroad.

Stiff competition for the tallest players has even led to recruiting foreign players at younger levels of the sport; high schools commonly use foreign exchange programs to fortify their teams with international talent. High school coaches are linked with foreign players through middlemen, like the Nigerian lawyer, Toyin Sonoiki, who spent $500,000 to send nine players to U.S. schools.

The role of middlemen is crucial in obtaining visas for the students. Another Nigerian lawyer, Lloyd Ukwu, lives in Washington, DC, and recruits on business trips back home. He started helping young Nigerians obtain U.S. visas in 1988. After meeting some players on a trip to Nigeria, he asked an assistant basketball coach at American University to write invitations for eight Nigerian players to visit the United States, and these letters were influential in helping them win visas. Word spread about Ukwu's recruiting efforts, and soon other universities were using his services.

The internationalization of the sport has changed the jobs of many American coaches and recruiters. For years, college recruiting has used tip sheets to describe U.S. high school players, but now there is one recruiting service that gives the scoop on foreign players as well. Dale Mock, a Georgia elementary-school physical-education teacher, runs International Scouting Service, begun in 1993. His tip sheets give subscribers the details about foreign players and contact information for $400 a year. Mock's subscriber list is up to 100, from a start of only 20 his first year. Dale Brown, Louisiana State's former coach, described the internationalization of the recruiting scene: "In the 1960s, I would go to the European championships, to the Asian games and all the rest—and I was the only American. Now, so many Americans are there it's like being in Grand Central Station."

SOURCES: International Scouting Service Web site, **http://www. inthoops.com** accessed November 9, 2002; and Marc Fisher and Ken Denlinger, "The Market for Imports Is Booming," *The Washington Post,* March 28, 1997, C1.

Table 15.4	World Tourism

Top 15 Tourism Destinations	Top 15 Tourism Earners	Top 15 Tourism Spenders
1. France	1. United States	1. United States
2. Spain	2. Spain	2. Germany
3. United States	3. France	3. United Kingdom
4. Italy	4. Italy	4. Japan
5. China	5. China	5. France
6. United Kingdom	6. Germany	6. Italy
7. Russian Federation	7. United Kingdom	7. China
8. Mexico	8. Austria	8. Netherlands
9. Canada	9. Canada	9. Canada
10. Austria	10. Greece	10. Belgium/Luxembourg
11. Germany	11. Turkey	11. Austria
12. Hungary	12. Mexico	12. Republic of Korea
13. Poland	13. Hong Kong (China)	13. Sweden
14. Hong Kong (China)	14. Australia	14. Switzerland
15. Greece	15. Switzerland	15. Taiwan (Pr. of China)

SOURCE: World Tourism Organization, *Facts and Figures*, **http://www.world-tourism.org**, accessed October 2, 2002.

ral resources and beauty offered by so many countries have already made tourism one of the most important services trade components. Table 15.4 shows the extent of tourism arrivals and receipts around the world.

A proper mix in international services might also be achieved by pairing the strengths of different partners. For example, information technology expertise from one country could be combined with financial resources from another. The strengths of both partners can then be used to obtain maximum benefits.

Combining international advantages in services may ultimately result in the development of an even newer and more drastic comparative lead. For example, if a firm has an international head start in such areas as high technology, information gathering, information processing, and information analysis, the major thrust of its international service might not rely on providing these service components individually but rather on enabling clients, based on all resources, to make better decisions. If better decision-making is transferable to a wide variety of international situations, that in itself might become the overriding future competitive advantage of the firm in the international market.

Starting to Market Services Internationally

For many firms, participation in the Internet will offer the most attractive starting point in marketing services internationally. Setting up a Web site will allow visitors from any place on the globe to come see the offering. Of course, the most important problem will be communicating the existence of the site and enticing visitors to come. For that, very traditional advertising and communication approaches often need to be used. In some countries, for example, rolling billboards announce Web sites and their benefits. Overall, however, we need to keep in mind that not everywhere do firms and individuals have access to or make use of the new e-commerce opportunities.

For services that are delivered mainly in the support of or in conjunction with goods, the most sensible approach for the international novice is to follow the path of the good. For years, many large accounting and banking firms have done so by determining where their major multinational clients have set up new operations and then following them. Smaller service marketers who cooperate closely with manufacturing firms can determine where the manufacturing firms are operating internationally. Ideally, of course, it would be possible to follow clusters of manufacturers in order to obtain economies of scale internationally while, at the same time, looking for entirely new client groups abroad.

For service providers whose activities are independent from goods, a different strategy is needed. These individuals and firms must search for market situations abroad that are similar to the domestic market. Such a search should concentrate in their area of expertise. For example, a design firm learning about construction projects abroad can investigate the possibility of rendering its design services. Similarly, a management consultant learning about the plans of a foreign country or firm to computerize operations can explore the possibility of overseeing a smooth transition from manual to computerized activities. What is required is the understanding that similar problems are likely to occur in similar situations.

Another opportunity consists of identifying and understanding points of transition abroad. Just as U.S. society has undergone change, foreign societies are subject to a changing domestic environment. If, for example, new transportation services are introduced, an expert in containerization may wish to consider whether to offer service to improve the efficiency of the new system. The *International Marketplace 15.3* shows how accounting problems may lead to an entire refurbishing of that global industry.

THE INTERNATIONAL MARKETPLACE 15.3

Accounting after Enron

The sudden collapse of U.S. energy giant Enron Corporation in 2002 has placed U.S. accounting practices under worldwide scrutiny. Enron, America's seventh largest company, was discovered to have released misleading financial information by manipulating the Generally Accepted Accounting Practices (GAAP). Confidence in the financial markets globally, and especially the U.S. market, has dropped, and investors are now more wary than ever of the financial information they receive. To restore investor faith in companies, countries are now seeking to create a global accounting standard which will make corporate accounts more transparent and accessible to investors worldwide. On a smaller scale, individual countries, especially the United States, are designing other ways to monitor financial reporting as well.

The exposure of Enron created panic in the investment field and caused investors to demand more information about the financial position of corporations. Many firms had to restate earnings. The worst case was perhaps WorldCom, which admitted to overstating revenues by $7.2 billion. Such findings have prompted foreign investors to question their investments around the world. Without the reliability of financial reports, investors are unwilling to risk their money.

To encourage investment globally, countries have decided that an international accounting standard is necessary. Not only should financial accounts be transparent and easy to understand, but comparisons between companies of different countries should be possible as well.

The European parliament announced recently that by 2007, all companies in the European Union will be required to use rules set by the International Accounting Standards Board (IASB). A number of countries, including Thailand, Tobago, Panama, and Peru, already employ the guidelines set by IASB. The GAAP have been under attack due to Enron's manipulation of reporting guidelines and U.S. firms may have to adjust to IASB rules.

In 2002, the U.S. Congress passed the Sarbane–Oxley Act, which prohibits auditors from selling nonaudit services to audit clients. Prior to this law, accounting firms provided a broad range of services that could be used to facilitate fraudulent practices. To comply with this new law, the remaining accounting firms have sold their consulting, legal, and other services. The Security and Exchange Commission has also established a five-member private-sector board to keep the auditing industry in check by using subpoena rights and disciplinary powers. Since accounting is a service that is offered globally, accountants must also be aware of the legislation of different countries. Perhaps better regulation of accounting and auditing practices in the future will restore global investor confidence in financial markets.

SOURCES: Paul Blustein, "Accounting's Rival Rules," *The Washington Post,* May 10, 2002; Paula Green, "Called to Account," *Global Finance,* April 2002, 31–33, *ABI/Inform Global,* online, August 28, 2002; "Swearing by the Numbers," *The Economist,* August 13, 2002: 1, *ABI/Inform Global,* online, September 6, 2002.

Leads for international service opportunities can also be gained by staying informed about international projects sponsored by domestic organizations such as the U.S. Agency for International Development, as well as international organizations such as the United Nations, the International Finance Corporation, or the World Bank. Very frequently, such projects are in need of support through services. Overall, the international service marketer needs to search for familiar situations or similar problems requiring similar solutions in order to formulate an effective international expansion strategy.

Strategic Implications of International Services Marketing

To be successful, the international service marketer must first determine the nature and the aim of the service offering—that is, whether the service will be aimed at people or at things, and whether the service act in itself will result in tangible or intangible actions. Figure 15.4 provides examples of such a classification that will help the marketer to better determine the position of the services effort.

During this determination, the marketer must consider other tactical variables that have an impact on the preparation of the service offering. The measurement of services capacity and delivery efficiency often remains highly qualitative rather

---

Figure 15.4   Understanding the Service Act

What Is the Nature of the Service Act?	Who or What is the Direct Recipient of the Service?	
	People	**Possessions**
Tangible Actions	*People processing* (services directed at people's bodies): Passenger transportation Healthcare Lodging Beauty salons Physical therapy Fitness center Restaurant/bars Barbers Funeral services	*Possession processing* (services directed at physical possessions): Freight transportation Repair and maintenance Warehousing/storage Office cleaning services Retail distribution Laundry and dry cleaning Refueling Landscaping/gardening Disposal/recycling
Intangible Actions	*Mental stimulus processing* (services directed at people's minds): Advertising/PR Arts and entertainment Broadcasting/cable Management consulting Education Information services Music concerts Psychotherapy Religion Voice telephone	*Information processing* (services directed at intangible assets): Accounting Banking Data processing Data transmission Insurance Legal services Programming Research Securities investment Software consulting

SOURCE: Christopher H. Lovelock, *Services Marketing: People, Technology, Strategy,* 4th ed., 38. © 2001. Reprinted by permission of Pearson Education, Inc., Upper Saddle River, NJ.

than quantitative. In the field of communications, the intangibility of the service reduces the marketer's ability to provide samples. This makes communicating the service offer much more difficult than communicating an offer for a good. Brochures or catalogs explaining services often must show a "proxy" for the service in order to provide the prospective customer with tangible clues. A cleaning service, for instance, can show a picture of an individual removing trash or cleaning a window. Yet the picture will not fully communicate the performance of the service. Because of the different needs and requirements of individual consumers, the marketer must pay very close attention to the two-way flow of communication. Mass communication must often be supported by intimate one-on-one follow-up.

The role of personnel deserves special consideration in the international marketing of services. Because the customer interface is intense, proper provisions need to be made for training personnel both domestically and internationally. Major emphasis must be placed on appearance. The person delivering the service—rather than the service itself—will communicate the spirit, value, and attitudes of the service corporation. The service person is both the producer and the marketer of the service. Therefore, recruitment and training techniques must focus on dimensions such as customer relationship management and image projection as well as competence in the design and delivery of the service.[18]

This close interaction with the consumer will also have organizational implications. Whereas tight control over personnel may be desired, the individual interaction that is required points toward the need for an international decentralization of service delivery. This, in turn, requires both delegation of large amounts of responsibility to individuals and service "subsidiaries" and a great deal of trust in all organizational units. This trust, of course, can be greatly enhanced through proper methods of training and supervision. Sole ownership also helps strengthen trust. Research has shown that service firms, in their international expansion, tend greatly to prefer the establishment of full-control ventures. Only when costs escalate and the company-specific advantage diminishes will service firms seek out shared-control ventures.[19]

The areas of pricing and financing require special attention. Because services cannot be stored, much greater responsiveness to demand fluctuation must exist, and therefore, much greater pricing flexibility must be maintained. At the same time, flexibility is countered by the desire to provide transparency for both the seller and the buyer of services in order to foster an ongoing relationship. The intangibility of services also makes financing more difficult. Frequently, even financial institutions with large amounts of international experience are less willing to provide financial support for international services than for products. The reasons are that the value of services is more difficult to assess, service performance is more difficult to monitor, and services are difficult to repossess. Therefore, customer complaints and difficulties in receiving payments are much more troublesome for a lender to evaluate for services than for products.

Finally, the distribution implications of international services must be considered. Usually, short and direct channels are required. Within these channels, closeness to the customer is of overriding importance in order to understand what the customer really wants, to trace the use of the service, and to aid the consumer in obtaining a truly tailor-made service.

Summary

Services are taking on an increasing importance in international marketing. They need to be considered separately from the marketing of goods because they no longer simply complement goods. Increasingly, goods complement services or are in competition with them. Because of service attributes such as intangibility, perishability, customization, and cultural sensitivity, the international marketing of services is frequently more complex than that of goods.

Services play a growing role in the global economy. As a result, international growth and competition in this sector outstrips that of merchandise trade and is likely to intensify in the future. Even though services are unlikely to replace production, the sector will account for the shaping of new comparative advantages internationally, particularly in light of new facilitating technologies that encourage electronic commerce.

The many service firms now operating domestically need to investigate the possibility of going global.

The historical patterns in which service providers followed manufacturers abroad have become obsolete as stand-alone services have become more important to world trade. Management must therefore assess its vulnerability to service competition from abroad and explore opportunities to provide its services internationally.

Key Terms

intangibility
perishability
service capacity
customer involvement

service consistency
market transparency
deregulation
barriers to entry

national security
infant industry
discriminatory regulations
nondiscriminatory regulations

Questions for Discussion

1. How has the Internet affected your service purchases?

2. Discuss the major reasons for the growth of international services.

3. How does the international sale of services differ from the sale of goods?

4. What are some of the international marketing implications of service intangibility?

5. Discuss the effects of cultural sensitivity on international services.

6. What are some ways for a firm to expand its services internationally?

7. How can a firm in a developing country participate in the international services boom?

8. Which services would be expected to migrate globally in the next decade? Why?

Internet Exercises

1. Find the most current data on the five leading export and import countries for commercial services. The information is available on the World Trade Organization site, **http://www.wto.org**. Click the statistics button.

2. What are the key U.S. services exports and imports? What is the current services trade balance? (**http://www.bea.doc.gov**).

Recommended Readings

Business Guide to the World Trading System. Geneva: International Trade Centre UNCTAD/WTO and London, Commonwealth Secretariat, 1999.

Cuadrado-Roura, Juan R., Luis Rubalcaba-Bermejo, John R. Bryson, and Witold J. Henisz (eds.). *Trading Services in the Global Economy.* Northampton, MA: Edward Elgar, 2002.

Hoffman, Douglas K., and John E. G. Bateson, *Essentials of Services Marketing.* Mason, OH: South-Western, 2002.

Lovelock, Christopher H. *Services Marketing: People, Technology, Strategy,* 4th ed. Upper Saddle River, NJ: Prentice-Hall, 2001.

Meyer, Anton, and Frank Dornach. *The German Customer Barometer,* Annual. Munich: FMG–Verlag, 2003.

Stern, Robert M. (ed.). *Services in the International Economy.* Ann Arbor: University of Michigan Press, 2001.

U.S. Coalition of Service Industries. Policy Issues and Links to Industries. **http://uscsi.org**.

U.S. Department of Commerce, International Trade Administration, Office of Service Industries. *Results of Services 2002.* Washington, DC, 2002.

Zeithaml, Valerie, and Mary Jo Bitner. *Services Marketing,* 3rd ed. New York: McGraw-Hill, 2003.

chapter 16

Global Pricing Strategies

THE INTERNATIONAL MARKETPLACE 16.1

A Global Tax War?

The U.S. Internal Revenue Service has begun to look more closely at transfer pricing on sales of goods and services among subsidiaries or between subsidiaries and the parent company. It has filed claims against hundreds of companies in recent years, claiming that multinational companies too often manipulate intracompany pricing to minimize their worldwide tax bills. Experts calculate that foreign-based multinationals evade at least $20 billion in U.S. taxes. Other countries have also strengthened their review systems. Japan has created specific transfer pricing legislation that penalizes marketers for not providing information in time to meet deadlines set by the government. German tax authorities are carefully checking intracompany charges to deem their appropriateness.

In its biggest known victory, the IRS made its case that Japan's Toyota had been systematically overcharging its U.S. subsidiary for years on most of the cars, trucks, and parts sold in the United States. What would have been profits in the United States were now accrued in Japan. Toyota denied improprieties but agreed to a reported $1 billion settlement, paid in part with tax rebates from the government of Japan.

And now Japan is striking back. The Japanese National Tax Administration Agency (NTAA) has charged the Coca-Cola Co. with a $145 million tax deficiency for 1990–1992. They also hit AIU Insurance Co., the Japanese subsidiary of giant American International Group Inc., with an $87 million bill that was later reduced to $37 million in a settlement. "There is clearly a war going on," says a Tokyo lawyer who advises foreign companies on Japanese tax laws. Some fear that the agency will target sectors in which U.S. firms are doing well, such as pharmaceuticals, computers, and chemicals, for retaliatory tax investigations. Companies would also be questioned over intangibles, such as R&D and marketing costs, which are typically higher for U.S. firms.

Other countries are also trying to tap into what they see as a potentially lucrative revenue stream. The German tax agency is heightening audit activity beyond what they ordinarily do. Fear is widespread, therefore, that an all-out tax war is about to erupt. To avoid that, the Organization for Economic Cooperation and Development (OECD) published its transfer-pricing guidelines in mid-1995, with periodic revisions since then. Experts also speculate that the European Court may move to standardize corporate tax rates within the EU, which would please high-taxing Germany and France but concern lower-taxing Britian and Ireland.

Until recently, countries such as Argentina, Brazil, and Mexico relied on other mechanisms, such as exchange controls, high import duties, and other nontariff barriers, to protect their tax bases. However, as those regimes are being abolished as part of multilateral and regional agreements, transfer pricing rules are being enacted to do the same job. Across emerging markets, governments are following the lead of the Europeans and North Americans in implementing and enforcing documentation requirements and backing them up with harsh penalties for violations.

Increasing communication among tax authorities is having a dramatic effect and will continue to accelerate, especially with the trend toward shifting profits. Historically, transfer pricing from the point of view of a U.S. company meant the shifting of income out of the United States, but with the corporate tax rate at 34 percent, many U.S. companies are now trying to use transfer pricing to shift profits into the country. Thus, U.S. multinationals must be prepared to justify transfer pricing policies on two or more fronts.

The entire tax equation has become more complicated because of changes in customs duties. In many countries, revenues from customs and indirect taxes are greater than revenue from corporate taxes. Authorities will jealously guard the income stream from customs taxes, and marketers could find gains on income taxes erased by losses on customs taxes.

Most multinationals are moving cautiously. Glen White, director of taxes at Dow Chemical, stresses this point. "I don't think anybody can afford to have a transfer-pricing system that cannot be revealed to all the relevant governments."

SOURCES: Peter H. Blessing, "U.S. Targets Foreign-Based Companies," International Tax Review 13 (no. 8, 2002): 29–31; Erika Morphy, "Asia Taxes: Beastly Burdens," Global Business, February 2000, 38–41; "Gimme Shelter: Is Tax Competition Among Countries a Good or Bad Thing?," The Economist, January 29, 2000; Erika Morphy, "Global Reaching," Export Today, May 1999, 60–76; "Transfer Pricing Problem," Journal of Commerce, November 14, 1997, 3A; "Here Comes the Great Global Tax War," Business Week, May 30, 1994, 55–56; "Pricing Yourself into a Market," Business Asia, December 21, 1992, 1; "The Corporate Shell Game," Newsweek, April 15, 1991, 48–49; and "Worldwide Tax Authorities Promise Increased Scrutiny of Transfer Pricing," Business International Money Report, February 22, 1988, 72. See **http://www.oecd.org** for The OECD Transfer Pricing Guidelines, 1998; see also **http://www.irs.ustreas.gov** for Development of IRC 482 Cases.

SUCCESSFUL PRICING IS A KEY ELEMENT in the marketing mix. Many executives believe that developing a pricing capability is essential to business survival and rank pricing as second only to the product variable in importance among the concerns to marketing managers.[1] This chapter will focus on price setting by multinational corporations that have direct inventories in other countries. This involves the pricing of sales to members of the corporate family as well as pricing within the individual markets in which the company operates. With increased economic integration and globalization of markets, the coordination of pricing strategies between markets becomes more important. At the same time, marketers may have to develop creative solutions through countertrade to situations in which buyers want to attach strings to their purchases due to the size of the sale or because they may not have the monetary means with which to buy.

Transfer Pricing

Transfer pricing, or intracorporate pricing, is the pricing of sales to members of the extended corporate family. With rapid globalization and consolidation across borders, estimates have up to two-thirds of world trade taking place between related parties, including shipments and transfers from parent company to affiliates as well as trade between alliance partners.[2] This means that transfer pricing has to be managed in a world characterized by different tax rates, different foreign exchange rates, varying governmental regulations, and other economic and social challenges, as seen in *The International Marketplace 16.1*. Allocation of resources among the various units of the multinational corporation requires the central management of the corporation to establish the appropriate transfer price to achieve these objectives:

1. Competitiveness in the international marketplace
2. Reduction of taxes and tariffs
3. Management of cash flows
4. Minimization of foreign exchange risks
5. Avoidance of conflicts with home and host governments
6. Internal concerns such as goal congruence and motivation of subsidiary managers[3]

Intracorporate sales can so easily change the consolidated global results that they compose one of the most important ongoing decision areas in the company. This is quite a change from the past when many executives dismissed internal pricing as the sole responsibility of the accounting department and as a compliance matter. Transfer pricing, when viewed from a company-wide perspective, enhances operational performance (including marketing), minimizes the overall tax burden, and reduces legal exposure both at home and abroad.[4] According to an annual survey, the portion of multinationals citing transfer pricing as the most important issue in terms of taxation has grown from one-half to two-thirds, and at the subsidiary level this importance is even more pronounced.[5]

Transfer prices can be based on costs or on market prices.[6] The cost approach uses an internally calculated cost with a percentage markup added. The market price approach is based on an established market selling price, and the products are usually sold at that price minus a discount to allow some margin of profit for the buying division. In general, cost-based prices are easier to manipulate because the cost base itself may be any one of these three: full cost, variable cost, or marginal cost.

Factors that have a major influence on intracompany prices are listed in Table 16.1. Market conditions in general, and those relating to the competitive situation

Table 16.1	Influences on Transfer Pricing Decisions

1. Market conditions in target countries
2. Competition in target countries
3. Corporate taxes at home and in target countries
4. Economic conditions in target countries
5. Import restrictions
6. Customs duties
7. Price controls
8. Exchange controls
9. Reasonable profit for foreign affiliates

SOURCE: Compiled from Robert Feinschreiber, *Transfer Pricing Handbook* (New York: John Wiley & Sons, 2002), chapter 1 (Business Facets of Transfer Pricing); and Jane O. Burns, "Transfer Pricing Decisions in U.S. Multinational Corporations," *Journal of International Business Studies* 11 (Fall 1980): 23–39.

in particular, are typically mentioned as key variables in balancing operational goals and tax considerations. In some markets, especially in the Far East, competition may prevent the international marketer from pricing at will. Prices may have to be adjusted to meet local competition with lower labor costs. This practice may provide entry to the market and a reasonable profit to the affiliate. However, in the long term, it may also become a subsidy to an inefficient business. Further, tax and customs authorities may object because underpricing means that the seller is earning less income than it would otherwise receive in the country of origin and is paying duties on a lower base price on entry to the destination country.

Economic conditions in a market, especially the imposition of controls on movements of funds, may require the use of transfer pricing to allow the company to repatriate revenues. As an example, a U.S.-based multinational corporation with central procurement facilities required its subsidiaries to buy all raw materials from the parent; it began charging a standard 7 percent for its services, which include guaranteeing on-time delivery and appropriate quality. The company estimates that its revenue remittances from a single Latin American country, which had placed restrictions on remittances from subsidiaries to parent companies, increased by $900,000 after the surcharge was put into effect.[7]

A new dimension is emerging with the increase in e-commerce activity. Given a lack of clear understanding and agreement of tax authorities on taxation of electronic transfer pricing activities, companies have to be particularly explicit on how pricing decisions are made to avoid transfer-price audits.[8]

International transfer pricing objectives may lead to conflicting objectives, especially if the influencing factors vary dramatically from one market to another. For example, it may be quite difficult to perfectly match subsidiary goals with the global goals of the multinational corporation. Specific policies should therefore exist that would motivate subsidiary managers to avoid making decisions that would be in conflict with overall corporate goals. If transfer pricing policies lead to an inaccurate financial measure of the subsidiary's performance, this should be taken into account when a performance evaluation is made.

Use of Transfer Prices to Achieve Corporate Objectives

Three philosophies of transfer pricing have emerged over time: (1) cost-based (direct cost or cost-plus), (2) market-based (discounted "dealer" price derived from end market prices), and (3) **arm's-length price,** or the price that unrelated parties would have reached on the same transaction. The rationale for transferring at cost is that it increases the profits of affiliates, and their profitability will eventually benefit the entire corporation. In most cases, cost-plus is used, requiring every affiliate to be a profit center. Deriving transfer prices from the market is the most marketing-oriented method because it takes local conditions into account. Arm's-length pricing is favored by many constituents, such as governments, to ensure proper intracompany pricing. However, the method becomes difficult when sales to outside parties do not occur in a product category. Additionally, it is often difficult to convince external authorities that true negotiation occurs between two entities controlled by the same parent. In a study of 32 U.S.-based multinational corporations operating in Latin America, a total of 57 percent stated that they use a strategy of arm's-length pricing for their shipments, while the others used negotiated prices, cost-plus, or some other method.[9] Generally tax authorities will honor agreements among companies provided those agreements are commercially reasonable and the companies abide by the agreements consistently.[10]

The effect of environmental influences in overseas markets can be alleviated by manipulating transfer prices at least in principle. High transfer prices on goods shipped to a subsidiary and low ones on goods imported from it will result in minimizing the tax liability of a subsidiary operating in a country with a high income tax. The effective corporate tax rate in the United States is 40 percent (35 percent federal), while the average rate in the EU is 32.5 percent, in Latin America 30.2 percent, and in Asia 31 percent.[11] This may give multinationals a reason to report higher profits outside of the United States. On the other hand, a higher transfer price may have an effect on the import duty, especially if it is assessed on an ad valorem basis. Exceeding a certain threshold may boost the duty substantially when the product is considered a luxury and will have a negative impact on the subsidiary's competitive posture. Adjusting transfer prices for the opposite effects of taxes and duties is, therefore, a delicate balancing act.

Transfer prices may be adjusted to balance the effects of fluctuating currencies when one partner is operating in a low-inflation environment and the other in one of rampant inflation. Economic restrictions such as controls on dividend remittances and allowable deductions for expenses incurred can also be blunted. For example, if certain services performed by corporate headquarters (such as product development or strategic planning assistance) cannot be charged to the subsidiaries, costs for these services can be recouped by increases in the transfer prices of other product components. A subsidiary's financial and competitive position can be manipulated by the use of lower transfer prices. Start-up costs can be lowered, a market niche carved more quickly, and long-term survival guaranteed. Ultimately, the entire transfer price and taxation question is best dealt with at a time when the company is considering a major expansion or restructuring of operations. For example, if it fits the overall plan, a portion of a unit's R&D and marketing activities could be funded in a relatively low tax jurisdiction.

Transfer pricing problems grow geometrically as all of the subsidiaries with differing environmental concerns are added to the planning exercise, calling for more detailed intracompany data for decision making. Further, fluctuating exchange rates make the planning even more challenging. However, to prevent double taxation and meet arm's-length requirements, it is essential that the corporation's pricing practices be uniform. Many have adopted a philosophy that calls for an obligation to maintain a good-citizen fiscal approach (that is, recognizing the liability to pay taxes and duties in every country of operation and to avoid artificial tax-avoidance schemes) and a belief that the primary goal of transfer pricing is to support and develop commercial activities.[12] Some companies make explicit mention of this obligation of good citizenship in their corporate codes of conduct.

Transfer Pricing Challenges

Transfer pricing policies face two general types of challenges. The first is internal to the multinational corporation and concerns the motivation of those affected by the pricing policies of the corporation. The second, an external one, deals with relations between the corporation and tax authorities in both the home country and the host countries.

Performance Measurement

Manipulating intracorporate prices complicates internal control measures and, without proper documentation, will cause major problems. If the firm operates on a profit center basis, some consideration must be given to the effect of transfer pricing on the subsidiary's apparent profit performance and its actual performance. To judge a subsidiary's profit performance as not satisfactory when it was targeted to be a net source of funds can easily create morale problems. The situation may be further complicated by cultural differences in the subsidiary's management, especially if the need to subsidize less-efficient members of the corporate family is not made clear. An adjustment in the control mechanism is called for to give appropriate credit to divisions for their actual contributions. The method may range from dual bookkeeping to compensation in budgets and profit plans. Regardless of the method, proper organizational communication is necessary to avoid conflict between subsidiaries and headquarters.

Taxation

Transfer prices will by definition involve the tax and regulatory jurisdictions of the countries in which the company does business, as is pointed out in *The International Marketplace 16.1*. Sales and transfers of tangible properties and transfers of intangibles such as patent rights and manufacturing know-how are subject to close review and to determinations about the adequacy of compensation received. This quite often puts the multinational corporation in a difficult position. U.S. authorities may think the transfer price is too low, whereas it may be perceived as too high by the foreign entity, especially if a less-developed country is involved. Section 482 of the Internal Revenue Code gives the Commissioner of the IRS vast authority to reallocate income between controlled foreign operations and U.S. parents and between U.S. operations of foreign corporations.

Before the early 1960s, the enforcement efforts under Section 482 were mostly domestic. However, since 1962, the U.S. government has attempted to stop U.S. companies from shifting U.S. income to their foreign subsidiaries in low- or no-tax jurisdictions and has affirmed the **arm's-length standard** as the principal basis for transfer pricing. Because unrelated parties normally sell products and services at a profit, an arm's-length price normally involves a profit to the seller.

A significant portion of Section 482 adjustments, including those resulting from the 1986 Tax Reform Act, have focused on licensing and other transfer of intangibles such as patents and trademarks. Historically, transfer pricing from a U.S. company's point of view has meant the shifting of income out of the United States, but, in cases of the U.S. having a lower corporate tax rate, the question now is how to use transfer pricing to shift profits into the United States. For example, Japan's corporate tax rate is 41 percent.

According to Section 482, there are four methods of determining an arm's-length price, and they are to be used in the following order:

1. The comparable uncontrolled price method
2. The resale price method
3. The cost-plus method
4. Any other reasonable method

Beginning with the 1994 tax return, U.S. firms have had to disclose the pricing method they use so that the IRS can ascertain that the price was established using the arm's-length principle.[13] Guidelines of the OECD for transfer pricing are similar to those used by U.S. authorities.[14] Some experts who argue that the arm's-length standard is only applicable for commodities businesses have proposed a simpler system that allocates profits by a formula such as that of the state of California that factors in percentages of world sales, assets, and other indicators. The rapid changes in international marketing caused by e-business will also have an impact on transfer pricing. Although transactions involving e-commerce represent new ways of conducting business, the fundamental economic relationships will remain the same. As a result, the existing principle of arm's length will probably be retained and adapted to address cross-border activities in a virtual economy.[15]

The starting point for testing the appropriateness of transfer prices is a comparison with *comparable uncontrolled* transactions, involving unrelated parties. Uncontrolled prices exist when (1) sales are made by members of the multinational corporation to unrelated parties, (2) purchases are made by members of the multinational corporation from unrelated parties, and (3) sales are made between two unrelated parties, neither of which is a member of the multinational corporation. In some cases, marketers have created third-party trading where none existed before. Instead of selling 100 percent of the product in a market to a related party, the seller can arrange a small number of direct transactions with unrelated parties to create a benchmark against which to measure related-party transactions.

If this method does not apply, the *resale* method can be used. This usually applies best to transfers to sales subsidiaries for ultimate distribution. The arm's-length approximation is arrived at by subtracting the subsidiary's profit from an uncontrolled selling price. The appropriateness of the amount is determined by comparison with a similar product being marketed by the multinational corporation.

The *cost-plus* approach is most applicable for transfers of components or unfinished goods to overseas subsidiaries. The arm's-length approximation is achieved by adding an appropriate markup for profit to the seller's total cost of the product.[16] The key is to apply such markups consistently over time and across markets.

Such comparisons, however, are not always possible even under the most favorable circumstances and may remain burdened with arbitrariness.[17] Comparisons are impossible for products that are unique or when goods are traded only with related parties. Adjusting price comparisons for differences in the product mix, or for the inherently different facts and circumstances surrounding specific transactions between unrelated parties, undermines the reliance that can be placed on any such comparisons. The most accepted of the other reasonable methods is the *functional analysis approach*. The functional analysis measures the profits of each of the related companies and compares them with the proportionate contribution to total income of the corporate group. It addresses the question of what profit would have been reported if the intercorporate transactions had involved unrelated parties. Understanding the functional interrelationships of the various parties (that is, which entity does what) is basic to determining each entity's economic contribution via-à-vis total income of the corporate group.

Since 1991, the Internal Revenue Service has been signing "advance pricing" agreements (APAs) with multinational corporations to stem the tide of unpaid U.S. income taxes. By January 1, 2002, a total of 349 such agreements were completed and 220 were under negotiation.[18] Since 1998, special provisions have been made for small and medium-sized companies to negotiate such arrangements. Agreement on transfer pricing is set ahead of time, thus eliminating court challenges and costly audits. The harsh penalties have also caused companies to consider APAs. In the United States, a transfer pricing violation can result in a 40 percent penalty on the amount of underpayment, whereas in Mexico the penalty can reach 100 percent. The main criticism of this approach is the exorbitant amounts of staff time that each agreement requires as well as the amount of information that may have to be disclosed.[19] Some also argue that such agreements may result in worse transfer pricing systems, from the corporate point of view, because companies with effective intracompany bargaining processes may have to replace them with poorly designed ones to satisfy the tax authorities.[20] Some companies have expressed concern about sitting down with tax authorities in general, for fear of some other issues emerging. Additionally, in many countries all information disclosed to tax authorities under an APA might become available to the public. In general, the costs and concerns about APAs have been reduced considerably in the recent past. For example, more of the data needed are online, and software has been developed to address the issue. A study can be had for $15,000, and many of the big accounting firms include these studies as part of their global tax strategy services.[21] In cases in which a company is doing business in a country that has a bilateral tax treaty with the home government (e.g., the United States and Germany), the company can seek a bilateral APA that is negotiated simultaneously with the tax authorities of both countries.

The most difficult of cases are those involving intangibles, because comparables are absent in most cases.[22] The IRS requires that the price or royalty rate for any cross-border transfer be commensurate with income; that is, it must result in a fair distribution of income between the units. This requires marketers to analyze and attach a value to each business function (R&D, manufacturing, assembly, marketing services, and distribution). Comparable transactions, when available—or, if absent, industry norms—should be used to calculate the rates of return for each function. Take, for example, a subsidiary that makes a $100 profit on the sale of a product manufactured with technology developed and licensed by the U.S. parent. If the firm identifies rates of return for manufacturing and distribution of 30 percent and 10 percent, then $40 of the profit must be allocated to the subsidiary. The remaining $60 would be taxable income to the parent.[23] Needless to say, many of the analyses have to be quite subjective, especially in cases that involve the transfer of intellectual property, and may lead to controversies and disputes with tax authorities.[24]

Pricing within Individual Markets

Pricing within the individual markets in which the company operates is determined by (1) corporate objectives, (2) costs, (3) customer behavior and market conditions, (4) market structure, and (5) environmental constraints.[25] Because all these factors vary among the countries in which the multinational corporation might have a presence, the pricing policy is under pressure to vary as well. With price holding a position of importance with customers, a market-driven firm must be informed and sensitive to customer views and realities.[26] This is especially critical for those marketers wanting to position their products as premium alternatives.

Although many global marketers, both U.S.-based[27] and foreign-based,[28] emphasize nonprice methods of competition, they rank pricing high as a marketing tool overseas, even though the nondomestic pricing decisions are made at the middle management level in a majority of firms. Pricing decisions also tend to be made more at the local level, with coordination from headquarters in more strategic decision situations.[29] With increased trade liberalization and advanced economic integration, this coordination is becoming more important.

Corporate Objectives

Global marketers must set and adjust their objectives, both financial (such as return on investment) and marketing-related (such as maintaining or increasing market share), based on the prevailing conditions in each of their markets. Pricing may well influence the overall strategic moves of the company as a whole. This is well illustrated by the decision of many foreign-based companies, automakers for example, to begin production in the United States rather than to continue exporting. To remain competitive in the market, many have had to increase the dollar component of their output. Apart from trade barriers, many have had their market shares erode because of higher wages in their home markets, increasing shipping costs, and unfavorable exchange rates. Market share very often plays a major role in pricing decisions in that marketers may be willing to sacrifice immediate earnings for market share gain or maintenance. This is especially true in highly competitive situations; for example, during a period of extremely high competitive activity in Japan in the computer sector, the local Fujitsu's one-year net income was only 5 percent of sales, compared with IBM's 12.7 percent worldwide and 7.6 percent in Japan.

Pricing decisions will also vary depending on the pricing situation. The basics of first-time pricing, price adjustment, and product line pricing as discussed earlier apply to pricing within nondomestic situations as well. For example, companies such as Kodak and Xerox, which introduce all of their new products worldwide within a very short time period, have an option of either skimming or penetration pricing. If the product is an innovation, the marketer may decide to charge a premium for the product. If, however, competition is keen or expected to increase in the near future, lower prices may be used to make the product more attractive to the buyers and the market less attractive to the competition. The Korean conglomerates (such as Daewoo, Goldstar, Hyundai, and Samsung) were able to penetrate and capture the low end of many consumer goods markets in both the United States and Europe based on price competitiveness over the past ten years (as shown in Table 16.2).

For the most part, the Koreans have competed in the world marketplace, especially against the Japanese, on price rather than product traits, with the major objective of capturing a foothold in various markets. For example, Samsung was able to gain access to U.S. markets when J.C. Penney was looking for lower-priced microwave ovens in the early 1980s. Samsung's ovens retailed for $299, whereas most models averaged between $350 and $400 at the time.[30] However, substantial strides in production technology and relentless marketing have started to make Korean products serious competitors in the medium to high price brackets as well.[31] In many cases, Koreans have been able to close the price gap and, in some cases, they have abandoned certain segments altogether. For example, in the compact refrigerator market, the Chinese have taken over.[32]

Price changes may be frequent if the company's objective is to undersell a major competitor. A marketer may, for example, decide to maintain a price level 10 to 20 percent below that of a major competitor; price changes would be necessary whenever the competitor made significant changes in its prices. Price changes may also be required because of changes in foreign exchange rates. Many marketers were forced to increase prices in the United States on goods of non-U.S. origin when the dollar weakened during the late 1980s and early to mid-1990s.

Table 16.2 South Korea's Price Edge over Japan

Product	Korean Brand				Japanese Brand			
	1985	1996	2000	2003	1985	1996	2000	2003
Subcompact autos	Excel/Accent (Hyundai) $5,500	$9,079	$9,699	$10,649	Sentra (Nissan) $7,600	$11,499	$11,649	$11,999
Videocassette recorders	Samsung $270	$260	$120	$80	Toshiba $350	$430	$199	$80
Compact refrigerators	Goldstar $149	$150	N/A	N/A	Sanyo $265	$180	$99	$149
13-inch color televisions	Samsung $148	$179	$170	$99	Hitachi $189	$229	$180	$90
Microwave ovens	Goldstar $149	$120	$130	$100	Toshiba $180	$140	$130	$95

SOURCE: Originally published in L. Helm, "The Koreans Are Coming," *Business Week*, December 23, 1985, 46–52; direct manufacturer/retailer inquiries, December 1996, March 2000, and January 2003. In the absence of information/availability, a similar make/model has been used based on *Consumer Reports* data.

With longer-term unfavorable currency changes, marketers have to improve their efficiency and/or shift production bases. For example, Japanese car manufacturers transplanted more manufacturing into the United States to ensure that yen-dollar changes did not have as sharp an impact as they once did. Furthermore, design and production was improved so that profitability could be maintained even at 80 or 85 yen to the dollar. When 1996 yen values were over 110 to the dollar, Japanese companies were able to cut prices 1.1 percent for the 1997 model year, while their U.S. competitors increased them by 2.8 percent on the average.[33]

Product line pricing occurs typically in conjunction with positioning decisions. The global marketer may have a premium line as well as a standard line and, in some cases, may sell directly to retailers for their private label sales. Products facing mass markets have keener competition and smaller profit margins than premium products, which may well be priced more liberally because there is less competition. For example, for decades, Caterpillar's big ticket items virtually sold themselves. But environmental factors, such as the U.S. budget deficit, the Gulf states oil crunch, and the Asian crisis, resulted in fewer large-scale highway and construction projects. The company then expanded to smaller equipment to remain competitive globally.

Costs

Costs are frequently used as a basis for price determination largely because they are easily measured and provide a floor under which prices cannot go in the long term. These include procurement, manufacturing, logistics, and marketing costs, as well as overhead. Quality at an affordable price drives most procurement systems. The decision to turn to offshore suppliers may often be influenced by their lower prices, which enable the marketer to remain competitive.[34] Locating manufacturing facilities in different parts of the world may lower various costs, such as labor or distribution costs, although this may create new challenges. While a market may be attractive as far as labor costs are concerned, issues such as productivity, additional costs (such as logistics), and political risk will have to be factored in. Furthermore, a country may lose its attraction due to increasing costs (for example, the average industrial wage rose 110 percent in Korea in the 1990s), and the marketer may have to start the cycle anew by going to new markets (such as Indonesia or Vietnam).

Varying inflation rates will have a major impact on the administration of prices, especially because they are usually accompanied by government controls. The task of the parent company is to aid subsidiaries in their planning to ensure reaching margin targets despite unfavorable market conditions. Most experienced companies in the emerging markets generally have strong country managers who create significant value through their understanding of the local environment. Their ability to be more agile in a turbulent environment is a significant competitive advantage. Inflationary environments call for constant price adjustments; in markets with hyperinflation, pricing may be in a stable currency such as the U.S. dollar or the euro with daily translation into the local currency. In such volatile environments, the marketer may want to shift supply arrangements to cost-effective alternatives, pursue rapid inventory turnovers, shorten credit terms, and make sure contracts have appropriate safety mechanisms against inflation (e.g., choice of currency or escalator clause).

The opposite scenario may also be encountered; that is, prices cannot be increased due to economic conditions. Inflation has been kept in check in developed economies for a number of reasons. Globalization has increased the number of competitors, and the Internet has made it easy for customers to shop for the lowest prices. Big intermediaries, such as Wal-Mart, are demanding prices at near cost from their suppliers. In Europe, the advent of the euro has made prices even more transparent.[35] Strategies for thriving in disinflationary times may include (1) target pricing, in which efficiencies are sought in production and marketing to meet price-driven costing; (2) value pricing, to move away from coupons, discounts, and promotions to everyday low prices; (3) stripping down products, to offer quality without all the frills; (4) adding value by introducing innovative products sold at a modest premium (accompanied by strong merchandising and promotion) but perceived by customers to be worth it; and (5) getting close to customers by using new technologies (such as the Internet and EDI) to track their needs and your costs more closely.[36] An example of Nike's adjustment to the new realities in Asia appears in *The International Marketplace 16.2*.

Internally, controversy may arise in determining which manufacturing and marketing costs to include. For example, controversy may arise over the amounts of research and development to charge to subsidiaries or over how to divide the costs of a pan-regional advertising campaign when costs are incurred primarily on satellite channels and viewership varies dramatically from one market to the next.

Demand and Market Factors

Demand will set a price ceiling in a given market. Despite the difficulties in obtaining data on foreign markets and forecasting potential demand, the global marketer must make judgments concerning the quantities that can be sold at different prices in each foreign market. The global marketer must understand the **price elasticity of consumer demand** to determine appropriate price levels, especially if cost structures change. A status-conscious market that insists on products with established reputations will be inelastic, allowing for far more pricing freedom than a market where price-consciousness drives demand. Many U.S. and European companies have regarded Japan as a place to sell premium products at premium prices. With the increased information and travel that globalization has brought about, status-consciousness is being replaced by a more practical consumerist sensibility: top quality at competitive prices.

The marketer's freedom in making pricing decisions is closely tied to customer perceptions of the product offering and the marketing communication tied to it. Toyota is able to outsell Chevys, which are identical and both produced by NUMMI Inc., which is a joint venture between Toyota and GM, even though its

THE INTERNATIONAL MARKETPLACE   16.2

Just Do It in a Recession!

Nike's international revenues have gradually grown to $4.4 billion, matching U.S. revenues of $4.7 billion (in 2001). While U.S. growth has been slower, Asia grew at a rate of 24 percent in the third quarter of 2002, with soccer footwear leading the way.

With the Asian recession having sapped purchasing power in Southeast Asia, Nike has targeted teens living in the region's rural and suburban areas with a range of "entry-level" footwear. The Nike Play Series line, launched in September 1999 in India, Indonesia, Singapore, and Thailand, retails for about $25, roughly half the price of most Nike shoes and far less than the $150 charged for its top-range products.

Asian kids in rural areas might be playing sports with no shoes at all, so they cannot relate to Nike's high-end products. Nike Play Series was created to introduce them to the concept of different shoes for different sports. Even among those who purchase luxury products, sales

have fallen 30 percent in the Asian markets hardest hit by the 1997–1998 Asian currency crisis.

Ads for the new product line use the slogan "It's My Turn" and depict young Asian athletes (such as Singaporean soccer sensation Aliff Shafaein and Philippine basketball star Alvin Patrimonio) alongside images of major sports stars. Nike also built branded Play Zones in new or refurbished urban centers such as Singapore, Kuala Lumpur, Bangkok, Manila, and Johor Bahru. Each includes a multicourt facility where kids play everything from badminton to basketball, highlighted by "event days" with tournaments. In rural areas, Nike donated equipment such as basketball hoops and football goal posts to raise the profile of the Nike Play Series.

SOURCES: "How Nike Got Its Game Back," *Business Week*, November 4, 2002, 129; Normandy Madden, "Nike Sells $25 Shoe Line in Recession-Hit Region," *Advertising Age*, November 1999, 17; and **http://nikebiz.com/community/gcastry.shtml**.

version (the Corolla) is priced $2,000 higher on the average. Similarly, Korean automakers have had a challenging time in shedding their image as a risky purchase. For example, consumers who liked the Hyundai Santa Fe said they would pay $10,000 less because it was a Hyundai.[37] Hyundai has made major inroads into improving quality perceptions with its ten-year drive train warranty policy (which is very expensive, however).

Prices have to be set keeping in mind not only the ultimate consumers but also the intermediaries involved. The success of a particular pricing strategy will depend on the willingness of both the manufacturer and the intermediary to cooperate. For example, if the marketer wants to undercut its competition, it has to make sure that retailers' margins remain adequate and competitive to ensure appropriate implementation. At the same time, there is enormous pressure on manufacturers' margins from the side of intermediaries who are growing in both size and global presence. These intermediaries, such as the French Carrefour and the British Marks & Spencer, demand low-cost, direct-supply contracts, which many manufacturers may not be willing or able to furnish.[38] The only other option may be to resort to alternate distribution modes, which may be impossible.

Market Structure and Competition

Competition helps set the price within the parameters of cost and demand. Depending on the marketer's objectives and competitive position, it may choose to compete directly on price or elect for nonprice measures. If a pricing response is sought, the marketer can offer bundled prices (e.g., value deals on a combination of products) or loyalty programs to insulate the firm from a price war. Price cuts can also be executed selectively rather than across the board. New products can be introduced to counter price challenges. For example, when Japanese Kao introduced a low-priced diskette to compete against 3M, rather than drop its prices 3M introduced a new brand, Highland, that effectively flanked Kao's competitive incursion. Simply dropping the price on the 3M brand could have badly diluted its image. On the nonprice front, the company can opt to fight back on quality by adding and promoting value-adding features.[39]

If a company's position is being eroded by competitors who focus on price, the marketer may have no choice but to respond. For example, IBM's operation in Japan lost market share in mainframes largely because competitors undersold the company. A Japanese mainframe was typically listed at 10 percent less than its IBM counterpart, and it frequently carried an additional 10 to 20 percent discount beyond that. This created an extremely competitive market. IBM's reaction was to respond in kind with aggressive promotion of its own, with the result that it began regaining its lost share. Motorola and Nokia, the leading mobile phone makers, are facing tough conditions in the Korean market. In addition to being competitive in price and quality, local companies such as Samsung and Goldstar are quick to come up with new models to satisfy the fast-changing needs of consumers while providing better after-sales service, free of charge or at a marginal price, than the two global players.[40]

In some cases, strategic realignment may be needed. To hold on to its eroding worldwide market share, Caterpillar has strived to shrink costs and move away from its old practice of competing only by building advanced, enduring machines and selling them at premium prices. Instead, the company has cut prices and has used strategic alliances overseas to produce competitive equipment to better suit local and regional needs.

Some marketers can fend off price competition by emphasizing other elements of the marketing mix, even if they are at an absolute disadvantage in price. Singer Sewing Machine Co., which gains nearly half its $500 million in non-U.S. sales from developing countries, emphasizes its established reputation, product quality, and liberal credit terms, as well as other services (such as sewing classes), rather than compete head-on with lower-cost producers.[41] At $40 to $60, jeans are not affordable to the masses in developing countries. Arvind, the world's fifth-largest denim maker, introduced "Ruf & Tuf" jeans—a ready-to-make kit of jeans components priced at $6 which could be assembled inexpensively by a local tailor.[42]

The pricing behavior of a global marketer may come under scrutiny in important market sectors, such as automobiles or retailing. If local companies lose significant market share to outsiders as a result of lower prices, they may ask for government interference against alleged dumping. Wal-Mart resigned from Mexico's National Retailers Association to protest an ethics code that members approved prohibiting price comparisons in ads by their members (on the basis of negative publicity for other retailers). Since ad campaigns are the key to Wal-Mart's "everyday low prices" strategy, it had no choice but to leave the organization.[43]

Environmental Constraints

Governments influence prices and pricing directly as well. In addition to the policy measures, such as tariffs and taxes, governments may also elect to directly control price levels. Once under **price controls,** the global marketer has to operate as it would in a regulated industry. Setting maximum prices has been defended primarily on political grounds: It stops inflation and an accelerating wage-price spiral, and consumers want it. Supporters also maintain that price controls raise the income of the poor. Operating in such circumstances is difficult. Achieving change in prices can be frustrating; for example, a company may wait 30 to 45 days for an acknowledgment of a price-increase petition.

To fight price controls, multinational corporations can demonstrate that they are getting an unacceptable return on investment and that, without an acceptable profit opportunity, future investments will not be made and production perhaps will be stopped. These have been the arguments of U.S. and European pharmaceutical marketers in China.[44] Cadbury Schweppes sold its plant in Kenya because price controls made its operation unprofitable. At one time, Coca-Cola and PepsiCo withdrew their products from the shelves in Mexico until they received a price increase. Pakistani milk producers terminated their business when they could not raise prices, and Glaxo Wellcome, a pharmaceutical manufacturer, canceled its expansion plans in Pakistan because of price controls.

In general, company representatives can cite these consequences in arguing against price controls: (1) the maximum price often becomes the minimum price if a sector is allowed a price increase, because all businesses in the sector will take it regardless of cost justification; (2) the wage-price spiral advances vigorously in anticipation of controls; (3) labor often turns against restrictions because they are usually accompanied by an income policy or wage restrictions; (4) noninflationary wage increases are forestalled; (5) government control not only creates a costly regulatory body but also is difficult to enforce; (6) authorities raise less in taxes because less money is made; and (7) a government may have to bail out many companies with cheap loans or make grants to prevent bankruptcies and unemployment.[45] Once price controls are invoked, management will have to devote much time to resolving the many difficulties that controls present. The best interest of multinational corporations is therefore served by working with governments, especially in the developing countries, to establish an economic policy centered on a relatively free market without price controls. This means, for example, that pharmaceutical firms need to convince governments that their products greatly benefit the public and that their prices are reasonable. If the companies can point to R&D focused on solving local challenges, the argument can be made more convincingly.

Pricing Coordination

The issue of standard worldwide pricing is mostly a theoretical one because of the influence of the factors already discussed. However, coordination of the pricing function is necessary, especially in larger, regional markets such as the European

Union, especially after the introduction of the euro. With the increasing level of integration efforts around the world, and even discussion of common currency elsewhere, control and coordination of global and regional pricing takes on a new meaning.

With more global and regional brands in the global marketer's offering, control in pricing is increasingly important. Of course, this has to be balanced against the need for allowing subsidiaries latitude in pricing so that they may quickly react to specific market conditions.

Studies have shown that foreign-based multinational corporations allow their U.S. subsidiaries considerable freedom in pricing. This has been explained by the size and unique features of the market. Further, it has been argued that these subsidiaries often control the North American market (that is, a Canadian customer cannot get a better deal in the United States, and vice versa) and that distances create a natural barrier against arbitrage practices that would be more likely to emerge in Europe, although even with the common currency, different rules and standards, economic disparities, and information differences may make deal-hunting difficult.[46] However, recent experience has shown that pricing coordination has to be worldwide because parallel imports will surface in any markets in which price discrepancies exist, regardless of distances.

The Euro and Marketing Strategy

On January 1, 1999, the euro (€) was officially launched by the European Union and it became the one and only currency of the 12 nations in the eurozone, or Euroland, January 1, 2002. Although the early focus was largely on managing the operational aspects of converting to the use of the euro for all business activities (such as preparing to account for sales and purchasing in euros as well as transforming internal accounting for areas such as R&D budgeting), the strategic issues are the most significant for the future.

In the longer term all firms will need to reexamine the positioning of their businesses. The potential advantages of a single-currency Europe (such as a more competitive market, both internally and externally) have been widely expounded, but the threats to businesses of all nationalities, sizes, and forms have not been so widely discussed. The threats are many. As barriers to the creation of a single domestic market are eliminated, more production and operating strategy decisions will be made on the basis of true-cost differentials (proximity to specific inputs, materials, immobile skills, or niche customers, for example). Consolidation will be the norm for many business units whose existence was in some way perpetuated by the uses of different currencies. This restructuring will have lasting effects on the European business landscape. For example, many marketers are streamlining their operations throughout Euroland and eliminating overlapping entities, such as distribution facilities.[47]

The euro will push national markets closer together. First and foremost in this area is the transparency to consumers of a single currency and a single cross-border price. The euro combined with the growing use of e-business, for example, will allow consumers in Barcelona to surf the Web for the cheapest source of fresh seafood delivered from anywhere within the EU12. Although theoretically possible before, the quotation of prices by individual currency and complexity of payment often posed a barrier—somewhat real, somewhat imagined—to cross-border purchasing. This barrier no longer exists, as consumers are now able to demand the highest quality product and service at the lowest price from businesses throughout the European community.

A more troublesome result is pricing, both within the firm and to the marketplace. Within the firm, the transfer prices between business units of the firm, whether in-country or cross-border, will now be held to an even more rigorous standard of no differentiation. Transfer prices internationally, however, are one of the key factors in how firms reposition profits in order to reduce their global tax burdens. Without this veil of differences in currency of denomination, any differences in transfer prices across multinational units will be even more apparent (and will not be allowed).

The pricing to the market and to the consumer is a more strategic concern. A price set for a particular demand segment, a pricing-point, in one currency such as the French franc will now need to be reset in euro. For example, imagine a French boutique's pricing of a Parisian cologne that has a long-established price of FF99. The euro price, which will now be posted on the boutique's shelf side by side with the franc price, will be:

$$\frac{FF99.00}{(FF6.55957/\text{€})} = \text{€}15.09.$$

But at €15.09, the consumer is faced with a qualitatively different price.[48] Should the Parisian boutique cut the franc price to FF98.33 (reducing the profit margin) so that the euro price is €14.99, or keep the price the same believing the consumer will continue to focus on the franc price first, the euro second? If the price is kept the same in francs, will this pricing in euro remain second in the minds of the consumer? Almost every pricing strategy both within and without the EU12 (U.S. or Japanese exporters who price product in local currency—now the euro—will have to likewise worry) will now have to be reevaluated.

Firms must plan strong promotional and educational materials for their products and services to allow consumers to adequately assess comparable qualities and characteristics given the transparency in pricing. Consumers in many of the EU12 are still figuring prices in the old currency and are wary that the euro conversion has allowed marketers to increase prices. Despite some isolated cases of increases, EU12 price indexes have not risen dramatically and no cause and effect has been shown with the introduction of the euro.[49]

The single currency has made prices completely transparent for all buyers. If discrepancies are not justifiable due to market differences such as consumption preferences, competition, or government interference, parallel importation may occur. The simplest solution would be to have one euro price throughout the market. However, given the huge differences of up to 100 percent at the present (as shown in Figure 16.1), that solution would lead to significant losses in sales and

Figure 16.1 | Price Differentials across European Consumer Goods Markets

Percent difference between highest and lowest

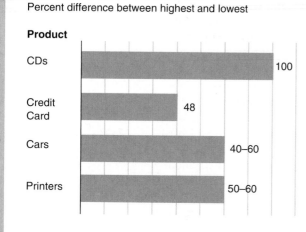

Product		Sample Size No. of countries	Highest price	Lowest price
CDs	100	6	France	Belgium
Credit Card	48	11	Austria	Spain
Cars	40–60	12	Varies by model and brand	
Printers	50–60	3	Italy	UK

SOURCE: Adapted from Johan Ahlberg, Nicklas Garemo, and Tomas Nauclér, "The Euro: How to Keep Your Prices Up and Your Competitors Down," *The McKinsey Quarterly* 35 (no. 2, 1999): 112–118.

profits, as a single price would likely be closer to the lower-priced countries' level. The recommended approach is a pricing corridor that considers existing country-specific prices while optimizing the profits at a pan-European level.[50] As described in *The International Marketplace 16.3*, such a corridor defines the maximum and minimum prices that country organizations can charge—enough to allow flexibility as a result of differences in price elasticities, competition, and positioning, but not enough to attract parallel imports that may start at price differences of 20 percent and higher.[51] This approach moves pricing authority away from country managers to regional management and requires changes in management systems and incentive structures.

In terms of specific pricing approaches, marketers should aim to lower prices as slowly as possible, especially for less price-sensitive customers. Alternatives include developing selective offers to price-sensitive customers using discounts and long-term contracts—measures that put considerably less downward pressure on prices across all customers. In addition, marketers can enhance the value of product and service offerings selectively, and thereby maintain price differentials across Europe.[52]

THE INTERNATIONAL MARKETPLACE 16.3

Coordinating Prices in Integrating Markets

Price differentials can survive across individual European Union markets only if marketers act decidedly. This calls for centralizing pricing authority and establishing "pricing corridors." Some marketers may have to pull out of low-margin markets where price increases cannot be sustained.

Future European price levels will be markedly lower than current ones, and firms must take quick action to avoid seeing prices fall to the lowest level prevailing in marginal markets. This is due to the large differentials that existed and continue to exist among EU member states. Prices in markets such as Portugal and Spain are often significantly lower than those in northern Europe markets, where consumers can afford much larger margins and where costs are higher. The differentials can range from 30 percent for natural yogurt to as much as 200 percent for pharmaceuticals. Even among northern nations, a 2001 European Commission study found that consumers in the United Kingdom were paying 66 percent more for the exact same car model as their counterparts in the Netherlands.

Parallel imports into affluent markets will force prices down as buyers simply go to the cheapest available source for their goods. If manufacturers leave it to market forces, prices may go down to the lowest level. For example, Portugal may influence prices in Germany through parallel imports. The parallel market in pharmaceuticals is worth $1 billion in the United Kingdom alone.

In order to avoid this, manufacturers must compromise now between the current policy of individually optimized prices and a uniform European price. Such a compromise will be possible because, even after the 1992 phenomenon and the introduction of the euro, Europe has not become a homogeneous market. Consumer habits will adjust gradually, allowing certain price differentials to be retained and defended.

Some experts recommend that manufacturers set up a European pricing corridor dropping high prices somewhat and raising low ones, creating a sustainable differential among markets in member states. The corridor would be much narrower for easily transportable items like photographic film than for heavy ones such as industrial machinery.

These changing market conditions imply a new focus on centralized price setting for Europe. The price corridor will be set by the head office, with local subsidiaries free to set prices within it. This approach runs contrary to the prevailing corporate culture, which is based on decentralization.

Manufacturers ought to consider pulling out of poorer markets where price hikes cannot be sustained. It is better to lose a small percentage of sales rather than see turnover, margins, and profits plummet. So far, however, there appears to be little movement toward more centralized pricing. Some experts are concerned by the lack of urgency apparently felt by many European executives, who seem content to wait and see what happens.

Indeed, a number of European industrialists argue that large price differences can be maintained in Europe through product differentiation. Simpler products could be sold into less-prosperous markets, whereas more elaborate items might go to those markets that are able to afford them.

In at least one industry—pharmaceuticals—executives fear that neither pricing corridors nor product differences will prevent prices from falling to the lowest level.

In markets such as France, Spain, and Portugal, prices for drugs are already very low because of national reimbursement schemes.

"We are sandwiched between the European Commission, which is determined to eliminate all trade barriers at whatever cost, and some national governments that are keeping pharmaceutical products artifically low," comments an executive at a major European drug maker. "In practice, the Commission has absolutely no control over the prices set by national governments." Pharmaceutical firms, which have heavy research and development costs, say they need high margins if they are to continue investing and competing with Japanese and U.S. companies. But if countries such as France, which accounts for a substantial part of the European drug market, continue to keep prices low, customers from other countries will simply buy their supplies in those markets. Manufacturers may well find themselves locked in an untenable position in an industry in which specifications are standardized, products cannot be differentiated, and suppliers cannot withdraw from the market for ethical reasons.

SOURCES: "Common Good," *The Economist—A Survey of European Business and the Euro*, December 1, 2001, 8–10; "Cure-All Wanted," *The Economist—A Survey of European Business and the Euro*, December 1, 2001, 13–14; "Car Prices in Britain Are Still the Highest in Europe," *Independent*, February 20, 2001, 11; Stephen A. Butscher, "Maximizing Profits in Euroland," *Journal of Commerce*, May 5, 1999, 5; "Pricing in Post 1992 EC: Expert Urges Fast Action to Protect Margins," *Business International*, August 24, 1992, 267; and **http://europa.eu.int/euro/quest**.

Multinational customers, such as Coca-Cola or IBM, like to drive hard bargains with their suppliers, seeking low and consistent prices worldwide. This can become a problem when some suppliers provide steep discounts in emerging markets such as China, while keeping prices higher in developed markets. Marketers should make sure that price differences reflect differences in quality or in the services provided. Many industrial companies try to coordinate panregional purchasing in Europe by empowering an individual or department to do so. However, many of them still have national structures whereby country organizations retain considerable say-so in what is bought. Marketers can take advantage of this separation of decision-making power and influence.

Countertrade

The Australian government declares that it will only purchase military aircraft from the United States if the U.S. navy and marine corps will buy lollipops from an Australian firm, Allen Sweets Ltd.[53] General Motors exchanged automobiles for a trainload of strawberries. The government of India has swapped palm oil from Sudan for the construction of a railroad link. All these are examples of countertrade activities carried out around the world.

Countertrade is a sale that encompasses more than an exchange of goods, services, or ideas for money. In the international market, countertrade transactions "are those transactions which have as a basic characteristic a linkage, legal or otherwise, between exports and imports of goods or services in addition to, or in place of, financial settlements."[54] Historically, countertrade was mainly conducted in the form of barter, which is a direct exchange of goods of approximately equal value, with no money involved. These transactions were the very essence of business at times when no money—that is, a common medium of exchange—existed or was available. Over time, money emerged to unlink transactions from individual parties and permit greater flexibility in trading activities. Repeatedly, however, we can see returns to the barter system as a result of economic circumstances. For example, because of tight financial constraints, Georgetown University, during its initial years of operation after 1789, charged its students part of the tuition in foodstuffs and required students to participate in the construction of university buildings. During periods of high inflation in Europe in the 1920s, goods such as bread, meat, and gold were seen as much more useful and secure than paper money, which decreased in real value every hour.

Countertrade transactions have therefore always arisen when economic circumstances have encouraged a direct exchange of goods rather than the use of money as an intermediary. Conditions that encourage such business activities are lack of money, lack of value of money, lack of acceptability of money as an exchange medium, or greater ease of transaction by using goods. However, the shrinking of established markets and the existence of a substantial product surplus are also conditions that foster countertrade.

These same reasons prevail in today's resurgence of countertrade activities. Throughout the past decades, the use of countertrade has steadily increased. In 1972, countertrade was used by only 15 countries. By 1983, the countries conducting countertrade transactions numbered 88, and by the late 1990s the number was more than 100. Estimates of the total global countertrade volume vary widely. The British government estimates that countertrade transactions make up between 10 percent and 15 percent of world trade.[55]

Why Countertrade?

Many countries are deciding that countertrade transactions are more beneficial to them than transactions based on financial exchange alone. A primary reason is that world debt crises and exchange rate volatility have made ordinary trade financing very risky. Many countries in the developing world cannot obtain the trade credit or financial assistance necessary to afford desired imports. Heavily indebted nations, faced with the possibility of not being able to afford imports at all, resort to countertrade to maintain product inflow.

The use of countertrade permits the covert reduction of prices and therefore allows firms and governments to circumvent price and exchange controls. Particularly in commodity markets with operative cartel arrangements, such as oil or agriculture, this benefit may be very useful to a producer. For example, by using oil as a countertraded product for industrial equipment, a surreptitious discount (by using a higher price for the acquired products) may expand market share. In a similar fashion, the countertrading of products at higher prices than their economic value has the potential to mask dumping activities.[56]

Countertrade is also often viewed by firms and nations alike as an excellent mechanism to gain entry into new markets. When a producer believes that marketing is not its strong suit, particularly in product areas that face strong international competition, it often sees countertrade as useful. The producer often hopes that the party receiving the goods will serve as a new distributor, opening up new international marketing channels and ultimately expanding the original market. Conversely, markets with high demand and little cash can provide major opportunities for firms if they are willing to accept countertrade. A firm that welcomes countertrade welcomes new buyers and sets itself apart from the competition.

Countertrade also can provide stability for long-term sales. For example, if a firm is tied to a countertrade agreement, it will need to source the product from a particular supplier, whether or not it wants to do so. This stability is often valued very highly because it eliminates, or at least reduces, vast swings in demand and thus allows for better planning.

Under certain conditions, countertrade can ensure the quality of an international transaction. In instances where the seller of technology is paid in output produced by the technology delivered, the seller's revenue depends on the success of the technology transfer and maintenance services in production. Therefore, the seller is more likely to be dedicated in the provision of services, maintenance, and general technology transfer.[57] In such instances, the second part of the transaction serves as a "hostage" that induces both trading partners to fulfill their contractual obligations. Particularly under conditions of limited legal and social protection, countertrade can be equated to an exchange of hostages that ensures that all parties involved live up to their agreement.[58]

In spite of all these apparent benefits of countertrade, there are strong economic arguments against this activity. These arguments are based mainly on efficiency grounds. As economist Paul Samuelson stated, "Instead of there being a double coincidence of wants, there is likely to be a want of coincidence; so that, unless a hungry tailor happens to find an undraped farmer, who has both food and a desire for a pair of pants, neither can make a trade."[59] Instead of trade balances being settled on a multilateral basis, with surpluses from one country being balanced by deficits with another, countertrade requires that accounts must now be settled on a country-by-country or even transaction-by-transaction basis. Trade then results only from the ability of two parties or countries to purchase specified goods from one another rather than from competition. As a result, uncompetitive goods may be marketed. In consequence, the ability of countries and their industries to adjust structurally to more efficient production may be restricted. Countertrade can therefore be seen as eroding the quality and efficiency of production and as lowering world consumption. These economic arguments notwithstanding, however, countries and companies increasingly see countertrade as an alternative that may be flawed but worthwhile to undertake. As far as the unilateral focus is concerned, it may well be that this restriction can be removed through electronic commerce. With growing ease of reach, it may well become possible to create an online global barter economy that addresses itself to those transactions that cannot be conducted on regular financial terms.

Types of Countertrade

Under the traditional types of **barter** arrangements, goods are exchanged directly for other goods of approximately equal value. However, simple barter transactions are less often used today.

Increasingly, participants in countertrade have resorted to more sophisticated versions of exchanging goods that often also include some use of money. Figure 16.2 provides an overview of the different forms of countertrade that are in use today. One refinement of simple barter is the **counterpurchase,** or parallel barter, agreement. The participating parties sign two separate contracts that specify the goods and services to be exchanged. Frequently, the exchange is not of precisely equal value; therefore, some amount of cash will be involved. However, because an exchange of goods for goods does take place, the transaction can rightfully be called barter.

Another common form of countertrade is the **buyback,** or compensation, arrangement. One party agrees to supply technology or equipment that enables the other party to produce goods with which the price of the supplied products or technology is repaid. One example of such a buyback arrangement is an agreement entered into by Levi Strauss and Hungary. The company transferred the know-how and the Levi's trademark to Hungary. A Hungarian firm began producing Levi's products. Some of the output is sold domestically, and the rest is marketed in Western Europe by Levi Strauss, in compensation for the know-how.

A more refined form of barter, aimed at reducing the effect of the immediacy of the transaction, is called **clearing arrangements.** Here, clearing accounts are established in which firms can deposit and withdraw the results of their countertrade activities. These currencies merely represent purchasing power, however, and are not directly withdrawable in cash. As a result, each party can agree in a single contract to purchase goods or services of a specified value. Although the account may be out of balance on a transaction-by-transaction basis, the agreement stipulates that over the long term, a balance in the account will be restored. Frequently, the goods available for purchase with clearing account funds are tightly stipulated. In fact, funds have on occasion been labeled "apple clearing dollars" or "horseradish clearing funds." Sometimes, additional flexibility is given to the clearing account by permitting **switch-trading,** in which credits in the account can be sold or transferred to a third party. Doing so can provide creative intermediaries with opportunities for deal making by identifying clearing account

Figure 16.2   Classification of Forms of Countertrade

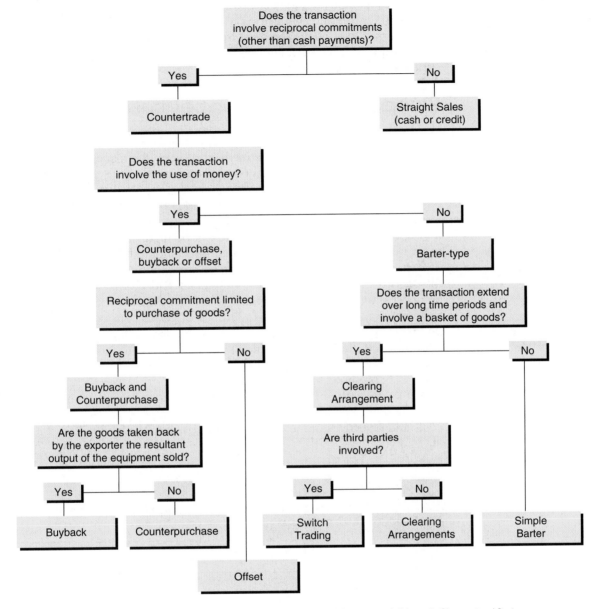

SOURCE: Adapted from Jean-François Hennart, "Some Empirical Dimensions of Countertrade," *Journal of International Business Studies* 21 (no. 2, 1990): 245.

relationships with major imbalances and structuring business transactions to reduce them.

Another key form of barter arrangement is called **offset,** which is the industrial compensation mandated by governments when purchasing defense-related goods and services in order to offset the effect of this purchase on the balance of payments. Offsets can include coproduction, licenses production, subcontractor production, technology transfer, or overseas investment. Typically, in order to secure the sale of military equipment, the selling companies have to offset the cost of the arms through investment in nonrelated industries. The offsets frequently reach or exceed the price of the defense equipment, to the delight of the buyer, but often to the chagrin of the home country government of the selling firms. U.S. weapons exporters alone are estimated to complete about $1 to $3 billion annually in defense offset transactions, which, according to some, may over time strengthen foreign competitors and adversely affect employment.[60]

With the increasing sophistication of countertrade, the original form of straight barter is used less today. The most frequently completed forms of countertrade are counterpurchase, buyback agreements and, due to continued major military expenditures around the world, offsets.

Preparing for Countertrade

Early on in the countertrade process a firm needs to decide whether it wishes to use an outside countertrade intermediary or keep the management of the transaction in-house. Assistance from intermediaries can be quite expensive but relieves the firm of the need to learn a new expertise. Table 16.3 provides a summary of the advantages and disadvantages of carrying out countertrade transactions within versus outsourcing them. If companies carry out countertrade transactions in-house, the profitability of countertrade can be high. However, developing an in-house capability for handling countertrade should be done with great caution.

First, the company needs to determine the import priorities of its products to the country or firm to which it is trying to sell. Goods that are highly desirable and necessary for a country mandating countertrade are less likely to be subject to countertrade requirements than imports of goods considered luxurious and unnecessary. As a next step, the company needs to incorporate possible countertrade cost into the pricing scheme. It is quite difficult to increase the price of goods once a "cash-deal" price has been quoted and a subsequent countertrade demand is presented.

At this stage, the most favored countertrade arrangement from the buyer's perspective should be identified. To do this, the company needs to determine the goals and objectives of the countertrading parties. As already discussed, these can

Table 16.3	**Organizing for Countertrade: In-House versus Third Parties**

Advantages	Disadvantages
In-House	
• More profitable	• Accounting and legal expertise required
• Customer contact	• Reselling problems
• Greater control	• Recruitment and training costs
• More flexibility	• Less objectivity
• More learning	• Unexpected risks and demands for countertrade
Third Parties	
• Export specialists	• May be expensive
• Customer contacts	• Distanced from customer
• Reselling contacts	• Less flexibility
• Legal and accounting expertise	• Less confidentiality
• More objectivity	• Less learning

SOURCE: Adapted from Charles W. Neale, David D. Shipley, and J. Colin Dodds, "The Countertrading Experience of British and Canadian Firms," *Management International Review* 31 (no. 1, 1991): 33.

consist of import substitution, a preservation of hard currency, export promotion, and so on.

The next step is to match the strengths of the firm with current and potential countertrade situations. The company should explore whether any internal sourcing needs can be used to fulfill a countertrade contract. This may mean that raw materials or intermediate products currently sourced from other suppliers could now be obtained from the countertrade partner. However, this assessment should not be restricted to the internal corporate use of a countertraded product. The company should also determine whether it can use, for example, its distribution capabilities or its contacts with other customers and suppliers to help in its countertrade transactions. Moreover, an increase in the use of mandated countertrade by governments, combined with a more proactive approach toward such transactions by firms, may well result in companies expecting their suppliers to share in the burdensome effects of countertrade. Based on the notion that the supplier benefits from the export taking place due to the countertrade, main contractors may demand that major suppliers participate in disposing of the countertraded goods. As a result, even companies that do not see themselves as international marketers may suddenly be confronted with countertrade demands.

At this point, the company can decide whether it should engage in countertrade transactions. The accounting and taxation aspects of the countertrade transactions should be considered because they can often be quite different from current procedures. The use of an accounting or tax professional is essential to comply with difficult and obscure tax regulations in this area.

Next, all of the risks involved in countertrade must be assessed. This means that the goods to be obtained need to be specified, that the delivery time for these goods needs to be determined, and that the reliability of the supplier and the quality and consistency of the goods need to be assessed. It is also useful to explore the impact of countertrade on future prices, both for the price of the specific goods obtained and for the world market price of the category of goods. For example, a countertrade transaction may appear to be quite profitable at the time of agreement. Because months or even years may pass before the transaction is actually consummated, however, a change in world market prices may severely affect the profitability. The effect of a countertrade transaction on the world market price should also be considered. In cases of large-volume transactions, the established price may be affected due to a glut of supply. Such a situation not only may affect the profitability of a transaction but also can result in possible legal actions, by other suppliers of similar products who feel injured by the price effects.

When evaluating the countertraded products, it is useful to determine the impact of the countertraded products on the sales and profits of other complementary product lines currently marketed by the firm. What, if any, repercussions will come about from outside groups should also be investigated. Such repercussions may consist of antidumping actions brought about by competitors or reactions from totally unsuspected quarters. For example, McDonnell Douglas ran into strong opposition when it bartered an airplane for ham used in its employee cafeteria and as Christmas gifts. The local meat-packers' union complained vociferously that McDonnell Douglas was threatening the jobs of its members and went on strike.

Using all of the information obtained, the company can finally evaluate the length of the intended relationship with the countertrading partner and the importance of this relationship for future plans and goals. These parameters will be decisive for the final action because they may form constraints overriding short-term economic effects. Overall, management needs to remember that, in most instances, a countertrade transaction should remain a means for successful international marketing and not become an end in itself.

Summary

In a world of increasing competition, government regulation, accelerating inflation, and widely fluctuating exchange rates, global marketers must spend increasing amounts of time planning pricing strategy. Because pricing is the only revenue-generating element of the marketing mix, its role in meeting corporate objectives is enhanced. However, it comes under increasing governmental scrutiny as well, as evidenced by intracompany transfer pricing.

The three philosophies of transfer pricing that have emerged over time are cost-based, market-based, and arm's-length. Transfer pricing concerns are both internal and external to the company. Internally, manipulating transfer prices may complicate control procedures and documentation. Externally, problems arise from the tax and regulatory entities of the countries involved.

Pricing decisions are typically left to the local managers; however, planning assistance is provided by the parent company. Pricing in individual markets comes under the influence of environmental variables, each market with its own unique set. This set consists of corporate objectives, costs, customer behavior and market conditions, market structure, and environmental constraints.

The individual impact of these variables and the result of their interaction must be thoroughly understood by the global marketer, especially if regional, or even worldwide, coordination is attempted. Control and coordination are becoming more important with increasing economic integration.

Corporations are increasingly using countertrade as a competitive tool to maintain or increase market share. The complexity of these transactions requires careful planning in order to avoid major corporate losses. Management must consider how the acquired merchandise will be disposed of, what the potential for market disruptions is, and to what extent the countertraded goods fit with the corporate mission.

Key Terms

arm's-length price
arm's-length standard
price elasticity of consumer demand
price controls
countertrade
barter

counterpurchase
buyback
clearing arrangements
switch-trading
offset

Questions for Discussion

1. Comment on the pricing philosophy "Sometimes price should be wrong by design."
2. The standard worldwide base price is most likely looked on by management as full-cost pricing, including an allowance for manufacturing overhead, general overhead, and selling expenses. What factors are overlooked?
3. In combating price controls, multinational corporations will deal with agency administrators rather than policymakers. How can they convince administrators that price relief is fair to the company and also in the best interest of the host country?
4. Which elements of pricing can be standardized?
5. Using the price differences presented in Figure 16.1 as a base, argue why such price differences will stay in place even with the euro.
6. Discuss the advantages and drawbacks of countertrade.

Internet Exercises

1. What is behind the euro as a common currency? Utilizing the discussion prepared by the European Commission at **http://www.europa.eu.int/ euro/quest/**, determine what made the euro a possibility. See also **http://www.captaineuro. com**.

2. The euro will be either a source of competitive advantage or a disadvantage for marketers. Using "Euro case study: Siemens," available at **http:// news.bbc.co.uk/hi/english/events/the_launch_ of_emu**, assess the validity of the two points of view.

3. Compare the services provided by the Asia Pacific Countertrade Association and those provided by the American Countertrade Association (**http://www.apcatrade.org**; **http://www.countertrade.org**).

Recommended Readings

Carrero Caldreon, Jose Manuel. *Advance Pricing Agreements: A Global Analysis*. Cambridge, MA: Kluwer Law International, 1999.

Chabot, Christian N. *Understanding the Euro: The Clear and Concise Guide to the New Trans-European Currency*. New York: McGraw-Hill, 1998.

Dolan, Robert J., and Hermann Simon. *Power Pricing: How Managing Price Transforms the Bottom Line*. New York: Free Press, 1997.

Engelson, Morris. *Pricing Strategy: An Interdisciplinary Approach*. New York: Joint Management Strategy, 1995.

Feinschreiber, Robert. *Transfer Pricing Handbook*. New York: John Wiley & Sons, 2002.

Nagle, Thomas T., and Reed K. Holden. *The Strategy and Tactics of Pricing: A Guide to Profitable Decision Making*. New York: Pearson, 1994.

Tang, Y. W. *Current Trends and Corporate Cases in Transfer Pricing*. Westport, CT: Quorum Books, 2002.

Zurawicki, Leon. *International Countertrade*. New York: Pergamon Press, 2003.

chapter **17**

Logistics and
Supply Chain Management

THE INTERNATIONAL MARKETPLACE   17.1

How Does That HP Printer Get to Your Desk?

Picture the logistical task of sourcing 1 million printers and 7 million cartridges and distributing them to 600 wholesalers who service 50,000 merchants in 25 countries in Europe, the Middle East, and Africa. Then, imagine replicating this challenge to meet stringent transfer deadlines every month!

Sustaining this complex supply chain is the responsibility of Hewlett Packard's EMEA Regional Manufacturing and Distribution Operation located near Stuttgart, Germany. As Heinz Winkel, product completion manager, explains, "Our challenge is to ensure that we have the right products in the right locations at the right time. We are judged not just on the quality of our products but on our ability to deliver. Put simply, we aim to do exactly what we say we can do!"

So, just how does that new LaserJet arrive on your desk?

First, your order is broadcasted by the retailer via Electronic Data Interchange (EDI) and placed into HP's central data system, which is supervised by HP's global team of process technology managers. Your posting draws stocking information from ten independent European warehouses, and your order is confirmed.

Simultaneously, HP's Worldwide Product Generation Organization swings into action to assure availability. To effectively meet high demands with superior-quality products at competitive prices, HP taps the supply chain with contract manufacturing for activities that are outside its core competencies. Accordingly, your LaserJet's base engine will have already been assembled by a contracted manufacturer in China or Japan and shipped by an outsourced sea transporter to Europe via the Rotterdam. It arrives at one of the ten warehouses where local components are added. The localization and configuration not only ensures the functionality of the printers for local areas, but it also reduces HP's inventory expenses by 18 percent and shipping costs by the millions. Once the data system transmits your retailer's order to the appropriate warehouse, your LaserJet is transported to your retailer within two to seven days. Then, it's happy printing for you—all thanks to successful logistics and supply chain management.

SOURCE: "The HP Story: 60 Years of Innovation." **http://h40045.www4.hp.com/supply_chain_management/data/5980–8093EN.pdf**, accessed September 20, 2002.

FOR THE INTERNATIONAL FIRM, customer locations and sourcing opportunities are widely dispersed. The physical distribution and logistics aspects of international marketing therefore have great importance, as shown in *The International Marketplace 17.1*. To obtain and maintain favorable results from the complex international environment, the international logistics manager must coordinate activities globally, both within and outside of the firm. Neglect of logistics issues brings not only higher costs but also the risk of eventual noncompetitiveness due to diminished market share, more expensive supplies, or lower profits. In an era of new trade opportunities in regions that may be suffering from major shortcomings in logistical infrastructure, competent logistics management is more important than ever before.

This chapter will focus on international logistics and supply chain management. Primary areas of concentration will be the linkages between the firm, its suppliers, and its customers, as well as transportation, inventory, packaging, and storage issues. The logistics management problems and opportunities that are peculiar to international marketing will also be highlighted.

A Definition of International Logistics

International logistics is the design and management of a system that controls the flow of materials into, through, and out of the international corporation. It encompasses the total movement concept by covering the entire range of operations concerned with goods movement, including therefore both exports and imports simultaneously. By taking a systems approach, the firm explicitly recognizes the linkages among the traditionally separate logistics components within and outside of the corporation. By incorporating the interaction with outside organizations and individuals such as suppliers and customers, the firm is enabled to build on jointness of purpose by all partners in the areas of performance, quality, and timing. As a result of implementing these systems considerations successfully, the firm can develop just-in-time (JIT) delivery for lower inventory cost, electronic data interchange (EDI) for more efficient order processing, and early supplier involvement (ESI) for better planning of goods development and movement. In addition, the use of such a systems approach allows a firm to concentrate on its core competencies and to form outsourcing alliances with other companies. For example, a firm can choose to focus on manufacturing and leave all aspects of order filling and delivery to an outside provider. By working closely with customers such as retailers, firms can also develop efficient customer response (ECR) systems, which can track sales activity on the retail level. As a result, manufacturers can precisely coordinate production in response to actual shelf replenishment needs, rather than based on forecasts.

Two major phases in the movement of materials are of logistical importance. The first phase is **materials management,** or the timely movement of raw materials, parts, and supplies into and through the firm. The second phase is **physical distribution,** which involves the movement of the firm's finished product to its customers. In both phases, movement is seen within the context of the entire process. Stationary periods (storage and inventory) are therefore included. The basic goal of logistics management is the effective coordination of both phases and their various components to result in maximum cost-effectiveness while maintaining service goals and requirements.

The growth of logistics as a field has brought to the forefront three major concepts: the systems concept, the total cost concept, and the trade-off concept. The **systems concept** is based on the notion that materials-flow activities within and outside of the firm are so extensive and complex that they can be considered only in the context of their interaction. Instead of each corporate function, supplier, and customer operating with the goal of individual optimization, the systems concept stipulates that some components may have to work suboptimally to maximize the benefits of the system as a whole. The systems concept intends to provide the firm, its suppliers, and its customers, both domestic and foreign, with the benefits of synergism expected from the coordinated application of size.

In order for the systems concept to work, information flows and partnership trust are instrumental. Logistics capability is highly information dependent, since information availability is key to planning and to process implementation. Long-term partnership and trust are required in order to forge closer links between firms and managers.

A logical outgrowth of the systems concept is the development of the **total cost concept.** To evaluate and optimize logistical activities, cost is used as a basis for measurement. The purpose of the total cost concept is to minimize the firm's overall logistics cost by implementing the systems concept appropriately.

Implementation of the total cost concept requires that the members of the system understand the sources of costs. To develop such understanding, a system of activity-based costing has been developed, which is a technique designed to more accurately assign the indirect and direct resources of an organization to the activities performed based on consumption.[1] In the international arena, the total cost concept must also incorporate the consideration of total after-tax profit, by taking the impact of national tax policies on the logistics function into account. The objective is to maximize after-tax profits rather than minimizing total cost.

The **trade-off concept,** finally, recognizes the linkages within logistics systems that result from the interaction of their components. For example, locating a warehouse near the customer may reduce the cost of transportation. However, the new warehouse will lead to increased storage costs. Similarly, a reduction of inventories will save money but may increase the need for costly emergency shipments. Managers can maximize performance of logistics systems only by formulating decisions based on the recognition and analysis of such trade-offs. A trade-off of costs may go against one's immediate interests. Consider a manufacturer building several different goods. The goods all use one or both of two parts, A and B, which the manufacturer buys in roughly equal amounts. Most of the goods produced use both parts. The unit cost of part A is $7, of part B, $10. Part B has more capabilities than part A; in fact, B can replace A. If the manufacturer doubles its purchases of part B, it qualifies for a discounted $8 unit price. For products that incorporate both parts, substituting B for A makes sense to qualify for the discount, since the total parts cost is $17 using A and B, but only $16 using Bs only. Part B should therefore become a standard part for the manufacturer. But departments building products that only use part A may be reluctant to accept the substitute part B because, even discounted, the cost of B exceeds that of A. Use of the trade-off concept will solve the problem.[2]

Supply Chain Management

The integration of these three concepts has resulted in the new paradigm of **supply chain management,** where a series of value-adding activities connect a company's supply side with its demand side. This approach views the supply chain of the entire extended enterprise, beginning with the supplier's suppliers and ending with consumers or end users. The perspective encompasses the entire product and information and funds flow that form one cohesive link to acquire, purchase, convert/manufacture, assemble, and distribute goods and services to the ultimate consumers. The implementation effects of such supply chain management systems can be major. For example, it has permitted Wal-Mart, the largest U.S. retailer, to reduce inventories by 90 percent, which has saved the company hundreds of millions of dollars in inventory holding costs, and allows it to offer low prices to its customers.[3]

Advances in information technology have been crucial to progress in supply chain management. For example, companies such as GE and Pitney Bowes have implemented Web-based sourcing and payables systems. GE's Trading Process Network (**http://www.gxs.com**) allows GE Lighting's 25 production facilities and other buying facilities around the world to quickly find and purchase products from approved suppliers electronically. The electronic catalog information reflects the pricing and contract terms GE has negotiated with each of the suppliers and also ties in with GE's inventory and accounts payable systems. The result has been the virtual elimination of paper and mailing costs, a reduction in cycle time from 14 days to 1 day, 50 percent staff reduction, and 20 percent overall savings in the procurement process. Pitney Bowes' suppliers need only Internet access and a standard Web browser to be electronically linked to the manufacturer's supply system to see how many of their products are on hand and to indicate how many will be needed in the future. The site even includes data that small suppliers can use for production planning.

These developments open up supplier relationships for companies outside of the buyer's domestic market; however, the supplier's capability of providing satisfying goods and services will play the most critical role in securing long-term contracts. In addition, the physical delivery of goods often can be old-fashioned and slow. Nevertheless, the use of such strategic tools will be crucial for international managers to develop and maintain key competitive advantages. An overview of the international supply chain is shown in Figure 17.1.

Figure 17.1 The International Supply Chain

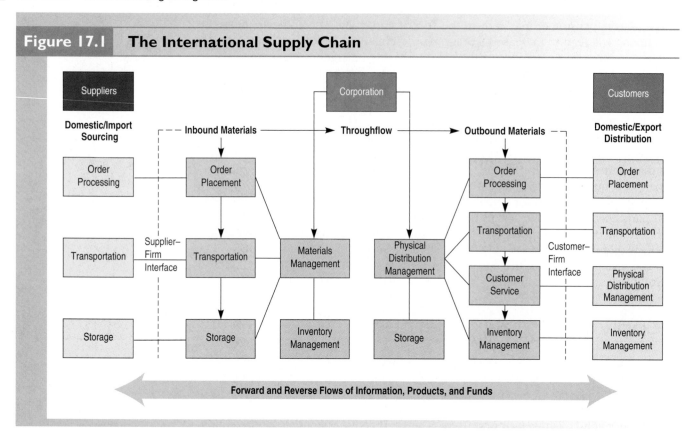

The Impact of International Logistics

Logistics costs comprise between 10 and 30 percent of the total landed cost of an international order.[4] International firms have already achieved many of the cost reductions that are possible in financing and production, and they are now looking at international logistics as a competitive tool. Research shows that the environment facing logistics managers in the next ten years will be dynamic and explosive. Technological advances and progress in communication systems and information-processing capabilities will be particularly significant in designing and managing logistics systems.

For example, close collaboration with suppliers is required in order to develop a just-in-time inventory system, which in turn may be crucial to maintain manufacturing costs at a globally competitive level. Yet without electronic data interchange, such collaborations or alliances are severely handicapped. While most industrialized countries can offer the technological infrastructure for such computer-to-computer exchange of business information, the application of such a system in the global environment may be severely restricted. Often, it is not just the lack of technology that forms the key obstacle to modern logistics management, but rather the entire business infrastructure, ranging from ways of doing business in fields such as accounting and inventory tracking, to the willingness of businesses to collaborate with one another. A contrast between the United States and Russia is useful here.

In the United States, more than 40 percent of shipments are made under a just-in-time/quick response regime. For the U.S. economy, the total cost of distribution is close to 11 percent of GNP. By contrast, Russia is only now beginning to learn about the rhythm of demand and the need to bring supply in line. The country is battling space constraints, poor lines of supply, nonexistent distribution and service centers, limited rolling stock, and insufficient transportation systems. Producers are uninformed about issues such as inventory carrying cost, store assortment efficiencies, and replenishment techniques. The need for information development and exchange systems for integrated supplier–distributor alliances and for efficient communication systems is only poorly understood. As a result, distribution cost remains at well above 30 percent of GNP, holding back the domestic economy and severely restricting its international competitiveness. Unless substantial improvements are made in the logistics area, major participation by Russian producers in world trade will be severely handicapped.[5] It is fair to say that logistics may well become the key dimension by which firms distinguish themselves internationally.

The New Dimensions of International Logistics

In domestic operations, logistics decisions are guided by the experience of the manager, possible industry comparison, an intimate knowledge of trends, and the development of heuristics—or rules of thumb. The logistics manager in the international firm, on the other hand, frequently has to depend on educated guesses to determine the steps required to obtain a desired service level. Variations in locale mean variations in environment. Lack of familiarity with these variations leads to uncertainty in the decision-making process. By applying decision rules developed at home, the firm will be unable to adapt well to the new environment, and the result will be inadequate profit performance. The long-term survival of international activities depends on an understanding of the differences inherent in the international logistics field.

Basic Differences

Basic differences in international logistics emerge because the corporation is active in more than one country. One example of a basic difference is distance. International marketing activities frequently require goods to be shipped farther to reach final customers. These distances in turn result in longer lead times, more opportunities for things to go wrong, more inventories—in short, greater complexity. **Currency variation** is a second basic difference in international logistics. The corporation must adjust its planning to incorporate different currencies and changes in exchange rates. The border-crossing process brings with it the need for conformance with national regulations, an inspection at customs, and proper documentation. As a result, additional intermediaries participate in the international logistics process. They include freight forwarders, customs agents, custom brokers, banks, and other financial intermediaries. Finally, the **transportation modes** may also be different. Most domestic transportation is either by truck or by rail, whereas the multinational corporation quite frequently ships its products by air or by sea. Airfreight and ocean freight have their own stipulations and rules that require new knowledge and skills.

Country-Specific Differences

Within each country, the firm faces specific logistical attributes that may be quite different from those experienced at home. Transportation systems and intermediaries may vary. The reliability of carriers may be different. The computation of freight rates may be unfamiliar. Packaging and labeling requirements differ from country to country. Management must consider all of these factors in order to develop an efficient international logistics operation.

International Transportation Issues

International transportation is of major concern to the international firm because transportation determines how and when goods will be received. The transportation issue can be divided into three components: infrastructure, the availability of modes, and the choice of modes.

Transportation Infrastructure

In industrialized nations, firms can count on an established transportation network. Internationally, however, major infrastructural variations may be encountered. Some countries may have excellent inbound and outbound transportation systems but weak transportation links within the country. This is particularly true in former colonies, where the original transportation systems were designed to maximize the extractive potential of the countries. In such instances, shipping to the market may be easy, but distribution within the market may represent a very difficult and time-consuming task.

The international marketer must therefore learn about existing and planned infrastructures abroad. In some countries, for example, railroads may be an excellent transportation mode, far surpassing the performance of trucking, whereas in others, the use of railroads for freight distribution may be a gamble at best. The future routing of pipelines must be determined before any major commitments are made to a particular location if the product is amenable to pipeline transportation. The transportation methods used to carry cargo to seaports or airports must also be investigated. Mistakes in the evaluation of transportation options can prove to be very costly. One researcher reported the case of a food processing firm that built a pineapple cannery at the delta of a river in Mexico. Since the pineapple plantation was located upstream, the company planned to float the ripe fruit down to the cannery on barges. To its dismay, the firm discovered that at harvest time the river current was far too strong for barge traffic. Since no other feasible alternative method of transportation existed, the plant was closed, and the new equipment was sold for a fraction of its original cost.[6]

Extreme variations also exist in the frequency of transportation services. For example, a particular port may not be visited by a ship for weeks or even months. Sometimes, only carriers with particular characteristics, such as small size, will serve a given location. All of these infrastructural concerns must be taken into account in the initial planning of the firm's transportation service.

Availability of Modes

Even though goods are shipped abroad by rail or truck, international transportation frequently requires ocean or airfreight modes, which many corporations only rarely use domestically. In addition, combinations such as land bridges or sea bridges frequently permit the transfer of freight among various modes of transportation, resulting in intermodal movements. The international marketer must understand the specific properties of the different modes in order to use them intelligently.

Ocean Shipping

Water transportation is a key mode for international freight movements. As *The International Marketplace 17.2* shows, an interruption of ocean-based transportation can have quite serious consequences for an economy. Three types of vessels operating in ocean shipping can be distinguished by their service: liner service, bulk service, and tramp or charter service. **Liner service** offers regularly scheduled passage on established routes. **Bulk service** mainly provides contractual services for individual voyages or for prolonged periods of time. **Tramp service** is available for irregular routes and is scheduled only on demand.

In addition to the services offered by ocean carriers, the type of cargo a vessel can carry is also important. Most common are conventional (break bulk) cargo vessels, container ships, and roll-on-roll-off vessels. Conventional cargo vessels are useful for oversized and unusual cargoes but may be less efficient in their port operations. It is a reflection of the premium assigned to speed and ease of handling that has caused a decline in the use of general cargo vessels and a sharp increase in the growth of **container ships,** which carry standardized containers that greatly facilitate the loading and unloading of cargo and intermodal transfers.

THE INTERNATIONAL MARKETPLACE   17.2

Port Closure Hurts Production and Produce

Perhaps the motto of the International Longshore and Warehouse Union (ILWU) says it best: "An injury to one is an injury to all." The labor dispute between the 10,500 members of the ILWU and the Pacific Maritime Association (PMA), which represents the shippers, and subsequent shutdown of the West Coast's 29 ports did more than merely injure the U.S. economy. Trade through these ports, which span from San Diego on the Mexican border to Seattle in the Northwest, amounted to $500 billion in 2001, or one-half of the nation's international trade. Experts estimated that a shutdown cost the U.S. economy $2 billion per day and nearly $50 billion over two weeks.

Ripples from the port delays reached well beyond the waters where the ships were anchored. Factories and retailers are susceptible more than ever to supply chain disruptions. Cargoes no longer rest in warehouses as they once did: Containers are transported from the ships directly to distribution centers, where they are broken down, repacked, and sent to final destinations within hours. Consequently, manufacturers and retailers no longer stock large quantities of parts and merchandise and rely heavily on frequent shipments to sustain production flows and inventory. Even if they wanted to store large quantities of goods, there would not be enough warehouse space to do so. Therefore, if supply lines are broken or stretched out for even short periods, companies quickly face a need to curtail or even halt production.

For the West Coast ports, major imports include industrial machinery, furniture, clothing, toys, computers, automotive goods, and electronics. The biggest exports include meat and poultry, industrial equipment, animal feed, automotive parts, chemicals, and fruits and vegetables. But those cargoes were bobbing offshore and idle on land all along the West Coast: Avocadoes from Central America sat in containers in the Port of Tacoma, Washington; televisions from Korea remained boxed in Southern California; and car parts destined for the General Motors/Toyota plant in Fremont, California, sat unloaded in the water off Oakland, idling 5,100 workers.

Imports weren't the only trade suffering. Exports were struggling just as much: In California, agricultural exports such as broccoli, oranges, grapes, and lettuce sat idle in ports, unable to get to customers in Taiwan, Hong Kong, and the Philippines and spoiling quickly.

Shippers had few alternatives for moving trans-Pacific goods. The ILWU operates all U.S. ports on the West Coast; ports in Canada and Mexico are too small to handle the large container vessels now used to transport goods from Asia to the United States, and most ships are also too large to fit through the Panama Canal or to dock at East Coast ports. Airfreight was an option—at costs many times higher than ocean vessels. For the average business using just-in-time inventory and just-in-time budgeting, such interruptions in the supply chain weren't easy to weather.

SOURCES: Nancy Cleeland et al., "Port Closures Start Taking Economic Toll," *Los Angeles Times,* October 1, 2002, 1, section 1; and Melinda Fulmer and Karen Robinson-Jacobs, "Trouble on the Waterfront," *Los Angeles Times,* October 3, 2002, 4, section 3.

As a result, the time the ship has to spend in port is reduced. Roll-on-roll-off (RORO) vessels are essentially oceangoing ferries. Trucks can drive onto built-in ramps and roll off at the destination. Another vessel similar to the RORO vessel is the LASH (lighter aboard ship) vessel. LASH vessels consist of barges stored on the ship and lowered at the point of destination. These individual barges can then operate on inland waterways, a feature that is particularly useful in shallow water.

The availability of a certain type of vessel, however, does not automatically mean that it can be used. The greatest constraint in international ocean shipping is the lack of ports and port services. For example, modern container ships cannot serve some ports because the local equipment is unable to handle the resulting traffic. This problem is often found in developing countries, where local authorities lack the funds to develop facilities. In some instances, governments purposely limit the development of ports to impede the inflow of imports. Increasingly, however, nations recognize the importance of appropriate port structures and are developing such facilities in spite of the heavy investments necessary. If such investments are accompanied by concurrent changes in the overall infrastructure, transportation efficiency should, in the long run, more than recoup the original investment.

Large investments in infrastructure are usually necessary to produce results. Selective allocation of funds to transportation tends to only shift bottlenecks to some other point in the infrastructure. If these bottlenecks are not removed, the consequences may be felt in the overall economic performance of the nation. A good example is provided by the Caribbean. Even though geographically close to the United States, many Caribbean nations are served poorly by ocean carriers. As a result, products that could be exported from the region to the United States are at a disadvantage because they take a long time to reach the U.S. market. For many products, quick delivery is essential because of required high levels of industry responsiveness to orders. From a regional perspective, maintaining adequate facilities is therefore imperative in order to remain on the list of areas and ports served by international carriers. Investment in leading-edge port technology can also provide an instrumental competitive edge and cause entire distribution systems to be reconfigured to take advantage of possible savings. Figure 17.2 shows how the ports of New York and New Jersey are upgrading their facilities to stay competitive.

Air Shipping

Airfreight is available to and from most countries. This includes the developing world, where it is often a matter of national prestige to operate a national airline. The tremendous growth in international airfreight is shown in Figure 17.3. The total volume of airfreight in relation to the total volume of shipping in international business remains quite small. Yet 40 percent of the world's manufactured exports by value travel by air.[7] Clearly, high-value items are more likely to be shipped by air, particularly if they have a high **density,** that is, a high weight-to-volume ratio.

Over the years, airlines have made major efforts to increase the volume of airfreight. Many of these activities have concentrated on developing better, more efficient ground facilities, introducing airfreight containers, and providing and marketing a wide variety of special services to shippers. In addition, some airfreight companies have specialized and become partners in the international logistics effort.

Changes have also taken place within the aircraft. Forty years ago, the holds of large propeller aircraft could take only about ten tons of cargo. Today's jumbo jets can load up to 105 metric tons of cargo with an available space of 636 cubic meters and can therefore transport bulky products, as Figure 17.4 shows.[8] In addition, aircraft manufacturers have responded to industry demands by developing both jumbo cargo planes and combination passenger and cargo aircraft. The latter carry passengers in one section of the main deck and freight in another. These hybrids can be used by carriers on routes that would be uneconomical for passengers or freight alone.

From the shipper's perspective, the products involved must be amenable to air shipment in terms of their size. In addition, the market situation for any given product must be evaluated. For example, airfreight may be needed if a product is perishable or if, for other reasons, it requires a short transit time. The level of customer service needs and expectations can also play a decisive role. For example, the shipment of an industrial product that is vital to the ongoing operations of a customer may be much more urgent than the shipment of packaged consumer products.

Choice of Modes

The international marketer must make the appropriate selection from the available modes of transportation. This decision, of course, will be heavily influenced by the needs of the firm and its customers. The manager must consider the performance

Figure 17.2   Advertisement for the Port Authority of New York/New Jersey

Figure 17.3 International Airfreight, 1960–2005

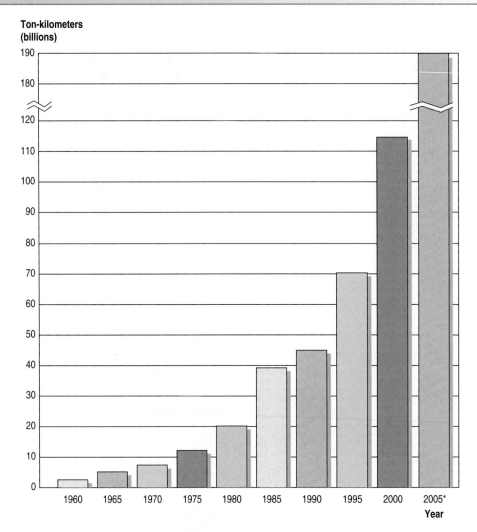

*Forecast

SOURCES: *Civil Aviation Statistics of the World* (Montreal: ICAO); **http://www.icao.org**; and Airbus Industries Global Market Forecast, 2001–2019, **http://www.airbus.com**, accessed November 15, 2002.

of each mode on four dimensions: transit time, predictability, cost, and noneconomic factors.

Transit Time

The period between departure and arrival of the carrier varies significantly between ocean freight and airfreight. For example, the 45-day transit time of an ocean shipment can be reduced to 24 hours if the firm chooses airfreight. The length of transit time will have a major impact on the overall operations of the firm. As an example, a short transit time may reduce or even eliminate the need for an overseas depot. Also, inventories can be significantly reduced if they are replenished frequently. As a result, capital can be freed up and used to finance other corporate opportunities. Transit time can also play a major role in emergency situations. For example, if the shipper is about to miss an important delivery date because of production delays, a shipment normally made by ocean freight can be made by air.

Figure 17.4　Loading a Train on a Plane

Shipping by airfreight has really taken off in the past 20 years. Even large and heavy items, such as this locomotive, are shipped to their destination by air.

SOURCE: Printed in the *Journal of Commerce.* Courtesy of Emery Worldwide.

Perishable products require shorter transit times. Rapid transportation prolongs the shelf life in the foreign market. For products with a short life span, air delivery may be the only way to enter foreign markets successfully. For example, international sales of cut flowers have reached their current volume only as a result of airfreight. At all times, the international marketing manager must understand the interactions between different components of the logistics process and their effect on transit times. Unless a smooth flow can be assured throughout the entire supply chain, bottlenecks will deny any timing benefits from specific improvements. For example, Levi Strauss, the blue jeans manufacturer, offered customers in some of its stores the chance to be measured by a body scanner to get custom-made jeans. Less than an hour after such measurement, a Levi factory began to cut the jeans of the customer's choice. Unfortunately, it then took ten days to get the finished product to the customer.[9]

Predictability

Providers of both ocean and airfreight service wrestle with the issue of **reliability.** Both modes are subject to the vagaries of nature, which may impose delays. Yet because reliability is a relative measure, the delay of one day for airfreight tends to be seen as much more severe and "unreliable" than the same delay for ocean freight. But delays tend to be shorter in absolute time for air shipments. As a result, arrival time via air is more predictable. This attribute has a major influence on corporate strategy. For example, because of the higher predictability of airfreight, inventory safety stock can be kept at lower levels. Greater predictability can also serve as a useful sales tool for foreign distributors, who are able to make more precise delivery promises to their customers. If inadequate port facilities exist, airfreight may again be the better alternative. Unloading operations from oceangoing vessels are more cumbersome and time-consuming than for planes.

Finally, merchandise shipped via air is likely to suffer less loss and damage from exposure of the cargo to movement. Therefore, once the merchandise arrives, it is more likely to be ready for immediate delivery—a facet that also enhances predictability.

Cost

A major consideration in choosing international transportation modes is the cost factor. International transportation services are usually priced on the basis of both cost of the service provided and value of the service to the shipper. Because of the high value of the products shipped by air, airfreight is often priced according to the value of the service. In this instance, of course, price becomes a function of market demand and the monopolistic power of the carrier.

The international marketer must decide whether the clearly higher cost of airfreight can be justified. In part, this will depend on the cargo's properties. For example, the physical density and the value of the cargo will affect the decision. Bulky products may be too expensive to ship by air, whereas very compact products may be more amenable to airfreight transportation. High-priced items can absorb transportation cost more easily than low-priced goods because the cost of transportation as a percentage of total product cost will be lower. As a result, sending diamonds by airfreight is easier to justify than sending coal by air. To keep cost down, a shipper can join groups such as shippers associations, which give the shipper more leverage in negotiations. Alternatively, a shipper can decide to mix modes of transportation in order to reduce overall cost and time delays. For example, part of the shipment route can be covered by air, while another portion can be covered by truck or ship.

Most important, however, are the overall logistical considerations of the firm. The manager must determine how important it is for merchandise to arrive on time, which will be different for regular garments than for high-fashion dresses. The effect of transportation cost on price and the need for product availability abroad must also be considered. For example, some firms may wish to use airfreight as a new tool for aggressive market expansion. Airfreight may also be considered a good way to begin operations in new markets without making sizable investments for warehouses and distribution centers.

Although costs are the major consideration in modal choice, an overall perspective must be employed. Simply comparing transportation modes on the basis of price alone is insufficient. The manager must factor in all corporate activities that are affected by modal choice and explore the total cost effects of each alternative. The final selection of a mode will depend on the importance of different modal dimensions to the markets under consideration. A useful overall comparison between different modes of transportation is provided in Table 17.1.

Noneconomic Factors

Often, noneconomic dimensions will enter into the selection process for a proper form of transportation. The transportation sector, nationally and internationally, both benefits and suffers from heavy government involvement. Carriers may be owned or heavily subsidized by governments. As a result, governmental pressure is exerted on shippers to use national carriers, even if more economical alternatives exist. Such preferential policies are most often enforced when government cargo is being transported. Restrictions are not limited to developing countries. For example, in the United States, all government cargo and all official government travelers must use national flag carriers when available.

For balance-of-payments reasons, international quota systems of transportation have been proposed. The United Nations Commission on International Trade and Development (UNCTAD), for example, has recommended a 40/40/20 treaty whereby 40 percent of the traffic between two nations is allocated to vessels of the exporting country, 40 percent to vessels of the importing country, and 20 percent

| Table 17.1 | Evaluating Transportation Choices |

Characteristics of Mode	Mode of Transportation				
	Air	Pipeline	Highway	Rail	Water
Speed (1 = fastest)	1	4	2	3	5
Cost (1 = highest)	1	4	2	3	5
Loss and Damage (1 = least)	3	1	4	5	2
Frequency* (1 = best)	3	1	2	4	5
Dependability (1 = best)	5	1	2	3	4
Capacity† (1 = best)	4	5	3	2	1
Availability (1 = best)	3	5	1	2	4

*Frequency: number of times mode is available during a given time period.
†Capacity: ability of mode to handle large or heavy goods.

SOURCE: Ronald H. Ballou, *Business Logistics Management,* 4th ed. © 1998. Reprinted by permission of Pearson Education, Inc., Upper Saddle River, NJ.

to third-country vessels (40/40/20). However, stiff international competition among carriers and the price sensitivity of customers frequently render such proposals ineffective, particularly for trade between industrialized countries.

The International Shipment

International shipments usually involve not just one carrier but multiple types of carriers. The shipment must be routed to the port of export, where it is transferred to another mode of transportation—for example, from truck or rail to vessel. Documentation for international shipments is universally perceived as so complicated, especially by smaller firms, that it can be a trade barrier. Recognizing the impact both in terms of time and money that documentation can have, the European Union has greatly simplified its required documentation for shipments. Whereas drivers earlier needed two pounds of documents on a route, for example, from Amsterdam to Lisbon, they now need only a single piece of paper. The savings on the elimination of this red tape are significant.

Few international marketers, especially small or medium-sized firms and those new to exporting, are familiar with the many and varied details involved in transportation. These may include arranging for shipment from the factory, transfer from train to vessel, securing of rates and space on vessels, clearing customs, stowing, delivery at the port of destination to docks, clearance through local customs, and finally, delivery to the buyer. Larger exporters have a separate department or staff to secure transportation services and proper documentation, whereas smaller firms rely on support agencies for this work.

Documentation

In the most simple form of exporting, the only documents needed are a bill of lading and an export declaration. In most countries, these documents are available either from the government or from transportation firms. For example, an export declaration can be obtained in the United States from the Census Bureau (**http://www.census.gov/foreign-trade/regulations/forms**). A bill of lading can be obtained in Canada from a shipper, for example, Manitoulin Transport (**http://www.manitoulintransport.com**).

Table 17.2   Documentation for an International Shipment

A. Documents Required by the U.S. Government
 1. Shipper's export declaration
 2. Export license
B. Commercial Documents
 1. Commercial invoice
 2. Packing list
 3. Inland bill of lading
 4. Dock receipt
 5. Bill of lading or airway bill
 6. Insurance policies or certificates
 7. Shipper's declaration for dangerous goods
C. Import Documents
 1. Import license
 2. Foreign exchange license
 3. Certificate of origin
 4. Consular invoice
 5. Customs invoice

SOURCES: Dun & Bradstreet, *Exporter's Encyclopedia* (New York: Dun & Bradstreet, 1985); Marta Ortiz-Buonafina, *Profitable Export Marketing* (Englewood Cliffs, NJ: Prentice-Hall, 1984), 218–246; and **http://www.ams.usda.gov**.

Most exports fit under a general license, which is a generalized authorization consisting simply of a number to be shown on the documents. Certain goods and data require a special validated license for export, as discussed in Chapter 5. For importation, the basic documents are a bill of lading and an invoice. Table 17.2 provides a summary of the main documents used in international shipments.

The **bill of lading** is the most important document to the shipper, the carrier, and the buyer. It acknowledges receipt of the goods, represents the basic contract between the shipper and the carrier, and serves as evidence of title to the goods for collection by the purchaser. Various types of bills of lading exist. The inland bill of lading is a contract between the inland carrier and the shipper. Bills of lading may be negotiable instruments in that they may be endorsed to other parties (order bill) or may be nonnegotiable (straight). The **shipper's export declaration** states proper authorization for export and serves as a means for governmental data collection efforts.

The packing list, if used, lists in some detail the contents, the gross and net weights, and the dimensions of each package. Some shipments, such as corrosives, flammables, and poisons, require a **shipper's declaration for dangerous goods.** When the international marketer is responsible for moving the goods to the port of export, a dock receipt (for ocean freight) or a warehouse receipt (if the goods are stored) is issued before the issuance of the bill of lading. Collection documents must also be produced and always include a commercial invoice (a detailed description of the transaction), often a **consular invoice** (required by certain countries for data collection purposes), and a **certificate of origin** (required by certain countries to ensure correct tariffs). Insurance documents are produced when stipulated by the transaction. In certain countries, especially in Latin America, two additional documents are needed. An **import license** may be required for certain types or amounts of particular goods, while a **foreign exchange license** allows the importer to secure the needed hard currency to pay for the shipment. The exporter has to provide the importer with the data needed to obtain these licenses from governmental authorities and should make sure, before the actual shipment, that the importer has indeed secured the documents.

Two guidelines are critical in dealing with customs anywhere in the world: sufficient knowledge or experience in dealing with the customs service in question and sufficient preparation for the process. Whatever the required documents, their proper preparation and timing is of crucial importance, particularly since the major terror attacks of 2001. Many governments expect detailed information about cargo well in advance of its arrival in port. Improper or missing documents can easily lead to difficulties that will delay payment or even prevent it. Furthermore, improper documentation may cause problems with customs. If a customs service seizes the merchandise, delays can be measured in weeks and may end up in a total financial loss for the particular shipment.

Assistance with International Shipments

Several intermediaries provide services in the physical movement of goods. One very important distribution decision an exporter makes is the selection of an international freight forwarder. Such an **international freight forwarder** acts as an agent for the marketer in moving cargo to the overseas destination. Independent freight forwarders are regulated and, in the United States, should be certified by the Federal Maritime Commission. The forwarder advises the marketer on shipping documentation and packing costs and will prepare and review the documents to ensure that they are in order. Forwarders will also book the necessary space aboard a carrier. They will make necessary arrangements to clear outbound goods with customs and, after clearance, forward the documents either to the customer or to the paying bank. A **customs broker** serves as an agent for an importer with authority to clear inbound goods through customs and ship them on to their destination. These functions are performed for a fee. Customs brokers are often regulated by their national customs service.

International Inventory Issues

Inventories tie up a major portion of corporate funds. As a result, capital used for inventory is not available for other corporate opportunities. Because annual **inventory carrying costs** (the expense of maintaining inventories) can easily comprise up to 25 percent or more of the value of the inventories themselves, proper inventory policies should be of major concern to the international marketing manager. Just-in-time inventory policies are increasingly adopted by multinational manufacturers. These policies minimize the volume of inventory by making it available only when it is needed for the production process. Firms using such a policy will choose suppliers on the basis of their delivery and inventory performance. Proper inventory management may therefore become a determinant variable in obtaining a sale.

In its international inventory management, the multinational corporation is faced not only with new situations that affect inventories negatively but also with new opportunities and alternatives. The purpose of establishing inventory—to maintain product movement in the delivery pipeline in order to satisfy demand—is the same for domestic and international inventory systems. The international environment, however, includes unique factors such as currency exchange rates, greater distances, and duties. At the same time, international operations provide the corporation with an opportunity to explore alternatives not available in a domestic setting, such as new sourcing or location alternatives. In international operations, the firm can make use of currency fluctuations by placing varying degrees of emphasis on inventory operations, depending on the stability of the currency of a specific country. Entire operations can be shifted to different nations to take advantage of newly emerging opportunities. International inventory management can therefore be much more flexible in its response to environmental changes.

In deciding the level of inventory to be maintained, the international marketer must consider three factors: the order cycle time, desired customer service levels, and use of inventories as a strategic tool.

Order Cycle Time

The total time that passes between the placement of an order and the receipt of the merchandise is referred to as order cycle time. Two dimensions are of major importance to inventory management: the length of the total order cycle and its consistency. In international marketing, the order cycle is frequently longer than in domestic business. It comprises the time involved in order transmission, order filling, packing and preparation for shipment, and transportation. Order transmission time varies greatly internationally depending on whether telephone, fax, mail, or electronic order placement is used in communicating. The order filling time may also be increased because lack of familiarity with a foreign market makes the anticipation of new orders more difficult. Packing and shipment preparation require more detailed attention. Finally, of course, transportation time increases with the distances involved. As a result, total order cycle time can frequently approach a hundred days or more. Larger inventories may have to be maintained both domestically and internationally to bridge these time gaps.

Consistency, the second dimension of order cycle time, is also more difficult to maintain in international marketing. Depending on the choice of transportation mode, delivery times may vary considerably from shipment to shipment. This variation requires the maintenance of larger safety stocks in order to be able to fill demand in periods when delays occur.

The international marketer should attempt to reduce order cycle time and increase its consistency without an increase in total costs. This objective can be accomplished by altering methods of transportation, changing inventory locations, or improving any of the other components of the order cycle time, such as the way orders are transmitted. By shifting order placement from mail to telephone or to electronic data interchange (EDI), for example, a firm can reduce the order cycle time substantially.

Customer Service Levels

The level of customer service denotes the responsiveness that inventory policies permit for any given situation. Customer service is therefore a management-determined constraint within the logistics system. A customer service level of 100 percent could be defined as the ability to fill all orders within a set time—for example, three days. If within these three days only 70 percent of the orders can be filled, the customer service level is 70 percent. The choice of customer service level for the firm has a major impact on the inventories needed. In their domestic operations, U.S. companies frequently aim to achieve customer service levels of 95 to 98 percent. Often, such "homegrown" rules of thumb are then used in international inventory operations as well.

Managers may not realize that standards determined heuristically and based on competitive activity in the home market are often inappropriate abroad. Different locales have country-specific customer service needs and requirements. Service levels should not be oriented primarily around cost or customary domestic standards. Rather, the level chosen for use internationally should be based on customer expectations encountered in each market. These expectations are dependent on past performance, product desirability, customer sophistication, the competitive status of the firm, and whether a buyers' or sellers' market exists.

Because high customer service levels are costly, the goal should not be the highest customer service level possible but rather an acceptable level. Different customers have different priorities. Some will be prepared to pay a premium for speed. In industrial marketing, for example, even an eight-hour delay may be unacceptable for the delivery of a crucial product component, since it may mean a shutdown of the production process. Other firms may put a higher value on flexibility, and another group may see low cost as the most important issue. Flexibility and speed are expensive, so it is wasteful to supply them to customers who do not value them highly. If, for example, foreign customers expect to receive their merchandise within 30 days, for the international corporation to promise delivery within 10 or 15 days does not make sense. Indeed, such delivery may result in storage problems. In addition, the higher prices associated with higher customer service levels may reduce the competitiveness of a firm's product.

Inventory as a Strategic Tool

International inventories can be used by the international corporation as a strategic tool in dealing with currency valuation changes or hedging against inflation. By increasing inventories before an imminent devaluation of a currency, instead of holding cash, the corporation may reduce its exposure to devaluation losses. Similarly, in the case of high inflation, large inventories can provide an important inflation hedge. In such circumstances, the international inventory manager must balance the cost of maintaining high levels of inventories with the benefits accruing to the firm from hedging against inflation or devaluation. Many countries, for example, charge a property tax on stored goods. If the increase in tax payments outweighs the hedging benefits to the corporation, it would be unwise to increase inventories before a devaluation.

Despite the benefits of reducing the firm's financial risk, inventory management must still fall in line with the overall corporate market strategy. Only by recognizing the trade-offs, which may result in less than optimal inventory policies, can the corporation maximize the overall benefit.

International Storage Issues

Although international logistics is discussed as a movement or flow of goods, a stationary period is involved when merchandise becomes inventory stored in warehouses. Heated arguments can arise within a firm over the need for and utility of warehousing internationally. On the one hand, customers expect quick responses to orders and rapid delivery. Accommodating the customer's expectation may require locating many distribution centers around the world. On the other hand, warehousing space is expensive. In addition, the larger volume of inventory increases the inventory carrying cost. The international marketer must consider the trade-offs between service and cost to determine the appropriate levels of warehousing. Other trade-offs also exist within the logistics function. As an example, fewer warehouses will allow for consolidation of transportation and therefore lower transportation rates to the warehouse. However, if the warehouses are located far from customers, the cost of outgoing transportation from the warehouse will increase.

Storage Facilities

One important location decision is how many distribution centers to have and where to locate them. The availability of facilities abroad will differ from the domestic situation. For example, whereas public storage is widely available in some countries, such facilities may be scarce or entirely lacking in others. Also, the standards and quality of facilities abroad may often not be comparable to those offered at home. As a result, the storage decision of the firm is often accompanied by the need for large-scale, long-term investments. Despite the high cost, international storage facilities should be established if they support the overall marketing effort. In many markets, adequate storage facilities are imperative in order to satisfy customer demands and to compete successfully.

Once the decision is made to utilize storage facilities abroad, the warehouse conditions must be carefully analyzed. As an example, in some countries, warehouses have low ceilings. Packaging developed for the high stacking of products is therefore unnecessary. In other countries, automated warehousing is available. Proper bar coding of products and the use of package dimensions acceptable to the warehousing system are basic requirements. In contrast, in warehouses still stocked manually, weight limitations will be of major concern.

To optimize the logistics system, the marketer should analyze international product sales and then rank products according to warehousing needs. Products that are most sensitive to delivery time may be classified as "A" products. "A" products would be stocked in all distribution centers, and safety stock levels would be kept high. Products for which immediate delivery is not urgent may be classified as "B" products. They would be stored only at selected distribution centers around the world. Finally, "C" products for which short delivery time is not important, or for which there is little demand, would be stocked only at headquarters. Should an urgent need for delivery arise, airfreight could be considered for rapid shipment. Classifying products through such an ABC analysis enables the international marketer to substantially reduce total international warehousing requirements and still maintain acceptable service levels.

Foreign Trade Zones

The existence of foreign trade zones can have a major effect on the international logistician, since production cost advantages may require a reconfiguration of storage, processing, and distribution strategies. Trade zones are considered, for purposes of tariff treatment, to be outside the customs territory of the country within which they are located. They are special areas and can be used for warehousing, packaging, inspection, labeling, exhibition, assembly, fabrication, or transshipment of imports without burdening the firm with duties.[10] Trade zones can be found at major ports of entry and also at inland locations near major production facilities. For example, Kansas City, Missouri, has one of the largest foreign trade zones in the United States.

Trade zones can be quite useful to the international firm. In some countries, the benefits derived from lower factor costs, such as labor, may be offset by high duties and tariffs. As a result, location of manufacturing and storage facilities in these countries may prove uneconomical. Foreign trade zones are designed to exclude the impact of duties from the location decision. This is done by exempting merchandise in the foreign trade zone from duty payment. The international firm can therefore import merchandise; store it in the foreign trade zone; and process, alter, test, or demonstrate it—all without paying duties. If the merchandise is subsequently shipped abroad (that is, reexported), no duty payments are ever due. Duty payments become due only if and when the merchandise is shipped into the country from the foreign trade zone.

Firms can also make use of sharp differentials in factor endowments, such as labor costs, between adjoining countries by locating close to their border. For instance, the **maquiladora program** between the United States and Mexico permits firms to carry out their labor-intensive operations in Mexico while sourcing raw materials or component parts from the United States, free of Mexican tariffs. Subsequently, the semifinished or assembled products are shipped to the U.S. market and are assessed duties only for the foreign labor component. The benefits of the maquiladora program are available for any firm that chooses to locate close to the border. For example, many Japanese firms have made use of this program.

One country that has used trade zones very successfully for its own economic development is China. Through the creation of *special economic zones* in which there are no tariffs, substantial tax incentives, and low prices for land and labor, the government has attracted many foreign investors bringing in billions of dollars. These investors have brought new equipment, technology, and managerial know-how and have therefore substantially increased the local economic prosperity.

Both parties to the arrangement benefit from foreign trade zones. The government maintaining the trade zone achieves increased employment. The firm using the trade zone obtains a spearhead in or close to the foreign market without incurring all of the costs customarily associated with such an activity. As a result, goods can be reassembled and large shipments can be broken down into smaller units. Also, goods can be repackaged when packaging weight becomes part of the duty assessment. Goods can also be given domestic "made-in" status if assembled in the foreign trade zone. Whenever use of a trade zone is examined, however, the marketer must keep the additional cost of storage, handling, and transportation in mind before making a decision.

International Packaging Issues

Packaging is instrumental in getting the merchandise to the ultimate destination in a safe, maintainable, and presentable condition. Packaging that is adequate for domestic shipping may be inadequate for international transportation because the shipment will be subject to the motions of the vessel on which it is carried. Added stress in international shipping also arises from the transfer of goods among different modes of transportation. Figure 17.5 provides examples of some sources of stress that are most frequently found in international transportation.

The responsibility for appropriate packaging rests with the shipper of goods. The U.S. Carriage of Goods by Sea Act of 1936 states: "Neither the carrier nor the ship shall be responsible for loss or damage arising or resulting from insufficiency of packing." The shipper must therefore ensure that the goods are prepared appropriately for international shipping. This is important because it has been found that "the losses that occur as a result of breakage, pilferage, and theft exceed the losses caused by major maritime casualties, which include fires, sinkings, and collision of vessels. Thus, the largest of these losses is a preventable loss."[11]

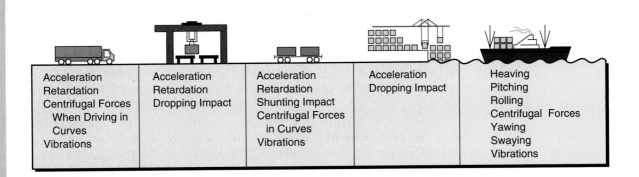

Figure 17.5   Stresses in Intermodal Movement

| Acceleration Retardation Centrifugal Forces When Driving in Curves Vibrations | Acceleration Retardation Dropping Impact | Acceleration Retardation Shunting Impact Centrifugal Forces in Curves Vibrations | Acceleration Dropping Impact | Heaving Pitching Rolling Centrifugal Forces Yawing Swaying Vibrations |

Note: Each transportation mode exerts a different set of stresses and strains on containerized cargoes. The most commonly overloaded are those associated with ocean transport.

SOURCE: Reprinted with permission from *Handling and Shipping Management*, September 1980 issue, p. 47; and David Greenfield, "Perfect Packing for Export." Copyright © 1980, Penton Publishing, Cleveland, OH.

Packaging decisions must also take into account differences in environmental conditions—for example, climate. When the ultimate destination is very humid or particularly cold, special provisions must be made to prevent damage to the product. The task becomes even more challenging when one considers that, in the course of long-distance transportation, dramatic changes in climate can take place. An example of a major packaging blunder was provided by a firm in Taiwan that shipped drinking glasses to the Middle East. The company used wooden crates and padded the glasses with hay. Most of the glasses, however, were broken by the time they reached their destination. As the crates traveled into the drier Middle East, the moisture content of the hay had dropped. By the time the crates were delivered, the thin straw offered almost no protection.[12]

Packaging issues also need to be closely linked to overall strategic plans. The individual responsible for international packaging should utilize transportation modes as efficiently as possible. This requires appropriate package design, which takes into account the storage properties of the product. For example, John Deere was shipping its combines from the United States to Australia for years, at a shipping cost of $2,500 each. Each combine took up much more space than its footprint, since the harvesting arm stuck out on its side. Once the company decided to ship the harvesting arm unmounted, shipping costs were reduced by $1,000 per combine.

The weight of packaging must also be considered, particularly when airfreight is used, since the cost of shipping is often based on weight. At the same time, packaging material must be sufficiently strong to permit stacking in international transportation. Another consideration is that, in some countries, duties are assessed according to the gross weight of shipments, which includes the weight of packaging. Obviously, the heavier the packaging, the higher the duties will be.

The shipper must pay sufficient attention to instructions provided by the customer for packaging. For example, requests by the customer that the weight of any one package should not exceed a certain limit, or that specific package dimensions should be adhered to, are usually made for a reason. Often they reflect limitations in transportation or handling facilities at the point of destination.

Although the packaging of a product is often used as a form of display abroad, international packaging can rarely serve the dual purpose of protection and display. Therefore, double packaging may be necessary. The display package is for future use at the point of destination; another package surrounds it for protective purposes.

One solution to the packaging problem in international logistics has been the development of intermodal containers—large metal boxes that fit on trucks, ships, railroad cars, and airplanes and ease the frequent transfer of goods in international shipments. In addition, containers offer greater safety from pilferage and damage. Of course, if merchandise from a containerized shipment is lost, frequently the entire container has been removed. Developed in different forms for both sea and air transportation, containers also offer better utilization of carrier space because of standardization of size. The shipper therefore may benefit from lower transportation rates.

Container traffic is heavily dependent on the existence of appropriate handling facilities, both domestically and internationally. In addition, the quality of inland transportation must be considered. If transportation for containers is not available and the merchandise must be removed and reloaded, the expected cost reductions may not materialize.

In some countries, rules for the handling of containers may be designed to maintain employment. For example, U.S. union rules obligate shippers to withhold containers from firms that do not employ members of the International Longshoreman Association for loading and unloading containers within a 50-mile radius of Atlantic or Gulf ports. Such restrictions can result in an onerous cost burden.

Overall, close attention must be paid to international packaging. The customer who ordered and paid for the merchandise expects it to arrive on time and in good condition. Even with replacements and insurance, the customer will not be satisfied if there are delays. This dissatisfaction will usually translate directly into lost sales.

Management of International Logistics

Because the very purpose of a multinational firm is to benefit from system synergism, a persuasive argument can be made for the coordination of international logistics at corporate headquarters. Without coordination, subsidiaries will tend to optimize their individual efficiency but jeopardize the overall performance of the firm.

Centralized Logistics Management

A significant characteristic of the centralized approach to international logistics is the existence of headquarters staff that retains decision-making power over logistics activities affecting international subsidiaries. Such an approach is particularly valuable in instances where corporations have become international by rapid growth and have lost the benefit of a cohesive strategy.

If headquarters exerts control, it must also take the primary responsibility for its decisions. Clearly, ill will may arise if local managers are appraised and rewarded on the basis of performance they do not control. This may be particularly problematic if headquarters staff suffers from a lack of information or expertise.

To avoid internal problems both headquarters staff and local logistics management should report to one person. This person, whether the vice president for international logistics or the president of the firm, can then become the final arbiter to decide the firm's priorities. Of course, this individual should also be in charge of determining appropriate rewards for managers, both at headquarters and abroad, so that corporate decisions that alter a manager's performance level will not affect the manager's appraisal and evaluation. Further, this individual can contribute an objective view when inevitable conflicts arise in international logistics coordination. The internationally centralized decision-making process leads to an overall logistics management perspective that can dramatically improve profitability.

Decentralized Logistics Management

When a firm serves many international markets that are diverse in nature, total centralization would leave the firm unresponsive to local adaptation needs. If each subsidiary is made a profit center in itself, each one carries the full responsibility for its performance, which can lead to greater local management satisfaction and to better adaptation to local market conditions. Yet often such decentralization deprives the logistics function of the benefits of coordination. For example, whereas headquarters, referring to its large volume of total international shipments, may be able to extract bottom rates from transportation firms, individual subsidiaries by themselves may not have similar bargaining power. The same argument applies also to the sourcing situation, where the coordination of shipments by the purchasing firm may be much more cost-effective than individual shipments from many small suppliers around the world.

Once products are within a specific market, however, increased input from local logistics operations should be expected and encouraged. At the very least, local managers should be able to provide input into the logistics decisions generated by headquarters. Ideally, within a frequent planning cycle, local managers can identify the logistics benefits and constraints existing in their particular market and communicate them to headquarters. Headquarters can then either adjust its international logistics strategy accordingly or can explain to the manager why system optimization requires actions different from the ones recommended. Such a justification process will greatly help in reducing the potential for animosity between local and headquarters operations.

Contract Logistics

While the choice is open to maintain either centralized or decentralized in-house logistical management, a growing preference among international firms is to outsource, which means to employ outside logistical expertise. Often referred to as contract, or "third-party," logistics, it is a rapidly expanding industry. More than 70 percent of Fortune 500 companies have outsourced at least one major logistics function such as transportation management, freight payment, warehouse management, shipment tracking, or other transportation-related functions.[13] The main thrust behind the idea is that individual firms are experts in their industry and should therefore concentrate only on their operations. Third-party logistics providers, on the other hand, are experts solely at logistics, with the knowledge and means to perform efficient and innovative services for those companies in need. The goal is improved service at equal or lower cost.

Logistics providers' services vary in scope. For instance, some may use their own assets in physical transportation, while others subcontract out portions of the job. Certain other providers are not involved as much with the actual transportation as they are with developing systems and databases or consulting on administrative management services. In many instances, the partnership consists of working closely with established transport providers such as Federal Express or UPS. The concept of improving service, cutting costs, and unloading the daily management onto willing experts is driving the momentum of contract logistics.

One of the greatest benefits of contracting out the logistics function in a foreign market is the ability to take advantage of an existing network complete with resources and experience. The local expertise and image are crucial when a business is just starting up. The prospect of newly entering a region such as Europe with different regions, business formats, and languages can be frightening without access to a seasoned and familiar logistics provider.

One of the main arguments leveled against contract logistics is the loss of the firm's control in the supply chain. Yet contract logistics does not and should not require the handing over of control. Rather, it offers concentration on one's specialization—a division of labor. The control and responsibility toward the customer remain with the firm, even though operations may move to a highly trained outside organization.

The Supply Chain and the Internet

Many firms still use their Web sites as a marketing and advertising tool without expanding them to order-taking capabilities. That is changing rapidly. Net e-commerce revenue in Europe alone reached $87.4 billion in 2000 out of a global total of $657 billion, which is expected to surpass $1.5 billion by 2004.[14]

Companies wishing to enter e-commerce will not have to do so on their own. Hub sites (also known as virtual malls or digital intermediaries) bring together buyers, sellers, distributors, and transaction payment processors in a single marketplace, making convenience the key attraction. Forrester Research estimates that B2B (business-to-business) e-commerce will surge past $1 *trillion* by 2003. The future is also growing brighter for hubs in the consumer-to-consumer market, where companies like eBay are setting high standards of profitability.[15]

When customers have the ability to access a company through the Internet, a company itself has to be prepared for 24-hour order-taking and customer service, and to have the regulatory and customs-handling expertise for international delivery. The instantaneous interactivity that users experience will also be translated into an expectation of expedient delivery of answers and products ordered.

Some companies elect to build their own international distribution networks. Both QVC, a televised shopping service, and amazon.com, an online retailer of books, have distribution centers in Britain and Germany to take advantage of the European Internet audience and to fulfill more quickly and cheaply the orders generated by their Web sites. Transactions and the information they provide about the buyers also allow for more customization and service by region, market, or even individual customer.

For industries such as music and motion pictures, the Internet is both an opportunity and a threat. The Web provides a new, efficient method of distribution and customization of products. At the same time, it can be a channel for intellectual property violation through unauthorized posting on other Web sites where these products can be downloaded.[16] For example, the music industry is very concerned about a shift in the balance of economic power: If artists can deliver their works directly to customers via technologies such as MP3, what will be the role of labels and distributors?

A number of hurdles and uncertainties may keep companies out of global markets or from exploiting them to their full potential. Some argue that the World Wide Web does not live up to its name, since it is mostly a tool for the United States and Europe. For all countries, but particularly developing nations, the issue of universal access to the Internet is crucial. Such access depends on the speed with which governments end their monopolistic structures in telecommunication and open their markets to competition. The 1997 World Trade Organization agreement on telecommunication accelerated the process of liberalization, while access to the Internet is undergoing major expansion through new technologies such as NetTV and Web phones. As Internet penetration levels increase in the near future due to technological advances, improvements in many countries' Web infrastructures, and customer acceptance, e-business will become truly global.

Logistics and Security

The entire field of supply chain management and logistics has been thoroughly affected by newly emerging security concerns. After the terrorist attacks of 2001, companies have had to learn that the pace of international transactions has slowed down and that formerly routine steps will now take longer. While in decades past many governmental efforts were devoted to speeding up transactions across borders, national security reasons are now forcing governments to erect new barriers and conduct new inspections. Logistics is one of the business activities most affected.[17]

Modern transportation systems have proved to be critical to terrorist activities. They provide the means for the perpetrators to quickly arrive at, and depart from, the sites of attacks. On occasion, terrorists have even used transportations systems themselves to carry out their crimes.

Logistics systems are often the targets of attacks. Consider the vulnerability of pipelines used for carrying oil, natural gas and other energy sources. Logistics systems also serve as the conduit for the weapons or people who are planning to carry out attacks. These systems are the true soft spots of vulnerability for both nations and firms. Take the issue of sea ports: Some 95 percent of all international trade shipments to the United States arrive by sea at 361 ports around the nation. Thousands of additional shipments arrive by truck and rail. In most instances, the containers are secured by nothing more than a ten-cent seal that easily can be broken.

The need to institute new safeguards for international shipments will affect the ability of firms to efficiently plan their international shipments. There is now more uncertainty and less control over the timing of arrivals and departures. There is also a much greater need for internal control and supervision of shipments. Cargo security will increasingly need not only to ensure that nothing goes missing, but also that nothing has been added to a shipment.

Firms with a just-in-time regimen are exploring alternative management strategies. Planning includes the shift of international shipments from air carriage to sea. Some U.S. firms are thinking about replacing international shipments with domestic ones, where transportation via truck would replace transborder movement altogether and eliminate the use of vulnerable ports. Further down the horizon are planning scenarios in which firms consider the effects of substantial and long-term interruptions of supplies or operations. Still, any actual move away from existing JIT systems is likely to be minor unless new large-scale interruptions occur.

Reverse Logistics

By using logistics, the international marketer can play an increasingly important role in allowing the firm to operate in an environmentally conscious way. Environmental laws, expectations, and self-imposed goals set by firms are difficult to adhere to without a logistics orientation that systematically takes these concerns into account. Since laws and regulations differ across the world, the firm's efforts need to be responsive to a wide variety of requirements. One logistics orientation that has grown in importance due to environmental concerns is the development of **reverse distribution systems.** Such systems are instrumental in ensuring that the firm not only delivers the product to the market, but also can retrieve it from the market for subsequent use, recycling, or disposal. To a growing degree, the ability to develop such reverse logistics is a key determinant for market acceptance and profitability.

Society is beginning to recognize that retrieval should not be restricted to short-term consumer goods, such as bottles. Rather, it may be even more important to devise systems that enable the retrieval and disposal of long-term capital goods, such as cars, refrigerators, air conditioners, and industrial goods, with the least possible burden on the environment. Increasingly, governments establish rules that hold the manufacturer responsible for the ultimate disposal of the product at the end of its economic life. In Germany, for example, car manufacturers are required to take back their used vehicles for dismantling and recycling. The design of such long-term systems across the world may well be one of the key challenges and opportunities for the logistician and will require close collaboration with all other functions in the firm, such as design, production, and marketing. *The International Marketplace 17.3* presents some of the major issues connected to the design of a reverse logistics system.

On the transportation side, logistics managers will need to expand their involvement in carrier and routing selection. Shippers of oil or other potentially hazardous materials are increasingly expected to ensure that the carriers used have excellent safety records and use only double-hulled ships. Society may even expect corporate involvement in choosing the route that the shipment will travel, preferring routes that are far from ecologically important and sensitive zones.

In the packaging field, environmental concerns are also growing on the part of individuals and governments. Increasingly, it is expected that the amount of packaging materials used is minimized and that the materials used are more environmentally friendly.

Companies need to learn how to simultaneously achieve environmental and economic goals. Esprit, the apparel maker, and The Body Shop, a British cosmetics producer, screen all their suppliers for environmental and socially responsible practices. ISO 14000 is a standard specifically targeted at encouraging international environmental practices by evaluating companies both at the organization level (management systems, environmental performance, and environmental auditing) and at the product level (life-cycle assessment, labeling, and product standards).[18] From the environmental perspective, those practices are desirable that bring about fewer shipments, less handling, and more direct movement. Such practices are to be weighed against optimal efficiency routings, including just-in-time inventory

THE INTERNATIONAL MARKETPLACE   17.3

Happy Returns

Product returns have always been a fact of business life, especially for catalog retailers, whose return rates can run to 35 percent for goods such as shoes and clothes. But with the growth of direct-to-consumer Internet sales, the reverse supply chain has exploded, amounting to over $100 billion per year—greater than the GDP of two-thirds of the world's countries! Industries facing the highest return volume are magazine/book publishing (50 percent), catalog retailers (18 to 35 percent), and greeting card companies (20 to 30 percent).

Reverse logistics is today's competitive differentiator. As firms are quickly realizing, providing excellent forward logistics—supplying the right products at the right quantities at the right time—is merely the price of admission for success, whereas reverse logistics may be a firm's potential profit center and competitive advantage. For example, in the early 1990s, Hallmark representatives collected and destroyed out-of-season merchandise, and no value was reclaimed. Today, however, Hallmark uses a reverse logistics firm to collect excess seasonal inventory and repackages it for resale in secondary markets.

Like forward logistics, reverse logistics requires quality information and processes, and the ability to track both at all times. Reverse logistics, however, is also a complex customer service, inventory control, information management, cost accounting, and disposal process. Customers don't want to wait weeks before charges are removed from their credit cards, and returned goods idling in warehouses cause both higher carrying costs and the risk of obsolescence and shrinkage.

Reverse logistics management is highly specialized. Return and reclamation rates vary drastically between industries such as cosmetics or pharmaceuticals. The objectives of successful reverse logistics are the same: recovering the greatest value possible from returns, maintaining customer loyalty, controlling costs, and harvesting information to help reduce future returns. Successful reverse logistics greatly affects a company's bottom line. Idle electronic and computer parts in inventory lose 12 percent of value each month. Conversely, efficient management of returns can reduce companies' annual logistics costs by as much as 10 percent.

With pollution control and good environmental management now on the corporate agenda, reverse logistics also entails an environmental dimension, yet another potential profit center. Returned items can be processed for scrap and recycled: As Xerox Corporation boasts, its Green World Alliance Recycling Program kept 160 million pounds of materials out of landfills in 2001. Further, 90 percent of Xerox-designed equipment can be re-manufactured. In one year alone, consumers worldwide returned more than 3 million cartridges for recycling. For returned items that range from obsolete or damaged, goods can be refurbished and resold, a practice both environmentally responsible and profitable. For example, IBM receives nearly 10,000 used machines each week in the United States alone and 16,000 per week globally. While operating recycling sites throughout the United States, Europe, Asia, and South Africa, IBM also auctions refurbished products on its own Web site, generating an additional $100 million in sales in only one year.

SOURCES: Bob Trebilcock, "Seven Deadly Sins of Reverse Logistics," *Logistics Management,* June 2002; and "Environment, Health and Safety," **http://www.xerox.com**, accessed November 7, 2002.

and quantity discount purchasing. For example, even though a just-in-time inventory system may connote highly desirable inventory savings, the resulting cost of frequent delivery, additional highway congestion, and incremental air pollution also need to be factored into the planning horizon. Despite the difficulty, firms will need to assert leadership in such trade-off considerations in order to provide society with a better quality of life.

Summary

The relevance of international logistics and supply chain management was not widely recognized in the past. As competitiveness is becoming increasingly dependent on cost efficiency, however, the field is emerging as one of major importance because international distribution comprises between 10 and 30 percent of the total landed cost of an international order.

International logistics is concerned with the flow of materials into, through, and out of the international corporation and therefore includes materials management as well as physical distribution. The logistician must recognize the total systems demands of the firm in order to develop trade-offs between various logistics components. By taking a supply chain perspective, the marketing manager can develop logistics systems that are highly customer-focused and very cost-efficient. Implementation of such a system requires close collaboration between all members of the supply chain.

International logistics differs from domestic activities in that it deals with greater distances, new variables, and greater complexity because of country-specific differences. One major factor to consider is transportation. The international marketer needs to understand transportation infrastructures in other countries and modes of transportation such as ocean shipping and airfreight. The choice among these modes will depend on the customer's demands and the firm's transit time, predictability, and cost requirements. In addition, noneconomic factors such as government regulations weigh heavily in this decision.

Inventory management is another major consideration. Inventories abroad are expensive to maintain yet often crucial for international success. The marketer must evaluate requirements for order cycle times and customer service levels in order to develop an international inventory policy that can also serve as a strategic management tool.

The marketer must also deal with international storage issues and determine where to locate inventories. International warehouse space will have to be leased or purchased and decisions made about utilizing foreign trade zones.

International packaging is important because it ensures arrival of the merchandise at the ultimate destination in safe condition. In developing packaging requirements, the marketer must consider environmental concerns as well as climate, freight, and handling conditions.

International logistics management is growing in importance. The international marketer must consider the benefits and the drawbacks that the information technology revolution has brought to supply chain and logistics activities. Increasingly, better implementation of change in logistics is key to defining a firm's competitiveness. Security concerns have also greatly affected the planning and implementation of the logistics interface. Companies also will have to think about the need to build reverse logistics systems, when customer returns and recycling activities make such systems a necessity.

Key Terms

materials management	bulk service	consular invoice
physical distribution	tramp service	certificate of origin
systems concept	container ships	import license
total cost concept	density	foreign exchange license
trade-off concept	reliability	international freight forwarder
supply chain management	bill of lading	customs broker
currency variation	shipper's export declaration	inventory carrying costs
transportation mode	shipper's declaration for dangerous	maquiladora program
liner service	goods	reverse distribution systems

Questions for Discussion

1. Contrast the use of ocean shipping to airfreight.
2. Explain the meaning of supply chain management.
3. What is the impact of transit time on international logistics and how can a firm improve its performance?
4. How can an international firm reduce its order cycle time?
5. Why should customer service levels differ internationally? Is it, for example, ethical to offer a lower customer service level in developing countries than in industrialized countries?
6. How can an improved logistics infrastructure contribute to the economic development of Eastern Europe?
7. What steps can logisticians take to make their effort more environmentally friendly?

Internet Exercises

1. What types of information are available to exporters on the Transport web? Go to the site, **http://www.transportweb.com** and give examples of transportation links that an exporter would find helpful and explain why.

2. Determine the length of transit time a shipment takes between two international destinations. What else should you know before making a shipping decision? Go to **http://www.apl.com** and click on "Schedules."

Recommended Readings

Anderson, David. *Mass Customization: The Ultimate Supply Chain Management and Lean Manufacturing Strategy*. London: CIM, 2002.

Burt, David, Donald Dobler, and Stephen Starling. *World Class Management: The Key to Supply Chain Management*. Boston: McGraw-Hill, 2003.

Monczka, Robert, Robert B. Handfield, and Robert J. Trent. *Purchasing and Supply Chain Management*. Mason, OH: South-Western, 2001.

Schechter, Damon, and Gordon F. Sander. *Delivering the Goods: The Art of Managing Your Supply Chain*. New York: John Wiley & Sons, 2002.

Simchi-Levi, David, Philip Kaminsky, and Edith Simchi-Levi. *Designing & Managing the Supply Chain: Concepts, Strategies, and Case Studies*. Boston: McGraw-Hill, 2003.

Stauss, Bernd, and Wolfgang Seidel. *Beschwerdemanagement* (complaint management), 3rd ed. Munich: Hanser, 2002.

Stock, James R., and Douglas M. Lambert. *Strategic Logistics Management,* 4th ed. Burr Ridge, IL: McGraw Hill, 2001.

Stroh, Michael. *A Practical Guide to Transportation and Logistics*. Dumont, NJ: Logistics Network, 2001.

chapter 18
Global
Promotional Strategies

THE INTERNATIONAL MARKETPLACE   18.1

Being a Good Sport Globally

In any given country, the majority of corporate sponsorship goes to sports. Of the nearly $25 billion spent worldwide in 2002, two-thirds was allocated to sports. Within sports, the two flagship events are the World Cup in soccer and the Olympic Games (both summer and winter). Sponsors want to align themselves with—and create—meaningful sports-related moments for consumers. At the same time, consumers associate sponsors of sports events with leadership, teamwork, and pursuit of excellence, as well as friendship.

Sponsorships have been a cornerstone of the Coca-Cola Company's marketing efforts for 100 years, having started with using sports stars such as world champion cyclist Bobby Walthour in ads in 1903. Presently, the company is the world's biggest sports sponsor, with total sponsorship-related expenses at $1 billion annually. These activities span different types of sports and various geographies (as shown below).

Coca-Cola spent $26 million for its sponsorship of the World Cup in 2002, which gave it the right to use the World Cup logo/trademarks, exclusive positioning and branding around the event, as well as premium perimeter advertising positions at every game. Sponsorships include a guarantee that no rival brands can be officially linked to the tournament or use the logo or trademarks. To assure exclusivity, FIFA (soccer's governing body) bought all key billboard advertising space around the main stadia for the tournament, and this space was offered to the sponsors first. In addition, every main sponsor got 250 tickets for each game of the tournament for promotional purposes or corporate entertainment (of key constituents, such as intermediaries or customers).

Each country organization within Coca-Cola decides which programs it wants to use during sponsorship depending on its goals, which are jointly set by local managers and headquarters. For example, in Rio de Janeiro, the company erected huge TV screens on which people could watch World Cup games. Given that Ecuador qualified for the tournament for the first time in its history, this fact was played up in local advertising. In Japan, the company used I-mode phones in addition to traditional media to create meaningful and relevant connections with the World Cup. Naturally, there is always substantial overlap in programs between markets, with headquarters' 20-person team in charge of the coordination effort. One example of this was an online World Cup game that headquarters created in conjunction with Yahoo! and then helped each interested country localize. Another global program was Coca-Cola Go! Stadium Art which allowed consumers and artists to compete to create ads that ran in the various stadia throughout the tournament. The company also joined forces with other sponsors for cross-promotional efforts, e.g., with Adidas to give away the Official Match Ball, with McDonald's for consumer promotions, and with Toshiba on a cyber cup tournament.

Although marketers have become far more demanding in terms of their sponsorships, the World Cup is one of the few global events available. Pulling out would mean a competitor stepping in (for example, when Vauxhall left in 1998, Hyundai took its place).

While measurement of the return on such investment is challenging, Coca-Cola evaluates such dimensions as the number of new corporate customers that sell Coke in their stores, the incremental amount of promotional/display activity, and new vending placement. The influence on the brand is the most difficult to establish; World Cup sponsorship has been suggested to have boosted its presence especially in the emerging and developing markets.

Coca-Cola's Sports Sponsorships

Olympics (since 1928)

- Supports athletes and teams in nearly 200 countries in exchange for exclusive rights in nonalcoholic beverage category through 2008
- Official soft/sports drink (Coca-Cola, PowerAde)
- Runs marketing programs in over 130 countries

Soccer

- FIFA partner since 1974—signed landmark eight-year agreement through 2006 to be official soft/sports drink at Men's World Cup 2002/2006, Women's World Cup 1999/2003, Confederation Cup competitions, under 20/under 17 World Youth Championships
- Also sponsors Copa America, Asian Football Confederation, over 40 national teams

Basketball

- Signed 100-year agreement in 1998 for Sprite to be official soft drink of NBA/WNBA
- Advertising in over 100 countries

Others

- Coca-Cola Classic: official soft drink of National Football League
- Surge/PowerAde: official sports drink of National Hockey League
- Coca-Cola Classic/PowerAde: official soft drink/sports drink of Rugby World Cup
- Sponsor of International Paralympics/Special Olympics

SOURCES: "Still Waiting for That Winning Kick," *Business Week*, October 21, 2002, 116–118; "The Best Global Brands," *Business Week*, August 5, 2002, 92–94; "World Cup: Sponsors Need to Get in the Game," *Business Week*, June 17, 2002, 52; "World Cup Marketing," *Advertising Age Global*, March 2002, 17–30; and "Too Many Players on the Field," *Advertising Age*, December 10, 2001, 3.

THE GENERAL REQUIREMENTS of effective marketing communications apply to the multinational corporation as well; however, the environments and the situations usually are more numerous and call for coordination of the promotional effort. Increasingly, marketers opt for varying degrees of panregional and integrative approaches to take advantage of similarities in markets they serve, as seen in *The International Marketplace 18.1.*

The technology is in place for global communication efforts, but difficult challenges still remain in the form of cultural, economic, ethnic, regulatory, and demographic differences in the various countries and regions. Standardization of any magnitude requires sound management systems and excellent communication to ensure uniform strategic and tactical thinking of all the professionals in the overseas marketing chain.[1] One marketer has suggested the development of a worldwide visual language that would be understandable and that would not offend cultural sensitivities.

This chapter will analyze the elements to be managed in promotional efforts in terms of environmental opportunities and constraints. A framework is provided for the planning of promotional campaigns. Although the discussion focuses mostly on advertising, other elements of the promotion mix, especially sales promotion and publicity, fit integrally into the planning model. Naturally, all of the mass selling methods have to be planned in conjunction with personal selling efforts. For example, personal selling often relies on updated direct mailing lists and promotional materials sent to prospects before the first sales call.

Planning Promotional Campaigns

The planning for promotional campaigns consists of the following seven stages, which usually overlap or take place concurrently, especially after the basics of the campaign have been agreed on:

1. Determine the target audience
2. Determine specific campaign objectives
3. Determine the budget
4. Determine media strategy
5. Determine the message
6. Determine the campaign approach
7. Determine campaign effectiveness[2]

The actual content of these stages will change by type of campaign situation; compare, for example, a local campaign for which headquarters provides support versus a global corporate image campaign.

The Target Audience

Global marketers face multiple audiences beyond customers. The expectations of these audiences have to be researched to ensure the appropriateness of campaign decision making. Consider the following publics with whom communication is necessary: suppliers, intermediaries, government, the local community, bankers and creditors, media organizations, shareholders, and employees. Each can be reached with an appropriate mix of tools. A multinational corporation that wants to boost its image with the government and the local community may sponsor events. One of the approaches available is **cause-related marketing,** in which the company, or one of its brands, is linked with a cause such as environmental protection or children's health. For example, Unilever's Funfit Program for its Persil washing powder brand in Europe creates resource packs for teachers to help boost children's fitness through physical education lessons. Microsoft launched a

Web site in Singapore to further the use of information technology. For every page hit within the site, Microsoft donated one cent to three local charities. This type of activity can benefit a brand but must be backed by a genuine effort within the company to behave responsibly.[3]

Some campaigns may be targeted at multiple audiences. For example, British Airways' "Manhattan Landing" campaign (in which Manhattan Island takes to the air and lands in London) was directed not only at international business travelers but also at employees, the travel industry, and potential stockholders (the campaign coincided with the privatization of the airline). Once the repositioning was achieved, the airline focused on establishing its global stature with the "Face" campaign and switched later to service enhancements with "Sweet Dreams."[4] As companies such as airlines become more internationally involved, target audience characteristics change. American Airlines, which enjoys a huge domestic market, had foreign routes generate 28 percent of passenger miles in 2001 compared with virtually none in 1980.[5]

An important aspect of research is to determine multimarket target audience similarities. If such exist, panregional or global campaigns can be attempted. Grey Advertising checks for commonalities in variables such as economic expectations, demographics, income, and education. Consumer needs and wants are assessed for common features. An increasing number of companies are engaging in **corporate image advertising** in support of their more traditional tactical product-specific and local advertising efforts.[6] Especially for multidivisional companies, an umbrella campaign may help either to boost the image of lesser-known product lines or make the company itself be understood correctly or perceived more positively. ABB, the global engineering and technology company, wants to be better known among its constituents and launched a major global campaign to ensure that (an example of which is provided in Figure 18.1). Canon, for example, is using the approach to reposition itself as an information technology specialist instead of just a manufacturer of office automation machines and as a serious contender to Xerox in the high end of the market.[7] Costs may also be saved in engaging in global image campaigning, especially if the same campaign or core concepts can be used across borders.

Often, however, problems may emerge. For example, Tang was marketed in the United States as an orange juice substitute, which did not succeed in testing abroad. In France, for example, Tang was repositioned as a refreshment because the French rarely drink orange juice at breakfast. In countries like the Philippines,

Figure 18.1   An Example of a Corporate Image Campaign

SOURCE: Courtesy of ABB; **http://www.abb.com**.

Tang could be marketed as a premium drink, whereas in Brazil, it was a low-priced item.[8] Audience similarities are more easily found in business markets.[9]

Campaign Objectives

Nothing is more essential to the planning of international promotional campaigns than the establishment of clearly defined, measurable objectives. These objectives can be divided into overall global and regional objectives as well as local objectives. The objectives that are set at the local level are more specific and set measurable targets for individual markets. These objectives may be product- or service-related or related to the entity itself. Typical goals are to increase awareness, enhance image, and improve market share in a particular market. Whatever the objective, it has to be measurable for control purposes.

While FedEx is one the top three transportation companies in Latin America, it is not the household name it is in North America. The company wanted to increase brand awareness among its target audience of small and medium-sized international shippers. Among large corporate clients, FedEx has no concerns and marketing to them is usually done through personal visits by the FedEx sales force. To reach the intended target, FedEx created a 30-second television spot featuring a soccer team's manager distressed over the fate of missing uniforms he had shipped to Madrid for a big match. Using soccer in the region is an effective way to cut through languages and cultures.[10]

There is a move by many governments to influence how their countries are perceived to gain commercial or political advantage.[11] After 9/11, for example, the United States has needed to build a new level of understanding of the country and its values and policies, especially in countries where resentment of its power and influence may be high. Part of this effort is a $10 million advertising campaign from McCann Erickson featuring stories of Muslim life in the United States. It ran on TV and radio from Indonesia through the Middle East. The campaign was based on the premise that Arab and U.S. cultures share family as a common core value. This campaign is also very much in the interest of U.S. marketers who have found that their brands are on the firing line as symbols of the United States.[12]

Local objectives are typically developed as a combination of headquarters (global or regional) and country organization involvement. Basic guidelines are initiated by headquarters, whereas local organizations set the actual country-specific goals. These goals are subject to headquarters approval, mainly to ensure consistency. Although some campaigns, especially global ones, may have more headquarters involvement than usual, local input is still quite important, especially to ensure appropriate implementation of the subsequent programs at the local level.

The Budget

The promotional budget links established objectives with media, message, and control decisions. Ideally, the budget would be set as a response to the objectives to be met, but resource constraints often preclude this approach. Many marketers use an objective task method, as a survey of 484 advertising managers for consumer goods in fifteen countries indicates (see Table 18.1); however, realities may force compromises between ideal choices and resources available.[13] As a matter of fact, available funds may dictate the basis from which the objective task method can start. Furthermore, advertising budgets should be set on a market-by-market basis because of competitive differences across markets. When it comes to global image campaigns, for example, headquarters should provide country organizations extra funds for their implementation.

Budgets can also be used as a control mechanism if headquarters retains final budget approval. In these cases, headquarters decision makers must have a clear understanding of cost and market differences to be able to make rational decisions.

In terms of worldwide ad spending, some of the leaders in 2001 were Procter & Gamble ($3.8 billion), Unilever ($3.0 billion), General Motors ($3.0 billion), Ford ($2.3 billion), Toyota ($2.2 billion), AOL Time Warner ($2.1 billion), and Philip

Table 18.1	Budgeting Methods for Promotional Programs

| Budgeting Method | Percentage of Respondents Using this Method* | Major Differences | |
		Lowest Percentages	Highest Percentages
Objective and task	64%	Sweden (36%) Argentina (44%)	Canada (87%) Singapore (86%)
Percentage of sales	48	Germany (31%)	Brazil (73%) Hong Kong (70%)
Executive judgment	33	Finland (8%) Germany (8%)	USA (64%) Denmark (51%) Brazil (46%) Great Britain (46%)
All-you-can-afford	12	Argentina (0%) Israel (0%)	Sweden (30%) Germany (25%) Great Britain (24%)
Matched competitors	12	Denmark (0%) Israel (0%)	Germany (33%) Sweden (33%) Great Britain (22%)
Same as last year plus a little more	9	Israel (0%)	
Same as last year	3		
Other	10	Finland (0%) Germany (0%) Israel (0%)	Canada (24%) Mexico (21%)

*Total exceeds 100 percent because respondents checked all budgeting methods that they used.

SOURCE: Nicolaos E. Synodinos, Charles F. Keown, and Laurence W. Jacobs, "Transnational Advertising Practices," *Journal of Advertising Research* 29 (April–May 1989): 43–50. © 1989, by the Advertising Research Foundation. Reprinted by permission.

Morris ($1.9 billion). Geographic differences exist in spending; for example, while Procter & Gamble spent 44 percent of its budget in the United States, Unilever's spending there was only 19 percent. The top 100 advertisers incurred nearly half of their spending in the United States, with Europe second at 34 percent. Asia-Pacific was a distant third, commanding only 13 percent of measured media bought.[14]

Media Strategy

Target audience characteristics, campaign objectives, and the budget form the basis for the choice between media vehicles and the development of a media schedule. The major factors determining the choice of the media vehicles to be used are (1) the availability of the media in a given market, (2) the product or service itself, and (3) media habits of the intended audience.

Media Availability

Media spending, which totaled $312 billion in 2002, varies dramatically around the world, as seen in Figure 18.2. In absolute terms, the United States spends more money on advertising than most of the other major advertising nations combined. Other major spenders are Japan, the United Kingdom, Germany, Canada, and France. The mature U.S. market anticipates continued growth in the future, but European integration and the development of the Pacific Rim's consumer markets are likely

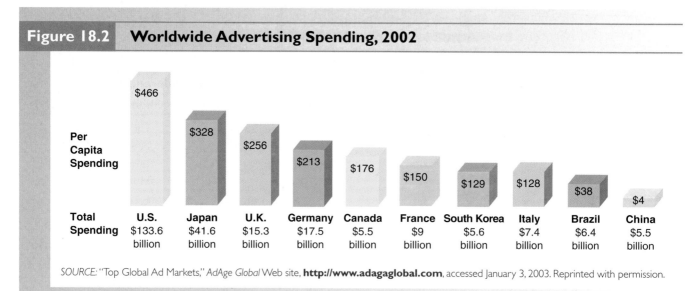

Figure 18.2 Worldwide Advertising Spending, 2002

Per Capita Spending

	U.S.	Japan	U.K.	Germany	Canada	France	South Korea	Italy	Brazil	China
Per Capita Spending	$466	$328	$256	$213	$176	$150	$129	$128	$38	$4
Total Spending	$133.6 billion	$41.6 billion	$15.3 billion	$17.5 billion	$5.5 billion	$9 billion	$5.6 billion	$7.4 billion	$6.4 billion	$5.5 billion

SOURCE: "Top Global Ad Markets," *AdAge Global* Web site, **http://www.adagaglobal.com**, accessed January 3, 2003. Reprinted with permission.

to fuel major growth after a two-year (2001–2002) advertising recession. The Athens Olympics (2004) are expected to provide a major boost to overall spending.[15]

Naturally, this spending varies by market. Countries devoting the highest percentage to television were Peru (84 percent), Mexico (73 percent), and Venezuela (67 percent). In some countries, the percentage devoted to print is still high: Kuwait (91 percent), Norway (77 percent), and Sweden (77 percent). Radio accounts for more than 20 percent of total measured media in only a few countries, such as Trinidad and Tobago, Nepal, and Honduras. Outdoor/transit advertising accounted for 48 percent of Bolivia's media spending but only 3 percent in Germany.[16] Cinema advertising is important in countries such as India and Nigeria. Until a few years ago, the prevailing advertising technique used by the Chinese consisted of outdoor boards and posters found outside factories; today, more new TV and radio stations are coming on-air. The Internet is well on the way to establishing itself as a complementary advertising medium in Europe and the Americas. In other parts of the world it has yet to make its mark. The projection is that the Internet may have a 5 percent market share in world advertising by 2002, with Internet ad spending reaching $17 billion, as shown in Table 18.2. The level is estimated to reach $28 billion by 2005 as other markets increase their volume as well. In addition to PCs, mobile phones and interactive TV will become delivery mechanisms.

The media available to the international marketer in major ad markets are summarized in Table 18.3. The breakdown by media points to the enormous diversity in how media are used in a given market. These figures do not tell the whole story, however, which emphasizes the need for careful homework on the part of the international manager charged with media strategy. As an example, Brazil has five television networks, but one of them—Globo TV—corners 50 percent of all television advertising spending. Throughout Latin America, the tendency is to allocate half or more of total advertising budgets to television, with the most coveted spots on prime-time soap operas that attract viewers from Mexico to Brazil. In general, advertising in Latin America requires flexibility and creativity. Inflation rates have caused advertising rates to increase dramatically in countries like Argentina. In Mexico, advertisers can use the "French Plan," which protects participating advertisers from price increases during the year and additionally gives the advertiser two spots for the price of one. For these concessions, the advertiser must pay for the year's entire advertising schedule by October of the year before.

The major problems affecting global promotional efforts involve conflicting national regulations. Even within the EU there is no uniform legal standard. Conditions do vary from country to country, and ads must comply with national regula-

| **Table 18.2** | **Global Online Advertising Spending by Region (in $ millions)** | | | | | | |

Region	1999	2000	2001	2002	2003	2004	2005
North America	$3,509	$5,390	$7,444	$9,768	$12,237	$14,623	$16,913
Europe	434	906	1,535	2,258	3,118	4,111	5,263
Asia	225	502	880	1,375	1,922	2,556	3,324
Latin America	52	127	240	402	628	888	1,168
Australia/New Zealand	24	74	135	208	288	373	462
Rest of the world	9	28	61	118	211	351	578
TOTAL	$4,253	$7,027	$10,296	$14,129	$18,402	$22,903	$27,708

SOURCE: Jupiter Media Matrix, Inc. in "International: Global Digital Divide Narrowest for Mobile Market," *Marketing News*, July 8, 2002, 19. Reprinted with permission.

tion. Most European countries either observe the Code of Advertising Practice of the International Chamber of Commerce or have their guidelines based on it.[17] Some of the regulations include limits on the amount of time available for advertisements; for example, in Italy, the state channels allow a maximum of 12 percent advertising per hour and 4 percent per week, and commercial stations allow 18 percent per hour and 15 percent per week. Furthermore, the leading Italian stations do not guarantee audience delivery when spots are bought. Strict separation between programs and commercials is almost a universal requirement, preventing U.S.-style sponsored programs. Restrictions on items such as comparative claims and gender stereotypes are prevalent; for example, Germany prohibits the use of superlatives such as "best."

Until now, with few exceptions, most nations have been very successful in controlling advertising that enters their borders. When commercials were not allowed on the state-run stations, advertisers in Belgium had been accustomed to placing their ads on the Luxembourg station. Radio Luxembourg has traditionally been used to beam messages to the United Kingdom. Currently, however, approximately half of the homes in Europe have access to additional television broadcasts through either cable or direct satellite, and television will no longer be restricted by national boundaries. The implications of this to global marketers are significant. The viewer's choice will be expanded, leading to competition among government-run public channels, competing state channels from neighboring countries, private channels, and pan-European channels.[18] This means that marketers need to make sure that advertising works not only within markets but across countries as well. As a consequence, media buying will become more challenging.

Product Influences

Marketers and advertising agencies are currently frustrated by wildly differing restrictions on how products can be advertised. Agencies often have to produce several separate versions to comply with various national regulations. Consumer protection in general has dominated the regulatory scene both in the European Union and the United States.[19] Changing and standardizing these regulations, even in an area like the EU, is a long and difficult process. While some countries have banned tobacco advertising altogether (e.g., France), some have voluntary restriction systems in place. For example, in the United Kingdom, tobacco advertising is not allowed in magazines aimed at very young women, but it is permitted in other women's magazines. Starting in 2003, tobacco companies are required to print vivid pictures of lung cancer victims and diseased organs on cigarette packets sold in the United Kingdom. The EU has tried to develop union-wide regulation and has proposed to ban all forms of cross-border tobacco advertising effective 2005.

Table 18.3   Global Media Breakdown

Market/Media Fact	United States	Japan	Germany	United Kingdom	France	Italy	Brazil	South Korea	Canada	China
Ad Spending, 2002 ($ billions)	$133.6	$41.6	$17.5	$15.3	$9	$7.4	$6.4	$6.1	$5.5	$5.5
Media Percentage										
Newspaper	32.9%	27.3%	43.5%	40.3%	43.5%	22%	35.4%	47%	39%	23%*
TV	38.0%	46.1%	24.3%	29.8%	24.3%	52%	48.4%	28%	39%	67%
Magazine	11.2%	9.6%	23.5%	17.5%	23.5%	16%	11.4%	4%	5%	—
Radio	14.2%	4.6%	3.8%	4.6%	3.8%	5%	3.1%	2%	13%	1%
Outdoor	3.7%	12.4%	3.9%	6.3%	3.9%	5%	1.7%	—	4%	9%
Cinema	—	—	1%	1.5%	1%	—	—	—	—	—
Top Advertiser ($ millions)	GM $2,188	Toyota $716	Ferrero $218	COI $216	France Telecom $310	Fiat $182	Imovel $85.3	SK Telecom $88.9	N/A	Taita $113
Top Ad Category ($ millions)	Auto $14,400	Food $2,730	Media $1,586	Finance $1,800	Retail $1,400	Food $976	Retail $1,976	Computer $629	Retail $653	Pharma $3,300
Online Ad Spending ($ millions)	$5,600	$600	$197	$254	$81	$93	$88	$94	$72	N/A
Technology Percentage										
Internet	58.7%	34%	42%	31%	20%	24%	8%	53%	69%	22%
PC	66.7%	46%	48.2%	48%	34%	37%	9%	54%	63%	27%
Mobile	45.4%	69%	65%	58%	62%	83%	16%	57%	49%	30%

*Includes all print media.

SOURCE: Compiled from "Top 10 Global Ad Markets," *Advertising Age Global*, April 2002, 18–23.

Table 18.4	Restrictions on Advertisements for Specific Products in Selected European Countries

Country	Cigarette and Tobacco Products	Alcoholic Beverages	Pharmaceutical Products
United Kingdom	Banned in broadcast; approval required for showing brands of tobacco companies in any sponsored events	Banned in broadcast during or adjacent to children's programs Broadcast permitted in non-children's program airtime, with many regulations	Advertisements for prescription drugs prohibited Restriction applies; e.g., no promotion by celebrities allowed
Ireland	Banned for all cigarette and tobacco products in all forms of advertising, including any sponsorship of events	Broadcast targeting adults is allowed with many rules	Advertisements for prescription drugs prohibited Strict guideline applies to nonprescription drugs
Denmark	Banned in all forms of advertising	Permitted for beverages with alcohol content of less than 2.8% Strict conditions apply	Banned in TV broadcast for both prescription-only and nonprescription medicines Radio broadcast is permitted with strict guidelines
Portugal	Banned in all forms of advertising, except in automobile sports events with international prestige	Banned in TV and radio broadcast between 7 A.M. and 10:30 P.M. Banned in sponsoring events in which minors participate	Advertisements for prescription drugs prohibited Strict guideline applies to nonprescription drugs

SOURCE: "Study on the Evolution of New Advertising Techniques in UK, Ireland, Denmark and Portugal," *Bird & Bird Brussels*, June 17, 2002. Reprinted with permission.

This would mean no tobacco advertising in print, as well as on radio, the Internet, and Formula One racing. Existing regulations ban TV advertising. Tobacco marketers would be allowed to advertise on cinema, poster, and billboard sites.[20] A summary of product-related regulations found in selected European countries is provided in Table 18.4. Tobacco products, alcoholic beverages, and pharmaceuticals are the most heavily regulated products in terms of promotion.

However, the manufacturers of these products have not abandoned their promotional efforts. Altria Group (formerly Philip Morris) engages in corporate image advertising using its cowboy spokesperson. Some European cigarette manufacturers have diversified into the entertainment business (restaurants, lounges, movie theaters) and named them after their cigarette brands. AstraZeneca, a leading global pharmaceutical, funded a TV campaign run by the French Migraine Association, which discussed medical advances but made no mention of the company. Novo Nordisk has set up an Internet page on diabetes separate from its home page and established the World Diabetes Foundation awareness group.[21]

Certain products are subject to special rules. In the United Kingdom, for example, advertisers cannot show a real person applying an underarm deodorant; the way around this problem is to show an animated person applying the product. What is and is not allowable is very much a reflection of the country imposing the rules. Explicit advertisements of contraceptives are commonplace in Sweden, for example, but far less frequent in most parts of the world. A number of countries have varying restrictions on advertising of toys; Greece bans them altogether, and Belgium restricts their use before and after children's programming.

Beyond the traditional media, the international marketer may also consider **product placement** in movies, TV shows, games, or Web sites. Although there is disagreement about the effectiveness of the method beyond creating brand awareness,[22] products from makers such as BMW, Omega, Nokia, and Heineken have been placed in movies to help both parties to the deal: to create a brand definition for the product and a dimension of reality for the film.[23] GM used the action feature film "XXX" to reintroduce its Pontiac GTO. In some markets, product placement may be an effective method of attracting attention due to constraints on traditional media. In China, for example, most commercials on Chinese state-run television are played back-to-back in ten-minute segments, making it difficult for any 30-second ad to be singled out. Placing products in soap operas, such as "Love Talks," has been found to be an effective way to get to the burgeoning middle class in the world's most populous country.[24] Some marketers have started to create stand-alone entertainment vehicles around a brand, such as the BMW film series on the Internet.[25]

Audience Characteristics

A major objective of media strategy is to reach the intended target audience with a minimum of waste. As an example, Amoco Oil Company wanted to launch a corporate image campaign in China in the hope of receiving drilling contracts. Identifying the appropriate decision makers was not difficult because they all work for the government. The selection of appropriate media proved to be equally simple because most of the decision makers overseeing petroleum exploration were found to read the vertical trade publications: *International Industrial Review, Petroleum Production,* and *Offshore Petroleum.*

If conditions are ideal, and they seldom are in international markets, the media strategist would need data on (1) media distribution, that is, the number of copies of the print medium or the number of sets for broadcast; (2) media audiences; and (3) advertising exposure. For instance, an advertiser interested in using television in Brazil would like to know that the top adult TV program is "O Clone," with an average audience share of 48 percent and a 30-second ad rate of $71,000. In markets where more sophisticated market research services are available, data on advertising perception and consumer response may be available. In many cases, advertisers have found circulation figures to be unreliable or even fabricated.

An issue related to audience characteristics is the move by some governments to protect their own national media from foreign ones. In Canada, for example, the government prevents foreign publishers from selling space to Canadian advertisers in so-called split-run editions that, in effect, have no local content. If U.S. publications, such as *Sports Illustrated,* were allowed to do it, Canadian publications would be threatened with insufficient amounts of advertising.[26]

Global Media

Media vehicles that have target audiences on at least three continents and for which the media buying takes place through a centralized office are considered to be **global media.**[27] Global media have traditionally been publications that, in addition to the worldwide edition, have provided advertisers the option of using regional editions. For example, *Time* provides 133 editions, enabling advertisers to reach a particular country, continent, or the world. In print media, global vehicles include dailies such as *International Herald Tribune,* weeklies such as *The Economist,* and monthlies such as *National Geographic.* Included on the broadcast side are BBC Worldwide TV, CNN, the Discovery Channel, and MTV. The Discovery Channel reaches more than 700 million subscribers in 155 countries in 33 languages through Discovery Channel–Europe, Discovery Channel–Latin America/Iberia, Discovery Channel–Asia, Discovery Canada, Discovery New Zealand, and several other language-tailored networks. The argument that global media drown out local content is not borne out in fact.[28] MTV as a global medium is profiled in *The International Marketplace 18.2.*

Advertising in global media is dominated by major consumer ad categories, particularly airlines, financial services, telecommunications, automobiles, and tobacco. The aircraft industry represents business market advertisers.[29] Companies spending in global media include AT&T, IBM, and General Motors. In choosing global media, media buyers consider the three most important media characteristics: targetability, client-compatible editorial, and editorial quality.[30] Some global publications have found that some parts of the globe are more appealing to advertisers than others; for example, some publications have eliminated editions in Africa (due to lack of advertising) and in Asia and Latin America (due to financial crises).

THE INTERNATIONAL MARKETPLACE 18.2

The World Wants Its MTV!

MTV has emerged as a significant global medium, with more than 375 million households in 164 countries subscribing to its services. The reason for its success is simple—MTV offers consistent, high-quality programming that reflects the tastes and lifestyle of young people.

Its balance of fashion, film, news, competitions, and comedy wrapped in the best music and strong visual identity has made it "the best bet to succeed as a pan-European thematic channel, with its aim to be in every household in Europe," according to *Music Week,* Britain's leading music trade paper. Given that 79 percent of the channel's viewers are in the elusive 16–34 age group, MTV is a force as an advertising medium for those who want to closely target their campaigns. MTV has proven to be the ultimate youth marketing vehicle for companies such as Wrangler, Wrigleys, Braun, Britvic, Levi Strauss, Pepsi, Pentax, and many others. Although many knockoffs have been started around the world, the enormous cost of building a worldwide music video channel will most likely protect MTV.

MTV's best response to threats from competition has been to make programming as local as possible. Its policy of 70 percent local content has resulted in some of the network's more creative shows, such as Brazil's month-long Rockgol which pitted musicians against record industry executives and Russia's Twelve Angry Viewers, a talk show focused on the latest videos.

Digital compression allows the number of services offered on a satellite feed to be multiplied. The network will use the new capacity to complement panregional programming and playlists, customizing them to local tastes in key areas. For example, MTV Asia has launched MTV India to have five hours of India-specific programming during the 24-hour satellite feed to the subcontinent.

Owned by Viacom, MTV's global network consists of the following entities:

- **MTV USA** is seen 24 hours a day on cable television in over 85 million U.S. television homes. Presented in stereo, MTV's overall on-air environment is unpredictable and irreverent, reflecting the cutting-edge spirit

of rock 'n' roll that is the heart of its programming. Through its graphic look, VJs, music news, promotions, interviews, concert tour information, specials, and documentaries, as well as its original strip programming, MTV has become an international institution of pop culture and the leading authority on rock music since it launched on August 1, 1981.

- **MTV Europe** reaches 43 territories (124 million households), 24 hours a day in stereo, via satellite, cable, and terrestrial distribution. The station acquires its own video clips, drawing from the domestic markets in individual European countries to discover bands making an international sound. It has its own team of VJs presenting shows specially tailored for the European market. The channel's programming mix reflects its diverse audience, with coverage of music, style, news, movie information, comedy, and more. MTV Europe has five local programming feeds and five local advertising windows—U.K./Ireland; MTV Central: (Austria, Germany, and Switzerland); MTV European (76 territories, including France and Israel); MTV Southern (Italy); and MTV Nordic (Sweden, Norway and others). It was launched August 1, 1987.

- **MTV Asia** was launched September 15, 1991. MTV reaches over 138 million households in 21 territories. Programming is tailored to the musical tastes, lifestyles, and sensibilities of Asian audiences in three regions: MTV Mandarin, MTV Southeast Asia, and MTV India.

- Although Japan was originally launched in October 1984 under a licensing agreement, it was reintroduced in 2001 as a wholly-owned entity of MTV Networks International. The 24-hour music television channel and Web site feature original Japanese-language programming and reach 2.8 million households.

- **MTV Latin America** reaches 28 million households in 21 countries and territories. The network features a mix of U.S. and Latin music, regional production, music

continued

and entertainment news, artist interviews, concert coverage, and specials.

- **MTV Internacional** is a one-hour weekly Spanish-language program. MTV Internacional is a mix of Spanish- and English-language videos, interviews, entertainment news, and on-location specials. The program is broadcast in the United States on the Telemundo Network and in various Latin American countries and is distributed by MTV Syndication Sales.
- **MTV Brazil** was launched in 1990 and is a joint venture of MTVNetworks and Abril S.A., Brazil's leading magazine publisher. The Portuguese-language network, viewed in 16 million households, is broadcast via UHF in São Paulo and via VHF in Rio de Janeiro.
- **MTV Russia,** launched in September 1998, is a free over-the-air service reaching more than 20 million homes in major cities. The entity was established with BIZ Enterprises in a multiyear licensing agreement. In 2000, MTV Networks International gained an equity position in MTV Russia. Programming includes music videos from Russian and international artists, as well as coverage of social issues relevant to Russian youth.

SOURCES: Claudia Penteado, "MTV Breaks New Ground," *Advertising Age Global*, March 2002, 8; "MTV's World," *Business Week*, February 18, 2002, 81–84; "MTV Asia's Hit Man," *Advertising Age Global*, December 2001, 10; "Focus: Trends in TV," *Advertising Age International*, January 11, 1999, 33; "MTV Fights Back from Nadir to Hit High Notes in India," *Advertising Age International*, March 30, 1998, 10; "High Tech helps MTV Evolve," *World Trade*, June 1996, 10; "Will MTV Have to Share the Stage?" *Business Week*, February 21, 1994, 38; and **http://www.mtv.com**.

In broadcast media, panregional radio stations have been joined by television as a result of satellite technology. The pan-European satellite channels, such as Sky Channel and Super Channel, were conceived from the very beginning as advertising media. Many are skeptical about the potential of these channels, especially in the short term, because of the challenges of developing a cross-cultural following in Europe's still highly nationalistic markets.[31] Pan-European channels have had to cut back, whereas native language satellite channels like Tele 5 in France and RTL Plus in Germany have increased their viewership. The launch of STAR TV (see Figure 18.3) has increased the use of regional advertising campaigns in Asia. While this medium is still regarded as a corporate advertising vehicle, it has nonetheless attracted the interest of consumer goods manufacturers as well.[32] The alternative showing the most immediate promise is cable channels that cater to universal segments with converging tastes, such as MTV, Animal Planet, or the Cartoon Network, all of which feature both local content and localized versions of foreign content.

The Internet provides the international marketer with a global medium. U.S. marketers have been slow to react to its potential because their domestic market is so dominant. They have also been reluctant to adapt their Web sites but are willing to repeat what happened in the United States in these regions. One simple way of getting started is to choose a few key languages for the Web site. For example, Gillette decided to add German and Japanese to its Mach3 Web site after studying the number of Internet users in those countries.[33] If the marketer elects to have a global site and region-specific sites (e.g., organized by country), they all should have a similar look, especially in terms of the level of sophistication. Another method is to join forces with Internet service providers. For example, Unilever has expanded its sponsorship of the Microsoft online network in the United States to France, Germany, and the United Kingdom.[34] Under the agreement, Unilever will provide banner ads, links, and sponsorship to MSN sites, particularly MSN Women. Premier sponsorship on the MSN sites will include logo placement at the top right corner of the Web pages, as shown in Figure 18.4.

The Promotional Message

The creative people must have a clear idea of the characteristics of the audience expected to be exposed to the message. In this sense, the principles of creating effective advertising are the same as in the domestic marketplace. The marketer must determine what the consumer is really buying—that is, the customer's motivations. These will vary, depending on the following:

Figure 18.3	Example of a Panregional Medium

Across Asia, we capture
the imagination of millions

63 million people' watch STAR every day. • From Mumbai to Taipei, from Dubai to Shanghai • Over 30 channels in entertainment, movies, sports, music, news and documentary. • Radio, internet and cable partnerships. • Setting the pace for a digitally connected Asia.

• • *just imagine* •

STAR CHINESE CHANNEL • STAR GOLD • STAR MANDARIN MOVIES • STAR MOVIES • STAR NEWS • STAR PLUS • STAR SPORTS • STAR WORLD • CHANNEL [V] • PHOENIX CHINESE CHANNEL • PHOENIX INFONEWS CHANNEL • PHOENIX EUROPE CHANNEL • PHOENIX MOVIES • PHOENIX NORTH AMERICA CHANNEL • ESPN • VIVA CINEMA • NATIONAL GEOGRAPHIC CHANNEL

SOURCE: Courtesy of STAR Group Limited.

1. The diffusion of the product or service into the market. For example, to penetrate Third World markets with business computers is difficult when few potential customers know how to type or with Internet advertising when the infrastructure is lacking.

2. The criteria on which the customer will evaluate the product. For example, in traditional societies, advertising the time-saving qualities of a product may not be the best approach, as Campbell Soup Company learned in Italy, Brazil, and Poland where women felt inadequate as homemakers if they did not make soups from scratch.

3. The product's positioning. For example, Parker Pen's upscale market image around the world may not be profitable enough in a market that is more or less a commodity business. The solution is to create an image for a commodity product and make the public pay for it—for example, the positioning of Perrier in the United States as a premium mineral water.

The ideal situation in developing message strategy is to have a world brand—a product that is manufactured, packaged, and positioned the same around the world. Companies that have been successful with the global approach have shown

Figure 18.4   Online Advertising

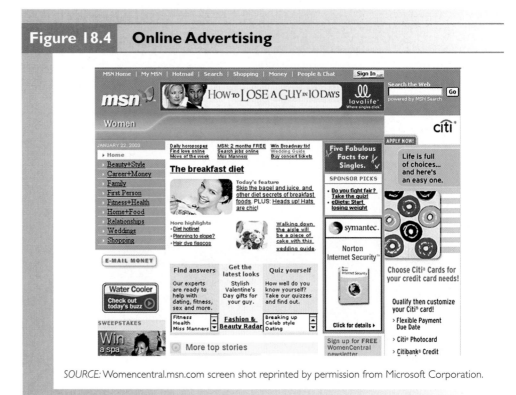

SOURCE: Womencentral.msn.com screen shot reprinted by permission from Microsoft Corporation.

flexibility in the execution of the campaigns. The idea may be global, but overseas subsidiaries then tailor the message to suit local market conditions and regulations. Executing an advertising campaign in multiple markets requires a balance between conveying the message and allowing for local nuances. The localization of global ideas can be achieved by various tactics, such as adopting a modular approach, localizing international symbols, and using international advertising agencies.[35]

Marketers may develop multiple broadcast and print ads from which country organizations can choose the most appropriate for their operations. This can provide local operations with cost savings and allow them to use their budgets on tactical campaigns (which may also be developed around the global idea). For example, the "Membership Has Its Privileges" campaign of American Express, which has run in 24 countries on TV and three more in print, was adjusted in some markets to make sure that "privileges" did not have a snob or elitist appeal, especially in countries with a strong caste or class system. An example of local adjustment in a global campaign for Marriott International is provided in Figure 18.5. While the ads share common graphic elements, two distinct approaches are evident. The top set of advertisements from the United States and Saudi Arabia is an example of a relatively standard approach, given the similarity in target audiences (i.e., the business traveler) and in the competitive conditions in the markets. The second set features ads for Latin American and German-speaking Europe. While the Latin advertisement stresses comfort, the German version focuses on results. While most of Marriott's ads translate the theme ("When you're comfortable you can do anything"), the German version keeps the original English-language theme.

Product-related regulations will affect advertising messages as well. When General Mills Toy Group's European subsidiary launched a product line related to G.I. Joe–type war toys and soldiers, it had to develop two television commercials, a general version for most European countries and another for countries that bar advertisements for products with military or violent themes. As a result, in the version running in Germany, Holland, and Belgium, Jeeps replaced the toy tanks, and guns were removed from the hands of the toy soldiers. Other countries, such as the United Kingdom, do not allow children to appear in advertisements.

Figure 18.5 Local Adjustments in a Global Campaign

SOURCE: Courtesy of Marriott International Inc. **http://www.marriott.com**.

Marketers may also want to localize their international symbols. Some of the most effective global advertising campaigns have capitalized on the popularity of pop music worldwide and used well-known artists in the commercials, such as Pepsi's use of Tina Turner. In some versions, local stars have been included with the international stars to localize the campaign. Aesthetics play a role in localizing campaigns. The global marketer does not want to chance the censoring of the company's ads or risk offending customers. For example, even though importers of perfumes into Saudi Arabia want to use the same campaigns as are used in Europe, they occasionally have to make adjustments dictated by moral standards. In one case, the European version shows a man's hand clutching a perfume bottle and a woman's hand seizing his bare forearm. In the Saudi Arabian version, the man's arm is clothed in a dark suit sleeve, and the woman's hand is merely brushing his hand.

The use of one agency—or only a few agencies—ensures consistency. The use of one agency allows for coordination, especially when the global marketer's operations are decentralized. It also makes the exchange of ideas easier and may therefore lead, for example, to wider application of a modification or a new idea. For example, Procter & Gamble has now moved all of its global brands under a single global agency. Pampers is handled by Publicis Group's Saatchi & Saatchi, while Charmin is with Bcom3 Group's D'Arcy Masius Benton & Bowles.[36]

The environmental influences that call for these modifications, or in some cases totally unique approaches, are culture, economic development, and lifestyles. It is quite evident that customers prefer localized to foreign-sourced advertising.[37] Of the cultural variables, language is most apparent in its influence on promotional campaigns. The European Union alone has eleven languages: English, Finnish, French, German, Dutch, Danish, Italian, Greek, Spanish, Swedish, and Portuguese. Advertisers in the Arab world have sometimes found that the voices in a TV commercial speak in the wrong Arabic dialect. The challenge of language is often most pronounced in translating themes. For example, Coca-Cola's worldwide theme "Can't Beat the Feeling" is the equivalent of "I Feel Coke" in Japan, "Unique Sensation" in Italy, and "The Feeling of Life" in Chile. In Germany, where no translation really worked, the original English language theme was used. One way of getting around this is to have no copy or very little copy and to use innovative approaches, such as pantomime. Using any type of symbolism will naturally require adequate copy testing to determine how the target market perceives the message.

The stage of economic development—and therefore the potential demand for and degree of awareness of the product—may vary and differentiate the message from one market to another. Whereas developed markets may require persuasive messages (to combat other alternatives), a developing market may require a purely informative campaign. Campaigns may also have to be dramatically adjusted to cater to lifestyle differences in regions that are demographically quite similar. For example, N. W. Ayer's Bahamas tourism campaign for the European market emphasized clean water, beaches, and air. The exceptions are in Germany, where it focuses on sports activities, and in the United Kingdom, where it features humor.

Unique market conditions may require localized approaches. Although IBM has utilized global campaigns (the Little Tramp campaign, for example), it has also used major local campaigns in Japan and Europe for specific purposes. In Japan, it used a popular television star in poster and door-board ads to tell viewers, "Friends, the time is ripe" (for buying an IBM personal computer). The campaign was designed to bolster the idea that the machine represents a class act from America. At the same time, IBM was trying to overcome a problem in Europe of being perceived as "too American." Stressing that IBM is actually a "European company," an advertising campaign told of IBM's large factories, research facilities, and tax-paying subsidiaries within the EU.

The Campaign Approach

Many multinational corporations are staffed and equipped to perform the full range of promotional activities. In most cases, however, they will rely on the outside expertise of advertising agencies and other promotions-related companies such as media-buying companies and specialty marketing firms. In the organization of promotional efforts, a company has two basic decisions to make: (1) what type of outside services to use and (2) how to establish decision-making authority for promotional efforts.

Outside Services

Of all the outside promotion-related services, advertising agencies are by far the most significant. A list of the world's top 50 agencies and agency groups is given in Table 18.5. Of the top 50 agencies, 26 are based in the United States, 9 in Japan, and the rest in the United Kingdom, France, Australia, South Korea, Italy, Canada, and Germany. Whereas the Japanese agencies tend to have few operations outside their home country, U.S. and European agencies are engaged in worldwide expansion. Size is measured in terms of gross income and billings. Billings are the cost of advertising time and space placed by the agency plus fees for certain extra services, which are converted by formula to correspond to media billings in terms of value of services performed. Agencies do not receive billings as income; in general, agency income is approximately 15 percent of billing.

Agencies form world groups for better coverage. One of the largest world holding groups, WPP Group, includes such entities as Ogilvy & Mather, J. Walter Thompson, Young & Rubicam, and Red Cell. Smaller advertising agencies have affiliated local agencies in foreign markets.

The choice of an agency will largely depend on the quality of coverage the agency will be able to give the multinational company. Global marketing requires global advertising, according to proponents of the globalization trend. The reason is not that significant cost savings can be realized through a single worldwide ad campaign but that such a global campaign is inseparable from the idea of global marketing. Some predict that the whole industry will be concentrated into a few huge multinational agencies. Agencies with networks too small to compete have become prime takeover targets in the creation of worldwide mega-agencies. Many believe that local, midsized agencies can compete in the face of globalization by developing local solutions and/or joining international networks.[38]

Although the forecast that six large agencies will eventually place most international advertising may be exaggerated, global marketing is the new wave and is having a strong impact on advertising. Major realignments of client–agency relationships have occurred due to mergers and to clients' reassessment of their own strategies toward more global or regional approaches.

Advertising agencies have gone through major geographic expansion in the last five years. The leader is McCann-Erickson, with advertising running in 130 countries, compared with 72 in 1991. In 2002, it handled the most international assignments of any group (a total of 62 accounts with 1,213 assignments).[39] Some agencies, such as DDB Worldwide, were domestically focused in the early 1990s but have been forced to rethink with the globalization of their clients. As a result, DDB Worldwide had doubled its country presence to 99 by 2002.[40] New markets are also emerging, and agencies are establishing their presence in them. For example, DDB Worldwide, which has been servicing its clients in the Chinese market from Hong Kong, formed a joint venture with the Chinese government in 1989.[41]

An example of an agency's client relationships is provided in Table 18.6. The J. Walter Thompson agency, which serves 90 countries worldwide, has 25 accounts that it serves in more than ten countries including Kimberly-Clark, Nestlé, and Unilever. On the client side, Unilever assigns more business on an international basis, working with nine agency networks from six holding groups, than any other global marketer. In a study of 40 multinational marketers, 32.5 percent are using a single agency worldwide, 20 percent are using two, 5 percent are using three,

Table 18.5   Top 50 Advertising Organizations Worldwide

Rank 2001	Rank 2000	Advertising Organization	Headquarters	Worldwide Gross Income ($M) 2001	Worldwide Billings ($M) 2001
1	2	WPP Group	London	$8,165.0	$75,711.0
2	1	Interpublic Group of Cos.	New York	7,981.4	66,689.1
3	3	Omnicom Group	New York	7,404.2	58,080.1
4	4	Publicis Groupe (includes Bcom3 Group)	Paris	4,769.9	52,892.2
5	5	Dentsu	Tokyo	2,795.5	20,847.8
6	6	Havas Advertising	Levallois-Perret, France	2,733.1	26,268.5
7	7	Grey Global Group	New York	1,863.6	12,105.7
8	8	Cordiant Communications Group	London	1,174.5	13,388.0
9	9	Hakuhodo	Tokyo	874.3	6,862.2
10	10	Asatsu-DK	Tokyo	394.6	3,500.6
11	11	TMP Worldwide	New York	358.5	1,705.6
12	12	Carlson Marketing Group	Minneapolis	356.1	2,611.1
13	17	Incepta Group	London	248.4	695.0
14	13	DigitasA	Boston	235.5	NA
15	15	Tokyu Agency	Tokyo	203.9	1,782.6
16	16	Daiko Advertising	Tokyo	203.0	1,585.0
17	14	Aspen Marketing Group	Los Angeles	189.2	1,262.2
18	18	Maxxcom	Toronto	177.1	386.7
19	20	Cheil Communications	Seoul	142.0	796.0
20	23	Doner	Southfield, MI	114.2	1,070.8
21	19	Ha-Lo Industries	Niles, IL	105.0	NA
22	22	Yomiko Advertising	Tokyo	102.2	1,022.2
23	21	SPAR Group	Tarrytown, NY	101.8	678.8
24	30	Cossette Communication Group	Quebec City	95.2	488.2
25	28	DVC Worldwide	Morristown, NJ	92.6	680.9
26	25	Clemenger Group	Melbourne, Australia	91.0	606.9
27	29	Rubin Postaer & Associates	Santa Monica, CA	90.3	851.4
28	27	Hawkeye Communications	New York	87.8	585.4
29	24	Panoramic Communications	New York	86.2	1,194.1
30	31	Richard Group	Dallas	84.5	570.5
31	26	Asahi Advertising	Tokyo	84.3	572.0
32	45	inChord Communications (Gerbig Snell/Weishemer)	Westerville, OH	76.1	630.1
33	35	Bartle Bogle Hegarty	London	73.9	581.3
34	32	Wieden & Kennedy	Portland, OR	73.8	777.2
35	38	Cramer-Krasselt	Chicago	72.7	478.2
36	37	M&C Saatchi Worldwide	London	71.7	577.1
37	34	LG Ad	Seoul	67.6	492.4
38	33	Nikkeisha	Tokyo	66.5	440.1
39	36	AKQA	San Francisco	66.0	264.0
40	40	Armando Testa Group	Turin, Italy	62.9	698.4
41	43	Sogei	Tokyo	61.3	437.2
42	48	Springer & Jacoby	Hamburg, Germany	60.6	404.4
43	47	ChoicePoint Direct	Peoria, IL	59.4	396.3
44	44	Gage	Minneapolis	58.6	391.1
45	39	Harte-Hanks Direct & Interactive	Langhome, PA	57.0	353.8
46	59	360 Youth	Cranberry, NJ	56.7	407.2
47	51	Ryan Partnership	Westport, CT	56.3	319.9
48	46	Envoy Communications Group	Toronto	54.8	NA
49	54	MARC USA	Pittsburgh	53.2	586.0
50	64	Data Marketing	Santa Clara, CA	52.8	NA

Table 18.6   Worldwide Agency–Client Relationships

Rank	Marketer	Dots/ Assignments	Armando Testa	Bartle Bogle Hegarty	Bates Worldwide	BBDO Worldwide	D'Arcy Masius Benton & Bowles	DDB Worldwide	Dentsu	Euro RSCG Worldwide	Foote, Cone & Belding Worldwide	Grey Worldwide	Hakuhodo	J. Walter Thompson Co.	Leagas Delaney	Leo Burnett Worldwide	Lowe & Partners Worldwide	McCann-Erickson Worldwide	Ogilvy & Mather Worldwide	Publicis Worldwide	Saatchi & Saatchi	TBWA Worldwide	Y&R Advertising
1	Unilever	385	•	•	•		•	•				•					•	•	•				
2	Nestlé	272					•	•	•			•						•	•	•			
3	Philip Morris Cos.	254								•	•	•				•			•			•	•
4	Pfizer	237			•						•												
5	Johnson & Johnson	226					•										•	•		•			
6	Gillette Co.	222				•											•	•	•				
7	Procter & Gamble Co.	205				•					•		•			•						•	
8	Mars	191				•						•										•	
9	L'Oreal	170										•							•				
10	Diageo	159	•			•					•		•		•					•			
11	Bayer Corp.	151				•		•			•		•			•							
12	Ford Motor Co.	144									•					•						•	
13	Coca-Cola Co.	135											•				•	•		•			
14	GlaxoSmithKline	124									•						•	•		•			
15	Sony Corp.	115				•		•					•				•	•		•	•	•	
16	General Motors Corp.	114					•										•	•					
17	Hewlett-Packard Co.	112							•										•				
17	British American Tobacco	112			•							•									•		
17	PepsiCo	112				•				•		•											•
20	Philips Electronics	105			•	•																	
21	Danone Group	103					•		•		•												•
22	Volkswagen	102		•			•							•									
23	Roche	100		•		•											•	•					
24	Reckitt Benckiser	93	•							•				•									
25	Siemens	92												•			•	•	•	•			

Ranking based on total assignments the top 25 advertisers awarded the agency networks in this report.

SOURCE: Reprinted with permission from the September 9, 2002, issue of *Advertising Age.* Copyright, Crain Communications Inc., 2002.

10 percent are using four, and 32.5 percent are using more than four agencies. Of the marketers using only one or two agencies, McCann-Erickson was the most popular with 17 percent of the companies.[42] While global media reviews (to consolidate all business to a single agency) are popular, most large companies typically use more than one agency, with the division of labor usually along product lines. For example, Matsushita Electric Industrial Company, an innovator in the consumer electronics industry, uses two major agencies. Backer Spielvogel Bates Worldwide handles everything involving portables, audio, VHS, and television. Grey Advertising handles the hi-fi area, the Technics label, and telephone products. Panasonic, one of Matsushita's U.S. brands, has a small agency for primarily nonconsumer items. Marketers are choosing specialized interactive shops over full-service agencies for Internet advertising. This is largely due to pragmatic reasons

due to conflicts, agencies' uneven coverage of the world (especially in emerging markets), and the marketers' own inability to make decisions from headquarters work on a global scale.[43]

The main concern arising from the use of mega-agencies is conflict. With only a few giant agencies to choose from, the global marketer may end up with the same agency as the main competitor. The mega-agencies believe they can meet any objections by structuring their companies as rigidly separate, watertight agency networks (such as the Interpublic Group) under the umbrella of a holding group. Following that logic, Procter & Gamble, a client of Saatchi & Saatchi Advertising Worldwide, and Colgate-Palmolive, a client of Ted Bates, should not worry about falling into the same network's client base. However, when the Saatchi & Saatchi network purchased Ted Bates, Colgate-Palmolive left the agency.

Despite the globalization trend, local agencies will survive as a result of governmental regulations. In Peru, for example, a law mandates that any commercial aired on Peruvian television must be 100 percent nationally produced. Local agencies also tend to forge ties with foreign agencies for better coverage and customer service and thus become part of the general globalization effort. A basic fear in the advertising industry is that accounts will be taken away from agencies that cannot handle world brands. An additional factor is contributing to the fear of losing accounts. In the past, many multinational corporations allowed local subsidiaries to make advertising decisions entirely on their own. Others gave subsidiaries an approved list of agencies and some guidance. Still others allowed local decisions subject only to headquarters' approval. Now the trend is toward centralization of all advertising decisions, including those concerning the creative product.

Decision-Making Authority

The alternatives for allocating decision-making authority range from complete centralization to decentralization. With complete centralization, the headquarters level is perceived to have all the right answers and has adequate power to impose its suggestions on all of its operating units. Decentralization involves relaxing most of the controls over foreign affiliates and allowing them to pursue their own promotional approaches.

Of 40 multinational marketers, 26 percent have centralized their advertising strategies, citing as their rationale the search for economies of scale, synergies, and brand consistency. Xerox's reason is that its technology is universal and opportunities abound for global messages. Centralization is also occurring at the regional level. GM's Opel division in Europe is seeking to unify its brand-building efforts with central direction. A total of 34 percent of the companies favor decentralization with regional input. This approach benefits from proximity to market, flexibility, cultural sensitivity, and faster response time. FedEx allows local teams to make advertising decisions as needed. The majority of marketers use central coordination with local input. While Ford Motor Company conceives brand strategy on a global level, ad execution is done at the regional level, and retail work is local.[44] However, multinational corporations are at various stages in their quest for centralization. Procter & Gamble and Gillette generally have an approved list of agencies, whereas Quaker Oats and Johnson & Johnson give autonomy to their local subsidiaries but will veto those decisions occasionally.

The important question is not who should make decisions but how advertising quality can be improved at the local level. Gaining approval in multinational corporations is an interactive approach using coordinated decentralization. This nine-step program, which is summarized in Figure 18.6, strives for development of common strategy but flexible execution. The approach maintains strong central control but at the same time capitalizes on the greatest asset of the individual markets: market knowledge. Interaction between the central authority and the local levels takes place at every single stage of the planning process. The central authority is charged with finding the commonalities in the data provided by the individual market areas. This procedure will avoid one of the most common problems

Figure 18.6   Coordinated Approach to Panregional Campaign Development

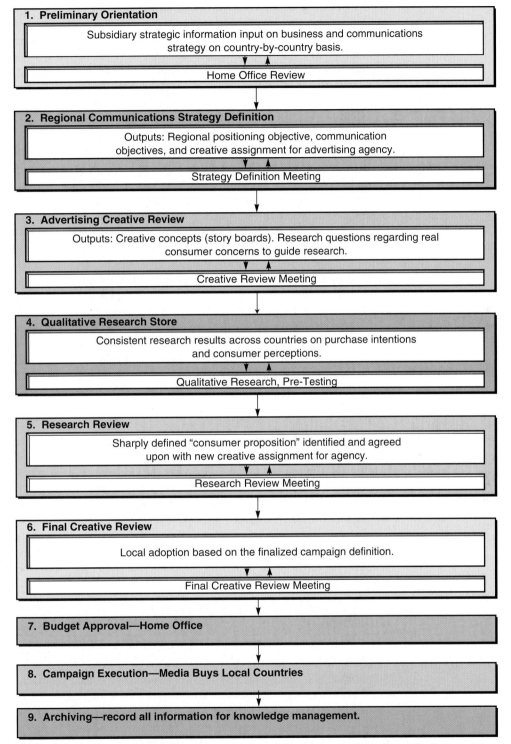

1. Preliminary Orientation

Subsidiary strategic information input on business and communications strategy on country-by-country basis.

Home Office Review

2. Regional Communications Strategy Definition

Outputs: Regional positioning objective, communication objectives, and creative assignment for advertising agency.

Strategy Definition Meeting

3. Advertising Creative Review

Outputs: Creative concepts (story boards). Research questions regarding real consumer concerns to guide research.

Creative Review Meeting

4. Qualitative Research Store

Consistent research results across countries on purchase intentions and consumer perceptions.

Qualitative Research, Pre-Testing

5. Research Review

Sharply defined "consumer proposition" identified and agreed upon with new creative assignment for agency.

Research Review Meeting

6. Final Creative Review

Local adoption based on the finalized campaign definition.

Final Creative Review Meeting

7. Budget Approval—Home Office

8. Campaign Execution—Media Buys Local Countries

9. Archiving—record all information for knowledge management.

SOURCES: Jae H. Pae, Saeed Samiee, and Susan Tai, "Global Advertising Strategy: The Moderating Role of Brand Familiarity and Execution Style," *International Marketing Review* 19 (no. 2, 2002): 176–189; Clive Nancarrow and Chris Woolston, "Pre-Testing International Press Advertising," *Qualitative Market Research: An International Journal* (1998): 25–38; and David A. Hanni, John K. Ryans, Jr., and Ivan R. Vernon, "Coordinating International Advertising: The Goodyear Case Revisited for Latin America," *Journal of International Marketing* 3 (no. 2, 1995): 83–98.

associated with acceptance of plans—the NIH syndrome (not invented here)—by allowing for local participation by the eventual implementers.

A good example of this approach was Eastman Kodak's launch of its Ektaprint copier-duplicator line in eleven separate markets in Europe. For economic and organizational reasons, Kodak did not want to deal with different campaigns or parameters. It wanted the same ad graphics in each country, accompanied by the theme "first name in photography, last word in copying." Translations varied slightly from country to country, but the campaign was identifiable from one country to another. A single agency directed the campaign, which was more economical than campaigns in each country would have been and was more unified and identifiable through Europe. The psychological benefit of association of the Kodak name with photography was not lost in the campaign.

Agencies are adjusting their operations to centrally run client operations. Many accounts are now handled by a lead agency, usually in the country where the client is based. More and more agencies are moving to a strong international supervisor for global accounts. This supervisor can overrule local agencies and make personnel changes. Specialty units have emerged as well. For example, Ogilvy & Mather established the Worldwide Client Service organization at headquarters in New York specializing in developing global campaigns for its clients.[45]

Measurement of Advertising Effectiveness

John Wanamaker reportedly said, "I know half the money I spend on advertising is wasted. Now, if I only knew which half." Whether or not advertising effectiveness can be measured, most companies engage in the attempt. Measures of advertising effectiveness should range from pretesting of copy appeal and recognition, to posttesting of recognition, all the way to sales effects. The measures most used are sales, awareness, recall, executive judgment, intention to buy, profitability, and coupon return, regardless of the medium used.[46]

The technical side of these measurement efforts does not differ from that in the domestic market, but the conditions are different. Very often, syndicated services, such as A.C. Nielsen, are not available to the global marketer. If available, their quality may not be at an acceptable level. Testing is also quite expensive and may not be undertaken for the smaller markets. Compared with costs in the U.S. market, the costs of research in the international market are higher in relation to the overall expenditure on advertising.[47] The biggest challenge to advertising research will come from the increase of global and regional campaigns. Comprehensive and reliable measures of campaigns for a mass European market, for example, are difficult because audience measurement techniques and analysis differ for each country. Advertisers are pushing for universally accepted parameters to compare audiences in one country to those in another.

Other Promotional Elements

Personal Selling

Advertising is often equated with the promotional effort; however, a number of other efforts are used to support advertising. The marketing of industrial goods, especially of high-priced items, requires strong personal selling efforts. In some cases, personal selling may be truly international; for example, Boeing and Northrop-Grumman salespeople engage in sales efforts around the world from their domestic bases. However, most personal selling is done by the subsidiaries, with varying degrees of headquarters' involvement. In cases in which personal selling constitutes the primary thrust of the corporate promotional effort and in which global customer groups can be identified, unified and coordinated sales practices may be called for. When distribution is intensive, channels are long, or markets have tradition-oriented distribution, headquarters' role should be less pronounced and should concentrate mostly on offering help and guidance.[48] A pivotal role is played by the field sales manager as the organizational link between headquarters and the salespeople.[49]

Eastman Kodak developed a line-of-business approach to allow for standardized strategy throughout a region.[50] In Europe, one person is placed in charge of the entire copier-duplicator program in each country. That person is responsible for all sales and service teams within the country. Typically, each customer is served by three representatives, each with a different responsibility. Sales representatives maintain ultimate responsibility for the account; they conduct demonstrations, analyze customer requirements, determine the right type of equipment for each installation, and obtain the orders. Service representatives install and maintain the equipment and retrofit new product improvements to existing equipment. Customer service representatives are the liaison between sales and service. They provide operator training on a continuing basis and handle routine questions and complaints. Each team is positioned to respond to any European customer within hours.

The training of the sales force usually takes place in the national markets, but multinational corporations' headquarters will have a say in the techniques used. For instance, when Kodak introduced the Ektaprint line, sales team members were selected carefully. U.S. copier personnel could be recruited from other Kodak divisions, but most European marketing personnel had to be recruited from outside the company and given intensive training. Sales managers and a select group of sales trainers were sent to the Rochester, New York, headquarters for six weeks of training. They then returned to Europe to set up programs for individual countries so that future teams could be trained there. To ensure continuity, all the U.S. training materials were translated into the languages of the individual countries. To maintain a unified program and overcome language barriers, Kodak created a service language consisting of 1,200 words commonly found in technical information.

Foreign companies entering the Japanese market face challenges in establishing a sales force. Recruitment poses the first major problem, since well-established, and usually local, entities have an advantage in attracting personnel. Many have, therefore, entered into joint ventures or distribution agreements to obtain a sales force. Companies can also expect to invest more in training and organizational culture-building activities than in the United States. These may bring long-term advantages in fostering loyalty to the company.[51]

Sales Promotion

Sales promotion has been used as the catchall term for promotion that does not fall under advertising, personal selling, or publicity. Sales promotion directed at consumers involves such activities as couponing, sampling, premiums, consumer education and demonstration activities, cents-off packs, point-of-purchase materials, and direct mail. The use of sales promotions as alternatives and as support for advertising is increasing worldwide. The appeal is related to several factors: cost and clutter of media advertising, simpler targeting of customers compared with advertising, and easier tracking of promotional effectiveness (for example, coupon returns provide a clear measure of effectiveness).

The success in Latin America of Tang, General Foods' presweetened powder juice substitute, is for the most part traceable to successful sales promotion efforts. One promotion involved trading Tang pouches for free popsicles from Kibon, General Foods' Brazilian subsidiary. Kibon also placed coupons for free groceries in Tang pouches. In Puerto Rico, General Foods ran Tang sweepstakes. In Argentina, in-store sampling featured Tang pitchers and girls in orange Tang dresses. Decorative Tang pitchers were a hit throughout Latin America. Sales promotion directed at intermediaries, also known as trade promotion, includes activities such as trade shows and exhibits, trade discounts, and cooperative advertising.

For sales promotion to be effective, the campaign planned by manufacturers, or their agencies, must gain the support of the local retailer population. Coupons from consumers, for example, have to be redeemed and sent to the manufacturer or to the company handling the promotion. A.C. Nielsen tried to introduce cents-off coupons in Chile and ran into trouble with the nation's supermarket union, which notified its members that it opposed the project and recommended that coupons not be accepted. The main complaint was that an intermediary, like Nielsen, would unnecessarily raise costs and thus the prices to be charged to consumers. Also, some critics felt that coupons would limit individual negotiations because Chileans often bargain for their purchases.

Global marketers are well advised to take advantage of local or regional opportunities. In Brazil, gas delivery people are used to distribute product samples to households by companies such as Nestlé, Johnson & Johnson, and Unilever. The delivery people are usually assigned to the same district for years and have, therefore, earned their clientele's trust. For the marketers, distributing samples this way is not only effective, it is very economical: they are charged five cents for each unit distributed. The gas companies benefit as well in that their relationship with customers is enhanced through these "presents."[52]

Sales promotion tools fall under varying regulations, as can be seen from Table 18.7. A particular level of incentive may be permissible in one market but illegal in another. The Northern European countries present the greatest difficulties in this respect because every promotion has to be approved by a government body. In France, a gift cannot be worth more than 4 percent of the retail value of the product being promoted, making certain promotions virtually impossible. Although competitions are allowed in most of Europe, to insist on receiving proofs of purchase as a condition of entry is not permitted in Germany.

Regulations such as these make truly global sales promotions rare and difficult to launch. Although only a few multinational brands have been promoted on a multiterritory basis, the approach can work. In general, such multicountry promotions may be suitable for products such as soft drinks, liquor, airlines, credit cards, and jeans, which span cultural divides. Naturally, local laws and cultural differences have to be taken into account at the planning stage. Although many of the promotions may be funded centrally, they will be implemented differently in each market so that they can be tied with the local company's other promotional activities. For example, Johnson & Johnson Vision Care offered trials of its one-day Acuvue contact lens throughout Europe, Africa, and the Middle East. The aim was to deliver the brand message of "Enhancing Everyday Experiences" and encourage consumers to book a sight test. The venue was a road-show event that adapted well to local market conditions. Professional lens fitters offered on-the-spot trials at gyms, sports clubs, and leisure centers. The program was devised and tested in Germany, and has since been executed in 18 different countries. The creative materials were translated into 14 languages and a virtual network using intranets ensured that all offices shared information and best practice.[53]

In the province of Quebec in Canada, advertisers must pay a tax on the value of the prizes they offer in a contest, whether the prize is a trip, money, or a car. The amount of the tax depends on the geographical extent of the contest. If it is open only to residents of Quebec, the tax is 10 percent; if open to all of Canada, 3 percent; if worldwide, 1 percent. Subtle distinctions are drawn in the regulations between a premium and a prize. As an example, the Manic soccer team was involved with both McDonald's and Provigo Food stores. The team offered a dollar off the price of four tickets, and the stubs could be cashed for a special at McDonald's. Provigo was involved in a contest offering a year's supply of groceries. The Manic-McDonald's offer was a premium that involved no special tax; Provigo, however, was taxed because it was involved in a contest. According to the regulation, a premium is available to everyone, whereas a prize is available to a certain number of people among those who participate. In some cases, industries may self-regulate the use of promotional items.

Table 18.7	Regulations Regarding Premiums, Gifts, and Competitions in Selected Countries

Country	Category	No Restrictions or Minor Ones	Authorized with Major Restrictions	General Ban with Important Exceptions	Almost Total Prohibition
Australia	Premiums	x			
	Gifts	x			
	Competitions		x		
Austria	Premiums				x
	Gifts		x		
	Competitions		x		
Canada	Premiums	x			
	Gifts	x			
	Competitions		x		
Denmark	Premiums			x	
	Gifts		x		
	Competitions			x	
France	Premiums	x			
	Gifts	x			
	Competitions	x			
Germany	Premiums				x
	Gifts		x		
	Competitions		x		
Hong Kong	Premiums	x			
	Gifts	x			
	Competitions	x			
Japan	Premiums		x		
	Gifts		x		
	Competitions		x		
Korea	Premiums		x		
	Gifts		x		
	Competitions		x		
United Kingdom	Premiums	x			
	Gifts	x			
	Competitions		x		
United States	Premiums	x			
	Gifts	x			
	Competitions	x			
Venezuela	Premiums		x		
	Gifts		x		
	Competitions		x		

SOURCE: Jean J. Boddewyn, *Premiums, Gifts, and Competitions,* 1988, published by International Advertising Association, 342 Madison Avenue, Suite 2000, NYC, NY 10017. Reprinted with permission.

Public Relations

Image—the way a multinational corporation relates to and is perceived by its key constituents—is a bottom-line issue for management. Public relations is the marketing communications function charged with executing programs to earn public understanding and acceptance, which means both internal and external communication. The function can further be divided into proactive and reactive forms.

Internal Public Relations

Especially in multinational corporations, internal communication is important to create an appropriate corporate culture.[54] The Japanese have perfected this in achieving a *wa* (we) spirit. Everyone in an organization is, in one way or another, in marketing and will require additional targeted information on issues not necessarily related to his or her day-to-day functions. A basic part of most internal programs is the employee publication produced and edited typically by the company's public relations or advertising department and usually provided in both hard-copy and electronic formats. Some have foreign-language versions. More often, as at ExxonMobil, each affiliate publishes its own employee publication. The better this vehicle can satisfy the information needs of employees, the less they will have to rely on others, especially informal sources such as the grapevine. Audiovisual media in the form of e-mails, films, videotapes, slides, and videoconferencing are being used, especially for training and indoctrination purposes. Some of the materials that are used internally can be provided to other publics as well; for example, booklets, manuals, and handbooks are provided to employees, distributors, and visitors to the company.

External Public Relations

External public relations (also known as marketing public relations) is focused on the interactions with customers. In the *proactive* context, marketers are concerned about establishing global identities to increase sales, differentiate products and services, and attract employees. These activities have been seen as necessary to compete against companies with strong local identities. External campaigns can be achieved through the use of corporate symbols, corporate advertising, customer relations programs, and publicity. For example, Black & Decker's corporate logo, which is in the shape and color of an orange hexagon, is used for all B&D products. Specific brand books are developed to guide marketing personnel worldwide on the proper use of these symbols to ensure a consistent global image. Figure 18.7 depicts an agricultural marketing publication, *The Furrow*, in three different language versions. This publication is mailed to agricultural customers worldwide.

Publicity, in particular, is of interest to the multinational corporation. Publicity is the securing of editorial space (as opposed to paid advertising) to further marketing objectives. Because it is editorial in content, the consuming public perceives it as more trustworthy than advertising. A good example of how publicity can be used to aid in advertising efforts was the introduction by Princess Lines of a new liner, the *Royal Princess*. Because of its innovative design and size, the *Royal Princess* was granted substantial press coverage, which was especially beneficial in the travel and leisure magazines. Such coverage does not come automatically but has to be coordinated and initiated by the public relations staff of the company.

Unanticipated developments in the marketplace can place the company in a position that requires *reactive* public relations, including anticipating and countering criticism. The criticisms range from general ones against all multinational corporations to more specific ones. They may be based on a market, for example, doing business with prison factories in China. They may concern a product, for example, Nestlé's practices of advertising and promoting infant formula in developing countries where infant mortality is unacceptably high. They may center on conduct in a given situation, for example, Union Carbide's perceived lack of response in the Bhopal disaster. The key concern is that, if not addressed, these

Figure 18.7   External Media: The Furrow

SOURCE: Courtesy of Deere & Co., Moline, IL, USA; **http://www.johndeere.com**.

criticisms can lead to more significant problems, such as the internationally orchestrated boycott of Nestlé's products. The six-year boycott did not so much harm earnings as it harmed image and employee morale.

Crisis management is becoming more formalized in companies, with specially assigned task forces ready to step in if problems arise. In general, companies must adopt policies that will allow them to effectively respond to pressure and criticism, which will continue to surface. Crisis management policies should have the following traits: (1) openness about corporate activities, with a focus on how these activities enhance social and economic performance; (2) preparedness to utilize the tremendous power of the multinational corporation in a responsible manner and, in the case of pressure, to counter criticisms swiftly; (3) integrity, which often means that the marketer must avoid not only actual wrongdoing but the mere appearance of it; and (4) clarity, which will help ameliorate hostility if a common language is used with those pressuring the corporation.[55] The marketer's role is one of enlightened self-interest; reasonable critics understand that the marketer cannot compromise the bottom line.

Complicating the situation often is the fact that groups in one market criticize what the marketer is doing in another market. For example, the Interfaith Center on Corporate Responsibility urged Colgate-Palmolive to stop marketing Darkie toothpaste under that brand name in Asia because of the term's offensiveness elsewhere in the world. Darkie toothpaste was sold in Thailand, Hong Kong, Singapore, Malaysia, and Taiwan and was packaged in a box that featured a likeness of Al Jolson in blackface.[56] Colgate-Palmolive redid the package and changed the brand name to Darlie. Levi Strauss decided to withdraw from $40 million worth of

Table 18.8 The Top Worldwide Public Relations Firms

Firm	2001 Net Fees	Employees
Weber Shandwick Worldwide (Interpublic Group of Cos.)	$426,572,018	3,000
Fleishman-Hillard (Omnicom Group)	345,098,241	2,288
Hill & Knowlton (WPP Group)	325,119,000	2,100
Incepta (Citigate et al.)	266,018,371	2,000
Burson-Marsteller (WPP Group)	259,112,000	2,000
Edelman PR Worldwide*	223,708,535	1,900
Ketchum (Omnicom Group)	185,221,000	1,400
Porter Novelli (Omnicom Group)	179,294,000	1,000
GCI Group/APCO Worldwide (Grey Global Group)	151,081,645	650
Ogilvy PR Worldwide (WPP Group)	145,949,285	1,200
Euro RSCG Corp. Comms. (Havas)*	124,158,504	900
Manning, Selvage Lee (Bcom3)	116,019,465	950
Golin/Harris International (Interpublic Group of Cos.)	113,247,644	696
Cordiant Communications Group (Morgen-Walke et al.)	90,655,000	500
Ruder Finn*	80,348,000	472
Brodeur Worldwide (Omnicom Group)	70,001,900	500
Waggener Edstrom*	59,890,800	475
Cohn & Wolfe (WPP Group)	57,779,000	410
Rowland Comms. Worldwide (Publicis)	42,666,000	277
Text 100 (One Monday Group)*	33,676,739	325
Publicis Dialog	28,631,788	155
Morgen-Walke Assocs	21,105,020	94
Noonan Russo/Presence	19,749,049	100
DeVries PR	12,475,762	58
Middleberg Euro RSCG	10,691,000	40

*Firms supplied CPA statements and other documents required for an O'Dwyer ranking.

SOURCE: J. R. O'Dwyer Co., Inc., "PR Operations Publishing Their Own Ratings," in O'Dwyer's Directory of Public Relations Firms (2002): A13; **http://www.odwyerpr.com**.

production contracts in China after consultations with a variety of sources, including human rights organizations, experts on China, and representatives of the U.S. government, led it to conclude that there was pervasive abuse of human rights.[57]

The public relations function can be handled in-house or with the assistance of an agency. The largest agencies and agency groups are presented in Table 18.8. The use and extent of public relations activity will vary by company and the type of activity needed. Product-marketing PR may work best with a strong component of control at the local level and a local PR firm, while crisis management—given the potential for worldwide adverse impact—will probably be controlled principally from a global center.[58] This has meant that global marketers funnel short-term projects to single offices for their local expertise while maintaining contact with the global agencies for their worldwide reach when a universal message is needed. Some multinational corporations maintain public relations staffs in their main offices around the world, while others use the services of firms such as Burson-Marsteller, Hill and Knowlton, and Porter Novelli on specific projects.

Sponsorship Marketing

Sponsorship involves the marketer's investment in events or causes. Sponsorship funds worldwide are directed for the most part at sports events (both individual and team sports) and cultural events (both in the popular and high-culture categories). Sponsorship spending is relatively even around the world: of the nearly $25 billion spent in 2002, North America contributed $9.6, Europe $7.1, Asia-Pacific $4.3, and Latin America $2.1 billion.[59] Examples range from Coca-Cola's sponsorship of the 2004 Olympic Games in Athens and MasterCard's sponsorship of World Cup Soccer in 2002 in Japan and South Korea to Visa's sponsoring of Eric Clapton's tour and Ford's sponsoring of the Montreux Detroit Jazz Festival. Sponsorship of events such as the Olympics is driven by the desire to be associated with a worldwide event that has a positive image, global reach, and a proven strategic positioning of excellence.

The challenge is that an event may become embroiled in controversy, thus hurting the sponsors' images as well. Furthermore, in light of the high expense of sponsorship, marketers worry about **ambush marketing** by competitors. Ambush marketing is the unauthorized use of an event without the permission of the event owner. For example, an advertising campaign could suggest a presumed sponsorship relationship. During the Atlanta Olympic Games in 1996, some of the sponsors' competitors garnered a higher profile than the sponsors themselves. For example, Pepsi erected stands outside venues and plastered the town with signs. Nike secured substantial amounts of air time on radio and TV stations. Fuji bought billboards on the route from the airport into downtown Atlanta. None of the three contributed anything to the International Olympic Committee during this time.[60]

Cause-related marketing is a combination of public relations, sales promotion, and corporate philanthropy. This activity should not be developed merely as a response to a crisis, nor should it be a fuzzy, piecemeal effort to generate publicity; instead, marketers should have a social vision and a planned long-term social policy. For example, in Casanare, Colombia, where it is developing oil interests, British Petroleum invests in activities that support its business plan and contribute to the region's development. This has meant an investment of $10 million in setting up a loan fund for entrepreneurs, giving students technical training, supporting a center for pregnant women and nursing mothers, working on reforestation, building aqueducts, and helping to create jobs outside the oil industry.[61] Examples of IBM's contributions to local communities are provided in *The International Marketplace 18.3*. Cisco Systems' Networking Academy is an example of how a marketer can link philanthropic strategy, its competitive advantage, and broader

THE INTERNATIONAL MARKETPLACE   18.3

Expanding the Social Vision: Global Community Relations

A recent Roper survey found that 92 percent of the respondents feel that it is important for marketers to seek out ways to become good corporate citizens, and they are most interested in those who get involved in environmental, educational, and health issues. Many are worried that globalization has brought about a decline in corporate conduct and responsibility. However, many marketers have seen it as completely the opposite. Community relations is, as one chief executive put it, "food for the soul of the organization." It has become a strategic aspect of business and a fundamental ingredient for the long-term health of the enterprise. As a global company, IBM has a network of staff responsible for corporate responsibility throughout the 152 countries of operation. Major initiatives that address environmental concerns, support programs for the disabled, and support education reform have been pioneered by IBM around the world.

IBM's policy of good corporate citizenship means accepting responsibility as a participant in community and national affairs and striving to be among the most-admired companies in its host countries. IBM sponsors Worldwide Initiatives in Volunteerism, a $1 million–plus program to fund projects worldwide and promote employee volunteerism. In Thailand, for example, IBM provides equipment and personnel to universities and donates money to the nation's wildlife fund and environmental protection agency. In 1986, the firm became one of only two companies with a U.S.-based parent to win the Garuda Award, which recognizes significant contributions to Thailand's social and economic development.

As part of its long-term strategy for growth in Latin America, IBM is investing millions of dollars in an initiative that brings the latest technology to local schools. IBM does not donate the computers (they are bought by governments, institutions, and other private firms), but it does provide the needed instruction and technological support. By 1993, some 800,000 children and 10,000 teachers had benefited from the program in ten countries. IBM Latin America's technology-in-education initiative is a creative combination of marketing, social responsibility, and long-term relationship building that fits in with the company's goal of becoming a "national asset" in Latin American countries. In Venezuela, IBM teamed with the government to bring computers to the K–12 environment to enhance the learning process through technology.

Increased privatization and government cutbacks in social services in many countries offer numerous opportunities for companies to make substantive contributions to solving various global, regional, and local problems. Conservative governments in Europe are welcoming private-sector programs to provide job training for inner-city youth, to meet the needs of immigrants, and to solve massive pollution problems. And in Eastern and Central Europe, where the lines between the private and public sectors are just now being drawn, corporations have a unique opportunity to take a leadership role in

shaping new societies. IBM Germany provided computer equipment and executive support to clean the heavily polluted River Elbe, which runs through the Czech Republic and Germany into the North Sea.

James Parkel, director of IBM's Office of Corporate Support Programs, summarizes the new expectations in the following way: "Employees don't want to work for companies that have no social conscience, customers don't want to do business with companies that pollute the environment or are notorious for shoddy products and practices, and communities don't welcome companies that are not good corporate citizens. Many shareholder issues are socially driven."

SOURCES: Michael E. Porter and Mark R. Kramer, "The Competitive Advantage of Corporate Philanthropy," *Harvard Business Review* 80 (December 2002): 56–68; Roger L. Martin, "The Virtue Matrix: Calculating the Return on Corporate Responsibility," *Harvard Business Review* 80 (March 2002): 68–75; Bradley K. Googins, "Why Community Relations Is a Strategic Imperative," *Strategy and Business* (third quarter, 1997): 64–67; "Consumers Note Marketers' Good Causes: Roper," *Advertising Age*, November 11, 1996, 51; Paul N. Bloom, Pattie Yu Hussein, and Lisa R. Szykman, "Benefiting Society and the Bottom Line," *Marketing Management*, Winter 1995, 8–18; and **http://www.ibm.com**.

social good. To address a chronic deficit in IT job applicants, the company created The Network Academy concept whereby it contributes networking equipment to schools. Cisco now operates 9,000 academies in secondary schools, community colleges, and community-based organizations in 147 countries. As the leading player in the field, Cisco stands to benefit the most from this improved labor pool. At the same time, Cisco has attracted worldwide recognition for this program, boosted its employee morale and partner goodwill, as well as generated a reputation for leadership in philanthropy.[62]

Increasingly, the United Nations is promoting programs to partner multinationals and NGOs (nongovernmental organizations) to tackle issues such as healthcare, energy, and biodiversity. For example, Merck and GlaxoSmithKline have partnered with UNICEF and the World Bank to improve access to AIDS care in the hardest hit regions of the world.[63]

Summary

As multinational corporations manage the various elements of the promotions mix in differing environmental conditions, decisions must be made about channels to be used in communication, the message, who is to execute or help execute the program, and how the success of the endeavor is to be measured. The trend is toward more harmonization of strategy, at the same time allowing for flexibility at the local level and early incorporation of local needs into the promotional plans.

The effective implementation of the promotional program is a key ingredient in the marketing success of the firm. The promotional tools must be used within the opportunities and constraints posed by the communications channels as well as by the laws and regulations governing marketing communications.

Advertising agencies are key facilitators in communicating with the firm's constituent groups. Many multinational corporations are realigning their accounts worldwide in an attempt to streamline their promotional efforts and achieve a global approach.

The use of other promotional tools, especially personal selling, tends to be more localized to fit the conditions of the individual markets. Decisions concerning recruitment, training, motivation, and evaluation must be made at the affiliate level, with general guidance from headquarters.

An area of increasing challenge to multinational corporations is public relations. Multinationals, by their very design, draw attention to their activities. The best interest of the marketer lies in anticipating problems with both internal and external constituencies and managing them, through communications, to the satisfaction of all parties.

Key Terms

cause-related marketing
corporate image advertising
product placement

global media
ambush marketing

Questions for Discussion

1. MasterCard sponsors the World Cup and Visa the Olympics. Who gets the "better deal" since the expense of sponsorship is about the same for both?

2. Comment on the opinion that "practically speaking, neither an entirely standardized nor an entirely localized advertising approach is necessarily best."

3. What type of adjustments must advertising agencies make as more companies want "one sight, one sound, one sell" campaigns?

4. Assess the programmed management approach for coordinating international advertising efforts.

5. Discuss problems associated with measuring advertising effectiveness in foreign markets.

6. Is international personal selling a reality? Or is all personal selling national, regardless of who performs it?

Internet Exercises

1. Rumors are one of the most difficult problems faced by public relations personnel, especially if they spread worldwide or occur in multiple-country markets. Procter & Gamble faced a rumor that it was associated with "forces of the dark side" and that its corporate logo was proof of that. Using Procter & Gamble's Web site (**http://www.pg.com**) and its "Trademark Facts," assess the company's efforts to eliminate the problem.

2. A company wishing to engage global markets through the Internet has to make sure that its regional/local Web sites are of the same caliber as its global site. Using Kodak as an example (**http://www.kodak.com**), evaluate whether its sites abroad satisfy this criterion.

Recommended Readings

Anholt, Simon. *Another One Bites the Grass: Making Sense of International Advertising*. New York: John Wiley & Sons, 2000.

Bly, Robert W. *Advertising Manager's Handbook*. New York: Aspen Publishers, 2002.

Burnett, Leo. *Worldwide Advertising and Media Fact Book*. Chicago, IL: Triumph Books, 1994.

De Mooij, Marieke K. *Global Marketing and Advertising: Understanding Cultural Paradoxes*. San Francisco: Sage Publications, 1997.

Grey, Anne-Marie, and Kim Skildum-Reid. *The Sponsorship Seeker's Toolkit*. New York: McGraw-Hill, 1999.

Jones, John Philip. *International Advertising: Realities and Myths*. San Francisco: Sage Publications, 1999.

Monye, Sylvester O., ed. *The Handbook of International Marketing Communications*. Cambridge, MA: Blackwell Publishers, 2000.

Moses, Elissa. *The $100 Billion Allowance: How to Get Your Share of the Global Teen Market*. New York: John Wiley & Sons, 2000.

Niefeld, Jaye S. *The Making of an Advertising Campaign: The Silk of China*. Englewood Cliffs, NJ: Prentice Hall, 1989.

Peebles, Dean M., and John K. Ryans. *Management of International Advertising: A Marketing Approach*. Boston: Allyn & Bacon, 1984.

Roberts, Mary-Lou, and Robert D. Berger. *Direct Marketing Management*. Englewood Cliffs, NJ: Prentice Hall, 1999.

Schultz, Don E., and Philip J. Kitchen. *Communicating Globally: An Integrated Marketing Approach*. New York: McGraw-Hill, 2000.

Shimp, Terence A. *Advertising, Promotion, and Supplemental Aspects of Integrated Marketing Communications*. Mason, OH: South-Western, 2003.

Zenith Media. *Advertising Expenditure Forecasts*. London: Zenith Media, December 2002.

chapter **19**

Marketing Organization, Implementation, and Control

© PHOTODISC, VOL. 22

© CORBIS

THE INTERNATIONAL MARKETPLACE   19.1

Procter & Gamble: Organization 2005

Globalization is at the heart of Procter & Gamble's restructuring of its organization, code-named Organization 2005. Organization 2005 recognizes that there is a big difference between selling products in 140 countries around the world and truly planning and managing lines of business on a global basis.

There are five key elements to Organization 2005:

- Global Business Units (GBUs). P&G is moving from four business units based on geographic regions to four GBUs based on product lines. This will drive greater innovation and speed by centering global strategy and profit responsibility on brands, rather than on geographics.
- Market Development Organizations (MDOs). The company is establishing seven MDO regions that will tailor global programs to local markets and develop marketing strategies to build P&G's entire business based on superior local consumer and customer knowledge.
- Global Business Services (GBS). GBS brings business activities such as accounting, human resource systems, order management, and information technology into a single global organization to provide these services to all P&G business units at best-in-class quality, cost, and speed. They will be in the following locations: Americas (San Jose, Costa Rica); Europe, Middle East, Africa (Newcastle, United Kingdom); and Asia (Manila, Philippines).
- Corporate Functions. P&G has redefined the role of corporate staff. Most have moved into new business units, with the remaining staff refocused on developing cutting-edge new knowledge and serving corporate needs. For example, the company decentralized its 3,600-person information technology department so that 97 percent of its members now work in P&G's individual product, market, and business teams or are

part of GBS, which provides shared services such as infrastructure to P&G units. The remaining 3 percent are still in corporate IT. In addition, 54 "change agents" have been assigned to work across the four GBUs to lead cultural and business change by helping teams work together more effectively through greater use of IT, in particular, real-time collaboration tools. Future plans have called for some of these functions to be outsourced.

- Culture. Changes to P&G's culture should create an environment that produces bolder, mind-stretching goals and plans; bigger innovations; and greater speed. For example, the reward system has been redesigned to better link executive compensation with new business goals and results.

A good example of the increased use of collaborative technology is a product called Swiffer, a dust sweeper with disposal cloths electrostatically charged to attract dust and dirt. Swiffer, which was introduced to the market in August 1999, represents collaboration among multiple P&G product groups, including paper and chemicals. Swiffer took just 18 months to go from test market to global availability. In the past, when a product was introduced, it might have taken years for it to be available worldwide, since management in each region was responsible for the product's launch there, including everything from test marketing to getting products onto retailers' shelves. Collaborative technologies, including chat rooms on the company's intranet, are transforming the company's conservative culture to one that encourages employees to be candid, test boundaries, and take chances.

Not all has gone smoothly with the planned changes, however. The major overlooked factor was the personal upheaval that the changes have created. More of the executives at the various levels are in new jobs. Physical

The New Procter & Gamble

Global Business Units	Market Development Organizations	Global Business Services	Corporate Functions
• Baby, Feminine, and Family Care • Fabric & Home Care • Food & Beverage • Health & Beauty Care	• North America • Latin America • Western Europe • Central Eastern Europe/ Middle East/Africa • ASEAN/India/Australia • Northeast Asia • Greater China	• Global Enabling Team • Regional Leadership Team • Global Process Owners	• Customer Business Development • Finance & Accounting • IT • Legal • Product Supply • R&D • Human Resources • Marketing • Consumer & Market Knowledge

transfers were significant as well; for example, 1,000 people were moved to Geneva from around Europe and another 200 to Singapore from various Asian locations. Furthermore, the changed reporting structures raised concerns as well. Food and Beverage managers, who are mostly in Cincinnati, report to a president in Caracas, Venezuela, while everyone in Fabric and Home Care reports to Brussels. Personnel transferred to MDOs suddenly had no brands to manage and had to think across borders. The change from a U.S.-centric company to a global one was a substantial demand in a short period of time and has required adjustments by those affected and in the timetables set.

© THE PROCTER & GAMBLE COMPANY

SOURCES: "Think Globally, Act Locally," available at **http://www.pg.com**, accessed November 24, 2002; Jack Neff, "Does P&G Still Matter?" *Advertising Age*, September 25, 2000, 48–56; "Rallying the Troops at P&G," *The Wall Street Journal*, August 31, 2000, B1, B4; "P&G Jump-Starts Corporate Change," *Internetweek*, November 1, 1999, 30; "All around the World," *Traffic World*, October 11, 1999, 22–24; "Organization 2005 Drive for Accelerated Growth Enters Next Phase," *P&G News Releases*, June 9, 1999, 1–5; and "Procter & Gamble Moves Forward with Reorganization," *Chemical Market Reporter*, February 1, 1999, 12.

AS COMPANIES EVOLVE from purely domestic entities to multinationals, their organizational structure and control systems must change to reflect new strategies. With growth comes diversity in terms of products and services, geographic markets, and personnel, leading to a set of challenges for the company. Two critical issues are basic to addressing these challenges: (1) the type of organization that provides the best framework for developing worldwide strategies while at the same time maintaining flexibility with respect to individual markets and operations, and (2) the type and degree of control to be exercised from headquarters to maximize total effort. Organizational structures and control systems have to be adjusted as market conditions change, as seen in *The International Marketplace 19.1*. While some units are charged with the development of strong global brands, others are charged with local adaptation and creating synergies across programs.

This chapter will focus on the advantages and disadvantages of the organizational structures available as well as their appropriateness at various stages of internationalization. A determining factor is where decision-making authority within the organizational structures will be placed. The roles of different entities of the organization need to be defined, including how to achieve collaboration among these units for the benefit of the entire global organization. The chapter will also outline the need for devising a control system to oversee the international operations of the company, emphasizing the control instruments needed in addition to those used in domestic business, as well as the control strategies of multinational corporations. The appropriateness and eventual cost of the various control approaches will vary as the firm expands its international operations. Overall, the objective of the chapter is to study intraorganizational relationships in the firm's attempt to optimize competitive response in areas most critical to its business.

Organizational Structure

The basic functions of an organization are to provide (1) a route and locus of decision making and coordination, and (2) a system for reporting and communications. Increasingly, the coordination and communication dimensions have to include learning from the global marketplace through the company's different units.[1] These networks are typically depicted in the organizational chart.

Organizational Designs

The basic configurations of international organizations correspond to those of purely domestic ones; the greater the degree of internationalization, the more complex the structures can become. The core building block is the individual company operating in its particular market. However, these individual companies need to work together for maximum effectiveness—thus, the need for organizational design. The types of structures that companies use to manage foreign activities can be divided into three categories based on the degree of internationalization:

1. Little or no formal organizational recognition of international activities of the firm. This category ranges from domestic operations handling an occasional international transaction on an ad hoc basis to separate export departments.
2. International division. Firms in this category recognize the ever-growing importance of international involvement.
3. Global organizations. These can be structured by product, area, function, process, or customer.

Hybrid structures may exist as well, in which one market may be structured by product, another by area. Matrix organizations have emerged in large multinational corporations to combine product, regional, and functional expertise. As worldwide competition has increased dramatically in many industries, the latest organizational response is networked global organizations in which heavy flows of technology, personnel, and communication take place between strategically interdependent units to establish greater global integration. The ability to identify and disseminate best practices throughout the organization is an important competitive advantage for global companies. For example, a U.S. automaker found that in the face of distinctive challenges presented by the local environment, Brazilian engineers developed superior seals, which the company then incorporated in all its models worldwide.[2]

Little or No Formal Organization

In the very early stages of international involvement, domestic operations assume responsibility for international marketing activities. The share of international operations in the sales and profits of the corporation is initially so minor that no organizational adjustment takes place. No consolidation of information or authority over international sales is undertaken or is necessary. Transactions are conducted on a case-by-case basis either by the resident expert or quite often with the help of facilitating agents, such as freight forwarders.

As demand from the international marketplace grows and interest within the firm expands, the organizational structure will reflect it. An export department appears as a separate entity. This may be an outside export management company—that is, an independent company that becomes the de facto export department of the firm. This is an indirect approach to international involvement in that very little experience is accumulated within the firm itself. Alternatively, a firm may establish its own export department, hiring a few seasoned individuals to take full responsibility for international activities. Organizationally, the department may be a subdepartment of marketing (as shown in Figure 19.1) or may have equal ranking with the various functional departments. This choice will depend on the importance assigned to overseas activities by the firm. Because the export department is the first real step for internationalizing the organizational structure, it should be a full-fledged marketing organization and not merely a sales organization; i.e., it should have the resources for market research and market-development activities (such as trade show participation).

Licensing is the international entry mode for some firms. Responsibility for licensing may be assigned to the R&D function despite its importance to the overall international strategy of the firm. A formal liaison among the export, marketing, production, and R&D functions should be formed for the maximum utilization of licensing.[3] A separate manager should be appointed if licensing becomes a major activity for the firm.

Figure 19.1 The Export Department Structure (TAL Apparel)

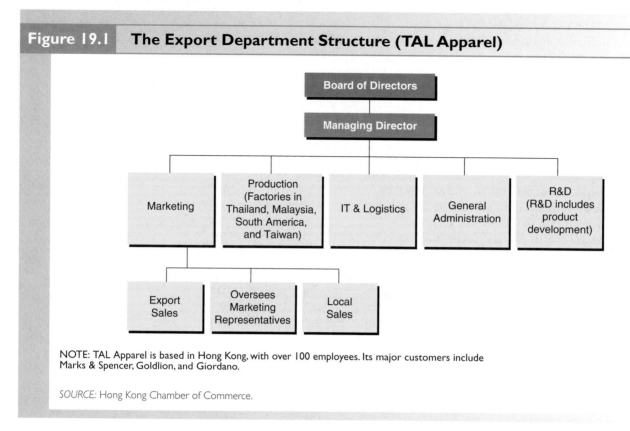

NOTE: TAL Apparel is based in Hong Kong, with over 100 employees. Its major customers include Marks & Spencer, Goldlion, and Giordano.

SOURCE: Hong Kong Chamber of Commerce.

As the firm becomes more involved in foreign markets, the export department structure will become obsolete. The firm may then undertake joint ventures or direct foreign investment, which require those involved to have functional experience. The firm therefore typically establishes an international division.

Some firms that acquire foreign production facilities pass through an additional stage in which foreign subsidiaries report directly to the president or to a manager specifically assigned this duty. However, the amount of coordination and control that is required quickly establishes the need for a more formal international organization in the firm.

The International Division

The international division centralizes in one entity, with or without separate incorporation, all of the responsibility for international activities, as illustrated in Figure 19.2. The approach aims to eliminate a possible bias against international operations that may exist if domestic divisions are allowed to independently serve international customers. In some cases, international markets have been found to be treated as secondary to domestic markets. The international division concentrates international expertise, information flows concerning foreign market opportunities, and authority over international activities. However, manufacturing and other related functions remain with the domestic divisions in order to take advantage of economies of scale.

To avoid situations in which the international division is at a disadvantage in competing for production, personnel, and corporate services, corporations need to coordinate between domestic and international operations. Coordination can be achieved through a joint staff or by requiring domestic and international divisions to interact in strategic planning and to submit the plans to headquarters. Further, many corporations require and encourage frequent interaction between domestic and international personnel to discuss common challenges in areas such as product planning. Coordination is also important because domestic operations may be

Figure 19.2   The International Division Structure (Timberland)

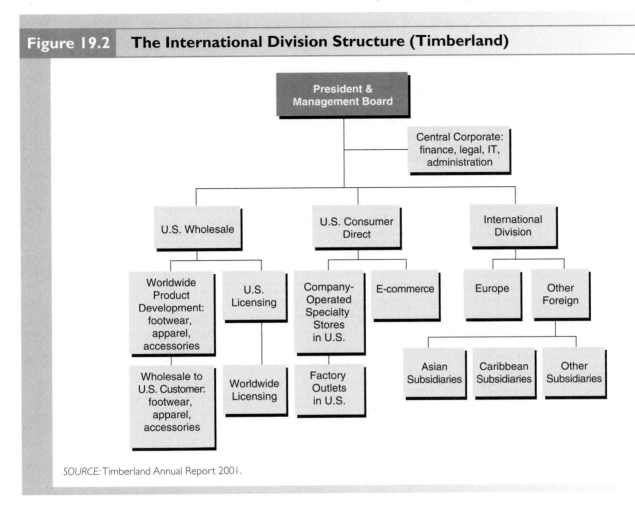

SOURCE: Timberland Annual Report 2001.

organized along product or functional lines, whereas international divisions are geographically oriented.

International divisions best serve firms with few products that do not vary significantly in terms of their environmental sensitivity, and when international sales and profits are still quite insignificant compared with those of the domestic divisions.[4] Companies may outgrow their international divisions as their international sales grow in significance, diversity, and complexity. European companies used international divisions far less than their U.S. counterparts due to the relatively small size of their domestic markets. N.V. Philips, for example, would have never grown to its current prominence by relying on the Dutch market alone. While international divisions were still popular among U.S. companies in the 1980s and 1990s, globalization of markets and the increased share of overseas sales have made international divisions less suitable than global structures.[5] For example, Loctite, a leading marketer of sealants, adhesives, and coatings, moved from having an international division to being a global structure in which the company is managed by market channel (e.g., industrial automotive and electronics industry), to enable Loctite employees to synergize efforts and expertise worldwide.[6]

Global Organizational Structures

Global structures have grown out of competitive necessity. In many industries, competition is on a global basis, with the result that companies must have a high degree of reactive capability.

Five basic types of global structures are available:

1. Global product structure, in which product divisions are responsible for all manufacture and marketing worldwide

2. Global area structure, in which geographic divisions are responsible for all manufacture and marketing in their respective areas

3. Global functional structure, in which the functional areas (such as production, marketing, finance, and personnel) are responsible for the worldwide operations of their own functional areas

4. Global customer structure, in which operations are structured based on distinct worldwide customer groups

5. Mixed—or hybrid—structure, which may combine the other alternatives

Product Structure The **product structure** is the one that is most used by multinational corporations.[7] This approach gives worldwide responsibility to strategic business units for the marketing of their product lines, as shown in Figure 19.3. Most consumer product firms utilize some form of this approach, mainly because of the diversity of their products. One of the major benefits of the approach is improved cost efficiency through centralization of manufacturing facilities. This is crucial in industries in which competitive position is determined by world market share, which in turn is often determined by the degree to which manufacturing is rationalized.[8] Adaptation to this approach may cause problems because it is usually accompanied by consolidation of operations and plant closings. A good example is Black & Decker, which rationalized many of its operations in its worldwide competitive effort against Makita, the Japanese power tool manufacturer. Similarly, Goodyear reorganized itself into a single global organization with a complete business team approach for tires and general products. The move was largely prompted by tightening worldwide competition.[9] In a similar move, Ford merged its large and culturally distinct European and North American auto operations by

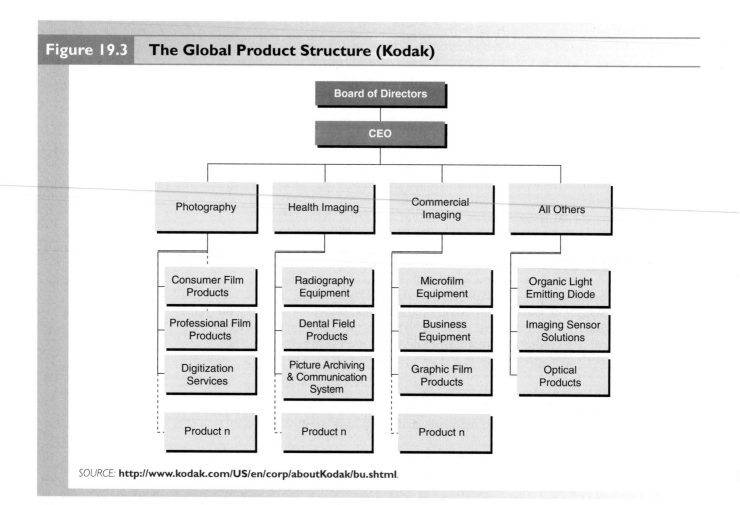

Figure 19.3   The Global Product Structure (Kodak)

SOURCE: **http://www.kodak.com/US/en/corp/aboutKodak/bu.shtml**.

vehicle platform type to make more efficient use of its engineering and product development resources against rapidly globalizing rivals.[10] The Ford Focus, Ford's compact car introduced in 1999, was designed by one team of engineers for worldwide markets.

Another benefit is the ability to balance the functional inputs needed by a product and to react quickly to product-specific problems in the marketplace. Even smaller brands receive individual attention. Product-specific attention is important because products vary in terms of the adaptation they need for different foreign markets. All in all, the product approach ideally brings about the development of a global strategic focus in response to global competition.

At the same time, this structure fragments international expertise within the firm because a central pool of international experience no longer exists. The structure assumes that managers will have adequate regional experience or advice to allow them to make balanced decisions. Coordination of activities among the various product groups operating in the same markets is crucial to avoid unnecessary duplication of basic tasks. For some of these tasks, such as market research, special staff functions may be created and then hired by the product divisions when needed. If product managers lack an appreciation for the international dimension, they may focus their attention on only the larger markets, often with emphasis on the domestic markets, and fail to take the long-term view.

Area Structure   The second most frequently adopted approach is the **area structure,** illustrated in Figure 19.4. The firm is organized on the basis of geographical areas; for example, operations may be divided into those dealing with North America, the Far East, Latin America, and Europe. Regional aggregation may play a major role in this structuring; for example, many multinational corporations have located their European headquarters in Brussels, where the EU has its

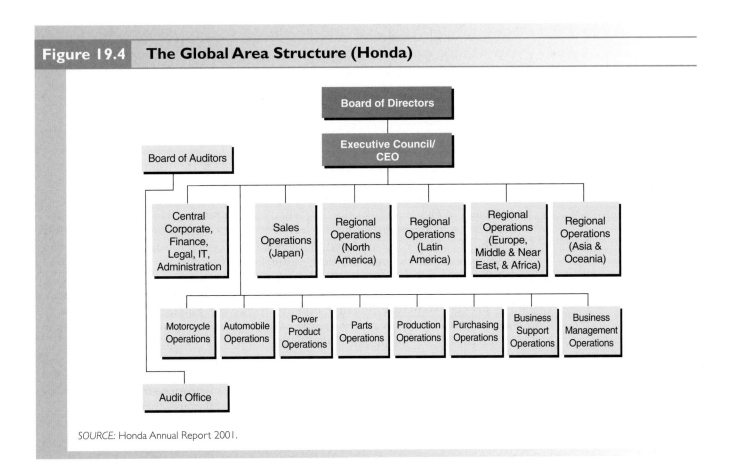

Figure 19.4   The Global Area Structure (Honda)

SOURCE: Honda Annual Report 2001.

headquarters. The inevitability of a North American trading bloc led to the creation of Campbell Soup Co.'s North American division, which replaced the U.S. operation as the power center of the company. Organizational changes were also made at 3M Company as a result of NAFTA, with the focus on three concepts: simplification, linkage, and empowerment. As an example, this means that new-product launches are coordinated throughout North America, with standardization of as many elements as is feasible and prudent.[11] The driver of the choice can also be cultural similarity, such as in the case of Asia, or historic connections between countries, such as in the case of combining Europe with the Middle East and Africa. Ideally, no special preference is given to the region in which the headquarters is located—for example, North America or Europe. Central staffs are responsible for providing coordination support for worldwide planning and control activities performed at headquarters.

The area approach follows the marketing concept most closely because individual areas and markets are given concentrated attention. If market conditions with respect to product acceptance and operating conditions vary dramatically, the area approach is the one to choose. Companies opting for this alternative typically have relatively narrow product lines with similar end uses and end users. However, expertise is most needed in adapting the product and its marketing to local market conditions. Once again, to avoid duplication of effort in product management and in functional areas, staff specialists—for product categories, for example—may be used.

Without appropriate coordination from the staff, essential information and experience may not be transferred from one regional entity to another. Also, if the company expands in terms of product lines, and if end markets begin to diversify, the area structure may become inappropriate.

Some marketers may feel that going into a global product structure may be too much too quickly and opt, therefore, to have a regional organization for planning and reporting purposes. The objective may also be to keep profit or sales centers of similar size at similar levels in the corporate hierarchy. If a group of countries has small sales compared with other country operations, they can be consolidated into a region. The benefits of a regional operation and regional headquarters are more efficient coordination of programs across the region (as opposed to globally), a management more sensitized to country-market operations in the region, and the ability for the region's voice to be heard more clearly at global headquarters (as compared to what an individual, especially smaller, country operation could achieve).[12]

Functional Structure

Of all the approaches, the **functional structure** is the most simple from the administrative viewpoint because it emphasizes the basic tasks of the firm—for example, manufacturing, sales, and research and development. This approach, illustrated in Figure 19.5, works best when both products and customers are relatively few and similar in nature. Because coordination is typically the key problem, staff functions have been created to interact between the functional areas. Otherwise, the company's marketing and regional expertise may not be exploited to the fullest extent.

A variation of this approach is one that uses processes as a basis for structure. The **process structure** is common in the energy and mining industries, where one corporate entity may be in charge of exploration worldwide and another may be responsible for the actual mining operation.

Customer Structure

Firms may also organize their operations using the **customer structure,** especially if the customer groups they serve are dramatically different—for example, consumers versus businesses versus governments. Catering to these diverse groups may require the concentration of specialists in particular divisions. The product

Figure 19.5   The Global Functional Structure (NetLogic Microsystem)

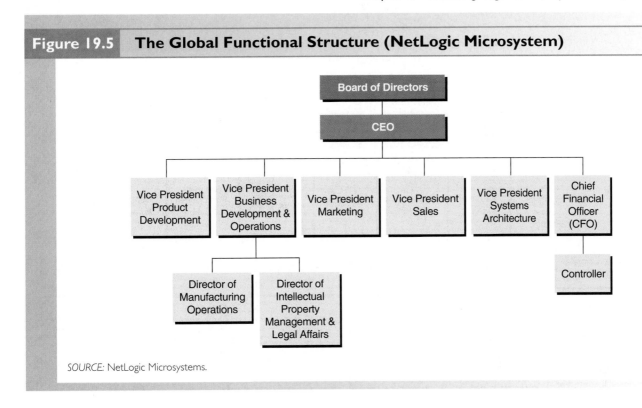

SOURCE: NetLogic Microsystems.

may be the same, but the buying processes of the various customer groups may differ. Governmental buying is characterized by bidding, in which price plays a larger role than when businesses are the buyers.

Mixed Structure

Mixed, or hybrid, organizations also exist. A **mixed structure,** such as the one in Figure 19.6, combines two or more organizational dimensions simultaneously. It permits attention to be focused on products, areas, or functions, as needed. This approach may occur in a transitionary period after a merger or an acquisition, or it may come about because of a unique customer group or product line (such as military hardware). It may also provide a useful structure before the implementation of the matrix structure.[13]

Organization structures are, of course, never as clear-cut and simple as they have been presented here. Whatever the basic format, inputs are needed for product, area, and function. One alternative, for example, might be an initial product structure that would eventually have regional groupings. Another alternative might be an initial area structure with eventual product groupings. However, in the long term, coordination and control across such structures become tedious.

Matrix Structure

Many multinational corporations—in an attempt to facilitate planning, organizing, and controlling interdependent businesses, critical resources, strategies, and geographic regions—have adopted the **matrix structure.**[14] Business is driven by a worldwide business unit (for example, photographic products or commercial and information systems) and implemented by a geographic unit (for example, Europe or Latin America). The geographical units, as well as their country subsidiaries, serve as the "glue" between autonomous product operations.

Organizational matrices integrate the various approaches already discussed, as the Philips example in Figure 19.7 illustrates. The product divisions (which are then divided into 60 product groups) have rationalized manufacturing to provide products for continent-wide markets rather than lines of products for individual

Figure 19.6   The Global Mixed Structure (DaimlerChrysler)

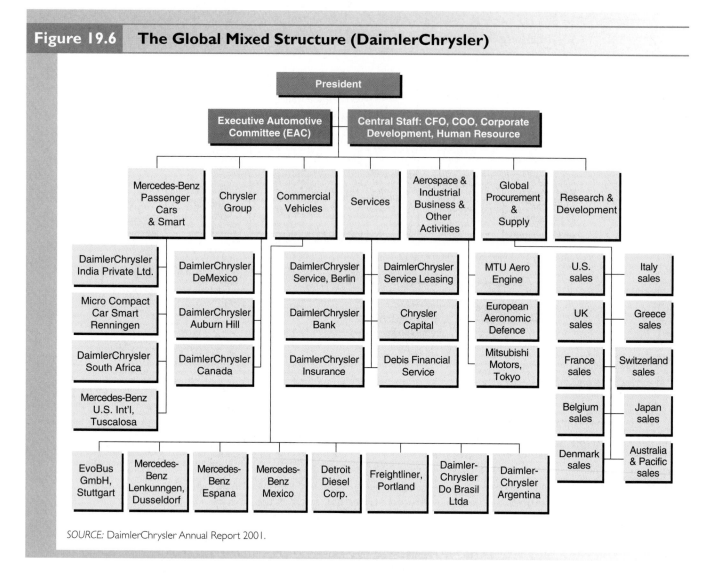

SOURCE: DaimlerChrysler Annual Report 2001.

markets. These product groups adjust to changing market conditions; for example, the components division has been slated to be merged into the other divisions due to lack of stand-alone profitability.[15] Philips has three general types of country organizations: In "key" markets, such as the United States, France, and Japan, product divisions manage their own marketing as well as manufacturing. In "local business" countries, such as Nigeria and Peru, the organizations function as importers from product divisions, and if manufacturing occurs, it is purely for the local market. In "large" markets, such as Brazil, Spain, and Taiwan, a hybrid arrangement is used depending on the size and situation. The product divisions and the national subsidiaries interact together in a matrix-like configuration with the product divisions responsible for the globalization dimension and the national subsidiaries responsible for local representation and coordination of common areas of interest, such as recruiting. The matrix structure manager has functional, product, and resource managers reporting to him or her. The approach is based on team building and multiple command, each team specializing in its own area of expertise. It provides a mechanism for cooperation among country managers, business managers, and functional managers on a worldwide basis through increased communication, control, and attention to balance in the organization.

The matrices used vary according to the number of dimensions needed. For example, Dow Chemical's matrix is three-dimensional, consisting of six geographic

Figure 19.7   The Global Matrix Structure (Philips)

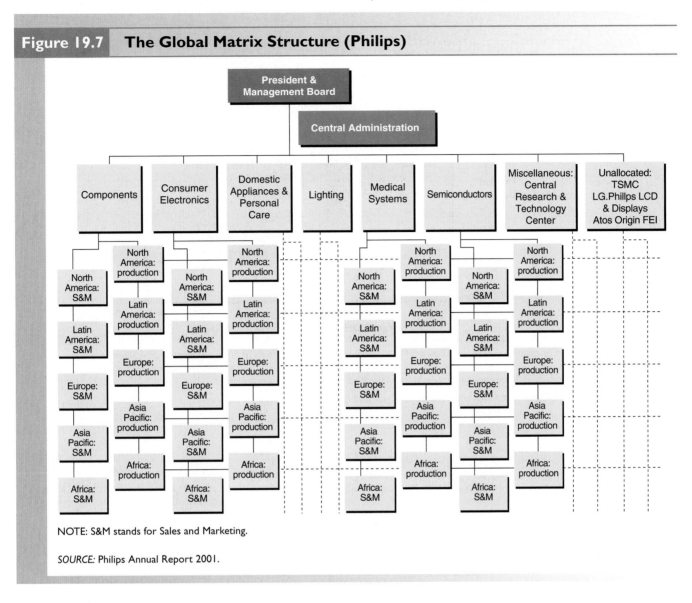

NOTE: S&M stands for Sales and Marketing.

SOURCE: Philips Annual Report 2001.

areas, three major functions (marketing, manufacturing, and research), and more than 70 products. The matrix approach helps cut through enormous organizational complexities by building in a provision for cooperation among business managers, functional managers, and strategy managers. However, the matrix requires sensitive, well-trained middle managers who can cope with problems that arise from reporting to two bosses—for example, a product line manager and an area manager. For example, every management unit may have some sort of multidimensional reporting relationship, which may cross functional, regional, or operational lines. On a regional basis, group managers in Europe, for example, report administratively to a vice president of operations for Europe. But functionally, they report to group vice presidents at global headquarters.

Many companies have found the matrix structure problematic. The dual reporting channel easily causes conflict; complex issues are forced into a two-dimensional decision framework; and even minor issues may have to be resolved through committee discussion.[16] Ideally, managers should solve problems themselves through formal and informal communication; however, physical and psychic distance often make that impossible. Especially when competitive conditions require quick reaction, the matrix, with its inherent complexity, may actually lower

Figure 19.8 Evolution of International Structures

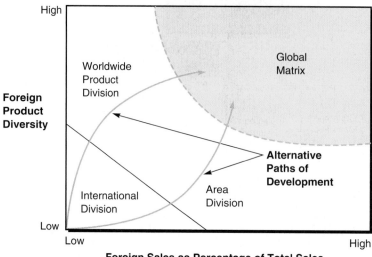

the reaction speed of the company. As a result, authority has started to shift in many organizations from area to product although the matrix may still officially be used.

Evolution of Organizational Structures

Companies develop new structures in stages as their product diversity develops and the share of foreign sales increases.[17] At the first stage are autonomous subsidiaries reporting directly to top management, followed by the establishment of an international division. With increases in product diversity and in the importance of the foreign marketplace, companies develop global structures to coordinate subsidiary operations and rationalize worldwide production. As multinational corporations have faced pressures to adapt to local market conditions while trying to rationalize production and globalize competitive reaction, many have opted for the matrix structure. The matrix structure probably allows a corporation to best meet the challenges of global markets: to be global and local, big and small, decentralized with centralized reporting by allowing the optimizing of businesses globally and maximizing performance in every country of operation.[18] The evolutionary process is summarized in Figure 19.8.

Whatever the choice of organizational arrangement may be, the challenge of people having to work in silos remains. Employee knowledge tends to be fragmented with one unit's experience and know-how inaccessible to other units. Therefore, the wheel gets reinvented at considerable cost to the company and frustration to those charged with tasks. Information technology can be used to synchronize knowledge across even the most complicated and diverse organizations.[19] At Procter & Gamble, for example, brand managers have use of a standardized, worldwide ad-testing system which allows them access to every ad the company has ever run, providing examples for the needs that may have to be met at a particular time.

Implementation

Organizational structures provide the frameworks for carrying out marketing decision making. However, for marketing to be effective, a series of organizational initiatives are needed to develop marketing strategy to its full potential; that is, secure implementation of such strategies at the national level and across markets.[20]

Locus of Decision Making

Organizational structures themselves do not indicate where the authority for decision making and control rests within the organization nor will they reveal the level of coordination between units. The different levels of coordination between country units are summarized in Table 19.1. Once a suitable form of structure has been found, it has to be made to work by finding a balance between the center and the country organizations.

If subsidiaries are granted a high degree of autonomy, the result is termed **decentralization.** In decentralized systems, controls are relatively loose and simple, and the flows between headquarters and subsidiaries are mainly financial; that is, each subsidiary operates as a profit center. On the other hand, if controls are tight and if strategic decision making is concentrated at headquarters, the result is termed **centralization.** Firms are typically neither totally centralized nor totally decentralized. Some functions, such as finance, lend themselves to more centralized decision making, whereas other functions, such as promotional decisions, lend themselves to far less. Research and development is typically centralized in terms of both decision making and location, especially when basic research work is involved. Partly because of governmental pressures, some companies have added R&D functions on a regional or local basis. In many cases, however, variations in decision making are product- and market-based; for example, Corning Glass Works' television tube marketing strategy requires global decision making for pricing and local decisions for service and delivery.

Allowing maximum flexibility at the country-market level takes advantage of the fact that subsidiary management knows its market and can react to changes quickly. Problems of motivation and acceptance are avoided when decision makers are also the implementors of the strategy. On the other hand, many multinational companies faced with global competitive threats and opportunities have adopted global strategy formulation, which by definition requires some degree of

Table 19.1   Levels of Coordination

Level	Description
5. Central control	No national structures
4. Central direction	Central functional heads have line authority over national functions
3. Central coordination	Central staff functions in coordinating role
2. Coordinating mechanisms	Formal committees and systems
1. Informal cooperation	Functional meetings: exchange of information
0. National autonomy	No coordination between decentralized units, which may even compete in export markets

Level 5 = highest; Level 0 = lowest. Most commonly found levels are 1–4.

SOURCE: Norman Blackwell, Jean-Pierre Bizet, Peter Child, and David Hensley, "Creating European Organizations That Work," in *Readings in Global Marketing*, Michael R. Czinkota and Ilkka A. Ronkainen, eds. (London: The Dryden Press, 1995), 376–385.

centralization. What has emerged as a result can be called **coordinated decentralization.** This means that overall corporate strategy is provided from headquarters, but subsidiaries are free to implement it within the range established in consultation between headquarters and the subsidiaries.

However, moving into this new mode may raise significant challenges. Among these systemic difficulties are a lack of widespread commitment to dismantling traditional national structures, driven by an inadequate understanding of the larger, global forces at work. Power barriers—especially if the personal roles of national managers are under threat of being consolidated into regional organizations—can lead to proposals being challenged without valid reason. Finally, some organizational initiatives (such as multicultural teams or corporate chat rooms) may be jeopardized by the fact that people do not have the necessary skills (e.g., language ability) or that an infrastructure (e.g., intranet) may not exist in an appropriate format.[21]

One particular case is of special interest. Organizationally, the forces of globalization are changing the country manager's role significantly. With profit-and-loss responsibility, oversight of multiple functions, and the benefit of distance from headquarters, country managers enjoyed considerable decision-making autonomy as well as entrepreneurial initiative. Today, however, many companies have to emphasize the product dimension of the product-geography matrix, which means that the power has to shift at least to some extent from country managers to worldwide strategic business unit and product line managers. Many of the previously local decisions are now subordinated to global strategic moves. However, regional and local brands still require an effective local management component. Therefore, the future country manager will have to have diverse skills (such as government relations and managing entrepreneurial teamwork) and wear many hats in balancing the needs of the operation for which the manager is directly responsible with those of the entire region or strategic business unit.[22] To emphasize the importance of the global/regional dimension in the country manager's portfolio, many companies have tied the country manager's compensation to the way the company performs globally or regionally, not just in the market for which the manager is responsible.

Factors Affecting Structure and Decision Making

The organizational structure and locus of decision making in multinational corporations are determined by a number of factors. They include (1) the degree of involvement in international operations, (2) the business(es) in which the firm is engaged (in terms, for example, of products marketed), (3) the size and importance of the markets, and (4) the human resource capability of the firm.[23]

The effect of the degree of involvement on structure and decision making was discussed earlier in the chapter. With low degrees of involvement by the parent company, subsidiaries can enjoy high degrees of autonomy as long as they meet their profit targets. The same situation can occur in even the most globally involved companies, but within a different framework. As an example, consider Philips USA, which generates 20 percent of the company's worldwide sales. Even more important, it serves a market that is on the leading edge of digital media development. Therefore, it enjoys an independent status in terms of local policy setting and managerial practices but is nevertheless within the parent company's planning and control system.

The firm's country of origin and the political history of the area can also affect organizational structure and decision making. For example, Swiss-based Nestlé, with only 3 to 4 percent of its sales in the small domestic market, has traditionally had a highly decentralized organization. Moreover, events of the past 90 years, particularly during the two world wars, have often forced subsidiaries of European-based companies to act independently in order to survive.

The type and variety of products marketed will have an effect on organizational decisions. Companies that market consumer products typically have product organizations with high degrees of decentralization, allowing for maximum local flexibility. On the other hand, companies that market technologically sophisticated products, such as General Electric's turbines, display centralized organizations with worldwide product responsibilities.

Going global has recently meant transferring world headquarters of important business units abroad. For example, Philips has moved headquarters of several of its global business units to the United States, including taking its Digital Video Group, Optimal Storage, and Flat Panel Display activities to Silicon Valley.

Apart from situations that require the development of an area structure, the characteristics of certain markets or regions may require separate arrangements for the firm. Upon entry, AT&T China was made the only one of 20 divisions in the world to be based on geography rather than on product or service line. Furthermore, it was the only one to report directly to the CEO.[24]

The human factor in any organization is critical. Managers both at headquarters and in the subsidiaries must bridge the physical and psychic distances separating them. If subsidiaries have competent managers who rarely need to consult headquarters about their problems, they may be granted high degrees of autonomy. In the case of global organizations, subsidiary management must understand the corporate culture because subsidiaries must sometimes make decisions that meet the long-term objectives of the firm as a whole but that are not optimal for the local market.

The Networked Global Organization

No international structure is ideal, and some have challenged the wisdom of even looking for an ideal one. They have called attention to new processes that would, in a given structure, develop new perspectives and attitudes to reflect and respond to complex demands of the opposite forces of global integration and local responsiveness. Rather than a question of which structural alternative is best, the question is thus one of how best to take into account the different perspectives of various corporate entities when making decisions. In structural terms, nothing may change. As a matter of fact, Philips still has its basic matrix structure, yet major changes have occurred in internal relations. The basic change was from a decentralized federation model to a networked global organization; the effects are depicted in Figure 19.9. This approach allows for the internal **glocalization** of strategic planning and implementation.[25]

Companies that have adopted the approach have incorporated the following three dimensions into their organizations: (1) the development and communication of a clear corporate vision, (2) the effective management of human resource tools to broaden individual perspectives and develop identification with corporate goals, and (3) the integration of individual thinking and activities into the broad corporate agenda.[26] The first dimension relates to a clear and consistent long-term corporate mission that guides individuals wherever they may work in the organization. Examples of this are Johnson & Johnson's corporate credo of customer focus and NEC's C&C (computers and communication). The second relates both to developing global managers who can find opportunities in spite of environmental challenges and to creating a global perspective among country managers. The last dimension refers to tackling the "not-invented-here" syndrome to co-opt possibly isolated, even adversarial managers into the corporate agenda.

For example, in an area structure, units (such as Europe and North America) may operate quite independently, sharing little expertise and information with the others. While they are supposed to build links to headquarters and other units, they may actually be building walls. To tackle this problem, Nissan established four management committees, meeting once a month, to supervise regional

| Figure 19.9 | **The Networked Global Organization** |

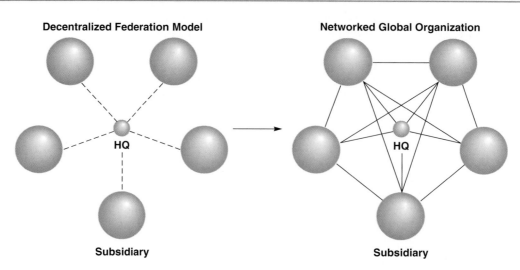

SOURCE: Reprinted with permission of Thomas Gross, Ernie Turner, and Lars Cederholm, "Building Teams for Global Operations," *Management Review*, June 1987, 34; permission conveyed through Copyright Clearance Center, Inc.

operations. Each committee includes representatives of the major functions (e.g., manufacturing, marketing, and finance), and the committees (for Japan, Europe, the United States, and general overseas markets) are chaired by Nissan executive vice presidents based in Japan. The CEO attends the committee meetings periodically but regularly.[27]

The network avoids the problems of duplication of effort, inefficiency, and resistance to ideas developed elsewhere by giving subsidiaries the latitude, encouragement, and tools to pursue local business development within the framework of the global strategy. Headquarters considers each unit as a source of ideas, skills, capabilities, and knowledge that can be utilized for the benefit of the entire organization. This means that the subsidiaries must be upgraded from the role of implementation and adaptation to that of contribution and partnership in the development and execution of worldwide strategies. Efficient plants may be converted into international production centers, innovative R&D units may become centers of excellence (and thus role models), and leading subsidiary groups may be given a leadership role in developing new strategy for the entire corporation.

Centers of excellence can emerge in three formats: charismatic, focused, or virtual. Charismatic centers of excellence are individuals who are internationally recognized for their expertise in a function or an area. The objective is primarily to build through an expert via a mentoring relationship a capability in the firm that has been lacking. The most common types are focused centers of excellence which are based on a single area of expertise, be it technological or product-based. The center has an identifiable location from which members provide advice and training. In virtual centers of excellence, the core individuals live and work around the world and keep in touch through electronic means and meetings. The knowledge of dispersed individuals is brought together, integrated into a coherent whole, and disseminated throughout the firm.[28]

Promoting Internal Cooperation

The global marketing entity in today's environment can be successful only if it is able to move intellectual capital within the organization; i.e., take ideas and move them around faster and faster.[29]

| Table 19.2 | Teaching Programs at Ford Motor Co. |

Program	Participants	Teachers	Components
Capstone	24 senior executives at a time	The leadership team	• Conducted once a year • About 20 days of teaching and discussion • Teams given six months to solve major strategic challenges • 360-degree feedback • Community service
Business Leadership Initiative	All Ford salaried employees—100,000 by 2002	The participants' managers	• Three days of teaching and discussion • Teams assigned to 100-day projects • Community service • 360-degree feedback • Exercises contrasting old and new Ford
Executive Partnering	Promising young managers	The leadership team	• Eight weeks shadowing seven senior executives
Let's Chat about the Business	Everyone who receives e-mail at Ford—about 100,000 employees	CEO	• Weekly e-mails describing Ford's new approach to business
Customer-Driven Six-Sigma	1,900 full-time employees awarded "Black Belt" in 2001	The leadership team	• 5 days of intensive instruction • "Learn-by-doing" model • Teams assigned multiple problem-solving projects

SOURCES: *Ford Motor Company Annual Report 2001* and *Corporate Citizenship Report* available at **http://www.ford.com**, accessed November 25, 2002; and Suzy Wetlaufer, "Driving Change: An Interview with Ford Motor Company's Jacques Nasser," *Harvard Business Review* 77 (March–April 1999): 76–88.

One of the tools for moving ideas is teaching. For example, at Ford Motor Company, teaching takes three distinct forms, as shown in Table 19.2. Ford's approach is similar to those undertaken at many leading global marketing companies. The focus is on teachable points of view, i.e., an explanation of what a person knows and believes about what it takes to succeed in his or her business.[30] For example, GE's Jack Welch coined the term "boundarylessness" to describe the way people can act without regard to status or functional loyalty and look for better ideas from anywhere. Top leadership of GE spends considerable time at training centers interacting with up-and-comers from all over the company. Each training class is given a real, current company problem to solve, and the reports can be career makers (or breakers).[31]

A number of benefits arise from this approach. A powerful teachable point of view can reach the entire company within a reasonable period by having students become teachers themselves. At PepsiCo, the CEO passed his teachable point on to 110 executives, who then passed it on to 20,000 people within 18 months. Second, participants in teaching situations are encouraged to maintain the international networks they develop during the sessions.

Teachers do not necessarily need to be top managers. When General Electric launched a massive effort to embrace e-commerce, many managers found that they knew little about the Internet. Following a London-based manager's idea to have an Internet mentor, GE encourages all managers to have one for a period of training each week.[32]

Another method to promote internal cooperation for global marketing implementation is the use of international teams or councils. In the case of a new product or program an international team of managers may be assembled to develop strategy. Although final direction may come from headquarters, the input has included information on local conditions, and implementation of the strategy is enhanced because local managers were involved from the beginning. This approach has worked even in cases that, offhand, would seem impossible because of market differences. Both Procter & Gamble and Henkel have successfully introduced pan-European brands for which strategy was developed by European strategy teams. These teams consisted of local managers and staff personnel to smooth eventual implementation and to avoid unnecessarily long and disruptive discussion about the fit of a new product to individual markets.

On a broader and longer-term basis, companies use councils to share **best practice,** an idea that may have saved money or time, or a process that is more efficient than existing ones. Most professionals at the leading global marketing companies are members of multiple councils.

While technology has made teamwork of this kind possible wherever the individual participants may be, technology alone may not bring about the desired results; "high-tech" approaches inherently mean "low touch," sometimes at the expense of results. Human relationships are still paramount.[33] A common purpose is what binds team members to a particular task and can only be achieved through trust, achievable through face-to-face meetings. At the start of its 777 project, Boeing brought members of the design team from a dozen different countries to Everett, Washington, giving them the opportunity to work together for up to 18 months. Beyond learning to function effectively within the company's project management system, they also shared experiences that, in turn, engendered a level of trust between individuals that later enabled them to overcome obstacles raised by physical separation. The result was a design and launch in 40 percent less time than for comparable projects.

The term *network* also implies two-way communications between headquarters and subsidiaries and between subsidiaries themselves. This translates into intercultural communication efforts focused on developing relationships.[34] While this communication can take the form of newsletters or regular and periodic meetings of appropriate personnel, new technologies are allowing marketers to link far-flung entities and eliminate traditional barriers of time and distance. **Intranets** integrate a company's information assets into a single and accessible system using Internet-based technologies such as e-mail, newsgroups, and the World Wide Web. For example, employees at Levi Strauss & Co. can join an electronic discussion group with colleagues around the world, watch the latest Levi's commercials, or comment on the latest marketing program or plan.[35] "Let's Chat about the Business" e-mails go out at Ford every Friday at 5 P.M. to about 100,000 employees to share as much information as possible throughout the company and encourage dialogue. In many companies, the annual videotaped greeting from management has been replaced by regular and frequent e-mails (called e-briefs at GE). The benefits of intranets are (1) increased productivity in that there is no longer lag time between an idea and the information needed to implement it; (2) enhanced knowledge capital that is constantly updated and upgraded; (3) facilitated teamwork enabling online communication at insignificant expense; and (4) incorporation of best practice at a moment's notice by allowing marketing managers and sales personnel to make to-the-minute decisions anywhere in the world.

As the discussion indicates, the networked approach is not a structural adaptation but a procedural one that requires a change in management mentality. Adjustment is primarily in the coordination and control functions of the firm. While there is still considerable disagreement as to which of the approaches works, some measures have been shown to correlate with success, as seen in *The International Marketplace 19.2.*

THE INTERNATIONAL MARKETPLACE   19.2

Characteristics of Success

A survey of chief executive officers of 43 leading U.S. consumer companies, made by McKinsey & Co., sheds light on organizational features that distinguish internationally successful companies. Companies were classified as more or less successful compared to their specific industry average, using international sales and profit growth over a five-year period as the most important indicators of success.

The survey results indicate certain distinctive traits that are correlated with high performance in international markets. The following are moves that companies can make to enhance prospects for international success:

- Differentiate treatment of international subsidiaries
- Let product managers in subsidiaries report to the country general manager
- Have a worldwide management development program
- Make international experience a condition for promotion to top management
- Have a more multinational management group
- Support international managers with global electronic networking capabilities
- Manage cross-border acquisitions particularly well
- Have overseas R&D centers
- Remain open to organizational change and continuous self-renewal

In general, successful companies coordinate their international decision making globally, with more central direction than less successful competitors, as seen in the following exhibit. This difference is most marked in brand positioning, package design, and price setting. The one notable exception is an increasing tendency to decentralize product development.

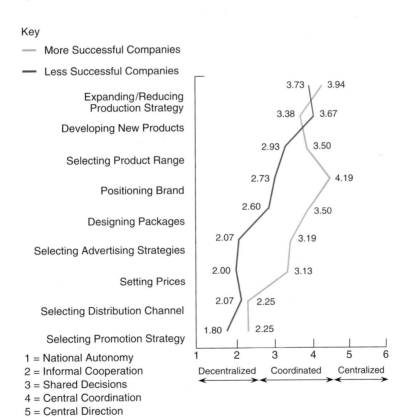

Key
— More Successful Companies
— Less Successful Companies

	Less Successful	More Successful
Expanding/Reducing Production Strategy	3.73	3.94
Developing New Products	3.38	3.67
Selecting Product Range	2.93	3.50
Positioning Brand	2.73	4.19
Designing Packages	2.60	3.50
Selecting Advertising Strategies	2.07	3.19
Setting Prices	2.00	3.13
Selecting Distribution Channel	2.07	2.25
Selecting Promotion Strategy	1.80	2.25

1 = National Autonomy
2 = Informal Cooperation
3 = Shared Decisions
4 = Central Coordination
5 = Central Direction
6 = Central Control

Decentralized   Coordinated   Centralized

SOURCE: Adapted from Ingo Theuerkauf, David Ernst, and Amir Mahini, "Think Local, Organize . . . ?" in *Best Practices in International Business,* Michael R. Czinkota and Ilkka A. Ronkainen, eds. (Mason, OH: South-Western, 2001), 249–255.

Figure 19.10 | Roles for Country Organizations

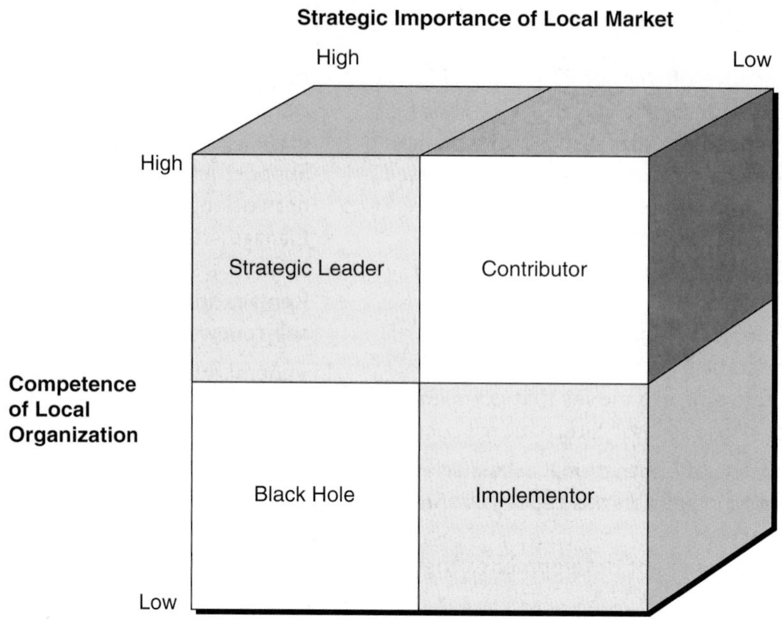

Strategic Importance of Local Market

	High	Low
High	Strategic Leader	Contributor
Competence of Local Organization — **Low**	Black Hole	Implementor

The Role of Country Organizations

Country organizations should be treated as a source of supply as much as they are considered a source of demand. Quite often, however, headquarters managers see their role as the coordinators of key decisions and controllers of resources and perceive subsidiaries as implementors and adapters of global strategy in their respective local markets. Furthermore, all country organizations may be seen as the same. This view severely limits the utilization of the firm's resources by not using country organizations as resources and by depriving country managers of possibilities of exercising their creativity.[36]

The role that a particular country organization can play depends naturally on that market's overall strategic importance as well as the competencies of its organization. From these criteria, four different roles emerge (see Figure 19.10).

The role of **strategic leader** can be played by a highly competent national subsidiary located in a strategically critical market. The country organization serves as a partner of headquarters in developing and implementing strategy. For example, a strategic leader market may have products designed specifically with it in mind. Nissan's Z-cars have always been designated primarily for the U.S. market, starting with the 240Z in the 1970s to the 350Z introduced in 2002.[37]

A **contributor** is a country organization with a distinctive competence, such as product development or regional expertise. Increasingly, country organizations are the source of new products. These range from IBM's breakthroughs in superconductivity research, generated in its Zurich lab, to low-end innovations like Procter & Gamble's liquid Tide, made with a fabric-softening compound developed in Europe. Similarly, country organizations may be assigned as worldwide centers of excellence for a particular product category, for example, ABB Strömberg in Finland for electric drives, a category for which it is a recognized world leader.[38]

Similarly, companies such as Carrier, IBM, and Hewlett-Packard use their units in Finland to penetrate the Russian market.[39]

The critical mass for the international marketing effort is provided by **implementors.** These country organizations may exist in smaller, less-developed countries in which corporate commitment to market development is less. Although most entities are given this role, it should not be slighted: Implementors provide the opportunity to capture economies of scale and scope that are the basis of a global strategy.

The **black hole** is a situation that the international marketer has to work out of. A company may be in a "black hole" situation because it has read the market incorrectly (for example, penetration of the beverage market in Japan may require a local partner) or because government may restrict its activities (for example, foreign banks restricted in terms of activities and geography in China). If possible, the marketer can use strategic alliances or acquisitions to change its competitive position. Whirlpool established itself in the European Union by acquiring Philips' white goods' operation and has used joint ventures to penetrate the Chinese market. If governmental regulations hinder the scale of operations, the firm may use its presence in a major market as an observation post to keep up with developments before a major thrust for entry is executed (for example, with China's WTO membership, the banking sector should start opening up).

Depending on the role, the relationship between headquarters and the country organization will vary from loose control based mostly on support to tighter control in making sure strategies are implemented appropriately. Yet in each of these cases, it is imperative that country organizations have enough operating independence to cater to local needs and to provide motivation to the country managers. For example, an implementor should provide input in the development of a regional or a global strategy or program. Strategy formulation should ensure that appropriate implementation can be achieved at the country level.

Good ideas can, and should, come from any country organization. To take full advantage of this, individuals at the country level have to feel that they have the authority to pursue ideas in the first place and that they see their concepts through to commercialization.[40] In some cases, this may mean that subsidiaries are allowed to experiment with projects that would not be seen as feasible by headquarters. For example, developing products for small-scale power generation using renewable resources may not generate interest in Honeywell's major markets and subsidiaries but may well be something that one of its developing-country subsidiaries should investigate.

Control

The function of the organizational structure is to provide a framework in which objectives can be met. A set of instruments and processes is needed, however, to influence the behavior and performance of organization members to meet the goals. Controls focus on actions to verify and correct actions that differ from established plans. Compliance needs to be secured from subordinates through various means of coordinating specialized and interdependent parts of the organization.[41] Within an organization, control serves as an integrating mechanism. Controls are designed to reduce uncertainty, increase predictability, and ensure that behaviors originating in separate parts of the organization are compatible and in support of common organizational goals despite physical, psychic, and temporal distances.

The critical issue is the same as with organizational structure: What is the ideal amount of control? On the one hand, headquarters needs information to ensure that international activities contribute maximum benefit to the overall organization. On the other hand, controls should not be construed as a code of law and allowed to stifle local initiative.

This section will focus on the design and functions of control instruments available for the international marketer, along with an assessment of their appropriateness. Emphasis will be placed on the degree of formality of controls used.

Types of Controls

Most organizations display some administrative flexibility, as demonstrated by variations in the application of management directives, corporate objectives, or measurement systems. A distinction should be made, however, between variations that have emerged by design and those that are the result of autonomy. The one is the result of management decision, whereas the other has typically grown without central direction and is based on emerging practices. In both instances, some type of control will be exercised. Here, we are concerned only with controls that are the result of headquarters initiative rather than consequences of tolerated practices. Firms that wait for self-emerging controls often find that such an orientation may lead to rapid international growth but may eventually result in problems in areas of product-line performance, program coordination, and strategic planning.[42]

Whatever the system, it is important in today's competitive environment to have internal benchmarking. Benchmarking relays organizational learning and sharing of best practices throughout the corporate system to avoid the costs of reinventing solutions that have already been discovered. A description of the knowledge transfer process by which this occurs is provided in *The International Marketplace 19.3*.

Three critical features are necessary in sharing best practice. First, there needs to be a device for organizational memory. For example, at Xerox, contributors to solutions can send their ideas to an electronic library where they are indexed and provided to potential adopters in the corporate family. Second, best practice must be updated and adjusted to new situations. For example, best practice adopted by the company's Chinese office will be modified and customized, and this learning should then become part of the database. Finally, best practice must be legitimized. This calls for a shared understanding that exchanging knowledge across units is valued in the organization and that these systems are important mechanisms for knowledge exchange. An assessment of how effectively employees share information with colleagues and utilize the databases can also be included in employee performance evaluations.

In the design of the control system, a major decision concerns the object of control. Two major objects are typically identified: output and behavior.[43] Output controls consist of balance sheets, sales data, production data, product line growth, or a performance review of personnel. Measures of output are accumulated at regular intervals and forwarded from the foreign operation to headquarters, where they are evaluated and critiqued based on comparisons to the plan or budget. Behavioral controls require the exertion of influence over behavior after, or ideally before, it leads to action. This influence can be achieved, for example, by providing sales manuals to subsidiary personnel or by fitting new employees into the corporate culture.

To institute either of these measures, corporate officials must decide on instruments of control. The general alternatives are bureaucratic/formalized control or cultural control. **Bureaucratic controls** consist of a limited and explicit set of regulations and rules that outline desired levels of performance. **Cultural controls,** on the other hand, are much less formal and are the result of shared beliefs and expectations among the members of an organization. A comparison of the two types of controls and their objectives is provided in Table 19.3. It can be argued that instilling the marketing approach (i.e., customer orientation) will have to rely more on behavioral dimensions since an approach focused on outputs may put undue pressure on short-term profits.[44]

Bureaucratic/Formalized Control

The elements of bureaucratic/formalized controls are (1) an international budget and planning system, (2) the functional reporting system, and (3) policy manuals

THE INTERNATIONAL MARKETPLACE   19.3

International Best Practice Exchange

As growing competitive pressures challenge many global firms, strategies to improve the transfer of best practice across geographically dispersed units and time zones becomes critical. The premise is that a company with the same product range targeting the same markets pan-regionally should be able to use knowledge gained in one market throughout the organization. The fact is, however, that companies use only 20 percent of their most precious resources—knowledge, in the form of technical information, market data, internal know-how, and processes and procedures. Trying to transfer best practices internationally amplifies the problem even more.

U.K.-based copier maker Xerox (formerly Rank Xerox), with over 60 subsidiaries, is working hard to make better use of the knowledge, corporatewide. A 35-person group identified nine practices that could be applicable throughout the group. These ranged from the way the Australian subsidiary retains customers to Italy's method of gathering competitive intelligence to a procedure for handling new major accounts in Spain. These practices were thought to be easier to "sell" to other operating companies, were considered easy to implement, and would provide a good return on investment.

Three countries were much quicker in introducing new products successfully than others. In the case of France, this was related to the training given to employees. The subsidiary gave its sales staff three days of hands-on practice, including competitive benchmarking. Before they attended the course, salespeople were given reading materials and were tested when they arrived. Those remaining were evaluated again at the end of the course, and performance reports were sent to their managers.

The difficult task is to achieve buy-in from the other country organizations. Six months might be spent in making detailed presentations of the best practices to all the companies and an additional three years helping them implement the needed changes. It is imperative that the country manager is behind the proposal in each subsidiary's case. However, implementation cannot be left to the country organizations after the concept has been presented. This may result in the dilution of both time and urgency and with possible country-specific customization that negate comparisons and jeopardize the success of the change.

With time, these projects become codified into programs. Focus 500 allows the company's top 500 executives to share information on their interactions with customers and industry partners. Project Library details costs, resources, and cycle times of more than 2,000 projects, making it a vital resource in assuring Six Sigma in project management. PROFIT allows salespeople to submit hot selling tips—with cash incentives for doing so.

SOURCES: Kristine Ellis, "Sharing Best Practices Globally," *Training*, July 2001, 34–38; Michael McGann, "Chase Harnesses Data with Lotus Notes," *Bank Systems and Technology* 34 (May 1997): 38; "Rank Xerox Aims at Sharing Knowledge," *Crossborder Monitor* (September 18, 1996): 8; "World-Wise: Effective Networking Distinguishes These 25 Global Companies," *Computerworld*, August 26, 1996, 7; and **http://www.rankxerox.co.uk**.

Table 19.3	Comparison of Bureaucratic and Cultural Control Mechanisms

| Object of Control | Type of Control | | Characteristics of Control |
	Pure Bureaucratic/ Formalized Control	Pure Cultural Control	
Output	Formal performance reports	Shared norms of performance	HQ sets short-term performance target and requires frequent reports from subsidiaries
Behavior	Company policies, manuals	Shared philosophy of management	Active participation of HQ in strategy formulation of subsidiaries

SOURCES: Peter J. Kidger, "Management Structure in Multinational Enterprises: Responding to Globalization," *Employee Relations*, August 2001, 69–85; and B. R. Baliga and Alfred M. Jaeger, "Multinational Corporations: Control Systems and Delegation Issues," *Journal of International Business Studies* 15 (Fall 1984): 28.

used to direct functional performance. **Budgets** are short-term guidelines in such areas as investment, cash, and personnel, whereas **plans** refer to formalized long-range programs with more than a one-year horizon. The budget and planning process is the major control instrument in headquarters-subsidiary relationships. Although systems and their execution vary, the objective is to achieve the best fit possible with the objectives and characteristics of the firm and its environment.

The budgetary period is typically one year because budgets are tied to the accounting systems of the company. The budget system is used for four main purposes: (1) allocation of funds among subsidiaries; (2) planning and coordination of global production capacity and supplies; (3) evaluation of subsidiary performance; and (4) communication and information exchange among subsidiaries, product organizations, and corporate headquarters.[45] Long-range plans, on the other hand, extend over periods of two to ten years, and their content is more qualitative and judgmental in nature than that of budgets. Shorter periods, such as two years, are the norm because of the uncertainty of diverse foreign environments.

Although firms strive for uniformity, this may be comparable to trying to design a suit to fit the average person. The budget and planning processes themselves are formalized in terms of the schedules to be followed.

Control can also be seen as a mechanism to secure cooperation of local units. For example, while a company may grant substantial autonomy to a country organization in terms of strategies, headquarters may use allocation of production volume as a powerful tool to ensure compliance. Some of the ways for headquarters to gain cooperation of country organizations are summarized in Figure 19.11. Some of the methods used are formal, such as approval of strategic plans and personnel selection, while some are more informal, including personal contact and relationships as well as international networking.[46]

Since the frequency and types of reports to be furnished by subsidiaries are likely to increase due to globalization, it is essential that subsidiaries see the rationale for the often time-consuming task. Two approaches, used in tandem, can facilitate the process: participation and feedback. Involving the preparers of reports in their ultimate use serves to avoid the perception at subsidiary levels that reports are "art for art's sake." When this is not possible, feedback about results and consequences is an alternative. Through this process, communication is also enhanced.

On the behavioral front, headquarters may want to guide the way in which subsidiaries make decisions and implement agreed-upon strategies. U.S.-based multi-

---

Figure 19.11 | **Securing Country-Organization Cooperation**

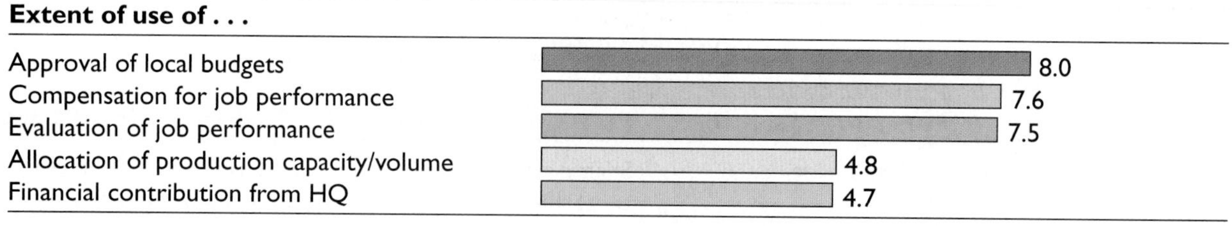

Extent of use of . . .

Approval of local budgets	8.0
Compensation for job performance	7.6
Evaluation of job performance	7.5
Allocation of production capacity/volume	4.8
Financial contribution from HQ	4.7

Among 35 MNCs.
0 to 10 scale (0 = "Never used" and 10 = "Always used")

SOURCE: Henry P. Conn and George S. Yip, "Global Transfer of Critical Capabilities," in *Best Practices in International Business,* Michael R. Czinkota and Ilkka A. Ronkainen, eds. (Mason, OH: South-Western, 2001): 256–274.

national companies, relying heavily on manuals for all major functions, tend to be far more formalized than their Japanese and European counterparts.[47] The manuals are for functions such as personnel policies for recruitment, training, motivation, and dismissal. The use of policy manuals as a control instrument correlates with the level of reports required from subsidiaries.

Cultural Control

In countries other than the United States, less emphasis is placed on formal controls, which are viewed as rigid and too quantitatively oriented. Rather, the emphasis is on corporate values and culture, and evaluations are based on the extent to which an individual or entity fits in. Cultural controls require an extensive socialization process, and informal, personal interaction is central to the process. Substantial resources must be spent to train the individual to share the corporate culture, that is, "the way things are done at the company."[48] To build common vision and values, managers spend a substantial amount of their first months at Matsushita in what the company calls "cultural and spiritual training." They study the company credo, the "Seven Spirits of Matsushita," and the philosophy of the founder, Konosuke Matsushita. Then they learn how to translate these internalized lessons into daily behavior and operational decisions. Although more prevalent in Japanese organizations, many Western entities have similar programs, for example, Philips' "organization cohesion training" and Unilever's "indoctrination." This corporate acculturation will be critical to achieve the acceptance of possible transfers of best practice within the organization.[49]

The primary instruments of cultural control are the careful selection and training of corporate personnel and the institution of self-control. The choice of cultural controls rather than bureaucratic controls can be justified if the company enjoys a low turnover rate. Cultural controls are thus applied, for example, when companies offer lifetime or long-term employment, as many Japanese firms do.

In selecting home country nationals and, to some extent, third-country nationals, multinational companies are exercising cultural control. They assume that these managers have already internalized the norms and values of the company and that they tend to run a country operation with a more global view. In some cases, the use of headquarters personnel to ensure uniformity in decision making may be advisable; for example, for the position of financial officer, Volvo uses a home country national. Expatriates are used in subsidiaries not only for control purposes but also for initiating change and to develop local talent. Companies control the efforts of management specifically through compensation, promotion, and replacement policies.

When the expatriate corps is small, headquarters can exercise control through other means. Management training programs for overseas managers as well as visits to headquarters will indoctrinate individuals to the company's way of doing things. Similarly, visits to subsidiaries by headquarters teams will promote a sense of belonging. These may be on a formal basis, as for a strategy audit, or less formal—for example, to launch a new product. Some innovative global marketers assemble temporary teams of their best talent to build local skills. IBM, for example, drafted 50 engineers from its facilities in Italy, Japan, New York, and North Carolina to run three-week to six-month training courses on all operations carried on at its Shenzhen facility in China. After the trainers left the country, they stayed in touch by e-mail, so whenever the Chinese managers have a problem, they know they can reach someone for help. The continuation of support has been as important as the training itself.[50]

Corporations rarely use one pure control mechanism. Rather, emphasis is placed on both quantitative and qualitative measures. Corporations are likely, however, to place different levels of emphasis on the types of performance measures and on the way the measures are taken.

Exercising Control

Within most corporations, different functional areas are subject to different guidelines. The reason is that each function is subject to different constraints and varying degrees of those constraints. For example, marketing as a function has traditionally been seen as incorporating many more behavioral dimensions than does manufacturing or finance. As a result, many multinational corporations employ control systems that are responsive to the needs of the function. Yet such differentiation is sometimes based less on appropriateness than on personality. One researcher hypothesized that manufacturing subsidiaries are controlled more intensively than sales subsidiaries because production more readily lends itself to centralized direction, and technicians and engineers adhere more firmly to standards and regulations than do salespeople.[51]

Similarly, the degree of control imposed will vary by subsidiary characteristics, including its location. For example, since Malaysia is an emerging economy in which managerial talent is in short supply, headquarters may want to participate more in all facets of decision making. If a country-market witnesses economic or political turmoil, controls may also be tightened to ensure the management of risk.[52]

In their international operations, U.S.-based multinational corporations place major emphasis on obtaining quantitative data. Although this allows for good centralized comparisons against standards and benchmarks, or cross-comparisons between different corporate units, several drawbacks are associated with the undertaking. In the international environment, new dimensions—such as inflation, differing rates of taxation, and exchange rate fluctuations—may distort the performance evaluation of any given individual or organizational unit.

For the global corporation, measuring whether a business unit in a particular country is earning a superior return on investment relative to risk may be irrelevant to the contribution an investment may make worldwide or to the long-term results of the firm. In the short term, the return may even be negative.[53] Therefore, the control mechanism may quite inappropriately indicate reward or punishment. Standardizing the information received may be difficult if the environment fluctuates and requires frequent and major adaptations. Further complicating the issue is the fact that, although quantitative information may be collected monthly, or at least quarterly, environmental data may be acquired annually or "now and then," especially when crisis seems to loom on the horizon.

To design a control system that is acceptable not only to headquarters but also to the organization and individuals abroad, a firm must take great care to use only relevant data. Major concerns, therefore, are the data collection process and the analysis and utilization of data. Evaluators need management information systems that provide for maximum comparability and equity in administering controls. The more behaviorally based and culture-oriented controls are, the more care that needs to be taken.

In designing a control system, management must consider the costs of establishing and maintaining it and weigh the costs against the benefits to be gained. Any control system will require investment in a management structure and in systems design. As an example, consider the costs associated with cultural controls: Personal interaction, use of expatriates, and training programs are all quite expensive. Yet these expenses may be justified in savings through lower employee turnover, an extensive worldwide information system, and a potentially improved control system.[54] Moreover, the impact goes beyond the administrative component. If controls are erroneous or too time-consuming, they can slow or misguide the strategy implementation process and thus the overall capability of the firm. The result will be lost opportunity or, worse, increased threats. In addition, time spent on reporting takes time away from other tasks. If reports are seen as marginally useful, the motivation to prepare them will be low. A parsimonious design is therefore imperative. The control system should collect all the information required and trigger all the intervention necessary but should not create a situation that resembles the pulling of strings by a puppeteer.

The impact of the environment must also be taken into account when designing controls. First, the control system should measure only dimensions over which the organization has control. Rewards or sanctions make little sense if they are based on dimensions that may be relevant for overall corporate performance but over which no influence can be exerted, for example, price controls. Neglecting the factor of individual performance capability would send wrong signals and severely impede the motivation of personnel. Second, control systems should harmonize with local regulations and customs. In some cases, however, corporate behavioral controls have to be exercised against local customs even though overall operations may be affected negatively. This type of situation occurs, for example, when a subsidiary operates in markets where unauthorized facilitating payments are a common business practice.

Corporations are faced with major challenges to appropriate and adequate control systems in today's business environment. With an increase in local (government) demands for a share in the control of companies established, controls can become tedious, especially if the multinational company is a minority partner. Even in a merger, such as the one between Daimler-Benz and Chrysler—or in a new entity formed by two companies as when Toyota and GM formed NUMMI—the backgrounds of the partners may be sufficiently different to cause problems in terms of the controls.

Summary

The structures and control mechanisms needed to operate internationally define relationships between the firm's headquarters and subsidiaries and provide the channels through which these relationships develop. The most fundamental test of organizational design is whether there is a fit with the company's overall marketing strategy and it reflects the strengths of the entities within the organization.[55]

International firms can choose from a variety of organizational structures, ranging from a domestic operation that handles ad hoc export orders to a full-fledged global organization. The choice will depend primarily on the degree of internationalization of the firm, the diversity of international activities, and the relative importance of product, area, function, and customer variables in the process. Another determining factor is the degree to which headquarters wants to decide important issues concerning the corporation as a whole or the subsidiaries individually. Organizations that function effectively still need to be reviewed periodically to ensure that they will remain responsive to changing environments. Some of the responses may not take the form of structural changes but rather are changes in internal relations. Of these, the primary one is the use of subsidiaries as resources, not merely as implementors of headquarters' strategy.

The control function is of increasing importance because of the high variability in performance that results from divergent local environments and the need to reconcile local objectives with the corporate goal of synergism. It is important to grant autonomy to country organizations so that they can be responsive to local market needs, but it is equally important to ensure close cooperation between units.

Control can be exercised through bureaucratic means, emphasizing formal reporting and evaluation of benchmark data. It can also be exercised through a cultural control process in which norms and values are understood by individuals and entities that compose the corporation. U.S. firms typically rely more on bureaucratic controls, whereas multinational corporations headquartered in other countries frequently control operations abroad through informal means and rely less on stringent measures.

The implementation of controls requires great sensitivity to behavioral dimensions and to the environment. The measurements used must be appropriate and must reflect actual performance rather than marketplace vagaries. Entities should be measured only on factors over which they have some degree of control.

Key Terms

product structure
area structure
functional structure
process structure
customer structure
mixed structure
matrix structure
decentralization
centralization
coordinated decentralization
glocalization

best practice
intranet
strategic leader
contributor
implementors
black hole
bureaucratic controls
cultural controls
budgets
plans

Questions for Discussion

1. Firms differ, often substantially, in their organizational structures even within the same industry. What accounts for these differences in their approaches?

2. Discuss the benefits gained in adopting a matrix approach in terms of organizational structure.

3. What changes in the firm and/or in the environment might cause a firm to abandon the functional approach?

4. Is there more to the "not-invented-here" syndrome than simply hurt feelings on the part of those who believe they are being dictated to by headquarters?

5. One of the most efficient means of control is self-control. What type of program would you prepare for an incoming employee?

6. "Implementors are the most important country organizations in terms of buy-in for effective global marketing strategy implementation." Comment.

Internet Exercises

1. Improving internal communications is an objective for networked global organizations. Using the Web site of the Lotus Development Corporation (**http://www.lotus.com**) and its section on solutions and success stories, outline how marketers have used Lotus Notes to interactively share information.

2. Using company and product information available on their Web sites, determine why Dow (**http://www.dow.com**) and Siemens (**http://www.siemens.com**) have opted for global product/business structures for their organizations.

Recommended Readings

Bartlett, Christopher, and Sumantra Ghoshal. *Managing across Borders*. Cambridge, MA: Harvard Business School Press, 1998.

Bartlett, Christopher, and Sumantra Ghoshal. *Transnational Management: Text, Cases, and Readings in Cross-Border Management*. New York: McGraw-Hill, 2000.

Cairncross, Frances. *The Company of the Future*. Cambridge, MA: Harvard Business School Press, 2002.

Chisholm, Rupert F. *Developing Network Organizations: Learning from Practice and Theory*. Boston: Addison-Wesley, 1997.

Doz, Yves, Jose Santos, and Peter Williamson. *From Global to Metanational: How Companies Win in the Knowledge Economy*. Cambridge, MA: Harvard Business School Press, 2001.

Ghoshal, Sumantra, and Christopher Bartlett. *The Individualized Corporation: A Fundamentally New Approach to Management*. New York: Harper Business, 1999.

Govindarajan, Vijay, Anil K. Gupta, and C. K. Prahalad. *The Quest for Global Dominance: Transforming Global Presence into Global Competitive Advantage*. New York: Jossey-Bass, 2001.

Govindarajan, Vijay, and Robert Newton. *Management Control Systems*. New York: McGraw-Hill/Irwin, 2000.

Humes, Samuel. *Managing the Multinational: Confronting the Global-Local Dilemma*. London: Prentice Hall, 1993.

McCall, Morgan W., and George P. Hollenbeck. *Developing Global Executives*. Cambridge, MA: Harvard Business School Press, 2002.

Moran, Robert T., Philip R. Harris, and William G. Stripp. *Developing the Global Organization*. Houston, TX: Gulf Publishing Co., 1993.

Pasternak, Bruce A., and Albert J. Viscio. *The Centerless Corporation: A New Model for Transforming our Organization for Growth and Prosperity*. New York: Simon and Schuster, 1998.

Pfeffer, Jeffrey, and Robert I. Sutton. *The Knowing-Doing Gap: How Smart Companies Turn Knowledge into Action*. Cambridge, MA: Harvard Business School Press, 1999.

Stewart, Thomas A. *The Wealth of Knowledge: Intellectual Capital and the Twenty-first Century Organization*. New York: Doubleday, 2001.

Transforming the Global Corporation. New York: The Economist Intelligence Unit, 1994.

chapter **20**

The Future

© PHOTODISC, VOL. 22

© PHOTODISC/GETTY IMAGES

THE INTERNATIONAL MARKETPLACE   20.1

Marketing Overseas—Excellent for Career Advancement

Overseas experience is beneficial and lucrative not only to companies that have gone international, but also to the marketing employees in those companies. In an increasingly internationalized world, job opportunities for marketers have become global. Companies are forced to meet a variety of consumer preferences, which are mainly attributed to different cultural and societal values. One way in which companies can attain a better understanding of others' cultural values is through the overseas experience of personnel.

Working overseas provides an opportunity to see how people live, how other countries market products and services, and to understand and gauge political and economic situations in other countries. This experience can be a great way to build a resumé and climb the corporate ladder. For example, Ian Cook joined New York–based Colgate-Palmolive Company in its London office in 1976. Since then he has worked in marketing positions around the world, including in the Philippines and in the Nordic countries, with a total of 19 years of overseas experience. Today, Cook is the president of Colgate-Palmolive North America, proving that overseas experience leads to career advancement.

Overseas experience does not have to be through corporate transfers. It may be difficult to find work abroad independently. For example, Beth Rehman, currently an account executive at TSI Communications Worldwide in New York, decided shortly after college to work in France and landed a six-month internship with Saatchi Healthcom in Paris. After getting married, Rehman went back to Paris for 18 months and worked as a marketer for a high-tech public-relations firm, Rumeur Publique. Her corporate career has shown that career advancement can be achieved transferring from firm to firm.

With more companies expanding to the world market, it is becoming a requirement for those in senior executive–level positions in multinational corporations to have had prior overseas experiences. Today, with more and more companies engaged in international business, it is necessary and, as an added incentive, gives marketing employees the edge for career advancement.

SOURCE: Lisa Bertagnolli, "Marketing Overseas Excellent for Career," *Marketing News*, June 4, 2001, 4, 6.

INTERNATIONAL MARKETERS are constantly faced with global change. This is not a new situation, nor one to be feared, because change provides the opportunity for the emergence of new market positions. Recognizing the importance of change and adapting creatively to new situations are the daily bread of marketing professionals and offer a chance for advancement, as the *International Marketplace 20.1* shows.

Recently, however, changes are occurring more frequently and more rapidly and have a more severe impact. Due to growing real-time access to knowledge about and for customers, suppliers, and competitors, the international marketing environment is increasingly characterized by high speed bordering on instantaneity.[1] In consequence, the past has lost much of its value as a predictor of the future. What occurs today may be not only altered in the future but completely overturned or reversed. For example, new technologies can alter ways of doing business. As a result, some countries can find that their major export industries, highly competitive for decades, can lose their international edge within a very short time. A nation's political stability can be completely disrupted over the course of a few months. In all, international marketers today face complex and rapidly changing economic and political conditions.

This chapter will discuss possible future developments in the international marketing environment, highlight the implications of these changes for international marketing management, and offer suggestions for a creative response. The chapter will also explore the meaning of strategic changes to the reader, with particular emphasis on career choice and career path alternatives in international marketing.

The International Marketing Environment

This section analyzes the international marketing environment by looking at political, financial, societal, and technological conditions of change and providing a glimpse of possible future developments as envisioned by a panel of experts.

The Political Environment

The international political environment is undergoing a substantial transformation characterized by the reshaping of existing political blocks, the formation of new groupings, and the breakup of old coalitions.

Planned versus Market Economies

The second half of the last century was shaped by the political, economic, and military competition between the United States and the Soviet Union, which resulted in the creation of two virtually separate economic systems. This key adversarial posture has now largely disappeared, with market-based economic thinking emerging as the front-runner. Virtually all of the former centrally planned economies are undergoing a transition with the goal of becoming market oriented.

International marketing has made important contributions to this transition process. Trade and investment have offered the populace in these nations a new perspective, new choices, new jobs, and new alternatives for marketing their products and services. At the same time, the bringing together of two separate economic and business systems has resulted in new, and sometimes devastating competition, a loss of government-ordained trade relationships, and substantial dislocations and pain during the adjustment process.

Over the next few years the countries of Eastern and Central Europe will continue to be attractive for international investment due to relatively low labor cost, low-priced input factors, and large unused production capacities. This attractiveness, however, will translate mainly into growing investment from Western Europe for reasons of geographic proximity and attractive outsourcing opportunities.[2] Even these investment flows, however, are likely to take place only selectively, resulting in very unbalanced economic conditions in the region. Firms and governments outside of Western Europe are likely to be much more reluctant to invest in Eastern Europe. This aversion is not so much driven by caution about a potential resurgence of Communism or fear of economic and political instability, but mainly due to attractive investment alternatives elsewhere.

Russia and the other nations of the former Soviet Union face great difficulty. The collapse of the ruble and repeated setbacks in economic development have led to a paradox faced by Russia and the world. Russia today is the world's sixth most populous country, a key nuclear power, and the holder of a permanent seat on the UN Security Council. Its economic health and creditworthiness, however, place it in the same tier of global powers as the Sudan. Economic recovery and participation in world trade are likely to be very gradual. Governments need to find market-oriented ways to reduce the flight of capital abroad.

Overall, many business activities will be subject to regional economic and political instability, increasing the risk of international partners. Progress toward the institution of market-based economies may be halted or even reversed as large population segments are exposed to growing hardship during the transformation process. It will be important to develop institutions and processes internally which assure domestic and foreign investors that there will be protection from public and private corruption and respect for property rights and contractual arrangements.

The North–South Relationship

The distinction between developed and less-developed countries (LDCs) is unlikely to change. The ongoing disparity between developed and developing nations is likely to be based, in part, on continuing debt burdens and problems with satisfying basic needs. As a result, political uncertainty may well result in increased polarization between the haves and have-nots, with growing potential for political and economic conflict. Demands for political solutions for economic problems are likely to increase. According to Mike Moore, former director general of the World Trade Organization, 2.6 billion people live on less than $2 per day.[3] Some countries may consider migration as a key solution to population-growth problems, yet many emigrants may encounter government barriers to their migration. There may well be more investment by firms bringing their labor-intensive manufacturing operations to these countries.

The fact that many countries, particularly in Africa, seem left out from the expansion of international prosperity is partly due to prevailing uncertainty and productivity limitations that have made firms reluctant to expand in these areas. Where there is substantial increase in stability, accompanied by local institutions desiring peace and economic development, the international production expansion might well extend to the less developed nations. Today's trickle of investment and purchasing in poorer countries could well become a torrent from firms in search of new opportunities. Those concerned with enforcing the peace in regions that might breed terrorists would be well served to consider such peace as a key instrument for the economic growth and prosperity in disadvantaged nations.[4]

An emphasis on education and training and the development of a supportive infrastructure are crucial, since that is where the investments and jobs go.[5] It is not enough to expect a rising tide to raise all boats. There must also be significant effort expended to ensure the seaworthiness of the boat, the functioning of its sails, and the capability of its crew. Market-oriented performance will be critical to succeed in the longer run.

The issue of **environmental protection** will also be a major force shaping the relationship between the developed and the developing world. In light of the need and desire to grow their economies, however, there may be much disagreement on the part of the industrializing nations as to what approaches to take. Of key concern will be the answer to the question: Who pays? For example, simply placing large areas of land out of bounds for development will be difficult to accept for nations that intend to pursue all options for further economic progress. Corporations in turn are likely to be more involved in protective measures, since they are aware of their constituents' expectations and the repercussions of not meeting those expectations. Corporations recognize that by being environmentally responsible, a company can build trust and improve its image—therefore becoming more competitive. For example, in the early 1990s the first annual corporate environmental report was published; now over 2,000 companies a year publish such reports.[6]

In light of divergent trends by different groups, three possible scenarios emerge. One scenario is that of continued international cooperation. The developed countries could relinquish part of their economic power to less-developed ones, thus contributing actively to their economic growth through a sharing of resources and technology. Although such cross-subsidization will be useful and necessary for the development of LDCs, it may reduce the rate of growth of the standard of living in the more developed countries. It would, however, increase trade flows between developed and less-developed countries and precipitate the emergence of new international business opportunities.

A second scenario is that of confrontation. Due to an unwillingness to share resources and technology sufficiently (or excessively, depending on the point of view), the developing and the developed areas of the world may become increasingly hostile toward one another. As a result, the volume of international activities, both by mandate of governments and by choice of the private sector, could be severely reduced.

A third scenario is that of isolation. Although there may be some cooperation between them, both groups, in order to achieve their domestic and international goals, may choose to remain economically isolated. This alternative may be particularly attractive if each region believes that it faces unique problems and therefore must seek its own solutions.

The Asia Pacific region is likely to regain its growth in the next decade. For the industrialized nations, this development will offer a significant opportunity for exports and investment, but it will also diminish, in the longer term, the basis for their status and influence in the world economy. While the nations in the region are likely to collaborate, they are not expected to form a bloc of the same type as the European Union or NAFTA. Rather, their relationship is likely to be defined in terms of trade and investment flows (e.g., Japan) and social contacts (e.g., the Chinese business community). A cohesive bloc may only emerge as a reaction to a perceived threat by other major blocs, as explained in *The International Marketplace 20.2*.

In light of China's membership in the World Trade Organization (WTO), its continued emergence as a trade power is likely to be the economic event of the decade. Despite innumerable risks, experts see Chinese pragmatism prevailing. Companies already present in the market and those willing to make significant investments are likely to be the main beneficiaries of growth. Long-term commitment, willingness to transfer technology, and an ability to partner either with local firms through joint ventures or with overseas Chinese-run firms are considered crucial for success. The strategic impact of Chinese trade participation is also likely to change. Due to WTO rules, the recipients of Chinese goods will be less able to exclude them with higher tariffs or nontariff barriers. China, in turn, is likely to assume a much higher profile in its trading activities. For example, rather than be the supplier of goods which are then marketed internationally under a Japanese or U.S. label, Chinese firms will increasingly develop their own brand names and fight for their own name recognition, customer loyalty, and market share.[7]

Among the other promising emerging markets are Korea and India. Korea could emerge as a participant in worldwide competition, while India is considered more important for the size of its potential market. Korean firms must still improve their ability to adopt a global mindset. In addition, the possible impact of the reunification of the Korean peninsula on the country's globalization efforts must be taken into account.

With the considerable liberalization that took place in India during the 1990s, many expect it to offer major international marketing opportunities due to its size, its significant natural wealth, and its large, highly educated middle class. While many experts believe that political conflict, both domestic and regional, nationalism, and class structure may temper the ability of Indian companies to emerge as a worldwide competitive force, there is strong agreement that India's disproportionately large and specialized workforce in engineering and computer sciences makes the nation a power to be reckoned with.

Overall, the growth potential of these emerging economies may be threatened by uncertainty in terms of international relations and domestic policies, as well as social and political dimensions, particularly those pertaining to income distribution. Concerns also exist about infrastructural inadequacies, both physical—such as transportation—and societal—such as legal systems. The consensus of experts is, however, that growth in these countries will be significant.

A Divergence of Values

It might well be that different nations or cultures become increasingly disparate in terms of values and priorities. For example, in some countries, the aim for financial progress and an improved quantitative standard of living may well give way to priorities based on religion or the environment. Even if nations share similar values, their priorities among these values may differ strongly. For example, within a market-oriented system, some countries may prioritize profits and efficiency, while others may place social harmony first, even at the cost of maintaining inefficient industries.

THE INTERNATIONAL MARKETPLACE   20.2

The Future of East Asian Integration

The East Asia Economic Summit of 2002, held in Kuala Lumpur, Malaysia, marked the renewal of commitments by many East Asian leaders to increase regional and global integration in the near future. Whether the effort focused upon strengthening the already existent trade bloc, ASEAN, or creating a free-trade area between the ASEAN nations and China or India, most members of the summit agreed to prioritize the push for integration.

The key reason for such a surge in liberal trade policy: competitiveness. The Asian nations are currently in a strong position to become global economic contenders along with a strong United States and a strengthening Europe, which they see as both potential partners and aggressive competitors. "We should push ahead with greater integration of East Asian economies. It will put us in better stead to respond to the formation of large economic blocs in Europe and the Americas," said Goh Chok Tong, prime minister of Singapore.

Prime Minister Thaksin Shinawatra of Thailand made a call for the development of stronger financial institutions, including developing an Asian bond market. Prime Minister Goh Chok Tong closed the summit by refocusing attention on the actual institutions and processes that could be used to further the task of Asian integration. Such processes include, first, increased regional cooperation via ASEAN and neighbor states like China and India, and subsequently, an effort to integrate globally. Finally, Prime Minister Mahathir bin Mohamad of Malaysia further underscored the need for Asians to work together as well as the need for Asians to support efforts to join in multilateral efforts such as the World Trade Organization.

The leaders of the leading East Asian nations have made strides toward regional integration through ASEAN and have demonstrated their future commitment to a more global presence at the Kuala Lumpur Summit, but commitments of current leaders will not be enough to carry East Asia into the global economy. The next genera-tion, those young leaders of tomorrow, must demonstrate their commitment to global integration.

While the Kuala Lumpur Summit stressed the goals of the traditional regional leaders, the World Economic Forum's Global Leaders for Tomorrow has created the New Asian Leaders Initiative to stress the goals of the leaders of tomorrow. Unlike modern Europe, which is marked by a noticeably aging population, Asia is home to very young societies, in which youth are taking on an in-creasing role in setting the regional agenda. There seems to be a growing understanding of the key role that *both* generations must play in guaranteeing the long-term via-bility of East Asian integration.

The role of the initiative is to "enhance the capacity of Asia's new generation of leaders . . . to confront chal-lenges and provide the leadership and vision needed in Asia." The initiative's mission statement proclaims its ob-jective "to provide young Asian leaders with a platform where [they] can exchange ideas which will enable [them] to put forward to the current leadership of [their] respective countries the view that the voices of the younger generation should be considered when national regional policies for the future are being formulated."

The New Asian Leaders Initiative guarantees that the current commitment to global integration will not die with current leaders. The initiative proves that this com-mitment is not being forced from the top down, but that the next generation of leaders also supports the push for regional and global integration. By joining forces across national borders, young leaders will set a precedent for their national leaders to do the same. By joining forces early in the integration process, young leaders are ensur-ing that the effort will be accomplished in the long run.

SOURCES: East Asia Summit 2002, "Renewing Asia's Foundations of Growth: Building on Diversity," *World Economic Forum,* **http://www. weforum.org/site/homepublic.nsf/Content/East+Asia+ Economic+Summit+2002** accessed October 28, 2002.

Such a divergence of values will require a major readjustment of the activities of the international corporation. A continuous scanning of newly emerging national values thus becomes imperative for the international executive.

The International Financial Environment

Debt constraints and low commodity prices create slow growth prospects for many developing countries. They will be forced to reduce their levels of imports and to exert more pressure on industrialized nations to open up their markets. Even if the markets are opened, however, demand for most primary products will be far lower than supply. Ensuing competition for market share will therefore continue to depress prices.

Developed nations have a strong incentive to help the debtor nations. The incentive consists of the market opportunities that economically healthy developing countries can offer and of national security concerns. As a result, industrialized nations may very well find that funds transfers to debtor nations, accompanied by debt-relief measures such as debt forgiveness, are necessary to achieve economic stimulation at home.

The dollar will remain one of the major international currencies with little probability of gold returning to its former status in the near future. Some international transaction volume in both trade and finance is increasingly likely to be denominated in nondollar terms, using particularly the euro. The system of floating currencies will likely continue, with occasional attempts by nations to manage exchange rate relationships or at least reduce the volatility of swings in currency values. Given the vast flows of financial resources across borders, it would appear that market forces rather than government action will be the key determinant of a currency's value. Factors such as investor trust, economic conditions, earnings perceptions, and political stability are therefore likely to have a much greater effect on the international value of currencies than domestic monetary and fiscal experimentation.

Given the close links among financial markets, shocks in one market will quickly translate into rapid shifts in others and easily overpower the financial resources of individual governments. Even if there should be a decision by governments to pursue closely coordinated fiscal and monetary policies, they are unlikely to be able to negate long-term market effects in response to changes in economic fundamentals.

A looming concern in the international financial environment will be the international debt load of the United States. Both domestically and internationally, the United States is incurring debt that would have been inconceivable only a few decades ago. The United States entered the new century with an international debt burden of more than $2 trillion. This debt level makes the United States the largest debtor nation in the world, owing more to other nations than all the developing nations combined. In light of ongoing trade deficits, it is projected by some that this net negative investment position may grow to $4 trillion by 2005. Others argue against an unsustainable scenario, believing that there are special mitigating circumstances which let the U.S. tolerate this burden, such as the fact that most of the debts are denominated in U.S. dollars and that, even at such a large debt volume, U.S. debt-service requirements are only a relatively small portion of GNP.[8] Yet this accumulation of foreign debt may very well introduce entirely new dimensions into the international business relationships of individuals and nations. Once debt has reached a certain level, the creditor as well as the debtor is hostage to the loans.

To some degree, foreign holders of dollars may choose to convert their financial holdings into real property and investments in the United States. This will result in an entirely new pluralism in U.S. society. It will become increasingly difficult and, perhaps, even unnecessary to distinguish between domestic and foreign products—as is already the case with Hondas made in Ohio. Members of Congress, governors, municipalities, and unions will gradually be faced with conflicting concerns in trying to develop a national consensus on international trade and investment.

Population Patterns

The population discrepancy between less-developed nations and the industrialized countries will continue to increase. In the industrialized world, population growth will become a national priority, given the fact that in many countries, particularly in Western Europe, the population is shrinking rather than increasing. This shrinkage may lead to labor shortages and to major societal difficulties when a shrinking number of workers has to provide for a growing elderly population. As *The International Marketplace 20.3* shows, large-scale migration flows may well be an important alternative to the dangers of a population decline.

THE INTERNATIONAL MARKETPLACE   20.3

Migration: A Double Blessing

An estimated 2.5 percent of the world's population, or 150 million people, had migrated from their mother country by the start of the new millennium. A variety of reasons, both push and pull factors, cause migrants to settle in a foreign country. Push factors include human rights violations, political oppression, economic hardships, crime, and violence, and pull factors include economic opportunities, political freedom, physical safety, and security.

International migration has benefits to both the sending country and the receiving country. For the receiving country, migrants, whether skilled or unskilled, provide a larger pool of laborers. When labor shortages occur, foreign workers are especially valued because they may meet the demand of a specific sector, for example, information technology or seasonal agriculture.

The recent surge of migration from Latin America to the United States can be used to illustrate the benefits migration may bring to both the sending and receiving country. Fifteen million Latin Americans are now living in the United States, allowing the American economy to expand without worrying about labor shortages, as do many other countries.

Migrants also help the United States by raising fertility rates, preventing population decline and correcting uneven age-distribution in the population. In industrialized countries such as the United States and Europe, the fertility rate, or average number of children born per woman, is below replacement level. Not only does this lead to a decrease in the labor force, it also reduces the ratio of working-age people to retired people and increases the burden of retirement. Migrants increase the population of the United States directly; they also increase the population indirectly by raising the fertility

rate. The higher fertility rate of Latinos at 3.0 children per woman will raise the fertility rate of the United States, increasing births and reducing the aging problem.

On the other hand, sending countries also benefit from migration. Remittance, or sending money back to one's home country, is one of the primary ways in which migrants help their home country. The Federal Reserve in Chicago estimates that in 2000, recorded remittances in the form of checks or money transfers from the United States totaled $20 billion. In many countries, remittances even exceed foreign investment, exports, or foreign aid and serve as the main source of support for many families. While the majority of remittances are used to provide survival necessities such as food and health care, the impact of remittances spent in the form of investments is just as valuable and extensive by creating jobs.

Migrants may also improve their home country by returning with skills and connections acquired in the United States. Some migrants contribute to the development of their mother country by starting joint ventures. In 1992, Colombia created a network of expatriate researchers and engineers from 30 countries. Other migrants help by using their position in the United States to persuade multinational firms to invest in their home country. Others, such as Bolivian native Virginia Sanchez, a New York banker, encourage the Bolivian-American Chamber of Commerce to assist Bolivian emigrants to ease their adjustment in the United States.

SOURCES: "Half a Billion Americans?" *The Economist,* August 24, 2002; Susan Martin, "Heavy Traffic: International Migration in an Era of Globalization," *The Brookings Review,* Fall 2001, 41–44; *ABI/Inform Global,* Online, September 6, 2002; and Kenneth Tom, "Making the Most of an Exodus," *The Economist,* February 23, 2002.

In the developing world, **population stabilization** will continue to be one of the major challenges of governmental policy. In spite of well-intentioned economic planning, continued rapid increases in population will make it more difficult to ensure that the pace of economic development exceeds population growth. If we determine the standard of living of a nation by dividing the GNP by its population, any increase in the denominator will require equal increases in the numerator to maintain the standard of living. Therefore, if the population's rate of growth continues at its current pace, even greater efforts must be made to increase the economic activity within these nations. This task becomes even more complex when we consider that within countries with high population increases, large migration flows take place from rural to urban areas.[9] The increasing number of mega-cities of more than 8 million inhabitants illustrates the change. In 1950, only two cities, London and New York, were that size. In 2015, the projected number of mega-cities is 36, 30 of them in the developing world and most (22) in Asia. Table 20.1 shows the ten largest urban areas in 2002.

Table 20.1 The Ten Largest Urban Areas in the World, 2002

Area	Population (Millions)
Tokyo (Japan)	35.1
New York (USA)	21.7
Seoul (South Korea)	21.4
Mexico City (Mexico)	21.0
São Paulo (Brazil)	19.9
Bombay (India)	18.4
Osaka (Japan)	18.1
Delhi (India)	17.5
Los Angeles (USA)	16.9

SOURCE: Thomas Brinkhoff, "The Principal Agglomerations around the World," **http://www.citypopulation.de**, accessed December 6, 2002.

Urbanization is taking place at different speeds on different continents. In North America, the number of city dwellers overtook the rural population before 1940. In Europe, this happened after 1950 and in Latin America at the beginning of the 1960s. Today, these three continents are almost equally urbanized; 75 percent of Europeans and Latin Americans are city dwellers and 77 percent of North Americans, according to UN estimates. A similar process is occurring in Africa and Asia, which are still mainly rural. Their proportion of city dwellers rose from 25 percent in 1975 to a little more than 37 percent in 2001.[10] The turning point, when the figure will top 50 percent, is predicted to occur around 2025. Such movements and concentrations of people are likely to place significant stress on economic activity and the provision of services but will also make it easier for marketers to direct their activities toward customers. Of key concern in some countries is **population balance.** Technology has made it possible to predict with high accuracy the gender of a child. In many countries where family growth has been restricted, parents have developed a preference for male heirs. Over time, the result has been a skewed population in which males substantially outnumber females. Particularly for younger generations, this development has led to much greater difficulties in finding a partner for marriage. In consequence, some key cultural dimensions have changed. For example, it has been reported that in the state of Haryana, India, there are just 820 girls born for every 1,000 boys. Girls of marriageable age are in such short supply that some parents are not only dropping their demands for wedding dowries (which have a centuries-old cultural tradition) but are offering a "bride price" to families of prospective mates for their sons.[11] One can also argue that over time such imbalances can drive a society to develop family models such as polyandry—in which one woman may have more than one husband. It might also be possible that societies with a large surplus of young men are more prone to engage in wars.

Another problem of many less-developed countries is an **expectation-reality gap** felt by their population. Because the persistence of unfulfilled expectations fosters discontent, these countries must close the gap. This can be accomplished either by improving economic reality—that is, offering more goods at lower prices and increasing the general standard of living—or by reducing the expectations. Although nations will attempt to improve the living standards of their people, substantial efforts to reduce expectations also appear quite likely. These efforts may require the use of de-marketing techniques on a national level.

The Technological Environment

The concept of the global village is commonly accepted today and indicates the importance of communication and technology. Worldwide, the estimated number of people online in March 2002 was 533 million.[12] That number is expected to grow to more than 945 million by 2004. By 2007, the number is expected to grow to 1.12 billion.[13] The United States had the highest number of Internet users, at more than 166 million. However, users in the United States and Canada now represent only a third of the global Internet community—which means that the rest of the world is catching up. Nonetheless, there is a wide digital gap around the globe, for in some nations, such as Yemen, 14,000 users or fewer are hooked up to the Internet.[14]

For both consumer services and business-to-business relations, the Internet is democratizing global business. It has made it easier for new global retail brands—like amazon.com and CDnow.com—to emerge. The Internet is also helping specialists like Australia's high-sensitivity hearing aids manufacturer Cochlear to reach target customers around the world without having to invest in a distribution network in each country. The ability to reach a worldwide audience economically via the Internet spells success for niche marketers who could never make money by just servicing their niches in the domestic market. The Internet also allows customers, especially those in emerging markets, to access global brands at more competitive prices than those offered by exclusive national distributors.[15]

Starting a new business will be much easier, allowing a far greater number of suppliers to enter a market. Small and medium-sized enterprises, as well as large multinational corporations, will now be full participants in the global marketplace. Businesses in developing countries can now overcome many of the obstacles of infrastructure and transport that limited their economic potential in the past. The global services economy will be a knowledge-based economy and its most precious resource will be information and ideas. Unlike the classical factors of production—land, labor, and capital—information and knowledge are not bound to any region or country but are almost infinitely mobile and infinitely capable of expansion.[16] This wide availability, of course, also brings new risks to firms. For example, unlike the past, today one complaint can easily be developed into millions of complaints by e-mail.[17] In consequence, firms are subject to much more scrutiny and customer response on an international level.

Changes in technology also make available vast amounts of data worldwide. Therefore the management of information becomes as important as the information itself. The premium will be on the organization, maintenance, and use of huge, current, and accurate databases covering customers, vendors, regulations, and standards. Knowledge distribution experts will form an entire new profession with two distinct specializations: Knowledge Focusers will be in charge of ensuring that the right kind of information is provided. Knowledge Erasers will concentrate on weeding out old or outdated data, in order to limit capacity constraints of information storage and to delete corporate information that may lead to future interpretation problems. Due to rising public concerns about the dissemination of information, the role of privacy experts will also be on the increase.

High technology will be one of the more volatile and controversial areas of economic activity internationally. Developments in biotechnology are already transforming agriculture, medicine, and chemistry. Chemically engineered foods, patient-specific pharmaceuticals, gene therapy, and even genetically engineered organs are on the horizon. Innovations such as these will change what we eat, how we treat illness, and how we evolve as a civilization.[18] However, skepticism of such technological innovations is rampant. In many instances, people are opposed to such changes due to religious or cultural reasons, or simply because they do not want to be exposed to such "artificial" products. Achieving agreement on what constitutes safe products and procedures, of defining the border between what is natural and what is not, will constitute one of the great areas of debate in the years to come. Firms and their managers must remain keenly aware of popular perceptions and misperceptions and of government regulations in order to remain successful participants in markets.

Even firms and countries that are at the leading edge of technology will find it increasingly difficult to marshal the funds necessary for further advancements. For example, investments in semiconductor technology are measured in billions rather than millions of dollars and do not bring any assurance of success. Not to engage in the race, however, will mean falling behind quickly in all areas of manufacturing when virtually every industrial and consumer product is "smart" due to its chip technology.

To spread the necessary financial commitments and to reduce the risk of permanent losses by participants in the race, firms will increasingly share technology provided that payment is made for shared information. In addition, industry consolidation, cooperative agreements, joint ventures, and strategic partnerings will proliferate. Concurrently, governments will increase their spending on research and development and further techno-nationalism through the creation of more sources of technological innovation within their boundaries. Government-sponsored collaborative research ventures are likely to increase across industries and country groupings. However, difficulties may emerge when global firms threaten to internationalize rapidly any gains from such regionalized research ventures.

The Trade Framework

The formation of the WTO concluded a lengthy and sometimes acrimonious round of global trade negotiations. However, key disagreements among major trading partners are likely to persist. Ongoing major imbalances in trade flows will tempt nations to apply their own national trade remedies, particularly in the antidumping field. Even though WTO rules permit for a retaliation against unfair trade practices, such actions would only result in an ever-increasing spiral of adverse trade relations.

A key question will be whether nations and their citizens are willing to abrogate some of their sovereignty even during difficult economic times. An affirmative answer will strengthen the multilateral trade system and enhance the flow of trade. However, if key trading nations resort to the development of insidious nontariff barriers, unilateral actions, and bilateral negotiations, protectionism will increase on a global scale and the volume of international trade is likely to decline. The danger is real. Popular support for international trade agreements appears to be on the wane. The public demonstrations in Seattle and other cities during the WTO meetings indicate that there is much ambivalence by individuals and nongovernmental organizations about trade. It is here where international business experts are, or should be, the guardians who separate fact from fiction in international trade policy discussions. Qualified not by weight of office but by expertise, international business experts are the indirect guarantors of and guides toward free and open markets. Without their input and impact, public apathy and ignorance may well result in missteps in trade policy.[19]

International trade relations also will be shaped by new participants whose market entry will restructure the composition of global trade. For example, new players with exceptionally large productive potential, such as the People's Republic of China and Central Europe, will substantially alter world trade flows. And while both governments and firms will be required to change many trade policies and practices as a result, they will also benefit in terms of market opportunities and sourcing alternatives.

Finally, the efforts of governments to achieve self-sufficiency in economic sectors, particularly in agriculture and heavy industries, have ensured the creation of long-term, worldwide oversupply of some commodities and products, many of which historically had been traded widely. As a result, after some period of intense market share competition aided by subsidies and governmental support, a gradual and painful restructuring of these economic sectors will have to take place. This will be particularly true for agricultural cash crops such as wheat, corn, and dairy products and industrial products such as steel, chemicals, and automobiles. These adjustments will need to be made rapidly and thoroughly if a new and effective world trade order is to result.

Governmental Policy

A worldwide trend exists toward increased management of trade by governments. International trade activity now affects domestic policy more than in the past. Governments, in their desire to structure their domestic economic activity, will feel forced to intervene more frequently in international markets. For example, trade flows can cause major structural shifts in employment with subsequent downstream effects. Changes in automobile production will also affect the steel and plastics industries, and shifts in the sourcing of textiles will affect the cotton industry. As a result, changes in international trade will require many industries to restructure their activities and their employment because of productivity gains and competitive pressures. Yet such restructuring is not necessarily negative. For example, since the beginning of the last century, farm sector employment in the United States dropped from more than 40 percent of the population to less than 3 percent. At the same time, the farm industry feeds 280 million people in the United States and produces large surpluses. A restructuring of industries can therefore greatly increase productivity and competitiveness and can provide the opportunity for resource allocation to newly emerging sectors of an economy.

Governments cannot be expected, for the sake of the theoretical ideal of "free trade," to sit back and watch the effects of deindustrialization on their countries. The most that can be expected is that they will permit an open market orientation, subject to the needs of domestic policy. Even an open market orientation will be maintained only if governments can provide reasonable assurances to their firms and citizens that this openness applies not only to their own markets but to foreign markets as well. Therefore, unfair trade practices, such as governmental subsidization, dumping, and industrial targeting, will be examined more closely, and retaliation for such activities will be increasingly swift and harsh.

Increasingly, governments will attempt to coordinate policies that affect the international marketing environment. At the same time, governments will find it more difficult to achieve a consensus. In the Western world, the period from 1945 to 1990 was characterized by a commonality of purpose. The common defense against the communist enemy relegated trade relations to second place and provided a bond that encouraged collaboration. With the common threat gone, however, the bonds have also been diminished, if not dissolved, and the priority of economic performance has increased. Unless a new key jointness of purpose can be found by governments, collaborative approaches will become increasingly difficult.

Governmental policymakers must understand the international repercussions of domestic legislation. For example, the imposition of special taxes (such as a surcharge on the chemical industry designed to provide for the cleanup of toxic waste products) will need to be carefully considered in light of its repercussions on the international competitiveness of industry. Similarly, antitrust laws should be revised if these laws hinder the international competitiveness of domestic firms.

Policymakers also need a better understanding of the nature of the international trade issues confronting them. Most countries today face both short-term and long-term trade problems. Trade balance issues, for example, are short-term in nature, whereas competitiveness issues are much more long-term. All too often, however, short-term issues are attacked with long-term trade policy mechanisms, and vice versa. In the United States, for example, the desire to "level the international play-ing field" by negotiating a further opening of Japan's market to foreign corpora-tions will have only a minor immediate effect on that country's trade surplus or the U.S. trade deficit.[20] Yet it is the expectation and hope of many in both the pub-lic and the private sectors that such immediate changes will occur. For the sake of the credibility of policymakers, it therefore becomes increasingly imperative to identify precisely the nature of the problem, to design and use policy measures that are appropriate for its resolution, and to communicate the hoped-for results.

In the years to come, governments will be faced with an accelerating technolog-ical race and with emerging problems that seem insurmountable by individual firms alone, such as pollution of the environment and global warming. As a result, it seems likely that the concepts of administrative guidance and **government–corporate collaboration** will increasingly become part of the policy behavior of governments heretofore pledged to believe only in the invisible hand of the free market. Governments can be expected to offer a variety of supporting postures toward the international marketer. The international marketer in turn will have to spend more time and effort dealing with governments and with macro rather than micro issues.

The Future of International Marketing Management

International change results in an increase in international risk. One shortsighted alternative for risk-averse managers would be the termination of international activities altogether. Yet businesses will not achieve long-term success by engaging only in risk-free actions.

International markets continue to be a source of high profits. International cus-tomers help cushion slack in domestic sales resulting from recessionary or adverse domestic market conditions. International activities provide firms with foreign experience that helps them compete more successfully with foreign firms in the domestic market. International activities are also necessary to compensate for for-eign product and service inflows into an economy. As long as supply potential exceeds demand on an international level, an inherent economic motivation will exist for international marketing.

Markets and marketing were affected in a major way by the terrorist attacks of September 11, 2001. America's sense of stability, feeling of security, and attitudes toward the world were profoundly changed by the events of a few hours. The emotional reaction was immediate and felt throughout the world, and the eco-nomic impact of the terrorist attacks continues.

Directly or indirectly, virtually all business activities have been affected by these events. Overall consumer demand went into shock worldwide, and in some indus-tries, particularly for luxury goods, it declined precipitously. The marginal cus-tomers who had gradually become important to many industries dropped out in droves as they hunkered down to observe everyone else's reactions. Airlines, air-ports, concession stands, hotels, and travel agents experienced massive disloca-tions. Since it is the purpose of this section to identify concerns and forecast changes in international marketing, we will use the findings from a large scale study carried out at Georgetown University[21] to specifically comment on how the terrorist attacks are likely to affect international marketing.

Overall, we found that a new global age of common sense seems to be emerg-ing, characterized by five key dimensions: vulnerability, outrage, collaboration, politics, and connection.

Vulnerability
The events of September 11 and subsequent attacks have underscored that terror-ism can affect not only those who fly or those who live and work beneath aviation

routes—anyone who is present or participates in any activity within any country is at risk. Protection is difficult, if not impossible, and there are ample and varied tools that might be used for another attack.

Outrage

The attacks of September 11 do not represent a condition of moral ambivalence, in which differing viewpoints lead to interpretations favoring one perspective over another. The self-righteous cruelty of the attacks repels almost all nations and touches the global community like a cold wind that makes one shiver.

Collaboration

Ever since the demise of the Soviet Union as a competing superpower, even the closest allies of the United States have been reluctant to embrace a joint direction or a common interest. Following September 11, we found a new understanding of the need to work together, to identify mutual goals, and to have a vision of a shared future. The rapid building of a coalition on the political level in support of the hunt for terrorists is only one indication of this sense of collaboration. Equally indicative on the policy side are agreements on implementation, such as how to identify bank accounts held by terrorist organizations and how to freeze them.

Collaboration also is rising on the business side. In the foreign exchange arena, for example, firms suffered for decades from exchange-rate volatility, spending large amounts to protect themselves, mainly by forward purchases in the foreign-exchange markets in order to hedge the risk. Since September 11, however, risk-sharing agreements are on the upswing, in which corporations see themselves as partners and agree to share the effects of major currency movements. Such agreements have been prevalent but were used less frequently after unilateral contractual hedging came into fashion. Firms with long-standing customer–supplier relationships across borders seem to be returning to some of the old ways of keeping friends.

Politics

For more than 40 years after World War II, the Coordinating Committee for Multi-lateral Export Controls (COCOM), an organization of sixteen Western nations, had largely denied or at least delayed the transfer of Western technology to unfriendly countries. During the 1990s, however, disagreement about what items required international export control was rampant in policy forums. The fact that an item or a technology was available in neutral countries or could be used for civilian as well as military purposes became an excuse for relinquishing control altogether rather than designing more effective controls. Since September 11, the easing of export control has been questioned in light of the dangers of nuclear proliferation and international terrorism. We found that, as far as technology is concerned, closer collaboration among partner countries has actually resulted in an easing of export-control policies. A tightening of the restrictions of questionable exports to dubious customers seems to have eased the way for exports to friendly countries.

The agreement to a new round of trade talks, reached at the end of the World Trade Organization's 2001 meeting in Doha, further demonstrates this trend. Several highly controversial issues, such as agricultural subsidies, dumping regulations, property rights, and investment rules were placed on the table in spite of dire predictions by trade-policy naysayers. The new round of talks does not mean U.S. allies will be pushovers in trade negotiations, but that mutual respect and collaboration have opened the road toward progress.

Connection

Finally, there is a new sense of what nations have in common. For quite some time, when global issues were addressed, local concerns were emphasized. Countries focused on the customs and products that make them different from one another and possibly separate them. Now we think more of the issues that make us behave alike and strengthen the bonds between us.

These five features of common sense bode well for a future of international negotiations, policy directives, and formulation of joint approaches to the progress of globalization.

International Planning and Research

Focus on the customer will remain a major factor in marketing. The international marketer must continue to serve customers well. At the same time, governmental demands will increasingly intrude in the international marketing arena. This means that the international marketing manager will have to take general governmental concerns much more into account when planning a marketing strategy. In light of a greater security focus, firms now focus more on where to sell, what to sell, and to whom to sell, rather than just selling wherever possible. Managers are developing an appreciation for the type and degree of risk exposure in certain regions of the world. Leading risk factors include the policies of home and host governments, exchange rate fluctuations, and economic turmoil.

More firms are developing trade portfolios that allocate effort and limits in different regions of the world. These portfolios are intended to achieve two goals: (1) limit dependence on any region or customer in order to reduce a firm's exposure to conflict or unexpected interruptions, and (2) systematically develop markets to balance existing exposure, to diversify a firm's risk, and to offer a fallback position.

There is also a greater scrutiny now of the alternative opportunities presented by foreign direct investment and exporting. Foreign direct investment demonstrates the long-term nature of a firm's objectives and makes use of local advantages. It also facilitates collaboration and reduces the firm's exposure to the vagaries of border-crossing transactions. At the same time, it renders the firm vulnerable to the effects of government policies and any divergence between home and host country. Some firms are beginning to look beyond the strict economic dimensions of foreign direct investment. They are using it to signal full confidence in an area or a partner, thus demonstrating commitment. Such a relationship focus may well alter some of the approaches used by government agencies in charge of encouraging foreign direct investment inflow.

Exporting, in turn, permits a broader and quicker coverage of world markets with the ability to respond to changes. Risks are lower, but costs tend to be higher because of transshipment and transaction expenses. Even though an export orientation is seen to be less risky, many firms are not as aggressive as they used to be in seeking new business or new accounts. A new desire to deal with old, established customers, with "people who we know and with whom we have developed a feeling of trust" has emerged. An export approach appears to be the preferred method of new market entry these days. It may remain the principal tool of international expansion for firms new to the global market or those highly concerned about international risk.

The diverging needs of foreign consumers will result in more available niches in which firms can create a distinct international competence. This points toward increased specialization and segmentation. Firms will attempt to fill very narrow and specific demands or to resolve very specific problems for their international customers. Identifying and filling these niches will be easier in the future because of the greater availability of international research tools and information. At the same time, the greater availability of information will make it tougher to compete, since many more competitors will become active globally.

The international marketer will also increasingly encounter high standards of social responsibility on the part of both governments and individuals. Governments will demand that private marketing practices not increase public costs and will expect marketers to serve their customers equally and nondiscriminately. This concept runs directly counter to marketers' desire to serve first the markets that are most profitable and least costly.

Public outrage can depress sales or block permits for new facilities, while public approval of a company's association with good causes can create customer and public goodwill and even allay local concerns about foreign companies. British Airways collects change for UNICEF on international flights. Timberland has created City Year Gear, casual clothing reflecting its support of City Year, a youth service corps. EDS, a large systems integration company, has run a Global Volunteer Day (GVD) since 1993; in India the new relationships and positive aura created by GVD were a main factor in successful market entry. IBM's Reinventing Education initiative puts IBM engineers, systems integrators, and consultants on significant projects in partnership with public schools, such as developing new voice recognition technology to teach reading. In Brazil, IBM teams up with local companies to improve education. These activities bear no resemblance to traditional charity; they apply a company's skills and innovation processes to increase quality of life.[22] The result is new opportunities for both customers and firms.

International marketers will therefore be torn in many directions. In order to provide results that are acceptable to governments, customers, and the societies they serve, they must walk a fine line, balancing the public and the private good.

Reputation management, or the strategy of building reputation as a corporate asset, is likely to gain prominence in the years ahead as pressure on corporations to be good corporate citizens grows.[23] Internationally, the acceptance of market thinking can only work if accompanied by managerial and corporate virtue, vision, and veracity. Unless the world can believe in what firms and managers say and do, it will be nearly impossible to forge a global commitment between those doing the marketing and those being marketed to. It is therefore of vital interest to the proponents of globalization to ensure that corruption, bribery, lack of transparency, and the misleading of stakeholders are relegated to the scrap heap of history. Perhaps the WTO should take steps to ensure a commitment to long-term thinking and truthfulness on the part of international marketers.[24]

Product and Production Policy

One key issue affecting product planning will be environmental concerns. Major public attention paid to the natural environment, environmental pollution, and global warming will provide many new product opportunities and affect existing products to a large degree. For example, manufacturers will increasingly be expected to take responsibility for their products from cradle to grave, and be intimately involved in product disposal and recycling. Although some consumers show a growing interest in truly "natural" products, even if they are less convenient, consumers in most industrialized nations will require products that are environmentally friendly but at the same time do not require too much compromise on performance and value. Management is likely to resist the additional business cost and taxes required for environmental protection, at least until investors and other constituent groups assure executives that environmental concern is acceptable even if it cuts into profit.

Worldwide introduction of products will occur much more rapidly in the future. Already, **international product life cycles** have accelerated substantially. Whereas product introduction could previously be spread out over several years, firms now must prepare for product life cycles that can be measured in months or even weeks.[25] As a result, firms must design products and plan even their domestic marketing strategies with the international product cycle in mind. Product introduction will grow more complex, more expensive, and more risky, yet the rewards to be reaped from a successful product will have to be accumulated more quickly.

Early incorporation of the global dimension into product planning, however, does not point toward increased standardization. On the contrary, companies will have to be ready to deliver more mass customization. Customers are no longer satisfied with simply having a product: They want it to precisely meet their needs and preferences. **Mass customization** requires working with existing product technology, often in modular form, to create specific product bundles for a particular customer.

Factor endowment advantages have a significant impact on the decisions of international marketers. Given the acceleration of product life cycles, nations with low production costs will be able to replicate products more quickly and cheaply. Countries such as China, India, and the Philippines offer large pools of skilled people at labor rates much lower than in Europe, Japan, or the United States. All this talent also results in a much wider dissemination of technological creativity, a factor that will affect the innovative capability of firms. For example, in 2002, nearly half of all the patents in the United States were granted to foreign entities. Table 20.2 provides an overview of the patents granted to foreign inventors.

Table 20.2	U.S. Patents Granted to Foreign Inventors in 2002 (counts include utility, design, plant, and reissue patents, and statutory invention registrations)

Country	Total	Country	Total
Algeria	1	Finland	769
Arab Emirates	6	France	4,456
Argentina	58	French Polynesia	1
Armenia	1	Georgia (Republic of)	2
Aruba	1	Germany	11,895
Australia	1,031	Greece	26
Austria	632	Hungary	61
The Bahamas	10	Iceland	21
Barbados	4	India	179
Belarus	7	Indonesia	10
Belgium	796	Iran	2
Bermuda	4	Ireland	166
Bosnia and Herzegovina	1	Israel	1,031
Brazil	125	Italy	1,978
Brunei	1	Jamaica	1
Bulgaria	5	Japan	34,891
Canada	4,063	Jordan	3
Cayman Islands	4	Kazakhstan	3
Chile	15	Kenya	4
China, Hong Kong SAR	620	Kuwait	6
China, People's Republic	266	Kyrgyzstan	1
Colombia	14	Latvia	1
Costa Rica	12	Lebanon	2
Croatia	8	Liechtenstein	24
Cuba	4	Lithuania	4
Cyprus	1	Luxembourg	48
Czech Republic	23	Madagascar	2
Czechoslovakia	7	Malaysia	56
Denmark	556	Malta	2
Dominica	2	Mexico	87
Ecuador	4	Monaco	18
Egypt	6	Morocco	1
El Salvador	3	Netherlands	1,494
Estonia	2	New Zealand	160

Table 20.2   (continued)

Country	Total	Country	Total
Nigeria	1	Syria	1
Norway	283	Taiwan	6,545
Pakistan	2	Tanzania	1
Panama	1	Thailand	47
Peru	6	Trinidad/Tobago	4
Philippines	15	Turkey	14
Poland	16	Turks & Caicos Islands	1
Portugal	16	Uganda	1
Romania	10	Ukraine	21
Russian Federation	239	United Kingdom	4,356
Saint Kitts & Nevis	2	Uzbekistan	2
Saudi Arabia	12	Venezuela	28
Singapore	304	Vietnam	1
Slovakia	1	Virgin (British Islands)	1
Slovenia	21	Yugoslavia	4
South Africa	137	Zimbabwe	1
South Korea	3,763		
Spain	340		
Sri Lanka	3	Total, All Foreign	85,391
Suriname	1	Total, All U.S. States	98,666
Sweden	1,935	Total, All Countries	184,057
Switzerland	1,557	All Foreign as percentage of total	46.4%

SOURCE: U.S. Patent and Trademark Office/TAF Data Base, **http://www.uspto.gov**, accessed December 10, 2002.

This indicates that firms need to make such foreign know-how part of their production strategies, or they need to develop consistent comparative advantages in production technology in order to stay ahead of the game. Similarly, workers engaged in the productive process must attempt, through training and skill enhancement, to stay ahead of foreign workers who are willing to charge less for their time.

An increase will occur in the trend toward strategic alliances, or partnerings, permitting the formation of collaborative arrangements between firms. These alliances will enable firms to take risks that they could not afford to take alone, facilitate technological advancement, and ensure continued international market access. These partners do not need to be large in order to make a major contribution. Depending on the type of product, very small firms can serve as coordinating subcontractors and collaborate in product and service development, production, and distribution.

On the production management side, security concerns now make it imperative to identify and manage one's dependence on international inputs. Industrial customers, in particular, are often seen as pushing for local sourcing. A domestic source simply provides a greater feeling of comfort. As a typical executive said, "When we tell our customers their goods will be produced in West Virginia or Kentucky, they feel so much better than when we inform them about the shipments coming from Argentina, Greece, or Venezuela. They're worried about interruptions or other problems."

Some firms also report a new meaning associated with the *made-in* dimension in country-of-origin labeling. In the past, this dimension was viewed as enhancing products, such as perfumes made in France or cars made in Germany. Lately, the made-in dimension of some countries may create an exclusionary context by making both industrial customers and consumers reject products from specific regions. As a result, negative effects may result from geographic proximity to terrorists, as has been claimed by some about textile imports from Pakistan.

The bottom line still matters. After all, money needs to be made and international marketing tends to be quite profitable. However, the issue of dependability of supplies is raised at many senior-management meetings, and a premium is now associated with having a known and long-term supplier. In the future, foreign suppliers may have to be recommended by existing customers or partners and be able to cope with contingencies before their products are even considered.

International Communications

Advances in international communications will have a profound impact on the international marketer. Entire industries are becoming more footloose in their operations; that is, they are less tied to their current location in their interaction with markets. Most affected by these advances will be members of the services industry. By easily bridging distances, service providers will mainly be concerned about the right to operate rather than the right to establish themselves in the global arena. Why build a large bank or insurance edifice and combat local regulations if a computer linkage with the customer will do? Best Western Hotels in the United States has channeled its entire reservation system through a toll-free number that is being serviced out of the prison system in Utah. Companies could as easily concentrate their communications activities in other countries. Communications for worldwide operations, for example, could be located in Africa or Asia and not impair international corporate activities.

For manufacturers, staff in different countries not only can talk together but also can share pictures and data on their computer screens. These simultaneous interactions with different parts of the world will strengthen research and development efforts. Faster knowledge transfer will allow for the concentration of product expertise, increased division of labor, and a proliferation of global operations.

Distribution and Logistics Strategies

Innovative distribution approaches will determine new ways of serving markets. For example, television through QVC has already created a $3.9 billion shopping mall available in more than 125.6 million homes worldwide.[25] Over time, self-sustaining consumer–distributor relationships will emerge. For example, refrigerators will report directly to grocery store computers that they are running low on supplies and require a home delivery billed to the customer's account. Firms that are not part of such a system will then simply not be able to have their offer be considered for the transaction.

The link to distribution systems will also be crucial to international marketers on the business-to-business level. As large retailers develop sophisticated inventory tracking and reordering systems, only the firms able to interact with such systems will remain eligible suppliers. Therefore, firms need to create their own distribution systems that are able to respond to information technology requirements around the globe.

Companies have already accepted that the international pipeline has slowed down, and that customary steps will now take longer in a new security environment. But the structure of the pipeline and the scrutiny given to the materials going through the pipeline have become important.

Firms that had developed elaborate just-in-time delivery systems for their international supplies were severely affected by the border and port closures immediately following the September 11 attacks. These firms and their service providers continue to be affected by increased security measures. Firms are also focusing more on internal security and need to demonstrate externally how much more security-oriented they have become. In many instances, government authorities require evidence of threat-reduction efforts to speed shipments along. Also, insurance companies have increased their premiums substantially for firms that are exposed to increased risk.

In the past, cargo security measures concentrated on reducing theft and pilferage from a shipment. Since September 11, additional measures concentrate on possible undesirable accompaniments to incoming shipments. With this new approach, international cargo security starts well before the shipping even begins. One result—perhaps unintended—of these changes is a better description of shipment content and a more precise assessment of duties and other shipping fees.

Carriers with sophisticated hub-and-spoke systems have discovered that transshipments between the different spokes may add to delays because of the time needed to re-scrutinize packages. While larger "clean areas" within ports may help reduce this problem, a redesign of distribution systems may lead to fewer hubs and more direct connections.

Firms with a just-in-time system are also exploring alternative management strategies, such as shifting international shipments from air to sea. More dramatically, some firms are considering replacing international shipments with domestic ones, in which truck transport would replace transborder movement altogether and eliminate the use of vulnerable ports. Future scenarios also accommodate the effects of substantial and long-term interruptions of supplies or operations. Still, any actual move away from existing just-in-time systems is likely to be minor unless new large-scale interruptions occur.

Many new positions have been created in the corporate security field, focusing on new production sites, alternative distribution methods, server mobility, and new linkages with customers. In some instances, key customers have been involved in the development of emergency procedures to keep operations going.

In spite of these measures, however, vulnerability to attack continues to be high. For example, 43 percent of all the maritime containers that arrived in the United States in 2001 came through the ports of Los Angeles and Long Beach. There are no required security standards governing the loading or transport of an intermodal container. Most are "sealed" with a 50-cent lead tag. An explosive device in a single container might well gridlock the entire flow and loading systems.[27]

International Pricing

Many products, as they become distributed more widely throughout the world, will take on commodity characteristics, as semiconductors did in the 1980s. Therefore, small price differentials per unit may become crucial in making international sales. For new products and technologies, firms will increasingly be forced to engage in **forward pricing** by distributing development cost over the anticipated volume of sales. This task will be difficult and controversial because demand levels for totally new products are impossible to predict accurately. As a result, firms will be open to charges of dumping.

Even for consumer products, price competition will be substantial. Because of the increased dissemination of technology, the firm that introduces a product will not be able to justify higher prices for long; domestically produced products will soon be of similar quality. As a result, exchange rate movements may play more significant roles in maintaining the competitiveness of the international firm. Firms can be expected to prevail on their government to manage the country's currency to maintain a favorable exchange rate. Technology also allows much closer interaction on pricing between producer and customer. The success of electronic commerce providers such as eBay (**http://www.ebay.com**) or Priceline (**http://www.priceline.com**) demonstrates how auctioning and bidding, alone or in competition with others, offers new perspectives on the global price mechanism.

Government management of trade will continue to influence international pricing in other ways. Through subsidization, targeting, and government contracts, nations will attempt to stimulate their international competitiveness. Because of the price sensitivity of many products, the international marketer will be forced to identify such unfair practices quickly, communicate them to his or her government, and insist on either similar benefits or government negotiation of an internationally level playing field.

Concurrently, however, international marketers will continue to differentiate themselves in the market on a nonprice basis. Major efforts will be undertaken to appeal to the market via services, quality, or other special aspects rather than on price alone. By accomplishing such an objective successfully, a firm can buy itself freedom from short-term fluctuations in its business relationships.

Careers in International Marketing

The reader of this book, it is hoped, has learned about the intricacies, complexities, and thrills of international marketing. Of course, a career in international marketing does not consist only of jet-setting travel between Rome, London, and Paris. It is hard work and requires knowledge and expertise. Globalists need to be well versed in the specific business functions and may wish to work at summer internships abroad, take language courses, and travel not simply for pleasure but to observe business operations abroad and to gain a greater understanding of different peoples and cultures. Taking on and successfully completing an international assignment is seen by managers as crucial for the development of professional, managerial, and intercultural skills and is highly likely to affect career advancement.[28]

Further Training

One option for the student on the road to more international involvement is to obtain further in-depth training by enrolling in graduate business school programs that specialize in international business education. A substantial number of universities in the United States and around the world specialize in training international managers. According to the Institute of International Education, the number of U.S. students studying for a degree at universities abroad rose to more than 154,000 students in 2001. Furthermore, American students increasingly go abroad for business and economics degrees, not just for a semester or two. At the same time, business and management are the most popular fields of study for the 583,000 international students at American universities.[29] A review of college catalogues and of materials from groups such as the Academy of International Business will be useful here.

In addition, as the world becomes more global, more organizations are able to assist students interested in studying abroad or in gathering foreign work experience.

Apart from individual universities and their programs for study abroad, many nonprofit institutions stand ready to help and to provide informative materials. Table 20.3 provides rich information about programs and institutions that can help with finding an international job.

For those ready to enter or rejoin the "real world," different employment opportunities need to be evaluated.

Employment with a Large Firm

One career alternative in international marketing is to work for a large multinational corporation. These firms constantly search for personnel to help them in

Table 20.3	Web Sites Useful in Gaining International Employment

AVOTEK Headhunters
Nieuwe Markt 54
6511 XL Nijmegen,
NETHERLANDS
Telephone: (31) 24 3221367
Fax: (31) 24 3240467
Web site: **http://www.avotek.nl**
Lists Web sites and addresses of jobs and agencies worldwide. Offers sale publications and other free reference materials.

Council Exchanges
Council on International Educational Exchange
633 3rd Avenue
New York, NY 10017
Telephone: (212) 822-2600
Fax: (212) 822-2649
Web site: **http://www.councilexchanges.org**
Paid work and internships overseas for college students and recent graduates. Also offers international volunteer projects, as well as teaching positions.

Dialogue with Citizens
Internal Market Directorate General
MARKT A/04, C107 03/52
European Commission
Rue de la Loi, 200
B-1049 Brussels
BELGIUM
Telephone: (011) 322 299 5804
Fax: (011) 322 295 6695
Web site: **http://europa.eu.int/citizens**
Factsheets on EU citizens' rights regarding residence, education, working conditions and social security, rights as a consumer, and ways of enforcing these rights, etc. Easy-to-use guides that give a general outline of EU citizens' rights and the possibilities offered by the European Single Market. A Signpost Service for citizens' practical problems.

Ed-U-Link Services
PO Box 2076
Prescott, AZ 86302
Telephone: (520) 778-5581
Fax: (520) 776-0611
Web site: **http://www.edulink.com**
Provides listings of and assistance in locating teaching jobs abroad.

80 Days
Web site: **http://www.80days.com**
Links to Web sites with job listings worldwide, including volunteer work and teaching English as a foreign language. Has special section on Europe.

The Employment Guide's CareerWeb
150 West Brambleton Avenue
Norfolk, VA 23510
Telephone: (800) 871-0800
Fax: (757) 616-1593
Web site: **http://www.cweb.com**
Online employment source with international listings, guides, publications, etc.

Escape Artist
EscapeArtist.com Inc.
Suite 832–1245
World Trade Center
Panama
Republic of PANAMA
Fax: (011) 507 317 0139
Web site: **http://www.escapeartist.com**
Web site for U.S. expatriates. Contains links on overseas jobs, living abroad, offshore investing, free magazine, etc.

EURopean Employment Services—EURES
Employment and Social Affairs Directorate General
EMPL A/03, BU33 02/24
European Commission
Rue de la Loi, 200
B-1049 Brussels
BELGIUM
Telephone: (011) 322 299 6106
Fax: (011) 322 299 0508 or 295 7609
Web site: **http://europa.eu.int/eures**
Aims to facilitate the free movement of workers within the 17 countries of the European Economic Area. Partners in the network include public employment services, trade unions, and employer organizations. The Partnership is coordinated by the European Commission. For citizens of these 17 countries, provides job listings, background information, links to employment services, and other job-related Web sites in Europe.

Expat Network
International House
500 Purley Way
Croydon
Surrey CRO 4NZ
UK
Telephone: (44) 20 8760 5100
Fax: (44) 20 8760 0469
Web site: **http://www.expatnetwork.com**
Dedicated to expatriates worldwide, linking to overseas jobs, country profiles, healthcare, expatriate, gift and bookshop plus in-depth articles and industry reports on issues that affect expatriates. Over 5,000 members. Access is restricted for nonmembers.

Table 20.3 (*continued*)

Federation of European Employers (FedEE)
Superla House
127 Chiltern Drive
Surbiton
Surrey, KT5 8LS
UK
Telephone: (44) 20 8339 4134
Fax: (44) 13 5926 9900
Web site: **http://www.fedee.com**
FedEE's European Personnel Resource Centre is the most comprehensive and up-to-date source of pan-European national pay, employment law, and collective-bargaining data on the Web.

FlipDog.com
3210 North Canyon Road
Suite 300
Provo, UT 84604
Telephone: (801) 418-7199 or (877) 887-3547
Fax: (801) 818-0879
Web site: **http://www.flipdog.com**
Constitutes the Internet's largest job collection. In addition to U.S. coverage, includes 82,000 or so vacancies abroad. One of the most comprehensive employment search engines on the Internet.

HotJobs.com
Hotjobs.com, Ltd.
406 West 31st Street
New York, NY 10001
Telephone: (212) 699-5300
Fax: (212) 944-8962
Web site: **http://hotjobs.yahoo.com**
Contains international job listings, including Europe.

Jobpilot
75 Cannon Street
London C4N 5BN
UK
Telephone: (44) 20 7556 7044
Fax: (44) 20 7556 7501
Web site: **http://www.jobpilot.com**
"Europe's unlimited career market on the Internet."

Monster.com
TMP Worldwide Global Headquarters
1633 Broadway
33rd Floor
New York, NY 10019
Telephone: 1 800 MONSTER or (212) 977-4200
Fax: (212) 956-2142
Web site: **http://www.monster.com**
Global online network for careers and working abroad. Career resources (including message boards and daily chats).

OverseasJobs.com
AboutJobs.com Network
12 Robinson Road
Sagamore Beach, MA 02562
Telephone: (508) 888-6889
Web site: **http://www.overseasjobs.com**
Job seekers can search the database by keywords or locations and post a resume online for employers to view.

PlanetRecruit.com
PlanetRecruit Ltd.
Alexandria House
Covent Garden
Cambridge CB1 2HR
UK
Telephone: (44) 87 0321 3660
Fax: (44) 87 0321 3661
Web site: **http://www.planetrecruit.com**
One of the world's largest UK and international recruitment networks. Features accounting and finance, administrative and clerical, engineering, graduate and trainee, IT, media, new media and sales, marketing and public-relations jobs from about 60 countries.

The Riley Guide
Margaret F. Dikel
11218 Ashley Drive
Rockville, MD 20852
Telephone: (301) 984-4229
Fax: (301) 984-6390
Web site: **http://www.rileyguide.com**
It is a directory of employment and career information sources and services on the Internet, providing instruction for job seekers and recruiters on how to use the Internet to their best advantage. Includes a section on working abroad, including in Europe.

SCI-IVS USA
814 NE 40th Street
Seattle, WA 98105
Telephone: (206) 545-6585
Fax: (206) 545-6585
Web site: **http://www.sci-ivs.org**
Through various noncommercial partner organizations worldwide and through SCI international, national, and regional branch development, the U.S. branch of SCI participates in the SCI network which exchanges over 5,000 volunteers each year in short-term (2–4 week) international group workcamps and in long-term (3–12 months) volunteer postings in over 60 countries.

Table 20.3   (continued)

Transitions Abroad Online: Work Abroad
PO Box 1300
Amherst, MA 01004-1300
Telephone: (800) 293-0373 or (413) 256-3414
Fax: (413) 256-0373
Web site: **http://www.transitionsabroad.com**
Contains articles from its bimonthly magazine; a listing of work abroad resources (including links); lists of key employers, internship programs, volunteer programs, and English-teaching openings.

Vacation Work Publications
9 Park End Street
Oxford, OX1 1HJ
UK
Web site: **http://www.vacationwork.co.uk**
Lists job openings abroad, in addition to publishing many books on the topic. Has an information exchange section and a links section.

Upseek.com
Telephone: (877) 587-5627
Web site: **http://www.upseek.com**
A global search engine that empowers job seekers in the online job search market. Provides job opportunities from the top career and corporate sites with some European listings.

WWOOF International
PO Box 2675
Lewes BN7 1RB,
UK
Web site: **http://www.wwoof.org**
WWOOF INTERNATIONAL is dedicated to helping those who would like to work as volunteers on organic farms internationally.

SOURCE: European Union, **http://www.eurunion.org**.

their international operations. For example, a Procter & Gamble recruiting advertisement published in a university's student newspaper is reproduced in Figure 20.1.

Many multinational firms, while seeking specialized knowledge like languages, expect employees to be firmly grounded in the practice and management of business. Rarely, if ever, will a firm hire a new employee at the starting level and immediately place him or her in a position of international responsibility. Usually, a new employee is expected to become thoroughly familiar with the company's internal operations before being considered for an international position. The reason a manager is sent abroad is that the company expects him or her to reflect the corporate spirit, to be tightly wed to the corporate culture, and to be able to communicate well with both local and corporate management personnel. In this liaison position, the manager will have to be exceptionally sensitive to both headquarters and local operations. As an intermediary, the expatriate must be empathetic and understanding, and yet fully prepared to implement the goals set by headquarters.

It is very expensive for companies to send an employee overseas. Typically, the annual cost of maintaining a manager overseas is about three times the cost of hiring a local manager. Companies want to be sure that the expenditure is worth the benefit they will receive, even though certainty is never possible.

Even if a position opens up in international operations, there is some truth in the saying that the best place to be in international business is on the same floor as the chairman at headquarters. Employees of firms that have taken the international route often come back to headquarters to find only a few positions available for them. Such encounters lead, of course, to organizational difficulties, as well as to financial pressures and family problems, all of which may add up to significant executive stress. Because family re-entry angst is one reason 25 percent of expatriates quit within one year of their return, companies are paying increasing attention to the spouses and children of employees. For example, about 15 percent of Fortune 500 firms offer support for children of employees relocated abroad.[30]

Figure 20.1 Advertisement Recruiting New Graduates for Employment in International Operations

---

EN BUSCA DE SU TALENTO

Procter & Gamble
División de Peru/Latino America

¤ Más de 40 productos de consumo en Latino America como Pampers, Ace, Ariel, Crest, Head & Shoulders, Camay y Vicks.

¤El area tiene el mayor volumen de ventas entre todas las divisiones Internacionales de P&G.

¤Oportunidades de desarrollar una carrera profesional en areas como Mercadeo, Finanzas, Computación, Ventas, etc.

Buscamos individuos con Talento, Empuje, Liderazgo, y continuo afán de superación para posiciones permanentes o practicas de verano en Peru, Puerto Rico, México, Colombia, Venezuela, Brazil, Chile, etc.

Es muy importante que envies tu RESUME pronto
ya que estaremos visitando tu Universidad
en la primera semana de Noviembre.

¿QUE DEBES HACER?
Envia tu resume tan pronto como sea posible a la atencion de Ms. Cynthia Huddleston (MBA Career Services) antes del 18 de Octubre.

SOURCE: The Procter & Gamble Company. Used by permission.

Employment with a Small or Medium-Sized Firm

A second alternative is to begin work in a small or medium-sized firm. Very often, these firms have only recently developed an international outlook, and the new employee will arrive on the "ground floor." Initial involvement will normally be in the export field—evaluating potential foreign customers, preparing quotes, and dealing with mundane activities such as shipping and transportation. With a very limited budget, the export manager will only occasionally visit foreign markets to discuss marketing strategy with foreign distributors. Most of the work will be done by e-mail, by fax, or by telephone. The hours are often long because of the need to reach contacts overseas, for example, during business hours in Hong Kong. Yet the possibilities for implementing creative business methods are virtually limitless, and the contribution made by the successful export manager will be visible in the firm's growing export volume.

Alternatively, international work in a small firm may involve importing—finding new low-cost sources for domestically sourced products. Decisions often must be based on limited information, and the import manager is faced with many uncertainties. Often, things do not work out as planned. Shipments are delayed, letters of credit are canceled, and products almost never arrive in exactly the form and shape anticipated. Yet the problems are always new and offer an ongoing challenge.

As a training ground for international marketing activities, there is probably no better place than a smaller firm. Ideally, the person with some experience may find work with an export-training or export-management company, resolving other people's problems and concentrating virtually exclusively on the international arena.

Self-Employment

A third alternative is to hang up a consultant's shingle or to establish a trading firm. Many companies are in dire need of help for their international marketing effort and are quite prepared to part with a portion of their profits to receive it. Yet in-depth knowledge and broad experience are required to make a major contribution to a company's international marketing effort or to run a trading firm successfully. Specialized services that might be offered by a consultant include international market research, international strategic planning, or, particularly desirable, beginning-to-end assistance in international market entry or international marketing negotiations.

The up-front costs in offering such a service are substantial and are not covered by turnover but rather have to be covered by profits. Yet the rewards are there. For an international marketing expert, the hourly billable rate typically is as high as $400 for experienced principals and $150 for staff. Whenever international travel is required, overseas activities are often billed at the daily rate of $3,000 plus expenses. The latter can add up quickly as the cost-per-diem map on page 624 shows. When trading on one's own, income and risk can be limitless. Even at these relatively high rates, solid groundwork must be completed before all the overhead is paid. The advantage is the opportunity to become a true international entrepreneur. Consultants and owners of trading firms will work at a higher degree of risk than employees, but with the opportunity for higher rewards.

Opportunities for Women in Global Firms

As firms become more and more involved in global business activities, the need for skilled global managers is growing. Concurrent with this increase in business activity is the ever growing presence and managerial role of women in international business.

Research conducted during the mid-1980s[31] indicated that women held 3.3 percent of the overseas positions in U.S. business firms. Five years prior to that time, almost no women were global managers in either expatriate or professional travel status. Thus, the 3.3 percent figure represented a significant increase. By 2000, 13 percent of expatriates in U.S. corporations were women.[32] The reason for the low

The Cost Per Diem in the World's Major Business Cities
(in U.S. dollars)

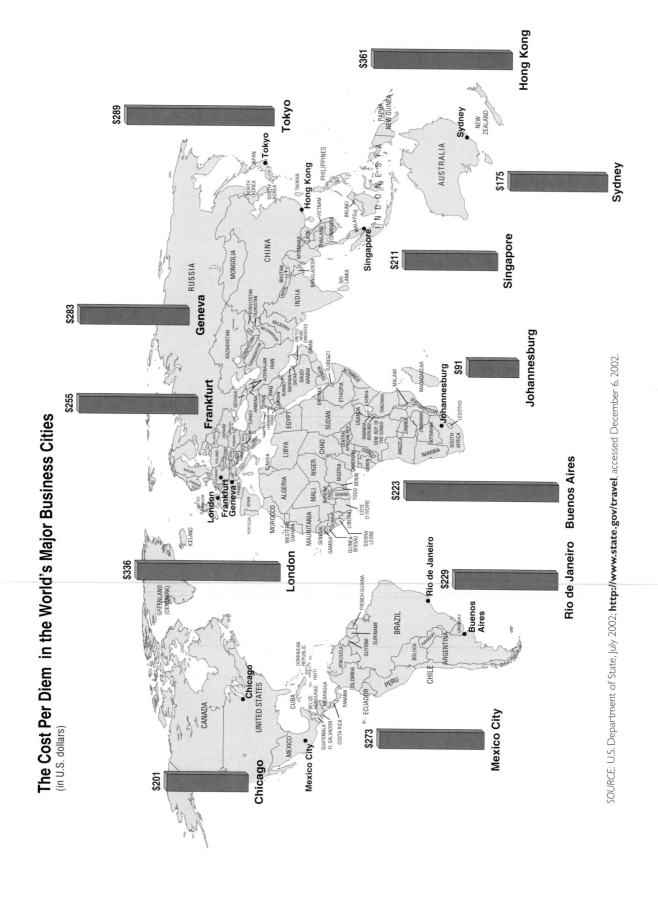

Chicago $201

London $336

Frankfurt $255

Geneva $283

Tokyo $289

Hong Kong $361

Sydney $175

Singapore $211

Johannesburg $91

Buenos Aires $223

Rio de Janeiro $229

Mexico City $273

SOURCE: U.S. Department of State, July 2002; **http://www.state.gov/travel**, accessed December 6, 2002.

participation of women in global management roles seems to have been the assumption that because of the subservient roles of women in Japan, Latin America, and the Middle East, neither local nor expatriate women would be allowed to succeed as managers. The error is that expatriates are not seen as local women, but rather as "foreigners who happen to be women," thus solving many of the problems that would be encountered by a local woman manager.

There appear to be some distinct advantages for a woman in a management position overseas. Among them are the advantages of added visibility and increased access to clients. Clients tend to assume that "expatriate women must be excellent, or else their companies would not have sent them."

It also appears that companies that are larger in terms of sales, assets, income, and employees send more women overseas than smaller organizations. Further, the number of women expatriates is not evenly distributed among industry groups. Industry groups that utilize greater numbers or percentages of women expatriates include banking, electronics, petroleum, publishing, diversified corporations, pharmaceuticals, and retailing and apparel.

For the future, it is anticipated that the upward trend previously cited reflects increased participation of women in global management roles in the future.

Summary

This chapter has provided an overview of the global changes facing international marketers and alternative managerial responses to these changes. International marketing is a complex and difficult activity, yet it affords many challenges and opportunities. "May you live in interesting times" is an ancient Chinese curse. For the international marketer, this curse is a call to action. Observing changes and analyzing how best to incorporate them in the international marketing mission are the bread and butter of the international marketer. If the international environment were constant, there would be little challenge. The frequent changes are precisely what make international marketing so fascinating to those who are active in the field. It must have been international marketers who were targeted by the old Indian proverb, "When storms come about little birds seek to shelter, while eagles soar." May you be an eagle!

Key Terms

environmental protection
population stabilization
population balance
expectation-reality gap
government–corporate collaboration

reputation management
international product life cycles
mass customization
forward pricing

Questions for Discussion

1. For many developing countries, debt repayment and trade are closely interlinked. What does protectionism mean to them?
2. Is international marketing segmentation ethical if it deprives the poor of products?
3. How do security concerns change the way international markets do business?
4. Do you agree that regional trade groupings like the EU and APEC (Asia Pacific Economic Cooperation Forum) will cause a fundamental change in the movement of goods and services across borders?

To what extent does this affect the marketing strategies of MNCs?

5. Some people argue that in the next decade a successful corporate marketing strategy must take into account the promotion of public goods (such as contributing to reducing environmental pollution and global warming). Do you agree with this and why?
6. What do you think are the qualifications needed to successfully locate a good job in international marketing in the next decade?

Internet Exercises

1. Using the Web site of Living Abroad (**http://www.livingabroad. com**), research several international schools that may interest you. What are the most interesting links to other Web sites concerning international issues? Why are you particularly interested in them?

2. The Web site **http://www.overseasjobs.com** provides valuable information for those interested in jobs overseas. What skills do international employers seem to value most? Peruse the job-listings and find several jobs that you might be interested in. Also, take a look at the profiles of several international companies that you might be interested in working for. What characteristics do the international firms listed here possess?

Recommended Readings

Adler, Nancy. *From Boston to Beijing*. Cincinnati, OH: South-Western College Publishing, 2002.

Buckley, Peter, and Mark Casson. *The Future of the Multinational Enterprise*. New York: Palgrave Macmillan, 2002.

Clifford, Mark, and Supachai Panitchpadki. *China and the WTO: Changing China, Changing World Trade*. Singapore: John Wiley & Sons, 2002.

Condon, Bradly. *NAFTA, WTO, and Global Business Strategy: How Aids, Trade and Terrorism Affect Our Economic Future*. Westport, CT: Quorom Books, 2002.

Cornelius, Peter, and Klaus Schwab, eds. *The Global Competitiveness Report 2002–2003*. Oxford, UK: Oxford University Press, 2002.

Czinkota, Michael R., and Ilkka A. Ronkainen, eds. *Best Practices in International Marketing*. Mason, OH: Thomson, 2002.

Friedman, Thomas L. *The Lexus and the Olive Tree*. Wilmington, NC: Anchor Books, 2000.

Gilpin, Robert. *The Challenge of Global Capitalism: The World Economy in the 21st Century*. Princeton, NJ: Princeton University Press, 2002.

Hollenbeck, George P., and Morgan W. McCall, Jr. *Developing Global Executives*. Boston, MA: Harvard Business School Press, 2002.

Omae, Kenichi. *The Invisible Continent: Four Strategic Imperatives of the New Economy*. New York: Harperbusiness, 2001.

Chupa Chups Vending: "Choose Your Flavor"

Andrew Lewis was a 37-year-old Welshman. After six years of marketing experience with multinational consumer goods companies, he had graduated with an MBA from IESE in 1993, shortly afterwards getting married to his Catalan wife. For the past five years he had been employed by the confectionery company Chupa Chups S.A., based in their Barcelona headquarters as area manager responsible for commercial and marketing activity in key European markets, including Spain. In September 2001, Andrew left Chupa Chups due to internal reorganization. He had been offered a position at the UK subsidiary as marketing director, but he declined for personal reasons. The separation was amicable on both sides, and Andrew still had many good friends at the company.

Now he had been asked to join a large and prestigious Catalan alcoholic beverage company. The firm was the market leader in Spain in its segment and had significant international sales. The job was based in Barcelona, with responsibility for international marketing.

Only three weeks before, Andrew had entered into detailed discussions with a small Spanish manufacturing company named Discapa. The firm manufactured vending equipment, and some months earlier had launched internationally a new lollipop vending machine, marketed in collaboration with Andrews' previous employer Chupa Chups S.A. Andrew had been offered the opportunity to work as a freelance commercial agent, heading up the worldwide commercialization of the new lollipop vending machine.

Chupa Chups S.A.

Chupa Chups S.A. is a Spanish confectionery company founded in 1958 by Enric Bernat. With its headquarters in Barcelona, the company defines itself as a "Catalan Multinational," 100 percent family-owned, and selling its products in more than 125 countries worldwide.

With the aid of market research, Bernat had confirmed his views that two-thirds of all candy consumption was, quite literally, in the hands of children under 16. Particularly among the youngest groups, sticky hands resulted in grubby kids and desperate parents. Based on new developments in the sugar-refining process, Enric Bernat created a universal sweet capable of keeping both children and their long-suffering parents happy, which was "like eating a sweet with a fork." Thus was born the world-famous Chupa Chups lollipop.

Bernat was also innovative in the way he went to market. He employed a direct sales force covering all of Spain and developed a revolutionary counter display within reach of the customers' hands. This was of fundamental importance for an impulse purchase product. Bernat also established the "1 Chupa Chups, 1 peseta" price point to fund advertising campaigns to build the brand.

SOURCE: Case contributed and written by Gary Andrew Lewis, Francesca Parés, and Lluís G. Renart at IESE Business School, Universidad de Navarra, Barcelona, Spain. Reprinted with permission from IESE Publishing, Av. Pearson, 21, 08034 Barcelona–Spain.

Figure 1 Product Display, "1 peseta"

By the late 1960s, Chupa Chups had become equally popular among teenagers and young adults as among kids, and sold equally well in bars and in traditional candy shops. At that time, Enric Bernat began to expand his company internationally, beginning in France where a factory was established. Throughout the 1970s international expansion continued with great success, something very unusual at that time for a Spanish company. Spain was still very much a closed economy as a result of the Franco regime and did not become a full member of the European Union until 1986. During this period, Chupa Chups S.A. export sales grew in importance, from representing just 10 percent of total company sales in 1970 to more than 90 percent by the early 1980s.

Products would often initially be sold into new countries on an ad hoc basis. A suitable local distributor would be sought, and the sales and marketing of the brand carried out on a more organized basis. As sales developed, Chupa Chups S.A. would often seek to establish a small representative office. With one or two employees, the office would work closely with the local distributor to provide sales and marketing support, coordinate product supply, and ensure that the distributor was sufficiently focused on the Chupa Chups brand. In the key markets where the investment could be justified, the local distributor would

eventually be replaced and a full sales and marketing subsidiary established. Finally, in a few cases in which it was considered viable, Chupa Chups S.A. even began to carry out local manufacturing of their lollipops, establishing their own factory either in collaboration with a local partner or on its own.

By 2001, the brand was distributed in more than 125 countries, and the company was selling around 4,000 million lollipops annually, or more than 10 million every day, accounting for approximately 35 percent of the worldwide lollipop market. In addition to the two factories in Spain and one in France, production also took place in China, Mexico, and Russia—the last being the single biggest market worldwide for Chupa Chups lollipops. In addition to these countries, there were full sales and marketing subsidiaries established in Germany, the United Kingdom, the United States, and Brazil, as well as a number of representative offices in many other countries including Italy, South Africa, Japan, Argentina, Canada, and Australia. Turnover was approximately 414 million euros, more than 90 percent of which came from sales outside of Chupa Chups' home market. Enric Bernat, aided by his five children, was still active in influencing company policy.

Discapa S.A.

Discapa was based in Calaf, a small inland town about an hour's drive west of Barcelona. The firm was founded in 1992 by two partners, Miguel Delgado and Joan Carles Jimenez, who both had backgrounds in the vending industry. The company was established to manufacture and sell vending machines to the "leisure" segment of the vending market. The main product was machines that dispensed plastic capsules filled with toys and other surprises specifically targeted at children. The innovation they brought to the market when they began in 1992 was to introduce the 100-mm spherical capsule, much larger than anything then available. This permitted the use of a wider range and a higher quality of gifts and toys.

The innovation was well received, and the machines and surprise capsules proved popular with both vending operators and children alike. The company grew steadily and, by 2001, employed 33 people. The machines and filled capsules were being exported to more than 30 countries. By 2001 annual sales had reached 6.6 million euros. More than 60 percent of sales were made to customers outside of their home market of Spain.[1]

Table 1	Chupa Chups Sales Share by Region (estimate)	
Region	Estimated Share, Percentage of Total Lollipop Sales 2000	Key Countries (Sales > 10 Million Lollipops Annually)
Africa & Middle East	4%	South Africa, Lebanon, Egypt
America	9	Mexico, Brazil, US, Canada
Asia	17	Japan, China, Australia, New Zealand, India
Spain	6	
Eastern Europe	21	Russia, Poland, Czech Republic, Baltics
Northern Europe	22	UK, France, Germany, Scandinavia, Holland, Ireland, Belgium, Switzerland, Austria
Southern Europe	21	Italy, Portugal, Greece
Total	100%	

Discapa did not operate any machines, but focused its activity on the manufacture and commercialization of the vending machines and capsules. The machines were of their own designs, with production of the parts usually outsourced and assembly taking place in their factory in Calaf. The toys and surprises were purchased directly from toy manufacturers, often based in Asia, and inserted into the capsules in Discapa's facilities.

The main customers for Discapa machines and capsules were small vending operators, typically either individuals or small family-run companies who would invest their money to build up a small network of machines. They would periodically refill the machines, service them, take the cash, and give a percentage of the income to the owner of the site. In order to maximize the profitability of their vending sites, the operators would often work simultaneously with other complementary types of vending machines such as gum ball or bouncing ball machines, electric crane machines, or kiddie rides. Machines would be placed in a wide variety of locations such as gas stations, theme parks, sports centers, bars, restaurants, and shopping malls.

The business philosophy of Discapa expressed by Miguel Delgado was "We are in business for the long term. Our first goal therefore is that our customers should make money. Our second goal is that our suppliers should make money. Only after having achieved this should we ensure our own profit." Discapa strove to implement this credo in the reliability of its machines, the quality and variety of its capsules collections, its competitive prices, and its sales and technical service.

The Chupa Chups Lollipop Vending Machine: "Choose Your Flavor"

It was at one of the initial meetings toward the end of 1998 when the opportunity of developing a vending machine specifically to sell the Chupa Chups lollipop, loose and not in a capsule, was first discussed.

There existed at that point in time no machine on the market exclusively designed for the sale of lollipops, since lollipops were very much a niche product and difficult to vend due to the awkward shape of the stick. Nonetheless, the team considered that such a machine had tremendous potential, not only because it would be a novelty within the vending market, but also because of its possible international dimension. It would have the potential to capitalize on the strength of the Chupa Chups brand worldwide and to generate a real alternative distribution channel for Chupa Chups lollipops in all markets where the brand was present, i.e., some 125 countries!

Initial Agreement

The two companies quickly agreed that Discapa was to develop such a lollipop vending machine using its own resources. Chupa Chups agreed to allow Discapa to use its brand. However, the lollipop project would differ from the capsule project, in which Discapa was responsible for both machine and ongoing capsule sales to all customers in all countries. In this new project,

Discapa would limit its involvement solely to the sale of the machine. Once the machine was in the hands of the operators, each operator in his own country would have to buy the Chupa Chups lollipops locally, either directly from the local distributor or even from a cash-and-carry or similar retail outlet. The long-term involvement of Discapa in the project was therefore limited, and the commercial success in each country would depend to a degree on the collaboration of the Chupa Chups organization and their distributors with each of the operators (i.e., ensuring sufficiently competitive prices, offering promotions, etc.). As Miguel Delgado commented: "Discapa will build the gas stations, but Chupa Chups will sell the gas."

The Mission

A mission statement was quickly drawn up, and work began on the technical development. The following points were considered the most important to be taken into account:

1. The machine should be able to be located in a wide variety of places. It should therefore be mechanical, without need for electricity, be of a manageable size, and be either freestanding or on countertops or on wall brackets.

2. Chupa Chups was fundamentally an impulse purchase product. To fully capitalize on the strength of the brand, the machine should be recognizable and attractive, displaying the product in an optimal way.

3. Chupa Chups lollipops were known and loved for their wide variety of flavors, with consumers having their particular favorites. The machine should allow consumers to choose the particular flavors they wished to purchase.

4. The machine should be adjusted to the exact size and dimensions of the Chupa Chups lollipop. This would limit, although not eliminate, the possibility of operators refilling the machine with other brands of cheaper lollipops.

5. Finally, a key factor to convince a vending operator to invest in a particular machine was the period of time he would need to pay back the cost of machine, i.e., to recover his initial investment. A period of nine months was normally considered acceptable, although obviously the shorter the better. Having done a few numbers on margins and likely rates of sale, the team concluded that the machine should have a cost to the operator of approximately 200 euros.

Figure 2 **Chupa Chups "Choose Your Flavor" Machine**

The "Choose Your Flavor" Machine

By January 2000 a prototype was produced. Many adjustments still had to be made and it was only by the end of the year that the machine was considered operational.

The machine was christened "Choose Your Flavor" by the Chupa Chups marketing team. It consisted of a base and a rotating carousel of 21 columns each of 16 lollipops, i.e., a total of 336 lollipops, each of which had to be loaded individually by the operator into the machine. The columns were to be filled by flavor and the carousel to be rotated by the consumer until they had positioned the desired flavor of lollipop above the exit chute. Subsequently the coin was inserted into the mechanism and the handle turned in order to retrieve the Chupa Chups. The machine could be configured to work with one or two coins, and could dispense either one or two lollipops.

The machine was to have a list price of 195 euros to the final operator, plus another 63 euros for the optional stand.[2] This pricing permitted the application of promotional discounts, and typically the offer of "10 + 1 free" was to be made during the launch period. Similarly, sales made to Discapa distributors or other vending equipment distributors in other countries would have significant discounts, as would any sales made directly to any Chupa Chups company or subsidiary.

Launch and Initial Feedback

The machine was officially presented for the first time at a large international leisure industry trade fair in London at the end of January 2001. It generated great interest and first orders, especially from UK customers, who were the majority visitors at the fair. However, it was another few months before the first machines were manufactured and shipped. The UK was the first market where the machines were to be sited in any number, thus serving as a test market.

Initial feedback was good. The rates of sale achieved were more than acceptable, averaging between 500 and 600 lollipops per machine per month. Margins for the operators were also good, with the lollipop vending at 20 pence, twice the normal sweet-shop price of 10 pence. The lollipop had a cost to the operator of approximately 5 pence. With a typical commission of 25 percent paid to the site, each machine was generating a gross margin of around 50 pounds (i.e., approximately 80 euros) per month.

No significant problems were encountered in the first few months, although the machines were certainly not completely problem-free. There were isolated incidences of lollipops jamming in the mechanism, as well as cases of "missed vends" (i.e., the lollipop was not expelled even though the coin had been inserted). Both problems were due either to misshaped lollipops or the result of the mechanism having been turned too quickly by the consumer. A problem became evident in machines of high rotation or those exposed to great heat. In these machines the constant action of the mechanism against the lollipops, especially when sticky, tended to peel off the wrappers, thus dirtying the machine with sugar deposits and impeding correct functioning until the machine had been withdrawn and properly cleaned. However, the machines were relatively easy to clean and Discapa was studying ways to reduce the number of these incidents.

Situation by the End of 2001

Throughout the remainder of 2001, there was an extremely high interest in the machine from both Discapa's vending customers, as well as from Chupa Chups subsidiaries and distributors around the world, all eager to try what could potentially

Table 2	Machine Sales by Country, 2001
Country	**Number of Machines**
Spain	884
United Kingdom	600
Italy	334
Canada/United States	275
Mexico	250
Uruguay	131
Australia	110
Norway	105
Lebanon	75
France	70
Greece	55
Lithuania	35
Dominican Republic	30
Letonia	25
Switzerland	15
Estonia	15
Belgium	8
Sweden	8
Kenya	5
Germany	3
Malaysia	3
Philippines	3
Ireland	2
Holland	2
Austria	2
Thailand	2
Puerto Rico	2
Hong Kong	2
Czech Republic	1
Venezuela	1
Chile	1
Total	3,054

be an important new sales channel for Chupa Chups lollipops.

By the end of the year, a total of some 3,000 machines had been sold by Discapa to more than 30 countries. Both Discapa and Chupa Chups considered this an acceptable result, especially as many customers would take only a small initial number of machines in order to carry out trials. Moreover, in European markets, demand was significantly dampened by the imminent launch of the new euro currency set for January 2002. Many potential customers preferred to await the arrival of the new coins in order to avoid the need for converting the coin mechanism.

Evaluating the Situation

It was against this background that Andrew was now contemplating his future—to follow his up-to-now traditional career path and accept the offer to join the prestigious Catalan alcoholic drinks company, or alternatively, to accept the invitation of Discapa and to involve himself fully in the Choose Your Flavor project.

To evaluate the offers, he obviously had to consider the economic aspects. There were other noneconomic criteria that were also important and needed to be taken into account, such as job security, opportunity for career development, professional interest, and not least his family situation. Barcelona was now very much Andrew's home, with his wife being Catalana and their two small children aged three and five.

Option 1: Employee, Marketing—International Alcoholic Drinks Company

The company in question was very well established and a market leader in Spain within its segment. It was family-owned for many generations, and very professionally run by both family and nonfamily members. It was in a phase of investment and expansion and had significant plans for new product and brand development as well as for growth of its international business. Accepting this post would be a natural progression of his career in marketing for branded consumer goods companies.

The position offered a salary, including bonus, of around 75,000 euros annually. Under normal circumstances he could anticipate these conditions to continue over the first two or three years, changing only with inflation. Afterwards, depending on his performance and opportunities within the company, there could be the possibility of a promotion, either to marketing director or to a position of similar responsibility within a subsidiary. Then he could anticipate perhaps a salary package of around 120,000 euros.

Option 2: Freelance, Commercial Agent—Vending Machine Manufacturer

Andrew knew that Choose Your Flavor was an extremely important project to Discapa. It was its first major product launch beyond the traditional capsule business, in which management hoped to achieve its short- to mid-term sales growth. He also knew that despite having its own commercial department, Discapa was keen to involve him due

to his professional experience, his language skills, and specifically his knowledge and contacts within both the confectionery industry and the Chupa Chups company.

Collaborating on a freelance commission basis would expose him to personal and financial risk that was unfamiliar to him. In addition, Discapa was a much smaller company than Andrew's previous employers. Accepting the offer would be a significant change of focus in his up-to-now steady career path. Working on a freelance basis would also mean that if necessary, he could manage his time so as to become involved in other projects as opportunities presented themselves.

After some initial discussions to investigate different formulas for working with Discapa, the proposal was for Andrew to become an external commercial agent working specifically on the Choose Your Flavor project. He would work primarily from his home to generate and follow up sales leads and orders for the Choose Your Flavor machine, both among existing Discapa customers as well as potential new customers worldwide. Discapa would then manufacture and ship the machines to order, invoice the customer, and take responsibility for all after-sales services. In return, Andrew was to receive a percentage commission on invoiced sales.

To evaluate the offer, Andrew decided to estimate a commission of 5 percent, and a scenario in which he would be responsible for the greater part of his own expenses, which he estimated at approximately 1,500 euros monthly. He also had to estimate the average invoicing price of the machine, which would sometimes be sold with stands, and sometimes without. Different discounts would be applied depending on the customer, quantities being purchased, and promotions being applied; however, he reasoned that the average invoiced amount for each machine/stand combination would be about 200 euros.

He also estimated the number of machines that could be sold. The internal budget set by Discapa for 2002 was for 10,000 machines, which given the sales achieved in 2001 did not seem unrealistic. For the longer term he thought of the 12,000 Chupa Chups capsule machines which had been sold since their launch in 1998, knowing that Choose Your Flavor had by comparison far more potential. It was a machine that could be located in far more sites than the capsule machine and was relevant to many more countries around the world. Finally, he considered the 4,000 million lollipops sold by Chupa Chups each year. If only 15 percent of these sales were to be made via the Choose Your Flavor vending machine, this would indicate total machines sales of around 100,000.

Additionally, he considered the lifespan of the project. Sales would probably be strong through the first three years or so, after which they would probably begin to tail off considerably as operators built up their networks and possible competitive machines were developed.

The obvious starting point was the traditional *vending channel* and specifically the existing Discapa customers, a great number of whom could very likely be persuaded to at least try the Choose Your Flavor machine alongside their capsule machines. Specifically he also contemplated operators of hot-drink machines and envisaged the Choose Your Flavor machine being located alongside them in offices, factories, and canteens. This idea could be especially relevant to the Spanish market, where a high percentage of the population were smokers, and smoking at work was increasingly being discouraged.

He considered that there might also be an opportunity to promote the machine as a business opportunity to *new investors,* i.e., people new to the vending sector and willing to invest their money to build up a network of machines to become operators, either as a new business initiative or as a complement to an existing business.

Finally, it was also clear to him that the long-term success of the project depended a great deal on the support of Chupa Chups S.A. Not only would its collaboration be needed in order to ensure an efficient and correctly priced supply of lollipops to the operators in each country, but active and positive involvement in the project could open up sales to many potential customers worldwide currently unknown to Discapa.

In summary, accepting the offer from Discapa would be to embark on an adventure, but he had to seriously consider whether this was the correct time for such a decision. As his wife reminded him, she was currently not employed, having decided to dedicate a few years to bringing up their two small children. If the decision were left to her, he would soon be indulging himself in the international alcohol market, leaving Chupa Chups to his friends and colleagues!

Notes

1. The success of Discapa was soon copied by other vending equipment manufacturers, both inside and outside of Spain, who produced similar vending machines and similar ranges of 100-mm capsules. While Discapa was generally regarded as the market leader in terms of product quality and innovation, competition was strong, and it was not unknown for Discapa machines to be seen filled with capsules from other suppliers, or vice versa.

2. For all countries other than Spain, the list prices were ex works, so all handling and transport costs were to be added. For Spanish customers, the prices were CIF.

Nova Scotia

The U.S. Market for Canadian Travel Services

The more than 15.5 million Americans who travel to Canada annually constitute 30 percent of all departures from the United States. The U.S. market is of crucial importance to the Canadian tourism industry because 95 percent of all tourists are Americans, who spend approximately $6.5 billion a year on these trips.

The 1980s witnessed a major escalation in campaigns that try to lure tourists to a particular state or foreign country. The Canadian Tourism Commission, the government tourist organization, launched a campaign with the theme "Come to the world next door" as an umbrella campaign for Canada as a whole. The provinces conduct their own independent campaigns to segments they deem most attractive and profitable. For example, ads for Manitoba are mostly written for the outdoor vacationer.

The Commission sponsored a large-scale benefit-segmentation study of the American market for pleasure travel to Canada, the results of which are

summarized in Table 1. Segmenting the market by benefits provides many advantages over other methods. Segmenting by attitude toward Canada or by geographic area would be feasible if substantial variation occurred. This is not the case, however. Segmenting by benefits reveals what consumers were and are seeking in their vacations. Knowing this is central to planning effective marketing programs.

A Benefit-Matching Model

Table 2 summarizes a strategic view for understanding tourism behavior and developing a marketing campaign. The model emphasizes the dominant need to define markets by benefits sought and the fact that separate markets seek unique benefits or activity packages. Membership in the segments will fluctuate from year to year; the same individuals may seek rest and relaxation one year and foreign adventure the next.

Identifying benefits is not enough, however. Competition (that is, other countries or areas) may present the same type of benefits to the consumers. Because travelers seriously consider only a few destinations, a sharp focus is needed for promoting a destination. This also means that a destination should avoid trying to be "everything to everybody" by promoting too many benefits. Combining all of these concerns calls for positioning, that is, generating a unique, differentiated image in the mind of the consumer.

SOURCE: This case was written by Arch G. Woodside and Ilkka A. Ronkainen for discussion purposes and not to exemplify correct or incorrect decision-making. The case is largely based on Arch G. Woodside, "Positioning a Province Using Travel Research," *Journal of Travel Research* 20 (Winter 1982): 2–6. For additional information, please see **http://www.gov.ns.ca**.

Table 1	**Benefit Segments of U.S. Travelers to Canada**		
Segment	**Segment Contents**	**Size**	**Segment Objective**
I.	Friends and relatives—nonactive visitor	29%	Seek familiar surroundings where they can visit friends.
II.	Friends and relatives—active city visitor	12%	Seek familiar surroundings where they can visit friends and relatives but are more inclined to participate in activities (i.e., sightseeing, shopping, cultural, entertainment).
III.	Family sightseers	6%	Look for new vacation place that would be a treat for the children and an enriching experience.
IV.	Outdoor vacationer	19%	Seek clean air, rest, quiet, and beautiful scenery. Many are campers, and availability of recreation facilities is important. Children also an important factor.
V.	Resort vacationer	19%	Most interested in water sports (for example, swimming) and good weather. Prefer a popular place with a big-city atmosphere.
VI.	Foreign vacationer	26%	Look for a place they have never been before with a foreign atmosphere and beautiful scenery. Money is not of major concern but good accommodation and service are. They want an exciting, enriching experience.

SOURCE: Shirley Young, Leland Ott, and Barbara Feigin, "Some Practical Considerations in Market Segmentation," *Journal of Marketing Research* 15 (August 1978): 405–412. Reprinted with permission.

Three destinations are shown in Table 2. Each destination provides unique as well as similar benefits for travelers. Marketers have the opportunity to select one or two specific benefits from a set of benefits when developing a marketing program to attract visitors. The benefits selected for promotion can match or mismatch the benefits sought by specific market segments. The letters S, M, and N in the table express the degree of fit between the benefits provided and those sought. For example, a mismatch is promoting the wrong benefit to the wrong market, such as promoting the scenic mountain beauty of North Carolina to Tennessee residents.

The Case of Nova Scotia

Nova Scotia is one of ten provinces and two territories that make up Canada. Given its location, it is known as Canada's Ocean Playground (see Figure 1). For many Nova Scotians the sea is their main source of livelihood and leisure. For 200 years the sea has played an integral role in the history and economy of the province (see Table 3). It was the abundant fisheries that drew settlers into the area. Today, many of their descendants work in a variety of professions related to the water, including tourism. The importance of tourism has increased with both the mining and fishing sectors

Table 2	**Benefit-Matching Model**			
Markets	**Benefits Sought**	**Benefit Match**	**Benefits Provided**	**Destinations**
A $\longrightarrow$	$A_s, B_s \longrightarrow$	S $\longleftarrow$	$A_p, B_p \longleftarrow$	X
B $\longrightarrow$	$B_s, C_s \longrightarrow$	M $\longleftarrow$	$C_p, D_p \longleftarrow$	Y
C $\longrightarrow$	$C_s, D_s \longrightarrow$	N $\longleftarrow$	$E_p, F_p \longleftarrow$	Z

SOURCE: Arch G. Woodside, "Positioning a Province Using Travel Research," *Journal of Travel Research* 20 (Winter 1982): 3.

Figure 1 · Nova Scotia and Its Main Travel Markets

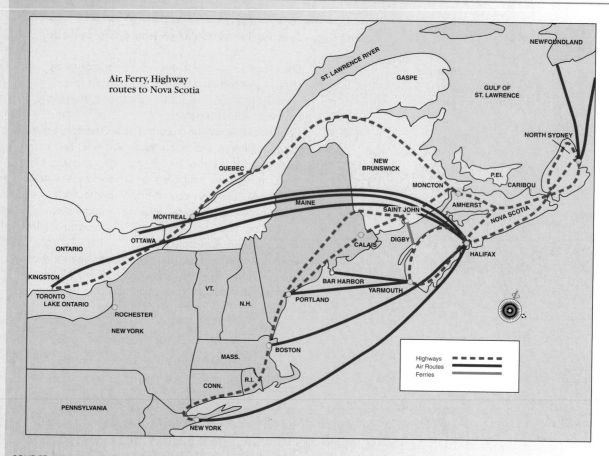

Air, Ferry, Highway routes to Nova Scotia

Highways — — —
Air Routes ———
Ferries ———

SOURCE: "Nova Scotia," *Travel Agent*, February 27, 1986, 14.

having difficulties from their resources drying up. Total tourism receipts exceed $1.22 billion and over 33,500 workers are employed directly and in spin-off jobs. More than a million people visit the province every year, with almost a quarter of these coming from outside of Canada, mainly the United States.

Canada as a whole has a rather vague and diffused image among Americans. This is particularly true of the Atlantic provinces. The majority of Nova Scotia's nonresident travelers reside in New England and the mid-Atlantic states of New York, Pennsylvania, and New Jersey. Most of these travelers include households with married couples having incomes substantially above the U.S. national average, that is, $50,000 and above. Such households represent a huge, accessible market— 10 million households that are one to two and a half days' drive from Halifax, the capital. Most households in this market have not visited the Atlantic provinces and have no plans to do so. Thus, the market exhibits three of the four require-

ments necessary to be a very profitable customer base for the province: size, accessibility, and purchasing power. The market lacks the intention to visit for most of the households described. Nova Scotia is not one of the destinations considered when the next vacation or pleasure trip is being planned. Worse still, Nova Scotia does not exist in the minds of its largest potential market.

In the past, Nova Scotia had a number of diverse marketing themes, such as "Good times are here," "International gathering of the clans," "The 375th anniversary of Acadia," "Seaside spectacular," and the most recent, "There's so much to sea." These almost annual changes in marketing strategy contributed to the present situation both by confusing the consumer as to what Nova Scotia is all about and by failing to create a focused image based on the relative strengths of the province. Some critics argue that Nova Scotia is not being promoted on its unique features but on benefits that other locations can provide as well or better.

Table 3	Nova Scotia Facts

The Land

Nova Scotia is surrounded by four bodies of water—the Atlantic, the Bay of Fundy, the Northumberland Strait, and the Gulf of St. Lawrence. Its average width of 70 miles (128 kilometers) means that no part of the province is far from the sea. Nova Scotia lies in the northern temperate zone and although it is surrounded by water, the climate is continental rather than maritime. The temperature extremes are moderated, however, by the ocean.

The History

The Micmac Indians inhabited Nova Scotia long before the first explorers arrived from Europe. The first visitors were Norsemen (in 1000), and, in 1497, Italian explorer John Cabot had noted the rich fishing grounds in the area. In the seventeenth century, all of Nova Scotia was settled by the French and formed a larger area known as Acadia. Feuds between the British and the French resulted in all of Acadia being ceded to the British in 1713. The British perceived the Acadians as a security threat and expelled them to Virginia and Louisiana. In 1783, there was an influx of loyalists from the newly independent New England states. Nova Scotia and three other provinces joined a federation called the Dominion of Canada in 1867. At the time, the province was known for international shipbuilding and trade in fish and lumber. The First and Second World Wars emphasized the importance of Halifax, Nova Scotia's capital, as a staging point for convoys and confirmed it as one of the world's major ports.

The People

Over 80 percent of Nova Scotia's population of 937,800 trace their ancestry to the British Isles, while 18 percent of residents are of French ancestry. The next largest groups by ancestry are German and Dutch. Almost 22,000 residents have Indian roots, primarily belonging to the Micmac nation.

The Economy

Nova Scotia's economy is highly diversified, having evolved from resource-based employment to manufacturing as well as business and personal services. The breakdown is as follows: (1) manufacturing/fish, 62 percent; (2) tourism, 12 percent; (3) forestry, 10 percent; (4) mining, 7 percent; (5) fishing, 5 percent; and (6) agriculture, 3 percent.

SOURCE: "Canadian Provinces and Territories," **http://www.canada.gc.ca.**

Examples of Successful Positioning

Most North Atlantic passengers flying to Europe used to have a vague impression of Belgium. This presented a problem to the tourism authorities, who wanted travelers to stay for longer periods. Part of the problem was a former "Gateway to Europe" campaign that had positioned Belgium as a country to pass through on the way to somewhere else.

The idea for new positioning was found in the *Michelin Guides,* which rate cities as they do restaurants. The Benelux countries have six three-star cities (the highest ranking), of which five are in Belgium and only one (Amsterdam) is in the Netherlands. The theme generated was "In Belgium, there are five Amsterdams." This strategy was correct in three different ways: (1) it related Belgium to a destination that was known to the traveler, Amsterdam; (2) the *Michelin Guides,* another entity already known to the traveler, gave the concept credibility; and (3) the "five cities to visit" made Belgium a bona fide destination.[1]

The state of Florida attracts far more eastern North American beach seekers than does South Carolina. Tourism officials in South Carolina had to find a way in which the state could be positioned against Florida.

The positioning theme generated was "You get two more days in the sun by coming to Myrtle Beach, South Carolina, instead of Florida." Florida's major beaches are a one-day drive beyond the Grand Strand of South Carolina—and one additional day back. Most travelers to Florida go in the May-to-October season when the weather is similar to that in South Carolina. Thus, more beach time and less driving time became the central benefit provided by the state.

Positioning Nova Scotia

The benefits of Nova Scotia as a Canadian travel destination cover segments III to VI of U.S. travelers (see Table 1). Those providing input to the planning process point out water activities, seaside activities, camping, or scenic activities. The segment interested in foreign adventure could be lured by festivals and other related activities.

The planners' argument centers not so much on which benefits to promote but on which should be emphasized if differentiation is desired. The decision is important because of (1) the importance of the industry to the province and (2) the overall rise in competition for the travelers in Nova Scotia's market, especially competition by U.S. states.

Questions for Discussion

1. How would you position Nova Scotia to potential American travelers? Use the benefit-matching model to achieve your supermatch.
2. Constructively criticize past positioning attempts, such as "There's so much to sea."
3. What other variables, apart from positioning, will determine whether Americans will choose Nova Scotia as a destination?

Note

1. Al Ries and Jack Trout, *Positioning: The Battle for Your Mind* (New York: McGraw-Hill, 2000), 171–178.

Customer Service Online: The HP DesignJet

At the beginning of September 1997, Ignacio Fonts, marketing director of the Barcelona Division of Hewlett-Packard Española, S.A., had a number of decisions to make regarding the start-up of the **http://www.designjet-online.hp.com** project, a relationship-marketing program that would allow HP to communicate on an interactive basis with the users of its large-format printers.

Hewlett-Packard (HP) was a multinational company with a presence in more than 120 countries worldwide whose activities included the manufacture and sale of personal and business computing products. In Europe it had 11 manufacturing sites, including one in the town of Sant Cugat del Vallés, near Barcelona (Spain), where it designed and manufactured large-format printers for the world market. HP was the undisputed world leader in this product category, with a market share of over 50 percent.

The Barcelona Division (HP-BCD) already had a Web presence at **http://www.hp.com/go/designjet**, but the new proposal Fonts was considering would entail major changes. Fonts had to carefully consider all the implications. The target visitors of the new Web site would not be the general public, or even potential customers; rather, the site would be very specifically aimed at existing users of the approximately 500,000 HP large-format printers in use around the world. The problem, however, was that only around 50,000 of these users had been identified and registered.

For the first time, HP-BCD would try to interact directly with the end users of its large-format printers scattered around the world, and at the same time offer them new technical support tools. As the project advanced, the situation turned out to be considerably more complicated than expected.

One of Fonts's concerns was that, for the project to succeed, it was vital to get the Technical Support Organization and the Territorial Sales Organization involved (both operated at a global level and with total independence within HP). It was vital that they accepted the new Web site as a useful marketing tool that also served their interests and not as an intrusion into their respective areas of responsibility.

Fonts had just returned from his summer holiday and had a meeting with his team planned for the coming Monday. At that meeting they would have to decide whether or not to go ahead and set up the new site. If they chose to go ahead, they would have to decide on the definitive content of the site, what measures would have to be taken to ensure its smooth operation, and which team member should be appointed as manager of the new Web site. If the new Web site were set up, it would be possible for any end user of large-format printers to start talking directly to "the manufacturer." Various departments within the HP organization, both within Fonts's direct area of responsibility and beyond it, therefore, would have to respond effectively for the service to gen-

SOURCE: Case of the Research Department at IESE. Prepared by Professors Lluís G. Renart and José Antonio Segarra, and Lecturer Francisco Pares, October 1999. Copyright © 1999, IESE. This is a condensed version of the case "Hewlett-Packard: DesignJet Online." The complete version is available from IESE PUBLISHING (Phone: 34 93 253 42 42, e-mail: iesep@iesep.com, web: **http://www.iesep.com**).

erate added value for the customer. Fonts thought that if any part of the HP organization was not properly prepared to communicate appropriately with the end users, it might be better to postpone the project or limit its scope so as not to harm the current excellent image of both HP Barcelona Division and its products in the world market.

Large-Format Printers

By 1997 there had been, for several years, a number of computer programs capable of creating and manipulating images by computer. CAD (Computer Assisted Design) and similar applications were regularly used by architects, engineers, and graphic designers to create two- and three-dimensional drawings. Large-format printers were a type of computer peripheral capable of printing the on-screen designs onto paper or other similar media more than one meter wide and almost unlimited length.

The earliest users of large-format printers were the pioneers of CAD in the fields of engineering and architecture. Later, graphic designers started to experiment, generating and printing large poster-size images. The CAD market initially used plotters, which could print large formats but were limited to line drawings and could not print large shaded areas (patterns or halftones) or solid color, which were often needed in graphic design. By 1997, most manufacturers had stopped using the term "plotter" for their machines, using the term "printer" instead. The performance of the machines had improved considerably and some models were capable of producing photo-quality prints. There were different types of large-format printers, using different printing technologies. All of HP's large-format printers used the inkjet printing system.

The purchasing process of large-format inkjet printers differed in important respects from that of the usual small desktop printers, which were regarded as consumer items. Large-format printers required an investment of between $2,000 and $12,000, depending on the model and the features. The decisive purchasing factors were quality and printing speed, based above all on reliability and robustness. For the end users it was particularly important that the printer worked smoothly, without unevenness between one print and another, making as little noise as possible, and if necessary for many hours at a stretch. Printing jobs often had to be done in a rush, just before the deadline for delivery of a project. If a printer broke down, a technician had to go to the user's premises to repair it. Only very rarely did the printer have to be transported to a repair shop.

Large-format printers had a useful life of over ten years, but in practice they became outdated within five years due to technological obsolescence resulting from the rapid pace of innovation. They were sold with a one-year warranty. When customers needed a large-format printer, they tended to go to their regular computer equipment supplier and to think the decision over much more carefully than they would normally do in the case of conventional office computing equipment. Most HP distributors were multibrand and sold to all types of customers. If a particular market warranted it, HP would have one or two large-format printer specialists in that country's sales organization, who would visit the distributors and respond to any requests for help from end users.

Figure 1 shows a model of one of the large-format inkjet printers developed and manufactured by HP Barcelona Division for the world market. The different models were sold under names that consisted of the expression "HP DesignJet," which was common to all, followed by a number or combination of numbers and letters, such as "HP DesignJet 450" and "HP DesignJet 750C Plus."

Figure 1 **A Large-Format Hewlett-Packard Printer**

SOURCE: © 1994–2003 Hewlett-Packard Company. All Rights Reserved.

The World Market for Large-Format Printers

Almost all architectural and engineering firms already had one or more large-format printers, or at least a plotter, and the number of new firms needing CAD equipment was growing very slowly. Also, the motivation to buy a new high-quality graphic printer was low, as there was no demand for spectacular improvements in performance or print quality in this sector. This was, therefore, basically a replacement market segment.

In contrast, the graphic design segment of large-format printer users continued to grow rapidly. Customers in this segment appreciated the cost reductions and the enhanced print quality and performance offered by large-format inkjet printers. Higher printing speeds and a more robust design had stimulated the demand for this type of printer by such users as advertising agencies, poster producers, industrial designers, interior designers, printers, design schools, and design departments in companies.

The graphic design market segment had two types of purchasers: (1) companies that used the printers in-house and (2) print shop service providers—shops where anyone who had created an on-screen graphic design could get it printed, paying a price per copy. The main suppliers of large-format printers in 1997 in the world are as shown in Table 1.

HP was the undisputed leader in large-format printers, with a market penetration in 1996 of more than 50 percent of the installed base. None of its competitors had as much as 20 percent of the world market, which was estimated at some

$1 billion per year at manufacturers' selling prices. HP's competitors in the large-format printer market were generally companies with more specific products for specialist uses, such as large-format printers for printing on fabric to be used as weather protection to cover scaffolding during renovation work on buildings in large cities, which was also used as a gigantic advertising medium. HP maintained one entry barrier that gave it a competitive advantage in the sector: its constant investment in research and development aimed at continuous improvement, which could be justified economically only by having a high market share.

Hewlett-Packard (HP)

In 1997, HP was a multinational company present in some 120 countries, with more than 120,000 employees and net revenue of more than $40 billion. It specialized in the manufacture and sale of personal and business computing products, peripherals, products for the world of electronics, test and measurement products, networking products, medical electronic equipment, chemical analysis, handheld calculators, and electronic components. It had 141 sales and support offices spread across 27 countries, which, together with 95 national distributors, supported a network of more than 600 retail distributors. HP had 111 manufacturing centers in Europe, including the facility in Sant Cugat del Vallés in the province of Barcelona (Spain).

HP's Operations in Spain

Under a single legal identity (HP Española, S.A.), three different and separate operational organizations each had a different functional relationship to the parent company as shown in Table 2.

The *Territorial Sales Organization* was responsible for selling Hewlett-Packard's product lines in Spain, with its head office in Madrid. Its global headquarters was located in Geneva, Switzerland. The Territorial Sales Organization was responsible for developing and strengthening the network of local distributors and agents, some of which were exclusive HP agents who sold to large companies or specialists, although most were shops selling computer equipment for office use. HP provided specialized area managers and sales engineers for particular products if the market warranted it. In Spain two specialist sales representatives for

Table 1	Key Suppliers of Large-Format Printers	
Name	Graphic Applications Focus	Graphic and CAD Application Focus
Hewlett-Packard	XXX	
Encad	XXX	
Calcomp		XXX
Xerox		XXX
Scitex	XXX	
Epson	XXX	
Mutoh	XXX	
Roland	XXX	
SELEX		XXX

<table>
<tr><td colspan="2">Table 2</td><td colspan="3">Organizations Legally Integrated in Hewlett-Packard Española, S.A.</td></tr>
</table>

Name	Deployment	Description	Headquarters
Territorial Sales Organization	Territorial lines	Multiproduct	Geneva, Switzerland
Technical Support Organization	Territorial lines	Territorial lines	Boise, Idaho
Barcelona Division	Worldwide	Design and manufacture of large-format printers for the world market	San Diego, California

large-format printers visited the agents and called on potential customers with them. In addition to maintaining the network of distributors and agents, the Territorial Sales Organization was responsible for implementing the entire marketing plan for Spain, following general guidelines laid down by each product division while adapting them to the domestic market. Thus, the Territorial Sales Organization decided on prices, promotional and advertising campaigns, and so on, and kept in touch with the local market. Each product division's marketing department would suggest marketing campaigns and plans, even prices, but ultimately each country was responsible for its own decisions and for the results of HP's general sales plan.

The *Technical Support Organization* also had its head office in Madrid, but reported to its own headquarters in Boise, Idaho. It was responsible for providing technical assistance for all the products and equipment of all of HP's product divisions established in Spain. It had technicians and specialized workshops to attend to the needs of the users of the equipment. It also organized the official technical assistance services through associated technical service centers. Besides carrying out repairs under warranty, which were charged to the corresponding product division, it offered its customers maintenance plans and charged for all its services, including those provided by telephone, when the products and equipment were out of warranty.

The Territorial Sales Organization and the Technical Support Organization coexisted in all those countries in which HP had a direct market presence. In other countries, or in smaller or less developed territories, their functions were performed by one or more independent importer-distributors.

The third operational organization in Spain was *HP Barcelona Division* (HP-BCD). Located in Sant Cugat del Vallés, near Barcelona, HP-BCD designed and manufactured large-format printers, reporting to HP Inkjet Products Group, with its headquarters in San Diego, California.

HP Barcelona Division (HP-BCD)

Founded in 1985, HP-BCD was responsible for performing the research and development (R&D), marketing, and manufacturing functions for the entire range of HP large-format printers for the entire world market. It also manufactured a range of HP inkjet products for Europe. In 1997, HP-BCD had about 1,250 employees. Most of them were directly involved in the production processes, which for most of the year were carried out in four shifts (three shifts per day plus Saturdays and Sundays). The general management of HP-BCD oversaw six departments:

- Research and Development
- Marketing
- Finance
- Human Resources
- Production
- Internal Services

With exports of more than 90 billion pesetas, HP-BCD was one of Spain's largest exporters of computer products.

Under Ignacio Fonts's management, the marketing department at HP-BCD designed and monitored the global marketing strategy for the products manufactured by the division. It employed around 70 people. It was responsible for applying the funds corresponding to the total marketing campaign budget for large-format printers, and it negotiated with each country the specific campaigns each wanted to run. The marketing department was organized into four sections:

1. *Product marketing.* This section had two main functions: (1) To propose new products, which involved visiting customers and distributors to detect new needs, adding whatever qualitative data were needed, and (2) to work closely with the R&D department to ensure that products under development matched the established specifications.

2. *Market development.* This section developed the market for HP-BCD's products. It gave each Territorial Sales Organization guidelines on

a. Communication (advertising, publications, public-relations campaigns, etc.)

b. Prices (a price level for each country—normally a price band)

c. Promotions (for example, the Renewal Plan, whereby an old large-format printer would be accepted as a partial exchange for a new one with a variable discount depending on the age of the machine to be replaced, whether it was an HP machine or not, etc. This plan had recently been accepted by a large number of countries with great success.)

d. Product (which accessories should be included as standard).

3. *Technical support.* This third section of the marketing department was responsible for developing easy and effective technical support or assistance systems to be used by the Technical Support Organization in each country. The local Technical Support Organization in each country (reporting to Boise, Idaho) provided on-site technical assistance for all types of HP equipment. The technical support section of the marketing department at HP-BCD, however, dealt exclusively with large-format printers and acted only through the Technical Support Organization of each country.

   The technical support section of the marketing department at HP-BCD also trained repair technicians (support engineers), both those employed by HP and those employed by the distributors; monitored warranties; and even resolved technical problems that were too complex for the Technical Support Organizations to handle. For example, when a customer used a printer in very special conditions (such as an unusual software environment or special print media), the Technical Support Organization might not be able to respond appropriately and the limitations of the product under extreme conditions of use might be brought to light. By studying and and classifying the technical problems that emerged, the technical support section could help design and propose improvement plans for the development of future generations of printers.

4. *Strategic planning.* The main task of this section was to supply the marketing management with information and data relating to sales and marketing. To do this it closely monitored data on sales, installed customer base, reasons for purchasing HP products, and competition at world level. It was also responsible for planning sales and negotiating targets with the Territorial Sales Organizations.

The Origins of the New Web Site Project

In January 1997, a group of managers from the marketing department at HP-BCD discussed the possibility of communicating directly with the end users of HP's large-format printers. There was an installed base of some 500,000 of these printers scattered around the world. Very frequently, these end users were working in very diverse computing environments, often unlike those of typical users of HP products. The idea of offering this group of users a tool to communicate directly and at any time with HP-BCD seemed an excellent marketing opportunity. The initial idea was to publish a printed newsletter, in various languages, that would be mailed to all end users of HP large-format printers. This new channel of communication would complement the messages that were already being sent through HP distributors and the sales and technical support organizations. It would also complement the advertising messages and news that the end users of large-format printers received through the traditional mass media. The problem was that of the 500,000 printers sold, only 50,000 end users had registered when they purchased their large-format printer. HP-BCD did not have a complete and unified database with the names and addresses of the end users of the printers.

The Focus Groups

Before proceeding with the newsletter idea, six focus groups were organized with end users (two in Germany, two in the United States, and two in the United Kingdom), and the project was explained to them. The reaction of the participants in the focus groups was unanimous: what most concerned them was technical assistance.

The Web Site Project

From the outset, the possibility of using the World Wide Web as the channel for communicating directly with end users had been considered. This idea had been discarded on the grounds that many end users did not have Internet access and so would effectively be excluded. The pros and cons of using electronic media rather than print were now reconsidered. In the United States in 1996, around 70 percent of the users of large-format printers of any brand had Internet access; in 1997 in the world as a whole, the figure was 55 percent. In light of these findings, the idea of using paper was abandoned and the development of a new Web site was seen as the best alternative. After a number of brainstorming sessions involving various departments at Sant Cugat, the project began to take shape. It was assigned to Joan* Miró from strategic planning, who in a report dated July 1997 summed up the conclusions reached so far.

Description of the DesignJet Online Project

Target of the program: Users of HP DesignJet printers (not retailers or potential customers). Definition of the program's main objectives:

- Stimulate and speed up renewal of the installed base.
- Increase HP's involvement in the sale of consumables.
- Strengthen and increase the loyalty of our customers.
- Increase our knowledge of the market.

The main criterion for including services in this Web site will be whether they offer anything that may be considered to be "of added value" to the end user. Another important feature of the program is its interactive nature: We must allow the users of our printers to talk to us and ask us questions, and we must talk to them, proactively and continuously, whenever possible.

Services Included in the Program

For Your Eyes Only. This service will inform users directly of the appearance of any new HP product. Registered users will receive an e-mail on the date of the launch of a new product and will be able to visit the Web site if they want more information.
HP DesignJet Speaking! Online discussion forum for users. HP will not take part in the discussion. The messages will be 100 percent from users. In the future, when the necessary internal resources are available, we will have to try to reply to all the messages.
Feedback. Users will send in messages about the products and the solutions that HP offers. HP will reply, thanking each user for the message, but it will not give a personalized reply. In the future, if the volume of messages allows it, we should try to develop a team capable of answering them.

Quarterly Newsletter: *Big Impressions*. Quarterly publication by HP to keep its customers informed of important events in their business or field of activity. Registered users will receive an e-mail containing a list of the subjects covered in each newsletter as it is published, and will be able to visit the Web site if they want to read the full text of the articles.
Success Stories. Users will be able to share their positive experiences with their DesignJets. Each month, the best story will be rewarded with an HP polo shirt.
Warranty Status. Information on the coverage provided by the HP warranty.
Technical Assistance Information. List of Technical Assistance services available at HP. Contact addresses and telephone numbers for all countries.
Diagnostics for DesignJets. Online tool for breakdowns. (An interactive tool enabling users to resolve some technical problems affecting their printers themselves.)
Pass the word on! Users invite a colleague to visit the web site. (Positive word-of-mouth advertising, "member invites member.")
Driver Upgrades. Users will be able to download the latest versions of the drivers for HP DesignJets. Besides all the above-mentioned services, HP will at regular intervals send users an e-mail containing:

- Information on new products and drivers
- Update on the content of the Web site
- Newsletter: list of articles
- General news: Y2K effect, printing the new Euro symbol, etc.

Under the plan, it is estimated that each user will receive around 10 e-mails per year.

The Budget

The preliminary budget for printing the newsletter on paper had been put at $1 million per year. The same budget was maintained for the Web site project. More than 50 percent of this amount was earmarked for the development and subsequent maintenance of the computer program. The rest would be devoted to promotional material and other derivative costs. The figure of $1 million, though large, was acceptable within HP-BCD's general marketing budget.

How to Get the Rest of the HP Organization Involved?

Although HP-BCD had assigned two people full-time to the project and planned to continue to do so, other people in HP outside the Barcelona Divi-

Joan is the male name equivalent to *John* in the local Catalan language spoken in Barcelona and its surroundings.

sion needed to be actively involved. Joan Miró explained:

> Initially, there was no plan to reply to the e-mails from users. But we'd like the Technical Support Organization to e-mail a reply to all the messages that come in via the Web site. And we'd like the Territorial Sales Organizations throughout the world to publicize the Web site and inform people about it in all their publications. Also, we'd like them to pass on to us any recent information that may be of interest to their users, so that we can keep the site up-to-date and attractive.

What all these ideas that emerged during the various stages of project development amounted to was an organizational challenge. The project would require the collaboration of a large part of the structure of HP. It went beyond the scope of responsibility of the marketing department of HP-BCD.

The Reaction of HP's Other Organizational Units

The Technical Support Organization, which was responsible for Technical Assistance, had its headquarters in the United States. It was totally independent and had its own budgets. The collaboration of the Technical Support Organization was vital. The Web site was supposed to improve customer satisfaction, so what was needed was not just an attractive array of pull information on the Web site, such as self-solve tools, a driver library, Frequently Asked Questions (FAQ), and so on, but also giving the customers professional expertise in e-mails that provided tailored solutions to specific problems. "The Web site had to be connected to specific support groups that would answer the customers' e-mails in 24 hours and free of charge," said Joan Miró. "All of this had to be done in a variety of languages. Initially, we thought of using six languages: English, German, French, Italian, Portuguese, and Spanish. We at HP-BCD said that our program had to be free of charge; we argued that the Internet had created a low-cost standard, and we couldn't charge customers for the service."

One thing was clear: large-format printers accounted for only 3.5 percent of the Technical Support Organization's revenue. Their overall financial results were not going to be seriously affected if they did not charge for the assistance they provided over the Internet. But they could

not allow this practice to set a precedent for other HP products to stop charging for all of their services. It was also important to bear in mind that some distributors had their own profitable technical assistance organizations, whose interests the Web site could conceivably damage.

With the Territorial Sales Organization the problem was even more complicated. Being close to the customer in each territory, it welcomed the idea of giving better service. But who would decide the content of the marketing messages to be sent to end users—HP-BCD? Would HP-BCD tell the users what they wanted when they wanted? For the Territorial Sales Organization it was very important that its permission be sought first, but how? How could they impose territorial limits on the Web site? How could the new channel of communication be coordinated with the marketing and sales campaigns in each individual country? And what about distributors? How would the distributors react to the project? Should they be consulted? Would they feel threatened?

The Decision

Ignacio Fonts had no doubt that it would be difficult to secure the formal approval of all the organizations affected. He also fully realized that, to work well, the project would require sufficient financial and human resources and a great effort of coordination and communication, both internal and external. He was convinced that HP-BCD and he himself as marketing director had the power and the resources to set up the new Web site. But the risks, both internal and external, were not to be underestimated.

Was it worth the effort? HP-BCD's marketing department already issued guidelines for large-format printers to all the Territorial Sales and Technical Support Organizations, and they adapted the guidelines to the circumstances in their countries. But the marketing department had never been directly in touch with HP customers before, which prompted some reservations.

Within the marketing department, Fonts was not even sure who should develop and maintain the Web site. Initially, the project had been assigned to strategic planning, but should that section continue to be in charge of the development or start-up of the new project? All the heads of the four sections of the marketing department agreed that the new project should go ahead, but their opinions did not coincide exactly, as can be seen from the following comments:

- *Product marketing:* "There's no doubt that it may be a very effective tool for our work.

It is essential for us to know our customers' future needs, and this project will help us achieve that. Even before we launch a new project, when we do the beta test it will be easy for us to identify the users who we want to test out prototypes. Right now, it is difficult for us to find the most appropriate users for our tests."

- *Market development:* "Essentially, it is a tool for developing the market and our department. The culture of horizontal and vertical communication is very well established in HP. Deciding what relationship we should have with other departments and divisions is a challenge for us; although we don't have the means or the experience of communicating as intensely as this, communication has always been part of our job."

- *Technical support:* "It is very clearly a question of improving the satisfaction of the users of our printers, and we've always played a key role in that. We need to ensure that the support units get involved at an international level. It may not depend on us alone, but judging by the results of the focus groups, we are undoubtedly one of the keys to success."

- *Strategic planning:* "The Web site is a window through which users will be able to make contact with HP, and they won't be familiar with our internal organization. They'll want answers, and we'll try to ensure that the messages we receive are answered by those in our organization responsible for doing so, whatever department or division they belong to. Coordinating between the different departments is part of my regular job."

Creating ideas is easy up to a point, but making them work is more difficult, thought Fonts. Are we about to jeopardize the prestige of HP-BCD? Are there any changes we ought to make? Would the users even appreciate the new Web site? Would they value all the services offered? If the services were not well received, would HP be able to change its mind and back out, once the site had been launched and publicized?

All these doubts crowded into Fonts's mind as he prepared for the meeting with the heads of his department and drew up the following list of the subjects that would have to be discussed before deciding whether or not to give the project his final approval.

HP-BCD Marketing Department Meeting
Monday, September 8, 1997
Room GD 124, 9:30 A.M.

- Analysis of costs, risks, and benefits of this new Web project
- Key success factors; ways to measure and to ensure success
- Internal marketing plan: How to secure the collaboration of the territorial organizations
- Approval or suggestions for change of the new Web site contents
- Budget and organizational matters
- Appointment of Web manager responsible for site launch, development and upkeep.

Questions for Discussion

1. What is your evaluation of the costs and benefits of this project?
2. How could the HP-BCD marketing team measure the level of success of the new Web site?
3. What action plans could the marketing team design and implement in order to increase the Web site's success?
4. What could be done to further involve and commit the HP Sales and Technical Support Organizations?
5. Would you suggest any changes in the specific contents of the new Web pages? Which ones? Why?
6. In your opinion, will the new Web project generate further changes in the HP organization?
7. Who should be designated as Web master, to be in charge of the new Web site? What should be the new job description?

The F-18 Hornet Offset

In May 1992, the Finnish government's selection of the F/A-18 Hornet over the Swedish JAS-39 Gripen, the French Mirage 2000–5, and fellow American F-16 to modernize the fighter fleet of its air force was a major boost to McDonnell Douglas (MDC) in an otherwise quiet market. The deal would involve the sale of 57 F-18 Cs and 7 F-18 Ds at a cost of FIM 9.5 billion (approximately $2 billion). The Finnish version will have an "F" for "fighter" (rather than F/A) because the attack dimension is not included. Deliveries would take place between 1995 and 2000. Armaments would add another $1 billion to the deal.

SOURCES: This case study was written by Ilkka A. Ronkainen and funded in part by a grant from the Business and International Education Program of the U.S. Department of Education. The assistance of the various organizations cited in the case is appreciated. Special thanks to David Danjczek of the Manufacturers Alliance. For more information, see **http://www.boeing.com/defense-space/military/fa18/fa18.htm**; **http://geae.net/geenginecenter/service_militaryavi.html**; **http://www.northgrum.com**; **http://www.hughes.com**.

Winning the contract was critical since MDC had been on the losing side of two major aircraft competitions in the United States in 1991. In addition, one of its major projects with the U.S. Navy had been terminated (the A-12), and the government of the Republic of Korea had changed its mind to buy F-16 aircraft after it already had an agreement with MDC for F/A-18 Hornets.

However, the $2 billion will not be earned without strings attached. Contractually, McDonnell Douglas and its main subcontractors (Northrop, General Electric, and General Motors's subsidiary Hughes), the "F-18 Team," are obligated to facilitate an equivalent amount of business for Finnish industry over a ten-year period (1992–2002) using various offset arrangements.

Offsets

Offsets are various forms of industrial and business activities required as a condition of purchase. They are an obligation imposed on the seller in major (most often military hardware) purchases by or for foreign governments to minimize any trade imbalance or other adverse economic impact caused by the outflow of currency required to pay for such purchases. In wealthier countries, it is often used for establishing infrastructure. Two basic types of offset arrangements exist: direct and indirect (as seen in Figure 1). Although offsets have long been associated only with the defense sector, there are now increasing demands for offsets in commercial sales where the government is the purchaser or user.

647

Figure I   The Offset Process

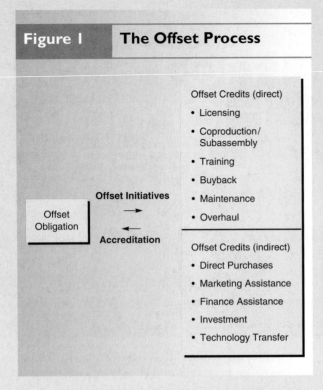

Offset Obligation

Offset Initiatives →
← **Accreditation**

Offset Credits (direct)
- Licensing
- Coproduction/ Subassembly
- Training
- Buyback
- Maintenance
- Overhaul

Offset Credits (indirect)
- Direct Purchases
- Marketing Assistance
- Finance Assistance
- Investment
- Technology Transfer

From 1993 to 1998, 279 new offset agreements totaling $21 billion were reported by U.S. defense exporters. These supported $35 billion in U.S. export sales. The average term for completing the offset agreements was 84 months. The agreements were concluded with a total of 30 nations, with 70 percent attributed to European nations. Although the average offset requirement is 82 percent for Europe, many countries require 100 percent. Outside of Europe, the overall requirement is 37 percent; however, there are exceptions, such as Canada's 168 percent average.

Direct offset consists of product-related manufacturing or assembly either for the purposes of the project in question only or for a longer-term partnership. The purchase, therefore, enables the purchaser to be involved in the manufacturing process. Various Spanish companies produce dorsal covers, rudders, aft fuselage panels, and speed brakes for the F/A-18s designated for the Spanish Air Force. In addition to coproduction arrangements, licensed production is prominent. Examples include Egypt producing U.S. M1-A1 tanks, China producing MDC's MD-82 aircraft, and Korea assembling the F-16 fighter. An integral part of these arrangements is the training of the local employees. Training is not only for production/ assembly purposes but also for maintenance and overhaul of the equipment in the longer term. Some offsets have buyback provisions; that is, the seller is obligated to purchase output from the facility or operations it has set up or licensed. For example, Westland takes up an agreed level

of parts and components from the Korean plant that produces Lynx Helicopters under license. In practice, therefore, direct offsets amount to technology transfer.

Indirect offsets are deals that involve products, investments, and so forth that are not to be used in the original sales contract but will satisfy part of the seller's "local" obligation. Direct purchases of raw materials, equipment, or supplies by the seller or its suppliers from the offset customer country present the clearest case of indirect offsets. These offset arrangements are analogous to counterpurchases and switch trading. Sellers faced with offset obligations work closely with their supplier base, some having goals of increasing supplier participation in excess of 50 percent. Teamwork does make the process more effective and efficient. There are various business activities taking place and procurement decisions being made by one of the sellers or its suppliers without offset needs that others may be able to use as offset credit to satisfy an indirect obligation.

Many governments see offsets as a mechanism to develop their indigenous business and industrial sectors. Training in management techniques may be attractive to both parties. The upgrading of skills may be seen by the government as more critical for improving international competitiveness than efforts focused only on hardware. For the seller, training is relatively inexpensive, but it provides good credits because of its political benefit.

An important dimension of the developmental effort will relate to exports. This may involve the analysis of business sectors showing the greatest foreign market potential, improving organizational and product readiness, conducting market research (e.g., estimating demand or assessing competition), identifying buyers or partners for foreign market development, or assisting in the export process (e.g., company visits, support in negotiations and reaching a final agreement, facilitating trial/sample shipments, handling documentation needs).

Sales are often won or lost on the availability of financing and favorable credit terms to the buyer. Financing packages put together by one of the seller's entities, if it is critical in winning the bid, will earn offset credits.

Buyer nations focusing on industrial development and technology transfer have negotiated contracts that call for offsetting the cost of their purchases through investments. Saudi Arabian purchases of military technology have recently been tied to sellers' willingness to invest in manufacturing plants, defense-related industries, or special-interest projects in the country. British Aerospace, for example, has agreed to invest in factories for the production of farm feed and sanitary ware.

Most often, the final offset deal includes a combination of activities, both direct and indirect vis-à-vis the sale, and no two offset deals are alike. With increasing frequency, governments may require "pre-deal counterpurchases" as a sign of commitment and ability to deliver should they be awarded the contract. Some companies, such as United Technologies, argue that there is limited advantage in carrying out offset activities in advance of the contract, unless the buyer agrees to a firm commitment. While none of the bidders may like it, buyer's market conditions give them

very little choice to argue. Even if a bidder loses the deal, it can always attempt to sell its offset credits to the winner or use the credits in conjunction with other sales that one of its divisions may have. Some of the companies involved in the bidding in Finland maintain offset accounts with the Finnish government.

McDonnell's Deal with the Finnish Air Force

The F/A-18 Hornet is a twin-engine, twin-tail, multi-mission tactical aircraft that can be operated from aircraft carriers or from land bases (see Table 1).

Table 1   F/A-18 Hornet Strike Fighter

Prime contractor	McDonnell Douglas
Principal subcontractor	Northrop Corporation
Type	Single- (C) and two-seat (D), twin-turbofan for fighter and attack missions
Power Plant	Two General Electric F404-GE-402 (enhanced performance engine)
Thrust	4,800 kp each (approx.)
Afterburning thrust	8,000 kp each (approx.)
Dimensions	
Length	17.07 m
Span	11.43 m
Wing area	37.16 m^2
Height	4.66 m
Weights	
Empty	10,455 kg
Normal takeoff	16,650 kg
Maximum takeoff	22,328 kg
Wing loading	450 kg/m^2
Fuel (internal)	6,435 litre (4,925 kg)
Fuel (with external tanks)	7,687 litre
Armament	
Cannon	One General Electric M61A-1 Vulcan rotary-barrel 20-mm
Missiles	Six AIM-9 Sidewinder air-to-air
	Four AIM-7 Sparrow
	Six AIM-120 AMRAAM
Radar	AN/APG-73 multi-mode air-to-air and air-to-surface
Performance	
Takeoff distance	430 m
Landing distance	850 m
Fighter-mission radius	> 740 km
Maximum speed	1.8 Mach (1,915 km/h) at high altitude
	1.0 Mach at intermediate power
Service ceiling	15,240 m
Payload	7,710 kg
Used since	1983
Expected manufacturing lifetime	2000+
Users	USA, Australia, Canada, Spain, Switzerland, and Kuwait
Ordered quantity	1,168

It is both a fighter (air-to-air) and an attack (air-to-ground) aircraft. McDonnell Aircraft Company, a division of MDC, is the prime contractor for the F/A-18. Subcontractors include General Electric for the Hornet's smokeless F404 low-bypass turbofan engines, Hughes Aircraft Company for the APG-73 radar, and Northrop Corporation for the airframe. Approximately 1,100 F/A-18s have been delivered worldwide. Although it had been in use by the United States since 1983, it had been (and can continue to be) upgraded during its operational lifetime. Furthermore, it had proven its combat readiness in the Gulf War.

Only since June 1990 has the F/A-18 been available to countries that are not members of the North Atlantic Treaty Organization (NATO). The change in U.S. government position resulted from the rapidly changed East-West political situation. The attractive deals available in neutral countries such as Switzerland and Finland helped push the government as well. When the Finnish Air Force initiated its program in 1986, MDC was not invited to (and would not have been able to) offer a bid because of U.S. government restrictions. Finland is prohibited by World War II peace accords from having attack aircraft, hence the designation F-18.

The Finnish Government Position

The Finnish government's role in the deal had two critical dimensions: one related to the choice of the aircraft, the other related to managing the offset agreement in a fashion to maximize the benefit to the country's industry for the long term.

Selecting the Fighter

In 1986, the Finnish Air Force (FAF) decided to replace its aging Swedish-made Drakens and Soviet-made MIG-21s, which made up three fighter squadrons. At that time, the remaining service life of these aircraft was estimated to be 15 years, calling for the new squadrons to be operational by the year 2000 and to be up-to-date even in 2025. Finland, due to its strategic geographic location, has always needed a reliable air defense system. The position of neutrality adopted by Finland had favored split procurement between Eastern and Western suppliers until the collapse of the Soviet Union in December 1991 made it politically possible to purchase fighters from a single Western supplier.

The first significant contacts with potential bidders were made in 1988, and in February 1990, the FAF requested proposals from the French

Dassault-Breguet, Sweden's Industrigruppen JAS, and General Dynamics in the United States for 40 fighters and trainer aircraft. In January 1991, the bid was amended to 60 fighters and seven trainers. Three months later, MDC joined the bidding, and by July 1991, binding bids were received from all four manufacturers.

During the evaluative period, the four bidders tried to gain favor for their alternative. One approach was the provision of deals for Finnish companies as "pre-deal counterpurchases." For example, General Dynamics negotiated for Vaisala (a major Finnish electronics firm) to become a subcontractor of specialty sensors for the F-16. Before the final decision, the Swedish bidder had arranged for deals worth $250 million for Finnish companies, the French for over $100 million, and General Dynamics for $40 million. MDC, due to its later start, had none to speak of. Other tactics were used as well. The Swedes pointed out to long ties that the countries have had, and especially to the possibilities to develop them further on the economic front. As a matter of fact, offsets were the main appeal of the Swedish bid since the aircraft itself was facing development cost overruns and delays. The French reminded the Finnish government that choosing a European fighter might help in Finland's bid to join the European Union (EU) in 1995. Since the FAF prefers the U.S. AMRAAM missile system for its new fighters, the U.S. government cautioned that its availability depended on the choice of the fighter. The companies themselves also worked on making their bid sweeter: Just before the official announcement, General Dynamics improved its offer to include 67 aircraft for the budgeted sum and a guarantee of 125 percent offsets; that is, the amount of in-country participation would be 125 percent of the sale price paid by the Finnish government for the aircraft.

After extensive flight testing both in the producers' countries and in Finland (especially for winter conditions), the Hornet was chosen as the winner. Despite the high absolute cost of the aircraft (only 57 will be bought versus 60), the Hornet's cost-effectiveness relative to performance was high. The other alternatives were each perceived to have problems: The JAS-39 Gripen had the teething problems of a brand-new aircraft; the Mirage's model 2000–5 has not yet been produced; and the F-16 may be coming to the end of its product life cycle. The MIG-29 from the Soviet Union/Russia was never seriously in the running due to the political turmoil in that country. Some did propose purchasing the needed three squadrons from the stockpiles of the defunct East Germany (and they could have been had quite economically), but the uncertainties were too great for a strategically important product.

Working Out the Offsets

Typically, a specific committee is set up by the government to evaluate which arrangements qualify as part of the offset. In Finland's case, the Finnish Offset Committee (FOC) consists of five members with the Ministries of Defense, Foreign Affairs, and Industry and Trade represented. Its task is to provide recommendations as to which export contracts qualify and which do not. The Technical Working Group was set up to support its decision making, especially in cases concerning technology transfer. From 1977 to 1991, the procedures and final decisions were made by the Ministry of Defense; since then, the responsibility has been transferred to the Ministry of Trade and Industry (see Figure 2). The transfer was logical given the increased demands and expectations on the trade and technology fronts of the F/A-18 deal.

When the committee was established in 1977 in conjunction with a major military purchase, almost all contracts qualified until an export developmental role for offsets was outlined. The Finnish exporter is required to show that the offset agreement played a pivotal role in securing its particular contract.

Two different approaches are taken by the government to attain its developmental objective. First, the government will not make available (or give offset credit for) counterpurchasing goods that already have established market positions unless the counterpurchaser can show that the particular sale would not have materialized without its support (e.g., through distribution or financing). Second, the government will use compensation "multipliers" for the first time. While previous deals were executed on a one-on-one basis, the government now wants, through the use of multipliers, direct purchases to certain industries or types of companies. For example, in the case of small or medium-sized companies, a multiplier of two may be used; that is, a purchase of $500,000 from such a firm will satisfy a $1 million share of the counterpurchaser's requirement. Attractive multipliers also may be used that may generate long-term export opportunities or support Finland's indigenous arms or other targeted industry. Similarly, the seller may also insist on the use of multipliers. In the case of technology transfer, the seller may request a high multiplier because of the high initial cost of research and development that may have gone into the technology licensed or provided to the joint venture as well as its relative importance to the recipient country's economic development.

Finnish industry is working closely with the government on two fronts. The Finnish Industrial Offset Consortium (FINDOC) was established to collaborate with the Finnish Foreign Trade Association (a quasi-governmental organization) on trade development. FINDOC's 21 members represent 15 main business areas (e.g., aircraft, shipbuilding,

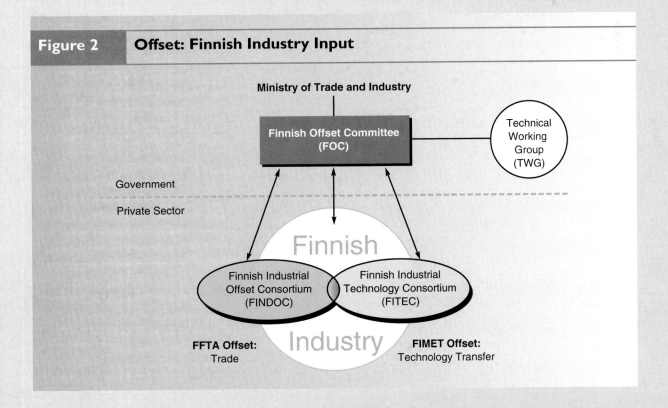

Figure 2   Offset: Finnish Industry Input

pulp and paper machinery, and metal and engineering) and are among the main Finnish exporters. Their consortium was set up to take advantage of offset opportunities more efficiently and to provide a focal point for the F-18 Team's efforts. For example, MDC and FINDOC arranged for a familiarization trip to the United States for interested Finnish businesses in the fall of 1992. For those companies not in FINDOC, it is the task of the FFTA to provide information on possibilities to benefit from the deal. The Finnish Industrial Technology Consortium (FITEC) was established to facilitate technology transfer to and from the Finnish metal and engineering industries.

The F-18 Team's Position

The monies related to offset management and associated development are not generally allowed as a separate cost in the sales contract. Profit margins for aircraft sales are narrow, and any additional costs must be watched closely. Extraordinary demands by the buyer make bidding more challenging and time-consuming. For example, the customer may want extensive changes in the product without changes in the final price. Switzerland wanted major alterations made to the airframe and additional equipment, which made its total cost per plane higher than the price in Finland. In the experience of high-tech firms, the add-on for direct offsets ranges from 3 to 8 percent, which has to be incorporated into the feasibility plans. Offsets have to make good business sense and, once agreed to, successfully executed.

Competing for the Deal

In accepting the offer to bid for the FAF deal, the F-18 Team believed it had only a 5 percent chance to win the deal but, given its size, decided to go ahead. From the time it received a request to bid from the FAF, MDC had three months to prepare its proposal. The only main negative factor from the short preparation time was MDC's inability to arrange for "prepurchase" deals and generate goodwill with the constituents.

After two fact-finding missions to Finland, MDC established an office in Helsinki in August 1991. The decision to have a full-time office in Finland (compared to the competitors whose representatives were in Helsinki two days a week on the average) was made based on the experiences from Korea and Switzerland. MDC's approach was to be ready and able to help the customer in terms of information and be involved with all the constituents of the process, such as the testing groups of the FAF, the Ministry of Defense (owners of the program), and the Parliament (supporters of the program).

Beyond the technical merits of the Hornet, MDC's capabilities in meeting the pending offset obligations were a critical factor in winning the deal. MDC had by 1992 a total of 100 offset programs in 25 countries with a value of $8 billion, and its track record in administering them was excellent. Another factor in MDC's favor was its long-term relationship with Finnair, the national airline. Finnair's aircraft have predominantly come from MDC, from the DC-2 in 1941 to the MD-11 aircraft delivered in 1991.

Satisfying the Offset Obligation

Offset deals are not barter where the seller and the buyer swap products of equal value over a relatively short time period. The F-18 Team members had to complete the offset program by the year 2002 through a number of different elements including marketing assistance, export development, technology transfer, team purchases, and investment financing. One of the major beneficiaries of the offset arrangement was Patria Finnavitec, the only major aircraft manufacturer in Finland. Patria Finnavitec assembled the 57 C-versions in Finland and also counted on the F-18 Team's connections to open markets for its Redigo trainer aircraft. The F-18 Team worked with Finnish companies to develop exports for their products and services by identifying potential buyers and introducing the two parties to each other. Purchases could come from within the contractor companies, suppliers to the F-18 contractors, and third parties. The motivation for completing offset projects was financial penalties for the prime team members if they do not meet contract deadlines.

However, no one in the F-18 Team or among its suppliers was obligated to engage in a given transaction just because Finland purchased fighters from McDonnell Douglas. The key point was that products must meet specifications, delivery dates, and price criteria to be successfully sold in any market. After an appropriate purchase had taken place, the F-18 Team received offset credit based on the Finnish-manufactured content of the transaction value as approved by the Finnish Offset Committee. For example, when Finnyards won the bid to build a passenger ferry for the Danish Stena Line, Northrop received offset credits due to its role in financing Finnyard's bid.

The offset obligations were not limited to the United States. The team had offset partners all over the world because the members operate worldwide. Furthermore, given the long time frame involved, there were no pressing time constraints on the members to earn offset credits.

Since 1992, the MDC office in Helsinki had two officers: one in charge of the aircraft, the other focused in offsets. Due to the worst recession in recent Finnish history, the response to the offset program was unprecedented, and the office was inundated with requests for information and deals.

Results

By October 2002 the program was complete, with Boeing having delivered all of the 64 aircraft early and satisfied the offset obligations ahead of schedule. A total of $3.345 billion of credits had been granted against the required minimum of $3 billion. Direct offsets accounted for 15 percent and indirect offsets 85 percent of the credits earned. Nearly 600 business transactions had been part of the indirect credits originating from 210 Finnish companies, 114 of which were small and medium-sized enterprises (SMEs). Exports had been directed at 30 different countries.

Politically, the deal enhanced Finnish–U.S. relations at a time of spectacular changes. Finnish industry was supported at a time when major shifts occurred in markets and their potential. The United States is currently Finland's fourth largest trading partner, having surpassed Russia. While FINDOC companies generated, as expected, a substantial share (48 percent) of the business transactions, SMEs benefited as well. They generated 140 projects, for a total of nearly $500 million in sales. Some broke into world markets as a result of the offset deal.

Exports accounted for nearly two-thirds of the indirect offset credits. However, significant activity also centered on technology transfer and investments. For example, Aker Finnyards received technology transfers to allow it to move into the hovercraft market where it has already done well with its prototype vessel for the Finnish Navy. SMEs benefited through marketing assistance programs (which constituted 10 percent of the total credits). For example, groups of SME managers were able to use the facilities of General Electric Trading in New York while getting accustomed to the U.S. business climate and establishing relationships with intermediaries and clients.

Questions for Discussion

1. Why would the members of the F-18 Team, McDonnell Douglas, Northrop, General Electric, and Hughes agree to such a deal rather than insist on a money-based transaction?
2. After the deal was signed, many Finnish companies expected that contracts and money would start rolling in by merely calling up McDonnell Douglas. What are the fundamental flaws of this thinking?
3. Why do Eastern governments typically take an unsupportive stance on countertrade arrangements?
4. Comment on this statement: "Offset arrangements involving overseas production that permits a foreign government or producer to acquire the technical information to manufacture all or part of a U.S.-origin article trade short-term sales for long-term loss of market position."

Recommended Readings

"Countertrade's Growth Continues." *BarterNews* 27 (1993): 54–55.

"Offsets in the Aerospace Industry." *BarterNews* 27 (1993): 56–57.

"Investing, Licensing, and Trading Conditions Abroad: Saudi Arabia." *Business International,* May 15, 1990, 5.

Jakubik, Maria, Irina Kabirova, Tapani Koivunen, Päivi Lähtevänoja, and Denice Stanfors. *Finnish Air Force Buying Fighters.* Helsinki School of Economics, September 24, 1993.

State Audit Office. *Offsets in the Procurement of Hornet Fighters.* Helsinki, Finland: Edita, 1999, chapter 1.

U.S. Department of Commerce. *Offsets in Defense Trade.* Washington, DC: Office of Strategic Industries and Economic Security, May 2001, overview.

Kadimi Group of Companies (India): Exports

itting in his comfortable office in New Delhi's busy commercial district, Rakesh Gupta, one of two partners at Kadimi, reflected on the meeting he had that morning with Rajiv Agarwal, partner and managing director. Of late, the export department of the company had been receiving an unusually high number of complaints from its overseas customers. Previously, such complaints had been sporadic and had been dealt with on a case-by-case basis by the two partners. However, the new spate of export-related complaints as well as growing consistency among worldwide complaints had put into question Kadimi's fluid policies and practices with regard to export complaint management. As he grappled with the ideas and concerns that were put forth in the meeting, Gupta wondered if Kadimi needed to adopt a complaint management system that would address the complaints in a consistent manner.

The Firm's Activities

The Kadimi Group began operations in 1977 with the incorporation of its first division, Kadimi International. Functioning solely as a distributor, the division represented some of the leading fastener-related international companies to serve India's growing fastener and electronic component indus-

tries. Then, in 1984, Kadimi obtained technical collaboration with OSG Corporation, Japan to manufacture thread-rolling dies in India. In 1991, a new facility for manufacturing self-tapping screws was added.

By 1993, the company had developed a strong competence in manufacturing. The directors now desired to diversify the manufacturing activities by entering a new industry. At this time, the popularity of natural stones (slates, sandstones, and quartzites) was increasing in many parts of the world as an alternative to marble and granite for interior and exterior building facades and flooring. Kadimi decided to set up a new plant to process natural stone and create stone tiles and blocks. As opposed to their engineering products, however, the stone products were strictly intended for exports due to limited demand for natural stone in India.

Since then, the company has enjoyed phenomenal success, especially with exports of stone products. Exports have been growing steadily at approximately 15 percent per year and will soon become the main source of revenue for the company. Recently, the company acquired a third plant to add capacity for natural stone processing, as well as to set up new capabilities in marble and granite processing for both the domestic and foreign markets.

With offices in New Delhi, Madras, and Singapore, Kadimi International today supplies India's fastener and electronic component industries with nut/bolt-making machinery, thread-rolling dies, cold heading quality steel, taps, endmills, and coil-winding machines imported from manufacturers in Korea, Japan, Taiwan, Singapore, Brazil, Italy, and

SOURCE: MBA Candidates Rahul Agarwal, Raphael Moreau, and Dixie Wang prepared this case under the supervision of Professor Michael Czinkota © 2001 as the basis for class discussion rather than to illustrate either effective or ineffective handling of an administrative situation.

the United States. The export department within the division is responsible for handling exports of products and components sourced externally (machinery, castor oil, and certain cutting tools), as well as manufactured in-house (self-tapping screws, thread-rolling dies, and stone products).

Exports

Kadimi's exports could be broken down into two major product groups: engineering components and stone products. The engineering components that were exported included thread-rolling dies and self-tapping screws, both of which were manufactured at Kadimi's plant in New Delhi. High-quality steel was imported from Korea and Thailand to manufacture these components. Manufacturing assistance had been obtained from a Japanese firm, and by 1996, multiple quality control mechanisms were in place to produce high-quality components. As such, complaints from overseas Original Equipment Manufacturers (OEMs) were rare. Quality was far more important than price in the purchasing decision for industrial components, and Kadimi had priced their products at a slight premium with respect to domestic competitors and at par with foreign competitors. Nevertheless, sales were steady and customers were pressuring Kadimi to increase the scope of their operations to include more components.

Stone products, however, were a new addition to the Kadimi family and brought with them a whole new set of manufacturing processes and marketing issues. The stone tile industry, unlike the engineering component industry, was rife with competitors, all producing a relatively similar product. Competition was especially pronounced in the ceramic tile industry, where the major players were now attempting to woo the market with superior designs. Kadimi was facing intense pressure to compete on price or offer new and differentiated products.

Despite the difficulties it encountered in stone exports, Kadimi was heavily dependent on its exporting activities. In 1996, almost 50 percent of Kadimi's revenues and 60 percent of its profits came from the export division. Of the export revenues, almost 90 percent were from exports of stone products.

Stone Industry

The natural stone industry was dominated by relatively few producers in select countries of Europe and Asia. This geographic concentration was a direct consequence of the availability of natural stone mines (slates, sandstones, and quartzites) that were scattered mainly in Southern Europe, India, and Indonesia. Success in this industry was dependent on an uninterrupted supply of natural stone from the mines. Not surprisingly, most producers owned mines themselves, or had exclusive arrangements with certain mine owners. However, along with stone availability, stone variability was also a success factor. Natural stone was mined straight from the earth and, very often, fluctuations in the earth's temperature and topography produced dramatic variations in stone colors and textures. Unusual stone colors and textures fetched a premium on world markets. Sometimes, however, the mined stone possessed faults such as spots or cracks that impaired the marketability of the finished product.

Kadimi sourced its stone from a number of quarries located in northern and southern India. For each stone variety, the company typically maintained a single supplier. Distances between the quarries and Kadimi's plant were significant. Road transportation was the most economical and practical option. It took from two to four days for the raw stone to be transported in trucks from the mines to the plant. The company had permanently stationed a company representative at each of the leading quarries to ensure monitoring of stone quality, timely ordering, and safe delivery to the plant. Kadimi also maintained limited stocks of the most popular stones, but due to storage and mining constraints, could not maintain stocks for very long.

Based upon its experience over a few years, Kadimi had developed an extensive nomenclature for its slate, sandstone, and quartzite varieties, despite the existence of variations within each variety. Stones that were mined in the same region or that possessed similar qualities (strength, color, recommended use, etc.) were grouped into families. For instance, the Peacock range of slates was multicolored and was obtained from the same mine in northern India. Other groupings within slates, sandstones, and quartzites included the Spectra range, the Everest range, and the Kanchan range. Several stones did not fit into any category and were marketed as unique stones. In all, Kadimi stocked 36 varieties of stones and was in constant search of new varieties to add to its stone repertoire. However, the addition of new stones was dependent on sufficient and regular availability of the stone, as well as favorable customer response to it. Therefore, Kadimi was very careful in selecting new stones and very often tested the response to a new stone at stone fairs before deciding to stock it.

The company marketed both its engineering and stone products at industrial and consumer fairs held worldwide at different times during the year. Engineering exports were primarily directed at key electronic and textile manufacturing facilities located in Asia. The company regularly participated in the annual industrial fairs held in Singapore, Japan, Korea, and Taiwan. By 1996, however, the company had developed a large base of regular customers for its engineering components and marketing was not as extensively required as before.

Stone products, on the other hand, required intensive and continuous marketing efforts. Kadimi was a regular participant in stone fairs held in Orlando, Nuremberg, Madrid, Verona, and Tokyo. Besides providing increased visibility for Kadimi products to worldwide customers, these fairs were strategically used by the company to introduce new products (such as new finishes, new stones, and new applications) and to perceive emerging trends in stone processing technology.

Kadimi's strategy in the stone business was to become the innovator and create new value for the commoditized industry. It did so by:

- Offering new and unusual stones to worldwide buyers
- Creating new stone textures and finishes (e.g., honed, polished, and calibrated)
- Developing customized stone applications (e.g., flooring and wall designs) for each client.

As a result of these efforts, Kadimi soon became the leading stone exporter in India. With its unique product finishes and stone offerings, it also managed to raise the bar for all local stone exporters, most of whom were fly-by-night producers with low-key operations. The company's mission was to compete globally and create value-added services in the stone industry.

The Export Process

The small number of engineering component exports was shipped directly to the OEM within a few days of order placement. Lead times were short, and product specifications did not require extensive retooling. Billing and handling was managed entirely by the Singapore office. Bulk purchases made by the small number of regular clients had enabled the Singapore office to set up individual accounts with the largest buyers. Export-related complaints were also handled largely by the Singapore office, which had developed long-standing relationships with the buyers in the Asia/Pacific region.

Stone exports presented a more complicated scenario. Unlike component exports, both distributors and retailers as well as individual customers demanded stone products. Due to economic efficiencies derived from bulk shipping, Kadimi was unable to directly serve individual customers and many small retailers, who all wanted small quantities. In the future, Kadimi anticipated having local distributors for its products in several countries. However, for the time being, only wholesaler orders were entertained.

Typically, a wholesaler placed an order with Kadimi at a stone fair or within a few months of a fair. In either case, orders were placed in terms of "containers."[1] Stone tiles were packed into wooden crates that were then loaded into containers at a port. Each container had capacity for 16 crates, each of which held approximately 50–250 tiles, depending on the size and thickness of the tiles. Kadimi did not encourage orders for less than a full container unless the buyer was willing to bear the shipping cost for the entire container. (Bundling of several small orders into a single container was not allowed by the Indian port authorities.) Once the order was placed, the buyer then had to open a Letter of Credit (LC) with his bank that would guarantee payment to Kadimi. As opposed to some local competitors, Kadimi relied solely on the LC method of payment. There was no flexibility in this policy. Once the LC was opened, the order was executed with a 45-day lead time (not including the shipping time). All activities related to production and packaging were handled at the same plant. Once the crates were ready, they were transported by trucks to the Indian port city of Madras for shipment. The shipping agreement was always Free-On-Board, Madras.[2] Hamburg was the most frequent destination for Kadimi's large European customer base, and average shipping times were in excess of a month. In all, the company had about 50 worldwide customers, and the average transaction amount per container ranged from $4,000 to $15,000, with a median around $6,000.[3] Since 1994, the number of containers shipped annually had increased every year to reach 95 containers in 1996, and was expected to climb to 150 containers in 1997. The company enjoyed a very healthy 22 percent margin (average) on its stone exports, mainly as a result of its differentiation strategy.

Export Complaints

Complaints, if any, were usually received by Kadimi upon receipt of the shipment by the customer (approximately 45 days after shipment from

India). Complaints were typically about product defects (70 percent) or shipping (30 percent). Almost all the product defect complaints were about the quality of the mined stone. Foreign customers were particularly conscious about spots or blemishes on the stone. Most of the times, these marks were created in the mining process. Shipping complaints were mainly about improper wooden crate packaging that had resulted in damage to certain tiles. Kadimi had not been able to develop packaging materials that were both safe and cost-efficient. Recently, reinforced fiberglass crates were being explored as a packaging alternative, although it was uncertain whether the new packaging could be obtained quickly and in bulk from local suppliers.

Complaints were received from about 5 percent of all customers. Letters and faxes were the primary media for communication, although Kadimi's recently developed Web site was becoming very popular as both a marketing and feedback channel.

Once a complaint was received, it was directed to the attention of either of the two partners. Depending upon the nature of the complaint (product vs. delivery), relationship to the customer (transaction vs. repeat), and shipment size, the complaint would be settled by either issuing a discount or replacing the product in a future shipment. In reaching a decision, the partners typically consulted with the export department manager. Kadimi's intention was to make instant reparation to the dissatisfied client, especially if he was perceived to be a repeat customer. Information about customer complaints circulated freely among the company's employees. However, only the relevant personnel (production/delivery/sales managers) were formally made aware of such shortcomings in their respective tasks.

Once the complaint was resolved, the matter was over for all practical purposes. Unless a particular complaint manifested itself again and again, past complaints were usually buried under the paperwork. There was no export complaint system in place to assimilate the complaint data and highlight existing problem areas or forecast emerging ones. The company was inundated with orders and priority was given for order fulfillment, rather than problem solving. In the past year alone, the company had achieved 50 percent export sales growth and was poised for even greater growth in 1997.

The Decision

After refreshing his mind with all these facts, Gupta considered the decision at hand. The meeting that morning between the partners and functional managers had lasted two hours and two opposing viewpoints had emerged.

The production and delivery managers both agreed that corporate infrastructure was lacking to cater to the increased exporting requirements placed on the company. While the former wanted Kadimi to invest in additional machinery for the value-added finishes (polishing, honing, and calibrating), the delivery manager complained about the use of Madras as a shipping point. He argued that Bombay was much closer and that reduced transportation times would mean reduced lead times for customers. Both managers were of the view that a complaint management system would impair the current flexibility Kadimi enjoyed with respect to settling customer complaints. They added that increased capacity and better products would far better satisfy foreign clients than a consistent policy framework for complaint resolution.

The sales and export managers both agreed that enhancing capacity was important. However, they proposed that establishing trust and building relationships with foreign customers was more important to ensure continued growth. Inconsistency in dealing with customer complaints was creating confusion among foreign buyers regarding corporate policies for product or delivery shortcomings. This was undermining the credibility and reliability of Kadimi's managers in their dealings with foreign clients. A complaint management system, they argued, would be a first step in assuring their customers that the company's policies were fair and consistent. Later on, they added, a similar system could be instituted for the pricing function as well.

As he thought about the discussion, Gupta wondered how he would prioritize the company's problems. The whir of the fax machine broke his train of thought and he glanced over to look at the message he was receiving. It was from his representative at the Himachal quarries. A truckload of Kanchan red slates was on its way to New Delhi. However, the stones were slightly spotted.

Gupta sprang from his chair and made his way to Agarwal's office. He knew what had to be done.

Questions for Discussion

1. How can Kadimi position itself better for global competitiveness?
2. How can a complaint management system help Kadimi improve its competitiveness?

3. What key issues would you consider in designing such a system for Kadimi?

4. How should Kadimi address the European situation?

Notes

1. "Containers" were hollow rectangular metal boxes that safeguarded materials on ships.

2. Kadimi was responsible for product delivery up to the port city of Madras, located approximately 1,100 miles from New Delhi. Once the product was loaded into a container on the ship, responsibility over the product shifted to the buyer.

3. With the addition of higher value-added stone processing techniques, these amounts were increasing every year; the median was expected to reach $10,000 by 1998.

Parker Pen Company

arker Pen Company, the manufacturer of writing instruments based in Janesville, Wisconsin, is one of the world's best-known companies in its field. It sells its products in 154 countries and considers itself number one in "quality writing instruments," a market that consists of pens selling for $3 or more.

In early 1984, the company launched a global marketing campaign in which everything was to have "one look, one voice," and with all planning to take place at headquarters. Everything connected with the selling effort was to be standardized. This was a grand experiment of a widely debated concept. A number of international companies were eager to learn from Parker's experiences.

Results became evident quickly. In February 1985, the globalization experiment was ended, and most of the masterminds of the strategy either left the company or were fired. In January 1986, the writing division of Parker Pen was sold for $100 million to a group of Parker's international managers and a London venture-capital company. The U.S. division was given a year to fix its operation or close.

SOURCES: This case was prepared by Ilkka A. Ronkainen for discussion purposes and not to exemplify correct or incorrect decision-making. The case draws facts from Joseph M. Winski and Laurel Wentz, "Parker Pen: What Went Wrong?" *Advertising Age*, June 2, 1986, 1, 60–61, 71; and Lori Kesler, "Parker Rebuilds a Quality Image," *Advertising Age*, March 21, 1988, 49. For a comprehensive discussion on globalization, see George S. Yip, *Total Global Strategy II*, (Upper Saddle River, NJ: Prentice-Hall, 2002).

Globalization

Globalization is a business initiative based on the conviction that the world is becoming more homogeneous and that distinctions between national markets are not only fading but, for some products, they will eventually disappear. Some products, such as Coca-Cola and Levi's, have already proven the existence of universal appeal. Coke's "one sight, one sound, one sell" approach is a legend in the world of global marketers. Other companies have some products that can be "world products," and some that cannot and should not be. For example, if cultural and competitive differences are less important than their similarities, a single advertising approach can exploit these similarities to stimulate sales everywhere, and at far lower cost than if campaigns were developed for each individual market.

Compared with the multidomestic approach, globalization differs in these three basic ways:

1. The global approach looks for similarities between markets. The multidomestic approach ignores similarities.
2. The global approach actively seeks homogeneity in products, image, marketing, and advertising message. The multidomestic approach produces unnecessary differences from market to market.
3. The global approach asks, "Should this product or process be for world consumption?" The multidomestic approach, relying solely on local autonomy, never asks the question.

Globalization requires many internal modifications as well. Changes in philosophy concerning local autonomy, concern for local operating results rather than corporate performance, and local strategies designed for local—rather than global—competitors are all delicate issues to be solved. By design, globalization calls for centralized decision-making; therefore, the "not-invented-here" syndrome becomes a problem. This can be solved by involving those having to implement the globalization strategy at every possible stage as well as keeping lines of communication open.

Globalization at Parker Pen Company

In January 1982, James R. Peterson became the president and CEO of Parker Pen. At that time, the company was struggling, and global marketing was one of the key measures to be used to revive the company. While at R. J. Reynolds, Peterson had been impressed with the industry's success with globalization. He wanted for Parker Pen nothing less than the writing instrument equivalent of the Marlboro man.

For the previous few years, a weak dollar had lulled Parker Pen into a false sense of security. About 80 percent of the company's sales were abroad, which meant that when local currency profits were translated into dollars, big profits were recorded.

The market was changing, however. The Japanese had started marketing inexpensive disposable pens with considerable success through mass marketers. Brands such as Paper Mate, Bic, Pilot, and Pentel each had greater sales, causing Parker's overall market share to plummet to 6 percent. Parker Pen, meanwhile, stayed with its previous strategy and continued marketing its top-of-the-line pens through department stores and stationery stores. Even in this segment, Parker Pen's market share was eroding because of the efforts of A. T. Cross Company and Montblanc of Germany.

Subsidiaries enjoyed a high degree of autonomy in marketing operations, which resulted in broad and diverse product lines and 40 different advertising agencies handling the Parker Pen account worldwide.

When the dollar's value skyrocketed in the 1980s, Parker's profits plunged and the loss of market share became painfully evident.

Peterson moved quickly upon his arrival. He trimmed the payroll, chopped the product line to 100 (from 500), consolidated manufacturing operations, and ordered an overhaul of the main plant to make it a state-of-the-art facility. Ogilvy & Mather

was hired to take sole control of Parker Pen advertising worldwide. The logic behind going with one agency instead of the 40 formerly employed was cost savings and the ability to coordinate strategies on a worldwide basis. Among the many agencies terminated was Lowe Howard-Spink in London, which had produced some of the best advertising for Parker Pen's most profitable subsidiary. The immediate impact was a noticeable decline in employee morale and some expressed bitterness at the subsidiary being dictated to by a subsidiary that had been cross-subsidizing the American operations over the years.

A decision was also made to go aggressively after the low end of the market. The company would sell an upscale line called Premier, mainly as a positioning device. The biggest profits were to come from a roller-ball pen called Vector, selling for $2.98. Plans were drawn to sell an even cheaper pen called Itala—a disposable pen never thought possible at Parker.

Three new managers, to be known as Group Marketing, were brought in. All three had extensive marketing experience, most of it in international markets. Richard Swart, who became marketing vice president for writing instruments, had handled 3M's image advertising worldwide and taught company managers the ins and outs of marketing planning. Jack Marks became head of writing instruments advertising. At Gillette, he had orchestrated the worldwide marketing of Silkience hair-care products. Carlos Del Nero, brought in to be Parker's manager of global marketing planning, had gained broad international experience at Fisher-Price. The concept of marketing by centralized direction was approved.

The idea of selling pens the same way everywhere did not sit well with many Parker subsidiaries and distributors. Pens were indeed the same, but markets, they believed, were different: France and Italy fancied expensive fountain pens; Scandinavia was a ballpoint market. In some markets, Parker could assume an above-the-fray stance; in others it had to get into the trenches and compete on price. Nonetheless, headquarters communicated to them all:

Advertising for Parker Pens (no matter model or mode) will be based on a common creative strategy and positioning. The worldwide advertising theme, "Make Your Mark With Parker," has been adopted. It will utilize similar graphic layout and photography. It will utilize an agreed-upon typeface. It will utilize the approved Parker logo/design. It will be adapted from centrally supplied materials.

Figure I — Ads for Parker's Global Campaign

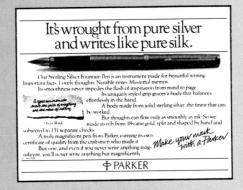

SOURCE: Joseph M. Winski and Laurel Wentz, "Parker Pen: What Went Wrong?" *Advertising Age*, June 2, 1986, 1, 60.

Swart insisted that the directives were to be used only as "starting points" and that they allowed for ample local flexibility. The subsidiaries perceived them differently. The U.K. subsidiary, especially, fought the scheme all the way. Ogilvy & Mather London strongly opposed the "one world, one brand, one advertisement" dictum. Conflict arose, with Swart allegedly shouting at one of the meetings: "Yours is not to reason why; yours is to implement." Local flexibility in advertising was out of the question (see Figure 1).

The London-created "Make Your Mark" campaign was launched in October 1984. Except for language, it was essentially the same: long copy, horizontal layout, illustrations in precisely the same place, the Parker logo at the bottom, and the tag line or local equivalent in the lower right-hand corner. Swart once went to the extreme of suggesting that Parker ads avoid long copy and use just one big picture.

Problems arose on the manufacturing side. The new $15 million plant broke down repeatedly.

Costs soared, and the factory turned out defective products in unacceptable numbers. In addition, the new marketing approach started causing problems as well. Although Parker never abandoned its high-end position in foreign markets, its concentration on low-priced, mass distribution products in the United States caused dilution of its image and ultimately losses of $22 million in 1985. Conflict was evident internally, and the board of directors began to turn against the concept of globalization.

In January 1985, Peterson resigned. Del Nero left the company in April; Swart was fired in May, Marks in June. When Michael Fromstein became CEO of the company, he assembled the company's country managers in Janesville and announced: "Global marketing is dead. You are free again."

Questions for Discussion

1. Should the merits of global marketing be judged by what happened at Parker Pen Company?
2. Was the globalization strategy sound for writing instruments? If yes, what was wrong in the implementation? If not, why not?
3. What marketing miscalculations were made by the advocates of the globalization effort at Parker Pen?
4. The task is to "fix it or close it." What should be done?

Whirlpool and the Global Appliance Industry

ithin a few months after becoming CEO of Whirlpool Corp. in 1987, David Whitwam met with his senior managers to plot a strategy for securing future company growth. At the time, Whirlpool was the market leader among U.S. appliance makers, but it generated only weak sales outside North America. Operating in a mature market, it faced the same low profit margins as major competitors like General Electric and Maytag. In addition to price wars, especially in mature markets, the industry had started to consolidate, and consumers were demanding more environmentally friendly products.

Whirlpool and Its Options

Whitwam and his management team explored several growth options, including diversifying into other industries experiencing more rapid growth, such as furniture or garden products; restructuring the company financially; and expanding vertically and horizontally. The group sharpened its focus to

SOURCES: This case was compiled by Ilkka Ronkainen. Portions of this case were researched from material available at **http://www. whirlpool.com**. The Global Success Factors section is derived from a report on the global appliance industry by John Bonds, German Estrada, Peter Jacobs, Jorge Harb-Kallab, Paul Kunzer, and Karin Toth at Georgetown University, March 2000. See also Ilkka A. Ronkainen and Ivan Menezes, "Implementing Global Marketing Strategy," *International Marketing Review* 13 (no. 3, 1996): 56–63; and "The Right Way to Go Global: An Interview with Whirlpool CEO David Whitwam," *Harvard Business Review* 72 (March–April 1994): 134–145.

consider opportunities for expanding the appliance business beyond North American markets. After all, the basics of managing the appliance business and the product technologies are similar in Europe, North America, Asia, and Latin America. As Whitwam put it, "We were very good at what we did. What we needed was to enter appliance markets in other parts of the world and learn how to satisfy different kinds of customers."

Whirlpool industry data predicted that, over time, appliance manufacturing would become a global industry. As Whitwam saw it, his company had three options: "We could ignore the inevitable—a decision that would have condemned Whirlpool to a slow death. We could wait for globalization to begin and then try to react, which would have put us in a catch-up mode, technologically and organizationally. Or we could control our own destiny and try to shape the very nature of globalization in our industry. In short, we could force our competitors to respond to us."

Whitwam and his team chose the third option and set out on a mission to make Whirlpool "one company worldwide." They aimed much higher than simply marketing products or operating around the globe. For decades, Whirlpool had sold some appliances in other countries to buyers who could afford them. Whitwam wanted to expand this reach by establishing a vision of a company that could leverage global resources to gain a long-term competitive advantage. In his words, this effort meant "having the best technologies and processes for designing, manufacturing, selling, and servicing your products at the lowest

663

possible costs. Our vision at Whirlpool is to integrate our geographical businesses wherever possible, so that our most advanced expertise in any given area—whether it's refrigeration technology or distribution strategy—isn't confined to one location or one division. We want to be able to take the best capabilities we have and leverage them in all of our operations worldwide."

As its first step in transforming a largely domestic operation into a global powerhouse, Whirlpool purchased the European appliance business of Dutch consumer-goods giant, Philips Electronics. Philips had been losing market share for years, running its European operations as independent regional companies that made different appliances for individual markets. "When we bought this business," Whitwam recalls, "we had two automatic washer designs, one built in Italy and one built in Germany. If you as a consumer looked at them, they were basically the same machines. But there wasn't anything common about those two machines. There wasn't even a common screw."

The Whirlpool strategy called for reversing the decline in European market share and improving profitability by changing product designs and manufacturing processes and by switching to centralized purchasing. The change reorganized the national design and research staffs inherited from Philips into European product teams that worked closely with Whirlpool's U.S. designers. Redesigned models shared more parts, and inventory costs fell when Whirlpool consolidated warehouses from 36 to 8. The transformation trimmed Philips's list of 1,600 suppliers by 50 percent, and it converted the national operations to regional companies.

Whitwam believed that the drive to become one company worldwide required making Whirlpool a global brand—a formidable task in Europe, where the name was not well-known. The company rebranded the Philips product lines, supported by a $135 million pan-European advertising campaign that initially presented both the Philips and Whirlpool names and eventually converted to Whirlpool alone.

Another important component of the Whirlpool global strategy—product innovation—sought to develop superior products based on consumer needs and wants. "We have to provide a compelling reason other than price for consumers to buy Whirlpool-built products," says Whitwam. "We can do that only by understanding the consumer better than anyone else does and then translating our understanding into clearly superior product designs, features, and after-sales support. Our goal is for consumers to prefer the Whirlpool brand because it offers greater overall value than competing products."

One successful product innovation led to the Whirlpool Crispwave microwave oven. Extensive research with European consumers revealed a desire for a microwave that could brown and crisp food. In response, Whirlpool engineers designed the VIP Crispwave, which can fry crispy bacon and cook a pizza with a crisp crust. The new microwave proved successful in Europe, and Whirlpool later introduced it in the United States.

Whirlpool's global strategy includes a goal to become the market leader in Asia, which will be the world's largest appliance market in the twenty-first century. In 1988, it began setting up sales and distribution systems in Asia to help it serve Asian markets and to make the firm more familiar with those markets and potential customers. The company established three regional offices: one in Singapore to serve Southeast Asia, a second in Hong Kong to handle the Chinese market, and a Tokyo office for Japan. Through careful analysis, Whirlpool marketers sought to match specific current products with Asian consumers. They studied existing and emerging trade channels and assessed the relative strengths and weaknesses of competitors in the Asian markets. The company set up joint ventures with five Asian manufacturers for four appliance lines with the highest market potential: refrigerators, washers, air conditioners, and microwave ovens. With a controlling interest in each of the joint ventures, the newly global company confidently expects to excel in the world's fastest-growing market.

Whirlpool has come a long way since embarking on its global strategy. By 2000, revenues had doubled to more than $10 billion. The company now reaches markets in more than 170 countries, leading the markets in both North America and Latin America. Whirlpool is number three in Europe and the largest Western appliance company in Asia. For building its integrated global network, "Whirlpool gets very high marks," says an industry analyst. "They are outpacing the industry dramatically."

Global Success Factors

From a global perspective, there are two success factors that affect all of the different geographic regions. The first key success factor on a global scale is successful branding. Each of the large global manufacturers has been very successful in developing a branding strategy. Most of these players sell a variety of brands, where each is targeted to certain quality and price levels. In addition, the strong brand reputation has been necessary for the major manufacturers either to expand operations into new regions or to launch new product lines. For example, Maytag did not have a line of products in the dishwasher category but had a large brand presence in the washer/dryer category. To expand its product line, Maytag decided to launch a new line of products in the dishwasher segment. Through a successful branding campaign, in less than two years Maytag captured the second-largest market share in the segment. It leveraged its successful brand image in one segment to quickly steal share from less successful competitors.

The second key success factor on a global scale is price sensitivity. Given the large cost of these goods, large-scale manufacturers have been able to lower prices to meet the demand of customers. While there is little price elasticity, some manufacturers have been able to raise prices on their high-end goods, but for the most part, most manufacturers have lowered prices, and thus margins, to stay competitive with other brands. With razor-thin margins across each segment, only manufacturers that have the size to realize economies of scale have been able to remain competitive and lower prices to meet demands of their customers. This price sensitivity and the need to continually lower prices made up one of the major forces driving the consolidation within the industry. Many smaller brands were not able to compete and therefore were sold to the larger appliance brands.

China and Asia

Aside from the global key success factors, two key success factors within China and Asia are very important. First, appliance manufacturers must have access to distribution channels and therefore the ability to provide the products across several different Chinese regions. The access to Chinese distribution channels can be very limiting for international corporations, whereas China-based companies, such as Kelon and Haier, have a definite competitive advantage.

Second, large appliance manufacturers must have a large scope of products for success. Specifically, it is the number of different segments in which a company sells products that will lead to success in China, not the scope of products within a given segment. Kelon manufactures 112 different types of air conditioners, but it is not a full-line supplier of appliances to its customers. Contrarily, Haier is a full-line supplier that manufactures products in each product segment and so provides its customers with a variety of appliances under one brand name.

The Japanese market has a different set of criteria for success than China and the rest of Asia. Instead, the Japanese market closely resembles certain aspects of the European and U.S. markets. Aside from the global success factors, success in the Japanese market is based on two key factors. First, due to the size of dwellings in Japan, innovation with regard to product size is very important. Japanese customers are looking for product innovations that will fit into smaller spaces while providing the most use of cabinet space. Second, to be successful in Japan, a manufacturer must sell a product that is very high in quality. Japanese customers are very demanding in regard to product quality, and they expect their products to last decades. Therefore, manufacturers selling products that are very high in quality will have a competitive advantage.

United States

Within the United States, two key success factors outside of the global factors are necessary for a company's success. First, a company must develop innovative products that incorporate new features while still operating efficiently. U.S. customers are very aware that energy consumption of a product will have a long-term effect on their utility bills, so they look for products that operate more efficiently. In addition, customers are willing to pay a premium for innovative features on a high-end product. Many manufacturers were surprised that Maytag was able to raise its prices for its front-loading washer not once, but twice. Customers were not as concerned with the price as they were concerned with the convenience of the product.

The second key success factor within the U.S. market is product quality, in respect to durability. U.S. consumers are willing to pay more for a product, but they expect it to operate for well over a decade with little to no maintenance. Therefore, for an appliance manufacturer to succeed in the United States, it must deliver products that are of high quality and of innovative design.

Europe

Outside of the two global success factors, the European market has two distinct factors that are required for success. First, to succeed in Europe, manufacturers must develop innovative products. In this context, innovative products are defined as products that are efficient and environmentally friendly. The "green" movement within Europe is very strong, and therefore a manufacturer that does not sell "eco-products" will not succeed when compared to a company that offers that type of product.

Second, quality is a key success factor for Europe. Similar to other markets, in this context quality refers to durability. European consumers are looking for products that are durable and will last over a long period of time. In this regard, the European market is very similar to the U.S., Japanese, and Latin American markets.

Latin America

Within Latin America, there are two additional success factors for a manufacturer to consider outside the global success factors. First, Latin American companies that provide excellent service to customers will have an advantage over the competition. The amount of time that the average consumer owns an appliance in Latin America is somewhat longer than in other global regions, so consumers are looking for excellent service. The economy in Latin America has had several challenges in recent history, and so consumers would much rather repair an existing product than buy a new appliance.

Second, quality is another success factor for Latin America. This key success factor ties directly into the service success factor. Initially, Latin Americans are looking for a durable product that will last for over a decade; then through customer service, the product will be repaired to extend its life for several more years.

Questions for Discussion

1. Whirlpool's marketing goal is to leverage resources across borders. How is this evident in its marketing approach? Consult **http://www.whirlpool.com** for additional information.

2. The challenge facing Whirlpool is not only external in catering to local customers' needs worldwide, but also internal—all the regional and local units have to "buy in" to the global vision. What types of particular issues (such as product or technology transfers) may arise, and how should they be dealt with?

3. Visit the Web site of the Association of Home Appliance Manufacturers, **http://www.aham.org**, and suggest some of the global trends among the major manufacturers of household appliances.

Chapter 1

1. Robert W. Armstrong and Jill Sweeney, "Industrial Type, Culture, Mode of Entry, and Perceptions of International Marketing Ethics Problems: A Cross-Culture Comparison," *Journal of Business Ethics* 13, 10: 775–785.
2. World Trade Organization, *International Trade Statistics,* **http://www.wto.org,** accessed February 13, 2002.
3. Michael R. Czinkota, Ilkka Ronkainen, and Bob Donath, *Mastering Global Markets* (Cincinnati: Thomson, 2003).
4. Marcelo Izquierdo, "Argentina: The Epidemic Spreads in Latin America," *Proceso,* June 30, 2002.
5. Eugene H. Fram and Riad Ajami, "Globalization of Markets and Shopping Stress: Cross-Country Comparisons," *Business Horizons* (January–February 1994): 17–23.
6. John J. Sviokla and Jeffrey F. Rayport, "Mapping the Marketspace: Information Technology and the New Marketing Environment," *Harvard Business School Bulletin* 71 (June 1995): 49–51.
7. Michael R. Czinkota and Sarah McCue, *The STAT-USA Companion to International Business,* Economics and Statistics Administration (U.S. Department of Commerce, Washington, DC, 2001), 16.
8. World Trade Organization, *International Trade Statistics 2001,* **http://www.wto.org,** accessed September 17, 2002.
9. Charlene Barshefsky, "The Transatlantic Groundwork for Global Prosperity," An Address before the American Council on Germany, Alexandria, VA, June 15, 2001.
10. Peter R. Dickson and Michael R. Czinkota, "How the U.S. Can Be Number One Again: Resurrecting the Industrial Policy Debate," *The Columbia Journal of World Business* 31, 3 (Fall 1996): 76–87.
11. Howard Lewis III and J. David Richardson, *Why Global Commitment Really Matters* (Washington, DC: Institute for International Economics, 2001).
12. *Cognetics,* Cambridge, MA, 1993.
13. Exporter Data Base, U.S. Department of Commerce and Small Business Administration, Washington, DC, April 2002.
14. Michael Kutschker, "Internationalisierung der Wirtschaft," *Perspektiven der Internationalen Wirtschaft,* Wiesbaden, Gabler GmbH, 1999: 22.

Appendix A

1. Marketing Definitions, **http://MarketingPower.com,** Web site of the American Marketing Association, accessed November 1, 2002.

2. Philip Kotler presents the eight Os in the eighth edition of *Marketing Management: Analysis, Planning, and Control* (Englewood Cliffs, NJ: Prentice-Hall, 1994), 174–175.
3. The four Ps were popularized by E. Jerome McCarthy. See William Perreault and E. Jerome McCarthy, *Basic Marketing: A Managerial Approach,* 14th ed. (Burr Ridge, IL: Irwin/McGraw-Hill, 2002).
4. Bert Rosenbloom, *Marketing Channels: A Management View,* 6th ed. (Fort Worth, TX: The Dryden Press, 1999).
5. Robert Bartels, "Are Domestic and International Marketing Dissimilar?" *Journal of Marketing* 36 (July 1968): 56–61.

Chapter 2

1. Henri Pirenne, *Economic and Social History of Medieval Europe* (New York: Harcourt, Brace, and World, 1933), 142–146.
2. Margaret P. Doxey, *Economic Sanctions and International Enforcement* (New York: Oxford University Press, 1980), 10.
3. For more information about the World Trade Organization refer to the following Web site: **http://www.wto.org.**
4. Thomas R. Graham, "Global Trade: War and Peace," *Foreign Policy* (Spring 1983): 124–137.
5. WTO Trade Policy Review of the United States 2001, WTO Secretariat Summary, Press Release, September 17, 2001. **http://www.wto.org/wto,** accessed September 3, 2002.
6. *Business Guide to the Uruguay Round,* International Trade Centre and Commonwealth Secretariat, Geneva, 1995. **http://www.intracen.org.**
7. "Michael R. Czinkota, "The World Trade Organization—Perspectives and Prospects," *Journal of International Marketing* 3 (no. 1, 1995): 85–92.
8. Remarks by Mr. Mike Moore, Director General, WTO, Geneva, June 25, 2002.
9. For more information about the International Monetary Fund, refer to the following Web site: **http://www.imf.org.**
10. **www.imf.org/external/np/sec/pr/2002/pr0240.htm.**
11. For more information about the World Bank, refer to the following Web site: **http://www.worldbank.org.**
12. Mordechai E. Kreinin, *International Economics: A Policy Approach,* 5th ed. (New York: Harcourt Brace Jovanovich, 1987), 12.
13. Kreinin, *International Economics,* 6.
14. Estimate based on Bureau of Economic Analysis, U.S. Department of Commerce, Washington, DC. **http://www.bea.doc.gov,** accessed Sep-

tember 24, 2002, extrapolations for 2002.
15. Catherine L. Mann, *Is the U.S. Trade Deficit Sustainable?* September 1999, **http://www.iie.com.**
16. *U.S. Jobs Supported by Exports of Goods and Services,* U.S. Department of Commerce, Washington, DC.
17. Michael R. Czinkota, "A National Export Development Strategy for New and Growing Businesses," remarks delivered to the National Economic Council, Washington, DC, August 6, 1993.
18. Gary Clyde Hufbauer and Kimberly Ann Elliott, *Measuring the Costs of Protection in the United States* (Washington, DC: Institute for International Economics, 1994).
19. *Die Aussenwirtschaftsförderung der wichtigsten Konkurrenzländer der Bundesrepublik Deutschland—Ein internationaler Vergleich* (The export promotion of the most important countries competing with the Federal Republic of Germany—An international comparison) (Berlin: Deutsches Institut für Wirtschaftsforschung, June 1991).
20. Masaaki Kotabe and Michael R. Czinkota, "State Government Promotion of Manufacturing Exports: A Gap Analysis," *Journal of International Business Studies* (Winter 1992): 637–658.
21. *2000 U.S. Master Tax Guide* (Chicago: CCH Inc., 2000), 572.

Chapter 3

1. Ernest Dichter, "The World Consumer," *Harvard Business Review* 40 (July–August 1962): 113–122; and Kenichi Ohmae, *Triad Power—The Coming Shape of Global Competition* (New York: The Free Press, 1985), 22–27.
2. "Rule No. 1: Don't Diss the Locals," *Business Week,* May 15, 1995, 8.
3. Warren Stugatch, "Make Way for the Euroconsumer," *World Trade,* February 1993, 46–50.
4. Mary O'Hara-Devereaux and Robert Johansen, *Global Work: Bridging Distance, Culture, and Time* (San Francisco: Jossey-Bass Publishers, 1994), 11.
5. Carla Rapoport, "Nestlé's Brand Building Machine," *Fortune,* September 19, 1994, 147–156.
6. Alfred Kroeber and Clyde Kluckhohn, *Culture: A Critical Review of Concepts and Definitions* (New York: Random House, 1985), 11.
7. Geert Hofstede, "National Cultures Revisited," *Asia-Pacific Journal of Management* 1 (September 1984): 22–24.
8. Robert L. Kohls, *Survival Kit for Overseas Living* (Chicago: Intercultural Press, 1979), 3.

9. Edward T. Hall, *Beyond Culture* (Garden City, NY: Anchor Press, 1976), 15.

10. **http://www.mcdonalds.com.**

11. Marita von Oldenborgh, "What's Next for India?" *International Business,* January 1996, 44–47; and Ravi Vijh, "Think Global, Act Indian," *Export Today,* June 1996, 27–28.

12. Michael T. Malloy, "America, Go Home," *The Wall Street Journal,* March 26, 1993, R7.

13. "Culture Wars," *The Economist,* September 12, 1998, 97–99.

14. George P. Mundak, "The Common Denominator of Cultures," in *The Science of Man in the World,* ed. Ralph Linton (New York: Columbia University Press, 1945), 123–142.

15. Philip R. Harris and Robert T. Moran, *Managing Cultural Differences* (Houston, TX: Gulf, 1987), 201.

16. David A. Ricks, *Blunders in International Business* (Malden, MA: Blackwell Publishers, 2000), Chapter 1.

17. David A. Hanni, John K. Ryans, and Ivan R. Vernon, "Coordinating International Advertising: The Goodyear Case Revisited for Latin America," *Journal of International Marketing* 3 (no. 2, 1995): 83–98.

18. "For His Next Trick, He'll Help Trade Negotiators Communicate," *The Wall Street Journal,* December 1, 1992, B1.

19. "France: Mind Your Language," *The Economist,* March 23, 1996, 70–71.

20. Rory Cowan, "The **e** Does Not Stand for English," *Global Business,* March 2000, L/22.

21. Margareta Bowen, "Business Translation," *Jerome Quarterly* 8 (August– September 1993): 5–9.

22. "Nokia Veti Pois Mainoskampanjansa," *Uutislehti 100,* June 15, 1998, 5.

23. "Sticky Issue," *The Economist,* August 24, 2002, 51.

24. Edward T. Hall, "The Silent Language of Overseas Business," *Harvard Business Review* 38 (May–June 1960): 87–96.

25. *World Almanac and the Book of Facts* (Mahwah, NJ: Funk & Wagnalls, 1995), 734.

26. Nora Fitzgerald, "Oceans Apart, but Closer than You Think," *World Trade,* February 1996, 58.

27. Mushtaq Luqmami, Zahir A. Quraeshi, and Linda Delene, "Marketing in Islamic Countries: A Viewpoint," *MSU Business Topics* 23 (Summer 1980): 17–24.

28. "Islamic Banking: Faith and Creativity," *The New York Times,* April 8, 1994, D1, D6.

29. Roger D. Blackwell, Paul W. Miniard, and James F. Engel, *Consumer Behavior* (Mason, OH: Thomson, 2001), Chapter 10.

30. Y. H. Wong and Ricky Yee-kwong, "Relationship Marketing in China: Guanxi, Favoritism and Adaptation," *Journal of Business Ethics* 22 (no. 2, 1999): 107–118; and Tim Ambler, "Reflections in China: Re-Orienting Images of Marketing," *Marketing Management* 4 (no. 1, 1995): 23–30.

31. "Iran Unveils Islamic Twin Dolls to Fight Culture War," *AP Worldstream,* March 5, 2002.

32. Douglas McGray, "Japan's Gross National Cool," *Foreign Policy,* May/ June 2002, 44.

33. Earl P. Spencer, "EuroDisney—What Happened?" *Journal of International Marketing* 3 (no. 3, 1995): 103–114.

34. Sergey Frank, "Global Negotiations: Vive Les Differences!" *Sales & Marketing Management* 144 (May 1992): 64–69.

35. See, for example, Terri Morrison, *Kiss, Bow, or Shake Hands: How to Do Business in Sixty Countries* (Holbrook, MA: Adams Media, 1994), or Roger Axtell, *Do's and Taboos around the World* (New York: John Wiley & Sons, 1993). For holiday observances, see **http://www.religioustolerance.org/main_day.htm#cal** and **http://www.yahoo.com/society_and_culture/holidays_and_observances.**

36. James A. Gingrich, "Five Rules for Winning Emerging Market Consumers," *Strategy and Business* (second quarter, 1999): 68–76.

37. "Feng Shui Strikes Chord," available at **http://www.cnnfn.com/1999/09/11/life/q_fengshui/.**

38. "Feng Shui Man Orders Sculpture out of the Hotel," *South China Morning Post,* July 27, 1992, 4.

39. "The New Life of O'Reilly," *Business Week,* June 13, 1994, 64–66; and "Heinz Aims to Export Taste for Ketchup," *The Wall Street Journal,* November 20, 1992, B1, B10.

40. "U.S. Superstores Find Japanese Are a Hard Sell," *The Wall Street Journal,* February 14, 2000, B1, B4.

41. The results of the Gallup study are available in "What the Chinese Want," *Fortune,* October 11, 1999, 229–234.

42. Kenichi Ohmae, "Managing in a Borderless World," *Harvard Business Review* 67 (May–June 1989): 152–161.

43. Joe Agnew, "Cultural Differences Probed to Create Product Identity," *Marketing News,* October 24, 1986, 22.

44. Joseph A. McKinney, "Joint Ventures of United States Firms in Japan: A Survey," *Venture Japan* 1 (no. 2, 1988): 14–19.

45. Peter MacInnis, "Guanxi or Contract: A Way to Understand and Predict Conflict between Chinese and Western Senior Managers in China-Based Joint Ventures," in Daniel E. McCarthy and Stanley J. Hille, eds., *Multinational Business Management and Internationalization of Business Enterprises* (Nanjing, China: Nanjing University Press, 1993), 345–351.

46. Tim Ambler, "Reflections in China: Re-Orienting Images of Marketing," *Marketing Management* 4 (Summer 1995): 23–30.

47. James H. Sood and Patrick Adams, "Model of Management Learning Styles as a Predictor of Export Behavior and Performance," *Journal of Business Research* 12 (June 1984): 169–182.

48. Jagdish N. Sheth and S. Prakash Sethi, "A Theory of Cross-Cultural Buying Behavior," in *Consumer and Industrial Buying Behavior,* eds. Arch G. Woodside, Jagdish N. Sheth, and Peter D. Bennett (New York: Elsevier North-Holland, 1977), 369–386.

49. Geert Hofstede, *Culture's Consequences: International Differences in Work-Related Values* (Beverly Hills, CA: Sage Publications, 1984).

50. Geert Hofstede and Michael H. Bond, "The Confucius Connection: From Cultural Roots to Economic Growth," *Organizational Dynamics* 16 (Spring 1988): 4–21.

51. Sudhir H. Kale, "Grouping Eurocon- sumers: A Culture-Based Clustering Approach," *Journal of International Marketing* 3 (no. 3, 1995): 35–48.

52. Jan-Benedict Steenkamp and Frenkel ter Hofstede, "A Cross-National Investigation into the Individual and National Cultural Antecedents of Consumer Innovativeness," *Journal of Marketing* 63 (April 1999): 55–69.

53. Sudhir H. Kale, "Culture-Specific Marketing Communications: An Analytical Approach," *International Marketing Review* 8 (no. 2, 1991): 18–30.

54. Hong Cheng and John C. Schweitzer, "Cultural Values Reflected in Chinese and U.S. Television Commercials," *Journal of Advertising Research* 36 (May/June 1996): 27–45.

55. Sudhir H. Kale, "Distribution Channel Relationships in Diverse Cultures," *International Marketing Review* 8 (no. 3, 1991): 31–45.

56. "Exploring Differences in Japan, U.S. Culture," *Advertising Age International,* September 18, 1995, I-8.

57. James A. Lee, "Cultural Analysis in Overseas Operations," *Harvard Business Review* 44 (March–April 1966): 106–114.

58. Peter B. Fitzpatrick and Alan S. Zimmerman, *Essentials of Export Marketing* (New York: American Management Organization, 1985), 16.

59. "Expansion Abroad: The New Direction for European Firms," *International Management* 41 (November 1986): 20–26.

60. W. Chan Kim and R. A. Mauborgne, "Cross-Cultural Strategies," *Journal of Business Strategy* 7 (Spring 1987): 28–37.

61. Mauricio Lorence, "Assignment USA: The Japanese Solution," *Sales & Marketing Management* 144 (October 1992): 60–66.

62. Rosalie Tung, "Selection and Training of Personnel for Overseas Assignments," *Columbia Journal of World Business* 16 (Spring 1981): 68–78.

63. "The Loneliness of the Hyundai Manager," *Business Week,* August 19, 1996, 12E4–6.

64. "Special Interest Group Operations," available at **http://www.samsung.com;** and "Sensitivity Kick," *The Wall Street Journal* (December 30, 1996), 1, 4.

65. Harris and Moran, *Managing Cultural Differences,* 267–295.

66. Simcha Ronen, "Training the International Assignee," in *Training and Career Development,* ed. I. Goldstein (San Francisco: Jossey-Bass, 1989), 426–440.

67. See, for example, Johnson & Johnson's credo at **www.jnj.com/our_company/our_credo/index.htm.**

68. 3M examples are adopted from John R. Engen, "Far Eastern Front," *World Trade,* December 1994, 20–24.

Chapter 4

1. Global Business Policy Council, *Globalization Ledger* (Washington, DC: A. T. Kearney, 2000), 3.

2. "African Debt, European Doubt," *Economist,* April 8, 2000, 46.

3. C. K. Prahalad and Stuart L. Hart, "The Fortune at the Bottom of the Pyramid," *Strategy and Business,* (first quarter, 2002): 35–47.

4. "Who Will Join Europe's Club—and When?" *Economist,* April 8, 2000, 53–54.

5. Rahul Jacob, "The Big Rise,"*Fortune,* May 30, 1994, 74–90.

6. Roger D. Blackwell, Paul W. Miniard, and James F. Engel, *Consumer Behavior* (Mason, OH: Thomson, 2001), 283.

7. *European Marketing Data and Statistics 2001* (London: Euromonitor, 2002), 380.

8. The World Bank, *World Development Indicators* (Washington, DC, 2000), 85. See also **http://www.worldbank.org/data/wdi2000.**

9. "In India, Luxury Is Within Reach of Many," *The Wall Street Journal,* October 17, 1995, A17.

10. Victor H. Frank, Jr., "Living with Price Control Abroad," *Harvard Business Review* 62 (March–April 1984): 137–142.

11. Bob Meyer, "The Original Meaning of Trade Meets the Future in Barter," *World Trade,* January 2000, 46–50.

12. Edward Tse, "The Right Way to Achieve Profitable Growth in the Chinese Market," *Strategy and Business* (second quarter, 1998): 10–21.

13. "Unplugging Data," *Advertising Age,* March 6, 2000, 50.

14. *Internet Domain Survey, June 2002,* available at **http://www.isc.org.**

15. *How Many Online?,* available at **http://www.nua.ie/surveys/how_many_online/index.html.**

16. "The Mad Grab for Piece of Air," *Business Week,* April 17, 2000, 152–154; and "Hello, Internet," *Business Week,* May 3, 1999, 170–175.

17. Jesse Berst, "It's Back: How Interactive TV Is Sneaking Back into Your Living Room," available at **http://www.zdnet.com/anchordesk/story/story_3368.html.**

18. Rahul Jacob, "Asian Infrastructure: The Biggest Bet on Earth," *Fortune,* October 31, 1994, 139–150.

19. Global Business Policy Council, *Globalization Ledger* (Washington, DC: A.T. Kearney, April 2000).

20. Ben Crow and Alan Thomas, *Third World Atlas* (Milton Keynes, England: Open University Press, 1984), 85.

21. John S. Hill and Richard R. Still, "Effects of Urbanization on Multinational Product Planning: Markets in Lesser-Developed Countries," *Columbia Journal of World Business* 19 (Summer 1984): 62–67.

22. The World Bank, *World Development Report 1982* (New York: Oxford University Press, 1982), 63.

23. Ilkka A. Ronkainen, "Trading Blocs: Opportunity or Demise for International Trade?" *Multinational Business Review* 1 (Spring 1993): 1–9.

24. *The European Union: A Guide for Americans* (Washington, DC: Delegation of the European Commission to the United States, 2002), chapter 2. See **http://www.eurunion.org/infores/euguide/euguide.htm.**

25. See **http://secretariat.efta.int.**

26. "For U.S. Small Biz, Fertile Soil in Europe," *Business Week,* April 1, 2002, 55–56.

27. Gary C. Hufbauer and Jeffrey J. Schott, *NAFTA: An Eight-Year Appraisal* (Washington, DC: Institute for International Economics, 2003), Chapter 1.

28. Sidney Weintraub, *NAFTA at Three: A Progress Report* (Washington, DC: Center for Strategic and International Studies, 1997), 17–18.

29. John Cavanagh, Sarah Anderson, Jaime Serra, and J. Enrique Espinosa, "Happily Ever NAFTA," *Foreign Policy,* September/October 2002, 58–65.

30. For annual trade information, see **http://www.census.gov/foreign-trade.**

31. "U.S. Trade with Mexico during the Third NAFTA Year," *International Economic Review* (Washington, DC: International Trade Commission, April 1997): 11.

32. "Fox and Bush, for Richer, for Poorer," *The Economist,* February 3, 2001, 37–38.

33. "Aerospace Suppliers Gravitate to Mexico," *The Wall Street Journal,* January 23, 2002, A17.

34. Laura Heller, "The Latin Market Never Looked So Bueno," *DSN Retailing Today,* June 10, 2002, 125–126.

35. "Retail Oasis," *Business Mexico,* April 2001, 15.

36. Lara L. Sowinski, "Maquiladoras," *World Trade,* September 2000, 88–92.

37. "The Decline of the Maquiladora," *Business Week,* April 29, 2002, 59.

38. "NAFTA's Scorecard: So Far, So Good," *Business Week,* July 9, 2001, 54–56.

39. "Hogtied," *The Economist,* January 17, 2002, 35.

40. "Localizing Production," *Global Commerce,* August 20, 1997, 1.

41. "Latin America Fears Stagnation in Trade Talks with the United States," *The New York Times,* April 19, 1998, D1.

42. "Mexico, EU Sign Free-Trade Agreement," *The Wall Street Journal,* March 24, 2000, A15.

43. "Latin Lesson," *Far Eastern Economic Review,* January 4, 2001, 109.

44. "The Americas: A Cautious Yes to Pan-American Trade," *The Economist,* April 28, 2001, 35–36.

45. "Regional Commonalities Help Global Ad Campaigns Succeed in Latin America," *Business International,* February 17, 1992, 47–52; and "Ripping Down the Walls across the Americas," *Business Week,* December 26, 1994, 78–80.

46. Paul Krugman, "A Global Economy Is Not the Wave of the Future," *Financial Executive* 8 (March–April 1992): 10–13.

47. Michael R. Czinkota and Masaaki Kotabe, "America's New World Trade Order," *Marketing Management* 1 (Summer 1992): 49–56.

48. Robert Scollay, "The Changing Outlook for Asia-Pacific Regionalism," *The World Economy* 24 (September 2001): 1135–1160.

49. "Afrabet Soup," *The Economist,* February 10, 2001, 77.

50. "Try, Try Again," *The Economist,* July 13, 2002, 41.

51. Eric Friberg, Risto Perttunen, Christian Caspar, and Dan Pittard, "The Challenges of Europe 1992," *The McKinsey Quarterly* 21 (no. 2, 1988): 3–15.

52. "Lean, Mean, European," *The Economist,* April 29, 2000, 5–7.

53. Gianluigi Guido, "Implementing a Pan-European Marketing Strategy," *Long Range Planning* 24 (no. 5, 1991): 23–33.

54. "TABD Uses Virtual Organization for Trade Lobbying," *Crossborder Monitor,* July 2, 1997, 1.

55. Pam Woodall, "Survey: East Asian Economies: Six Deadly Sins," *Economist,* March 7, 1998, S12–14.

56. "Latin America and the Market," *Economist,* November 21, 1998, 23–25.

57. "In Argentina, Going Without," *The Washington Post,* February 19, 2002, E1–E2.

58. Swee Hoon Ang, Siew Meng Leong, and Philip Kotler, "The Asian Apocalypse: Crisis Marketing for Consumers and Businesses," *Long Range Planning* 33 (February 2000): 97–119.

59. "Asia's Sinking Middle Class," *Far Eastern Economic Review,* April 9, 1998, 12–13.

Chapter 5

1. Quoted in Philippe Dollinger, *The German Hansa* (Stanford, CA: Stanford University Press, 1970), 49.

2. Robin Renwick, *Economic Sanctions* (Cambridge, MA: Harvard University Press, 1981), 11.

3. Margaret P. Doxey, *Economic Sanctions and International Enforcement* (New York: Oxford University Press, 1980), 10.

4. George E. Shambaugh, *States, Firms, and Power: Successful Sanctions in United States Foreign Policy* (Albany: State University of New York Press, 1999), 202.

5. Gary Clyde Hufbauer, Jeffrey J. Schott, and Kimberly Elliott, *Economic Sanctions Reconsidered,* 3rd ed. (Washington, DC: Institute for International Economics, 2002).

6. Michael R. Czinkota and Erwin Dichtl, "Export Controls and Global Changes," *Der Markt* 37, 5 (1996): 148–155.

7. We are grateful to David Danjczek of Manufacturer's Alliance for his helpful comments.

8. E. M. Hucko, *Aussenwirtschaftsrecht-Kriegswaffenkontrollrecht, Textsammlung mit Einführung,* 4th ed. (Köln, Germany: Bundesanzeiger, 1993).

9. Michael R. Czinkota, "From Bowling Alone to Standing Together," *Marketing Management,* March/April 2002, 12–16.

10. Gary Clyde Hufbauer, Jeffrey J. Schott, and Barbara Oegg, *Using Sanctions to Fight Terrorism* (Washington, DC: Institute for International Economics, November 2001), 1.

11. James R. Hines, Jr., *Forbidden Payment: Foreign Bribery and American Business after 1977,* working paper 5266 (Cambridge, MA: National Bureau of Economic Research, September 1995), 1.

12. Magoroh Maruyama, "Bribing in Historical Context: The Case of Japan," *Human Systems Management* 15 (1996): 138–142.

13. **http://www.investorwords.com,** accessed December 18, 2002.

14. Michael G. Harvey, "A Survey of Corporate Programs for Managing Terrorist Threats," *Journal of International Business Studies* (third quarter, 1993): 465–478.

15. Harvey J. Iglarsh, "Terrorism and Corporate Costs," *Terrorism* 10 (1987): 227–230.

16. Michael Minor, "LDCs, TNCs, and Expropriation in the 1980s," *CTC Reporter,* Spring 1988, 53.

17. Overseas Private Investment Corporation (OPIC), Washington, DC, **http://www.opic.gov.** September 30, 2002.

18. *Investment Insurance Handbook* (Washington, DC: Overseas Private Investment Corporation, 1991).

19. Stuart M. Chemtob, Glen S. Fukushima, and Richard H. Wohl, *Practice by Foreign Lawyers in Japan* (Chicago: American Bar Association, 1989), 9.

20. Surya Prakash Sinha, *What Is Law? The Differing Theories of Jurisprudence* (New York: Paragon House, 1989).

21. *National Trade Estimate Report on Foreign Trade Barriers* (Washington, DC, Office of the United States Trade Representative, 2002), **http://www.ustr.gov.**

22. Michael R. Czinkota, "The Policy Gap in International Marketing," *Journal of International Marketing,* 8 (no. 1, 2000): 99–111.

23. We are grateful to Professor Ed Soule of Georgetown University for this example.

24. Michael R. Czinkota, "International Information Needs for U.S. Competitiveness," *Business Horizons* 34 (November–December 1991): 86–91.

Chapter 6

1. Naresh K. Malhotra, Mark Peterson, and Susan Bardi Kleiser, "Marketing Research: A State-of-the-Art Review and Directions for the Twenty-First Century," *Journal of the Academy of Marketing Science* 27 (no. 2, 1999): 160–183.

2. Marketing Definitions, **http://MarketingPower.com,** Web site of the American Marketing Association, accessed October 8, 2002.

3. Naresh K. Malhotra, *Marketing Research: An Applied Orientation,* 4th ed. (Upper Saddle River, NJ: Prentice-Hall, 2003.)

4. Jan-Benedict E. M. Steenkamp, "The Role of National Culture in International Marketing Research," *International Marketing Review* 18 (no. 1, 2001): 30–44.

5. C. Samuel Craig and Susan P. Douglas, *International Marketing Research,* 2nd ed. (Chichester: John Wiley and Sons, 2000).

6. Nina L. Reynolds, "Benchmarking International Marketing Research Practice in UK Agencies—Preliminary Evidence," *Benchmarking,* 7 (no. 5, 2000): 343–359.

7. For an excellent exposition on measuring the value of research, see Gilbert A. Churchill, Jr., and Dawn Iacobucci, *Marketing Research: Methodological Foundations,* 8th ed. (Mason, OH: South-Western, 2002).

8. For an excellent diagnostic tool, see Tamer Cavusgil's "Company Readiness to Export," Michigan State University, **http://globaledge.msu.edu,** accessed October 9, 2002.

9. Michael R. Czinkota, "International Information Cross-Fertilization in Marketing: An Empirical Assessment," *European Journal of Marketing,* 34 (2000).

10. "EU Vote Relaxes E-Privacy Rules," Reuters, May 31, 2002, **http://zdnet.com.com/2102-1105-929605.html,** accessed October 10, 2002.

11. Elizabeth De Bony, "EU, U.S. Plug Away at Data Privacy Accord," *Industry Standard,* December 10, 1998, 45–46.

12. European Society for Opinion and Marketing Research (ESOMAR), Annual Study of the Market Research Industry, **http://www.esomar.nl,** accessed October 11, 2002.

13. Salah S. Hassan and A. Coskun Samli, "The New Frontiers of Intermarket Segmentation," in *Global Marketing: Perspectives and Cases,* eds. Salah S. Hassan and Roger D. Blackwell (Fort Worth, TX: The Dryden Press, 1994), 76–100.

14. Michael R. Czinkota and Masaaki Kotabe, "Product Development the Japanese Way," in *Trends in International Business: Critical Perspectives,* eds. M. Czinkota and M. Kotabe (Oxford, England: Blackwell Publishers, 1998), 153–158.

15. R. Nishikawa, "New Product Planning at Hitachi," *Long Range Planning* 22 (1989): 20–24.

16. For an excellent example, see Alan Dubinsky, Marvin Jolson, Masaaki Kotabe, and Chae Lim, "A Cross-National Investigation of Industrial Salespeople's Ethical Perceptions," *Journal of International Business Studies* 22 (1991): 651–670.

17. Jussaume and Yamada, 222.

18. Sydney Verba, "Cross-National Survey Research: The Problem of Credibility," in *Comparative Methods in Sociology: Essays on Trends and Applications,* ed. I. Vallier (Berkeley: University of California Press, 1971), 322–323.

19. Camille P. Schuster and Michael J. Copeland, "Global Business Exchanges: Similarities and Differences around the World," *Journal of International Marketing* (Number 2, 1999): 63–80.

20. Kavil Ramachandran, "Data Collection for Management Research in Developing Countries," in *The Management Research Handbook*, eds. N. Craig Smith and Paul Dainty (London: Routledge, 1991), 304.

21. Gilbert A. Churchill, Jr., and Dawn Iacobucci, *Marketing Research: Methodological Foundations,* 8th ed. (Mason, OH: South-Western, 2002).

22. Kathleen Brewer Doran, "Lessons Learned in Cross-Cultural Research of Chinese and North American Consumers," *Journal of Business Research,* 55 (2002): 823–829.

23. C. Samuel Craig and Susan P. Douglas, *International Marketing Research,* 2nd ed. (Chichester: John Wiley and Sons, 2000).

24. C. Samuel Craig and Susan P. Douglas, "Conducting International Marketing Research in the Twenty-First Century," *International Marketing Review* 18 (no. 1, 2001): 80–90.

25. Janet Ilieva, Steve Baron, and Nigel M. Healey, "On-line Surveys in Marketing Research: Pros and Cons," *International Journal of Marketing Research* 44 (no. 3, 2002): 361–376.

26. David Luna, Laura A. Peracchio, and Maria D. de Juan, "Cross-Cultural and Cognitive Aspects of Web Site Navigation," *Journal of the Academy of Marketing Science* 30 (no. 4, 2002): 397–410.

27. William D. Neal, "Still Got It: Shortcomings Plague the Industry," *Marketing News,* September 16, 2002, 37.

28. Thomas C. Kinnear and James R. Taylor, *Marketing Research: An Applied Approach,* 5th ed. (New York: McGraw-Hill, 1996).

29. Winter and Prohaska, "Methodological Problems," 429.

30. Peter Clarke, "The Echelon Questions," *Electronic Engineering Times,* March 6, 2000, 36.

31. Andre L. Delbecq, Andrew H. Van de Ven, and David H. Gustafson, *Group Techniques for Program Planning* (Glenview, IL: Scott, Foresman, 1975), 83.

32. David Rutenberg, "Playful Plans," Queen's University working paper, 1991.

Chapter 7

1. Howard Lewis III and J. David Richardson, *Why Global Commitment Really Matters!* (Washington, DC: Institute for International Economics, 2001).

2. Michael R. Czinkota, "U.S. Exporters in the Global Marketplace: An Analysis of the Strengths and Vulnerabilities of Small and Medium-Sized Manufacturers," Testimony before the 107th Congress of the United States, House of Representatives, Committee on Small Business, Washington, DC, April 24, 2002.

3. *The 2002 National Export Strategy,* Trade Promotion Coordination Committee, Washington, DC, 2002, 24.

4. S. Tamer Cavusgil and Shaoming Zou, "Marketing Strategy–Performance Relationship: An Investigation of the Empirical Link in Export Marketing Ventures," *Journal of Marketing* 58 (no. 1, 1994): 1–21.

5. Masaaki Kotabe and Michael R. Czinkota, "State Government Promotion of Manufacturing Exports: A Gap Analysis," *Trends in International Business* (Malden: Blackwell, 1998), 78–96.

6. Tiger Li, "The Impact of the Marketing-R&D Interface on New Product Export Performance: A Contingency Analysis," *Journal of International Marketing* 7 (no. 1, 1999): 10–33.

7. Yoo S. Yang, Robert P. Leone, and Dana L. Alden, "A Market Expansion Ability Approach to Identify Potential Exporters," *Journal of Marketing* 56 (January 1992): 84–96.

8. Michael L. Ursic and Michael R. Czinkota, "An Experience Curve Explanation of Export Expansion," in *International Marketing Strategy: Environmental Assessment and Entry Strategies* (Fort Worth, TX: The Dryden Press, 1994), 133–141.

9. C. P. Rao, M. Krishna Erramilli, and Gopala K. Ganesh, "Impact of Domestic Recession on Export Marketing Behaviour," *International Marketing Review* 7 (1990): 54–65.

10. Shawna O'Grady and Henry W. Lane, "The Psychic Distance Paradox," *Journal of International Business Studies* 27 (no. 2, 1996): 309–333.

11. Aviv Shoham and Gerald S. Albaum, "Reducing the Impact of Barriers to Exporting: A Managerial Perspective," *Journal of International Marketing* 3 (no. 4, 1995): 85–105.

12. Shaoming Zou and S. Tamer Cavusgil, "The GMS: A Broad Conceptualization of Global Marketing Strategy and Its Effect on Firm Performance," *Journal of Marketing,* October 2002, 40–56.

13. Michael R. Czinkota, "Export Promotion: A Framework for Finding Opportunity in Change," *Thunderbird International Business Review,* May–June 2002, 315–324.

14. Daniel C. Bello and Nicholas C. Williamson, "Contractual Arrangement and Marketing Practices in the Indirect Export Channel," *Journal of International Business Studies* 16 (Summer 1985): 65–82.

15. Mike W. Peng and Anne Y. Ilinitch, "Export Intermediary Firms: A Note on Export Development Research," *Journal of International Business Studies* 3 (1998): 609–620.

16. Vanessa Bachman, Office of Export Trading Companies, U.S. Department of Commerce, Washington, DC, October 23, 2002.

17. Oystein Moen and Per Servais, "Born Global or Gradual Global? Examining the Export Behavior of Small and Medium-Sized Enterprises," *Journal of International Marketing* 10 (no. 3, 2002): 49–72.

18. Masaaki Kotabe and Michael R. Czinkota, "State Government Promotion of Manufacturing Exports: A Gap Analysis," *Journal of International Business Studies* (Winter 1992): 637–658.

19. Yoo S. Yang, Robert P. Leone, and Dana L. Alden, "A Market Expansion Ability Approach to Identify Potential Exporters," *Journal of Marketing* 56 (January 1992): 84–96.

20. Andrew B. Bernard and J. Bradford Jensen, *Exceptional Exporter Performance: Cause Effect or Both,* Census Research Data Center, Pittsburgh, Carnegie Mellon University, 1997.

21. Farok J. Contractor and Sumit K. Kundu, "Franchising versus Company-Run Operations: Modal Choice in the Global Hotel Sector," *Journal of International Marketing* 6 (no. 2, 1998): 28–53.

22. Martin F. Connor, "International Technology Licensing," Seminars in International Trade, National Center for Export-Import Studies, Washington, DC

23. Pamela M. Deese and Sean Wooden, "Managing Intellectual Property in Licensing Agreements," *Franchising World* 33 (September 2001): 66–67.

24. *Global Franchising Statistics,* International Franchise Association, Washington DC, 2002.

25. Josh Martin, "Profitable Supply Chain Supporting Franchises," *Journal of Commerce,* Global Commerce Section (March 11, 1998): 1C.

26. George W. Russell, "Into the Frying Pan," *Asian Business* 37 (October 2001): 28–29.

27. Leonard N. Swartz, "International Trends in Retailing," Arthur Andersen, December 1999.

28. Farok J. Contractor, "Economic and Environmental Reasons for the Continuing Growth in Alliances and Interfirm Cooperation," *Emerging Issues in International Business Research,* eds. M. Kotabe and P. Aulakh (Northampton, MA: Elgar Publishing, 2002).

29. Farok J. Contractor, ibid.

30. Marko Grünhagen and Carl L. Witte, "Franchising as an Export Product and Its Role as an Economic Development Tool for Emerging Economies," *Enhancing Knowledge Development in Marketing*, vol. 13, eds. W. Kehoe and J. Lindgren, Jr. (Chicago: American Marketing Association, 2002), 414–415.

31. Jonathan L. Calof and Wilma Viviers, "Internationalization Behavior of Small- and Medium-Sized South African Enterprises," *Journal of Small Business Management* 33 (no. 4, 1995): 71–79.

32. Michael R. Czinkota, "A National Export Assistance Policy for New and Growing Businesses," in *Best Practices in International Business*, eds. M. Czinkota and I. Ronkainen (Cincinnati: South-Western, 2001), 35–45.

Chapter 8

1. Jeffrey E. Garten, "Globalization without Tears: A New Social Compact for CEOs," *Strategy and Business* (fourth quarter, 2002): 36–45.

2. "For U.S. Small Biz, Fertile Soil in Europe," *Business Week*, April 1, 2002, 57.

3. Jill G. Klein, Richard Ettenson, and Marlene Morris, "The Animosity Model of Foreign Product Purchase: An Empirical Test in the People's Republic of China," *Journal of Marketing* 62 (January 1998): 89–100.

4. **http://www.levistrauss.com/brands/dockers.htm**.

5. Stephanie Nall, "American Exports Chicken Out," *World Trade*, September 1998, 44–45.

6. Thomas L. Friedman, *The Lexus and the Olive Tree: Understanding Globalization* (New York: Anchor Books, 2000), chapters 3 and 15.

7. S. Tamer Cavusgil and Shaoming Zou, "Marketing Strategy–Performance Relationship: An Investigation of the Empirical Link in Export Market Ventures," *Journal of Marketing* 58 (January 1994): 1–21.

8. Dana James, "B2–4B Spells Profits," *Marketing News*, November 5, 2001, 1, 11–12.

9. Jean-Noël Kapferer, *Survey among 210 European Brand Managers* (Paris: Euro-RSCG, 1998).

10. Carl A. Sohlberg, "The Perennial Issue of Adaptation or Standardization of International Marketing Communication: Organizational Contingencies and Performance," *Journal of International Marketing* 10 (no. 3, 2002): 1–21.

11. "EU/Country Briefing," *Business Europe*, April 21, 1999, 9–11.

12. "Trading Places," *The Economist*, November 22, 2001, 58.

13. "U.S. and EU at Odds over Jet Noise," *The Washington Post*, January 19, 2000, E1, E10.

14. Erika Morphy, "Cutting the Cost of Compliance," *Export Today* 12 (January 1996): 14–18.

15. James D. Southwick, "Addressing Market Access Barriers in Japan through the WTO: A Survey of Typical Japan Market Access Issues and the Possibility to Address Them through WTP Dispute Resolution Procedures," *Law and Policy in International Business* 31 (Spring 2000): 923–976.

16. "EU Nears Stricter GMO Food Labels," *The Wall Street Journal*, July 5, 2002, A8.

17. Davis Goodman, "Thinking Export? Think ISO 9000," *World Trade*, August 1998, 48–49.

18. *ISO Survey 2001*, available at **http://www.iso.ch**.

19. Enrique Sierra, "The New ISO 14000 Series: What Exporters Should Know," *Trade Forum* (no. 3, 1996): 16–31.

20. Kirk Loncar, "Look Before You Leap," *World Trade*, June 1997, 92–93.

21. Drew Martin and Paul Herbig, "Marketing Implications of Japan's Social-Cultural Underpinnings," *Journal of Brand Management* 9 (January 2002): 171–179.

22. Jennifer Aaker, "Dimensions of Measuring Brand Personality," *Journal of Marketing Research* 34 (August 1997): 347–356.

23. **http://www.ctw.org**.

24. James A. Gingrich, "Five Rules for Winning Emerging Market Consumers," *Strategy and Business* (second quarter, 1999): 35–42.

25. "Holding the Fries—At the Border," *Business Week*, December 14, 1998, 8.

26. "Exporting to Survive," *Time Global Business*, September 2002, A20–A22.

27. Robert Gray, "Local on a Global Scale," *Marketing*, September 27, 2001, 22–23.

28. Jean-Noël Kapferer, "Is There Really No Hope for Local Brands?" *Journal of Brand Management* 9 (January 2002): 163–170.

29. Alan Mitchell, "Few Brands Can Achieve a Truly Global Presence," *Marketing Week*, February 7, 2002, 32–33.

30. "The Best Global Brands," *Business Week*, August 5, 2002, 92–108.

31. "Mozart's Genius Extends to Selling Lederhosen in Japan," *The Wall Street Journal Europe*, January 6, 1992, Section 1.1.

32. NameLab, Inc. (**http://www.namelab.com**).

33. Barry M. Tarnef, "How to Protect Your Goods in Transit without Going Along for a Ride," *Export Today* 9 (May 1993): 55–57.

34. Jesse Wilson, "Are Your Spanish Translations Culturally Correct?" *Export Today* 10 (May 1994): 68–69.

35. Dan McGinn, "Vodka with Punch," **http://mbajungle.com**, September/October 2002, 34–36.

36. **http://www.tetrapak.com**.

37. "Waste Not," *Business Europe*, February 20, 2002, 4.

38. Thomas J. Madden, Kelly Hewett, and Martin S. Roth, "Managing Images in Different Cultures: A Cross-National Study of Color Meanings and Preferences," *Journal of International Marketing* 8 (no. 4, 2000): 90–107.

39. "Riding the Theme Park Wave," *World Trade*, October 1999, 86.

40. "Why Don't We Use the Metric System?" *Fortune*, May 29, 2000, 56–57.

41. Carla Kruytbosch, "The Minds behind the Winners," *International Business*, January 1994, 56–70.

42. "Awash in Export Sales," *Export Today* 5 (February 1989): 11.

43. Dana James, "B2–4B Spells Profits," *Marketing News*, November 5, 2001, 1, 11–12.

44. Ian Wilkinson and Nigel Barrett, "In Search of Excellence in Exports: An Analysis of the 1986 Australian Export Award Winners," paper given at the Australian Export Award presentations, Sydney, November 28, 1986.

45. Thomas H. Stevenson and Frank C. Barnes, "Fourteen Years of ISO 9000: Impact, Criticisms, Costs, and Benefits," *Business Horizons* 44 (May/June 2001): 45–51.

46. "Keeping Cool in China," *The Economist*, April 6, 1996, 73–74.

47. Martin S. Roth and Jean B. Romeo, "Matching Product Category and Country Image Perceptions: A Framework for Managing Country-of-Origin Effects," *Journal of International Business Studies* 23 (third quarter, 1992): 477–497.

48. Warren J. Bilkey and Erik Nes, "Country-of-Origin Effects on Product Evaluations," *Journal of International Business Studies* 13 (Spring–Summer 1982): 88–99.

49. Johny K. Johansson, Ilkka A. Ronkainen, and Michael R. Czinkota, "Negative Country-of-Origin Effects: The Case of the New Russia," *Journal of International Business Studies* 25 (first quarter, 1994): 1–21.

50. Johny K. Johansson, "Determinants and Effects of the Use of 'Made in' Labels," *International Marketing Review* 6 (1989): 47–58.

51. Philip Kotler and David Gertner, "Country as Brand, Product, and Beyond: A Place Marketing and Brand Management Perspective," *Journal of Brand Management* 9 (April 2002): 249–261.

52. Arnold Schuh, "Global Standardization as a Success Formula for Marketing in Central Eastern Europe," *Journal of*

World Business 35 (Summer 2000): 133–148.

53. Business Software Alliance, *Seventh Annual BSA Global Software Piracy Study* (Washington, DC: BSA, 2002), 1; see also **http://www.bsa.org**.

54. Ilkka A. Ronkainen, "Imitation as the Worst Kind of Flattery: Product Counterfeiting," *Trade Analyst* 2 (July–August 1986): 2.

55. Ilkka A. Ronkainen and Jose-Luis Guerrero-Cusumano, "Correlates of Intellectual Property Violation," *Multinational Business Review* 9 (no. 1, 2001): 59–65.

56. "In Pursuit of Pokémon Pirates," *The Wall Street Journal*, November 8, 1999, B1, B4.

57. **http://www.wipo.org**.

58. "Patently Problematic," *The Economist*, September 14, 2002, 86.

59. "Lubricating a Crackdown," *Export Today*, June 1999, 29.

60. Michael G. Harvey and Ilkka A. Ronkainen, "International Counterfeiters: Marketing Success without the Cost and the Risk," *Columbia Journal of World Business* 20 (Fall 1985): 37–45.

61. Pankaj Ghemawat, "Distance Still Matters: The Hard Reality of Global Expansion," *Harvard Business Review* 79 (September 2001): 137–147.

Chapter 9

1. "The Secret of U.S. Exports: Great Products," *Fortune*, January 10, 2000, 154A–J.

2. James A. Gingrich, "Five Rules for Winning Emerging Market Consumers," *Strategy and Business* (second quarter, 1999), 35–46.

3. David Arnold, "Seven Rules of International Distribution," *Harvard Business Review* 78 (November/December 2000): 131–137.

4. Matthew B. Myers, and S. Tamer Cavusgil, "Export Pricing Strategy-Performance Relationship: A Conceptual Framework," *Advances in International Marketing* 8 (1996): 159–178.

5. Howard Forman and Richard A. Lancioni, "International Industrial Pricing Strategic Decisions and the Pricing Manager: Some Key Issues," *Professional Pricing Society*, October 9, 1999, at **http:www.pricing-advisor.com/jour_article2.htm**.

6. John A. Boyd, "How One Company Solved Its Export Pricing Problems," *Small Business Forum*, Fall 1995, 28–38.

7. S. Tamer Cavusgil, "Unraveling the Mystique of Export Pricing," *Business Horizons* 31 (May–June 1988): 54–63.

8. Thomas T. Nagle and Reed K. Holden, *The Strategy and Tactics of Pricing: A Guide to Profitable Decision Making*

(Englewood Cliffs, NJ: Prentice-Hall, 2002), chapter 3.

9. Mary Anne Raymond, John F. Tanner, Jr., and Jonghoon Kim, "Cost Complexity of Pricing Decisions for Exporters in Developing and Emerging Markets," *Journal of International Marketing* 9 (no. 3, 2001): 19–40.

10. Barbara Stöttinger, "Strategic Export Pricing: A Long and Winding Road," *Journal of International Marketing* 9 (no. 1, 2001): 40–63.

11. "Keeping Time with the Global Market," *World Trade*, December 1999, 82–83.

12. "What's in a Name," *Economist*, February 2, 1991, 60.

13. Al D'Amico, "Duty Drawback: An Overlooked Customs Refund Program," *Export Today* 9 (May 1993): 46–48. See also **http://www.customs.treas.gov**.

14. Michael D. White, "Money-Back Guarantees," *World Trade*, September 1999, 74–77.

15. International Chambers of Commerce, *Incoterms 2000* (Paris: ICC Publishing, 2000). See also **http://www.iccwbo.org**.

16. Kevin Maloney, "Incoterms: Clarity at the Profit Margin," *Export Today* 6 (November–December 1990): 45–46.

17. Alexandra Woznik and Edward G. Hinkelman, *A Basic Guide to Exporting* (Novate, CA: World Trade Press, 2000), chapter 10.

18. "Getting Paid: Or What's a Transaction For?" *World Trade*, September 1999, 42–52; and Chase Manhattan Bank, *Dynamics of Trade Finance* (New York: Chase Manhattan Bank, 1984): 10–11.

19. David K. Eiteman, Arthur I. Stonehill, and Michael H. Moffett, *Multinational Business Finance* (Reading, MA: Addison-Wesley, 2001), 460–488.

20. International Chamber of Commerce, *Uniform Customs and Practice for Documentary Credits* (New York: ICC Publishing Corp., 2002).

21. Vincent M. Maulella, "Payment Pitfalls for the Unwary," *World Trade*, April 1999, 76–79.

22. Erika Morphy, "Form vs. Format," *Export Today*, 15 (August 1999): 47–52.

23. Erika Morphy, "Paper's Last Stand," *Global Business*, May 2001, 36–39.

24. "Ready Cash?" *Global Business*, September 2000, 45. See also **http://www.tradecard.com**.

25. **http://www.cofacerating.com**.

26. Michael S. Tomczyk, "How Do You Collect When Foreign Customers Don't Pay?" *Export Today* 9 (November–December 1993): 33–35.

27. James Welsh, "Covering Your Bets on Credit and Collections," *World*

Trade, February 1999, 28–29; and Ron Siegel and Mark Stoyas, "Foreign Collections," *Export Today* 11 (April 1995): 44–46.

28. Saied Mahdavi, "Do German, Japanese, and U.S. Export Prices Asymmetrically Respond to Exchange Rate Changes?" *Contemporary Economic Policy* 18 (January 2000): 70–81.

29. Paul R. Krugman, "Pricing-to-Market When the Exchange Rate Changes," in S. W. Arndt and J. D. Robinson, eds., *Real-Financial Linkages among Open Economies* (Cambridge, MA: MIT Press, 1987), 49–70.

30. "Did U.S. Car Makers Err by Raising Prices When the Yen Rose?" *The Wall Street Journal*, April 18, 1988, A1, A14.

31. Michael H. Moffett, "Harley Davidson: Hedging Hogs," in Michael R. Czinkota, Ilkka A. Ronkainen, and Michael H. Moffett, *International Business 2003 Update* (Mason, OH: Thomson, 2003), 634–637.

32. "Turning Small into a Big Advantage," *Business Week*, July 13, 1998, 42–44.

33. "Competitive Exports, Sky High Imports," *Financial Mail*, October 2, 1998, 19.

34. Chi Lo, "Asia's Competitive Endgame: Life after China's WTO Entry," *The China Business Review*, January–February 2002, 22–36.

35. See, for example, **http://www.jetro.org**.

36. Miles Maguire, "Reading Your Bank's Correspondence," *Export Today* 11 (November/December 1995): 27–31.

37. Miles Maguire, "Mergers and Money," *Export Today*, 11 (September 1995): 24–30.

38. Lawrence W. Tuller, "Beyond the LC," *Export Today*, 12 (August 1996): 70–74.

39. Daniel S. Levine, "Factoring Pays Off," *World Trade*, September 1998, 79–80.

40. Ray Pereira, "International Factoring," *World Trade*, December 1999, 68–69.

41. Mary Ann Ring, "Innovative Export Financing," *Business America*, January 11, 1993, 12–14.

42. The authors acknowledge the assistance of Craig O'Connor of the Export-Import Bank of the United States.

43. "EXIM-Bank Program Summary," in *Export-Import Bank of the United States* (Washington, DC: EXIM Bank, 1985), 1; updated for 2002.

44. Robert Frewen, "Are Your International Credit Terms Cutting Your Throat?" *World Trade*, January 2001, 71–73.

45. Claude Cellich, "Business Negotiations: Making the First Offer," *International Trade Forum* 14 (no. 2, 2000): 12–16.

46. Pricewaterhousecoopers, *State of the Industry Report 2002* (Fairfax, VA:

Equipment Leasing and Finance Foundation, 2002), 9; see also **http://www.elaonline.com**.

47. Elnora M. Uzzelle, "American Equipment Leasing Companies Should Consider the International Arena," *Business America,* June 28, 1993, 11–12.

48. **http://www.elcamino.com**.

49. "Steeling Jobs," *Time Global Business,* February 2002, B6–B12.

50. "EU Charges Asian Fiber Dumping," *Textile World,* May 1999, 134.

51. Paul Magnusson, "Bring Anti-Dumping Laws Up to Date," *Business Week,* July 19, 1999, 45.

52. **http://www.wto.org**.

53. "A U.S. Trade Ploy That Is Starting to Boomerang," *Business Week,* July 29, 2002, 64–65.

54. Delener Nejdet, "An Ethical and Legal Synthesis of Dumping: Growing Concerns in International Marketing," *Journal of Business Ethics* 17 (November 1998): 1747–1753.

Chapter 10

1. Wilbur Schramm and Donald F. Roberts, *The Process and Effects of Mass Communications* (Urbana: University of Illinois Press, 1971), 12–17.

2. John L. Graham and Persa Economou, "Introduction to the Symposium on International Business Negotiations," *Journal of International Business Studies* 29 (no. 4, 1998): 661–663.

3. Joel Reedy, Shauna Schullo, and Kenneth Zimmerman, *Electronic Marketing* (Mason, OH: South-Western, 2003), chapter 17.

4. "What's Working for Other American Companies," *International Sales & Marketing,* November 22, 1996, 5.

5. George Field, Hotaka Katahira, and Jerry Wind, *Leveraging Japan: Marketing to the New Asia* (Hoboken, NJ: Jossey-Bass, 1999), chapter 10.

6. John A. Quelch and Lisa R. Klein, "The Internet and International Marketing," *Sloan Management Review* 38 (Spring 1996): 60–75.

7. Terence Brake, Danielle Walker, and Thomas Walker, *Doing Business Internationally: The Guide to Cross-Cultural Success* (New York: McGraw-Hill Trade, 1994), chapters 1 and 2.

8. Courtney Fingan, "Table Manners," *Global Business,* July 2000, 48–52.

9. Nurit Zaidman, "Stereotypes of International Managers: Content and Impact on Business Interactions," *Group and Organization Management* 25 (March 2000): 45–66.

10. Stephen E. Weiss, "Negotiating with the Romans — Part I," *Sloan Management Review* 36 (Spring 1994): 85–99.

11. Arnold Pachtman, "Getting to 'Hao!'" *International Business,* July/August 1998, 24–26.

12. Claude Cellich, "FAQ . . . About Business Negotiations on the Internet," *International Trade Forum,* 15 (no. 1, 2001): 10–11.

13. Pervez N. Ghauri, "Guidelines for International Business Negotiations," *International Marketing Review* 4 (Autumn 1986): 72–82.

14. "Negotiating in Europe," *Hemispheres,* July 1994, 43–47.

15. Virginia J. Rehberg, "Kuwait: Reality Sets In," *Export Today* 7 (December 1991): 56–58.

16. Catherine H. Tinsley and Madan M. Pillutla, "Negotiating in the United States and Hong Kong," *Journal of International Business Studies* 29 (no. 4, 1998): 711–728.

17. Claude Cellich, "Negotiations for Export Business: Elements for Success," *International Trade Forum* 9 (no. 4, 1995): 20–27.

18. Jackie Mayfield, Milton Mayfield, Drew Martin, and Paul Herbig, "How Location Impacts International Business Negotiations," *Review of Business* 19 (Winter 1998): 21–24.

19. "Stay-at-Home" Careers?" *Global Business,* January 2001, 62.

20. Framework for this section adapted from John L. Graham and Roy A. Herberger, Jr., "Negotiators Abroad—Don't Shoot from the Hip," *Harvard Business Review* 61 (July–August 1983): 160–168.

21. Sally Stewart and Charles F. Keown, "Talking with the Dragon: Negotiating in the People's Republic of China," *Columbia Journal of World Business* 24 (Fall 1989): 68–72.

22. Hokey Min and William P. Galle, "International Negotiation Strategies of U.S. Purchasing Professionals," *International Journal of Purchasing and Materials Management* 29 (Summer 1993): 41–53.

23. Frank L. Acuff, "Just Call Me Mr. Ishmael," *Export Today* 11 (July 1995): 14–15.

24. Andrea Kirby, "Doing Business in Asia," *Credit Management,* October 2002, 24–25.

25. Kathy Schmidt, "How to Speak So You're Open to Interpretation," *Presentations* 13 (December 1999): 126–127.

26. Berry J. Kesselman and Bryan Batson, "China: Clause and Effect," *Export Today* 12 (June 1996): 18–26.

27. Ilkka A. Ronkainen, "Project Exports and the CMEA," in *International Marketing Management,* ed. Erdener Kaynak (New York: Praeger, 1984), 305–317.

28. Richard D. Lewis, *When Cultures Collide* (London: Nicholas Brealey Publishing, 2000), chapter 17.

29. Y. H. Wong and Thomas K. Leung, *Guanxi: Relationship Marketing in a Chinese Context* (Binghamton, NY: Haworth Press, 2001), chapter 3.

30. Richard W. Lewis, *Absolut Book: The Absolut Vodka Advertising Story* (New York: Journey Editions, 1996). For the latest ads in the series, see **http://www.absolut.com**.

31. "2002 State of the Industry Report," *Beverage Industry,* June 2002, 38–40.

32. "TBWA/Chiat/Day to Serve Competing Spirits Giants," *Advertising Age,* April 8, 2002, 45.

33. Gary Levin, "Russian Vodka Plans U.S. Rollout," *Advertising Age,* November 11, 1991, 4.

34. John Helyar, "Will Harley-Davidson Hit the Wall?" *Fortune,* August 12, 2002, 120–124.

35. Lara Sowinski, "Breaking All the Rules," *World Trade,* May 2002, 16–19. See also **http://www.ernieball.com**.

36. **http://www.cnewsusa.com**.

37. **http://guiaexport.bellsouth.com**.

38. Sean Callahan, "McCann-Erickson Offers B-to-B Clients the World," *Business Marketing,* January 2000, 35.

39. *The Handbook of International Direct and E-Marketing* (London: Kogan Page Ltd., 2001), chapter 1.

40. Hope Katz Gibbs, "Mediums for the Message," *Export Today,* 15 (June 1999): 22–27.

41. Deborah Begum, "U.S. Retailers Find Mail-Order Happiness in Japan," *World Trade,* 13 (May 1996): 22–25.

42. William McDonald, "International Direct Marketing in a Rapidly Changing World," *Direct Marketing* 61 (March 1999): 44–47.

43. Hope Katz Gibbs, "It's Your Call," *Export Today* 13 (May 1997): 46–51. For examples, see Brendan Reid, "Call Center Showcase," *Call Center Magazine* 15 (March 2002): 40–41.

44. Sam Bloomfield, "Reach Out and Touch Someone Far, Far Away," *World Trade,* April 1999, 80–84.

45. Roger Hickey, "Toll-Free Europe: Continental Call Centers," *Export Today,* 11 (January 1995): 20–21.

46. Rolf Rykken, "Call Waiting?" *Export Today,* 14 (November 1998): 55–57.

47. For a discussion on marketing on the Internet, see K. Douglas Hoffman, Michael R. Czinkota, Peter R. Dickson, Patrick Dunne, Abbie Griffith, Michael D. Hutt, John H. Lindgren, Robert F. Lusch, Ilkka A. Ronkainen, Bert Rosenbloom, Jagdish N. Sheth, Terence A. Shimp, Judy A. Siguaw, Penny M. Simpson, Thomas W. Speh, and Joel E. Urbany, *Marketing: Best Practices* (Mason, OH: South-Western, 2003), chapter 15.

48. P. Rajan Varadarajan and Manjit Yadav, "Marketing Strategy and the Internet," *Academy of Marketing Science* 30 (Fall 2002): 296–312.

49. "International in Internet Closes U.S. Lead," *Marketing News*, February 14, 2000, 7.

50. Carl R. Jacobsen, "How Connecticut Companies Use the Internet for Exporting," *Business America*, January 1998, 17.

51. Gerry Dempsey, "A Hands-On Guide for Multilingual Web Sites," *World Trade*, September 1999, 68–70.

52. V. Kanti Prasad, K. Ramamurthy, and G. M. Naidu, "The Influence of Internet-Marketing Integration on Marketing Competencies and Export Performance," *Journal of International Marketing* 9 (no. 4, 2001): 82–110.

53. Lewis Rose, "Before You Advertise on the Net—Check the International Marketing Laws," *Bank Marketing*, May 1996, 40–42.

54. Thomas V. Bonoma, "Get More Out of Your Trade Shows," *Harvard Business Review* 61 (January–February 1983): 137–145.

55. Kathleen V. Schmidt, "Trading Plätze," *Marketing News*, July 19, 1999, 11.

56. Richard B. Golik, "The Lure of Foreign Trade Shows," *International Business*, March 1996, 16–20.

57. **http://www.messe.de/27711** for "Trade Shows as a B2B Communication Tool."

58. "IMB '97 a Hit: Cologne Show Draws 30,000 Manufacturers from 100 Countries," *Apparel Industry Magazine*, August 1997, 16–26.

59. Bob Lamons, "Involve Your Staff in Trade Shows for Better Results," *Marketing News*, March 1, 1999, 9–10.

60. **http://www.buyusa.com/cgi-bin/ db2www.exe/trade_res/virt_ tradeshow.d2w/input.**

61. Charlene Solomon, "Managing an Overseas Sales Force," *World Trade*, April 1999, S4–S6.

62. For a detailed discussion of the expatriate phenomenon, see Michael R. Czinkota, Ilkka A. Ronkainen, and Michael H. Moffett, *International Business: 2003 Update* (Mason, OH: South-Western, 2003), chapter 18.

63. Lisa Bertagnoli, "Selling Overseas Complex Endeavor," *Marketing News*, July 30, 2001, 4.

Chapter 11

1. Donald V. Fites, "Make Your Dealers Your Partners," *Harvard Business Review* 74 (March/April 1996): 84–95.

2. Rod B. McNaughton, "Foreign Market Channel Integration Decisions of Canadian Computer Software Firms," *International Business Review* 5 (no. 1, 1996): 23–52.

3. Peter N. O'Farrell, Paul A. Wood, and Jiang Zheng, "Internationalization of Business Services: An Interegional Analysis," *Regional Studies* 30 (no. 2, 1998): 101–118.

4. Rajiv Vaidyanathan and Praveen Aggarwal, "Strategic Brand Alliance: Implications of Ingredient Branding for National and Private Label Brands," *The Journal of Product and Brand Management* 9 (no. 4, 2000): 214–228.

5. Erin Anderson, George S. Day, and V. Kasturi Rangan, "Strategic Channel Design," *Sloan Management Review* 39 (Summer 1997): 59–69.

6. The Boston Consulting Group, December 21, 1999; available at **http://www.bcg.com.**

7. Rajshkhtar Javalgi and Rosemary Ramsey, "Strategic Issues of E-Commerce as an Alternative Global Distribution System," *International Marketing Review* 18 (no. 4, 2001): 376–391.

8. Michael R. Czinkota and Jon Woronoff, *Unlocking Japan's Market* (Rutland, VT: Tuttle Co., 1993).

9. Stephen J. Arnold and John Fernie, "Wal-Mart in Europe: Prospects for the UK," *International Marketing Review* 17 (nos. 4 and 5, 2000): 416–432.

10. "China's Car Makers: Flattened by Falling Tariffs," *Business Week*, December 3, 2001, 51; and Mike Dunne, "Card Loans: Ready, Set, Go?" *Automotive News International*, September 1, 2000, 33.

11. Nicholas Alexander and Hayley Myers, "The Retail Internationalization Process," *International Marketing Review* 17 (nos. 4 and 5, 2000): 334–353.

12. "European Retailing: French Fusion," *The Economist*, September 4, 1999, 68–69.

13. Vijay Govindarajan and Anil K. Gupta, "Taking Wal-Mart Global: Lessons from Retailing's Giant," *Strategy and Business* 4 (fourth quarter, 1999): 14–25.

14. "For U.S. Internet Portals, the Next Big Battleground Is Overseas," *The Wall Street Journal*, March 23, 2000, B1, B4.

15. Rod B. McNaughton, "The Use of Multiple Channels by Small Knowledge-Intensive Firms," *International Marketing Review* 19 (no. 2, 2002): 190–203.

16. **http://www.expert.org.**

17. Sandra Dolbow, "Benetton Bounces Back," *Brandweek*, February 12, 2001, 1, 8.

18. Erin Anderson and Hubert Gatignon, "Modes of Foreign Entry: A Transaction Cost Analysis and Propositions," *Journal of International Business Studies* 17 (Fall 1986): 1–26.

19. Erin Anderson and Anne T. Coughlan, "International Market Entry and Expansion via Independent or Integrated Channels of Distribution," *Journal of Marketing* 51 (January 1987): 71–82.

20. We are indebted to Dr. James H. Sood of the American University for this example.

21. Michael R. Czinkota, "Distribution of Consumer Products in Japan: An Overview," in *International Marketing Strategy: Environmental Assessment and Entry Strategies*, Michael R. Czinkota and Ilkka A. Ronkainen, eds. (Ft. Worth, TX: The Dryden Press, 1994), 293–307.

22. Andrea Knox, "The European Minefield," *World Trade*, November 1999, 36–40.

23. Soumava Banbdyopadhyay and Robert H. Robicheaux, "Dealer Satisfaction through Relationship Marketing across Cultures," *Journal of Marketing Channels* 6 (no. 2, 1997): 35–55.

24. Daniel C. Bello and David I. Gilliland, "The Effect of Output Controls, Process Controls, and Flexibility on Export Channel Performance," *Journal of Marketing* 61 (January 1997): 22–38.

25. For a discussion of the basic forms, see **http://www.usatrade.gov.**

26. "It Could Be Worse," *International Business*, April 1996, 8.

27. Peter B. Fitzpatrick and Alan S. Zimmerman, *Essentials of Export Marketing* (New York: American Management Association, 1985), 43.

28. S. Tamer Cavusgil, Poh-Lin Yeoh, and Michel Mitri, "Selecting Foreign Distributors: An Export Systems Approach," *Industrial Marketing Management* 24 (Winter 1995): 297–304.

29. Sherrie E. Zhan, "Booting Up in Santiago," *World Trade*, July 1999, 30–34.

30. "Five Steps to Finding the Right Business Partners Abroad," *World Trade*, March 1999, 86–87.

31. Both TOP and CDIC are available on the National Trade Data Bank at **http://www.stat-usa.gov.**

32. U.S. Department of Commerce, *2002 Export Programs Guide* (Washington, D.C.: Department of Commerce, 2002). Also available through **http://www.ita.doc.gov/tic.**

33. Nick Wreden, "Internet Opens Markets Abroad," *Information Week*, November 16, 1998, 46–48.

34. Joseph V. Barks, "Penetrating Latin America," *International Business*, February 1996, 78–80.

35. Lara L. Sowinski, "Pernod Ricard Toasts Its U.S. Distribution Partners," *World Trade*, August 2002, 24–25.

36. Keysuk Kim and Changho Oh, "On Distributor Commitment in Marketing Channels for Industrial Products: Contrast between the United States and Japan," *Journal of International Marketing* 10 (no. 1, 2002): 72–97.

37. For a detailed discussion, see International Chambers of Commerce, *The ICC Model Distributorship Contract* (Paris: ICC Publishing, 2002), chapters 1–3; **http://www.iccwbo.org.**

38. Michael G. Harvey and Ilkka A. Ron-kainen, "The Three Faces of the Foreign Corrupt Practices Act: Retain, Reform, or Repeal," in *1984 AMA Educators' Proceedings* (Chicago: American Marketing Association, 1984), 290–294.

39. Gary L. Frazier, James D. Gill, and Sudhir H. Kale, "Dealer Dependence Levels and Reciprocal Actions in a Channel of Distribution in a Developing Country," *Journal of Marketing* 53 (January 1989): 50–69.

40. Leonidas C. Leonidou, Constantine S. Katsikeas, and John Hadjimarcou, "Building Successful Export Business Relationships: A Behavioral Perspective," *Journal of International Marketing* 10 (no. 3, 2002): 96–115.

41. Bert Rosenbloom, *Marketing Channels: A Management View,* 6th ed. (Mason, OH: South-Western, 1999), Chapter 9.

42. Sudhir H. Kale and Roger P. McIntyre, "Distribution Channel Relationships in Diverse Cultures," *International Marketing Review* 8 (1991): 31–45.

43. Constantine S. Katsikeas and Tevfik Dalgic, "Importing Problems Experienced by Distributors: The Importance of Level-of-Import Development," *Journal of International Marketing* 3 (no. 2, 1995): 51–70.

44. David Arnold, "Seven Rules of International Distribution," *Harvard Business Review* 78 (November–December 2000): 131–137.

45. Ilkka A. Ronkainen and Linda van de Gucht, "Making a Case for Gray Markets," *Journal of Commerce,* January 6, 1987, 13A. See also **http://www.antigraymarket.org**.

46. Jeff Prine, "Time On-Line, the New Global Grey Market," *Modern Jeweler,* November 1998, 45–48.

47. Frank V. Cespedes, E. Raymond Corey, and V. Kasturi Rangan, "Gray Markets: Causes and Cures," *Harvard Business Review* 66 (July–August 1988): 75–82.

48. "The Earth Is Shifting under Heavy Equipment," *Business Week,* April 6, 1998, 44.

49. "How the Gray Marketeers Are Cashing In on DRAM Shortages," *Electronic Business,* June 1, 1988, 18–19.

50. Peggy E. Chaudry and Michael G. Walsh, "Managing the Gray Market in the European Union: The Case of the Pharmaceutical Industry," *Journal of International Marketing* 3 (no. 3, 1995): 11–33; and "Parallel Trade and Comparative Pricing of Medicines: Poor Choice for Patients," *Pfizer Forum,* 1996.

51. "European Court Supports Levi Strauss in Tesco Case," *The Wall Street Journal,* November 21, 2001, A11.

52. "A Red-Letter Day for Gray Marketeers," *Business Week,* June 13, 1988, 30.

53. Ellen Klein and J. D. Howard, "Strings Attached," *North American International Business* 6 (May 1991): 54–55.

54. For a comprehensive discussion on remedies, see Robert E. Weigand, "Parallel Import Channel—Options for Preserving Territorial Integrity," *Columbia Journal of World Business* 26 (Spring 1991): 53–60; and S. Tamer Cavusgil and Ed Sikora, "How Multinationals Can Counter Gray Market Imports," *Columbia Journal of World Business* 23 (Winter 1988): 75–85.

55. Hong Liu and Yen Po Wang, "Co-ordination of International Channel Relationships," *Journal of Business and Industrial Marketing* 14 (no. 2, 1999): 130–150.

56. Erika Morphy, "Making Cash Flow," *Export Today* 14 (July 1998): 22–29.

57. Miles Maguire, "Spinning the Web," *Export Today* 14 (January 1998): 28–32.

58. "Shopping for a Marketplace," *Global Business,* February 2001, 36–37.

59. Rolf Rykken, "Opening the Gate," *Export Today* 15 (February 1999): 35–42.

60. Eryn Brown, "Nine Ways to Win on the Web," *Fortune,* May 24, 1999, 112–125.

61. Hope Katz Gibbs, "Taking Global Local," *Global Business,* December 1999, 44–50.

62. Richard Prem, "Plan Your e-Commerce Tax Strategy," *e-Business Advisor,* April 1999, 36.

63. Erika Morphy, "The Geography of e-Commerce," *Global Business,* November 1999, 26–33.

64. "E-Commerce Firms Start to Rethink Opposition to Privacy Regulation as Abuses, Anger Rise," *The Wall Street Journal,* January 6, 2000, A24.

65. Amy Zuckerman, "Order in the Courts?" *World Trade,* September 2001, 26–28.

66. "Music Piracy Poses a Threat to Regional Artists," *The Wall Street Journal,* June 4, 2002, B10.

Chapter 12

1. Theodore Levitt, *The Marketing Imagination* (New York: Free Press, 1983), 20–49.

2. Jonathan Sprague, "China's Manufacturing Beachhead," *Fortune,* October 28, 2002, 1192A–J.

3. This section draws from George S. Yip, *Total Global Strategy II* (Upper Saddle River, NJ: Prentice Hall, 2002), chapters 1 and 2; Jagdish N. Sheth and Atul Parvatiyar, "The Antecedents and Consequences of Integrated Global Marketing," *International Marketing Review* 18 (no. 1, 2001): 16–29; George S. Yip, "Global Strategy . . . In a World of Nations?" *Sloan Management Review* 31 (Fall 1989): 29–41; and Susan P. Douglas and C. Samuel Craig, "Evolution of Global Marketing Strategy: Scale, Scope, and Synergy," *Columbia Journal of World Business* 24 (Fall 1989): 47–58.

4. Ernst Dichter, "The World Customer," *Harvard Business Review* 40 (July–August 1962): 113–122.

5. Kenichi Ohmae, *The Invisible Continent: Four Strategic Imperatives of the New Economy* (New York: Harper Business, 2001), chapter 1; Kenichi Ohmae, *The Borderless World: Power and Strategy in the Interlinked Economy* (New York: Harper Business, 1999), chapter 1; and Kenichi Ohmae, *Triad Power: The Coming Shape of Global Competition* (New York: Free Press, 1985), 22–27.

6. Luciano Catoni, Nora Förisdal Larssen, James Nayor, and Andrea Zocchi, "Travel Tips for Retailers" *The McKinsey Quarterly* 38 (no. 3, 2002): 88–98.

7. Catherine George and J. Michael Pearson, "Riding the Pharma Roller Coaster," *The McKinsey Quarterly* 38 (no. 4, 2002): 89–98.

8. "Finnish Paper Concern to Buy Champion," *The Wall Street Journal,* February 18, 2000, A3, A6.

9. Stuart Crainer, "And the New Economy Winner Is . . . Europe," *Strategy and Business* 6 (second quarter, 2001): 40–47.

10. Suzy Wetlaufer, "Driving Change: An Interview with Ford Motor Company's Jacques Nasser," *Harvard Business Review* 77 (March–April 1999): 76–88.

11. "Telecommunications," *The Economist,* April 4, 2002, 102.

12. Gary Knight, "Entrepreneurship and Marketing Strategy: The SME under Globalization," *Journal of International Marketing* 8 (no. 2, 2000): 12–32.

13. "A Dedicated Enemy of Fashion: Nestlé," *The Economist,* August 31, 2002, 51.

14. Jordan D. Lewis, *Trusted Partners: How Companies Build Mutual Trust and Win Together* (New York: The Free Press, 2000), 157.

15. Cait Murphy, "The Hunt for Globalization That Works," *Fortune,* October 28, 2002, 67–72.

16. "3 Big Carmakers to Create Net Site for Buying Parts," *The Washington Post,* February 26, 2000, E1, E8.

17. Myung-Su Chae and John S. Hill, "Determinants and Benefits of Global Strategic Planning Formality," *International Marketing Review* 17 (no. 6, 2000): 538–562.

18. "Computing's New Shape," *The Economist,* November 23, 2002, 11–12.

19. C. Samuel Craig and Susan P. Douglas, "Configural Advantage in Global Markets," *Journal of International Marketing* 8 (no. 1, 2000): 6–26.

20. Michael E. Porter, *Competitive Strategy: Techniques for Analyzing Industries and*

Competitors (New York: Free Press, 1998), chapter 1.

21. "Europe's Car Makers Expect Tidy Profits," *The Wall Street Journal,* January 27, 2000, A16.

22. Lori Ioannou, "It's a Small World After All," *International Business,* February 1994, 82–88.

23. "Nokia Widens Gap with Its Rivals," *The Wall Street Journal,* August 20, 2002, B6.

24. Michael Porter, *Competitive Advantage: Creating and Sustaining Superior Performance* (New York: Free Press, 1998), chapter 1.

25. Robert M. Grant, *Contemporary Strategy Analysis: Concepts, Techniques, Applications* (Oxford, England: Blackwell, 2002), chapter 8.

26. George S. Yip, *Total Global Strategy II* (Upper Saddle River, NJ: Prentice Hall, 2002), chapter 10.

27. The models referred to are GE/McKinsey, Shell International, and A. D. Little portfolio models.

28. "Company CV: Cereal Partners Worldwide," *Marketing,* November 29, 2001, 50.

29. "The Fight for Digital Dominance," *The Economist,* November 23, 2002, 61–62.

30. "Tissue Titans Target Globally with Key Brands," *Advertising Age,* December 20, 1999, 4.

31. Richard Tomlinson, "Europe's New Computer Game," *Fortune,* February 21, 2000, 219–224.

32. Saeed Samiee and Kendall Roth, "The Influence of Global Marketing Standardization on Performance," *Journal of Marketing* 56 (April 1992): 1–17.

33. "Euroteen Market Grabs U.S. Attention," *Marketing News,* October 22, 2001, 15.

34. "The American Connection," *The Washington Post,* May 25, 2002, E1–E2.

35. Peter N. Child, Suzanne Heywood, and Michael Kliger, "Do Retail Brands Travel?" *The McKinsey Quarterly* 38 (no. 1, 2002): 73–77.

36. Aruna Chandra and John K. Ryans, "Why India Now?" *Marketing Management,* March/April 2002, 43–45.

37. Imad B. Baalbaki and Naresh K. Malhotra, "Marketing Management Bases for International Market Segmentation: An Alternate Look at the Standardization/Customization Debate," *International Marketing Review* 10 (no. 1, 1993): 19–44.

38. Rahul Jacob, "The Big Rise," *Fortune,* May 30, 1994, 74–90.

39. "Whirlpool's Platform for Growth," *Financial Times,* March 26, 1998, 8.

40. "Shania Reigns," *Time,* December 9, 2002, 80–85.

41. Larry Greenemeier, "Offshore Outsourcing Grows to Global Propor-

tions," *Information Week,* February 2002, 56–58.

42. W. Chan Kim and R. A. Mauborgne, "Becoming an Effective Global Competitor," *Journal of Business Strategy* 8 (January–February 1988): 33–37.

43. Gary Hamel and C. K. Prahalad, "Do You Really Have a Global Strategy?" *Harvard Business Review* 63 (July–August 1985): 75–82.

44. "Nokia Widens Lead in Wireless Market While Motorola, Ericsson Fall Back," *The Wall Street Journal,* February 8, 2000, B8.

45. Andreas F. Grein, C. Samuel Craig, and Hirokazu Takada, "Integration and Responsiveness: Marketing Strategies of Japanese and European Automobile Manufacturers," *Journal of International Marketing* 9 (no. 2, 2001): 19–50.

46. James A. Gingrich, "Five Rules for Winning Emerging Market Consumers," *Strategy and Business* (second quarter, 1999): 19–33.

47. "Does Globalization Have Staying Power?" *Marketing Management,* March/April 2002, 18–23.

48. Kamran Kashani, "Beware the Pitfalls of Global Marketing," *Harvard Business Review* 67 (September–October 1989): 91–98.

49. George S. Yip, Pierre M. Loewe, and Michael Y. Yoshino, "How to Take Your Company to the Global Market," *Columbia Journal of World Business* 23 (Winter 1988): 28–40.

50. George S. Yip and Tammy L. Madsen, "Global Account Management: The New Frontier in Relationship Marketing," *International Marketing Review* 13 (no. 3, 1996): 24–42.

51. David B. Montgomery and George S. Yip, "The Challenge of Global Customer Management," *Marketing Management,* Winter 2000, 22–29.

52. John A. Quelch and Helen Bloom, "Ten Steps to Global Human Resources Strategy," *Strategy and Business* 4 (first quarter, 1999): 18–29.

53. Sharon O'Donnell and Insik Jeong, "Marketing Standardization within Global Industries," *International Marketing Review* 17 (no. 1, 2000): 19–33.

Chapter 13

1. United Nations, World Investment Report 1998, New York, United Nations, 2001, XVIII. **http://www.un.org**.

2. *Survey of Current Business,* U.S. Department of Commerce, Bureau of Economic Analysis, October 2002; **http://www.bea.doc.gov**.

3. *Multinational Corporations in World Development* (New York: United Nations, 1973), 23.

4. Bernard L. Simonin, "Transfer of Marketing Know-How in International Strategic Alliances: An Empirical

Investigation of the Role and Antecedents of Knowledge Ambiguity," *Journal of International Business Studies* 30 (no. 3, 1999): 463–490.

5. Lenn Gomes and Kannan Ramaswamy, "An Empirical Examination of the Form of the Relationship between Multinationality and Performance," *Journal of International Business Studies* 30 (no. 1, 1999): 173–188.

6. Howard Lewis III and David Richardson, *Why Global Commitment Really Matters!* (Washington, DC: Institute for International Economics, 2001).

7. Detlev Nitsch, Paul Beamish, and Shige Makino, "Characteristics and Performance of Japanese Foreign Direct Investment in Europe," *European Management Journal* 13 (no. 3, 1995): 276–285.

8. Michael R. Czinkota, "From Bowling Alone to Standing Together," *Marketing Management,* March/April 2002, 12–16.

9. Jack N. Behrman, "Transnational Corporations in the New International Economic Order," *Journal of International Business Studies* 12 (Spring–Summer 1981): 29–42.

10. John M. Mezias, "How to Identify Liabilities of Foreignness and Assess Their Effects on Multinational Corporations," *Journal of International Management,* 8 (no. 3, 2002): 265–282.

11. Michael R. Czinkota, "Success of Globalization Rests on Good Business Reputations," *The Japan Times,* October 12, 2002, 19.

12. Prasad Padmanabhan and Kang Rae Cho, "Decision Specific Experience in Foreign Ownership and Establishment Strategies: Evidence from Japanese Firms," *Journal of International Business Studies* 30 (no. 1, 1999): 25–44.

13. Richard H. Holton, "Making International Joint Ventures Work," presented at the seminar on the Management of Headquarters/Subsidiary Relationships in Transnational Corporations, Stockholm School of Economics, June 2–4, 1980, 4.

14. Isaiah Frank, *Foreign Enterprise in Developing Countries* (Baltimore: Johns Hopkins University, 1980).

15. W. G. Friedman and G. Kalmanoff, *Joint International Business Ventures* (New York: Columbia University Press, 1961).

16. Holton, "Making International Joint Ventures Work," 5.

17. Oded Shenkar and Shmuel Ellis, "Death of the 'Organization Man': Temporal Relations in Strategic Alliances," *The International Executive* 37 (no. 6, November/December 1995): 537–553.

18. Holton, "Making International Joint Ventures Work," 7.

19. Jordan D. Lewis, *Partnerships for Profit: Structuring and Managing Strategic Alliances* (New York: Free Press, 1990), 85–87.

20. Vijay Pothukuchi, Fariborz Demnnpour, Jaepil Choi, Chao C. Chen, and Seung Ho Park, "National and Organizational Culture Differences and International Joint Venture Performance," *Journal of International Business Studies,* 33 (second quarter, 2002): 243–265.

21. Manuel G. Serapio, Jr., and Wayne F. Cascio, "End-Games in International Alliances," *Academy of Management Executive* 10 (no. 1, 1996): 62–73.

22. **http://www.eads.com**, accessed November 13, 2002.

23. Richard Gibson, "Cereal Venture Is Planning Honey of a Battle in Europe," *The Wall Street Journal,* November 14, 1990, B1, B8.

24. Lawrence S. Welch and Anubis Pacifico, "Management Contracts: A Role in Internationalization?" *International Marketing Review* 7 (1990): 64–74.

25. Richard W. Wright and Colin Russel, "Joint Ventures in Developing Countries: Realities and Responses," *Columbia Journal of World Business* 10 (Spring 1975): 74–80.

Chapter 14

1. "Tailoring World's Cars to U.S. Tastes," *The Wall Street Journal,* January 15, 2001, B1; and "Auto Marketers Gas Up for World Car Drive," *Advertising Age,* January 16, 1995, 1–16.

2. *Introducing Unilever,* available at **http://www.unilever.com**.

3. Black & Decker's 2002 Vision Statement is available at **http://www.bdk.com/vision_statement.htm**. See also "Black & Decker's Gamble on 'Globalization,'" *Fortune,* May 14, 1984, 40–48.

4. "The Zen of Nissan," *Business Week,* July 22, 2002, 18–20.

5. "Blade-runner," *The Economist,* April 10, 1993, 68.

6. Bill Saporito, "Behind the Tumult at P&G," *Fortune,* March 7, 1994, 74–82.

7. Edward Tse, "Competing in China: An Integrated Approach," *Strategy and Business* 3 (fourth quarter, 1998): 45–52.

8. Ben Van Houten, "Foreign Interpreter," *Restaurant Business,* November 1, 1999, 32.

9. Eric von Hippel, *The Sources of Innovation* (Oxford, England: Oxford University Press, 1997), chapter 1.

10. Eric von Hippel, Stefan Thomke, and Mary Sonnack, "Creating Breakthroughs at 3M," *Harvard Business Review* 77 (September–October 1999): 47–57.

11. "Could America Afford the Transistor Today?" *Business Week,* March 7, 1994, 80–84.

12. Eric von Hippel and Ralph Katz, "Shifting Innovation to Users via Toolkits," *Management Science* 48 (July 2002): 821–833.

13. David DeVoss, "The $3 Billion Question," *World Trade,* September 1998, 34–39.

14. Laurel Wentz, "World Brands," *Advertising Age International,* September 1996, i1–i21.

15. Edward Tse, "The Right Way to Achieve Profitable Growth in the Chinese Market," *Strategy & Business* 3 (second quarter, 1998): 10–21.

16. "The Stateless Corporation," *Business Week,* May 14, 1990, 98–106; see also "The World of Otis," available at **http://www.otis.com**.

17. "A Car Is Born," *Economist,* September 13, 1997, 68–69.

18. Ilkka A. Ronkainen, "Product Development in the Multinational Firm," *International Marketing Review* 1 (Winter 1983): 24–30.

19. Durward K. Sobek, Jeffrey K. Liker, and Allen C. Ward, "Another Look at How Toyota Integrates Product Development," *Harvard Business Review* 76 (July–August 1998): 36–49.

20. Edward G. Krubasik, "Customize Your Product Development," *Harvard Business Review* 66 (November–December 1988): 46–52.

21. Georges LeRoy, *Multinational Product Strategies: A Typology for Analysis of Worldwide Product Innovation Diffusion* (New York: Praeger, 1976), 1–3.

22. "In the Labs, the Fight to Spend Less, Get More," *Business Week,* June 28, 1993, 102–104.

23. "For Best Results, Decentralize R&D," *Business Week,* June 28, 1993, 134.

24. Alphonso O. Ogbuehi and Ralph A. Bellas, Jr., "Decentralized R&D for Global Product Development: Strategic Implications for the Multinational Corporation," *International Marketing Review* 9 (no. 5, 1992): 60–70.

25. Susan Moffat, "Picking Japan's Research Brain," *Fortune,* March 25, 1991, 84–96.

26. "Savi Launches Global R&D Center in Singapore," *Transportation & Distribution,* July 2002, 16.

27. Robert Ronstadt, "International R&D: The Establishment and Evolution of Research and Development Abroad by U.S. Multinationals," *Journal of International Business Studies* 9 (Spring–Summer 1978): 7–24.

28. Guido Reger, "Internationalization of Research and Development in Western European, Japanese, and North American Multinationals," *International Journal of Entrepreneurship and Innova-*

tion Management 2 (nos. 2/3, 2002): 164–185.

29. Manuel G. Serapio and Donald H. Dalton, "Foreign R&D Facilities in the United States," *Research and Technology Management,* November–December 1993, 33–39.

30. Michelle Fellman, "Auto Researchers' Focus on Customers Can Help Drive Sales in Other Industries," *Marketing News,* January 4, 1999, 12.

31. C. K. Prahalad and Allen Hammond, "Serving the World's Poor, Profitably," *Harvard Business Review* 80 (September 2002): 48–57.

32. "Sharp Puts the Consumer on Its New-Product Team," *Business International,* December 14, 1992, 401–402.

33. Lester C. Krogh, "Managing R&D Globally: People and Financial Considerations," *Research & Technology Management* 14 (July–August 1994): 25–28.

34. Rajesh Sethi, Daniel Smith, and C. Whan Park, "Cross-Functional Product Development Teams, Creativity, and the Innovativeness of New Consumer Products," *Journal of Marketing Research* 38 (February 2001): 73–85.

35. Julian Birkinshaw, "Managing Internal R&D Networks in Global Firms—What Sort of Knowledge Is Involved?" *Long Range Planning* 35 (June 2002): 245–267.

36. "Manufacturers Strive to Slice Time Needed to Develop Products," *The Wall Street Journal,* February 23, 1988, 1, 24.

37. "Consortium Forms RFID Center of Excellence," *Transportation & Distribution,* August 2002, 10.

38. A.C. Nielsen, "New-Product Introduction—Successful Innovation /Failure: Fragile Boundary," *A.C. Nielsen BASES,* June 24, 1999, 1; Robert G. Cooper and Elko J. Kleinschmidt, "New Product Processes at Leading Industrial Firms," *Industrial Marketing Management* 14 (May 1991): 137–147; and David S. Hopkins, "Survey Finds 67% of New Products Fail," *Marketing News,* February 8, 1986, 1.

39. Eric Berggren and Thomas Nacher, "Introducing New Products Can Be Hazardous to Your Company," *The Academy of Management Executive* 15 (August 2001): 92–101.

40. Laurel Wentz, "Mars Widens Its Line in U.K.," *Advertising Age,* May 16, 1988, 37.

41. Veronica Wong, "Antecedents of International New Product Rollout Timeliness," *International Marketing Review* 19 (no. 2, 2002): 120–132; Robert Michelet and Laura Elmore, "Launching Your Product Globally,"

Export Today 6 (September 1990): 13–15; and Laura Elmore and Robert Michelet, "The Global Product Launch," *Export Today* 6 (November–December 1990): 49–52.

42. George S. Day, "Diagnosing the Product Portfolio," *Journal of Marketing* 41 (April 1977): 9–19.

43. "Even Rivals Concede GM Has Deftly Steered Road to Success in Brazil," *The Wall Street Journal,* February 25, 1999, A1, A8.

44. Susan P. Douglas and C. Samuel Craig, "Global Portfolio Planning and Market Interconnectedness," *Journal of International Marketing* 4 (no. 1, 1996): 93–110.

45. Andrew J. Parsons, "Nestlé: The Visions of Local Managers," *The McKinsey Quarterly* 36 (no. 2, 1996): 5–29.

46. C. Samuel Craig and Susan P. Douglas, "Configural Advantage in Global Markets," *Journal of International Marketing* 8 (no. 1, 2000): 6–26.

47. "Will Renault Go for Broke in Asia?" *Business Week,* February 28, 2000; and "Ford, GM Square Off over Daewoo Motor: The Question Is Why?" *The Wall Street Journal,* February 14, 2000, A1, A13.

48. "Whirlpool Expected Easy Going in Europe, And It Got a Big Shock," *The Wall Street Journal,* April 10, 1998, A1, A6.

49. David C. Court, Anthony Freeling, Mark G. Leiter, and Andrew J. Parsons, "Uncovering the Value of Brands," *The McKinsey Quarterly* 32 (no. 4, 1996): 176–178.

50. Christine Bittar, "Cutting Edge," *Brandweek,* February 4, 2002, 16.

51. David C. Court, Mark G. Leiter, and Mark A. Loch, "Brand Leverage," *The McKinsey Quarterly* 35 (no. 2, 1999): 100–110.

52. Tobi Elkin, "Intel Inside at 10," *Advertising Age,* April 30, 2001, 4, 31.

53. "Starbucks: Keeping the Brew Hot," *Business Week Online,* August 6, 2001.

54. David A. Aaker, *Managing Brand Equity: Capitalizing on the Value of a Brand Name* (New York: Free Press, 1995), 21–33.

55. "The Top Brand Portfolios," *Business Week,* August 6, 2001, 64.

56. **http://www.nestle.com/html/ brands/breakfast.asp**.

57. Bernd Schmitt and Alexander Simonson, *Marketing Aesthetics: The Strategic Management of Brands, Identity, and Image* (New York: Free Press, 1997), chapter 1.

58. David Aaker and Erich Joachimsthaler, "The Lure of Global Branding," *Harvard Business Review* 77 (November/ December 1999): 137–144.

59. Colin Mitchell, "Selling the Brand Inside," *Harvard Business Review* 80 (January 2002): 99–105.

60. Andrew J. Parsons, "Nestlé: The Visions of Local Managers," *The McKinsey Quarterly* 36 (no. 2, 1996): 5–29.

61. Richard Tomlinson, "L'Oreal's Global Makeover," *Fortune,* September 30, 2002, 141–146.

62. Ilkka A. Ronkainen and Ivan Menezes, "Implementing Global Marketing Strategy: An Interview with Whirlpool Corporation," *International Marketing Review* 13 (no. 3, 1996): 56–63.

63. "Unilever's Goal: Power Brands," *Advertising Age,* January 3, 2000, 1, 12; and "Why Unilever B-Brands Must Be Cast Aside," *Marketing,* June 10, 1999, 13.

64. Jean-Noël Kapferer, "Is There Really No Hope for Local Brands?" *Journal of Brand Management* 9 (January 2002): 163–170.

65. David Dunne and Chakravarthi Narasimhan, "The New Appeal of Private Labels," *Harvard Business Review* 77 (May–June 1999): 41–52; and John A. Quelch and David Harding, "Brands versus Private Labels," *Harvard Business Review* 74 (January– February 1996): 99–109.

66. "Shoot Out at the Check-Out," *The Economist,* June 5, 1993, 69–72.

67. François Glémet and Rafael Mira, "The Brand Leader's Dilemma," *The McKinsey Quarterly* 33 (no. 2, 1993): 3–15.

68. "Like My Pants? Pssst, They're Wal-Mart," *The Wall Street Journal,* September 3, 2002, B1.

69. Varun Mudgil, "The Big Two Build on Private Label," *Retail World,* July 22, 2002, 3.

70. Alan Treadgold, "ALDI—A Four-Letter Word That Promises Fierce Competition," *Retail World,* August 16, 2002, 6; see also **http://www.ALDIfoods. com/what_is_aldi.htm**.

71. "Nestlé Set to Enter Euro Own-Label Market," *Marketing Week,* August 9, 2001, 7.

Chapter 15

1. Leonard L. Berry, "Services Marketing Is Different," in *Services Marketing,* ed. Christopher H. Lovelock (Englewood Cliffs, NJ: Prentice-Hall, 1984), 30.

2. Christian Grönroos, "Marketing Services: The Case of a Missing Product," *Journal of Business & Industrial Marketing* 13 (no. 4/5, 1998): 322–338.

3. Pierre Berthon, Leyland Pitt, Constantine S. Katsikeas, and Jean Paul Berthon, "Virtual Services Go International: International Services in the Marketspace," *Journal of International Marketing* 7 (no. 3, 1999): 84–106.

4. globalEDGE, Country Insights, **http://globaledge.msu.edu/ibrd/ ibrd.asp**, accessed October 23, 2002.

5. The World Bank, *World Data File,* **http://www.worldbank.org.data**.

6. U.S. Department of Commerce, Bureau of Economic Analysis. **http:// www.economicindicators.gov**, accessed March 3, 2003.

7. U.S. Department of Commerce, Bureau of Economic Analysis, **http:// www.economicindicators.doc. gov**, accessed March 3, 2003.

8. 2002 Bechtel Global Report, Bechtel Group, Inc., **http://www.bechtel. com**.

9. U.S. Department of Commerce, Bureau of Economic Analysis, **http:// www.economicindicators.gov**, accessed March 3, 2003.

10. *The World Factbook* 2002, **http:// www.cia.gov**, accessed October 30, 2002.

11. International Trade Centre, Geneva, **http://www.intracen.org/ servicexport**, September 1999.

12. Terry Clark, Daniel Rajaratnam, and Timothy Smith, "Toward a Theory of International Services: Marketing Intangibles in a World of Nations," *Journal of International Marketing* 4 (no. 2, 1995): 9–28.

13. World Trade Organization, *Doha Development Agenda,* **http://www. wto.org**, accessed October 30, 2002.

14. Dorothy Riddle, "Using the Internet for Service Exporting: Tips for Service Firms," *International Trade Forum,* 1 (1999): 19–23.

15. Alex Garden, "Why Multi-Lingual Makes Sense," NetInsites, **http:// www.bzone.co.nx**, accessed October 2, 2002.

16. "Engineering, Technical, and Other Services to Industry," Synthesis Report, Organization for Economic Cooperation and Development, Paris, 1988.

17. Business Line, "Software Exports to U.S. up 32pc," July 23, 2002, **http:// www.blonnet.com/2002/07/04/ stories/2002070401220600.htm**, accessed October 30, 2002.

18. Paul G. Patterson and Muris Cicic, "A Typology of Service Firms in International Markets: An Empirical Investigation," *Journal of International Marketing* 3 (no. 4, 1995): 57–83.

19. M. Krishna Erramilli and C. P. Rao, "Service Firms' International Entry-Mode Choice: A Modified Transaction–Cost Analysis Approach," *Journal of Marketing* 57 (July 1993): 19–38.

Chapter 16

1. Shantanu Dutta, Mark Bergen, Daniel Levy, Mark Ritson, and Mark Zbaracki, "Pricing as a Strategic Capability," *Sloan Management Review* 43 (Spring 2002): 61–66; and Saeed Samiee, "Elements of Marketing Strategy: A Comparative Study of U.S. and Non-U.S. Based Companies," *International Marketing Review* 1 (Summer 1982): 119–126.

2. Victor H. Miesel, Harlow H. Higinbotham, and Chun W. Yi, "International Transfer Pricing: Practical Solutions for Intercompany Pricing," *International Tax Journal* 28 (Fall 2002): 1–22.

3. Wagdy M. Abdallah, "How to Motivate and Evaluate Managers with International Transfer Pricing Systems," *Management International Review* 29 (1989): 65–71.

4. Sherif Assef and Surjya Mitra, "Making the Most of Transfer Pricing," *Insurance Executive*, Summer 1999, 2–4.

5. Ernst & Young, *Transfer Pricing 2002 Global Survey* (New York: Ernst & Young, August 2002), available at **http://www.ey.com.**

6. Robert Feinschreiber, *Transfer Pricing Handbook* (New York: John Wiley & Sons, 2002), chapter 2 ("Practical Aspects of Transfer Pricing").

7. "How to Free Blocked Funds via Supplier Surcharges," *Business International*, December 7, 1984, 387.

8. Wagdy Abdallah, "Global Transfer Pricing of Multinationals and E-Commerce in the 21st Century," *Multinational Business Review* 10 (Fall 2002): 62–71.

9. Robert Grosse, "Financial Transfers in the MNE: The Latin American Case," *Management International Review* 26 (1986): 33–44.

10. Erika Morphy, "Spend and Tax Politics," *Export Today* 15 (April 1999): 50–56.

11. KPMG, *Corporate Tax Rate Survey* (New York: KPMG, January 2002), available at **http://www.kpmg.com.**

12. Michael P. Casey, "International Transfer Pricing," *Management Accounting* 66 (October 1985): 31–35.

13. Weston Anson, "An Arm's Length View of Transfer Pricing," *International Tax Review* (December 1999): 7–9; and "Pricing Foreign Transactions," *Small Business Reports* (April 1993): 65–66.

14. Organization for Economic Cooperation and Development, *Transfer Pricing Guidelines for Multinational Enterprises and Tax Administrations* (Paris, France, 1999), 14–15.

15. Brad Rolph and Jay Niederhoffer, "Transfer Pricing and E-Commerce," *International Tax Review* (September 1999): 34–39.

16. Robert B. Stack, Maria de Castello, and Natan J. Leyva, "Transfer Pricing in the United States and Latin America," *Tax Management International Journal* 31 (no. 1, 2002): 24–43.

17. Victor H. Miesel, Harlow H. Higinbotham, and Chun W. Yi, "International Transfer Pricing: Practical Solutions for Intercompany Pricing—Part II," *International Tax Journal* 29 (Winter 2003): 1–23.

18. Internal Revenue Service, *Assessment and Report Concerning Advance Pricing Agreements* (Washington, DC: Department of the Treasury, March 29, 2002), 8.

19. Stephane Gelin and Alan Baudeneau, "France Updates Transfer Pricing Rules," *Global Business*, February 2000, 62.

20. "Pricing Yourself into a Market," *Business Asia*, December 21, 1992, 1.

21. "Knocking on the IRS's Door," *Export Today* 15 (April 1999): 52–53.

22. Paul Burns, "U.S. Transfer Pricing Developments," *International Tax Review* 13 (no. 4, 2002): 48–49.

23. "MNCs Face Tighter Net over Transfer Pricing Rules," *Business International*, October 31, 1988, 337–338.

24. John P. Fraedrich and Rae Bateman, "Transfer Pricing by Multinational Marketers: Risky Business," *Business Horizons* 39 (January–February 1996): 17–22.

25. Kent B. Monroe, *Pricing: Making Profitable Decisions* (New York: McGraw-Hill, 2003), 12.

26. Douglas W. Vorhies, Michael Harker, and C. P. Rao, "The Capabilities and Performance Advantages of Market-Driven Firms," *European Journal of Marketing* 33 (nos. 11/12, 1999): 1171–1202.

27. J. J. Boddewyn, Robin Soehl, and Jacques Picard, "Standardization in International Marketing: Is Ted Levitt in Fact Right?" *Business Horizons* 29 (November–December 1986): 69–75.

28. Saeed Samiee, "Pricing in Marketing Strategies of U.S.- and Foreign-Based Companies," *Journal of Business Research* 15 (March 1987): 17–30.

29. For an example of pricing processes by multinational marketers, see John U. Farley, James M. Hulbert, and David Weinstein, "Price Setting and Volume Planning by Two European Industrial Companies: A Study and Comparison of Decision Processes," *Journal of Marketing* 44 (Winter 1980): 46–54.

30. Ira C. Magaziner and Mark Patinkin, "Fast Heat: How Korea Won the Microwave War," *Harvard Business Review* 67 (January–February 1989): 83–92.

31. "Ford, GM Square Off over Daewoo Motor; The Question Is: Why?" *The Wall Street Journal*, February 14, 2000, A1, A13.

32. Jonathan Sprague, "Haier Reaches Higher," *Fortune*, September 16, 2002, 43–46.

33. "Detroit Is Getting Sideswiped by the Yen," *Business Week*, November 11, 1996, 54.

34. Janet Purdy Levaux, "Now It Is Time to Think about Expanding Overseas Sourcing," *World Trade*, June 2000, 52–56.

35. "The Price Is Wrong," *The Economist*, May 25, 2002, 59.

36. "Stuck!" *Business Week*, November 15, 1993, 146–155.

37. "Hyundai Gets Hot," *Business Week*, December 17, 2001, 84–86.

38. Richard Tomlinson, "Who's Afraid of Wal-Mart?" *Fortune*, June 26, 2000, 58–62.

39. Akshay R. Rao, Mark E. Bergen, and Scott Davis, "How to Fight a Price War," *Harvard Business Review* 78 (March–April 2000): 107–116.

40. "Domestic Electronic Products Overtaking Foreign Goods," *Korea Times*, May 12, 1996, 8.

41. Louis Kraar, "How to Sell to Cashless Buyers," *Fortune*, November 7, 1988, 147–154.

42. C. K. Prahalad and Stuart L. Hart, "The Fortune at the Bottom of the Pyramid," *Strategy and Business* 7 (first quarter, 2002): 35–47.

43. "Wal-Mart Quits Retailers Group," *Advertising Age*, October 21, 2002, 16.

44. Wang Yuguan and Jiang Song, "China: A Future Star for Foreign Pharma Companies," *Pharmaceutical Executive*, August 1999, 78–87.

45. Victor H. Frank, "Living with Price Control Abroad," *Harvard Business Review* 63 (March–April 1984): 137–142.

46. "Borders and Barriers," *The Economist—A Survey of European Business and the Euro*, December 1, 2001, 10–11.

47. "One Currency—But 15 Economies," *Business Week*, December 31, 2001, 59.

48. Apart from the strategic pricing decision, there are also simple rounding decisions to be made to report two different currency values or prices side by side. The EU has an official rounding practice that requires rounding to the nearest cent; with EUR 1.455, it is rounded up to EUR 1.46; with 1.454 to 1.45. See **http://europa.eu.int/euro/quest.**

49. "Hold the Foie Gras," *The Economist*, May 25, 2002, 60.

50. "Even After Shift to Euro, One Price Won't Fit All," *The Wall Street Journal Europe*, December 28, 1998, 1.

51. Stephen A. Butscher, "Maximizing Profits in Euroland," *Journal of Commerce*, May 5, 1999, 5.

52. Johan Ahlberg, Nicklas Garemo, and Tomas Nauclér, "The Euro: How to Keep Your Prices Up and Your Competitors Down," *The McKinsey Quarterly* 35 (no. 2, 1999): 112–118.

53. Travis K. Taylor, "Using Offsets in Procurement as an Economic Development Strategy," Working Paper for presentation at the International Conference on Defence Offsets and Economic Development, Alfred University, College of Business, September 2002.

54. "Current Activities of International Organizations in the Field of Barter and Barter-like Transactions," *Report of the Secretary General,* United Nations, General Assembly, 1984, 4.

55. Trade Partners UK, **http://www. tradepartners.gov.uk/ countertrade/introduction/ about_countertrade/introduction. shtml,** accessed February 4, 2003.

56. Dorothy A. Paun, Larry D. Compeau, and Dhruv Grewal, "A Model of the Influence of Marketing Objectives on Pricing Strategies in International Countertrade," *Journal of Public Policy and Marketing* 16 (no. 1, 1997): 69–82.

57. Rolf Mirus and Bernard Yeung, "Why Countertrade? An Economic Perspective," *The International Trade Journal* 7 (no. 4, 1993): 409–433.

58. Chong Ju Choi, Soo Hee Lee, and Jai Boem Kim, "A Note on Countertrade: Contractual Uncertainty and Transaction Governance in Emerging Economies," *Journal of International Business Studies* 30 (no. 1, 1999): 189–202.

59. Paul Samuelson, *Economics,* 11th ed. (New York: McGraw-Hill, 1980), 260.

60. Edward H. Phillips, " 'Offset' Threat," *Aviation Week & Space Technology,* February 26, 2001.

Chapter 17

1. Bernard LaLonde and James Ginter, "Activity-Based Costing: Best Practices," *Paper #606,* The Supply Chain Management Research Group, Ohio State University, September 1996.

2. Toshiro Hiromoto, "Another Hidden Edge: Japanese Management Accounting," in *Trends in International Business: Critical Perspectives,* ed. M. Czinkota and M. Kotabe (Oxford, England: Blackwell, 1998), 217–222.

3. Perry A. Trunick, "CLM: Breakthrough of Champions, Council of Logistics Management's 1994 Conference," *Transportation and Distribution,* December 1994.

4. Richard T. Hise, "The Implications of Time-Based Competition on International Logistics Strategies," *Business Horizons,* September/October 1995, 39–45.

5. Michael R. Czinkota, "Global Neighbors, Poor Relations," in *Trends in International Business: Critical Perspectives,* ed. M. Czinkota and M. Kotabe (Oxford, England: Blackwell, 1998), 20–27.

6. David A. Ricks, *Blunders in International Business,* 3rd ed. (Oxford, England: Blackwell, 2000), 20.

7. **http://www.iata.org,** accessed October 15, 2002.

8. Ian Putzger, "Pricing: Based on Volume or Weight?" *Journal of Commerce,* February 15, 2000, 10.

9. "Survey: E-Management," *The Economist,* November 11, 2000, 36.

10. Patriya S. Tansuhaj and George C. Jackson, "Foreign Trade Zones: A Comparative Analysis of Users and Non-Users," *Journal of Business Logistics* 10 (1989): 15–30.

11. Charles A. Taft, *Management of Physical Distribution and Transportation,* 7th ed. (Homewood, IL: Irwin, 1984), 324.

12. David A. Ricks, *Blunders in International Business,* 3rd ed. (Oxford, England: Blackwell, 2000), 29.

13. Tim Wilson, "Outsourcing Cuts Logistics Complexity," *Internet Week,* November 2001, **http://www. internetweek.com,** accessed November 18, 2002.

14. From Christopher Hobley, "Just Numbers," *European Commission's Electronic Commerce Team,* **http://europa.eu. int,** accessed November 2002.

15. Mohanbir Sawhney, "Let's Get Vertical," *Business 2.0,* September 2000, **http:www.business2.com,** accessed November 2002.

16. Jodi Mardesich, "How the Internet Hits Big Music," *Fortune,* May 10, 1999, 96–102.

17. For more detail, see Gary A. Knight, Michael R. Czinkota, and Peter W. Liesch, "Terrorism and the International Firm," Working Paper, College of Business, Florida State University, January 10, 2003.

18. Haw-Jan Wu and Steven C. Dunn, "Environmentally Responsible Logistics Systems," *International Journal of Physical Distribution and Logistics Management* 2 (1995): 20–38.

Chapter 18

1. Carl Arthur Sohlberg, "The Perennial Issue of Adaptation or Standardization of International Marketing Communication: Organizational Contingencies and Performance," *Journal of International Marketing* 10 (no. 3, 2002): 1–21.

2. Framework adapted from Dean M. Peebles and John K. Ryans, *Management of International Advertising: A Marketing Approach* (Boston: Allyn & Bacon, 1984), 72–73.

3. "Why P&G Is Linking Brands to Good Causes," *Marketing,* August 26, 1999, 11; and "Microsoft's Singapore Site Ties Page Views to Charity," *Advertising Age International,* October 1999, 4.

4. "The Material Years 1982–1992," *Marketing,* July 4, 2002, 22–23.

5. **http://www.amrcorp.com/ar2001/ pdf/notes.pdf.**

6. "Corporate Campaigns Attract Bigger Slices of Advertising Pie," *Advertising Age International,* March 8, 1999, 2.

7. "Global Marketing Campaigns with a Local Touch," *Business International,* July 4, 1988, 205–210.

8. Robert E. Hite and Cynthia Fraser, "International Advertising Strategies of Multinational Corporations," *Journal of Advertising Research* 28 (August–September 1988): 9–17.

9. William J. Holstein, "Canon Takes Aim at Xerox," *Fortune,* October 14, 2002, 215–220.

10. Paula Andruss, "FedEx Kicks Up Brand through Humor," *Marketing News,* July 30, 2001, 4–5.

11. Chris Powell, "Are Countries Brands?" *Advertising Age Global,* December 2001, 5.

12. Ira Tenowitz, "Beers Draws Mixed Reviews after One Year," *Advertising Age,* September 23, 2002, 3, 57.

13. J. Enrique Bigne, "Advertising Budget Practices: A Review," *Journal of Current Issues and Research in Advertising* 17 (Fall 1995): 17–32.

14. "Top 100 Global Marketers," *Advertising Age,* November 11, 2002, 2.

15. "Signs of Recovery," *Zenith Optimedia,* December 9, 2002, available at **http:// www.zenithmedia.com.**

16. Compiled from Leo Burnett, *Worldwide Advertising and Media Fact Book* (Chicago: Triumph Books, 1994).

17. **http://www.iccwbo.org/home/ statements_rules/rules/1997/ advercod.asp.**

18. European Media: Flirtation and Frustration," *The Economist,* December 9, 1999, 85–86.

19. Ross D. Petty, "Advertising Law in the United States and European Union," *Journal of Public Policy and Marketing* 16 (Spring 1997): 2–13.

20. "EU Ministers Vote to Ban Tobacco Ads," *Advertising Age Global,* December 3, 2002, available at **http://www. adageglobal.com.**

21. "Pushing Pills: In Europe, Prescription-Drug Ads Are Banned," *The Wall Street Journal,* March 15, 2002, B1.

22. Pola B. Gupta and Kenneth R. Lord, "Product Placement in Movies: The Effect of Prominence and Mode on Audience Recall," *Journal of Current Issues and Research in Advertising* 20 (Spring 1998): 47–60.

23. Allyson Stewart-Allen, "Product Placement Helps Sell Brand," *Marketing News,* February 15, 1999, 8.

24. "Chinese TV Discovers Product Placement," *The Wall Street Journal,* January 26, 2000, B12.

25. Hank Kim, "Madison Avenue Melds Pitches and Content," *Advertising Age,* October 7, 2002, 1, 14–16.

26. "Canada Moves toward New Laws on Magazines," *Advertising Age International,* January 11, 1999, 29.

27. "Global Media," *Advertising Age International,* February 8, 1999, 23.

28. Benjamin Compaine, "Global Media," *Foreign Policy,* November/December 2002, 20–28.

29. "Marketers Take New Look at Trying Panregional TV," *Advertising Age International,* March 30, 1999, 2.

30. David W. Stewart and Kevin J. Mc-Auliffe, "Determinants of International Media Buying," *Journal of Advertising* 17 (Fall 1988): 22–26.

31. "Eurosport Posts Big Victory: First Profit Since Rocky Start," *Advertising Age International,* March 30, 1998, 17.

32. Michael Cooper, "TV: The Local Imperative," *Campaign,* April 21, 2000, 44–45.

33. "The Internet," *Advertising Age International,* June 1999, 42.

34. "Unilever, Microsoft in European Net Deal," *The Wall Street Journal,* February 2, 2000, B8.

35. "Global Marketing Campaigns with a Local Touch," *Business International,* July 4, 1988, 205–210.

36. Jack Neff, "P&G Flexes Muscle for Global Branding," *Advertising Age,* June 3, 2002, 53.

37. Jae H. Pae, Saeed Samiee, and Susan Tai, "Global Advertising Strategy: The Moderating Role of Brand Familiarity and Execution Style," *International Marketing Review* 19 (no. 2, 2002): 176–189.

38. "So What Was the Fuss About?" *The Economist,* June 22, 1996, 59–60.

39. "Global Accounts Ranks Unilever First," *Advertising Age,* September 9, 2002, 16. See also **http://www.mccann.com.**

40. Laurel Wentz and Sasha Emmons, "AAI Charts Show Yearly Growth, Consolidation," *Advertising Age International,* September 1996, 1–33. See also **http://www.ddb.com.**

41. Nancy Giges, "DDB Needham to Enter China for Asian Growth," *Advertising Age,* May 1, 1989, 57–58.

42. "U.S. Multinationals," *Advertising Age International,* June 1999, 39.

43. Richard Linnett, "Global Media Reviews Not So Worldly," *Advertising Age,* August 19, 2002, 1, 32.

44. "Centralization," *Advertising Age International,* June 1999, 40.

45. *Global Vision* (New York: Ogilvy & Mather, 1994), 8. See also **http://www.ogilvy.com.**

46. Debra A. Williamson, "ARF to Spearhead Study on Measuring Web Ads," *Advertising Age,* February 10, 1997, 8; and Gerard J. Tellis and Doyle L. Weiss, "Does TV Advertising Really Affect Sales? The Role of Measures, Models, and Data Aggregation," *Journal of Advertising* 24 (Fall 1995): 1–12.

47. Joseph T. Plummer, "The Role of Copy Research in Multinational Advertising," *Journal of Advertising Research* 26 (October–November 1986): 11–15.

48. John S. Hill, Richard R. Still, and Unal O. Boya, "Managing the Multinational Sales Force," *International Marketing Review* 8 (1991): 19–31.

49. Artur Baldauf, David W. Cravens, and Nigel F. Piercy, "Examining the Consequences of Sales Management Control Strategies in European Field Sales Organizations," *International Marketing Review* 18 (no. 5, 2001): 474–508.

50. Joseph A. Lawton, "Kodak Penetrates the European Copier Market with Customized Marketing Strategy and Product Changes," *Marketing News,* August 3, 1984, 1, 6. See also **http://www.kodak.com**.

51. Robert B. Money and John L. Graham, "Salesperson Performance, Pay, and Job Satisfaction: Tests of a Model Using Data Collected in the United States and Japan," *Journal of International Business Studies* 30 (no. 1, 1999): 149–172.

52. "Fuel and Freebies," *The Wall Street Journal,* June 10, 2002, B1, B6.

53. Robert McLuhan, "Face to Face with Global Consumers," *Marketing,* August 22, 2002, 34.

54. Tim R. V. Davis, "Integrating Internal Marketing with Participative Management," *Management Decision* 39 (no. 2, 2001): 121–138.

55. Oliver Williams, "Who Cast the First Stone?" *Harvard Business Review* 62 (September–October 1984): 151–160.

56. "Church Group Gnashes Colgate-Palmolive," *Advertising Age,* March 24, 1986, 46.

57. "Levi to Sever Link with China; Critics Contend It's Just a PR Move," *Marketing News,* June 7, 1993, 10.

58. Michael Carberry, "Global Public Relations," keynote speech at Public Relations Association of Puerto Rico's Annual Convention, San Juan, September 17, 1993.

59. Data by IEG made available in "Event/Sponsorships," *Marketing News,* July 8, 2002, 23.

60. "Olympic Torch Burns Sponsors' Fingers," *Financial Times,* December 13, 1999, 6.

61. Bradley K. Googins, "Why Community Relations Is a Strategic Imperative," *Strategy and Business* 2 (third quarter, 1997): 64–67.

62. Michael E. Porter and Mark R. Kramer, "The Competitive Advantage of Corporate Philanthropy," *Harvard Business Review* 80 (December 2002): 56–68.

63. "Business Scales World Summit," *The Wall Street Journal,* August 28, 2002, A12, A13.

Chapter 19

1. Lawrence M. Fischer, "Thought Leader," *Strategy and Business* 7 (fourth quarter, 2002): 115–123.

2. Robert J. Flanagan, "Knowledge Management in Global Organizations in the 21st Century," *HR Magazine* 44 (no. 11, 1999): 54–55.

3. Michael Z. Brooke, *International Management: A Review of Strategies and Operations* (London: Hutchinson, 1986), 173–174; and "Running a Licensing Deparment," *Business International,* June 13, 1988, 177–178.

4. Jay R. Galbraith, *Designing the Global Corporation* (New York: Jossey-Bass, 2000), chapter 3.

5. William H. Davidson and Philippe C. Haspeslagh, "Shaping a Global Product Organization," *Harvard Business Review* 59 (March–April 1982): 69–76.

6. **http://www.loctite.com/about/global_reach.html.**

7. See, for example, Samuel Humes, *Managing the Multinational: Confronting the Global–Local Dilemma* (London, Prentice Hall, 1993), chapter 1.

8. Vijay Govindarajan, Anil K. Gupta, and C. K. Prahalad, *The Quest for Global Dominance: Transforming Global Presence into Global Competitive Advantage* (New York: Jossey-Bass, 2001), chapters 1 and 2.

9. "How Goodyear Sharpened Organization and Production for a Tough World Market," *Business International,* January 16, 1989, 11–14.

10. Michael J. Mol, *Ford Mondeo: A Model T World Car?* (Hershey, PA: Idea Group Publishing), 1–21.

11. 3M Annual Report 2000, 1–3, 15; and "3M Restructuring for NAFTA," *Business Latin America,* July 19, 1993, 6–7.

12. Philippe Lasserre, "Regional Headquarters: The Spearhead for Asia Pacific Markets," *Long Range Planning* 29 (February 1996): 30–37; and John D. Daniels, "Bridging National and Global Marketing Strategies through Regional Operations," *International Marketing Review* 4 (Autumn 1987): 29–44.

13. Daniel Robey, *Designing Organizations: A Macro Perspective* (Homewood, IL: Irwin, 1982), 327.

14. Christopher A. Bartlett and Sumantra Ghoshal, *Managing across Borders* (Cambridge, MA: Harvard Business School Press, 2002), chapter 10.
15. Spencer Chin, "Philips Shores Up the Dike," *EBN*, October 14, 2002, 4.
16. Milton Harris and Artur Raviv, "Organization Design," *Management Science* 48 (July 2002): 852–865.
17. John P. Workman, Jr., Christian Homburg, and Kjell Gruner, "Marketing Organization: Framework of Dimensions and Determinants," *Journal of Marketing* 62 (July 1998): 21–41; and John U. Farley, "Looking Ahead at the Marketplace: It's Global and It's Changing," in *Reflections on the Futures of Marketing*, Donald R. Lehman and Katherine E. Jocz, eds. (Cambridge, MA: Marketing Science Institute, 1995), 15–35.
18. William Taylor, "The Logic of Global Business," *Harvard Business Review* 68 (March–April 1990): 91–105.
19. Mohanbir Sawhney, "Don't Homogenize, Synchronize," *Harvard Business Review* 79 (July–August 2001): 100–108.
20. Ilkka A. Ronkainen, "Thinking Globally, Implementing Successfully," *International Marketing Review* 13 (no. 3, 1996): 4–6.
21. Russell Eisenstat, Nathaniel Foote, Jay Galbraith, and Danny Miller, "Beyond the Business Unit," *The McKinsey Quarterly* 37 (no. 1, 2001): 180–195.
22. "Country Managers," *Business Europe*, October 16, 2002, 3; John A. Quelch and Helen Bloom, "The Return of the Country Manager," *The McKinsey Quarterly* 33 (no. 2, 1996): 31–43; and Jon I. Martinez and John A. Quelch, "Country Managers: The Next Generation," *International Marketing Review* 13 (no. 3, 1996): 43–55.
23. Rodman Drake and Lee M. Caudill, "Management of the Large Multinational: Trends and Future Challenges," *Business Horizons* 24 (May–June 1981): 83–91.
24. Joe Studwell, *The China Dream* (New York: Atlantic Monthly Press, 2002), 104–105.
25. Goran Svensson, "'Glocalization' of Business Activities: A 'Glocal Strategy' Approach," *Management Decision* 39 (no. 1, 2001): 6–13.
26. Christopher A. Bartlett and Sumantra Ghoshal, "Matrix Management: Not a Structure, a Frame of Mind," *Harvard Business Review* 68 (July–August 1990): 138–145.
27. Carlos Ghosn, "Saving the Business without Losing the Company," *Harvard Business Review* 80 (January 2002): 37–45.
28. Karl Moore and Julian Birkinshaw, "Managing Knowledge in Global Service Firms," *Academy of Management Executive* 12 (no. 4, 1998): 81–92.
29. Julian Birkinshaw and Tony Sheehan, "Managing the Knowledge Life Cycle," *Sloan Management Review* 44 (Fall 2002): 75–83.
30. Noel Tichy, "The Teachable Point of View: A Primer," *Harvard Business Review* 77 (March–April 1999): 82–83.
31. "See Jack. See Jack Run Europe," *Fortune*, September 27, 1999, 127–136.
32. "GE Mentoring Program Turns Underlings into Teachers of the Web," *The Wall Street Journal*, February 15, 2000, B1, B16.
33. Richard Benson-Armer and Tsun-Yan Hsieh, "Teamwork across Time and Space," *The McKinsey Quarterly* 33 (no. 4, 1997): 18–27.
34. David A. Griffith and Michael G. Harvey, "An Intercultural Communication Model for Use in Global Interorganizational Networks," *Journal of International Marketing* 9 (no. 3, 2001): 87–103.
35. "Internet Software Poses Big Threat to Notes, IBM's Stake in Lotus," *The Wall Street Journal*, November 7, 1995, A1–5.
36. Christopher A. Bartlett and Sumantra Ghoshal, "Tap Your Subsidiaries for Global Reach," *Harvard Business Review* 64 (November–December 1986): 87–94.
37. "The Zen of Nissan," *Business Week*, July 22, 2002, 46–49.
38. "Percy Barnevik's Global Crusade," *Business Week Enterprise 1993*, 204–211.
39. Michael D. White, "The Finnish Springboard," *World Trade*, January 1999, 48–49.
40. Julian Birkinshaw and Neil Hood, "Unleash Innovation in Foreign Subsidiaries," *Harvard Business Review* 79 (March 2001): 131–137; and Julian Birkinshaw and Nick Fry, "Subsidiary Initiatives to Develop New Markets," *Sloan Management Review* 39 (Spring 1998): 51–61.
41. Vijay Govindarajan and Robert Newton, *Management Control Systems* (New York: McGraw-Hill/Irwin, 2000), chapter 1.
42. Anil Gupta and Vijay Govindarajan, "Organizing for Knowledge within MNCs," *International Business Review* 3 (no. 4, 1994): 443–457.
43. William G. Ouchi, "The Relationship between Organizational Structure and Organizational Control," *Administrative Science Quarterly* 22 (March 1977): 95–112.
44. Cheryl Nakata, "Activating the Marketing Concept in a Global Context," *International Marketing Review* 19 (no. 1, 2002): 39–64.
45. Laurent Leksell, *Headquarters-Subsidiary Relationships in Multinational Corporations* (Stockholm, Sweden: Stockholm School of Economics, 1981), chapter 5.
46. Henry P. Conn and George S. Yip, "Global Transfer of Critical Capabilities," *Business Horizons* 38 (January/February 1997): 22–31.
47. Arant R. Negandhi and Martin Welge, *Beyond Theory Z* (Greenwich, CT: JAI Press, 1984), 16.
48. Richard Pascale, "Fitting New Employees into the Company Culture," *Fortune*, May 28, 1994, 28–40.
49. Michael R. Czinkota and Ilkka A. Ronkainen, "International Business and Trade in the Next Decade: Report from a Delphi Study," *Journal of International Business Studies* 28 (no. 4, 1997): 676–694.
50. Tsun-Yan Hsieh, Johanne La Voie, and Robert A. P. Samek, "Think Global, Hire Local," *The McKinsey Quarterly* 35 (no. 4, 1999): 92–101.
51. R. J. Alsegg, *Control Relationships between American Corporations and Their European Subsidiaries*, AMA Research Study No. 107 (New York: American Management Association, 1971), 7.
52. Ron Edwards, Adlina Ahmad, and Simon Moss, "Subsidiary Autonomy: The Case of Multinational Subsidiaries in Malaysia," *Journal of International Business Studies* 33 (no. 1, 2002): 183–191.
53. John J. Dyment, "Strategies and Management Controls for Global Corporations," *Journal of Business Strategy* 7 (Spring 1987): 20–26.
54. Alfred M. Jaeger, "The Transfer of Organizational Culture Overseas: An Approach to Control in the Multinational Corporation," *Journal of International Business Studies* 14 (Fall 1983): 91–106.
55. Michael Goold and Andrew Campbell, "Do You Have a Well-Designed Organization?" *Harvard Business Review* 80 (March 2002): 117–124.

Chapter 20

1. William Lazer and Eric H. Shaw, "Global Marketing Management: At the Dawn of the New Millennium," *Journal of International Marketing* 8 (no. 1, 2000): 65–77.
2. Reiner Springer and Michael R. Czinkota, "Marketing's Contribution to the Transformation of Central and Eastern Europe," *Thunderbird International Business Review* 41 (no. 1, 1999): 29–48.
3. Speech by Mike Moore, "Preparations for the Fourth WTO Ministerial Conference," Paris, October 9, 2001, **http://www.wto.org**.
4. Michael R. Czinkota, Ilkka A. Ronkainen, and Bob Donath, *Mastering*

Global Markets (Cincinnati: Thomson, 2003).

5. "Business and Political Leaders Discuss Digital Divide," *World Economic Forum*, Davos, **http://www.worldeconomicforum.org,** February 2, 2001.

6. "The Corporation and the Public: Open for Inspection," *World Economic Forum*, January 27, 2001, **http://www.worldeconomicforum.org,** February 2, 2001.

7. John Pomfret, "Chinese Industry Races to Make Global Name for Itself," *The Washington Post*, April 23, 2000, H1.

8. Catherine L. Mann, "Is the U.S. Trade Deficit Still Sustainable?" *Institute for International Economics*, March 1, 2001.

9. Murray Weidenbaum, "All the World's a Stage," *Management Review*, October 1999, 42–48.

10. UN Population Division, *World Urbanization Prospects*, **http://www.un.org/esa/population,** accessed December 10, 2002.

11. John Lancaster, "The Desperate Bachelors," *The Washington Post*, December 2, 2002, A1, A17.

12. **http://www.cyberatlas.com,** accessed December 5, 2002; CyberAtlas is an Internet research company that gathers data from such sources as *CIA World Factbook* and Nielsen's Net Ratings services as well as authoritative sources in 50 countries around the world.

13. *Computer Industry Almanac*, **http://www.c-i-a.com/pr032102.htm,** accessed December 5, 2002.

14. *CIA World Factbook*, **http://www.cia.gov/cia/publications/factbook/index.html,** accessed December 5, 2002.

15. John Quelch, "Global Village People," *Worldlink Magazine*, January/February 1999, **http://www.worldlink.co.uk.**

16. Renato Ruggiero, "The New Frontier," *WorldLink Magazine*, January/February 1998, **http://www.worldlink.co.uk.**

17. Minoru Makihara, Co-Chairman of the Annual Meeting of the World Economic Forum, Davos 2001, **http://www.worldeconomicforum.org.**

18. Polly Campbell, "Trend Watch 2001," *The Edward Lowe Report*, January 2001, 1–3.

19. Michael R. Czinkota, "The Policy Gap in International Marketing," *Journal of International Marketing* 8 (no. 1, 2000): 99–111.

20. Michael R. Czinkota and Masaaki Kotabe, "The Role of Japanese Distribution Strategies," in *Japanese Distribution Strategy*, M. R. Czinkota and M. Kotabe, eds. (London: Business Press, 2000), 6–16.

21. Michael R. Czinkota, "From Bowling Alone to Standing Together," *Marketing Management*, March/April 2002, 12–16.

22. Rosabeth Moss Kanter, "Six Strategic Challenges," *Worldlink Magazine*, January/February 1998; **http://www.worldlink.co.uk.**

23. "The Corporation and the Public: Open for Inspection," World Economic Forum, **http://www.**

worldeconomicforum.org, accessed February 2, 2001.

24. Michael R. Czinkota, "Success of Globalization Rests on Good Business Reputations," *The Japan Times*, October 12, 2002, 9.

25. Michael R. Czinkota and Masaaki Kotabe, "Product Development the Japanese Way," in M. Czinkota and Masaaki Kotabe, *Trends in International Business: Critical Perspectives* (Oxford, England: Blackwell Business, 1998), 153–158.

26. Business Overview of QVC, Inc., **http://www.qvc.com,** accessed December 6, 2002.

27. Gary Hart and Warren B. Rudman (Stephen E. Flynn, Project Director), *America Still Unprepared—America Still in Danger* (New York, Council on Foreign Relations, December 6, 2002).

28. Gunter K. Stahl, Edwin L. Miller, and Rosalie L. Tung, "Toward the Boundaryless Career: A Closer Look at the Expatriate Career Concept and the Perceived Implications of an International Assignment," *Journal of World Business* 37 (2002): 216–227.

29. Institute of International Education, *Open Doors*, Internet Document, November 18, 2002. **http://www.iie.org.**

30. Joann S. Lublin, "To Smooth a Transfer Abroad, a New Focus on Kids," *The Wall Street Journal*, January 26, 1999, B1, B14.

A

absorption   A pricing approach in which foreign currency appreciation/depreciation is not reflected (either entirely or partially) in the target market price.

accidental exporters   Firms which become international due to unsolicited orders, such as those placed via a Web site, requiring export; unplanned participation in the international market.

acculturation   Adjusting and adapting to a specific culture other than one's own.

agent   An intermediary for the distribution of goods who earns a commission on sales. *See also* distributor

ambush marketing   The unauthorized use of an event without the permission of the event owner; for example, an advertising campaign that suggests a sponsorship relationship.

analysis   Collecting data and using various quantitative and qualitative techniques of marketing research to investigate an issue.

antidumping duty   A duty imposed on imports alleged to be "dumped"—or sold at less than fair market value—on a domestic marketplace.

antidumping laws   Laws prohibiting below-cost sales of products.

area structure   An approach to organization based on geographical areas.

area studies   Environmental briefings and cultural orientation programs; factual preparation for living or working in another culture.

arm's-length price   A basis for intracompany transfer pricing: The price that unrelated parties would have arrived at for the same transaction.

arm's-length standard   A principle basis for transfer pricing favored by governments to stop companies from shifting income to foreign subsidiaries in low- or no-tax jurisdictions.

augmented features   Elements added to a core product or service that serve to distinguish it from competing products or services.

B

back-translation   The translation of a foreign language version back to the original language by a person different from the one who made the first translation; an approach used to detect omissions and avoid language blunders.

backward innovation   Simplifying a product or service due to lack of purchasing power or usage conditions.

banker's acceptance   A method of payment for exported goods: When a time draft, with a specified term of maturity, is drawn on and accepted by a bank, it becomes a banker's acceptance, which is sold in the short-term money market. *See also* documentary collection; discounting

barriers to entry   Obstacles to trade created by governments and market conditions.

barter   Exchange of goods for other goods of equal value.

best practice   An idea which has saved money or time, or a process that is more efficient than existing ones; best practices are usually established by councils appointed by a company.

bilateral negotiations   Trade agreements carried out mainly between two nations.

bill of lading   A document that acknowledges receipt of the goods, represents the basic contract between the shipper and the carrier, and serves as evidence of title to the goods for collection by the purchaser; required for export.

black hole   A situation that the international marketer has to work its way out of; a company may be in a "black hole" because it has read the market incorrectly or because government may restrict its activities.

born global   Newly founded firm that, from its inception, is established as an international business.

boycotts   Refusing to purchase from or trade with a company because of political or ideological differences.

brain drain   Foreign direct investors attracting the best and brightest employees from a domestic firm; said to be depriving domestic firms of talent.

brand   Name, term, symbol, sign, or design used by a firm to differentiate its offerings from those of its competitors.

budgets   Short-term financial guidelines in such areas as investment, cash, and personnel. *See also* plans

built environment   The structures created by human activities; most evident in cities.

bulk service   Ocean freight service that mainly provides contractual services for individual voyages for prolonged periods of time.

bureaucratic controls   A limited and explicit set of regulations and rules that outline desired levels of performance. *See also* cultural controls

buyback   A form of countertrade: A compensation arrangement whereby one party agrees to supply technology or equipment that enables the other party to produce goods with which the price of the supplied technology or equipment is repaid.

C

cash in advance   A method of payment for exported goods: The most favorable term to the exporter; not widely used, except for smaller, custom orders, or first-time transactions, or situations in which the exporter has reason to doubt the importer's ability to pay.

cause-related marketing   Marketing that links a company or brand with a cause, such as environmental protection or children's health.

centralization   When a firm maintains tight controls and strategic decision making is concentrated at headquarters. *See also* coordinated decentralization

certificate of origin   A document required by certain countries to ensure correct tariffs are paid.

change agent   The introduction into a culture of new products or ideas or practices, which may lead to changes in consumption.

clearing arrangements   Clearing accounts for deposit and withdrawal of results of countertrade activities.

climate   A natural feature that has profound impact on economic activity within a place.

code law   A comprehensive set of written statutes; countries with code law try to spell out all possible legal rules explicitly; based on Roman law and found in a majority of nations.

commercial risk   Term referring primarily to an overseas buyer suspected of insolvency or protracted payment default.

commissionario   An intermediary for the distribution of goods who may sell in its own name (as a distributor would), but for an undisclosed principal (an agency concept).

common law   Based on tradition and depends less on written statutes and codes than on precedent and custom.

common market   Goods and services, including labor, capital, and technology, are freely exchanged among member countries; restrictions are removed on immigration and cross-border investment; member countries adopt common trade policies with nonmembers.

computer-aided design (CAD)   A combination of hardware and software that allows for the design of products.

concentration   A market expansion policy characterized by focusing on and developing a small number of markets. *See also* diversification

confiscation   Transfer of ownership from a foreign firm to the host country without compensation to the owner.

consignment selling   A method of payment that allows the importer to defer payment until the imported goods are actually sold.

consular invoice   A document required by certain countries for data collection purposes, to track exports/imports.

container ships   Cargo vessels that carry standardized containers, which greatly facilitate the loading and unloading of cargo and intermodal transfers.

content analysis   A research technique investigating the content of communication in a society; for example, counting the number of times preselected words, themes, symbols, or pictures appear in a given medium.

contributor   A role of a country organization; a subsidiary with a distinctive competence, such as product development or regional expertise.

control mechanisms   Tools to monitor environmental forces, competitors, channel participants, and customer receptiveness; includes short-term control tools and long-term control tools, such as auditing.

coordinated decentralization   Overall corporate strategy is provided from headquarters (centralized decision making) but subsidiaries are free to implement it within the range established in consultation between headquarters and the subsidiaries.

core product   Product or service in its simplest, generic state; other tangible and augmented features may be added to distinguish a core product or service from its competitors.

corporate image advertising   An umbrella marketing communications plan to make the company itself be correctly understood or perceived more positively.

cost-plus method   A pricing strategy based on the true cost of a product (inclusive of domestic and foreign marketing costs).

counterpurchase   A form of countertrade that is a parallel barter agreement: The participating parties sign two separate contracts that specify goods and services to be exchanged (some cash may be exchanged to compensate for differences in value).

countertrade   Transactions in which purchases are tied to sales and sales to purchases.

countervailing duties   A duty imposed on imports alleged to be priced at less than fair market value, due to subsidization of an industry by a foreign government.

cross-subsidization   The use of resources accumulated in one part of the world to compete for market share in another part of the world.

cultural assimilator   A program in which trainees must respond to scenarios of specific situations in a particular country.

cultural controls   Informal rules and regulations that are the result of shared beliefs and expectations among the members of an organization. *See also* bureaucratic controls

cultural convergence   The growing similarity of attitudes and behaviors across cultures.

cultural knowledge   Broad, multifaceted knowledge acquired through living in a certain culture.

cultural universals   Characteristics common to all cultures, such as body adornments, courtship, etiquette, family gestures, joking, mealtimes, music, personal names, status differentiation, and so on.

culture   An integrated system of learned behavior patterns that are distinguishing characteristics of members of any given society.

currency flows   Transfer of capital across national boundaries.

currency variation   Changes in exchange rates which can affect the purchases and profitability of the international firm.

customer involvement   The degree of participation of the recipient in the production of a service.

customer relationship management   Exporter's strategy to increase perceived attention to the foreign customer through call-center technologies, customer-service departments, and the compnay's Web site.

customer structure   An approach to organization that is based on the customer groups that are served—for example, consumers versus businesses versus governments.

customs broker   An agent for an importer with authority to clear inbound goods through customs and ship them on to their destination.

customs union   Nation members of customs unions agree to set aside trade barriers and also establish common trade policies with nonmember nations.

D

database marketing   Promotional tool combining telemarketing with data on the purchasing habits of a customer; allows the creation of an individual relationship with each customer or prospect.

debt problem   Developing countries can be burdened with loans from international sources or other countries, which can crush a nation's buying power and force imports down and exports up to meet interest payments.

decentralization   When a firm grants its subsidiaries a high degree of autonomy; controls are relatively loose and simple. *See also* coordinated decentralization

decoding   The process by which the receiver of a message transforms an "encoded" message from symbols into thought.

del credere agent   An intermediary for the distribution of goods who guarantees the solvency of the customer and may therefore be responsible to the supplier for payment by the customer.

density   Weight-to-volume ratio of a good; high-density goods are more likely to be shipped as airfreight, rather than ocean freight.

deregulation   Reduction of governmental involvement in the marketplace.

derived demand   Business opportunities resulting from the move abroad by established customers and suppliers.

direct exporting   A distribution channel in which the marketer takes direct responsibility for its products abroad by either selling directly to the foreign customer or finding a local representative to sell its products in the market. *See also* indirect exporting

discounting   When a time draft, a method of payment for exported goods with a specified term of maturity, is drawn on and accepted by a bank, it may be converted into cash by the exporter by discounting; the draft is sold to a bank at a discount from face value. *See also* banker's acceptance

discretionary product adaptation   Conforming a product or service to meet prevailing social, economic, and climactic conditions in the market.

discriminatory regulations   Rules and laws that impose larger operating costs on foreign firms than on local competitors, that provide subsidies to local firms only, or that deny competitive opportunities to foreign suppliers.

distribution culture   Existing channel structures and philosophies for distribution of goods.

distributor   An intermediary that purchases goods for resale through its own channels. *See also* agent.

diversification   A market expansion policy characterized by growth in a relatively large number of markets. *See also* concentration

documentary collection   A method of payment for exported goods: The seller ships the goods and the shipping documents and the draft demanding payment are presented to the importer through a bank acting as the seller's agent; the draft, also known as the bill of exchange, may be a sight draft or a time draft.

domestication   Gaining control over the assets of a foreign firm by demanding partial transfer of ownership and management responsibility to the host country.

draft   A method of payment for exported goods: Similar to a personal check; an order by one party to pay another; "documentary" drafts must be accompanied by specified shipping documents; "clean" drafts do not require documentation; also known as the "bill of exchange." *See also* documentary collection

dual pricing   Differentiation of domestic and export prices.

dual-use items   Goods that are useful for both military and civilian purposes.

duty drawbacks   A refund of up to 99 percent of duties paid on imports when they are re-exported or incorporated into articles that are subsequently exported within five years of the importation.

E

economic blocs   Groups of nations that integrate economic and political activities.

economic union   Integration of economic policies among member countries; monetary policies, taxation, and government spending are harmonized.

economies of scale   Production condition where an increase in the quantity of the product results in a decrease of the production cost per unit.

efficiency seekers   Firms that attempt to obtain the most economic sources of production in their foreign direct investment strategy.

embargoes   Governmental actions that terminate the free flow of trade in goods, services, or ideas, imposed for adversarial and political purposes.

encoding   The process by which a sender converts a message into a symbolic form that will be properly understood by the receiver.

environmental protection   A major force shaping the relationship between the developed and developing world; Being environmentally responsible may help a company to build trust and improve its image, but may be contradictory to a developing nation's need to expand into undeveloped areas and exploit its resources.

Environmental Superfund   A fund to cover the costs of domestic safety regulations and made up from fees imposed on U.S. chemical manufacturers, based upon volume of production.

ethnocentrism   The belief that one's own culture is superior to others.

European Union   Effective January 1, 1994; formed by the ratification of the Maastricht Treaty; set the foundation for economic and monetary union among member countries and the establishment of the euro, a common currency.

exchange rates   Price of a currency expressed in units of another currency, e.g., yen per euro.

expectation-reality gap   Divergence between hoped-for and achieved conditions, frequently experienced with the standard of living in less-developed nations; countries must either lower expectations or make more goods available at lower prices.

experiential knowledge   Knowledge acquired only by being involved in a culture other than one's own.

experimental exporter   A stage in which a domestic firm chooses to engage in limited export, usually to countries that are "psychologically close," without yet having evaluated whether and how an international strategy makes sense.

exploratory stage   A stage in which a firm begins to explore the feasibility of exporting or otherwise engaging in international trade.

export adaptation   An experienced export firm which is able to adjust its activities to keep pace with changing exchange rates, tariffs, and other variables in the international market.

export consortia   Legislation that permits domestic firms to work together, in a manner similar to Japanese *sogo-shoshas,* to overcome trade barriers through cooperative efforts.

export control systems   Governmental policy designed to deny or at least delay the acquisition of strategically important goods by adversaries.

export license   Written authorization to send a product abroad.

export trading company (ETC)   Legal construct designed to encourage small and medium-sized companies that are encouraged to participate in the international marketplace.

expropriation   Seizure of foreign assets by a government with payment of compensation to the owners.

Exterritorial Income Tax Exclusion (ETI)   A tax mechanism that provides exporting firms with certain tax concessions, thus making international marketing activities more profitable.

F

facilitating payments   Small fees paid to expedite paperwork through customs; also called "grease"; not considered in violation of the Foreign Corrupt Practices Act or OECD guidelines.

factor mobility   The loosening of restrictions on the trade of capital, labor, and technology among nations.

factoring   A trade financing method; companies known as factoring houses may purchase an exporter's receivables for a discounted price; factors also provide the exporter with a complete financial package combining credit protection, accounts-receivable bookkeeping, and collection services.

factual information   Objective knowledge of a culture obtained from others through communication, research, and education.

feedback   Responses to communications that seek to generate awareness, evoke a positive attitude, or increase purchases; collection and analysis of feedback is necessary to analyze the success of communication efforts.

field experience   Placing a trainee in a different cultural environment for a limited time; for example, living with a host family of the nationality to which the trainee will be assigned.

financial incentives   Special funding legislated by government to attract foreign investments.

fiscal incentives   Special funding legislated by government to attract foreign investments.

focus groups   Eight to twelve consumers representing the proposed target market audience, brought together to discuss motivations and behavior.

forced distribution tests   A group of consumers reports on new products they encounter in normal retail outlets. *See also* laboratory test markets; microtest marketing

foreign affiliate A U.S. firm of which foreign entities own at least 10 percent.

foreign availability High-technology products that are available worldwide, from many sources.

foreign direct investment Capital funds flow from abroad; company is held by noncitizens; foreign ownership is typically undertaken for longer-term participation in an economic activity.

foreign exchange license A license that may be required by certain countries for an importer to secure the needed hard currency to pay for an import shipment; the exporter has to provide the importer with the data needed to obtain these licenses from governmental authorities and should make sure that the importer has indeed secured the documents.

foreign market opportunity analysis Basic information needed to identify and compare key alternatives when a firm plans to launch international activities.

forfaiting A trade financing technique; the importer pays the exporter with bills of exchange or promissory notes guaranteed by a leading bank in the importer's country; the exporter can sell them to a third party at a discount from their face value for immediate cash.

Fortress Europe Term expressing the fear that unified European nations will raise barriers to trade with other nations, including setting rules about domestic content and restricting imports.

forward exchange market A method used to counter challenges in currency movements; the exporter enters into an agreement for a rate at which it will buy the foreign currency at a future date; the rate is expressed as either a premium or a discount on the current spot rate.

forward pricing Distributing development costs over the anticipated volume of future sales of a product.

Free Trade Area of the Americas (FTAA) A proposed free trade zone reaching from Point Barrow, Alaska, to Patagonia; negotiations and an agreement planned for 2005.

free trade area The least restrictive and loosest form of economic integration among nations; goods and services are freely traded among member countries.

functional lubrication Bribes that are not imposed by individual greed, but that serve to "grease the wheels" of bureaucratic processes; amounts tend to be small, the "express fee" is standardized, and the money is passed along to the party in charge of processing a document.

functional structure An approach to organization that emphasizes the basic tasks of the firm—for example, manufacturing, sales, and research and development.

futures A method used to counter problems of currency movements; in the currency futures market, for example, a buyer agrees to buy futures on the British pound sterling, which implies an obligation to buy in the future at a prespecified price. *See also* option

G

Generalized System of Preferences (GSP) A method by which many developed countries help developing nations to improve their economic condition by providing for the duty-free importation of a wide range of products.

geologic characteristics The characteristics of a place relating to its natural attributes.

global account management Account programs extended across countries, typically for the most important customers, to build relationships.

global media Media vehicles that have target audiences on at least three continents.

glocalization Building in organizational flexibility to allow for local/regional adjustments in global strategic planning and implementation; uniformity is sought in strategic elements such as positioning of a product; care is taken to localize tactical elements, such as distribution.

government–corporate collaboration The accelerating technological race and emerging key concerns, such as environmental pollution and global warming, may lead to increased cooperation between policymakers and business executives.

gray market Distribution channels uncontrolled by producers; goods may enter the marketplace in ways not desired by their manufacturers.

Group of Five Five industrialized nations regarded as economic superpowers: The United States, Britain, France, Germany, and Japan.

Group of Seven Seven industrialized nations regarded as economic superpowers: The United States, Britain, France, Germany, Japan, Italy, and Canada.

Group of Ten Ten industrialized nations regarded as economic superpowers: The United States, Britain, France, Germany, Japan, Italy, Canada, the Netherlands, Belgium, and Sweden.

H

high context cultures Cultures in which the context is at least as important as what is actually said; for example, Japan and Saudi Arabia have cultures in which what is not said can carry more meaning than what is said.

household All the persons, both related and unrelated, who occupy a housing unit.

hydrology Rivers, lakes, and other bodies of water influence the kinds of economic activities that occur in a place.

I

implementation The actual carrying out of the planned marketing activity.

implementors A role of a country organization; although implementors are usually placed in smaller, less-developed countries, they provide the opportunity to capture economies of scale and scope that are the basis of a global strategy.

import license A license that may be required by certain countries for particular types or amounts of imported goods.

import substitution A policy that requires a nation to produce goods that were formerly imported.

Incoterms Internationally accepted standard definitions for terms of sale, covering variable methods of transportation and delivery between country of origin and country of destination, and set by the International Chamber of Commerce (ICC) since 1936.

indirect exporting A distribution channel that requires dealing with another domestic firm that acts as a sales intermediary for the marketer, often taking over the international side of the marketer's operations. *See also* direct exporting

infant industry Relatively new firms are sometimes seen as deserving of protection which allows the industry to "grow up" before having to compete with "adult" global industries.

inflation The increase in consumer prices compared with a previous period.

infrastructures Economic, social, financial, and marketing support systems, from housing to banking systems to communications networks.

innate exporters   Start-up exporters; firms founded for the express purpose of marketing abroad; also described as "born global."

intangibility   Cannot be seen, touched, or held. A key difference between goods and services.

integrated distribution   An export marketing strategy in which the marketer makes an investment into the foreign market for the purpose of selling its products.

integrated marketing communications   Coordinating various promotional strategies according to target market and product characteristics, the size of budget, the type of international involvement, and control considerations.

intellectual property rights   Safeguarding rights by providing the originators of an idea or process with a proprietary compensation, at least, in order to encourage quick dissemination of innovations.

intermediaries   Independent distributors of goods, operating primarily at a local level. See also distributor; agent

international comparative research   Research carried out between nations, particularly those with similar environments, where the impact of uncontrollable macrovariables is limited.

international freight forwarder   An agent who provides services in moving cargo to an overseas destination; independent freight forwarders are regulated in the United States and should be certified by the Federal Maritime Commission.

international marketing   The process of planning and conducting transactions across national borders to create exchanges that satisfy the objectives of individuals and the organizations.

international product life cycles   The length of market viability of a product; cycles are shorter than in previous decades and firms must prepare for product introductions over months, or even weeks, rather than spread out over several years.

interpretive knowledge   Knowledge that requires comprehensive fact finding and preparation, and an ability to appreciate the nuances of different cultural traits and patterns.

intranet   A company network that integrates a company's information assets into a single and accessible system using Internet-based technologies such as e-mail, newsgroups, and the World Wide Web.

inventory carrying costs   The expense of maintaining inventories.

L

laboratory test markets   Participants are exposed to a product and their reactions measured in a controlled environment. See also microtest marketing; forced distribution tests

lead users   Companies, organizations, or individuals who are ahead of trends or have needs that go beyond what is available at the present time.

letter of credit   A method of payment for exported goods: an instrument issued by a bank at the request of a buyer; the bank promises to pay a specified amount of money on presentation of documents stipulated in the letter of credit, usually the bill of lading, consular invoice, and a description of the goods.

liner service   Ocean freight service that offers regular scheduled passage on established routes.

low context cultures   Cultures in which most information is contained explicitly in words; for example, North American cultures.

M

management contract   An agreement where the supplier brings together a package of skills that will provide for the ongoing operation of the client's facilities.

mandatory product adaptation   Conforming a product or service to meet prevailing legal and regulatory conditions in the market.

maquiladora program   An agreement between the United States and Mexico that permits firms to carry out labor-intensive operations in Mexico while sourcing raw materials or component parts from the United States, free of Mexican tariffs.

maquiladoras   Mexican plants that make goods and parts or process food for export to the United States.

marginal cost method   A pricing strategy that considers only the direct cost of producing and selling products for export as the floor beneath which prices cannot be set; overhead costs are disregarded, allowing an exporter to lower prices to be competitive in markets that otherwise might not be accessed.

market pricing   Determining the initial price of a product by comparison to competitors' prices.

market seekers   Firms that search for better opportunities for entry and expansion in their foreign direct investment strategy.

market transparency   Clarity of the offering made to the customer; transparency in service delivery is often difficult to ensure, because services may be customized to individual needs.

market-differentiated pricing   Export pricing based on the dynamic, changing conditions of each marketplace.

mass customization   Manufacturing that meets customers' growing desires for products that precisely meet their needs and preferences; requires working with existing technology, often in modular form, to produce large quantities of base products which are then adapted and refined.

master franchising system   A system wherein foreign partners are selected and awarded the franchising rights to territory in which they, in turn, can subfranchise.

materials management   The timely movement of raw materials, parts, and supplies into and through a firm.

matrix structure   An approach to organization based on the coordination of product and geographic dimensions of planning and implementing strategy.

microtest marketing   A panel of consumers is exposed to new products through a retail grocery operated by a research agency. See also laboratory test markets; forced distribution tests

mixed aid credits   Loans to domestic businesses designed to overcome barriers to export and composed partially of commercial interest rates and partially of highly subsidized developmental aid interest rates.

mixed structure   An approach to organization that combines one or more possible structures (see product, functional, process, and customer structures); also called a hybrid structure.

multilateral negotiations   Trade agreements carried out among a number of nations.

N

national security   Protecting the welfare—economic, cultural, or military—of a nation's people; tariffs, barriers to entry, and other obstacles to trade often are established to ensure such protection.

noise   Extraneous and distracting stimuli that interfere with the communication of a message.

nondiscriminatory regulations   Rules and laws that may be inconvenient and hamper business operations, but that are imposed in an even-handed manner, without discriminating between local and foreign suppliers.

nonfinancial incentives   Support such as guaranteed government purchases; special protection from competition through tariffs; import quotas, and local content requirements designed to attract foreign investments.

nontariff barriers   Barriers to trade that are more subtle than tariff barriers; for example, these barriers may be government or private-sector "buy domestic" campaigns, preferential treatment of domestic bidders over foreign bidders, or the establishment of standards that are not common to foreign goods or services.

not-invented-here syndrome (NIH)   Local resistance or decline in morale caused by the perception that headquarters is not sensitive to local needs.

offset   A form of countertrade: Industrial compensation mandated by governments when purchasing defense-related goods and services in order to equalize the effect of the purchase on the balance of payments.

open account   A method of payment, also known as open terms; exporter selling on open account removes both real and psychological barriers to importing; however, no written evidence of the debt exists and there is no guarantee of payment.

operating risk   Exposing ongoing operations of a firm to political risk in another nation.

opportunity costs   Costs resulting from the foreclosure of other sources of profit, such as exports or direct investment; for example, when licensing eliminates options.

option   A method used to counter challenges in currency movements; gives the holder the right to buy or sell foreign currency at a prespecified price on or up to a prespecified date. *See also* futures

outcome   The results of meeting objectives that seek to generate awareness, evoke a positive attitude, or increase purchases.

overinvest   Tendency in the initial acquisition process to buy more land, space, and equipment than is needed immediately to accommodate future growth.

ownership risk   Exposing property and life to political risk in another nation.

P

parallel importation   Authentic and legitimately manufactured trademark items that are produced and purchased abroad but imported or diverted to the markets by bypassing designated channels; also called "gray market."

partially interested exporter   A firm that becomes involved in a very limited way in global trade, by choosing to respond to unsolicited overseas orders, or otherwise responding to international market stimuli.

pass-through   A pricing approach in which foreign currency appreciation/depreciation is reflected in a commensurate amount in the target market price.

Pax Romana   "The Roman Peace," referring to the common coinage, trading activities, and communication networks established and protected throughout a vast empire.

penetration pricing   Introducing a product at an initial low price to generate sales volume and achieve high market share.

perishability   The rapidity with which a service or good loses value or becomes worthless; unused capacity in the form of an empty seat on an airplane, for example, quickly becomes nonsaleable.

physical distribution   The movement of a firm's finished product to its customers.

Physical Quality of Life Index (PQLI)   A composite measure of the level of welfare in a country, including life expectancy, infant mortality, and adult literacy rates.

place   Distribution policy covers the place variable of the marketing mix and has two components: channel management and logistics management.

planning   The blueprint generated to react to and exploit the opportunities in the marketplace, involving both long-term strategies and short-term tactics.

plans   Formalized long-range financial programs with more than a one-year horizon. *See also* budget

political risk   Term referring to a factor beyond the control of an exporter or importer; for example, a foreign buyer may be willing to pay but the local government may delay methods of payment.

political risk   The risk of loss when investing in a given country caused by changes in a country's political structure or policies, such as tax laws, tariffs, expropriation of assets, or restriction in repatriation of profits.

political union   Unification of policies among member nations and establishment of common institutions.

population   The human element of the environment.

population balance   The proportion of male to female children in a population; in many countries, male heirs are preferred, and the result of technologies that can predict the sex of a child has been that populations are skewed toward males, resulting in a gender inequality.

population stabilization   Reducing sharp population growth; important in determining and predicting the standard of living (measured by dividing a nation's GDP by its population).

positioning   The presentation of a product or service to evoke a positive and differentiated mental image in the consumers' perception.

predatory dumping   Dumping—or selling goods overseas for less than in the exporter's home market or at a price below the cost of production, or both—that is termed "predatory" because it is used deliberately to increase the exporter's market share and undermine domestic industries.

price   The revenue-generating element of the marketing mix.

price controls   Government regulations that set maximum or minimum prices; governmental imposition of limits on price changes.

price elasticity of consumer demand   Adjusting prices to current conditions: for example, a status-conscious market that insists on products with established reputations will be inelastic, allowing for more pricing freedom than a price-conscious market.

price escalation   The higher cost of a product resulting from the costs of exporting and marketing in a foreign country.

price manipulation   Adjusting prices of exported goods to compensate for changing currency rates.

pricing-to-market   Destination-specific adjustment of mark-ups in response to exchange-rate changes. *See also* pass-through; absorption

process structure   An approach to organization that uses processes as a basis for structure; common in the energy and mining industries, where one entity may be in charge of exploration worldwide and another may be responsible for the actual mining operation.

product policy   Covers all the elements that make up the good, service, or idea that is offered by the marketer, including tangible (product) and intangible (service) characteristics.

product placement   Creating brand awareness by arranging to have a product shown or used in visual media such as movies, television, games, or Web sites.

product structure   An approach to organization that gives worldwide responsibility to strategic business units for the marketing of their product lines.

profit repatriation   Transfer of business gains from a local market to another country by the foreign direct investor.

promotion tools   Communications policy uses promotion tools such as advertising, sales promotion, personal selling, and publicity to interact with customers, middlemen, and the public.

promotional mix   The tools an international marketer has available to form a total communications program for use in a targeted market: advertising, personal selling, publicity, sales promotion, and sponsorship.

protectionistic legislation   An important bargaining tool; however, legislated protectionism can result in the destruction of the international trade and investment framework.

proxy variable   A substitute for a variable that one cannot directly measure.

psychological distance   Perceived distance from a firm to a foreign market, caused by cultural variables, legal factors, and other societal norms; a market that is geographically close may seem to be psychologically distant.

pull strategies   Promotional strategies in a targeted market relying primarily on mass communication tools, mainly advertising; appropriate for consumer-oriented products with large target audiences and long channels of distribution.

purchasing power parities (PPP)   A measure of how many units of currency are needed in one country to buy the amount of goods and services that one unit of currency will buy in another country.

push strategies   Promotional strategies in a targeted market relying primarily on personal selling; higher cost per contact, but appropriate for selling where there are shorter channels of distribution and smaller target populations.

Q

qualitative data   Data is gathered to better understand situations, behavioral patterns, and underlying dimensions.

quantitative data   Data is amassed to assess statistical significance; surveys are appropriate research instruments.

quota systems   Control of imports through quantitative restraints.

R

R&D consortia   Companies that collaborate in long-term research and development projects to create technologies without the threat of antitrust suits.

R&D costs   Costs resulting from the research and development of licensed technology.

realism check   A step in the analysis of data in which the researcher determines what facts may have inadvertently skewed the responses; for example, if Italian responders report that very little spaghetti is consumed in Italy, the researcher may find that the responders were distinguishing between store-bought and homemade spaghetti.

reference groups   A person or group of people that significantly influences an individual's attitude and behavior.

reliability   The vagaries of nature can impose delays on transportation services; these delays tend to be shorter in absolute time for air shipments, which are considered more predictable.

reputation management   The strategy of building a corporate reputation for virtue, vision, and veracity, the attributes of a good corporate citizen.

research consortia   Joint industry efforts in the research and development of new products to combat the high costs and risks of innovation; often supported by governments.

research specifications   In the centralized approach to coordinating international marketing, specifications such as focus, thrust, and design are directed by the home office to the local country operations for implementation.

resource seekers   Firms that search for either natural resources or human resources in their foreign direct investment strategy.

reverse distribution systems   Logistics that ensure that a firm can retrieve its goods from the market for subsequent use, recycling, or disposal.

S

safety-valve activity   The use of overseas sales as a way to balance inventories or compensate for overproduction in the short term.

scenario analysis   Evaluating corporate plans under different conditions, such as variations in economic growth rates, import penetration, population growth, and political stability over medium- to long-term periods.

self-reference criterion   The unconscious reference to one's own cultural values in comparison to other cultures.

seminar missions   Promotional event in which eight to ten firms are invited to participate in a one- to four-day forum; a soft-sell approach aimed at expanding sales abroad.

sensitivity training   An approach based on the assumption that understanding and accepting oneself is critical to understanding a person from another culture.

service capacity   Ability to supply service on demand, including the planning of backup during peak periods; similar to an inventory of goods.

service consistency   Uniformity or standardization in the offering of a service; unlike products, services are often subject to individual influences and the need to customize to satisfy unique customer interactions.

shipper's declaration for dangerous goods   Required for shipments such as corrosives, flammables, and poisons.

shipper's export declaration   A document that states proper authorization for export and serves as a means for governmental data collection efforts.

Single European Act   Ratified in 1987 by twelve European countries to free the exchange of goods, services, capital, and people among member countries.

skimming   Offering a product at an initial high price to achieve the highest possible sales contribution in a short time period; as more market segments are identified, the price is gradually lowered.

social stratification   The division of a particular population into classes.

sogoshosha   Large Japanese trading companies, such as Sumitomo, Mitsubishi, Mutsui, and C. Itoh.

solo exhibitions   Promotional event, generally limited to one or a few product themes and held only when market conditions warrant them; aimed at expanding sales abroad.

standard worldwide pricing A price-setting strategy in which a product is offered at the same price regardless of the geography of the buyer.

strategic leader A role of a country organization; a highly competent national subsidiary located in a strategically critical market.

supply chain management An integration of the three major concepts of the logistics in which a series of value-adding activities connect a company's supply side with its demand side. See also systems concept; total cost concept; and trade-off concept.

switch-trading Credits in a clearing account (established for countertrading) can be sold or transferred to a third party.

systems concept One of three major concepts of the logistics of international management, based on the notion that materials-flow activities within and outside of the firm are so extensive and complex that they can be considered only in the context of their interaction. See also total cost concept and trade-off concept

T

telemarketing Promotional tool that is growing worldwide as customers become more accustomed to calling toll-free numbers and more willing to receive calls from marketers.

terrain The geology of a place expressed in terms of its regional characteristics; terrain plays a role in population, resources, travel, and trade.

theocracy A legal perspective that holds faith and belief as its key focus and is a mix of societal, legal, and spiritual guidelines.

total cost concept One of three major concepts of the logistics of international management, in which cost is used as a basis for measurement; the purpose of the total cost concept is to minimize the firm's overall logistics cost by implementing the systems concept appropriately. See also systems concept and trade-off concept.

trade deficit A trade deficit occurs when a country imports more goods and services than it exports.

trade missions A promotional event aimed at expanding sales abroad; may be a country-specific, industry-organized, or government-approved event. See also seminar missions

trade promotion authority Assures that the U.S. executive branch may reach international agreements that will not be subject to minute amendments by Congress; gives Congress the right to accept or reject trade treaties and agreements.

trade sanctions Governmental actions that inhibit the free flow of trade in goods, services, or ideas, imposed for adversarial and political purposes.

trademark licensing The ownership of the name or logo of a designer, literary character, sports team, or movie star, for example, which can be used on merchandise.

trade-off concept One of three major concepts of the logistics of international management, which recognizes that linkages within logistics systems lead to interactions; for example, locating a warehouse near the customer may reduce the cost of transportation, but requires investment in a new warehouse. See also systems concept and total cost concept.

tramp service Ocean freight service that is available for irregular routes and is scheduled only on demand.

transfer costs Costs incurred in negotiating licensing agreements; all variable costs resulting from transfer of a technology to a licensee, and all ongoing costs of maintaining the agreement.

transfer risk Exposing the transfer of funds to political risk across international borders.

translation-retranslation approach Reducing problems in the wording of questions by translating the question into a foreign language and having a second translator return the foreign text to the researcher's native language.

transportation mode Choices among airfreight and ocean freight, pipeline, rail, and trucking.

triad The megamarkets of North American, Europe, and Asia-Pacific.

turnkey operation A complete operational system, together with the skills investment sufficient to allow unassisted maintenance and operation of the system following its completion.

U

unintentional dumping Dumping—or selling goods overseas for less than in the exporter's home market or at a price below the cost of production, or both—that is termed "unintentional" because the lower price is due to currency fluctuations

urbanization Descriptions of urbanization range from densely-populated cities to built-up areas to small towns with proclaimed legal limits.

V

value-added tax (VAT) A tax on the value added to goods and services charged as a percentage of price at each stage in the production and distribution chain.

VAT. See value-added tax

video/catalog exhibitions Promotional tool coordinating product presentations from several companies in one catalog or video; aimed at expanding sales abroad.

virtual trade shows Electronic promotional tool enabling exporters to promote their products and services over the Internet and to have electronic presence without actually attending an overseas trade show; aimed at expanding U.S. sales abroad.

A

Aaker, David A., 463, R-13 14n54, R-13 14n58
Aaker, Jennifer, R-6 8n22
Ab, Oy Canon, 360
Abdallah, Wagdy M., R-14 16n3, R-14 16n8
Absolut vodka, 312–313
Absorption, 294
Accidental exporters, 232
Accounting services, 477
Accounting standards, 480
Acculturalization, 59
Acuff, Frank L., R-8 10n23
Adams, Eric J., 329
Adams, Patrick, R-2 3n47
Adaptation, 250–252, 253, 280, 441; and consumer goods, 251–252, 266
Adler, Nancy, 626
Adoption tendencies, 80–81
Advance pricing agreements (APAs), 490–491, 552–553
Advertising. See also Advertising agencies; Promotional campaigns: color in, 73; cultural factors and, 80–81, 552; deceptive practices, 151; effectiveness of, 558; foreign language, culture and, 63–64; for intermediaries, 349; in international markets, 312–313, 541–546, 552; job recruitment and, 622; and marketing services, 479–480; music in, 73; rates and regulations for, 543, 545–546; regional markets and, 124; restrictions on, 545–546; sex in, 73; spending for, worldwide, 541–542; spending of corporations, 540–541; sports sponsorship, 537
Advertising agencies, 553–556. See also Advertising; and client relationships, 553, 555–558; top 50, 554
Aerotek International, 273
Aesthetics, 73
AFL-CIO, Web site, 128
Africa, 601; economic integration in, 113, 122; indebtedness of, 91; rainforest in, 24
African Union (AU), 122
Agents, 345
Aggarwal, Praveen, R-9 11n4
Agnew, Joe, R-2 3n43
Agricultural cooperatives, 182–183
Agricultural regions, 28
Agriculture, 8, 11, 106; organic, 183
Ahlberg, Johan, 498, R-15 16n52
Ahmad, Adlina, R-17 19n52
AIDS, 566
Airbus Industries, 434
Air routes, 323, 520
Air shipping (freight), 516, 518–519
Ajami, Riad, R-1 1n5
Albaum, Gerald, S., R-5 7n11
Alcoholic beverages, 312–313, 339, 545
Alden, Dana L., R-5 7n7
Alden, Edward, 166
Aldi Group, 115
Alexander, Nicholas, R-9 11n11
Allen, Mike, 166
Al Muhairy Group, 238
Alon, Ilan, 245
Alsegg, R. J., R-17 19n51

Aluminum industry, 23
Ambler, Tim, R-2 3n46
Ambush marketing, 565
America Leads on Trade, Web site, 128
American Chamber of Commerce, 194
American Countertrade Association, Web site, 507
American firms and European Union, 115, 116
American Hospital Supply, 259
American Marketing Association (AMA), 18, 188
American Plywood Association, 52
Analysis (of marketing research), **20**
Andean Common Market (ANCOM), 113, 120, 123
Anderson, David, 535
Anderson, Erin, R-9 11n5, R-9 11n18, R-9 11n19
Anderson, Sarah, R-3 4n29
Andruss, Paula, R-15 18n10
Ang, Swee Hoon, 126, R-4 4n58
Anheuser-Busch, 132, 336
Anholt, Simon, 567
Annan, Kofi, 465
Anson, Weston, R-14 16n13
Anti-dumping. See also Dumping
Antidumping duty, 301
Antidumping laws, 151
Anti-globalization forces, 3
Anti-Gray Market Alliance, Web site, 367
Antitrust statutes, 49, 141
Anti-Western sentiment, 146
AOL, 333
Appliance industry, 397–398, 663–666. See also Electrical appliances
Aquaculture, 180
Arab League, 112, 133
Arab Maghreb Union, 122
Area guides, 76
Area structure, 575, 583
Area studies, 76, 82
Argentina, 6, 69, 125
Armament exports, 135
Arm's-length price, 487–488
Arms-length standard, 489
Armstrong, Robert W., R-1 1n1
Arndt, S. W., R-7 9n29
Arnold, David, 362, R-7 9n3, R-10 11n44
Arnold, Stephen J., R-9 11n9
Aronson, Brad, 331
Art (painting), international market for, 9
Asbill, Richard M., 245
ASEAN (Association of South East Asian Nations) Free Trade Area (AFTA), 113, 121, 123
ASEAN Free Trade Area (AFTA), 121, 123
Asia, 602; appliance industry in, 665; brand names in, 262; economic crisis in, 6, 494; financial crisis in, 124, 125, 258–259; integration of, 113, 121, 123; population of, 95; soup sales in, 71; spending patterns in, 100, 101
Asia Pacific Countertrade Association, Web site, 507
Asia Pacific Economic Cooperation, 123
Association of Southeast Asian Nations (ASEAN), 6, 121

Atacs Products, Inc., 305
Athletes, professional recruitment services, 478
Audited reports, 289
Augmented features, 248
Auto industry, 11, 280–281; in China, 170–173; distribution system for, 338; export and, 294–295; and international trade, 9; in Korea, 454; and nonconforming import cars, 386–388; and U.S. imports, 386–388
Axtell, Roger E., 86, R-2 3n35
Ayal, Igal, 408

B

Baalbaki, Imad B., 410, R-11 12n37
Bachman, Vanessa, R-5 7n16
Back-translation, 64
Backward innovation, 258
Baerwald, Thomas J., 21
Baker, John, 389–390
Baldauf, Artur, R-16 18n49
Baldwin, Richard E., 129
Baliga, B. R., 591
Bamford, James, 437
Banbdyopadhyay, Soumava, R-9 11n23
Bangladesh, 23, 90
Banker's acceptance, 288
Banking services, 476
Bank of America, 124
Banks, as agents of change, 232
Barbie and Ken dolls, 68
Barks, Joseph V., 333, R-9 11n34
Barnes, Frank C., R-6 8n45
Barnevic, Percy, R-17 19n38
Barnevik, Percy, 447
Baron, Steve, R-5 6n25
Barrett, Nigel, R-6 8n44
Barriers to entry, 475
Barshefsky, Charlene, R-1 1n9
Barter, 502, 504
Barth, Steven, 329
Bartlett, Christopher A., 580, 588, 596, R-17 19n14, R-17 19n26, R-17 19n36
Basketball, 7, 478
Bateman, Rae, R-14 16n24
Bateson, John E. G., 483
Batson, Bryan, R-8 10n26
Baudeneau, Alan, R-14 16n19
Bavaria, 240
B2B (business to business), 286, 607
Beamish, Paul, R-11 13n7
Becker, Helmut, 275, 279
Bedbury, Scott, 463
Beer industry, 240
Begum, Deborah, R-8 10n41
Behrman, Jack N., R-11 13n9
Belarus tractors, 265–266
Bellas, Ralph A. Jr., R-12 14n24
Bello, Daniel C., R-5 7n14, R09 11n24
Bennett, Peter D., R-2 3n48
Benson-Armer, Richard, R-17 19n33
Bergen, Mark, R-14 16n1
Bergen, Mark E., R-14 16n39
Berger, Robert D., 567
Berggren, Eric, R-12 14n39
Bernard, Andrew B., R-5 7n20
Bernat, Enric, 627, 628
Berry, Leonard L., R-13 15n1

Berst, Jesse, R-3 4n17
Bertaglioni, Lisa, R-9 10n63
Bertagnolli, Lisa, 599
Berthon, Jean Paul, R-13 15n3
Berthon, Pierre, R-13 15n3
Bestfoods, 131; Web site, 418
Best practice, 586, 591
Beverage industry, 43, 240, 376–377, 454
Big emerging markets, map of, 91
Bigne, J. Enrique, R-15 18n13
Bilateral free trade agreements, 110
Bilateral negotiations, 51
Bilateral political relations, 153, 154
Bilingualism, 261–262
Bilkey, Warren J., R-6 8n48
Bill of lading, 522
Biotechnology, 607–608
Birkinshaw, Julian, 418, 447, R-12 14n35, R-17 19n28, R-17 19n29, R-17 19n40
Bitner, Mary Jo, 483
Bittar, Christine, R-13 14n50
Bizet, Jean-Pierre, 581
Black, J. Stewart, 83
Black & Decker, 441, 458, 574
Black hole, 589
Blackwell, Norman, 581
Blackwell, Roger D., R-2 3n29, R-3 4n6, R-4 6n13
Bleeke, Joel, 433
Blessing, Peter H., 485
Bloom, Helen, R-11 12n52, R-17 19n22
Bloomfield, Sam, R-8 10n44
Blustein, Paul, 480
Bly, Robert W., 567
Boddewyn, J. J., R-14 16n27
Boddewyn, Jean J., 561
Body language, 65
Body Shop, The, 532
Boeing aircraft, 80, 247, 248, 254
Bond, Michael H., R-2 3n50
Bonoma, Thomas V., R-9 10n54
Boone, Louis E., 389
"Born global", 41, 401
Botswana, 90
Bottled water industry, 376–380
Bowen, Harry, 54
Bowen, Margareta, R-2 3n21
Boya, Unal O., R-16 18n48
Boycotts, 141
Boyd, John A., R-7 9n6
Brain drain, 427
Brake, Terence, R-8 10n7
Brand, 68–69, 260. See also Brand names
Branding. See Brand names
Brand names, 260–261, 262. See also Brand; importance of, 455–456; 100 most valuable, 456; private (intermediary) brands, 460–462; value of, 456, 457
Brand portfolio, 451–462. See also Product portfolio; marketing strategy and, 456–460
Braunstein, Ruth L., 368
Brazil, 6–8, 69, 256; Amazon Basin in, 22, 24; financial crisis in, 124, 125; iron ore in, 23, television networks, 543
Breakfast foods, 63–64, 81, 255–256
Bribery, 142–143; frequency of, by country, 143–144

Brinkhoff, Thomas, 606
Brislin, R. W., 86
Britt, Steuart Henderson, 256
Britton, Terry A., 271
Broder, John M., 368
Brooke, Michael Z., R-16 19n3
Brookes, Richard, 214
Brown, Agnes, 303, 331
Brown, Eryn, R-10 11n60
Bruno, Philippe, 247
Bryson, John R., 483
Buckley, Peter, 437, 626
Buddhism, 65, 67–68
Budgets, 592
Built environment, 24
Bulk service, 514
Bureaucratic controls, 590, 591, 592–593
Bureau of Economic Analysis, Web site, 436
Burgi, Peter T., 84
Burnett, Leo, 567, R-15 18n16
Burns, Paul, R-14 16n22
Burr, Pete, 373
Burt, David, 535
Bush, George W., 161–162, 164
Business journals, 316–317
Business marketing, 17
Business Software Alliance, Web site, 271
Business Week Online, 3
Butscher, Stephen A., 500, R-14 16n51
Buying American, 421
Buyback, 502
BuyUSA.com, 225

C

Cadbury Schweppes, 259
Cairncross, Frances, 596
Caldreon, Carrero, 507
California, and almond exports, 9
Callahan, Sean, R-8 10n38
Call centers, 319–320
Calof, Jonathan L., R-6 7n31
Campbell, Andrew, R-17 19n55
Campbell, Polly, R-18 20n18
Campbell Soup, 70, 71
Canada, 634–638; grain exports and, 24; and NAFTA, 116; and United States, 229; wood-products industry and, 52
Canadian Anti-Dumping Tribunal, 300–301
Canon, 360, 361
Capehart, Thomas, 373
Carberry, Michael, R-16 18n58
Careers, 600, 618–625; international Web sites for, 619–621; and language skills, 621; with large firms, 618, 621; with small and medium firms, 623; for women, 623, 625
Caribbean Community and Common Market (CARICOM), 113, 123
Carrefour, 115
Cascio, Wayne F., R-12 13n21
Casey, Michael P., R-14 16n12
Cash in advance, 284
Caspar, Christian, R-3 4n51
Casson, Mark, 626
Catalogs, 318
Catoni, Luciano, R-10 12n6

Caudill, Lee M., R-17 19n23
Cause-related marketing, 538, 565–566
Cavanagh, John, R-3 4n29
Cavusgil, Tamer, 192, 276, 294, R-4 6n8, R-5 7n4, R-5 7n12, R-6 8n7, R-7 9n4, R-7 9n7, R-9 11n28, R-10 11n54
CD-ROMs, 195
CeBIT, 326
Cederholm, Lars, 584
Cellich, Claude, R-7 9n45, R-8 10n12, R-8 10n17
Center for International and Area Studies (Brigham Young University), 76
Centers of Excellence, 447
Central American Common Market (CACM), 113, 123
Central Europe, 91, 608–609; European Union and, 114
Centralization, 415
Centralization (Decision-making), **581**
Certificate of origin, 522
Cespedes, Frank V., R-10 11n47
Chabot, Christian, 507
Chae, Myung-Su, R-10 12n17
Chamber of Commerce, 151, 194
Chandler, Clay, 166
Chandra, Aruna, R-11 12n36
Change agent, 60, 230, 232; external, 232–233; internal, 230–232; new developments as, 231
Channel adjustment, 357
Channel configurations, 335
Channel design, 336, 340–341, 344
Channel intermediaries, 361–363
Channels of distribution. See Distribution channels; unauthorized, 358
Channel structure, 334–335
Channel system, culture and, 79, 337–339
Charles-Parker, Nancy, 238
Chaudry, Peggy E., R-10 11n50
Chemical industry, 43
Chemically engineered food, 607
Chemtob, Stuart M., R-4 5n19
Chen, Chao C., R-12 13n20
Cheng, Hong, R-2 3n54
Chernobyl nuclear accident, 25
Chicago Mercantile Exchange, 293
Child, Peter N., 581, R-11 12n35
Chile, 23, 120
Chin, Spencer, R-17 19n15
China, 5, 602; appliance industry in, 665; auto industry in, 170–173; average income in, 171; car financing in, 170–173; consumer credit in, 170–173; consumption patterns in, 73, 101–102; currency in, 168; economic growth in, 167–168, 169; foreign direct investment in, 168, 426; gift giving in, 70; intellectual property rights and, 132; international trade and, 608–609; isolationism in, 32; market research in, 187; multinational corporations in, 168–169; personal computers in, 101–102; political change in, 167, 169; private sector in, 167; railway system in, 106; research and development in, 447–448; and tobacco industry, 370–371; U.S. sanctions against, 137;

values and attitudes in, 68; and WTO, 152, 167–171

Chisholm, Rupert F., 596

Cho, Kang Rae, R-11 13n12

Choi, Chong Ju, R-15 16n58

Choi, Jaepil, R-12 13n20

Chopsticks industry, 391–393

Christianity, 65, 67

Chupa Chups S.A., 627–633

Churchill, Gilbert A., Jr., 214, R-4 6n7, R-5 6n21

Cicic, Muris, R-13 15n18

CIF (cost, insurance freight), 279, 283

Cifra, 118

Cisco Systems, 565–566

Cities. See also Urbanization: growth of, 24; ten largest, 606

City-nations, 32

Clark, Terry, R-13 15n12

Clarke, Peter, R-5 6n30

Clearing arrangements, 502

Cleeland, Nancy, 515

Clement, Norris C., 128

Clifford, Mark, 626

Climate, 23–24, 259

Clocks, 9

CNN, 6

Coalitions, 152

Coca-Cola, 90, 240, 257, 485, 537

Cochlear, 401

Code law, 150–151

Coface Group, 290

Coffee production, 6; and fair trade, 182–183; specialty coffee, 183

Cohen, Daniel, 129

Coil, James, 214

Cold War, 33, 600

Coleman, Joseph, 150

Colgate-Palmolive, 115

Colonialism, 146

Commercial banks, 296–297

Commercial News USA, 347

Commercial risk, 289

Commercial transactions, 289–292

Commissionario, 346

Committee for Foreign Investments in the United States, 44

Commodity Credit Corporation, 371–372

Common law, 150–151

Common market, 111

Common Market for East and Southern Africa (COMESA), 113, 122

Commonwealth nations, 112

Communication policy, 19

Communications, 306; cultural factors and, 80; and manufacturing industry, 616; in marketing, 306–308; and service industry, 616

Communications and marketing strategy, 312–316

Communication systems, 26, 106–107; and multinational corporations, 27

Communication technology and globalization, 6–7

Communist countries, 91

Community relations, 565–566, 613

Compaine, Benjamin, R-16 18n28

Compeau, Larry D., R-15 16n56

Competition, 6, 114, 402, 405–406; channels and, 339–340; global markets and, 413–414; in international markets and, 189, 228, 259, 454; pricing and, 495–496

Competitive advantage, 406

Competitors as agents of change, 232

Computer-aided design, 443

Computer industry, 11, 43, 107, 137; distribution of, 341; and world trade, 9

Computer services, 477

Computer technology, history of, 8

Concentration, 408

Condon, Bradly, 626

Confiscation, 147

Confucianism, 65, 67–68

Conn, Henry P., R-17 19n46

Connor, Martin F., R-5 7n22

Conrad Hotels. See Hilton Hotels

Consignment selling, 289

Consular invoice, 522

Consumer boycotts, 61

Consumer confidence, financial crises and, 125–127

Consumerism, 18–19

Consumer Price Index, 104

Consumer products and channels of distribution, 335

Consumers, 612; and Internet, 607; tastes and preferences of, 189–190

Consumer spending, 100

Consumption patterns, 100–106, 256

Container ships, 514

Content analysis, 211

Contino, Richard M., 303

Contract logistics, 530

Contract manufacturing, 434

Contractor, Farok J., R-5 7n21, R-5 7n28, R-5 7n29

Contributor, 588

Control mechanisms, 20, 593, 594

Controls, 589–595

Cooney, Terry, 305

Cooper, Michael, R-16 18n32

Cooper, Robert G., 463

Cooperative agreements, 11

Coordinated decentralization, 582

Coordinating Committee for Multilateral Export Controls (COCOM), 611

Copeland, Lennie, 86

Copeland, Michael J., 331, R-5 6n19

Core product, 248

Corey, E. Raymond, R-10 11n47

Cornelius, Peter, 626

Corporate citizenship, 565–566

Corporate culture, 417

Corporate executives. See Managers

Corporate image, 562

Corporate image advertising, 539

Corporations, 40 largest, 423

Corruption, 142–143

Cosmetics industry, 337–338

Cost of living, per diem, 624

Cost-plus method, 277, 490

Costume industry, 157–160

Coughlan, Anne T., R-9 11n19

Council for Mutual Economic Assistance (USSR), 33

Council for Trade in Services, 475

Counterfeit products, law enforcement and, 267

Counterpurchase, 502

Countertrade, 500–505; classification of forms of, 502, 503; in-house vs. third parties, 504

Counterveiling duties, 301

Country-market choice, 406–409

Country of origin, 131, 265–266, 616; gray markets and, 360

Country organizations, 588–589; and corporate headquarters, 589, 592

Court, David C., R-13 14n51, R-13 14n49

Court cases: *Traveler Trading Co. v. United States,* 157, 158

Cowan, Rory, R-2 3n20

Craig, C. Samuel, 214, 453, R-4 6n5, R-5 6n23, R-5 6n24, R-10 12n3, R-10 12n19, R-11 12n45, R-13 14n44, R-13 14n46

Crainer, Stuart, R-10 12n9

Cravens, David W., R-16 18n49

Credit reports, 289, 290, 291

Crisis management, 563–564

Cromwell, Erbin, 183

Cross-cultural behavior, 77–78

Cross-cultural differences, 60

Cross-cultural training methods, 83

Cross-marketing, 434

Cross-subsidization, 413–414

Crow, Ben, R-3 4n20

Cuadrado-Roura, Juan R., 483

Cuba, 153

Culpan, Refik, 437

Cultural analysis, 77–81

Cultural assimilator, 82–83

Cultural attitudes of teenagers, 68–69

Cultural controls, 590, 591, 593

Cultural convergence, 73

Cultural diversity, 59

Cultural imperialism, 57–59, 60

Cultural knowledge, 75–77

Cultural noise, 307–308

Cultural segmentation, 79–80, 80

Cultural sensitivity, 69, 82

Cultural training, online, 84

Cultural universals, 61

Cultural values: and market segmentation, 411; and research and development, 448; United States and Japan, 150

Culture, defined, **59;** and globalization, 7

Culture consulting, 77

Cuneo, Alice Z., 416

Currencies, 603–604; and exports, 273, 293–294, 295–296

Currency flows, 9

Currency risk. See Foreign exchange risk

Currency valuation and inventory, 525

Currency variation, 513

Customer involvement, 469

Customer relationship management, 328

Customers, 229, 255–258, 336–337; and marketing, 612

Customer service, 320, 328–329, 524–525

Customer structure, 576

Customs, 522

Customs broker, 523

Customs union, 111
Czinkota, Ilona, 241
Czinkota, Michael R., 3, 52, 161, 166, 179, 280, 337, 368, 374, 376, 391, 626, R-1 2n7, R-3 4n47, R-4 5n6, R-4 5n9, R-4 5n22, R-4 5n24, R-4 6n9, R-4 6n14, R-5 7n2, R-5 7n5, R-5 7n8, R-5 7n13, R-5 7n18, R-6 7n32, R-6 8n49, R-7 9n31, R-8 10n47, R-9 10n62, R-9 11n8, R-9 11n21, R-11 13n8, R-11 13n11, R-15 17n2, R-15 17n5, R-15 17n17, R-17 19n49, R-17 20n2, R-17 20n4, R-18 20n21, R-18 20n24, R-18 20n25

D
Daihatsu, 126
DaimlerChrysler, 578
Dalgic, Tevfik, R-10 11n43
Dalton, Donald H., R-12 14n29
Damar International, 374–375
D'Amico, Al, R-7 9n13
Daniels, John D., R-16 19n12
Danjczek, David, R-4 5n7
Das, Bhagirath Lal, 54
Data. *See also* Research: analysis of, 208; evaluation of, 196; and future forecasting, 211; government sources of, 194; importance of, 209–210; international sources of, 194; marketing research, 190; primary, 208; secondary sources of, 193–196; transmission technology, world map of, 206
Database marketing, 320
Databases, list of, 219–220
Data collection, 208; and service industry, 474
Data industry, 477–478
Data privacy, 197
Dataram Corp., 329
David, K., 87
Davidson, William H., R-16 19n5
Davis, Scott, R-14 16n39
Davis, Tim R. V., R-16 18n54
Day, George S, R-9 11n5, R-13 14n42
De Beers, 70
De Bony, Elizabeth, R-4 6n11
Debt problem, 103, 105–106, 604; by country, 105–106
De Castello, Maria, R-14 16n16
Decentralization (decision-making), **581**
Decision-making, 581–583
Deere & Co., 126, 283, 563
Deese, Pamela M., R-5 7n23
De Juan, Maria D., R-5 6n26
Delamaide, Darrell, 21, 29
De la Torre, José, 145
Delbeq, Andre L., R-5 6n31
Del credere agent, 346
Delene, Linda R., R-2 3n27, R-2 23n27
Dell Computers, 102
Del Monte Foods, 349
DeLozier, Wayne, 312
Delphi studies, 211–212
Demnnpour, Fariborz, R-12 13n20
Demographics, 96. *See also* Population; U.S. Census Bureau and, 211
DeMooij, Marieke K., 567
Dempsey, Gerry, R-9 10n51

Denlinger, Ken, 478
Density, 516
Deregulation, 123, 473; of service industry, 473–474
Derived demand, 425
Deschamps, Jean-Philippe, 463
Deutsche Bank, 124
Deutsche Telekom, 108, 123
Developing countries: cities in, 24; population of, 37
DeVoss, David, R-12 14n13
DeWalt (brand), 458
Dichter, Ernst, R-1 3n1, R-10 12n4
Dichtl, Erwin, R-4 5n6
Dickinson, Rink, 183
Dickson, Peter R., R-1 1n10, R-8 10n47
Digital gap, 607
Direct exports, 327–328
Direct mail, 318–319
Direct marketing, 318–320
Directories, 195, 316–317, 317, 347; Internet addresses, 218
Discapa S.A., 628–633
Discounting, 289
Discretionary product adaptation, 252
Discriminatory regulations, 475
Disney, 57
Disneyland, 69
Distribution alternatives, 341
Distribution channels. *See also* Distribution systems: capital required for, 341–342; control of, 343–344; cost of, 342; coverage (geography), 342–343; information and, 344–345
Distribution culture, 337
Distribution policy, 19
Distribution systems, 337, 616–617. *See also* Distribution channels; in Latin America, 333; laws and regulations for, 357
Distributor, 345. *See also* Intermediaries; as agents of change, 232; exclusivity and, 343; partnerships and, 340–341; promotion and, 312–314
Distributor Agreement, 353–355, 361–363
Diversification, 408
Dobler, Donald, 535
Documentary collection, 286, 288
Documentation, 521–523
Dolan, Robert J., 507
Dolbow, Sandra, R-9 11n17
Dollar, value of, 604
Dollinger, Philippe, R-4 5n1
Domestication, 147
Domestic economies: growth rates and trade, 6; laws and regulations, 132
Domestic markets, 89–90; saturation of, 229
Domestic policy, 8–10
Dominican Republic, 23
Donath, Bob, R-1 1n3, R-17 20n4
Doran, Kathleen Brewer, R-5 6n22
Dornach, Frank, 483
Douglas, Susan P., 214, 453, R-4 6n5, R-5 6n23, R-5 6n24, R-10 12n3, R-10 12n19, R-13 14n44, R-13 14n46

Dow, Web site, 596
Doxey, Margaret P., R-1 2n2, R-4 5n3
Doz, Yves L., 419, 596
Draft, 286
Drake, Rodman, R-17 19n23
Drinking water. *See* Bottled water industry
Duales System Deuschland, Web site, 271
Dual pricing, 277
Dual-use items, 135
Dubinsky, Alan, R-4 6n16
Dumping, 300–301. *See also* Anti-dumping
Dun & Bradstreet, 291
Dunn, Steven C., R-15 17n18
Dunne, David, R-13 14n65
Dunne, Mike, 167, 170, R-9 11n10
Dunne, Patrick, R-8 10n47
Dutta, Shantanu, R-14 16n1
Duty drawbacks, 281
Dykehouse, Brant R., 84
Dyment, John J., R-17 19n53

E
East African Community (EAC), 122
East Asia Economic Group (EAEG), 121
Eastern Europe, 91; spending patterns in, 100, 101
E-commerce, 363–366. *See also* Internet; business to business, 31; in emerging markets, 365; and globalization, 41, 225; government regulations of, 364–365; language and, 364; letter of credit and, 286; privacy issues and, 366; revenue from, 363; service industry and, 476; supply chain and, 530–531; transfer pricing and, 487; value of, 31
Economic blocs, 37–38
Economic coercion, 33
Economic Community of Central African States (CEEAC), 122
Economic Community of the Great Lakes Countries, 122
Economic community of West African States (ECOWAS), 113, 122, 123
Economic development of overseas markets, 258–259
Economic Free Trade Association (EFTA), 114
Economic infrastructure, 72
Economic integration, 109–121; and company reorganization, 124; East Asian countries, 603; and governmental regulation, 253–254; history of, 109–110; and international marketing, 122, 123–124; less-developed countries and, 601–602; maps of, 112–113
Economic isolationism, 4, 11. *See also* Protectionist legislation
Economic union, 111
Economies of scale, 42, 114, 228, 476, 480
Economist Intelligence Unit, 76
Economou, Persa, R-8 10n2
Education: and business careers, 618; and culture, 74
Edwards, Ron, R-17 19n52
Efficiency seekers, 425
Eisenstat, Russell, R-17 19n21
Eiteman, David K., R-7 9n19

Elashmawi, Farid, 86
El Camino Resources International, 300
Electrical appliances, 94, 102, 103, 264, 397–398. See also Appliance industry
Electricity, use of, 94, 107, 108
Electrolux, 63
Electronic Data Interchange (EDI), 509
Electronic industry, 43
Electronic information services, 195–196, 206. See also Internet
Elite readers, 197–198
Elkin, Tobi, R-13 14n52
Elliott, Kimberly Ann, 156, R-1 2n18, R-4 5n5
Ellis, Kristine, 591
Ellis, Shmuel, R-11 13n17
Elmore, Laura, R-12 14n41, R-13 14n41
Emerging markets, 5, 365, 602
Emmons, Sasha, R-16 18n40
Employees, training of, 593
Employment opportunities, 619–621
Encoding, 306
Encyclopedias, Internet addresses, 218
Energy consumption, 106
Engel, James F., R-2 3n29, R-3 4n6
Engel's laws, 100
Engelson, Morris, 507
Engen, John R., R-3 3n68
Enron, 480
Ensign, Prescott, 447
Entertainment industry, 60
Environmentalism, 532, 533
Environmental protection, 601
Environmental Protection Agency (EPA), 379
Environmental quality, 25
Environmental regulations, 132
Environmental scanning (social, economic and political), 210–211
Environmental Superfund, 132
Environment (social, legal, political, economic, cultural, etc.), 532, 533; and globalization, 400–401; marketing research, 188–190
Equal Exchange, Inc., 182–183
Ernst, David, 433, 587
Erramilli, M. Krishna, R-5 7n9, R-13 15n19
Espinosa, J. Enrique, R-3 4n29
E-tailers, 3
Ethnocentrism, 81
Ettenson, Richard, R-6 8n3
Euro, 114, 124, 497–498; and export payments, 292; future of, 604; Web site, 506
Europe. See also European Union: agricultural subsidies in, 181; appliance industry in, 665–666; data sources in, 194; economic integration of, 112; price differentials in, 498–499; regions of, 29
European Aeronautic Defense and Space Agency (EADS), 434
European Coal and Steel Community, 38
European Community (EC), 111, 124
European Court of Justice, 253
European Economic Area (EEA), 114, 247
European Free Trade Area (EFTA), 110, 123
European Parliament, 124

European Union (EU), 6, 111, 112, 114, 115, 123. See also Europe; and data privacy, 197; and e-commerce, 31; and entertainment industry, 60; export standards of, 247; history of, 38, 111; marketing strategies and, 497–500; and parallel importation, 359; population of, 95; and programming quotas, 60; regulatory activity of, 141, 247; and secondary data sources, 194; and United States, 9; Web site, 128
Europe integration, 111–116
Evans, Jody, 339
Eveready, 333
Excess capacity, 229
Exchange controls, 147
Exchange rates, 9
Excite!, 108
Ex-Im Bank, 298–299; Web site, 245
Expectation-reality gap, 606
Experiential knowledge, 75, 76
Experimental exporter, 236
Exploratory stage, 236
Export adaptation, 236
Export Administration Act, 135
Export consortia, 49
Export control systems, 135; international conflicts and, 137; and terrorism, 137, 140; value of, 42–44, 137
Export credit agencies (ECAs), 298
Exporters, Web sites of, 533
Export-import Bank of the United States, 49, 298–299
Export intermediaries. See Intermediaries
Export license, 135, 135
Export management companies (EMC), 233–234
Export price escalation, 279
Export pricing, 276–281. See also Pricing
Exports, 38–39, 612; costs of, 278–281, 283; cultural and psychological factors for, 255–257; currency swings and, 273, 293–294; and economic integration, 116; financing of, 49, 296–299; and foreign demand, 232; government financing of, 298–299; government restrictions on, 191; and local behaviors, 255; and local currency, 290; marketing research and, 191–192; motives for, 231–232; payment for, 289–292; price stability and, 295; pricing of, 299–300; promotion of, 48–50; term of credit for, 284, 286, 288–289; and tobacco industry, 368–372, 368–373; transportation and, 283; of U.S. entertainment, 60; of U.S. goods and services, 471
Export Trading Company Act of 1892, 49–50, 141
Expropriation, 146–147
Exterritorial Income Tax Exclusion (ETI), 227
Exxon Valdez, 211

F

Facilitating payments, 355
Factoring, 297
Factor mobility, 111
Factual information, 75, 76

Fair trade, 182–183
Fallen, Admiral William J., 150
Family planning, 96
Farley, John U., R-14 16n29, R-17 19n17
Farmer, Richard N., 10
Farmers and international markets, 11
Fast track authority, 35
Fedders International, 429
Feedback, 308
Feinschreiber, Robert, 507, R-14 16n6
Feist, William R., 419
Fellman, Michelle, R-12 14n30
Fernie, John, R-9 11n9
Ferraris, 386–388
Ferraris, Dr. Carl J., 180
Feudalism, 32
F-18 Hornet strike fighter, 647–653
Field, George, R-8 10n5
Field experience, 83
Film industry, 57–58, 60
Films, 57–58
Financial centers and computer technology, 27
Financial crises, 105–106, 124–127. See also Recessions; consumer and marketer adjustments to, 126
Financial incentives, 427
Financial infrastructure, 72
Financial institutions, 476
Financial markets, 604
Financial reports, 289
Fingan, Courtney, R-8 10n8
Finger, Michael J., 54
Finland, 381–385, 647–653
Firms, 11, 14, 242–244. See also Multinational corporation; going global, 235–237; as information source, 196; internal factors and, 229–230; marketing problems of, 11; motives for international business, 226–230; service-oriented, 229–230; small, 11
First Boston Group/Credit Suisse, 477
Fiscal incentives, 427
Fischer, Lawrence M., R-16 19n1
Fisher, Marc, 478
Fites, Donald V., R-9 11n1
Fitzgerald, Nora, R-2 3n26
Fitzpatrick, Peter B., 346, R-2 3n58, R-9 11n27
Flanagan, Robert J., R-16 19n2
Flannery, Russell, 398
Focus groups, 72, 202–203
Food and Drug Administration (FDA), 379–380; and catfish farming, 181
Food industry in Europe, 115
Foote, Nathaniel, R-17 19n21
Forced distribution tests, 450
Ford, John, 346
Ford Motor Co., teaching program of, 585
Foreign affiliate, 42, 42–43, 115
Foreign availability, 136
Foreign Corrupt Practices Act, 142
Foreign demand, 232
Foreign direct investment, 42–44, 421–434, 612; in China, 168, 426; corporate ownership and, 421; criticisms of, 427–428; government incentives for, 425–427; guidelines for, 428; incentives for, 422–427; multinational

Foreign direct investment (*cont.*)
corporations and, 422, 423; restrictions on, 44; and types of ownership, 428–434; value of, 422
Foreign exchange license, 522
Foreign exchange risk, 292–296
Foreign market opportunity analysis, 191
Foreign markets, criteria for identification of, 94
Foreign policy and international marketing and trade, 33
Foreman, Linda, 373
Forfaiting, 297
Formalized control. See Bureaucratic control
Forman, Andrew, 181
Forman, Howard, 275, R-7 9n5
Forrest, Edward, 214
Fortress Europe, 116
Fortune 500 firms, 621; Web site, 436
Forward exchange market, 293
Forward pricing, 617
Foster, Faren L., 285
Fraedrich, John P., R-14 16n24
Fram, Eugene H., R-1 1n5
France, 48, 57, 131
France Telecom, 108
Franchising, 240–242
Francis, June N. P., 262
Franc Zone, 113
Frank, Isaiah, R-11 13n14
Frank, Robert, 400
Frank, Sergey, R-2 3n34
Frank, Victor H., Jr., R-3 4n10, R-14 16n45
Frankel, Glenn, 368
Fraser, Cynthia, R-15 18n8
Fraser, Jane, 403
Frazier, Gary L., R-10 11n39
Freeling, Anthony, R-13 14n49
Free trade: and catfish farming, 179–181; projected financial benefits of, 35; and steel industry, 164
Free trade area, 28, 110
Free Trade Area of the Americas (FTAA), 120
French Guiana, 24
French West Africa, 154
French wine, 131
Frewen, Robert, R-7 9n44
Friberg, Eric, R-3 4n51
Friedman, Thomas L., 626, R-6 8n6
Friedman, W. G., R-11 13n15, R-15 13n15
Frost, Tony, 447
Fry, Nick, R-17 19n40
Fukushima, Glen S., R-4 5n19
Full ownership, 428–430
Fulmer, Melinda, 515
Functional lubrication, 142
Functional structure, 576
Furniture retailing, 176
Futures, 293

G

Gabrielson, Mika, 341
Gagnon, Joseph A., 294
Galbraith, Jay R., R-16 19n4, R-17 19n21
Gale, H. Frederick, Jr., 373
Galle, William P., R-8 10n22

Ganesh, Gopala K., R-5 7n9
Garden, Alex, R-13 15n15
Garemo, Nicklas, 498, R-15 16n52
Garreau, Joel, 28, 29
Garten, Jeffrey E., R-6 8n1
Gatignon, Hubert, R-9 11n18
Gelin, Stephane, R-14 16n19
General Agreement on Tariffs and Trade (GATT), 370. See also World Trade Organization; Kennedy Round, 34; Tokyo Round, 34; Uruguay Round, 35
General Agreement on Tariffs in Services (GATS), 35
General Electric, 108, 511, 585
General Foods, 69
Generalized System of Preferences, 268
General Mills, 124
General Motors, 126; in China, 172–173
Geography, 21, 22, 259; human features, 24; natural features, 23–24; transportation systems and, 26–27
Geologic characteristics, 23
Geology, 23
George, Catherine, R-10 12n7
Germany: and auto exports, 9, 294; small firms in, 11
Gertner, David, R-6 8n51
Ghauri, Pervez N., 437, R-8 10n13
Ghemwat, Pankaj, R-7 8n61
Ghoshal, Sumantra, 588, 596, R-17 19n14, R-17 19n36
Ghosn, Carlos, R-17 19n27
Giannini, Valerio, 326
Gibbs, Hope Katz, R-8 10n40, R-8 10n43, R-10 11n61
Gibson, Richard, R-12 13n23
Gibson-Thomson ruling, 131
Gift giving, 70
Giges, Nancy, R-16 18n41
Gill, James D., R-10 11n39
Gill, Mark, 391
Gillette, 260, 439–440, 441; Web site, 463
Gilliland, David I., R-9 11n24
Gilpin, Robert, 626
Gingrich, James A., R-2 3n36, R-6 8n24, R-7 9n2, R-11 12n46
Ginter, James, R-15 17n1
Glemit, Francois, R-13 14n67
Global account management, 417
Global brands, 68–69
Global Business Dialogue on Electronic Commerce, 31
Global Business Policy Council, 3
Global cooperation, 134
Global customer, 58
Global environment, 143; and acid deposition, 47; deforestation and, 46, 47; desertification, 46
Global expansion, 3, 398; competitive strategy for, 402, 405–411; core strategy for, 402–405; cost factors and, 399–400; country-market choice, 406–409; critique of, 3; and home appliances, 397–398; internal analysis for, 405; market analysis for, 404–405; market factors for, 399; marketing strategy for, 405–411; market potential of, 402–403

Global investment strategies, 8
Globalization, 402–403. See also International business; International marketing; case studies of, 659–662, 663–666; and corporate culture, 417; and decision-making authority, 415, 581–583; and domestic policy repercussions, 8–10; and economic growth, 3; governments and, 609–610; and industrial extinction, 14; management processes, 415, 582; organizational structures, 416–417, 570–581, 582, 589–595; tax policy and, 485, 486–491; vulnerability of, 610–611
Globalization drivers, 399–402
Global linkages, 6–8
Global market expansion: contractual arrangements and, 434–435; direct foreign investment and, 421–434
Global marketing: and adaptation, 412, 413; and local differences, 414; and product development, 412–414, 441–450; and standardization of product, 412, 413
Global media, 546–548
Global product development, 412–414, 441–450; adaptability and, 441; organization of, 448–449
Global product launch, 439–440, 450–451
Global product structure, 574–575
Global program management, 444
Global village, 607
Global warming, 143
Glocalization, 412, 583
Goldman, Steven M., 245
Goldstein, I, R-3 3n66
Golik, Richard B., R-9 10n56
Gomes, Lenn, R-11 13n5
Goodman, Davis, R-6 8n17
Goods and services, interaction of, 465, 467
Googins, Bradley K., R-16 18n61
Google, 108
Goold, Michael, R-17 19n55
Gooley, Toby B., 283
Gorchels, Linda, 271, 463
Gould, Laura M., 374
Government, as agent of change, 232–233
Government consortia, 433–434
Government-corporate collaboration, 610
Government publications, 317
Governments, as data source, 193
Govindarajan, Vijay, 118, 596, 597, R-9 11n13, R-16 19n8, R-17 19n41, R-17 19n42
Graham, John L., R-8 10n2, R-8 10n20, R-16 18n51
Graham, Thomas R., R-1 2n4
Grameen-Phone Ltd., 90
Gramm, Senator Phil, 180
Grant, Linda, 71
Grant, Robert M., 404, 419, R-11 12n25
Gray, Robert, R-6 8n27
Gray market, 36, 132, 357–360, 387
Greed, 142
Green, Paula L., 273, 480
Greenemeier, Larry, R-11 12n41
Green Mountain Coffee, 183

Gregory, James R., 463
Grein, Andreas F., R-11 12n45
Grewal, Dhruv, R-15 16n56
Grey, Anne-Marie, 567
Griffith, Abbie, R-8 10n47
Griffith, David A., R-17 19n34
Griggs, L., 86
Gritzinger, Bob, 386
Gronroos, Christian, R-13 15n2
Gross, Thomas, 584
Gross Domestic Product: and inter-
    national trade, 12–13; per capita,
    97–98
Grosse, Robert, R-14 16n9
Group of Five, 90–91
Group of Seven (G7 nations), **90**–91,
    195
Group of Ten, 90–91, **90**–91
Gruner, Kjell, R-17 19n17
Grunhagen, Marko, R-6 7n30
Grupo Gigante, 117, 118
Guangzhou Market Research Co. (GMR),
    187
Guerrero-Cusumano, Jose-Luis, R-7 8n55
Guido, Gianluigi, R-3 4n53
Gulati, Ranjay, 340
Gulf Cooperation Council (GCC), 38,
    112, 122, 123
Gupta, Anil K., 118, 596, R-9 11n13, R-16
    19n8, R-17 19n42
Gupta, Pola B., R-15 18n22
Gustafson, David H., R-5 6n31
Gutterman, Alan, 437

H
Haas, Richard, 156
Hadjimarcou, John, R-10 11n40
Hakim, Danny, 167
Hall, Edward T., 59, 86, R-2 3n9, R-2 3n24
Hall, Mildred Reed, 86
Hallmark, 533
Halloween, 157–158
Hamel, Gary, R-11 12n43
Hammond, Allan, R-12 14n31
Hampden-Turner, Charles, 87
Han, Jin K., 262
Handfield, Robert B., 535
Hanni, David A., 557, R-2 3n17
Harding, David, R-13 14n65
Harker, Michael, R-14 16n26
Harley-Davidson Company, 48, 295,
    356–357
Harmonized Tariff Schedule of the United
    States (HTSUS), 157, 158
Harrell, Gilbert D., 407
Harris, Milton, R-17 19n16
Harris, Philip R., 86, 597, R-2 3n15
Hart, Gary, R-18 20n27
Hart, Stuart L., 90, R-3 4n3, R-14 16n42
Harvey, Michael G., R-5 5n14, R-7 8n60,
    R-10 11n38, R-17 19n34
Haspeslagh, Philippe C., R-16 19n5
Hassan, Salah S., R-4 6n13
Hauser, John, 271
Healey, Nigel M., R-5 6n25
Heely, James A., 419
Heinrich von Thünen, 28
Heller, Laura, R-3 4n34
Helm, L., 492

Helms-Burton Act, 153
Hendon, Donald W., 331
Hendon, Rebecca A., 331
Henisz, Witold J., 3, 483
Henkel, 73, 115, 416–417
Hensley, David, 581
Herath, Hamantha S. B., 440
Herberger, Roy A., Jr., R-8 10n20
Herbig, Paul, 331, R-6 8n21, R-8 10n18
Hermes Kreditanstalt, 149
Heslop, Louise A., 271
Hewett, Kelly, R-6 8n38
Hewlett-Packard, 89, 121, 509
Heylar, John, R-8 10n34
Heywood, Suzanne, R-11 12n35
Hickey, Roger, R-8 10n45
Higginbotham, Harlow H., R-14 16n2,
    R-14 16n17
High context cultures, 59
Hill, John S., R-3 4n21, R-10 12n17, R-16
    18n48
Hilton Hotels, 70–71
Hinduism, 65, 67–68
Hines, James R., Jr., R-4 5n11
Hinkelman, Edward G., 245, 303, R-7 9n17
Hiromoto, Toshiro, R-15 17n2
Hirschorn, Eric, 156
Hise, Richard T., R-15 17n4
Hite, Robert E., R-15 18n8
H.J. Heinz Company, 72, 106, 115
Hobley, Christopher, R-15 17n14
Hodge, Sheila, 331
Hoecklin, Lisa, 86
Hoff, Edward J., 413
Hoffman, K. Douglas, R-8 10n47
Hofstede, Frenkelter, R-2 3n52
Hofstede, Geert, 59, 79, 86, R-1 3n7, R-2
    3n49, R-2 3n50
Holden, Reed K., 303, 507, R-7 9n8
Hollander, Abraham, 54
Hollenbeck, George P., 597, 626
Hollywood films, 57–58
Holstein, William J., R-15 18n9
Holton, Richard H., R-11 13n13
Homburg, Christian, R-17 19n17
Homogeneous cultures, 60
Honda, 575
Hong, F.C., 262
Hong Kong and Shanghai Banking
    Corporation, 76
Hood, Neil, 437, R-17 19n40
Hopkins, David S., R-12 14n38
Hory, Bill, 305
Host country, culture of, 189
Household, 96, 103
Hovhannisyan, Armen S., 161, 179
Howard, J. D., R-10 11n53
Hsieh, Tsun-Yan, R-17 19n33, R-17 19n50
Hub-and-spoke system, 617
Hucko, E. M., R-4 5n8
Hufbauer, Gary Clyde, 134, 156, 166, R-1
    2n18, R-3 4n27, R-4 5n5, R-4 5n10
Huffman, Sarah, 340
Hulbert, James M., R-14 16n29
Human capital, 37
Humes, Samuel, 597, R-16 19n7
Hutchins, Lynn S., 285
Hutt, Michael D., 367, R-8 10n47

Hydroelectric power, 23
Hydrology, 23

I
Iacobucci, Dawn, 214, R-4 6n7, R-5 6n21
IBM, 565–566
Iceland, bottled water from, 376, 380
ICI, 333
Ideas, marketing of, 17
Iglarsh, Harvey J., R-4 5n15
IKEA: international expansion of, 174,
    175; marketing strategy of, 175–177;
    in the United States, 177–178
Ilieva, Janet, R-5 6n25
Ilinitch, Anne Y., R-5 7n15
Implementation, 20
Implementors, 589
Import barriers, cost of, 48
Import controls, 140–141
Import license, 522
Imports, 42; and automobile industry,
    386–388; government regulations
    and, 389–390; restrictions on, 44–45,
    48, 147; voluntary restraints on,
    45, 48
Import substitution, 120
Incandela, Denise, 339, 340
Income, 97–100
Incoterms (Trade terms), **281,** 282–283,
    293
Indexes to literature, Internet addresses,
    218
India, 602; and data entry services,
    477–478; gift giving in, 70
Indirect exporting, 327, 345
Individualism, 79–80
Indonesia, imports from, 374–375
Industrialized countries, map of, 91
Industrial products and channels of
    distribution, 335
Industrial property, 154
Industrial regions, 28
Industrial sector, employment rate by,
    470
Infant industry, 475
Inflation, 103, 148; and pricing
    decisions, 493
Information, 199, 415, 607
Information sources, marketing issues,
    215–220. *See also* Internet addresses;
    company registers, 220; directories,
    218; encyclopedias and handbooks,
    218; European Union, 215–216; news-
    papers and magazines, 218–219; for
    price information, 220; for selected
    organizations, 216–218; for shipping
    information, 220; and standards, 220;
    statistics, 220; for tariffs and trade
    regulations, 220; and trade, 220,
    346–349; trade publications and data-
    bases, 219–220
Information technology, 326
Infrastructures, 72, 106–108; agricul-
    ture and, 106; data on, 108; and mar-
    keting opportunities, 107, 108; rural
    areas and, 109; social development
    and, 109
Innate exporters, 236
Insurance industry, health and life, 471

Intangibility, 468

Integrated distribution, 345

Integrated exports, 327, 328–329

Integrated marketing communications, 314

Intellectual property rights, 132, 237, 267, 269

Intellectual Property Rights Improvement Act, 269

Intellectual property rights protection, 270

Interactions of physical and human features, 25

Inter-American Convention for Trademark Protection, 154

Interest rates, 8

Interfaith Center on Corporate Responsibility, 563

Intermediaries: selection of, 357

Intermediaries, 334, 345–347, 349–352. See also Distributors; and distribution channels, 343; performance of, 351–352, 356; professionalism of, 352; screening of, 350–351; sources of, 346–347, 349, 350; termination of, 361–363

Intermodal containers, 528

Internal Revenue Service (IRS), 485; and transfer pricing, 315–316, 489, 490–491

International Anti-Counterfeiting Coalition, 269

International Bank for Reconstruction and Development. See World Bank

International business. See also Globalization; International marketing: behavior, ethics and, 143; economic integration and, 114–115; entry into, 235–237; government and, 609–610; and innovation and change, 77–78; local firms and, 127; motivations for, 226–230, 415–516; regulations, rules, laws and, 141–143, 144, 151–152, 252, 255

International careers, 74, 618–625

International Chamber of Commerce, 269, 281

International Company Profiles (ICP), 291, 348

International comparative research, 205

International Convention for the Protection of Industrial Property, 154

International cooperation, 611

International Data Corporation, 102

International finance, 42–44, 603–604

International Financial Statistical Yearbook, 6

International freight forwarder, 523

International information systems, 209–210. See also Data; Research

International law, 153–154

International logistics. See also Logistics strategy: basic differences (by country) and, 513; and contract logistics, 530; cost of, per order, 512; defined, 509–511; impact of, 512–513; Internet and, 530–531; inventory and, 523–525; management of, 529–530; packaging issues, 527–529; security issues and, 531–532; shipping and, 521–523, 527;

storage issues, 525–527; transportation and, 513–521

International Longshore and Warehouse Union (ILWU), 515

International marketing, 4, 600. See also Globalization; International business; careers in, 600, 618–625; challenges to, 3; competition and, 189; definition of, 4–5; and foreign policy, 33; politics and, 10; war on terrorism and, 10; and world peace, 10

International marketplace, access to, 225–226

International Monetary Fund (IMF), 6, 33, 36; financial crises and, 125; history of, 36; Web site of, 194

International negotiations, 308–312. See also Negotiations; dangers of, 308; Internet and, 308–309

International Organization for Standardization, 247, 254–255

International product life cycles, 613

International shipment, 521–523. See also Transportation

International standardization programs, 247

International supply chain, 512

International teams (councils), 586

International trade, 5. See also Trade; World trade; and foreign policy, 33; and Gross Domestic Product, 12–13

International Trade Administration and Patent and Trademark Office, 269

International Trade Commission (ITC), 161, 163, 266

International Trade Organization (ITO), 33

International transactions, 5

International travel, cost of, 624

Internet, 6, 107, 548, 607. See also E-commerce; and digital colonialism, 108; English language and, 64, 321; and internal communications, 320–321; and marketing services, 479–480; and negotiations, 308–309; portals to, 108, 321, 456; and research, 209; sales promotion and, 320–321; users, worldwide, 607

Internet addresses, 55. See also Information sources, marketing issues; European Union, 215–216; selected organizations, 216–218; United Nations, 216; U.S. Government, 216

Internet portals, 321

Interpretive knowledge, 77

Interstate Commerce Commission (ICC), 475

InterTrend Communications, 77

Interviews, 202–203

Intracultural differences, 60

Intranets, 586

Inventory, 523–525; and currency valuation, 525; customer service and, 524–525

Inventory carrying costs, 523

Investment, 422, 423. See also Foreign direct investment; impact of, 42–44

Ioannou, Lori, R-11 12n22

Iran and relations with U.S., 153

Iraq, 33; invasion of Kuwait, 134

Irrigation, 25

Irwin, Douglas A., 419

Isabella, Lynn A., 437

Islam, 65, 67

Izquierdo, Marcelo, R-1 1n4

J

Jackson, George, R-15 17n10

Jackson, John H., 303

Jacob, Rahul, R-3 4n18, R-11 12n38

Jacobs, Laurence W., 541

Jacobsen, Carl R., R-9 10n50

Jacobson, David, 305

Jaeger, Alfred M., 591, R-17 19n54

Jagoe, John R., 303, 331

Jakubik, Maria, 653

Jamaica, 23

James, Dana, 90, R-6 8n8, R-6 8n43, R-8 8n8

Japan, 69, 121; and automotive exports, 294; cosmetics industry in, 337–338; distribution system in, 81; gift giving in, 70; and imported chopsticks, 391–393; product positioning in, 257; sogoshosha, 49, 234–235; soup sales in, 71; and trade with United States, 52, 121; transfer pricing and, 485

Jarvis, Steve, 203

Javalgi, Rajshkhatar, R-9 11n7

Jensen, J. Bradford, R-5 7n20

Jensen, Paul, 247

Jeong, Insik, R-11 12n53

Joachimsthaler, Erich, 463, R-13 14n58

Jocz, Katherine E., R-17 19n17

Joemarin Oy (sailboats), 381–385

Johansen, Robert, 87, R-1 3n4

Johansson, Johny K., R-6 8n49, R-6 8n50

Johnson, Thomas E., 245, 303

Joint List of the European Union, 135

Joint ventures, 430–431, 432, 433

Joko, Inc., 89

Jolson, Marvin, R-4 6n16

Jones, Chip, 368

Jones, John Philip, 567

Joyner, Nelson T., 245

Jurisdiction clause, 154

Just-in-time (JIT) delivery (supply) system, 27, 510, 512, 532, 616–617

K

Kabirova, Irina, 653

Kaikati, Jack, 358

Kale, Sudhir H., 80, R-2 3n51, R-2 3n53, R-2 3n55, R-10 11n39, R-10 11n42

Kalmanoff, G., R-11 13n15

Kaminsky, Philip, 535

Kamprad, Ingvar, 174

Kanter, Rosabeth Moss, 419, R-18 20n22

Kapferer, Jean-Noel, 463, R-6 8n9, R-6 8n28, R-13 14n64

Kashani, Kamran, R-11 12n48

Katahira, Hotaka, R-8 10n5

Katsikeas, Constantine S., R-10 11n40, R-10 11n43, R-13 15n3

Katz, Ralph, R-12 14n12

Kaufman, Marc, 373

Kaynak, Erdener, R-8 10n27

Kazakhstan, 24

Keegan, Warren J., 271
Kehoe, W., R-6 7n30
Keller, Kevin L., 463
Kelley, Bill, 174
Kenna, Peggy, 86
Kentucky Fried Chicken, 60
Kenya, 72
Keown, Charles F., 541, R-8 10n21
Kesler, Lori, 659
Kesselman, Berry J., R-8 10n26
Kidger, Peter J., 591
Kiefer, Richard O., 407
Kim, Hank, R-16 18n25
Kim, Jai Boem, R-15 16n58
Kim, Jonghoon, R-7 9n9
Kim, Keysuk, R-9 11n36
Kim, W. Chan, 251, R-3 3n60, R-11 12n42
Kimberly-Clark, 96
Kinnear, Thomas C., R-5 6n28
Kirby, Andrea, R-8 10n24
Kirpalani, V. H. Manek, 341
Kitchen, Philip J., 567
Kitcho, Catherine, 463
Klein, Alec, 386
Klein, Ellen, R-10 11n53
Klein, Jill G., R-6 8n3
Klein, Lisa R., R-8 10n6
Kleinschmidt, Elko, R-12 14n38
Kleiser, Susan Bardi, R-4 6n1
Kliger, Michael, R-11 12n35
Kluckhohn, Clyde, 59, R-1 3n6
Knetter, Michael M., 294
Knight, Gary, 401, R-10 12n12, R-15 17n17
Knox, Andrea, R-9 11n22
Kobrin, Stephen J., 76
Kodak, 121, 574; Web site, 567
Kohls, Robert L., R-1 3n8
Koivunen, Tapani, 653
Korea, 454, 602; and globalization, 82; and Japanese, 492
Kotabe, Masaaki, 463, R-1 2n20, R-3 4n47, R-4 6n14, R-4 6n16, R-5 7n5, R-5 7n18, R-15 17n2, R-18 20n25
Kotler, Philip, 126, 249, R-4 4n58, R-6 8n51
Kraar, Louis, R-14 16n41
Kramer, Mark R., R-16 18n62
Kreinin, Mordechai E., R-1 2n12, R-1 2n13
Krienke, Mary, 174
Kroeber, Alfred, 59, R-1 3n6
Krogh, Lester C., R-12 14n33
Krubasik, Edward G., R-12 14n20
Krugman, Paul, R-3 4n46, R-7 9n29
Kruytbosch, Carla, R-6 8n41
Kuala Lumpur Summit, 603
Kundu, Sumit K., R-5 7n21
Kurlantzick, Joshua, 398
Kurtz, David L., 389
Kutschker, Michael, R-1 1n14

L

Labeling, 151, 261–262; bilingualism and, 261–262
Laboratory test markets, 450
Lacy, Sondra, 86
Lakewood Forest Products, 391–393
LaLonde, Bernard, R-15 17n1
Lam, Janet P.Y., 262

Lambert, Douglas M., 535
Lamons, Bob, R-9 10n59
Lancaster, John, R-18 20n11
Lancioni, Richard A., 275, R-7 9n5
Landlords, 7
Lane, Henry W., R-5 7n10
Languages, 61–64, 310; and international marketing, 63–64, 621; and Internet, 364; and marketing research, 189; Web sites and, 64; word meaning of, 63, 64
Laos, 90
Larssen, Nora Forisdal, R-10 12n6
Lasalle, Diane, 271
Lasserre, Philippe, R-16 19n12
Latin America, 24, 38, 120–121; appliance industry in, 667; debt crisis in, 105–106; distribution systems in, 333; economic crisis in, 6
Latin American Integration Association, 123
Lau, Min H., 419
Laura Ashley, 239–240
La Voie, Johanne, R-17 19n50
Lawton, Joseph A., R-16 18n50
Lazer, William, R-17 20n1
Lead users, 442
League of Nations, 133
Leasing of equipment, 300
Leather industry, 11
Lee, Barton, 187
Lee, James A., R-2 3n57
Lee, James E., 81
Lee, Soo Hee, R-15 16n58
Legal services, 477
Legal system, 149–150, 189
Leggett, Karby, 426
Lehman, Donald R., R-17 19n17
Leiter, Mark G., R-13 14n49, R-13 14n51
Leksell, Laurent, R-17 19n45
Leone, Robert P., R-5 7n7, R-5 7n19
Leong, Siew Meng, 126, R-2 3n54, R-4 4n58
Leonidou, Leonidas C., R-10 11n40
LeRoy, Georges, R-12 14n21
Less-developed countries, 600–602; and expectation-reality gap, 606; map of, 91
Letterman, Gregory G., 54
Letter of credit, 284, 285, 286–287
Leung, Thamals, R-8 10n29
Levaux, Janet Purdy, R-14 16n34
Levin, Gary, R-8 10n33
Levine, Daniel S., R-7 9n39
Levi Strauss & Co., 416
Levitt, Theodore, 271, R-10 12n1
Levy, Daniel, R-14 16n1
Lewis, Gary Andrew, 627
Lewis, Howard III, R-1 1n11, R-5 7n1, R-11 13n6
Lewis, Jordan D., R-10 12n14, R-12 13n19
Lewis, Richard D., 86, R-8 10n28
Lewis, Richard W., R-8 10n30
Leyva, Natan J., R-14 16n16
Li, Tiger, R-5 7n6
Libya, 136
Licensing, 237–240, 571; and counterfeit products, 269; criticisms of, 238–239; negotiations for, 239; trademarks, 239–240
Liesch, Peter, R-15 17n17

Lighter aboard ship (LASH) vessels, 515
Liker, Jeffrey K., R-12 14n19
Lim, Chae, R-4 6n16
Lin, Jennifer, 174
Lindgren, J., Jr., R-6 7n30
Lindgren, John H., R-8 10n47
Lindsey, Brink, 419
Liner service, 514
Linguistic diversity, 64
Linnett, Richard, R-16 18n43
Linton, Ralph, R-2 3n14
Liu, Hong, R-10 11n55
Living Abroad Web site, 626
Lo, Chi, 168, R-7 9n34
Lobbying, 124, 152–153, 180
Local firms, 127
Local managers, 83
Local markets, 414–415
Local retailers and free trade, 117
Local sourcing, 615
Location, 22
Loch, Mark A., R-13 14n51
Loewe, Peirre M., R-11 12n49
Logistics strategy, 616–617. See also International logistics
Loncar, Kirk, R-6 8n20
Lonner, W. J., 86
Loomis, Judi E., 333
Loral Space, 136
Lord, Kenneth R., R-15 18n22
Lorence, Mauricio, R-3 3n61
Lorenz, C., 271
Los Angeles, water resources in, 23
Lotus Development Corporation, Web site, 596
Lovelock, Christopher H., 483
Low context cultures, 59
Lowell, Julia, 303
Lublin, Joann S., R-18 20n30
Luna, David, R-5 6n26
Luostarinen, Reijo, 327, 341
Luqmami, Mustaq, R-2 3n26
Lusch, Robert F., R-8 10n47

M

3M, 84–85, 115
MacAvoy, Thomas C., 437
MacInnis, Peter, R-2 3n45
Macrae, Chris, 463
Madden, Normandy, 494
Madden, Thomas J, R-6 8n38
Madrid Arrangement for International Registration of Trademarks, 154
Madsen, Tammy L., R-11 12n50
Magaziner, Ira C., R-14 16n30
Magee, John F., 115
Magnusson, Paul, R-8 9n51
Maguire, Miles, R-7 9n36, R-7 9n37, R-10 11n57
Mahdavi, Saied, R-7 9n28
Mahini, Amir, 587
Mail-order, 318–319
Makihara, Minoru, R-18 20n17
Makino, Shige, R-11 13n7
Makito, Noda, 128
Malaysia, 268, 603
Malhotra, Naresh, R-11 12n37
Malhotra, Naresh K., 410, R-4 6n3
Malloy, Michael T., R-2 3n12

Maloney, Kevin, R-7 9n16

Management consulting services, 478

Management contract, 434, 435

Manager, 75, 76; and employee recruitment, 74; and foreign environment, 189–190; and foreign languages, 62–63, 64, 621; globalization and, 582; and government ministers, 14; and international competence, 41; international expertise of, 75, 76; international interests of, 227, 230–231; and local employees, 83; of logistics, 513; and negotiations, 310–312; public image of, 144; training of, 81–83, 593

Mandatory product adaptation, 252

Mann, Catherine L., R-1 2n15, R-18 20n8

Mann, Michael, 166

Manner and customs, 69–70, 72

Mano River Union, 122

Manuel, Jose, 507

Manufacturing: communications and, 616; and service industry, 479–480

Manufacturing processes, 7–8, 281

Manufacturing products, 43

Maquiladoras, 28, 117–119

Marber, Peter, 128

Mardesich, Jodi, R-15 17n16

Marginal cost method, 277

Market, 306; segment of, 19

Market analysis, 20

Market-differentiated pricing, 278

Market economy, 3; vs. planned economy, 600

Market implementation, 20

Marketing: cultural best practices, 84–85; definition of, 18; demographics and, 18; the eight Os of, 17–19; government regulations of, 252–255; and price, 274–275

Marketing infrastructure, 72

Marketing management, 610–612

Marketing-mix development, 79

Marketing potential and economic development, 258–259

Marketing process, 19–20

Marketing public relations, 562–564

Marketing research, 20, 72, 187. See also Research; and appropriate markets, 191, 192; benefits of, 190–192; defined, 188; domestic, 187; environment (social/political, etc.), 188–190; exports and, 191–192, 192; imports and, 192; and market expansion, 192; objectives of, 190–193, 193

Market management, 19

Market planning, 20

Market-portfolio mix, 407

Market pricing, 274–275

Market research. See Marketing research

Market seekers, 425

Market tastes, 454

Market transparency, 469

Marriot International, 551

Marsh, Peter, 165, 166

Martenson, Rita, 174, 177

Martin, Drew, R-6 8n21, R-8 10n18

Martin, Josh, R-5 7n25

Martin, Susan, 605

Martinez, Jon I., R-17 19n22

Maruyama, Magoroh, R-4 5n12

Marx, Elizabeth, 87

Marxism-Leninism, 65

Mass customization, 614

Master franchising system, 242

Materials management, 510

Matrix structure, 571, 577–580

Mauborgne, R. A., 251, R-3 3n60, R-11 12n42

Maulella, Vincent M., R-7 9n21

Mavondo, Felix T., 339

Mayer, Charles S., 271

Mayfield, Jackie, R-8 10n18

Mayfield, Milton, R-8 10n18

McAuliffe, Kevin J., R-16 18n30

McCall, Morgan W., 597, 626

McConville, Daniel, 231

McCue, Sarah S., 54, 245, R-1 1n7

McDonald, William, R-8 10n42

McDonald's, 60, 73, 75

McDonnell Douglas, 647, 649–650, 652–653

McGann, Michael, 591

McGinn, Dan, R-6 8n35

McGray, Douglas, R-2 3n32

McIntyre, Roger P., R-10 11n42

McKinney, Joseph A., R-2 3n44

McKinsey & Co., 587

McLaughlin, Kathleen, 339, 340

McLuhan, Robert, R-16 18n53

McNaughton, Rod B., R-9 11n2, R-9 11n15

Media, worldwide, 542, 543, 544, 546–548

Medical journals, 465

Mendelsohn, Martin, 245

Mendenhall, Mark, 83

Menezes, Ivan, R-13 14n62

Mercosur (Southern Common Market), 6, 38, 113, 120, 123, 349

Message channel, 306–307

Messerlin, Patrick A., 54

Messner, Stephen C., 247

Metal industry, 43

Mexico, 6, 117, 124, 125; gift giving in, 70; and NAFTA, 116–119; retail stores in, 118; and trade with U.S., 117, 119

Meyer, Anton, 483

Meyer, Bob, R-3 4n11

Mezias, John M., R-11 13n10

Michelet, Robert, R-12 14n41, R-13 14n41

Michelin, 126–127

Microtest marketing, 450

Middle East, economic integration in, 112, 122

Middle-income developing countries, map of, 91

Miesel, Victor H., R-14 16n2, R-14 16n17

Migration, 605

Miles, Gregory L., 283

Military defense and export controls, 136–137

Miller, Danny, R-17 19n21

Miller, Edwin L., R-18 20n28

Miller, Tom, 411

Min, Hokey, R-8 10n22

Mineral (nonmetallic) products, 43

Miniard, Paul W., R-2 3n29, R-3 4n6

Minimum wage legislation, 132

"Mininationals," 401

Minor, Michael, R-4 5n16

Mira, Rafael, R-13 14n67

Mirus, Rolf, R-15 16n57

Mitchell, Alan, R-6 8n29

Mitchell, Colin, R-13 14n59

Mitra, Surjya, R-14 16n4

Mitri, Michel, R-9 11n28

Mixed aid credits, 49

Mixed structure, 577

Mobile phones, 72

Moen, Oystein, R-5 7n17

Moffat, Susan, R-12 14n25

Moffett, Michael H., R-7 9n19, R-7 9n31, R-9 10n62

Mol, Michael J., R-16 19n10

Monczka, Robert, 535

Money, Robert B., R-16 18n51

Monopolies, 114, 123

Monroe, Kent B., 303, R-14 16n25

Montgomery, David B., R-11 12n51

Monye, Sylvester O., 331, 567

Moore, Karl, 447, R-17 19n28

Moore, Mike, 601, R-1 2n8, R-17 20n3

Moral behavior, 143

Moran, Robert T., 597, R-2 3n15

Morphy, Erika, 247, 273, 333, 485, R-6 8n14, R-7 9n22, R-7 9n23, R-10 11n56, R-10 11n63, R-14 16n10

Morris, Marlene, R-6 8n3

Morrison, Terri, R-2 3n35

Morton, Roger, 333

Moses, Elissa, 567

Moss, Simon, R-17 19n52

Most-Favored Nation (MFN) clause, 34, 152

Motion Picture Association of America, 268

Motivation, 226–228, 228–230

Motorola, 108, 333

MTV, 547–548

Mudgil, Varun, R-13 14n69

Multidisciplinary teams, 445, 448

Multilateral Agreement on Investment, 60

Multilateral negotiations, 51, 109

Multinational corporation, 571–580, 583, 613. See also Firms; area structure of, 575–576, 583–584; as change agents, 109; and community relations, 565–566, 613; customer structure of, 576–577; decision-making in, 415, 581–583; export department of, 571, 572; foreign direct investment and, 422, 423; functional structure of, 576; global product structure, 574–575; headquarters of, 583, 589; and internal cooperation, 584–586; international structures and, 580–581; keys to success of, 587; licensing and, 571; matrix structure of, 571, 577–580; mixed structure of, 577; networking within, 583–584; organizational structure of, 570–581, 589–595; and research, 200, 202; subsidiaries, control of, 594–595; training programs of, 81–83; transfer pricing and, 485, 486–491; and U.S. subsidiaries, 497

Multipurpose vehicles, 280–281

Mundak, George P., R-2 3n14

Munitions Control Act, 135

Murjani, 240

Murphy, Cait, R-10 12n15
Murphy, Kate, 70
Murphy, Paul R., 535
Murray, Inc., 247
Mutual recognition agreements (MRAs), 124
Myers, Hayley, R-9 11n11
Myers, Matthew B, R-7 9n4

N

Nacher, Thomas, R-12 14n39
Nagahama, Masaoki, 373
Nagle, Thomas T., 303, 507, R-7 9n8
Naidu, G. M., R-9 10n52
Nakata, Cheryl, R-17 19n44
Nall, Stephanie, R-6 8n5
NameLab, 261
Nancarrow, Clive, 557
Narasimhan, Chakravarthi, R-13 14n65
National Cooperative Research Act, 448–449
National Highway Traffic Safety Administration (NHTSA), 386–388
Nationalism, 148
National security, 475
National Trade Data Bank (NTDB), 55, 195
Nation states, sovereignty of, 9, 10, 608–609
NATO, export controls and, 137
Nauclér, Tomas, 498, R-15 16n52
Nayak, P. Raganath, 463
Nayor, James, R-10 12n6
Neal, William D., R-5 6n27
Necessary, Sandra, 238
Neckar, David H., 145
Neff, Jack, 440, R-16 18n36
Negandhi, Arant R., R-17 19n47
Negotiations, 305, 308–312. See also International negotiations; advice for, 310–312; cultural factors and, 69, 79–80, 309, 310; and pricing, 299–300; process of, 309–310
Nejdet, Delener, R-8 9n54
Nelson, Carl A., 271
Nelson, Gary, 340
Nersesian, Roy L., 419
Nes, Erik, R-6 8n48
Nestlé, 59, 124, 259, 452, 458–460
Netherlands, 9, 25
NetLet Microsystem, 577
Networking and global organizations, 583–584, 586
Neupert, Kent E., 419
Newly industrialized countries (NIC), 90–91
New products, 6–7; pricing of, 275; testing of, 449–450
Newsletters, 195
New Superregions of Europe, The (Delamaide), 29
Newton, Robert, 597, R-17 19n41
NGOs (Nongovernmental organizations), 566
Niche marketing, 144, 259
Niche players, 124
Niederhofer, Jay, R-14 16n15
Niefeld, Jaye S., 567
Nielsen, A. C., R-12 14n38
Nigeria, 37, 478

Nike, 494
Nine Nations of North America, The (Garreau), 28
Nishikawa, R., R-4 6n15
Nissan USA, 75
Nitsch, Detlev, R-11 13n7
NLR (No license required) conditions, 135
Noise, 307
Nokia, 64
Nondiscriminatory regulations, 475
Nonfinancial incentives, 427
Nontariff barriers, 48, 254–255
Nonverbal language, 64–65
Noonan, Chris, 245
Norman, Richard, 174, 176
North American Agreement on Labor Cooperation (NAALC), 117; and intellectual property rights, 269
North American Free Trade Agreement (NAFTA), 6, 29, 38, 110, 116–119, 123; arbitration panel and, 119; Asia and, 119; and country of origin, 131; future of, 119–120; job loss/gain and, 116, 117; map of, 113; Mexico and, 117, 118; opposition to, 116, 117; pharmaceutical industry and, 124
North American integration, 116–120
North Carolina, Research Triangle Park, 446
North-South relationship, 600–602
Not-invented-here syndrome (NIH), 414
Nova Scotia, 634–638
Nuclear weapons, 136
N.V. Philips Company, 573, 577, 578–579, 583

O

Objective information, 75
Observation, 203–204
Ocean shipping, 514–515
O'Connor, Craig, 299, R-7 9n42
O'Donnell, Sharon, R-11 12n53
Oegg, Barbara, 134, R-4 5n10
O'Farrell, Peter N., R-9 11n3
Office buildings, 8
Office of the U.S. Trade Representative (USTR), 370–371
Offset, 503, 647–649, 651, 652
Ogbuehi, Alphonso O., R-12 14n24
O'Grady, Shawna, R-5 7n10
Oh, Changho, R-9 11n36
O'Hara-Devereaux, Mary, R-1 3n4
O'Hara-Devereux, Mary, 87
Ohmae, Kenichi, 128, R-1 3n1, R-2 3n42, R-10 12n5
Oil-exporting countries, map of, 91
Oil industry, 26
Olajuwon, Hakeem, 478
Omae, Kenichi, 626
Omnibus Tariff and Trade Act of 1984, 267, 269
Ong, Hoon Meng, 331
Open account, 289
Operating risk, 144
Operating systems, 264
Oppenheim, Jeremy, 403
Opportunity costs, 239

Option, 293
Order-cycle time, 524
Orecklin, Michele, 416
Organic agriculture, and coffee production, 183
Organization for Economic Cooperation and Development (OECD), 112, 121, 142, 194
Organization of African Unity (OAU), 133
Organization of American States (OAS), 133, 142
Organization of Arab Petroleum Exporting Countries (OAPEC), 112
Organization of Economic and Development (OECD), 485
Organization of Petroleum Exporting Countries (OPEC), 90–91, 112
Ortiz-Buonafina, Marta, 522
Ortley, John, 225
Oster, Lee, 278
Oster, Patrick, 247
O'Sullivan, Meghan L., 156
Otis Elevator, Inc., 443
Ouchi, William G., R-17 19n43
Outcome (communications), **308**
Outsourcing, 119, 615
"Over-invest," 148
Overproduction, 228
Overseas Business Reports, 108
Overseas jobs, Web site on, 626
Overseas Private Investment Corporation, Web site, 245
Overseas Private Investment Corporation (OPIC), 149
Overtook Computer Corporation, 225
Ownership, 428–434
Ownership risk, 144
Oxenfeld, Alfred R., 276
Øystein, Moen, 401

P

Pachtman, Arnold, R-8 10n11
Pacifico, Anubis, R-12 13n24
Packaging, 73, 261–263; aesthetics of, 262–263, 263; and culture, 70; and intermodal containers, 528; and labeling, 261–262; recycling of, 263; for shipping, 527–529; size of, 263; technology for, 263
Padmanabhan, Prasad, R-11 13n12
Pae, Jae H., 557, R-16 18n37
Pagers, 108
Palmer, Howard, 303
Panitchpakdi, Supachai, 626
Papadopoulos, Nicolas, 271
Paper industry, 400
Parallel importation, 357, 359
Parés, Francesca, 627
Park, C. Whan, R-12 14n34
Park, Chan S., 440
Park, Seung Ho, R-12 13n20
Parker, Barbara, 87
Parker Pen Company, 659–662
Parsons, Andrew J., R-13 14n45, R-13 14n49, R-13 14n60
Partially interested exporter, 236
Partnerships, 340–341
Parvatiyar, Atul, R-10 12n3
Pascale, Richard, R-17 19n48

Pass-through, 294
Pasternak, Bruce A., 597
Patent protection, 124
Patents and foreign investors, 614–615
Paterson, Jerry, 231
Patinkin, Mark, R-14 16n30
Patterson, Paul G., R-13 15n18
Paun, Dorothy A., R-15 16n56
Pax Romana, 32
Payment, terms of, 284–286, 288–289
Pearlstein, Steven, 166
Pearson, J. Michael, R-10 12n7
Pecotich, Anthony, 262
Peebles, Dean M., 567, R-15 18n2
Penetration pricing, 275
Peng, Mike W., R-5 7n15
Penteado, Claudia, 548
Peracchio, Laura A., R-5 6n26
Per capita income, world economic
    pyramid and, 89
Pereira, Ray, R-7 9n40
Periodic reports (newspapers, magazines),
    Internet addresses of, 218–219
Perishability, 468
Perishable products, 519
Personal rapport, 65
Personal selling, 314, 326, 329–330,
    558–559; automation and, 329
Perttunen, Risto, R-3 4n51
Peterson, Mark, R-4 6n1
Petty, Ross D., R-15 18n19
Pfeffer, Jeffrey, 597
Pharmaceutical industry, 124, 151, **269,**
    359, 545; and world trade, 9
Philadelphia Stock Market, 293
Phillips, Edward H., R-15 16n60
Physical distribution, 510
**Physical Quality of Life Index
    (PQLI), 109.** See also Quality of life
Picard, Jacques, R-14 16n27
Piercy, Nigel F., R-16 18n49
Pier 1 Imports, 389–390
Pillutla, Madan M., R-8 10n16
Pirenne, Henri, R-1 2n1
Pitt, Leyland, R-13 15n3
Pittard, Dan, R-3 4n51
Place, 19, 22–24
Planned economy vs. market economy,
    600
Planning, 20; and research, 612–613
Plans, 592
Platt, Gordon, 273
Plummer, Joseph T., R-16 18n47
Poggi, Walter, 247
Pokémon, 61
Policy, 44
Political risk, 144–149, 289; corpora-
    tions and, 148–149; insurance against,
    148–149
Political union, 114
Political violence, 146–147
Politics, 611; domestic, 151–153; inter-
    national, 153
Pollution control, 532, 533
Pomfret, John, R-18 20n7
Pope, Greg, 238
Population, 24, 95–96, 604. See also
    Demographics; and age distribution, 96;
    as human feature, 24; and life

expectancy, 96; migration of, 605; zero
    growth, 96
Population balance, 606
Population stabilization, 605
Populism, 3
Port Authority of New York and New
    Jersey, 517
Porter, Michael, 406, 419, R-10 12n20
Porter, Michael E., R-11 12n24, R-16 18n62
Ports, proximity to, 229
Positioning, 256, 637, 638
Pothukuchi, Vijay, R-12 13n20
Poverty, 89–90, 91, 601
Powell, Chris, R-15 18n11
Power tool manufacturers, 441
Prahalad, C. K., 90, 419, 596, R-3 4n3, R-11
    12n43, R-12 14n31, R-14 16n42, R-16
    19n8
Prasad, V. Kanti, R-9 10n52
Predatory dumping, 301
Prem, Richard, R-10 11n62
Price, 19. See also Pricing
Price changes, 492
Price controls, 148, 496
**Price elasticity of consumer
    demand, 494**
Price escalation, 278
Price manipulation, 295
Price negotiations, 299–300
Price stability, 295
Pricing, 274–275, 491–496, 617–618.
    See also Export pricing; Price; Transfer
    pricing; coordination of, 496–497,
    499–500; corporate objectives and,
    491–493; costs and, 493–494; demand
    and market factors, 494–495; euro
    and, 497–498; exports and, 276–278;
    government and, 496, 617–618; gray
    markets and, 360; Internet and,
    617–618; market structure and com-
    petition, 495–496; multinationals and,
    497; strategies for, 277–278
Pricing decisions, 274–275
Pricing policy, 19
Pricing-to-market, 295
Prine, Jeff, R-10 11n46
Prison labor, 143
Privacy issues, 197, 366
Private brands, 460–462
Private consumption per capita, 37
Process structure, 576
Procter & Gamble, 68, 81, 187, 569–570,
    622; Web site, 567
Product. See also Product development:
    elements of, 249; and legal, religious
    and social taboos, 260; management
    of, 451–455; and production policy,
    613–616; quality of, 264–265; service/
    repairs of, 265; standardization of, 412
Product adaptation, 278, 280
Product characteristics, 259–266,
    312–313; and distribution channel, 341
Product counterfeiting, 266–267, 269–270
Product development. See also Product:
    data banks for, 443; process of,
    442–445; source of ideas for, 442
Product failures, rate of, 449
Product-market portfolio, 451, 452

Product policy, 19
Product portfolio, 453–455. See also
    Brand portfolio; analysis of, 451–452
Product positioning, 256–257, 258
Product placement, 546
Product returns, 533
Product saturation (diffusion), 102, 103
Product structure, 574
Product usage and foreign markets, 264
Product variables, 248–249
Profit repatriation, 429
Profits and internationalization,
    243–244
Promotional campaigns, 542, 543. See also
    Advertising; Sales promotion; budget
    for, 540–541; government restrictions
    on, 545–546, 550; media and, 541–543,
    550; message strategy and, 548–550,
    552; multinational corporations and,
    552–553; objectives of, 540; and per-
    sonal selling, 558–559; product place-
    ment and, 546; and public relations,
    562–564; research for, 538, 539; and
    sales promotion, 559–560; and spon-
    sorship marketing, 564–566; and spon-
    sorship of events, 538–539, 564–565;
    and target audience, 538–540, 546,
    548–549, 552
Promotional mix, 314
Promotion tools, 19
Protectionist legislation, 10, 33, 50,
    151. See also Economic isolationism;
    Tariffs; and catfish, 179–181; and steel
    industry, 161–165
Protestantism, 65, 67
Proxy variable, 196
Psychological distance, 229
Publicity, 314, 562–564
Public libraries, 109
Public relations, 562; and community rela-
    tions, 565–566, 613; and crisis man-
    agement, 563–564; external, 562–564;
    internal, 562; leading firms (worldwide),
    564; and reputation management,
    613
Pull strategies, 314
Purchasing power parities (PPP), 98;
    and gross domestic product, 99
Push strategies, 314
Putzger, Ian, R-15 17n8

Q
Qualitative data, 204, 205, 595
Quality of life. See also Physical Quality of
    Life Index (PQLI)
Quantitative data, 204
Quebec, 64
Quelch, John A., 362, 413, R-8 10n6, R-11
    12n52, R-13 14n65, R-17 19n22, R-18
    20n15
Questionnaires. See Survey questionnaires
Quota systems, 140
Quraeshi, Zahir A., R-2 3n27

R
Rahul, Jacob, R-3 4n5
Railroads, 322–323
Rainforest, 25, 143
Rajaratnam, Daniel, R-13 15n12

Ramachandran, Kavil, R-5 6n20
Ramamurthy, K., R-9 10n52
Ramaswamy, Kannan, R-11 13n5
Ramirez, Rafael, 174, 176
Ramsey, Rosemary, R-9 11n7
Rangan, V. Kasturi, R-9 11n5, R-10 11n47
Rao, Akshay R., R-14 16n39
Rao, C. P., R-5 7n9, R-13 15n19, R-14 16n26
Rapoport, Carla, R-1 3n5
Raviv, Artur, R-17 19n16
Raymond, Mary Anne, R-7 9n9
Rayport, Jeffrey F., R-1 1n6
R&D consortia, 449. *See also* Research and development
R&D costs, 239. *See also* Research and development
Reagan Administration, 370
Realism check, 208
Recession, 89–90, 494. *See also* Financial crises
Recycling, 263, 533
Reedy, Joel, 331, R-8 10n3
Reference groups, 74
Reger, Guido, R-12 14n28
Regional integration, 38, 123
Regions, 28–29
Registered importers (RI), 386, 387
Regulations, discriminatory and non-discriminatory, 475
Rehberg, Virginia J., R-8 10n15
Reid, Brendan, R-8 10n43
Reid, T. R., 421
Reliability, 518
Religion, 65, 67–68; holidays of, 67; map of worlds', 66; and products and services, 67; women and, 67
Renart, Luís G., 627
Renner, Sandra L., 271
Rennie, Michael W., 401
Renwick, Robin, R-4 5n2
Reputation management, 613
Research. *See also* Data; Marketing research: administration of, 198–199; expenditures for, 197; and formulating questions, 198; industrial vs. consumer, 198; and local conditions, 203; presentation of, 208; review of, 208–209; subcontracting to outside firms, 199–202; web technology and, 209
Research and development, 433–434; in European Union (EU), 449; globalization and, 400; investment for, 446; location of, 445–448; and product development, 443, 445–448
Research consortia, 433
Research organizations, 201
Research specifications, 198
Research techniques, 202–208
Resellers. *See* Gray market
Resource seekers, 425
Retail industry, 342
Retail outlets, 72; internationalization of, 338–339; and NAFTA, 117
Reverse distribution systems, 532, 533
Reynolds, Nina L., R-4 6n6
Richardson, J. David, 3, R-1 1n11, R-5 7n1, R-11 13n6

Ricks, David A., R-2 3n16, R-15 17n6, R-15 17n12
Riddle, Dorothy, R-13 15n14
Ries, Al, 463
Ries, Laura, 463
Rifkin, Glenn, 440
Rindal, Karin, 3
Ring, Mary Ann, R-7 9n41
Risks, political, 144–149
Risks of internationalization, 243–244, 610–612
Ritson, Mark, R-14 16n1
Roads, 106, 109, 322
Roberts, Donald F., R-8 10n1
Roberts, Mary-Lou, 567
Robey, Daniel, R-16 19n13
Robicheaux, Robert H., R-9 11n23
Robinson, J. D., R-7 9n29
Robinson, Michael, 437
Robinson-Jacobs, Karen, 515
Rocky Mountain Chocolate Factory, Inc., 238
Rodkin, Henry, 271
Rodwedder, Detlev, 145
Rolex, 360–361
Roll-on-roll-off (RORO) vessels, 515
Rolph, Brad, R-14 16n15
Roman Catholicism, 65
Roman Empire, 32
Roman law, 150–151
Romeo, Jean B., R-6 8n47
Ronen, Simcha, R-3 3n66
Ronkainen, Ilkka A., 3, 167, 174, 386, 626, 634, 647, 659, R-3 4n23, R-6 7n32, R-6 8n49, R-7 8n608, R-7 8n54, R-7 8n55, R-7 9n31, R-8 10n27, R-8 10n47, R-9 10n62, R-9 11n21, R-9 11n38, R-10 11n45, R-12 14n18, R-13 14n62, R-17 19n20, R-17 19n49, R-17 20n4
Ronstadt, Robert, R-12 14n27
Rose, Lewis, R-9 10n53
Rosenbloom, Arthur H., 437
Rosenbloom, Bert, 367, R-8 10n47, R-10 11n41
Rosensweig, Jeffrey, 419
Rosson, Philip J., 356
Roth, Kendall, R-11 12n32
Roth, Martin S., R-6 8n47
Rubalcaba-Bermejo, Luis, 483
Rubie's Costume Co., 157–160
Rudman, Warren B., R-18 20n27
Ruggiero, Renato, R-18 20n16
Runzheimer International, 76
Russel, Colin, R-12 13n25
Russell, George W., R-5 7n26
Russia, 5, 600. *See also* Soviet Union; coal deposits in, 23; financial crisis in, 124–125; grain exports and, 24; negotiators in, 69
Rutenberg, David, R-5 6n32
Ryans, John K., 128, 557, 567, R-2 3n17, R-11 12n36, R-15 18n2
Rykken, Rolf, R-8 10n46, R-10 11n59

S
Sachs, Jeffrey, 10, 419
Safe Drinking Water Act, 379
Safety regulations, 132, 143
Safety-valve activity, 228

Saklani, Soumya, 187
Sale, terms of, 281–284
Sales and motive for international business, 228
Sales force automation (SFA), 329
Sales promotion, 559–560. *See also* Promotional campaigns; by premiums, gifts and competitions, 561; regulations and, 560, 561
Samek, Robert A. P., R-17 19n50
Samiee, Saeed, 557, R-11 12n32, R-14 16n1, R-14 16n28, R-16 18n37
Samli, A. Coskun, R-4 6n13
Sampling, 207–208
Samuelson, Paul, 500–501, R-15 16n59
Sanctions, cost of, 134
Saner, Raymond, 305
Santos, Jose, 596
Saporito, Bill, 174, R-12 14n6
Satellite broadcasting, 548
Satellite (space) industry, 137
Sauder, Maynard, 231
Sauder Woodworking Company, 231
Saudi Arabia, 23, 70
Sawhney, Mohanbir, R-15 17n15, R-17 19n19
Scenario analysis, 212
Scenario building, 212–213
Schmidt, Kathleen V., 329, R-9 10n55
Schmidt, Kathy, R-8 10n25
Schmitt, Bernd, 463, R-13 14n57
Schott, Jeffrey J., 134, 156, R-3 4n27, R-4 5n5, R-4 5n10
Schramm, Wilbur, R-8 10n1
Schuh Arnold, R-6 8n52
Schullo, Shauna, 331, R-8 10n3
Schultz, Clifford J., 262
Schultz, Don E., 567
Schuster, Camille P., 331, R-5 6n19
Schwab, Klaus, 419, 626
Schwartz, John, 368
Schweitzer, John C., R-2 3n54
Scollay, Robert, R-3 4n48
Scott, Allen J., 419
Sea routes, 323
Sears, 77
Secondary data, 196
Securities and Exchange Commission, 475
Security issues, 615, 617; and shipping ports, 617
Segmentation, 409–411
Seidel, Wolfgang, 535
Seifert, Bruce, 346
Seiko, 357, 358
Self-employment, 623
Self-reference criteria, 81
Semiconductor Chip Protection Act of 1984, 269
Semiconductors, 9
Semiconductor trade agreements, 301
Seminar missions, 325
Sensitivity training, 83
September 11, 2001, 134, 137, 610–611
Serapio, Manuel G., Jr., R-12 13n21, R-12 14n29
Serra, Jaime, R-3 4n29
Servais, Per, 401, R-5 7n17
Service capacity, 468–469

Service industry, 476–479, 481–482; and channels of distribution, 335, 482; communications and, 616; cultural factors and, 470; and customer interaction, 469; data collection and, 474; distribution of, 469–470; e-commerce and, 476; globalization and, 473–474; and goods, 465, 467; and gross domestic product (map), 466; and international organizations, 481; pricing for, 482; regulation of, 475; technological advances, 473; trade and, 8; and U.S. economy, 470–472; and world economy, 472–473
Service (of product), 265
Service organizations, 194
Sethi, Rajesh, R-12 14n34
Sethi, S. Prakash, 78, R-2 3n48
Shambaugh, George E., 156, R-4 5n4
Shannon, Victoria, 31
Sharp, 262
Shaw, Eric H., R-17 20n1
Sheehan, Tony, R-17 19n29
Shenkar, Oded, R-11 13n17
Sheth, Jagdish N., 78, R-2 3n48, R-8 10n47, R-10 12n3
Shimp, Terence A., 307, 331, 567, R-8 10n47
Shipper's declaration of dangerous goods, 522
Shipper's export declaration, 522
Shipping, Web sites about, 534
Shipping port, 515
Shishkin, Philip, 166
Shoham, Aviv, R-5 7n11
Siegel, Ron, R-7 9n27
Sierra, Enrique, R-6 8n19
Siguaw, Judy A., R-8 10n47
Sikora, Ed, R-10 11n54
Silicon Valley (California), 446
Simchi-Levi, David, 535
Simchi-Levi, Edith, 535
Simon, Hermann, 507
Simonin, Bernard L., R-11 13n4
Simonson, Alexander, 463, R-13 14n57
Simpson, Penny M., R-8 10n47
Singapore, 22
Single European Act in 1987, 114
Sinha, Surya Prakash, R-4 5n20
Sivadas, Eugene, 262
Skildum-Reid, Kim, 567
Skimming, 274
Smith, Christiana, 339, 340
Smith, Daniel, R-12 14n34
Smith, Timothy, R-13 15n12
Smoot-Hawley Act, 33
Sobek, Durward K., R-12 14n19
Social change, 109
Social infrastructure, 72
Social institutions, 74–75
Socially responsible firms, 3
Social marketing, 96
Social organization, 74–75
Social problems, 109
Social stratification, 74
Socrates, 4
Soehl, Robin, R-14 16n27
Sogoshosha trading companies (Japan), 49, **234–235**

Sohlberg, Carl A., R-6 8n10, R-15 18n1
Soils and agriculture production, 24
Solo exhibitions, 325
Solomon, Charlene, R-9 10n61
Sondergaard, Mikael, 305
Song, Jiang, R-14 16n44
Sonnack, Mary, R-12 14n10
Sood, James H., 381, R-2 3n47, R-9 11n20
Soros, George, 419
Soule, Ed, R-4 5n23
Soup industry, 71
South Africa, mineral wealth in, 23
South African Development Community (SADC), 113, 122
South Asian Association for Regional Cooperation (SAARC), 121, 123
Southern African Customs Union (SACU), 122, 123
Southern Common Market. See Mercosur
Southwick, James D., R-6 8n15
Sovereignty, 9, 10, 608–609
Soviet Union. See also Russia: and Eastern Bloc countries, 33
Sowinski, Lara L., R-3 4n36, R-8 10n35, R-9 11n35
Space exploration, 24
Speh, Thomas W., 367, R-8 10n47
Speier, Cheri, 329
Spekman, Robert E., 437
Spencer, Earl P., R-2 3n33
Sponsorship marketing, 314, 537, 538–539, 565–566
Sports, 7, 478; advertising and, 537
Sprague, Jonathan, 398, R-10 12n2, R-14 16n32
Springer, Reiner, R-17 20n2
Sroades, James, 273
Stack, Robert B., R-14 16n16
Stagnant sales, 228–229
Stahl, Gunter K., R-18 20n28
Standardization, 249–252; brand names and, 260–261; cost of, 254; franchising and, 241; and globalization, 441, 613–614; vs. adaptation, 250–252
Standard Rate & Data Service, 318
Standards, 124
Standard worldwide pricing, 277
Starbucks, 183, 340
Starling, Stephen, 535
Statistical Yearbook, The, 193
Stauss, Bernd, 535
Steel industry, 11, 24, 45, 88, 300–301, 301; production, by country, 163; protectionism vs. free trade and, 161–165; recent history of, 162–164, 163–164
Steenkamp, Jan-Benedict, R-2 3n52, R-4 6n4
Stern, Robert M., 483
Stevenson, Thomas H., R-6 8n45
Stewart, David W., R-16 18n30
Stewart, Sally, R-8 10n21
Stewart, Thomas A., 597
Stewart-Allen, Allyson, R-16 18n23
Stiglitz, Joseph E., 419
Still, Richard R., R-3 4n21, R-16 18n48
Stock, James R., 535
Stonehill, Arthur I., R-7 9n19
Storage facilities, 525–526

Stöttinger, Barbara, 276, R-7 9n10
Stoyas, Mark, R-7 9n27
Strategic alliances, 432–433, 615
Strikes (work stoppages), 515
Stripp, William G., 597
Stroh, Michael, 535
Studwell, Joe, 167, R-17 19n24
Stugatch, Warren, R-1 3n3
Sueo, Sekiguchi, 128
Sullivan, Andy, 31
Supercomputers, 137
Supermarkets and private brands and, 461–462
Supply-chain management, 511; security issues and, 531–532
Survey questionnaires, 205, 207
Surveys, 204–205
Sutton, Robert I., 597
Svensson, Goran, R-17 19n25
Sviokla, John J., R-1 1n6
Swartz, Leonard N., R-5 7n27
Sweden, 383–384
Sweeney, Jill, R-1 1n1
Switch-trading, 502
Swoboda, Frank, 166
Synodinos, Nicolaos E., 541
Systems concept, 510

T

Taft, Charles A., R-15 17n11
Tai, Susan, 557, R-16 18n37
TAL Apparel, 572
Tang, Y. W., 507
Tanner, John F., Jr., R-7 9n9
Tansuhaj, Patriya S., R-15 17n10
Target market selection, 17–19
Tariffs, 33, 278, 280. See also Protectionist legislation; and catfish farming, 179–181; and costume industry, 157–160; and steel industry, 161–166; and textile industry, 159–160
Tarnef, Barry M., R-6 8n33
Tatterson, David, 187
Tavassoli, Nader, 262
Tax benefits for international business, 227–228
Taxes and multinational corporations, 485, 486–491
Tax evasion, 207
Tax rates, 148
Taylor, Charles, 3
Taylor, James R., R-5 6n28
Taylor, Travis K., R15 16n53
Taylor, William, R-17 19n18
Teaching services, 478
Teamster Union, 119
Technological advantage, 227
Technology, 607–608; and cultural change, 73; foreign availability of, 136; marketing and, 8; for military use, 136–137; problems of, 25; and use by terrorists, 136–137
Teenagers, 62, 68–69
Telecommunications, 27, 107, 108
TeleGea, 259
Telemarketing, 319
Telephones, 106–107, 107, 108, 473
Television, 57–58, 61, 73; Spanish-language, 58

Tellis, Gerard J., R-16 18n46

Tenowitz, Ira, R-15 18n12

Terpstra, Vern, 87

Terrain, 23

Terra Networks, S.A., 108

Terrorism, 10, 138–139, 146–147, 610–611; export controls and, 136, 140; incidents over time, 146–147; international logistics and, 531–532; map of global incidents, 138–139; state sponsored, 133; United States and, 133–134

Tetra Pak International, 263

Texas Instruments, 432

Textile industry, 11; tariffs and, 10, 159–160; and WTO, 158

Thailand, 603; financial crisis in, 125

Theocracy, 150

Theuerkauf, Ingo, 587

Thomas, Alan, R-3 4n20

Thomke, Stefan, R-12 14n10

Thorndike, R. M., 86

Thurmond, Molly, 303

Tichy, Noel, R-17 19n30

Timberland, 573

Time Warner, 108

Tinsley, Catherine, H., R-8 10n16

Tobacco industry, 43, 143, 368–373; government regulations of, 370–372, 545; leading brands of, 370; and U.S. trade policy, 370–371

Tom, Kenneth, 605

Tomlinson, Richard, R.11 12n31, R-13 14n61, R-14 16n38

Tonczyk, Michael S., R-7 9n26

Torry, Saundra, 368

Total cost concept, 510

Tourism, 478–479

Tracy, Eleanor Johnson, 174

Trade, 608–609. See also International trade; government regulations and, 609–610; history of, 31–33; impact of, 41–42; nontariff barriers, 48; restrictions on, 424

Trade, terms of (Incoterms), 281–283, 293; cost and freight (FR), 282; delivered duty paid (DD), 282, 283; ex-works (EX), 281; free alongside ship (FAS), 281; free on board (FOB), 282; undelivered duty paid (DUD), 282

1988 Trade Act, 142

Trade agreements, 10

Trade and travel networks, map of, 322–323

Trade associations, 108, 151, 194–195; as agents of change, 232

Trade barriers, 45

Trade deficit, 42

Trade directories, 347

Trade fair, 326

Trade finance, 298–299

Trade flows, 9

Trade journals, 316–317

Trademark Counterfeiting Act of 1984, 269

Trademarks, protection of, 154

Trade missions, 325–326

Trade-off concept, 510

Trade promotion authority, 50

Trade-Related Intellectual Investment Measures (TRIMS), 35

Trade-Related Intellectual Property Rights (TRIPS), 35, 269

Trade sanctions, 132–134; in history, 133

Trade shows, 321, 324–325

Trading companies, 234–235

Trailmobile Company, 430

Training programs, 81–83, 585, 618; and corporate culture, 593; cultural assimilator program, 82–83; and field experience, 83; and intercultural competence, 81–83; language training, 82–83, 621; for sales force, 559; and sensitivity training, 83

Tramp service, 514

Transaction costs, 114, 520–521

Transcultural similarities, 65

Transfer costs, 239

Transfer pricing, 485, 486–491. See also Pricing; corporate objectives and, 487–488; cost-plus approach, 490; E-commerce and, 487; functional analysis approach to, 490; performance measurement and, 489; taxation and, 489

Transfer risk, 144

Translation-retranslation approach, 207

Transparency International (TI), 143

Transportation, 26–27, 521. See also International shipment; cost of, 520; exports and, 283; geographic location and, 26–27; government involvement in, 520–521; infrastructure and, 106, 514, 516; international issues and, 513–521; predictability of, 519–520; roads, 106, 109; transit time of, 518–519

Transportation equipment industry, 43

Transportation linkages, 28

Transportation modes, 513, 514–521, 527; stresses and, 527; Web sites about, 534

Treadgold, Alan, 339, R-13 14n70

Treaties of friendship, commerce, and navigation (FAN), 154

Trebilcock, Bob, 533

Trent, Amelia, 373

Trent, Robert J., 535

Trompenaars, Fons, 87

Tropical environment, 25, 46

Trucking industry, NAFTA and, 119

Trunick, Perry A., R-15 17n3

Tse, Edward, R-3 4n12, R-12 14n7, R-12 14n15

Tulips, 9

Tuller, Lawrence W., 271, R-7 9n38

Tung, Rosalie, R-3 3n62, R-18 20n28

Tuominen, Jouko, 360

Turner, Ernie, 584

Turnkey operation, 435

Tussie, Diane, 331

U

Ukraine, grain exports and, 24

UNICEF, 566

Unilever, Web site, 418

Unintentional dumping, 301

Union Carbide Corporation, and Bhopal disaster, 212

Unions, 515

United Arab Emirates (UAE), 238

United Nations, 133; information sources, marketing issues, 216–217

United Nations Center on Transnational Corporations, 193

United Nations Commission on International Trade and Development (UNCTAD), 520–521

United Nations Conference on Trade and Development (UNCTAD), 193, 238

United States: appliance industry in, 665; Asia and, 8; catfish farming in, 179–181; China and, 426; Civil War, 33; cultural dominance of, 60; debt load of, 604; education and global business, 41; European Union and, 9; export controls and, 135, 136–137; exports and, 141; grain exports and, 24; Iran and, 153; Mexico and, 117, 119; regulations against entry and, 475; and sanctions against terrorism, 133, 134; and service industry, 470–472; submarine-Japanese fishing boat incident, 150; tobacco industry and, 368–372; trade deficit of, 391; trade policy of, 40–41, 44–45, 48, 50; urbanization in, 97; Vietnam and, 179–181; world trade and, 8, 40–41, 50–51

United States Trade Promotion Coordinating Committee (TPCC), member Internet addresses, 55

Urban, Glen L., 271

Urbanization, 96–97, 605–606. See also Cities; in Europe, 181

Urbany, Joel, R-8 10n47

Ursic, Michael L., R-5 7n8

U.S. Carriage of Goods by Sea Act of 1936, 527

U.S. Census Bureau, 211

U.S. Chamber of Commerce, Trade Opportunities Program (TOP), 347

U.S. Coalition of Service Industries, Web site, 483

U. S. Commercial Service, Web site, 367

U.S. Commercial Service, guides, 221–223

U.S. Custom Service, 280

U.S. Department of Agriculture, 371–372; Economic Research Service, 370; and tobacco industry, 370, 371–372

U.S. Department of Commerce, 135; as agent of change, 232–233; Commercial Service of, 49; Country Directories of International Contacts (CDIC), 347; country guides, 76; International Company Profiles (ICP), 290; International Trade Administration, 301; National Trade Data Bank (NTDB), 195; Trade Promotion Coordination Committee, 49; Web site, 214

U.S. Department of State, 135; and international business, 41

U.S. Department of Transportation, 386

U.S. dollar, 64; exports and, 273, 293

U.S. Exporters Yellow Pages, 331, 347

U.S. government information sources, marketing issues, 216

USS *Greeneville*, 150
U.S-Vietnam Trade Council, 180
Uzzelle, Elnora M., R-8 9n47

V

Vaidyanthan, Rajiv, R-9 11n4
Vallier, I., R-4 6n18
Valmis, Tony, 303
Value-added activities, 412– 413
Value-added tax (VAT), 279
Values, 68, 602–603
Van de Gucht, Linda, R-10 11n45
Van deVen, Andrew H., R-5 6n31
Van Houten, Ben, R-12 14n8
Varadarajan, P. Rajan, R-8 10n48
Vehicle import guidelines, 386
Venables, Anthony, 129
Vending machines, 628–633
Venedikian, Harry M., 303
Venkatesh, Viswanath, 329
Verba, Sydney, R-4 6n18
Vermulst, Edwin A., 303
Verne, Jules, 27
Vernon, Ivan R., 557
Video/catalog exhibitions, 325
Video pirates, 268
Vietnam, 179–181, 240
Virtual trade shows, 325
Viscio, Albert J., 597
Viviers, Wilma, R-6 7n31
Von Hippel, Eric, R-12 14n9, R-12 14n10, R-12 14n12
Von Oldenborgh, Marita, R-2 3n11
Vorhies, Douglas W., R-14 16n26

W

Waddle, Commander Scott, 150
Walker, Danielle, R-8 10n7
Walker, Thomas, R-8 10n7
Walls, Jan, 262
Wal-Mart, 511; and Mexico, 118
Walsh, Michael G., R-10 11n50
Wang, Yen Po, R-10 11n55
Ward, Allen C., R-12 14n19
Ward, Ian, 391–393
Wardlow, Daniel L., 535
Warfield, Gerald A., 303
WatchGuard Technologies, 116
Wayne, Leslie, 166
Weapons, 135, 137–138
Webber, Robert, 271
Webb-Pomerene Act of 1918, 141
Weigand, Robert E., R-10 11n54
Weinstein, David, R-14 16n29
Weinstock, Geoff, 166
Weintraub, Sidney, R-3 4n28
Weiss, Doyle L., R-16 18n46
Weiss, Stephen E., R-8 10n10
Welch, Jack, 585
Welch, Lawrence, 327, R-12 13n24
Welge, Martin, R-17 19n47
Wells, Melanie, 433
Welsh, James, R-7 9n27

Wentz, Laurel, 447, 659, R-12 14n14, R-12 14n40, R-16 18n40
Western culture, consumer boycotts of, 61
Western Europe, spending patters in, 100, 101
Westernization, 69
Wetlaufer, Suzy, 58, R-10 12n10
Whirlpool Corp., 663–666
White, Michael D., R-7 9n14, R-17 19n39
Wiechman, Jack G., 463
Wilbon, Michael, 7
Wilkinson, Ian, R-6 8n44
Will, George F., 166
Williams, Oliver, R-16 18n55
Williamson, Debra A., R-16 18n46
Williamson, Nicholas C., R-5 7n14
Williamson, Peter, 596
Wilson, Jesse, R-6 8n34
Wilson, Tim, R-15 17n13
Wind, Jerry, R-8 10n5
Wine industry, 24
Winget, W. Gary, 271
Winnebago Industries, 248
Winski, Joseph M., 659
Winter resorts, 25
Wireless technology, 106–107
Witte, Carl L., R-6 7n30
Wohl, Richard H., R-4 5n19
Women, 67, 109; and international careers, 623, 625; in workforce, 198
Wonacott, Peter, 426
Wong, Veronica, R-12 14n41
Wong, Y. H., R-2 3n30, R-8 10n29
Wood, Donald F., 535
Wood, Paul A., R-9 11n3
Woodall, Pam, R-4 4n55
Wooden, Sean, R-5 7n23
Wood-products industry, 52
Woodside, Arch G., 634, R-2 3n48
Woolston, Chris, 557
Workers, 3; average work week, 73; wages of, 11
Workman, John P, Jr., R-17 19n17
World Atlas, 194
World Bank, 33, 36–37, 566; and International Monetary Fund, 37; international trade and GNP, 12–13; and poverty, 37
World economies (by GDP), map of, 92–93
World economy, service industry and, 472–473
World Health Organization (WHO), 465
World population, map of, 95
World trade, 40. See also International trade; Trade; employment and, 42–43; exports and gross domestic product, 40; exports and imports per capita, 40; international perspective on, 51; merchandise exports and imports, 39;

United States and, 50–51; value of, 5–6
World Trade Organization (WTO), 194, 602, 608–609. See also General Agreements on Tariffs and Trade (GATT); China and, 167–171; Doha Round, 35, 50, 611; dumping and, 301; future of, 608–609; history of, 33–35; intellectual property rights and, 237, 269; international law and, 153–154; international trade agreements, 10; national sovereignty and, 608–609; and telecommunications, 531; Web site of, 483
World Wide Web, 531
Woronoff, Jon, R-9 11n8
Worthington, Roger, 391
Woznick, Alexandra, 245, 303
Woznik, Alexandra, R-7 9n17
Wreden, Nick, R-9 11n33
Wright, Richard W., R-12 13n25
Wu, Haw-Jan, R-15 17n18
Wyche, Steve, 7

X

Xerox, 591

Y

Yadav, Manjit, R-8 10n48
Yager, Loren, 256, 303
Yahoo!, 108
Yang, Yoo S., R-5 7n7, R-5 7n19
Yee-kwong, Ricky, R-2 3n30
Yeoh, Poh-Lin, R-9 11n28
Yeung, Bernard, R-15 16n57
Yi, Chun W., R-14 16n2, R-14 16n17
Yip, George S., 398, R-10 12n3, R-11 12n26, R-11 12n49, R-11 12n50, R-11 12n51, R-17 19n46
Yiu, Lichia, 305
Yorio, V., 94, 253
Yoshino, Michael Y., R-11 12n49
Young, Stephen, 437
Yuguan, Wang, R-14 16n44

Z

Zaidman, Nurit, R-8 10n9
Zbaracki, Mark, R-14 16n1
Zeff, Robbin Lee, 331
Zeithaml, Valerie, 483
Zhan, Sherrie E., 305, R-9 11n29
Zheng, Jiang, R-9 11n3
Zhenzheng, Gong, 167
Zif, Jehiel, 408
Zimmerman, Alan S., 346, R-2 3n58, R-9 11n27
Zimmerman, Jan, 331
Zimmerman, Kenneth, 331, R-8 10n3
Zocci, Andrea, R-10 12n6
Zou, Shaoming, R-5 7n4, R-5 7n12, R-6 8n7
Zuckerman, Amy, R-10 11n65
Zurawicki, Leon, 507